This is number one hundred and sixteen in the
second numbered series of the
Miegunyah Volumes
made possible by the
Miegunyah Fund
established by bequests
under the wills of
Sir Russell and Lady Grimwade.

'Miegunyah' was the home of
Mab and Russell Grimwade
from 1911 to 1955.

'Cobbers' by Peter Corlett of Melbourne.
The 2.1 metre bronze group is the centrepiece of the Australian Memorial Park at Fromelles, and was unveiled there on 5 July 1998. This is the second casting and is at the Melbourne Shrine of Remembrance and was unveiled on 19 July 2008.
PHOTO J CORFIELD, 19 JULY 2008

Don’t forget me, cobber

The Battle of Fromelles

‘the definitive account’—Les Carlyon

Robin S Corfield

THE MIEGUNYAH PRESS
An imprint of Melbourne University Publishing Limited
187 Grattan Street, Carlton, Victoria 3053, Australia
mup-info@unimelb.edu.au
www.mup.com.au

This book is a reissued and updated edition of *Don't forget me, cobber*, published by Corfield & Company in July 2000.
This edition published 2009

Designed by Robin S Corfield
Typeset by Justin J Corfield
Printed in China by Imago

National Library of Australia Cataloguing-in-Publication entry

Corfield, Robin S., 1929-
The Battle of Fromelles

Rev. ed.

9780522855296 (hbk)

Includes index.
Bibliography.

McCay, J. W.
Hitler, Adolf, 1889-1945.
Fromelles, Battle of, Fromelles, France, 1916.
World War, 1914-1918——Campaigns——France——Fromelles.
World War, 1914-1918——Participation, Australian.
World War, 1914-1918——France——Fleurbaix.
World War, 1914-1918——Prisoners and prisons.

940.4272

for Justin

and in memory of all those who fought in the battle of Fromelles ...

Probably in the early summer of 1919, in the wild grass then covering the battlefield of Fromelles, Father Louis Dahiez the vicar of Fromelles from 1919 to 1922, solemnly kneels before the remains of an English or Australian soldier, killed in the battle of 19/20 July 1916, and still unburied.
COURTESY M DELEBARRE

‘Robin S Corfield’s *Don’t forget me, cobber*, published in 2000, is the definitive account of Fromelles’
—Les Carlyon, The Great War (2006).

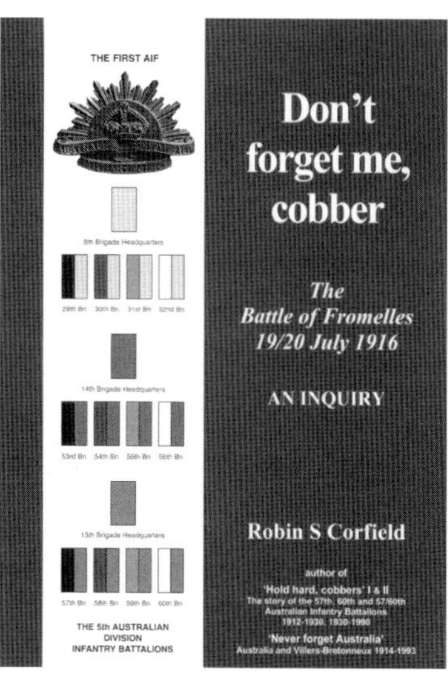

THE FIRST AIF
THE 5th AUSTRALIAN DIVISION INFANTRY BATTALIONS
Don’t forget me, cobber
The Battle of Fromelles 19/20 July 1916
AN INQUIRY
Robin S Corfield
author of
‘Hold hard, cobbers’ I & II
The story of the 57th, 60th and 57/60th Australian Infantry Battalions 1912-1930, 1930-1990
‘Never forget Australia’
Australia and Villers-Bretonneux 1914-1993

When the battle of Fromelles was over, the Germans counted some 2000 bodies lying before their defences: of these, some 1700 were Australian, the rest British. Of the 1700, some 350 were members of the 60th Bn, a further 400 had been wounded. It was the worst loss by any Australian Battalion in WW1, in a single action.

It fell to the 57th Bn to be the stretcher bearers for the 60th in this first major battle in France for the AIF. One of those stretcher bearers back in July 1916 was Sgt Simon Fraser, a 40-year-old farmer from Byaduk, Victoria, and he wrote of his work which is, in a very real sense, the pulse of this history:

> we found a fine haul of wounded and brought them in; but it was not where I heard this fellow calling, so I had another shot for it, and came across a splendid specimen of humanity trying to wriggle into a trench with a big wound in his thigh. He was about 14 stone weight, and I could not lift him on my back; but I managed to get him into an old trench, and told him to lie quiet while I got a stretcher. Then another man about 30 yards out sang out, ‘Don’t forget me, cobber.’ I went in and got four volunteers with stretchers, and we got both men in safely. Next morning at daylight, whilst observing over the parapet, I saw two figures in their shirts and no hats, running about half way between our lines and the Germans. They were our captains, Cameron and Marshall, hunting for more wounded.

For the reader about to embark on the journey from 1916 to the present, Fraser’s letter is given as introduction, an encouragement even, to read on.

Cobber: probably derived from the English dialect (some say Yorkshire, others Somerset) verb—to cob, meaning ‘to take a liking to’. Hence the form—to cobber up with. Leading to the noun cobber—a companion, a friend, a mate, or more emphatically a tried and trusted pal. The Macquarie Dictionary draws attention to the Yiddish word for comrade—chaber.

Contents

The Cross of Sacrifice
VC Corner Australian Cemetery,
Fromelles, 11 November 1994

Foreword

Fromelles is a pretty village in French Flanders that still moves to the rhythms of the land, even though most of its residents now work elsewhere. At first there seems little to tell the visitor that terrible things once happened in the night here. The village is too charming, particularly on a summer evening. Red geraniums sway in the window boxes. Elderly couples poke around their vegetable gardens before penning the ducks for the night and one hears the diesel knock of a tractor as a farmer makes one last pass for the day. Fromelles sits on a little frown of a ridge that looks down on a plain of heavy clay: ripening corn, wheat stubble, potato stalks wilting in the sun, ponies grazing in a field behind a war cemetery.

PHOTOGRAPH L & A LIGHT

A cemetery, an Australian cemetery: here is the first clue. And nearby one comes upon a sculpture, perhaps the most affecting memorial along the line of the old Western Front, a bronze of an Australian carrying in a wounded man, the cobber he didn't forget. These things tell you this place is not Arcady, never can be, because of what happened on this plain during the Great War. Other clues poke through the fallow and lie beneath the tasselled corn: mortar shells, grenades, a soldier's comb that has given up its teeth, rifle rounds splotched with lurid green mould, rusting curls of barbed wire, shrapnel balls, hanks of webbing, a tobacco tin. The debris won't go away. Neither will the memories.

Australian life changed on this plain. Here, during one night, more than 1900 Australians died and another 3100 were wounded in an attack that made no sense then and still doesn't. Here, near that drain, died a medical student from Colac, a Duntroon graduate, an architecture student from Melbourne, a wool buyer from Geelong, a detective from Sydney and hundreds of others: fathers, sons, husbands, sweethearts. Here is the setting for what may fairly be described as the worst night in Australian history, July 19, 1916.

Yet for eighty-four years Fromelles remained outside the folklore. We heard about Gallipoli and Poziéres and Passchendaele, as well as Kokoda and El Alamein. Fromelles was an orphan.

Until 2000, that is, when Robin Corfield's *Don't forget me, cobber* first appeared. Robin Corfield is a thorough man. He assembles facts like a barrister building a case, going back and forth over documents, thousands of them—diaries, letters, books, German records, trench maps, photographs—sifting and testing, comparing one version with another, looking for inconsistencies and corroborating witnesses, and asking questions, always asking questions. This is not a conventional narrative. Rather, as the author tells us, it is an inquiry, an attempt to find out what happened at Fromelles and why.

But if the approach is forensic, this is first of all a human story with a rich cast: Richard Haking, the deluded British corps commander; James McCay, the Australian divisional commander, cranky and high-handed and unready for what he was being asked to do; the young Adolf Hitler, gawky and with dead eyes, somewhere in the German lines facing the Australians; the fabled Australian brigade commander Pompey Elliott; Walter Cass, the hero who never received the recognition he deserved; the poet Geoffrey McCrae, kind and gentle, killed in no-man's land; and Simon Fraser, the sergeant depicted carrying in the wounded man in Peter Corlett's bronze.

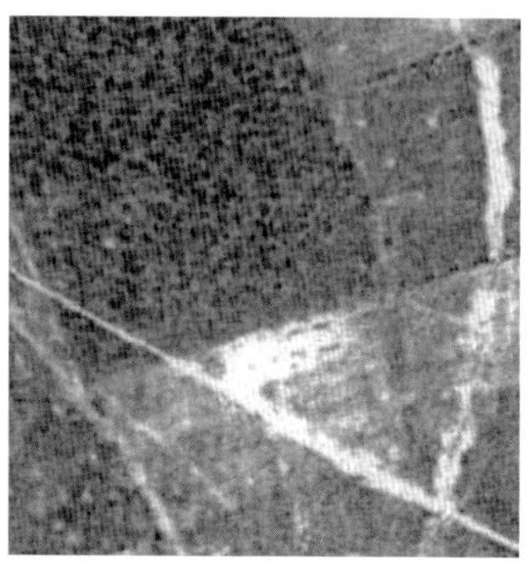

The pits behind the Pheasant Wood, 29 July 1916
PHOTO ROYAL FLYING CORPS

Also reproduced here is a long extract from the diary of Private William Barry, wounded and taken prisoner at Fromelles. This contains a brief reference to Germans throwing Australian bodies into a pit. Those two sentences became the starting point for the search to find the bodies of the Australian missing at Fromelles.

Robin Corfield's achievement is simply that he has told us, better than anyone before him, what happened at Fromelles and why Fromelles matters.

Les Carlyon

Prologue

By Lambis Englezos

In 1991, on the 75th anniversary of the Battle of Fromelles, Robin Corfield and Major John Bradley, a Shrine Trustee, organised a service of commemoration at the Victorian Shrine of Remembrance. It was there that I introduced myself to Robin. A man of great knowledge and empathy, it was Robin who saw the need to write a book about Fromelles and the terrible tragedy of its 'missing' soldiers.

That book, *Don't forget me, cobber*, was published in 2000. In its pages Robin mentioned a Lieut J C Bowden of the 59th Battalion and the possibility that Pheasant Wood, near the battleground at Fromelles, was a burial ground for Australian soldiers. This planted a seed in my mind and, on a visit to Fromelles in April 2002, I began to ask some questions about the 'missing'.

On one memorable afternoon of that visit, I walked the length of 'no man's land' with Martial Delebarre, curator of the Fromelles Museum. We started in what were the 8th Brigade lines and made our way to the Sugarloaf Salient. There was the usual assortment of battlefield debris—cartridge cases, shattered shell casings of various sizes, barbed wire, dented bullets and shrapnel, occasional live ordnance and grenades. There is a constant harvest. At the Sugarloaf we found a sandbag; the hessian pattern was evident on its solid shape. It was a remarkable find. During our walk, I asked Martial about Pheasant Wood, whether he knew where it was. Martial pointed, extending both arms towards the village of Fromelles.

As we walked, I wondered and speculated: were there any unrecovered bodies?

I had met survivors of the Battle of Fromelles, '19th of July men'. Men like Tom Brain, the last of the 60th Battalion. He was a regular at our services and tough and feisty; qualities that probably got him through the war years. At Fromelles, his best friend was killed at his side. The same shell burst gave him 'a smack in the mouth'. At one of our Pompey Elliott services, he laid a wreath, stepped back, snapped a salute to his Brigadier General and said, 'this one's from the boys'.

Charlie Henderson was with the 57th Battalion. He observed the battle and the aftermath. In the days after the battle he went out into 'no man's land' at great personal risk to recover the wounded. As many as thirty Australians were killed doing this work. They could not resist the call of their wounded 'cobbers'. If only Major General McCay had agreed to the generous offer of a truce on the morning after the battle. By showing some consideration for his men, the dead and wounded could have been gathered.

Bill Boyce, the wonderful Bill Boyce, said that McCay was 'not popular'. Of course, a General need not be popular, however McCay stands condemned for his lack of judgement and acumen, and, in this case, for his lack of compassion. Bill Boyce and I would talk about many things, his childhood days, his interest in fishing and local history. On one occasion I asked if I could tape one of our conversations. He agreed. Like other veterans he had been reluctant to talk about his war years. He had kept the scars, physical and emotional, to himself. In his eighties, he finally spoke with his daughters about his experiences. He was a true and loving man; his immaculate room had many framed photos of his children, grandchildren, and great grandchildren.

At Fromelles, Bill went into battle with digging implements. He was to extend the Rhondda sap across 'no man's land'. They drew heavy fire. The orders were, if any were killed, to roll the killed to one side and spread them with lime to help build up the defences. When they withdrew the following morning, he found that his uniform had been creased and riddled with holes from bullets and shrapnel. He also had a vivid memory of a weeping Brigadier General Pompey Elliott acknowledging the shattered remnants of his Brigade. At the end of our taped conversation we stood up and spontaneously reached out and hugged each other.

I consider myself very fortunate to have met and shared the company of our veterans. They are our living history. The call to commemorate and remember, to make a pilgrimage, is not confined to those who have blood relations who were there. It became very personal for me. These '19th of July men' are the motivation for what I wanted to achieve at Fromelles.

For many years, I went about seeking information and documentation to support my contention that Australian soldiers were buried at Pheasant Wood; the number of Australian soldiers who died at Fromelles and the numbers recorded at the VC Corner Cemetery just didn't add up.

There are 1299 names etched on the Honour Roll at VC Corner. There should be 1335. In July 2003, after the

Commonwealth War Graves Commission investigated the proposition, they came up with a figure of 163 unaccounted for 'missing'. A reconciliation of the local cemetery registers and official records provided this figure. The Australian War Memorial at Villers-Bretonneux lists thirty-six 'missing' from the Battle of Fromelles. After researching those listed at Villers-Bretonneux, the figure went to 175. Through the research, we also learnt that another soldier was not listed on either Honour Roll. (We have asked about the possibility of an addendum panel to be placed at VC Corner. It would be a pity if a clerical error left these soldiers unlisted with their cobbers at Fromelles.) With further scrutiny the 'official' figure of Australian 'missing' is 191. The shovel would tell whether all of the 191 'missing' Australians and 329 'missing' English are at Pheasant Wood. I suspect that there are other sites.

I sought archival aerial photos of the ground behind the German frontline. Clearly, they must have had to clear their lines. Those English and Australians who had been killed at or beyond the so-called objective must have been gathered and buried. The German photo of 'Englander' stacked on train carriages supported this view. I received the photos, looking for anomalies in the ground. I found them.

Belgian archivist Jeroen Huygelier told me about the Red Cross Wounded and Missing Files. Using the Honour Roll in Robin's book, I went through the files of each of the 'missing'—the 1299 names etched into the stone of VC Corner Cemetery. It was a long process; the files varied in size and there was a constant element of anguish. The letters from home were heartbreaking, mothers and fathers seeking information, hoping against hope that there might be some encouraging news. Perhaps 'he' might be in a hospital, a prisoner of war. Others sought information, news, details about 'his' death. Some news, anything. The files also included accounts of death. Some of the information was blurred, some of it conflicting. Perhaps there was some deliberate misinformation to ease or veil the details of death.

There was one constant and specific archival note. Those who were recovered and buried by the Germans had an accompanying document. It stated the name and battalion of each soldier that they buried. The Germans had removed the ID discs of each soldier, collected the personal effects and returned the items to families back in Australia. A remarkable process. We now had them by name. There was no more guessing. The total of German documented burials equated almost exactly with the unaccounted for 'missing'.

There was never any secrecy about the research I undertook. I was ably assisted by a group who were collectively and affectionately dubbed 'Lambis' mob'. The founding members were Ward Selby and John Fielding. I met Ward and Jo Selby at VC Corner, at Fromelles, in 2002. Ward's grandfather, Norm, was a '19th of July man' who survived the tragic and ill-fated assault by two Companies of the 58th Battalion at 9 pm that evening. John Fielding, a high school Deputy Principal and an Army Reserve Lieutenant Colonel, had made contact after some press coverage of our efforts.

The team worked tirelessly to build a case for Canberra to investigate the fate of the 'missing' soldiers of Fromelles. There was active discouragement from Canberra, but we persisted.

I did not take the decision to go public with my suspicions about Pheasant Wood lightly. I was aware that it might raise renewed family hopes. But I was frustrated pursuing 'official' channels, so I went to the press and sought political pressure. It worked, and eventually I and other members of 'Lambis' mob' presented evidence to an expert panel in Canberra in 2005.

In July 2005, Peter Barton, an English author and historian was visiting Melbourne, and Ward and I introduced ourselves. Peter had extensive World War One battlefield experience and listened to our proposition. I forwarded him our research and kept him informed of developments. Peter offered to take the proposition to the British All Parliamentary War Graves and Battlefield Heritage Group, if I could provide a strong case.

Also around this time, I saw a TV programme, *Two Men In A Trench*. Through the show's producers I found Tony Pollard, one of the show's presenters. I rang, then emailed him, made my introduction and sent him some background information. Would he be interested in investigating the proposal?

Resistance to the idea of an undiscovered burial site at Pheasant Wood centred around the incredulity that such a large site had not been discovered and recovered by the Graves Registration Unit (GRU) which had been established after the War. The GRU had scoured the battlefields seeking the 'missing'. When a body was recovered, they documented its point of recovery and where it was reburied.

When I learned about the existence of these records in mid 2006, I rang London. I introduced myself to an archivist at the Imperial War Museum, gave him the map reference for Pheasant Wood and said that I would ring back in two hours. When I did, I was informed that there was a 'nil' return in the recovery team's records for Pheasant Wood: the team had looked for the site in

1920, but found nothing because it was overgrown. This provided a strong, if circumstantial, piece of evidence that Pheasant Wood could be an undiscovered burial ground.

We had put forward a strong case to the panel in Canberra and, in 2007, the Glasgow University Archaeological Research Division (GUARD) was finally sent to Pheasant Wood to investigate. I had full confidence in Tony Pollard, who was also team leader at GUARD, and his team. They had official approval and, for what it was worth, they had my full confidence.

It was my choice to make the trip to Fromelles in 2007 for the investigation at Pheasant Wood; resolution was close and I felt compelled to be there. But I was in Fromelles for almost two weeks before I went down to Pheasant Wood to make my first ever visit.

I had walked past it many, many times, I felt familiar with the ground. The site was overgrown, the grass was almost knee high. Undulations in the growth were evident; the light and breeze indicated a rise and fall in the ground. In my strictly amateur way, I had convinced myself that this was a strong indication that it was still a burial ground. I wasn't sure how I'd feel walking the ground; there was some apprehension, nervousness and, ultimately, some comfort. I felt that I was in good company. I felt, sensed, if you like, that the boys were still there.

The day before my visit to Pheasant Wood, I had made my way to Rue Petillon Cemetery. As I picked my way through the headstones, I paused and, looking across, saw that I was beside Reverend Maxted who had been the padre to the 54th Battalion. It was a warm day and I had walked a fair distance. I lay down for a rest. I fancy that I may have gone into a conversational mode. I fancy that I may have informed the Reverend about Pheasant Wood. I fancy that I may have sought a blessing for the work to be done and the possible outcome. It was the first of many ongoing visits.

The team from GUARD used a variety of technology to determine whether the site was of interest. Somehow, the processes they used, the exacting science, the clever machinery, the shovelling, the stretching of the hamstrings, the repetition, the bagging of items, the flicking of mosquitoes, the toil, made a romantic amalgam. I never knew that archaeology could be so enervating.

The team were there for three weeks. Towards the end they did a surface scan of the site using a metal detector. They plotted every bullet, every shrapnel ball, every item found. This process indicated that there was a general and consistent scatter pattern across the site. The ground had not been disturbed.

Among the items recovered from the site was a medallion with the words 'Shire of Alberton' engraved on it. Each departing soldier from that district had been given a medallion and a prayer book; three soldiers from the district were killed that night.

The recovered medallion belonged to Private Harry Willis, the only one whose body was recovered by the Germans and buried at Pheasant Wood. His is not among the etched names on the VC Corner Cemetery Honour Roll; he is among those listed at Villers-Bretonneux. It was a remarkable find, an absolutely crucial link.

A further significance of the find was that Private Harry Willis was the great uncle of one of the 'mob' who had been working with me since 2006, Tim Whitford. The Willis family came from the Yarram district in Gippsland, Victoria. Harry was one of fourteen children and had three brothers who had already volunteered. He received a white feather in the mail, forged his mother's signature and followed his brothers.

Tim had seen the *60 Minutes* story about the 'missing' of Fromelles, which went to air on 18 July 2006. He had found my number and called me that night and I had invited him to our annual Fromelles service at the Shrine the following day. We kept in regular touch with each other and he also came to several planning meetings with Ward and me. Tim had served in the Army for fourteen years and his Uncle Harry had been a constant thought. Tim's grandmother had pleaded with him not to become a soldier. When the medallion was found, I rang and emailed Tim: 'Please call'.

On the last day of the preliminary investigation, the Mayor came down to the site. He pulled some plastic cups, bottles of wine and apple juice from his backpack. We toasted and thanked one another; speeches were made. I had asked Tony Pollard if he could give me a 'nudge, nudge, wink, wink' before I got on the plane home, to give me some idea as to the status of the ground. He called me aside and suggested that the ground was of interest.

I made my way to VC Corner Cemetery. I had made the walk many, many other times. This time at VC Corner was especially significant. I said hello to the 'boys' (I can't help it, every time I walk into VC Corner, I greet the 'boys') and sat at the Cross of Sacrifice, facing the etched names. I confess to an emotional release.

After the investigative dig in 2007, a decision was made to return to Pheasant Wood to determine whether it was still a burial site.

(Tony Pollard and his GUARD team would later do a second dig in late May 2008.)

I returned to France for the dig. On the first day I was taken onto the site to view the work. The topsoil had been removed and the edges of the pit had been exposed. There was a distinct variation in the colour of the clay. The edges of the pit were clearly defined, there was an almost pencil line straightness to the edges. The pits had not been disturbed, they were intact.

Late on the second day of the dig, journalist Paola Totaro was convinced that something had been found. Paola prowled and paced the fenced-off press and visitor's tent area, looking across at the increased activity around pit five. Phone calls were being made, discussions were being had. Extended viewing activity and a distinct lack of eye contact as the site was being closed down for the evening led her to believe that they had found remains.

When I arrived at the site on Wednesday morning, the third day of the dig, I was told that remains had been found. However, the 'official' announcement back home had to be made. When the team arrived, I received absolute confirmation. Tony Pollard greeted me with 'give me a hug big fella' (or words to that effect). It was a nice moment.

There was a lot of activity at the site. The police arrived to view the remains and to determine that work could proceed. Much to the consternation of the Mayor, one of the local's dogs also followed them in. There was a certain vigour and excitement and a lot of press activity. I had hoped and suggested that when remains were found that the ground would be consecrated and the work blessed by a military chaplain and local priest but that would come later.

The GUARD team had been asked to determine the status of the site and now they were to determine the state of the remains. Careful digging with trowels was the next step, as the topsoil needed to be removed from the other pits.

I saw the first remains uncovered. An arm emerged from the clay. His hand had been blown off. The human tragedy and the nature of the work to follow became more tangible. I was to make another visit to Rev. Maxted at Rue Pettilon Cemetery.

Pheasant Wood will be recovered. The soldiers buried there will be given the dignity of individual reburial. Hopefully, they will also be given back their identities, perhaps through being procedurally tested for DNA.

In time, I believe it will be revealed that the 'missing' are not all at Pheasant Wood; I contend that there are other burial sites in the Fromelles area. Given the results of Peter Barton's research in Geneva in the archives of the Red Cross, the resolve of authorities and the precedents established at Pheasant Wood will be tested.

I believe that our war dead should be recovered. Cost and inconvenience should not allow the 'missing' to be left in anonymous ground. The locals have demonstrated their awareness of the sacrifices of the 'missing' of Pheasant Wood and we can rest assured that the bodies will lie together forever in dignified burial in the care and custody of a village that will look after them. The new Pheasant Wood Cemetery at Fromelles will become a site of pilgrimage as will other sites across France and Belgium, when and if they are discovered.

Robin and I have had a long association. We have collaborated and shared our thoughts, applying them to a variety of commemorative work. I confess my fondness for Robin and have welcomed his counsel. Certainly I have needed it.

It is largely because of the work of Robin Corfield, Fromelles is no longer the 'Forgotten Front'. While the awareness of the 'missing' is ongoing and the process of recording and commemorating continues, I acknowledge Robin as the instigator.

As highly as I recommend this book, I recommend its author even more so. Thank you, Robin.

Hindsight

'A thing I remember about Anzac Day was after the service the men would put their arms around each other, and cry.'
—Manning Clark

When it became apparent that such a highly respected publisher as MUP was interested in doing a reprint of a book that had been privately published nine years earlier, one wondered. Some looking back was unavoidable.

An application to the Australian War Memorial in 1994 for a grant was successful on the basis that somebody there liked *Hold hard, cobbers*. So I had enough to get to France and back. The rest was down to me.

The first edition was subtitled 'An Inquiry'. The scope and size of it was dictated only by what was found. It remains so, and more material from the last ten years has been added, and that in connection with the 'Missing at Fromelles' is of particular importance. This grew from the interest in Fromelles that Lambis Englezos and I shared from our first meeting in 1991, and with the exhumation and reburial of the Missing set down for 2009–2010, it is very relevant. As Lambis has said, '*Robin planted the flag and I picked it up and ran with it.*' He found the 'Missing at Fromelles'. However it was Lambis's 'gut feeling' that was the main accelerant that the fire extinguishers in Canberra and elsewhere could not subdue. This is good news for all 'amateur historians': a label that Lambis and I proudly and joyfully wear.

There are other flags planted in this book that need runners —the Missing Papers of Fromelles, the 21st July casualties, and why and by whom, mention of Fromelles was so effectively suppressed in the inter-war years.

Hindsight, that great and necessary solace for the human spirit, and perhaps the one benefit of getting old, tells me that the subtitle of the original edition of this book *The Battle of Fromelles 19/20 July 1916* should have been *The Tragedy of Fromelles 1916–1998*. This would make it necessary to subtitle this edition *'updated to 2009'*. Why so the reader is entitled to ask, the Great War from which there are but one or two survivors is long gone. But tragedies unlike battles have no end: the trauma endures, that is the great burden of memory. A compelling example of this is given in the margin *Four generations of my family*. As the concerned mother confessed to me, '... *at least I will know where it all started*'. Reviewing the past, as somebody said, is the only way to cope with the future.

Back in 1920, on the anniversary of the battle, the family of Andrew Murray Perry 2095, 32nd Bn, placed an 'In memoriam' notice in *The Register* in Adelaide:

FOUR GENERATIONS OF MY FAMILY

It is important to record this note about 'The Battle of Fromelles' but in a real sense it belongs to every battle, of every war—civil or otherwise, every killing. An inquirer phoned this writer asking if she could purchase a copy of *Don't forget me, cobber*. After taking her address and details I enquired what was her interest. Without pause and solemnly she answered '*The battle of Fromelles has ruined four generations of my family*'. I asked how.

Her husband's grandfather was in the battle of Fromelles and so badly wounded that he was returned to Australia, and lived in Adelaide. Fromelles had been his only battle. The pain, trauma and frustration of being a semi-invalid drove him to drink. He married and added violence to his behaviour beating up and abusing his wife and their son. When the son turned 16, the earliest age he could leave home, he fled to Sydney to make a life. He eventually married and had a son. But his father's behaviour and terrible abuse took its toll—he killed himself. His son was the husband of the woman on the phone. I did not need to ask her how all that had gone before affected her, but I asked about the fourth generation. '*My children found it difficult to cope when they learnt of their terrible great grandfather, the suicide of their grandfather, and their father's state of mind ... that makes the four generations.*' The tone of this last confession left me in no doubt about the severity of her problem with her children. She concluded, '*When I've got your book at least I will know where it all started*'.

THE MISSING INTELLIGENCE SUMMARIES AND MUCH ELSE
In the surviving files of 5th Division the daily (6 am to 6 am) Intelligence Summaries begin with No. 22 covering 31 July/1 August. The files are complete from 22 onwards and the Summaries prior—taking records back to 10/11 July—are all missing. These two or three page reports give a valuable amount of detail on enemy operations—machine guns, artillery, front and support lines, patrols, shelling, condition of the ground, signalling, aircraft, balloons, ruses and intelligence matters. The missing Summaries would have revealed what 5th Division knew about the enemy some nine days before the battle and what went on the twelve days after.

The absence of all the July summaries is difficult to explain. Certainly the ones prior to the battle may have been passed to the British or the Anzac Corps for information, but when nothing happened after the battle, why pass to anybody else the summaries for the rest of July? Did they reflect badly on the management of the Division? Were there items in those summaries which if they had been seen by more people would have reduced the losses and/or the extent of the disaster? Surely if they reflected well on the conduct of Divisional HQ they would be preserved. But then they are not the only items missing for this period.

Except for McCay's and the Artillery, Engineers and Medical Reports and some tables of Divisional strength, and the typed up incoming and outgoing messages during the battle, there are no pieces of paper referring to the battle and afterwards in the file. The War Diaries record nothing concerning the enemy except the attempted truce on 20 July, and that a bombardment on 29 July set Fleurbaix church on fire. The impression is that after Wagstaff filed a message timed 5 am on 20 July passing on the instructions for withdrawal nothing happened until 6 am on 31 July.

> Perry. In loving memory of our dear brother, Private A M Perry of Naracoorte, killed at Fleurbaix, on 19 July 1916.
> *'Some day we will understand'.*

Thanks to the German records for the Missing found by Lambis, we now know that in one of the great graves behind the Pheasant Wood, is Andrew Perry of Naracoorte.

With the finding of the Missing, we understand much much more. We know how careful the German victors were in what must have been a terrible task of carrying hundreds of bodies, terribly broken, stinking and fly-blown, and laying them in pits in as good order as they could manage. One has to ask oneself, would I have done that well? Would I? Could I have collected their possessions, taken off their identity discs and parcelled them up for the Red Cross? The reality is that if those Germans had not done that work, we would not know about those in the pits behind the Pheasant Wood. The records that were made then have half-solved another mystery. The margin note 'Cover up?' draws attention to a group of missing whose given date of death was wrong, and they were left off the VC Corner Memorial. One of these men—Pte H V Willis 983 31st Bn—is among the Missing buried behind the Pheasant Wood. His story—see page 443—is rather special for this reason.

Now for another part of the tragedy of Fromelles: '*The Missing Papers*' that would tell us exactly what went on. The item in the margin *The Missing Intelligence* gave my concerns in 2000, and which remain. The greatest '*need to know*' is what happened to so much of HQ's paperwork from the battle, especially the Daily Intelligence Reports. Were they among the papers that McCay, the commander of the 5th Australian Division, burned in his back garden after he had been all but 'pardoned' in C E W Bean's Official History of the War? Is there another set somewhere? Perhaps, hopefully misfiled so they were not collected up; or perhaps in some British file, files that were locked up for 50 years and thus out of reach. These Reports would tell us what was known about the German defences. They would reveal how it all was up to the 18th of July ... and what happened on the 19th/20th and the rest of July. It is certain that in the relatively quiet days after the battle, the activities of the Germans clearing their own and our dead would have been recorded. If, as was reported in August, the arrival of timber and gangs of workers to repair the German positions were seen, it is most unlikely that the light railway freight carriers loaded with dead were not seen in July. And prior to the catastrophe, how could they have missed the machine gun posts well out in front of the Sugarloaf? Such evidence, if shared with Elliott, would not have allowed him to tell his men, '*... you won't find a German in these trenches when you get there.*' Instead his men walked straight into those German machine guns. Elliott made his share of mistakes and, sad to say, some of his judgements at Fromelles were very flawed, by lying he never did.

Who was it in the final analysis that judged the drainage channels behind the German lines to be trenches? It does not hold up that by mid 1916 'reading' aerial photographs was so amateurish, when taking them was so professional and clearly judged to be important.

Then there is knowledge from at least 7 July that the Germans could listen into the Allied phones and telegraphs, surely ending all the estaminet gossip about spies. One supposes we could listen into their phones and that the battle strategy would reflect the knowledge so gained. But we get no hint of any adjustment to the tactics at any time. And from the prisoners taken by the Germans, we get a distinct feeling of disillusion with their Higher Authorities.

Hindsight also demands that one reviews one's own work. I have corrected names, places, dates and spelling - there were not a lot, and some probably still survive. But more important is correcting mistakes, omissions and wrong judgements. Boxed panels titled 'Hindsight' give revised interpretations or corrections as need be. However, I have to confess that after ten years, nothing I have read causes me to revise my opinion of McCay. He stays where I put him then, in the dock awaiting trial! A searching study of Brudenell White's conduct would, I am sure, produce a case for him to answer. Research I have done since has caused me to think more deeply about Elliott, a complex character who in an age when '*real men did not cry*', wept openly in view of his men, and none thought any less of him for it.

Robin Corfield

COVER UP?
THE 21st JULY CASUALTIES

One of the reasons this inquiry concerns itself with lists of dead, prisoners and unit strengths is to detect cover-ups or maladministration. For instance in the Roll of Honour of 31st Bn, 40 men (but no officers) are shown as killed in action, 21 July. The Military Orders after the battle only listed 19 of these men, all shown as KIA on 21 July (see page 433). We know via Tivey's message to Wagstaff that the 31st (and 32nd) were back in their lines around 5 am on 20 July. According to the Battalion War Diary the Bn then went out of the line to billets in Fleurbaix. There is no mention anywhere of any action of any size on the 21st. To produce 40 dead it would have also produced at least 80 wounded, that is casualties of the order of the raid on 58th Bn on 15 July, an event which both sides regarded as very noteworthy.

Of the 40 killed on 21 July, 17 are in marked graves, 13 of these are in the early casualty lists. The rest—23 have no grave (6 of these were in the early lists) and are noted on the Villers-Bretonneux Memorial.

Unless there was some disaster on 21 July that has been effectively concealed, these men must have died in the battle of 19/20, and therefore their names should be on the VC Corner Memorial, taking its total into the 1300s, as against 1299. Could that be the reason? Or were they accidentally left off some list and the only way of squaring the books was to change the date of death? Or did something happen in Fleurbaix on 21 July 1916? Either way the missing of the 31st Bn have been deprived of their proper memorial—on the screen wall at VC Corner.

AND SOME 18 JULY DEATHS

Another group of unexplained casualties is eight men of 13th Bde AFA listed as killed in action on 18 July, when in fact there was no action. Perhaps a gun or ammunition dump blew up. Whatever the cause, they are listed in the Rolls of Honour on page 449.

PART OF THE WESTERN FRONT DECEMBER 1914

The thick black line shows a small part of the Western Front, so called because the Germans also had an Eastern Front—with Russia—and the section shown here is largely under British control: the Belgians holding the section from Ypres north to the coast, and the French from Albert to Switzerland.

The dot-dash line shows the Belgian–French border dividing the area known as Flanders, an ethnic region covering western Belgium, together with adjoining sections of France and Holland predating the creation of Belgium in 1830 as an independent nation; the language spoken being Dutch or Flemish. As a result of the war, Flanders took on an identity of its own. It would be the wild red poppy so familiar in Flanders' fields that would become the most evocative and lasting symbol of the Great War, assisted greatly of course by the lines of the Canadian medical officer, Colonel John McCrae:

In Flanders' fields the poppies blow
Between the crosses, row on row,
That mark our place: and in the sky
The larks, still bravely singing, fly,
Scarce heard amid the guns below.

We are the Dead. Short days ago
We lived, felt dawn, saw sunset glow,
Loved and were loved, and now we lie
In Flanders' fields.

Take up our quarrel with the foe;
To you from failing hands we throw
The torch: be yours to hold it high.
If ye break faith with us who die
We shall not sleep, though poppies grow
In Flanders' fields.

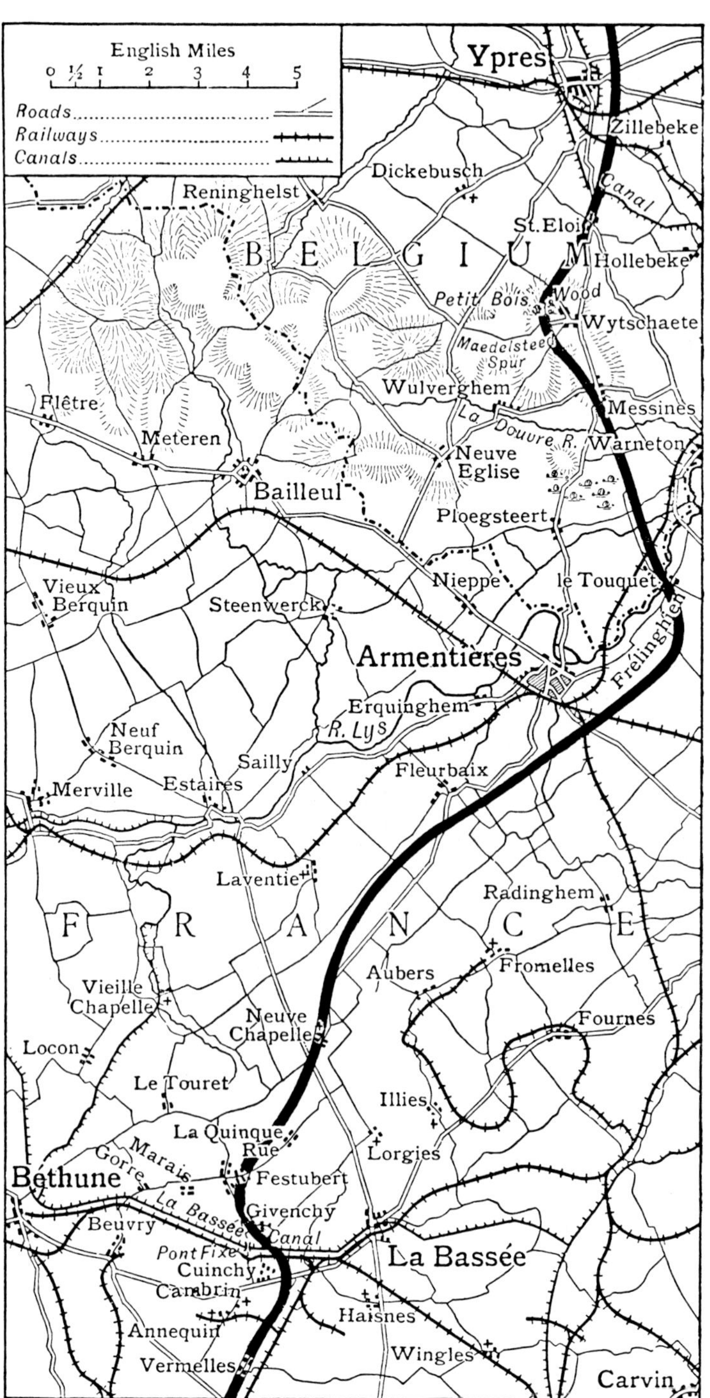

1

To reason why

Theirs not to make reply,
Theirs not to reason why,
Theirs but to do and die

— Alfred, Lord Tennyson in
The Charge of the Light Brigade

Very, very few of the hundreds of memorials in Australian cities and towns dedicated to the dead of the Great War carry the name—Fromelles, pronounced 'Fro-mell'. Not one of the twelve battalions that fought there has it as a battle honour. All because, it was said, Fromelles was not a victory. But that criteria never applied to Gallipoli which is on just about every memorial and is a battle honour for numerous battalions, and certainly was no victory. As a matter of comparison, the Australian casualties in the Anzac campaign over nine months totalled 26,094 and the loss at Fromelles over one night was 5533.

For the reader unfamiliar with the importance, or even the existence of the Battle of Fromelles on 19/20 July 1916, perhaps a few paragraphs of background would be useful.

When the German army invaded Belgium and France in August 1914 it moved with great speed and was by the end of September, to generalise, in possession of Amiens, within sight of Paris but held well in front of Ypres by the Belgians and the British and at Verdun by the French. Then followed the unforgiving Battle of the Marne which with pressures all along the Western Front, as it became known, caused the Germans to fall back. They left Amiens and Albert, retreated beyond Soissons and Reims and although by this time they occupied most of Belgium, Ypres remained in Allied hands but the Germans held Lille. Fromelles was only 17 miles (27 kms) south of Ypres and 10 miles (16 kms) west of Lille, and so was in an area of real importance to the Germans. Between the early fighting in 1914–15 and July 1916 they fortified their line extensively, regarding the defence of Lille as of paramount importance. Curiously the British called this 'a nursery sector' and so used it to introduce new divisions to the tests and trials of the Western Front. But it was not always so.

The British had, since late 1914, been heavily involved with the Germans in the area of Fromelles—from Armentières in the north, to Bethune—La Bassée in the south. Throughout 1915 numerous British and Indian regiments had been all but

THE REMOVED BATTLE OF FROMELLES

Someone however planned a sharp attack on Lille. It was really the predecessor of the battle of Neuve Chapelle and should be called perhaps the battle of Fromelles. But it was completely abortive and the details were removed from public news—the first and last night attack of its kind. The date was exactly one week before Christmas (1914), and looking at that narrow strip of No-Man's Land in which the attack spent itself, one realises afresh how ineffectual were all these little battles of the war. Men died: that was all their effect.

The attack was timed to start at six in the evening ... The night was black as pitch and full of the unknown. It was not long before the enemy began to fire, and men dropped rapidly ... the affair lasted all night long, and scarcely anyone knew where anyone else was. But back and forth they ranged in that fatal width of eighty yards of No-Man's Land, and in one battalion alone a hundred and eighty men were lost ... Lille was safe as ever. Little Fromelles, just behind the enemy lines, was safe as Lille. The dead lay in front of the German trenches, and the foe carried some of them to the graveyard at Fromelles and buried them. But seven days later, on the Christmas Day armistice, many still lay green on the green earth where they had fallen.

—Stephen Graham
The Challenge of the Dead (1921)

General Sir Charles C Monro, 1915.

LACKED THE MORAL COURAGE
But before their (ANZAC Corps) translation from the Flanders front, 5th Australian Division was committed with the British 61st in a venture ill-devised by Haig to tap the enemy front to see whether, owing to the reinforcement demands on Prince Rupprecht's army for the Somme, it was hollow. General Sir Charles Monro believed that the best way to do this was a full frontal attack in full daylight with a singular lack of co-ordination between either of the attacking infantry forces or their artillery. He had the opportunity, as the weather was bad, to cancel the operation—Haig left the decision in his hands. But he lacked the moral courage to do so. Australian and English battalions advanced to their doom across the waterlogged ground.

—A H Farrar-Hockley
The Somme (1964)

AN IMPERIAL WAR
No attempt has been made in this work to change Imperial measurements to metric because it would involve altering letters, diaries and everything else to conform. As it was an Imperial war, the Australian Imperial Force used miles, yards, feet and inches. The things it carried or fired were mostly weighed in tons, cwts, pounds or ounces. The AIF was paid in pounds, shillings and pence and for the most part kept its timekeeping to AM and PM.

annihilated along this line, and as a guide to the scale of the fighting some 43 VCs were awarded in the area during this period (see pages 360–61). The British leader was Lieut General Sir Richard C B Haking commanding the XI Corps which at July 1916 was made up of the 61st British Division and the 5th Australian Division, together with Artillery and other units.

The 61st Division (South Midlands Territorial) had been brought together in September 1915 and was trained through the winter as much of the weather, shortage of equipment and absence of experienced officers would allow. The GOC was Major General C J Mackenzie who had wide experience in the Empire, and came from a strong military family. He retained command of the 61st until 1918. Although it has often been stated that the 61st was seriously under strength, when it landed in France in the last week of May it was at full strength. The fact that two months later it went into action at little over half that strength is one of the conundrums of this story. With 1547 casualties out of an assaulting force of around 2400 the 61st Division suffered heavily, indeed very heavily.

The Battle of Fromelles was the first major conflict in Western Europe for the Australian Imperial Force (AIF). The 5th Australian Division under the command of Major General the Hon. J W McCay (rhymes with 'sky') had been formed in Egypt five months earlier and consisted of seasoned survivors of Gallipoli and fresh reinforcements every one, in the Australian tradition, a volunteer. The Division arrived in France at the end of June and within three weeks half of that Division were casualties: 1917 dead, 3146 wounded and 470 taken prisoner. And almost all of that happened between 6 pm on 19 July and 9 am on 20 July. These losses were the highest for one Australian Division in one day in the whole war, the 60th Bn's losses the highest for any Australian battalion in a single action.

This combined force on a front of 4300 yards (3930 metres) measured down the centre of No-Man's Land, but 4725 yards (4320 metres) of actual front line, was facing the 6th Bavarian Reserve Division, a strong, well-disciplined and experienced German army group which knew the area very well, they had been there for over a year, and built a formidable line of desence. When the Australians and British had broken through the German frontline made accessible by a massive bombardment that would cut the wire entanglements, and reduce the German parapets, they would push on to a second and third line of trenches, and there await further orders. However the artillery did much damage to the Australian trenches as well as to those of the enemy, the wire was only cut in a few places and there was no third line of trenches anyway. What had been seen on the aerial photographs were just deserted ditches. As it turned out, two of the three Australian brigades did make it across the German line and found themselves in a completely undefendable position. The fact that McCay, '*through inexperience*', to use the Official Historian's words, left nobody to garrison the front line they had smashed through was the Australians' undoing.

Haking had been asked by his superiors '*to put forward a scheme*' which would persuade the Germans that a large offensive was a real possibility and therefore they should not denude their forces around Lille and nearby in order to reinforce their army in the Battle of the Somme which had begun on 1 July. Haking had in May 1915 commanded 1st Division (part of I Corps under Lieut General Sir Charles C Monro) in an assault against Aubers Ridge, coming around the south of Neuve Chapelle, thus some five miles SW of Fromelles. In this same attempt it was the 8th Division (Major General F J Davies) from IV Corps commanded by Lieut General Sir Henry S Rawlinson that was the assaulting force at Fromelles. This is only important in that it reveals, contrary to popular opinion, Haking was not involved in the assault against Fromelles in May 1915, and in fact was in a different army. However the heavy defeat of the whole British line, for reasons briefly described later, might well explain the fixation that Haking was said to have about Aubers Ridge. And perhaps the possibility of doing it another way a year later was more likely to succeed, so he suggested it again, and now from the much stronger position he now had, as Corps Commander. Haking, however, was told that an attack of that magnitude was not contemplated, instead there would be a preliminary bombardment which should '*give the impression of an impending offensive operation on a large scale*', and in fact be limited to an infantry attack on the German front line. It should be noted that:

> the scene of operations partly coincided with that of the Battle of Aubers Ridge fought in May 1915: indeed the 8th Division had attacked over the same ground as the 5th Australian Division was about to do, and against the same opponents.

When one notes Haking's original intention, it is clear that the attack now planned had no real destination so to speak. Earlier at Neuve Chapelle the battle was to take the town, but this attack was not about taking anywhere. When the men got over the German front line, what were they to do? 'Walk to Berlin?', as one veteran of the battle put it over seventy years later.

THE INDIAN CONTINGENT

From mid-September 1914 Indian troops were beginning to arrive at Marseilles, and from 19 October Indian regiments were sent into the Neuve Chapelle area, in the line west of that town and east of Estaires. On 28 October they went into battle, the first time Indian troops had fought in Europe. Wrote *The Times: They were required to take part in an offensive against a strong position held by a force of the regular army of the greatest military power in Europe. They responded splendidly. The objective was the village of Neuve Chapelle, a position of great tactical importance. Our trenches here presented something of a salient and could be enfiladed ... It was necessary to take the village and straighten up the line.*

Then on 31 October, 1 and 2 November, the German artillery and infantry broke the attack with huge casualties on both sides. Within a week all the Indian hospitals in France were full. Although rather coy about actual numbers *The Times* took pride in describing the hospital ships taking the Indians from Boulogne to England: *The Indian contingent consisted of four ships of the Castle Line and two of the Peninsular and Oriental, vessels averaging some 8000 tons, with provision for from 300 to 500 wounded.* The Indian wounded went to hospitals at Brighton and in the New Forest, *The original plan of subsidiary hospitals at Marseilles and Alexandria was wisely abandoned, and the English people were given the opportunity of showing in a more practical form their appreciation of the sepoys' loyal services.*

Near Festubert another battle began in the last week of November when the Germans attempted to change the *status quo*. This time they lost to the Indians.

CAPTAIN A D ELLIS (1885–1963)
Alexander Donaldson Ellis was born 5 September 1885 at Oxley, Victoria, and educated at Queen's College, Maryborough and University of Melbourne. He was Inter-varsity sprint champion 1910–14 and a teacher at University High School 1914–15, enlisting 3 April 1915 in 31st Bn, transferring to 29th Bn 6 June in Egypt. Commissioned 6 July in France, and promoted to Capt., 31 March 1917. On 7 November he was MID and received the MC 5 March 1918. Ellis married Dymphna Kirkcaidie 16 August 1918 and returned to Australia December 1919. He read Law at the University of Melbourne adding to his BA, an LLB and later in life a DLitt. He was admitted to the Bar in 1922.

This timetable indicates Ellis wrote *The Story of the Fifth Australian Division* in England, and perhaps was assembling material while still on service in France. He must have worked closely with the staff of Australian War Records then preparing material for shipment to Australia. To put together in well under a year, a 200,000-word highly detailed record plus Rolls of Honour and Decorations of a whole division, one fifth of the AIF, was a very remarkable achievement. Ellis acknowledged the assistance of Lieut T E Stapleton, 29th Bn, for doing the Rolls and other appendices, and [continued opposite]

This is the nub of the events at Fromelles. Given that it was a feint designed to deceive the Germans, the moment it failed or was called off exposed the ruse. Sending men to their death in an effort to capture some village or hill was one thing, but sending them to certain annihilation in some charade about fooling the enemy for an afternoon was something else. The difference was well understood by Mackenzie who held back most of his men from the senseless sacrifice, but not understood at all by McCay, who sent every available man into the line. Mackenzie saw it for what it was, an attack without any enduring result. McCay, on the other hand, was fighting a battle which would have some definite outcome.

Haking's position is clear: he was not allowed to do what he wanted to do, he was stuck with two inexperienced divisions away from the mainstream of the war, and his earlier failures could not be redeemed here at Fromelles whatever happened. Looking at him in hindsight it is clear that in any book of Haking's life, '*the subsidiary attack at Fromelles*', as the British Official Historian called it, may not even receive a mention. After all it took up barely two weeks of his 83 years.

The horrendous slaughter of the Australians at Pozières started a few days later and the disaster at Fromelles was effectively lost to public view. The casualty lists in the newspapers gave a clear picture of the size of the losses, but at this time the papers stopped putting totals on the lists. The authorities and newspapers never went beyond such words as '*heavy*', '*severe*', '*significant*' to describe the casualties. On 12 August when questioned about the rumours of heavy casualties, the Minister for Defence, G F Pearce, said they were '*quite unfounded*'. This, some believe, had to do with the forthcoming referendum on conscription announced in August and held in October, and which was the very special project of the Minister for Defence.

It was not until 1920, when Pearce was no longer in a position to control all the information, that questions about Fromelles first surfaced, partly due to next of kin trying to find out about 1299 of the 1917 dead of whom no identifiable trace was found, and as a consequence had no grave. And at that point, no memorial.

When the first account of the Battle of Fromelles (sometimes called the Battle of Fleurbaix by diggers remembering the town they knew, rather than the town they never reached) was published in early 1920 in *The Story of the Fifth Australian Division*, the author Capt. A D Ellis, an officer in

29th Bn, provided the first public viewing of the other major loss at Fromelles: the loss of trust between the Australians and the British. He began his chapter quoting the British Official Communique of 20 July:

> Yesterday evening, south of Armentières, we carried out some important raids on a front of two miles in which Australian troops took part. About 140 German prisoners were captured.

Then he quoted in contrast the German Official Communiques, first of 20 July:

> Considerable British forces attacked our positions north and west of Fromelles. They were repulsed and wherever they succeeded in penetrating our trenches they were ejected by counter-attacks, in which we captured over 300 prisoners, among them being some officers.

Then the German Official Communique of 21 July:

> The English attack in the region of Fromelles on Wednesday was carried out, as we have ascertained by two strong Divisions. The brave Bavarian Division, against whose front the attack was made, counted on the ground in front of them more than 2000 enemy corpses. We have brought in so far 481 prisoners, including ten officers, together with 16 machine guns.

Ellis pointed out the strategic necessity to tell lies in communiques '*to preserve civilian morale during a period of tension*'. But now with the war won Ellis ventured this criticism:

> ... this official distortion of the facts of the Battle of Fromelles has resulted in a general and profound misconception of its purpose and gravity, and there are few incidents of the war which deserve a closer attention from the Australian public.

This writer first became interested in the Battle of Fromelles by way of the 15th Brigade consisting of the 57th, 58th, 59th and 60th Battalions all of whose origins were in Victoria, Australia. It seemed to be, at first examination, no more than the usual Great War disaster involving appalling casualties and achieving nothing. But research soon revealed all manner of stories related to Fromelles, almost a folklore about what happened existed among the survivors. For instance, virtually every Australian who fought in and thought about the battle, was sure the Germans had been supplied with intelligence by French spies. Many diggers '*recalled*' the summary execution of a French farmer or postman after the battle, and there was a story written by H Scanlon of 59th Bn, who was a casualty at Fromelles, about the girl friend of one of the diggers from a nearby farm being the source of the Germans' intelligence and that she and her 'father' were shot by the Australians for this

CAPTAIN A D ELLIS (contd)

'several officers' in the final revision of the manuscript. But Lieut General J J T Hobbs in his introduction only acknowledged Ellis.

There are several curious aspects to these events. Ellis ignores Bean in the author's note, yet quite how Ellis used the records that Bean was packing ready for the Official History, without Bean's help is difficult to imagine. Ellis, by the very nature of his book, obviously had access to all the 5th Division records and would have been the first to go through them. We know the records were in Australia by October 1919, meaning they left England around August. Thus Ellis must have finished his manuscript by then. This fits in with a schedule for setting, proofing, correcting, printing and the binding of a book of that size and complexity for a publication date of January 1920, in London. The book was on offer in Melbourne in April 1920, when Ellis presented to the Melbourne Public Library the original of Foch's message which is the Foreword in the book. The reviews of that time centred largely about 'The Battle of Fromelles' as Ellis called it, never considering that it could be known as anything else. The speed with which Ellis brought out his book and the detail it contains may well have had something to do with the lack of Battalion histories from 5th Division: only two—the 30th and 53rd were published between the wars.

When Bean brought out his Volume III which contains his story of Fromelles, Ellis' book was listed in the preface and Ellis in one footnote, and there does not seem to be any correspondence between the two in Bean's papers. Strange, when one considers the thoroughness of Ellis, and that Ellis lived in Melbourne and Bean in Canberra in the 1920s.

Ellis went on to become a Judge and moved to Sydney where he took up residence at 29 Suffolk Avenue, Collaroy Beach prior to 1950.

Bean, in 1956, moved to 24 Suffolk Avenue. Ellis died on 15 August 1963.

A MOST CURIOUS MILITARY DELUSION

The same vintage as Haking, Lieut General Sir Aylmer Haldane was also a corps commander. Judged by Denis Winter in *Haig's Command* to be a first-rate soldier, he knew about GHQ and its failings. Thus Tim Travers in *The Killing Ground* felt it worthwhile quoting him: *The fact is that GHQ is without a policy. The tail wags the dog, and Army Commanders who have their own advancement in sight, submit schemes, instead of GHQ ... so that what is ordered may fit in with the general policy. But there being no general policy except that of frittering away and trying to exhaust the enemy, GHQ seems to cling to any straw that offers.*

Travers then observed that indeed, senior commanders did seem to be given *carte blanche* to a large degree, for example, Haking's attack at Fromelles which was criticised in 1937 by Capt. Philip Landon on the staff of 182nd Infantry Brigade.

The weakness of GHQ lay in not seeing that a Corps Commander, left to himself, would also be tempted to win glory for his Corps by a spectacular success, and would be prodigal in using the Divisions that passed through his hands for this purpose.

That captain was, according to Travers, not only supporting Haldane's opinion of 1916 but also Liddell-Hart's verdict in his well reasoned book of 1930, *The Real War 1914–18*. There he makes an important comment on the 'planning' behind Fromelles, clearly the inevitable result of no policy and ambitious generals: *He [Haig] ordered, however, a number of local attacks in the north as a means to fix the enemy's attention and keep his reserves there, and away from the Somme. The method reveals a most curious military delusion, for while simulated preparations for a large-scale offensive would cause the enemy natural apprehension, the actual delivery of a narrow-fronted local attack would merely disclose the bluff. One consequence was the shattering of the 5th Australian Division in an absurdly advertised attack at Fromelles, an attack which was the final link of an almost incredibly muddled chain of causation.*

treachery after a pseudo courts-martial. All rather melodramatic. Whereas in the British sector the source of German intelligence about the forthcoming attack was said to have been from papers describing it as a feint, found on a captured or dead British officer. This was later stated in the history of the 17th Bavarian Reserve Infantry Regiment which faced the British. This could have happened during the disastrous raid by the 2/4th Berkshires on the night of 13/14 July when all the officers were either killed or wounded. In the British sector after the battle the British themselves became aware of a security breach. Referring to a 'find' in their trenches there is this entry in the 183rd British Brigade War Diary, where it had been for some 80 years, albeit 50 of those years in secret:

> 26 July. German listening apparatus discovered.

As early as 7 July 5th Australian Division HQ was aware that:

> captured documents and the examination of prisoners have shown beyond all possibility of doubt that information regarding our attack was obtained by the Germans through overhearing telephone messages. We have not yet got full details of the German system for overhearing but there is clear evidence that it is both accurate and extends over large areas. (per Major D M King)

And by August when it was too late, the capacity of the Germans' listening apparatus was at last assessed:

> It has been established that the enemy can intercept buzzer [morse] signals passing within two miles, and speech over telephone within 600 yards of their line.

From the great distance of eighty years since this small piece of intelligence was recorded, one has to wonder if perhaps this, not the 'fumbling' generals, was the true cause of the early disasters.

But at Fromelles, all these sources of information probably only confirmed what the Germans already knew by way of their well placed observation towers on the higher ground of Aubers Ridge, and balloons, let alone aircraft. No effort was made by either the British or Australians to conceal their arrival and the bringing forward of the equipment and supplies, partly, so it was said, to intimidate the Germans and partly because to make such arrangements secretly on flat farm land in less than 10 days would have been impossible anyway.

The 5th Division made Intelligence Summaries which were observations of the enemy's activities between 6 am on one day and 6 am on the next. Counting backwards from No. 22, the first of the surviving summaries, these reports should have begun on 10/11 July. All the July summaries are missing, and there is almost no piece of paper in the Divisional files relating to what happened after 5 am 20 July to 6 am 31 July (see margin: page xiv).

This is of small account compared to the different interpretations by the two divisional commanders of the original order. The British XI Corps Order No. 57 was received on 15 July by the 61st British Division:

> With the object of preventing the enemy withdrawing troops from our front, offensive operations are to be carried out by troops of XI Corps and 2nd A&NZC under the command of GOC XI Corps.
>
> The 61st Division and the 5th Australian Division will capture and hold the German front line and support trenches on the front opposite our trenches from the Fauquissart-Trivelet Road (M.24.b.8.8.) to south of Cordonnerie Farm (N.10.c.8.7.).
>
> The Division will attack with three Brigades in line, each Brigade with two assaulting Battalions and two Battalions in reserve: the two reserve Battalions in each Brigade are not to be employed for the attack without the permission of the Corps Commander.

Together with this came '*verbal instructions*' if we are to believe the General of the Division, Major General C J Mackenzie, when he wrote his Report after the battle on 22 July. Those instructions were:

> ... that it was not intended to employ more than 6 battalions for the assault in order that the Division might be kept intact for future operations.

From this order the British Army did not deviate, nor is there any evidence in the Unit War Diaries that they seriously sought to do so.

There is no evidence in the surviving papers that any such '*verbal instruction*' accompanied Corps Orders to the HQ of the 5th Australian Division. Instead we learn from McCay's own report of 25 July that the conference of 14 July (re: XI Corps Order No. 57) he clearly recorded the basic order: note that McCay claims the meeting was on the 14th, whilst Mackenzie remembers it as being on the 15th, but it appears they were briefed separately, curious in itself.

There is absolutely no mention about keeping the 5th Australian Division intact for future operations, and McCay's Report clearly states that the Corps Commander's permission is required before extra battalions are used. This is quite at variance with the secret 5th Australian Division Order No. 31 of 16 July which although over Major King's name had the authority of McCay. He had changed the emphasis thus:

Sir JAMES McCAY (1864–1930)
James Whiteside McCay was born 21 December 1864 at Ballynure, Antrim, Ireland and came to Australia the following year with his parents. Because McCay is a major part of this inquiry, these notes give but an outline of his early life, leaving detailed examination of his later career, character and reputation to the body of this book.

McCay's father was the Presbyterian Minister in Castlemaine, a keen student of theology and history and married to Esther who spoke seven languages fluently. James, the eldest of ten children, at the age of 12 won a scholarship to Scotch College in Melbourne and was Dux of the school in 1880. He entered the University of Melbourne and excelled in classics, logic and English. In 1883 he took up teaching and in 1885 bought Castlemaine Grammar School, where he taught, and employed his mother. In 1892 he went back to his degree studies concentrating on maths, then in 1897 he graduated in Law. A year earlier he had married a Catholic and they had two daughters: one became a nun, the other married George Reid, a Victorian politician. McCay began his legal practice in Castlemaine whilst still teaching and had received a commission in 4th Bn, Victorian Rifles. He also entered local politics and was elected to the council and after that to State Parliament. When McCay opposed the sending of a Victorian contingent to the [continued next page]

Sir JAMES McCAY (contd)
South African War he lost support, and was not re-elected. However he bounced back, supported Federation, and gained a seat in the first Federal Parliament—all by 1903, and he was not yet 40. As a Lieut Colonel since 1900, together with his interest in and knowledge of defence matters, he became Minister for Defence and so presided over the Council of Defence, but McCay's style was not suited to committees. In the 1906 election he was soundly defeated and became disillusioned with politics, but not sufficiently to stop him running for the Senate in 1910. However he already had a job, from 1907, as Commander of the new Australian Intelligence Corps. He was fired from this position in 1913 due to offending the Military Board and staff. After a trip to Europe he returned to the appointment as Censor on the outbreak of war. He had been succeeded as Minister for Defence, and later as Censor by George Pearce, and now Pearce appointed McCay to command 2nd Brigade, which he took to Gallipoli. McCay led them at the landing. In the opening hours he lost control of himself, drew his revolver against his men to enforce his will, and within two days half the brigade were casualties. Later, on 8 May, he led the survivors at Krithia, showing some personal bravery, some might say bravado, in an attack that was hopeless and badly planned. He was wounded and evacuated, but returned in June for a month when his leg snapped. He was invalided to Australia, his wife and father had died in his absence and within two weeks Pearce had appointed him Inspector General of the AIF with the rank of temporary Major General: one unkind critic drew attention to the fact that McCay had seen only five weeks of action.

Then going against the advice of General Birdwood, Pearce appointed McCay to command the new 5th Australian Division being formed in Egypt. McCay arrived there on 22 March 1916 and remained in command until 18 December when he *went to England under medical orders*, to quote the 5th Division War Diary. Later McCay was transferred to command the Australian base in the UK.

> ... the two reserve battalions in each brigade will be at the disposal of the Divisional Commander ... the two reserve battalions in each Brigade will not be used for assaulting the position without orders from GOC Division.

No mention of the Corps Commander!

It is almost certain from all the surviving papers that the Brigadiers and certainly the Lieut Colonels commanding British regiments were aware of the limits placed on the operation, the assaulting battalions were designated well before the battle began. To have not been aware of this at Brigade and Battalion level would have made it impossible to give meaningful orders.

So whilst no town was to be taken, and certainly no assault on Aubers Ridge contemplated, there was a clear understanding that ground was to be gained, and held until the order to withdraw was given. As an example, the 184th Bde:

> was ordered to attack, capture and hold with 2 Battalions (2 Bucks and 4 Royal Berks) the German Front and Support Lines from N14 a 6.2½ to N8 d 9½.1. Two companies of the 4 Oxfords were placed at the disposal of the Brigadier to occupy the Front Line in the event of all companies of the Assaulting Battalions being absorbed in the same: the 5 Glosters and remaining 2 Coys of 4 Oxfords were in Divisional Reserve.

And orders to other Brigades were the same. The infantry assault began at 6 pm and when, after 6.30 pm, messages came in that the attack had largely failed, Mackenzie arranged over the next hour to bring forward three reserve battalions, '*placed at disposal of Brigadiers, to support*' a second attack. This would follow the heavy bombardment then scheduled to go on to 9 pm. However according to Mackenzie:

> GOC XI Corps telephoned, about 8.20 pm, that the assault should not be renewed, and troops withdrawn from captured trenches after dark ... Artillery fire on both sides died down about 9.30 pm.

Having fluctuated between making a second assault, then withdrawing everybody, Haking was on the telephone to Mackenzie at 11.10 pm ordering a night attack by two companies from 184th Bde on the fortified German strong point—the Sugarloaf. But the 184th was so badly knocked about that it could not re-organise before dawn: so that attack was cancelled. At 12.10 am Haking was again on the phone to Mackenzie about another assault in the morning. Mackenzie went through the motions of ordering up new battalions and more ammunition, only to learn at 5 am, '*that the attack would not be resumed.*'

All of which could indicate that despite his alleged expectations Haking never really seriously considered a second attack either feasible or even necessary: but the pretence, not just for the sake of the Germans, had to be maintained, because that is what the whole action was—a pretence. Perhaps only Mackenzie took it for what it was.

McCay, however, was a very different person. At 10 pm Haking's Chief of Staff came to McCay's HQ to discuss events, and the decisions were, according the Australian Official Historian C E W Bean, that the British would attack again during the night and meanwhile the Australians were to hold and consolidate their gains. To do this McCay got authorisation to employ '*half of each of his last three reserve battalions*'. The files give no mention of this meeting, nor does McCay's Report. All we have is a handwritten message to his Brigades and Artillery by Major General McCay. Across the top of this document is written: '*This is to be kept carefully. J W McCay*', then underneath that '*Not to be destroyed by order of GOC*'. It is timed 11.25 pm (19 July) and was '*Read to BGGS XI Corps*'. The second sentence of that message is:

> Brigadiers are each authorised to use three battalions for fighting and a half battalion for carrying and digging, holding our old front system parapet and 300 yards line with remaining half battalion each.

How come Haking let McCay go ahead with such an incredibly reckless decision the result of which was to put the entire Australian Division at the front line, whereas only half of the British Division was so committed? Unless Haking had been misled he must have realised that McCay's requirement left the Australian front defended by six companies at most, and by the time the men went out there were less than that. So what was going on?

In the Report of the CO of the 2/4th Gloucestershire Regiment, the battalion which was part of the 183rd, it is clearly stated that they knew the assault on Sugarloaf by the 184th had failed after 15 minutes, that is at 6.15 pm 19 July. It is interesting that this Report, by Lieut Col Tupman, probably the first battalion report completed, was found carefully misfiled under September, and marked 'certified true copy 3.9.16'. This might have been because of Tupman's being evacuated to hospital on the afternoon of the 20th, and later to England, preparing and submitting his Report from there: but it was, in actual fact, dated 20 July.

At the 5th Australian Division HQ, what was the motivation behind McCay's message of 11.25 pm and its preservation? Many hours earlier, by his own account he had given permission for two extra companies to go forward in the 8th and 14th Brigade sectors. About these McCay wrote: '*Authority was*

CHARLES E W BEAN (1879-1968)
Charles Edwin Woodrow Bean was born 18 November 1879 at Bathurst, NSW, the first of three sons of Edwin and Lucy Bean, Edwin being headmaster of All Saints' College, Bathurst. In 1889 the family sailed to Britain. Charles went to Oxford in 1898 and took BA in 1902, BCL in 1904 and MA in 1905, returning to Australia the same year where he attempted a legal career without much success. In 1908, having decided to be a writer, he joined the *Sydney Morning Herald* and two years later was appointed the paper's London correspondent. Back in Australia in 1913, with two books published, he was in September 1914 elected by the Australian Journalists' Association to be the official correspondent with the AIF. The other major candidate was Keith Murdoch, who later took on the role of a roving reporter and whose influence behind the scenes was very considerable: first exposing the shambles of Gallipoli and later the inadequacies of sections of the High Command in France. He was, it would seem, the main opponent of McCay's appointment as GOC of the AIF in 1918, pushing for Monash whom Bean opposed in favour of White. That said, the two war correspondents in their different ways guided, for want of a better word, the sometimes lost politicians and always bewildered general public. Bean in his role as correspondent sent despatches that [continued next page]

CHARLES E W BEAN (contd)
tried, often desperately hard, to convey what really happened in defiance of the censor's blue pencil. Murdoch on the other hand dispensed his opinions and colourful observations with all the vigour of a man who was sure he had got it right. Anybody truly interested in the subject must reflect on what sort of history Murdoch would have written.

Pearce must have been very content with Bean's appointment because in 1909 Bean had published *With the flagship in the south*, as the result of being a correspondent on a Royal Navy ship. One of Bean's conclusions was that Australia should have its own navy, and this was an early project of Pearce's which he later achieved.

Bean went with the first contingent of the AIF, and he had the rank of Captain. From Cairo where he had access to all the characters and personalities of the ANZAC Corps, he went to Gallipoli on 25 April 1915, going ashore around 10 am. He remained on the peninsula until December, being Mentioned in Despatches for rescuing wounded men under fire, then wounded himself, but all the while taking copious notes and sending reports. He was alongside McCay in the trench at Krithia when the Lieut Col said, *I suppose I have to do the damned heroic act* and called upon the Australians to follow him. Bean's writing of this episode reveals his admiration for the thrusting upfront conduct of McCay in the field, but none the less he felt it necessary to say quite plainly that McCay's attitude towards his men was wrong.

As a result of the Gallipoli experience, Bean brought together *The Anzac Book* (1916). In France he moved about with the AIF, covering an extraordinary number of events from the front line, and by now was well known and hugely respected by the main characters in the AIF.

In 1917 he published *Letters from France*, which contained some of his despatches and was dedicated to the men who fought at Fromelles. It was, one might say, the first chapter of his history, as his selection, with the benefit of hindsight, reveals how his [continued opposite]

asked for and given'. This is not endorsed by the surviving papers.

The situation with the 15th Bde was very different. By 7 pm it was apparent they could go no further: according to McCay he learned at 7.30 pm that the British assault against Sugarloaf had failed, and another attack was scheduled for 9 pm. McCay wrote at the time:

> The 15th Brigade were asked to co-operate and authority was given to use half the 58th Battalion for this attack.

But, as we shall see, McCay two days earlier had already decided on a role for the 58th, before the battle began. In his own handwritten notes of 15 July McCay wrote '*Is the 58th still fit to be an assaulting Bn*', referring to the raid of that day, which decimated that Bn. Due to these losses and the heavy workload of the 57th and 58th Bns had had in establishing themselves, they were withdrawn from the line on the 17th and replaced by the 59th and 60th.

Mackenzie in his Report says that:

> GOC XI Corps telephoned, about 8.20 pm, that the assault should not be renewed.

It is difficult to believe that Haking did not also phone McCay at the same time. The 5th Divisional HQ was at Sailly (since 12 July) no more than 3 miles from the 15th Bde HQ and they had at least half an hour to get a message through to them. This would have saved what was left of the 58th and 59th Bns from annihilation. Wrote McCay afterwards:

> Meanwhile information had been received that the attack of the 61st Division would not take place, but the information could not reach the 58th in time.

The 15th Bde Report says the message reached them at 9.37 pm. Thus on the face of it the message had taken an hour and a quarter to go three miles by telegraph. The times on the vast majority of the messages indicate they were received between two and fifteen minutes of being initiated. C E W Bean presumably after investigation, put down the lateness of the message to the lack of realization by 5th Div HQ of its importance and being unaware that 15th Bde was tied into a 9 pm assault. But clearly McCay was aware of it as he had authorized the use of the 58th Bn for the assault. When Bean went to Fromelles on the afternoon of 20 July he noted in his diary that McCay came to Brig. General Elliott, GOC 15th Brigade, and was agitated about the 58th Bn. Wrote Bean at the time:

> McCay was also, I thought, anxious about an order which he and Elliott had given for 2 Coys of the 58th Bn to support between the 14th Bde and the British.

On the 17 July, the day the battered 58th were relieved, Elliott had received a message from McCay via Lieut Col Wagstaff of Divisional HQ:

> Divisional commander wishes me to say that if the 58th want to get even with the enemy that battalion might be left in the line and we will give them a chance.

The curious use of the first and third person to establish who is instructing whom is unique in all the messages of the period. Elliott's response came next day at 11.55 pm on 18 July:

> 58th Bn withdrawn to Billets in Sailly.

It could be argued that these messages from McCay about 58th Bn were no more than 'for discussion' between McCay and Elliott. As McCay was aware of the weakness of 58th Bn why push them forward? Why not use the much better-led and intact 57th? There is something not entirely straight-forward about the whole arrangement, which is hinted at in Bean's note. Then, on the 19 July, it was noted that at 4.45 pm, that '*58th Bn is in position 300 yards line except ½ company now in VC Avenue'*, and that they all reached the 300 yards line by 5 pm. The next note about the 58th Bn to McCay was timed at 9.10 pm '*58th Bn sent in to support attack ... Am co-operating with 61st Division at 9.00 pm.*'

Some fourteen years later Elliott explained the event thus:

> When the British reported they would renew their attack at 9 pm, and wanted help, I at once arranged with General McCay to take two companies of the 58th under a splendid Duntroon boy, Major Hutchinson ... Unfortunately the British troops could not start ... A message was sent to me to stop Hutchinson's attack, but this did not reach me till half an hour after he had gone forward ... Proper liaison measures should have prevented this catastrophe.

Whose liaison measures, one has to ask? Elliott's? McCay's? Haking's?

And there is one other curious episode about this last dash by the 58th. In the 5th Division file there is a sheet recommending Major A J S Hutchinson for the VC. It is clearly initiated, marked and signed by McCay. It is noted as being supported by Lieut H J Boyd and 2/Lieut L H Dardier, and there are details of Hutchinson's action, or rather, the manner of his death. Usually such recommendations, if they failed, or the man was

CHARLES E W BEAN (contd)

understanding had evolved: to use his own words *the only memorial which could be worthy of them (AIF) was the bare and uncoloured story of their part in the war.*

Following up this belief Bean organised the collection of material needed for the history, and was sharp enough at the time to arrange for copies to be made of all the British documents he needed before the British locked them away for 50 years or longer. The earnestness and devotion Bean showed got him the historian's job which he expected would take him four years: it took twenty-four years, plus the four collecting the experiences. The achievement provided Australia with a record that is commensurate with the sacrifice in as much as any chronicle can be, but also intimately related to the actual participants from privates to generals, in a way no other history ever attempted, and thus is unique.

At the beginning of his work Bean married Ethel Young, a nursing sister, in January 1921 and as his health was never robust, her care for him through the years of the history was most important. The first volume about Gallipoli was published in 1921, the second in 1924. He wrote four about the campaigns in France, jointly worked on the photograph volume with Gullett, and advised the writers of the other five volumes in the 12 volume set, the last of which, Volume VI, appeared in 1942. They sold well. For instance the photograph volume, which first came out in November 1923, ran through 15 reprints totalling 27,500 copies, and today they are very difficult to find.

Bean apparently declined a knighthood twice, avoided publicity, but associated himself with educational projects and helped set up the Commonwealth Archives, and was never too proud to admit he had changed his views on all sorts of issues and people. His stated recreation was walking.

At the age of 84, in 1964 C E W Bean was admitted to Concord Repatriation Hospital where he remained for four and a half years. He died there on 30 August 1968.

Sir GEORGE F PEARCE (1870–1952)
George Foster Pearce was born 14 January 1870 at Mt Barker, West Australia. He attended school until age 11 and then started work, first on farms, later as a carpenter. He married Eliza Maud Barrett in 1897 and they had four children. The 1891 Depression introduced him to further hard times, and until 1900 he was active in the Trade Union movement. Then Pearce entered politics: he was a Senator for 35 years and a Minister for 25 of those years. His career, in as far as it concerns this volume, covered the Federation, the establishment of the Australian Armed Forces, the First World War and the repatriation of the 1st AIF. As he entered politics on the left it is not surprising that he was against strong ties with the Empire and spoke against Australia assisting Britain in the South African War. Not from the left, but as one with Pearce on this was McCay, a 'protectionist', whereas Pearce was a 'free trader'. Pearce was within a couple of years to move to the right, change to being a protectionist and become extremely interested in defence matters, so that in 1906 he became Minister for Defence. He took over the portfolio from none other than McCay, who had lost his seat in Parliament, but who within a year had been appointed to establish the Australian Intelligence Corps.

Pearce's work in the next years included the establishment of the [continued opposite]

killed, were noted with a Mentioned in Despatches. Hutchinson received nothing at all.

After the battle, around noon on 20 July, there was an attempt at a truce so that the wounded might be rescued and the dead buried. It was initiated by an officer of the 104th Saxon Regiment, which had in the early morning come to assist the 21st Bavarian Regiment opposite 8th Australian Bde. When comparing the first edition of C E W Bean's *Official History of Australia in the War 1914–1918* Volume III with later editions, it can be seen that Bean rewrote his piece about the proposed truce at Fromelles: another event in which McCay was implicated, in the view of the men there at the time. The officer involved, Major A W Murdoch, whom Bean had trusted, deliberately gave him a false version of the event. When Bean was directed to Lieut Col J McArthur for better information, McArthur was silenced by the fact that he was still a serving officer, but Bean did now mention his presence in the event. As we shall see, Bean could not include McArthur's barbed comment about who was responsible for stopping the armistice.

This is much more troubling as there was no doubt in McArthur's mind that McCay was at fault. McCay later replied to Bean's questioning on who prevented the truce with slippery 'legalese', and Bean did not pursue it, curiously. The Military Law of the time expressly permitted a suspension of arms for the purposes of removing the wounded and dead, and the procedures and even the language used by the Saxon officer who initiated the negotiations were exactly within the internationally agreed rules. The neglect of the welfare of the men, under the same rules, was a punishable offence for junior officers: but perhaps not for generals.

Then there was the famous affair of Colonel Pope: a hero of Gallipoli, sacked by McCay for being drunk on duty even though he was asleep and the battle was over. Or was this more to do with Pope's failure to obey an order a few days earlier because, as he told Divisional HQ, it was badly expressed? However, Bean's observation of Pope on that day was one of disgust, but of course he could never commit his comment to print.

All of these items and more have a strong input from the 5th Australian Divisional HQ, and in particular Major General McCay, whom Bean went out of his way to clear of all blame for the Fromelles disaster. But however hard one searches Bean's papers, it is impossible to find who cleared McCay of blame for Fromelles other than McCay himself as Bean never corresponded with the British generals concerned, getting all his information and guidance from Brig. General Edmonds, the British Official Historian. All this is curious especially as Bean was well aware of McCay's defects as well as General Birdwood's judgement on McCay when McCay tried in 1918 to get control of the 3rd Division. Said Birdwood, '*I told him I didn't want the 3rd Division ruined like he had ruined the 5th.*'

Known to all the Australians who served under his command as 'Butcher' McCay, the intensity of the men's hatred continued well beyond McCay's death in 1930. At that death *The Bulletin*'s eulogy had the theme '*the most detested officer in the AIF*'. When asked about McCay, some old diggers remembered the time when at St Kilda's Army and Navy Club prior to a visit by McCay, there was written on the pavement in blood red paint 'Butcher McCay'. The same diggers when speaking in admiration for Capt. Jacka VC related another event at the same club when Jacka refused to shake McCay's extended hand and pointedly snubbed him. As there is no doubt about the intense hatred the men had for McCay, the question to ask is why, and then to assess whether or not it was justified.

As this work will reveal, McCay's influence in Australia was very considerable. Having been a lawyer, a politician, Minister for Defence, Head of Intelligence and Censor before going to Egypt at the end of 1914, McCay was never without a substantial appointment for the rest of his life, and when he returned to Australia severely wounded in 1915, his good and great friend, George Foster Pearce, Minister for Defence, did not fail him. Pearce overrode General Birdwood GOC of the ANZAC Corps, who wanted McCay to command 3rd Division being formed in Australia, and gave McCay command of 5th Division in Egypt. McCay had exploited the Government's desire to have the overseas division led by an Australian: but in truth McCay, had he been anybody else, would not have been passed fit by the Medical Board. As it turned out, McCay's health broke down after only six months in France. And this was *not* the only time Pearce overruled Birdwood in connection with McCay.

Other people also sought Pearce's patronage. Even the great Monash asked McCay to intercede on his behalf with Pearce: and Monash coaxed his own wife to cultivate her relative, Mrs Pearce!

And.

It was the Hon G F Pearce who told C E W Bean that he would be the Official Historian of Australia's involvement in

Sir GEORGE F PEARCE (contd)
Australian Navy and Army, and, by 1912, the flying school at Point Cook, all of which were supported by the compulsory training schemes brought in as a result of Kitchener's Report of 1910.

The compulsory training scheme was not a popular political project, and Pearce's former Labor colleagues accused him of being too close to the military establishment. Pearce, however, as a result of a world tour was certain that Britain and Germany would go to war, and that the next threat would be Japan. These convictions confirmed his determination to push on with what had to be done.

At the outbreak of war McCay was appointed in charge of censorship and Pearce began his ministry, which survived throughout the war despite numerous changes in government. When McCay left for Gallipoli, Pearce took on the censorship role after Monash had had charge of the department for a month, and whilst perhaps no worse than the British censors, he was regarded as unnecessarily restrictive and too inclined to 'protect the public' from the full truth.

When McCay returned wounded from Gallipoli, Pearce appointed him Inspector General, a position he retained until Pearce overrode Birdwood and made McCay a Major General and gave him the 5th Division.

To the suspicious, Pearce's censorship of the Fromelles disaster, deliberately mixing it up with Pozières, might have had something to do with his commitment to McCay. It also had a lot to do with the forthcoming Conscription Referendum of which Pearce was the chief architect. It was announced a week after Fromelles and was voted upon and lost as the Battle of the Somme came to an end. Pearce persevered with the conscription idea and tried again in 1917, but his timing was equally bad: Passchendaele occurred just prior to that Referendum, which was also lost.

Pearce arrived in London late March 1919, his main task to work with Monash on the repatriation of the AIF and some 15,000 dependants. He was [continued next page]

Sir GEORGE F PEARCE (contd)
there until September and doubtless assisted Bean in his collection of material for the Official History and the projected War Museum: from the timing, that material might well have been on the same Australia-bound ship as Pearce because the history, and the historian, were also projects largely initiated by Pearce in 1914.

Pearce's political career continued until 1937, and his public career went on until 1947. He died in Melbourne on 24 June 1952.

ADOLF HITLER: FROMELLES 1916
He was born 20 April 1889 at Braunan on the Austrian-German border, the son of a minor Customs official, who died when Hitler was 13. Of the five children his mother bore only two survived, Adolf and a sister Paula; the mother died in 1907. As a student Hitler was interested in architecture, art and music while in Vienna, later surviving by doing postcards, posters and other commercial art. He moved to Munich in 1913, and there in August 1914, enlisted in the Bavarian Infantry, with which he served for over four years.

the War 1914–18, and saw through all the arrangements for the great project. It was Pearce who supported Bean's collection of documents, records and anything else useful to both the history and the eventual War Museum.

Pearce's foresight in this and much else marks him out as one of the major political figures of this period of Australian history. But one has to wonder if Bean's loyalty to Pearce did not impinge on his published assessment of McCay, when his actual notes of the time have no such bias. Bean's verdict in his private diary was not ambiguous, calling McCay along with Legge and Anderson '*crooked*' and ranged against the '*straight men*' White, Birdwood and Griffiths.

Also Bean owed an enormous amount of his success to Brudenell White who was very close to Pearce with whom, he and Bridges, created, for the want of a better word, the AIF and all that flowed from that.

Clearly it was not Bean's style nor job to denigrate anybody in the AIF. Lawsuits stemming from such comments, let alone political pressure would have quickly put an end to his work. Whilst it has long been popular to explain all the disasters of the Great War by calling British generals butchers and much else, it has yet to be proven that the British Army had exclusive recruitment rights to such people. Unpleasant as it may be to the national psyche, the AIF had its fair share and there is no doubt that McCay was one. Bean's excusing of McCay for Fromelles was published when McCay was still alive, but his generosity dried up in Volume VI published in 1942. There Bean discusses the calamity that nearly overtook the AIF when Birdwood was to leave and McCay with Pearce's support was next in line: but due to intense lobbying Monash took charge of the AIF. Wrote Bean on McCay then: '*whose capacity was great but whose judgement and powers of leadership were not trusted*'—which is exactly the conclusion the men of the 5th Division had come to by sunset on 20 July 1916.

Then.

On the other side of the barbed wire there was Adolf Hitler. The influence of his experiences at Fromelles shaped much of his philosophy, and a friend he had at that time was crucial to his political success, and they remained friends right to the end. After France surrendered in 1940 Hitler headed for Fromelles with, among others, two of his old comrades of 1914-18 and they toured the area in an open car reviving old memories.

Much more important than such historical footnotes was the determination of Bean and the British never to put into print the actual German losses, although the figures were known to Bean, and generalise with 'around 1500 to 2000'. Doubtless to admit that only 501 Germans died and 943 were wounded at Fromelles on the day when the British and Australians had 2436 dead and 4123 wounded would have caused some real questions to be asked, and it would have been impossible to attribute the disparity solely to Haking: so it would have to come to rest on McCay's shoulders, an eventuality that Bean went to extraordinary lengths to prevent.

It is discoveries like these that make research rewarding, stimulating and thus a little addictive and that is how this volume has come to be an inquiry, rather than a history. And while the main accent of this work is Australian, the British contribution is not ignored, nor the German defence. Although the main chapters take the action from 1915 to the present, there are throughout separate, self-contained stories. One or two are included at length because they are interesting, but the rest are presented as evidence in the inquiry and placed at the end of the chapter to which they refer. In this way they are complete and not moulded or shortened to fit into the flow of the narrative. This style of presentation means that some items of evidence or opinion are duplicated. The reader is asked to accept this because to edit out such sections would seriously affect the continuity of some narratives. And there are many short pieces in the margins, asides so to speak, which illustrate an event or a point of view, emphasise an opinion or show an emotion which would be not apparent otherwise.

Thus it is hoped that the diary entries, letters, quotations, poems and epitaphs are not robbed of their own special part in the story of Fromelles. As they are all voices of people affected one way or another by the experience they deserve to be heard, and here they have their place.

Before embarking on the inquiry, a brief review of the strategy used and the material collected.

We will first quickly examine the overall situation on the Western Front up to July 1916, this is to place Fromelles in a sequence of events which the British Command at the time were trying desperately to control, but with only limited success. It is relevant to deal then with the campaigns in the Fromelles region prior to July 1916, because of the lessons that they provided, but from which nothing was learnt.

We then search the days before the battle for indications of the character and capacity of the British and Australian Divisions before giving descriptions of their participation in

EARLY BATTLES OF FROMELLES

Very early in the war Fromelles was in the front line, revealed in outline in *British Campaigns in Europe 1914–18* by A C Doyle (c. 1930):

21 October 1914

It (the 19th Bde, Gordons) ... had been ordered to occupy Fromelles, and so close the gap which existed between the left of the Second and the right of the Third Corps, situated respectively at Aubers and Radinghem. The chief fighting occurred at the village of Le Maisnil, close to Fromelles. The village was occupied by the 2nd Argylls and half 1st Middlesex, but they were driven out by severe shellfire followed by infantry advance. The Brigade fell back in good order, the battalions engaged having lost 300 men.

22 October 1914

... not only had Smith-Dorrien (Second Corps) experienced this hold up upon his right flank, but his left flank had become more vulnerable, because the French had been heavily attacked at Fromelles, and had been driven out of the village.

THE RIGHT MAN

Shortly after the outbreak of war there was a general election in Australia. The Cook ministry was overthrown and a Labour government, under Mr Andrew Fisher, succeeded it. Apprehension was entertained in some quarters in Australia lest the Labour government should be less keen on giving assistance in the war than its predecessor. This fear was wholly groundless. The Labour leaders during the election pledged themselves in the most complete fashion. Mr Andrew Fisher declared at the beginning of the war that Australia should support Great Britain with her last man and her last shilling. When he became prime minister he acted on the declaration. Senator Pearce was made Minister for Defence, and showed himself the right man for the place.

—Sir John Hammerton
Popular History of the Great War
(c. 1932)

THE SONS AND THE FATHER
Richard Gibbs was in the fourth year of his medical studies at University of Melbourne when he enlisted, and he had earned his University Blue for football. Gibbs was born on 4 February 1892 at Colac where his father practised as a doctor. Richard had a very meritorious school career at Caulfield Grammar. When he arrived in Egypt in January 1916 as a Lieut in 6th Bn, he was 'talent spotted' by Brig. Gen. Elliott and joined 59th Bn. With them he went to Fromelles and his death. His body was never found and his name is on the screen wall at VC Corner. He was posthumously awarded the Military Cross (see page 289).

But the war had not yet finished with the Gibbs family. Richard's younger brother, Cpl John (Jack) Gibbs came back to Australia with a disease contracted on Gallipoli. His father took care of him in Colac but after only four weeks, he died in August 1917. Dr Gibbs, his two sons gone, left Colac and took the position of senior surgeon at the Macleod Military Hospital, Mont Park, where his considerable medical skills and his '*highly esteemed kindly personal qualities*' could help alleviate the suffering of those maimed physically and mentally by the war. In the late afternoon of 12 July 1919, a Saturday, Dr Gibbs was on a tram going down St Kilda Road. When it swung around the corner into Domain Road, Dr Gibbs who was standing on the rear platform, lost his grip and was thrown onto the road. Unconscious, he was taken to Caulfield Military Hospital where he died early next morning.

In one of those curiosities of life, the father of one of the acknowledged heroes of Fromelles was fatally injured on the very corner where, 89 years later, almost to the day, the *Cobbers* statue commemorating that terrible day in 1916 was unveiled in what has now become the Shrine Reserve (see page 427).

the battle. The German narratives of the event follow: these now benefit greatly from the information found in the German Archives at Munich in connection with the search for the missing, and this is dealt with in the new last chapter. After the German chapter, we then come to the immediate aftermath of the battle, the medical work, the padres, the burials and a full account of the attempted armistice. This story, perhaps better than the battle itself, reveals the character of the men and their generals. The known heroes are the subject of the next section. Then, to the plight of the POWs (together with a full listing) and the missing with a long memoir of a badly wounded man taken prisoner by the Germans.

The last period of the war in so far as it affected Fromelles is then briefly dealt with. The cemeteries and memorials, their establishment and character over the years and what the French keep in memory of the battle form the next chapter.

Next, a comparison in the years afterwards between official views and popular views of what actually happened. Suppressed inquiries, the historians' problems in finding the facts and owning some that they did find.

Then, to the next of kin and the survivors, the reunions and anniversaries, the wrath of Elliott and the silence of the others.

The next chapter brings together the thoughts that such a search as this provokes, perfectly collected, so to speak, in the sculpture *'Cobbers'* by Peter Corlett. That centrepiece of the Australian Memorial Park at Fromelles was dedicated on 5 July 1998, eighty-two years almost to the day when men of the 5th Australian Division first glimpsed the battlefield which so many never left. That same inspiring bronze—its second casting—now stands in the reserve of Melbourne's Shrine of Remembrance, unveiled on 19 July 2008, the 92nd anniversary.

The story of the Missing of Fromelles, no longer missing, forms the last chapter. How the indefatigable enthusiast wove his way through the maze of the unimaginative and uncooperative adds a new phase to the Battle of Fromelles. But by no means the last, this writer believes.

The Rolls of Honour conclude the inquiry. Here for the first time are collected the names of all who were killed or died of wounds at Fromelles, except for three regiments of the 6th Bavarian Division. It is hoped that the publication of this book will unearth these lists

The Notes and Index are provided as assistance to those who might wish to make their own inquiry into the Battle of Fromelles.

Fromelles—an historical note

The extent to which Fromelles and the region around Lille has been at the crossroads of history and at the mercy of passing armies is emphasised by an examination of the history of Flanders.

Although ancient pottery shards, and remains of Roman villas have been found around Fromelles, the history of the modern town of Fromelles can only be traced back to Norman times—Formellas (sic) was recorded in a document from 1119. At that time the region was controlled by the Count of Flanders, who was dependent on the King of France. Less than 30 kms away was the western border of the Holy Roman Empire.

Over succeeding generations the name Formeles (1169, 1174, 1210) and Fourmielles (1272, 1281, 1330, 1407, 1449) is recorded in surviving documents. The battle of Bouvines in 1214, where the King of France defeated the English King John, forcing him to withdraw from northern France, was some 30 kms south-east of Fromelles.

During the first years of the fourteenth century, the King of France, Philip IV, tried to extend his rule over neighbouring and squabbling duchies. The Battle of the Golden Spurs near Kortrijk (Courtrai), some 25 kms from Fromelles, resulted in a defeat for the Count of Flanders who, two years later, acknowledged the King of France as his ruler. French garrisons were placed in Lille and Douai. At this time Fromelles was beginning to rely heavily on the wool trade—Lille rapidly becoming one of the major cities in the trade of Flemish woollen cloth.

In 1337 the Hundred Years' War between England and France broke out, but hostilities ended with the Peace of Brétigny in 1360. When the conflict was resumed in 1369, the French, needing extra soldiers, withdrew their garrisons from Lille and Douai. In the next seven years the English were driven from most of France leaving the region around Fromelles in peace.

When the heiress to the Count of Flanders married Philip the Bold, Duke of Burgundy, in 1384, Fromelles became a part of the extensive lands of the Dukes of Burgundy. Although Philip was the brother of the King of France, he was effectively the ruler of a separate state, so Fromelles remained a part of their lands until 1482.

In 1415 the Hundred Years' War had resumed, and the battle of Agincourt, in which the English King Henry V defeated a massive French army, was fought less than 60 kms from Fromelles. However, by the 1430s the French were once again winning the war, and in 1453 the English were reduced to holding Calais.

In 1483, Lille and the area around Fromelles passed into the hands of the Holy Roman Empire, and then, with the whole of the southern Netherlands, effectively under the control of the King of Spain.

The name 'Fromelles' is noted for the first time in 1543, and repeated again in documents from 1591 and 1688.

In 1618 the Thirty Years' War broke out, and in 1635 France declared war on Spain leading to further fighting throughout the region. In 1650, actually two years after the Thirty Years' War had ended, the Duke of Broglie who commanded La Bassée on behalf of the King of France, burned Aubers and four neighbouring villages for their part in the war.

When the French King Louis XIV embarked on the war against the Spanish Netherlands, he besieged Lille. After capturing it on 28 August 1667, Louis XIV in person established Lille as the capital of Walloon Flanders, and the region, including Fromelles, became French in the first Treaty of Aix la Chapelle in May 1668.

In 1789 when the French Revolution broke out the Seigneur of Fromelles was Julien-Louis-François Bide, with the curate, Charles Salembié, in charge of the church, the cemetery and the local school.

On 14 December 1789 a decree removed the rights of the Seigneur, and established the power of the office of the Mayor. Auguste Alexandre Dubrulle became the first Mayor, presiding over a town of 1350 people, with five officials, twelve notables and an attorney. At the end of 1793 the Church was closed, but was reopened in 1802 when Napoleon, as First Consul, concluded the Concordat with the Vatican. The new vicar was Pierre Joseph Chavattes.

After the battle of Waterloo in 1815 (some 120 kms from Fromelles), Flanders had its longest period of peace. The population had reached its peak in 1841—1399 people.

After about 1830 Fromelles started to have a flourishing linen industry, but when the windmill was destroyed in 1879, it was never repaired.

The rich farming land sustained the town, supplying vegetables, sugar beet and grain to an increasingly prosperous France. At Fromelles in 1877 Jules Descamps, a well-established young farmer, became mayor, a position he held until 1919 (see page 344).

One of the aspects of the changing times was the demand for woollen clothing, and the need to import raw wool to be processed, spun and made into cloth by the mills of Flanders. Interestingly, one of the results of this was that wool buyers from Flanders in general, and Tourcoing and Roubaix in particular, went to Australia and set up businesses there in the late 1890s, thus establishing close links between Flanders and Australia well before 1916.

INFORMATION COURTESY M DELEBARRE

Fromelles—before the war

In 1900 the population of Fromelles was 1106 people living in 225 houses. The railway came to the town in 1902 with the establishment of the station 'Le Michon', 500 metres southwest of the town. This addition meant that one of the major events of the period—the Eucharist Congress of the Canton of La Basée could be held at Fromelles. As the postcards of the time show, the choir of 60 children lead the Cross to the Calvary on rue des Rouges Bancs, the altar being set up in the adjacent field which belonged to Jules Descamps, the Mayor.

Electricity was available to houses and businesses in the main street in 1914, and to the rest of the town in 1928.

By 1913 Fromelles, like country towns everywhere, was losing people to the cities: the population was down to 955 in 217 houses. There were only nine marriages that year, and 23 births and 19 deaths. Some 67 farms, 22 shops, a laundry, a distillery and a brewery supplied jobs, and early in 1914 a weaving mill was established.

INFORMATION AND PHOTOGRAPHS COURTESY M DELEBARRE

Fromelles—before the war

The *Annual Review* of 1914 has a list from which one can gauge the style of the town. The first name was the Mayor—Jules Descamps. Then there was his assistant and secretary. The next was the vicar, Father Dervaux, and after him the tax collector, who was at Fournes. Then the school master and school mistress, followed by the Rural Constable. From then on various trades and occupations were: two butchers, two bakers, one brewer, nineteen taverns, five carpenters and joiners, one wheelwright, five shoemakers, about thirty-five farmers, eleven grocers, four seedsmen, one blacksmith, one doctor, three painters, about twelve shopkeepers, two locksmiths, one tobacconist and two tailors.

The annual community fête was held on the second Sunday in July.

Fromelles (Nord). — Chapelle et Route d'Aubers à Fournes et Hanbourdin.

FROMELLES — Rue de l'Ommerie

FROMELLES (Nord) - Avant la guerre - Rue des Veaulx
Lefebvre, photo, Ascq

INFORMATION AND PHOTOGRAPHS COURTESY M DELEBARRE

Fromelles—before the war

The old church at Fromelles is thought to date back to the late 14th or early 15th century. A storm on 27 March 1606 partly demolished it. In 1738 lightning struck the tower and severely damaged the bell, and again in 1815 the bell was struck by lightning. The church was almost totally wrecked by the end of 1915 and reduced to a ruin by 1918.

These photographs show the dominant position of the church and the views from the tower, first looking south into the town, and secondly looking north towards Rouge Bancs and beyond there to what was to become the battlefield in July 1916.

The town centre is about 25 metres above sea level, the high ground behind it, Aubers Ridge 35m, statistics which emphasise the flat character of Flanders with its rich damp soil.

INFORMATION AND PHOTOGRAPHS COURTESY M DELEBARRE

2

They shall not pass

Ils ne passeront pas

—Maréchal Pétain, at Verdun February 1916

In the long tradition of Imperialism, whose armies were inevitably led by Princes and Royal Dukes, much of the action was dictated by life at the Court. At the beginning of 1915 troops of both sides were still wearing colourful uniforms, carrying noble standards and behaving as they had been trained to behave, years before. The Commanders by dint of connection and breeding were entirely motivated by their perceived duty to their Supreme Commander—the King. Thus the German High Command in search of a birthday present for the Kaiser—he would be 56 on 27 January—renewed their offensive on 25 January 1915, hoping that Ypres might be one present. But the French then defending that front drove them off. Further south, before Bethune, Prince Rupprecht with his Bavarian Division began a feint at Neuve Chapelle before a strong assault on Bethune, deemed to be another suitable present: but the Germans gained little.

This was a section of the Western Front along with Perthes, near Reims and Eparges between Metz and Verdun which the French High Command thought were the principal places to break through the German line, therefore when the reverse happened, the allies were caught quite unprepared. And so began the battle for this area which went on and off for most of 1915 with fearful losses of men on both sides and very little territory changing hands.

Neuve Chapelle, a village on the crossroads between Bethune and La Bassée and Armentières was occupied by the Germans in early October 1914, the British took it back on 16 October and lost it again on 27 October. It was of strategic importance as the launching point for an assault on Aubers Ridge, and the capture of that—the opening of a possible liberation of Lille.

Another of the objectives of the French and English at this time was to so harass the Germans that they could not withdraw troops to the Russian front, and to this end the British had been preparing for an assault of their own at Neuve Chapelle in mid-March when conditions were more favourable weatherwise

Verdun n'est pas seulement la grande fortresse d'est destiné à barrer la route à l'invasion, c'est le boulevard moral de la France.

—Maréchal Pétain

THEIR FIRST EXPERIENCE OF EUROPEAN WARFARE

In August 1914 Lord Kitchener, Secretary of State, issued instructions to Sir John French: something of a public declaration it had among its 500 words a few sentences applicable to the subject of this volume.

It must be recognised from the outset that the numerical strength of the British Force and its contingent reinforcement is strictly limited, and with this consideration kept steadily in view it will be obvious that the greatest care must be exercised towards a minimum of losses and wastage.

And further on:

In minor operations you should be careful that your subordinates understand that risk of serious losses should only be taken where such risk is authoritatively considered to be commensurate with the object in view.

And:

... officers may well be reminded that in this their first experience of European warfare, a greater measure of caution must be employed than under former conditions of hostilities against an untrained adversary.

Sir JOHN FRENCH (1852–1925)
Had the Great War begun some years earlier French would have brought some vision and experience to the job of commanding the British Army. In 1905 French was testing trenches and breastworks in the Chiltern Hills, after working on embarkation and disembarkment techniques the year before. In 1906 he turned to testing wireless, field telegraph and signals, together with the problems of moving large numbers of troops by rail. In subsequent years he travelled widely in Europe and the Empire studying armies and their organisation: even the Kaiser showed him how the German Army trained. French, after returning from the South African War in 1902, had concluded it was only a matter of time before Britain went to war with Germany.

Having resigned in March 1914 over a crisis in Ulster, he was recalled by Kitchener at the outbreak of war and went to France in August 1914 as a Field Marshal and C in C. Unable to do anything about the initial German advance and the Mons retreat, but the successful October counterattack along the Marne included his work and ideas, and then in early 1915 came the stand at Ypres and the moves of Neuve Chapelle, which were as much hindered by lack of supplies, men and shells as by the lack of experience around the table at HQ.

French, the son of an Irish naval Captain and a Scottish woman, was born on 28 Sept 1852, and thus 9 years older than Haig, 10 years older than Haking, but only a year younger than Foch, and the same age as Joffre. The last two he got on well with, the first two assisted by others, knifed him in the back. And interestingly they never did much better on the battlefield than French. But as the age table signifies, the rivalry was not about military skills, but purely a generation conflict, between men at the top and end of their careers and those who had one last chance. No corporation board room, academic council or political committee was, or is, any different.

and their arrangements more in order. The 7th and 8th British Divisions, together with two Indian Divisions, the Meerut and Lahore, were to break through the German line and go on to capture Lille, while another British Corps would take back La Bassée. As one historian wrote:

> In military history it stands as the first battle of the war which was deliberately planned for some time in advance and was preceded by adequate artillery preparation ...

The Commander of the British, Sir John French, had 48,000 men at his command, but they were poorly equipped and ammunition was in short supply. All this is important when seen as an earlier version of the Battle of Fromelles 19/20 July 1916. The Germans held Neuve Chapelle and had extensive wire on the west. The British artillery was to cut the entanglements and batter the German trench. At the outset some of the Indians were sent in the wrong direction so ending up against uncut wire. Other wire was only partly destroyed and leading British companies were badly hit. The Middlesex Regiment was thought to have got through '*for not a man came back to report otherwise. The men of this first wave were afterwards found lying dead in the formations in which they had advanced.*' Almost precisely what happened to the Australians in front of the Sugarloaf a year and a bit later. Also in this early echo, the British rushing forward into captured trenches were too fast for their own artillery and suffered severely from it. However, unlike Fromelles, Neuve Chapelle was taken on 10 March. A breakdown in communications and contrary views in High Command as to what to do next, gave the Germans some five hours to sort out their arrangements, which included a determination to take back the town. General Sir Douglas Haig, the senior corps commander in 1914 and now in command of the 1st Army, who was making the overall decisions, ordered an advance because '*it appears that the enemy before us is in no great strength ...*'

The British observers had missed the new German line '*in the rear of their strong points the day before*', so as the British set off the German artillery on Aubers Ridge put down three hours of shells right along the British line, blew them and their communications to pieces and waited for the next victims. The German reinforcements, lifting their numbers to 16,000 men, arrived in the evening of 12 March. At 10.40 am the next day they made their first attempt to take back Neuve Chapelle. But they were stopped on the edge of the village, exhausted, starving and all their officers dead. Haig now turned his artillery on

Aubers Ridge and ordered the infantry to storm the ridge. The Germans had machine guns everywhere and as more British tried to get to Aubers they were cut down and then there were just no more reserves to call upon, and the battle came to an end. The British had lost 583 officers and 12,309 other ranks and achieved nothing except one would have hoped, a very healthy respect for the German artillery on Aubers Ridge. But apparently not.

Less than two months later, on 9 May, there began another attack on Aubers Ridge. The line was from Bois Grenier south to Festubert, with the greatest thrust at Rouges Bancs just in front of Fromelles. Beginning at 5 am on Sunday morning with a bombardment which was much less than it should have been because ammunition was in short supply, it was an attack that never had a chance of success. Since the last attempt, the Germans had worked hard at improving their defence system.

> They had specially manufactured barbed cables of much heavier gauge than usual which could not be severed with ordinary cutters, and which resisted shrapnel fire. To make these cable entanglements more difficult to reduction by artillery, the Germans had thrown up banks, looking like trench parapets, behind which extended the entanglement area protecting the real trench. All that advancing troops could do when faced by an unbroken and uncuttable barbed cable defence of this kind, was to cast their overcoats upon the barbed edge, and then try to clamber over it while the German machine-guns were playing upon them. As well as this strong wiring the Germans had been working hard to render their machine-gun posts impregnable and to give their troops in the line protection from gun fire by means of dugouts and strong parapets.
>
> There was a varying space, often less than two hundred yards wide, between the British and German trenches. In many places the sandbag barricades, built man-high on the marshy lowland soil, were close enough for the opposing troops to hear each other talking, so very narrow was the long strip of No-Man's Land running between the khaki-coloured sandbags on the British side and the piebald, black and white sandbags of the Germans.

That was an almost perfect description, less the benefit of another year's work by the Germans, of what the Australians would face on 19/20 July 1916.

However at this time, May 1915, it was British, and again Indian troops, who would assault Aubers Ridge at 6 am where it was Monro's I Corps operation (with 1st Division under Haking, 2nd Division, 47th London Division, and 1st Canadian). Whilst opposite Fromelles further north was IV Corps under Rawlinson, with 7th and 8th British Divisions and Indian Corps of three divisions. Haig again was directing the attack, as a man he did not attach real importance to machine-guns, '*the machine-gun is a much over-rated weapon and two per battalion*

NO LARGER THAN A MODERATE FARM

Arthur Conan Doyle, creator of Sherlock Holmes, had been a war correspondent during the South African Wars 1899–1902. His despatches were very much to the point, not given over to heroics. He took up pen and despatch pad again. His book *The British Campaign in France and Flanders 1915* was published by Hodder and Stoughton in 1917. The following extracts from Chapter 2 'Neuve Chapelle and Hill 60' sum up that campaign very well, especially the final sentence.

With the breaking of the spring and the drying out of the water-soaked meadows of Flanders, an era of larger more ambitious operations had set in, involving, this time, little change of position, but far larger forces on the side of the British. The first hammer-blow of Sir John French was directed, upon March 10 (1915), against the village of Neuve Chapelle which had ... changed hands several times, and eventually remained with the Germans during the hard fighting ... in the last week of October (1914). The British trenches had been drawn a few hundred yards to the west of the village, and there had been no change during the last four months. Behind the village was the Aubers Ridge, and behind that again the whole great plain of Lille and Turcoing. This was the spot upon which the British General had determined to try the effects of his new artillery.

The troops chosen for the assault were Rawlinson's Fourth Army Corps upon the left and the India Corps upon the right, upon a front of half a mile, which as the operation developed broadened to three thousand yards. The object was not the mere occupation of the village, but an advance to the farthest point attainable.

The obstacle in front of the Army was a most serious one. The barbed wire entanglements were on an immense scale, the trenches bustling with machine guns, and the village in the rear contained several outlying houses with walls and orchards, each of which had been converted into a fortress.

[continued next page]

NO LARGER THAN A MODERATE FARM (contd)

After a huge artillery barrage by some three hundred guns firing without pause for 30 minutes, the infantry went forward. Those on the right got to the German trenches, and then to the village. Those on the left however found much of the wire intact and suffered horrendous losses, some battalions reduced to 150 or less, and most of the officers killed. The Indian Corps in their first large scale attack had no better luck, and yet it was 3rd Brigade of Gurkhas and the rifles of the 25th English Brigade that took the town by midday. The British and Indians pushed on before being halted near the Laies River. They had gained a thousand yards.

On 11 March a thick all day mist prevented any artillery work or infantry advance. It however provided the Germans with a very necessary opportunity to rebuild and reinforce. The 12th was a better day weatherwise and the Germans made several strong counterattacks, but decided to settle into new positions - roughly the position that they were in when the Battle of Fromelles began on 14 (sic) July 1916.

The losses at Neuve Chapelle were for the British 562 officers and 12,239 men: 7,500 from the Fourth Corps, 4,000 from the Indian Corps. The Germans lost in the vicinity of 18,000. The reward was a slice of ground no larger than a moderate farm.

MORE THAN ANNIHILATED

What was wrong with the British armies is perfectly explained by Conan Doyle in his book describing the events in France and Flanders in 1915:

... so insatiable are the demands of modern warfare that already after eight months the whole of the regiments of the original expeditionary force would have absolutely disappeared but for the frequent replenishments ... they had been far more than annihilated, for many of the veteran corps had lost from one and a half times their numbers. The 1st Hants at this date had lost 2,700 out of an original force of 1,200 men, and its case was by no means an exceptional one.

is more than sufficient' (14 April 1915). Haig was to find after two hours that the German general relied almost totally on them, with spectacular success. So after desperate efforts throughout the day, at 5 pm the offensive was called off and the British and Indians counted the cost—10,000 officers and men. This abject failure was put down to a lack of high explosive shells, and as a result of *The Times* correspondent reporting this fact, a great turmoil began in the British government, culminating in a huge shake-up in munitions manufacture and supply, and the government itself.

But it did nothing to save the rest of British and Indian assault further south. There was a breakthrough at Festubert at very high cost to both sides, the Germans desperate to check any incursion onto Aubers Ridge. It was 18 May before the British were relieved by Canadians, who in five days time were sent into attack but failed also to break the German resolve. On 25 May Sir John French ordered Haig to hold the line, so that the French army could be supported elsewhere. The Battle of Festubert casualties now totalled 710 officers and 15,938 other ranks.

Interestingly in all the accounts of this battle there were continual references to the preparedness of the Germans, and their uncanny accuracy in knowing the time of the attack. In one case a prisoner told the British that an attack '*had only come a quarter of an hour before it was expected*'. This too would have an echo on 19/20 July 1916.

Both of these assaults were directed by Haig, both were total failures, but curiously Haig got away from them without a blemish to his reputation. One of his senior officers at this time was Haking, and he likewise was never held accountable for the lamentable planning. He had had command of 1st Division during the first half of 1915 and then, as Lieut General Haking, took XI Corps on 29 August.

In June, near Givenchy, Haig put forward yet another scheme for another attack, although well aware that there was not sufficient ammunition to prepare the way for the infantry. Three attempts were made to push the Germans back. All failed. British success was no better anywhere else, all the way north to Ypres and south to Arras every action was a disaster.

However, after months of planning the battle of Loos in September appeared to have some chance of success. The French and the British were cooperating closely, huge quantities of ammunition were now available (three to four million shells), every piece of railway equipment was mobilised to bring in men and supplies. The prize would be Lens, the coalfields, and then Lille. But the Germans were not idle either: both sides had gas at their disposal and the new German *Flammenwerfers* were another threat.

The full story of the battle of Loos is not the concern of this volume: but the weather was the first upset, then the terrain and extensive bogs. Heavy mist hindered aerial observation, and untried gas equipment were other handicaps. The conduct of the battle was once again in the hands of Haig with overall control with Sir John French and General Joffre. If any battle of the British army in the Great War endorses the German officer's remark about '*Lions being led by donkeys*', the Battle of Loos was it. Regiment after regiment was sent to oblivion: new men, seasoned soldiers on both sides were wasted in huge numbers. The British 1st Army had another go at Aubers Ridge via Rouges Bancs and Fromelles, and the Indians were again sent forward at Neuve Chapelle, and despite initial small advances they could do no better than the earlier efforts and no ground was won along the front that concerns this volume, but the British took Loos and an area to its north. The battle which began on 25 September and ceased on 16 October took the lives of some 800 British officers and 15,000 men, with 1,200 officers and over 33,000 men wounded.

What is most important about the Battle of Loos in so far as the Battle of Fromelles is concerned, is Haking's role at Loos. Here we can see him for the first time in charge of a Corps—the XI, consisting initially of the 21st and 24th Divisions, later the 12th and 46th plus the Guards and 3rd Cavalry. A considerable upgrade from just the 1st Division at Aubers Ridge six months earlier. What Haking did with this command is worth a few paragraphs because it clearly and without any ambiguity establishes what he brought to Fromelles and what was on the record. The only authority we have for Haking's deeds, as distinct from his character, is the official British history. Edmonds has no real criticism of Haking at Aubers and Neuve Chapelle. These disasters had other causes. It was Edmond's proposition, arising out of the Neuve Chapelle and Festubert experiences that one of the lessons was '*how quickly troops became exhausted and how soon fresh divisions were required to carry the attack forward; it had further shown the need for taking immediate advantage of the first success.*' This statement by Edmonds established early on where he stood in the differences between the C-in-C Sir John French and GOC 1st Army Sir Douglas Haig. Haig advised French to move forward

ANTHONY WILDING (1883–1915)
Among the dead of May 1915 at Neuve Chapelle was Captain Anthony Wilding, the New Zealand born (31 October 1883) Wimbledon champion for 1910, 11, 12 and 13 and finalist (defeated by Norman Brookes) in 1914. Of the 30 Davis Cup rubbers he played, he won 21, usually with Brookes and representing 'Australasia'.

A Cambridge law graduate and generally regarded as one of the great tennis players of all time, Wilding joined the Royal Marines, Armoured Car Division, and was killed on 9 May at the age of 31. His grave (11.D.37) is in the Rue-des-Berceaux Military Cemetery, Richebourg-l'Avoué.

THE GERMANS DID NOT FOLLOW
In front of the German second position between Bois Hugo and Hulluch, isolated groups of officers and men of the 24th Division—about five hundred in all—who had not joined in the retirement (from the Lens Road, 26 Sept 1915) continued to hold on in the hope that reinforcements would eventually arrive.

Behind this screen of scattered parties which, lying in the long grass, could not be seen from the British lines, the retirement was carried out unmolested. They came back at a walk, but without order of formation … the remainder re-crossed the great open space of the Loos valley, and then moved up the slope to the Lone Tree ridge.

The Germans did not follow in pursuit, but from Hulluch about 2 pm they sent out medical personnel and stretcher bearers, who, regardless of shelling, worked at binding up the British wounded, sending all who could walk or crawl back to the British lines.

—*Military Operations, France and Belgium 1915*
Vol II, p333–34. Edmonds (1928)

THE BRITISH ARMIES
Whilst there was but one British army there were a number of Armies: First, Second, Third, Fourth. Each of these had two Corps designated by Roman numerals I, II, III, IV, V, etc. Each Corps had 2 or 3 Divisions numbered 1st, 2nd, 3rd up to 87th. There were also 9 mounted divisions. These divisions could be both British, or might be Indian, Canadian or Anzac, and there might be Cavalry, Guard, Artillery Divisions also part of a Corps which was brought together for a particular battle or task. Each Division had three Brigades, and each Brigade had between four and six battalions, but at the end of the war most had only three.

For Fromelles, the operation was the task of the Third Army (General C C Monro), who designated the XI Corps (Lieut General RCB Haking) to bring together divisions etc. for the battle. The available divisions were the British 61st 'borrowed' from General Plumer's Second Army and the Australian 5th Division then part of very recently assembled I Anzac Corps.

The flexibility of movement within the British army was therefore considerable and designed to provide for decisions and mobility to meet both opportunities and emergencies quickly. Perhaps the real weakness was that the 'minimum unit' in this system was a division ie some 20,000 men, not all that easy to move without drawing attention to itself, blocking up the roads, and creating supply and equipment demands of, say, a whole town.

IN HAKING'S DEFENCE
It might be said in Haking's defence that his elevation to Corps Commander on 29 August (1915) and the assembly the next day of HQ Staff, '*composed of officers who had never previously worked together or served on a Corps staff*' was something of a handicap in the forthcoming—25 September—battle of Loos.

—*History of the Great War Medical Services* (1923)

Haking's XI Army so as to be in a position to follow the initial expected success of Haig's Ist Army and Rawlinson's IVth. But French did not agree and ordered Haking's Corps to remain back. It would seem certain that Haking put this approach to Haig who promoted it to French, causing Edmonds to comment about Haking '*his position was a most embarrassing one*'.

As the battle began, Haig wanted Haking's 21st and 24th Divisions to move forward with the first assault, but French only agreed after '*two valuable hours had ... been lost*'. There was then an exchange of messages between the three, until it was decided at 1.20 pm that Haking's Division was under Haig who '*was embarrassed by their not being handed over to him as early as he expected*'. An hour later, Haig ordered Haking '*to push forward*'. But the Germans were in better shape than Haig thought, and the traffic in and out to the battle area was forever congested so that Haking's men were exhausted before they reached the front line. '*The rain came down in torrents as in failing light the four brigades of 21st and 24th Div began to form up*' so as to march through the night into Loos Valley. The men had only been in France three weeks and seen no action at all.

The general turn of events caused French, in Edmonds' words, to comment '*very strongly*' to Haig '*on the futility of pushing reserves through a narrow gap in the enemy's defences*'. Thus the two egos were on collision course: and Haking backed Haig.

The appalling destruction of the 21st and 24th Divisions, in basic figures: 21st—4051; 24th—4178 was the outcome. Wrote Edmonds: '*many legends have grown up as regards to the failure of 21st and 24th Div at Loos: in particular, that thrust into action worn out by continuous night marching and unfed, they disgraced themselves and the New Army by retiring before the enemy. The men were certainly subjected to unnecessary hardship and kept longer hours on the road than was intended, owing to inadequate road control and the inexperience of the staff in dealing with the road system ...*' Edmonds then goes on for over two pages about how others put up with the same difficulties but got through, and that food and water distribution failure were largely due to inexperienced staff. But nowhere is there any comment about the man in charge of the carnage. The nearest shot Edmonds fires in Haking's direction is this: '*the putting of the cookers under divisional control, by the Corps, was absolutely contrary to all experience*'. All the rest was down to the officers inexperienced in staff work and team work.

The 21st and 24th now destroyed and sent back, Haking got another two divisions, 12th and 46th, to form a '*reconstituted XI Corps*': both had been at Ypres for some months. And for the last part of the Battle of Loos, Edmonds never again mentions Haking's name, but instead unlike earlier accounts he makes a point of naming virtually every Brigade and Battalion commander under Haking's command. For instance the 46th Div. Major General E J Montagu-Stuart-Wortley after '*examination of the ground, was of the opinion that the best course to proceed, as in siege warfare, by bombing attack and approaching the position trench by trench, but in this he was overruled*'. But by whom there is no mention. The shambles that followed caused the Division 6,537 casualties. Overall Haking's command of XI Corps in this battle accounted for 16,830 casualties out of the 59,247 British loses. The Germans had 19,836 casualties. What more needs to be said? Except that with 1st Division losses at Aubers of 3,968, that gives Haking a total of 20,798 casualties in under six months.

Whilst many have written with great passion about this event, perhaps some extracts from Alan Clark's *The Donkeys* are the most succinct and historically telling:

> In contrast to the attack of the previous day—which had, at least, been preceded by a four-day artillery bombardment and a half hour discharge of gas along the entire front, and had moreover, been carried out by four selected divisions trained for the assault in every detail for weeks beforehand—the hapless 21st and 24th Divisions were expected to cross No-Man's Land in broad daylight with no gas or smoke cloud to cover them, with no artillery support below divisional level, and attack a position as strongly manned as had been the front defences and protected by a formidable and intact barbed wire entanglement.

The Germans were active adjusting their defences, strengthening their positions, getting organised for the next attack.

> These, and other minor local counter attacks carried out by the Germans with the intention of improving their defensive position, must surely have given 1st Army HQ, and to both Haig and Haking, ample warning that an unprepared attack by two untrained divisions was unlikely to succeed. But the question of revising the order in light of Intelligence reports does not seem to have been considered.

As usual the Official History noted that the men were delighted at the prospect of getting at the enemy, but as Clark points out, forgets to note that the men had no sleep for 48 hours and almost no food. Clark again:

> Punctually at eleven o'clock the British rose out of the ground ... and formed up in a dense mass ... sheer weight of numbers must, it seemed,

MANY SUFFERINGS
Each new man posted to the battalion is posted to the historical and spiritual inheritance of the battalion also ... The battalion gives him its style, its stamp and impression, and as he breathes the regimental air he swears the regimental oaths. The spirit, however, is borne of many sufferings and endless patience.

—Stephen Graham
A private in the Guards (1919)

CROWNED WITH SUCCESS
Counter Attack at Cuinchy. January–February 1915. Special credit due: (1) To Major General Haking, commanding 1st Division for the prompt manner in which he arranged this counter attack and for the general plan of action, which was crowned with success. (2) GSO Brigades. (3) Officers, NCOs, men of 2nd Coldstream Guards and Irish Guards.

—General Sir Douglas Haig

DOING THE WRONG THING
The British officer has sometimes failed in war because he has been afraid, not of the enemy, or of being shot, but of doing the wrong thing. The result has been that he has done little or nothing, and has allowed the enemy to do what he pleases.

—Col R C B Haking
Staff Rides and Regimental Tours (c. 1906)

This is the story of the destruction of an army—the old professional army of the United Kingdom that always won the last battle, whose regiments had fought at Quebec, Corunna, in the Indies, were trained in musketry at Hythe, drilled on the parched earth at Chuddapore, and were machine-gunned, gassed and finally buried in 1915.

—Alan Clark
The Donkeys (1961)

> carry the British through the thinly spread German outposts ... For fully ten minutes the Germans held their fire as the two divisions deployed in columns of extended line and started obediently off ... at the range of 1,000 yards, the order to fire was given.

Then follows descriptions of how the Germans could not grasp that the British would act with such disregard for the realities of the situation, then when the battlefield was covered with dead and dying and the attack was over:

> no shot was fired at them from the German trenches for the rest of the day, so great was the feeling of compassion and mercy for the enemy after such a victory.

That short sharp massacre of three and a half hours cost the British 385 officers and 7,861 men, whereas the Germans do not seem to have lost a single man.

When the survivors of the divisions met with Haking—'*they seemed rather done in, but steady*', he remarked before—asking them '*What went wrong?*' As one would expect in Edmonds' History, the troops confessed it was all their fault. '*We did not understand what it was like; we will do all right next time.*' Of course it should have been the other way round: the men should have marched on Haking and asked him, '*What went wrong?*' and he should have been the one who got it right next time. But he did not, because his 'next time' was the Battle of Fromelles.

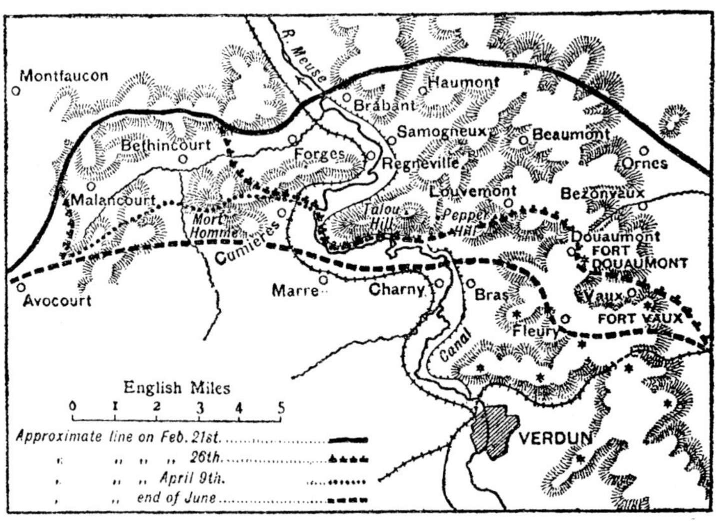

VERDUN—showing the successive lines taken up by the defence under the pressure of German attacks between February and June 1916. After the war the estimate of the losses at Verdun were French: 362,000; German: 336,000.

Sir DOUGLAS HAIG (1861–1928)
Born at Edinburgh, 19 June 1861, youngest son of John a wealthy whisky distiller, Haig was brought up largely by his mother and elder sister. He was educated at Clifton College (1875–79) and Brasenose College, Oxford (1880–83) before going to Sandhurst in 1884. Two years later he was in India with 7th Hussars, becoming one of its best polo players. During his ten years in India he took leave often in France and Germany, and was fluent in both languages. Haig entered Staff College in 1896 for two years before going to the Sudan, and a year after that to South Africa for four years. All this distinguished activity caught the eye of Kitchener, and in 1904 age 43 he was promoted Major General. The next year when at Windsor Castle, as guest of King Edward VII, he met the Hon. Dorothy Vivian Crespigny, one of the Queen's ladies-in-waiting. They were married in 1905: it was Haig's best career move, and gave him a calling card at Court for the rest of his life. There were two daughters and a son from the marriage.

In the years until 1914 Haig had a number of responsible jobs giving him wide experience. A Lieut General since 1910, Haig took the 1st Army Corps to France in August 1914. From then on he was engaged in virtually every major decision until early 1918 when Foch took overall command.

Back in Britain in 1919 he was still a hero and was created an Earl, conferred with the OM, already having GCB, GCVO and Knight of the Thistle: he publicly announced he would accept no more honours, but Parliament voted him £100,000. In the 1920s Haig devoted himself to ex-servicemen's organisations. On 30 January 1928 he died suddenly in London, which liberated the critics who homed in on his many defects. By his own admission Haig re-wrote his diaries for publication, but even that precaution did not impress his detractors. The astute Lord Beaverbrook found them *a self-revealing document: frank, truthful, egotistical, self-confident and malicious. His spear knew no brother.*

Asked about his long record of losing battles, Haig is said to have replied without any anger—*we won the war.*

Perhaps the most extraordinary consequence of this campaign, is that Sir John French was replaced by Haig, and with the advent of 1916, General Sir Douglas Haig became the C-in-C, loyally attended by such men as Haking who had been participants in, witnesses of, and planners of many of the disasters these last pages have dealt with. Perhaps their mutual association in the campaign against French and in the failures, gave them a special bond.

What they did with that experience now concerns us.

As the winter of 1915–1916 began to lift, in February the German offensive at Verdun was reactified with a new ferocity culminating in the fall of the fortress of Douaumont on 25 Feb: the French would not recapture it until 24 Oct 1916. In this action the French had taken losses on such a scale that it was doubtful if they could hold Verdun. But they did and that was forever remembered by Pétain's order—'*They shall not pass.*'

The Medal struck to commemorate the French victory at Verdun.

It would be fair to say that all the Allied forces were entirely new to the fast moving ruthless opening, and the scale of the war. Likewise the Germans, who sometimes went too far, too fast and had to pull back to consolidate along a more defensible line.

The British forces, like all the rest, were also entirely new to the near-stationary trench war that followed the first rush, and especially to opponents equipped as well as they were, or better. Fighting Afghans, Zulus, the Ashanti and Burmese had been very unequal battles and that certainly revealed itself as the British blundered their way through the early days of the war. The French used to putting down the Riffs, the Congolese, Ubangi pygmies and the Sudanese were no better, and did no better. Indeed had the Germans not been haemorrhaging badly

Marshal HENRI-PHILIPPE PETAIN (1856–1951)

To compare a biographical note on Pétain written before 1940 with one written, say, after 1945, reveals dramatically the fall of this French hero of the Great War.

Born at Cauchy-a-la-Tour, Pas-de-Calais, 24 April 1856, he entered St Cyr Military School in 1876, passing out in 1878. By 1902 he was an instructor in musketry, and in 1906 at the same School—Chalons—under Foch. In 1912 he had command of the 33rd Regiment of Arras, and in 1914 in command of 4th Infantry Brigade. In the first years of the war he was continually in action with, like most other generals, mixed success. However his skill with artillery often gave him the edge so that in February 1916 he was placed in command of the defences of Verdun. It was there in the grimmest days of the war that his organisational skills won through, and he became a hero of France. He was appointed Commander in Chief in March 1918 when Foch took over the whole Allied effort from Haig. At the end of the war he was made a Marshal of France.

As a man of such stature it was not surprising that as France once again stood before the German army in 1940, the government of the day called upon Pétain in an effort to rally public opinion. The old, not to say ancient, hero was no match for Hitler and his puppets, and Pétain's establishment of a regime of collaboration with the Nazis brought its just desserts. After the war he was put on trial and sentenced to death. However, his earlier status doubtless saved him from execution and he was put in prison where he died on 23 July 1951, then aged 95.

THE FATE OF THE WORLD

While we hung on the news from Verdun—it seemed as though the fate of the world were in Fort Douaumont—our own lists of death grew longer.

—Philip Gibbs
Realities of War (1920)

OUR VERDUN

Rightly understood, the battle of the Somme was not a greater battle than that of Verdun. It was similar; it was our Verdun battle.

—Stephen Graham
The Challenge of the Dead (1921)

B H LIDDELL HART (1895–1970)
Born in Paris 31 October 1895, son of a Wesleyan minister in that city, Basil Henry Liddell Hart was educated at St Paul's School, London, before going to Cambridge in 1913 to read history. In 1914 with a temporary commission in King's Own Yorkshire Light Infantry, he went to France where he was wounded at Ypres. After recovery in England he returned to the Somme where he was gassed. He did not return to action, but instead went to training units where he worked out original new battle tactics. He later transferred to Army Education Corps
[continued opposite]

on their front with Russia they would have been much more successful.

But in the end they too came up against that same factor as the British and French had faced in their Empires: that element that often drives people to defend their own land regardless of how hopeless the battle looks and is, simply because it is their own land.

The important part of the Verdun epic was the realisation by the French, that this was it: if Verdun goes, it all goes. Such a possibility wonderfully focused the minds of the French politicians and High Command. And equally important, also realising what the loss of Verdun would mean, the British High Command blind as it often was to reality, saw clearly the resulting fate of the fifty or so British Divisions then in France.

But having such a realisation did not equip them with the perception of what best to do: or how best to do it. After many ungraceful, not to say disgraceful displays of rank, ego and outright arrogance between the generals, the Allied command decided upon a huge thrust on the Somme, to relieve the pressure at Verdun. The French then would break out of Verdun thus tying up large German forces, and keep up the pressure along their front, all the way to Albert. The British would attempt the same along the line from Albert to the Channel: but the principal event would be the Battle of the Somme. In true British orderliness it was set down to start at 7.30 am on 1 July: a week's intensive

The Battle of the Somme
1 July – 20 November 1916

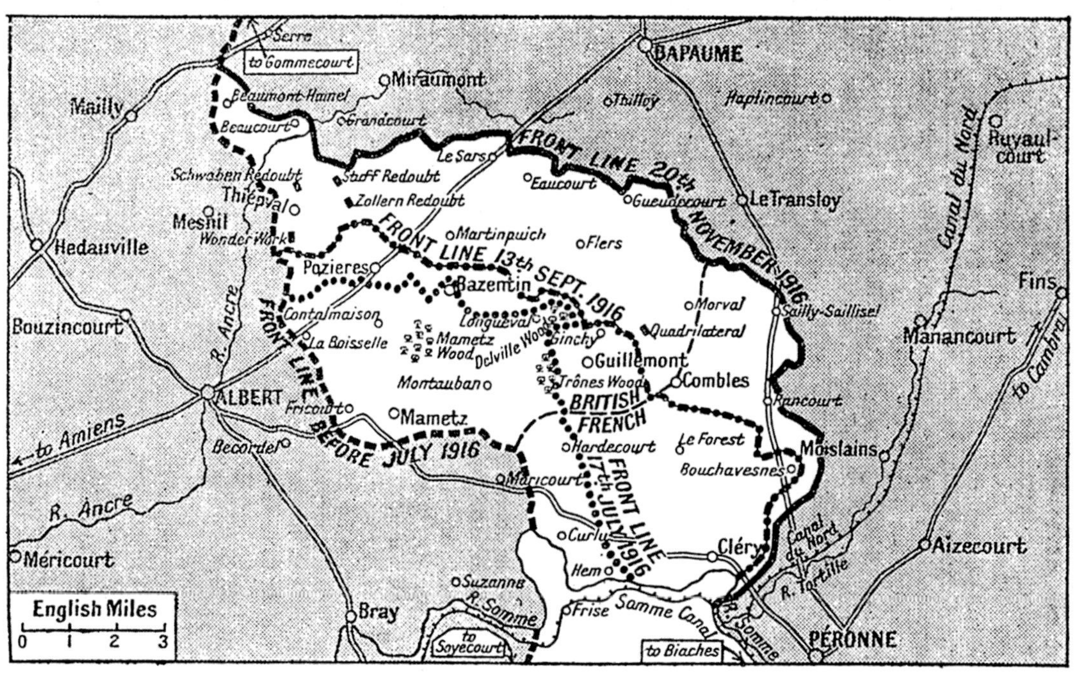

bombardment preceding it. Two British armies would deal with the top half and two French armies with the lower half of the battle area.

The French, badly damaged by the events of 1915 and early 1916 needed time to consolidate and reorganise: their losses of experienced officers meant that this was not easy. The British set deadlines and refused to budge from them. When the French pleaded for an extra day, General Haig refused and as Liddell Hart describes it:

> Haig's anger was unconcealed, and in the face of his objection to any postponement Foch did not argue the point. Then on the 28th (June), when part of Haig's assaulting troops had already moved up to the trenches, the rain came down and flooded the trenches, and Haig was forced to concede to General Rain the postponement that he was inclined to withhold from General Foch.

Haig knew that the Germans had built during 1915 and 1916 a defence line largely based on concrete block houses, well protected supply routes and massive stores safe in underground bunkers that would enable the invaders to hold their ground.

However, so convinced were the Germans of their security and British commonsense that:

> It is recorded that the Germans were unable to believe that the British seriously intended to develop their main attack against the Somme defences. Rather did they think that the elaborate preparations which they observed were but a blind with which to force the German High Command to denude its front farther north of reserves and to concentrate them in the region of Douai and Bapaume.

Haig's own knowledge of the depth and strength of the German line is clearly revealed in his own dispatch on the subject, which is in part:

> During nearly two years' preparation he (the enemy) had spared no pains to render these defences impregnable. The first and second systems each consisted of several lines of deep trenches, well provided with bomb-proof shelters and with numerous communication trenches connecting them. The front of the trenches in each system was protected by wire entanglements, many of them in two belts forty yards broad, built of iron stakes interlaced with barbed wire, often almost as thick as a man's finger.
>
> The numerous woods and villages in and between these systems of defence had been turned into veritable fortresses. The deep cellars usually to be found in the villages, and the numerous pits and quarries common to a chalk country, were used to provide cover for machine guns and trench mortars. The existing cellars were supplemented by elaborate dugouts, sometimes in two storeys, and these were connected up by passages as much as thirty feet below the surface of the ground. The salients in the enemy's line, from which he could bring enfilade

B H LIDDELL HART (contd)

where he remained until 1927. His ideas and the depth of his thinking on military matters interested many, as did his regular newspaper contributions and biographies of men such as Scipio Africanus, General Sherman, Foch, and TE Lawrence. In 1930 in *The Real War* he was the first to question the reputation of Haig, at that time not a popular theme.

As the second world war drew closer, Liddell Hart found himself on the side of compromise with Hitler, believing that he had signalled the rise of such a regime years earlier but had been ignored, and now there was no sensible option. Curiously after the war he was allowed to interview some German generals who had, they said, benefited from reading Liddell Hart's texts!

Liddell Hart's philosophical approach to the subject of war and the waging of it, equips his comments with a special depth very useful in understanding in particular the Great War, where the two antagonists were basically equal intellectually and militarily, and thus the victory belonged to the side who thought out the consequences of the action taken more thoroughly than the other. Typical of this, which seems so obvious, is his comment about the feint at Fromelles, or anywhere else for that matter. That is, that as soon as the feint is over, it is shown for that and the enemy is then free to do what he wishes. Perhaps this turn of mind is what makes Liddell Hart's *Foch* so interesting and his *TE Lawrence* so perceptive: one does not have to like or loathe either subject, but both men brought thinking to military combat situations with some real success.

Liddell Hart married firstly in 1918, there was a son, the marriage was later dissolved and in 1942 he married again. In 1966 he was given a Knighthood. He died on 29 January 1970 and his papers passed to King's College, London, an archive of particular interests accumulated by a man who truly tried to understand what happened on the Western Front between 1914 and 1918.

fire across his front, were made into self-contained forts and often protected by mine fields; while strong redoubts and concrete machine gun emplacements had been constructed in positions from which he could sweep his own trenches, should they be taken.

These various systems of defence, with the fortified localities and other supporting points between them, were cunningly sited to afford each other mutual assistance and to admit of the utmost possible development of enfilade and flanking fire by machine guns and artillery. They formed in short, not merely a series of successive lines, but one composite system of enormous depth and strength.

Against that line Haig knowingly sent his infantry, some so laden with gear (their packs weighed 66 lbs/30 kgs) that they had to hold their heavy rifle out in front of them to give them balance as they walked across No-Man's Land, watched through the sights of German machine guns until they were within 1000 yards. And then the massacre began. The battle went on at peak for two and a half months, when it should have taken that many weeks. Or as some would suggest that many days for what it achieved. The Germans suffered as much at the hands of their High Command as did the British, their officers threatened with court martial if they lost a trench. And in the south driving against Peronne and Chaulnes the two French armies had no easy time: at the end their casualties were 195,000; as against the British 481,842; and the Germans 236,194.

Two weeks into the Battle of the Somme the 1st, 2nd and 4th Divisions of the AIF, the 1 ANZAC Corps, were moved from the Armentières region towards the battlefield where they would be given the task of taking Pozières beginning on 23 July.

In the meantime Haig's attention had been drawn to intelligence reports which indicated the Germans were taking battalions from the Lille area to reinforce their line in the Somme battle. Things were going so badly for the British that it would be easy to make a case for preventing even one battalion from joining the defenders, but it was said at least nine had been seen entraining at Lille for the front.

We, now of necessity, turn our backs on the Somme while never forgetting that it is, as it were, the background noise and pressure to what happens at Fromelles. In simple terms, if some action can be maintained in that region near Fromelles, the Germans would be foolish to deplete their strength, for if they did, the British might grab the opportunity to move on Lille. This style of bluff and counter-bluff had many critics but the maintenancc of it as a strategy helped build many a military career.

THE GERMAN GUNNERS ... BECKONED THEM ON

They had, as instructed, formed into a line, rifles held across their chests, bayonets at the ready; they advanced slowly in a disciplined way—they could do little else carrying six stone packs. They walked and watched. They presented a facile target. The German gunners laughed and beckoned them on. As men fell, their comrades still carried on in the same way, slowly, walking in line. There was almost no panic. They felt terror and anger but they were numbed. The survivors of the first wave, the first of six tragic waves carried on walking in a line ...

—M Middlebrook
First Day on the Somme (1971)

THE HEAVIEST DAY'S LOSS

After a week's bombardment the great assault was delivered at 7.30 am on July 1st—a day of fiery heat. Thirteen British Divisions, with six more close up, began to advance at a stately pace which gave the enemy time, where ever No-Man's Land was wide, to bring out their machine-guns from shelter after the barrage lifted. In the furnace of their fire British lines melted with tragic swiftness. Sixty thousand men fell on that one day, the heaviest day's loss in the history of the British army. And for little result.

—B H Liddell Hart
Foch (1937)

Actual figures: 21,392 dead, 35,493 wounded. It took seven days and 58 packed hospital trains to clear the wounded.

The Battalion with the highest casualties on 1 July was 10th Bn West Yorkshire with 306 killed, 404 wounded.

The 60th Australian Bn, the most damaged at Fromelles, had 398 killed and around 360 wounded.

3

Except by attack

... in modern war, however good the commanders and their staff may be, no one can win the battle except the infantry soldier, and he cannot win except by attack.

—Brig. General R C B Haking (1913)

Right from the beginning the British called the action at Fromelles, an attack. They never regarded the event as a battle and none of the regiments involved have it as a battle honour. *The British Official History 1916* (compiled by Capt. Wilfred Miles: preface by Brig. General Sir James Edmonds) Chapter V has the title 'The Subsidiary Attack at Fromelles' which downgrades it even further, and extraordinarily there is no Fromelles nor Fleurbaix in the index. And as it was the last official account written, this relegation can only be a direct comment by Edmonds on Bean's elevation of the event to a battle. The description occupies a mere 16 pages plus a full page map and was first published in 1938, nine years after Bean, and eighteen years after Ellis: and the first Bavarian Regiment histories pre-dated the British effort by fifteen years, the last one by six. This should have surely meant that the British account would have been the last word, the final chance to deal properly with Fromelles.

Instead we note considerable reliance on Bean and the Bavarian historians rather than digging deep into the British files, and that is not surprising when one examines the style and content of the British history. Unlike Bean it makes no judgements on people or events, and does not deal in individuals. In the Fromelles chapter the lowest rank mentioned is Major G G McCrae, CO of 60th Bn AIF and that only because he was killed: Lieut Colonels are only mentioned by name if they are wounded or killed. Lieut Col Tupman of 2/5th Gloucesters whose heroism and initiative brought him promotion to Brigadier a month later is ignored. Given this basic intellectual and social handicap, one reads the British version of Fromelles with some caution. How much caution will be apparent as we trace the action with the help of the War Diaries, which incidentally were not open to the public until 1965. Some other War Diaries, the Public Record Office on its public handout notes: '*are closed to general public inspection for 100 years*'.

THE PITY OF IT

The pity of it was that the action need not have been fought since the First Army had perfect liberty to cancel it.

—Sir John Edmonds, British Official Historian, on Fromelles

61ST DIVISION HEADQUARTERS

GOC: Maj. Gen. C J Mackenzie
ADC: Capt. W M Baird
ADC: Lieut T Coats
GSO1: Lieut Col Sir H Wake
GSO2: Major C G Stansfield
GSO3: Capt. R Mostyn Owen
AA & QMG: Lieut Col C C Marindin
DAA & QMG: Major C L Porter
DAQMG: Major E P Blencowe
CRA: Brig. Gen. R C Coates
CRE: Lieut Col S William

FIRST SECOND LINE DIVISION TO GO ABROAD

The Story of the 2/4th Oxfordshire and Buckinghamshire Light Infantry by Captain G K Rose MC was published in 1920. A slim volume based on a series of articles in the *Oxford Times* during the summer of 1919 it had an introduction by the then Brigadier General Ames. As leader of the regiment at Fromelles Ames 'left' soon after that battle, being one of many colonels who 'left' their units after Fromelles. Rose, the Adjutant is noted as being invalided to England 'early in July', so one assumes he was not at Fromelles. All this may account for the rather secondhand feel of his entry pertaining to the events of 19/20 July. Whether or not Rose had access to the War Diaries of the unit is difficult to judge because uniquely of those involved at Fromelles the 2/4th Diaries are skeletal, even shoddy, when compared with the order and style of the others of this period.

As the Diaries start at Laventie in June 1916 there is also no way of checking what Ames says in his introduction. Curiously in that introduction Ames omits any reference to his first and only battle with the battalion, and restricts himself to three paragraphs about preparation.

At the end of October 1915, I consider that the battalion reached its zenith and its efficiency during its home service. It was a great pity that the Division could not have been sent abroad then. Instead, each battalion was reduced in November to a strength of 17 Officers and 600 men. Individual training recommenced until specialist training of every kind flourished and multiplied.

In January 1916, the Battalion had recently been made up of untrained recruits moved to Parkhouse Camp, Salisbury Plain to complete its training with the rest of the Division.

The Division was speedily completed for foreign service, new rifles were issued (previously they had Japanese guns). We were made up to strength with drafts from the Liverpool, Welsh, Dorset, Cambridge and Hertfordshire Regiments, were inspected by the King and embarked as a unit of the first second line Division to go abroad.

[continued opposite]

At this point a paragraph on the British Official Historian is not out of place. General Sir James Edmonds was born in 1861 so was aged 65 when corresponding with Bean on the subject of Fromelles, and aged around 76 when compiling the chapter. A cynic and manipulator *par excellence* Edmonds outlived almost everybody about whom he wrote, he finished the history in 1947, and died in 1956 aged 94. His many letters to Bean reveal a highly intelligent and deeply unpleasant man, barking out instructions to an unruly colonial. However, for the great good fortune of Australia, Bean was not an army officer, so Edmonds' orders were, to Bean, only opinions and he rejected most of them as far as Fromelles was concerned. This aspect will be fully dealt with in later chapters; here we confine ourselves to the British contribution at Fromelles. Edmonds summed up the objective thus:

> ... the operation was to be a purely local attack intended to hold the enemy to his ground and to teach him that he could not, with impunity, reinforce the main battle by thinning his line on this front.

Whilst this was the objective of the original idea submitted to Haig, it was soon apparent that General Haking, commander of the XI Corps of the British First Army was again pressing to take Aubers Ridge, or at least try for it. Edmonds draws attention to the fact that:

> The scene of operation partly coincided with that of the Battle of Aubers Ridge fought in May 1915: indeed, the 8th Division had then attacked over the same ground as the 5th Australian Division was about to do, and against the same opponents.

Since May 1915, '*the Germans had ample opportunity to strengthen their breastwork defences, which now included many machine gun emplacements constructed of concrete, well-sited and concealed*', whilst '*the actual numbers of guns and howitzers at Aubers Ridge 1915 was almost the same as at Fromelles 1916*': a combination of events not very encouraging to those around Haking and who now sought to call off the attack.

Right up to 16 July Haking was still floating the idea of getting to Aubers Ridge but Haig seems to have been absolutely against it. It was a pity he did not express himself with the same resolution instead of the ambiguous couple of sentences he wrote on the Report for the attack, '*Approved except that infantry should not be sent in unless an adequate supply of guns and ammunition for counter-battery work is provided. This depends partly on what guns enemy shows.*'

It is obvious, and in a sense acceptable, that in the overall British history, Fromelles was of little account. Their attack changed nothing—no territory won or lost, and only cost 1,547 British casualties (519 killed, 977 wounded, 51 POWs) which in the first month of the Battle of the Somme with losses in the 100,000s, certainly made Fromelles no more than an 'attack'. Disinterest is one thing, but misinformation is something else.

The British contingent at Fromelles was the 61st Division described as 'The 2nd line South Midland Territorial Division', and according to the British Official Historian assembled at Northampton in January 1915. However, the War Diaries of the three Brigades and twelve battalions that formed the Division that went to France, begin in July/August 1915, and training is noted as beginning mostly in September. This is important because it was these men who fought at Fromelles and to give the impression as the Official British History does, that the men had the benefit of 18 months training prior to Fromelles is a serious misrepresentation of the situation. It is also a grave insult to the men in those units who served and died.

The War Diaries also reveal rather obviously that training during winter was extremely limited.

Whereas the Official History says this of the Division's early days:

> Its training had been delayed owing to lack of arms and equipment, and interrupted by the necessity of supplying drafts to the top line division: also by its responsibilities as part of the home defence forces.

This cannot be described or even checked as the War Diaries of the Brigades and Battalions for February, March and April 1916 are all missing. The absence of these, yet the survival of all the others, is curious. Suspicious may be another description. Perhaps a few sentences about the surviving War Diaries might be of interest here. They are kept at the Public Record Office at Kew near London in stout cardboard boxes. For the most part they are written or typed on the usual War Diary/Intelligence Report paper—foolscap size, landscape format. Prepared by the HQ company, they are signed (and thus, one assumes, read and approved) by the duty officer for the month. Their content varies hugely depending on the literary capacity and observation skills of those involved. Sometimes one is very aware that the writer is making sure significant events are being recorded, at other times it is clear that keeping the diary is an onerous, but required duty. In preparing the diaries none of the writers would have been particularly aware that these sheets might become the only surviving record of the events. Few soldiers in the line had

THE FIRST SECOND LINE DIVISION TO GO ABROAD (contd)

Rose devotes one paragraph to the events of 19 July.

This harassing warfare had a crisis in July. The operations of July 19, which were shared with the 61st Division by the 5th Australian holding trenches further north, were designed as a demonstration to assist our attack upon the Somme and to hold opposite to the XI Corps certain German reserves, which, it was feared, would entrain at Lille and be sent south. That object was achieved, but at the cost of severe casualties to the divisions engaged, which were launched in daylight after artillery preparation, which results proved to have been inadequate, against a trench-system strongly manned and garrisoned by very numerous machine-guns. The objectives assigned to the 61st Division were not captured, while the Australians further north, after entering the German trenches and taking prisoners, though they held on tenaciously under heavy counter-attacks, were eventually forced to withdraw. 'The staff work,' said the farewell message from the XI Corps to the 61st Division three months later, 'for these operations was excellent.' Men and officers alike did their utmost to make the attack of July 19 a success, and it behoves all to remember the sacrifice of those who fell with appropriate gratitude. It was probably the last occasion on which large parties of storming infantry were sent forward through 'sally ports'. The Battalion was in reserve for the attack. C Company, which formed a carrying party during the fighting, lost rather heavily, but the rest of the Battalion, though moved hither and thither under heavy shelling, suffered few casualties. When the battle was over, companies relieved part of the line and held the trenches until normal conditions returned.

The next paragraph of Rose's history is more to the point.

Soon after these events the Battalion was unlucky to be deprived of Colonel Ames, a leader whose energy and common sense could ill be spared. This was the first change which the Bn had in its Commanding Officer, and it was much regretted.

such a feeling of self-importance. It would have never occurred to them that what they wrote at the time would be locked up for 50 years, thus depriving the vast majority of those affected by the events from ever finding out about them, except through the Official History, which by the time it had taken had become irrelevant for this purpose anyway.

That said, it is important now to describe the 61st British Division as it prepared itself—*For the Imperial Force*, that is to go into action abroad.

The Division had three Brigades. The 182nd consisted of four battalions of the Royal Warwickshire Regiment—2/5th, 2/6th, 2/7th and 2/8th. Originally formed in 1675 the regiment achieved its Royal title in 1832. The 183rd Brigade was made up of the 2/4th and 2/6th Gloucestershire Regiment—another long established unit distinguished by its Sphinx badge since 1801. The other two battalions in the 183rd were the 2/6th and 2/7th Worcestershire Regiment dating from 1694. During its training period the 183rd was under the command of Colonel Sir John Barnsley VD, whose forceful early reports were written in a strong and stylish hand, almost suggesting he used a quill. Sir John did not go to France with the Brigade and his successor was sacked a week after Fromelles. The 184th Brigade was formed by the 2/1st Buckinghamshire and 2/4th Oxfordshire and Buckinghamshire, 2/5th Gloucestershire and 2/4th Royal Berkshire with formation dates of 1908, 1741, 1801 and 1782 respectively. Thus all but one had long traditions.The fact that by the end of the war most of the units were but skeletons, while by February 1918 the 2/4th, 2/6th Glosters and the 2/1st Bucks had been disbanded, is another story.

As the Division's title implies, the men serving with it were from Birmingham, Coventry, Northampton and that general area, together with Warwickshire, Gloucestershire and Worcestershire. At this stage of the war regiments were still very territorial, but later when huge losses virtually wiped out battalions this demarcation could not be sustained.

The Brigades trained in different places on a rotation basis. The 182nd began at Northampton and Danbury, the 183rd at Epping and Brentwood, the 184th near Chelmsford and Colchester. After the restrictions due to bad weather and resulting sickness, the next concern of Brigade Headquarters seems to have been the lack of weapons and ammunition to train with, plus 'a supply of recruits of the right sort'.

Conscription began on 2 March 1916 in England, the Compulsory Service Act having been passed on 24 January, so those already in the 61st Division were volunteers. At this time

A NARROWNESS OF OUTLOOK

A reviewer in the influential *United Services Magazine* in 1920 of 'The Story of the 2/4th Oxfordshire and Buckinghamshire Light Infantry' had nothing to say about the early actions of the battalion, but this about the author:

Captain Rose has produced an interesting account, though his comments on the Regular Army and on matters strategical argue some narrowness of outlook and want of appreciation of essentials.

However it should be noted that Capt. Rose did receive a Bar to his MC on 18 May 1917.

REAL WAR RIBBONS

Sir Colin Mackenzie KCB had commanded the 61st Division through many difficult vicissitudes. His watchful eye and quiet manner gained everywhere the confidence and admiration of his regimental subordinates, who saw in him great soldierly qualities. The General's bearing and his string of real war-ribbons made many an eye rove at an inspection. By a wound he was obliged in June 1918, to retire from command of the Division. He was much missed.

—Capt. G K Rose MC 1920
2/4th Oxford and Bucks

While on the subject of the 61st Division it is fair to quote the entire entry as far as Fromelles is concerned from *The Territorial Divisions* by J Stirling (1922): *The Division went to France in May 1916. On 19/20 July they and an Australian Division made an attack in the Neuve Chapelle district. Ground was gained but could not be held as the guns on Aubers Ridge had command of it.*

The divisional sign of the 61st British Division which originates from Roman numerals LXI.

they acquired Major General Colin Mackenzie on 4 February 1916 as GOC, with Brig. Gen. A F Gordon heading up 182nd Bde on 13 February, Brig. Gen. C G Stewart commanding 183rd Bde from 3 May, and Brig. Gen. C H P Carter commanding 184th Bde from 7 May.

As already noted, there are no surviving War Diaries for February, March and April for any of the units. But most of the May War Diaries survive and are important because it was then that the Division packed up its kit and horses, and embarked for France. Some of the detail is worth recording.

In the case of the 2/6th Royal Warwickshire there were 33 officers, 936 ORs, 21 vehicles, 64 animals, 9 bicycles and 4 Lewis guns. The 2/7th had 33 officers, 965 ORs, 12 riding horses, 64 draught animals, 4 two-wheeled vehicles and 17 with four wheels. The 2/8th was much the same, but had 8 bicycles and no riding horses. The 2/1st Buckinghamshire set sail with 35 officers, 897 ORs, 3 officers' chargers, 9 riding horses, 17 heavy draught, 2 light draught, 24 mules, 9 pack ponies, plus 2 GS wagons, 9 GS limbers, 4 travelling kitchens, 2 water carts, 1 officer's mess cart, 1 Maltese cart and 9 bicycles. Apart from general interest these figures reveal that the British units were not, on embarkation, seriously under-strength, a point often pleaded for their later failure, and it is difficult to reconcile these near full strength numbers with the 550 or less that were given as 'fighting strength' prior to the battle. In the War Diaries there is no indication that some 300 men were casualties in every British Battalion, even though the 'fighting strength' given by Mackenzie in his Battle Report implies this.

The Division made its way towards Southampton and beginning 21 May, and over the next four days, sailed to Le

(continued page 40)

2/4TH ROYAL BERKSHIRE
Officers—Chelmsford 1915

Back Row: 2nd Lieut R Holland, 2nd Lieut T C Keble, 2nd Lieut G S R Webb, 2nd Lieut J H Skene †, 2nd Lieut W O Down, 2nd Lieut G A Brooke*, Lieut O J Dowson*, Lieut & QM C G H Smith.

Second Row: 2nd Lieut E O Lambart, 2nd Lieut N G Hunt, 2nd Lieut H J Gale*, Lieut H C Meysey-Thompson, Lieut G T Simonds, Lieut F W Dilke, 2nd Lieut J F Duff, Capt A N Palmer, 2nd Lieut G H Hawkes, Lieut R V C Freeth †, Lieut F M J White.

Sitting: Capt. E P Lucas*, Capt. J C Hammond, Capt. T Shields*, Major J H Simonds, Lieut Col M Wheeler, Major C Bartram, Capt. R Whittaker, Capt. C J D Cave, Capt. F L Hadden.

On Ground: 2nd Lieut M D Walker, 2nd Lieut C E Brooke, 2nd Lieut R G Imray, 2nd Lieut A Bartram, 2nd Lieut A A Austen-Leigh.

† Killed in Action. * Wounded. July 1916.

COURTESY THE ROYAL GLOUCESTERSHIRE, BERKSHIRE & WILTSHIRE REGIMENT (SALISBURY) MUSEUM

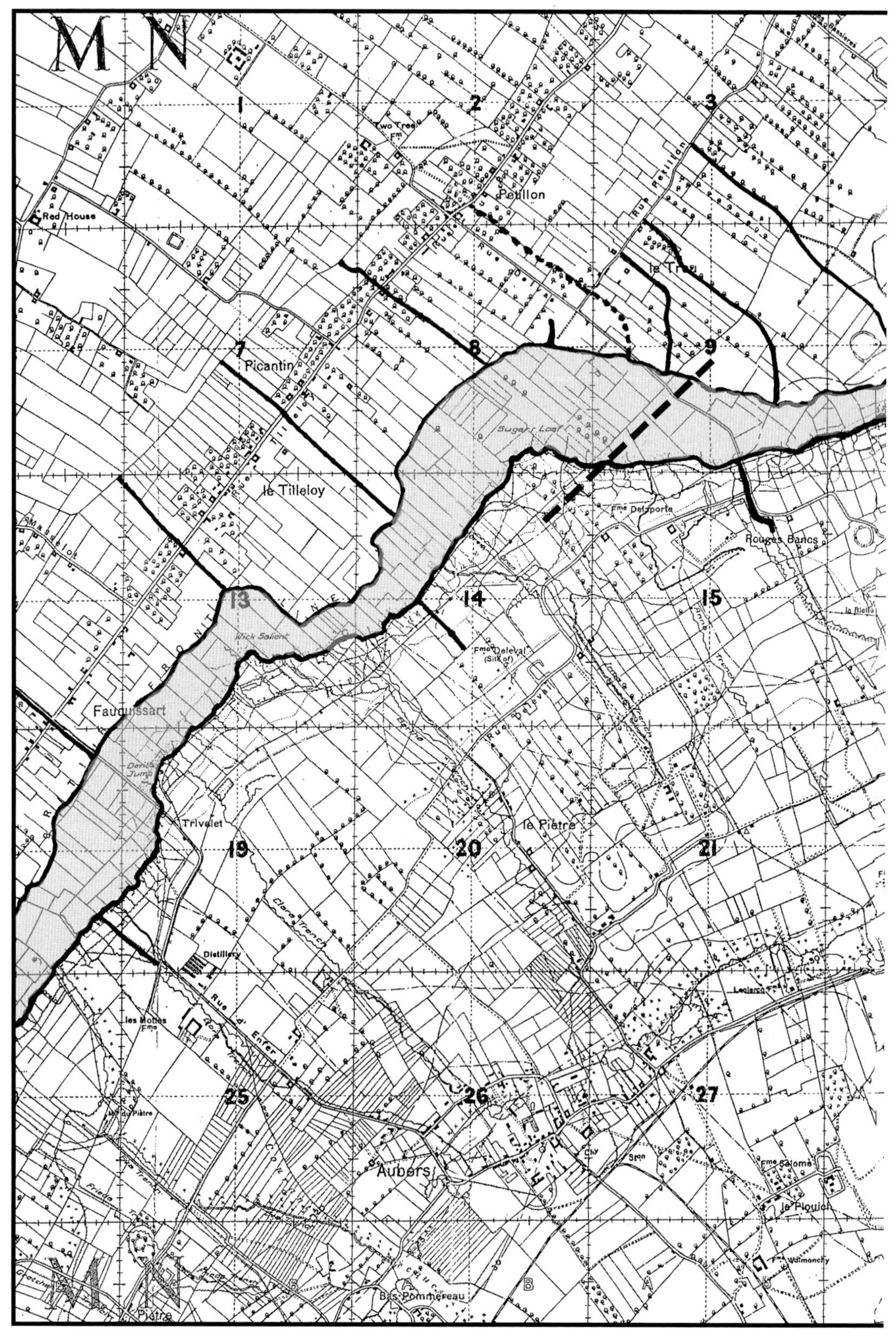
M N
1
2
3
Two Tree Fm
Petillon
Red House
Rue Petillon
le Trou
7
Picantin
8
9
Sugar Loaf
le Tilleloy
Fme Delaporte
Rouges Bancs
13
14
15
Wick Salient
Fme Deleval (Site of)
Fauquissart
Devils Jump
Trivelet
le Piètre
19
20
21
Distillery
Rue d'Enfer
les Mottes Fme
Leclercq Fme
25
26
27
Aubers
Fme Salomé
le Plouich
Fme Wamonchy
Bas Pommereau
Piètre

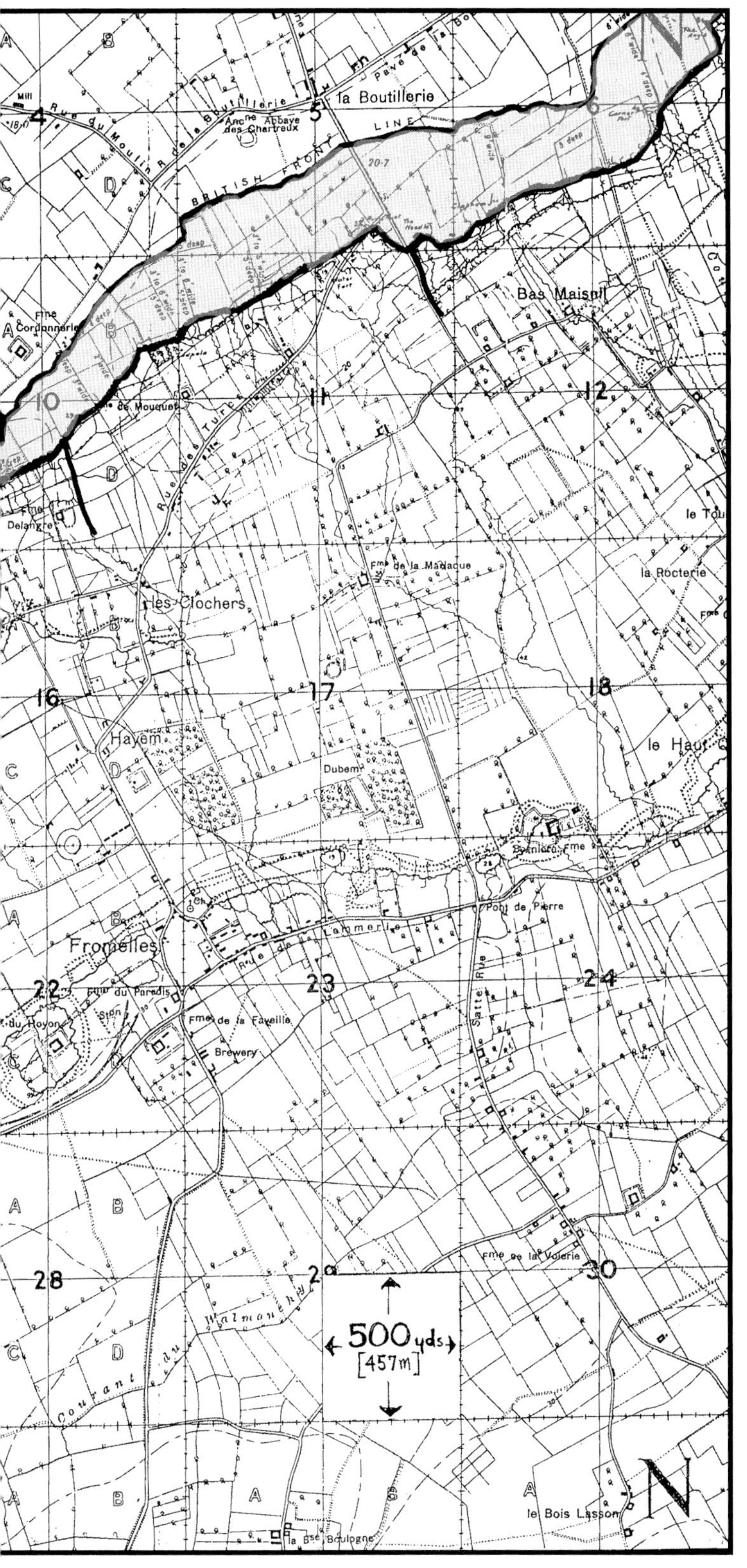

THE BRITISH TRENCH MAP 1916

This is not the map used for the battle, a copy of which could not be located, but is a composite of two British Army Maps. The left hand side from Aubers, Map 36 SW1 '*corrected to 31.8.16 with minor corrections to 5.9.16*', and the right hand side from Radinghem, Map 36 SW2 '*corrected to 5.5.16*'. The substantial reduction and combining has required the painting out of some lines and the enlargement of some names, together with some emphasis on lines to show the front lines and Brigade sectors. When viewed with the composite photograph on pages 106–7 it can be seen that the front lines changed little between May and October 1916. There is some disparity between some map references from quoted sources in the text and the apparent location of those points on the map, but no corrections have been made and no explanation attempted.

- 182nd Bde from the thick line just south of Fauquissart to the next thick line.
- 183rd Bde to the next thick line, known as Sutherland Avenue.
- 184th Bde to the next thick line, known as Bond Street.
- 15th Bde MG Coy occupied the next section—to the short thick line.
- 15th Bde to the next thick line known as Pinney's Avenue (after Brig. Gen. R J Pinney, 23rd Bde 8th British Division). The dotted line in this sector is VC Avenue communication trench. The thick dash line is the Laies across No-Man's Land.
- 14th Bde covers the area to the next thick line—Brompton Road.
- 8th Bde to the next thick line—Cellar Farm Lane.
- 60th British Brigade and the New Zealand Division are beyond that line.
- On the German side the 17th covers from below Trivelet to near Ferme Deleval. The 16th from there to rue Delvas. The 21st from there to just beyond Ferme Delangré, and 20th to the next thick line.

A MOST DANGEROUS SITUATION

The question of the enemy overhearing telephone conversations in the forward area arose in June 1915. Intelligence reports, deductions and experiment all combined to show the leakage of information to the enemy, which was known to have taken place, was connected with the extension of the telephone system to the front. It was learnt in August 1915 that the French, who were troubled with the same problem, had established a listening station, well forward in their own lines, and were overhearing scraps of German conversation. Various precautions and restrictions in the use of the telephone were instituted, but were difficult to enforce, and as the enemy could undoubtedly overhear messages sent through a badly insulated line laid on or in the earth, the menace of his obtaining information in this manner created a most dangerous situation, although code names and position calls for units had been introduced.

That the alarm was not unfounded was proved on 2 July 1916, when British troops, on entering Ovillers la Boisselle, found pasted up in a dug-out the copy of a portion of a British order which had been overheard and gave clear warning of imminent attack. Investigation showed that this order had been repeated by a brigade-major over the telephone to a battalion.

—*Military Operations: France & Belgium 1916*, Vol 1 (1932)

The much later research of Douglas Porch in *The French Secret Services* (1997), provides an excellent description of French technology which was much the same as the earlier German system:

More common were devices which amplified conversations on the one-way trench wires, allowing German-speaking French teams to eavesdrop on enemy telephone conversations. The listening devices were comprised of a series of insulated wires which radiated out from a switchboard placed in the front lines. Each sought to pick up the currents of a telephone line passing through the soil from a specific 'search ground'. When

[continued opposite]

Havre. They proceeded to billets at Laventie, Gonneham, La Valleè and Le Sart—in the vicinity of Estaires. It was a journey not without incident. The 183rd held a big inquiry after, on the train from Le Havre, a man opened the door of a horse box to shout for help to control the horses, and a panic-stricken horse bolted for the door and took four men with it: the horse died, but the men survived. This generated considerable paperwork but nobody was blamed or court martialled. But the Courts-Martial would be busy by July with men falling asleep at their posts while on duty. The Staff Captain of the 183rd pointed out that '*the men have had to do two or more turns*' and without saying so directly, were close to exhaustion. This was due to route marches, training and moving supplies up to the front line, not forgetting the stress of now being under fire. Since 28 May the British were being concentrated in the Laventie-Neuve Chapelle area, some in trenches, some in billets. Then in the closing days of May they moved into the front line, or rather half of them did, while the other half was in reserve.

The reader is directed to the map on pages 38–39 which shows the placement of the British regiments, and also reveals that the British and Australian troops were facing south-east and south respectively, quite unusual on the Western Front.

Mackenzie's Report, dated 22 July, paragraph two, details the limits of the attack fairly concisely:

> The method of the attack and this disposition of Battalions were according to Corps Orders No. 57 para 5 attached and supplemented by verbal instructions that it was not intended to employ more than 6 battalions for the assault, in order that the Division might be kept intact for future operations.

If what Major General Mackenzie wrote in his Divisional Report on the battle was true, the six battalions that went to the front line were presumably the best battalions in the Division—the assaulting battalions.

In the 182nd Bde sector these were the 2/6th and 2/7th Warwicks, in the 183rd Bde sector the 2/4th and 2/6th Glosters, and in the 184th Bde sector the 2/1st Bucks and 2/4th Royal Berks. This deployment was never changed or revised, which meant that these six battalions were for all of June and most of July under considerable stress, but apparently not used for carrying and other such jobs.

The War Diary entries for June vividly portray the variety of the new experiences of being in action. That of the 2/1st Bucks is remarkable in its detail, already reflected in their embarkation listing. It is this diary that records the first action, on 11 June: *Battalion had its first casualty—man killed coming back from*

Listening Post near Red Lamp Corner. No. 4378 Pte Davies H (C Coy). Lieut Col H M Williams, the Battalion's CO who signed the Diaries was keen that every casualty would be named, and for a time this was possible. This is quite unique, naming of ORs in War Diaries, when it is usually only officers whose wounding or death was recorded by name. When on 16 June an officer was killed, the first, precise burial details were also given in the War Diary. Williams, as we will see, was dedicated to his men, and they to him.

On 12 June the 182nd Brigade sent 4 officers, 264 ORs representing its four battalions under command of Major Capper of 2/5th Warwicks to be attached to 3rd Australian Tunnelling Coy at La Gorgue. This seems to be the first mention of an Australian presence in the area. The second mention is in the 61st Division diary under 16 June:

> At 11.30 pm the gas alarm sounded and the two Bdes in the front line stood to arms. The gas was slight over Laventie and La Gorgue for 1 hour, having blown by a NE wind from the front of the ANZAC Corps.

Then this curious sequence of events:

> 17 June. Another gas alarm occurred in Laventie at 11 pm, without any cause. It was started by Australian Corps. 18 June. During the day 875 gas cylinders were moved into position. 2500 men were employed ... the whole action was completed without casualties and without arousing the enemy's suspicion. 19 June. A further 626 gas cylinders were moved into Fauquissart section (1500 in all).

Supporting this, the 18 June entry by 182nd Brigade:

> All units furnished working parties for special RE work placing cylinders in Fauquissart section.

As to be expected, on 19 June the 2/1st Bucks provided some interesting detail:

> The Regiment provided working parties of 480 men, 18 Sgts and 12 officers both yesterday and today to take up gas cylinders to the trenches in the left sub-section Fauquissart section. It was done without a single casualty. Working parties from 2 Brigades were required (about 1,800 men). Each cylinder was carried up by a party of 4—2 carrying and 2 resting.

It would seem that having got the gas into position the tactic was to start raids on the German lines, assisted by artillery support. The big raids were disasters. First to go was the 184th Brigade on 21 June. The unit was badly knocked about by German artillery fire before leaving. The cost was high and Brigadier General C H P Carter, Brigade Commander, was highly critical of Col Ames of 2/4th Oxford and Bucks, but no conclusion was

A MOST DANGEROUS SITUATION (contd)

amplified the conversations became audible ... They proved a valuable source of tactical intelligence—advance warning of trench raids and artillery bombardments, the location of enemy batteries—much appreciated in the armies even if GHQ found it uninteresting.

LISTENING IN

When the New Zealand Division reached the Fromelles area in late May 1916, it was not long before they became aware of German listening devices (see page 76)—'*also found a telephone cable running from No-Man's Land under the German wire*'. This may well have been what the 183rd Bde also found. The system worked by utilising the water table and soil conductivity with uninsulated wires or rods, so that the power output from the poorly insulated British telephone cables could be picked up and thus messages intercepted without any indication that security had been breached. This provided the Germans with a massive advantage.

It was when in early 1916 that the French found a German listening post during a raid near Arras that this system was then understood. The Allies turned to making their own version, and trying to be more careful with their own signals. They too found that '*enemy telephone conversations could be heard over distances as great as 300 yards*'—the Germans probably had had that capacity for almost two years.

In 1916 the British Fullerphone was introduced, which cut down the opportunities for intercept considerably. Later the Power Buzzer Amplifier was developed by the French. This worked by earth wires, firstly only providing a one-way service, but later two-way. It had a range of 2000 yards, and the Germans were also thought to have had similar apparatus with this long range capability. However, by mid-1917, due to interference and jamming, the Power Buzzer Amplifier system fell into disuse, as telephone lines had become much more secure.

Information courtesy of Tim Gellel
Royal Australian Corps of Signals.

given, nor survives in the file at Kew. However, the history of the 2/4th Oxfordshire and Buckinghamshire Light Infantry (1920) was introduced by Ames, and the historian wrote '*Soon after these events the Battalion was unlucky to be deprived of Col Ames ...*'—Army shorthand for 'being fired'? or in view of Ames later returning to command the brigade, does this mean he saw through Carter early on. Carter himself was fired after Fromelles, and sent back to England.

Second into the valley of death, so to speak, was the 182nd Brigade on 26 June. The Brigade carried out a raid, and Lieut Col E C Cadman (CO 2/8th Warwicks) reported:

> ... that they (the enemy) were fully prepared for the attack and they had, or had brought up, very much more artillery than we foresaw ... if their shooting had been better we should have suffered much more ... considerable damage was done to our trenches.

Cadman's handwritten note is accompanied by another from Brigade Major J R Heelis:

> Dear General, The Germans were absolutely ready. Directly our bombardment started they overwhelmed the party with heavy shell and lighter guns. Two platoons and Col Cadman got about halfway across J(?) field and a few men are reported to have got into the trenches and found them empty. This requires confirmation. Estimated losses: 4 killed, 20 wounded, 3 missing [Later: 2 officers killed, 5 wounded: 16 ORs killed, 71 wounded and 2 missing]. Col Cadman says the men did their best but the Hun Artillery fire was too heavy.

The later Bde report gives greater detail but does not change the facts: it was a disaster <u>not</u> because of bad planning only, but because the Germans were so well established and their wire was uncut.

Third to the slaughter was 183rd Brigade on 4/5 July, a much smaller affair involving 4 officers and 138 ORs. One officer was killed and one wounded, 2 ORs killed, 8 missing and 29 wounded. All these were from 2/4th Glosters and the raid was the subject of a spirited report by Lieut Col J A Tupman, the CO of 2/4th. He personally watched the raid and, unlike the larger earlier raids, this one was something of a success. A proud Tupman wrote:

> Captain Hanham cleared one bay with his revolver and a fierce bomb fight occurred which I could see from where I was, and during which, all there agree, 15 to 20 Germans were killed. About 1.30 Captain Hanham was hit in the leg with a bullet and had to be carried out by Pte May and Pte Allen.

Tupman went on in some detail to describe the courage and coolness of others, before concluding:

Lieut Colonel E C Cadman DSO Commanding 2/8th Royal Warwickshire Regiment 1916–18.

At the age of 43, Edward Cadman Cadman was killed in action, 27 May 1918 when commanding 10th Bn Cheshire Regiment at the beginning of the battles around Soissons. His name on the Memorial there, is one of nearly 4000 who have no known grave and were casualties of the battles the Aisne and the Marne, May to August 1918.

PHOTO COURTESY ROYAL REGIMENT OF FUSILIERS MUSEUM

> I desire to recommend Captain Frederick J Hanham who died from his wound soon after reaching our trenches for the Victoria Cross, as it was undoubtedly due to his splendid dash and courage and noble example that our party reached the enemy's parapet.

The file contains two statements from fellow officers, and presumably Tupman supplied the third sworn statement necessary for a VC recommendation to go forward. 2/Lieut F A Ridler was put forward for the MC, and this was awarded on 29 July. Tupman was also put forward for an award, his DSO might have been for this action, and in October was given command of the Brigade. Hanham, it would appear, got nothing.

All this background is deemed important to give a wider picture of the conduct and experiences of the British units prior to the 'attack' at Fromelles. It clearly reveals that the Germans were very solidly established, had excellent intelligence sources, overwhelming fire power, and this superiority was well known to the British commanders in the field. Their reports to their superiors never gloss over these realities, so there can be no possibility that the High Command was ignorant of the difficulties ahead, unless they chose to be.

At the far right on 4 July the 182nd issued order No. 17 marked 'Very Secret', *The 3rd Australian Mining Company will explode a mine north of Birdcage at 11.25 pm*. The work of this group—sometimes called Tunnelling, other times Mining—is noted a few times in the British War Diaries and by the poet Ivor Gurney (see page 342–43), their work was as dangerous as it was important, and much of it was concerned with digging saps across No-Man's Land, especially the extension of the Rhondda Sap in front of the Sugarloaf.

All activity prior to the 14/15 July was of course routine, there being no attack scheduled. So on 6 July the main event for the 182nd and its battalions was to do with gas. Prior to any gas being released smoke was sent out to test the wind strength and direction: on this day it was once more unfavourable. The War Diaries note 'Gas helmet alerts', but as there is no mention of German gas, all the drama is about the British gas, which in the final analysis proved to be a total liability. On 13 July the 182nd tried again, but the wind was not helpful, so at 11.30 pm it was cancelled. On 16 July, then only 24 hours away from the scheduled attack the following entry in the War Diary:

> A gas attack was ordered for 8.30 pm. Owing to reliefs by 31st Division being completed and the 2/7th Warwicks being in a front where cylinders were installed smoke and gas were not let off quite in accordance with the table. The attack was stopped however ¼ hour after it had started

THE RHONDDA SAP

The Rhondda Sap (so called because it was started by Welsh men) had been used much earlier in a manoeuvre to reduce the width of No-Man's Land. It would be pushed out some 200 yards and then joined left and right with other trenches, which when well established would become the new British front line. But the water table, let alone the machine gunners of the Sugarloaf, had made the task impossible. That it should be started up again in the battle which was to be very dependent on its success, makes one wonder how intelligent were the Intelligence Staff?

Much of the original work on the Sap was done by the Australian Tunnellers, and the sad fact that more Australians were lost on this pitiless task, and that many were buried in it, makes it of special importance.

ONE IDIOT OF A SAPPER

The gas event with the 2/7th Warwickshire was clearly something of a drama. It was described by Capt. G B Donaldson in a letter home, albeit in less official terms than the War Diary:

I can tell you that in the ½ hour before the attack started, I came nearer to ... losing my nerve than has ever been the case before ... the RE officer responsible for letting off the gas on my frontage told me he had done several such stunts, but he thought the wind rather weak and did not like doing it in daylight as the Boche could shell more accurately. At 8.30 pm the show started. I had all the men in the trench out of dugouts and we all had our gas helmets on. It was like an appalling nightmare as you look like some horrible kind of demon or goblin in these masks. There were words of command along the line from the RE and then a loud hissing sound as the taps were turning on and the deadly greenish white vapour poured out of the jets and slowly blew in a great rolling cloud towards the opposite line of trenches.

In the next bay to me, one idiot of a sapper turned the jet in the wrong direction, and filled our trenches with gas in slewing it round over the parapet.

The Australian Tunnellers

One of the more extraordinary groups of men in the AIF were the three Australian Tunnelling Coys, made up of 15 officers and 400 men each, and set up with the blessing of Pearce in October 1915. Only the 3rd ATC concerns us here and the men in that company were mainly from Queensland, Tasmania and Western Australia. Their first commander was Lieut Leslie J Coulter, a mining engineer aged 27, with his 2/IC Lieut Alexander Sanderson, a consulting engineer and mine manager aged 35. After their arrival in France in May they were attached to the 1st Army, and had worked under Haking further south at the Boar's Head Salient.

They probably looked somewhat different to the average infantry man in that French summer. The Routine Orders of 27 July detailed their clothing, which also gives a good idea of the conditions under which they worked:

Waterproof Hats, souwester. Frocks, oilskin. Trousers, oilskin. Boots, Gum, thigh and short. Donkeys, khaki. Frocks, drill. Trousers, drill. Canvas suits.

With the early planning of the attack at Fromelles the 3rd ATC was brought up to work against the Sugarloaf. The idea was to cut a trench across the huge expanse of No-Man's Land by pushing a pipe filled with explosive out of what already existed of the Rhondda Sap, and creating a series of long craters which could quickly be dug out and connected to form the trench.

The Germans, however, saw what was going on at 3 pm on 19 July and put down a bombardment on the area. Coulter and six men were wounded, and others including Sanderson had to fire the charges, which they did with some success. The British recorded the event sparsely. Mackenzie first:

At Zillebecke, Hill 60, near Ypres.

'At 4.30 pm a pipe which had been pushed out by 3rd Australian Mining Co from the end of the Rhondda Sap, was exploded after four attempts by Major Coulter, commanding Company, who was wounded.'

Contrast this with the 184th Brigade Report, the area where Coulter was working:

'Arrangements were made for a party of the 3rd Australian Mining Co under Major Coulter to blow up by means of an ammonial pipe a continuation of the Rhondda Sap, after this had been affected ...'

The same number of words, but leaving distinctly different impressions. Others thought more of Coulter's efforts and he was awarded the DSO.

Later the 3rd ATC went onto Hill 70 a mile and a half north west of Lens. After months of secret digging and enormous danger on both sides, they clashed in a raid on 28 June 1917. Coulter was killed and Sanderson who was then in command survived. He received the DSO for his action, and went on to get the MC and two bars.

Hersin Communal Cemetery Extension—the graves of fifty-five AIF Tunnellers; fifty-four belong to the 3rd Australian Tunnelling Company: Coulter is buried here.

> but not before a considerable amount had been discharged from 2/7th Warwicks front.

That was how the Brigade saw it, but the War Diarist of the 2/7th Warwicks (an attacking battalion on the right) had something extra to add:

> Some of our men were gassed by the RE (Royal Engineers) in the afternoon who turned on the taps by mistake. Machine gun fire was very heavy.

The 2/6th Warwicks (an attacking battalion on the left) meantime had on 6 July taken up to the front line trenches '250 boxes of P bombs, 850 smoke candles ... 250 boxes of fuses ... 500 Brock lighters. And on 16 July, the somewhat hard pressed War Diarist noted:

> Working parties and carrying parties supplied with sudden orders received to move into trenches and take over line N.13.C.3½.3¼—N.B.C.9.0 thereby leaving a part to 2/7th Warwicks. Orders received to prepare for offensive on Wick salient. On arrival in trenches supplies of ammunition, bombs etc. was found to be insufficient and large working and carrying parties had to be organized to carry some to the line, also water, wire cutters etc.
>
> (Back at Riez Bailleul) Other large working parties organized—8 officers and 310 ORs, 12 officers and 410 ORs.

As an aside, this entry gives an important check on the strength of the 2/6th—i.e. 20 officers and 720 ORs being available for carrying parties, this being quite contrary to what Mackenzie would later write in his Report. It also reveals the amazing situation of last minute arrangements, which is fully backed up by *The History of the 2/6th* (1929).

> On July 16th the Battalion received sudden orders to take over the same part of the line as previously held, and, although but scanty details were yet to hand, orders were received that the Battalion would attack early the following morning ... the attack was postponed ... [and] ... would not even take place the following day. It will easily be understood by anyone who has experienced waiting for an attack to take place what a strain this constant postponement was to all ranks. Rumours were current in Laventie and La Gorgue amongst the civilian population that an attack was taking place on July 19th, and it is possible that this information was somehow conveyed to the Germans ... There can have been no doubt in the Germans' minds as to our intentions, and each postponement had given them more time in which to prepare for the assault. Everything had to be done in such haste that to hide our movements was impossible.

For the 2/6th Warwicks A and C companies were in the front line, B in support and D in reserve, and the historian wrote: *Many batteries of Artillery had only reached their positions during the previous night, and under great difficulty attempted*

AN OFFICER IS A DIFFERENT THING

One of the great talents lost at Fromelles was Geoffrey Boles Donaldson, a captain in the 2/7th Warwickshire. The only child of late Dr Donaldson of Londonderry, he was killed on 19 July, aged 22. After leaving Oundle School he went to Caius College, Cambridge intending to be a botanist, taking first class honours in Natural Science in June 1914. On the outbreak of war he joined up, thus missing his final year at Cambridge. By March 1916 he was a Captain and on arrival in France commander of C Company. His story is wonderfully told by Malcolm Brown in *The Imperial War Museum Book of the Western Front.* When we read the letter where Donaldson tells his mother about '*the larks singing at dawn ... over No-Man's Land, of wild flowers, poppies, roses, larkspur and monkshood, clematis-covered gateway*', and he encloses a piece of Lysimacia, we know of course that he is doomed and soon all she will have is the letter and the sprig of Lysimacia.

The sensitivity Donaldson had for

nature as one might expect included the men around him, being acutely aware of their exhaustion and the tension of constant movement. He understood the psychology of the leaders and the led, describing the necessity of sending two officers stricken with nerves out of the line, '*as it is essential that they should not be near the men while the sort of ague, which is the outward and visible*

[continued next page]

AN OFFICER IS A DIFFERENT THING (contd)

sign of the disease, is upon them. Some of the men had it too, but I allowed none of them to go back. An officer is a different thing, because on him depends so largely the nerves of the men.'

So with two officers down before the action, Donaldson and Capt. T H Bethell, the other company commander, took on the task of taking the men into No-Man's Land, and with some success. The 2/7th Warwickshire did get into the German trenches, the only British battalion that did, but at a cost. Both Donaldson and Bethell died. His Colonel said of him, '*he was always a most reliable and painstaking person, no work was too much for him and I shall always feel that what he did during our training greatly helped in bringing my battalion to a high state of efficiency.*' The 1920 records have Donaldson dying as a prisoner of war, whilst Bethell was killed in action. A very considerable number of men also lost their lives—around 85.

Donaldson had written '*urgent need of drastic measures on our front to hold back Hun reinforcements for the South and to do this certain troops had to be, well, more or less sacrificed. That is war, of course, and all in a day's work.*'

Donaldson is remembered on the Ploegsteert Memorial.

Capt. Thomas Henry Bethell of 2/7th Warwicks was the son of Thomas and Annie Bethell of Coventry. He was aged 31 and his name is on the Ploegsteert Memorial (Panels 2 & 3).

Capt. W Simms, 2/6th Warwicks was the son of William and Mary Simms of Wellington, Somerset, and was aged 29 when killed 19 July 1916. His grave is in Aubers Ridge British Cemetery (VI B 9).

to register on their targets, and it is no exaggeration to state that many of them had not succeeded when zero hour was reached. Then, near 6 pm, 19 July, as the battalion stood ready, this:

> Whilst waiting ... for the attack to commence, Bairnsfather's famous cartoon was amply confirmed, for a special corps enquiry was received by DRLS at Battalion HQ ... as to the number of empty pickle jars returned to store during the previous month.

When A and C companies led the attack they were cut down in seconds by shells and machine guns *while B company climbing over their dead and wounded comrades made their way out ... to form the second line ... following at 100 yards distance, were treated alike, all officers being killed or wounded at once. Only two platoons were left intact enough to carry out the final assault, but they, in face of tremendous odds, were unable to hold their ground.* And so it ended, the few survivors were withdrawn to be ready for another attack later, but at 9.45 pm the 2/7th learned that the 2/8th would take over the line and *by one am the last of the Battalion had left the line, with the exception of a small party of D company who ... remained to bring in our dead and wounded. Throughout the night they toiled incessantly, assisted by parties of 2/8th.*

Writing from the 182nd Bde perspective Brig. Gen. Gordon stated the disaster simply:

> When the bombardment lifted the first line of the 2/6th Warwicks were within 80 yards of the Wick and the leaders were seen to be inside the wire, when machine guns handled with the greatest bravery by the Germans were raised on the parapet and mowed down the attackers ... our losses—killed 22, wounded 381, missing 253, 4 Vickers and 6 Lewis guns ...

Among the dead were three company commanders, Captains W Simms, A E Coulton and T S Wathes: the fourth, Capt. M C Wade was wounded.

The two assaulting companies of 2/7th were C (left) under Capt. G B Donaldson, and D (right) under Capt. T H Bethell: B Coy was in support under Capt. L A Edwards and A in reserve under Capt. Hills. The Brigade Report noted that at *5.31 pm C and D Coys commenced to file out through sally ports and succeeded in deploying all four lines in No-Man's Land opposite without being fired upon.* At 6.00 pm under cover of the bombardment *moving with great dash reached the enemy's front line ... and about ten minutes later reported by artillery observers to be in the second line.*

This attack was in four waves, 50 yards apart with Coy Bombers behind first wave, Lewis gunners behind second wave, and Bn Bombers behind third, and a section of 182nd MG Coy behind fourth.

At 6.31 pm a message arrived by runner from 2/6th reached the 2/7th: *The 7th are across; our men won't face it, send reinforcements.* At 9.45 Lieut Crombie reported that *those who went over first are no more.* All the messages had been by runners because *telephone instruments, cable and office smashed up before the party got away ... operator shot through the head almost immediately.*

In the quick success of the early move, about 100 Germans were taken prisoner and in moving back such a large number at speed over No-Man's Land, they were thought to be attackers and shot down by the British, only 30 or so surviving. B Coy had gone out after the other two but had been caught by very effective enfilade machine gun fire and got nowhere. When orders were received to withdraw at 8.10 pm only A Company returned, with some wounded but there was no news of the other three. Donaldson and Bethell had been killed, as had most of their men. The early casualty returns showed: 1 officer was dead, 9 wounded, 2 believed dead and another missing, while 200 ORs were wounded and 170 missing. No ORs were by 21 July listed as dead, they had all disappeared.

Colonel H J Nutt CO of 2/7th wrote in his Report dated '*21 July 1916. In the Field Major A Welsh reports to me that the waves went over in perfect order and that the final push from about 40 yards of the German line was carried out with great dash and exactly as it had been arranged.*' Nutt had observed earlier that:

'*I am of the opinion that had the 2/6th been able to get in, it still would have been impossible to have held the enemy line without further support as he appeared to be in greater strength than was anticipated ... it would be necessary to have a greater number of men than that which we were able to put forward.*'

The 2/7th Warwicks War Diary had some precise information worth noting:

> 18 July. Preparation continue for the attack. New officers reported for duty in trenches which A Coy took over for the night giving D Coy and its officers a complete rest. A Coy cut wire opposite 2 sally ports during night.
>
> 19 July. B and C Coys moved from Rue Ballieul. Major Welsh took up his position in Front Line near Advance Signal Station. 21 Officers only allowed for the attack. The remainder returned to La Gorgue 11 am. Attack commenced at 6 pm. Withdrawal commenced 8–10 pm. Casualties 13 officer, 305 NCOs and men. Capt. Bethell reported missing presumed killed. Capt. Donaldson reported killed. 2/Lieut Wood reported killed.

Colonel Herbert John Nutt (1861–1940). A 2nd Lieut in the Volunteer Forces in 1888, later commanding 7th Bn, Royal Warwickshire Regiment till 1913. He raised and commanded 2/7th Bn and took it to France in 1916. At Fromelles he was awarded the DSO and MID. From August 1917 onwards he commanded Training Camps and Areas in France.

COURTESY ROYAL REGIMENT OF FUSILIERS MUSEUM

2/7TH ROYAL WARWICKSHIRE OFFICER LOST AT FROMELLES

Capt. Thomas Sidney Wathes was first reported missing believed killed, but it was later established that he had been shot in the head and killed while leading his men close to the German trenches. Thomas, whose brother was also a Captain in 2/7th Royal Warwickshires, was aged 28 when he died on 19 July. He had been educated at King Edward's School, Birmingham, and Wadham College, Oxford. Commissioned as Lieutenant in November 1914, he left a widow and child. He is remembered on the Ploegsteert Memorial.

ORDER OF BATTLE

182nd British Brigade
GOC: Brig. Gen. A F Gordon
Bde Major: Major J R Heelis
SC: Capt. P A Landon
RMO: Capt. A H Chovil

2/7th Royal Warwicks (assaulting/right)
CO: Lieut Col H J Nutt
SC: Capt. C La Trobe
D Coy (right): Capt. T H Bethell †
C Coy (left): Capt. G B Donaldson †
B Coy (support): Capt. L A Edwards
A Coy (reserve): Capt. R T Hills

2/6th Royal Warwicks (assaulting/left)
CO: Lieut Col J J Shannessy
SC:
C Coy (right): Capt. A E Coulton †
A Coy (left): Capt. W Simms †
B Coy (support): Capt. T S Wathes †
D Coy (reserve): Capt. M C Wade*

2/5th Royal Warwicks (support)
CO: Lieut Col P L Coates

2/8th Royal Warwicks (reserve)
CO: Lieut Col E C Cadman
SC: Capt. E G Davis

B & C Coys: Capt. T E Lefroy

Also:
A Coy: 1/5th Duke of Cornwall
2 Coys: 2/8th Warwicks
1 section of 182nd MG Coy and
TM Battery
- all at La Gorgue

† Killed in Action. * Wounded. July 1916.

Capt. W Simms,
British Aubers Ridge Cemetery.
PHOTOGRAPH L & A LIGHT

The 2/8th Warwicks (the part support, part reserve, battalion, along with 2/5th) whose war diaries are sparse to put it politely, noted on 11 July that two men were in hospital with self-inflicted wounds where a Courts Martial was held: '*CM repealed*' was the concluding observation.

However, the 2/8th had an historian, H T Chidgey, who in 1924 well before other histories, and while his memory was good, gave in his *Black Square Memories* some important detail. On 3 July the 2/8th was in the centre sector in front of Rue Tilleloy, and a week later moved to the right, the 182nd Bde taking up the area vacated by 31st British Division which moved to the west side of the Fauquissart Road. Chidgey noted:

> In this sector, as in the right sector, mining operations were a special feature. Australian tunnelling companies were engaged in preparing and blowing up mines under the enemy front line, the Boche retaliating, as opportunity offered, in the same manner under our front line: we had had to supply a considerable party of men to work with one of these tunnelling companies ...

After losing their Intelligence Officer on 13 July, the battalion on 15 July was relieved and went back to billets at La Gorgue, but were only there a day when told to move back to Rue Masselot '*a road running parallel with the front line ... pick up gas cylinders and carry them to the troops in the front line ... then the news leaked out, there was to be an attack on the 17th, and much additional artillery had been brought up and got into position.*'

Then Chidgey outlined his understanding of what the 'show', as he called it, was to do: and this clearly reveals the British understanding:

> The attack had as its objective the enemy second line trench system, which was to be held for a time, if reached, but not permanently.

Those last three words are of course important in judging the British battle plan. With some bluntness Chidgey recalled the 'show':

> ... the 19th of July, a date which will always remain a memorable one to all those taking part in the affair. The artillery preparation was very intense and produced a heavy retaliation. At the appointed moment our barrage lifted and the troops went over the top and through the various sally ports—all well known to the enemy by his aeroplane photographs. The Boche rifleman and machine gunners having retired to their strong concrete shelters, where they remained in safety during the bombardment, emerged as soon as the barrage lifted and blazed away with rifles and machine guns ... the hostile fire was very effective ... at many points of the attacked trenches an entry into the enemy's line was effected, and the objective, in some cases reached, and even

> passed ... there is not the slightest doubt that our casualties, in what was officially described as a 'successful raid' were far heavier than the enemy's, running, as they did, into the neighbourhood of six thousand between the two attacking divisions.

With regard to the German's concrete shelters: in a memo from Capt W A Greene 61st Division to 182nd Bde, there was this warning: '*Fauquissart Section, German Machine Gun Emplacements. 31 positions listed including 3 'not confirmed'.* these final observations: *'Four Vicker machine guns and six Lewis guns were also lost ... of these, it is believed that some are in No-Man's Land and may be recovered. The signalling communications were extraordinarily good throughout ... I hope to bring to notice a number of officers, NCOs and men who were conspicuous for their gallantry and coolness ... attackers.*'

In his history Chidgey wrote movingly of the conclusion of the Warwick's day at Fromelles:

> The remaining companies ... were rushed up in the early evening by motor buses to Laventie, and after dark went into the line and relieved the remainder of the 2/6th and 2/7th. It will be impossible to forget the scene of destruction and havoc ... everywhere apparent ... Many good fellows were lost that day ... Padre Bennett whose rescue work among the wounded ... will always be remembered ... was awarded the MC—the first in the battalion.

In the laconic style of the War Diarist, the 2/8th: '*On 20th July, parties patrolled for killed and wounded ... many bodies buried. Night of 21 July, many bodies recovered from No-Man's Land including Capt Simms (2/6th Warwicks) and Lieut Fison (2/6th Gloucesters). 22 July, Recovery of bodies continued. One wounded fetched from No-Man's Land by three men of C Coy, in daylight.*' (The graves of Simms and Fison are now at Aubers Ridge British Cemetery which was behind the German lines during most of the war.)

At the centre of the British line the 183rd Bde was caught up in the gas manoeuvres on its right on 15 July.

> 1pm. Informed that gas to be let off if wind held NW. 1.05pm Made arrangements to let gas off, this very difficult owing to reliefs going on ... 8.30pm. Gas let off in part of Div Front, not on part held by this Bde. Told to stand by to try and let off remainder during the night. No success however, a disagreeable night. Some of the gas that was let off blew back over our trenches. The men were absolutely steady. The wind was unfavourable and too light. The reliefs much interrupted by the Gas operation completed at last about 1.30am on 16th.

There is every reason to believe that this was the gas episode noted in the history of 17th BRIR who were opposite. As a result of it the Germans lost four dead and 21 gassed and as

ORDER OF BATTLE

183rd British Brigade
GOC: Brig Gen C G Stewart
Bde Major: Capt. M M Parry-Jones
SC: Capt. R B Stevenson

2/6th Gloucestershire (assaulting/right)
CO: Lieut Col F A C Hamilton*
SC:
A Coy:
B Coy:
C Coy:
D Coy:

2/4th Gloucestershire (assaulting/left)
CO: Lieut Col J A Tupman
2IC: Major R E Boulton
SC: Capt. D G Barnsley
D Coy (right): Capt. R H K Byers †
A Coy (left): Capt. E H E Woodward *
B Coy (support):
C Coy (reserve):

2/6th Worcesters (support)
CO: ..

2/7th Worcesters (reserve)
CO: Lieut Col L C Dorman

2/8th Worcesters (reserve)
CO: Major L L Briton.
MG Coy + TM Bty:

† Killed in Action. * Wounded. July 1916.

61st DIVISION ARTILLERY (RFA)
305 Bde: Lieut Col H A Koebel
306 Bde: Lieut Col F G Willcock
307 Bde: Lieut Col F Hilder
308 Bde: Lieut E W Furze

ROYAL ENGINEERS (RE)
All South Midland
1/3 Field Coy: Major C B Hosegood
2/2 Field Coy: Major O R Langley
3/1 Field Coy: Major O S Davies

FIELD AMBULANCES (FA)
2/1: Major G Mackie
2/2: Lieut Col G W Craig
2/3: Lieut Col P Moxey

2/4TH GLOUCESTERSHIRE OFFICER LOST AT FROMELLES

Capt. R H Knight Byers. At the early age of 13 he took First Class Honours in the Senior Cambridge locals and afterwards in Senior Oxford locals, being first of all England in chemistry and taking First Class Honours in mathematics and theology. He obtained a scholarship to Manchester University, but had to wait till he was 16 before going to the School of Technology there. In his first year he was head of the school, took his intermediate BSc and won four events at University sports. He obtained his commission through OTC in September 1914 and soon became Lieutenant. In July 1915 he went to the Front, where he saw much fighting and became Captain. Byers was aged 20 when killed 20 July whilst with 2/4th Gloucestershire. His Sergeant Major wrote that: '*The men had implicit confidence in him and would follow him anywhere.*'

2/6TH GLOUCESTERSHIRE OFFICERS LOST AT FROMELLES

2nd Lieut J W Gorrie was killed on 19 July when serving with 2/6th Glosters. He was the youngest son of Mr H T Gorrie of Auckland, New Zealand, and had been educated at King's College, Auckland. A well-known polo player and cross country rider, Gorrie came to England in June 1915 and joined the Inns of Court OTC and from there gazetted to the Worcester Regiment. His Major wrote of him: '*He was a splendid officer and we all loved him: he died a gallant death.*' His grave is in the Pozières British Cemetery.

Lieut Frank Henry Fison of 2/6th Glosters was the son of George and Elizabeth Fison, and a native of Brandon, Suffolk. He was 22 when killed 19 July 1916. His grave is in the Aubers Ridge British Cemetery (III B 16).

prisoners later told them there were men killed and wounded when the gas was blown back over the British lines. According to their records the Brigade coped with the postponement to the 17 and then to the 19 by making '*further preparations*'. Because there are hardly any records from the Gloucestershire Regiments involved, we must rely on the Brigade entry for 19 July. By way of preface the 2/4th Glosters were on the right: their CO was Lieut Col J A Tupman, with their D Coy on the right under command of Capt. R H K Byers and A Coy on the left under Capt. E H E Woodward. B Coy in support and C Coy in reserve. On the left was 2/6th Glosters whose CO Lieut Col F A C Hamilton, but other details have not been traced. In overall charge of the Brigade was Brig. General C G Stewart who one assumes approved the following:

> 19 July (Laventie). Zero time for operation fixed for 11 am. Preliminary Bombardment carried out as scheduled. 5.31 pm 2/6th Glosters filed out of sally ports to take up positions in open for the Assault. Lost a large number of officers and men in this operation. The Assault broke down under heavy MG fire and shrapnel, only one or two small parties reaching the enemy wire. These were wiped out. The four companies detailed for the assault lost 21 officers and 327 ORs. Some of these were lost during the enemy retaliation to our bombardment. A second Assault was organized for 9 pm. This however was cancelled by DHQ. The 7th Worcesters relieved the 4 and 6 Glosters in the trenches. During the night of 19/20 Orders were received to assault again next day, this however was again cancelled about 6 o'clock on 20th.
>
> 20 July. Day spent cleaning up trenches. BM to trenches. Little material damage but terrible chaos as regards salvage and the immense quantity of stores taken to trenches for the attack. The matter will be in hand by the afternoon. One or two very creditable pieces of work by officers and men of 7th Worcester in getting in wounded during daylight.

When this writer was researching material in the Public Records Office at Kew there were only skeletal notes from the 2/4th Glosters, and nothing at all from 2/6th Glosters, and later the Soldiers of Gloucestershire Museum were unable to locate anything of consequence.

However one item at Kew escaped whoever it was who plundered the files, simply because it was filed under September and that fact in itself seems not to have been entirely accidental.

The 2/4th Gloucester Regiment Report by Lieut Col J A Tupman CO was written 20 July 1916 but filed in September, because that is when it was returned by 61st Division Headquarters, although at the top it is written '*For attachment to War Diary 2/4th Gloucester Regt for month of July 1916*'. In the margin is a note 'Certified True Copy 3/9/16, D G Barnsley(?)

Capt. and Acting Adjutant 2/4th Bn Gloucester Regiment.' Tupman on the afternoon of 20 July went to hospital in Merville (Command taken over by Major R E Boulton), then to England, sick. A note in the file says he (Tupman) has copy (of the Report) in his possession. Tupman returned to the Battalion in September (he signed the War Diary for that month) and on 4 October 'proceeded to Brigade as A/Brigadier.'

Tupman's report which follows, unedited, is of immense importance because it was this battalion, together with the 2/6th Glosters that was on the left of those who had to take the Sugarloaf. From it we learn that at 6.15 Tupman knew that the 184th Bde assault had failed. Next to them, of course, was the Australian 15th Brigade, at that time still sending men 'over the bags' with 400 yards of No-Man's Land to cross. If the adjacent British Bdes were aware of each others' positions, how come the British and Australians never had such liaison? The historian of 2nd Bucks explained it simply: '*the Australians on the left of the Bucks, but owing to the salient unable to keep in touch*'. With the two assaulting British units effectively disposed of in the first 15 minutes of the Battle, the German gunners at the Sugarloaf could concentrate on the Australians, which they did to terrible effect.

> *With reference to the operations of the 19th inst. I have to make the following report.*
>
> *At 5.31 pm the time ordered for deployment in No-Man's Land, A Coy (the left assault) filed out through Sap 7a and successfully deployed 3 platoons in accordance with my orders. D Coy (the Right assault) was delayed for a few minutes, and by 5.50 pm had its leading platoon well deployed in No-Man's Land, the next platoon of this forming the 2nd wave were partly out. At this point in the operations a heavy machine gun fire was opened on D Coy in the open, and the men were driven back on me into the Sally Port of Sap 9 where I was standing. This machine gun fire was particularly heavy and appeared to come from the Front, and Right Front from at least 5 or 6 MGs.*
>
> *At 5.55 pm I received a report saying A Coy was pushing on all right and I at once ordered the 2nd, 3rd and 4th waves of D Coy to be moved to the other Sally Port (No. 7a), and gave the officers orders to push out there as rapidly as possible and to work up to the right of A Coy. I then went to the Sally Port (7a) and on arriving there found that A Coy by that time 6.10 pm had also been driven back. I then ordered that the men should be collected and all to be ready for a push forward should the opportunity occur. At that time I considered further attempt to advance in the face of this MG fire useless.*
>
> *I communicated with the 6th Glosters on my right, these events as they occurred.*
>
> *At 6.15 pm I received information that the attack on my left had also failed, and I was unable to ascertain the state of affairs on my right.*
>
> *At 8.0 pm I received an order to attack again at 9.0 pm, with the Companies not previously engaged—this was done, but only 1 Lewis*

THEY KNOW WHAT YOU ARE WORTH

This letter to his wife from 2nd Lieut Francis Saxon Snell of the Royal Berkshire Regiment was marked simply: France. Summer, 1916. Snell, a private tutor, educated at Felsted and King's College, Cambridge, was killed in action on 11 July 1916 as the unit was preparing for Fromelles. He was aged 29.

... I have to deal with men whose response to noble impulses has been strong enough to make them give up their homes and everything they value, from motives that must be almost wholly unselfish. Nothing is more remarkable than the absence of hatred or lust of battle in these fellows, whose one hope is to go back to "Blighty" "after the duration"—or before if it is possible even with a wound;—in spite of all they are full of courage and cheerfulness. They are so intensely human. I can tell you I break all rules impressed on me in lectures at the Inns of Court and elsewhere as regards the proper deportment of an officer before his men.

One must not be weak or vulgar, or toadying, or showing off, or sickly sentimental of course, but neither would one be those things with one's own social and military equals.

One may stand in relation to these men as a father or an elder brother, in some cases; but such relations exist between commissioned officers also. And quite as often the boot is on the other foot, even as officers and men. Nothing is more fatuous than the old military precept, that the officer must by every subterfuge keep up an appearance of omniscience, and that if he is "caught out" or reveals his ignorance on any point, his hold over his men will be gone.

Any sort of bluff of that kind will be detected by these men in an instant and they will despise you for it:—and serve you right too! They know what you are worth, and if you are fit to lead them they will follow you. But even if not, and you are honest, and sympathetic, and do your best—your level best—they'll lead you.

[continued next page]

Gun could be found available, 3 being out in No-Man's Land, of the other 3, 1 was in the reserve trench (under orders to come up), 1 was ready and the 3rd was hung up to the Right Sally Port. These guns have all been recovered with the exception of 1 left in the trench last night, and which has been sent for.

The behaviour of both Officers and men, under very trying circumstances was excellent and I very much regret A and D Coy did not get an opportunity of proving their mettle, as they went forward for the assault in a most gallant manner. The conduct of their officers, Captain E H E Woodward (wounded) and Lieutenants R G Scrase and J C James (both killed) in particular, being beyond praise.

After we had been driven back, there were many instances of men going out to assist to bring in the wounded. When it got dark I also sent out 2 patrols.

Of the 30 trained Lewis Gunners there are only 20 left. The 13 Lewis Gunners who went out with the 2 guns of A Coy were reduced to three, and I desire to bring to your notice the devotion to duty shewn by L/Cpl Porter, and Privates Burge and Denning, in remaining near their guns till after dark and then bringing them in. Lieutenant S J Stotesbury was acting as Staff Officer to me during the operation and was of the greatest assistance.

I also desire to bring to your notice the gallantry and devotion to duty shewn by Corporal Squance, who went out at 4.15 pm during a very heavy bombardment and again about 10 pm, also under fire to repair the telephone wire from my HQrs. to the Firing Line.

Our casualties yesterday were 7 Officers and 155 Other Ranks, approximately. I consider that as the casualties during the recent operations are approaching 50% of our trench strength, an opportunity should be taken, as soon as possible, to give the time necessary for a complete reorganisation.

20.7.16
(Signed) J A Tupman Lt Col Comdg
2/4th Gloucestershire Regiment

Back at Brigade level, as already noted, there was the finding of the '*German listening apparatus*' on 26 July, and on the 28th '*General Stewart left Bde. Major Porter commanding Bde until arrival of new Brigadier (Brig Gen Spooner).*' No mention anywhere that Lieut Col F A C Hamilton CO of the 2/6th Glosters had been severely wounded, or that Tupman had been evacuated ill and who had taken over their commands. The brusqueness of 28 July entry is clearly a comment, as well as a record.

At the left, the 184th Bde, those next to the Australians, however did record some useful information, rather better described in the 2/4th Royal Berks Regimental history than the War Diary. On the night 13/14 July an elaborate raid was made up of ten parties from 2/4th Royal Berks under Capt. Lucas with Lieut Dawson, 2nd Lieuts Skene and Brooke, and 100 men. The raiding party reached enemy trenches, but the Bangalore

THEY KNOW WHAT YOU ARE WORTH (contd)

I think many, I hope most of them like me, and I am getting much more confident in grasping situations and organising what has to be done ...

R. and F. are such ripping fellows, and yet they look upon the "Bosch" as just so much unutterable vermin; they have no sort of pity or compunction for them; the more they kill the better. Once L. came into our mess, and he said in his open boyish way, "And you know there was a rather rotten story about that raid last night" (it was a raid on the German trenches). What was that?" said R. and F. "Why," said L., "they captured a German officer, and were taking him back to our lines and he had his hands tied behind his back, and a chance bullet hit one of the men forming his escort, so they turned on him and killed him."

"I don't see anything rotten about that," said R. (and F. backed him up). "More Bosch you kill the better."

"But," expostulated little L., "he was a prisoner; and it was only a stray bullet that hit his escort, and his hands were tied behind his back; and he could not defend himself; and they simply killed him just as he was." "And a damned good job too," says R.

It's rather awful that, you know, for it means this;—that not only hard cruel uncharitable men like some we have met—but even lots of awfully nice chaps, have simply put the Germans outside the range of all human sympathies whatever; not in the heat of anger, but deliberately, in their calm considered moments.

There is no question whatever about a man like R. being affected by, or of his catching feelings from, the crowd of other people. And there must be thousands and thousands like him ...

ILL BEGOTTEN

We soon learned that the Germans greatly disliked the appellation of 'Bosche' which apparently was not absolutely meaningless but meant 'ill-begotten' or something of the sort.

—Stephen Graham,
A Private in the Guards (1919)

Torpedo (a tube filled with explosive that is pushed under the wire entanglements and detonated) they took with them could not be used because the fuse was lost when the carriers were wounded. Wrote Lucas:

> Owing to the heavy casualties amongst officers, it would appear that at this period a lack of leadership was apparent amongst NCOs and consequently the first wave was not supported by the succeeding waves. Gallant attempts, however, were undoubtedly made to force a way through the wire under a galling fire from four or five machine guns. 2nd Lieut Skene and 11 other ranks forming the first wave very gallantly penetrated the enemy's first line under severe opposition.

The historian's comment was: 'The casualties in this rather unfortunate raid were specially heavy among officers, every one of whom was either killed or wounded.' These included Lieut Freeth who had gone into No-Man's Land to help the wounded, and was killed, as was Skene. The historian noted that of the ORs, 6 were killed, 15 wounded and 11 were missing. The event itself is worth noting in detail for what it reveals: in terms of leadership, the considerable adverse effects that such a costly and totally abortive raid had, and most importantly it showed the tenacity of the enemy.

On 15 July the Bde received orders that an attack was to be made on 17 July, so at 2pm it closed Bde HQ at La Gorgue and opened at M.6.a.5.8. noting the next day, '*183rd on our right and 15th Australian Bde on our left. Oxford and Glosters engaged all day carrying up material.*' Then again showing the lack of time in the preparations allowed: '*16 July 11.45 pm. Zero hour will be at 4am unless orders to contrary are issued.*' Then under 8pm, which clearly should be 8am: '*The operations detailed in Bde Order No. 16 will not take place on 17 or 18 July. Preparations and movements of stores as arranged will be continued today.*'

Of the battalions in the 184th Bde the 2/4th Royal Berkshire kept a good record. It moved to Laventie on 16 July losing 1 officer killed, 1 wounded and 8 ORs wounded by shelling. On the 17 July it was noted:

> Attack cancelled owing to guns being prevented from registering on account of misty weather. In afternoon Bn returned to positions occupied 15/16. 8 ORs wounded.

This indicates—together with the entry of 18 July—that this assaulting Bn did not stay in the trenches, but only came forward for the attack, endorsing the other Bde reports that reliefs were getting into place late on the 16th. In the 2/1st Bucks on the 18 July *The Bn resumed its position in the trenches* is the

ORDER OF BATTLE

184th British Brigade
GOC: Brig. Gen. C H P Carter
Bde Major: Major E C Gepp
SC: Major R W Harking

2/4th Royal Berkshire (assaulting/right)
CO: Lieut Col J H Beer †
2IC: Major R E Boulton
B Coy (right):
A Coy (left):
C Coy (support):
D Coy (reserve):

2/1st Bucks (assaulting/left)
CO: Lieut Col H M Williams
A Coy (right): Capt. H Church †
D Coy (left): Capt. I Stewart-Liberty*
C Coy (support): Capt. H S G Buckmaster
B Coy (reserve): Capt R F Symonds

2/1st Royal Berkshire (support)
CO: Lieut Col P Balfour

2/4th Oxford & Bucks: 2 Coys (support)
CO: Lieut Col W H Ames

2/5th Gloucestershire (reserve)
CO: Lieut Col M Wheeler

Also:
B Coy: 1/5th Duke of Cornwall
3rd Field Coy, Royal Engineers, and MG Coy, and TM Bty

† Killed in Action. * Wounded. July 1916.

SO MISLEADING IN DETAIL

Historian Denis Winter's (*Death's Men, The First of the Few, 25 April 1915, Making the Legend* and *Haig's Command*) assessment of Edmonds gained from trawling through the Edmonds–Bean correspondence and much else sums up Edmonds thus: *Only a profoundly knowledgeable man could have produced an Official History so misleading in detail and yet with that ring of plausibility which has led to a general acceptance so long.*

STRAGGLERS
The Staff Captain will arrange for Battle Police, 4 NCOs and 8 men to collect stragglers. The stragglers will be taken to Battalion Battle HQ.

—184th Bde Battle Orders, 16 July 1916

IN QUICK TIME
At the time for the assault the Infantry will advance each Coy in 4 waves about 50 yds apart. Platoons will be led by their commanders and NCOs in the rear must see that the line is kept straight. A signal will be arranged so that the waves rise simultaneously, start in quick time and rush if fired upon. No man to fire in No-Man's Land unless obstructed by wire.

—184th Bde Battle Orders, 16 July 1916

SPECIAL PEOPLE
Commanding officers will impress upon their men the necessity of pushing forward to their objective regardless of the progress of units on their flanks. He will also make it known to them that the care of the wounded is not their business as special people are detailed for this purpose.

—184th Bde Battle Orders, 16 July 1916

FLASHING MIRRORS
The Assaulting Infantry will notify their front position in the enemy's trenches to aeroplanes of the RFC by means of flashing mirrors and flares at 8.00 (1 hour after assault), 9.00 (2 hours after assault) and at intervals of 1 hour subsequently during daylight.

—184th Bde Battle Orders, 16 July 1916

way it is described. This strategy of only bringing forward the assaulting battalions shortly before to the attack was general practice in the 61st Division, whilst others were engaged in carrying in supplies and, in this particular situation, carrying out gas cylinders. The weather being uncooperative every effort was now made to get the cylinders out. It proved impossible to clear them before the 17th and the men had to live with the consequences of a German shell landing on the gas cylinders. But with the cancellation of the 17th, it did not need the Germans. Wrote Mackenzie:

> About 10 am on 18th, 70 men of the 184th Bde on the left were gassed by the bursting of 2 cylinders hit by shell fire from within our own or the Australian lines.
>
> The order to remove the gas cylinders installed in the front trenches was received about 5 pm. Every available man except those detailed for the assault was engaged in the work, and by daylight on 19th 470 cylinders had been removed to railhead, leaving 670 still in the trenches. The men were completely exhausted, and nothing more could be done.

The affected Brigade made this note:

> A shell breaks one of the gas cylinders in the trenches held by the 2/1st Berks with the result that 1 officer and 78 men are effected (sic) by it. Orders received that attack will take place on 19th inst.

We now follow the work of the 184th Brigade under the command of Brig. General C H P Carter, like Gordon and Stewart, a veteran of battles around the Empire. He had lost an eye in Africa, and was the oldest of the trio. His task was quite the most difficult with the probable exception of Brig. General H E Elliott, commanding the 15th Australian Brigade on his left.

As this is the most critical sector in the battle, it is best we examine Carter's battle plan first. In his Report of 21 July Carter explained the objective: '*on 19 July the Brigade was ordered to attack, capture and hold with 2 battalions (2 Bucks and 4 Royal Berks) the German Front and Support Lines from N.14.a.6.2½ to N.8.d.9½.1.*' This, of course, included the entire Sugarloaf salient plus 350 yards to its west. One glance at the map shows that the attack would not be front on and the guns of the Sugarloaf covered the entire brigade area. Carter then detailed the strategy: '*Two companies of 4 Oxfords were placed at the disposal of the Brigadier to occupy our front line in the event of all companies in the Assaulting Battalion being absorbed in the same: the 5 Glosters and remaining 2 Coys of 4 Oxfords were in Divisional Reserve. The following were also placed at the disposal of the Brigadier, 3rd Field Coy RE and B Coy 1/5th Duke of Cornwall's Light Infantry (Pioneers).'*

By 9 am everybody was in position including two Vickers Machine Guns in the front line to support the attack and another four which would follow the assaulting troops '*on the positions being captured*', while another six Vickers were at Jock's Lodge, some 400 yards behind the front line and thus about 575 yards from the Sugarloaf. Then Carter wrote: '*Owing to the difficulty of coming within effective range, only one Stokes Mortar was detailed to bombard the Sugarloaf, it was arranged for 4 Stokes Mortars to follow the Assaulting Companies. The Assaulting Companies 1 and 2 were ordered to attack in 4 waves at 50 yards distance. The third company was to follow as soon as the position was reported captured carrying consolidating material. Each consolidating company had 4 RE and 4 Pioneer detailed to accompany same. An RE and Pioneer Officer were also detailed to supervise work of consolidation.*'

At this point it is interesting to note that Carter placed three Companies up front, and in both the 2 Bucks and 4 Royal Berks the third company was in the centre. Carter was the only Brigadier to make this arrangement, and it must have been this that led to the early disaster described simply by him as follows:

> Up to 5.30 pm owing chiefly to the crowded condition of our Front line trenches, considerable casualties had taken place, amounting to 100 killed and wounded in 2 Bucks and 40 killed and wounded in 4 Royal Berks. This necessitated reorganization of the Assaulting and Consolidating companies.

Carter sent forward two platoons from the Reserve Companies to reinforce the Assaulting Battalions. From there on it was all downhill to disaster. Absolute disaster. Although he was writing two days after the event, Carter's Report has no word of praise for the men he sacrificed and only one word of praise for an officer, '*ably led by Captain Church*'. It has the feeling of having been written in a comfortable living room miles away from the action: and it may well have been.

So we have to turn to somebody who was there and cared, Lieut Col H M Williams CO of 2/1st Bucks, the Battalion whose task it was to take the Sugarloaf. It is no surprise to learn from the Unit History that Williams was in the front line throughout the action. What follows is his description. The reader is directed to the margin story '*A very special war diary*' for the other dimension of this terrible tale:

> 18 July. The Bn resumed its position in the Trenches—holding a front of 300 yards, with three Coys 'UP' and one coy in Reserve Trenches.

2/1st BUCKINGHAMSHIRE OFFICERS LOST AT FROMELLES

Lieut Charles Percy Phipps was killed on 20 July while serving with 2/1st Bucks. He was the second son of Rev. Canon and Mrs Constantine Osborne Phipps of Lee Vicarage, Bucks. Educated at Winchester, he enlisted in October 1914. He was 20 years old. He is remembered on the Loos Memorial (Panel 83–85).

Lieut Geoffrey William Atkinson was in his 20th year when killed on 19 July while leading his men in an attack on the enemy trenches. Educated at Berkhamstead, Atkinson later joined the Inns of Court OTC and was commissioned January 1915, going to the Front with the 2/1st Bucks in May 1916. His Colonel wrote: '*He was wounded and when binding up a wound of one of his men, he was hit again and killed.*' His name is on the Loos Memorial (Panels 83–85).

Capt. Harold Church, OC of B Coy, 2/1st Bucks was killed on the approaches to the Sugarloaf at Fromelles on 19 July. Born in London on 24 March 1883, he was at Trinity College Oxford and a prominent Rugby player there in 1902. He was a barrister-at-law and resided at Chesham, Buckinghamshire and was married. His grave is in Laventie Military Cemetery (II E 23).

Lieut D G Chadwick was gazetted 2/Lieut 31 Oct 1914, promoted Lieut 18 Aug 1915. He died of wounds on 20 July 1916 and was buried in Merville Community Cemetery.

2/Lieut Roland Burton Hudson at the outbreak of war joined the Public Schools Bn of Royal Fusiliers and obtained a commission on 26 June 1915. He was killed in action on 19 July 1916 and was aged 25. His name is on the Loos Memorial.

2/Lieut Harold Ronald Nelson Brewin was probably born in India, attached from Wiltshire Regiment, commissioned 22 Dec 1915. He was killed 19 July 1916, aged 21. His grave is in Laventie Military Cemetery (II E 22).

2/Lieut Frederick Richard Parker, attached from Wiltshire Regiment, was killed on 19 July 1916. His name is on the Loos Memorial.

A VERY SPECIAL WAR DIARY
The contents of the July War Diary of the 2/1st Bucks are interwoven in the story of the battle of Fromelles. But the Diary itself needs to be described because there is something special, indeed highly important about it. It presently is kept in a cardboard box at the Public Records Office at Kew, near London, together with other diaries of the unit from September 1915 to February 1918 when the 2/1st was disbanded.
[continued opposite]

Lieut Col H M Williams
2/1st Bucks, 1915
COURTESY OXFORDSHIRE & BUCKINGHAMSHIRE LIGHT INFANTRY MUSEUM, OXFORD

19 July: Zero was at 11 am, and at that hour our Bombardment started. [5.30 pm]. By 5.30 pm we had lost nearly 100 men killed and wounded by shell fire. This was serious as on July 18 A Coy (which was the one holding the Bn front) lost 78 men gassed—owing to one of OUR [their capitals] shells having burst a gas cylinder in our trenches. The Bn went into action with 20 officers and 622 other ranks. This was reduced by casualties suffered during the action to 6 officers and 300 ORs. [5.40 pm] What was left of A & D Coys (the assaulting Coys) about 120 men—filed out into No-Man's Land by Rhondda Sap and lay down in 4 waves. [6 pm] With a cheer, the four waves leapt up and assaulted the enemy's trenches. Even before 5.40 pm the enemy's machine guns had become busy: and at 6 pm they mowed down our advancing waves, so that only a few men actually reached the German parapet. These did not return.

Telephone communication between Bn Battle HQ and Front Line was soon cut (about 1 pm). After many gallant attempts to mend the wire, success was obtained at exactly 5.40 pm, and from 5.40 pm till 9.30 pm the telephone was in constant use and saved many lives—in that Runners were spared.

Reports that flowed in over the Telephone were sent on—as they came in—straight to BDE HQ, and were very contradictory. Owing to the distance between the trenches and to the continuous bombardment —and smoke, the officers who were observing found their task almost impossible of fulfilment with any degree of accuracy. Seeing our men actually on the German parapet—it was concluded that a certain number must have got in. But it is certain that very few survived the enemy's machine gun fire, and whether they got in or not, they never returned. C Coy (the coy which carried over RE material for consolidating purposes) went out into No-Man's Land at 6.10 pm but, again, the enemy's machine gun fire prevented any advance without extermination.

[6.30 pm] By 6.30 pm it was clear that 1) the attack could not succeed without more men. 2) that given more men (say two coys) the attack must have succeeded. No reserves however were available and the CO of the Bn was ordered to reorganize and to attack again at 8.30 pm. This order was received at a time when every man [their underlining], save a few telephone operators, orderlies and wounded, was in No-Man's Land. Gradually about 80 men (of A, C & D Coys) were reorganized and 40 men of B Coy (the Reserve Coy) were added. [7.30 pm] The order came to postpone attack till 9 pm. [8 pm] And at 8 pm the order came through that no further attack would take place that night. Every officer who went out with the Assaulting Coys was either killed or wounded & Capt. H S G Buckmaster was the only officer who went out into No-Man's Land who came back physically unhurt. During the 18th and 19th July the Battalion lost 322 ALL RANKS.

Then follow the names of 4 Officers killed, 1 DOW, 2 missing and 8 wounded. Other Ranks: killed 62, wounded 180, missing 65. The statistics of the event now dealt with, Lieut Col Williams decided to offer some opinions, and although these notes bear Williams' signature, they are not in his handwriting.

The whole attack was unsuccessful in that the enemy's trenches, though penetrated were not consolidated and held—but a very great measure of success was obtained in that 1) the enemy suffered severe casualties, 2) he was and will be prevented from withdrawing either Infantry or Guns for support of his forces further south on the Somme.

One of the most striking lessons to be learnt from this attack is that the very greatly superior method of holding trenches adopted by the German should at once be followed by the British and French Armies. Whereas on our Bn front, the Regt had NOT ONE [their capitals] Bombproof shelter, and lost 100 casualties from shelling alone, the Germans appeared to have about 6 teams of machine gunners and very few infantry and even after seven hours of bombardment by our guns, these six teams of machine gunners appeared intact—firing over the parapet—at our assaulting infantry. By crowding three companies with three hundred yards of front, our casualties from shell fire were more heavy.

The Diary concludes thus:

The Bn was relieved by 2/4 Oxfords at 1 am 20 July, and at 10 pm went by Motorbus into billet at Estaires. 22 July: the Bn was inspected by Major Gen Colin Mackenzie CB GOC 61st Div. Major H L C Barrett and Capt. H S G Buckmaster were invalided home to England. Thus all four Coy Commanders have gone. The Battalion has now 19 officers and 545 other ranks (on paper).

Lieut Col H M Williams signed the War Diary 'in the field'. Then follow Appendices A (detailed order to attack 17 July), B: Objectives, C: Plan of Attack; D: the usual thanks and tributes from Regimental, Bde, Division and Haking.

As near as Carter could come to a conclusion was:

A good proportion of this Coy (perhaps B Coy) ably led by Capt. H Church (who was killed just before the glacis to enemy's breastworks) got into the German trenches. (This has since been substantiated by reports of the Right Battalion of the 15th Australian Brigade.) Owing to the 4 Royal Berks having been driven back on their right and the same thing having occurred to the Right Battalion of the 15th Australian Brigade on their left—this lack of support on their flanks seriously impaired what chances the 2 Bucks had of capturing the Sugarloaf. The CO is of the opinion (with which I concur) that if 2 Reserve Companies had been available at this period for throwing into the assault—a substantial lodgement would have undoubtedly been effected in the Sugarloaf. 61 missing NCOs and men in this Battalion testifies to the belief that a considerable proportion of the left company of this Battalion got into the German trenches.

The other victim of this sector was 2/4th Royal Berkshires under the command of Lieut Col J H Beer. He joined the unit on 27 June when the War Diary noted: '*Lieut Col M Wheeler relieved of his command by Major J H Beer, 2/8th Warwicks who assumes command from this day.*'

When the time came to describe the battle it was just as matter of fact, giving at first the position of the Battalion and others on its left and right and concluding with casualties: '*Officers 3 killed (Lt Col Beer and 2/Lieuts G S Abbott and*

(contd page 62)

A VERY SPECIAL WAR DIARY (contd)

As already noted the June 1916 Diary was crammed with detail about casualties and duties. It like every other monthly diary, except that of July, has loose paper covers. The July War Diary is however bound with cord in a manilla folder, so that the carefully numbered, 32 pages, all on War Diary paper, should not get out of order or be lost. There was something very purposeful about the way this file was put together at the end of July 1916. No more than three people wrote the 9 pages of diary and the 23 pages of appendices. It is signed by Lieut Col H M Williams, CO of the 2/1st Bucks.

After reading the contents it is not difficult to imagine that this folder was thrown down on the desk of some 'Higher Authority' probably Brig. General Carter GOC of 184th Bde, subsequently fired, with anger, and a remark like, 'that, sir is what happened to my men, who were denied support when they had given everything a man can give.'

To find this folder intact after eighty years, and then to read the contents and learn what happened, much of which explains the catastrophe in front of the Sugarloaf is what makes historical research exciting and satisfying. But then to open the next paper covered file and read this, the first entry of August 1916, is the proper ending to the story.

Lieut Col H M Williams gave up his command of the Battalion, which command was resumed by Major G Christie-Miller. August 1, 1 am, Lieut Col H M Williams left by motorcar for Boulogne and England. His loss is deeply felt by the whole Battalion.

After leaving the 2nd Bucks, Lieut Col Williams '*held a staff appointment in France*' until March 1919. He then returned to his civilian occupation as an outdoor assistant carriage superintendent of the London & North Western Railway at Wolverton. A year later, on 30 April 1920, he retired after 47 years with the company.

… nothing left to attack with …

Since publication of the first edition, a number of interesting items have been received, but none compare with the unpublished memoirs of Major Geoffry Christie-Miller 2IC, 2/1st Bucks at Fromelles. These memoirs are at the Imperial War Museum, and if the rest of his memoirs are as candid as the chapter on Fromelles, it is not difficult to understand why they remained unpublished. The Fromelles section is around 3000 words and deals with the period 15/16 July to 20/21 July. Most of the historical material he gives ties in with the unit's war diaries and unit history, where, of course, there was no place for assessments of the conduct and style of individuals. The memoirs seem to date from the early 1920s, and as far as Fromelles is concerned, he consulted with Capt. I Stewart-Liberty, which reinforces their worth. Some sections are quoted at length, especially his view of the artillery arrangements, or rather lack of them. He treats Mackenzie and Carter more harshly than this writer, but the conclusions are the same. Haking appears but once as the distant Higher Authority intent on doing it 'by the book'—as it turns out, his own book! His often quoted remarks 'that next time the 61st Division should do better', Christie-Miller personally witnessed.

The 2/1st Buckinghamshires were part of the British 184th Bde which was on the right of the Australian 15th Bde, and it was their 'failure' to assist in an attack on the Sugarloaf some hours after the first assault that has been blamed by some for the massacre of the 58th Bn that night. This writer, however, does not subscribe to this view, believing that Brig. Gen. Elliott should have reconfirmed the arrangements of some hours earlier, knowing as he did that the whole event had gone terribly wrong. Anyway, sending a third battalion, which under Battle Orders should have been manning the Australian Line, into the black night which had already swallowed up the 59th and 60th battalions was a serious error of judgement. Christie-Miller's work shows very clearly why the 184th could not have gone ahead in a second attack, and that was known well before Elliott sent the 58th into No-Man's Land.

Capt. G Christie-Miller

Preparations for 19th

My recollections are that from the moment we reached this Laventie North area again, the troops were practically engaged every night in the line or on working parties, in preparation for an attack to be launched on the morning of the 17th (Monday).

I may be asked what should necessitate all this work and why should the assaulting troops be worn out doing it? The second question I cannot answer. The first I should like to be able to answer in detail. Suffice it to say that some hundreds of preserved rations and tins of water, thousands of Mills Bombs, wire and picquets in profusion, and last but not least, an abundance of trench mortar ammunition, heavy, medium and light, if prepared on such a scale can provide a respectable carrying load for a couple of Battalions for a couple of nights.

In addition, extensive revetting arrangements for the consolidation of captured positions were made, and endless TM Emplacements were built.

The details are wanting, but it is a fair general statement that practically none of the troops detailed for the attack, had a decent night's rest from that at Richbourg on the Wednesday (a clear week) before the attack, and then only had one after coming out of a tour in the line.

The Battalion were accommodated on the road to the right of and parallel with the railway running from Laventie Station.

(It was a curious coincidence that September 29th, 1918 I went up the same road with the Gloucesters to attack Junction Post not 1000 yds from the scene of the Bucks attack of July 19, and that the men killed that day were buried beside their comrades of July 1916.)

The Battalion went into the line on Sunday July 16th, for the attack next day, but the attack was postponed as the preparations were incomplete.

The next day two of the assaulting Coys were withdrawn from the line to rest, and accommodated in an old Strong point between Rouge de Bout and the Red House.

The concentration of Artillery was extensive. It was estimated that on 18th and 19th over 300 guns were engaged.

The artillery were packed into every possible and impossible position, and those in the latter suffered heavily notably "00" Battery RHA who had come up from the Somme where they had been heavily engaged. They were put in action in the open in full view of Aubers Ridge. Their services on 19th were naturally of short duration.

Every road towards the line from Laventie was packed with wheel transport, mostly artillery limbers, and columns of traffic often stood for hours without movement.

The concentration must have been obvious, and why it was not interfered with and why the roads were not searched by enemy artillery I have never understood.

The Battalion went into action with four officers per Coy, 4 at Bn HQ and 622 ORS, the remaining ten Officers principally the new comers, being put "into store" at the Town Hall Estaires.

A small (much too small) reserve of other ranks was sent to the transport lines behind Laventie.

When the Monday attack was postponed some of the officers were withdrawn from Store including Ranger and myself—the former to do intelligence and orderly work for the CO, and myself to take charge of the Battalion battle HQ, while the CO was in the line.

It should be said here that some of the artillery shooting was bad, notably an Australian Battery. This could not clear our front line, and on the 18th after dropping several HE shells in our front line dropped one onto a gas cylinder in A Coy, which of course burst and, with an enfilade wind, spread gas down the line instantly causing between 70 and 80 casualties, including one officer, Lieut Pitcher, and some of the best NCOs. In addition, Capt. Church and his CSM, Arthur Brown, got a slight dose but did not report sick.

This disorganized one of the Coys for the attack. To some extent the gaps were filled by sending for the Coy reserve, and a new draft of 38 which had joined the Battalion two days before and had been left at the transport lines.

As far as I can remember, part of C Coy were sent over with A Coy to make them up.

The "19th"

Accurate details of the action cannot be given from memory without the orders or a trench map, but roughly the Battalion was to attack on about 800 yds front in the neighbourhood of Bond St—Picantin Avenue, with 2/4th Royal Berks on right and 5th Australian Division on our left, the attack on our right being extended about as far as Fauquissart by 183rd Brigade.

A seven hours preparation with our 300 odd guns and every description of trench mortar was to take place.

At "zero—20 minutes" the assaulting Battalions were to move out into No-man's Land and form up in waves under cover of our own Barrage which was to smother everything in the Hun line and neutralise his machine gun fire.

We were forbidden to go over the top of the trench, and narrow and inconvenient sally ports were ordered by higher authorities to be used. This of course necessitated the forming up in No-man's Land before zero, as of course it would be impossible to deploy a Battalion in an instant through low and inconvenient sally ports, through which men in attack order would crawl slowly.

The orders for the Barrage included some picturesque details something on the following lines, "at zero hrs the Barrage will lift from the enemy front line. He will think you are attacking, the troops in the front line will show their bayonets over the top and cheer. The enemy will reinforce. The artillery will then shell his communication trenches and the ground between his front line and support line, and mow down his supports".

As far as I can remember, the process was repeated hourly during the 7 hours of the bombardment which no doubt gave a Biblical flavour to the proceedings, while the shouting and the waving of bayonets took one back to the destruction of the Walls of Jericho.

The attack was to be carried to the support line near the River Laies, and a line to be consolidated with strong points in rear of it, for which the RE were to be responsible.

Enthusiastic memos were sent from Corps describing the annihilating effect of our 300 guns, the powerlessness of the enemy artillery, the demolition of his MG emplacements, and gruelling of his infantry after 7 hours of hell etc.

So much for the intention, now for the reality. Our artillery fire grew in intensity during the 17th, 18th and 19th, and was to become intense from 11 am, 19th until zero which was fixed for 6 pm, 19th.

Various explanations had been given as to orders against Registration by our gunners, also there is no doubt that the OPs on Rue Tilleloy were heavily pounded by the enemy during 18th and more especially during 19th, and that any fire control depending on these must have been far from efficient. The gunner officers who flocked to these OPs suffered heavy casualties. The wires in working order must have been few and far between.

Capt. H S Buckmaster

As a result of these and other contributing causes, no effective destructive or neutralising of the Hun infantry, artillery or MGs took place. The total effect of our artillery preparation on the Hun resistance was nil.

The enemy reply on our front line and communications and his counter battery work, were vigorous and effective during the whole day.

Our front line was battered about and being packed with troops during this 7 hours counter bombardment. The casualties were heavy: in our case estimated at over 100.

Not only were the casualties heavy, but the effect on assaulting troops was bound to be bad.

When the time came at zero—20 minutes for the assaulting infantry to move out, the sally ports were effectively covered by machine gun fire and progress was impossible.

The Berks lost a lot of men persevering, and few men of the Battalion were seen to reach No-man's Land.

The Bucks found a way into No-man's Land in dead ground down the Rhonda Sap, and succeeded in forming up with slight loss.

At zero the Battalion advanced. The advance has been described to me as magnificent, not a man was seen to waiver.

The fire brought to bear was annihilating. Hardly a man, if any, reached the German parapet—it was said that one man L/Cpl Stevens of D Coy was seen to reach it.

About 300 men must have gone over, allowing for the 100 casualties during the day, and less than a hundred got back.

Of the officers, all 3 of A and also of C Coy were killed, of D Coy all three were wounded.

The only Coy officer of the three assaulting Coys left, was Capt. H S Buckmaster who collapsed under the strain.

At 7.30 the situation was that the CO was in the line with B Coy fairly intact, but definitely marked for garrison duty; a handful out of the three assaulting companies who had survived the assault were in No-man's Land awaiting darkness to get back. The situation having been duly reported to Division, a fresh attack was ordered for 8.30.

Capt. H Church

It proved next to impossible to persuade the Authorities that there was nothing left to attack with, the Battalion or what was left of it, being mostly in No-man's Land, and our trenches still under intense bombardment.

Eventually it was agreed that a further attack should be postponed until midnight, when the Oxfords had taken over. This was subsequently put back for lack of preparation until 3 am and finally abandoned.

Captain Stewart-Liberty who was commanding D Coy in this action reminds me that the dispositions were:

A	D
C	

Lieut R B Hudson

with half C Coy following A Coy, and B moving into the line to hold and garrison it at zero.

Actually A and D were reduced by casualties to two lines each before zero, and C Coy went over with A Coy.

Taking the action as a whole on the front of the two Divisions who were attacking, we understood that a party of Worcesters on the right opposite Fauquissart met with less opposition and got into the enemy's line but could not be supported and few got out, and that one Battalion of Australian 5th Division on our left met with a similar fate, and that on no other part of the line was any impression made.

And after

As to casualties, we understood that the 5th Australian Div. lost nearly 5000 men and ours about 2000 as well as the considerable casualties to the artillery.

The Bucks must have lost: OR killed 62, wounded 180, missing 65, and the following officers: killed, Capt. Church, Lieut Hudson, Lieut D G Chadwick, Lieut C P Phipps, Lieut H Brewin, Lieut J Parker, Lieut G W Atkinson; wounded, Lieut Drakes, Lieut Relf, Capt. Stewart-Liberty, Lieut Pitcher.

The loss of these in addition to 2 CSMs (Arthur Brown and Ralph Brown) and most of the best NCOs, including Sgt Crump and L G Sgt, and Moon the Bombing Sergeant who was gassed, practically broke up three of our four Coys from a fighting point of view.

After this action the remnants of the Battalion were withdrawn that night to their previous billets north of Laventie, and were the following day withdrawn to Estaires for rest and refit.

The whole Battalion was billeted there in one large house and the remnants of the officers established a central mess at the Cafe d'Hotel de Ville.

The first parade held at Estaires, when the Coys paraded as they had come out of the line, was one of the saddest I have ever attended.

B Coy were a fair sized Coy, C Coy had two fair platoons and the rest of the Battalion was represented by a handful of men and practically without NCOs.

Lieut C P Phipps

Of the officers, practically all those with experience including all four Company Commanders had gone and, except for B Coy, those present were the new ones who had just joined.

The Divisional Commander (Maj. General C J Mackenzie) addressed the Battalion in a hesitating speech in which I for one could see no point, unless it was that in the next action perhaps we should do better.

Awards

As it is well known, no recognition could be asked for many gallant and devoted officers and men who fell on this date. The regulations only allowed of awards to the survivors.

MCs were awarded to Capt. Ivor Stewart-Liberty who commanded D Coy in the attack and was severely wounded. He was brought in during the night by Sgt Petty (and nearly

Capt. J E S Wilson

brought into the Hun lines in error); Lieut B H Drakes of D Coy also badly wounded; Capt. J E S Wilson who for 12 hours worked unceasingly at his RAP in the open near Rue Tilleloy under the fire of our guns and the enemy's alternately; Lieut A H Phillips and V W G Ranger (the latter being slightly wounded), who were in the line, and in No-man's Land obtaining intelligence and communicating with the flank Battalions. Both assisted in the reorganization of the Battalion after the attack; Capt. G E W Bowyer —as Adjutant—and subsequently reorganizing the Battalion (this was awarded as a half-yearly honour).

DCMs were awarded to RSM Jones for reorganizing the Battalion after the attack; Corpl Gurney, for gallantry when A Coy were badly gassed on 18th.

MMs were awarded to Sgt Petty, Sigs Franklore and Oldroyd, Corpl Hayers and Pte J W Saunders for gallantry as stretcher bearers.

After three days at Estaires we were moved into a little camp near "Cockshy House" west of Laventie for a week, after which the Coys were put into a line of posts behind Neuve Chapelle, while HQ were left in the same camp to proceed with reorganization and refitting.

It is difficult to describe the amount of reorganization required when a Battalion is knocked out in this manner.

The officers and NCOs have to be re-sorted and equalised between Coys, a process which always leads to much searching of heart. Large numbers of NCOs have to be found out of a number of inexperienced privates.

The whole of the fighting and other kits is invariably lost, and has to be supplied afresh.

The personnel of Coys has to be reconstituted and reorganized.

Innumerable conundrums arise about conduct sheets, pay roll, officers' mess accounts, Sgts mess accounts, canteen debts, and endless queries as to missing men etc.

War has become so complicated that organization takes a conspicuous place in it. A Company no longer consists of so many riflemen, but the organization of Lewis gunners, bombers, rifle grenadiers has to be complete, as well as arrangements for instruction in the general duties of physical training, bayonet fighting and musketry. A Company which does not include an officer and NCO instructors in all these is at a serious disadvantage.

A sequel to the unsuccessful attack of "July 19th" was the selection of a proper complement of "victims".

This complement was not in any way reduced by the fact that all orders complete in detail came from Corps, and no opportunity was given to any subordinate commander to initiate any operation on his own.

Even the instructions about deploying from the sally ports instead of over the parapet came from the Corps Commander (Haking).

The victims included the GSO I who subsequently obtained a reprieve, the Brigadier (Carter) Col H M Williams of the Bucks and Col W H Ames of the 2/4th Ox. and Bucks.

The departure of the last 2 completed the process started by the Divisional staff in March of getting rid of all Territorial COs. (The CRE Col Williams, survived these two by about a month.)

It is outside of the scope of these notes to comment on the fate of the other victims, but of Col Williams, I say without hesitation, after close personal contact with him for almost two years, that he was by far the best CO in the Division. A close study of tactics and military organization added to his sound business ability, and power of administration fitted him in every way for command of a Battalion. It cannot be contradicted that the state of the Battalion when he took it to France was sufficient demonstration (in spite of the interference of the higher authorities with the training) of his fitness to command.

If any criticism was to be made (and if such should be considered a fault) he was a little too exacting and in expecting a great deal from his subordinates, inclined too often to back up the fault finding of the higher authorities, who were wholly ignorant of the difficulties to be encountered—the greatest of which was invariably inexperience.

The support he invariably accorded to higher authority sometimes had the effect of putting him out of sympathy with his officers. This was notably the case in the strenuous and difficult days at Park House.

When once the Battalion came to France nothing could have exceeded his consideration for and his confidence in his officers, and it is true to say that at no time did he stand better with all ranks of the Battalion than the day he was sent home with the victims.

His reputation was enhanced by his gallant conduct during the 7 hours bombardment on the "19th", during the whole of which time he was under fire in the front line, and by his presence of mind and composure during the subsequent action, and his personal reorganization of the Battalion in the line after the attack.

Of the Brigadier one can only say that great sympathy was felt for him in being sent home for the failure of a plan in which he had no share, but the brigade were heartily glad to be rid of a Commander in whom they had no confidence, who demonstrated daily his ignorance of the require-ments of war, and who as far as I know, made no friend in the brigade in the three months of his command and left no one regretting his departure.

COURTESY R JEFFS

TEN MEN OF THE LEE
The parish of The Lee, Great Missenden, is in Buckinghamshire, and from its modest population of some 750, about 150 men had enlisted by mid-1916. Some 40% of those joined one of the county regiments—the Bucks Yeomanry or Oxford and Bucks Light Infantry—which had two battalions, 1st and 2/1st, the latter recruiting from the Aylesbury, Chesham and Chiltern areas. Men from The Lee thus formed a significant part of the 2/1st, officers and men, so it is not suprising that of the thirty soldiers killed in the war and remembered on the village war memorial, ten died at Fromelles: A Brown, R W Brown (brothers), H Church, S Dwight, H Harding, A Morris, C Phipps, H Pratt, P Price and E Sharp.

INFORMATION FROM *ONE HUNDRED YEARS IN THE LEE*, edited by B USBORNE (c.1998).

F C D Williams), 2 wounded. ORs 35 killed, 115 wounded and 8 shellshock. Bn relieved by 2/4th Oxfords and Bucks LI at 10.30 pm. Marched back into billets at Rue de la Lys. The War Diary for July is in fact written up as June.

The account in the Battalion history introduces nothing that is not in Carter's Report. Indeed it stays with his casualty figures: 3 officers killed and 2 wounded, with 22 ORs killed, 123 wounded and 9 missing. This seems to answer the question about any Unit Report being prepared. There was nothing in the file when this research was done in 1994.

As a footnote the 2/4th Oxon and Bucks, the reserve battalion made one sad entry: '*19 July. After the relief, all coys occupied in getting in the dead and wounded of their own and of other two battalions. ORs killed 14, missing 1, wounded 43.*'

A note with regard to the MG Companies: considering the huge success of this weapon in the hands of the Germans and the vital need to do something about the Sugarloaf, we only have to read Carter's two paragraphs to realise, like Haig and the rest, the British Army regarded them as a bit of a waste of time—unedited:

Officers of the 2/1st Bucks Territorial Battalion of the Oxfordshire & Buckinghamshire Light Infantry at Parkhouse Camp, Salisbury Plain, England, in May 1916 (prior to embarkation to France).

L–R. Back Row: Lieut P E Wells, 2/Lieut T J Relf (Devon Regt), Lieut & QM D Waller, 2/Lieut A T Pitcher, 2/Lieut J B Quayle, 2/Lieut T S Markham (Hunts Regt).

Second Row: Capt. W A Cummins, Capt. V W Ranger, Lieut R F Symonds, Lieut A Tubbs, Capt. G T Hankin, Capt. Rev. J Foster, Lieut J E S Wilson (RAMC)†, Lieut G W Atkinson†, Lieut C P Phipps†, Lieut D G Chadwick†, Capt. G C Stevens.

Seated: Capt. W A Greene, Capt. I Stewart-Liberty, Capt. H S Buckmaster, Major J Chadwick, Lieut Col H M Williams, Capt. G E W Bowyer, Capt. G Christie-Miller, Major H L C Barrett, Capt. H Church†.

Front Row: Lieut E M Letts, Lieut R B Hudson†, Lieut E W Long, 2/Lieut C P Quayle†, 2/Lieut F R Floyd (Devon Regt), Lieut A A Ionides (Devon Regt). Absent 2/Lieut A H Phillips

† denotes killed in action or died of wounds, July 1916.

PHOTO COURTESY R JEFFS

184 Machine Gun Company. The machine gun company fired 30,000 rounds with indirect fire and supporting infantry attack. 3 of their guns were put out of action by bullets. They endeavoured to silence the enemy guns.

184 Light Trench Mortars. The one gun in the front line at 4.30 pm fired 30 rounds on the Sugarloaf obtaining direct hits.

The MG Coy had 1 Officer and 15 ORs wounded, the Mortars 1 OR killed, 1 Officer wounded, 6 ORs wounded.

Perhaps a summary of staff changes is the best conclusion of this sorry episode. Stewart 'left' the 183rd on 28 July, Carter 'left' the 184th on 31 July (he did not have time to sign the July War Diary!). Of the six Lieut Cols commanding the assault battalions one was dead, two were in hospital, one had resigned and two were untouched. Of the twelve Captains leading assault companies, at least six were killed, and most of the others wounded.

Only one other matter, left till last and isolated because of its Australian content, is the activities of the 3rd Australian Tunnelling Company, called Mining Company by Carter. Already partly constructed in earlier campaigns was the Rhondda Sap, a communication trench being dug across No-Man's Land with the ambitious objective of reaching the Sugarloaf.

It was down this trench that Williams' men went, which is doubtless why the gallant few got to the Sugarloaf. By all accounts the Rhondda got about halfway across despite furious work. For the most part, this was done by exploding ammonal pipes to cause a trench which would then be dug out connecting where practical with shell holes. Prior to and during the battle the 3rd Australian Tunnelling Company under Major Coulter were working at this, continually under fire. Carter had members of the 1/5th Duke of Cornwall's and some engineers to assist. We know that there was a section from 58th Bn also there, and that they worked all night in darkness and under bombardment from both sides, but their task was unachievable. As Bill Boyce of the 58th explained: '*we never knew how far we got, how far we had to go, or even sometimes if we were going in the right direction.*' It was his reward, and he did not regard it lightly, that when he emerged from the Sap at dawn on 20 July, his Brigadier, Brig. General H E Elliott, was there to greet him and the others, tears streaming down his face.

Those notes present a picture of the British units up to and including 19/20 July, so we now turn to a general review of the British position. It has always been said that the 61st Division was seriously under-strength at Fromelles and this was one of

2/4th ROYAL BERKSHIRE OFFICERS LOST AT FROMELLES

Lieut Col John Henry Beer: second son of Mr and Mrs K A Beer of Kenton, Devon. He served in 27th Coy, Imperial Yeomanry in the South African War and in August 1914 obtained a commission in the Sussex Yeomanry. In 1915 he proceeded to France as a major in the Bengal Lancers with whom he remained for six months, returning to England in October and rejoining the Sussex Yeomanry. In March 1916 he was appointed 2IC of the 2/8th Royal Warwickshire Regiment with whom he went to the front and only a few weeks before his death on 19 July he was given command of the unit—2/4th Royal Berks—at whose head he fell fighting. Lieut Col Beer was born in Devon, 6 September 1879, and had been a farmer at Kenton. His grave is in Laventie Military Cemetery (II E 17).

2nd Lieut Francis Christopher Dallas Williams of the East Surrey Regiment was killed in action, 19 July. Aged 21 Williams was leading a platoon of 2/4th Royal Berks and was one of four brothers, sons of Rev. E O Williams of Leeds. Williams, who was born at Paoning, West China, was intending to proceed to Keble College, Oxford, with the intention of taking Holy Orders when war broke out, and he enlisted. He was remembered as spending '*the whole day (19 July) cheering up his men, continually bandaging the wounded, and then in the same cheerful manner he went out to his death. The last words he was heard to speak were to Colonel Beer: 'Shall I go out now, sir?' 'Yes now Mr Williams'. He and the Colonel were killed almost simultaneously.*' Williams was buried at Laventie Military Cemetery (II E 21).

61st DIVISION STRENGTH 29 MAY - 21 JULY 1916

	29 May (Embarkation)		3 June (France)		18 July (Mackenzie's Report)		21 July (after Battle)	
	Officers	ORs	Officers	ORs	Officers	ORs	Officers	ORs
182 Bde								
2/5 Royal Warwick			33	936			25	745
2/6 Royal Warwick	33	936	33	931	20	500	30	569
2/7 Royal Warwick	33	965	32	954	20	530	17	523
2/8 Royal Warwick	32	987	32	982			29	832
182nd MG Coy							5	104
183 Bde								
2/4 Gloucester	34	861	34	885	20	550		
2/6 Gloucester					20	600		
2/6 Worcester								
2/7 Worcester								
183rd MG Coy								
184 Bde								
2/4 Royal Berks	35	948			20	540		
2/1 Bucks	35	897			20	550	19	545
2/5 Gloucester	34	881						
2/4 Oxford & Bucks	34	889						
184 MG Coy								

the reasons why it was overwhelmed, or could not support the later attempts to renew the attack.

Using figures given in the War Diaries over the period, it can be seen from the table above that none of the battalions were on departure for France really under-strength. Then taking the figures of the 182nd Bde as typical, strength was maintained in France. The next War Diary figures are those of 21 July, after the battle, and again taking the 182nd as typical, it is clearly seen that the two assaulting battalions, 2/6th and 2/7th Warwickshire lost heavily and the supporting battalion 2/5th proportionately. The 2/8th reserve battalion's losses over the 6 weeks were modest.

The list of figures of 18 July are those supplied by Mackenzie in his report to Haking. On the face of it, after the loss of around 250 men the Battalions each still had over 500 men left, and in the case of 2/7th, at least half their officers. This is clearly suspect. Add some 250 to the survivors of the 2/6th and 2/7th to arrive at 819 and 773, remarkably close to the 'untouched' 2/8th with 832.

The excuse of a shortage of men thus disposed of, we turn to the question why the British units were not used at full strength in the battle. This is an aspect of the event that has never been discussed before. It is possible to establish reasonably accurately how many men the 61st put into the assault. There are three basic

NONE GOT BACK

At 6pm with a cheer the four waves leaped up and assaulted the enemy's trenches. The advance was described by an officer of the RAF, observing for the Artillery, as magnificent. Not a man was seen to waver, but the fire brought to bear was annihilating. Even before 5.40 pm the enemy machine guns had begun to get busy, and at 6 pm they literally mowed down the advancing waves; only a few men actually reached the German parapet, some were seen actually on the parapet, and may have got in, but none got back.

By 6.30 it was evident that the attack had failed, but it has been asserted that success could have been secured had it been possible to bring two fresh companies to the assault. No reserves, however, were available.

—J C Swann

History of the 2nd Bucks Bn 1914–18

checks: the War Diaries of the Units, then the published casualty list (c. 1920) and Major General C J Mackenzie's 'Report of Operations 15th to 19th July 1916'. The first two sources need no explanation except to note that the published casualty lists were for dead only, whereas Mackenzie's list was a mix of dead, missing and wounded. Mackenzie's Report was a 5 page typed document, set out in well-spaced paragraphs with appendices, and submitted to Haking on 22 July.

In Mackenzie's 'Remarks', a summary of results, performance etc. he draws attention to Appendix C which:

> shows the trench strength before the action of the battalions engaged ... the number actually engaged in the assault was approximately 2400, and it will be seen that their casualties were nearly 50 per cent, a high test for comparatively inexperienced troops.

Interestingly both figures were filled in by pen after the typing of the document.

The trench strengths that Mackenzie quotes are under a heading *Approximate fighting strength on 18th.* He then gives 20 officers in six battalions as 140 (an error in addition!) actually 120, and ORs at between 500 and 600 per battalion to give a total of 3270, a figure that is curiously low—6 battalions with about 800 men each, would provide 4800. His own admission that around 2400 were engaged in the assault raises the question: what happened overnight to the 870 difference? Were they held back as nucleus or support?

This is the first real hint that Mackenzie is not telling the truth, nor even feeling it necessary to provide Haking with an explanation. But the main exposure of Mackenzie's 'false' figures can be traced through the well documented 2/6th Warwickshire. It lands in France with 33 officers and 931 ORs. According to Mackenzie its fighting strength after six weeks is 20 officers and 500 ORs. Curiously 24 hours after the battle in which the Regiment lost about 6 officers killed and 86 ORs killed, plus wounded of approximately 160, ie a total of 252, it has 30 officers and 569 ORs—on the face of it more men than it sent into battle! But add the 5 dead officers to 30, equals 35, add the 246 killed and wounded to 569 for 815—interestingly close figures to those on arrival in France, bearing in mind the losses in the earlier raids etc.

Further evidence of Mackenzie's 'false' figures is the 2/8th Warwickshire which was in reserve. On 21 July it had 29 of its original 32 officers, and 832 of its 982 original ORs, the same proportions as the figures in the 2/6th which was in the battle.

THE SACRIFICE DIVISION

The wastage from 61st Division which might account for the disparity of numbers between the embarkation and 19 July was their losses in the month they were in the area ahead of the Australians. Add in the gas accidents and the daily toll by German gunners and snipers, and the losses would have been substantial.

'Within a month, the 61st Division had launched eight raids ... the results were mixed and the cost high. German shelling savaged a raiding party from 2/4 Ox. and Bucks just before it went over the top on 21 June and smashed a raid by 2/8 Warwicks five days later. 2/4 Glosters actually got into German trenches on 4-5 July and 2/5 Warwicks attacked in daylight on 9 July. 2/4 Royal Berks had their turn on 13 July but the Bangalore torpedo party was hit on the way across and only the first wave of eleven men got through the German wire ... on 12 July a stokes mortar fired without warning near D Coy, 2/4 Ox. and Bucks. Replying instantly, the Germans cleaned up an entire platoon.'

—Fromelles. Peter Pederson, 2004.

And as already noted, this was called 'The Nursery Sector' by the British. No wonder then, when Horatio Bottomley, the outspoken 'tell it as it is' journalist heard of the Fromelles story, he gave the 61st Division the sad title—'The Sacrifice Division'.

HINDSIGHT

Based on further reading, the rather harsh judgement of Mackenzie given in the text needs comment. Nothing has been found to contradict the embarkation figures. It is what happened in the seven weeks before 19 July that was missed. The list above gives an indication of the raids. From the interrogation by the Germans of 45 prisoners of 2/8th Warwicks, we learn that the weakness of the attackers was because of losses of an average of 50 men per company, and when gas was released on 15 July, some blew back and 'ten men in C Coy were gassed.' We know about the gas 'accident' on 18 July when the total casualties were 1 officer and 70 men. So wastage could have easily been 500, another reason why, according to one of the Warwicks, another battalion was brought in a week before the attack as reinforcement.

HAIG TO HAKING

Please convey to the troops engaged last night my appreciation of their gallant effort, and of the careful and thorough preparedness made for it. I wish them to realise that their enterprise has not been by any means in vain and that the gallantry with which they carried out the attack is fully recognised.

—General Sir Douglas Haig

HAKING TO MACKENZIE

I wish to convey to all ranks of your Division my appreciation of the gallant attack carried out yesterday by them. Although they were unable to consolidate the ground gained, the effect on the enemy will be far-reaching, and will prevent him from moving troops away from our front to the South.

I wish you all in your next attack a more complete and permanent victory, and that you may reap the full fruit of the energy and skill displayed by all Commands and their Staffs in the execution of their task.

—R Haking, Lieut General
Commanding XI Corps,
20 July 1916

MACKENZIE TO HIS DIVISION

The Division not only fought gallantly but all ranks of every arm and service have carried out in a most exemplary and devoted manner, working day and night, an amount of labour which has highly tested their endurance and discipline, and merits my unqualified praise.

—Colin Mackenzie CB
Commanding 61st Division
20 July 1916

JOIN HANDS WITH THE AUSTRALIANS

As soon as the Front line trench is captured by the 2 Bucks a party will bomb down the Front line Trench from N8.d.4½.2. to join hands with the Australians. The OC 2 Bucks will see the OC Right Battalion of the Australian Division and settle all details.

—184th Bde Battle Orders,
16 July 1916

Having established that Mackenzie is feeding Haking with obviously inaccurate material, one has to ask why, and to what ends? Having proven that each battalion prior to the battle has around 30 officers and 800 ORs, we note that the trench strength of 18 July of 20 officers and 550 ORs represents almost precisely two-thirds of what was available. If Mackenzie was telling the truth about sending in 2400, that is remarkably close to half strength! Too close, one might suggest, to be a coincidence. Clearly Mackenzie had made some very specific arrangements.

With or without Haking's knowledge, Mackenzie made the decision to use only half of his available strength in the attack. Perhaps he was keeping the other half for the second assault, but then his 18 July figures would not support that. Perhaps Mackenzie personally thought the attack was a stupid operation anyway and decided to conserve his men, or he had had experience of Haking's style before and decided to make his own judgement in this way. Or Mackenzie may have been entirely straightforward and taken full advantage of that earlier quoted remark about his receipt of the original battle order:

> ... supplemented by verbal instructions that it was not intended to employ more than 6 battalions for the assault, in order that the Division might be kept intact for future operations.

The 5th Australian Divisional Commander, General McCay, made no record of such a supplementary verbal instruction and clearly acted in a way which indicates no restriction on his operations: he did however receive the same instructions about only using six battalions. There is no debate about who was the more experienced military man, Mackenzie or McCay, and therefore it is possible that McCay misunderstood the whole operation and went in 'boots and all', which was his style.

There is of course an alternative, that Mackenzie made the arrangement with the full knowledge and consent of Haking. If this were so, then there are indeed very, very serious implications. One would be that one standard was applied to the British Division, and another to the Australian. If so, then almost all of the blame for the massacre of the 5th Australian Division has to be put at the feet of Haking.

Regardless of how harshly one might judge the British generals for their lack of vision and caring, it is difficult to saddle them with such callousness that they would apply one set of rules to a British Division and another to a Colonial Division, ensuring one is kept intact and the other is nearly annihilated. However, we have to remember how Haking and his group

to quote the British *Dictionary of National Biography* (DNB):

His work there as a teacher of tactics and strategy was of great value and his contribution to the preparation of the army for war was substantial: he was a clear thinker and expositor and taught on sound lines. His 'Company Training (1913)' was a most useful and helpful book.

Haking was a Brigadier General in 1908 and GOC of 5th Bde in 1911 until 1914; CB in 1910 and Major General in 1914.

And the rest of that biographical note can find no fault with Haking; he is always on the edge of success but 'not supported'. He was at Mons in 1914 commanding the 5th Bde which:

established itself on the ridge of the Chemin des Dames, but, being unsupported, had to come back.

Haking was wounded the next day, evacuated to England only to return to France in December as Major General of the 1st Division. The conflicts on Givenchy-Cuinchy front began early 1915 extending to Rue du Bois on 9 May 1915, all of course near Fromelles: and Haking was there.

In August 1915 Lieut General Haking was given XI Corps:

but at Loos he had little chance of handling it, the divisions being taken from him and thrown into the battle piecemeal.

He was closely associated with the Hohenzollern Redoubt in the Loos action: this according to Denis Winter, helped earn Haking the title of 'Butcher'.

Haking's very rapid promotion has been ascribed to his support for Haig against Field Marshal French, as well as to his distinguished conduct on the field, despatches 8 times, or as one would have it:

Haking was promoted to the Army Command over the head of Sir Henry Wilson, his senior, among others. This was a sharp move by Haig to keep the post for his friend General Lord Horne, to whom he gave it, sending Haking back to his corps.

Others even more cynical, suppose that Haking received promotions and decorations to compensate him for the terrible losses his army suffered. In Haking's case this is absolutely what happened.

Now a Lieutenant General, as was the custom, Haking was knighted early in 1916. Then followed the battle of Fromelles, doubtless if the biographer had thought it worth mentioning by name, it too failed due to lack of support. Instead this piece: *Subsequently the corps (XI) took over the left of the First Army's front, roughly from Vermelles to Laventie, with headquarters at Hinges, and this line it was to hold almost unchanged until the autumn of 1917. The corps was not called upon to undertake any major operations and Haking was thus denied the opportunities he might have been relied upon to turn to good account.*

Lieut Gen. Sir Richard C B Haking

To reduce the battle at Fromelles to such a triviality seems extraordinary, but that is the British view, and because it is, it is important to record it here. It is also important to note that Haking's failure at Fromelles is thus not noted officially.

The XI Corps in November 1917 went to Italy, returning to France in March 1918 when it went into action again. This year saw Haking with a KCMG. The DNB description does not let the rest of the entry down:

... did much to check the German exploitation of their original success, holding on in front of Nieppe Forest and Hazebrouck. Subsequently it carried out in June a very successful local recovery of ground.

And so on!

After the war Haking was chief British representative on the Allied Armistice Commission, chief of the British military mission to Russia and Baltic provinces, and High Commissioner for the League of Nations to Danzig. In 1921 he added a GBE to his collection. He was in command of British troops in Egypt from 1923–27, becoming a general in 1925. He retired in 1927, and became the colonel of his old regiment.

His wife Rachel, daughter of Sir H J B Hancock, sometime Chief Justice of Gibraltar, whom Haking married in 1891, died in 1939. There were no children. Haking died at Bulford, Salisbury, 9 June 1945. There was no shortage of tributes, for example:

A man of practical capacity and high intellectual ability with an equable and well-balanced mind, Haking did admirable work, as a teacher before the war, in command of troops during the war, and the diplomatic and political duties entrusted to him after it.

Whatever Haking did was well thought out and well carried out.

The judgements from later on appear in the text. He is variously described as a 'Butcher', 'a vindictive bully, untruthful, and incompetent'. He 'always scorned the defensive and glorified the aggressive', he thought 'war was a great adventure' and that 'he had an obsession with Aubers Ridge'.

Perhaps because Richard Haking lived till he was 83 and died during the Second World War, detailed objective biographical material is difficult to find. It should be noted that the entry in the prestigious *DNB* follows very, very closely the *The Times* obituary of 11 June 1945. Haking's entry in *Who's Who* over which he had control while he was alive declines to name his parents, his place of birth or education, his recreations and whether or not he had children. The Hakings lived at Mill Cottage, Bulford, and their other address was the Army and Navy Club.

THE COMMANDER OF THE BRITISH DIVISION

Major General C J MACKENZIE
(Age at Fromelles—55)

Colin John Mackenzie was born on 26 November, 1861, the son of Major General Colin Mackenzie, and was educated in Edinburgh and at Sandhurst. He entered the army in 1881. He married, in 1898, Ethel Ross, daughter of an India civil servant. There were no children from the marriage. He was ADC to Lord Roberts when Roberts was C-in-C in India. For a time he was director of Military Intelligence in South Africa, and at other times served in Egypt, Burma, Hunza-Nagar, Gilgit, Waziristan, the Nile Expedition including Khartoum and the South African war, collecting medals and despatches at them all. He was Director of Staff Duties at the War Office in 1915 and then called to command the 61st Division from 1916 to 1918. He was wounded, mentioned in despatches five times and knighted KCB in 1918. He retired in 1920 and became Col of Seaforth Highlanders till 1931. His recreations unsurprisingly were shooting, fishing, hunting, cricket and golf. He held for a time the record for highest score for first wicket in India. We know that Mackenzie remained close to his division throughout his life. He was at Laventie on 21 April 1935 to unveil a plaque at the Town Hall in memory

Major Gen. Sir Colin J Mackenzie at Laventie, 21 April 1935
COURTESY M DELEBARRE

of the Division's dead in the battles of July 1916, and 9 April onwards in 1918. He died on 7 July 1956.

Whilst Bean gives details of many of the British senior officers, curiously he omits any biographical note on Maj. General C J Mackenzie GOC 61st Division, surely, as far as the Australians at Fromelles were concerned, the most important senior British General after Haking. Edmonds who was rather pleased that Bean had found space for notes on Butler, Barrow, Franks and others, had nothing to say on Mackenzie's behalf: nor does Bean seem to have ever canvassed Mackenzie, or sought to. Bean's sole mention of Mackenzie is a footnote in Volume 3, page 394 and it even omits Mackenzie's awards, not done in the cases of Butler etc.

THE COMMANDERS OF THE BRITISH BRIGADES

Brig. General A F GORDON
182nd Brigade
(Age at Fromelles—44)

Alister Fraser Gordon was born Feb 1872, third son of W Gordon of Inverness shire. He joined Gordon Highlanders Nov 1890 and with them saw service in India, West Africa and South Africa. In 1895 he was with the Relief of Chitral, received medal and clasp, and during Tirah Campaign of 1897–8 he was present at Chagru Kotal and Dargai as well as at the capture of the Sampagha and Arhunga Passes, and took part in the Waran and Bara Valleys, for which he was MID. In West Africa in 1900 he was in the Ashanti operation, DSO and MID, proceeding to South Africa 1901–02 where he acted for a time as Railway Staff Officer and Station Staff Officer. He then took part in operations in Transvaal. He received

Brig. Gen. A F Gordon CMG DSO

the Queen's Medal and 3 clasps. He was in action in France 19 October 1914, again MID. He was wounded at Festubert May 1915, and later appointed to command 182nd Bde and his services were rewarded with a CMG. He died of wounds on 31 July 1917 and was buried at Lijssenthock Military Cemetery. In 1908 Gordon had married Pilar Mary Edmonstoune-Cranstoun of Lanarkshire and they had three children.

Brig. General C G STEWART
183rd Brigade

(Age at Fromelles—47)

Cosmo Gordon Stewart was born on 21 November 1869, the eighth son of Sir J M Stewart, 3rd Bart. He was thus of Irish descent and the family motto was 'Forward'. He entered the army in 1888, was a qualified German interpreter from the Royal Military Academy, then going to India serving in the Kurran Expedition and the Relief of Chitral in 1895, where he was awarded the DSO. As Lieutenant, Stewart had charge of artillery and he was described by a fellow officer as the most bloodthirsty individual he had ever met. The extraordinary tale of the relief of Chitral, '*one of the sagas of the Empire*', and Stewart's part in it clearly reveals his courage and drive, and that his 'people skills' were poor, if existent at all.

As a Captain he transferred to the Egyptian Army serving in the Sudan, Nile Expedition and then to South Africa. In 1916 he was appointed to command 183rd Brigade of the 61st Division. He 'left' on 28 July 1916. After Fromelles he transferred to the 33rd Division to command a field artillery brigade, and there was very severely wounded. He later commanded the artillery of the 33rd Division. Made CMG in 1915 and Croix de Guerre, Stewart

Lieut (later Brig. Gen.) C G Stewart with the Eastern Relief force at Chitral, 1895

had six despatches. After the war he commanded the Allahabad Brigade Area from 1921–25, when he retired. There was one son from Stewart's marriage in 1911 to Gladys, daughter of Dr Honeyman of Auckland, New Zealand. Stewart also was CB. He died at Haselmere, 19 April 1948.

Brig. General C H P CARTER
184th Brigade

(Age at Fromelles—52)

Charles Herbert Philips Carter was born 14 Feb 1864 in County Galway. He was educated at Cheltenham College and became a naval cadet in 1878 but ten years later entered Black Watch. With them he served in the Benin Expedition of 1897 and subsequently in Nigeria, Ashanti—the Relief of Kumasi. He commanded part of the West African Frontier Force in 1900 when he led a force of 350, plus one 7-pounder and his own fox terrier. The party was ambushed and nearly wiped out even though the dog ran around barking at the concealed snipers. Carter was severely wounded (in his left eye) and the first relief party was also ambushed. The second relief party was marginally more successful. However Carter, perhaps disorientated by his wound, misread the orders and this led to another disaster. Carter however got out and was invalided to the UK. He returned to West Africa in 1909, gazetted Lieut Col 1911, Commandant of Nigeria Regiment 1913. At the outbreak of the war he was in the German Cameroons. In 1915 he was given district command at home, and appointed GOC 184th Bde May 1916, but he 'relinquished' command after Fromelles. Thereafter he had the Welsh Reserve Infantry Bde and then the South Wales Infantry Bde until Jan 1917. Mentioned in despatches, Carter was CB, CMG and CBE (1919). He died as the result of an accident on 22 October 1943.

Charles Carter at Cheltenham College, 1879
COURTESY CHELTENHAM COLLEGE

Haking's Philosophy of Attack

As the instigator and planner of 'The Attack at Fromelles', Lieut General Haking's philosophy of war as expounded in his much praised book *Company Training* provides important insights into the man and is very relevant to this inquiry. The book first appeared in 1913 and was reprinted regularly throughout the war (15,000 copies by November 1915). A neat volume, only fractionally larger than a present day paperback, with 470 pages, including index (approximately 140,000 words, no charts, tables or maps), it is full of the military discipline of the time, but none of the jargon. There is nothing slick or intellectual about it, indeed it is full of commonsense but somewhat long-winded. Overall it reads like the transcription of lectures, and was doubtless based on Haking's lectures at Staff College. Such comments as, 'Nothing can excuse carelessness', 'Thoughtless orders lead to counter orders', 'Revenge is not a Christian emotion' and 'It is proverbial that all that is best and all that is worst come out in a human being in war', abound.

The problem with Haking's book and thus his ideas, and all such guides to conduct, is that they are taken up by the unimaginative to be the full limit of conduct, rather than a start. Haking makes this point forcibly in his preface:

It is not suggested for a moment that the solutions recommended in this book are the best; the most that can be claimed for them is that the author has tried them all with actual troops on the ground and found them at least of practical, though by no means of universal, application.

Haking is referring to his service in South Africa, although it is clear from his first chapter 'Human nature in war' that he is expecting something else soon.

Do not let us leave it until war comes; do not let us think, in a vague sort of way, that in war we shall be all right and do as well as most people. We know that we are not gifted with tremendous personal courage, and we know that, whatever happens, we shall not run away. But that is not enough. We must train ourselves to understand that unless in the day of trial we can harden our hearts, assume the initiative in a most obscure situation, and retain it by constant advance and constant attack, avoiding all such sophistries as the offensive defensive, the delaying action, the waiting for reinforcements, &c., we cannot hope to play a dominating part even in a humble sphere on the battlefield.

Such passages, and the first chapter is full of them, do not show Haking as an out of touch academic or fanatical commander. He is a thoughtful man much given to examining his fellows and getting the best of them, by example, persuasion, discipline and respect. His very first page clarifies this abundantly.

No methods of training are thoroughly effective unless the strength and weakness of human nature are understood by the instructor. It is desirable, therefore, before entering into details regarding the various operations which have to be carried out by the infantry soldier in war, to consider how far human nature is likely to hinder and how far it will assist us in our task.

The idea of turning a man into a machine, by means of strict discipline, and thus making him more afraid of disobeying orders than of anything the enemy can do to him, has long since proved to be abortive. This method of training was only possible when infantry fought in close formation, when words of command were given by a battalion commander, and when it was easy to obey, because large bodies of infantry moved forward in great masses; one of the axioms of human nature being 'to go with the crowd'.

In modern war we are dependent for success upon the individual action of the infantry solider. This action is greatly influenced by his state of mind at the moment, and by the power that can be exercised over his mind by his comrades and by those who are leading him.

The strengths and weaknesses he summarises a few paragraphs further on:

the characteristics or emotions of the human mind which, from the military point of view, require the most serious consideration are courage and fear, surprise, respect and disrespect, cheerfulness and dejection, comradeship, emulation and esprit de corps.

Whilst recognising that some are fearful, some are stupid, some are grumblers, nowhere does Haking underestimate the possible development of the ordinary soldier, and therefore the ordinary man. He accepts that some are born with a better start than others:

but it is a mistake to suppose that a man must remain through life with the same amount of character that he brought into it. The attributes of the human mind, such as determination, bravery, ambition, energy, &c., are all capable of improvement and also of deterioration. These are totally different from gifts or talents, such as the power of painting, the art of music, the gift of tongues, &c., which come easily to some people under proper instruction, but which others are incapable of learning to the extent of producing satisfactory results.

Haking is well aware of the failures due to long periods of inaction or peace on military discipline, where there is no real urgency:

Perhaps the worst of all military habits, to use a slang expression, is to 'let things slide', or to wait on events. This habit, if indulged in, becomes part of our character and is allied to the worst form of the 'kismet' of Eastern nations.

Hence it is no surprise that the basic thrust of Haking's ideas is 'The Attack'. It is this which brings the best out of the commanders, the men, and rather obviously wins the battle of war.

There is one rule which can never be departed from and which will alone lead to success, and that is always to push forward, always to attack.

In so far as 'The Attack at Fromelles' is concerned, it is perhaps in Chapter VI 'The Company in Attack', that provides some real guide to Haking's style and values, and why he acted as he did at Fromelles.

The importance of the attack, as compared with any other form of military operation, is so vast that it practically swamps the remainder. The service of security is necessary and the defence is necessary, but they are only means to an end, the main object of any first-rate commander is to use them with two definite objects.

To which, a page or so further on, Haking adds this:

Furthermore, that this attack, unless pressed home with the utmost vigour and with every man thrown into the fight, and unless continued and maintained by every commander, high or low, and every company, is not really an attack at all, but merely another of those spurious operations of the offensive defensive nature which rarely lead to success.

That goes a long way to explain Haking's attitude to mounting attacks and his thoughts on the infantry are an important adjunct to this view.

Let us remember the great part that is played by the infantry soldier in war. The artillery help us, the cavalry help us, and the engineers are there to confirm our success and overcome obstacles, but it is the infantry solider, officer and man, who must bear the great stress of battle. He has no immovable gun to serve, and no horse to carry him forward; of his own initiative he advances against the enemy's position with a fixed determination to drive him back and defeat him. It is not generally considered that he requires any very high training, and yet his training in the correct use of the ground and of his rifle, in the dire stress of battle, is more complicated and more difficult than that of any other arm of the service. He is more influenced than any other soldier by those characteristics of the human mind which are adverse to success; ground is never the same and can never be treated in the same way, and therefore we can give him no fixed rules to work by.

It could be argued that all this thinking, based as it was, on Haking's experience with considerably inferior enemies, and with the world's best army behind him, rather than in front, all this is not truly applicable to the Western Front of 1915 or 1916. But what is best confirmed by these extracts is Haking's faith in a fully committed, well trained, properly equipped infantryman in a correctly planned attack. He develops this theme, and classifies attacks into seven categories, and it is the first of these that mirrors Fromelles:

The attack is a battle against an enemy holding a defensive position, where the company is part of a much larger force and is required to advance for a long distance exposed to the enemy's artillery fire, and subsequently to his artillery and infantry fire, before the assault can be delivered. This is what might be called the stereotyped form of attack.

In this type of attack there is usually plenty of time for preparation, and this could have been so at Fromelles, but proceedings were stupidly rushed: Haking acting contrary to all his first premises. Yet this is how he would develop an attack in ideal conditions.

In the first-mentioned type of attack there is usually plenty of time for preparation. Orders have been issued by all commanders, the situation has been explained to the officer commanding the company, and the direction of advance and objective of the company have been pointed out to him on the ground. He knows that the attack will be carried out in five stages. First he must advance exposed to hostile artillery fire only, the distance from the enemy's position being too great for the men to use their rifles with effect. He will, in consequence, adopt formations which are difficult for the enemy's artillery to deal with, he will move rapidly over ground where the enemy's shells are bursting in great numbers, he will halt for rest in places where the enemy cannot see him, and he will move at a walk over ground which is not being fired at by the enemy's guns. His main object will be to get forward as rapidly as possible without suffering more casualties than can be helped and without exhausting his men.

The second stage of the attack commences when the enemy's position is sufficiently close for the men to use their rifles, and ends when the company has reached a fire position where it comes under such a heavy fire from the enemy that further advance is impossible until that fire has been reduced. During this advance the company will be exposed to both the artillery and infantry fire of the defence, formations must be in extended order, and it will be necessary to reinforce the firing line to help it forward. The great object of the company will be to go forward from one good fire position to another, to pass over ground exposed to the enemy's bullets as rapidly as possible, and move at a walk over ground which is not so exposed. The object being still to husband the energies of the men so as to keep them fresh for the great fire fight which is now about to commence.

The third stage of the attack is the struggle for superiority of fire.

The fourth stage is the advance from this position after the enemy's fire has been reduced so as to gain a locality close enough to the enemy's position to deliver the assault.

The fifth stage is the assault with the bayonet.

All wonderful in theory, but there is no mention or allowance for machine guns, enfilade fire, concrete blockhouses, or even barbed wire, and certainly not the effect on the men of 50 per cent or more casualties around them. It is all about advancing.

In his next chapter Haking goes into detail about the elements of the attack—some 150 pages in fact—before he describes the Company in Defence. In so far as what he writes reveals more about Fromelles, perhaps the whole operation failed due to his first precept not being fulfilled by Haking himself:

We must first impress upon the recruit the vast importance of the attack, as compared with any other operation in war (and bring home to him the fact that no battles can be won without attack). It is the same when two men are boxing; if one man always defends and never hits back, he will never knock the other man down and win the contest. It is the same at football, cricket, or any other game; if one side contents itself with keeping the ball out of their goal or wicket, and never hits out to make runs or presses forward to kick goals, onlookers will regard that side with contempt.

The first question we must ask is, 'What are we trying to do when the company commences the attack?'

We are trying to drive back the enemy from some position which he is holding, or from some ground which he is advancing over.

'Which is the most important from our point of view, the ground which the enemy is holding, or the enemy's troops themselves?'

There is no real indication anywhere from Haig down to the British or Australian Brigadiers that they were told or were convinced that 'The Attack at Fromelles' was in any way important.

The enemy's troops, wherever they may be, or whatever they may be doing, are the sole object of our attack. If we confine ourselves to attacking some particular locality, which it is believed that the enemy is defending or advancing across, we may find, later on, that he is in some other locality, and we must at once make the necessary changes in our dispositions to meet the new situation. Ground comes into our operations to a very great extent, but it is never the ground that we are attacking, but always the enemy's soldiers, whom we must defeat and drive back wherever we find them. The only way in which we can defeat them and drive them back is to close up to them with the bayonet and compel them to break and run.

If these two commanding attitudes did not permeate the attacking force, all the rest of Haking's theories are without substance. For instance, he deals at length with the role of the artillery and the gunner in the attack, all supposing that everybody is familiar with the range and capacity of the guns being used. When we know that at Fromelles the Australian artillery for the most part had no such knowledge or experience, or even proper equipment, one wonders why Haking ignored this huge segment of his attack philosophy. Could it be that he was never told the true state of the Australian artillery? Perhaps McCay concealed from him the real situation in some happy assurance that 'it would be right on the night'. Haking's high estimate of the value of the artillery, especially after its failure, cost him the battle at Chemin des Dames where he commanded the 5th Bde, makes it almost unbelievable that he would have attacked at Fromelles with such an incompetent artillery sector. McCay knew the true state of the Australian artillery, but to admit it was inadequate, or well nigh useless, would have been a severe criticism of his own leadership, and self-criticism was not part of McCay's nature.

Haking places great confidence in the use of the rifle, being of the persuasion that the infantryman rushing forward firing his rifle is thus distracted from fear, nearby casualties and any emotion other than 'attacking'. Advancing over open ground under the surveillance of the enemy Haking deals with but it was what he called 'a civilised enemy' in South Africa. So civilised in fact they had no machine guns, barbed wire or concrete blockhouses! He deals in passing with enfilade fire from rifles, the enfilade fire from the German machine guns at or near the Sugarloaf was something else, and changed the whole event at Fromelles.

It would seem therefore that Haking did not develop with the times, his lack of success throughout the war confirms this, we cannot put down these failures as the faults of others. With studying his basic rules of warfare so eloquently espoused in *Company Training* we come to the conclusion that the teacher forgot what he was teaching, and that in no way makes Haking unique.

Haking's concluding remarks, reprinted here in full, reveal a man much different to the caricature 'Colonel Blimp', a part callous, part nit wit, that debunkers of the British Command revel in. It is not a case of whether Haking's values were correct or not, but an assessment of their relevance then. This extract does give an idealistic view of the whole operation of an army, but pays no account to having an enemy that is its equal or better, something of course the British of Haking's era never had to concern themselves.: that is, until 1914:

We have now followed the company through many days' training, we have considered the moral aspect of most problems that the regimental officer, non-commissioned officer and man is likely to meet with in war; the difficulties and dangers have been brought out into the full light of day, efforts have been made to show how some of them can be reduced, and perhaps we can think of similar methods to suit other situations and other ground.

The training of an infantry company for war, considered by the uninitiated as one of the simplest things in the world, is in reality the most complex; it is one constant struggle against human nature, and incessant variations of the tactical situation and of the ground, to say nothing of the frequent changes in the company as regards the junior officers and non-commissioned officers; whilst, to the Britisher, perhaps the greatest difficulty of all is the make-belief inseparable from all forms of peace training. We have to imagine so much without the bullet, and sometimes our imagination fails us, while sometimes it runs riot; in either case the teaching is apt to suffer, but we soon discover our mistake and apply common-sense theories and practices which must always be the great stand-by of every soldier in war.

In spite of all these difficulties, our company commanders have every reason to be proud of their handiwork, because it is carved on human faces and human figures all over the world. Put a subaltern in the most remote corner of the Empire, and give him the most unpromising material to work with, and we shall find that with the assistance of a few non-commissioned officers of his own flesh and blood he will produce in a short time a company of men that will face the bullets in war, but who only a few months earlier would have fled for their lives before any threatened danger. The reason is to be found in the extraordinary faith possessed by every British officer in the excellence of any human beings who are placed under his control. Whatever other companies or regiments may do he is perfectly certain that his own company is all right. He has confidence in himself and in his men, and his confidence is conveyed in some telepathic manner to those under his command and increase enormously their military value. He is a gentleman himself, and he treats his men as gentlemen, whatever race they may belong to, but directly they lose their claim to this high title he lets them know it, and the evil influence, whatever it may be, does not flourish or bear fruit.

In many cases he has fought with his men alongside him in war, and each has learnt to value and respect the military qualities of the other. We know that some of us are braver than others, but we are all ready to fight, and those who are least brave have a harder task than the heroes. Our company commanders are proud to be the keepers of the Empire, and it is a satisfaction to them to know that this is truly the case, because in modern war, however good the commanders and their staff may be, no one can win the battle except the infantry soldier, and he cannot win except by attack.

Could it have been this 'Club' idealism that was the real problem of Haking and the rest? If he asked McCay a question he expected a truthful answer. McCay who had spent most of his life as a lawyer and politician had a record of only presenting a position to suit whatever the case demanded.

Haking's *Company Training* was of course no handbook to the Western Front, but its enthusiastic acceptance by the commanders of the time (this author's copy once belonged to Lieut Gen. Sir Sydney Rowell) means that it guided much of the thinking and tactics employed. Fromelles was perhaps the classic example of how battles cannot be won from books.

NOT FOR THE LAZY OR UNINTELLIGENT

The defenders of Haking always referred the later doubters to *Company Training* as proof of the man's quality. The review in the *United Service Magazine* (Volume 47 1913, page 348)) gives an interesting contemporary assessment of it. Haking also wrote *Staff Rides and Regimental Tours* (1908).

Company Training by Brigadier General R C B Haking, CB, *p.s.c.*, Commanding 5th Infantry Brigade. London: Hugh Rees, Ltd., 5, Regent Street, S.W. 1913. Price 5*s*. net.

To the lazy or unintelligent officer this manual can be of no use; its pages are not intended to be read to the men as a means of saving the trouble of preparing lectures. On the contrary, the aim of the author is evidently to furnish useful elementary instruction for the officers themselves, leaving the latter to extract from it matters to put before their men in their own words. The view taken of the functions of a company in action is a wide one; and this is as it should be, because the far too general tendency is in the opposite direction. If company commanders fail to realise fully how the success or failure of the battalion, or even of the brigade, may in an emergency depend upon the action of a single company, it is not to be expected that section leaders and others shall think and act as they ought, within the company itself.

The officer who profits intelligently by the study of Brigadier General Haking's little book, will find himself a competent company commander—if he has in him those qualities with which only nature, zeal and experience can endow him—and being such will have no difficulty in training his men on sound lines. The book is in effect a manual of minor tactics, furnishing a reliable mentor.

The New Zealand Division at Fromelles

As the 'other half' of ANZAC, this division's total independence came in Egypt in January 1916 when there were sufficient men to form a New Zealand Division. The NZ Division with the 1st and 2nd Australian Divisions formed the I ANZAC Corps and under Birdwood went to France in April 1916.

It was east of Armentières on 20 May that the New Zealanders occupied their first trench system facing the well fortified German line protecting Lille. When the II ANZAC Corps arrived at the end of June the New Zealand Division moved to that Corps, while the I ANZAC Corps (1, 2 and 4 Divs) prepared for the Somme. The effect of this change was to extend the New Zealand front from 4 miles to 8½ miles, including Bois Grenier which, in the words of their historian '*normally occupied by 2 Divisions, threw a considerable strain both on the fighting troops and administrative services.*'

The Division carried out raids and bombardments from the beginning of July as part of the effort to keep the Germans alert. This activity culminated in five heavy attacks on the German line, the nights 10/11 July, 11/12 July, 12/13 July, 13/14 and 14/15 July all except the last were costly failures. The New Zealand historian had a theory why: *such was the uncanny promptitude and deadly accuracy of the enemy retaliation that it seemed certain that the Germans had acquired information through unguarded conversation either in a town estaminet—for Armentières was not without its German agents—or over the telephone.*

In the history of the Maori units in the war, members of whom were in the raiding parties, there is a note about '*having located an enemy listening post and also found a telephone cable running from No-Man's Land under the German wire*'.

When the preparations for 19/20 July were finished, the 60th British Bde moved in between the 8th Aust Bde and the New Zealanders for reasons not entirely clear, but that

A New Zealand Division Field Ambulance Station

did not exclude the New Zealand Division from making a contribution.

'*To assist the enterprise by way of diversion, smoke and gas were discharged on the night of the 19/20 on the New Zealand front, and a violent bombardment, in which the corps 'heavies' cooperated was directed from 8pm till 11 pm on the whole of the enemy's trenches, billets and batteries. In addition, 2 raiding enterprises were carried out ... The ammunition expended on this night by the Divisional artillery alone in connection with these activities exceeded 12000 rounds. Assistance was given to the 5th Australian Division in the evacuation of their heavy casualties.*'

In return for this work the New Zealanders received: *'The enemy bombardment was of exceptional fury, 8000 shells being flung into the area exclusive of trench mortar projectiles. The whole ground was turned over as if by a volcanic upheaval, and the local features altered so as to be unrecognisable.'*

After some movements in the general area, the New Zealanders returned to Sailly on 13 October, and began to relieve the 5th Australian Division with 1st Bde HQ at Rouge de Bout and the 3rd Bde in Fleurbaix. The historian's description of the territory gives an interesting contrast to the turmoil of earlier days: and the last couple of sentences reveal a little of the aftermath.

'*The Sailly sector extended for 3 miles in flat pleasantly wooded country before the German positions at Fromelles and on the Aubers Ridge, which guarded the south western approach to Lille and had looked down on the slaughter of Neuve Chapelle and the XI Corps repulse in July. The front area was crossed by a network of several sluggish streams and drains running back among the hedgerows to the Lys. The principal of these was the Laies. All were now considerably swollen by the late autumn rains, and broad tracts along their banks were little better than marshes ... Across these streams ran the continuous breastworks of the front line and the derelict close support line. This latter, though not manned, was maintained in outward repair, and in it men occasionally showed themselves and fires were kindled in order to give the enemy the impression of occupation and to attract shelling The real support line lay somewhat in the rear, in a series of small garrison posts connected laterally by a continuous fire trench. Further again in the rear were the series of defended localities, Charred, Windy, Winter's Night Posts and others, that formed the third or subsidiary line of the front system. These were joined by a rudimentary trench, which was in a few places fire-stepped and revetted.*

For the protection and maintenance of this whole system the Division was responsible ... the village of Fleurbaix was extensively protected by a ring of such redoubts ... Several of the subsidiary line garrisons ... could boast of a habitation in abandoned pumphouses, but generally the accommodation was inadequate. The relieved Australian battalions had been of weak strength, and the first urgent task was to provide shelter for all the troops in the line.'

4

They'll get used to it

They'll get used to it
—Major General J W McCay
to Brigadier General E Tivey in the
trenches, dawn 20 July 1916

To properly understand many of the events concerning the 5th Australian Division at Fromelles, it is necessary to examine the manner of its formation and the conduct of its command from the first days. In the margin is the official description from the Divisional War Diary. It was written in the same hand and at the same time as the rest of the War Diary of the period and appears to have been done to tidy up the rather complicated genesis of the division, and avoid any contentious issues.

Quite naturally it omits the prelude to formation, that is the determined efforts by Australia to set up its own army, with Australian command. The case 'for' was fought by Major General Brudenell White and the case 'against' by General Sir Archibald Murray in command of the Mediterranean Expeditionary Force, whose view of the issue was '*The Australian Training Depot in Egypt has always found the greatest difficulty in producing officers of any value, and non-commissioned officers of any sort at all*'. But as C E W Bean put it '*Murray was not seized of the principles of colonial self-government*'. However, the resolution of White who, to quote Bean again, made '*a strong statement of the case for Australian self-government*' so that it was agreed at the end of January 1916 Generals Birdwood and White should '*temporarily have control of the whole Anzac force and commence reorganization*'.

That reorganisation brought about the formation in Egypt of the 1st, 2nd, 4th and 5th Divisions. (The 3rd Division was under formation in Australia.) One of the early concerns of Murray was who could command the Australian divisions.

At this point the opinion of Major General William Birdwood was canvassed, on the basis that he had been in command of the Anzac forces on Gallipoli. Birdwood wished to hold on to the services of some experienced, if old, British Generals, recommending that McCay who had been invalided to Australia, take the 3rd Division. Birdwood was overruled by the Minister of Defence in Melbourne, G F Pearce. McCay had been going to command the 1st Division in July 1915 but, due to an earlier wound, his leg snapped the day before he was to

A GOOD FIGHTING FORCE
The 5th Australian Division was formed as follows: After the evacuation from the Gallipoli Peninsula the 1st, 2nd and NZ–Australia Divisions, the latter containing 4th Inf. Bde, returned to Egypt. Large numbers of reinforcements were available and after completing the existing units to WE it was found that many thousands were still left over. In consequence, the new formations were taken in hand in February and 1st Inf. Bde, then under command of Brig. Gen. Smyth VC, took over command of this, and Colonel Elliott (late 7th Bn) took over 1st Inf. Bde. 1st Australian Division was at Serapeum at this time with the exception of 1st Inf. Bde. At Serapeum the old 2nd Inf. Bde was also split in two—the new Bde forming 15th Inf. Bde and Brig. Gen. Irving took over command of this. He had lately arrived from Australia. The remaining Inf. Bde of the Division was now the 8th Inf. Bde under command of Brig. Gen. Tivey DSO and at this period they were holding the front line some seven miles east of the canal. The 3 Bdes were collected at Tel el Kebir, and Gen. Smyth VC temporarily commanded the 5th Australian Division. An exchange was later effected and Gen. Smyth VC rejoined 1st Inf. Bde. Colonel Elliott went to 15th Inf. Bde and Brig. Gen. Irving took 14th Inf. Bde. Major Gen. McCay CB arrived from Australia, a staff was appointed by HQ Aust and NZ Forces (Ismailia) and Brig. Gen. Christian was made Divisional Artillery Commander.

On the departure of 2nd Australian Division to France the new 5th Division moved, mostly by route march, to Ferry Post, Ismailia and there took over the line called 'B' subsection of No. 2 Section of the Defences ... The [continued next page]

A GOOD FIGHTING FORCE (contd)
Division rapidly developed into a good fighting force and the energy of all ranks was maintained at a high standard by the prospects of an early move to France. About May 20th we knew pretty well that the 4th Division at Serapeum was to sail on June 1st and the 5th Division on June 10th.

THE MINISTER REMAINED FIRM
Knowing their reputation (Generals Cox and Lawrence) Birdwood was anxious to secure both, and on January 31 submitted their names to the Australian Government for the command of the new divisions in Egypt, adding a hope that McCay would be given the command of that forming in Australia.

To the Minister and military staff in Australia the fact that no Australian brigadier, even after the experience of Gallipoli, was considered capable of commanding a division, came as a surprise and disappointment. Senator Pearce telegraphed to this effect, and expressed a desire that McCay, who was now fairly fit, should receive one of the Egyptian commands. Meanwhile he accepted Cox and Lawrence on the condition one of them awaited the arrival of the 3rd Division from Australia. Birdwood, recognising this would lose him Lawrence, continued to press his recommendation that McCay should take the 3rd, but the Minister remained firm.

—C E W Bean
Official History Volume III page 45

WHITE AND MCCAY ON THE DESERT MARCH
While preparing Volume III of his history, Bean corresponded with White, 27 May 1926, asking about the march. White's reply of 1 June 1926 was:

I do not know who ordered the test march. Birdwood certainly did not, Godley may have. McGlinn thinks GHQ ordered it that at that time there was a shortage of railway rolling stock. I will by inquiry see if I can find out anything for you.

White must have contacted McCay on this issue, because McCay wrote to Bean:
[continued opposite]

take up the appointment. Being the senior Brigadier General it was to be expected he would get a Division, but that he should be appointed over Birdwood's wishes revealed for the first time the extent of his power base. His long history of conflict and abrasiveness in positions of authority and an extraordinarily brief active service record of five weeks, hardly qualified him for such special treatment. Only one other 'Australian' was deemed qualified to lead a division and that was Major General J G Legge who was given the 2nd. The 1st went to Major General H B Walker and the 4th to Major General H V Cox, both English. Later in the year when the 3rd came to England and was given to Major General John Monash, it was technically the only AIF division commanded by a 'dinky-di', that is a person born in Australia, McCay and Legge both being born elsewhere.

To deal with the Turkish presence in Palestine an Australian Mounted Division was also formed. The New Zealanders under Major General A J Godley, another Englishman, now had their own Division and that went to France in early April.

We now turn to the 5th Division. McCay arrived in Egypt and on 22 March took command. Much of the organisation had been done and training was to start in earnest while in front line positions along the Suez Canal where Turkish raids could be expected. McCay learned that the division in three 'flights' would have to march from its present camp at Tel-el-Kebir to the canal, a three day march along a desert road and beginning in a week's time. It seems a distinct possibility that this was an established way of moving troops over a short distance when there was no emergency.

There now follows a fairly detailed examination of the Desert March because it reveals for the first time McCay in charge of over 17,000 men. McCay never, in either his civil or military career, had charge of a group of anything like this size and complexity. He had not, like Legge for instance, served his apprenticeship in administration. McCay was notoriously bad with committees and boards, as well as being *very* aware that he had been a high ranking officer for the last sixteen years. By his own account McCay consulted the British High Command in regards to the arrangements and was told that there was a shortage of railway rolling stock, which necessitated the march. In actual fact, four railway trucks *were* provided for each 'flight' anyway.

Brig. General G G Irving, a 49 year old professional soldier from Victoria who had been in temporary command of the Division before McCay's arrival had asked High Command if the march could be done at night, but was told it would '*interfere with other Echelons'*, which seems to indicate other units were using the route at night.

In view of this Irving and his staff had gone to some pains to organise camel trains to carry heavy gear, kit and extra water. There were to be in fact 250 camels and 15 horse drawn wagons to each brigade or 'flight'. Irving had been made aware that many men had only recently been inoculated, that many were new arrivals suffering from the climate and various illnesses, and most importantly, the vast majority were wearing old boots.

Perhaps to accommodate these problems Irving arranged the march over three days of modest distances, 15 miles, 15 miles and 9 miles. Such marches were not bad things in themselves: used as a toughening up process they also bonded together the men into the beginnings of a unit through a significant shared experience.

For reasons never actually dealt with by Bean or anybody else, McCay decided to change the character of the march. The men would carry full packs, waterproof sheets, rations, one full water bottle, 120 rounds of ammunition and a rifle. They would wear wool uniforms, puttees and British issue 'pith' helmets: this, called '*full marching order*', meant that the men carried around 93 lbs (42 kgs), and the temperature was in excess of 100°F (38°C). The camels would carry officers' kit, cooking utensils and two blankets per man, '*5% of the camels were without load*'. At the end of the second day of each 'flight' the camels were returned to Tel-el-Kebir, their loads going the third day by road transport. A curious operation to put it mildly, but reading the orders one is sure that it was a regular arrangement.

On 25 March McCay's order (over the signature of Lieut Col C M Wagstaff, GSO1) set out the march procedure, including the facts that supplies would be '*drawn at Mahsama and Moascar from depots at those places*' and '*Drinking water up to 4500 gallons per diem is being provided at Mahsama. OC of each Echelon will arrange for its distribution*'. Then some preparedness about the casualties. '*Ambulances are being established at Mahsama and Moascar for the reception and evacuation of sick unable to continue marching. Cases which fall out on the road will be dealt with by the Field Ambulances accompanying each Echelon. OCs ... will report at the end of the move the numbers of each unit which fell out.*'

In view of what happened these instructions were remarkably perceptive, accurately alerting the possible problems, but the accounts of this march given by Ellis, Bean,

WHITE AND MCCAY ON THE DESERT MARCH (contd)

White has spoken to me about the march to Moascar of two of the 5th Div. brigades, which some people have spoken of as being a 'test' march, and I enclose a note on that point also. With Kind Regards, Yours Sincerely, J W McCay.

(1) Orders came from Corps GHQ (Gen Godley's command) that the infantry brigades of the 5th Div were to march to Moascar.
(2) I objected to this verbally at Corps HQ and was told it was an order.
(3) I then went to GHQ and was told it was an order and that train transport was not available. Nothing was said about 'tests'.
(4) I then issued order accordingly.
(5) The 15th Bde did the march all right but the 14th had a bad time.
(6) Then the 8th Bde was brought by train.
(7) GHQ despite the matter being raised by me, were wholly responsible.
(8) I am aware that it has been said in the 'yellow press' that I ordered the march or asked for it as a test. That is a malicious untruth. The facts are set out above. 6.6.26 McCay.

McCay's legal training once again was his refuge, he was obeying orders. But it was the conduct of the march that was the issue, *not* the march itself. Likewise the Battle: it was the conduct of McCay that was the concern, *not* the orders he received. Were Bean, White and others deliberately asking the wrong question so as to allow McCay to escape proper examination?

THE FLIGHTS

The first 'flight' under Brig. General Irving consisted of 114 Officers, 3475 ORs, 250 camels, 15 Limber GS wagons and 4 railway trucks.

The second 'flight' under Colonel H E Elliott consisted of 97 Officers, 3750 ORs, 250 camels, 15 Limber GS wagons and 4 railway trucks.

The third 'flight' under Lieut Col O F Phillips consisted of 44 Officers, 1525 ORs, 250 camels, 7 Limber GS wagons and 4 railway trucks.

Irving and Colonel Shepherd OC 8th Field Ambulance, almost describe four different events.

Ellis gives precise details of the 'flights' leaving 27 March, 28 March and 1 April pointing out that an advanced party of 8th Bde went on 22 March and the Bde itself by train on 23 March. Of 14th Bde Ellis wrote positively of Irving's arrangements:

> *In order to enjoy the full benefit of the cool hours of the early morning General Irving wisely provided for an early start.*

Ellis describes how they marched until 3 pm when they reached Mahsama, exhausted and in bad state. The next day was particularly hot and by 10.30 am men were beginning to drop, but they pushed on till 3 pm to within a few miles of Moascar.

> *Here news of the plight of the remainder reached General McCay. Water supplies were immediately requisitioned and sent out along the route, and the men, half dead with exhaustion or distracted by thirst, were gradually collected and restored.*

Ellis then tells how on the third and '*easiest day*' the 14th Bde reached Ferry Post. Next he relates the 15th Bde's journey under the watchful eye of Elliott, '*arriving in Moascar in good order although suffering fairly severely. They had marched only in the morning and in the evening*'.

Bean, on the other hand, deals at length with Irving's 'flight', but ignores Elliott's semi-success entirely. He points out that when the 4th Division made the same journey General Cox permitted his men '*to pack their rations ... and their waterproof sheets upon the camels*' being '*slightly more lenient in his march orders than McCay*'. Bean has no friendly word for Irving and quotes a couple of lines from his Report of 5 April to McCay:

> *Scores, including officers and NCOs, literally dropped down, the officers and NCOs from the extra fatigue they had experienced in looking after and exhorting their men.*

These few phrases are from a 1600-word compassionate account by Irving of what happened, and some other extracts are important to note. The first day:

> *Actual time of marching ... 4 hours 23 minutes. The nature of the ground was good throughout ... fresh water was carefully guarded and men were with difficulty kept clear of the Freshwater Canal. An inspection of all men by RMOs was ordered. After tea, the whole column soon settled down and all was quiet for the night.*

KEPT THEM GOING

Sunday, 26 March: went for route march about seven miles, pretty hot, not too much struck on the marching business. Monday, 27 March: Went to physical exercises in morning and for route march in afternoon about five miles. Tuesday, 28 March: had day of rest, packed up all belongings ready for route march. Parades of kit in afternoon. Webb Robertson came over in evening said 14th Brigade got a bad start on route march. Watch went bung. Wed. 29 March: Left Tel-el-Kebir for Ferry Post 39 miles. Left Tel-el-Kebir at 7 am. 1st spell very good, travelling last run to midday. Men dropping out everywhere. Left for march at 4 pm and bivouacked for night very sore and stiff, did 15 miles. Thurs. 30 March: was on rear guard to bring on stragglers, started dropping out in front—kept them going, had midday bivouac at 11, started again at three. Reached Moascar camp and bivouacked for night just at dark. Friday, 31 March: Finished up march from Tel-el-Kebir to Ferry Post 39 miles. Bivouacked at Moascar night before, had fine march through Ismailia, beautiful avenue of trees for about three miles. Left Moascar at 6 reached Ferry Post at 11, went to canal for bath at 4. Saturday, 1 April: Went for bathing parade to Suez Canal, cleaned up lines, received 50 piastres pay and 175 piastres extra duty pay for eight days, mounted as Sgt of quarter guard at quarter to six with 12 men and Stan Evans as Corporal.

—Sgt Simon Fraser 3101, 57th Bn.

BLISTERED FEET

I consider that the men of 54th Bn will not be fit for ordinary parades for 2 or 3 days especially if hot weather continues. The march was undertaken too soon after inoculation which weakened the men to a certain extent. The majority of men have blistered feet which will be well in 2 to 3 days if men are rested.

—F M Farrer, Captain
RMO 54th Bn 29.3.16

B Coy, 60th Bn about to start on the Desert March, 29 March 1916
COURTESY M WOOD

Next morning after a 5 am Reveille and 7 am start, Irving noted that:

> *... 41 men by MOs orders and 42 cooks etc. leaving by train.*

So there was a train available after all for some. The day was a disaster, and after the majority had reached Moascar, Irving wrote:

> *... went back to cheer up and get together those who perforce had to fall out and remained out till nearly 8 pm when all I believe had been brought in thanks to the assistance of the New Zealanders, with water and men. ... by the morning it was ascertained that 19 were in Ambulances and 13 others unaccounted for but believed to be in camp with the New Zealanders.*

The next morning the camels were returned to Tel-el-Kebir and wheeled transport was provided. Irving concluded that:

> *No other cases admitted to hospital other than those mentioned at Moascar.*

What Irving did not mention was that on the 26 March the CO of 8th Field Ambulance and others had had a meeting to discuss how to deal with what was clearly going to be a difficult exercise. Col Shepherd wrote later:

> *A number of infantrymen fell out in the first mile and within the first two hours a large number of men had fallen out. I and the Brigade Major ... decided ... to send them back to Tel-el-Kebir ... 150 were collected ... A second depot at Qassasin ... 120 men were left. 28.3.1916 ... 60 men had been weeded out by RMOs ... during the morning probably 40 men dropped and, but from this time till midday halt ... they dropped out by scores, so that the Ambulances could not deal with them. [At Moascar]*

THE CAMELS BOLTED

Those who took part in the march from Tel-el-Kebir will not forget it in a hurry. The camels bolted with our water and we only had our water-bottles in the march across the desert. By the time we reached the Sweet Water Canal we were panting like dogs, our tongues swollen and hanging out, our lips cracked and bleeding ... we were warned that the Sweet Water Canal was full of germs and that to drink it might possibly mean death, but most of us were too far gone ... and we threw ourselves down and lapped it up like dogs. Fortunately there were few ill effects, and the medical staff was not overworked because of it. There might have been many casualties, though, if it had not been for the New Zealanders, who, hearing of our plight, came out with water carts and ambulances and picked up those who had fallen by the way.

—R H Knyvett, 59th Bn
Over there with the Australians (1918)

THE MEN HAD NO TIME FOR HIM

The camp at Ferry Post was like the camp at Tel-el-Kebir, on a sandy desert, on the Asia side of the canal ... The flies, like in Egypt were in millions and most unbearable ... The next day ... orders had come through that we were to leave our camp and proceed back to Moascar and we had to parade with all our kit. After marching to the parade ground with all our belongings, a fatigue party went through the tents and everything we left behind was seized and burnt ... it was a disgrace to see the quantity of clothing etc. that was destroyed by burning.

Sunday morning saw 8th Bde ... moving out of camp. As we were in full marching order and the sand very soft, it was heavy marching but when we crossed the pontoon bridge we were once more on a good hard road going towards Ismailia ... we expected a spell when the canal was crossed, but our luck was out for who should come along on horseback but McCay, who was in command of 5th Division and I might here mention that very few of his men had any time for him. We never got the spell we expected, and to make things worse, we were passing a division of Tommies who were going out to relieve us and they were enjoying a rest on the roadside. When my company passed McCay he had dismounted and had his watch out taking the time as we marched past.

Without any spell we reached Moascar and had to set to work pitching tents, but the job did not take very long so we had the rest of the day to ourselves. Monday morning we were roused at 3 am ... the order came along the line to fall in, with full marching order. When we fell in we were told that McCay was disgusted at the way the Bde marched past the Tommies yesterday and we were to be punished by having to do three route marches ... if he only knew what the men said about him ... (they) had no time for him ... and for three mornings we were up at 3 am, did our route marches through the sand and were back in camp tired out by 9 am.

We had been camped at Moascar about eight days when we were told the

[continued opposite]

> *My Medical officers reported that the condition of most of the troops was very serious on account of lack of water, so I made arrangements with Engineers to supply a water cart to each battalion to send out to troops, but found it was impossible to get the carts through the camp, as the men rushed them ... a water cart passed me and was immediately rushed by the men. Mr Hamilton (Colonel Hamilton of NZASC) and myself fought the men off it, and despatched it through the lines at a gallop, and it got off. The men in camp were out of hand altogether, and took notice of neither commands nor entreaties on behalf of their Commander.*

When Shepherd came to summing up the reasons for the 'March Breakdown', he first pointed out that his unit did not have sufficient riding horses and so was unable to get around quickly to the men in distress, he then made notes on the lack of fitness etc. and that early morning and late afternoon moves would have made it all easier. His last observation was:

> *I have never seen men sweat to such an extent as these troops. Many of the packs picked up were almost wet through.*

Another account on this aspect reported that the uniforms were all damp and the boots wet through when the march began due to the heavy desert dew. As they dried out through the day the uniforms shrank, and the boots went hard.

Both Irving's and Shepherd's Reports were written in response to a document called G3/1403(?), which is not in the file. What does survive however is a close typed page from Headquarters signed by McCay and dated by him 29 March 1916, and marked for distribution to the 53rd, 54th, 55th and 56th Bns, to be read to the men by their COs. In the Divisional Administration file on another copy over the signature of Brigade Major King there is this note in King's hand and undated:

> *This was handed to Brig. General Irving, commanding 14th Bde on completion of his march from Tel-el-Kebir to Moascar.*

Some passages from the 450 word tirade are as follows:

> *When troops are ordered to make marches it is for some definite purpose, and it is always necessary that the troops reach their destination as formed bodies capable of immediate action: for example taking part in a battle, forming an outpost line, or in the easiest case forming a camp. The 14th Bde did not answer this test on any of the 3 days ... It might be excused for the first day's march ... but there is no excuse ... for what happened in the final stage of the 3rd day's march, when large numbers of the Brigade fell out without authority ... indeed some officers and NCOs were offenders and the Bde struggled into its Camp without cohesion, and for the time without value. A soldier's duty is to do what he is told in the time and manner appointed and to persevere to the limits of his endurance.*

McCay went on to detail his great disappointment and blame the regimental officers, NCOs and men and concluded:

> *... until a great improvement takes place I shall not be able to report the 14th Bde as fit for active service.*

Perhaps he should have waited until he received the Report of Col Shepherd.

Bean summed up the event, also noting that neither Monash nor Glasfurd who also took brigades on this route were immune to errors. He wrote that the 5th's arrival at Moascar was '*like the remnant of a broken army*', and that: '*Many of the men felt bitterly that they and their units had been unnecessarily humiliated by subjection to so severe a trial. Irving, whose arrangements for the march were in McCay's opinion very defective, was replaced in the command of the 14th Bde by Colonel Pope of 16th Bn.*'

The way Bean deals with the Desert March and McCay is one of his least satisfactory efforts, and the more one reads around the subject, the clearer it becomes that Bean is being very economical with the truth. And one wonders precisely what he really knew when he resorted to this footnote with its 'triple negative':

> *A rumour was afterwards current that, as a result of this march, several men had died. Though the available records contain no evidence to support this statement, it is not therefore necessarily incorrect.*

And Ellis mentioned Irving's departure in a curious way:

> *There were a few important changes in command during April and May, but Colonel Pope relieved General Irving at 14th Bde HQ, while ...*

One wonders about Ellis' use of the word '*but*'. The War Diary notes that on 1 May Irving came to the Ferry Post HQ '*to see GOC*' and on 6 May it notes that Irving had '*gone to Tel-el-Kebir*'. The Nominal Roll of the AIF says Irving returned to Australia 1st May! When he did return to Australia he had administrative jobs in Victoria, South Australia and Queensland.

The War Diary's only detailed entry on the Desert March was as follows:

> *28.3.16 1st Flight 14th Inf. Bde and details arrived at Moascar. Many hundreds fell out in the last 4 miles owing to the great heat and lack of march discipline. The NZ Division gave assistance in furnishing water carts and ambulance wagons.*

There then followed references to the eventual arrival of all of the 5th Division at the Canal largely without comment.

THE MEN HAD NO TIME FOR HIM (contd)

only things that we were to have, had to be put in our packs, everything else had to be thrown out. This order was carried out by the men to a certain extent and our khaki was put in our kit bags and sent to a siding for a couple of days. Imagine our surprise when one morning to see a couple of transports come into camp loaded with clothing etc.—these loads were dumped and rooted over by the boys to try and find their personal property. For it turned out that taking our kit bags to the siding to be put on the train for embarkation was only a bluff. All the bags were broken open and everything except one uniform was thrown out and destroyed ... I lost a pair of boots, one uniform that had never been used and three pairs of socks ... this is one of the reasons for the enormous expense of the war ... like all the lads I went to the dump to see if there was anything worth picking up and there were silver back hair brushes, periscopes, razors and all sorts of articles ... I was lucky in getting a pair of Zeiss field glasses ... The natives had the time of their lives ... (one) had no less than five coats and six hats ... wearing them all at once.

—Pte W C Barry, 2514, 29th Bn

NOT A GOOD WORD

Friday, March 31. At Ferry Post. Have seen a lot of the 14th Bde after their awful march. They look even worse than did the troops upon their return from Gallipoli, and we have heard much of their trying experience. They have not a good word for those responsible for the march, but they are full of praise for the New Zealanders who went out voluntarily from Moascar and helped them in. The 15th Bde arrived today and, although they had a better march, they all looked knocked up. They rub it into us about being 'Tivey's Chocolates', but I fail to see how the inhuman treatment they have received will make them any better in action than we 'Chocolates'.

—R E Lording (A Tiveychoc)
There and Back (1935)

WITHOUT STEP OR BEARING
Today the 8th Brigade (the yellow brigade whose colours I have never seen before) passed this hospital. They seemed to be big men and they mostly wore the British helmet—but they marched worse than any Australian or New Zealand troops I have ever seen—on the wrong side of the road, on both sides of the road and from side to side of it, without step or bearing. It had probably been a long march, but it didn't seem to me like our last 3 divisions.
—C E W Bean, 23 March 1916. Cairo

TIVEY CHOCS
There was a good deal of rivalry between us (15th Bde) and another brigade (8th) known as 'The Chocolate Soldiers'. They received this nickname because they were the most completely equipped unit that ever left Australia. They were commanded by a well-known public man, and the womenfolk had seen that they lacked nothing in sweaters or bed socks. They had a band for every battalion ...
—R H Knyvett, 59th Bn
Over there with the Australians (1918)

OUR DISGRACEFUL CONDUCT
Some days later the Battalion was paraded and we had read to us a lengthy screed on the march, from the divisional commander, Maj. Gen. McCay. In scathing terms he described what had been reported to him as our 'disgraceful conduct'. This made the men in the ranks scapegoats for somebody's blunder.
As punishment, for mornings after, the battalion was marched round and round in a great circle under full packs for two hours, to teach us march discipline.
—H R Williams, 56th Bn
The Gallant Company (1933)

A MAD THING
'Yesterday Somerville told us of the march ... of 5th Div. (McCay's and Irving's Brigade) which came to disaster ... I had heard before I left that it was a mad thing to attempt. Somerville brings news of the result. It was like a retreat from Moscow ... Sturdee, who is one of the best men in Egypt collapsed when he got in.'
—C E W Bean,
c. 7 April 1916. France

When cornered years later about his repeated failures, McCay always held to the position that he had to obey orders. But as far as the Desert March was concerned, the only order was that the Australians had to march. It was entirely in McCay's ambit to arrange that march in any way he wished. The fact that he chose to turn it into '*I'll show you who's in charge*' exercise was entirely his decision.

He was under no battle stress, fresh from a five week voyage, at the top of his career with a staff beyond his wildest dreams. He had huge influential support in Australia and plenty of friends in Cairo, and for the second, or was it the third time, he failed his men. In hindsight there is no doubt that almost all of the suffering and consequent disaffection could have been avoided. Three hours in early morning, three hours in late afternoon were sufficient for the march. Camels, some with water, others with the capacity to take on kit men could no longer carry, and a consultation with the RMOs beforehand would have solved most of the problems. The Desert March was a clear warning that, like the performance on the beach on 25 April 1915, and at Krithia a little later, it was always *somebody else's orders* that were at fault. No such excuse, however, could pardon a verbal lashing given 2nd Brigade after their New Year's celebrations in 1915. A W Keown in *Forward with the 5th* recalled it bitterly: '*New Year's morning saw the four battalions drawn up on the sand ... listening with amazement to the torrent of invective poured over their heads by the irate Brigadier. It was an unmerited stricture, that rankled deeply in the minds of all, and the crowning insult of 'sots, whoremongers and blackguards' deeply wounded the decent minded men who were in the majority.*'

During the early period on the canal McCay made a detailed examination of the defences and prepared a Report dated 10 April on what he thought was wrong with them, and how they could be improved. Two days later 2nd Anzac Corps had a reply back on McCay's desk virtually rejecting all his ideas and correcting some of McCay's terminology. So in his secret memo of 13 April McCay noted, among much else, phrases lifted directly from the 2nd Anzac reply but not attributed to them, and '*It has consequently been decided to hold the outer line as an outpost position, and keep up the works that have actually been prepared*'. The same works McCay wanted demolished.

Training proceeded along the canal until mid June. No Turks appeared, and every effort was made to get the division presentable, as the Ordnance Report vividly reveals (see margin opposite: *Presentable Clothing*).

The enthusiastic War Diarist, the same person from the beginning in Egypt, started the June diary and notes about McCay inspecting 13th Field Artillery Bde at Moascar:

> *GOC was very pleased ... We are gradually getting everything fixed up for the big move to which we are all looking forward.*

On 31 May, from Ferry Post, HQ issued its 'Order of Battle' detailing for the first time all the commands from McCay at the top to QM and Hon. Lieut W Thom, Field Butchery at the end of the page.

The C-in-C had reviewed the Division on 25 May, then on 28 May the memorandum was issued: '*The 5th Australian Division will entrain at Moascar Station commencing about the 6 June 1916, and will proceed to a point of embarkation for service overseas*'.

On 2 June it was noted that McCay and his senior staff were going to Cairo on short leave. '*We move Divisional HQ tomorrow so everything is being packed up*'.

When the Division started to leave Egypt on 16 June there were fourteen ships in Alexandria harbour for the job. One of the first was the *SS Kalyan* which was to carry 47 officers, 1248 ORs, 238 horses, 115 vehicles, 12 guns and 280 tons of baggage. The records give no breakdown by battalion, only brigades. For instance the 15th Bde, including HQ, had 137 officers, 4234 ORs, 62 officers' chargers, 5 riding horses, 47 bicycles, 16 two-wheeled vehicles, 49 limbers and 16 other four-wheeled vehicles. Divided by four, these figures provide an interesting comparison with the equipment taken by British battalions (see page 37). All the heavy draught and light draught horses were allocated to artillery and the like—the division had 450 heavy and 600 light draught horses on its roll so to speak, plus 352 officers' chargers and 331 riding horses.

As the last of the convoy left Egyptian waters on 23 June the first of the same convoy was arriving at Marseilles: and this continued till 30 June.

The voyage was without incident: there were some submarine alerts and a couple of ships diverted to Malta as a result. The War Diarist wrote that there were no offences committed during the voyage and the landing in France and entraining for the front seems to have not just gone without disturbance but with such good conduct that the British Commandant in Marseilles was moved to write to McCay (see page 86).

The 5th Division Headquarters which had embarked on 17 June, (an advance party had already left on 5 June) arrived at Marseilles on 22 June and moved directly to Blaringhem,

PRESENTABLE CLOTHING

One of the appendices in the June Divisional files is titled '*Notes regarding the equipping of the 5th Australian Division from the Ordnance point of view*', undated and unsigned, it describes the state of the equipment till the day the Division embarked for France. It is a sorry tale:

> *At that time (6.3.16) no unit of the Division was in possession of mobilisation stores of any importance excepting rifles, bayonets and a quantity of web and leather equipment, but all the rifles were of the low velocity type. The vehicles of the Division were practically nil, all work being done on borrowed wagons. The equipment of the men was very poor, and the clothing was in bad condition. The Artillery was short of guns, horses and limbers ... In the weeks ending 13, 20 and 27 March very little stores were received that made any appreciable difference to the state of the Division ...*

The Report (at nearly 1700 words it is much more than notes) goes on to detail the problems involved in getting spare parts for artillery pieces, having all the low velocity rifles replaced, exchanging all the rifle ammunition (3 million rounds; all of which the men had carried across the desert for no purpose—it was all now dumped at Ismailia), finding and reconditioning harness (without which of course horses and mules were unusable) and another fairly basic item—taps for water carts. Clearly it was more a case of huge demand on what was available, rather than inefficiency, and one senses from the Report's last paragraph that after a Herculean effort something was achieved.

The state of the Division for embarkation was as follows:

> *All ranks were clothed with presentable clothing, the equipment throughout the Division was of a 1908 pattern and every unit was practically complete ... The only exception to this was in the case of the 51st and 60th Batteries of Artillery which had no guns or equipment. Of Howitzers, the Division had none although in possession of all their stores. With regard to Officers' equipment the Division was very short of binoculars, revolvers and compasses.*

6 miles (10 kms) west of Hazebrouck and was established on the 25th. Whilst the voyage had been invigorating, the countryside of France was, in every diary that described it, a sort of Garden of Eden. W H Downing of 57th Bn wrote of the journey north thus:

> *It was summer, and France was buried in green leaves. Every road was a grove, and the fields were smooth lawns where white roads wandered. On distant slopes the cornfields were vermilion with poppies, the barley purple with cornflowers; there were yellow squares where 'mustard flowers' grew. The hills were green and in the distance blue ... All this contrasted vividly with the blazing sands and the dark fertility of Egypt. It was still early morning as we passed through Lyons on a viaduct above the sunny cobbled squares and the canals ... Beneath the belfries of Dijon, Dames de la Croix Rouge gave us roses, smiling kindly. Before night we saw the Cathedral of Amiens; at morning St. Wulfran's Church in Abbeville. After midnight we detrained at Steenbecque near Hazebrouck. It was raining. We marched to a muddy little camp!*

Upon arrival Simon Fraser, 57th Bn, noted:

> *... at Marseilles, this place is beautiful ... marched to camp about a mile, complimented by Major Denehy on behaviour on boat ... lady conductors manage trams here ... passed through lovely country, crops in among hills ... French people very enthusiastic about Australians.*

To Harry Goeby of 59th Bn, it was:

> *... just a mass of beautiful green, amid which one can see red-tiled roofs of houses; and churches with high towers ... nice green fields, white roads, clean white cement-like house—this cement is stone ... all along the line we have the salutations of the villagers as we pass through.*

Lieut Walter Vaile of 59th Bn:

> *we have arrived in France at last ... no wild dream is sufficiently comprehensive or imaginative to suggest such a paradise as this land is ... the Rhône Valley, a veritable Garden of Eden ... the colouring is lovely ... the poppies, red-roofed houses and bright spots against the greens of the trees, crops and grasses. The celebrated Palace of Versailles ... is close to the railway ... the train considerately stopped at the right time to let us have a look at it. It is hard to imagine that the place is real and not some halucination.*

When they arrived at the edge of the war, Bill Barry of 29th Bn was struck by other things:

> *... the French people were years behind the times ... to see farmers cutting their crops with a scythe reminded me of fairy tales. Another thing I noticed was ... a large wooden wheel around twelve feet in diameter. A dog about the size of a cattle dog was put inside the wheel and started trotting ... it was the means the French had of getting power to grind corn or churn butter when there was no water power available. We were able to buy from the people fresh white bread, butter, eggs and coffee and many a good feed of fried eggs did I enjoy at some of these farm houses.*

AND TWO LADIES

Prior to the main shipment of the Division, the 5th Division Advance Party left on the PT *Oriana* on 7 June. The list details 19 Officers (led by Bde Major King) and 19 ORs, obviously the Officers' batmen, then there was one Officer and 72 ORs from British regiments, three Australian Chaplains—Milne, Rentoul and Crookston. Finally this group:

'Indulgence for UK 14 Officers, 2 ORs and 2 Ladies.' No other ship in the convoy carried Ladies.

PLEASING TO ME

McCay received a note from Col Tinley, Commandant of the British Base at Marseilles:

Dear General McCay,

The last details of your Division are gone and I trust all will reach you safely. It gives me genuine pleasure to be able to tell you that the conduct of the Division during its passage through this place has been exemplary. Notwithstanding the many and varied attractions and temptations of this huge seaport, I am glad to say that not a single case of misbehaviour or lack of discipline has been brought to my notice. It is a record and one the Division may be proud of. The Officers and men of the Divisional Guard commanded by Major Beardsmore performed their duties in a soldierlike, firm and tactful manner, and their smartness was very noticeable. I am personally indebted to Major King of your staff for the very valuable assistance which in many ways he afforded me, and it is a pleasure to tell you so. The good work of the Divisional AMLOs and RTOs deserve mention also.

The best of good luck to you and your fine Division.

Another letter from Lieut Col Pope of DADRT Marseilles was equally complimentary mentioning Lieut Chapman of 30th Bn, Lieut Stuchberry of 55th Bn and Captain Harris of 57th.

McCay sent copies of the letters to 1st ANZAC with the request that they be shown to Birdwood because: '*it is naturally pleasing to me to find the Division so well spoken of*'. There is no evidence that he circulated the praise to the Brigades, let alone the men.

So the war had begun for the 5th Australian Division. It was now 27 June, and 15th Bde was at Steenbecque. The day before 8th Bde were in Morbecque whilst it was the 30 June before 14th Bde arrived at their billets in Thiennes. The Pioneers were at Lynde but the Artillery and Divisional train had stopped at Abbeville for equipment, arriving early in July at Lynde. Thus the Division was all in the region some 4 miles east of Blaringhem. The front line was about 12 miles to the east, an easy day's march.

Visé Paris nº 3 ARMENTIÈRES.
Vue panoramique vers Lille. — LL.

The previous Australian presence in the region is dealt with by Ellis and Bean only in terms of units taking over one from another. But there was considerable personal contact between the men as well as between officers. People went in search of their brothers or friends and in letters, wrote, '*saw Jim, he looked well*'. That got past the censor. But it would be foolish to suppose that the men coming in did not ask those they were replacing what the situation was, what they had been through, what they had heard and seen. After all, it was around here that Australians had first been killed in France, not by artillery, but many on raids in what was loosely called 'Armentières' but which included Messines well north, down through Bois Grenier to Fleurbaix.

Given the perspicacity of the diggers in the experienced 1st, 2nd and 4th Divisions, it is extremely unlikely that they did not have considerable ground knowledge to pass on to the newcomers of the 5th. For instance, the 2nd Division had on 8 April taken over the line south of Armentières where the German positions had hardly altered since 25 October 1914, when they took Fromelles and Aubers and established their line of defence in front of Lille. The 2nd had been relieved by the 4th

HAD A ROUGH TIME

28 June. Arrived at Marseilles Harbour. Very hilly and rocky, rather pretty place. Left for the front same night. Put in three nights and days in ordinary carriage without corridor, eight men to a compartment. On guard at our latest camp not far from firing line. Camped at a place called Steenbecque. Can hear bombardment at night. 8 July. Left Steenbecque, marched to another village named Sailly, had a rough time, one stretch of 2 hours without rest. Finished up with terribly blistered feet. Within range of German guns. Common thing to see them shooting at aeroplanes. Billeted in a building which shows signs of rifle and shell fire. 10 July. Preparing to march up close to firing line. Arrived at new billet at half past twelve and went straight on guard. Big guns and rockets going all night. 16 July. Left Croix Blanche (White Cross) 2 o'clock in the morning doing work and movements in the night. 17 July. Moved up and close to firing line. Kept going preparing for advance. 19 July. Went in from row of trenches at half past two in afternoon. Shelter on the way down sap leading to trench. Platoon commander killed. Half past six made a bayonet charge, got shot in hip. Laid in shell hole for 3 hours. Shells bursting all round. When dark, started to crawl back in own trench. Progress slow taking six hours to get back. Laid for 12 hours in our trench waiting for stretcher. Got shifted at 3 o'clock next day. Had long train journey. In hospital somewhere in Calais. Probably go to England. 26 July. Left Calais for England. Took train for Leeds. Doing well. Expect to go under operation shortly. 5 August. Had bullet extracted. Doing well. Later: 19 July. Had seven of my pals killed in one charge including: Fred Bradshaw, Owen Clarke, Charlie Dicker, Tim O'Halloran, Jack Edney, Goldby and Alan Russell.

From the diary of Pte W C Bright 4742 D Coy 59th Bn.

COURTESY DONALD GRANT

THE FIRST AUSTRALIAN ACTIONS IN FRANCE

The German line protecting Lille was designed to be permanent, and by the time the Australians arrived it was well and truly that. The British line of course was not, because they had the fond hope of driving the Germans back and therefore to set up permanent lines would be a denial of that ambition. So, when the Australians came they inherited for the most part, open pits, breastworks with little rear protection and communication trenches hardly worthy of the name. One unit took over some trenches dug by the British Bantam Brigade (under 5 foot 2 inches) and found that this presented the German snipers with perfect targets until the trenches were considerably deepened.

From late April 1916 there were Australians in the Sailly area, battalions of the 4th Division mainly, with others from the 1st and 2nd, together with New Zealanders, under General Birdwood and titled 1 Anzac Corps. The first significant losses were in 20th Bn (2nd Div., 5th Bde, NSW) with over 100 casualties, including some taken prisoner on 5 May. These were the prisoners who were paraded in Lille and, so the story goes , cheered and offered chocolates and cigarettes by the locals much to the Germans' dismay. However, it was the loss by 20th Bn of 2 Stokes Mortars, a new weapon much valued by the British, that projected this German raid into the history books. The OC 20th Bn being sent back to Australia as punishment.

Raids continued, but it was the end of May when the next serious loss occurred: 11th Bn (1st Div., 3rd Bde, WA) lost 131 men. Throughout June and early July other battalions went on raids or were raided often with little achieved and unnecessary casualties. But the AIF was learning its trade. In this period, to strike a positive note, south-east of Bois Grenier on the night of 25/26 June, a volunteer raiding party from 5th Bde was formed. In its ranks was 19 year old William Jackson (No. 588, 17th Bn, NSW): his heroism in rescuing wounded earned him a VC, the first for an Australian on the Western Front.

In the first week of July there were a number of changes, principally 12th and [continued opposite]

in mid-June and the 5th took over from them beginning 10 July. For an idea of the cost of these early, largely neglected operations (see margin, *The First Australian actions in France*).

Another area totally neglected by 'official histories' is an assessment of how much the officers and men knew of the war and its general progress. Newspapers from Britain and Australia are often referred to in letters, but that news was sanitised by phrases like 'somewhere in France'. The always existent human grapevine with all its gossip and rumours must have been important. What also does not survive is any actual reference to intelligence being passed on from the outgoing unit to the incoming one.

But the fact that there had been much fighting in this area during the previous 18 months did not escape some individuals in the ranks who saw the destruction and the graves along the roads that they had to march in early July 1916. W H Downing, 57th Bn, noted:

> The graves of Englishmen lay everywhere; the dates on the little crosses had almost faded since 'December, 1914', 'February', 'October 1915'. Most of the graves were nameless.

The three brigades of the Division began to move closer to the front line on 9 July, mainly to the Estaires-Sailly area, by route marches. The new boots and the cobblestone roads were not a good combination, and many men dropped out: in 57th Bn some 150. Arthur Ebdon of 57th Bn had a strong memory of this: '*The boots were English and the high sides got your ankles*'. Ebdon remembered one stop when the sergeant called for '*All men with 3 or more blisters to fall out ... I had 13*'. Lieut Col Stewart, CO of 57th, insisted that his men march on, but the RMO refused to clear the men for further duty. The upshot of this, as Ebdon

remembered, was the later issue of Australian-made boots largely due to the influence of Brig. General Elliott.

But it was more than sore feet that made progress slow, and the Divisional War Diary recorded that considerable congestion and delays occur: '... *when a formation as large as a Brigade marches into a town with narrow streets and many crossings*'. The 5th taking over the 4th Division HQ at Sailly also was not easy, and the War Diarist observed also that, '*5 enemy balloons were up most of the day—possibly they saw the movements*'. Late in the day machine guns and automatic rifles were issued. On 10 July the 8th Bde relieved the 4th Bde in the left section, on 11 July the 14th relieved the 12th in the centre section, and on 12 July the 15th relieved 13th Bde in the right section. These dates are very important, revealing in an instant how little time the units had to prepare for the attack.

Throughout the re-writes of the story of Fromelles over the years, there has crept into the narratives the phrase 'a nursery sector' implying in effect that this area was some sort of quiet training ground where inexperienced troops might learn their trade. Whoever introduced this expression, it was not Ellis, Bean nor Edmonds, was well off the mark. The placement of the 6th Bavarian Reserve Division there and the extent of the fortifications surely indicated how important it was to the Germans: and it certainly was no 'nursery sector' for them. And nor had it been, as has been detailed, for the British in earlier days.

While the men were being moved forward there had been considerable activity at the various headquarters. On 5 July it was 'noted' that the Germans opposite were sending men south to reinforce their army in the battle of the Somme. This was, after the war, found to be a false assumption. The traffic through Lille Station was from elsewhere and none of the units in defence of Lille went to the Somme. Pretty obvious why—without Lille being absolutely secure the great rail junction facility could not be used to move men and equipment towards the south. However the British reaction to this was to order raids and small offensive attacks along the line north of the Somme which would persuade the Germans that any weakening of other parts of their line might be dangerous. As already noted the Germans in the early days of the battle of the Somme could not believe the stupidity of the action and were quite sure it was a ruse for something else, probably a big offensive around Ypres, as well as some relief for Verdun.

Unphased by the horrendous losses on the first days, Haig on 2 July wrote: '... *total casualties are estimated at over*

THE FIRST AUSTRALIAN ACTIONS IN FRANCE (contd)

13th Bdes relieving 1st and 3rd Bdes. At this time some battalions were badly damaged by bombardments, not least the 51st Bn (13th Bde, WA) with 151 casualties: an event ignored by Bean. In another 13th Bde battalion, the 47th Bn Pte William Elsdale (No. 4484, Qld) was killed in action at Fleurbaix on 7 July. A full-blood Aboriginal from Queensland he may have well been the first of his people to be killed on the Western Front.

THE AUSTRALIAN BOOT

A soldier's boots are arguably his most essential piece of equipment, and when the main way of moving men was by route march, no wonder there developed the great boot debate: the English boot versus the Australian boot. Not surprisingly to the Australians, their boots became very popular. By the end of the war they were standard issue to the Gurkhas in India and Sudanese police in Egypt: the boot being lighter than its British counterpart, it was also most successful in Palestine. However, early on, Australian boots were said to wear out after two marches, and after soaking would fall apart; but the use of heavier leathers and, with the watertight tongue made higher, the Australian boot became much sought after. Production was around 100,000 a month, made by appointed manufacturers, and it would seem there were always ample supplies.

Grim as the thought may be, the photograph on page 189 showing the heap of Australian and English dead, clearly reveals some bare feet, perhaps indicating that some boots have been salvaged by the Bavarians. The German Army was, by all accounts, poorly shod.

British Infantry Regulation Boot of early 1916 showing high sides about which the Australians complained.

40,000 to date. This cannot be considered severe in view of the numbers engaged and the length of front attacked. By nightfall, the situation is much more favourable than when we started today.' On 5 July Haig issued an order:

> The First and Second Armies should each select a front on which to attempt to make a break in the enemy lines, and to widen it subsequently.

It might be said that these few lines in the hands of various generals gave rise to the battle of Fromelles. What Haig actually thought only his 'private private papers' could reveal: his published 'private papers' omit any reference to the period 4 July to 21 July, as they do any reference to the battle of Fromelles, Haking at Fromelles and all. It is important to note that the British Historian did no more than rephrase Bean when he could have quite easily (in 1938) added some new substance to this matter. And only Bean introduces General Godley into the preplanning period of Fromelles. Godley GOC II Anzac Corps according to Bean issued an order that seems on the face of it quite stupid. He knew better than anybody on 7 July that the 5th Division had no experience and the other half of his corps, the New Zealand Division (see page 76) was already severely overstretched. His order, as Bean decided to publish it, was:

> It is imperative that raids and all possible offensive should be undertaken at once by both divisions of the corps in order to make a certainty of holding on our front such German troops as may now be there.
>
> Raids must therefore take place immediately and must be on a larger scale than has hitherto been attempted—about 200 men or a company ... The Corps Commander wishes to impress on divisional commanders and begs them to impress it on their subordinates, that we must fight now, at once, in order to give help to our comrades fighting desperately in the south, and that however little we may be ready, or however difficult it may be, we should never forgive ourselves if we did not make the necessary effort, and, if necessary, sacrifice, to help them.

It must have been the briefing concerning this order that Bean questioned McCay about in his letter of 2 May 1926 and drew a bad-tempered reply (see margin: *The Cancelled Raids*). McCay totally unable to admit he had been influenced by anybody was not being truthful: Tivey, Pope and probably Elliott had all gone on record that as the men had never been in a trench at that point, they would not have the faintest idea what to do.

Bean who clearly wanted to get the sequence of orders and commands correct did justice to this period, the only historian who did, and it is interesting to see how he converted McCay's disclaimer:

THE CANCELLED RAIDS

Following on from stories he had heard, Bean tackled McCay again on 2 May 1926 about:

A raid was to have been undertaken by the 5th Div. as soon as it entered the line. Do you recollect whether this was abandoned because of the brigadiers' objections that the troops were too new, or because the orders for the main attack were received (I think the raid was to have come off before the orders were received), or for some other reason?

Bean perhaps to remind McCay that he had not yet answered these questions, wrote again on 10 July:

The story of the battle is finished, except for such corrections as these. It has been a most difficult job.

McCay now replied after 'asking McGlinn and others to help or verify my recollections'.

No intended raid was abandoned through any objection by brigadiers or others. I knew of the intention to make an attack some days before any orders were issued to me. This I knew of course confidentially, and therefore quietly postponed any minor plans, such as a raid etc. That is why any raiding intention 'ceased to be'.

SAUCE AND PICKLES

Not everything was of earth shattering importance: on 11 July—under Condiments (2nd ANZAC 16590).591.

It has been notified from War Office that occasions may arise on which it may be necessary to ship Worcester or other sauce in lieu of pickles. The Medical Authorities have fixed the equivalent scale of issues at 1 oz of sauce—3 oz of pickles, and whenever sauce is received from the Base this scale of issue will be adopted.

TELLING THE TIME

On 15 July Routine Orders made the following pronouncement:

TIME ... In future the AM and PM method will be adopted by all formations to denote time.

> Such instructions obviously imposed upon the divisional commanders the duty of straining every nerve to undertake immediate operations, even if these were likely to involve loss. Although the 5th Division had not at that time reached the front area, its commander, General McCay, consented to launch one or more raids with his inexperienced troops. Subsequent events caused this intention to be abandoned, and the whole raid-programme of the corps during the next ten days had to be provided by the New Zealand Division.

From here on the debate over what to do concerns at the very least Generals Haig, Plumer, Monro, Major Generals Butler, Harrington, Barrow, Franks and Gwynn, not forgetting Generals Haking, Godley, Birdwood, White, Mackenzie and McCay, and probably another half a dozen in the wings. The only one who had good knowledge of the Aubers Ridge areas was Haking.

General Monro, as a result of a letter from Plumer, summoned his Corps Commanders on 8 July and instructed Haking to suggest a campaign. If we are to believe McCay's account of these early days, this information was already with him. What detail Haking, or anybody else, confided to him, we will never know. Bean, again the only authority on these early stages, makes a point of emphasising that Haking put forward a scheme on 9 July:

> which was an ambitious one, aiming at the capture, partly by means of a feint—of the Fromelles-Aubers Ridge, a mile behind the enemy's front ... It was, however, rejected, Monro being of the opinion that the capture ... would be of little assistance ... Haking was accordingly informed on 12 July that he would not be ordered to carry out his project.

Nothing could be clearer than that. It was on the next day that 'information' came to GHQ that nine battalions of Germans had left the Lille area for the Somme and that was now the stimulus to do something quickly. If the allies knew of German movements south, it is fair to presume that the Gemans may have been aware of allied movements south also, and would thus know that the experienced Australian Divisions that had been in the general Armentières region for up to three months were being replaced by the 5th which had no battle experience. And where had the experienced Australians gone? To the Somme, just like the Germans! We can assume that the Germans were talented enough to draw certain conclusions from this change over, especially as it can now be admitted their intelligence gathering was exceptionally good. How good, was the subject of Memo 3, dated 7 July, by 5th Division Major King (see page 6). Perhaps nobody read it. This fact is never a consideration for Ellis, Bean nor Edmonds: nor is the tactical skill and equipment superiority

HAD TO FALL OUT

Pte Leonard Charles Western 3562 of 60th, and later 59th Bn, enlisted 3 August 1915, returning to Australia 12 March, 1918.

His sparse diary for the first three weeks in France show the speed of preparation and his long days of 19 and 20 July.

2 July. Arrived Steenbecque 2.30 pm after 2 days train journey. 8 July. Marched from Steenbecque to Estaires. Marched for 1½ hours without a spell. Had to fall out .
12 July. Marched to Sailly at night. 14 July. Fatigue in supports. 18 July. Took over from 57th Bn at about 4.30 pm. 19 July. Hop-over. Bombardment commenced at about 1.30 pm, over at 6.30. On same night took post till morning of 20th. 20 July. Relieved at about 11.30 am. On guard at 8 pm till 12 noon next day. Rest till Sunday (23rd). 23 July. Fatigue in supports at about 12.30 pm till 4.30-5.00 pm. 24 July. Fatigue. 25 July. Fatigue. Fatigues till 30th.

COURTESY LEN WESTERN

WE COULD NOT RESPOND

On one of our first moves towards Caudescure we came for the first time upon several hundreds of Australians and New Zealanders. Dare-devil experience was written in their faces. I thought many of them were of the bush-ranger type, with an easy play of muscle, and a fine horsey air. They had the names of their towns written on their slouch hats, such as 'Oomalong'. Their uniforms were a dusty grey-white. they walked along anyhow, hands in great coat pockets, shoulder straps undone, saluting nobody. They were sunburnt, and we heard they had come from Egypt, and some of them had fought at Gallipoli. A crowd of them raised a great cheer for the Black Watch. We could not respond, as we were marching at attention, but the cheer gave us immense delight. It was the first we had had since we left Dundee so long before.

—W L Andrews of Black Watch
Haunting Years (nd)

THE 5TH AUSTRALIAN DIVISION JULY 1916

5th Division HQ
5th Divisional Artillery HQ
5th Pioneer Battalion
5th Divisional Sanitary Section
5th (10th) HQ Coy Signal Corps
5th Divisional Ammunition Column
5th Divisional Train
5th Divisional Trench Mortar Battery
5th Machine Gun Coy
5th Divisional Engineers
5th Divisional Traffic Control

8th Brigade HQ
29th Infantry Battalion
30th Infantry Battalion
31st Infantry Battalion
32nd Infantry Battalion
8th Machine Gun Coy
8th Field Coy Engineers
8th Field Ambulance
18th Coy Signal Corps
8th Light Trench Mortar

14th Brigade HQ
53rd Infantry Battalion
54th Infantry Battalion
55th Infantry Battalion
56th Infantry Battalion
14th Machine Gun Coy
14th Field Coy Engineers
14th Field Ambulance
28th Coy Signal Corps
14th Light Trench Mortar

15th Brigade HQ
57th Infantry Battalion
58th Infantry Battalion
59th Infantry Battalion
60th Infantry Battalion
15th Machine Gun Coy
15th Field Coy Engineers
15th Field Ambulance
29th Coy Signal Corps
15th Light Trench Mortar

13th Brigade AFA HQ
49th Battery AFA
50th Battery AFA
51st Battery AFA
113th Howitzer Battery AFA

14th Brigade AFA HQ
53rd Battery AFA
54th Battery AFA
55th Battery AFA
114th Howitzer Battery AFA

of the Germans. Supplementing this point it was suggested by Bean that '*nothing would be more likely to prevent further transfers (by the Germans) than a threat, made by the First and Second Armies, of a British advance on Lille*'. Again assuming that German intelligence was reasonable, they would know the calibre of the allied divisions facing their long experienced, well-fortified line, and not feel all that threatened.

With all the 'wisdom of hindsight', the British historian wrote an excellent paragraph years after the battle which is used here purely as an observation, because it includes nothing that was not abundantly obvious at the time of the battle:

> Thus the troops acting under the XI Corps were committed to a short advance across the flat water-logged Flanders country under the eyes of the enemy on Aubers Ridge whence, during daylight hours, he could watch all the preparations for attack. As little fighting had taken place in this region for the past fourteen months, the Germans had had ample opportunity to strengthen their breastwork defences, which now included many machine-gun emplacements constructed of concrete, well-sited and concealed. Whilst all depended upon the destructive effect of the British bombardment and the rapid advance of the infantry, success would but bring the British front line under still closer enemy observation. Consolidation, which meant the construction of sand-bag breastworks, since digging soon reached water-level, was bound to be difficult; and as no further offensive action was contemplated—or indeed, feasible with the forces available—the retention of the ground won would present a problem of its own.

That said, we turn to the plight of the 5th Australian Division being sucked into an event that was unpardonable in its stupidity, criminally negligent in its planning and totally ineffective militarily. Already the speed of the events was getting on top of them. For instance the first casualties in the Division on 11 July were not noted: five men of 57th Bn were killed and eight wounded by shellfire. But movements were meticulously recorded. The 8th Bde came forward, via Estaires, on 8 July, Erquinghem then to Bois Grenier on 13 July; their HQ was established at Croix Blanche the next day. The 14th came via Thiennes, Estaires, Sailly and to Fleurbaix: 14th HQ was at Le Croix Discornex. The 15th came via Estaires, Sailly to Rouge du Bout where HQ were established on 14 July.

Now as the men were put into billets in villages and on farms, life became a little less attractive. Often the quarters were stables, farm outbuildings, pig pens and cow-sheds. The toilet arrangements were those of the peasantry and fresh water was often difficult to find. The comparison to the hygiene standards of their own camps at Tel-el-Kebir and Ferry Post many noted in their letters home. But something else they noted was the welcome by the populace which included sharing a meal around the kitchen table, helping out with farm chores and enjoying the French summer. It had been raining heavily early in the month so the ground was soft and muddy and remained so up to and after the battle. But the days before were mostly good, often very good.

On 13 July Monro was visited by Butler, Haig's messenger, with the suggestion that by taking two divisions and concentrating them along a small front, a strong artillery bombardment (starting on 14 July) could be followed by an infantry assault three days later, and this would have the desired effect of stopping the Germans sending any more men south.

If all these dates are correct, it must mean that Haking, at the behest of Monro, prepared this attack strategy in what was left of 13 July (he got his orders at 6.30 pm) and before he met with McCay at 11 pm. He must have had some meeting with Mackenzie also, but the 5th Division file never mentions him. At 9.45 am on 14 July Haking met with McCay at Hinges, HQ of XI Corps, and gave him the details of the attack, British XI Corps Order No 57. Amazingly Mackenzie, so he said, received his details the next day. It is quite clear what the objectives were and they did not include advancing on Fromelles or Aubers Ridge, but it was also very clear that there was no ultimate objective, and the position was totally unsustainable. The order in part read:

> With the object of preventing the enemy withdrawing troops from our front, offensive operations are to be carried out by troops of XI Corps and 2nd A&NZC under the command of GOC XI Corps.
>
> The 61st Division and the 5th Division will capture and hold the German front line and support trenches on the front opposite our trenches from the Fauquissart-Trivelet Road (M.24.b.8.8.) to south of Cordonnerie Farm (N.10.c.8.7.)
>
> The Division will attack with three Brigades in line, each Brigade and two assaulting Battalions and two Battalions in reserve: the two reserve Battalions in each Brigade are not to be employed for the attack without the permission of the Corps Commander.

McCay, as already noted, said he was aware of the planning prior to the issue of the order from talking with the various people involved, but he never claimed to have had any input into the planning. For a person with such a long record of advocating causes it seems unlikely he just accepted the order without attempting some input. But this was, in later years, exactly what he said happened, so that he would not be associated with an action which was a token sacrifice, in the style that Godley had described.

THE 5TH AUSTRALIAN DIVISION JULY 1916 (contd)

15th Brigade AFA HQ
57th Battery AFA
58th Battery AFA
59th Battery AFA
(No Howitzer Battery)

25th Brigade AFA HQ
52nd Battery AFA
56th Battery AFA
60th Battery AFA
115th Howitzer Battery

Aust. Army Medical Corps
Aust. Army Veterinary Corps
Aust. Army Pay Corps
Aust. Provost Corps
Aust. Army Ordnance Corps
Aust. Army Salvage Corps

Chaplains' Department

SPIES ... ALL OVER THE PLACE

We moved one night to Fleurbaix and were billeted there. Then more conferences and some vague details of what was to come. We split into our little parties and made our way up the various avenues to reconnoitre the lay of the ground, Cellar Farm, York, Mine and VC Avenues—up these we went, looking about us, getting lost, then on the right track again till we returned home with the conviction that we knew all we had to know. 'Secrecy must be strictly observed' we were told and we told the men this, but in every estaminet in the neighbourhood there was nothing else to be heard but the 'stunt'. Even the M'selles asked us when it was coming off. Dumps sprang up here and there, and every time one went up the CTs they passed men carrying ammunition and plum puddings. The Bosche couldn't have helped seeing all these preparations, for his planes were over often enough, and spies seemed all over the place. Even the farm where we were billeted in had a girl who we understood was under observation as a suspected spy.

—Captain W H Zander (born 1892) 30th Bn

ORDER OF BATTLE
5TH AUSTRALIAN DIVISION

GOC	Major General the Right Honourable J W McCay
ADC1	Lieut W L Hamilton
ADC2	Lieut H F Moore
GSO1	Lieut Col C M Wagstaff
GSO2	Major D M King
GSO3	Capt. A J Boase
AA & QMG	Lieut Col J P McGlinn
DAA & QMG	Major R P Varwell
DAQMG	Capt. G D Smith

KNOWN AS VC CORNER
2/Lieut L W Elliott of C Coy 57th Bn arrived in Egypt 19 December 1915 and was promoted Lieut at the end of May 1916. His diary for the year reveals an extremely observant and conscientious officer. His entry for 12 July:

Went the rounds this morning. Examined dumps ... Bombardment pretty heavy ... Can hear heavy guns going all night at La Bassée and Neuve Chapelle. The ground we occupy is just near Two Tree Farm where Pte O'Leary won his VC early in the war. The spot is known as VC Corner. Heavy MG fire tonight, practically no gunfire. MGs trying to feel out each other's positions.

This reference to VC Corner underscores the fact that the area had some heroic connections long before the establishment of the VC Corner Cemetery in 1919. Elliott was incorrect, however, about O'Leary whose exploits became a legend: he was in action near Cuinchy, about 8 miles south, when he captured an enemy position virtually single handed, thus earning his VC (see page 361).
COURTESY G H ELLIOTT

JULY 1916

M	T	W	T	F	S	S
					1	2
3	4	5	6	7	8	9
10	11	12	13	14	15	16
17	18	19	20	21	22	23
24	25	26	27	28	29	30
31						

As a result of the meeting at La Motte, HQ of 2nd Anzac Corps on 13 July, a '*partial withdrawal of Brigades from the line with view to prospective attack*' was ordered for 14 July and then McCay got to work on some of his own ideas. In his secret memo to 'The Commanders of Infantry Brigades', dated 15 July, McCay set out his ideas for the attack, most of which dealt with how to organise the assault. But paragraph 6 revealed that already McCay was bending the rules and not following standing orders. This is a most damning document in regards to McCay:

> It is hoped that the attack and the holding of enemy trench may succeed with two Battalions of each Brigade but perhaps Brigadiers will use their third Battalion to hold the enemy trenches if captured, but not to take them, if first two battalions fail. If this suggestion is altered Brigades will be notified. They will not let anyone except Brigade Majors know this. It would be bad for morale if even Battalion Commanders of 3rd and 4th Battalions knew they were not being definitely expected to attack.

Clearly McCay did not agree with nor understand the original order which was utterly specific about two battalions attacking. As for misleading the Battalion Commanders, Mackenzie had, as we have seen, designated the battalions to assault right from the beginning, but McCay seemed to want all twelve battalions kept on their toes all of the time, which meant of course, unlike the 61st Division, any battalions assigned to reserve and backup work in the 5th Division could not be appointed without contravening McCay's order. In the most rudimentary tasks this was a planning disaster, which can in no way be blamed on Haking.

McCay's next 'Instruction for Infantry Brigadiers' goes on for two-and-half pages of theory on how the second wave will take on the duties of the first wave if it falls etc, etc. It does not consider for a second that everything may not go to plan.

Meanwhile we learn from Bean that on 14 July a member of Haig's staff, Major Howard, visited '*the Chiefs of Staff of the First and Second Armies*', and discussed the arrangements agreed with Butler the day before. He then visited the front line with Brig. General Elliott and was shown the huge expanse of No-Man's Land over which Elliott had to send his men. Bean writes this of his reaction:

> Considering the artillery and ammunition available, [Howard] formed the opinion that the attack could hardly fail to end in disaster.

After the war Elliott remembered Howard's verdict as being that the result would be '*a bloody holocaust*'. When Bean recounted Elliott's memory, he came under heavy attack from Edmonds for daring to mention that a Staff Officer expressed an opinion outside of HQ! (See Chapter 12).

On 15 July in Secret Order No 30, the 5th Division was advised '*Arrangements are being made for an attack on the enemy's front line system from Trivelet to Fme Delangre*'. From this the 5th Division was allotted from: '*Bond Street (exclusive) N.8.d.½.8 to Cellar Farm Avenue (inclusive) N.10.b.9½.1.*', it then detailed the operational areas of each brigade (see margin page 39). This placed the whole Division on a '*war footing*', and from here on everything was deadly serious. How serious was proven that evening.

On the night of 15 July for two hours from 9.30 pm the Germans put down a heavy bombardment on the Cellar Farm and Mine Avenue area where A and B Coys of 58th Bn were about to be relieved by the 6th Oxfords from the incoming 60th British Bde, who were going to hold the sector on the left of 5th Division. The barrage wrecked the dugouts, killed many and was cover for a German raiding party (2 officers, 95 ORs of 21st Bavarian RIR).They lost 10 killed and 22 wounded and left the 58th with one officer and 41 ORs dead, and one officer and 102 ORs wounded. Four men were missing, three being a 58th Lewis gun team complete with weapon: all were taken prisoner —the main purpose of the raid. The Germans thus learned that the 5th Australian Division was in front of them and had been there three days. The German report on the raid said they got no indication of a forthcoming attack either from their excursion into the allied trenches or from their prisoners.

However, it was the methodical registration and wire-cutting action of the artillery next day which alerted the Germans that something was planned. Doubtless their listening devices would have confirmed some of these suspicions. Destructive as this raid was on two companies of the 58th, the other two companies, were unaware of it. The raid would soon be overshadowed by the Battle, but for some the raid would always remain the main event: see margin story '*Together ever since*'.

The first days of the 5th Division in the line saw from 8th Bde, far left; 29th and 30th Bns in line with 31st and 32nd in reserve. In centre, 14th Bde with 55th and 56th Bns in line, and 53rd and 54th in reserve. On the right for 15th Bde 57th and 58th Bns in line with 59th and 60th in reserve.

The extraordinary haste with which the assault was being put together is well-illustrated throughout the War Diary of the 5th Division. But perhaps the following exchange tells best how shoddy the planning was in 5th Division HQ. Over Wagstaff's signature a SECRET briefing note went out to all three brigades

Ernest King, 58th Bn, 1994

TOGETHER EVER SINCE

When Ernest King, 3571, 58th Bn, was visited in 1994 he produced a photograph of himself in uniform, a young soldier all of 19, going to the war. It was in a silver frame with glass. So that it might be copied he was asked if it could be removed for a minute or two, 'Yes,' Ernest said. Beneath his photograph was another and Ernest was a little surprised, he had not seen it for some years and had quite forgotten about it. It was of another teenage digger of 1915, his school friend Alfred J Wootton, 3668, 58th Bn, somewhat silverfished round the edges. They had enlisted together, gone away together, trained together in Egypt and at Fromelles almost died together. Alfred was killed during the German raid on the 58th on 15 July 1916, and was buried at Rue Petillon Military Cemetery with 31 others, casualties of the raid, and Ernest was wounded. But as photographs, the two had been together ever since. Ernest King died on 19 November 1996, three months short of his 100th birthday.

Alfred Wootton, 58th Bn, 1915

on 16 July, probably mid-afternoon, and addresses itself to an assault at 7 am on the morning of 17 July. First: '*Para 4 VERY SECRET. To act on, but not necessarily, tell to anyone but Senior Officers till tomorrow morning—zero time is 4 am, unless weather compels postponement on account of Artillery.*' This is preceded by Para 3 which says: '*Give the two assaulting Battalions a good meal and a good rest tonight (16th). Also a good meal before 10am tomorrow (17th).*' Then there is this: '*Para 5. First two waves to be deployed in No-Man's Land before 7.0 after zero time.*'

Quite how anybody could judge the next day's weather at 4 am is one thing, how the men could be rested, fed and deployed on the given schedule is something else. However, as there was no assault on the 17 July, one assumes it all fell into place at the expense of the men, as always. What did not fall into place was the finding by McCay that Col Pope had not submitted a Report on the condition of the barbed wire between the 14th Bde and the Germans. The exchange between the two reveals a degree of incompetence all round and perhaps helped Pope lose his job. The 15th Bde did at least try, and Elliott advised McCay it '*was unable to inspect the wire due to heavy shelling from our own guns and the Germans having watch posts well forward.*'

As the time ticked away, McCay, via both Wagstaff and King, started issuing directives.

The Secret Order No. 31 of 16 July (12.30 pm) is quite explicit in regard to the assaulting battalions:

> The Division will attack with three Brigades in line, each Brigade with two assaulting Battalions and two battalions in reserve; the two reserve Battalions in each Brigade will be at the disposal of the Divisional commander. These will be assembled within Brigade sectors as follows: One battalion per brigade on the line of rue du Quesne; one battalion per brigade on the line of du Quesne. The two reserve Battalions in each Brigade will not be used for assaulting the position without orders from GOC Division.

All of this duplicated Haking's order except the last two words —changed from GOC Corps (ie Haking) to GOC Division (ie McCay).

Now it might be offered in McCay's defence that as far as his Brigadiers were concerned, they were answerable to him and not Haking, hence the change. And that may be so, but the implications of the change are that he has ultimate control. In fact as will be seen, this is how he played it. But, of course, when McCay submitted his Report on the Battle to Haking, the phrase 'Corps Commander' returned.

A GIFT FROM THE BOYS

While billetted in the Rue de Quesnes, Fleurbaix, prior to the Battle of Fromelles the officers of C Coy, 30th Bn, which I at that time commanded, had been living mostly on tinned 'stuff', and decided that, as some of us would in all probability 'go west' in the coming fight, to have a real meal on the night before the battle. Arranging with Marie at our billet to provide for us 1 lb of steak and 1 lb of onions per man, we accepted her assurance that she knew how to serve grilled steak and fried onions.

After waiting till late in the evening we had given up hope of getting our steak and onions, and were on the point of obtaining something tinned, when Marie announced that the cooking was completed, and we sat down in anticipation of a really good square meal. Alas, we did not know then, as we came to learn later, that the cooking ability of the French peasantry appeared to be limited to eggs and chips, omelettes, &c. Our 6 lbs of steak was served in one piece and to this day I have never been able to decide how it was cooked. It was tough and appeared to be partly boiled and partly baked. The onions, partly boiled, were served whole. Our disappointment can be imagined.

The same party never again sat down to a meal together, for in the next day's fight all five of my officers became casualties—Lieuts A Mitchell and J Parker, killed; and Capt. B A Wark and Lieuts I G Fullarton and E Haviland, wounded.

On the morning after the battle, the 30th Bn was withdrawn into reserve at Croix Blanche and, after the calling of the roll, the issuing of rum and the attending as far as possible to the comfort of my men, I sat down on the roadside to have my breakfast. There were plenty of rations, sufficient bread and bully beef having been received for a full company, while only about 30 all told remained.

Two of my men (I have forgotten their names) asked permission to visit the billets we had left the previous day and on their return handed me two small bottles of champagne—a gift from [continued opposite]

Seemingly out of the blue, there arrived on Elliott's table, timed 2.35 pm on 17 July, a message written and signed by Wagstaff (the original is in the Divisional file, there is no copy in the Bde file), the complete text follows:

> Reference Gra 22 Divisional Commander wishes me to say that if the 58th want to get even with the enemy that battalion might be left in the line and we will give them a chance.

The specifying of Wagstaff as the messenger and McCay as the originator of the message is quite unique. Apart from McCay's orders, as the GOC, personalities do not usually intrude. So why for this? There is no record either in the Divisional, Brigade or Battalion files of any direct reaction to this suggestion. The War Diary entry for 18 July, signed by Bde Major Wieck, recorded a specific decision:

> Owing to the losses sustained by the 58th Bn it was considered advisable to withdraw them from the assault. It was then decided that as the 57th Bn had been in the trenches for so long it would be as well to replace them in the assault so that the original plan was modified and the 59th and 60th Bns will assault ...

From battalion sources we know that the 59th took over the line from 10.22 pm and 60th moved in from Rouge de Bout and the first reply to McCay's idea was a message at 11.55 pm on 18 July (received 19 minutes later at DHQ – ie, early morning on the day of the battle):

> 58th Bn withdrawn to billets in Sailly.

The fact that Elliott did not place on record his reaction to McCay's idea is one point of interest, and the quite inappropriate use of this depleted battalion in the second stage of the battle is another. But the truly critical question which will be fully dealt with in its proper place, ie after the battle, is why McCay came to Elliott on the afternoon of 20 July and was seen to be anxious about that use of the 58th.

With the absence of the Intelligence Summaries we can form no real idea of what McCay and others were using to guide their deliberations. The one 'intelligence' matter that survives in the files refers to the aerial photographs which were used first to plan the attack, and later for the post mortem. Hence Secret Order No 38 of 18 July is of interest:

> ... For the operations of 19th July 1916, No. 10 Squadron RFC is to provide machines for reconnaissance and liaison work. No. 16 Squadron RFC is to co-operate with 5th Divisional Artillery.

The photographs taken by RFC, of the Australian lines, are assembled on pages 106–107, which shows the varying width

A GIFT FROM THE BOYS (contd)

the boys. I therefore made my breakfast on bully beef, dry bread and champagne—truly a strange mixture, but I should like any of those who were present on that morning 20 years ago, to know that I then appreciated and have never forgotten the kindly spirit of comradeship which prompted this gift.

—Lieut Col M Purser
Reveille, 1 July 1936

WHAT A PITY

Another time, I had to go to the 6th Brigade near Fleurbaix. On returning, I noticed a field of buttercups and daisies. It was a beautiful sight in the war area, and I went over to have a look. It was so peaceful. I lay down amongst the flowers. Suddenly, I heard a lark singing in the sky and my thoughts went back to my dear old home in Queensland. I remembered my father telling me about the fields of flowers in Yorkshire and a lark singing in the sky. As I stood up, a bullet whirred past me. I dropped back to the ground and crawled for cover. 'What a pity,' I thought, 'that this beautiful spot and this lovely, fair land of France, should be so ravaged by war.' Our wonderful continent Australia, surrounded by blue seas, had never heard the sound of guns, and I pray our beautiful island in the sun will always be spared the horror of war.

—Harold Hinckfuss
Memories of a Signaller (1983).

Cpl Harold C Hinckfuss MM & Bar, 640, 2nd Div Signal Co (1893–1983).
COURTESY C HINCKFUSS

Lieut R H Knyvett, 59th Bn c1917

THREE LINES OF GERMAN TRENCHES

Our Company Commanders gathered us in small groups and carefully explained the plan of attack. We were to take the three lines of German trenches that were clearly discernible on the aeroplane photograph which was shown us: the first wave was to take the first trench, the second jumping over their heads, and attacking the second German line, the third going on to the third German line. When all the Germans had been killed in the first trench, those left of the first wave were to follow to the third line. Unfortunately this photograph misled us, as one of the supposed trenches proved to be a ditch, and a great number of men were lost by going too far into enemy territory, seeking the supposed third line.

I have seen an actual photograph taken by an aeroplane during this battle, that shows a fight going on five miles behind the German lines. Many of the boys had sworn not to be taken prisoners, and though they knew they were cut off, they fought on until every last one of them was killed.

—R H Knyvett, 59th Bn
Over there with the Australians (1918)

of No-Man's Land dramatically. It is clear from various reports that HQ examined earlier photographs to locate the second and third lines behind the main German line, because these were where the attackers would dig in. Sgt R H Knyvett with 15th Bde Intelligence, seems to be the only one who openly commented on this aspect of Intelligence, see margin '*Three lines of German Trenches*'. One thing he got wrong was that the Australians were five miles behind the lines, which would have placed them beyond Aubers Ridge, and there is no evidence for that.

Issued at 4 pm on 18 July, thus some 26 hours before the battle began, was Secret Order No. 39 giving details of dates. McCay here describes in detail how the '*3rd battalion will be employed*'. Up to half of the battalion will form carrying parties and move into the line immediately the fourth wave of the assaulting infantry have left. The rest will be at the 300 yard line. The '4th battalion will form a Divisional Reserve' and move into the positions vacated by the 3rd. There are also orders for active patrolling of No-Man's Land on this night, cutting ways through our own wire, putting ladders in place and '*All commanders will ensure that all ranks have a good breakfast and a good midday meal on 19th inst. Assaulting troops will be rested as much as possible during the night and during the 19th.*'

That and half a dozen other instructions formed the last order before the battle.

That general outline established, it is now sensible to examine, so to speak, the fine print. Examination of the full 5th Divisional files, there are two—Operational and Administrative, reveals that on 31 July/1 August Intelligence Summary No. 22 was issued. These two or three page reports cover the 24 hours between 6 am one day and 6 am the next, and report on enemy activities in great detail. The noise of trains, arrival of timber, dogs barking, different types of uniform seen, the number of balloons, aircraft, artillery activity and anything else that may give a clue to a forthcoming attack, or the enemy reclaiming or extending some fortification, a change over of regiments, arrival of supplies. As No. 22 is the first of the surviving Intelligence Summaries, a simple calculation would confirm that No. 1 would have been 10/11 July, the day the first of the Brigades moved into the line. The fact is, the first 21 Intelligence Summaries are missing, which alerts one to what else is missing.

Around 30 June, Capt. Boase of HQ staff had issued 'Notes for Battalion Observers'. The twenty points he gave very closely formed the headings in the Intelligence Summaries that survive. The absence of all information about the enemy prior to the 19/20 July, and indeed for the rest of July is suspicious. There are attached to the 5th Divisional file for the Battle 279 pages of Appendices, each page is numbered and there are no gaps, however all the Appendices are basically orders and outward going information. Apart from McCay passing on the congratulations of the British Commandant at Marseilles to 2nd Anzac, there is almost nothing from outside sources ie Haking or 61st Division. A substantial quantity of 'Messages and Signals' survive, mostly from 15 July onwards, and in general terms they form three groups: the exchange between McCay and Pope; some battalion movements of the 15th Bde and several notes between the 61st and 5th Divisions of almost no consequence. It is this last area that is most surprising and it persists throughout the entire period. In short, the July records look very tidy, almost too tidy considering the huge amount of work to introduce into some four square miles over 17,200 men in three days. Compared with the care taken to type up about 150 incoming and 98 outgoing messages during the battle, the pre-battle files are very empty.

There now follows brief biographical notes of the Australian Higher Authorities to give an idea of their experience and background.

IN THE EVENT OF HEAVY CASUALTIES

In McCay's Routine Orders of 13 July, under the heading of 'Burials' he draws the attention of Chaplains to instructions '*issued by the Adjutant-General 1916—Location and Registration of graves*', and that '*a supply of Army Forms W3314 has been issued to Divisional Artillery, Infantry Brigades and Pioneer Battalion for use of Chaplains as required*'.

Then under graves: Identification of—

In order to facilitate the identification of graves, the following will be the procedure in the event of heavy casualties:

(i) Bodies will be collected by the burying party, the identification discs will be removed after the particulars have been noted on a label supplied for the purpose. This label will be securely attached to the body.

(ii) Chaplains or others conducting the funeral services will make careful note of the names of those whom they bury in common graves.

(iii) The position of each grave will be marked by a piece of wood or anything suitable. On this will be written the Chaplain's initials and a number. He will thus have a tally.

(iv) He will send the position of the grave on the map and a description of the marks identifying it as soon as possible to Graves Registration Unit No. 1 Bailleul with a list of the men buried in the said grave.

(v) These orders only take effect when the normal method of registering and identifying graves cannot be used.

Example: The Rev. AB buries 22 men in a common grave. He notes position in the 1/40000 map and places on the grave a piece of wood with AB1 written on it. His communication to the Graves Registration Unit will be like this: On … 1916 I buried 22 men (names as follows) in grave marked AB1 at x 12.d.5.4. and Map 91D 1/40000.
Sgd A B.

The Australian Higher Authorities

It was not until Monash's appointment in 1918 that any Australian General had any degree of autonomy over the AIF, or any other force in Europe. As both Birdwood and Godley were British, their training, thinking and careers were of the British Army. Imagination, innovation and lateral thinking had been bashed out of them, and most of the others, on the parade grounds of the Empire years ago. And it certainly showed at Fromelles.

Of the Australians noted here only one was a professional soldier, Christian, and it could be said his contribution to Fromelles was the worst. Of the others, only Pope had experience in organising large groups of men—in the railways, the rest were from small offices, and as a result seemed incapable of appointing 'good managers'. This was the area in which Monash excelled, marking him out from all the rest.

THE COMMANDER OF THE I ANZAC CORPS

General W R BIRDWOOD

(Age at Fromelles—51)

William Riddell Birdwood was born at Poona, India 13 September 1865, his father being the Under-Secretary to the government of Bombay. His mother, Edith was from the Impey family, then with some three generations of service in India. Birdwood went to Clifton College and then Sandhurst, where at the age of nineteen he received his Commission and within two months—July 1885—he was in India, a Lieutenant in XII Royal Lancers. This being a rich man's regiment, Birdwood transferred to the XI Bengal Lancers and did not leave India again until 1899. In 1894 he married Jeanette Gonville and they had three children. He went to South Africa and was on Kitchener's staff, and by 1911 a Major General. In November 1914 Birdwood was appointed to command the Anzac forces then being prepared for Europe. That changed to commanding them in Egypt.

Birdwood, with Brudenell White, planned the Anzac landing, and both were conspicuous all through the campaign, Birdwood being opposed to quitting, but then working hard to make the evacuation a total success.

In France, then in command of 1st Anzac Corps, Birdwood expressed disapproval of the objectives of Fromelles and its organisation, but that was all. Up against tough men he never fought his corner. It was sufficient that people took into account who he was and then to express his views and let events

Gen. Sir William Birdwood, c. 1915

prove or disprove them. He could have made a great difference to what happened at Fromelles had he been resolute. That said 'Birdie' was always popular with Australians and he would have been greatly welcomed as Governor-General, and would have welcomed the appointment, but the Scullin Government wanted an Australian. Birdwood went on to become C-in-C in India, and later Lord Birdwood of Anzac and Totnes.

When the time came for Birdwood to turn to compiling his memoirs, one of the sentences in the first chapter was a revealing remark not just about the autobiography, but the man himself.

'*... I have a strong instinctive distaste for writing anything in criticism of others; yet it seems to me that a book of memoirs can be of little value, historical or otherwise, unless the writer is prepared to give frank and outspoken opinions.*'

He did not, so Birdwood's book *Khaki and Gown* (1941) is a bland, cheery, pleasant recollection of an interesting life populated by charming and decent people! Although obviously ambitious and hugely successful, Birdwood seems to have been genuinely surprised by the wonderful receptions given him by old comrades: which may well be the reason why he got such receptions.

THE COMMANDER OF THE II ANZAC CORPS

General A J GODLEY

(Age at Fromelles—49)

Alexander John Godley was born 4 February 1867, eldest son of Lieut Col W A Godley of County Leitrim, Ireland. Educated at the Royal Naval School before transferring to Haileybury and thence to Sandhurst and United Services College. In August 1886 he was Lieut in Royal Dublin Fusiliers. In 1898 he married Louisa Fowler, sister of Lieut Gen. Sir John Fowler, later Director of Army Signals at GHQ in France 1914–18. There were no children from the marriage.

Lieut Gen. Sir A J Godley, c. 1918

Godley as a special intelligence officer went to the South African War and was in the siege of Mafeking, after which he joined Colonel (later Field Marshal) Plumer's staff. From then until 1910 he worked mainly at Aldershot re-organising army procedures in line with the lessons learned in South Africa.

In October 1910 he was appointed to command the New Zealand Military Forces and worked on that until 1914 when in co-operation with the Australian Military Forces he took the New Zealand Division to Egypt at the end of 1914. Now a Major General he went with Birdwood's Anzac Corps to Gallipoli, later taking command. Back in Egypt in 1916 Godley was given command of II Anzac Corps which was at the outset one New Zealand Division and one Australian division (the 1st Division), which he took to France in March 1916, guiding them into position and action south of Armentières. At the time of Fromelles as Chief of II Anzac Corps his New Zealand Division was on the left of the 5th Australian Division and his prior experience of the area meant that he appeared at McCay's HQ on occasion, and his personal contacts with Plumer made him important behind the scenes. For instance it was on Godley's recommendation that Brig. Gen. C J Hobkirk of Essex Regiment took over from Pope.

Always viewed as tall, lean, aloof, but thorough and alert Godley collected honours from Britain, France, Belgium, Serbia, Spain and Morocco, plus 11 Mentions in Despatches. He was seen by New Zealanders as being with them but never of them.

Godley was promoted General in 1923 and from 1928 to 1932 was Governor of Gibraltar. During the Second World War he commanded a platoon of the Home Guard. Colonel of the Royal Ulster Rifles, Godley was also Colonel of Otago Mounted Rifles and the North Auckland Regiment. He died at Oxford 6 March 1957, aged 90.

AUSTRALIAN IMPERIAL FORCE CHIEF OF THE GENERAL STAFF

General C B B WHITE

(Age at Fromelles—40)

Cyril Brudenell Bingham White was born at St Arnaud, Victoria, 23 September 1876; his father had been an army officer. It is perhaps not surprising that following his education in Queensland White, after three years as a trainee in a bank, joined the permanent artillery. Going with the Queensland contingent to South Africa White arrived just as the war ended. He then spent time on Thursday Island as an officer in the garrison there. In 1904 he was ADC to General Hutton and two years later in England, first at Staff College, later in training operations—a total of five years. Returning to Australia he became Director of Military Operations and at the outbreak of the war was Acting Chief of the General Staff. In this capacity White with the Minister for Defence G F Pearce, Generals Bridges and Legge, created the AIF. He went to Gallipoli as Bridges' Chief of Staff, and after Bridges' death was with Birdwood. White, whose planning of the landing went astray for reasons still being debated, masterminded the evacuation—introducing periods of silence, during one of which the successful quitting of Anzac was finally accomplished.

White, not for the last time, was now canvassed as a candidate to command a division, but fortunately for the AIF his capacity for organisation was recognised as being more important, and he remained the brains behind the scene. As it turned out this was the role he kept to and thus nobody was ever sure how many or which of the blunders or successes were due to his directives. He became a faceless man but one whom it would seem every senior officer in the AIF turned to for an opinion. It would not be an exaggeration to say Bean idolized him. It was from White that Bean borrowed a car to go to Fleurbaix on the morning of 20 July 1916, having discussed the event with him over breakfast. White's evasive silence in connection with Fromelles is important—see p388–89—and his unexpected death in an aircraft accident on 13 August 1940 meant that no memoirs were ever written. It is unlikely that he would have written anything historically valuable anyway: his diaries, which he kept daily from 1895, give no evidence of any ability with the pen. His courtly nature, secretive style and the enormous power wielded by his friends meant his conduct and views were never examined publicly.

GOC AIF ARTILLERY

Brig. General S E CHRISTIAN

(Age at Fromelles—48)

Sydney Ernest Christian was born on 17 April 1868 at Tenterfield, NSW, son of a pastoralist. Educated at Geelong Grammar School, he commanded the School Cadet Corps and wrote essays on military matters. For example in 1885: '*The day may come when the enemy may be at our gate, when we may have to fight for our common country against a common foe. It is then that the lessons of obedience, of discipline and of skill learnt in the School Cadet Corps will be of service to Australia …*'

Brig. Gen. S E Christian, 1920s

Christian duly qualified for Sandhurst, but instead he returned to the family property. He was in a volunteer unit in 1891 and in 1895 as Lieutenant joined 'A' Field Battery of the New South Wales Permanent Military Forces. With them in 1900–1 he served in South Africa and was wounded at Springfontein.

Christian studied artillery procedures in England and in 1909 back in Sydney trained and later commanded the 1st Field Artillery Brigade. He took them to Egypt and in May 1915 to Gallipoli where they were with the British. For this work he was appointed CMG, awarded Legion d'Honneur and MID. In February 1916, now temporary Brig. Gen. Christian was given the task of raising and training the artillery of 5th Australian Division. He had very few experienced officers and most of the men were formerly infantry or lighthorsemen. He was also given the artillery of 4th Division. With almost no equipment and four months in the desert as background, these units were shipped to France and it could be said, with about ten days to get ready for battle, nobody could have done much better than Christian. Overall the artillery at Fromelles was a near total disaster, and how much of this was Christian's fault, or that of the other artillery commanders will never be known. But the heavy casualties in the Australian lines from their own 'shorts' tell their own sad story. Christian remained in Flanders with the New Zealand Division the rest of 1916. In January 1917 he was evacuated ill, and in April invalided to Australia. This deterioration in health probably had much to do with the death of his wife in London at the same time. They had married in Sydney in 1902, she was his cousin Edith and they were noted as a devoted couple. They had no children, so Christian lived the rest of his life at the Australian Club in Sydney until he died of pneumonia on 17 May 1931.

Upon his death one of his staff recounted memories of Christian, one of which might indicate more than any listing of military tributes. At Helles a long-time associate was shot dead beside him … *'he appeared to be unconcerned and refused to attend the burial: but as the burial party was withdrawing from the grave, Colonel Christian's figure was seen alone and hatless, behind an olive tree, literally stricken with grief*'.

THE COMMANDERS OF AUSTRALIAN BRIGADES

Brig. General E TIVEY
8th Brigade

(Age at Fromelles—50)

Edwin Tivey was born at Inglewood, Victoria, 19 September 1866, educated at Wesley College, he started work as an accountant and later became a stockbroker. Tivey was successful and well-regarded, and had been very active in Militia Forces since his early twenties. He was commissioned in the Victorian Rangers in 1889 and promoted Captain in 1891. He went to South Africa in 1900 with the 4th Victorian (Imperial) Regiment earning a DSO, two MIDs and the Queen's Medal (four clasps). He was 'Pompey' Elliott's senior officer. Tivey married Annie Robb in 1906, and there was

Brig. Gen. E Tivey, c. 1918

a son and a daughter from the union: the son died of wounds whilst a prisoner of the Italians after the battle of El Alamein in 1943.

In July 1915 now as Colonel, Tivey was first to command the new 8th Bde, raising it in Adelaide. He took it to Egypt in early December 1915, and in February 1916 they were in position on the Suez Canal: the 8th Bde had gone by train, whereas the other Brigades of the 5th Division marched. This event, and others, caused the members of the brigade to be known as Tivey's Chocs! Tivey remained in command of the 8th for most of the war, except at the end of 1918 when briefly taking command of 5th Division. Tivey was wounded in action December 1916 and again in October 1917. He was gassed in May 1918. Mentioned in Despatches six times, he was appointed CB and CMG. The long association with the brigade engendered loyalty both ways and Tivey used his authority and experience for the benefit of his men during and after the war. Interestingly Bean makes no character assessment of Tivey, whereas Ellis, whose Brigadier he was, was full of praise and information.

In later life Tivey became rich and advised Monash, White and others on their investments: he never lost his soldierly bearing. Tivey died on 19 May 1947 and was buried in Brighton Cemetery.

Colonel H POPE
14th Brigade

(Age at Fromelles—42)

Harold Pope was born at Ealing, Middlesex on 16 October 1873, the son of a solicitor. He was educated in England, joining the clerical staff of the Great Northern Railway when 16. He emigrated to Perth, Australia in 1895 to work for the railways. Married in 1896 to Susan Slater at Albany, he joined the Western Australian Military forces four years later and was a Lieut Colonel in 1908.

At the Landing, 25 April 1915, he led the 16th Bn, and at nightfall they executed an important move in an area later called Pope's Hill. His conduct on Gallipoli throughout the campaign was spoken of with unreserved admiration: Monash thought highly of him, the men swore by him, '*a popular figure … with confident bearing, strong face and kindly eyes*' was one description. Near the end of the campaign he was appointed CB and in October was evacuated ill.

Appointed by McCay to command 14th Bde, Pope, now temporary Colonel, was blessed with experienced battalion commanders

Colonel H Pope, late 1920s
COURTESY THE ARMY MUSEUM OF WA

and at Fromelles was the most successful brigade commander in the battle.

When he went to sleep after lunch on 20 July after some sixty hours of high tension and little rest, he could not be awakened. McCay sacked him and shipped him back to Australia: see Dismissal of Col Pope, page 260.

When McCay was out of the way, Birdwood who had dodged the affair earlier on, backtracked and with Hobbs brought Pope back to France and in command of 52nd Bn. On 7 June 1917 he was wounded at Messines. Later MID, Pope was invalided home in February 1918. From then until the end of the war, he worked on organising troopships. Hobbs, a man never afraid to stand up and be counted wrote '... *there are few who enjoy more the respect and admiration of their friends than yourself.*'

After the war, Pope returned to Perth and was Commissioner of Railways 1920–28 facing many financial and administrative problems which he *'attacked with verve'*. He retired in October 1928 due to ill-health. He had been, from 1925-30, Hon. Colonel of the 16th Bn and ADC to the Governor-General in 1926. He died 13 May 1938, survived by his wife, three sons and two daughters. He was buried at Karrakatta Cemetery.

Brig. General H E ELLIOTT
15th Brigade

(Age at Fromelles—38)

Harold Edward Elliott was born 19 June 1878 at West Charlton, Victoria. His father was a farmer. Educated at Ballarat College, Elliott entered the University of Melbourne to read Law. These studies he left in 1900 to go to South Africa with 4th Victorian (Imperial) Regiment. While serving with them he earned a DCM. Later he was commissioned in the 2nd Royal Berks, served with the Border Scouts and was MID.

In 1909 Elliott married Catherine Campbell and they had a daughter and a son. Catherine died in 1938, the son was killed by natives in New Guinea, and the daughter (together with W Jamieson, formerly of 7th Bn) sorted her father's papers and gave them to the Australian War Memorial.

After South Africa, Elliott returned to his studies with considerable success and in 1907 was called to the Bar of Victoria. His military career continued from 1904 as 2/Lieut in the 5th Infantry Regiment and in 1913 he took command of 58th Bn at the commencement of compulsory military training. A year later at the outbreak of war he was given command of 7th Bn and took them to Gallipoli on 25 April 1915. He was wounded that day and evacuated, returning in June. In August he led the 7th at Lone Pine where four of his men were awarded VCs. Elliott received nothing, somebody crossed his name off the top of the list of recommendations. After Anzac Elliott went to Egypt and in February 1916 was first given command of 1st Bde, then on 1 March promoted to Brig. General and given 15th Bde. He worked hard to bring it up to battlefield readiness. His resolute ideas on how this should be done did not please everybody but began the extraordinary *esprit de corps* of 15th Bde.

In France, Elliott soon became aware of the impossible nature of the attack at Fromelles. French Military Documents about not attempting to cross a No-Man's Land wider than 150 yards, supported his view as did one of Haig's staff officers. But to no avail. However he threw himself and his men into the battle with an optimism that was at variance with his prior view and when it all went wrong, he learned the lesson. For the rest of the war he argued his case, fired off memos and reports to generals who often ordered their destruction. The upshot of this was that he was never given a division, and there is no doubt that Brudenell White saw to that.

'Pompey' Elliott (his nickname is thought to be derived from the same named football coach of Carlton whom he greatly resembled) led the 15th Bde right to the end with real success. Back in Melbourne in 1919, Elliott returned to his legal practice and became a Senator, a position he held for two terms. His battles

Brig. Gen. H E Elliott, 1921

with Pearce, White and Birdwood continued until 1925, but in 1926 with General Sir Harry Chauvel as Chief of General Staff he was given command again of 15th Bde and the next year 3rd Division and promoted to Major General.

But the bitterness persisted, and together with the strain and sorrow of the Depression and the deterioration of the society he had seen so many die for, he was driven to suicide on 23 March 1931. He was buried at Burwood Cemetery.

The Artillery at Fromelles: Part One

Having now described the first brushes with the enemy and the general preparation for the battle, it is essential to consider the positioning and importance of the artillery, it being very much a British area of command. The 5th Australian Divisional Artillery came from Egypt without equipment, and very little training, and therefore were very much dependent on the British.

One of the most mystifying aspects of Fromelles is the misjudgement by Haking of the capacity of the artillery he had assembled. His long-held view that the artillery assault came before the infantry assault underscores the fact that he was not a recent convert, even though the strategy had failed him earlier. McCay on the other hand had no real experience of artillery, and if one judges his conduct at Fromelles from this standpoint, it is clear that it was never in the front of his mind. He was an infantry man and judging by his report on the battle, the role of the artillery was simply wire cutting and providing the creeping barrage behind which the infantry would cross No-Man's Land, then the enemy lines and then enter and hold the support lines. There is a curious lack of intent to pulverise such strong points as the Sugarloaf.

Much hope of success was placed in the artillery which, while the British Historian stated to be almost the same as in the Aubers Ridge fiasco of 1915, was:

now a more powerful artillery, with more ammunition, besides trench mortars to help in cutting the German wire.

The First Army, from its line further south, contributed the following heavy and siege artillery: sixteen 60 pounders, six 6 inch howitzers, three 12 inch howitzers, two 6 inch guns, one 12 inch gun. The Second Army's contribution was: twenty-four 60 pounders, sixteen 6 inch howitzers, eight 9.2 inch howitzers, two 12 inch howitzers - making a total of 78 heavy pieces for which 4,350 rounds of ammunition were allocated. And there was no shortage of heavy artillery, wrote the British Historian:

The proportion of guns to frontage of attack was more than that of the Fourth Army for the opening of the Somme offensive on 1 July.

He was referring to the 31st British Division's twenty-eight 18 pounders and sixteen 4.5 inch howitzers, the 61st British Division's ninety-six 18 pounders and twenty-four 4.5 inch howitzers, the 4th Australian Division's forty-eight 18 pounders and twelve 4.5 inch howitzers, the 5th Australian Division's forty-eight 18 pounders and twelve 4.5 inch howitzers. For the field guns 200,000 rounds were available and for the 4.5 inch howitzers 15,000 rounds.

Other support came in mortars: the 6th British Division contributed eight 2 inch mortars, the 50th British Division 4, the 1st Canadian Division 4 and the 3rd Canadian Division 4. The 61st British Division had 40 (12 were kept in reserve) together with two 9.2 inch mortars and 5th Australian Division another twenty 2 inch mortars.

One way and another, according to the British, there were 296 field pieces, and as Haking said:

... the narrow depth of the attack should make it possible, with the ammunition available, to reduce the defenders to a state of collapse before the assault.

Clearly it did not, and the failure of the artillery to do what Haking expected is a major factor in the battle.

The story of the 5th Division Artillery, with hindsight, reveals all that was wrong with the Fromelles operation. Wrote Ellis, probably with a tinge of sarcasm:

During the Blaringhem period, the structure of the Division underwent some important modifications. Trench mortar batteries were formed. On the 5th July each infantry brigade proceeded to form its own light trench mortar battery ... The battery strength was raised by voluntary transfer from the infantry battalions and, as none of the men had had any previous training in the work, instructors were furnished by 1st Australian Division ... About the same period the Divisional Artillery was instructed to form one heavy and three medium trench mortar batteries ... the formation commenced 5th July, on which date a number of officers and other ranks were sent to a course of instruction ... The three light trench mortars were brigade troops and operated under the command of infantry brigadiers, while the one heavy and three medium trench mortar batteries were artillery units purely, and acted under command of the CRA. The Divisional Trench Mortar Brigade assembled on 13 July at Winter's Night near Fleurbaix.

On 7 July an important modification in the composition of the artillery brigades was effected ... The effect of the change was to distribute the howitzer batteries through three of the four brigades instead of keeping them all as one brigade.

Ellis offers no rationale for the changes, but this state of flux going on within a few days of the battle has to be kept in mind. Well experienced, highly qualified gunners would have taken such movements in their stride, but not some 2,000 ex-infantry and light horse men who put their hands up a few months earlier in Egypt and who now formed the rank and file of the Australian Artillery. Likewise, the younger officers who would by the very nature of their new responsibility be less decisive, less able to adapt to or take advantage of new situations. This problem is hinted at by the Courts-Martial charges in the Artillery where a considerable number of men had quarrelled with officers' decisions or orders.

Ellis was mindful of the problems:

The new batteries had to travel to the sector and take up battery positions; the whole force had to be regrouped into three groups, one to support each assaulting infantry brigade, and the registration on new targets and barrage lines to be completed. For this latter work the assistance of two squadrons, the 10th and the 16th, of the Royal Flying Corps, was obtained, and although their work was considerably hampered by a succession of misty mornings, the clear hours were crowded by busy registration. This had to be done in two days and in such a way, if possible, that the enemy would not suspect that an offensive action was impending. In addition to the artillery batteries, five medium trench mortar batteries, two of them Canadian, were placed at the disposal of the Division for the operation. Positions had to be found for these and ammunition carried to them before they could commence their work of registration and wire cutting.

All this merely draws attention to the problems of getting ready without addressing the extra problems of the command structure. In charge of the Australian Artillery was Brig. General S E Christian, then 48, who had served in South Africa with distinction and later at Gallipoli commanded 1st Field Artillery Bde. Christian earns no compliments from either Bean or Ellis, only the mandatory mentions of command. Only Ellis attempts to deal with the complex command structure of the artillery, but it fell to others much later to comment on the difficulties encountered, there being:

... No artillery command function at Corps level i.e. the level at which the battle was commanded. The senior artillery officer at XI Corps HQ the Brig. General Royal Artillery had merely advisory status.

Bean in his account of Fromelles, gives most of his information about the artillery in a half page footnote where he notes almost casually that the quantity of artillery which he calculated to be 258 field guns and howitzers, 64 heavy pieces and 70 medium trench mortars, represented: *a field gun or howitzer to every 15 yards of the front and 800 rounds to each field piece.*

Only from Ellis however can we learn the deployment: Bean must have thought it was not particularly important. Christian organised his artillery into three groups: On the right supporting 15th Bde under Lieut Col O F Phillips, the centre under Lieut Col H O Caddy supporting 14th Bde, and on the left under Lieut Col H J Cox-Taylor supporting 8th Bde. Equally divided over these three groups were the 15th Artillery under Lieut Col J W S Lucas, the 4th Divisional Artillery's 10th Bde, 9th and 11th Bdes right to left. The contribution from the 171st British Bde was also split three ways. The 4th Div and 171st were armed on 15 July with final orders 11 am, 18 July:

The three groups were thus of similar strength and composition, each consisting of nine 18 pounders, and two 4.5 howitzer batteries.

Only Ellis records that:

a small force of heavy artillery with definitely allotted targets operated under Corps control throughout the fight. It included a small number of 6 inch guns, two batteries of 9.2 inch and two 12 inch howitzers on railway trucks. The five trench mortar batteries lent to the Division for the operation, were placed under Major Sir J Keane RFA who acted as DTMO throughout the battle. The officers and personnel of 5th Divisional Trench Mortar Batteries, who had not yet had a fortnight's experience of their new arm, were distributed among the loaned batteries to assist wherever possible and to learn all they could of their new work.

So before a shot is fired in anger we can see the fragmentation of command and experience, and there is no evidence to show that there was any contact between the artillery commands of the British and Australians. Perhaps the most extraordinary evidence of this is the surviving 'bombardment' map in the 5th Division files, which clearly shows the areas set aside for each of the three groups and on the far right the Australian area stops some 70 yards short of the Sugarloaf. The British, one assumes therefore entirely responsible for the bombardment of the 'fortress' that controlled most of the sector. The Australian MG posts in the area between the divisions were directly opposite the Sugarloaf where No-Man's Land was widest—450 yards, which in the circumstances does not seem to have been a cooperative decision: and a misunderstanding of the formidability of the Sugarloaf. And nobody had to go very far to get first hand comment on that subject: the 60th British Bde on the left of the Australians, previously as part of the earlier British Army, had spent weeks in front of it.

Such procedures seem to indicate that the battle was fought not by one Corps, but by two divisions and as we shall see when this became an infantry matter, real problems surfaced. The almost total failure of the artillery to deliver the things it was required to do, ie cut wire, make a demoralised and shell-shocked enemy, silence enemy artillery and provide a protective curtain for the allied infantry will be addressed in the chapter on the battle itself. Suffice it to say that the back room chaos already described explains most of the failures.

The artillery behind the British lines is seldom commented upon in the unit histories. The 2nd Bucks is an exception: '*The preliminary bombardment which lasted for three days was carried out by some 350 guns of all calibres, RFA and RHA Batteries being pushed up to within a short distance of Tilleloy Street, many of them in exposed positions, where they suffered heavy casualties.*'

Part Two, and map—pages 154–56.

This composite is made from six Royal Flying Corps photographs of 1916 as follows: L–R: A – July; B – 10 October; C, D, E – 19 July; F – 10 October

The Fromelles' No-Man's Land from the air

Bean published two other aerial photographs in his Vol III: 31 and 32. 31 is surely upside down in regard to his caption, but anyway the trench he draws attention to is well outside 8th Bde sector and follows roughly the same line as the trench shown in F and thus not as well defined as in Bean's photo. It must be 'the new front line' trench described on page 118. Plate 32 dramatically illustrates the sweep and thrust of the 14th Field Coy.

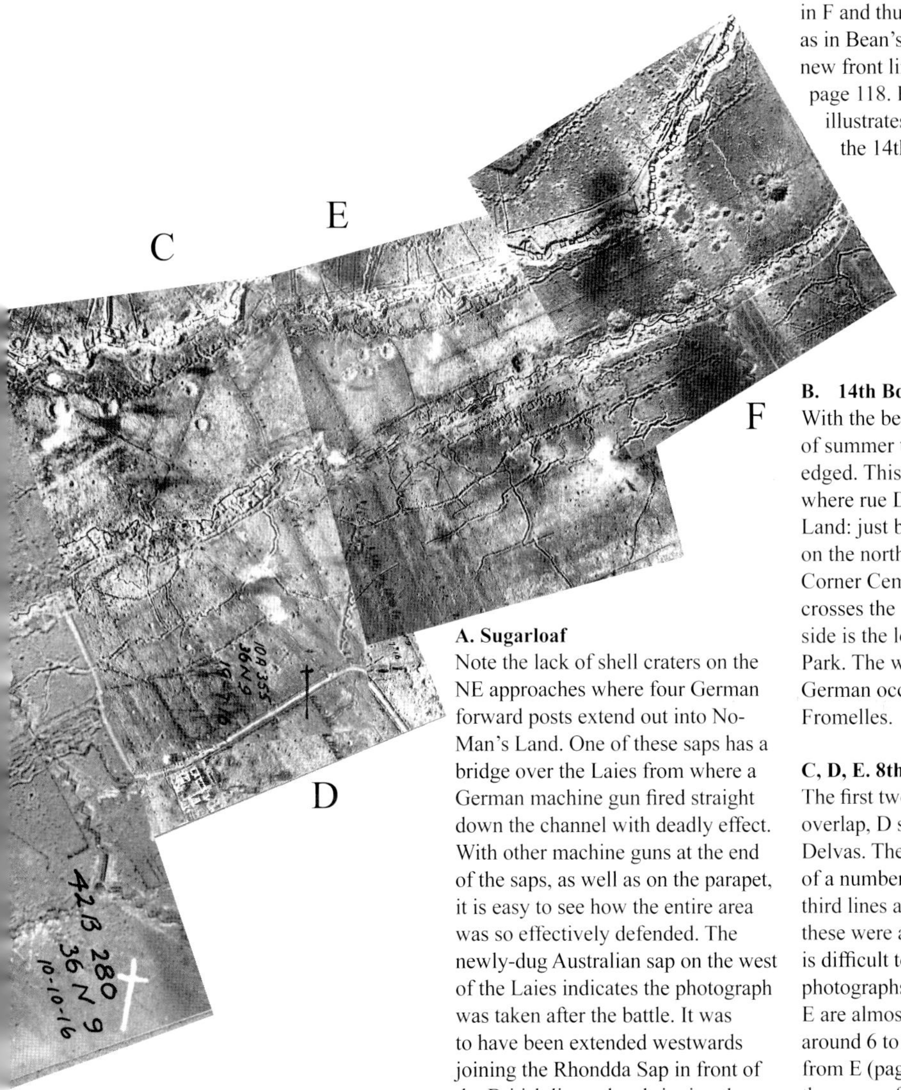

C

E

F

D

A. Sugarloaf
Note the lack of shell craters on the NE approaches where four German forward posts extend out into No-Man's Land. One of these saps has a bridge over the Laies from where a German machine gun fired straight down the channel with deadly effect. With other machine guns at the end of the saps, as well as on the parapet, it is easy to see how the entire area was so effectively defended. The newly-dug Australian sap on the west of the Laies indicates the photograph was taken after the battle. It was to have been extended westwards joining the Rhondda Sap in front of the British lines, thus bringing the British front line almost half way across No-Man's Land. Behind the British lines the effect of precise German shelling can be seen along what was Bond Street. The very wide VC Avenue, with many craters where it enters the front line is another example. The huge number of craters in open country tell their own story.

B. 14th Bde Sector
With the benefit of three months of summer the craters are less hard edged. This photograph shows where rue Delvas crosses No-Man's Land: just before it turns south, on the north side is the site of VC Corner Cemetery, and where it crosses the German line, on the east side is the location of the Memorial Park. The well used road in the German occupied area leads to Fromelles.

C, D, E. 8th Bde Sector
The first two photographs heavily overlap, D showing more of rue Delvas. The size, layout and style of a number of German second and third lines and the later wisdom that these were all abandoned ditches is difficult to reconcile from these photographs. The shadows of C, D, E are almost identical and thus all around 6 to 6.30 pm, 19 July. Details from E (pages 116 and 117) provide the reason for this assumption. The large crater on the eastern edge must be the result of the mine exploded around 6 pm (page 114).

F. Divisional Boundary
This also has the 6 pm crater and there are feint lines where the 8th Bde sap across No-Man's Land would have been, but now seemingly filled in and grassed over.

AWM.A B-42B280. C-10A355. D-10A351. E-J00278 F-J03376

THE SUGARLOAF SALIENT AWM E05990
Bean described this photograph as being taken before the battle, but is this so? The Rhondda Sap and the trench dug by the Australians on 19 July are in about the same state as in photos A and B on page 106. And all the major craters in the other photographs are visible. More important, however, is the well-marked track going forward from Rhondda Sap to the Sugarloaf. Or is it down *from* the Sugarloaf ? Is this evidence that the British got to the ramparts, or that the Germans later wore a path coming down to bury them? Taken over British-held territory, looking southeast, this photograph gives a view of Aubers Ridge and beyond, as far as (R–L) Herlies, Fournes and Beaucamps-Ligny—the road connecting them marked by the row of trees. The prominent straight road running up from the bottom of the photograph is rue Delvas, thus the present day location of VC Corner Cemetery is just beyond where it meets the Australian trenches. Where the road cuts through the German lines is the location of the Australian Memorial Park. The road then continues to the town of Fromelles, at the centre of the photograph.

5

Dreadful day

19 July. 15 Bde attacked Fromelles front—self cracked in shoulder and on ribs—casualties 60th Bn 800—Capt Evans, Lieut Rhind killed. Only one Sgt left in B Coy. Dreadful day.

—Lieut Tom Kerr, 60th Bn, Diary 19 July 1916

It would be doubtful whether any battle could be better described and more compassionately remembered than Bean's account of Fromelles. Partly because the battle was of short duration, on a narrow front and ended conclusively, it made a compact story. Bean's Fromelles runs to 119 pages (50,000 words) and by the nature of the event, it was nearly all new research. On the other hand Ellis' account introduces little personal non-official material and for the most part concerns officers only. Bean made much use of German Unit histories, the books themselves in the Australia War Memorial Reference Library have his notes and translations written in the margins, and those same phrases appear in his work. It is also clear that Fromelles had some real personal importance to Bean. Perhaps some of those killed or changed by the event were special friends from the months on Gallipoli, perhaps he was annoyed with himself for not being there, and doubtless the size and extent of the disaster disturbed him profoundly. And there is little doubt that he was aware that there was another side to the official story.

Lieut T Kerr
COURTESY M WOOD

If it had been possible, Bean's two chapters would have been included in this work as an appendix. The reader is directed to them if, after finishing this volume, more detailed information is required. Bean mentions by name over 280 participants in the battle, all with some biographical material, and is remarkably balanced between the brigades.

Examination of his working papers show how he plotted every significant event in the battle by canvassing accounts from various vantage points and trying to confirm each claim or statement by asking other witnesses. He would write to them: '*I have an account of ...* ' and then ask '*whether you have a memory of ...* ' The replies were often helpful, in some cases pages long with maps, diagrams and the names of others who could also help. But other replies were angry, bitter and from men whose lives the battle had ruined absolutely. All this material ended up in two files; the main one is a green spring-back folder and is titled 'The Battle of Fromelles'. It has, as do all his files, the 'Bean Label' (see margin *With Great*

IT DID NOT EXIST

... the infantry showed magnificent courage, but their lack of training was their undoing ... The Australian Artillery did splendidly. The staff work all through could not be criticised, for it did not exist.

—Lieut Col Charles MacLaurin, AMC Fromelles
Sydney Morning Herald 26 July 1919

MENTIONED IN BEAN

There are over 280 individuals mentioned by name, excluding Generals, in Bean's account of Fromelles. The balance in relation to work done is very fair: 8th Bde—92; 14th Bde—107 and 15th Bde—54. The remainder are Medical, Chaplains, Pioneers, Tunnellers and attached British Officers.

WITH GREAT CAUTION
Diaries and Notes of C E W Bean concerning the War of 1914–1918

The use of these diaries and notes is subject to conditions laid down in the terms of gift to the Australian War Memorial. But, apart from those terms, I wish the following circumstances and considerations to be brought to the notice of every reader and writer who may use them.

These writings represent only what at the moment of making them I believed to be true. The diaries were jotted down almost daily with the object of recording what was then in the writer's mind. Often he wrote them when very tired and half asleep; also, not infrequently, what he believed to be true was not so—but it does not follow that he always discovered this, or remembered to correct the mistakes when discovered. Indeed, he could not always remember that he had written them.

These records should, therefore, be used with great caution, as relating only what their author, at the time of writing, believed. Further, he cannot, of course, vouch for the accuracy of statements made to him by others and here recorded. But he did try to ensure such accuracy by consulting, as far as possible, those who had seen or otherwise taken part in the events. The constant falsity of second-hand evidence (on which a large proportion of war stories are founded) was impressed upon him by the second or third day of the Gallipoli campaign, notwithstanding that those who passed on such stories usually themselves believed them to be true. All second-hand evidence herein should be read with this in mind.

—C E W Bean
16 Sept 1946

Caution). The file begins with the typescript of Bean's article for *Reveille* June/July 1931, the 15th Anniversary. In this piece Bean basically blames Haking for adopting the position that the artillery was sufficient and concluded '*it is little wonder that July 19 has since been looked upon as one of the saddest anniversaries of the AIF calendar*'. Then follow notes among much other material by or about Lieut Col Toll of 31st Bn, and notes from conversations with Lieut Col Cass of 54th Bn. From Bean's notes, asides really, it is clear that he was not sure about statements Cass made. Cass was much war-damaged and bitter against Australian HQ, and Bean dodged strong opinions as a rule, and also the blunt presentation of events. There was of course good reason for Cass to be bitter, and anyway bitterness does not imply untruthfulness.

The account that follows pays full attention to Bean's cautionary statement, but if Bean in his diary or notes wrote his immediate observations, this writer regards them as such, but where Bean is told something by somebody else that is covered by his 'let out' clause. This is why great store is placed on such an event as Bean witnessing and recording McCay and Elliott's meeting after the battle, an event which was, of course, outside the purpose of his history, but which is very much the concern of this work.

What criticism there was of Bean's chapters on Fromelles centred about his neglect of the artillery, engineers, medical and other services in favour of the infantry. That Bean saw the battle as an infantry event is in itself an important point. Ellis began his description with the artillery because that is how the battle began and then took the reader through the various brigades, battalions and services largely as they emerged from

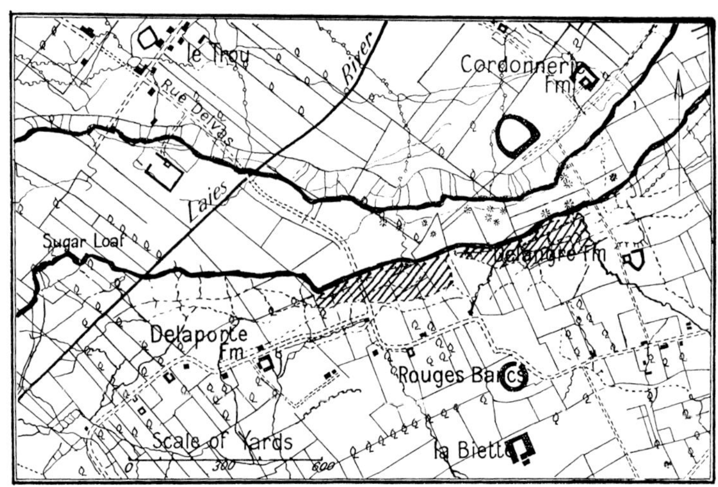

The Australian Sector in the Battle. The shaded areas were those occupied during the night of 19/20 July 1916. The Official History used this map and 54 small sectional maps to illustrate Bean's narrative.

the 'Official Sources' ie War Diaries and their Appendices from which he worked.

Before starting on the battle it is well to examine the basic situation in which the 5th Australian Division found itself, and to remember that it is not the classic stark Great War scenery. Due to recent rains and being summer, it was hot and humid, and much of the battlefield was covered with wild grass or abandoned crops two to three feet high. Only Ellis really credits the Germans with brains, skill and good judgement. He took time to understand their positioning:

> ... it may be said that the typical German position consisted of a considerable width of low-lying ground, trenched, wired and studded with strong points, behind which rose in tiers ridge after ridge of higher ground, culminating in a feature that conferred command over all the adjacent terrain for miles. And in the Flanders area particularly it should be added that this command was derived not so much from any great height of the ridges themselves as from the utter flatness of the rest of the country.

Given this careful planning and the technical superiority of German artillery, together with the firm establishment of the line at Fromelles, none of which were secrets, the allied plans seem in retrospect totally bizarre. After barrages and bombardment, inevitably on the hour, or half hour, always in the same time sequence would come the juvenile manoeuvre of showing hats, bayonets and dummy figures over the parapet to encourage the Germans to man their parapets and so fall victim to the next artillery barrage. Oh, that it was all that simple. It may have worked against the Zulus, but the 8th Bavarian Reserve Division was somewhat more sophisticated.

Neither Ellis, nor Bean, really concerned themselves with the fact that the British and Australians in open trenches were sitting targets for the German artillery. The disaster of the 183rd and 184th British Brigades has already been described and the 8th Australian Brigade suffered as badly. The open trenches coupled with the terrible overcrowding of forward positions explains some of the early problems. Only Sloan in his history of 30th Bn raises this point, so it is well to examine this issue prior to describing the fate of the three Australian brigades. It is merely the mathematics concerning the number of men and the length of the line. First, the British: 182nd Bde had 1070 Officers and men on a 950 yard front, 183rd Bde had 1190 Officers and men on a 1000 yard front, while the 184th Bde had 1130 Officers and men on 850 yards. The Australians: 15th Bde had about 1600 Officers and men on 550 yards, the 14th Bde had some 1550 Officers and men on 550 yards, and the

THEY KISSED US AND HUGGED US ALL THE WAY ...

Because the horror of 19/20 July so overwhelmed their lives, some men forgot, except in their diaries, that a few days prior as representatives of the 5th Australian Division (2 officers and 100 ORs) they had gone to Paris to be part of the 14 July celebrations. It was, compared with what was to come, the last happiness. Hector Brewer of 56th Bn in his diary wrote of those days:

13 July. Reached Paris. Marched to the Caserne Pepenière Barracks. Crowds of people lined the streets.
14 July. Left barracks at 7 am and marched to the Esplanades Invalides where all the allied troops were drawn up. From there the procession began headed by the Belgians and ended at the Place de la Republique. We got back to barracks about 1 pm. Leave was granted from 2.30 pm to 8 pm. An English lady showed several of us a few of the fine sights of Paris. Great British advance on the River Somme. Weighed 11.7.
15 July. Leave granted to all hands, I had a good stroll round Paris streets. British still advancing.
16 July. British enter German third line of defence. British cavalry in action for the first time since 1914. No leave granted today. Great disappointment in barracks as we all have someone to see. Soldiers are lionized in Paris especially British soldiers on account of their good work on the Somme. We had a great march to the station. Thousands of people lined the street to see us all off. They kissed us and hugged us all the way to the Railway Gates. Reached Abbeville Station next morning about 8.30 am. Had a sleep.
17 July. All the boys talking about their experiences in Paris. Left Abbeville again at 8.30 pm, entrained and reached Steenwerk next day about 2.30 pm.
18 July. All detachments joined their units. I was glad to be back with the boys again. I shall never forget gay Paree. The people are loveable. All the men are talking of their first experience in the firing line. Some of them got a rough time evidently. Expecting to make a big attack here shortly.

SUCH WERE OUR ORDERS

It is useful to record at the outset some of the precise instructions given on 16 July to 8th Bde battalion commanders:

Each brigade will attack with two assaulting battalions in reserve. The two reserve battalions will be at the disposal of the Divisional Commander, and will assemble within the brigade sector as follows: 30th Bn on the line Rue de Quesne; 29th Bn on line Rue de Quesnoy.

The brigade will move into position as follows: 31st and 32nd Bns, each one company less one platoon, in the front line. One platoon from each of the above companies in 70 yards (support) line. Remainder of 31st and 32nd in 300 yards (reserve) line.

The method of attack will be: each battalion of the assaulting battalions will have two companies in the first and second waves, and two companies in the 3rd and 4th waves. Companies distributed in depth—that is, two platoons in front and two platoons of same company in rear.

A little before the bombardment of enemy parapets finally lifts, (it will lift to support trenches and return to parapet several times) the 1st and 2nd waves will cross our parapet and take up a position in No-Man's Land as near as possible to the enemy wire, with an interval between sections. One wave to go through the enemy wire before next wave reaches it, unless front wave breaks up.

Such were our orders for the 'feint' which afterwards became known as the Battle of Fromelles ... in accordance with the orders issued, the attacking battalions of our brigade were formed into four waves, each consisting of approximately 400 men ...

—Lieut Col H Sloan
The Purple and Gold: A history of the 30th Battalion (1938)

8th Bde with over 1200 Officers and men was on 600 yards. Between the two divisions there was a 300 yard gap covered by '*four machine guns of 15th Bde and five Lewis guns of 58th Bn with the duty of sweeping the parapet of the Sugarloaf until the advancing lines gradually masked their fire*'. This wedge shaped sector on the outside of the elbow of the line would disappear if everybody involved could or would be allowed to proceed straight ahead unhindered by craters, barbed wire, artillery barrages or machine gun fire. The folly of such an idea is beyond belief – and if the 184th and 15th Brigade men did nicely converge on the Sugarloaf, how could the 15th Bde machine guns keep up useful covering fire without risking hitting their own men in the back?

Anyway from the figures alone it is obvious that the British brigades with about one quarter less men, had almost double the front line. It also shows that the British had in general terms one man to a yard, whereas the Australians had almost three. Such overcrowding in open trenches and along clearly visible communication trenches reveals that McCay and/or his staff had no real idea what they were doing. This perhaps should not be a surprise because none of them had ever taken part in such an operation before. For comparison, and to highlight the general style of the front it is important to note that the German Regiments of around 1100 Officers and men had between 1600 and 1700 yards each.

The style of this description of the part played in the battle by the 5th Australian Division follows that of the chapters on the British, and German armies—that is by Brigades and from the beginning to the end of the action.

The Secret Order No. 30 of 13 July detailed the Brigade Fronts—see map on pages 38-39 and the Attack Orders were issued on 16 July, see margin '*Such Were Our Orders*'.

At the far left of the Australian front was 8th Brigade, under command of Brig. Gen. Tivey who although he had a DSO from the South African war, had not gone to Gallipoli, and so this was his first real battle. While some of his senior officers had been through the Anzac campaign, the ranks were largely without battle experience. The two assaulting battalions were, to quote Bean:

> Composed of his older and most hardened men: the 32nd containing many Western and South Australian miners and farmers, occupied the most difficult position on the left of the whole attack; the 31st partly composed of Queensland miners and bush workers next to it. Whilst the 31st had two days at the front, the 32nd had less than a day.

The 32nd was led by Lieut Col D W R Coghill, a 45-year-old school teacher from South Australia, the 31st by Lieut Col F W Toll, aged 44, veteran of the South African war and New Guinea. His son had been killed a year earlier on Gallipoli.

The 29th and 30th had been in the line for a few days at the beginning and taken some losses, not a few due to 'shorts' from the Australian artillery. No-Man's Land in front of the 8th was about 120 yards wide so shells directed at cutting the wire in front of the German trenches had to be very accurately placed. Many were not, and in the history of 30th Bn there was this judgement:

> The divisional trench mortar batteries had been in existence for no more than two weeks, while a large portion of the artillery personnel had been but recently transferred from the infantry ... and it is easy to realise that numbers of our men dreaded the effects of our own artillery to a greater extent than that of the enemy. Quite a number of casualties thus occurred, the most notable perhaps being the destruction of a party of the 8th Field Company Engineers who were engaged in cutting a sally port through their own parapet. The losses of the 8th Brigade in this respect were greater than those in other units ...

Ellis, himself a member of 8th Bde, who was perhaps not in the front line at Fromelles, wrote '*on General Tivey's front the casualties had been severe before the assault*', but does not detail them, and never mentions our 'shorts' doing damage. But Bean did, and also noted, '*the ammunition and bomb dump of 31st Bn was blown up and the battalion Commander, Lieut Col Toll and most of his signallers, messengers and medical staff of the battalion were wounded*'. The ordnance had taken 3 days to carry in and could not be replaced. In his own notes he gives the times: ... *HQ was blown out about noon, whole of signallers except one killed or wounded. Stretcher bearers and AMC details were knocked out 4.30 pm including medical officer ... The assault Coys were in position at 4.00 and throughout the next German barrage that went till near 5 pm, mixed in with our own artillery 'shorts'*. Curiously Ellis omits all such detail and there can be no doubt he had seen Lieut Col Toll's Report, which was damning:

> At 4.10 pm ... our artillery no effect on sector ... our shells landing in rear of enemy's parapets ... 4.30 pm our shells still falling in rear of enemy parapets ... their wires still intact ... at 4.30 wire in sector N10C43 to N10C75 badly damaged, also parapets. Enemy shelling lightly on front trenches but very heavy on support trenches. Reports were then received that our shells were dropping on our own parapets causing casualties and at 4.56 pm the request was made for our artillery to lift ... this was not carried out ... but became worse, shells falling behind the whole

ORDER OF BATTLE
8th Australian Brigade
(29th Victoria, 30th NSW,
31st Queensland & Victoria,
32nd SA/WA)
GOC: Brig. Gen. E Tivey
Bde Major: Major C S Davies (Leicester Regt)
SC: Capt. J F Wootten

32nd Bn (assaulting left)
CO: Lieut Col D W R Coghill *
2IC: Major J J Hughes (later POW)*
A Coy (left): Major J A Higgon †
C Coy (right):
D Coy (support): Capt. A R White
B Coy (reserve):

31st Bn (assaulting/right)
CO: Lieut Col F W Toll*
2IC: Major R R Hockley
A Coy (left): Major P A M Eckersley
B Coy (right): Capt. C Mills (later POW)*
C Coy (support):
D Coy (reserve): Capt. F Drayton

30th Bn (support)
CO: Lieut Col J W Clark
SC:
A Coy: Major R H Beardsmore*
B Coy: Capt. F Street
C Coy: Major M Purser
D Coy: Capt. W Cheeseman

29th Bn (reserve)
CO: Lieut Col A W Bennett
SC: 2IC Major H M Duigan
A Coy: Capt. K Mortimer †
B Coy:
C Coy:
D Coy:

8th MG Coy
CO: Capt. T R Marsden

8th Field Coy
CO: Lieut C P Tenbosch †
(then Major V A H Sturdee)

† Killed in Action. * Wounded. July 1916.

THE ENEMY'S FRONT SYSTEM
This unedited document of c. 5 July found in the 5th Division Artillery file reveals instantly the quality of the intelligence available and raises the questions of (a) why it was not used and (b) why it has been weeded out of the divisional headquarters file.

Report of Enemy's Defences: about Sugar Loaf.
Reference Sheet—36 SW 1 and 2

1. Front System (i). The enemy's front system forms a salient and is protected by a chain of strong points across the base of the triangle. These are:

(a) N 14 b 4 3. Not very strong and not known to be wired. Probably contains machine guns. Enemy working here on 8th June 1916.
(b) Ferme Delaporte. Very strong—and backed by earthworks at N 15 b 0.3 to N 15 b 4.4. Earthworks and farm wired and contain machine guns—vicinity much knocked about by artillery, but farm itself and earthworks appear to have escaped damage. Strong system of trenches run from farm to road junction N 15 b 4½ 8½.
(c) Ferme Delangré. Protected by earthworks to North and by strong point in NW corner of farm. Backed by very strong system of earthworks from road junction N 16 a 8½ 5½ to Hayem–Les Clochers road which are heavily wired and are nearly untouched by our artillery. Earthworks containing machine guns to west of Hayem Village form an additional line in rear. A strong point at Les Clochers flanks these two works. It contains machine guns—it is probably wired, though there is no information on the point. Aeroplane photos show it much knocked about by our artillery.

[continued opposite]

> frontage held by us, very heavy casualties eventuating, and at 5.10 pm a very urgent wire was sent ... 'Please ask Artillery to lift another 100 yards on sectors A, B and C. Shells falling behind our parapet. 5.00 pm: The situation was not improved ...

Toll then went on to describe the desperate situation of getting ready for the assault, lamenting '*our casualties ... were heavy and unfortunately very many must be accounted to our own artillery dropping short*'.

This long passage about the difficulties before the attack began is to reveal the shambles of planning and operation that the infantry had to endure for hours before facing the enemy. The problems thus created meant that much had to be reorganised. Already early on, two of the companies in the front line had been withdrawn due to shelling, but after lunch they were filtered back, Toll wounded in the head during the bombardment, now tried to organise the four waves for the attack, and found he had barely enough men for three, and whilst all were hopeful that the German wire was cut, they were at this stage unsure.

On the left of 8th Bde was the 60th British Brigade, and next to them the New Zealand Division rather thinly spread and facing the 20th BRIR sector, and who would offer continuous artillery support, stand to and as it turned out, provide much needed assistance with the wounded after the 8th Bde Dressing Station had been destroyed. The 60th Brigade of whom part was 1/6th Oxon and Bucks, had been for some weeks earlier in position opposite the Sugarloaf and were familiar with the area and the habits of the Bavarians. At this time the 2nd Australian Tunnellers were working on a huge mine—1200 lbs of ammonal—set near the enemy front line just beyond the flank. It was timed for 6 pm, and according to Bean designed to throw up a pile of earth that might hinder German machine gun fire. However, 1/6th Oxon and Bucks noted that after the explosion the German set up a parapet in front of Delangré Farm and were undeterred. Quite what the huge explosion did for the morale, let alone nerves, of the men of 32nd Bn only a few yards away is not mentioned in either the War Diaries of the 32nd or the 31st, next to them.

Waiting behind the 8th Bde infantry were the engineers and others who were, the moment after the assault began, to begin digging a fire trench and communication trench across No-Man's Land. The official time for the assault was 6 pm, but the 32nd left at 5.53 and the 31st at 5.58, perhaps to be ahead of the explosion. But Ellis makes a point of saying the assault and the explosion were *meant* to happen together.

The job of the 32nd Bn on the flank was by far the most difficult, protecting itself, advancing and at the same time blocking off the German line on its left so that the Germans could not come around behind them. This it would seem on the face of it was another blunder, that is not putting the battle experienced Toll on the left. With two inexperienced groups that with the best Commander would surely be the strongest. Each 8th Bde man, as those in 14th and 15th Bdes went forward with his rifle and bayonet, 120 rounds of ammunition, 2 grenades, 2 sandbags, and every third man had either a pick or shovel.

'*After many casualties ... finally reached the German front line*' wrote Toll. It would seem that the defenders were either dead, hiding or somewhere else and the Australians passed over the much ruined earthworks noting the complex of intact concrete lined dugouts and shelters. They had rounded up 35 prisoners, but had no men to spare to take them back to Australian lines, so they had to be guarded all night and when the 8th Bde withdrew in the morning, the prisoners went with them.

One of the major blunders of McCay now surfaced. Bean delicately describes it '*through inexperience*'. This is little comfort considering the ramifications of the decision not to garrison the German front line but to leave it and rush on. McCay gave specific orders not to consolidate the captured front line but to make for the support line seen on aerial photographs and turn this into a defensive position, ideally before dark. As they searched for the nonexistent support line the German machine guns at the Tadpole, Delangré Farm and de Mouquet Farm '*swept the whole field with their deadly traverse fire*'. It is difficult to understand why no special attention was paid to information such as *'The Enemy's Front System'* (see margin). All the machine gun posts were noted early on and been checked from the air. One has to wonder why such a document is not in the 5th Division HQ file, or in the 15th Bde file, and why all such intelligence is missing.

In this regard the ability to observe activity in the German held territory is dramatically revealed by an example quoted by Bean. '*At 7 pm an artillery observer reported that 150 of our infantry came out of Rouges Bancs farm and walked into hostile trenches ... They appeared to have men in dark uniforms, probably prisoners*'. If such detail could be observed in the heat of battle, clearly the Intelligence Summaries must have had a wealth of important observations.

We turn to Lieut Col Toll for the opening phase:

THE ENEMY'S FRONT SYSTEM (contd)

Front Line (ii). Strong wire entanglement on wooden posts 5 ft high visible behind Sugar Loaf.

(a) Machine Guns. The whole of the Sugar Loaf salient in N 8 d is well built and well furnished with machine guns, which have been located at N 14 b 1½ 8½, N 8 d 3½ 2, N 8 d 5½ 2, and N 8 d 7½ 1½. The last named is a strong point in front line. Machine guns have also been located at N 9 c 5 1, N 9 d 3 1, N 10 c 1½ 3 and in the maze of trenches in rear of the craters in N 10 c. This maze of trenches is strongly fortified. There is a strong series of works about Fme de Mouquet and the Tadpole containing machine guns, whence flanking fire could be brought to bear to South West.

(b) Trench Mortars. Located at: N 8 d 5½ 2, N 9 c 1 1, N 9 d 3½ 1½, N 9 d 9 1½, N 15 b 7 5½ (Rouges Bancs), N 11 a 3 5½ (Tadpole)

(c) The two communication trenches from Les Clochers NW to Front Line have been given overhead cover throughout.

2. Rear Line Defence

A very strong and heavily wired second line runs from Aubers–LeClercq Farm–Fme Dy Hoyon–Fromelles–Bernière Farm–Le Haut Quesnoy. The trench line and wire are virtually continuous, but the defence is contained in strong points. Of these, Leclerq Farm and Fme du Hoyon are very strong, organised for flank defence, and thickly wired. Machine Guns do not fire from these points but they contain many emplacements. Machine guns are said to have fired from Fromelles Church. Bernière Farm is another very strong point, and the gap thence to Fromelles is a mass of wire and trenches.

S B Pope, Captain for Brig. General, General Staff
2nd A & NZ Army Corps

> Unfortunately many officers were struck down in the early stage together with senior NCOs and in many instances were without leaders. Our wire was well cut and there was no difficulty in getting through. No-Man's Land was fairly easy to cross, although badly cut up by large craters and ditches full of water. No-Man's Land was swept mostly by MG fire. The enemy's first line was won and thoroughly cleared, many Germans were killed and prisoners taken. The dugouts were thoroughly searched by bombs. A temporary search was made for communication trenches but could not be found except in one instance. Only sufficient men were left behind to assist the Lewis gunners in establishing posts. The remainder swept on with the intention of capturing the second and third trenches in the first line system, but we went on and on but no trace could be found of same. It now appeared evident that the information supplied as to enemy defences and aerial photographs were incorrect and misleading. The ground was flat, covered with fairly long grass, the trenches shown on aerial photos were nothing but ditches full of water, along which were straight lines of trees.

But there is a case to be made that they had gone far too far and should have settled in the second line, and garrisoned the front line behind them and dug in. This way they would have had the shelter of the German positions and a safe rear. At best one could blame the short time allowed for planning, at worst the near total incompetence of HQ.

These 'misleading' photographs will be a recurring theme, or a convenient excuse for further incompetence at British and Australian HQs. As there is confirmation at the time of all three Australian brigades having seen the photographs, it cannot be blamed solely on the British, but we do not know exactly which aerial photographs were examined.

Lieut Col Sloan, however, in his history of 30th Bn, indicates that they were working from maps made from photographs and not the photographs themselves, and there are other casual remarks that could be taken to indicate while such people as Knyvett in 15th Bde Intelligence section may have viewed a photograph, the Commanders in the field were working with British Trench Maps not dissimilar to that on pages 38–39. This map '*corrected to 31.8.16*' does show other trench lines and the 'Kastenweg'.

The composite on pages 106–107 is made up of those photographs held by the Australian War Memorial, and while some are from October 1916, some during the battle, none are before the battle. According to Bean the general view on page 108, 'lent' to the AWM by McCay was before the battle, but this may not be so. However if that was the photograph the second and third line defences were identified in, then there can be no surprise about the mistakes made. But supposing the photographs that they worked from were at least as good as

At the top, men of 54th Bn advancing over open country, and lower down men of 31st Bn in a trench. Fromelles is about 1500 yards to the left, the German front line 300 yards to the right. AWM J00278

those taken during the battle, then other questions have to be asked, because everything is clearly visible.

Of the photographs in the composite the fifth from the left, for this part of the story is a vital piece of evidence. When Bean reproduced part of this in his photographic volume he also supplied a key, identifying men of the 31st and 54th Bns then in ditches behind the German front line, saying the photograph was taken about 6 pm. The photographic volume was published in 1923 well before Bean had researched Fromelles, which could account for this estimate. In his Volume III Bean reproduced others which show the trenches dug across No-Man's Land on the night of 19/20 July, so are thus post-battle photographs. It is reasonable to suppose that the Intelligence Summaries prior to the battle would have had some comment on the second and third line because they were *the* objectives of the attack and every effort should have been made to establish that they were suitable objectives. But as the battle was merely a '*pretence*', a '*ruse*', a '*diversion*', as it was variously described at the time, was real work not done in case it might expose the absence of the objectives and thus expose it all as a 'suicide mission'? Is this why the Intelligence Summaries are missing?

However, to enshrine this slice of Australian history so to speak, enlarged and fine screen reproductions of this split-second are given here. The diggers of 14th Bde, their shadows long in the late afternoon summer sun are crossing No-Man's Land, whilst opposite, others, probably of 54th and 31st Bn, are already in ditches some 300 yards behind the German front line. So it might be nearer 6.30 pm.

The men of the 31st and 32nd had reached similar positions by 6.30 pm and decided to dig in: but it was near impossible, they had insufficient sand bags, Capt. White of 32nd confessing that the ditch had '*1 to 2 feet of mud and slush in the bottom. The soil was very 'gluey' and most difficult to work*'. According to Toll it was not until about an hour later contact was established between the two, and only after that was contact with 54th Bn on the right established, and later with 55th Bn on their right. So for a moment in the battle there was a sort of Australian line, an extraordinary success considering the situation. Toll at this time sent a pigeon back with the message that, '*Four waves well over 200 yards beyond enemy's parapets, no enemy works found yet, so am digging in*'. All the men '*were rallied and opened out and instructed to dig in about 250 yards from the enemy's front line*'.

As that was being done Toll and his staff went on some 350 to 400 yards until they were 150 yards from '*What appeared to*

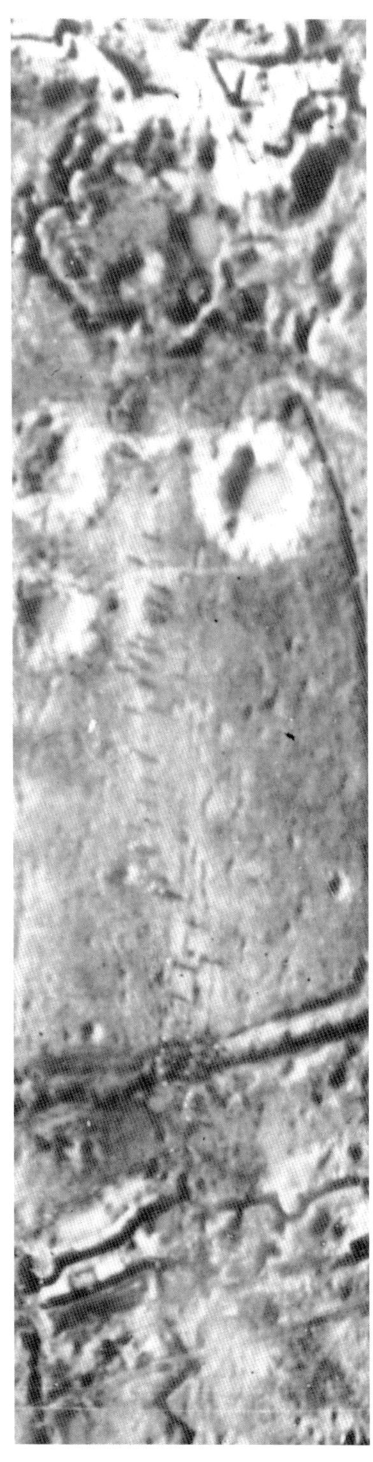

Men of 14th Bde crossing No-Man's Land: the Australian front line is at the top of the picture, the German at the foot. AWM J00278

Lieut Col F W TOLL
Frederick William Toll was born in Bowen, Queensland, 18 January 1872. In 1888 while at Brisbane Grammar he joined the cadets and four years later he had a commission in the Kennedy Regiment. He became an accountant and married in 1894: there was a son and daughter from the marriage. In 1897 Toll was Captain and two years later volunteered for service in South Africa. While he went as a special service officer in 2nd Queensland Contingent, once there he joined the British Army. He returned to Brisbane in 1901, perhaps due to the death of his wife. He returned to South Africa as 2IC 5th Queensland Contingent now as a Major. He was captured by the Boers just before the end of the war. He had been MID and was awarded the Queen's South Africa medal (with 5 clasps) and the King's Medal (with 2 clasps).

Toll married again in 1904, managed a saw mill, and on 7 Nov 1914 enlisted again. He served first in the Rabaul Campaign before joining 8th Bde and getting command of 31st Bn. Toll led them at Fromelles, receiving the DSO. Later he received a bar to the DSO. He was badly wounded and gassed at Polygon Wood, so moved to London January 1918 and served with Administrative HQ. In December 1917 Bean had met up with Toll and in his notes recorded this opinion:

'[he] was another man who was in the thick of it at Fromelles and Ypres, but he is full of consciousness of it – can't help telling you how he walked up and down the parapet at Fromelles after the men retired, in full sight of the Germans. He must be a brave man and an aggressive hard fighting one also, but he is not a type that attracts one as Norman Marshall [60th Bn] does.'

An accomplished sportsman and athlete, Toll was a foundation member of the RSSILA. His health broke in 1930, but he continued to work and was appointed MBE in 1939. He died on 6 Nov 1955 at Brisbane, aged 83.

be a strong and important enemy position. It was protected in front by high heavy barbed wire entanglements some five feet high and would have been a difficult position to storm and was intact from our own gunfire'. It was most probably a fortified position called Grashof. The Australian line by now was under fire from the Germans on three sides and '*also from our own artillery, as it was impossible to post them as to our position*'. The line was under command of Major Eckersley and Toll noted that '*the men were cheerful and worked willingly*', but the woeful scarcity of Officers and NCOs soon made it necessary to pull back. So at 7.14 pm a pigeon flew off bearing this sad message:

> No works to hold, so fell back to enemy first line. Send ammunition across urgently. Machine guns and crews required. Am strengthening parados: will require entrenching tools, picks, shovels, sandbags. Many casualties but cannot estimate until first count after reorganizing.

The 32nd had reached the same decision but had the advantage of a phone line, and so when they asked for artillery assistance, they got it. They also got instructions after asking for reinforcements, that '*the trenches were to be held at all costs*'. The supplies of sandbags and tools were brought forward via the newly dug sap.

Since the moment the assault began the 8th Field Coy Engineers, with others, began digging this trench across No-Man's Land. Lieut Tenbosch, the engineer in charge, had been killed at the outset and 36 others of this little group were also casualties. They worked all night and just before first light had only 25 yards to go—the trench being 175 yards long over all, the diggers had it 6 ft deep at the Australian end and 3 ft 6 inches at the German wire. But then the Germans saw what was happening and concentrated fire on it, and in Ellis' words it became '*blocked with dead and further work was impossible*'.

Apart from this trench there was another further left, beyond 8th Bde's front which according to Bean was *'not a communication trench but part of the new front line'*. This seems to have been McCay's idea, his Report is the only place it is mentioned at the time, and is another instance of his disregard of Corps orders. How 'ad hoc' it was we shall never know for sure, but as the area was beyond 8th Bde's jurisdiction the Australian wire had not been cut in readiness the previous night. When the hapless diggers got through this obstacle a Sgt Garland was equipped with a signpost to plant on the German parapet so that the men digging the new front line would not lose direction.

Before he got to his objective Garland was shot dead, and then systematically over the next hours so were most of the others involved in this hare-brain scheme. Ellis gave it a sentence whereas Bean spent a page describing it but carefully avoided any comment on the basic idea and the resultant casualties.

Around 8.30 the Germans counter-attacked. Their own account of this clearly acknowledges the first failure and the high losses, but then when totally dark they had more success: doubtless because they knew their own lines well. After almost three hours at 8.50 pm Toll and Coghill, now desperately short of men pleaded for reinforcements and '*authority was granted for the use of half of 30th Bn*'.

Whether or not this ever happened was challenged in 1935 by then Lieut Col M Purser, who in 1916 was Major and leading C Coy of 30th Bn. He noted that Ellis wrote '*that a company of 29th Bn was sent up to carry stores, and that C and D Coys of 30th Bn were ordered to reinforce the attack*'. To this Purser countered:

> I distinctly remember a company of 29th Bn under Capt Mortimer (who was killed) being sent to reinforce (not to carry stores, although, at my request they took extra ammunition with them), but have no recollection of any of the companies of 30th Bn being ordered to reinforce. C Coy certainly was not, and in its case prompt fulfilment of such an order would have been impossible as the men were in small carrying parties going and coming across No-Man's Land ... they had been reduced in numbers to little more than a platoon at the time Capt Mortimer's company reinforced.

If Purser's recollection was correct, it explains much of the forthcoming chaos. Earlier, the 8th MG Coy under Capt. Marsden had got a number of guns across, at a terrible cost, and was as darkness fell providing some cover for the infantry. Aware that their own men were not there or vulnerable, the German artillery deluged the sector.

Toll had been asked to report on the sections of enemy trenches held so that the artillery could bombard the rest. The message concluded '*Give exact boundaries for artillery guidance. The portions captured will be held onto*'. One has to wonder what Toll's private thoughts were on the possibility of the artillery succeeding in such a task, but publicly his message was confident, '*have captured enemy's first line opposite Brigade Sector but doubtful as to exact location*'. Five minutes later perhaps fearful of the bombardment, he sent: '*Uncertain as to exact area captured, have not seen 32nd. 54th on my right ... have no communications except telephone to Col Cass (54th)*'.

FROM WHAT I HEARD

One would almost have believed that the enemy knew the exact moment that all the units were in position, for when our trenches were packed with men his artillery and machine guns activity increased considerably ... we in the 300 yd line suffered many casualties. One of them was my batman (Pte Charlie Dodds) and I suppose I thereupon became one of the most helpless being in the war—an officer without a batman.

Moving along the communication trench—Cellar Farm Avenue—we found it blown in near its junction with Mine Avenue, damage which was later in the night repaired by 5th Pioneer Bn. This necessitated climbing out of the trench and passing the obstruction in the open under very heavy artillery and machine gun fire, from which we suffered additional casualties.

From the front line which in this sector consisted of sandbag breast works, my platoons went across No-Man's Land at short intervals with SAA and bombs. Capt. B A Wark (2IC) accompanying the first platoon to supervise the establishment of a dump. It was not long before ... Capt. Wark was wounded, and that two of my platoon commanders, Lieuts A Mitchell and J Parker had been killed ... While standing near a front line ammunition dump, I was temporarily dazed by a shell burst ... and signal man Sgt Facey, seeing I was a bit shaky, gave me a nip of rum. I having forgotten (I know this is hard to believe, Diggers, but it is nevertheless true!) that in my pocket I had a flask filled from a bottle given me by Madame just before we left billets.

A runner, Pte W Barrett, suggested I should change places with him ... I was liable to be hit where I was sitting. I declined, as the suggested change would place him in a dangerous situation, to which he replied that it would be better for him to be hit than me, as my life was the more valuable ... the following day Barrett had shown conspicuous bravery throughout the fight, and from my own knowledge and from what I heard, he certainly earned the DCM he was awarded.

—Lieut Col M Purser, 30th Bn
Reveille, 1 July, 1935

The rear of front line breastworks at Fleurbaix early 1916.

THE JOB ENTAILED HARD WORK

The breastworks were really like castle walls built of sandbags running along the moat which was No-Man's Land. The problem of infantry attacking from behind such fortifications meant that they presented an easy target as they scrambled over the wall to get into No-Man's Land. To let them back gaps had to be made: so the PBI (poor bloody infantry) were not well catered for. Twenty years after the battle, writing in *Reveille*, Lieut W Smith of 53rd Bn, who had been a sapper in 14th Field Coy at Fromelles, recalled the difficulties:

Scaling ladders were placed in each bay to enable our boys to climb over our breastwork, which was 9 to 10 ft high ... the majority of the men were new troops ... awaiting the moment when they would mount the parapet and advance to what, for many of them, meant certain death: and yet they passed each order along the line more correctly than they would have done on parade.

Smith's squad began with having to cut through the breastwork where the 14th Bde communication trench was to start *'to cut through ... the men had to work at the top of the parapet, which was frequently swept by machine gun fire, and as the breastwork was some 10 ft high and about 14 ft thick at the bottom, the job entailed hard work ...'* While they were engaged in this the Germans turned a searchlight on them so that their machine guns might do positive damage.

SOMETHING TO DO

In one of the letters to Bean from a correspondent, this story: *'A tall man came to Allen shaking all over with shell shock and said, 'I'm not afraid, give me something to do!' Allen gave him an ammunition box and he took it on. A Coy was largely sailors, an overflow from the Naval Bridging Team.'*

It should be no surprise that when the artillery recommenced its activity, despite Toll's careful replies, their shells were still falling on the Australians. To alleviate this McCay *'ordered both the left and centre of field artillery to increase their range by 200 yards'*. But complaints were still made, and the range extended by 500 yards. *'By 8.15'*, Bean wrote rather grimly, *'it was noted that the complaints of short shooting had, for the time being, ceased; but the artillery could now give little assistance'*.

Such machine guns that survived were now ordered back across No-Man's Land and the situation became desperate. The Germans had reformed and moved on the flanks of the beleaguered survivors. Toll's messages assumed a more bewildered tone. At 8.55 pm:

> Thick curtain of smoke in front, cannot observe. Strengthening parados of first captured enemy's line. Battalion broken up, reorganization at present impossible. Send as many stretcher bearers as possible. Ammunition required: also picks, shovels, sand bags and duck boards.

With great tenacity Toll kept sending back messages—by runners (in particular Pte D O'Connor 460, who made the journey three times) asking especially for a telephone wire. He was somewhat heartened when a small party of 29th Bn *'no more than 2 platoons'* got through and as he put it *'were a welcome and useful addition to our small garrison'*. Toll estimated that there were about 200 men of his Bn together and others mixed up with the 32nd and 54th, out on the line.

The authorisation of the use of half of 30th Bn is mentioned by McCay in his Report after the battle, but in the Divisional files there is no record of request to or approval by Corps Commander Haking. Whereas there is a record about an hour later of Elliott's request and granting his use of 58th Bn. Perhaps due to constant pleading by Tivey as he watched his beloved brigade butchered, granting him reinforcements was irresistible, even if just to shut him up. Had anybody told Tivey that many of his men had already made their own decision and joined the garrison, other questions would have been asked. But perhaps Tivey, like McCay, had no real idea of what was going on, and how to bring some order to the chaos. Unless McCay had been misled by Tivey he would have known that 8th Bde could not hold on: they simply did not have the numbers to do so. And at a time like this McCay with all his well documented character defects was unlikely to listen carefully or act rationally. Under this appalling handicap the heroes of Fromelles like Lieut Col Toll kept going.

Toll did not know until later that the smoke to which he had referred came from the 8th Bde and 14th Bde ammunition dumps which were on fire. But he was told that reinforcements, tools, ammunition and machine guns were going forward. Although a decision had been taken that 8th Bde was to hold on regardless at 9.40, the plight of the '*small garrison*' was clearly given in this message:

> Front line cannot be held unless strong reinforcements are sent. Enemy's machine gunners are creeping up. No star shells. The artillery is not giving support. Sand bags required in thousands. Men bringing sand bags are being wounded in the back. Water urgently required.

Curiously this message and all the others from 31st Bn, back to the one of 8.55 about 'curtain of smoke' were all marked into Division HQ at 10.20. The messages from 32nd Bn are all together and timed at 10.10. In amongst all this is a message from Major D M King who '*represented the divisional staff in the 8th Bde sector*', timed at 10.55:

> Have been round old line. 32nd Bn require one company reinforcements due to casualties. 30th and 31st doing well. A well-officered fatigue party of about 30 required to take over ammunition, sand bags and bombs—the last is urgent. Send motor car to Tivey's Headquarters to wait for me. Must see you.

Bean published that message, less the final lines about the car and seeing McCay. Bean notes that King was bringing the benefit of his Gallipoli experience to the '*previously untried staff of 8th Bde*'. Why was there a special watching brief over Tivey? King's words to McCay, '*must see you*' open up the imagination to all sorts of possibilities. King was a full-time soldier and could be expected to bring some realistic judgements to the situation. It is highly unlikely that he did not see the real

WHY HAD MEN BEEN WASTED?
The general deceit of the operation disturbed Major M Purser, 30th Bn. In 1935 he wrote:

> *In Cellar Farm Avenue I met General Tivey on his way to the front line. His lip showed a spot of blood, as though he had been biting it, and he remarked to me that it had been a 'great fight'. It had, but it gave us food for thought, when we were told later, that it was never intended to hold the line attacked. If that were so, why had men been wasted in digging fire and communication trenches, and why were all carrying parties ordered to leave their emergency rations on the other side of No-Man's Land, with the object of forming the nucleus of a ration dump for those who were to hold the new line?*

No wonder Purser felt let down. When he brought his C Company together at Croix Blanche on the 20 July, he was the only officer out of 6 who was neither killed or wounded, and 30 ORs survived from the 181 who went out. He wrote of the last meal they had together—*A gift from the boys*—page 96—published 20 years after the battle and a poignant reminder of the depth of the Fromelles experience.

... STOOD APART
Even the uniform stood apart. The Australians' was of pure wool, dusty grey in colour and with vest and useful pockets. A bush hat, brim curled in a variety of ways and with home town badges fastened to it, set the whole thing off.

—Denis Winter
Death's Men (1978)

COVERED IN BLOOD
One man who was near Toll at the end, and was taken prisoner, later noted: '*Col Toll's head was covered in blood. I don't know how he got back to our lines.*'

IN NO WAY RESPONSIBLE

General Tivey hurried down on hearing of the retirement, and could not restrain his tears when he saw the plight of his beloved men, it is sufficient to say that General Tivey was in no way responsible for the ill-advised attack. The four trenches that were dug out into NML were also full of dead and wounded.

—Pte Joseph H Case
3037 2nd Pioneer Bn.

SEVEREST TEST

Men who had fought on Gallipoli from the Landing to the Evacuation, admitted freely that Fromelles was the severest test they had seen.

—H R Williams, 56th Bn
The Gallant Company (1933)

THEY HUNG ON

It was noted in the 32nd Bn War Diary of 21 July *'Lieut Col D W R Coghill, relinquished command of Bn. Capt A R White acting in command.* Ellis noted, without comment, that *'Major R H Beardsmore succeeded Lieut Col Coghill'.*

Capt White, a 30 year old draughtsman from West Australia, prepared the Bn Report. It was handwritten, two and a half pages and compared to Toll's was a gross insult to the battalion. Not a single name is given, not a single heroic deed noted, and comment is superficial beyond belief. All of which must have something to do with the shamefully short honours list of 32nd Bn. For the battalion with the second highest losses, 90 taken prisoner, 8 Officers dead, at least 15 wounded, one has to wonder why. Tivey's tidy little Report did no better, for the 32nd or any of his other battalions. Half of all he wrote about the 32nd was:

They hung on to their positions until the counter attack of the enemy rolled up their left flank. The Battalion when it retired only numbered some 200 men.

Coghill returned to Australia 23 May 1917 and died a little over five years later when he was 51.

danger of the collapse of the 8th Bde, but more dangerous was the now lightly held Australian line. Quite who would have come to the rescue if the Germans overran the line has never been discussed. We already know one company of 30th Bn is engaged in digging '*the new front line*' and another company has already become reinforcements when, as Bean described it, it became '*absorbed into the struggle in spite of orders to the contrary*'.

We know that a portion of 29th carrying much needed supplies over No-Man's Land had joined Toll's garrison. Thus probably at most two companies of 29th were left to hold the 8th Bde line. The ammunition dump was burning, the casualty station had been blown up and the communication trench—the one safe way back for the heroes holding the line—was unusable. Tivey was clearly well out of his depth, and Bean, apropos nothing at all, slips in this remark, that there was '*a dangerous vagueness as to the steps to be taken*'. And ahead was the '*pitch dark night*' as the historian of the 21st BRIR opposite described it.

Having examined in some detail the passage of Lieut Col Toll and the 31st Bn through the first hours, we turn to Lieut Col Coghill and the 32nd, who had the most difficult job. Whilst we have a good record of the deeds of 31st Bn, thanks to Reports by Toll and others, what happened to the 32nd is much less clear. The Battle Report was by Capt. A R White *'for the CO of 32nd Bn'* and of little use (see margin *They Hung On*), and due to the casualties including a large number taken prisoner, other information seems to have been very scarce. Bean relied a good deal on White and there are some large grey areas in the story.

At the start Major Higgon, an officer of the British Regular Army (Pembroke Yeomanry) and now in the AIF, led A Coy and was shot down in the first minute. Ellis remembered him being shot dead, Bean said he died of wounds later, confirmed perhaps by the date on his headstone, 20 July: and this is typical of the variance in information. Who led C Coy, and then B and D, which formed the 3rd and 4th waves, was not stated. This is important because it would have given an idea of who survived the crossing and thus what officer strength the 32nd had as they battled on. It is only much later that Ellis notes that before dawn only Capt. White and Capt. Geddes (D Coy) who with Coghill, were unwounded:

> ... the company Commanders and their seconds in command of the other three companies were all either killed or wounded and with them most of their subalterns.

We know that Major Hughes 2IC of the Bn was active behind the German lines for a while before being wounded and taken prisoner, but where was Lieut Col Coghill? Ellis hardly mentions him, and Bean's three mentions are praiseworthy implying that Coghill was quite a hero. He notes that Coghill once crawled back across No-Man's Land to get some message through, and during the night around 10 pm, he was right in the thick of it. '*Despite his age*' wrote Bean forgetting that Coghill was only a year older than Toll, he '*struggled through the mud around almost the whole front of the brigade, regarded apprehensively the formidable enemy position of Ferme Delangré immediately beyond his left*'.

Coghill reported that the fortified hulk dominated the position, and others reported hearing German Officers and NCOs shouting orders to reinforcements who had rallied there. After this Bean noted another exploit of Coghill's, trying to connect with the 31st Bn. He then disappears: he was not on the wounded or missing list, and White takes over and gives no information.

The loss of Coghill, or more accurately the change of command, might explain the lack of information about the sizeable, solidly constructed communication trench that the Germans built to the west of the road that ran from the front line past Delangré Farm. The Germans called it 'Kastenweg', literally 'chest way', because it was walled with earth filled ammunition chests. As will be seen in the German accounts this was an important element in their defence strategy. In this regard Bean made this note which seems to undermine the importance of photographic evidence versus the official map:

> This (Kastenweg) was easily discernible in the aeroplane photographs from which the British trench maps were drawn, and could have been discovered, had there been time for close study, even by the inexperienced staff of the 5th Australian Division; but the British general staff had been slow to develop specialist instruction in the interpretation of air-photographs, and the abandoned trenches had consequently been shown on the map as if they were part of the enemy's main occupied system.

Reproduced in the margin is part of the Kastenweg—no water filled ditch, that is certain. Another piece of evidence that it was maps, not photographs, that McCay had used? The attempts of various 8th Bde officers and men to clear the 'Kastenweg' are well documented, but it caused many heavy losses and in the end was not occupied because the Germans had it covered from every angle. Typical of these attempts was one by Capt. F L Krinks of 30th Bn who came over with a carrying party and

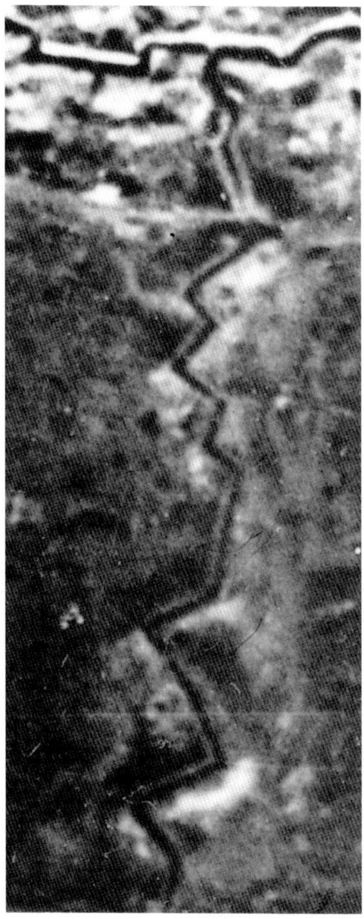

The Kastenweg (Chest Way) shown here much enlarged from a photograph of 10 October 1916: it connects with the German front line at the top of the picture.
AWM J3376

WHAT A JOB

One veteran of Fromelles remembered the Trench Police without any bitterness, but with the understanding of how terrible it was, saying simply, '*somebody had to do it*.'

These were the men who ordered, forced, coerced, shamed, helped or pushed timid, terrified, bewildered men over the top or through the sally ports into the battle. '*What a job*,' he reflected, '*but it was the only way lots of us got started.*'

For the record: CO of 5th Div. Police was Major E J F Langley.

KRINKS' ELEVEN

Frank Leslie Krinks was born in Newtown, NSW, 1 June 1894 and was a furniture warehouseman living in Hurstville when he enlisted. He was described by Bean as a '*hardened and determined young officer*', and as a Captain in 30th Bn, reached the German lines leading a carrying party. He soon saw the predicament of the 32nd Bn and after trying to block off the Kastenweg, set up his men as snipers in nearby shell holes while he went back to the Australian lines to ask Lieut Col Clark, CO of 30th, for two Lewis guns. These, with crews, he took back to the shell holes and harassed the enemy all night as they sought to clear Kastenweg to aid their counter attack. For the next part of the story our only source is Bean. Curiously in the 30th Bn history Bean's version is almost exactly transcribed and there is not a single new word or phrase about the initiative or bravery Krinks showed, from the compiler of the history, Lieut Col Sloan. And although an Officer, Ellis does not mention him, but then Ellis' sanitised history could hardly cope with the conclusion of this story.

Being out on their own, Krinks' party of eleven were at dawn both unidentified by the Germans and forgotten by the Australians. Thus they found themselves behind the Germans and cut off. After discussion they decided to run for it, this necessitating jumping over two trenches filled with Germans, and then racing across No-Man's Land. They elected to go as a group so that if anything happened to any of their number, the others could do something about it. At the first trench two were seized. The other nine stopped and turned on the Germans, secured their comrades and then all escaped into No-Man's Land, but two of the party once clear of the wire fell, one shot, the other injured. As soon as it was dusk on 20 July Krinks and three others with a stretcher went out for the two, whom they found and brought in. As they approached the 8th Bde lines a sentry fired a single shot and killed two of the stretcher bearers.

with some men entered the Kastenweg and attempted to block it off by pulling down some of the ammunition boxes. Well aimed German grenades drove them out and Krinks set up snipers in shell holes to keep the Germans from advancing while he went all the way back to the Australian line to get two Lewis guns which he now returned with, via part of the Kastenweg, and set them up in the shell holes. All through the night Krinks and his party harassed the enemy in their attempt to use the Kastenweg and with some success (see page 184). How Krinks' Fromelles finished is described in the margin: *Krinks' Eleven*, and has to be one of the saddest stories of the battle.

Considering the closeness of the 8th Bde, a quality that Tivey had nurtured since its creation, it was not surprising that it would appear everybody wanted to help get supplies across to Toll and Coghill. The alarming proof of this is the Roll of Prisoners taken (see page 329–32), the 29th who in theory should not have left the Australian lines losing as many as the 31st who were in the thick of it all the time.

Lieut Col Clark of 30th who had been sending carrying parties over was confronted with the reality at 10.10 when he noted:

> All my men who have gone forward with ammunition have not returned. I have not even one section left.

It was fairly certain Clark could not have stopped the volunteers anyway. A typical excuse was put forward by Sgt H H Stevenson 1213, 30th Bn:

> We did not mind going forward with our load, and thus face enemy fire, but the thought of being hit in the back on the return journey was too much for most of us, hence our inclination to remain with the fighting troops.

The Germans had by now also made No-Man's Land an artillery target so as to stop supplies and withdrawal, meaning that while Toll's group was in the front German trenches, Coghill's group was almost 100 yards further out, under the shadow so to speak, of Delangré Farm. Late orders had excluded this from the objectives of the attack. Bean suggests this order may not have got through to the battalion commanders. Higher up however there was much confusion. McCay, we are told, had '*been given to understand that it was in Australian hands*' and thus did not shell it early on. However, at 10.30 when the fact that the Australians were not in possession was confirmed, McCay gave orders for it to be heavily shelled: but it was too late now to be of any real assistance to 32nd Bn. They were badly positioned in the rear of the German line, so that there were empty German trenches behind them. McCay as already noted, had not provided a garrison there. But the Germans, not fully aware of the advantage they had, edged forward.

As it neared midnight and the calls for reinforcements and supplies grew more shrill, Lieut Col Clark, '*sent forward the whole of the two companies of the 29th Bn which had been given to him to garrison the old Australian front*'.

At 11.35 he reported:

> I have now no men left at all. There was no other option.

Around 2.15 am the Germans began to assemble at the Delangré Farm. As we now know, due to their heavy losses the 21st BRIR was being reinforced by 104th Saxon Regiment and it must have been this that gave them the energy and edge for the next phase. It was only a matter of time. The 32nd was totally surrounded but not aware of this. Capt Mortimer of 29th who had noted that the Germans were now between this group and the German front line went to the Kastenweg, perhaps to see if that was a way out. He was never seen again. Krinks and his gallant band were holding on, but separated from the main group and thus able later to escape. '*Unsupervised parties began to break back across No-Man's Land, and the sector was rapidly emptied*', but apart from the dead left behind, some 182 were taken prisoner, many badly wounded. Despite the gravity of it all, Tivey telephoned McCay to ask '*What instructions should be sent to the Bde—to hold on ... or withdraw?*'. The men had already made up their own minds, as they had earlier on to go the other way. Lieut Col Toll and his party not being surrounded, with some loss, made it back to the Australian lines, but this withdrawal left 55th Bn very open and bringing into prominence the deeds of Capt. Gibbins, one of the other heroes of Fromelles.

Ellis, not a man to hand out compliments, however had to say something about Toll:

> Lieut Col Toll was the last to leave the enemy trench and he strode back contemptuously through the enemy fire, maintaining to the end of the action the soldierly bearing and disregard of personal safety that had characterised his conduct throughout the operation.

Another aspect of the 8th Bde *esprit de corps* Ellis had to comment on was Tivey, who while not the character that Elliott was, did have a strong personal following:

> It is no wonder that General Tivey, hurrying to the front line at the first moment he could be spared from Bde HQ, stood for a moment stricken silent with grief at the spectacle he saw. Above all other things he was

Lieut Col J W CLARK

Born in Newcastle, NSW, 7 Sept 1877, James William Clark became a Lieut Col in 1914, and he was appointed to command 30th Bn on 22 July 1915. In September 1916 he had command of 8th Bde in Tivey's absence, being the senior Colonel. He received DSO at beginning of 1917, again taking Bde command at that time, and in October. He was in command of 30th Bn for Morlancourt in July 1918, but then left the front line to head a training Bde. After the war as a shipping merchant, he lived in and near Sydney. He was living at Terrigal when he died 8 Feb 1958.

THE WORST INSTRUMENT

A small item perhaps, but to S K Donnan in the Engineers as important as a good rifle. He complained strongly about the Stanley Level's technical design, and then about it being polished.

When our chaps got into the German trenches the latter turned on the waterworks from somewhere in the rise behind their line, and flooded them out. Subsequently I was given a job of running lines of levels along the drains among our first and second lines and support trenches. I was issued with a Stanley Level to do the job with. It was absolutely the worst instrument that could have been chosen for the job ... Instead of being dull and inconspicuous it was burnished bright. Working on one side of the valley with the Germans on the other I think I must have been taken by them as someone trying to send a message by heliograph, otherwise I wouldn't have been here today. Just what purpose the levels were for I am unable to say, but I hope it was a useful and substantial one.

MEN OF 53RD BN

A group of photographs from Charles Henry Lorking of Park Dairy, Wentworth Falls, NSW, attracted Bean's attention and he wrote to him.

On 7 July, 1922, Lorking, who had a DCM from a later action, replied,

... regarding the photographs of the bombardment of the German

(contd next page)

MEN OF 53RD BN (contd)
trenches ten minutes before the commencement of the attack. I had to get out into No-Man's Land to secure it. Firstly for fear of an officer seeing me with a camera, secondly because the parapet was swept with very accurate machine gun fire from 'Parapet Joe', a name given to the German machine gunner owing to his accuracy if a head showed above the parapet. It was taken about 5.30. I think we hopped over at 13 minutes to six. I took it myself with one or two others which you returned.

Lorking's more famous photographs were those of Section 2, A Coy 53rd Bn during the last rest and smoke before donning equipment. Bean recorded, that of the group of eight, only three came out of the action alive and all were wounded.

Shortly after the first publication of this book, the writer was contacted by the son of Pte Frederick Turvey 4923 53rd Bn to say that it was his father smoking the cigarette in the photograph on the left, adding that he never stopped smoking.

AWM A03042 and H16396

characterised by a loving attachment to his men, and he was deeply moved as he picked his way carefully through the front line among the bodies of the men he had loved so well.

But Bean concluded his treatment of 8th Brigade with a melancholy paragraph:

> The mere sight of men of their own side running towards the rear always came as a rude and hateful shock to those in neighbouring sectors. They could not realise that the men they saw running were not necessarily panic-stricken, but sometimes included, as on this occasion, troops who rather than submit to capture, were making a desperate attempt to regain their own lines.

It was, of course, impossible for Bean to include in his account Cass' description of 8th Bde in retreat, but with several awards to members of the 14th Bde being given for work on helping the retreating 8th, and letters and diaries describing it, what Cass said, it would seem, was the perfect description:

> like a crowd running across a field at the end of a football match.

Meanwhile with the approach of dawn McCay went to Haking at Sailly and at 5 am the conference began. With the sure knowledge that 8th Bde was finished, that 15th Bde had got nowhere, and 14th Bde isolated in the middle had to be withdrawn, the messages began to go out at 5.15.

Only the 14th Australian Brigade, in the centre position of the Australian line could be described as being anywhere near successful in the Battle of Fromelles. They did most of what they were asked, and as their leader reminded Bean rather bitterly after the battle '*we were really the only brigade who didn't come back 'til we were told to*'. This confident tone of Colonel H Pope was typical of the whole Brigade whose toughness was perhaps best symbolised by the action of Sgt C H Lorking 3373a, 53rd Bn. Fifteen minutes before the battle began, dodging officers, he took photographs of his cobbers in the trench, the view over the sandbags and from No-Man's Land, tucked the camera in his pocket, survived the next twelve hours and then the rest of the war.

No-Man's Land in front of 14th Bde was 250 yards at its widest and their front was from near where the river Laies crossed the Australian line to Brompton Road. Running NW to SE across No-Man's Land was what remained of rue Delvas, the northern portion of this road ran back deep into 5th Divisional territory whereas that south of No-Man's Land was part of the road directly to Fromelles. It could be no surprise then that given such an accessible route the Germans had considerably fortified their positions beside the road, and the area to the east which was not within the range of enfilade fire from the Sugarloaf.

The 14th Bde Commander had been a Lieut-Col in West Australia from 1908 and led 16th Bn at the Gallipoli landing with some distinction. There seems to be no doubt that Col H Pope was a capable and imaginative leader of men. Opinions of those who knew what he did at Anzac were full of unqualified praise. Since McCay fired Irving after the Desert March, Pope had been in charge and he retained all the battalion COs he inherited, three of whom were decorated men from the Gallipoli Campaign.

For the attack it was designated that on the left would be 54th Bn under Lieut Col W E H Cass, and on the right 53rd Bn under Lieut Col I B Norris.

In support would be 55th Bn under Lieut Col D McF McConaghy, whilst in reserve was 56th Bn under Lt Col A H Scott. All battalions had been raised in NSW and about 25% were '*well-seasoned men*' to use Bean's phrase, and the majority of the Officers and NCOs were at Anzac.

ORDER OF BATTLE
14th Australian Brigade (all NSW)
GOC: Col H Pope
Bde Major: Major N K Charteris (Royal Scots)
SC: Capt. G A Street

54th Bn (assaulting/left)
CO: Lieut Col W E H Cass *
2IC: Major R Harrison †
then Major R O Cowey
Adj: Capt. M J Lowe
A Coy (left): Capt. C S Lecky *
B Coy (right): Lieut A O Thompson *
C Coy (support): Capt. J Hansen *
D Coy (reserve): Capt. H Taylor †
*See below

53rd Bn (assaulting/right)
CO: Lieut Col I B Norris †
2IC: Major O M Croshaw
SC:
Adj: Lieut H L Moffitt †
A Coy (left): Capt. D Thomson †
B Coy (right): Capt. J J Murray
C Coy (support): Major V H B Sampson †
D Coy (reserve): Capt. C Arblaster †

55th Bn (support)
CO: Lieut Col D McF McConaghy
2IC:
Adj: Capt. P W Woods
A Coy: Capt. N Gibbins †
B Coy:
C Coy:
D Coy:

56th Bn (reserve)
CO: Lieut Col A H Scott
2IC:
SC:
A Coy: Capt. W R Sheen
B Coy: Capt. H A Roberts
C Coy: Capt. C R Lucas
D Coy: Capt. F Fanning

14th MG Coy
CO: Lieut C M Spier *
then Capt. W T Dick

14th Field Coy
CO: Major H Bachtold

† Killed in Action. * Wounded. July 1916.

*54th Bn A Coy: CO Capt. H Taylor, mortally wounded before attack. Coy taken over by Lecky also wounded before attack. Lieut H R Lovejoy led A Coy. B Coy: Hansen wounded before attack, led by Thompson. C Coy: Major R D Holman wounded before attack, Lieut A H Hirst took over command. D Coy: Capt. B Jack wounded in No-Man's Land. Lieut A G Morris led them over.
This information, courtesy of Ross St Claire, updates the Order of Battle that the 54th Bn originally had, and gives some detail to the losses noted on p.145.

Lieut Col W E H CASS
Walter Edmund Hutchinson Cass was born at Albury, NSW, on 28 August 1876 and educated there. He joined the Victorian Dept of Public Instruction as a trainee teacher in October 1890, serving in several country schools.

In 1901 he enlisted in 5th Victorian Mounted Rifles and went to South Africa. After a year, and as sergeant, he returned to teaching. Then in June 1906 he became a full-time soldier and by 1913 was a major. He went to Anzac Cove as Bde Major to 2nd Bde, McCay's brigade. Acting on McCay's orders he took charge of 7th Bn at Krithia 8 May 1915, and was wounded twice. He recovered, returned and was at the evacuation, then as Lieut Col. He was appointed CMG for his work at Krithia, which '*saved the situation*'.

In Egypt in February 1916 he was given command of 54th Bn and took them through Fromelles after which his health broke down and he was evacuated to England. There he recovered sufficiently to work briefly in AIF Administration, and to be married. He and his wife Helena returned to Australia early in 1917 and Cass became director of military training in Melbourne until 1921, when he began a series of army appointments in Queensland, Hobart, Melbourne, Adelaide and then back to Melbourne in September 1931. He was a prominent Freemason and now Brigadier. On 6 November 1931 he died in the Caulfield Military Hospital as the result of an appendix operation.
[continued opposite]

There is no evidence that Pope had queried the viability of the whole operation, he went methodically ahead getting things organised. He, however, had a brush with McCay on several occasions. Firstly, over the earlier proposed raids by unexperienced troops, which in the end did not eventuate, and on 17 July about not sending in reports on the state of the wire. Pope, who took a fairly pedantic line on the way the order was worded, had not surveyed the wire, and told McCay his order was badly expressed. It would not be difficult to imagine that Pope regarded (probably correctly) that his work at Anzac was somewhat better than McCay's, and as he had been among men and in action for many months, he was a better judge of situations and what one could reasonably expect from men, areas in which McCay was abysmally ignorant.

Throughout the battle Pope kept McCay well informed of developments and the messages reflect a much firmer command structure than 8th Bde and none of their special pleading, or the early unsubstantiated confidence of 15th Bde. Right from the start it has to be said that it seems only Pope understood and followed the Battle Order about using two battalions in assault, and the other two for support and reserve. Although there is no evidence to prove such a point, one must wonder if this was a factor in McCay's turning on Pope after the battle. It is easy to imagine Pope telling McCay that he did not know what he was doing: and he would have had support from such as Lieut Col Cass.

Cass was not a man to bite his tongue and he described to Bean in some detail his early concerns about the way the preliminaries were managed:

> When the 53rd and 54th went into the line on Sunday night for the original attack which was to have taken place on Monday (at 11 am) they had never before been in the trenches in France. That is to say, they were going new into the trenches to make this attack. When the attack was postponed they were brought out and put in again on Wednesday morning to make the attack that evening. A great number of officers and men were hit before ever the hour of the attack came.

Lieut Col Cass also discussed with Bean the secrecy or rather the lack of it regarding the forthcoming attack. Cass said the men were told openly in the estaminets that they were going to attack German trenches, and this was a deliberate campaign, so that the information would be conveyed to the Germans, and thus they had to keep their men in position all the time. Somebody in HQ was sure the security covering the build up was so good that the Germans had little knowledge of it, so some purposeful leak had to be organised. Bean's judgement on this, Cass's opinion, was that Cass was attacking McCay. Cass knew McCay well, he had been alongside him at Krithia and it is odd that Bean should bother to record his reaction to Cass in such an emotional way:

> I must say this seems too foolish to be true, even of the commanders at that time. To tell the Germans that our men are going to attack when the attack itself would put them aware of the same fact six or twelve hours later would be a crime even the stupidest General would scarcely commit, and McCay was not stupid.

But surely Bean missed Cass's point entirely. Cass was questioning the tactic, which could well have been no more than the fault of some officers then newly aware of what was ahead. On 19 July at 9am at Brigade HQ Pope assembled his battalion commanders and '*zero time was received from 5th Div at 11 am. Plans for the attack were discussed. Divisional orders read and also all instructions issued by 5th Div were explained ... all time tables and instructions were carefully and thoroughly carried out ...*'

Like 8th Bde, 14th Bde had one experienced and one unexperienced battalion leader; Lieut Col Cass had been on Gallipoli and earlier in South Africa, while Lieut Col I B Norris had never been in action. Therefore it is not surprising that the assembly and movement forward of 53rd Bn was something of a shambles, whereas the 54th got to position in reasonable order despite the ravages of the German artillery. However, the movement across No-Man's Land and into the German trenches was catastrophic for the 54th. The second-in-command Major R Harrison was killed and all four company commanders, all their seconds-in-command and six junior officers were killed or wounded in the first few minutes. Cass got through and found the German line easy to take, '*the whole wave of the 54th swept over the enemy's parapet without trouble*' wrote Bean, and he could have added 'and without officers'. It would seem that from now on the '*well-seasoned*' NCOs had to make many of the decisions.

The first wave hunted the Germans from the trenches and bunkers while the next three waves went on in search of the line which had to be held. Like the 8th on their left they found nothing but ditches, and there was nothing that could be converted into a firing line in all of the 300 yards up to the Rouges Bancs Road. The 54th therefore came back to a line of deserted earthworks 150 yards behind the front line and worked to put up a parapet and so be in a position to deal with the inevitable German counter-attack. Everybody had been

Lieut Col W E H CASS (contd)
He was buried in Melbourne General Cemetery (310M:913). His wife, who was from Nova Scotia, and their daughter survived him.

Within a few weeks, the November issue of *Reveille* carried Bean's tribute: it was extraordinarily detailed about Cass and McCay at Krithia, and had only one paragraph concerning Fromelles. Bean wrote in conclusion: '*his subordinates knew him as a friend, and his seniors as one whom they could rely to the utmost, be the trial ever so severe.*' And Gordon Bennett offered this: '*In peace time he endeared himself to all ... his capacity as an instructor left its mark on many young officers.*'

THE FLYING MACHINES
On 18 July, only the War Diary of 56th Bn noted aircraft activity. At 12.30 pm '*friendly aircraft active*' but by 6.30 it was '*friendly aircraft extraordinarily active. 7 machines being seen from Bn HQ over our lines.*'

Advice was given on 18 July that on 19 July the 5th Division artillery would be assisted by No. 16 Squadron RFC whose '*machines*' could be distinguished '*by two black bands, one just in front and the other just behind the pilot's seat. In between two black bands on both sides of the machine a blue circle with a red bull.*' Whilst reconnaissance and liaison work would be in the hands of No. 10 Squadron RFC whose '*machines*' had '*a broad black stripe two feet wide outside the usual rings on the lower planes*'.

advised on this matter on 18 July. A memo came from Haking, prefaced by a note:

> The Corps Commander has made the following remarks as regards details to be attended to in consolidating the captured German trenches. A copy is to be issued to each company commander.

Then Haking's advice:

> Don't let the position go when you have once got it. Above all look after and block and wire the enemy's communication trenches leading into the position and prevent the enemy from bombing you out there. A counter-stroke across the open you can easily repel with rifle and machine gun and with your artillery. Set your communications across the new line as rapidly as possible in the early part of the night, and have a good fire position along the whole front ready by daylight on the 20th. Have this order conveyed to all ranks.
>
> When this has been read to the troops, please ensure that all copies are burnt.

Cass set up HQ in a German dugout. Bean shows the position of this as about the centre of the 54th Bn sector, thus some 100 yards to the west of the row of surviving blockhouses that now form part of the Australian Memorial Park at Fromelles. These blockhouses were built after July 1916, however Cass's own description (see margin: *The German Front Line*), as distinct from Bean's rewriting of it, provides an interesting glimpse of how the Germans lived at the front line, and is an aid to the imagination for the present day visitor to that place.

When the prisoners had been sent back, those who had cleared the German line now joined those preparing the new line. So, like the 8th, the German's strongest and best thought out defence system was deserted. McCay had seen no value in garrisoning this, '*through inexperience*', as already noted. Instead they tried to make a defence line out of the ditch, there being no obvious alternative.

Ellis described their dilemma '*a careful search ... failed to disclose anything ... at the place indicated on the aeroplane maps*': a curious expression further adding confusion to the question of what the battalion commanders had seen before the battle, and what they used in the battle. The origin of the water-filled ditches behind the German front line only Ellis seems to have thought about. He concluded they were probably used to take the water that was pumped out of the deep front line trenches, which would then find its way into the river. Obviously the water pumped out had to go somewhere and with German engineering skill this seems an appropriate explanation. Thus the later accusations that the Germans pumped water into their trenches is easily dealt with. The constant seepage

THE GERMAN FRONT LINE

The Front line is a breastwork about 8 feet high fitted with recesses. On the forward ground level were three machine gun emplacements of which one was destroyed by our shell fire. The other two guns remained in action until captured by the 54th Bn and the gunners killed or captured. There were no sleeping dugouts in this line as far as I saw. In the next line—about 10 yards in rear were placed dugouts for NCOs and men I should judge. In these we placed our wounded. They had about 5 feet of earth for a roof and were sunk in the ground about 4 feet. This gave an internal height of 6 to 7 feet.

In the third line, about 10 yards further back still, were much better dug-outs used as headquarters of sections officers, signal officers etc.

The one I used as headquarters was fitted with electric lights, had two sleeping berths end to end giving a length in the side of about 13 or 14 feet, height about 7'6", width 8 feet. Thickness of earth on top about 8 feet, depth (below ground level) of about 10 feet. It was reached by steps and had a passage for light to a window. It was strongly built and had an upright about 12" x 12" in the centre supporting a rafter of somewhat similar thickness. The ceiling appeared to be flat sheet iron papered with wall paper. The walls were papered and even decorated with gold moulding similar to picture frame moulding. It had table, armchair, heating stove, electric bell, electric light, acetylene gas lamp similar to bicycle lamp. In it were stored from 10 to 20 thousands rounds SAA, many flares, gas helmets, a special type of rubber bag with cast-iron cylinder probably for oxygen. Other dugouts in the line were similarly built.

The revetments of the trenches were strong timber with small mesh wire netting, walls vertical and grass grown. Trenches were narrow and difficult to get wounded through. Latrines were on pan system.

—Extract from 'Report on Condition of German Trenches' by Lieut Col W E H Cass, in the field, 22 July 1916

would continue and flood the dugouts if the pumping system was damaged or turned off. The high water table had proved a problem to 14th Field Coy during their upgrading of Brompton Road, and making the sap across No-Man's Land.

'*Taken altogether*', Ellis wrote, '*the situation in Col Pope's sector for a time appeared encouraging.*' He also noted that Capt Dick OC of 14th MG Coy '*succeeded in pushing across No-Man's Land ten of his guns and these were soon located in favourable positions in the captured ground*'. Bean did not note this. And early on the 55th, in line with original orders, took sandbags and ammunition over No-Man's Land.

As with 8th Bde, the moment the action began the 14th Field Coy under Major Bachtold started work on a sap across No-Man's Land. It was a continuation of Brompton Road, '*a sap which had been little used and was extensively repaired by 14th Field Coy*'. It was to be the only such sap that was completed and was hugely important to 14th Bde. It was also hugely difficult and hazardous: see margin: *A Trench Across No-Man's Land*. But digging a trench and filling sandbags were somewhat different tasks. The earth was slippery mud and many of those who brought the sandbags over, on seeing the work involved and the desperation of the situation stayed and helped, '*comparatively few of the 55th returned for a second load*', Bean observed. But some officers were intelligent enough to see that this was a ridiculous arrangement. Lieut N E F Pinkstone and his section went for further supplies and one of their number recalled later that he crossed No-Man's Land '*at least a dozen times*'.

Cass was well served by this type of initiative. Indeed had he succeeded in getting the majority of his officers into the German trench they would have had the organisation to make an even stronger stand than they did.

Before we follow the misfortunes of 53rd Bn, a piece of historical trivia remembered by one of them: '*Rum was issued—the front coys A & B had tin hats, C & D and Lewis Gun section only had felt hats.*' The shambles that introduced 53rd Bn to the battle was memorable. Whilst, despite the losses in early shelling the first waves got across No-Man's Land, the later waves—in particular the fourth veered to the right, climbing through partially cut wire to end up in the Pinney's Avenue communication trench which ran diagonally across and very close to where the river Laies entered No-Man's Land. The whole area was swept by German machine guns at the Sugarloaf. '*The ditch was full of wounded and dying men—like a butcher's shop—men groaning and crying and shrieking. Ammunition was carried up by pairs of men, the boxes being carried on sticks.*

A TRENCH ACROSS NO-MAN'S LAND

Late in 1933 Sidney Kenneth Donnan, formerly Pte 2386 in 1 Section 14th Field Coy Engineers, *wandered into the Sydney Public Reading Library and chanced to see an Official History of the Australian Imperial Force ... I wondered what was therein, about the July 19, 1916 stunt at Fleurbaix, otherwise Fromelles.*

As a result of what he found, Donnan wrote a long and detailed letter (dated 3.2.34) to Bean concerned with many issues. Donnan who had enlisted 7 August 1915 later transferred to Australian Flying Corps, returning to Australia 6 September 1919. At Fromelles he had been involved in the digging of the communication trench or sap across No-Man's Land in the 14th Bde sector. He felt that Bean's meagre – *At the same time a sap across the old No-Man's Land was already being dug by two sections of engineers of the 14th Field Company, under instructions of Major Bachtold and Lieutenants Fry and Ferguson about the centre of their brigade sector* – was insufficient. His account vividly describes one of the successes at Fromelles and thus worth noting:

I don't remember being instructed that it was the particular job of our Section No. 1 to get the communication trench across No-Man's Land in the 14th Brigade sector. We moved down the communication trench and arrived at the second line up to that time having been passed only by a few stretcher bearers and blanketed forms. But in the second line I realised it was the day of the 'big stunt'. All along the bays behind the parapets (no trenches much below ground level owing to water bearing ground) one could see troops preparing for the 'hop' from the second to front line. There was a precise and terrific barrage of machine gun and rifle bullets, shrapnel and high explosive. The latter I remember coming in salvos which worked from flank to flank and back again. I can truthfully say that at that time I had a sort of callous control of myself and was not at all fearful. I can remember older and more

[continued next page]

A TRENCH ACROSS NO-MAN'S LAND (contd)
sensitive minded men who were so, one in particular crying momentarily and hysterically for his mother. Several times the 'Jack Johnsons' shut daylight out for many seconds, but the only loss up to that point was my pipe which got under the duck-boards and flying debris. We hopped over the parapet at a given signal from Lieut Ferguson our section Commander, and made a dash for the front line. With the tape-drum and other tools and battle Order Kit (I think a pick axe) the run was too far for me, and I decided to walk the last quarter and hang the consequences. Arrived in front line I could see Lieut Ferguson had been hit in the neck and Sapper Saunders staunching the blood which spurted out of small wound at great pressure. The bleeding actually stopped and at that moment some German Prisoners (about four) seemed to come from nowhere. They ran into a dug-out to shelter from the heavy shelling. Lieut Ferguson, usually proper and precise, seemed to have gone light headed from what proved a fatal wound, was using lurid language as to what to do with the 'Fritzies'. There was a bit of humour then when a plumber chap about 5'4" high went to them and looking fierce and threatening addressed them with 'Come on you big b–s you have got to get out'. I don't think they had much intention of stopping however and made off toward the second line. There was no escort. Ferguson went back out of action accompanied by two or so men who apparently had had enough. By this time there were a number making back for the clearing stations ... We seemed to be at a dead end amongst the confusion and moved along the front line ...

The slaughter and confusion being worse than ever we decided to get over into the German lines and do something. Getting over the parapet we found No-Man's Land a sort of hell on earth mainly through the moans of the wounded who were too numerous to get away, and the barrage was too
[continued opposite]

One man would go down and crash would go the box into the water. Shelling was very heavy. The engineers were digging a communication trench ... the wounded were hopping over into this, and the engineers were having an awful time trying to dig the trench.'

The man, unnamed, who gave that account to Bean, also remembered that there were two gas alarms which came to nothing, and concluded his recollections thus:

> So many men were falling that things were clearly wrong; but, when the word about retiring came along, the men received it with: *'What-retreating? Not on your life!'* And at the same time things were so broken that they had a sort of fear, that it was true.

Those who got to the German front line had not had an easy time. The first waves had vanished in the smoke and dust and then Lieut Col Norris, his Adjutant Lieut Moffitt and staff followed. They reached the German parapets and it would seem clambered over them running and sliding down the other side. A well-sited German machine gun killed the lot. Major Sampson, the senior company commander following met a similar fate, meaning that when there was time to work it out, command of 53rd Bn was the responsibility of Capt. C Arblaster, a 21-year-old Duntroon graduate.

After his description of the early disasters of 14th Bde, Bean makes this observation:

> In spite of these difficulties the fairly numerous reports reaching McCay from most parts of his front about 7.30 were satisfactory.

Disregarding the messages prior to 6 pm, there are in fact in the Divisional file only 26 messages up to 7.30, and there is only one reference to '*heavy casualties*' and that from Elliott regarding 59th Bn. Not a single word, if we are to believe the carefully typed-up messages as being complete, to advise McCay that by now two battalion commanders were dead and probably five majors, eight captains and perhaps twenty lieutenants, and of course no hint of the 1000 or more men who must have '*gone west*' as the diggers described it. Only Elliott admits to having a rough time, and his rough time only really began at 6. The others had been battered since 4 at least. At this time Haking probably for the sake of Monro and others sent a copy of how he saw things to McCay:

> 5th Aust Div. report attack of right Bde appears successful and musketry fire by enemy practically ceased. Centre Bde occupy trenches in front of Rouges Bancs. Left Bde reported in enemy's trenches and their left battalion holding German communication trench leading up to Ferme Delangré.

In the 14th Bde file, timed at 7.36 is this entry:

> 54th Bn asked for reinforcements stating that the battalion of 8th Bde on its left had apparently withdrawn, but that it was consolidating its left. Permission was obtained from 5th Div to use 2 coys of 55th Bn to support 53rd and 54th. This half battalion of 55th was now in our old front line, its remainder having been used up for working parties. Col McConaghy was ordered to send one company in support of 53rd and one in support of 54th.

Then at 9.30 this entry:

> Report received from Col McConaghy that above order had been carried out successfully.

Interestingly there is no message about a request for or approval of reinforcements in McCay's file and it is not until 10.20 that 14th Bde advises him thus, as answers to the three questions, which are not on the file:

> 1. Present information is not definite. There was at 9.00 a gap between my left and 8th Bde right which I am trying to make good. 2. 53rd and 54th Battalions with 2 coys of 55th Bn plus carrying parties—about 400 of 55th Bn. 3. No.

The decision to use two companies of 55th for reinforcements meant in simple terms that now the whole battalion was in action. Earlier one company was ordered to assist 14th Field Coy with the communication trench and the other was carrying supplies over No-Man's Land and ended up staying here. This meant that A and B coys of 56th Bn now had custody of the 14th Bde front line. Later, due to the need to hurry the work on the trench B Coy of 56th joined that group. So three companies of 56th were all that was left north of No-Man's Land , and the battle was then not yet half way through.

Keeping in mind this background material we return to Lieut Col Cass in his ex-German dugout HQ. Major Croshaw who was the person to take over from Lieut Col Norris was now more involved with Bde liaison work and moved back and forth over No-Man's Land getting things organised. So leadership of the small band of 53rd Bn that remained was under Capt. Arblaster, who was on the extreme right, theoretically next to the German lines that should have been occupied by 60th Bn. But unknown to anybody, even their commander, Brig. General Elliott, they never got past the enemy parapet. So Arblaster's neighbours were the Germans. He was of course in a much worse position than Lieut Col Coghill of the 32nd, because he had absolutely no protection on that flank. Heroically the battalion had built in parts a barricade of sandbags joining with the same being constructed by the 54th ready for dawn

A TRENCH ACROSS NO-MAN'S LAND (contd)

heavy. I heard afterwards that there were stretcher bearers or perhaps impromptu stretcher bearers, who having sheltered in a dug-out openly admitted that they could not face the task. Any man's nerve was likely to desert him at any moment through such noise and carnage. On the way to the fighting front in fact as soon as we got into the German trenches which were a comparatively calm spot (no barrage) word was passed back for more bombs. We at once formed into a carrying party and made back to get some bombs. In our front line I came upon the Company O.C. Major Bachtold who asked me how things had gone with us. I told him that Lt Ferguson had been put out of action and that we were at present getting bombs up to the front for the infantry. He said that we had to get a trench across No-Man's Land under any circumstances and for me to get Lieut Fry of our company (another section) and ask him to see to it. I found Fry in the front line German Trench directing bomb carriers and others as to the way to where help was wanted. I then got the drum of tape from some place I had left it in and we lost no time in setting out a zig-zag trench across No-Man's Land missing a few bumps and utilising a few hollows. Any available infantry got on to the work and I am told a party from the 56th under Sgt Phillips arrived later. We all simply 'dug like Hades, one man to about 6'0" of trench. I went through a nightmare of hard work and vomiting and now and again comforting some moaning wounded digger. It was just about coming on dark when Fry and myself laid the tape out, as far as I can remember, and the trench was right across No-Man's Land before daybreak.

THE BARRISTER AS ARTILLERY MAN

Most artillery men were from an engineering or science background and thus had mathematical skills and interests. When S K Donnan, 14th Field Coy, had to 'locate' the position of an 18 pounder battery on a map for its commander, he was amazed at the officer's lack of map reading and mathematical skills. Donnan who had personally witnessed the havoc caused by 'shorts' from the Australian artillery was after 18 years still very angry:

At another time I was asked by our adjutant to call on a 18 pounder battery commander operating on the right hand side of road from Fleurbaix to Wye Farms. The commander was anxious to have the position of his guns on our map. Arrived there, it transpired that he was anxious to check his position on his own map. On the latter he scaled about 100 yds to the right of the road, and by stepping he made it 150 yds (or some such figures). He then produced a rough theodolite (an artillery director) and asked me would I check his position. He was the 150 yards from the road no doubt and I pointed out that such was the case without or regardless of any fancy method the distance might be measured by. I also pointed out that there were probably men under his command who could do the job better than myself, but he assured me that not one knew anything about a director. I ran a traverse from the Church Tower in the town and connected up with the battery and gave him the plan showing him of course to be 150 yds from the road. There was insufficient data to do anything else but he could not appreciate the fact. Later when I happened to be at Artillery Headquarters at Bac St Maur I found out what was his trouble. The French Ordinance Plans were inaccurate in detail as to roads etc. and Artillery H.Q. used to locate the correct positions of guns on maps issued to batteries. Thus this man's position was right relative to Trig. points such as the Church Tower

[continued next page]

when it was expected the Germans would rush head on against this wall and so be easily destroyed. Once again it would seem that everybody lost sight of the fact that behind them, between their new line and 'home' so to speak, were the largely empty German front line trenches and dugouts. The lack of any clear assessment of the real situation and underestimation of the intelligence and experience of the Germans, let alone the basic factor that they were operating in their own territory where they had been for over a year is the most incredible fact of the whole affair. And it was never better illustrated than the belief of the Australians that the Germans would sacrifice their men with the same abandon as they had been sacrificed.

That said we now follow what is to be one of the great attempts by huge-hearted, broad-shouldered volunteers to mount a defence that shows what can be done and what can be lost.

Bean in his history writes that: '*a report that 53rd were retiring reached McCay at Sailly shortly after 7 pm; but in the German trenches Col Cass of 54th, and even the rest of 53rd knew nothing of it.*' There is no such message nor indication in the Bde or Division files and Bean ties it to the event already mentioned when somebody shouted '*we are retiring*', made more bizarre by being shouted by a man who was not even out of the Australian line! As it was still daylight and the 55th Bn reinforcements had only just arrived it is very unclear how such a message could be sent to McCay and who would have sent it.

An hour and a half later, 9.30 pm, half of 55th Bn, '*made available by Gen. McCay*' wrote Bean, presented itself to Lieut Col Cass, who quickly sent one company under Gibbins to support the 54th on the left and the other under Capt. J H Matthews to assist the 53rd on the right. They found most of the rest of the 55th already there busy building the parapet and fighting off German attacks at both sides and in front. And all the night was yet ahead. They established a good line, however it no longer connected at the left with the 31st Bn who had pulled back to the German front line, leaving as already shown the 32nd on the same line as the 54th and 53rd but with a 250-yard gap between them. Despite this, of which he was only partly aware, Cass was confident and chirpy. We do not know the time he sent the message but perhaps an hour before it was received by 14th Bde HQ at 1.56 am.

> Sandbags are coming in good numbers ... have not at time of message received Verey pistols or flares but am using German flares. Enemy artillery strafing us pretty badly as it comes enfilade. I fancy some rifle grenades or similar things have just landed in my back yard. Cannot

> our artillery stop their guns as they are '*a source of danger to us*'. Am forwarding papers and books found in dugout here. They contain range tables and descriptions of Minenwerfer which might be useful, sorry we did not get the guns.

It would now seem that Arblaster, helped by the arrival of new men and thinking clearly delegated duties to other officers while he went to examine the situation at the left, basically at the place where rue Delvas crossed into German-held territory, checking on the Lewis guns that were facing down the road from where the Germans might begin their counter attack. Fairly obviously the Germans now began to take advantage of the darkness and move in on the flanks, unaware as already noted of how vulnerable the Australian line was due to the gap between the two brigades, but as they worked forward it became apparent thanks to a constant use of flares, and bombing parties who knew the layout of the trenches.

Arblaster having satisfied himself that his left was as secure as it could be, moved back to the right just about the time when the Germans were working to move in behind by re-occupying their front line. Assisted by a few men of extraordinary courage he began a desperate, hopeless defence. This began by trying to out bomb the enemy as their machine guns at the Sugarloaf and elsewhere swept the area. Lieut E M Farmer of 55th who had, with 30 men, been given the task by Arblaster to upgrade a communication trench as extra protection for the line, suddenly found themselves under German grenade attack. Farmer '*called for men experienced with bombs, and two of his party responded, but discovered that the bombs given to them had not been fused. Farmer thereupon set to work himself to fuse the grenades, and the enemy was then kept at bay for a time.*' Out on the right flank which was totally unsupported Arblaster '*constantly called for volunteers to bomb the Germans back*'. From one of these appeals a team of seven went forward with 25 bombs each and '*crawled unobserved over the open into shell holes from which, facing towards the Australian rear, they began to throw their grenades into the position occupied by the German bombers*'. But although they inflicted heavy casualties it was to no avail. After an hour the Australians pulled back, and held on, their bomb supplies almost gone. The Germans also badly damaged were regrouping.

While all this had been going on Lieut Col Cass in his HQ no more than 200 yards away was according to Bean '*entirely unaware*' of the Germans coming in on the right via their old front line. Shortly after 10 pm, Lieut Col McConaghy, who was now with his staff, went out to assess the situation and in

THE BARRISTER AS ARTILLERY MAN (contd)

and other conspicuous objects. The roads relative to his gun positions would scale wrongly on his map. Being outside his profession he could not appreciate the position, and I suppose there were many other mathematical points he could not appreciate, which cost other men their lives. I was told by my chainman that this chap was a Western Australian barrister though he may have been a bit astray in his observation or placing. I would say that there were fully half a dozen sappers in our company who would have been more capable artillery commanders than this man, whose lives were endangered or sacrificed whilst using the pick and shovel every day, and who were used as navvies and called 'Engineers'.

For the record: CO of AOD (Ordnance) was Capt. J M Rodd.

A MINENWERFER

Described as a trench bomb-throwing mortar this example was captured by the French early in 1916. *'The two attached cylinders, seen at either side of the mortar-barrel, contain the recoil apparatus, which is worked by means of compressed air and strong steel spiral springs which have to control and counter-balance the shock of the discharge within a very limited space, and are constructed of an exceptional stoutness.'*

—*Illustrated War News*, 12 April 1916

a classic Bean understatement '*at once received the impression that matters were far from well*'. This was an important opinion. McConaghy had been at the Landing and Lone Pine and as the war progressed he was to prove to be a man of great capacity. His second-in-command Major R Cowey, also a man of the Landing, was equally able and the trio set about trying to reclaim the night. Having located Arblaster and his garrison, assessed the dangers, they sent a small party west to explore the possibilities that 60th Bn was in the German trenches. The party was never seen again. The second party was driven back.

Meantime the 14th Field Coy had by midnight in spite of extraordinary difficulties finished the communication trench across No-Man's Land so the supply situation was considerably improved although it clashed as always with the never-ending stream of wounded walking, crawling, or being carried back to the Australian line.

Having come over via this trench McConaghy and his staff were obviously more in touch with actual events than Cass in his bunker, and next made it their duty to find out what was happening on the left where it was apparent the 8th Bde's 31st Bn had fallen back leaving the 54th open to a counter-attack that could easily lead to the same problem facing Arblaster. In charge on the left they found their Capt. N Gibbins. Bean's description of him was wonderful—'*six foot four inches in his boots, a gaunt, brave, humourous, cool-headed Australian, bank manager in civil life, older than most company officers* [38], *but an athlete, promoted from the ranks at Anzac.*'

The calibre of the man is revealed in one of his messages to McConaghy:

> We hold front line with 54th. CO 54th (Cass) in next trench in rear. 53rd on our right. 31st and 32nd on our left. Consolidating positions as fast as possible. Sending back to rear trench by parties of ten under NCOs for ammunition and sandbags. We want Very pistols, flares and sandbags (plenty). Have 54th Lewis guns and five of our own under Sergeant Colless for counter-attack. Each of my men have three bombs, but require more. Expect a counter-attack shortly. Anyway, we can hold them easily.
>
> N Gibbins, Capt., OC B Company
>
> Sergeant Colless doing good work—my officers also of course. Would like you to say something to this man (ie the bearer of the message). He is doing splendid work.

It must have been apparent to McConaghy within a short time that the dangers were the flanks, although Bean suggests that even up to near midnight Cass was not aware that 15th Bde had failed to get into the German line. Considering that the

UNDER THE NOSES OF THE FRENCH

One of the issues never really resolved about Fromelles was whether the official tactic was to try to conceal the preparation, or to make much of it so that the enemy was intimidated and kept on his toes. Bean opted for the first, which is why S K Donnan 14th Field Coy, took him to task in 1934.

In the first place I strongly disagree with any suggestion that any attempt was made to screen the attack. In fact I understood right from the start that we were to make as big a demonstration as possible in order to provide a feint to cover the Somme offensive. We, the 14th Co., were moved about a good deal just prior to the attack. We were taken out of one part of the front and moved to the right a few days before the start and then transferred back again. I may not be exactly right as to location. I think we were first on the front near Jay's Post, Tinbarn Av., and then transferred to Dead Dog and V.C. Avenue (Communication Trenches) and then moved back, all within a few days. I mean from billets behind one to billets behind the other trench. Remarking on how openly preparations were being conducted if there was to be an attack I can remember a general agreement with the 'Good Oil' among the troops that we were being moved about to give the impression of preparations on a large scale. I understood at the time that the infantry were being instructed and rehearsed within the hearing and under the noses of the French populace with the idea, partly, of spreading the news to the German lines. There were bound to be a few spies among them, amateur or professional.

signallers of 14th Bde had been much better at keeping a phone line open than those of 8th Bde, and that the sap was functioning well unlike its counterpart in the 8th Bde sector, it is difficult to sort out why accurate information on which the survival or otherwise of 14th Bde depended was so slow in going forward. Whether this was due to a collapse of operations at Pope's HQ or McCay's is not easy to establish. But the isolation of the garrison of 14th Bde must cause some hard questions to be asked. In all of Bean's brilliant, understanding and hugely well-organised version of this part of the battle there is no mention of Pope, although as we have seen Tivey's HQ was much involved in the affairs of 8th Bde, and as will be shown Elliott's HQ was even closer to its men.

Due to McCay's sacking of Pope the day after the battle, indeed at the very moment according to Pope that he was beginning his Report on the battle, we have no pieces of paper setting out what Pope did and knew. The 14th Bde War Diary is fairly meagre and Cass, probably because he was the senior colonel took it upon himself to supply two reports about '*the assault and capture and subsequent withdrawal*' and '*condition of German trenches*' under Brigade heading rather than 54th Bn.

Perhaps the only testimony needed for Pope has already been proven, that is the installation of Cass and McConaghy and the communication trench ready and usable in six hours. Anyhow Cass seems to have no doubt his Bde HQ as he always told it 'as it was', confident that was what was wanted. At 3 am a message, '*the Germans are coming...*' then at 3.22 am '*Position is serious. We have no grenades...*' and 3.45 am. '*Position very serious. 53rd are retiring. Enemy behind them and in their old front line and within 100 yards of my right...*'

In the obvious confusion rumours about retiring were again heard and Cass was unable to persuade some 53rd men now bereft of all their officers. However men of his 54th, perhaps inspired by the endurance of their leader and his staff took it upon themselves to try to hold back the German infiltrators with grenades. They '*flung their missiles like cricketers throwing at a wicket*' wrote Bean. And Major Cowey ran back to the Australian lines to find more reinforcements, whilst McConaghy argued with Cass about the sending of 55th Bn men across open ground to attack the advancing Germans. But Cass prevailed and ordered Lieut Denoon and some men to attack. Denoon and his party moved into No-Man's Land and crept around the German breastwork, and then surprised the Gemans in the trench. This caused sufficient damage and confusion to take the pressure off

COLONEL SPOKE VERY FEELINGLY TO US ALL

Hector Brewer of 56th Bn who had returned from Paris a few days earlier, continued his diary throughout the battle, and afterwards.

19 July. Our artillery heavily shelled the enemy trenches. About 6 pm our brigade charged the German trenches. Our casualties very heavy.
20 July. We had to retire on to our own trenches. The brigadier very pleased with our work and says we are not to blame for the failure of the Division to hold the trenches. Our battalion relieved this morning. We came back to the billet in the afternoon. Losses in the section: 3 killed, 1 wounded, 1 missing. Total 5. All NCOs casualties. I am acting section commander.
21 July. Went out last night with RSM Bramhall [B H Bramhall 525, 56th Bn] to bring in wounded. We got several poor fellows in. I got back to billet about 6.30 this morning.
22 July. Slept well last night. All feeling stiff, sore and tired. Colonel spoke very feelingly to us all yesterday afternoon. He thanked the battalion for their splendid behaviour first time under fire.
23 July. We left Bac St Maur about 10 pm and marched single file to the town of Fleur Baix. Despite the fact that the Germans shell the town occasionally, civilians, mostly women and old men and girls still live here. They go into the cellars when a shelling is on.
24 July. Fritz shelled the town this morning. Several houses, where our men were, hit.

COOKERS IN THE FRONT LINE

Looking back from the mud-holes of the Somme one soon realised that the land of the Pharaohs wasn't too bad, after all. But our turn was to come, and the late spring of 1916 found us across France and making steady progress towards the great stoush.

Our line of approach was via Hazebrouck, if I remember rightly, and eventually we fetched up at a village called Bac St Maur, a few miles behind the lines. It was from this village, by the way, that the 55th went not very [continued next page]

other areas and Arblaster in particular. Then at 4.20 am Cass advised Pope:

> Position almost desperate. Have got 55th and a few of 54th together and have temporarily checked enemy. But do get our guns to work at once, please. The 53rd have confidence temporarily and will not unwillingly stand their ground. Some appear to be breaking across No-Man's Land. If they give way to right rear, I must withdraw or be surrounded.

But all was not lost, yet.

The word spread back through the men working in and manning the communication trench and new supplies of grenades were rushed up via this route, together with a number of volunteers to throw them. Cowey also had others from 56th Bn and having cleared the Germans out of some eighty yards of their front line, set up '*a Herculean bomb fight*', to use Bean's words, confirmed so he noted by a Bavarian bomber who threw over 500. Somebody else advised Bean that '*there must have been nearly twelve bombs in the air at a time*'. The reader is directed to the citations for 14th Bde pages 279–86, for an idea of whom and what was involved in this event. The 14th Bde thus gained an hour or so, and it was now becoming light.

It was not until the first traces of dawn that Arblaster and his men became aware of figures moving to their right. They fired at them and then, perhaps half in hope thinking they may be 15th Bde men, held their fire. They were, of course, Bavarians and not only were they on the right but they were in the trenches behind them, evidenced a little while later as Australians began to be shot in the back. The situation was terrible. Arblaster seems to have been about the only officer not wounded, was '*singularly cool*' and made what was in a sense the only decision he could. What grenades were left he distributed to the survivors in the trench that they held all night whilst facing the Germans to the south and west. He then turned them around and led them north, out of their trench towards the original German front line suspecting no doubt, but not entirely sure, that it was now full of Germans. They had no hope and Arblaster was cut down, his men fell back into their trench and were all taken prisoner. Arblaster might well have been taken back to the trench and watched over by his men, for he survived for a few days before dying in the German hospital at Douai.

Facing catastrophe and this new day, the messages were more confusing. Pope in receipt of Cass's previous message advised Wagstaff. Bean wrote: '*Wagstaff had replied that the orders were to hold on, and, upon Pope's stating that he thought he could do so if reinforced, had authorized him to employ as*

COOKERS (contd)
long afterwards, to take its part in the ill-fated attack at Fromelles on July 19, 1916.

The village of Fleurbaix, where we usually came for our spell out of the line, was a couple of kilos further forward—roughly a mile behind the front line. So peaceful was this village in the ordinary way that the inhabitants continued in residence, and indeed did a very thriving trade, especially the several estaminets. One in particular possessed a gramophone, which I can almost hear now playing 'I'm on my way to dear old Dublin Bay'.

Many of the boys used to carry a bottle of vin blanc up the line with them, and, of course, sling the bottle away after finishing it. I can remember one occasion, in company with Frank Tate, Small and 'Puddin' Nelson, when we were on the rocks. We got a bag and made a 'backsheesh' trip up the line and collected 50 or 60 bottles, on which madame allowed 3d. each.

Our first trip into the front line was accomplished—not without a great deal of palaver and halts and false alarms, but we got in at last, and great was the surprise of the mob when they found no trenches—only built-up sandbags on the surface. This part of the front was reckoned a real 'rest home'—and so it was, until our stunt at Fromelles on July 19 altered it all. Our cookers were only just behind the actual front line, and across the way Fritz could be seen stoking up after stand-down in the morning. Rations and rum were obtainable without any difficulty, and were plentiful. Those were the days of 'two to a loaf'. Hidden in the mists of the future was the time when it was 'ten to a loaf'—and lucky to get that.

The days of carrying Carl Gough's containers with hot stew over three or four miles of knee-deep mud were yet to come. True, we had a few fatigues to do of a night. Sometimes pushing the ration truck up the little light railway, or perhaps a bit of mending up a broken parapet - but generally speaking, our nights were peaceful. 'Parapet Joe', the German machine-gunner, played a few tunes at intervals, [continued opposite]

reinforcement half of 56th Bn.' It was 5 o'clock in the morning and McCay went to Haking's temporary headquarters at Sailly. Ellis mentions that Monro was also there, but nobody mentions Mackenzie or 61st Division. It is clear that Wagstaff was at 5th Division Headquarters and it was during this period that Wagstaff spoke to Tivey to be confronted with the simple fact that the 31st and 32nd were now back in their own lines. Then, according to Bean, Wagstaff asked Tivey to phone Pope and advise him of his isolation while he, Wagstaff, spoke to McCay.

The moment Pope heard from Tivey, he sent a message to Cass '*appraising him of the fact that 8th Bde had withdrawn and 14th probably would*'. Pope concluded:

> Do not retire until you receive word. Machine guns should be brought back.

That message, according to Bean, reached Cass at 6.20 an hour after Pope sent it. Bean saw no point in explaining the delay, but Ellis did, '*none of the first seven runners succeeded in reaching Lieut Col Cass. The eighth runner had better success and Lieut Col Cass acknowledged receipt ... at 7.50.*' This important aside, and the lapse of time between 6.20 and 7.50 reveals the isolation of Cass and his garrison which was, for all intents and purposes at least an hour behind decisions taken at Sailly. Crossing however with Pope's message was Cass's of 6.15. '*Position much easier and improved. Have driven enemy back by counter-attack and grenades well out of bombing distance...*'

There then followed Pope's next message, Bean gives no time:

> Be prepared to withdraw on the order given. The old German front line will be held to the end. Make arrangements to dribble men in very small parties back through sap across No-Man's Land to our front line. Make no move until I send word: withdraw.

Cass ordered the machine-gunners home one at a time, and then set about establishing a rearguard party. Bean felt there was some confusion between the worn-out Cass and McConaghy at this point causing McConaghy immediately to send a note to Gibbins:

> Secret. Capt Gibbins and 55th Officers. You must prepare for an orderly retirement. We are unprotected on our flanks. Hold first Hun line until further order. 20.7.16. 6.30 am.

There now began the final act of the tragedy of the AIF at Fromelles. It was to shepherd out what remained of the last garrison and Capt. Gibbins saw his task with total clarity. He moved two Lewis guns to a position to cover where the

COOKERS (contd)

perhaps at Jim Magee coming in from one of his nightly prowls—he was the company's sniper. Small patrols went out occasionally, ready for trouble, but seldom finding any—Fritz didn't believe in spoiling a 'good thing'.

But a very few miles away the sky was lit up every night, and the roar of the guns was unceasing—that was Ypres, they told us. Our days were spent mostly in sleeping—with an occasional sentry posted here and there with a periscope. The heavy fatigues that were such a feature of the days at Gallipoli were absent here. Now and then our 18-pounders gave Fritz a bit of peppering, and he replied in kind—generally knocking a few more bricks off the old monastery, which was just in the rear of the line. We tried to reach Fritz's trenches with rifle grenades of a new pattern, and on occasions the Stokes mortar specialists, as was their custom, fired a dozen or so of their 'little beauties' and made a hasty 'get-away', leaving the P.B.I. to take the consequences.

We learned, among other things, what destruction could be done by a 'minenwerfer' (worse than any shell), and how best to dodge those accursed things. Looking back, it seems that Fleurbaix served the purpose of a kind of short apprenticeship for the more deadly parts of the front we were presently to visit.

So things went along quietly enough at Fleurbaix until July 19. Regarding that attack, the Official History has showed us what a ghastly mistake and tragedy it all was. My own impressions of it were the ridiculous ease with which the first objective was taken (on our sector, at any rate), and the hopeless 'left in the air' sort of feeling when we were finally withdrawn to our own old line, leaving so many good 'cobbers' behind. A company of the 56th was occupying the old line, and I heard an officer (who seemed boiling over with rage) say that he had a fresh company of men and they wouldn't let him counter-attack.

—H J Maynard 4843, C Coy, 55th Bn.
Reveille Feb 1935

Germans might be expected to rush forward when detecting a withdrawal and bombard the sap through which it was being made.

In the area of the road Capt. Murray saw a group of Australians being taken prisoner and apparently went to Cass, in Bean's words, '*represented that the troops in his sector were being gradually faced with a situation in which they could only die or surrender.*' In Bean's files covering this incident is the following version of the event by Major R O Cowey, McConaghy's 2IC, included because the episode reappears in the statements of 53rd men taken prisoner (see page 314):

> The officer who wanted to surrender was Capt Murray of the 53rd. I flourished my revolver at him and endeavoured to make him realize that I was more ferocious than any German. I did intend to have him arrested at the time in case he caused disaffection in the firing line: but thought that perhaps he'd had his nerves badly used and that my bullying would save court martial business. I was astonished later to see him wearing a MC for that engagement.

Cass in his Report, which was probably not unrelated to his confrontation with Murray, wrote:

> ... both these attacks caused the 53rd to break and crowd in on my right. Many of the men were demoralised and a mixed party surrendered. It would appear that at least six Germans in Australian uniform went over to the Germans from the vicinity of the right of the 53rd and others seeing this followed. I am informed also that four officers of the 53rd Bn surrendered at this time. But in the half light there may be some mistake about this. [Only two officers of 53rd were captured.]

Time dragged on, and as the above incident illustrates the strain was getting beyond the strongest of men. Bean's version of the last half hour or so is curiously unquestioning.

> While this force was thus being destroyed piecemeal, Cass was at 7.20 still waiting for the expected command. He reported that he had sent away the machine guns, and that the Lewis guns were following: '*please arrange artillery to create barrage right around us, as enemy bombing very heavily. His rifle fire is causing casualties, and I cannot get wounded away... No order to withdraw yet.*' For some reason the order for withdrawal seems not to have been received by the 14th Bde report centre until 7.30 or by Cass until 7.50. The barrage around his position had been ordered long before, and began to fall at 5.40; and to the long delay which followed must be attributed the loss of a great part of Cass's right flank. On receipt of the final order he at once passed the word for his men to move to the rear through the well-traversed trench across No-Man's Land ... now from four to six feet deep and duckboarded through to the old German front.

Few passages in Bean's story of Fromelles carry the extended footnote by him that this does. He noted '*the decision to*

[continued page 143]

THEY HAVE MURDERED MY BOYS

Although it is difficult to tie in with events as Cass reported them, one anecdote that surfaces often concerns his meeting with Pope after he, Cass, had come back from the German trenches. The most concise telling of the conversation comes from Lieut W Smith's article in *Reveille* of July 1936. However, his assertion that Pope had at some time crossed over No-Man's Land is not mentioned anywhere else, and unlikely to be true:

Just before daybreak Col Pope and Lieut Col Cass came along the new trench [this was the trench Smith had been working on all night] *and through our cutting in the breastwork. Both these officers had been across to the enemy lines. Col Cass was obviously overwrought and distressed. He and Pope were having a heated argument about the attack and Col Cass unburdened his mind. 'I tell you that it was wholesale murder, they have murdered my boys'. 'Oh pull yourself together man, this is war'. 'This is not war. They have murdered my boys.'*

Smith concluded, *I had served under Col Cass in 2nd Bn for three months on Gallipoli and my full sympathy went out to him.*

... TO BE CHOPPED UP...

Cass wrote to his wife-to-be on 29 July from a rest home in France where he had been since the battle. Again he did not disguise his feelings: *'... we got such a strafing that I honestly thought it was certain that I should get hit as they simply rained shells on us. And then both flanks retired and left me out there to be chopped up. And I was waiting and waiting for the order to withdraw and all the time Germany was smashing in on both sides. We beat them back again and again, despite their bombs and machine guns. My men were simply splendid and only when I gave the order did they come back ...'*

Will somebody take my papers ?

The death of Lieut Col Ignatius Bertram Norris of 53rd Bn in the first minutes of the battle was a grevious blow to the battalion; he had been their commander from the beginning of the unit in Egypt. Ellis recorded that his promotion in the NSW Militia Forces had been rapid and his work in the field soon revealed him as a fine soldier. Bean had no view, but noted he was almost 36 and a barrister of Sydney. Actually Norris was somewhat more interesting. Son of a banker, born 31 July 1880, his school career at St Ignatius College (Riverview) was '*distinguished*' and by 1908 he was admitted to the NSW Bar and built up a prosperous legal practice with professional associations, which included Representative of the Government in the Legislative Council. He was a very good tennis player, represented NSW in interstate hockey and better than average at both cricket and golf. He had joined the Irish Rifles and was soon second-in-command, and by the time the war began was major. He enlisted and was in Egypt by June 1915.

He had married Bessie Lane-Mullins in March 1915 and at sometime in the second half of the year Mrs Norris followed her husband to Cairo where she later gave birth to their son.

This unusual domestic arrangement must have had something to do with the wealth and influence of the Norrises. In Cairo Norris began with the 6th Infantry Training Bn, but his legal experience soon had him as Judge Advocate on Courts-Martial and in other judicial work. '*His capacity for organization and control found responsibility gravitating towards him, and at one time he was Camp Commandant of ANZAC Base details, comprising 10000 men of all arms and details, and at another time he was appointed acting Brigadier of ANZAC Reserve Bde, a brigade comprising about 12000, which was responsible for a large section of the Cairo Defence Scheme.*' But it was not what he wanted. '*I should like to get into the fight*', he wrote to a friend and was gazetted Lieut Col to command 22nd Bn but soon transferred to the 53rd. When they left for France at the end of June, Mrs Norris and their son sailed to London where she was when news of Col Norris's death was announced. The speed of the news was such that there was a photograph and obituary in the *Sydney Morning Herald* of 1 August, days before other Fromelles deaths were revealed.

One of those who witnessed Norris's death remembered him shouting to his men '*Come on lads! Only another trench to take*', as he moved over the German line. Then he was hit and fell, and his last words were, '*Here, I'm done, will somebody take my papers?*'

One of the tributes most revealing of the character of Norris was from a private in 53rd AMC. After describing the manner of death, he wrote:

He was a man in a million, a gentleman to speak to, and if anyone got into Crime Street, and came before him, he got sound advice and the minimum penalty. I had a chat with him on the morning of the charge, and he might have been a private, so nice and friendly he was to me. He received Holy Communion in his dug-out that morning: Father Kennedy told me he had done so regularly for some considerable time ... I attended the Requiem Mass in the town ... the large church was filled with soldiers of his battalion, and others as well.

The priest who conducted this Mass was, of course, Father J J Kennedy, whose work at Fromelles earned him the DSO. He wrote to Mrs Norris about her late husband:

It is with feelings of greatest sorrow and deepest sympathy that I write you this letter. I should have written to you some days ago, but I could not brace myself to write.

Lieut Col I B Norris, Sydney 1915

Your dear husband died a hero's death ... God knows how I pity you—but you have the great consolation of knowing that the Colonel was prepared to die. He was never ashamed of his Holy Faith. Every Sunday he received Holy Communion and often during the week since he was appointed to the Command of this regiment.

On the morning of the battle he knelt down before his men and received Holy Communion from me. He had successfully led his men to the second line of enemy trenches when a machine gun bullet struck him and killed him instantly ...

Oh, Mrs Norris, he died a hero's death, and you will be able to tell your child later how brave his father was, and above all, how noble and conscientious a Catholic.

Yesterday morning I offered a Solemn Requiem Mass for the soul of the late Colonel. May God comfort you.

Also in Sydney at St Mary's Cathedral there was a Requiem Mass celebrated for Ignatius Bertram Norris at which the Archbishop preached a panegyric.

The very end of all things

Captain Norman Gibbins' headstone (Grave I.A.5) in Anzac Cemetery, Sailly-sur-la-Lys carries the inscription: My beloved brother. Son of the late William Gibbins. CE Australia.' The original Register entry reads:

Gibbins, Capt Norman. 55th (formerly 3rd) Bn Australian Infantry. Killed in action 20 July 1916. Age 35. Son of Mary and the late William Gibbins. Native of Ararat, Victoria, Australia.

Whilst Gibbins' role in the battle is dealt with in the appropriate place, the effect of his death and lack of recognition of his heroism is an important event on its own. It would seem that Violet Gibbins, owner and Head Mistress of Osborne College for Girls in Epping, NSW, wrote to Bean in an effort to get something done in this regard; the letter is dated 3 May 1920:

With great reluctance I yield to the prompting of numerous friends of the late Captain Norman Gibbins and submit the accompanying letters from his comrades and relative to his death in action. My brother's friends are of the opinion that his fine services and heroic self-service at Fromelles (where he was killed) have been entirely ignored. Certainly I have not received any official recognition of them, but I am satisfied that this was due to the unfortunate change in higher command at the time of his death. My brother's comrades invariably meet this explanation on my part with the statement, 'well anyhow, it was a gross shame' and, they are fiercely indignant about it.

The letter continues with the opinion of others at Fromelles that Gibbins should have got a VC, and refers Bean to Ellis's description of Gibbins' exploits. She concludes:

Of course, I am inexpressibly proud of all he has done and the esteem he has won from brave comrades. If you have sisters of your own you will understand and sympathise, even, if I appear lacking in modesty concerning this "sisterly pride".

My brother was my lifelong comrade and dearest friend so his death to me was "the very end of all things". My only comfort is that future generations may benefit a little by my sacrifice, and, young Australians find inspiration in his most noble and unselfish life and death. With apologies, I am, yours faithfully, Violet Gibbins.

Her next letter of 21 December 1921 seems to be sent to ask Bean what has happened to the 200 letters from friends which she had sent to him, and she reminded Bean that Gibbins was at the Landing, wounded, continued on till being wounded again on 28 April and then sent to England. He later returned to the Peninsula and was *'among the last to leave'*.

One of Gibbins officers, Lieut (later Capt.) P W Chapman of B Coy, 55th Bn, a 20-year-old student from Orange, was close to his CO throughout the last hours. They were, during the night while sitting on the paradoes, suddenly aware of a figure crawling towards them from behind. '*It proved to be a German, dreadfully wounded, bathed in blood and almost senseless.*' Gibbins and Chapman led him, but when Chapman let go one of his hands, '*the poor mangled brute got up on his knees ... and started to pray. Oh cruel! cruel! said Gib ... and together we helped him along.*' Chapman's letter to Violet Gibbins of 27 July 1916 also told the end of the story, which was fortunate because Chapman himself was killed in action 12 March 1917.

... ever since the 55th has been formed, I have been a Lieut in his Company, and not only was he my superior officer, but my best friend... I have never known a braver or cooler man in action than he, the welfare of his men was his chief thought, and they realized it and would follow him anywhere ... when returning to our trenches he remained till the last and

while directing me through the CT, was shot through the head. I did not see his body, but those who did, say that he died with a smile on his lips. He is buried near our trenches, with a wooden cross over his grave.

Then on 3 April 1918 Bert White, writing from N Ward, Randwick Military Hospital, added a little to the story:

... I first came in contact with Captain Gibbins about 5 am. He was quite cheery when he showed me my position and was moving freely amongst his men, although at the time he was wearing a bandage around his head, on account of a wound he had received some time in the night.

White then concluded:

Trusting you will accept the little information I can give concerning the death of a 'Soldier and a Man'.
[continued opposite.]

withdraw was arrived at after 5.15. Cass had received warning of its probability by 6.30. There is no record of the issue by divisional headquarters of the formal order to withdraw, but at 6.18 a message was despatched to the 8th and 15th Bdes informing them of it, and it appears to have been forwarded by the 14th Bde HQ at 6.30, and by its advanced report-centre at 7.3, reaching Cass at 7.50.'

What makes all this important is that Bean has chosen this style to bring to the readers' attention that something was very amiss at 5th Divisional HQ, very amiss indeed. The surviving file of messages confirms the confusion. One message timed at 5.20 was received at 5.10 and related to something that happened at 2.15. The only incoming message from 14th Bde refers to them sending over '*two sandbags containing German books and maps captured by 54th Bn yesterday.*' It is timed in at 4.55. Perhaps what was distracting McCay from his real task of commanding the 5th Australian Division was the message in from XI Corps timed at 6.25, one has to assume a result of their 5.00 meeting. Note carefully the use of the personal pronoun, ie Haking. It reads in its entirety thus:

> 5th Australian Division reports that the left Bn of their right Bde retired about daylight being unable to consolidate their positions. GOC centre brigade reported he could no longer hold his ground and I sent orders for him to be withdrawn to our original line of defence.
>
> The night attack on Sugarloaf Salient by 61st Division could not be organised in time to complete it under cover of darkness. 61st Division is now holding the divisional line with three battalions in front line and three battalions in support all fresh. Remainder organising in rear.
>
> 5th Australian Division has used up several battalions reinforcing its front line and has 1½ battalions fresh holding the front line and 1½ battalions being used for carrying parties and remainder have been employed in attack or support of attack.
>
> In these circumstances I do not think it is feasible to renew the attack with these two divisions though I am of the opinion that they are both capable of continuing to hold the line especially with the strong artillery support they have in the rear. It is probable that the 5th Australian Division when reorganised will have plenty of men available.

Unknowing of all this, those still surviving in the outpost, made their way back. A lot did not make it, but a large number did, Cass and his adjutant Capt. Lowe among the last to leave. Their safety and that of many others had been greatly aided by the covering fire directed by Capt. Gibbins. Sgt B A White, 2035, 55th Bn, a Lewis gunner recalled for Bean, the last moments:

> We were being hard pressed all the time until the word came through to retire ... at that time Capt Gibbins was but a few yards from me, and most of the infantry had retired. I was suddenly brought back to my

THE VERY END OF ALL THINGS (contd)

Another member of B Coy, P W Lurbalestier wrote to Olivet Gibbins from Hurdcott on 21 January 1917:

We thought a lot of your brother, and would have followed him anywhere, in fact when going up to the front line, we met another Battalion coming back. 'No good', said their officer, 'we can't get up there.' 'The 55th can' said our skipper and we did. I was one of the old 3rds and was consequently under your brother a long while.

R G Metcalfe, also of B Coy, added something else which highlights another aspect of Gibbins:

I shall never forget the time we were going to the trenches to participate in the fighting, when our Captain read to us the Colonel's message—the last message to a great many of our comrades. The 'boys' remarked afterwards that they never heard a man read a farewell message as our 'dear old captain' read that message.

Bean's research had Gibbins born 22 April 1878 and thus 38, not 35 as his sister believed, and that he worked at Ipswich, Queensland. Bean was unable to do anything in connection with the recognition of Gibbins' bravery, but as the text shows, his praise for the captain was without bounds, all he could do in the circumstances, and revealing Bean at his best.

ONLY TREES?

Lieut Col Cass of 54th Bn one of many troubled by the accuracy of German artillery fire ventured this idea in his Report:

I believe that the Germans have some very accurate system of observing the rear of our position. It could be done by a telescope periscope (similar to a submarine's periscope) about 20 feet long and placed in a tree. The observer in that case could easily be in a dugout behind the tree observing everything and reporting to the guns when he saw a target. I know that on returning to Rue Petillon via York Avenue I had no sooner reached our 300 line with about

[continued next page]

ONLY TREES? (contd)
12 or 15 men than heavy shells rained on us and searched the avenue for about 50 yards. This could not have been done by chance as there had been no fire on this point for over 15 minutes prior to my arrival there. Similarly any party of 6 or 8 in the forward end of Brompton Road was similarly shelled by accurate fire, and yet only trees in the German area could be seen.

AWM E4046

While Cass may have had this explanation, when Bean visited the area on 11 November 1918 and all the leaves had fallen he photographed trees used by the Germans at Fromelles: no periscope, just a place for brave German observers at the top with a phone!

> senses by hearing Capt Gibbins call out: 'come on, all you gunners', I immediately picked up my spare parts and followed him.

Having seen the last of 14th Bde, including his own team on their way back to safety, Gibbins was the last to leave and entered the sap behind them. The communication trench was clogged with wounded so in a careless moment, he left its protection. Sgt White saw the result:

> I saw him reach the top of our trenches where he turned his head around sharply and was immediately struck in the head by a bullet and killed instantaneously.

It was a moment witnessed by many and never forgotten for all their lives. But such a death meant that Gibbins would be buried by his own men and in a marked grave, unlike so many of his comrades.

Ellis seems to have thought Gibbins died at his post rather than when seemingly safe after the moment of triumph. Instead, in general terms he wrote: '*one by one they fell at their posts, and of this gallant band scarce a man was left alive*'. Cass got it wrong too, in his Report written a few days later before he was taken away to hospital he blamed Gibbins for misunderstanding the orders and wrote that Gibbins had '*withdrawn his Company at once*'. The result of which was that the Germans '*rushed in between my front and rear*'. For the record, only Cass saw it that way.

As the list of prisoners in Chapter 9 attests, very many of 14th Bde did not escape, but did survive.

At 9.20 the Bavarian intelligence officer noted:

> The last of the Englishmen who were defending themselves have been captured.

This part of the story would not be complete without some of the last paragraphs of Lieut Col Cass's Report, the man who would be, by the end of the war, the only survivor of 14th Bde COs.

> ... there was no communication except by runners with Bde HQ and all seemed too dazed to send for help. Our communication trenches were being blown to pieces and not until I myself reached Bn HQ at Rue de Petillon about 11 am was I able to inform anyone of this most pressing need for doctors and trained stretcher bearers. I there saw Capt Cosgrove RMO and told him the position. He at once sent off 14 stretchers and three doctors but I was too exhausted to do anything more. At about 1 pm a cart came and took me away to the 14th Bde HQ at Les Croix Lecornex when I reported verbally to the OC 14th Inf Bde.

Lieut Col Cass was invalided to England, and never saw action again, and in fact never recovered from this day at Fromelles. Years later when Bean contacted Cass as he was preparing the story of the battle, Cass finished his reply thus:

> I hope you have a reliable account of this fight – I haven't read or heard one yet!

In contrast to the stories of the 8th and 14th Bdes, that of the 15th Bde is short and without feats of arms to match the deeds of Toll or Cass. In hindsight it is clear they were given a task that was not attainable and were subject to a number of orders which were emotional reactions rather than military decisions. Part of this was undoubtedly due to the style of Brig. Gen. H E 'Pompey' Elliott, but most because McCay was not being able to grasp the fact that due to the huge width of No-Man's Land in front of 15th Bde and the presence of the Sugarloaf dominating it, the same tactics as used for the 8th and 14th Bdes could not succeed here. An example was the task of digging a trench across 450 yards of No-Man's Land as against 150 yards, let alone the problems of moving men and supplies through a trench of that length in such a vulnerable situation. Nobody seems to have given such things a thought. McCay certainly did not. This has nothing to do with his excuse, after it was all over, that he was obeying orders. The orders were about the objective, not the method of obtaining it: McCay had no experience in such things and even though Elliott obeyed and cooperated with him at every level, between them there was no sign of initiative nor innovation. Understandable, as both were lawyers by training and thus governed by precedent (see margin: *An Efficient Foreman*). The fate of 15th Bde was also attributable to the lack of planning and cooperation between Mackenzie and McCay, and Carter and Elliott: all conducting themselves like strangers who had not been properly introduced. Was this Haking's failing, or was it just the style of the time?

The only memos issued in the days prior to the battle that show any initiative or what would now be called 'lateral thinking' were from Lieut Col C M Wagstaff, a British professional soldier now McCay's GSO1. His drafting of orders was precise, organised and readable. There can be no doubt that Wagstaff would have been appalled at the speed with which the attack was being thrown together and so took advantage of the postponement from 17th to 19th to tell the Bdes on 17 July that: '*Patrolling will be done in No-Man's Land to learn the terrain ... Bdes and units will now learn methods of, and arrange to use apparatus for communication with aeroplanes ... plans of enemy trenches should be laid out and parties of assaulting battalions, so far as they are not required to hold the trenches, will be exercised over them. On the plans, enemy strong points and machine gun positions should be marked.*' All implying that these basic tasks had not been done before.

CLEARING THE TRENCHES

Probably because he had not been battered by front line action at Fromelles, Lieut Col Scott of 56th wrote movingly of what his battalion did after the battle ended. No other War Diary handles this so clearly:

20 July. 12 noon. Enemy bombardment eased up, which considerably improved condition for bringing out the wounded from the front line trench, also the 300 yard trench. 3 pm. Parties commenced to arrive from 53rd, 54th and 55th Bns to assist 56th in collecting wounded men from No-Man's Land, during the night 20/21. Also a party arrived from Pioneer Bn to assist in carrying dead from the trenches ... during the night over 100 wounded men were brought in from No-Man's Land.
21 July 8 am ... remainder of day was devoted to clearing the trenches of dead, also bringing in wounded men who crawled in from No-Man's Land.

AN EFFICIENT FOREMAN

In a letter to Bean the noble 'Pompey' Elliott in the late 1920s as the clouds gathered, wrote this of himself:

'That I myself have my own grevious limitations I am free to admit. By training in law my mind has developed so that it instinctively looks to the past for enlightenment. I am everlastingly looking for a precedent. Had I like Sir John Monash had a training in Science and Engineering I might have done better.

The teaching of Science and Engineering tends to the evolution of new ideas to meet old difficulties. Monash's contribution to the Art of War is the use of the smoke barrage to screen movement and the exact synchronization of effort, both due to his engineering skill.

For myself a word will make it clear to me my leader's intention.
I am an efficient foreman—not the inventor, the designer of the new.'

ORDER OF BATTLE
15th Australian Brigade (all Victoria)
GOC: Brig. Gen. H E Elliott
Bde Major: Major G E G Wieck
SC: Capt. R G Legge

60th Bn (assaulting/left)
CO: Major G G McCrae †
2IC: Major T P Elliott †
Adj: Lieut H Wrigley *
A Coy (left): Capt. H McD Plowman †
B Coy (right): Capt. E A Evans †
C Coy: Capt. H C Piercy *
D Coy: Capt. H O Ground †

59th Bn (assaulting/right)
CO: Lieut Col E A Harris *
SC/2IC: Major H T C Layh
A Coy (left): Capt. A W Liddelow †
B Coy (right): Capt. K G McDonald *
C Coy:
D Coy:

58th Bn (support)
CO: Lieut Col A Jackson *
2IC: Major C A Denehy
A Coy: Major A J S Hutchinson †
B Coy:
C Coy:
D Coy:

57th Bn (reserve)
CO: Lieut Col J C Stewart
SC:
A Coy: Capt. N Marshall
B Coy: Capt. H G L Cameron
C Coy:
D Coy:

15th MG Coy
CO: Lieut S W Neale

15th Field Coy
CO: Major H Greenway

† Killed in Action. * Wounded. July 1916.

Major G G MCCRAE, 60th Bn
Geoffrey Gordon McCrae was born at Hawthorn, Victoria, on 18 Jan 1890, the son of George Gordon McCrae, the poet, novelist and artist, and brother of Dorothy Frances McCrae, another poet. He was at Melbourne Grammar School 1905-06 before studying architecture. After hours, he was a Lieutenant in 58th Bn at Essendon serving under Lieut Col H E Elliott. In 1914 he went away as [continued opposite.]

No-Man's Land in front of 15th Bde was between 400 and 450 yards wide and absolutely flat. It was this feature that both necessitated the building of the Sugarloaf and its paramount control over two thirds of the sector in the battle. And being on the outside of the elbow of the line ensured that a head-on attack was impossible to mount. This was endorsed when the plans were drawn up, having the 184th British Bde attacking one side and the 15th Australian Bde the other: and so what about the front? This was facing a gap of 300 yards where the four 15th Bde machine guns and five 58th Bn Lewis guns were positioned, the idea being that the British and Australians would come together on the parapets of the Sugarloaf which by then would have been pulverised by the artillery and the enemy demoralised by flashing bayonets and shouting.

There is no real evidence that the artillery did any important damage to the Sugarloaf if it did any at all. A glimpse of the Australian Artillery Map (page 154) shows that they did not have it as a target, and the aerial photograph gives scant evidence of shell holes in the vicinity. In short it can be said that the artillery did not do its job, because most of the wire was not cut and the German account gives no hint of being greatly inconvenienced prior to, or during the battle in the vicinity of Sugarloaf.

While Elliott became one of the great personalities of the AIF he was, at Fromelles, like the rest, learning. What was to make him unique was his command of the brigade for all the war, providing a consistency that could be understood and respected. Thus the *esprit de corps* that grew up around 15th Bde began with Fromelles, when the test was so severe that nothing could conceal the real character of the commanders, and the men they chose to be principal officers. The Brigade had some 25% of its officers and NCOs with experience on Gallipoli, and were '*well-seasoned*'. The Brigade was all Victorian which provided further cohesion.

The official boundaries of the 15th Bde sector were from the east side of Bond Street to a point between where rue Delvas and the Laies River crossed the Australian front line. This was longer than the lines held by 14th and 8th, because it included the 300 yards covered by 15th Bde machine guns. Although the brigade was expected to go forward directly south, all the fence lines, rows of trees or stumps from the old orchards, and the layout of the fields were at an oblique angle to the line of the advance, whereas all the British brigades were following these semi-natural lines. The 15th Bde was unique in having this obstacle which was of real consequence after dark, as was the river enlarged and distorted by shell holes, and another diagonal across their field of battle.

The afternoon bombardment of the Sugarloaf was seen to be ineffective by artillery observers and according to Bean at 2.35 instructions were given to increase the barrage so as to cut the wire. Then Bean remarks that the message was '*received only at 5.10, too late*'. It was another example of the near total shambles of the artillery operations at Fromelles. While the men who were new to the job might be excused, there can be none for the experienced senior artillery officers, British and Australian. Some have suggested the disorganisation stemmed from the fact that nobody was in charge of the artillery overall, and thus there was no coordination of effort. The patrols of 15th Bde had found during the night of 18/19 July that the German wire was undamaged and as the Germans had posts as far as 80 yards in front of their front line, so safely situated in a sea of barbed wire, there was no chance for the attackers to get close enough to do any damage, especially after having run, crawled and scrambled over 300 yards to get that far. Elliott's Report on 18 July: '*Patrols were unable to approach wire owing to our artillery fire. Enemy covering posts were found halfway across No-Man's Land. The wire was not inspected at any point.*' One can only guess the thoughts of the 15th Bde Staff Officer who wrote on the message '*Too late*', and an hour later watched his men go out.

Major G G McCrae,
Lemnos, Christmas Day 1915.
AWM C1190

The 15th Bde itself was well organised. The assaulting Bns were in position at 3.25 pm. On the right 59th Bn under command of Lieut Col E A Harris, a farmer, aged 36, and on the left 60th Bn under Major G G McCrae, an architectural apprentice aged 26. In support was 58th Bn under Lieut Col A Jackson, aged 29, and in reserve, 57th Bn commanded by Lieut Col J C Stewart, aged 32. All four were Gallipoli veterans, although only two, McCrae and Stewart, were Elliott appointments. The 59th Bn had been in the line earlier for a day, the 60th had '*not yet been in the front line.*'

In the period before the assault 15th Bde got some of the same treatment as the other two brigades. The Bde signals Officer around 5 pm: '*All communications forward of advanced report centre hopelessly torn up. Despatch Order Service will have to be established between here and Bde HQ*' and then from Elliott in his HQ. '*Assaulting Bns in position and enemy shelling with H E mainly directed at VC Avenue which appears to be blocked. Third Bn not yet in position owing to barrage. Will endeavour to expedite. MG Coys have suffered 17 casualties*

Major G G MCCRAE (contd)
Captain in 7th Bn of which Elliott was CO. McCrae was not at the landing, '*a source of lasting regret*' as he was organising transfers at sea. He became Major the next day, was severely wounded 17 May, then shell-shocked 12 July, but stayed until evacuation.

His conduct had so impressed Elliott that he was determined to have McCrae as a battalion commander in 15th Bde, and in May McCrae joined the 60th Bn. But it was not until the eve of Fromelles that Elliott was able to pass through the papers for McCrae to be gazetted as Lieut-Col.

So as Major, he led the fourth wave of 60th Bn on 19 July and was eighty yards out in No-Man's Land when shot in the neck and killed. His body was found by Capt. Norman Marshall of 57th Bn and brought back for burial in Rue-du-Bois Cemetery (Grave: I F 33).

NO ONE MOVING

There is in Bean's notes an account which might be related by Lieut Kerr of 60th Bn combined with observations by Capt. N Marshall of 57th and later CO of 60th Bn. Bean used very little of it, however it gives good detail not recorded elsewhere.

A and C Coys went first [A Coy was led by Capt. Plowman, with Lieuts Sterling and Smith—all killed. C Coy was led by Capt. Piercey with Lieuts Russell, Simpson and Hamilton all wounded.] ... *the Germans opened on the first wave when the third went over. They could see our men lying dead all over—the place—but no one moving. When Kerr with third wave* [B Coy led by Capt. Evans with Lieut Rhind – both killed] *got about three quarters way over they seemed to have passed all the dead of our men by that time. Kerr had a few with him. The Germans were standing at the parapet ... crossing the Laies where Kerr did there was about a foot of water and there was probably a machine gun for it. There were machine guns in front of the Sugarloaf. About an hour after the 60th went over the Germans began to shell No-Man's Land and our part of the line, and a lot of men were killed. Kerr and a few others got into a position where they got a little cover. They dug in with entrenching tools.*

McCrae with the last wave [D Coy led by Capt. Ground with Lieut McKinnon and Wright—both killed: Ground died of wounds] *as did Major Elliott* [2IC 60th Bn], *Capt. Wrigley* [Adjutant], *all BN HQ—except Orderly Room Sgt. McCrae was shot through the neck about 80 yards in front of the line, Elliott was shot through the chest and crawled back to about the same line as McCrae, but more to the left. Marshall came across him by accident later—he had taken his coat, revolver and all his kit off.*

Ground [leading D Coy] *lying out the next day about 2 pm sent in a message* 'If you want to do a Xtrian act send out a drop of water'. *Marshall slung a couple of water bottles over his shoulder and found Ground—hit in the groin. They got him in, though sniped at.*

on our right. Inform Neale. Assaulting Bns as yet have not suffered much. Enemy wire on our left has not suffered very much. Observation difficult.'

The heavy losses in the MG Coy at this early stage must have considerably upset their ability to cover the advance and as this was critical to the assault one wonders why Ellis and Bean omit to mention it. Unlike the other sectors nobody reported casualties from our own 'shorts', not a problem here, doubtless due to the width of No-Man's Land.

All battalions, except 58th were at full strength and morale was high as Elliott moved around the front line getting things in order, and pretending to be optimistic about it all when privately he knew it was hopeless. He had his field HQ at Trou Post, near the site of what is now Trou Aid Post Military Cemetery, and within easy walking distance of the front line, but providing no vantage point, thus reliance on telephones and telegraphs for information was a critical part of the operation.

The assaulting battalions moved out in front of the Australian breastworks forming up in waves, the first of which went forward at 5.45, under the protection of our artillery cover as well as under attack from German artillery. A message came back from Elliott at Trou Post to Bde HQ:

> Infantry advance commenced. Enemy opening fire, musketry and machine guns not very hot.

It was timed as being sent at 6.45, received 6.51 and then remarked as being received at 5.55. There is no evidence that the 15th Bde started an hour later than the other Bdes, and this is the first indication that their clock was an hour ahead. One considered explanation of this is that Elliott alone adopted a time scale based on hours after zero hour ie 11 am. The attack was to take place at 7 hours after zero, hence 6 for everybody else, but 7 for 15th Bde.

The four waves went over five minutes apart, the fourth wave led by McCrae had included the signalers with the telephones. But all were killed or wounded and the phone wires cut by shells, and from then on Elliott and others had to rely on what they could see or on messages brought back by battered, bewildered officers and men.

Every now and then some artillery observer would report a sighting of Australians, but well short of the German front line. Then as the sound of rifle and machine gun fire died down, Elliott took this to be an indication that his men must be in command of the German line. His mind could hardly be expected to attribute the silence to the grim reality that most of his men were dead or wounded, and therefore reported at 6.30 it appeared the '*attack seems to be successful.*'

Ten minutes later a battered Major H T C Layh came out of No-Man's Land to report, on instructions from Lieut Col Harris, that the 59th was only half way across and could go no further. Elliott, still unable to grasp the gravity of the situation, sent Layh back to Harris to tell him to make another attempt as it '*appeared the rest of the line had succeeded*'. This was not a helpful judgement: it was at best an optimistic guess, and had to be revised within half an hour. '*Report from 59th that they cannot get on. Trenches are full of enemy and every man who rises is shot down. Reports from wounded indicate the attack is failing for want of support.*' Then a little later at 7.50: '*Reinforcements appear to be badly needed along all our fronts. At present we are just hanging on with men in some places of the front trench. Greenway reports 59 and 60 casualties very severe.*'

Major Greenway, 15th Field Coy, was working in the communication trench and therefore had access to real information, which with no telephone wires open except to his HQ, Elliott sadly lacked. As there had been no word as yet from 60th Bn, Elliott sent out Lieut Doyle, 60th Bn Intelligence Officer, to find McCrae and ascertain what they were doing. Doyle found none of them, but only the 59th, and brought back a reply to Elliott's previous command, that a further advance was impossible. Within the hour Harris was blown up and had to be evacuated. Major Layh took over command of the 59th.

The 60th Bn did have one little pocket alive and reasonably optimistic, an event which Bean chose to ignore completely even though two of its number were awarded significant decorations for this work. It was led by Capt. T Kerr who went over in the third wave and according to Bean got within 150 yards of the German parapet. Bean consulted Kerr when writing his account and recorded Kerr's memory as that of a 'survivor'. Kerr had seen the Germans '*standing out shoulder high… looking as if they were wondering what was coming next*', and seems to have been the only 60th Bn officer to have got that far and returned to tell his story. He was in a hole well out in No-Man's Land with Pte R Poulter 2878 and three others, and needed to send a message back—the only piece of paper they had between them was the fly-leaf of a pocket New Testament which Poulter always carried. With difficulty Kerr wrote: '*here with 4 men, a few yards from parapet. Must have reinforcements. Useless going on without*'. Poulter buttoned the little book in his pocket and made his way back to the Australian lines. When darkness

ADVANCED DOWN VC SAP INTO HELL

Simon Fraser 3101, 57th Bn, kept a diary as well as writing letters. As sergeant in B Coy he had much to do in the days leading up to the battle:

17 July: went out with 10 men cutting entanglements, got wet through arrived in at 03.00. To hop parapet at 15.00 stunt, did not come off had quiet night and did duty from 1 to stand to at 3.15.

18 July: heavy bombardment on both sides some close calls for our chaps. Our company relieved out of the trenches by the 59th.

19 July. I stayed behind with Mr Edgar and 12 men to cut the wire entanglements. Left the support line and reached at 06.45, left in the warpath at 16.30. 59th hopped the parapet at 17.30 and occupied the German trenches. We waited in supports advanced down VC Sap into Hell, found the advance had been a failure. We occupied our old line and were shelled all night.

20 July: Jack Simons, Sgt Bull Robertson were killed, and dead and wounded everywhere. Next morning, the 60th were practically wiped out, 58th and 59th smashed up and 57th got Hell, the stretcher bearers going all day and wounded out in front to be brought in.

21 July: Foggy morning. Was going all night bringing in wounded. B Coy brought in 250, brought up packs from Rifle Villa and had good sleep—first for 3 nights.

22 July: Another quiet day. Saw Fred Hindes and brought up water for platoon. Had bundle of papers and some letters from home.

COURTESY R FRASER

... NOT ONLY OUR CAPTAIN ...
Aubrey W Liddelow was born 10 November 1876 in Gippsland and educated at Scotch College from where he matriculated in May 1893; then attended the University of Melbourne. He married Fanny Retallack in 1904 and became a school teacher gaining his early experience at state schools in Melbourne suburbs and country towns until he joined Melbourne High School in January 1914 as Second Master.

Capt A W Liddelow, 59th Bn

He enlisted 11 November 1914 and left for overseas as 2nd Lieut, in 8th Bn, in December. He was at the Landing, was wounded twice during the campaign, but was there for the evacuation. A photograph he took at the Landing remains at Melbourne High School. In Egypt in February 1916 he joined the 59th as Captain. At Fromelles he led A Coy, and afterwards was posted missing. His widow wrote of that time:

For many months we could gain no tiding of him: but, early in the new year, several wounded men of my husband's company returned to Australia, and one man said, 'I was with the Captain from the time he went over our parapet until it was all over... On going over our parapet, the Captain was wounded in the head: but he rose at once and led us on... He reached the German lines with only a handful of men left, and, in going over their parapet, he was again wounded—in the shoulder and then in the arm: but nothing daunted him. In order to spare the few men remaining,
[continued opposite.]

came down on the whole '*dreadful day*', as Kerr called it, he and his three men crawled back, well after midnight. Although wounded Kerr refused to be evacuated, and set about helping other survivors.

The 59th Bn also had lost most of its officers in the opening minutes. However Capt A Liddelow with a small group were thought to have reached the German parapet but '*the position there being hopeless, withdrew them into shell holes to await support*'. But of course support never came, and Liddelow, now with three wounds, refused to leave his post and was later killed, but some of his men got back and told as much as they knew (see margin: ... *Not Only Our Captain*...).

Bean provides a vivid description of how it was in No-Man's Land but his paragraphs are clearly the recollections of a number of men without attributions to anybody in particular. The only 'hard' evidence that any 15th Bde got through the wire and onto or near to the German parapet is from Liddelow's party. The only prisoner taken and surviving that first charge was from 59th Bn, and the identifiable remains that were found there after the armistice were also 59th and 58th. The 60th got no further than the uncut wire; if any were taken prisoner, they did not survive.

These events were not all known nor confirmed until later in the night, so we return to Elliott at around 7.30 when it was still daylight, and he believed that his men were 'in' the German lines.

According to Bean; at about 7.30, McCay authorised both 14th and 15th Bdes to use half of their support battalion as reinforcements for the assaulting troops. In fact the 14th were authorised at 7.34. As already examined this was 55th Bn under McConaghy, and for 15th Bde it would be the 58th under Major Hutchinson.

At 7.45 McCay advised '... *GOC 15th Bde to use rest of 3rd Bn to stiffen and go on with the assault bringing up ½ of his reserve Bn to hold his front and 300 yard line.*' Then at 8.50 pm to 15th Bde, '*You cannot have any more troops to assault with. You have three battalions to assault with.*'

What was Elliott going to do with his third battalion, the 58th? He believed there were men of his brigade in or near the German trenches and he had, at this point, heard nothing to confirm or deny this. He took the relative absence of musketry fire to be an indication that there had been some success and the 58th would be just what was needed to, in McCay's words, '*stiffen and go on with the assault*'. How he could support this decision without any evidence is one thing, and why McCay could approve it is something else. In the other two brigades it was all based on real knowledge: Elliott had nothing to go on.

Over and above the disasters swamping 15th Bde was the situation on its right, where 184th Bde had also assaulted the Sugarloaf and some of whose men, like those of 15th Bde, were thought to have got in. In support of these beleagured garrisons, although there was not a shred of evidence that they existed, the 184th was to make another assault at 9 o'clock (originally at 8.30). In fact the 184th had already reported via Haking at 8.00 that '*they have not taken any of the German trenches on their front ... the Germans still hold Sugarloaf*'. The new attack as Haking noted had another reason '*in order to help the Australians, whose Left Brigade had failed*'.

Quite how such an attack could have been entertained considering what had happened to the 184th is difficult to understand and perhaps due to its weakness, the 184th asked for help. We learn from Bean that '*the commander of 184th Bde sent at 7.52, through the headquarters of the two divisions, the following message to 15th Australian Bde: Am attacking at 9 pm. Can your right battalion co-operate?*' This was received by Elliott at 8.10.

In fact the time of receipt marked on that message is 8.02. This means it took 10 minutes in transmission from British Bde HQ to British Div HQ to Australian Div HQ to Australian Bde HQ. However the marked time of receipt 8.02 is in a circle on the face of the message, a characteristic of all the messages in the 15th Bde HQ file. Investigating this, one finds that all, *except* the three messages concerning the supporting of the 184th, which appear to be hand delivered, are 'retimed' just under an hour *before* they were sent ie. Elliott's first message from Trou Post to HQ about the battle was timed as being sent at 7.30, received at 7.40 and later marked as received at 6.44. This discovery caused close examination of the 15th Bde HQ files and there are some features that are troubling.

The request from 184th Bde surely required an answer. There is none in either the Bde or Div files. It is obvious many orders and messages in this situation would have to be given personally and were never written down. But that there are no instructions, references or notes about, or to or from, the MG and Field Companies concerning the 9 o'clock attack and/or the cooperation with the British seems very strange. Both were in the direct path of the action and had significant casualties, and their part in 15th Bde operations were very important. Elliott at 8.13 called forward 2 companies of 58th Bn. This message timed

... NOT ONLY OUR CAPTAIN ... (contd)

he withdrew us, and we took shelter in a shell crater until reinforcements should come ... I had been wounded by this time, and I had had quite enough, so I went to the Captain and begged him to return with me, as his wounds needed attention. But he said, 'I'll never walk back into safety and leave the men I have led into such grave danger! We'll wait for reinforcements.' He then ordered me back, but I had only gone about ten yards when a shell ended the life of a hero if ever there was one. Many of his men have since proved this statement perfectly, and all speak beautifully of their Captain. One man said, 'He was not only our Captain, but our friend and a Christian gentleman.'

Aubrey's youngest brother Roy was born near Maffra 22 April 1884 and became an accountant, marrying in 1912. He enlisted in 1915 and met up with his brother in Egypt in early 1916. Roy joined the 59th Bn there, and as 2nd Lieut went with the battalion to France. At Fromelles he was badly wounded when searching No-Man's Land for Aubrey, whose body was never found. Roy returned to Australia on 8 August 1918, and later joined the SEC becoming its General Manager 1946–49. He died in 1967.

INFORMATION AND PHOTOGRAPH COURTESY P LIDDELOW & MELBOURNE HIGH SCHOOL

15TH BRIGADE TELEPHONES

All telephone lines within 500 yards of the front trench were smashed during the earlier bombardment. One surface line was run out under fire, to Trou Post in the 300 yd line and was maintained throughout the action, also one from Trou Post to the front line. The enemy's fire barrage stopped nearly all communications with the assaulting line. Officers and runners were killed so no reliable information could be obtained.

—Brig. Gen. H E Elliott, 23 July 1916

THE MATTER OF TIME
No section of this work was more difficult to sort out than this. The starting point came from a chance observation in a letter from T C Whiteside, 59th Bn, that the battalion was subject to 'Summer Time' and that he thought this was a good enough idea to be copied in Australia. In a moment the disparity in a number of timings was explained. For example how a message sent at 7 pm arrived at shortly after 6 pm. Research revealed that Summer Time for the British came into being in the spring of 1916 as the result of an Act of Parliament, the Summer Time Act (1916), based on an idea suggested by a William Willett around 1907. In 1916 summer time began on 21 May and ran till 1 Oct; in 1917 from 8 April to 17 Sept and 1918 24 March to 30 Sept.

Bean, however, noted that '*the British and French advanced their clocks an hour on June 14*' which only adds to the confusion. And there is plenty of confusion. According to Bean the Germans had begun their Daylight Saving time before British Summer Time was adopted on the Western Front putting them two hours ahead until June 14, when they were one hour ahead. Their histories agree that for the Germans the battle of Fromelles began at 7 pm, which implies that the British 6 pm was Summer Time. Thus the battle really began at 5 pm 'true time' as Bean called Greenwich Mean Time. This might well explain the brightness shown in the '6.30' aerial view of the battlefield.

Doubtless there is some explanation to this confusion, but the issue is raised to help resolve the further one hour difference noted by Gen. Mackenzie, and by 15th Bde and its Battalions whose additional hour was out of line with *all* other Brigades and Battalions.

at 9 o'clock and 'retimed' at 8.13, read: '*Send ½ Bn to 300 yard trenches near VC Avenue. The Ave is practically destroyed so they will have to take the open road artillery formation. Warn them to be prepared to go up and hold front line and also help with fatigues. OC to report to me at Trou Post.*' This must refer to 57th Bn and not 58th Bn, and this message was followed by one timed at being sent at 9.50, received at 10 o'clock and 'retimed' at 9.07. '*Have sent 58th Bn into front line. They will be there now. Half 57th Bn have reported, am now organizing them. Have ordered Donohy to co operate with the Bde on his right at 10.00.*' Then from Wagstaff at 5th Division timed at 8.38 and received at 9.07, '*61st Div left has failed to get in. Fresh bombardment of Sugarloaf and line southwest being carried on and will continue till 9.00 pm when fresh attack will be made by 61st*', which seems to indicate that Wagstaff was ignorant of the 15th Bde input into the 9 o'clock attack. This could add weight to a view that Bean was incorrect in saying the original request came through the four HQs, and in fact went directly from the 184th Bde to 15th Bde. But this is not supported by later remarks by Wagstaff and others indicating that they were aware of the 184th's request.

No sequence of messages reveals more clearly the confusion. If the 184th Bde were attacking at 9 o'clock, Elliott was an hour late in his cooperation. Clearly this could be explained as already noted by Elliott using 'hours after zero' rather than clock time: but perhaps it had something to do with a misunderstanding about Summer Time and GMT? (See margin: *The Matter Of Time*.)

If we go back to Bean, his version of the period notes that at around 8.20, Haking, due to the bad news that was now filtering in, decided '*the best course was to bring back all elements of 183rd and 184th Brigades ... and to reconstitute its front line with troops of the third battalion. He countermanded the projected 9 o'clock attack, of which information at the moment reached him.*' Is Bean suggesting that Haking had not heard of the 9 o'clock attack before? He then says that 183rd and 184th were informed of the cancellation at 8.30 '*barely in time, if his reinforcing battalions had been punctual, to prevent them from launching the attempt*'.

With so much uncoordinated activity Bean's next sequence requires special attention:

> Haking had not directly informed the 5th Division of the cancellation (probably he was unaware that it had been asked to co-operate), but a message was despatched at 8.30 from the 61st Division.

Under instructions from Corps Commander am withdrawing from captured enemy line after dark.

This had been received at the 5th Divisional Headquarters at 8.35 [In fact it was marked in at 8.30], and it is just within the bounds of possibility that, had instant action been taken, the assault of the 15th Bde at 9 o'clock might have been stopped... But apparently there was a failure at the headquarters of 5th Australian Division to grasp either the meaning of the message or the importance of sending it on to General Elliott. Thus it was not until Haking's order was received at 9.10 that the information was forwarded by McCay to the 15th Bde as follows:

9.25 pm. 61st Division not attacking tonight. General Elliott may withdraw 59th Bn and its reinforcements if he thinks attack is not likely to succeed.

It was, of course, too late, the 58th had long since left and were now nearly all dead or wounded and it would be midnight before their fate was reported back to Elliott. In a memoir of a survivor it is mentioned that the Germans had a searchlight on the Sugarloaf and it was this, together with the flares, that enabled them to pick off the 58th and 59th.

But Bean's sequence does not hold together. At the beginning, the message about '*co-operating*' came via Mackenzie's and McCay's HQs, so both Divisional Staffs knew, thus Haking's knowledge or otherwise was not critical. If Elliott had replied to 184th in the affirmative there is no doubt they would have informed him directly. If he had said 'no', and there is such a message in the file, but untimed, that explains why 184th did not bother to tell him. At another level both Mackenzie and McCay had to get authorisation from Haking to use new battalions. Thus Haking should have known about McCay authorizing Elliott to use half of the 58th Bn because that was Haking's decision and now specially important because the 58th was to be used to support the 184th in the 9 o'clock attack. McCay's sanitised Report carefully deals with this: '*The 15th Bde were asked to co-operate and authority was given to use half of the 58th ...*' It can be safely assumed Haking was not privy to McCay's idea that the battalion should be put into the battle '*to get even with the enemy*'. But as will emerge later, it is almost certain that McCay did not consult Haking regarding using any of the third battalions and made the decisions himself, advising Haking later.

Regarding Bean's notion that this assault was in some ways initiated by 184th and 183rd Bdes, in Carter's Report, albeit scant, there is no indication of such an initiative. On the evidence of the state of the 184th, it is highly doubtful if Carter was able to initiate anything. Stewart's 183rd Bde was only in

[continued page 161]

IT IS EXPECTED THE PLACE WILL BE PRETTY STRONG

Lieut L W Elliott of 57th Bn, in reserve, was in a unique position to observe the preparations, having been in the line only two days earlier.

16 July. Preparation for big stunt. Our Bn and 58th to go forward in first line ... Great stores coming up. Expect to jump over 3 pm tomorrow. Very busy getting bombs ready.

The next day Elliott made a very interesting note about the Germans.

17 July. Very foggy. Stunt put off as artillery couldn't see to pick up range. Great preparation for attack, no attack has been made here for two years and it is expected the place will be pretty strong. Heavy bombardment by the enemy. 58th pretty badly knocked. We took over their frontage as well as our own.

He did not conceal his disappointment about the withdrawal of 57th.

18 July. Expect to go forward this morning. Heavily shelled. Stunt put off 24 hours. 59th and 60th relieve us, we are to act as divisional reserve. Very disappointing as we made all the preparations but right as our boys were so knocked about. We left the trenches at about 11 pm and marched back to Sailly to billets for the night ... had some supper, getting to bed at 1 am.

Lieut Elliott's entry for the next day, the day of the battle, is not easy to read but what can be deciphered is this: *19 July. Slept till 10 am. Felt much better. Had breakfast at Estaminet. Marched up to Windy Corner, our rendezvous. Attack made at 7 pm. First and second lines got nearly across (400 yards in open) ... could not hold what they had gained. The both Battalions of our Brigade were practically wiped out.*

Elliott (no kin to Pompey) remained with 57th Bn throughout the war earning a DSO in the victory at Villers-Bretonneux 24/25 April 1918.

COURTESY G H ELLIOTT

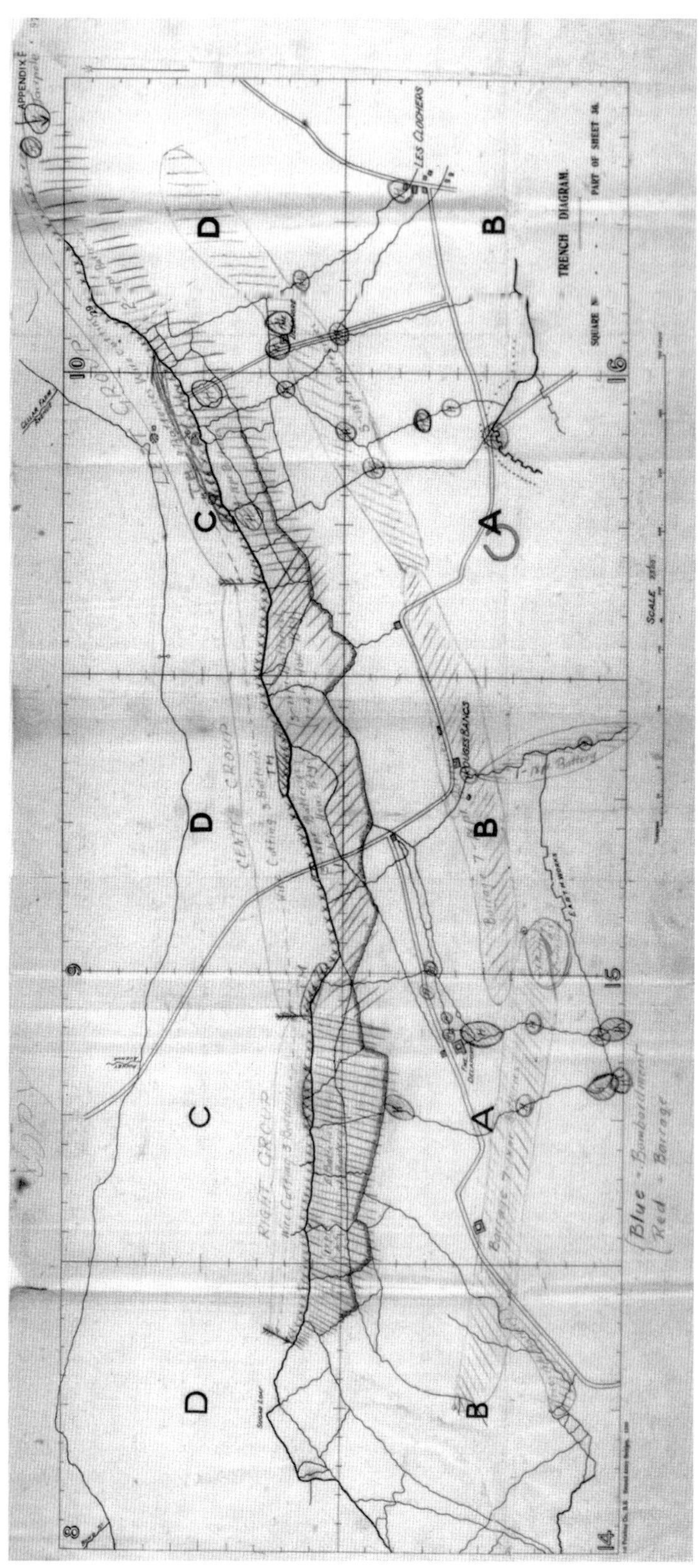

THE ARTILLERY AT FROMELLES
With the battle over Brig. General Christian prepared his report (about 400 words) on 24 July. He began by listing who was under his command: 5th Australian Divisional Artillery, 4th Divisional Artillery and 171st Brigade RFA including Medium Trench Mortars. The map given here is the one he used in his Report noting that the artillery was divided into three groups and '*given similar zones to those of the three infantry Brigades*'. These can be seen on the map by the different shading. It is clear that the Sugarloaf was outside the Australian area.

Christian then details the placement of five MT Mortars (2 from 6th Div, 1 from each of 50th Div, 1st and 3rd Canadian Divisions) and that Major Sir J Keane RFA had control of this group. The mortars were placed into protection as they arrived '*in the necessary emplacements being prepared for them in the trenches*'—but no dates given. However Christian says that 4th Div. and 171st arrived on 15 July and all the batteries of the division commenced registering and wire cutting on 16 July. During the days before the battle heavy enemy shelling required the 52nd Bty to move and the 110th was heavily shelled. On the morning of 19 July, the 48th and 51st Bty were shelled but not damaged. '*Generally*', observed Christian, '*the enemy seemed to have few guns*', and amplifying this remark he went on to say '*the communications during the day were good, though much has yet to be done in burying and protecting wires. Owing to the lack of the material and the short time at our disposal prior to the attack ... this could not be done, and it was due mainly to the ineffective artillery reply from the enemy that the communications were preserved intact—the enemy wire does not appear to have been an obstacle to our infantry and from reports received seems to have been well cut. The front parapet was also very heavily damaged*'. All very positive, so he kept the one negative to his last sentence: '*Our first false barrage apparently had no effect as the forward officer in the trenches reported that the enemy did not appear to man his parapet during the "lift"*'.

AWM 41.50.3.1642

The Artillery at Fromelles: Part Two

ORDER OF BATTLE
AUSTRALIAN ARTILLERY
GOC: Brig. Gen. S E Christian

13th AFA Bde. CO: Major H O Caddy
14th AFA Bde. CO: Lieut Col O F Phillips
15th AFA Bde. CO: Lieut Col J W S Lucas
25th AFA Bde. CO: Lieut Col H J Cox Taylor

5th Div Ammunition Column.
CO: Major F D W Thornthwaite

The pattern of artillery activity for 19 July was from 9 to 11 am registration and wire cutting. At 11 am—Zero hour—for half an hour, registration. Then from 1 pm to 6 pm wire cutting by 18 pounders and trench mortars, supplemented over the last three hours by the rest of the 18 pounders and 4.5" Howitzers. All this was equally distributed between the front and support lines in order to cut wire both on front of the line and support lines, and during the afternoon there were four 'lifts' to barrage lines at near to 3.30, 4.00, 4.30 and 5.30, and at 6 pm the whole of the fire lifted to barrage lines, protecting the infantry as they made their way over No-Man's Land. Paying attention to the different widths of No-Man's Land 15th Bde started first, 14th second, and 8th third, so that the whole German line was kept down until the infantry was well established.

Christian's Report notes that overall 1 officer and 11 ORs were killed, 5 officers and 28 ORs wounded. The only casualty to equipment was that an 18 pounder had one wheel blown off. Of the ammunition expended, in the four days prior to 19th, 16,501 of A and AX and 1,433 of BX. On the day of the battle these rose to 62,092 and 4,807 respectively.

One of the most contentious matters as far as the artillery was concerned were the shorts, '*the friendly fire*'. As already related, this was worst in 8th Bde sector, and had much to do with the narrowness of No-Man's Land. But defenders of the artillery felt this was exaggerated out of all proportion by the men of the 8th who were inexperienced. These people pointed out that the friendly fire that so damaged the 8th and 14th Bde men who had passed over the German line was because they had gone too far. Capt. Gatliff of 13th AFA after the battle wrote: '*After we had bombarded the trenches ... we lifted our fire so as to form a curtain between them and the enemy's reserve. They were told only to go for a certain distance but went on and ran into our fire—we had to lift three times to clear them*'. The map shows as shaded areas behind the German line where barrage fire was directed, revealing the fairly narrow area the infantry had to remain within, and how it was that those in search of the second or third line soon found themselves in trouble. What Gatliff might have mentioned, but perhaps when he wrote he did not know, that it was not just the friendly fire that was the problem, it was the delay between request and compliance.

In a fairly detailed and brightly written account published in *Reveille* May 1937, Capt. G H Wilson of 31st Bn, and at Fromelles OC X5A LTM Battery revealed an aspect of the operation not noted elsewhere, that is the Canadian participation beyond their own Divisional Mortar Batteries.

There were three Australian Medium Trench Mortar Batteries designated as X5A (8th Bde sector), Y5A (14th Bde Sector) and Z5A (15th Bde sector). They fired what they called 'Plum Puddings', but had so little experience that on the evening before the battle, Canadians were brought in '*to man the mortars, the Australians standing by as extra personnel*'. These mortars were aimed at the German wire early on the morning of 19 July, and Capt Wilson was told by men of 8th and 14th Bdes that the enemy wire was effectively cut. He observed that the operation was completed without German retaliation as far as his unit was concerned. He wrote:

> *The Canadians and ourselves withdrew with but one casualty, the death of a gunner in another battery ... The Canadians were cool and nonchalant, and did their job in splendid style. We Australians were naturally disappointed when we had to hand our guns over to them, but there is no doubt that we were inexperienced, and needed a little more training in actual shooting.*

The Canadian mortars, as described by Lieut W Smith of 53rd Bn '*... the large mortars ... were sending over football bombs each weighing 60 lbs at the rate of 8 to 10 per minute, while the Stokes mortars ... were firing a three inch cylindrical bomb, weighing about 12 lbs, at the rate of fifteen to twenty per minute.*'

Artillery experts have always wondered why there was no counter battery work at Fromelles, and some suggest it was because the allied gunners preferred not to provoke the Germans for fear of their superiority. The casualty rate among our artillery was extraordinarily light. The death of two of those, Capt. Wilson witnessed '*... early morning of 19 July ... one huge minenwerfer ... burst just behind our position, killing an officer and a man... both by concussion. We found no mark on the officer ...*'

Among those in the artillery at Fromelles was Lieut W C Scurry. It had been Sgt Scurry who invented the self-firing rifle on Gallipoli which enabled the evacuation to be done successfully. After that, in Egypt he transferred to 58th Bn and under Brig. General Elliott's guidance formed the 15th Light Trench Mortar Battery consisting of eight mortars. Ellis recorded that after Scurry had fired his first salvo of ten on the 15th Bde front, the battery evacuated very quickly before the Germans retaliated, earning a nickname '*the shoot and scatter mob*'.

While one can easily get indignant at the waste at Fromelles, the shambles of the artillery might have another aspect. As the whole attack was but a ruse, it did not actually matter how good or trained it was: this action could be the training. Without being too cynical, it could be argued that Haking, who knew all along that the attack was going nowhere, accepted assurances which he must have realised were without substance. Haking was not an idiot and would have known that no Divisional Artillery could be really functional in seven days, and there was no point in expecting it to be. This might help explain why he did not appoint an overall Artillery Commander, did not organise joint conferences, and did not insist on close co-operation between the Australian and British Artillery all through the attack. He did no better between Mackenzie and McCay.

The British artillery began its bombardment at 11 am and '*continued according to the programme—the infantry reported that the enemy's parapet was shattered all along the line, and that the wire presented practically no obstacle*', wrote Mackenzie in his Report, adding—'*as regards the enemy's parapet, the portion captured later by the 7 Warwicks on the right was so knocked about that it afforded them no cover when they got into it. Other portions of the line did not suffer so much, particularly the Sugarloaf and the Wick. The enemy machine guns were not destroyed by the bombardment.*'

The most extraordinary statistic concerning the artillery at Fromelles reveals that out of the 75 German reinforced dugouts, 60 were not hit at all; of the 15 others, eight were destroyed and seven slightly damaged. Add to this, only about half the wire was cut and the Sugarloaf never seriously hurt, so one wonders what happened to the 66,500 shells, 'plum puddings' and other projectiles the Australian artillery, with some Canadian assistance, fired off on 19 July, 1916, in the Australian half of the line. On the assumption no less were launched from the British Artillery, we know that they cut the wire quite successfully, but they too missed the Sugarloaf and it would seem most of the reinforced dugouts.

Part One on pages 104–105.

The Medium Trench Mortars at Fromelles

Lieut G H Wilson OC X5A Battery. *Reveille* May 1937

The work of the medium trench-mortars at Fromelles commenced a week or two prior to the date set for the battle. At the time we had no div. Trench-mortar officer in the 5th Division, and it was my luck to be the senior officer who had gone through the school at Berthen. Only five men in my battery had done a TM course, the remainder having come from the artillery and infantry. Lieut W H Hind, an infantry subaltern, was appointed as my second-in-command.

On being summoned to corps headquarters for instructions, I detailed certain requirements, as a result of which orders were 'phoned through to the engineers for supplies, and to the 5th Pioneer Battalion for a working party of 150 men—exactly one hundred more than I asked for. It was, however, no use arguing the point about it, so I took the 150, and left 100 spares to sit it out all that night. By daybreak the battery positions, as well as alternative ones, were completed. We placed two guns to a bay.

Three Australian medium trench-mortar batteries, firing the 'plum pudding' bombs, were engaged at Fromelles—X5A, Y5A and Z5A, covering the 8th, 14th, and 15th Infantry Brigades. The heavy battery (V5A) also operated with 'flying pigs'. Our batteries trained incessantly at Sailly, and afterwards came under the command of Capt. Miles, eventually to be appointed DTMO.

It will be remembered that the Fromelles battle was postponed, but during this spell my battery was visited by Major Sir John Keane, who had charge of all trench-mortars in the Second Army.

A day or two prior to the battle, a certain general paid us a call. After inquiring about our guns, he suggested that I should 'send one over'. I naturally gave good reasons why it would be inadvisable to do so, and his staff officer cordially agreed with me. After the party had moved on, one of the boys said, 'Why didn't you send a "pudding" across?'

'Well, you know the answer as well as I do,' I replied. 'Fritz would put something back, and we'd get skittled.'

'Yes,' he remarked, brightly, 'and so would the old ... too.'

Our TM units were all keyed up and ready when news came that Canadians would man the mortars, our men standing by as extra personnel. On the heels of this news came the Canadians, a fine crowd of chaps, too. I have a hazy recollection of dates, but I know that one of their officers spent a night in the line with us prior to the fight, and it happened to be that during which the 5th Pioneers fixed up the trench tram-line. While sitting together we noticed several of our Pioneers, a few feet away, get hit in the legs—our Canadian visitor humourlessly endeavouring to get a Blightly as well. But his luck was out. Capt. W J R Richardson (of Thirroul), who died in 1935, was one of those wounded.

The early morning of July 19, 1916, was one of comparative calm, so far as Fritz was concerned. One huge minenwerfer, however, burst just behind our position, killing an officer and a man—both by concussion. We found no mark on the officer. The other chap was killed in a peculiar manner, the force of the explosion bashing his head against the sandbags below [on] which he had been sitting.

Our artillery were not working into a frenzy. By 8 am an intense bombardment from all our guns had been opened on the German line. Simultaneously, like a shoal of huge tadpoles, over went a line of our plum-pudding bombs, which dropped into the German wire and exploded with what, we hoped, was devastating effect. At this stage, I might add that the 'extra' personnel, according to the needs of the moment, took up points of vantage.

The trench-mortar work was all over in half-an-hour or so, and the line was then left clear for the attacking infantry. Incidentally, spare TM bombs were lobbed into known machine-gun posts, which I had had previously marked for consideration. Fortunately, Fritz did not open fire on the mortars while they were in action; or, if he did so, his shooting was very bad, for the Canadians and ourselves withdrew with but one casualty, the death of a gunner in another battery. Fritz did not seriously molest the front line until later that day. He then did quite enough to make up for his earlier neglect.

I was told by men of the 8th and 14th Brigades that the enemy wire was so effectively cut that they had no obstructions in reaching the enemy trenches. Doubtless there were other influences besides our own working at this particular job, but in view of the extreme care we had taken in getting ranges and in siting the batteries, I feel that the units did fine work. The Canadians were cool and nonchalant, and did their job in splendid style. We Australians were naturally disappointed when we had to hand our guns over to them, but there is no doubt that we were inexperienced, and needed a little more training in actual shooting.

At 6 pm, the infantry went over, and we saw the fight from various points. Next morning, at the head of the trench tram-line, we came across a pile of Mills bomb boxes, and the men of X5A Battery immediately set to work to get them down to the front line. None of us knew how to fuse them, but, under the guidance of four battalions RSMs of the 8th Brigade, we set to work with a will, assisted by some lightly wounded men. The first truck-load was pushed down under fire by Bombardier A S Wilkes and Gunner Sam Power (of Gympie, Queensland, afterwards mortally wounded), who returned with two desperately wounded men in the truck. Other members of the battery followed their example, each time returning with two shattered men whom we quickly passed on to a nearby first aid post, and I cannot speak too highly of the courage of all of them.

Later an order came to send the bombs down, 'fused or unfused', so we loaded the truck and ran it down. Shortly afterwards the enemy completely destroyed the tram-line. I have since wondered whether the story of the unfused bombs at Fromelles originated here. At the foot of the tram-line, remnants of the 8th Brigade were having a hard fight. I had not slept for three nights and was worn out, so do not remember much more, except that I stumbled into a Fritz and passed him on to two of my chaps.

Later, when we passed through the shambles of our front line, things had quietened down. We stood by under orders, and helped in sundry ways to clean things up. My chaps made a dixie of tea for the survivors of the 30th Battalion, and I remember betting Capt. Sloan that a chap named ... would have come through. I'd helped this particular lad on a previous occasion, and felt sure he would survive. He had !

The Signallers at Fromelles

CO 5th Signal Coy: Major R A Stanley

Combining the sparse information on the signallers at Fromelles with references in Reports, it would seem that the main telephone lines survived well. That is those going back from Bde HQs to Divisional HQ and to the Artillery. Those forward of Bde HQs to Bns and to the front line and beyond were, it would seem seldom operative and never dependable.

The switchboards that were open were subject to heavy loads and thus considerable delays were experienced in a situation where two minutes were critical. Although nobody, quite obviously, in their Reports said so, it is clear the chaos in enemy territory would have been hugely eased if telephone lines had got through. Quite why the signallers were left to run over behind the last wave like an appendix to the operation defies logic. Surely they should have been shepherded, guided and helped across in some way to ensure there was a signals post on the other side. The classic case was 60th Bn, whose whole signal unit following behind the fourth wave of infantry was wiped out in the first minutes: and nobody ever knew what happened to the 60th Bn after that, and they got no help, no advice, no orders. This was an area where a competent general like Monash succeeded: probably the only time McCay thought about the signals was when his phone went dead.

The demands McCay made of his Divisional Signals Office is betrayed by the statistics: 505 sealed packets and 526 messages, which the Signals historian, Theo Barker, noted '*could have been handled without difficulty except for the fact that much of the traffic had high precedence gradings*'. One has no difficulty in accepting that everything McCay sent out was of special importance, in his judgement. More importantly his file of messages, even taking into account that some were copied to numerous units, falls well short of 500, well short.

[continued page 159]

Pigeons at Fromelles

The one area of signals which did not reason why were the carrier pigeons. Bean seems to have had a soft spot for them: '*another small service, but one destined at certain critical moments to be of unestimable value was ... added to the AIF ... that of carrier pigeons: a pigeon station was organised among signallers of each infantry brigade*'. One can only imagine the fright and stress of the birds released into the man-made hell of Fromelles, but some got through it.

A mobile field loft

The 'homing' instinct, coupled with a flying speed of up to 60 miles per hour (96 kms) over short distances, together with the practical aspects—portability, endurance, reliability and long service capacity, made the pigeon a very valuable signalling 'device'. The main problem was night flying: '*pigeons cannot be relied upon to home at night. If released after dark, they will almost certainly settle down to roost and resume their flight at daylight*'. (HMSO *Carrier Pigeons at War* 1918)

The signallers were in charge of pigeon stations in each Brigade, then when the action demanded it, in a Battalion. In the other services—Navy and Flying Corps, pigeons were also used, and they were also carried in tanks. The Germans also had an extensive pigeon service, as did the French.

The birds were kept well behind the front line in lofts, which were supplied by the British in the form of old London buses that had had an open top deck. Later in the same style special lofts were built, with towards the end of the war, some 150 mobile lofts in service and an uncounted number of 'permanent' lofts. The pigeons were carried from the lofts to the frontline in wicker 'Stock Baskets' by motorcycle. These were about 20" x 20" x 15" (51 x 51 x 38 cms) and could hold up to 16 birds. Once at the 'pigeon station', two birds would be transferred to every 'Trench Basket' available. These baskets, 12" x 11" x 10" (30 x 28 x 25 cms) were what the Signallers carried up to the frontline, and into No-Man's Land. The flights back to the loft in still weather would be at around 2,400 ft (730 metres), and in poor weather some 70 ft (21 metres), and instructions were that two birds should carry the same message every time, as one at least was certain to get through. Alternatively, the second pigeon released should, if carrying a new message, also carry the same message as the first bird. When the pigeon arrived back at the loft the staff transmitted the message by telephone to Divisional or Brigade HQ as required.

Fromelles is the first mentioned use of pigeons by Bean. '*The pigeons, of which both Toll (8th Bde) and Cass (14th Bde) sent several, were at the Divisional Pigeon Loft within 17 minutes of their despatch from the front line: this method of communication with headquarters was much the quickest.*'

At Fromelles as it did not get fully dark until around 10, and it was light at around 4, it would seem that the messages that got through were very early on the morning of 20 July. But the early messages from Toll and Cass were sent before it got dark, when they were both trying to find the German 'second line', which it later transpired never existed. A small party of 3 officers and one pigeoneer (Sgt R Eddie 663 31st Bn) went on further confirming that they were in the wrong place. Bean wrote, '*The pigeon messages, sent by Colonel Toll of 31st Bn during his journey out in the front line, had duly come to hand, together with another sent after his retirement ...*'. Thus both 8th and 14th Brigades were well served by the pigeons, but there is no reference to what happened with 15th Brigade.

Pte C R Kift 1954A 58th Bn and his wife

The 15th Bde Pigeoneer at Fromelles was Pte Charles Robert Kift 1954 58th Bn. Born at Ballarat on 21 March 1888, he enlisted in Melbourne on 25 February 1916 and served for 1,267 days of which 1,088 were overseas. A carpenter by trade, 5'6" in height with brown hair and grey eyes, Charles married May Mackay, also of Ballarat, on 17 January 1920 at Essendon. He died on 29 July 1973 at Heidelberg and was cremated at Fawkner Crematorium.

As a matter of interest, Bean mentions pigeon messages in connection with the Australians at Pozières, Mouquet Farm, Flers, First Bullecourt, Broodseinde, Passchendaele, Polygon Wood, Hamel, on 8 August 1918 and later, and some involve 5th Division or 15th Bde.

THE SIGNALLERS (contd from page 157)

Despatch riders also served between Divisional and Brigade HQs: Divisional HQ had ten, each brigade one, and artillery two. Wrote Barker on this, '*these numbers, although normally adequate were found to be insufficient in action and in fact, the despatch riders were so heavily taxed that the signals despatch service almost broke down. The cause of the trouble was the large number of priority despatches that were handed in for delivery immediately the battle began*'.

The Engineers at Fromelles

ORDER OF BATTLE
ENGINEERS/PIONEERS

CRE: Lieut Col A B Carey (Royal Engineers)
8th Field Coy. CO: Major V A H Sturdee
14th Field Coy. CO: Major H A Bachtold
15th Field Coy. CO: Major H Greenway
5th Pioneer Bn. CO: Major H G Carter

In a battle dominated by the endeavours of the Infantry the huge backup task of the Engineers is afforded only a paragraph by Ellis and as a group hardly a line by Bean, although of course he mentions many individuals. The tasks they were given and the degree of success under the circumstances warrants proper attention. In command of 5th Divisional Engineers was Lieut Col A B Carey of Royal Engineers, and his Report on the battle, in the style of a professional soldier/engineer is straightforward and full of information. He began by setting down exactly what they were expected to do:

The quantity of stores required was estimated on the basis that we should take and hold approximately 2000 yards each of the German front and support trenches and that, in addition to consolidating these, it would be necessary to construct two flank trenches communicating the two German lines, and also a left flank fire trench and three or four communication trenches across No-Man's Land.

By any standards this was a huge job, and further complicated by the high water table, the gluey mud and general inexperience all round. Donnan of 14th Field Coy in his description—pages 131–33—gives a ground level view of it all, but Carey's Report dealt with the wider picture.

'*A special type of Low Hurdle was provided for the rapid revetment of the communication trenches, also duck walks.*' Carey then detailed how three lorries '*laden with tools and special stores*' were kept ready to be sent forward at a moment's notice. He noted that one was called for early by 8th Bde: perhaps another example of how Tivey faced early with disaster called in everything and why Major King had to go to 8th Bde HQ to keep an eye on things. The tram line the Engineers built was also in 8th Bde's area, but it did not survive the battle.

The attention to water supply, without which no army can survive for long was carefully thought through, although of course in the actual battle water in the German trenches was in abundant supply and pumps for getting rid of it would have been perhaps equally useful.

Special water supply arrangements were made utilizing the mine shaft in the front line with their pumping gear and some 2000 petrol tins. Arrangements were also made for the rapid sinking of water holes in the German lines so as to avoid waste of labour and casualties in carrying water.

The men who would do these tasks were to follow the fourth wave of the infantry and upon arrival at the German front line set up positions for receiving the tools and supplies to enable the positions to be fortified. The other part of the Field Companies designated to dig the communication trenches had surveyed and examined the ground well prior to 19 July. It is worthwhile to reprint here Carey's descriptions of what was achieved in the digging of trenches. It is also interesting to note that he makes no reference to the '*new front line trench*' McCay had ordered on the extreme left and how he all but dismisses the 8th Bde trench, '*this work was supervised by Lieut Farr, 8th Field Coy who was considerably hampered by casualties and by the passing of munitions and stores through the trench*'. But for the other two there are real details not given elsewhere:

14th Bde Communication Trench laid out and supervised by Lieut H W Fry, 14th Field Coy. This trench was very well laid out and constructed. At dawn on the 20th, the trench was complete from end to end. Total length 195 yards, duck-boarded throughout except for 25 yards length near our own lines. The bottom of the trench varied from 4 ft to 6 ft below ground level, the excavated earth giving additional cover.

In the 15th Bde section the fire was too hot for digging in the open. Lieut L Noedl, although severely wounded at the start, carried on for some hours distributing the remaining men in various drains and sapping in both directions from each, resulting in a total length of 687 ft of sap from Pinney Avenue averaging 3 ft 6 ins deep, of which 180 ft was duck-boarded, and a second sap put out by the same company from VC Avenue was carried out 270 ft, of which 90 ft was duck-boarded.

Of casualties Carey generalized: 'one officer and thirty-four men per company', and signed off with this sentence, 'I could not wish for anything more efficient than the three Field Companies of the 5th Australian Division.'

... the Brigadier General cried ...

Cpl H B Goeby, 5388 of 59th Bn left a '*Diary of Events during the War*' which reads as if written up later from extensive notes. However, in the days leading up to Fromelles and later, his entries reveal aspects not in other diaries used in this work

July 12th. Weather very bad now. We are all living in tents and many of them are blowing down ... I rise now at 4.30 every morning, very wet and cold. Rations very poor, tinned meat rations used for breakfast, very awkward ... Over an inch of rain last night.

We have a parade today 18th, and ask for 50 volunteers, get 200, select 50, to go to the firing line at 3.30 this morning.

21st of July. Things seem to be moving a good deal at the front, many men leave here, some of my staff too. It was a few days ago the 19th, when the Australians had a very bad time; many of the men that left here on the 18th, were killed. It took place at Fleurbaix. General McCay tried to make a feint, so that the Germans would come away from Pozières where the 1st Division was going to make an attack. We advertised our attack (of the 5th Division) so much that when they did go 'over the top' the Germans were more than ready for us. Before the men had gone a few yards they were met with terrific fire both rifle and shot that mowed them down in thousands. We never reached the German lines, while our trenches being very shallow, were blown out of existence, giving us no shelter from the murderous fire that was concentrated on us. Many of our men were drowned in the little creek, or were killed in the valley.

To give some idea of this affair, my own Battalion, the 59th, went in 880 strong, and when they marched out a few hours later, the Brigadier General cried, for there was only about 87 fit men—this was his favorite Battalion. It withdrew a lot of the enemy from another place, but it was too great a price to pay—12,000 casualties in one day, and it was almost the first battle the Australians had had in France. I was down on the list to go to the front for this battle, but at the last moment, I was taken off it, to take up a position as Corporal Clerk in the orderly room—a position which I held for some time. Further details of the above show we had 420 guns on a 2 mile front. Men returning informed me that of the Battalions, either 59th or 60th had only 77 men at Roll Call. One shell killed 5 out of the 6 cooks of the 60th. The Australians appear to have had a very rough time.

We have sent up now a lot of reinforcements, 59th got special recommendation from General Haking, also from General Plumer. I am now learning the office work under Sgt Neville.

Wednesday, July 26th. Many men are reporting back from the Front, done up after the great smash up of the 59th and 60th Battalions—they report the field is nothing but a shambles. These men march in with all their equipment and clothing stained with mud and blood just as they left the line. I notice the machine gunners appear to have had the worst time.

Monday 31st of July. The latest report is that 64 of 59th, 40 of 60th, unwounded.

COURTESY G SEARLE

'All the officers of 59th Bn were photographed as a group at Moascar Camp, 20 June 1916'. So wrote Lieut W H Vaile on 20 June 1916 in a letter home. This copy was donated to the AWM by Mrs M Cousins. From another copy held by descendants of Lieut Bowden in the UK, a full listing has been obtained, courtesy of G Stocks (UK) and J Ingram (Australia). Back row, L-R: Lieuts J C Bowden †, R Liddelow, A C Anderson, H C Howard †, R H M Gibbs †, D W Fair, E M Young, A D Morrow †. Centre row: Lieuts W H Vaile †, J W Fenton, J S Mann, J D Haddow, F L Cousins †, E T W Carr †, G R Stockfeld, J B Sutherland, G S Smith, H A L Binder. Front row: Lieut W E Hammond, Capts G W Akeroyd, G M Parker (Medical Officer), A Liddelow †, Lieut Col E A Harris, Capts L L Hornby, D S Brumwell (Chaplain), F R Hewitt, K G McDonald, Lieut T F McL Bursey.

† denotes killed in action or died of wounds, July 1916.

marginally better state than 184th, and well aware that only two battalions were to be used in assault: and these had been used. The real situation was properly put by Lieut Col Williams of 2/1st Bucks (see page 56). '*No reserves were however available ... this order* [Haking's about the new 8.30 then 9.00 assault] *was received when every man ... was in No-Man's Land.*'

All this questions Bean's version of events. There is no evidence that a new assault was initiated by the British Brigadiers, but the command came from Haking, and was in effect 'returned' by Mackenzie as being impossible to implement. We learn from the CO of 2/4th Oxfords, who were to be the third battalion of the 184th Bde that it was not in position until 11–11.30 (see margin: *He Had No Material At All*).

This probing of the sad and totally useless sacrifice of 58th Bn shows how complex such an event can be, and how difficult it is to make sense of the documents that record it (see margin next page: *When Hutchinson Went Out ...*). Bean settled on the fact that it was a combination of neglect by 61st Division and lack of attention to detail by 5th Division HQ. Ellis had come to much the same conclusion. This writer however feels it is a little more involved than that, and that Elliott's impetuosity obscured the military reality: to send half of another battalion after two others who had for all intents and purposes vanished, was a wrong decision, and it could be argued that Elliott would not have done it unless egged on by McCay. Elliott's own estimate of himself—*An Efficient Foreman* page 145—surely confirms this. For McCay to undertake before the battle had even started to give the 58th '*a chance*' was typical of his irresponsible, cavalier behaviour. To dodge commenting on this it was highly convenient to weave it all in with British incompetence, and it allowed Bean to place some blame onto unnamed staff, rather than the person whose staff they were—McCay. Wrote McCay in his Report: '*meanwhile information had been received that the attack of the 61st Div would not take place, but the information could not reach the 58th in time.*'

But why? If the message requesting cooperation could go through four headquarters in ten minutes, another could have gone through two in under half an hour. Was McCay so committed to giving the 58th '*a chance*' that he had, to use the current expression, lost the plot? As we have seen he had lost the plot several times earlier. This writer's conclusion is that the times between the arrival of permission for Elliott to use 58th Bn, the specification that they were to assist the 59th and 60th, the request from the 184th for assistance and the sending out of the 58th Bn are all too close to settle a final judgement. It

HE HAD NO MATERIAL AT ALL

As noted in 'The First Second Line Division to go abroad' (pages 34–35). Col W H Ames CO of 2/4th Oxfordshire, the half support, half reserve battalion of 184th Bde 'left' his command after Fromelles. Whilst Rose gives no hint why in his history, there is in the Regiment Chronicle a narrative by Ames about the confusion behind the lines that comes closer than any other recollection to explaining why the 184th could not respond to Haking's exhortation to mount another attack. Not a mention of the 8.30/9.00 attack with which the hapless Australians were expected to co-operate: instead the revelation that the new men were not in place until 11.00! Then the revelation that the British were filing out for a 2.30 am assault.

An intense bombardment was kept up from 11 am till 6 pm, when the assault was delivered, but owing to the machine-gun fire of the enemy the assaulting Battalion could not get across No-Man's Land, and suffered heavy losses. About 7 pm the Battalion was loaded on to motor-buses and moved up towards the firing-line, and was sent up to take over the line held by the Berks and the Bucks. The relief was completed by 11, and at 11.30 the CO, who had been ordered to remain at the Battle Headquarters, received orders to organize an attack with two companies on the Sugar Loaf, being told that he would find a party of Engineers with consolidating material at a certain point for which he was to provide a carrying company. A and D Companies were selected for the attack, and at 2.15 am the Engineer party had not been discovered. The companies were filing out to take up their positions two minutes later, when the Engineer officer reported, and stated that he had no material at all. The CO just at that moment received an order from the Brigade Headquarters that unless everything was ready by 2.30 he was not to start, so the attack was cancelled.

The narrative continues telling of the cleaning up after the battle and, concludes, not surprisingly '*on 1st August went to Robermetz for divisional rest. That day Colonel Ames gave up command of the Battalion.*' The 2/4th had lost in July 24 ORs killed, 3 Officers and 96 ORs wounded.

is possible the 58th had gone before the 184th request arrived. There is no evidence from the time to conclusively prove that what everybody said after the battle was in fact true.

Ellis and Bean both mention that at 10 o'clock Haking's Chief of Staff visited McCay to agree what to do next. This meeting and its decisions are not mentioned in any 5th Division papers. Bean is careful to note that Wagstaff was also there, and one supposes that it was Wagstaff who told him about the arrangements, which in summary were, the Australians would hold on and the British would '*before dawn, endeavour to seize the Sugarloaf*'. As a result of this conference, Bean wrote that McCay '*asked leave to employ ... should he desire to do so—half of each of his last three reserve battalions. This was agreed to*'. Then without blushing, so to speak, Bean wrote:

> McCay, who had already sent forward—for works of repair behind the Australian line and for trench digging in No-Man's Land—half of the 5th Pioneers, at 11.40 gave his brigadiers half of the 29th, 56th and 57th Battalions directing that the old line should be held by the remaining halves, and adding—you are asked to take and hold the whole of the original objectives.

But at this point Elliott had not yet requested the Pioneers (he would at 11.15) and in the hour and a half before McCay authorised officially the use of the fourth battalions, much else happened.

At the 10 o'clock meeting, Haking's staff knew the 58th Bn had been sent over, they had been advised shortly after 9 o'clock. they also knew that there was no positive information about the 59th and 60th which had now been out in the battlefield for four hours. Compared with what was happening in the 8th and 14th Bde sectors this was totally different. 15th Bde HQ knew that the machine gun emplacement was a mere skeleton, that the Sap was proving very difficult work and the communication trenches were basically unusable. Coupled with this Elliott's Field HQ and the Bde HQ further back continued to operate on a time scale an hour ahead of everybody else. So Elliott, not yet in possession of any information from the meeting, advised his HQ at 9.31 (10.26 his time):

> It is impossible to say at present with any certainty which portions of the enemy's lines are being held. Communications have broken down with field front lines. Renewing attack now being made by 58th Bn. Enemy opened heavy musketry fire ... all organization broken down here.

Subsequent messages from Elliott reveal a deteriorating situation and the understandable trauma and stress of his Field HQ can be easily understood and factored into the confusion.

WHEN HUTCHINSON WENT OUT DID HIS WATCH READ 8.00, 9.00 OR 10.00

As already noted, this writer in pursuit of a rational explanation to the tragedy of 15th Bde at Fromelles found the altered times of all the messages at 15th Bde HQ troubling. Hours of checking them against Division and Battalion records could only resolve the puzzle one way. Some signals officer or clerk supposed that the time everybody else was using was GMT and so added an hour, believing that would provide Summer Time, the time the battle was being fought on, so to speak. The fact that Elliott went along with this is curious; the fact that Division HQ did not draw 15th Bde HQ's attention to it is even stranger. But however hard one looks, there is no evidence that 15th Bde started an hour late in the original attack.

What, however, must be asked is did this time confusion cause actual confusion: and if it did not, why not? After all who noted inside 15th Bde HQ that while the new attack was to be at 9.00, they would go out at 10.00. One can only assume they must have regarded everybody else as being incorrect, and just corrected the schedules within their own little group. How else could it have kept going? Strange as the alterations are, the fact that they were made and by Bde Major Wieck, gives them some validity, but we do not know how this other level of time was carried on by phone or verbal messages. For instance, when Hutchinson went out did his watch read 8.00, 9.00 or 10.00? When Elliott advised McCay of the content of Denehy's report his watch said 1 am: or was that the watch of his signaller, or the watch of the signaller who received the message? But for it to get to McCay at 12.20 clearly reveals it was sent at 12 not 1: yet it was marked 11.25. So did 5th Division automatically deduct an hour? We will never know, and while it may have had no significant effect on the general outcome, there are events it might have altered.

Haking advised Mackenzie at 8.20 about cancelling the second attack, [continued opposite]

But the message from McCay (actually signed by him—so it is the original in the file) timed at 10.30 and received by Elliott's HQ twenty minutes later, was hardly helpful and certainly untruthful. In full it read:

> Now learn 61st Div hold apex of Sugarloaf. They are endeavouring to take tonight from Sugarloaf to right of your objective. Has 59th got in or have you had to withdraw them? Is 60th still in and is 53rd in on its left? Can you seize and hold all your objective if I give you your reserve battalion?

Bean in his reporting of this *only* quoted the last sentence, deciding not to print McCay's deliberate misinformation. Haking, Mackenzie and Carter were all well aware long before this that there were no British in the Sugarloaf. The garrison, if there had ever been one, which is extremely doubtful, could hardly be expected to hold on till 2 am. And anyway, Haking had advised McCay at 9 o'clock: '*61st Division have been instructed to withdraw parties in enemy's front line ... with view to renewal of attack tomorrow.*'

So what could Elliott use half of 57th Bn for now?

The appalling state of communications is vividly displayed by that message which Elliott received at 10.50, a time by which all of the British troops were back in their own lines. Elliott had learned that 55th Bn had not made contact with 60th Bn and admitted '*I have not yet established direct communication with my battalions in advanced line*'. Yet later in response to McCay's suggestion he sent this message at 11.21 (12.16 Elliott's time).

> 59th Bn have not yet got in. I can get no information as to situation regarding 60th Bn but believe from accounts of wounded that they are still in. I cannot guarantee success of attack with 57th as enemy machine gun is very hot, but would try.

When that landed on McCay's desk somebody along the line had changed the last words to '*willing to try*'.

One can only explain this offer by Elliott as being the result of the stress of the time and his deference to his senior officer. But the reader's attention is drawn to Elliott's letter of four days later (see margin: *And Failure It Was ...)* where he wrote about 57th Bn '... *the reserve battalion which I was not allowed to employ ...*' to realise that it was not all exactly straightforward.

We now come to the most critical document of the middle period of the battle. The original draft in McCay's own handwriting is in the Divisional file. Across the top he has written '*This is to be kept carefully, J W McCay*'. Then, '*not to be destroyed by order of GOC*'. McCay made a number of

WHEN HUTCHINSON WENT OUT DID HIS WATCH READ 8.00, 9.00 OR 10.00 (contd)

then Mackenzie promptly (8.30) passed on a message to McCay on which no action was taken so we are told. If action had been taken the message would have arrived at Elliott's HQ around 8.37, which would be 9.37 his time, exactly when he said he got it. Had he got that message at 9.37 it would have been 10.37 his time. What is troubling is that whilst all the telegraph messages fit the pattern, the three, seemingly hand delivered messages, about cooperation with 184th Bde, do not. And it is only these that 'prove' McCay's version of events.

When 15th Bde HQ and all four battalions consistently stated in their War Diaries that the attack began at 7 pm, and the second attack at 10 pm, how did they synchronize with everybody else when all the orders from outside clearly said 6 and 9?

Bearing in mind the above, is it not possible that the 58th went out at 8 pm (Elliott's 9 pm)? Clearly something was amiss and one feels that Bean suspected it, hence his observation about the agitated McCay discussing the matter with Elliott the next morning.

MAJOR A J S HUTCHINSON

Arthur Justin Sandford Hutchinson was born at Wodonga, Victoria, 25 August 1894, the son of Rev Arthur Edward Hutchinson. After education at Launceston Church Grammar School, Hutchinson went to Duntroon. From November 1914 he was Lieut and OC of MG Section, 9th Light Horse and then went to Gallipoli. He was evacuated 14 September. He returned as Capt of 3rd LH MG Coy and evacuated again ill in late November. He then transferred to 8th LH as MG Officer: on 29 April 1916 he became 2IC of A Coy of 58th Bn. He was promoted to Major on 30 May and then Coy Commander. He is remembered at VC Corner Cemetery, his body never being identified.

AND FAILURE IT WAS

Elliott was a prolific letter writer and would in times of crisis pour out his feelings in a letter, and if we judge by his writing, he wrote at speed and seldom altered what he wrote. As far as Fromelles is concerned his letter to Mrs Edwards in England, a second cousin on his mother's side, dated 23 July 1916, there can be no mistaking his anger, and to whom it is directed. But his phrase about the 57th Bn *which I was not allowed to employ* rests uneasily with his concern and the certain knowledge that had the 57th been put into the battle, it too would have been decimated. A contrary view of this reference is that Elliott was merely telling Mrs Edwards that he was forbidden to use the 57th Bn, and not that he wished to use them but was not allowed to.

Dear Mrs Edwards, Since writing last my division has been engaged in a most bloody encounter with the enemy. God knows why this enterprise was ordered, apparently as a feint to distract the enemy's attention from the Somme Area. However it was the Division was hurled at the German trenches without anything like adequate preparation and although we broke the German line and captured nearly two hundred prisoners the slaughter was dreadful and at length we were ordered to retire. Of one Battalion of 900 strong in my Brigade I could only muster 106 men, most of whom were employed as machine gunners, signallers etc. who being in the rear did not actually reach the German trenches. The others suffered almost equally severely with the exception of the reserve battalion which I was not allowed to employ as it became speedily evident that the act of employing it would only add to the useless slaughter. I am glad to say that my poor boys behaved magnificently.

We have been labouring night and day to get in the wounded from No-Man's Land in spite of the constant fire from snipers by day and machine guns by night.

One of the best of my Commanding Officers was killed and practically all my best officers, the Anzac men who

[continued opposite]

alterations—the most significant being that '*and in conjunction with 15th Bde*', was deleted after Sugarloaf. McCay timed it at 11.25, and it was marked in at 15th Bde HQ at 12.25 am the full text follows:

> Sixty first Division are reported to hold apex of Sugar-Loaf and are to-night attacking. 61st Division are ordered to take from apex to junction of German trench with River Laies. Brigadiers are each authorised to use three Battalions for fighting, and a half Battalion for carrying and digging, holding our front system parapet and 300 yards line with remaining half Battalion each. You are asked to take and hold whole of original objectives. You will however avoid the error often committed in France of holding captured trenches too thickly as unnecessary casualties occur and men cannot dig or consolidate trenches. Corps Commander and I congratulate you on splendid work done. Addressed 8th, 14th and 15th Infantry Brigades—repeated C.R.A., C.R.E. XI Corps, 2nd Anzac.

Crossing with this message Elliott had at the same time advised his HQ; again the full text:

> Following message from Major Denehy indicates that the attack of the Bde has completely failed. Such men of the 60th as actually reached the enemy trench being killed or captured. The two companies of 58th were mown down when close to enemy's trench and very few came back. Message begins: Men of all bns are coming back from No-Man's Land and fully expect they will gradually drift back to the line. Many men are wounded, many are not. Very many officers are casualties including Majors McCrae, Elliott and Hutchinson, all of whom are reported dead, and seems impossible to re-organize. Sapping proceeding but how long it will be possible depends on the protection provided by the others. Report seems to be unanimous to the effect that not a single man of 15th Bde is now in enemy's trench as enemy's flares are coming from the whole front allotted to the Bde. I am now organizing the defence of our original trenches and on the front Pinney's Ave and VC. Ends. Please notify division and ask for instructions.

This was marked '*Urgent 1 am*' by Elliott at Trou Post, and re-timed 'midnight' at 15th Bn HQ. In the Divisional file it is clocked in at 12.20 and noted as being timed at 11.25. The only line changed by Bde HQ referred to the Saps, after 'proceeding' it now read '*but unless more protection is given against enemy artillery this cannot last.*'

15th Bde HQ advised 5th Div. twenty minutes later that it now had taken 41 prisoners. From where one has to ask? And who brought them in, and how through all the shot and shell? But that is of small account to what Capt. R G Legge reported on, sometime after 1 am:

> I have traversed the 15th Bde lines. 2 Coys of 57th with details hold the line from VC to Pinney. The line is not strongly held and my parapets are breached. The ammunition supply seems satisfactory. No position

information can be obtained ... but 59th and 58th appear to be drifting in. Patrols have been sent out by Major Denehy and Major Layh. The trenches are filled with wounded. The enemy's artillery fire is fairly heavy on our parapet and communications also ... sweeping machine gun fire. Any reinforcements sent will probably have to move over the open. I consider that the line at present could not be held against a counter especially at the junction with 14th Bde where it is impossible to find Officers or NCOs and very few whole men.

This must have caused some alarm, because an hour or so later Legge updated his observation:

After second inspection and sorting out and organizing, our line is fairly well held. The left is still rather weak but can be strengthened. Bombardment has eased off.

The Brigade now in its worst time was being well served by Capt. Legge and others. Elliott himself was trying to retrieve the situation. At 2 am he advised 5th Division: '*57th Bn is taking over front line and 59th and 60th Bns are being withdrawn. Have issued instructions for a trench to be dug towards 14th Bde. Hostile shell fire diminishing. Patrol sent to German trenches found only wounded men.*'

But at 3.05 am Capt. S W Neale in charge of that stand of machine guns in 300 yard gap, reported to Elliott that, '*two reliable men from 58th Bn Lewis Gun detachment set out at 12.45 am and returned at 3 am. They could not get in touch with 60th Bn and they say there is no established line. There would be no advantage to send Lewis Guns forward so I am holding them back ... will you advise me further please.*'

And shortly after that, Major Layh advised Elliott that, '*Capt. Legge and Engineers Officer are attending to sap to 14th Bde. Major Denehy and myself are organizing defence. It will be impossible to give any exact idea of our strength owing to darkness and the great number of wounded until dawn, but I will advise soon as possible.*'

Then somebody, at 5.05, when the battle ended, advised McCay:

Estimated casualties during last night's operation are 57th Bn—5%, 58th Bn—35%, 59th Bn—50%, 60th Bn—50% and 15th Field Coy Engineers 1 officer and 30 ORs.

However, Layh at 8.26 am when it was all over was a little more precise, as was his style:

... in addition to 57th Bn, the following unwounded troops were mustered in our firing line: 54th Bn—7 ORs, 59th Bn—5 Officers and 59 ORs, 60th Bn—1 officer and 57 ORs, 58th Bn—6 Officers and 189 ORs, but this battalion must have over 100 men in rear on working parties

AND FAILURE IT WAS (contd)

helped build up my Brigade in Egypt, are dead.

I presume there was some plan at the back of the attack but it is difficult to know what it was. One can only say—it was an order. I trust those who gave the order may be made to realise their responsibility.

I am as you may guess not particularly happy but I am consoled by the fact that none of my local arrangements went wrong and that the responsibility for the failure, and failure it was, rests entirely on higher authorities.

58TH BNS TRANSPORT OFFICER

George Norman Scott was born December 1894 and educated at the Pleasant Street State School, Kew, and later at Ballarat College. Scott worked for the Victorian Railways and left the position of assistant station master at Kew Station to enlist in 6th Bn on 17 August 1914. He went to Gallipoli where he was twice wounded. In Egypt in 1916 he joined 58th Bn, was commissioned 2nd Lieutenant and was transport officer. According to a family story, Norman met his younger brother, Bill, who was in the Hazebrouck area on 18 July 1916. He handed over money and letters saying that he did not expect to survive the next day's battle. He did not, and died in the late night charge by the 58th along with Major Hutchinson, Lieutenants Barnfather, Gray and others. Scott's body was never found.

If the family story is true it provides an interesting and revealing facet on the 58th's position. On the 18th it was in Sailly-sur-la-Lys and not officially due to go into action on 19 July. As transport officer, Scott would have been privy to whatever other arrangements McCay and/or Elliott had made for the Battalion. One of the least straightforward incidents involving 15th Brigade.

Information from *The History of the Richards of the Bombay and the Scotts of the Lightning 1852-1988*, Peter R Scott (Melbourne 1988) etc. There is no doubt a few more and some of the 60th Bn may be with 14th Bde. Can Major Duigan or other senior officer be spared for 60th Bn please.

And in a very real sense, as far as Fromelles was concerned, that was the end of it for 15th Bde, just over 400 still standing out of 2,500 that once formed the 58th, 59th and 60th Bns.

And years later the historian of the 16th Bavarian Reserve Infantry Regiment wrote: '... *no English came into the trenches of the Regiment this day, except as prisoners*'.

Having now followed the fate of the British and Australians to dawn on 20 July, we move to Haking's temporary HQ at Sailly. There at 5 am were assembled Haking, General Monro and his chief of staff, General Barrow, Mackenzie and McCay. It is curious in his account of this assembly Ellis does not mention Mackenzie, and once again Bean avoids using his name and refers to him as '*the Commander of the 61st*'. Thus in the whole story of the battle Mackenzie's name is *never* given in the text, only one footnote. One has to wonder why.

Anyway, according to Bean, Mackenzie explained to the others that he '*had found it impossible to place in position during the night the companies allotted for the attack on the Sugarloaf*'. Then according to Bean '*the conference was ... about to consider the renewal of the assault during the morning by the whole 61st Division, when McCay was called to the telephone to receive an urgent message from his headquarters, where Colonel Wagstaff had just received bad news from both the 8th and 14th Bdes*'.

What had happened was Pope, unable to hold on without further reinforcements, had been given half of 56th Bn. Having authorised this Wagstaff phoned Tivey only to find that the 8th Bde '*were back in their own lines*'. Wagstaff probably in anger told Tivey to phone Pope and tell him that he was now on his own, something Tivey should have done anyway. Bean dodges all this having Wagstaff, then Tivey, phoning McCay at 5.15 to find out what to do.

'*Upon McCay reporting the news to Monro and Haking it was immediately decided to abandon the attack and withdraw 14th Bde.*' Pope's reaction to this decision and its consequences has already been described. The event as Bean described it, the event that brought the Battle of Fromelles to an end, is not mentioned in the War Diary of 5th Division. The only reference to it in McCay's report is '*An Army Commander who was present, directed the withdrawal of this (14th) Brigade to our own line.*' McCay recorded no decision about the possible attack by the 61st or the end of the operation: perhaps he too just could

15th BDE MG COY

Capt. Neale had kept Elliott well informed throughout. At 5 pm he reported '*Company in position for the attack*', that meant 4 Vickers of the 15th MG Coy and 5 Lewis guns of the 58th. At 6.30: '*suffered 17 casualties ... two guns buried*'. At 7.50: '*withdrew rescue guns (4) that had given covering fire from right flank*', and fifteen minutes later, '*called on reserve machine gunners, suffered twenty-two casualties to this time*'. Then at 9.40 this: '*sent order to officer on left to stand by his guns in anticipation of move forward'.* Could this refer to supporting the 58th attack which on one time scale would be at 10 pm? There are no notes in the files, received or sent, but at 11.45 Neale sent this to Elliott: '*There is a big gap between us and Tommies and should Bde dig in where they are, I will not go forward for I can give better fire from here, our present firing line. Do you approve please? I have 11 guns in front line.*'

By 4.35 am, half an hour before the battle ended Neale's last report: '*I have the following fighting men—Front line—5 officers, 43 ORs, 9 guns. 300 yard line—6 ORs, 2 guns. Reserve—1 officer, 23 ORs, 4 guns ... my HQ is head of VC Ave in front line.*'

ABORIGINALS AT FROMELLES

Stirred by the knowledge that Pte Billy Elsdale, a full blood Aboriginal, was killed in action at Fleurbaix on 7 July 1916 when serving with 47th Bn (4th Division), a search was made to see if there were any Aboriginals in the 5th Division at Fromelles.

A probable candidate is Sgt George McDonald 695 58th Bn. Born at Lake Condah Aboriginal Mission, Victoria, on 26 November 1890, he enlisted on 11 February 1915 and joined 58th Bn on 4 April 1916. He survived the battle of Fromelles but as one of the two leaders in a raid on German lines on the night 17/18 September, in front of Fromelles, he was severely wounded and as a result lost a leg. He returned to Australia on 4 May 1917.

INFORMATION COURTESY D HUGGONSON

	c. 20 June (Embarkation in Egypt)		5 July (France)		18 July (into Battle)		21 July (after Battle)	
	Officers	ORs	Officers	ORs	Officers	ORs	Officers	ORs
8th Bde (total)	137 (140)	4132 (4137)	117	3796	131	3890	80	2096
29th Bn	30 (28)	991 (988)						
30th Bn	30 (30)	991 (951)			29	927	20	585
31st Bn	30 (29)	991 (992)					11	501
32nd Bn	30 (32)	991 (985)						
8th MG Coy	10 (10)	145 (143)						
Bde HQ	7 (11)	25 (78)						
14th Bde (total)	137 (140)	4134 (4138)	130	3877	135	3723	71	2164
53rd Bn	30 (33)	991 (987)			28	823	5	107
54th Bn	30 (31)	991 (992)					16	517
55th Bn	30 (32)	991 (976)						
56th Bn	30 (31)	991 (989)						
14th MG Coy	10 (9)	145 (143)						
Bde HQ	7 (4)	25 (51)						
15th Bde (total)	137 (131)	4134 (4102)	122	3881	134	3622	68	1970
57th Bn	30 (28)	991 (983)						
58th Bn	30 (29)	991 (979)						
59th Bn	30 (28)	991 (967)						
60th Bn	30 (30)	991 (975)						
15th MG Coy	10 (9)	145 (148)			8			
Bde HQ	7 (7)	25 (50)						
5th Division	Including Pioneers, Artillery, Signals		17843		17735 (18th July)		12394	

not find the words! Then neither could Wagstaff. His carefully typed four paragraph note about the decisions of the conference, timed and dated 5 am 20 July, in his own handwriting, was all the information Bean had. There were instructions for the artillery and permission for Pope to use whatever he required to cover his withdrawal.

Wagstaff seemingly spelling it all out so posterity would know who did what, wrote, '*General McCay directs that Col Pope ... might withdraw* and *that the operation was to be conducted by him.*'

It is little wonder that Cass felt the way he did, and Col Pope had a good stiff drink (if in fact he did) before having his first sleep in three days. The fact that McCay sacked him for doing so and *nobody* came to Pope's defence until it was safe, a year later, says much about McCay and the Australian Higher Authorities generally. Pope, the only commander to succeed, was thus the only man whose reputation officially suffered as the result of Fromelles.

THE EFFECTIVE STRENGTH OF 5th AUSTRALIAN DIVISION
Upon leaving Egypt enormous care was taken, as can be seen from this table, to have the official figures perfect. As such an arrangement was clearly impossible, why was it done, especially when real figures were available? By checking the 'sailed from Egypt' sheets in the Divisional File, we find more realistic figures: sheets for 11 of the 14 ships are in the file. These figures are in brackets. In France a couple of weeks later irregular figures take over, and perhaps reality: 42 Officers and 848 ORs are already elsewhere. It is strange that there was no breakdown by battalions on a regular basis. The few figures quoted are mostly from War Diaries. The Brigade figures are from the Divisional File.

... a short truce had been arranged ...

Robert Vernon Quick was born 16 January 1897 at Ballarat, his father was a quarryman and his mother a housemaid, themselves children of miners and subsistence farmers on the Goldfields. Robert left school at 14, worked as an apprentice to a boilermaker, then as delivery boy for a grocer, and then to Heinz Brothers butchers of Bridge Street, Ballarat. After two and a half years with them he joined up early 1915. He left for overseas in 4th Reinforcements for 7th Bn on 13 April 1915. After a short stay in Egypt, on 24 May he was at Lemnos and a few days later on Gallipoli. He became ill, was evacuated, and returned on 26 November, the beginning of days of rain, ice and blizzard '*... on the morning of 27th, when we woke the place was covered with about a foot of snow ... some men were frozen to death as they stood in the trenches.*'

Quick remained at Anzac Cove and was part of the final group of 7th Bn in the evacuation '*... it was 10 am when we arrived at Lemnos Island on the morning 20 December ... we were met by the CO and lots of words about bravery, courage, tradition, and all that Bull.*'

Back in Egypt, Robert Quick was transferred to 59th Bn but later organised a change to 58th Bn, with whom he went to France. His description of Fromelles, which follows, makes no reference to being with Hutchinson's two companies that went out at 9 pm. It would seem Quick was one of a number of bombing parties that went out to support the men of the 59th and 60th struggling to survive in No-Man's Land.

18 July ... our battalion (58th) was sent up into the front line that afternoon more as a show of force, than anything else, but we were caught in a communication trench and many were killed and wounded. (Someone had issued this order from HQ many miles behind who knew nothing of the situation.) On the way back we sheltered on the side of what had been a road, when a shell burst overhead. I drew my right foot up a bit and ... the nose cap of the shell ploughed into the ground where my foot had been ...

19 July. Early in the afternoon we were ordered forward again and moving along the road, men on each side with a distance of about ten to twelve feet between each party of six ... to minimise casualties ... we walked about 2 to 3 miles, then entered a communication trench and after moving some distance we came under shell fire ... It was some time before the front line was reached ... there were dead everywhere. You could never describe the scene and it was no wonder that some went insane. One had to be careful where you walked that you would not step on the dead or wounded. There were officers giving directions where to go and nothing about what to do. I don't think they knew themselves ... It was now late afternoon when I led 8 or 9 men into this holocaust. I was carrying 24 hours rations, water bottle and other bags containing 8 mills, grenades and a 45 service revolver, a gas mask besides my ordinary equipment, but no rifle. I was classed as a grenade thrower and a rifle would be in the way in throwing bombs ...

I ran as fast as I could and dropped into a small hole ... about 20 yards and all the time you could see the bullets from the German machine gun hitting the ground all around you. They seemed to be firing from every direction ... with great effort I got myself out of the shell hole and hurried ... towards the next ... but not seeing any I threw myself to the ground ... as I felt a terrific impact against my body in the region of my back. It seemed as if I was thrown over and over coming to earth on my stomach, unable to move my legs with my right hand underneath me. I do not know how long I laid like that, but when my mind cleared ... I realised I was ... near the enemy's line and hearing the rattle of machine gun fire. I saw one about 50 yards on my right in the open between the two lines

Pte R V Quick, 1861, 58th Bn Egypt 1915

making havoc with the advancing troops. I laid very still in case he saw me move ... I tried to get my revolver out but ... could not move my right arm ... I realised I was in a bad way. A thought raced through my mind was this the beginning of the end? It was some time later that a violent explosion shook the earth ... after the dust cleared away I never heard or saw anything of the machine gun or its crew. By this time the day was drawing to a close and with it my life. All around was dead and dying, the long shadows of the evening making the scene horrid and frightening. The piteous cry for help and stretcher bearers rose above the other noise of the battlefield. With the darkness came the awful feeling of loneliness and helplessness.

During the night I managed to remove my equipment ... and felt freer except for the lower part of my body which felt cold, dead and useless. I turned to crawl with my hands and elbows back to our lines ... not until I came to a ditch with water running in it and on the other side what was left of the enemy barbed wire I realised I had crawled the wrong way
[continued opposite]

Wagstaff's four paragraphs are the last sheet of paper about the battle in the files. From then on nothing happens except schools and lists of '*effective strength of the Division*'. Since their arrival in France there are no figures for individual battalions, only the tables prepared by the medical people of dead, wounded and missing.

Only the last paragraph of McCay's report admits anything happened after 5.15 am, 20 July. He completed it on 25 July after receiving reports from Artillery, Engineers and Medical. We are asked to believe that the next week wherein the War Diary dealt with the attempted armistice, the sacking of Pope, the appointment of his successor, conflicts that caused 36 casualties on 22 July, 26 on 23 July, 11 on 24 July, and so on every day, required no further explanation or even a memo.

The Administrative File however is full of Routine Orders covering the conduct of men, Courts-Martial, some promotions and the first batch of awards. There are still no Intelligence Summaries, however the serial number of the next one—31 July/1 August—reveals they were prepared. There are no orders, memos, or communications with anybody.

As the men came back from No-Man's Land they encountered devastation no less than that they had just left. Bodies and pieces of bodies were everywhere, screams of the demented and groans of the dying took over from the chatter of machine guns, and disoriented officers and bewildered NCOs trained to bring order out of chaos, tried to be helpful and useful but they were as one man put it, '*in as bad a state as the rest of us*'. No memoir recalls this period with anger, all reflected on it positively when the human spirit somehow understood, somehow coped, somehow kept a sense of proportion and humour. Even the man who found an officer cowering in a trench blanched with fear and his mind gone, only had sorrow. All who saw and heard the legless man calling for a passageway so that he might get himself to a Dressing Station, just marvelled in the witnessing of it. The officer who had to organise the clearing of corpses so that the living might pass was moved by '*the wounded clutching you as you passed*'. And what of the battalion who on returning to their billet found one of their number dead by his own hand. Wrote his friend, '*he was a very excitable sort, I suppose the whole thing got him down*'. How many of his cobbers would have denied him the place he has on the bronze tablets at the Australian War Memorial? One can only imagine the atmosphere in the billets while the survivors wait to see who will come in, and who will not.

A SHORT TRUCE (contd)

... I was able to cross and shelter under a bank so as to be protected from German fire ...

During the night a solder was passing by me and I called to him asking if he could help me to my feet ... he tried to help me with one hand, and when I asked him for the other he showed me a torn bloody sleeve but no arm. I told him to go as I was sure he was in greater trouble than I was. That night passed in delirium and most of next day the same ... I cannot remember anything of the day. The second night came and passed, and daylight filled the sky. It seemed very quiet and then I noticed men walking between the lines carrying bodies away. I made myself heard to an Australian with a Red Cross on his arms, he came over and carried me back to our lines ... where a doctor examined me after cutting off my tunic to reveal a wound on my right shoulder and neck, the steel helmet I was still wearing had part of the back rim blown off. I learned later that a short Armistice had been arranged in the area so that both sides could bury the dead.

That night we were carried to a hospital train ... at Estaires ... it was loaded with English and Australians ... and we arrived at Wimereux near Boulogne ... I stayed in this hospital until 1 August. I could not be moved because I was still haemorrhaging from the lungs ... From this hospital we were taken to the Norwich Community Hospital ...after about two weeks I was able to get up ... the extent of my injuries were a collapsed right lung, right shoulder and arm with very little movement...

Robert Quick returned to Australia on 2 July 1917. He died in Nhill in 1984.

INFORMATION AND PHOTOGRAPH COURTESY H QUICK

BROUGHT IN 370

These notes from Bean's file are the result of a conversation with Lieut Col J C Stewart CO of 57th Bn at Fromelles provide the astounding fact that well over half of the Australian line was for a time held by two companies.

At 2 am on 20 July, 57th Bn was instructed to take over defence line ... it was in a dreadful state, all saps blocked and full of dead and wounded. Enemy still shelling but mostly falling behind.

The 14th Bde was still in line – line right up to the back of 14th Bde was practically manned by 2 Coys of 57th Bn, under Marshall.

On 20 July nothing unusual in German line. If any of our parties went out to pick up wounded they turned machine guns on them and hit some during the day. During the night the 57th Bn brought in 200 wounded and 170 on night 21/22 July. As far as we know the Germans did nothing.

At 2 pm 21 July word was received that the Germans had manned their trenches. We stood to till 6 pm.

On 22 July we could see a wounded man. A party went out and brought him in. They brought him right up to the parapet and were just going to hand him over when the Germans shot and badly wounded one of the stretcher bearers and shot and killed the man on the stretcher. On 23rd one man wandering in front of the German line, apparently blind, was bombed by the Germans. For the next two days either our dead in our uniforms, or else dummies were put on top of the German parapet. Instructions were given to fire at these—they may have been used as a screen or under the idea that we would not fire on them.

Capt. Bean arrived at Sailly and 5th Division HQ at about 1.20 pm and '*went straight up to Wagstaff's room—there was a conference on and they were very busy*'. Bean's notes on this visit were extensive and included much information which needed revision, but the sentiment that emerges from his notes, his observations and direct experiences on this day are hugely important to this story.

The first man he met was the ADC at McCay's HQ who told him, '*we've had an awfully rough passage*', though he was '*clearly very pleased with the 8th Bde—his old brigade*'. The summary of the battle by this man was reasonably accurate, but when he told Bean that the battalion digging the sap for 8th Bde had lost 400 men, Bean wrote: '*Lost 400 men—400! Good God—they could take and keep Courcelette with losses like these*'. Bean had a conversation with somebody of 14th Bde from which he gleaned the fact that the German front trenches were '*almost unoccupied where they went in*'—and that the 14th had an easier task as '*both flanks were to some extent protected.*'

Bean also found '*that a Gallipoli officer who was in the action at Lone Pine*' had said '*that even then they never had shelling like this*', and another remarked '*the shell fire in Gallipoli was child's play to this*'.

Although Bean gives no times for his interviews with Tivey and Pope, it would seem he saw Tivey first who he found '*his eyes like boiled gooseberries. He had been up two nights and had been through the trenches today.*' He noted that '*the one thing he seemed anxious to assure himself of was that his Brigade had lost ... 1700—that's about as heavy as some brigades lost at the landing isn't it?*' Bean wrote: '*And it was*', leaving the reader with the distinct impression that Tivey saw the loss as some badge of honour.

Bean next called on Pope, who rather disgusted him by boasting and that he had '*been refreshing himself*' (see *The Dismissal of Col Pope*, page 260–61), but it was more likely to have been Pope's contempt for Elliott that forever turned Bean against Pope.

The full note of Bean's visit to Brig. General Elliott, whom he visited next, reads:

'*Old Elliott* [curiously everybody called Elliott old but he was the youngest Brigadier] *was dead asleep when I called—but McCay came in and woke him up. When Elliott came out I felt almost as if I were in the presence of a man who had just lost his wife. He looked down and could hardly speak—he was clearly terribly depressed and over wrought. McCay was also,*

I thought, anxious about an order which he and Elliott had given for 2 companies of 58th Bn to support between 14th Bde and the British. The British, McCay explained, reported at 9 pm that they had captured the cap of the salient and so Elliott with his full approval—sent in two companies of the 58th to fill in the gap'—Bean's comment, '*An important point if the gap had existed*'. Then Bean jotted down McCay's explanation, '*they had to be put into the gap as the 61st Division reported that it was in*'. Then Bean wrote, '*As a matter of fact it never had the cap of the salient ... if it got anything it got the part shaded!*' Here Bean drew a little map showing a small shaded patch on the right side (facing it) of the Sugarloaf.

From where McCay got an assurance about the British being in the Sugarloaf at 9 o'clock has escaped this writer, and McCay did not mention the 58th going in to help the new British attack, or to stiffen up the 59th, as McCay's and Elliott's reports later remembered. Curious, to use again a word already much used in this inquiry, or would the word 'revealing', or even 'troubling' be better?

When Bean left Sailly he went to Amiens to send a cable about the battle (see *Reporting Fromelles*, page 216–17) and then returned to Contay at 10 pm. His last notes of the day seem to bring it all to a sort of ending:

'The 1st Army told the correspondents that the Australians did quite well and would have held on if 61st Division had done so. The 61st Division they said, were rather second-rate territorials. Why do they put second-rate terriers in with our men on a job like this? They said our Australian Artillery was not quite so good—that it fired on 61st Division, hit a gas plant and gassed 70 men (may or may not be true—it may have come from rival artillery). 1st Army ... said that anyhow the attack had succeeded in its object. That is not true—it is the opposite.

Tomorrow is a more important attack—White told me.' And that was Pozières.

McCay issued his Report on 25 July. Of 20 pages, it is well-written and well-arranged, indeed a mini-history, taking the reader through the whole event from '*11am, 13 July, a short meeting ... when I was informed*' to the table of casualties then noted as 506 killed, 3327 wounded, 1700 missing—total 5533. Reports from Artillery, Engineers and Medical Services were attached, but none from Signals.

A number of meaningless notes from Haig, Haking and others followed. In the view of this writer the content of these has been taken too seriously. Apart from the naming of the 5th

IN ONE BILLET
60th Bn relieved by 57th at 7 am and survivors returned to former billets. Roll Call held at 9.30 am, 4 officers and 61 other ranks being present. Battalion concentrated in one billet 200 yards NNW of Brigade HQs. Order received 20 reinforcements to arrive at 6 pm: postponed.

—War Diary 60th Bn, 20 July 1916

VERY QUIET
21 July. The day was very quiet. Our parties brought in some more wounded. The Germans were seen to be helping our wounded men close to their parapet. The day was spent in clearing the kit and stores etc. from the trenches and repairing the parapets.

—War Diary 15th Bde, 21 July 1916

RETURN OF LABOUR
Return of Labour, skilled and unskilled, other than that provided by fighting troops or reinforcements on 21 July 1916.

French civilians with 5th Sanitary Section for 'Scavenging and Sanitary' Work—32. With 5th Divisional Engineers in 'Workshops and Stores'—292.

—5th Division Admin File, July 1916

CENSUS OF ANIMALS
To 31 July 1916 for 5th Australian Division.

Horses: Riders 1290.
Light Draught 1356
Heavy Draught 531
Pack 71
Mules: Light Draught 1638.
Pack 72.
Overall Total 4988

—5th Division Admin File, July 1916

For the record: CO of ADVS (Veterinary Service) was Major M Harvey.

and 61st Division, they could be made to refer to any battle with the change of no more than five words. Haig's vacuous phrases like '*the gallantry with which they carried out the attack is fully recognised*' are of no importance. But Haking's appalling effort showed how out of touch he was. The depth of his intellect is fully exposed in his concluding sentence: 'I wish you all a still more complete victory in your next attack and I hope I shall be somewhere near when it takes place'. One can imagine the Diggers' reaction to that when it was posted on the Notice Board!

The 5th Division stayed in the Fleurbaix area until October, it taking all that time to reorganise and rebuild.

The narrative of the battle from the British and Australian perspective completed, we turn to the German account.

THE SALVAGE OF FROMELLES

Apart from the waste of men there was of course material. At the end of July the 5th Divisional Salvage Corps put together a list of 85 items that they had collected in both serviceable and unserviceable condition. Some are very revealing like the rifles that were unserviceable, but repairable—1,500, and web equipment—2,000. Some 420 steel helmets were found but no felt hats, and whilst 351 pairs of unserviceable ankle boots were retrieved, odd boots filled five sacks. There were 61 sacks of useless saddlery, but the 9 sacks of horse muzzles were serviceable.

Sadder statistics were the 1,359 blankets that were deemed serviceable, and the 210 great coats, 10 sacks of tunics and breeches, 21 sacks of underclothing that were classified unserviceable. Also useless, but collected, were 226 pairs of puttees, 75 pairs of braces, 7 pairs of spurs and a sack of gumboots. But very serviceable were 48 SRD (Rum) jars, 8 latrine buckets and 6 picks.

Of Ordnance items retrieved but unusable, were a sack of horseshoes, 2 trench catapaults, one hurricane lamp and a quantity of horse rugs. Of the serviceable items there were 2 trumpets, one cleaver and case, 15 axe handles, 5 sickles, 3 wire cutters, and a pair of handcuffs.

Large amounts of ammunition salved included 247 boxes of small arms ammunition, 70 boxes of Mills grenades and 11 cases of cordite.

At the end of the list under supplies were 20 cases and 20 tins of biscuits and 24 cases of Bully Beef, then a sack of Hospital suits and a bundle of maps.

All this goes a little way towards understanding the full impact of the battle, such lists put together without any consideration that they are part of the history are always revealing. In the list there is one tin of Chloride of Lime left, a quantity of shoemaker's tools, 5 trench periscopes and a bell tent: each in its way noting an activity which the narrative has passed by.

Always conscientious and straightforward

Kenneth Malcolm Mortimer was born at Leneva West, Victoria on 9 October 1895: his father Australian born of Scottish descent, his mother from Derbyshire. Kenneth, one of six sons, attended the local Leneva State School obtaining a scholarship to Wangaratta Agricultural High School. He had a gift for mathematics, had photography as a hobby, was a good all-rounder at sports and handy with a rifle. He entered Duntroon Military College on 9 March 1913, having always had the ambition to be a professional soldier. Mortimer graduated 28 June 1915. From there, on 20 Sept 1914, he wrote:

Nearly everybody was glad here ... that Labor had beaten the Liberals ... as we knew then that Pearce would be made Minister of Defence ... Pearce has studied his work from the aspect of a military as well as a civil man, and he knows of 'the evils of civilian control' in wartime.

As Lieutenant he sailed for Egypt in November 1915 and became Battalion Signals Officer of 29th Bn in Egypt, being promoted Captain in February 1916. It has to be said that his letters from Egypt showed little imagination about that country or what was ahead, but the arrival in France captured Mortimer, as it did most Australians. The green and beautiful countryside, the historic buildings and welcoming French people were such a change after Egypt that it was another world.

By 16 July he had seen the other side of France, the war-torn landscape and told his mother, '*It wasn't bad at all up forward—quite an experience you know ...*' His last letter written on 18 July rejoiced in all the letters he had received from family and friends; '*Old Fritz was very quiet during our stay in the trenches so there is nothing at all to worry about.*' Like all the rest he had no real idea what was then just twenty-four hours away.

The assaulting battalions in the 8th Bde were the 31st and 32nd, with the 30th, the '3rd Bn' and the 29th (or 4th) reserve. Thus the 29th should not have been forward of the Australian line. However, as a result of McCay's mismanagement, Mortimer and many others from the 29th were sent forward. Mortimer was with Captain Tom Sheridan and one other who survived to relate to Mortimer's family what happened.

Captain Mortimer was last seen wounded and crawling along through the grass: neither he nor Sheridan were ever seen again, and no trace was ever found of either man.

There is a distinct possibility that Pte William Miles was Captain Mortimer's batman, and it was his search for Mortimer that introduced Miles to the Saxon Officer 'interested' in an armistice (pages 262–72). The curious situation of a 36-year-old ex-sailor from Wales, a South African War veteran and father of two looking after a 20-year-old captain, who until Fromelles had never heard a shot fired in anger nor ventured far away from his studies needs noting.

One POW claimed Sheridan had been captured. Writing from a POW camp on 22.8.17, CSM Ken F Newman (307) explained to Mrs Mortimer that he had asked around about Captain Mortimer and the conclusion was that he had died on the battlefield. He wrote:

I had the honour of serving under him in A Coy ... he was always most popular with all other ranks, because of his gentleness and goodness. Always conscientious and straight forward he has done his duty to the last, as we all know he would do.

What was Mortimer doing? According to Capt. Purser of 30th Bn, '*I distinctly remember a company of 29th Bn under Captain Mortimer (who was killed) being sent to reinforce (not to carry stores, although, at my request they took extra ammunition with them), but have no recollection of any of the companies of 30th Bn being ordered to reinforce.*'

K M Mortimer at Duntroon, 1913

This was in respect to Ellis' assertion that the 29th Company was sent up to carry stores: which was the duty of the reserve (4th) battalion: not as McCay chose, to be reinforcements.

Florence Mortimer in 1928 writing to Bean of her son '*a rather studious affectionate country lad*', still described him as '*wounded and missing*', there never having been proof of his death to satisfy her. She remained hopeful that he would return and life would go on from her last memory of him. That last memory was the farewell dance at Leneva when the dashing young officer in his Duntroon uniform danced with his mother before embarking on 'The Great Adventure'.

INFORMATION & PHOTO COURTESY OWEN MORTIMER

At the Front

by Corporal E A Hubbard,
from *The Evelyn Observer* 30 March 1917.

With the mists of night stealing over everywhere the stretcher-bearers worked like madmen, hundreds of the wounded being got through to the field dressing station. Many of them had lain out in all the fury of the day's fighting, unable to be removed owing to the communication trenches being blown in. During the night, however, fatigue parties had been working with all strength making a passage through the blown-in trenches and having finished, the wounded were removed with all speed. Many of them were suffering intense agony, but their courage was magnificent. Many of the wounded were removed on the trucks used for engineering, those in charge working under fire with great bravery.

Ernest Albert Hubbard, no 1961, 59th Bn
Egypt, July 1915

With the night coming on the terrific bombardment slackened slightly, but though the lighter guns were not so consistent, yet the heavy guns kept up their fire. They were shelling a strong German position known as the 'Sugar Loaf,' a concrete fortress that defied every effort to break it—one of the greatest mysteries of the German line, supposed to be full of guns and machine guns. At night the scene was one of terrible beauty. It is simply terrific and fascinating to watch the guns at night. The whole sky seemed to be ablaze, which resembled brilliant summer lightning. Infernal fires were flashing; flickering, swift tongues of flame were tossing burning feathers above, rosy smoke clouds were concentrating in an immense volume over the battlefield, where rockets, flares and star shells rose continuously. Away in the distance can be seen the village of ———; it is a mass of smoke, flames and ruins. The enemy's heavy guns had been bombarding it all day, and when night fell little remained - all a mass of ruins. The beautiful church, houses, etc., all are a mass of ruins over which the flickering tongues of fire leap and twine continuously.

To the rear of our transfer parties of men, under heavy fire, had been bringing up thousands of rounds of ammunition, bombs, flares, etc., for use in case of urgent need; but during the night a high-explosive shell from the enemy landed in the midst of the stack of ammunition, with a terrific result, for there was a terrible explosion, the concussion of which caused the ground to tremble and shake, while the air was filled with an awful tongue of flame.

Throughout that awful night we lined our ruined and shattered parapets, keeping a sharp look-out: for the failure of the day's charge, it was thought might tempt the enemy to attack our lines, under cover of darkness. Evidently the Germans had suffered severely from our bombardment; they were quite content to take a breather during the night, both sides keeping up a heavy rifle and machine gun fire throughout the night. There was the usual shelling, but it had slackened off considerably throughout the night. Along our line all was confusion. Units were all mixed up together, -th, -th, and -th Battalions all worked together throughout the night. There were very few men left of the -th and -th Battalions, these two having suffered heavily in the charge on the German trenches. As we watched along the parapets we could hear the wounded men lying out in No-Man's Land calling out for help; their coo-ees and cries were pitiful to listen to. From out [of] the darkness it was a continual call of 'For God's sake give me water,' 'Stretcher bearers.' In many cases the men had become delirious owing to the awful agony of their wounds, and they cursed, raved and moaned until they expired, or become unconscious.

It was impossible to stand by and listen to the awful sufferings of the wounded, and parties of men volunteered to go out in that fire-swept stretch of land in an attempt to bring any one they could in. All through the night, under the cover of darkness, these men worked, and many a man lying helpless out in that awful zone of fire owed his life to that gallant band of men who risked their lives for their suffering comrades. Since that happening many of the men have been awarded military crosses and medals in reward for their brave deeds. It was terrible to hear the wounded men, on the approach of their rescuers, begging piteously to be taken in. Many of the men were bearing terrible wounds; they had tried to bandage them up in a rough way to stay the flow of blood. Some of the men were just living, while for many a poor fellow the help so greatly called for had arrived too late, death having relieved him from his awful sufferings. Many a man who took part in that terrible assault will carry with him to his grave the remembrance of those awful horrors he passed through in that day and night.

Throughout the night signal rockets were constantly being fired into the air, red and green lights, all carrying some signal. Far to the rear of the enemy's trenches the shrill blasts of a horn rang out on the night air, and at the time we wondered what it meant. Since we have learnt that it is a signal for stretcher-bearers by the enemy. About midnight high into the air burst a green rocket, its brilliant green light illuminating the surroundings, in a splendour of beauty. Magnificent it looked, but it carried a warning that made every man move with rapidity. For was it not a signal for the warning to all that there was a great danger of the enemy launching a gas wave. Already we could hear the blast of a horn sound the Gas Alarm, while along the line could be heard the 'ding-dong' of the Gas Alarm bells along the trenches. As we rapidly adjusted our gas helmets over our heads, tucking them securely under the collars of our tunics, our thoughts flew to those unfortunate comrades still lying out in the open, helpless, unable to put their helmets on. For the space of a quarter of an hour in the helmets, then we received orders to remove them. The men on the Gas Alarm Post had mistaken the thick clouds of white smoke in the distance for gas, so had sounded the alarm.

Throughout the night we 'stood to' while we shivered with cold, the night being very chilly, while a dense, heavy fog crept over the battlefield, causing the enemy's trenches to be completely obliterated from view. The numbers of flares sent into the air was very great, the mist causing their light to show a dull yellow, which reflected faintly through the gloom. Under this fog in the early morn many parties of men scoured No-Man's Land in search of our wounded men, with the result that near a hundred of them were brought over the parapets, while many of the wounded, who had lain out all night, made another attempt to reach safety under the cover of the heavy fog. The latter was undoubtedly the means of saving many men's lives.

With the breaking of dawn the heavy mists passed silently from the battlefield and the welcome sunshine gleamed down upon us once more. Once again another day had broke[n] forth in all the beauties of a spring morning. But, alas! what a scene of carnage it dawned upon. Looking out into No-Man's Land it was a dreadful sight. Everywhere was to be seen the remnants of the rusted and torn barbed wire entanglements; the ground between the trenches was pitted with huge shell holes. There was no vestige of the true surface of the ground; the ground was completely churned up. Trees around had been struck by shell fire, their branches having been shattered as if they were paper. As one gazed through the periscope one could see the motionless khaki-clad forms of our dead dotted amongst the grass out in that awful strip of land owned by no one. Everywhere their rifles, equipments, etc., were scattered. Some of the bodies lay as they had fallen, their heads towards the enemy's lines. In many of the shell-craters could still be seen the forms of men, but whether living it was hard to say. Undoubtedly there were still many living out in those craters, awaiting chances to be brought in. Away in the distance the village of ——— was a shapeless heap of bricks and masonry.

With the breaking forth of another day many of us began to feel the pangs of hunger. The horrors of the previous day had caused us to forget all thoughts of food. Now we were beginning to feel the effects, after our strenuous time. We had some hard biscuits and some bully beef, and, after looking around, in an old broken dug-out—evidently once occupied by an officer—my mate and I found a tin of jam, a tin of condensed milk, and some bread from the previous day. Of these we made a decent meal.

As we walked along the remnants of our trenches, what a sight met our eyes. Everywhere lay our dead. The majority of them had been killed by shell fire. Many of the wounded had crawled into dug-outs, as they thought for safety; inside these many had died while waiting for attention to their wounds. Many of these dug-outs had been blown in, and underneath were the mangled bodies of many. Armless and legless corpses were laying everywhere. In a dug-out used as a dressing station were many dead. A pitiful story is that told by Pte ——— still with us. The lad, a mere boy of eighteen, had a trying experience; the following is it, as told by him later to us: 'Badly shaken up by the explosion of a high explosive shell, I crawled into a dug-out, late in the evening, inside of which were four, including myself. Late during the night a large shell burst, blowing in the dug-out on to us. Two were killed outright, while the third chap and myself were pinned up by the fallen sandbags. I suffered intense pain, while the groans of the other chap were awful to hear; he appeared to be in awful agony. In my cramped and terrible position I seemed to lose my senses. Suddenly I thought I must be in Heaven, for there broke out suddenly the hymn, 'Lead, Kindly Light', sung in a voice that was as clear as a bell. The singer finished, then there was silence. I must have become unconscious for I knew no more until I came to, to find the daylight had appeared once more. Over in the corner my mate of the night before was dead. Later I managed to attract the attention of an officer, and they dug me out. Except for my back being much hurt, I am all right otherwise. But never will I forget that night passed through in that dug-out, nor the hymn sung by that chap before he died.' Private ——— has now quite recovered from his injury and is still with the battalion. In one place I saw a number of our dead; they had been smothered by sandbags. One of the bodies, when we dug them out, was still clasping in his rigid hand his pocket bible. He had evidently been reading it when death overtook him, for the book was still half open. He belonged to the Field Engineers, for upon his shoulder he wore the purple colours.

Amongst a heap of broken woodwork and sandbags we got a terrible shock. Buried amongst the debris, almost to the neck, we came upon a body. Thinking him dead we were about to leave, when one of the men saw a movement of his eyes. At once he was dug out. And oh, what a sight! Both the legs had been blown off to the knees, but the mud had clogged around the jagged wounds and stayed the bleeding, thus saving the man's life. Quickly he was borne away upon a stretcher, still game to the last. He had been one of a machine gun crew, who, early in the fight, had been blown up with their machine, and he was the only survivor.

These are only a few of the incidents come across that morning, the reminder are too awful to think of and the sooner forgotten the better.

LEAD, KINDLY LIGHT

Lead, Kindly Light, amid the encircling gloom,
Lead thou me on,
The night is dark, and I am far from home;
Lead thou me on:
Keep thou my feet; I do not ask to see;
The distant scene; one step enough for me.

I was not ever thus, nor prayed that thou
shouldst lead me on;
I loved to choose and see my path but; now
Lead thou me on;
I loved the garish day, and in spite of fears,
Pride ruled my will; remember not past years.

So long thy power hath blest me, save it still
Will lead me on,
O'er manor and fen, o'er crag and torrent, til
The night is gone,
And with the morn those angel faces smile,
Which I have loved since and lost a while.

Ernest Albert Hubbard was born at Steel's Creek, Victoria in September 1894, probably out of wedlock and brought up by his father's mother. Known as 'Snowy', he was 20½ when he enlisted, embarking at Melbourne on the HMAT *Hororata* on 17 April 1915.

He was taken on strength of the 7th Bn at Gallipoli on 5 August and in the action at Lone Pine on 8/9 August wounded. He was evacuated to Egypt. On 24 February 1916 he transferred to 59th Bn and made Lance-Corporal 10 June.

A number of 'Snowy's' letters to his uncle, Ern Cary of Steel's Creek, were published in the *Evelyn Observer* from November 1916 to March 1917. He wrote of his time at Gallipoli, in Egypt, by the Suez Canal and arrival in France, then at Fromelles. The letter reproduced in full here is the third in a series of five describing the lead up, the battle and the aftermath.

Ernest Hubbard was made Corporal in August; he attended various Schools of Instruction becoming a Sergeant on 23 August 1917. A month later he was wounded at Polygon Wood, and on 16 October 1917 was killed in action at Passchendaele. He was buried at Tyne Cot Military Cemetery (Plot 34, Row C, Grave 5). His father died the same year.

ARTICLE, PHOTOGRAPH & INFORMATION
COURTESY KEITH McC HUBBARD.

... expecting the world to come to an end ...

As noted opposite, Cpl Ernest A Hubbard wrote five letters dealing with his time at Fromelles. The most significant, of course, is 'At the Front', the three extracts that follow refer to the opening of the battle and the aftermath, from his other letters: sadly all there is space to include.

As the hands of our watches pointed to the hour of twelve the bombardment opened up to the minute. Everything had been 'quiet' with no hint of anything extraordinary about to happen. But suddenly it began. No description can do justice to what followed. In my life I have never encountered anything to equal that bombardment. As a spectacle, for the splendour and power of it, I doubt if anything ever resembled what was on during that afternoon; the noise was awful. In our bay we crouched. One of our men Pte ——— lost his reason and his breakdown was pitiful to see. He was like a child stricken with fright, and he could not be controlled. The rest of the men crouched against the parapet expecting the world to come to an end. For me, I wished to shriek, to bite my fingers, to do I know not what. And all one could do was to crouch against the parapet and gasp. How many guns we had at work I do not know ... hundreds, thousands ... but they all began at once ... hurricanes, whirlwinds, thunderstorms and gigantic conflagrations: bring them altogether and concentrate them all in a ring of a few acres, and you have only a faint idea of what went on immediately before our eyes.

Later I was to learn that further along the line of trenches the havoc was awful, the trenches having been blown in on top of the men in them. In some places the enemy's shells had landed in the bays and burst causing frightful damage ... our supports and communication trenches were almost obliterated. Men caught in the awful fire were blown to pieces and the carnage was awful. The bombardment obliterated all our communication trenches and in places it was impossible to get reserves through ... telephone wires were smashed and in places communications were entirely cut off. But working in the open, under awful shell fire the men of the Signalling Corps repaired broken wires and ran the reels of new telephone wires, linking up communications with headquarters again. With what result? For as fast as they repaired it the wire was again broken. But these signallers never lost heart, working throughout the day with great bravery, earning the admiration of all.

... when wounded the first thing that a man thinks of is to get rid of his equipment and anything else he carries. The rifles in pieces, the woodwork smashed and splintered from the barrels and the bayonets broken to pieces were to be seen every few yards, while such things as mess tins, bandoleers, waterproof sheets, torn and bloodstained uniforms and helmets scattered along the way. But the most gruesome sight of all was those who had been caught by the explosion of the shells, and the result is best unwritten for their torn and shattered bodies were lying everywhere as they were hurled and twisted about, so there they laid, a sight enough to sicken one of this awful war.

Egypt 1916. L-R, Back Row: Lieuts M A Lillecrapp, J W Axtens, P R Sheppard. Front Row: Lieut A K Flack, Capt. T R Marsden, Lieut R Walker.
AWM H15414

OFFICERS OF 8TH MACHINE GUN COMPANY

As described on page 119, Capt. Marsden '*got a number of guns across, at a terrible cost*'. His team, of which these are some, were a diverse collection. Marsden, a soldier and much later a wing commander in the RAAF, was born in Kent in 1887, and was from Sydney. His work at Fromelles earned a DSO. He later headed 5th MG Bn when all the 5th Div. MG Coys were amalgamated. Lillecrapp and Sheppard went with him—Lillecrapp was a bank clerk from Adelaide, Sheppard from Beaudesert was wounded by an Australian shell in No-Man's Land. Flack, born in London, was an ironworker from NSW, his work was noted with a MC. Axtens became a Capt. with 30th Bn, and Walker, born in Dublin, and a labourer from Northern Territory, went to 29th Bn. All survived, only Sheppard coming home early—1917—perhaps due to his wounds.

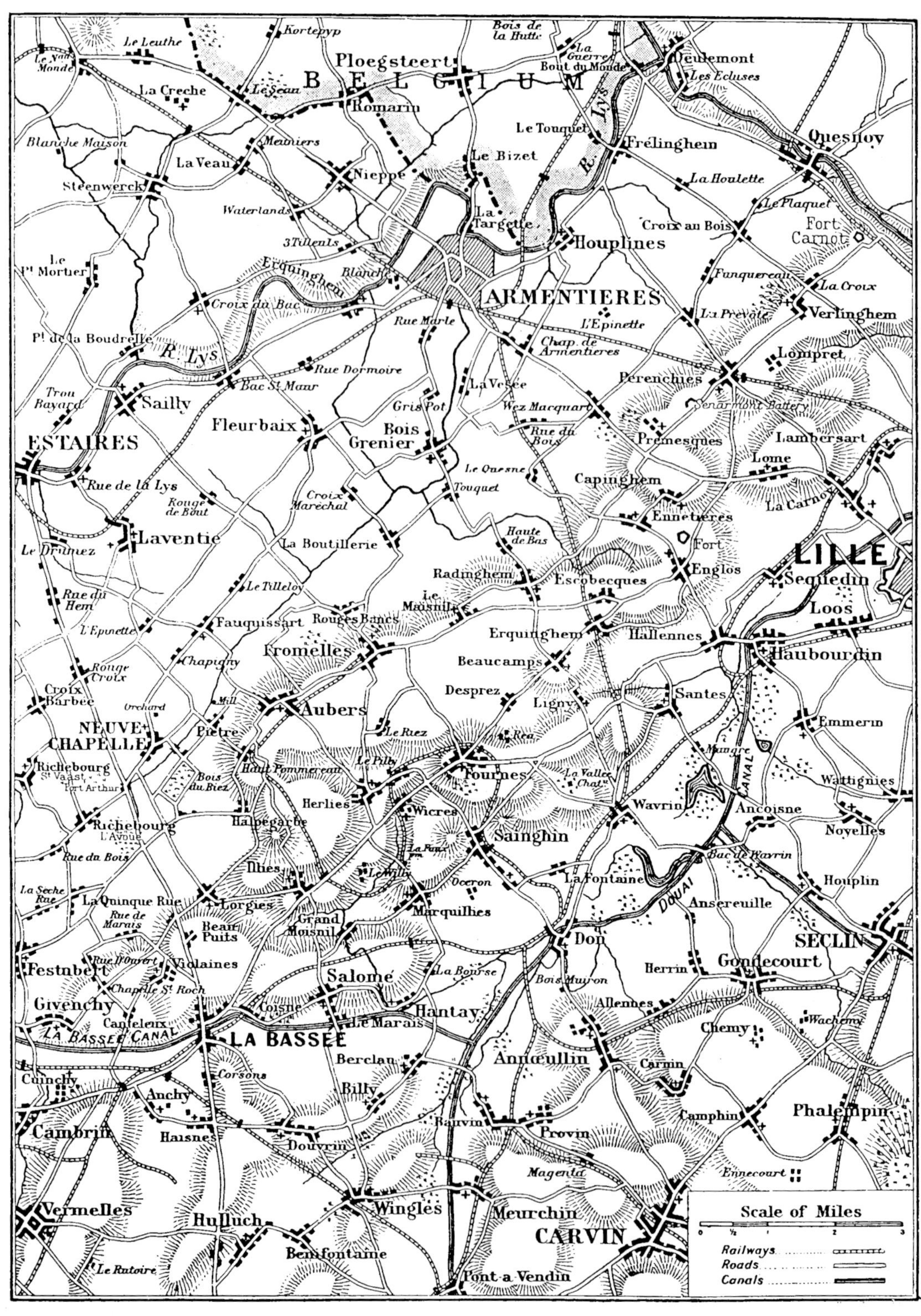

The Battle Front between Armentières and La Bassée showing the fortified ridge which formed a barrier to the attack on the German entrenchments before Lille

6

War forces one to think deeply

War forces one to think
deeply about human nature
—Adolf Hitler

The German army facing the British and Australians at Fromelles was the 6th Bavarian Reserve Division made up of 16th and 17th (12th Bde), 20th and 21st (14th Bde) Bavarian Reserve Infantry Regiments. It had been in service from October 1914, first in Flanders, then in March 1915 it was at Neuve Chapelle, back to Flanders, then to La Bassée and Arras for the rest of that year. In 1916 it remained in the same general area until moving south in September. The General in Command of the 6th Bavarian Reserve Division was Gustav Scanzoni von Lichtenfels, a career soldier, and he was 61 at the time of Fromelles. In view of the result of Fromelles, it is interesting to note that the German Commander was an accomplished artillery man.

The British Historian summarised the deployment thus:

> The whole front of attack fell within the sector of the 6th Bavarian Reserve Division, which extended, as it had in the Spring of 1915, from east of Aubers to a point south of Bois Grenier, a distance of about 4½ miles. All four regiments, 17th, 16th, 21st and 20th Bavarian Reserve from south to north, were in the line, each with one battalion in front, one in support, and one in either local or divisional reserve.

It was vital to this inquiry that some close examination of the German side be included. Obviously Ellis had no access to any German material and Bean, as far as Fromelles was concerned, used the unit histories of the 17th and 21st Bavarian Reserve Infantry Regiments (BRIR) both published in Munich in 1923, both of 120-odd pages, fairly austere and without a Roll of Honour or Nominal Roll. It is not clear whether Bean consulted the history of the 104th Saxons published in 1925: but on his page 442 he was in no doubt about the Saxon presence at the battle of Fromelles, but he avoids the word 'Saxon', and later on mentions that the truce was negotiated with a Bavarian officer (see pages 262–72). He also had access to the 16th BRIR records, but not their history.

The British Historian had access to the history of the 16th BRIR published in 1932, a nicely produced, well-illustrated

HIGH MORALE
Bean made this entry in his working papers on Fromelles, its origin not noted: '*6th Bavarian Reserve Division was undoubtedly a division of high morale. They greeted our men attacking across No-Man's Land with cheers*'.

LIEUT GENERAL GUSTAV SCANZONI VON LICHTENFELS (1855–1924)
Scanzoni—how he signed himself—was born in Wurzburg on 13 March 1855. At the age of 20 he enlisted voluntarily as a cadet in the 2nd Bavarian Field Artillery Regiment. He was promoted 2nd Lieutenant in 1877, and in 1906 he became commander of the 6th Field Artillery Brigade. In 1907 he was promoted Major General. He became commander of the 6th Bavarian Reserve Division on 24 December 1914, then in Flanders. Two weeks later on 11 January 1915 he was made Lieutenant General. On 14 November 1916 he was promoted to General of an Artillery Corps, but on 13 January 1917 at his own request he retired on the grounds of ill health. He died in Munich on 16 March 1924.

C E W Bean in his account of Fromelles had a General von Schleinitz in charge of the 6th Bavarians: the German Military Archives have no record of any such person.
INFORMATION COURTESY H TAPLIN

THE GERMAN ARMY

When the war began, a German Army Corps comprised of two divisions, each division of around 17,500 men. A division was then made up of two infantry brigades each of two regiments. Each regiment had three battalions, each of which had four companies.

During 1916 when the full ramifications of trench warfare had become apparent the formation was changed. A Division now had one Brigade Staff over three Regiments. Each Regiment as before had three battalions, each with four companies. In round terms this reduced Divisional strength by about a quarter but greatly simplified the chain of command and provided for the inclusion of heavy artillery, survey, mining, wireless and other services from the Division as the events demanded. Cavalry, field artillery, pioneers and divisional services such as telephones, transport, field hospitals and veterinary services were part of the basic Divisional establishment.

Each Regiment had an overall number, and also had a title, usually after a King, Prince or military identity. The three battalions were numbered I, II, III and the companies were numbered 1 to 12. Each battalion also had a machine gun company and these were numbered 1, 2 and 3. Each of the twelve companies was divided into three platoons, whilst each platoon had four sections—thus numbered 1 to 12 through each company. There was also a smaller subdivision called Group, consisting of a Lance Corporal with 8 ORs.

The approximate establishment of a German division was:

Divisional HQ	108
Infantry	8407
Cavalry	170
Artillery	1363
Pioneers	838
Divisional Troops	757
TOTAL	11,643

An infantry battalion had 23 officers, 3 RMOs and paymasters and 1050 ORs; with 59 horses and 19 vehicles completing the equipment. Later in 1917 the strength of a battalion was reduced to about 750.

book of 502 pages with tables of casualties and Roll of Honour, but, like Bean before him, refused to deal accurately with the numbers of German casualties when their histories gave quite definite figures.

From the other perspective, the German authors of the 17th and 21st histories had no access to British or Australian histories except Ellis. However, the author of the 16th history did use, and quote from Bean's Volume III. An inquiry to the Bavarian War Archives revealed the existence of a manuscript history of 20th BRIR, received, so it seems, at the Archives in 1964. There are 11 pages devoted to Fromelles and it is quoted at length here especially because it is very much a personal account, as well as describing the important part the regiment had in the action. The style and language could indicate it was written around the same time as the 17th and 21st histories (ie 1923). The opening paragraphs follow very closely some of those in the 21st BRIR book.

This writer knows no German language and so has relied entirely on translations, and extracts and comments that Bean and others made. Careful sifting through the Unit histories with translators, however, revealed a number of valuable observations and asides showing among much else that boredom, bureaucracy and incompetence were also familiar in the German army, and that comradeship together with the challenges of action were seen as positive sides of army life. As the German accounts of the action use their place names, the reader is directed to the German maps on pages 186 and 187, which, although neither is of July 1916, provide a guide to many of the names used. The authors of these narratives rely heavily on positions by giving Sector/Zone locations, and vary in style, but here are brought together into one system allied to the map on page 187. The map shows Sectors II, III and IV; each of these is divided into six Zones: a, b, c, d, e, f. Thus the Sugarloaf is Sector III Zone d: or IIId, and any unit there would be similarly classified. The Battalions are numbered by Roman numerals I, II, III etc, and the Companies 1st, 2nd, 3rd etc, and Reserve Companies A, B, C etc. German time is one hour ahead of Allied time.

We will examine the three German sectors, right to left, from the Unit histories, adding where appropriate cross-references to the Australian and British armies. But we begin with preparations for the raid a few days prior, which was to severely wound the 58th Battalion and was carried out by the 21st BRIR, both units were *then* at the eastern end of the sector.

14.7. Last minute preparations for a new operation 'Kulmbach', and establishing the range of the light and heavy batteries, and the mortars.

15.7. Carrying out the operation. Leader: Lieut Härder, 2nd Company. Assembly of patrols similar to 30.5. Purpose and duties: same as 30.5. Despite careful preparation the operation struggled from the beginning of its implementation with unfavourable circumstances of all kinds. Our own artillery landing short of the target, the loss of the leading group, a mishap with one of the mortars and a sudden gas attack. Nonetheless, and despite heavy retaliation from the enemy trenches, the operation was carried through to the end and three prisoners were taken. The blood toll of the enemy was great, but also our own losses from Härder's Company were high: they consisted of 10 dead (among them Lieut of the Reserves Kriechbaum), and 22 wounded. For those who on this occasion showed particular courage in the face of the enemy, the following were promoted: to vice sergeant major from corporal, the aspiring officer Otto Frank (11), and Corporal Walz (9): to corporal, senior privates Rittberger, and Huber (1), Ler (4) and Gerhauser (6). [Numbers after names are Companies.]

An Unknown German Soldier.
At Rue Petillon Military Cemetery this headstone stands in a row of 58th Bn headstones, all victims of the German raid of 15 July 1916.

From elsewhere we know that the raiding party consisted of 2 officers and about 95 ORs. Ellis wrote that it was well staged and successful, and worried that one or other of the prisoners might under stress of injury or concussion provide the Germans with some information about the forthcoming attack, then scheduled for the 17 July. However, any such information if they did get it, did not find its way into the records of the 21st BRIR. Whereas the 17th BRIR did admit to getting this information from a captured or dead British officer, an event dealt with on page 209.

The first account is from 20th BRIR, which was in Sector II, from the east side of Kastenweg to just west of Bas Maisnil, facing on the right the New Zealand Division, and on the left the 60th British Brigade. Here the account is slightly rearranged to provide a continuous timeline.

Erinnerungsblätter
deutscher Regimenter

Bayerische Armee

Das K. B. Reserve-
Infanterie-Regiment Nr. 21

Herausgegeben vom bayer. Kriegsarchiv

21st BRIR History.
The histories of the 17th and 21st, both published in 1923 have the same title page. The artwork is signed AH—Anton Hoffman, who also had drawings in the 16th BRIR history.

The bombardment reached the highest intensity on 19 July. From our trenches, we observed the incredible battering received by RIR 21 to our left ... Individual shots also fell in our IId ... about 140 were counted. Most of them went behind the trenches ... therefore they did not cause big losses. About 2 pm the bombardment lifted to become a heavy barrage. The English attacked first at about 7 pm ... The enemy—61st English and 5th Australian Divisions—were completely repelled by RIR 16. Only momentary success was achieved by the English against RIR 17. The Australians in comparison were more successful against the RIR 21, where with stronger forces they penetrated IIe. The artillery and mortars knocked out obstacles and opened up our defence installations. A great part of the trench crew were killed or wounded. Once through, the enemy moved towards the west but could only get as far as the middle of the sector ... he had more success in the east. He attacked along Kastenweg and on going through there drove more of our troops out.

The Australians went deep on this first attack—after going through Kastenweg to Toten Sau [Delangré Farm]—they moved towards the west ... coming near to Grashof and 200 metres from Brandhof. Our

PLACE NAMES
Although not used in the text, in German papers and documents, Fromelles is Petzstadt, Aubers is Buchheim, and Le Maisnil is Brandorf.

TIME
The times given in the German histories are of course their (Berlin) time, hence their attack began at 7.00 pm, but on the Allied side it was 6.00 pm.

A POSTSCRIPT:
A CONTINUOUS INFLUX
The material found in the Munich Archives in 2007 in connection with the action consists of Reports from Company Commanders and similar written two or so days after the action. Compared with the Unit Histories account on this and following pages, they add almost nothing, except names of individuals, to the overall story. There are also narratives from each of the Regiments which add little. This shows perhaps how widely researched (and remembered) the events were by the historians.

A few items in the Reports, almost personal observations by the officers concerned, add some human scale to the event.

20th BRIR. 20 July having got back to their front line, they were not left alone: '*Between 10.30 am and 12.30 pm, Sector 1d and rear area heavily shelled (about 55 rounds of 23.4 cms), resulting in [much] damage. The trench itself remained passable and in defensible condition. Clear-up work is in progress. The wire in centre and left sections is quite badly damaged.*'

21st BRIR. The Report was from Capt Schaaf, and begins dramatically: '*At 2.45 pm, 19 July ... received order to 'stand to' from the Colonel ... HQ left immediately for regimental command post at Fromelles (in a new concrete dugout) ... arrived 3.30 pm.*'

Later faced with a very dangerous situation, Schaaf recalled [continued opposite]

artillery and the precise fire from infantry and machine guns stood in the way of any further advance ... Our regiment took the necessary steps. Our 9th Company was brought forward from Le Maisnil ... to Depot Farm. Machine guns were set up there so they could effectively cover the area between the Farm and Türkenhauser, and the middle ground from there to the front lines ... another company moved to Schiatzergraben (south east of Depot Farm) ... I Battalion was being moved to Fournes.

The Commandant of RIR 21 informed his troops that the enemy had broken into his sector and was trying to widen his territory over Kastenweg. Türkenhauser was held by us with 4 platoons and two machine guns to stop the enemy moving to the east. Based on this, the 9th Company (Lieut Josef Schwarz) received orders to engage the enemy and disrupt further widening by them at all costs. The 10th Company now took over at Depot Farm. At the same time the Pioneer Company was ordered to have all available manpower and shock troops ready, and load up two ammunition trucks and a Pioneer truck with handgrenades and keep them ready under covers. A machine gun company was positioned at the Regiment's command post.

At 7.40 pm the 9th Company moved forward ... the company leader found that the Australians were in strength at Kastenweg and called for support but there were no spare forces available. The 9th was too weak to have any effect on the strong enemy force. It was also under fire from machine guns at Kastenweg and others further west ... 9th Company then joined with 6th Company RIR 21 in an attack. This included the area to the left of Kastenweg to Toten Sau—and would start at 12.35. However it began much later and only after parts of I Battalion had joined in the attacking force.

Meanwhile the battalion that had been ordered to march to Fournes was rerouted to Fromelles, and as they got near they suffered heavy casualties due to enemy artillery.

That first section of the 20th BRIR story reveals the extent to which 8th and 14th Bdes penetrated and how effective their attack was. As will be noted there is some duplication with that of 21st BRIR but this is retained to give a two-way view. The 20th BRIR historian continues:

> ... it became close to midnight and it was assumed that the enemy still with strong forces, held considerable parts of our positions ... it was also assumed that the RIR 16 supported by available units would attack from the left. The counter attack by the RIR 21 units did not happen, companies of their II Battalion on their way to forward positions fell under a heavy barrage and the positions, now declared too dangerous, were not used so the companies fell back. The Australians now received reinforcements and this posed a real danger to the II Battalion ... especially as it was known that the enemy had taken up a position in the area of Grashof. Two companies of our I Battalion – just the 3rd and later the 4th—would lead the attack against Grashof with three companies of RIR 16 already advancing from the left. At 11.50 our 3rd Company (Lieut Krieg) was ordered to move along Türkenhauser ... and support the attack. The company passing between Grashof and Brandhof found itself under heavy enemy artillery fire and received serious losses. Also considerable mistakes in action became obvious, partly due to the terrain, the dark night and the strange area, but soon

Portion of a German second line showing the sandbagged defences put in place probably by 8th Bde over the night 19/20 July. The earthworks on the right are probably those also shown in the photograph on page 205. Photograph taken by a German Intelligence Officer on the morning of 20 July.
AWM 1556

Grashof was declared free of enemy forces.

The whole company moved to the left of Grashof and using approach trenches made its way to some trees 150 metres beyond. There it encountered strong machine gun fire from the front and right: artillery fire was also concentrated on the woodland. Part of the company took the woodland and then sought out the rest of the company. The main part, upon crossing the road, came unexpectedly upon the Australians who were in weakly developed trenches. In a courageous attack the trenches were swiftly cleared. Now, with only about 40 men the company reached the tree line, 150 metres from Schmitzstrasse [leading to Rouges Bancs]. It was now 5 am, and there it came to an halt because to work through the ruined dugouts would be very hard as they were still very strongly held by the Australians. Especially strong was point 325 where a machine gun fired at the right flank of the company. Some 15 men were sent against it, but did not achieve anything, already some 50 were out of action. The exhausted men of the already depleted company lay there alone, further attack being impossible. More artillery was concentrated on the woodland and the company was ordered to dig in. It was easy to see the ruined dugouts, and as soon as possible they should be retaken and a push made for the trenches. The company waited there until after 10 am in the unceasing fire from the enemy artillery. Soon after that all went quiet. Immediately patrols were sent out and reported that the enemy had withdrawn. And to the east the enemy was not there anymore. The Australians had moved out during the heavy artillery fire. They did not know that our whole first line went around their back at the same time, cutting off their way back to their trenches. Those who did not fall in the later battles were taken prisoner.

That section clearly refers to the stand by Gibbins and his men holding off the Germans, until they left under the protection of the Australian artillery. The obvious success of this manoeuvre is clear. The historian now goes back in time to 12.35 am and to the far right position (from the German viewpoint) where Krinks and his men were having some success.

The fighting … of the surrounded enemy was the hardest and with the worst casualties. Strong forces held some trenches and more were

A CONTINUOUS INFLUX (contd)
the time and his personal gratitude to two of his officers:

The front line trench under very heavy artillery fire and was in a very poor state ... Capt Schaaf ... found himself compelled (as another attack by the enemy through the gaping holes in the trench defences would pose a great threat to our troops) to ask Regiment by telephone for reinforcements on right flank. At the same time he called for barrage fire on enemy front line trenches opposite the entrance of the Kastengraben, as the English were receiving a continuous influx of men and materiel from that point which ... were pouring through to the Kastenweg and Türkenecke.

A bombing party of pioneers ... arrived at around 5.30 am with about 25 men ... and the counter attack then began in earnest. Special praise ... due to Lieut Schwarz ... thanks to him and his men the Kastenweg was closed off and secured well before 2.00 am ... [Lieuts Schwarz and Friedrich] ... deserve the warmest recognition for their personal courage ...
I recommend them for the award of the Iron Cross, First Class.
Signed Schaaf.

These three biographical notes, together with another on page 194 come from *Kriegsgedentbuch der israelitischen kulturgemeinde Nürnberg* [A book to remember the war: from the Jewish Community of Nuremberg], published in Nuremberg in 1920.

ON THE BRINK OF BECOMING AN OFFICER

Alfred Bernhart was born on 13 February 1895 in Nuremberg the only child of the timber trade industrialist Phillip Bernhart and his wife Sophie. He went to the grammar school and took his leaving certificate on 15 July 1914. He intended to study chemistry because he had a gift for it; however, because of the outbreak of war he was not able to begin his degree. On 1 February he was called up to the army and on 18 October 1915 he came to the 21st BRIR, which was located in Fromelles. He started as a non-commissioned officer and officer cadet, was promoted to vice-sergeant and was on the brink of becoming an officer when he was shot in the head during heavy fighting around Fromelles on 19 July 1916. His body was buried in a mass-grave in the military cemetery in Beaucamps. The Field-Rabbi Dr Baerwald held the funeral service.

TRAINED TO BECOME A BAKER

Willy Weglein, was the son of trader Samuel Weglein and his wife Clothilde, and born in Erlangen (Geldersheim) on 20 November 1892. He went to primary school and after that he was trained to become a baker. Later he was an office worker with his last job in Nuremberg. Several times he was judged unfit for military service, but in 1915 he was called up to the army. He was trained as an infantryman; then at the end of March 1916 he came into the field and was allocated to the Mining Company of 6th Bavarian Reserve Division, which had to build trenches at the front. During the English offensive on 19 July 1916 the Mining Company had to support the 20th BRIR. During this fight he was killed by the bullets of a machinegun. He was buried in a mass grave in the cemetery in Beaucamps.

coming. Many machine guns set in those trenches strengthened the enemy lines unbelievably. The 9th and 6th Companies of RIR 21 could not force the enemy, without further help. At 2.00 am 4th Company (Lieut Schönborn) was sent forward ... but it lost its way due to the dark night and the lack of essentially correct directions... However it soon became apparent that they were in a good position, near Kastenweg. As it advanced to Toten Sau it came under heavy fire from a trench which Australians had hurriedly built.

There now follows an extraordinary account of the problems the Germans encountered at Kastenweg, almost certainly due to Lieut Krinks and his machine gunners (see page 124). The account now becomes detailed and personal, surely indicating that the author was in this action:

Determined, the company, intent on dislodging the enemy, set to attack Kastenweg. But the attack did not go forward. The right wing of the attack which was supposed to clean up Rodergraben by itself came unexpectedly upon units of RIR 21 that should have cleaned up Kastenweg a long time before, but they had lost their nerve due to the sustained barrages of the Australian machine guns and rifles. No leader would be capable of getting these troops into another fight had he lacked the strength and will of steel, and if he had not been able to demonstrate coolness and bravery himself. Lieut Schönhorn only needed to call *'Follow me .... '* and many soldiers found the strength to follow him.

The platoon leader Cpl Augermann, with some of his men, tried to move forward box by box in Kastenweg but the enemy opened with furious machine gun fire. Of the eight sabre-carrying officers of 4th Company, six were severely wounded as was the Company Commander, but he kept on encouraging his troops. Somebody else, due to the loss of officers, took charge and because of heavy fire from three sides, further frontal attack was not possible, so the Company pulled back to Toten Sau. Then some soldiers of the RIR 21 appeared and joined with 4th Company and the attack through Kastenweg was resumed. Hard work was ahead. An English sandbagged trench between Röder and Kastenweg had to be taken. With two groups Sgt Wilhelm Vetter stormed it, throwing hand grenades before the attack on the tough enemy, and made him surrender. Now the enemy could, step by step, be pushed back through Kastenweg. After cleaning out Kastenweg Vetter also took part in rushing a firing machine gun in Kampfgarben. He ran through the trenches to sack it after several attacks. He received the Silver Medal for Bravery; he fell on 29 March 1917 at La Bassée.

That closely observed narrative about the Australian machine gunners is now followed by what has to be an eyewitness account of the grenade battle already described on page 138.

As a result of the successful attack [on Kastenweg] there were now favourable conditions for the 9th and 6th Companies of RIR 21 to attack. These companies were in a long gunfire and hand grenade combat with a strong enemy who desperately defended himself and made three attacks of his own against the two companies. These companies suffered heavy losses. While it was now difficult for the Australians to draw on replacements from their trenches, ... we began the difficult task of clearing out our front line trenches, to the left and to the right.

Around 3 am the involvement of the 6th Reserve Pioneer Company was ordered … and they brought forward short range weapons and grenades which were much needed. The counter attack was not yet ready, but the Division was informed and the Prussian Jäger Battalion was put on alert … and sent to Fromelles.

But for one intervention in this battle, there is no more to say. Divisional orders stated that the last Reserve Companies, 1 and 2, should support the attack against the flanks and the part of Kastenweg still occupied. The leader of 2nd Company, Lieut Maier, was ordered to attack to the left. It was in these battles that Sgt Johann Wolfrum was especially noteworthy. At the front of the handgrenade group, he pushed the attacking Australians back again and again. He and his men came under fire from one of the flanking trenches, then when there was a lull they rushed the open ground in front of the enemy. Almost 90 Australians, surprised by this attack, dropped their weapons and were taken prisoner. Two machine guns were also taken. Wolfrum received the Silver Medal for Bravery.

Gradually the whole front line came again into our hands, even though there was still some fierce fighting. Our 4th Company still in the backline had few grenades left and had been pushed back, so … Josef Molz got his men to throw what grenades were left altogether and then storm the enemy shoulder to shoulder. This caused the enemy to move towards the RIR 16 … he had no choice but to flee, but some 30 prisoners were taken. Molz received the Gold Medal for Bravery.

The 1st Reserve Company (OC Lieut Sauber) did not engage the enemy, and 10th Company stayed at Depot Farm. Our machine gun platoon was stationary during the battle … it later moved to Turkenecke … it was to shoot at English planes.

Our Regiment's sector was surprisingly quiet during all the fighting. Enemy artillery fire was mainly directed at our left wing. Lieut Eichhorn, 6th Company, was killed by shrapnel in this area.

At 7.15 am all the front trenches had been taken back, what was left of the enemy … was cut off … and during the next few hours without fighting, discovered and taken prisoner. By about 11 am there were no more Australians behind or in German installations.

The enemy was beaten. Despite the fierceness with which it fought, and all the artillery barrages, over the short 4 km front the Australians and English could not achieve anything with their two divisions against our one division.

All units in our Regiment had a great and decisive part in the successful conclusion of the battle, especially the driving out of the enemy from the unbelievably toughly defended Kastenweg and clearing of the front trenches of the steadfast Australians.

The 19/20th July 1916 belongs to our Regiment's glorious history. Like all successes in war, this one also could only be achieved with heavy losses. Our losses were: 36 dead (amongst them Lieut Eichhorn of 6th Coy), 113 wounded (among them Lieut Schönhorn, Lieut Gulden, Lieut Maurer, Cpl Angermann of 4th Coy. 7 missing.

The next account, from the historian of 21st BRIR repeats some of the material from the 20th BRIR because they shared some operations.

Heavy artillery fire in the next few days was taken to be retaliation for our operation [15 July raid], however the enemy's use of munitions rose quite sharply on 17th, only the mortars were silent.

AN EXCELLENT PIANIST

Julius Schönberg was born the son of trader Louis Schönberg and his wife Amalie in Nuremberg on 25 February 1885. He went to the municipal school of commerce, to the new grammar school and to the normal secondary school. He got official permission to join the voluntary service for the period of one year. He could not finish the normal secondary school because his father became ill and he used the free periods during his apprenticeship for foreign language studies. He further improved his language skills during his stays in Geneva and London where he attended lectures at the university while working as a trader. He also played music and was an excellent pianist. Eventually he worked as a trader in his father's company. At the outbreak of war Julius immediately wanted to join the army voluntarily, but because of his situation at home he had to forget this idea, and had to wait for his call-up which came in March 1915, as a Landstürmmann because he had no prior military service experience. In January 1916, after he had finished a seminar for officer-cadets and non commissioned officers, he came to the 21st BRIR which was fighting near Lille. There he was promoted to a vice-sergeant and later recommended for lieutenant. But he became a victim of the English offensive on 20 July 1916. After several hours he died because of his severe wounds and was buried in the military cemetery in Beaucamps. Field-Rabbi Dr Baerwald conducted the funeral service. Later the body was transferred to his home and then to the new Jewish Cemetery in Nuremberg amongst the 'row of honour'.

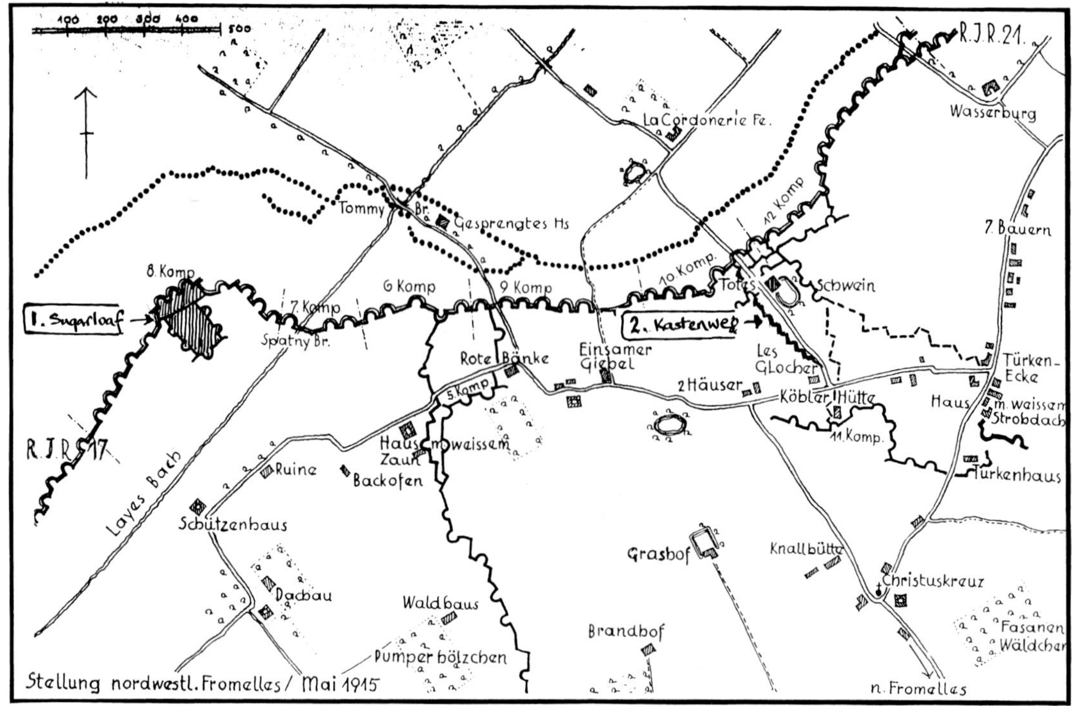

THE FROMELLES FRONT, MAY 1915
This map, featured in the 16th BRIR history, shows the outline plan of the Sugarloaf (1) which according to some sources resembled that of locally-baked sugar loaves, hence the name. (2) is Kastenweg, 'Chest-way', a communication trench, so named because it was largely lined with earth-filled ammunition chests. It was thus durable and passable in winter. Delangré Farm is the shaded box to the east, and called by the Germans 'Toten Sau' (dead pig).

GERMANS PUZZLED
London: 22 July 1916. The Amsterdam correspondent of the Central News says the German war correspondents are puzzled at the British attacks at Fromelles, south of Armentières, on Wednesday evening, in which two strong divisions were engaged. Some consider that they were to introduce a new offensive, and some serious attempt to advance towards Lille, while others think they were a demonstration to prevent the Germans sending troops to the menaced sectors at Hooge, near Ypres.
Hobart Mercury 24 July 1916.

18.7. Today very heavy and compared with yesterday even increased fire directed against the division's positions.

19.7. In the morning, very heavy artillery fire along the whole zone of the division; from 2 pm on it increased with heavy barrages from all calibres of artillery and mortars. The second line was put on urgent standby and the reserve brigade (1) was put on alert. Early on the telephone connections with the front line were broken, but contact with the command posts was maintained throughout with the use of dispatch runners.

At 7 pm an attack from several divisions on the three left zones of the division began. In Sector III it was totally repelled and in Sector IV it attained only temporary success. In contrast to that the enemy succeeded in advancing into Sector II (RIR 21) as well as at c (11th Company) where the enemy's artillery and heavy mortars swept aside all obstacles, levelled our defence installations and decimated the majority of our forces. From here the enemy spread to the south into sub-division d, where the 12th Company battled heroically to prevent further progress of the enemy. And to the north towards IIb the enemy gradually pushed back 10th Company while simultaneously attacking with new lines at the front, until our company found itself back over the front of the road to the barracks—Kastenweg [a communication trench].

Only here did the remainder of the 10th and 9th Companies, which were soon supported by the company of RIR 20 on the left wing, manage to block off the position. The enemy also advanced downhill, along *Kastenweg* up to *Toten Sau* and south west near *Hofgarten*, *Grashof* and even up to 200 metres near *Brandhof*. Then, however, all attempts to gain more room failed due to our artillery fire and the unerring and well-planned fire of our infantry and the machine guns from the positions *Toten Sau*, *Schmitzhof*, the left wing of *Türkenecke* and *Brandhof*. The *Frashof* position was unfortunately not finished and therefore unmanned.

Meanwhile, RIR 20 moved 1st Company of reserves to IIa, G Company (reserves of RIR 21) were moved forward to block off *Kastenweg* trench and *Sau* trench and as the two first companies of the brigade reserves were preparing to counter-attack from the direction of *Türkenhäuser-Schmitzhof*; F Company in *Brandhof* was to maintain contact with RIR 16 and support its counter-attack from the left. To this company the remainder of the 11th Company under 2nd Lieut Aal was attached. The effective barrage of the enemy's artillery and moved-up machine guns, nightfall and high losses caused the failure of the counter-attack. However, very soon a new attack was ordered, this time in particular against the enemy's left flank. H Company, which was relieved from the second position by parts of the infantry company of pioneers, was ordered to attack at *Türkenecke* along *Kastenweg* together with E Company, while all I Battalion supported by two companies of RIR 20 proceeded from the front trench via IIIa and the second line trenches to the point where *Kastenweg* meets the front line and to its shelters at the very front, in order to attack.

The difficulty of keeping up contact in the pitch dark night, made

GERMAN TRENCH MAP 1915
This clearly shows, when compared with the British map of a year later (pages 38–39) the unchanging nature of the front line, together with the locations of regiments *printed* on the map.
COURTESY H TAPLIN

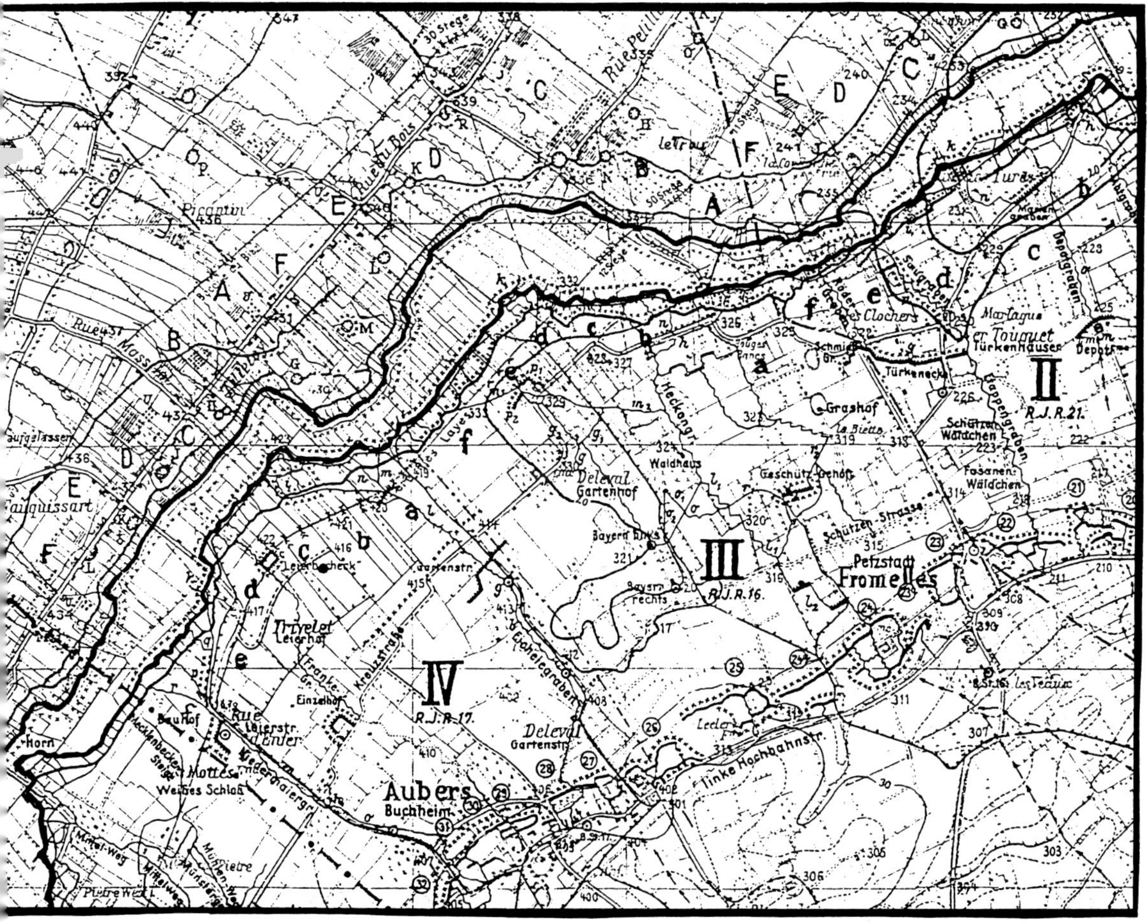

21ST BRIR AFTER THE BATTLE
23 July: Consecration of the new section of the cemetery (Beaucamps) and solemn burial of the casualties of the 19th and 20th took place in the presence of the Commanders of the Division and the Brigade, as well as the officers who were off duty in the neighbouring Regiment. Eight groups of III Bn under Lieut Echinger fired the salvos of honour.
27 July: Parade in front of His Royal Highness, the Crown Prince Rupprecht of Bavaria in Haubourdin. His Royal Highness greeted the Forces and expressed his appreciation for their action.
8 August: Promotions for bravery: Non-commissioned officer Eichenstaetter to Sgt Major. Privates Kuester and Schneider to Non-Commissioned Officers. All are from MG Coy.
27 August. The very first mounting of the newly concreted base 'Grashof' with two infantry groups and machine guns. Its position is very favourable ... the whole project was built by the Infantry Pioneer Coy with great skill ... under the rubble of the destroyed property ... so that the enemy did not notice any of the work being done.

—War Diaries of 21st BRIR
COURTESY H TAPLIN

THE NAME OF FAIR FIGHTERS
No armistice allowed so that the wounded simply have to chance to luck. Poor devils. Two 29th Bn volunteered as stretcher bearers and went out several times into No-Man's Land and brought in wounded one after another without getting a single crack. There's a rumour Saxons are now opposite us and I reckon they deserve the name of fair fighters when they will do that.

—Lieut Theodore M Pflaum (1898-1917), 32nd Bn

GERMAN CASUALTIES
7.5% of German troops were killed or died or wounds; 3.5% died of disease; 6% were rendered unfit for any service; and 6% of the wounded and ill were cleared for home service.

even more impenetrable by the smoke of exploding projectiles, and the high consumption of hand grenades delayed progress at first. Only when pioneers brought new ammunition could the attack progress, first more slowly, then more and more forcefully despite resistance from the enemy who entrenched himself and was continually bringing in new forces.

Curiously the 21st BRIR account of the morning of 20 July mentions a fog which no other accounts record. In fact Australian accounts point out how clear the morning after the battle was.

> 20.7. Around 7 am the whole position was again fully under our control. Very thick ground fog had made contact and overall view extremely difficult during combat in the morning, enabling RIR 16 to penetrate into Sector IIb in the second trench which they mistook for the first, without realising that the I Battalion of the RIR 21 had passed them in the front trench and so proceeded almost as far as the Tommy Street, on the left wing of IId, clearing their own position of the enemy. And neither did this regiment have any knowledge of the progress at its back by RIR 16. However, the fog prevented a large number of the enemy from grasping the situation, thus deciding too late to withdraw and finding their way back barred.

The summary of the losses and affects of the Battle on the 21st BRIR now concern their historian in one of the most telling sections of any of the unit histories. This was the worst damaged of the three Regiments by far, but compared to the losses of the two Australian Brigades (8th and 14th)—1024 killed and 2034 wounded—remarkably moderate. However, as their numbers were much less than the Australians, the losses represented real danger, and for this reason the 104th Saxon Infantry Regiment came to their assistance.

> Our losses were very high, particularly from the III Battalion; they consisted of 7 officers and acting officers, among them 2nd Lieuts Baumgärtel, Keim, Wolf and Wagner, and 288 corporals and men: 8 officers and 377 men were wounded; 1 officer and 94 men were reported missing, most of them probably buried under collapsed breastworks. The enemy's losses were much higher. There were 399 dead in the regiment's zone alone, in the area in front of that several hundred, polluting the air for weeks until our patrols sprinkled them with chlorine lime and covered them with soil in spite of the enemy's fire. Besides, in our zone alone the enemy lost more than 200 men taken prisoner, 8 machine guns and a great number of weapons, ammunition, food supplies and other equipment, the salvage of which took many more days.

The paragraph from the history of the 104th Saxon Infantry Regiment notes their urgent transfer to the front line, but makes no mention of the would-be armistice that one of their officers sought to arrange, adding more mystery to the event.

> Our III Battalion, which had been moved for 14 days for the purpose of exercise and which had been replaced by the Infantry Battalion 13, was to experience a special task. On 19 July it was suddenly alerted and sent

Casualties of the battle.
Bodies of English and Australians were loaded on the field railway and taken back for burial at Fournes behind the German lines.
FROM THE UNIT HISTORY OF 16TH BRIR, PHOTOGRAPHED BY HANS BAUER

Pte E MAIER, 7th COY, 16th BRIR
Eugen Maier was born at Karlsruhe, 30 March 1889 (Army records say April) and as educated at Rosenheim High School. After training, he worked as travelling salesman in the family business in Rosenheim. He enlisted in 1915 and in Feb 1916 he was assigned to the 16th BRIR. Maier qualified as a patrolman and was put in charge of all patrols. It was while on an observation patrol on 16 July 1916 that he was killed. Buried first at Fournes (see photo), his body was moved to Munich in Feb 1917. He was awarded the Iron Cross II Class and the Bavarian Military Service Cross with Crown and Swords.

to the 6th Bavarian Reserve Infantry Division, because a quite strong counter-attack was taking place in their sector. In the night of 19/20 July the III Battalion of RIR 104 was brought into action in the front line near Fromelles instead of the Bavarian Reserve Infantry Regiment 21 in expectation of further operations of the enemy.

As these did not occur, the Battalion returned on 22 July, having lost 4 killed and 4 wounded, to take over from the 13th Infantry Battalion on 24 July.

The summary of the days after the battle reveal one of the great unanswered questions of Fromelles—the desertion of their dead by the Australians.

Except for the great number of batteries that were quickly assembled from all sides, the Division beat back the attack by themselves. It was not necessary to deploy the III Battalion of RIR 104 [Saxons] and Machine Gun Company 134, which had been made available as well.

The enemy's artillery fire and our own only died away around noon. Nevertheless, the salvage of wounded and prisoners were already started in the morning. However, the rearrangement of troops could only be carried out in the course of the afternoon and late in the evening the III Battalion had to be relieved with respect to the great losses. After the battle, our own position and *Kastenweg* looked very bad, and so did the train tracks running behind the position. They had always been in need of repair, but now most sections had to be newly laid. The barricades, however, were thoroughly destroyed in the counter-attack by our own mortars and batteries. There was lots of work to be done.

In the night of 21 July, the III Battalion of RIR 104 relieved the III Battalion of RIR 21 in the front line; the II Battalion was put on stand by together with the 6th Battalion of RIR 20, which was put under its control. The I and III were Divisional reserves. The III Battalion could not be deployed in the front line for some time; it needed replenishment first.

For that period two companies of RIR 20 and one company of RIR 16 respectively were made available to the regiment.

Officers and serjeant-major-lieutenants needed to work with great care to salvage the killed, identify them in accordance with the rules and

> list their personal belongings. Again, the big graveyard in Beaucamps had to be extended considerably. The killed enemies were buried in mass graves behind the Pheasant Wood. Also two 'saps' had to be filled again. The enemy built them from his position to ours during the night of 19/20 July and they were filled with killed enemies; the enemy did not bother to salvage their dead, as usual.

The mass graves behind the Pheasant Wood, 16 September 1916.

The sector under the control of 16th BRIR was the front with 15th Australian, and 184th British brigades, and the strong point of their line, the Sugarloaf dominated this whole area, as well as much beyond it. No-Man's Land in front of the 16th BRIR was exceptionally wide and flat. The account of the Battle of Fromelles for the Unit history was written by Captain Friedrich Wiedemann, Adjutant of the Regiment, and later personal adjutant to Adolf Hitler. He also contributed other sections in the book, perhaps because he served with the Unit throughout the war, remained in contact afterwards and could write well, with understanding, balance and humour. The photographs in the book in relation to Fromelles, are mostly concerned with the Australian and British dead and prisoners. From the unit's earlier Fromelles campaign other photographs show casualties, buildings, churches and groups of soldiers. There are also many paintings and drawings by unit members together with maps. For some of his information Wiedemann acknowledged the help of the diaries of Alexander Weiss and Karl Gründig. In the first

The Sugarloaf. For all the trouble it caused the Allies and the huge success it was for the Germans, photographs of it at its peak seem non-existent. This, taken 14 Nov 1919, gives an idea of the low profile. The view is from the back looking north over No-Man's Land where the figure is standing. The Sugarloaf was one of some 700 blockhouses built by the Germans in the Fromelles–Aubers area between 1915 and 1917. Its complete eradication must have been an interesting exercise. AWM E5793

part of his section on Fromelles dealing with the period from May to July, the unit, and doubtless the entire Division, was preparing itself for the inevitable attack:

> At the beginning of May when the weather improved, the area between dried up and was accessible again: larger operations of the enemy were to be expected. The ever increasing artillery fire reminded us of this as well as memories of 9 May 1915 .... the enemy is fortifying his positions .... on 8 May 6th Company under 2nd Lieut of the Reserves Glunk was attacked by an English patrol.

After dealing in some detail with the results of that raid and staff appointments, Wiedemann reflected on what was going on opposite, when the front became stagnant:

> It was one of the effects of the long lasting positional warfare that troops at the front line sometimes felt strongly against 'orders from above' because they felt their superiors would not understand them. The 'battle for the Australians' position' fell into that category. It was fought in two ways: on the front line, patrols of the [German] companies were fighting the English for the area in between [the lines], and behind the lines staff in the various command offices were arguing about the adequate tactical approach.

House at Haubourdin (a detail)
There are no signs of war damage in this peaceful scene which Hitler painted, probably on 15 April 1916.

Then Wiedemann described, with some sarcasm, how the English/Australians tried to build new trenches and fortify their position. The Germans tried to prevent them from doing so. The regiment and battalion suggested the use of machine guns and artillery; the brigade ordered a patrol be sent to bomb the trench. The regiment and battalion doubted that this could be carried out successfully. Several trenches were bombed; artillery fire and *Minenwerfer* were used to drive back the construction troops; a great deal of reconnaissance was carried out, using planes, patrols and guards. After four weeks, fighting for and against the Australians' position ceased. Perhaps rather sanguine about these events, Wiedemann then wrote:

> This is the concluding sentence of the Regiment's Report which was now filed in a thick record labelled *Australians' position* and thus the staff's going through a lot of red tape on the matter came to an end at the end of June.
> *It definitely was not easy for the enemy to fortify the Australians' position, the reason why they succeeded nevertheless is to be found in the layout of our trenches as well as theirs, which greatly supported the enemy because he had the advantage of the outer line.*

The next passage which cannot by virtue of the dates refer to 5th Division, is most likely to be about a prisoner from a 4th Australian Division raid:

> On July 2 and 3, the English fired smoke grenades. Thick impenetrable fog came down in front of our position. On carpets and with blackened faces, the English crept over our barrier of barbed wire and threw hand grenades, seriously wounding 2nd Lieut Peters who had drawn

HITLER AT FROMELLES

Often in conversations with interviewers and others Hitler would reflect on his time in the trenches. His own stories were frequently about his survival which it would seem both amazed him and also endorsed his faith in his mission. Only H A Heinz in *Germany's Hitler* (1934) seems to relate a Fromelles episode. On the night of 14 July the British artillery barrage had cut all regimental telephones so runners had to be sent out, Hitler and another man '*in the face of almost certain death, peppered with shot and shell every metre of the way*'. They hid in shell holes and ditches and when the other man could go on no longer, Hitler dragged him back to their dugout.

many *Lister-Karten* [and was from Magdeburg]. An Australian who was taken prisoner stated that 5 to 6 men reported sick before the operation because they did not want to take part. According to him, the Australians had not known they were being sent to France; if the people in Australia knew what it was like here, there would not have been so many volunteers. In their position, they had to do a lot of hard trench work. Our machine guns were a great nuisance to them. All of them expected a major English attack.

Whilst, as already described, the British attempts at gas attacks were very mixed in their effectiveness, the 17th BRIR had been up until 13 July subject to 8 attacks '*without success*'. From the vantage point of the 16th BRIR the effect was noted in somebody's diary:

Gas emerged from the enemy's breastworks in separate small clouds, soon they thickened to form a continuous wall. The colour, a yellow or yellowish green, changed to whitish. At the same time the wall rose so that the high trees in the hinterland could no longer be seen. When the gas reached our position, the blank metal parts of our weapons were quickly covered by a layer of rust. By applying grease, the guns and machine guns were kept ready for use; firing them from time to time served the same purpose … It lasted approximately one hour … due to the use of gas masks the gas did not affect the troops.

At the end of this general review of the lead up to 'the Action near Fromelles'—in German 'Das Gefecht bei Fromelles'—Wiedemann had this final remark to make:

If we keep in mind that the battle on the river Somme had begun on June 24, it becomes obvious that the increased operations of the enemy at our front served as diversionary tactic. At first, operations by small patrols and an increase in artillery fire, then operations by large patrols combined with gas attacks and heavy methodical artillery and mortar fire, the climax of this being the battle at Fromelles on July 19 and 20.

German Observation Post and Artillery Headquarters on Aubers Ridge. Built in 1915 by a Bavarian unit some 400 metres south east of Aubers Church, it provides a view over the whole battlefield. The top photo was taken in the 1920s, and the lower one in 1997.
COURTESY M DELEBARRE

There then begins Wiedemann's narrative of the Battle. He notes that his sources are the Staff Report and the Diary of 2nd Lieut Gründig. Only one long paragraph of comparison between orders and tactics versus theory and fact is omitted.

The Battle near Fromelles on 19 and 20 July 1916
By the Adjutant of the Regiment, Hauptman Friedrich Wiedemann

On the morning of 19 July the Regiment was arranged as follows: III Battalion—Battalion of battle in the front line. Behind it II Battalion as support. I Battalion as brigade reserve in La Vallée. Staff of the Battalion in Wavrin.

The arrangement of the companies in the front line from right to left was as follows: 10th (2nd Lieut Bachschneider), 11th (2nd Lieut Plenge), 12th (2nd Lieut Holzfelder), 9th (2nd Lieut Reher).

Behind them as support company, on the right, 8th Company (2nd Lieut Hess) with two platoons in the bases Schützenhauswerk, Sendling, Dachau and Schwabing, on the left 7th Company (2nd Lieut Prechtl) in the bases and bullet proof dugouts on Rue Deleval, Starnberg, Rotes Haus and Kniehof.

Heavy German MG and crew as used at Fromelles. One of their techniques was to fire into an area rather than concentrate on selected targets. This had the effect of obscuring exactly from where the fire was coming, especially if three or four MG posts were using the same method at the same time.

These six companies except one platoon were under the control of the commander of the front line Captain Gebhardt.

One platoon of the 8th and the 6th Companies under 2nd Lieut Arnold, which in battle were united to form one company comprising 4 platoons, were laying as regimental reserve in Fromelles; 2nd Lieut Seelbach and his 5th Company were laying as security in a position on the ridge Fromelles-Aubers.

After there had already been strong artillery fire on the entire regiment sector on 16 and 18 July, the English artillery began on 19 July at 9 am to shoot the trenches and the rear ground. At 1.45 pm it turned into drumfire, from the right and from the left flank as well as from the front, heavy, moderate and light artillery fired accompanied by heavy and moderate mortars. The fire many times abated and intensified in many waves. Since Captain Gebhardt had the impression that the English would shoot our position until they could storm, he gave orders to keep up the observation at all cost and to get ready for an attack. At 5 in the afternoon Plenge reported some English in front of the Australian position who were fired on immediately by our artillery (Group Wurm) and thereupon ran back.

Since the telephone lines were cut shortly afterwards, the battalion commander sent scouts with orders to verify the situation in the front line under all circumstances. They reported back that there was heaviest drumfire on our trenches, that losses were tremendous and that there was heavy damage to our position.

At 6.45 pm in the entire regimental sector and on the right and on the left red signal rockets were fired by which the infantry signalled to the artillery to start their barrage. The English jumped over the ramparts of their trenches and started to storm our position. While they were trying to disentangle the thick throngs at the sally ports into thinner formations they were hit by the heavy fire of our infantry, our machine guns and artillery and had many casualties and became disorganised. Already several groups started to retreat; they were brought to a halt by shouting from their position. The second and third waves came out of the trenches only very slowly because of the hold-up of the front formations. Again and again the English tried to build up new lines and

WE HAVE NO FIGHT WITH YOU

At the age of 43 William Joseph Denny enlisted as a trooper in the 9th Light Horse, quite a change for a lawyer who had been Attorney General in the South Australian legislature. In early 1916, in Egypt, he transferred to 5th Division Artillery and went with the Division to France as 2/Lieutenant. He served at Fromelles and in 1919 published a book *The Diggers* wherein there is a short chapter on Fromelles. Although the book overall is shallow and predictable a couple of Denny's observations, not found elsewhere, are of interest. After the war he continued his political career up until 1933, when he retired.

The Hun appeared to know not only that the attack was to be made, but also the time and date, and he was well prepared. The Australians had not been long in the trenches before they were heralded with the not-altogether-unfriendly intimation, 'Australians, go back to your own country; we have no fight with you,' and when the attack was delayed another notice from their trenches was put up, 'Why so long?' You are twenty-four hours late'—and so it was. There is no doubt that the Germans had a cleverly devised spy-system in the Armentières sector. Many of the population were suspected of being either sympathetic with or in the pay of the Germans.

Aeroplane activity on both sides was very noticeable and planes appeared like small clouds in the heaven night and day. Their aerial movements are exceedingly graceful and rapid ... The German prisoners (many of whom spoke English well) expressed their surprise at the wonderfully sustained Australian attack.

IT IS WORTHWHILE
It would appear that Vice-Sgt-Major, Officer Cadet Robert Ziegel of 20th BRIR died of head wounds in Lille on 27 August 1916 and may therefore have been a casualty of the battle of 19 July. He had an Iron Cross (2nd Class), and was from Nuremberg where he had been born 21 January 1895. A lawyer before enlisting, these letters of his war experiences were published in Berlin in 1935 in *Kriegsbriefe gefallener Deutscher Juden* [War Letters of Fallen German Jews], and like those of Mayer on page 208–09, reveal much about the character of a young German officer who was also Jewish.

Wyschaete, 1 December 1914
Now that another period of time has past, the observer immediately has to ask the following questions: What did you gain from this war which you wanted so much? Is it really worth all the effort and suffering? The last question which is the easiest can be answered first. Those who went out into the world like us and were greeted with shouts and cheers by German men and women and those who saw the Rhine like us in the middle of its 'autumn-beauty'—those people know the following: it is worthwhile to give one's life for this country and for this nation. 'The power of the Rhine' is valuable, sweet and full of honour. We are part of 'home' here outside and this makes us proud and self-confident. Thus the war, though it has taken some strength has also given us very great strength. By the time this letter reaches you, the time of the Massabaer-festival will be approaching. And this year the thought of our brave forefathers will touch us more than usual. Elsbeth has already sent me some Hanukkah-Candles. However, I think that I am going to celebrate Hanukkah on my own this time. But I will celebrate Christmas with my comrades, not as a Christian but as a German feast.

07/04/1915 Trench west of Lille.
Thank you very much for sending me
[continued opposite]

advance but our infantry and machine gun salvos inflicted losses. In vain, courageous English officers with bayonets drawn tried to rally the troops by their example. They were shot down and the momentum of the attack diminished. Those not shot and able to move tried to return to their own trenches. Again our fire hit the retreating groups and caused bloody losses. Those not hit in the retreat by our bullets fell victim to shrapnel fire from our barrage. The English attack on the sector of the RIR 16 was repulsed before it could properly develop. No English came into the trenches of the Regiment this day except as prisoners. Credit for this outcome was mainly due to the observation posts of the III Battalion who dutifully stayed at the breastworks even in the heaviest drumfire. Wherever someone was wounded or shot another took his place without being ordered, pressed his body against the breastworks, staring with burning eyes through the smoke and dust of the fiery explosions to the greyish brown stripe of the enemy position in order not to miss the moment when the English would first commence their attack. Every man who loyally watched in this fire storm was at that time the personification of the German Army on the Western Front. None of the names of the observers who automatically did their duty is recorded. Still, the Fatherland owes them the greatest gratitude. The III Battalion suffered heavy losses from the death and wounding of these observers.

Immediately before our signals calling for protective curtain fire, the enemy moved its fire backwards to the support area and especially targeted the approach lines. Before the attack the enemy artillery's aim was to destroy the trenches ready for storming. Now they wanted to seal off the area where they broke in to hinder our support and reserves from coming into action.

An illustration of the ideas behind the attack is evidenced from an entry found in a diary showing how much the English thought they would smash our power of resistance by their artillery fire '*we are now going to take the German trenches, I think that will be very easy*'.

Our artillery curtain barrage fire was falling on the trenches of the enemy, especially the position of the Australians. It was supported by a single gun moved forward on the flank near Giesing.

The Regimental Commander who with his staff had moved onto the ridge to the command position in Meierhof at 5.30 pm at 7 pm received the message from the commander of the front line battalion that the English had broken through on the right at RIR 21 and also on the left at RIR 17 and was moving towards Grashof in the sector of RIR 21. At the same time one could hear heavy machine gun fire in the entire sector of the regiment especially on the right flank. Since the break in position at RIR 21 was close to our sector and it remained unclear how far the English had penetrated, the regiment had to secure the right flank. For this the front line battalion commander used the 8th Company (Hess) and a platoon of the 7th and the 6th Company (Arnold). 2nd Lieut Arnold was ordered to move to the extreme right flank through a hedged trench and depending on the situation to secure this flank with the united company or remove the enemy if they had broken in.

Little by little the situation cleared up as the break in at RIR 17 was not very serious although the English had broken in at RIR 21 in a width of three companies and were still advancing. According to Division orders the 14th Reserve Brigade should with one battalion of the division's reserve from the right and the 12th Reserve Brigade with a battalion of the brigade reserve from the left attack the English and throw them out. The 12th Brigade gave the leadership of the attack to the commander of RIR 16 and gave him three companies of our first battalion. The last company of this battalion (4th Company, 2nd Lieut Frobenius) was to remain as brigade reserve in Herlies.

In order to achieve unity in attack 2nd Lieut Arnold's 6th Company which had moved to the junction point Heckengraben-Grenzgraben was instructed to hold there until the employment of the three companies of the I Battalion (2nd Lieut Schmidt), to cover the right flank and to discover how far the English had penetrated. However, when 2nd Lieut Bachschneider asked for support, the 6th Company was at 11 pm moved to that area.

After the Regimental Commander had reached agreement with RIR 21 about the implementation of the attack. Lieut Schmidt (with 3 companies of I Battalion) received the following order for attack at 11.15 pm. *'The battalion Schmidt attacks the enemy in his right flank from the trenches between Schützenhauswerk and Dachau. The attack will be in three columns'*. The counter-attack was supposed to be a wide push or hit in the flank of the enemy, the implementation went on a little differently owing to the autonomous behaviour of the sub-leaders.

Let us follow the individual companies who were leading the counter-attacks, remembering the fact that everything was taking place in the dark of the night when human senses were more influenced by blurred shapes and forms than during the day.

2nd Lieut Bachschneider, when 2nd Lieut Arnold appeared with his company, had not only held his sector but also gained back 100 metres of the sector next to him. The remaining part of the next sector was taken by the enemy. 2nd Lieut Arnold had included the remarks *'excellent mood'* in his report indicating his arrival at Heckengraben. He was burning with pugnacity. By 2 am the three companies of the I Battalion had not yet arrived so Lieut Arnold decided to wait no longer. He attacked and broke into the trench taken by the English with a hand grenade troop of the 6th Company consisting of one non commissioned officer and eight men as well as men of his third platoon who had dug a flanking trench and brought hand grenades forward. Arnold himself led the storm troops first along the trench then together with Pte Kernbichl and Infantryman Christoph on the breastwork, with the remainder following along the so-called Verkehrsweg (communication trench) behind the front line. There were only a few of the enemy in the first 50 to 80 metres and a few prisoners were taken and also one machine gun. Then at 2.15 am the assault party or raiding patrol of the 1st Company of the I Battalion arrived with Company Commander 2nd Lieut Fuchs.

Shortly before midnight I Battalion had moved from its reserve position. The following units were to move according to battalion orders: 1st Company with one platoon in the combat trench and with two platoons in the covering trench; 2nd Company from Schützenhauswerk; 3rd Company from Dachau in a generally easterly direction. 2nd Lieut Dehn of 1st company who was supposed to move on with two platoons as second squadron found when he wanted to cross the Layesbach, the covering trenches full of water; he sent off Non-Commissioned Officer Wenzl and Pte Schmuck on patrol who then established that the trenches in the rear area up to the junction point with RIR 21 were free of the enemy. Lieut Dehn then moved along the Layesbach to the front line. The 2nd Company despite strong artillery fire proceeded eastwards reaching the junction point where it paused for a short period to regroup and close up to the right and left.

IT IS WORTHWHILE (contd)

the service for Hanukkah. I had almost expected the same. Only a few hours before I received it I had found the Hanukkah text from 1914 while searching for something in my bag. And I thought that there might be an order of service for the spring—and liberation—feast. By the way I celebrated Passover very little. I spent the Seder night without being aware that it was the Seder night. Only my observation of the sky during full moon indicated to me that it might be the time of the spring-feast. After the end of my patrol I wanted to have a look at my calendar, but when I came back to my dugout I fell asleep immediately. It was not until two days later on a bright spring day that thoughts and prayers of Passover came to my heart and lips. On Easter Sunday I was finally able to bless the Matzot which I got from home.

It might look ridiculous, but from time to time I wish to draw a parallel between our military rusk and the bread eaten by those fleeing Egypt.

23 September 1915

Yesterday I received a long letter from my brother which contained the content of your three Yom Kippur sermons. It was half past three during the night when I came back very tired from the trench.

In the trench for six hours in the morning and six hours in the evening we had to clear up the used explosives that our enemy had left behind and fires that were as big as those which destroyed Neuve Chapelle. While reading the letter I imagined the actual performance of the sermons:

I could feel love and death and my strong and steady faith in God, it was not until then that I really deeply celebrated the 'feast of reconciliation'. The celebration in Lille the other day did not really satisfy me. Only during the Kol Nidre hour and during the hour of the soul-celebration did I really feel the day's holiness but tonight I made up for it. Now death rushes again over the realms of Arras, over the fields and over the trenches at Armentières. My

[continued next page]

IT IS WORTHWHILE (contd)

hut shivers and the ground trembles, but my heart is strong and my courage is great. Maybe within the next few days I will face the most difficult days during this campaign. However, I have 60 arms and 60 people who trust me and who I know like me being their leader. I put my trust in God, I know that He will be with us.

25 September 1915. Hüttenfest
My dearest! Just a quick note to let you that I am fine. I was taken as a prisoner by the English today for six hours after I suffered from two light stabs from the bayonet but our enemy did not take care of me. The English had stormed into our trench today and the bloody fighting lasted for 7 hours until we managed to get rid of them again. My wounds have been taped by now. I have a flesh-wound in my wrist. My left breast almost lost no blood at all. I lead my company as usual, but we have lost half of our people. However, the losses on the English side are even worse. We were saved by the brave intervention of the Saxons. I will never give a description of this bloody day, at least not a written one ...

9 February 1916
Please keep on praying for our victory and for our lives. And in case your prayers are not being heard, then please try to bear it patiently and keep on praying! This is good for you and good for us.

Handgranatenwerfer.
Von Prof. Anton Hoffmann.

At this time a grenade hit the company and killed Company Leader 2nd Lieut Zeulmann [of Munich]. 2nd Lieut Ulrich who took over tried unsuccessfully to get in touch with 3rd Company on the right. 2nd Lieut Ulrich, who knew the order to attack only generally and had learned from a patrol that 1st Company was in the front line, thought he would be more successful if he cleaned out the combat trench with this patrol rather than moving on in the dark without contact on both the right and the left. Consequently the 2nd Company too moved onwards towards the combat trenches. Almost the same happened to the 3rd Company. Moving eastwards from Dachau 2nd Lieut Bindseil heard that the 6th Company had already moved on to the front line. So they too moved on to the front.

When 2nd Lieut Fuchs with his 1st Company assault troop reached 2nd Lieut Arnold about 2.15 am the situation was approximately the following: the English were still in the trenches of RIR 21 but had not got beyond the covering trench. It seems that the first English storm wave had settled in the covering trench, the second wave in the German front lines. In that part of the trench that the 6th Company had retaken and in the sector of the 10th Company next to it, were still the 6th and the 1st Companies who were about to throw the Tommies out of the neighbouring trenches on the right with hand grenades. The 2nd and 3rd Companies moved up at the same time in order to support the attack.

With 2nd Lieut Fuchs arrival the joint attack of the 6th and 1st Companies began. Arnold observed from the breastwork, Fuchs went forward in the communication trench throwing hand grenades. The English tried to hinder our people. From the heavy artillery fire of the enemy our trenches were heavily damaged and there were large holes in the breastwork. Our people had to overcome this by jumping in and out of the remaining portion of the trench. While doing this there was infantry and machine gun fire from the enemy position as well as from the English in our covering trench. Particularly annoying was an English machine gun set up behind the first trench which was controlling the approach lines and by which 2nd Lieut Kuttroff [of Baden] was shot dead. Ten men of 1st Company rendered it harmless with hand grenades. In the trench itself the English were defending themselves desperately. Little by little we took over parts of the trench in close combat. When moving with two strong columns separated by breastworks, it was not always easy to maintain unity of attack so that the leading groups maintained touch with each other. Subsequently some of our own people were hit by our own hand grenades which had a strong effect on morale and because of which the storm troops temporarily moved back.

All in all, we took over relatively quickly though it was necessary to exchange the assault troops because they were physically worn out by the throwing of hand grenades. After twenty or thirty throws the people had always to be relieved. The leaders of the hand grenade troops were almost all officers who volunteered for this task. Until the morning we had taken over several hundred metres of trenches. At this time the English who numbered about 120 men in front of us began a heavy counter-attack which 2nd Lieut Dehn who had the leadership of the storm troops put down. Since the hand grenade throwers of the first company—Zehentbauer, Sperber and Mittesmeier are mentioned in particular—little by little lost their strength 2nd Lieut Dehn thought it would be necessary to dam up the trench and to set up trench blocks. Since the supply of hand grenades and ammunition needed a lot of

Germans re-occupying their second line on the morning of 20 July, after the 14th Bde had withdrawn. Wrote Bean, 'The attempts to consolidate are evidenced by the deepening of the left side of the trench and piling of sandbags to form a parapet. Lying in the water and mud are some Australians who held the position'.
PHOTO TAKEN BY A GERMAN INTELLIGENCE OFFICER AWM 1562

people and the retaken trench had to be occupied, the 4th Company got the order at 4 am to move on from Herlies and come to the front line. Two companies of the RIR 17 were placed under the regiments command and the strong morning fog favoured the approach of the reserves.

In the meantime Battalion Leader Lieut Schmidt had moved on up to the front with Adjutant Sölch from the base Dachau in order to personally lead the combat. 2nd Lieut Frobenius, who had hurried ahead of his 4th Company wanted to relieve 2nd Lieut Ulrich at about 7 am of the leadership of the storm troops, was severely wounded whilst organising this. 2nd Lieut Bindseil of the 3rd Company took his place and was successful in throwing out the English entirely and linked up with comrades coming from the other flank from RIR 21 at 9.10 am. English who had still occupied one covering trench in the morning of 20 July were being fired on by their own artillery with whom they had no contact from the beginning of the day and from our own artillery. They surrendered by waving a white flag and came out of the trenches with their hands up.

We were again fully in possession of the position. The troops were rearranged and the reconstruction of the trench was begun. A volunteer patrol in the afternoon of the 2nd Lieuts Arnold, Dehn and Gramp into the hinterland confirmed the high number of English dead and wounded as well as the fact that the enemy had not crossed the covering trench.

We captured four machine guns and about 180 prisoners. The losses were 5 officers dead, 5 wounded, and in the ranks 86 dead, 284 wounded.

The prisoners were the subject of a series of photographs which later found their way into the Australian War Memorial Collection. Whilst a few prisoners are heavily bandaged most are shown standing or sitting in the sun prior to marching off.

The battle near Fromelles was a new leaf of victory in the history of the 16th Regiment. It showed the spirit of the volunteer regiment. It showed their bold will to go forward and attack, in spite of being exposed to positional warfare for a long period of time. The RIR 16 shared the not-at-all enviable experience with many Bavarian regiments of being deployed in the trenches mostly, and there is no denying the fact that this does not have a good influence on the mood and enthusiasm of the

A group of Australian prisoners and a German medical officer, 20 July 1916
AWM 1547

A POSTSCRIPT: MOUNTAINS OF DEAD

As Capt. Wiedemann was in the action and by 1932 when his account was published, he had a wide view of the event, some of the immediate detail—ie two days after the battle—found in the Munich Archives is worth adding into his account. But the great importance of this 'new' material is one of the concluding statements: '*Not one of the English troops entered the 16th BRIR sector*', which seems to end the discussion about some of the English or Australians getting into the Sugarloaf.

Capt. Gebhardt's short report in the Archives was clearly used in the history—some of it word for word—as were the narratives. A few incidents worth mentioning: '*19th July PM: In spite of intense drumfire, observation was maintained. Those men who were not observing, lay down on the floor of the trench or sought shelter in funk holes. Dressing stations were set up in mixed dugouts. A large number of shelters were destroyed ... and the trench levelled in places. 6.45 pm. The enemy artillery fire lifted once more to the rear and the enemy infantry left their trenches, some over the parapet, and others through previously prepared and carefully concealed sally ports. The enemy advanced ... in dense waves, carrying scrambling ramps and mats with them. In front of IIIa the enemy ignited several smoke pots. Our trench garrison was immediately alerted ... and hurried to the breastworks. A barrage of MG, small arms and artillery fire mowed down the* [continued opposite]

troops generally. People longed for the end of sameness, for the end of 'standing on guard', carrying materials, building trenches. People were easily angered by the garrison-like trivialities and the touch of barracks brought about by red tape nonsense and the effort of the long operation in the same place. They were missing out on the momentum and verve of action brought about by successfully pushing forward which conceals the ugly side of war. Therefore the fight brought in some kind of welcome relief. Finally, once they were allowed to attack instead of continuously serving as targets for English and American grenades! The companies were eager to start the fight and the officers of the I Battalion and the 6th Company were competing for the leadership in the attack. Maybe details concerning the attack could have been better organised and more orderly but it could not have been in a better spirit.

So ended the battle, Wiedemann's account then went on to detail casualties and reflect on the lessons learned. Although the losses of the 16th BRIR were nowhere near those of the Brigades they faced, what makes the next section so interesting is the analysis of the origins of the casualties, 50% from artillery and 50% in what one might term hand-to-hand fighting. The analysis of the success and quality of the concrete blockhouses, the fact only 8 out of 75 were completely destroyed, reveals their enormous value. Interestingly there is no particular reference to the Sugarloaf or its pivotal position and the shattering fact that 60 of the concrete installations were not even hit, says much about the British artillery and intelligence service.

The extraordinary achievement of the 16th BRIR in holding off two Brigades and surviving the worst the British artillery could deliver, cannot be ignored. And when one sets this success against the earlier achievement of Aubers Ridge, the question has to be asked why were not the Allies better informed: or was it they did not really care, as long as they had tens of thousands of men at their disposal? As far as Fromelles is concerned, the German conservation of their manpower is always apparent.

The Dambre Brewery and residence some 400 metres south of Fromelles Church on the road to Herlies. Here, early in the war it is deserted but reinforced by the Germans as a defence post: it was later destroyed. Madame Dambre was the sister of Jules Descamps, Mayor of Fromelles from 1877 to 1919

INFORMATION COURTESY A-M DESCAMPS-CARRÉ
PHOTOGRAPH COURTESY J-M BAILLEUL

Germans reoccupying a portion of their front line. Bodies covered with coats or blankets by the Germans can be seen in front of the parapet. Photo taken by a German Intelligence Officer on the morning of 20 July.
AWM AO1560

No wonder that not even Bean was prepared to list on one clear table the comparative losses: to do so would have been very revealing.

The III Battalion with 158 killed and wounded (amongst the dead—2nd Lieut Wesche from Hamburg and Lehr from Munich) and suffered the most. Next was the I Battalion with a total loss of 122, amongst them the modest Lieut Petz. He was from Nuremberg and a highly gifted assessor in Bavaria's Ministry of Finance, son of leading historian Petz. Meanwhile the II Battalion with 62 dead and wounded escaped lightly.

It is striking that the I Battalion which had to move through enemy artillery fire over open country during the night then with all companies counter-attacking had fewer casualties than the III Battalion which remained in cover and nipped the enemy's attack in the bud. One should reflect on the high casualties at Fromelles caused mainly by the above-ground trenches which provided only moderate security against artillery and that the combat trench was heavily manned as the tactical view at that time required. Previously issued Divisional orders said: '*When an infantry attack by the enemy is expected, and even trenches that are being heavily fired upon are not to be vacated ... During the night the vacating of the trenches under fire is out of the question.*'

As the matter stood on 19 July, the III Battalion could do nothing else but stay within the front trenches. All of the protective trenches were under water and could not be used. The time had not yet come for what was later called a moving defence because traditional tactical opinions make way for the force of war conditions only slowly. Only the tremendous use of ammunition by the enemy in the material battles of that year—first experienced by us on the river Somme—taught us to change from a steady defence to a subdivided moveable defence zone and not to counter great numbers of the heaviest grenades and mortars with the bodies of fearless soldiers tied to their position by order; taught us to move out of the way of concentration points of the enemy's fire and to regain with a counter-attack terrain that was lost.

MOUNTAINS OF DEAD (CONTD)
attacking enemy like a scythe. Only a small number reached our wire and were shot down there, while the remainder tried in vain to return.'

Then this, curiously placed at IIIa: '*10.15 pm the enemy in front of IIIa launched a second attack, again with very strong forces, which was snuffed out by our artillery barrage, MGs and small arms fire before it could develop.*' If this was the ill-fated attack by 58th Bn, its placement wall to the right of Sugarloaf adds a new question to the controversy.

Capt. Gebhardt's next paragraph is almost a memorial notice for 15th Bde. '*After the failure of this second attack, relative calm settled over Sector III ... During the night of 19/20 July sector III experienced only light searching and sweeping fire; the infantry remained completely quiet, and the day passed without incident.*'

Then, '*The English dead lying in front of our trenches are estimated to number at least a thousand. Daylight patrols on 21 July reported mountains of dead and wounded in the Rhondda Sap, the Obstgarten and Kirchmeiergraben.*'

The Chateau of Jules Descamps, Mayor of Fromelles 1877-1919, probably late 1918.
COURTESY A-M DESCAMPS-CARRÉ

A German Observation Post on the ridge Aubers–Perenchies near Le Maisnil. This photograph was taken on 11 November 1918.
AWM EO4040

There are less losses in energetic counter-attacks as soon as they are out of reach of the enemy's artillery. Of the 122 losses in I Battalion 63 were because of the artillery, 36 of the wounded were by rifle and machine gun fire and only 19 because of hand grenades and 4 from land mines. The difficulty of a task must not be judged from the number of casualties; on the contrary, our losses in close combat are less if the troop proceeds in a dashing manner.

Cavities in the combat trench that were built into the breastwork and which were secured by a 22 to 30 centimetre strong concrete cover served as shot secure dugouts. Out of 75 of such dugouts 60 were not hit, out of the rest only 1 was not damaged, 6 slightly damaged, 8 completely destroyed, namely 3 crushed from the top or hit by grenades and 5 shot down from the side. It is clear that trust in such hiding places was not great and the ranks were ordered to lie down on the floor of the trenches. Consequently in the future there should only be dugouts for security with 50 centimetre strong concrete. 2nd Lieut Arnold emphasised that it should be avoided that troops in the counter-attack storm column throw hand grenades from 5th or 6th position in the column, even though they are keen to fight or are nervous, as this puts the leader in the front in great danger. There should be more leaders in distances of ten to twelve men in the storm row. '*At each counter by the enemy there can occur a push back of the storm troop which can easily lead to panic if there are no sub leaders to prevent it.*'

Just like any battle, the events on 19 July showed that the first news about the advance of the enemy was exaggerated. According to news which the Regiment got in the evening the enemy would have pushed forward far into our hinterland while he did not get further than our covering trench. According to the II Battalion the wearing of caps—we did not have the steel helmets then—instead of helmets, led to unpleasant confusion with the English at night, while during close combat with hand grenades the tip of the helmet in particular is a distinctive feature as opposed to the mushroom-shaped steel helmets of the English.

Wiedemann's remarks about the prisoners taken are incorporated in Chapter 9. Following his narrative, Wiedemann then gave translations from the London *Daily Mail* of 23 and 24 July,

German Mortar Pit of 1916, photographed in 1997. It provided angle of fire of 45° giving a range of 450-900 metres. It is situated behind Delangré Farm. Map Ref N.10.d.2.1.
COURTESY M DELEBARRE

'Bayern Nord' Headquarters of 16th BRIR, situated some 600 metres south of Fromelles Church and 500 metres from the shelter below. Photographed in 1997.

German shelter for 77 mm artillery piece. Note the steel-lined arch and blast walls. Some 800 metres SSE of Fromelles Church. Photographed in 1997

COURTESY M DELEBARRE

the first from British Field Headquarters and the second from Capt. C E W Bean. Haking's secret order of 15 July is provided in German over the signatures of Haking as Commander of XI Corps, and surprisingly that of C H Wagstaff, described as the Commander of the 5th Australian Division. Does this prove that the copy the Germans had of the order came via an Australian prisoner and not British? Then follows Wiedemann's wide ranging comments on events in the sector. In early September the Bavarians noticed the English '*knocking apples off the trees with sticks, exercising with hand grenades hardly a hundred metres behind the front trench, playing some music*'. And at the same time '*24 officers and 722 men of III Battalion were sent for a swim at Henst on the North Sea, for a change*'.

Then on 28 September, Alexander Weiss wrote in his diary:

> ... the company marches through Fromelles for the last time. How much had the place changed, that is almost as familiar as home; houses destroyed by the enemy's artillery, the high steeple disappeared long

BREATHER

The attack was beaten off. Everybody had the feeling: they won't get through. That restored confidence in our strength. Like a tree defiantly reaching out its branches towards the sky in the morning after a thunder-storm, and, although windswept, seems to say: 'No matter how many stormy winds like that may come, I will hold out', so the regiment was now stronger than before.

Between the battle of Fromelles and the battle on the Somme by Adjutant of the Regiment Captain Friedrich Wiedemann.

Wiedemann's comment on the *Daily Mail* articles:

How glorious our regiment fought at Fromelles is shown by accounts in the English press, which during the war certainly was geared to raise the spirits of their own people and to show the actions of their compatriots in a favourable light.

ago, gardens and fields churned up by grenades! We already feel the tension of the big battle to come and we part with memories of quiet and bad days from the area, which we had held for 1½ years.

Wiedemann reflected also on the departure and the fate perhaps awaiting them all on the Somme.

APPLE STEW
The Germans' observations are echoed in the diary of Simon Fraser: *2 August ... Len and I got apples and got Alf Cripps to make a stew ...*
5 August ... got Alf Cripps to make another pear stew ...

FRONT LINE NOTICE
Germans erected the following notice in their front line at N.10.C.4½.4. *'Keep your heads down until 4th August'*.

—5th Div Intelligence Summary
2/3 August 1916

Two German postcards of 1915 showing the Church at Fromelles, and that it was a ruin well before the battle of 19 July 1916. These postcards were purchased by German troops in canteens or messes for sending home to confirm the extent of the German advance.
COURTESY M DELEBARRE

For weeks in Fromelles we had heard the thunder of artillery fire from the south, we were reading reports about the battle on the Somme and we were listening to what the troops had to say who were stationed there. The impression arose that on the Somme a whirlwind had come into existence which would attract anything, sweep it away at twilight or night and only after several days spew out the scattered remains of regiments. It was only a matter of time when we would be seized by this whirlwind. Something that reeked of fate was in the air.

UNHEALTHY TUESDAY AFTERNOONS
After a while we got to know that Fritz had a regular cut and dried system in the shelling of these trenches. He always took Mine Ave, Brompton Ave, and Pinney's Ave alternatively ... Weeks later I worked out the ... system ... and had such notices as this posted: 'Pinney's Ave, dangerous on Mondays 2 to 6 pm', 'VC unhealthy Tuesday afternoons' and so on. Of course there were times when ... he would shell anything indiscriminately. The god of the German is Method, and his goddess System, and it hurt his gunners sorely when we tried something new.

—R H Knyvett, 59th Bn
Over there with the Australians (1918)

We turn now to the 17th BRIR which faced on the far left of the German line, the British 182nd and 183rd Brigades.

15.7. On 15 July at 9.30 pm, the previous peace was followed by a gas attack on the Regiment's position. The gas rolled in from a number of

This 1915 German Postcard shows a chapel at Fromelles, which still stands at the corner of Rue de Verdun and Rue des Vaulx, 150 metres from Fromelles Museum.
COURTESY M DELEBARRE

positions; on the high corner at the boundary between Sector III and IV in the middle of Sector IV, both sides of the Leierstrasse and on the boundary of Sector IV Zones c and d. Half as high as the breast works, it formed thick green clouds, which oozed forwards as it spread, and quickly formed a wall of gas about 3 metres tall as it reached our position.

The gas lay in part over our forward positions, partly extending in the same direction back over Einzelhof to the High Street [trench line]; from there it spread with the wind from south west to north east, roughly along the position, and blew back from our forward positions from Sector II to the enemy trenches, so that the enemy, as we discovered later from prisoners of war, had their own soldiers killed and wounded by the gas. The [gas] release lasted about an hour, and was accompanied by smoke shells. In our position, the gas lasted about 1½ hours, but in nooks and crannies it could still be found the next morning. During the gas attack the enemy displayed little infantry activity; Sector III d was engaged with about 400 shrapnel shells, Sector IV b and c likewise with 50 mortar rounds. No enemy infantry attack followed. In our position the gas alarm took effect very quickly; masks were in place in a few seconds in silence, not a word was spoken. The resulting casualties—the Regiment lost four men dead and 21 gassed—were attributable in every case to mistakes that had occurred; some people masked too late or put their masks on incorrectly in the excitement, or breathed too soon, anticipating the 'all clear' while the attack was still in progress, or entered areas after the attack ended which had not been cleared of gas.

From 16.7 on, the firing increased on our position from mortars, rifle grenades and artillery (including flanking fire); it had recently been light, but it grew over the next few days to around 2000 shells [per day], and at 12.30 pm on 19 July, while five enemy pilots cruised over the Regiment's position, it developed into a real preparatory bombardment for the attack which began at 6.30 pm.

The front line of the position was occupied by III Battalion (Capt Petri); the companies occupied the trenches a–d in the order 11, 12, 9, 10. The Reaction Battalion (I) [literally 'Preparedness Bn'] had occupied the strong points behind the I Battalion's position with their 4th Company (e), 2nd Company (h). The second (security) position. 1st Company (f) was in Aubers and 3rd Company (g) in Herlies as

A POSTSCRIPT:
NEAR THE WILLOW TREES

The material in the Munich Archives related to 17th BRIR consists of Reports from Company Commanders—Keller (1st Coy), Lutterloh (4th Coy) and Neumüller (9th Coy). Lutterloh recorded one incident:

I attached myself to Kirmeier's group. After several rushes forward, we were met by MG fire and observed a party of about 20 English lying near the willow trees there. After a brief exchange of rifle fire, we approached, in spite of fierce MG fire, to within 30 m ... and threw several hand grenades ... I then called on ... the English troops to surrender... All 19 surviving members of the MG teams ... raised their hands, surrendered and moved out leaving behind several dead including a captain, who had been shot during the short engagement.

And Neumüller adds some detail to the setting up of 3 MGs by the English (page 206).

The smaller party, about 40 men, established a firm foothold with 3 MGs at the boundary of IVb/c from a concrete emplacement in the Salient ... firing on the enfilading position and Trivelet. Hatzelmann despatched a group ... to defend the MG emplacement on the Leierstrasse. The larger enemy contingent pressed forward ... in direction of the Frankengraben.

A storming party (3 officers, 10 men) advanced into the enfilading position ... and were fired on by the 3 MGs previously mentioned. The group built a sand bag barricade to provide cover while they engaged the MGs. They then rushed forward again, throwing hand grenades, captured the 3 MGs and cleared the Trench. About 23 prisoners were taken.

The dogs of No-Man's Land

In August and September 1916 while Hitler's unit, the 16th BRIR, was still in the line, the Intelligence Summaries of the 5th Australian Division noted on 4 August '*Germans appear to use a dog in one of their listening posts*'. And then on 28 August, '*A dog was again heard in the enemy forward listening post.*' On 7 September, '*a small brown dog was seen approaching a Sally Port ... it is suspected that the enemy uses this for locating Sally Ports*'. Then on 21 September, '*two dogs have been observed to stray into our lines from NML in the last two days*'.

Was one of them Foxl, Hitler's dog ?

Foxl (Fuchsl in German 'Little Fox') is generally thought to have been a mascot of a British officer and came across No-Man's Land probably near Neuve Chapelle. Of the several photographs of Hitler and his army comrades at the time Foxl is usually present. Hitler acquired the dog in January 1915 and it took some time to persuade it to stay with him. The photographs' location and date have now been established; Hitler still has his curled moustache which he dispensed with early in 1917.

By his own account Hitler would during times out of the line go on painting expeditions accompanied by Foxl which would guard the artist while he worked, and the satchel of paintings when Hitler dozed in the sun. When Foxl was lost or stolen during the urgent move which Hitler describes, so was his satchel of paintings.

It is an interesting reflection on the mind of Hitler that he shared fond, humorous memories of his dog with Bormann and others on the night of 22-23 January 1942, and at lunch next day with Himmler and others verbally set in motion 'The Final Solution' which had been given some administrative form on 20 January by Heydrich and his group, some 12 months after Eichmann's first Bulletin on the subject.

Foxl and friends, at Fournes-en-Weppes 1916: his owner sitting far right.

How many times, at Fromelles, during the first World War, I've studied my dog Foxl. When he came back from a walk with the huge bitch who was his companion, we found him covered with bites. We'd no sooner bandaged him, and had ceased to bother about him, than he would shake off this unwanted load.

A fly began buzzing. Foxl was stretched out at my side, with his muzzle between his paws. The fly came close to him. He quivered, with his eyes as if hypnotised. His face wrinkled up and acquired an old man's expression. Suddenly he leapt forward, barked and became agitated. I used to watch him as if he'd been a man—progressive stages of his anger, of the bile that took possession of him. He was a fine creature.

When I ate, he used to sit beside me and follow my gestures with his gaze. If by the fifth or sixth mouthful I hadn't given him anything, he used to sit up on his rump and look at me with an air of saying: 'And what about me, am I not here at all?' It was crazy how fond I was of the beast. Nobody could touch me without Foxl's instantly becoming furious. He would follow nobody but me. When gas-warfare started, I couldn't go on taking him into the front line. It was my comrades who fed him. When I returned after two days' absence, he would refuse to leave me again. Everybody in the trenches loved him. During marches he would run all round us, observing everything, not missing a detail. I used to share everything with him. In the evening he used to lie beside me.

To think that they stole him from me! I'd made a plan, if I got out of the war alive, to procure a female companion for him. I couldn't have parted from him. I've in my life never sold a dog. Foxl was a real circus dog. He knew all the tricks.

I remember, it was before we arrived at Colmar, the railway employee who coveted Foxl came again to our carriage and offered me two hundred marks. 'You could give me two hundred thousand, and you wouldn't get him!' When I left the train at Harpsheim, I suddenly noticed that the dog had disappeared. The column marched off, and it was impossible for me to stay behind!
[continued opposite]

THE DOGS OF NO-MAN'S LAND (CONTD)

The photograph opposite was taken in the courtyard of the Regimental Infirmary at Fournes-en-Weppes, the village where the Regiment HQ was located. It had previously been the village tax office in rue Faidherbe, the same street as Hitler's billet above the butcher's shop. In 1940 Hitler, Amann, Schmidt and others went straight to the old site and posed before the same wall: this time without Foxl !

I was desperate. The swine who stole my dog doesn't realise what he did to me.

It was in January 1915 that I got hold of Foxl. He was engaged in pursuing a rat that had jumped into our trench. He fought against me, and tried to bite me, but I didn't let go. I led him back with me to the rear. He constantly tried to escape. With exemplary patience (he didn't understand a word of German), I gradually got him used to me. At first I gave him only biscuits and chocolate (he'd acquired his habits with the English, who were better fed than we were). Then I began to train him. He never went an inch from my side. At that time, my comrades had no use at all for him. Not only was I fond of the beast, but it interested me to study his reactions. I finally taught him everything: how to jump over obstacles, how to climb up a ladder and down again. The essential thing is that a dog should always sleep beside its master. When I had to go up into the line, and there was a lot of shelling, I used to tie him up in the trench. My comrades told me that he took no interest in anyone during my absence. He would recognise me even from a distance. What an outburst of enthusiasm he would let loose in my honour! We called him Foxl. He went through all the Somme, the battle of Arras. He was not at all impressionable. When I was wounded, it was Karl Lanzhammer who took care of him. On my return, he hurled himself on me in frenzy.

When a dog looks in front of him in a vague fashion and with clouded eyes, one knows that images of the past are chasing each other through his memory.

WEAKNESS OF OUR COMMAND

I cannot tell you how greatly I suffered, during the Great War, from the weakness of our command. In a military sense we were not at all clever, and in a political sense we were so clumsy that I had a constant longing to intervene ...

If I were twenty to twenty five years younger, I'd be in the front line. I passionately loved soldiering.

—Adolf Hitler
24 July 1941

[continued from page 203]

Regimental Reserve. The II Battalion was deployed as Divisional Reserve in Sante. The heavy bombardment of the last few days had given notice of an impending attack, and a heightened degree of preparation was ordered for Divisional and Brigade Reserves from the evening of 18 July. As the situation grew threatening, the Reaction Battalion staff and the Regimental staff prepared to meet for orders; in doing so, the Regimental staff were held up by going on the Herlies–Aubers Road, and only reached Aubers at 8.10 pm, when the enemy attack was already under way.

As preparation for this attack, from 12.30 pm the enemy engaged our positions a, b, c, in several waves of fire, with breaks in between. The fire was heavy and accurate, supported by flanking observation from 5 am the most significant parts of the rear area, were engaged, as well

This view, taken by a German Intelligence Officer, is of the area behind the main German line, probably in the 8th Bde sector. It reveals the huge earthworks, the drainage ditch and debris strewn everywhere.
AWM 1558

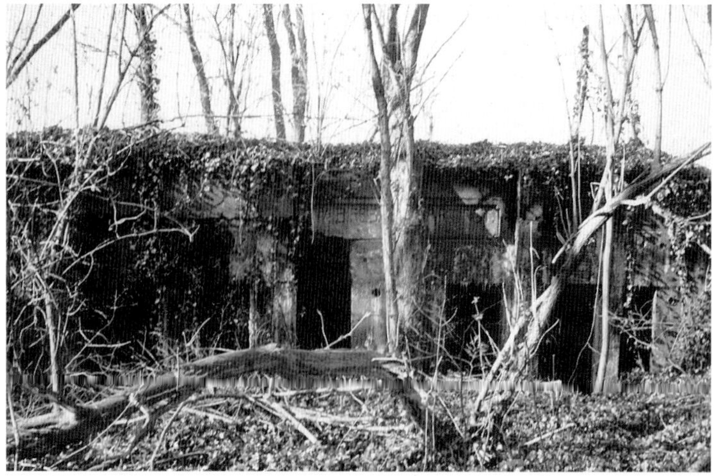

The ammunition dump of the 6th Bavarian Reserve Artillery. Some 1800 metres SE of Aubers Church. Completed in June 1916: this photograph is from 1997.
COURTESY M DELEBARRE

as the hamlets of Herlies and Aubers (this last particularly heavily) by aerial bombing; in the breaks in the shelling, the parapet in the front line were engaged with lighter weapons, rifles and machine guns. The enemy fire almost completely destroyed the barbed wire obstacle forward of our position, the path to shelters and dugouts buried in many places. Nearby, the enemy had blown a line of 200 mines (Bangalore torpedoes) forward of our position in a line diagonally opposite 'Trivelet Corner' toward the enemy position opposite our position Zone IV d, with a jumping off trench from their lines to our position. From midday our artillery responded strongly to the enemy fire; from 2 pm they were supported by the artillery of XXVII Reserve Corps, on our left. At 6 pm, the enemy fire strengthened into a bombardment (lit: Drum fire); soon afterwards, the enemy infantry commenced their attack while their artillery was still firing on our trenches. First, at 6.15 pm the projecting corner in Sector IV a was attacked from two sides. The Company Commander, Lieut Reichenhardt stood 11th Company to. With their 3 attached machine guns, they hurried to the parapet, happy that the agonising wait was over, to greet with shouts the advancing columns and skirmish lines of the advancing enemy, to drive him back to his trenches with heavy casualties, using artillery fire, rifle and machine gun and grenades. Without this effort, more than one would have made it beyond 50 metres from the point where they entered our trenches but none did. The left-hand Company, in Sector IV b, which was closing up, was given the alarm at the same time, and hurried to the parapet, saw no enemy and came under artillery fire, so they were ordered back under cover. At about 6.40 pm an enemy assault column of about 200 men had come up unnoticed under cover of the supporting fire close to our trenches in Sector IV b and c, crossed the destroyed wire obstacle and into the trenches, and divided into two groups. The smaller of these, with 3 machine guns, formed (and built) a sort of block position facing toward Trivelet between our first and second line, while the stronger group pressed on against the middle of IV b and towards the second line. The troops occupying the edge of the mined position on the left wing (flank) of Sector IV b could not be accomplished; some was recovered by storm, other parts were left in enemy hands after grenades had been thrown into the positions of 6th Company's two machine guns, one had been made unserviceable by fire, and the other found itself still in the

A MOST HOPEFUL LIFE
Justin Gerngross, was the son of businessman Phillip Gerngross and his wife Regina, and born in Nuremberg on 23 April 1883. He went to the municipal commercial school and to the secondary modern school in Gombrich. He got official permission to join the voluntary service for the period of one year. After that he started his career as an office worker. He spent a couple of years in Paris and Japan and after that he had a leading post in Nuremberg. In July 1915 he was called up to the army as a Landstürmmann as he had no prior military service. In August he came to the western front and the 21st BRIR with whom he took take part in fighting around Lille. He was slightly wounded several times. On 19 July he informed his family that he wanted to get away from the front because of his night blindness. On the same night he was severely wounded by a shell in a fight against the Australians in Fromelles. He died because of these wounds on 20 July 1916, and was buried in the military cemetery in Beaucamps together with some comrades who also died in the fight against the English. The Field-Rabbi Dr Baerwald held the funeral service together with the clergymen of the other denominations. Justin Gerngross's sergeant, Paul Weiss, [continued opposite]

mined area and was borrowed later. From the shreds of the right part of b Company, two Grenade Teams were formed; under the leadership of Sergeant Lachenmayr, these bombed their way from right to left, clearing the trenches as they went.

In Sector IV c, the enemy who had forced their way in were sealed off. Those assaulting the second line were engaged from the flank with machine gun fire, and a quick attack by Storm troops, under Lieut Schattenmann began to mop up the trench by bombing from the right hand end.

In Sector IV d, which was not immediately engaged, extensive help was given by the right and middle platoons with their dug-in machine guns giving flanking fire along the Fauquissart–Trivelet road against the back of the enemy attack waves. Also, from Sector IV a, where the enemy attack had been beaten off, the area occupied by the English was blocked from withdrawing by machine gun fire, so that the following waves of the attack were pinned down. In the meantime, the battalion commander in the forward line, Capt. Petri, had warned the nearest available forces and brought them forward. 4th Company was ordered to occupy the holding position (strong point); with the weakest of available forces, the Company Commander, Lieut Lutterloh had to block a further push of the enemy on the Leierstrasse. Since the Regimental staff, still on the way from Aubers, could not be reached, even by phone, Capt. Petri ordered 1st Company (still in Aubers as Regimental Reserve) to move forward by platoons to a forward assembly area; he ordered the first platoon to arrive (Sgt Herb) to move quickly via the Frank Trench to IV b, to reinforce the Company in Zone b. The next platoon was given the same task, the last was set to reinforce 9th Company in Sector IV c. Sgt Herb attacked toward the left in the trench in Sector IV b, moved to the front of his platoon with grenades against the English and drove them back from dugout to dugout. The rear half of his platoon pushed grenades forward, and, while Herb pushed forward, fired on the English, who fled from our trenches toward their own positions; the second platoon of 1st Company joined in as they arrived. Lieut Lutterloh pressed forward with his 42 available men in the trench in Sector IV c; he gave one group the task to make another push toward Trivelet to delay the English. With the remainder, he stormed the enemy strong point across the open field, after a short engagement with rifles, and despite enemy machine gun fire, he reached a point 30 metres from the machine gun, where the English commenced a grenade attack. From here, Lutterloh charged, cheering, into the enemy occupied front line, took a number of prisoners and met with the storm troops (assault force) from 9th and 1st Companies, under Lieut Schattenmann and Sgt Herb. The English, pinned down and engaged from three sides, surrendered. At 7.45 pm, the whole forward trench was once again in our hands – 47 unwounded and 14 wounded Englishmen were captured, as well as seven machine guns and sundry material. A great number of wounded and dead English lay in front of our position. Bandages (dressings) were ordered forward, the platoons which had been pushed in moved back into their positions and the responsibilities reallocated, the machine guns allocated anew and in IV b two captured machine guns were turned against the enemy.

On the alarm, 2nd Company (Security detachment) occupied second position and settled in with the Pioneer platoon of the I Battalion, and the Water Construction troops (Engineers). The position was not shelled, but was bombed repeatedly from the air; one bomb killed Officer

A MOST HOPEFUL LIFE (contd) told Justin's mother the following about her son:

'During the fight against the English and the Australians who stormed our trenches on 19 July your son gave his young and most hopeful life for his Fatherland. He was part of my company until a short while ago and I prized him highly as a friend and adviser. Oh how delighted he was when he found out he would be transferred from the front to the depot of the recruits in Haubourdin due to his eye-problems. I and everyone else were delighted for him that he was relieved from the suffering of the front which he had endured the last few weeks. However, to our surprise, he was transferred back to the company after the night of 2 July in which we had many losses. I almost did not trust my eyes when I saw him again. I am still wondering how he managed to keep up with the rest this stormy night. We came to lie next to each other several times during the breaks and had a short conversation between the heavy barrages. However, we lost each other again in the ongoing fight.
I think your son suffered his fatal wound as dawn broke. When he died one of our bravest and most eager comrades died. He was always a role model for us. Though he was still young, he was most fearless and quick-witted under shellfire. We will always keep his memory alive and honour him.

The Chapel at Fromelles as shown in the 16th BRIR History

… not ashamed of our tears

Lieut Fritz Mayer of 17th BRIR was killed in the Battle of Fromelles, 19 July 1916. This collection of his letters was published in Berlin in 1935 in a book entitled: *Kriegsbriefe gefallener Deutscher Juden* [War letters of Fallen German Jews]. Clearly the timing of the publication and the sentiment of the collection was not without another agenda, but Mayer's letters and those of Ziegel (pages 194–96) give a valuable view of the high morale of the German soldier and the patriotic resolve of German Jews. Mayer's description of his section of the front is important to this story. He was a Vice Sgt Major earlier and had an Iron Cross (3rd Class). Mayer was not quite 23 when he died, having been born at Gmünd, 23 August 1893.

I am delighted to be an advocate for the holy truth of our idea (now in bloody earnestness) and stronger than ever burns in us the love for our German Fatherland. It is a shame that the dishonourable slandering voices have not ceased yet, however, we will not be discouraged. It only makes us sad, very sad. What more could they possibly want than our blood? They may go on with their racial research on the blood which was shed by our dead brothers in faith. Our enemies' bullets do not care about such differences. Thank Heavens! But I will put away these bitter thoughts now. I fight because of the hate between the citizens and not in order to gain your thanks.

In the trench, 28/04/1915
Today's sunny and the calm afternoon put me in a state of dreamy thoughtfulness and I thought about our struggles and longings as German Jews. This induced me to give you a somehow unexpected report on a minor wartime experience which caused severe heartache to me. However, it also gave me cheerful strength which might bring sunshine to some sad moments in my later life. Our company commander had asked me to search for him and I had found him amongst the many dead people, who covered the muddy, marshy fields around the Flemish village of W. He had left the dugout of our seriously ill company commander an hour before, in order to get some Cognac for him from the nearby battalion quarters. He didn't come back from his errand and we feared that he might have got wounded on his way and could not manage to get back on his own. He did not lie far away from our trench While he was striding out he was shot and on his youthful and pretty face there was a slight expression of astonishment about the fact that death had greeted him so early. He had been one of the merriest and liveliest among us and often it was him who managed to cheer us up in the heavy fights because of his charming cheerfulness. Thus he became the favourite of the company and we were united in a special friendship because of the close Württenbergian Landsmannschaft. Thus my comrades to whom I reported his death, felt as I did, that his death amidst all the dead soldiers on the fields had taken the last glimmer of hope and we felt not ashamed of our tears. We thought our tears were devoted to all the young lives which were cheerfully given to the Fatherland in these hard times. Our comrade had had two letters with him: there was one from his mother which contained a copy of a medieval 'plea for protection' to the Saints. It said that the carrier of this talisman should be protected against any wounds caused by strokes, blows or shots. The other letter was from his wife and written with affectionate feeling and anxiety. His wife was a young French woman who he had met while he was working in Nice and to whom he was very much attached, regardless of the hate which existed between the nations. In the evening we buried him near to our quarters and we put a simple cross on his grave. I myself had made the cross by binding branches together. Now while shells were churning up the ground I granted our dead friend his last wishes according to our Jewish religious traditions. But when I prepared to leave the grave I sensed from the looks of my comrades that they were still missing something. Thus I loudly said the Lord's Prayer and they joined in full of faith. Their recognition was apparent in their eyes. However, above us, a wonderful sunset was glowing like the soft smile of a merciful woman. Do you now know why I am at last able to laugh about our neighbours' maliciousness?

27/12/1915
First of all thank you very much for your congratulations on my Iron Cross.
I have to ask you a favour: please do not wrongly interpret my wretched sounding letter and see it as a sign of my homesickness. Do not think that I am feeling miserable out here and that I am now having less eagerness and willingness to fight. That is absolutely not the case. My recklessness has never been stronger than now. You might see that from the fact that I am used to talking to the leader of our company till late into the night and that I even dance to zither music, which is forbidden at your place. It is like this: those parts of the original enthusiasm which disappeared have been replaced by habit. And now it seems to be difficult to imagine that these things were different once upon a time. 'Once upon a time there was ...' does not that sound like a fairy-tale? And finally the word 'home' is less of a geographical than an infinite term, which is appropriate anywhere where one uses one's strengths for one's compatriots. We think we are doing exactly this here. However, sometimes we feel an almost wild longing for all those things which now only belong to us in our holy memory. It could be compared to the longing of an old man for his childhood, who is
[continued opposite]

Candidate Hehl. The 3rd Company (Regimental Reserve–Herlies) got the order at 7.30 pm to move to Aubers. There, they were employed in moving ammunition forward and escorting prisoners away (from the battle area). The II Battalion (Divisional Reserve in Sante) was alerted at 7.30 pm and taken forward, partly by light (trench) railway, to Fournes; from here it was sent early on the morning of the 20 July to Sector III; 8th Company was moved into Sector III a, 5th Company behind them as a Reaction force, HQ, 6th and 7th Companies were at the ready in Fromelles. The Battalion took no more part in the battle; on the night of 20/21 July, they occupied the front line in Sector IV.

Apart from the attack in Sector IV, the enemy attack stretched 3½ km, into the Division's area in Sectors III and II; in Sector III, also, where he succeeded in breaking into the German trenches, he had been destroyed or captured. In Sector II he broke through the forward positions over a front of about 700 metres; however, he was immediately engaged by the Division's troops on both sides and attacked from the front. What was not recovered when the enemy withdrew was recaptured in the early morning in a continuing fight. By the morning of 20 July, the whole position had been reoccupied by the Division. In total, over 300 POW, including a number of officers, fell into our hands. According to previously captured orders, the enemy wanted by his attack to prevent the Germans sending reinforcement to the Somme. Our horseshoe position [the Wick Salient] threatened the English with flanking fire and left them exposed to the danger of a German gas attack, at least until our second line was captured. One would seize the convenient opportunity to attack if one believed that our line in this position had been weakened by withdrawal of troops for the Somme battle. The strongest artillery and mining should be used to break down the German position, machine guns and telephone systems destroyed; repeated breaks in fire employed to bring the defenders out of their dugouts, and then to chase them back with renewed firing, until he, tired of alarms, would regard the enemy attack very lightly.

The English had made seriously misleading assumptions even during the preparation stage for the attack, his troops had suffered considerable casualties from our artillery; some attacking units arrived late, or not at all, for the assault; others were bloodily turned back before our trenches; those who got through were thrown back with heavy losses, or taken prisoner.

The Commander of the 6th Army, Crown Prince Rupprecht, thanked the Division in Army Orders for its good composure and steadiness; His Majesty the Kaiser sent a telegram, praising and giving special recognition to their outstanding performance and their strong defence in the face of countless odds, outnumbered two to one.

The Regiment lost 3 officers and 56 men killed, and 5 officers and 166 men wounded, with 44 missing on the 19/20 July.

The countless English dead lying in front of our position were not recovered by the enemy. As the corpse-smell became more perceptible, the English bodies were sprinkled with lime. The German 'Barbarians' have never shrunk from danger or casualties to fetch their dead from in front of their positions and to give them a dignified burial.

The damage caused by the conflict on 19 July was considerable. The trenches in Sectors IVa and b were in large measure destroyed. Positions, machine gun posts and paths were ripped up; the right wing of IV c had been seriously damaged, the rear area of this Sector was destroyed in

NOT ASHAMED (contd)

reminded of his past by cheerful talks of children. It is the same for us when nice friends tell us about the happy and serious things we left behind.

In Position 06/04/1916
Your recognition of my lasting carefree attitude pleased me a lot. You are funny at home. Do you really think we have nothing else to do but to be depressed and to spend our time crying and with chattering teeth?
In theory you rave about Rousseau, but when someone puts his ideas into practice and even enjoys it, you shake your head in amazement. Not by a long shot. Here one experiences all the delights of a divine 'nature-rapture' and one feels full of strength, to be one with the spring. And here one could totally devote oneself to the spring, if it were not for the damned heroic death. But maybe it's death which acts as a special stimulus on the atmosphere. In these days I am once again a little King. I am the first hope of the Regiment in case of an attack. Together with my platoon we have occupied the first reserve position, and I have now made myself independent from my company which lies one kilometre behind.
It is pleasing to me to describe the surrounding Europe: 'All this is under me'. This surrounding Europe consists of 500 metres of trenches, 1/7 of a square kilometre of open land, two large former farms, the remains of a distillery, a little castle in the air next to a park and greenhouse and 500 metres of a national French street. There is also a similar sized conveyor belt on which the materials are transported to the first position and there is a creek.
I feel like Lord Muck with seven horses. The only thing that is missing is a harem. Instead of it, the English once in a while really trouble us and the rats and the mice which share my innocent camp are at least something alive. Thus you can see the form of address from Horace, you must employ in your next letter:
'O fortunate adulescens'
[O fortunate youth].

GERMAN CASUALTIES AT FROMELLES: 19-20 JULY 1916

	Officers KIA & DOW	ORs KIA & DOW	Officers Wounded	ORs Wounded	Officers Missing/ POW	ORs Missing/ POW	Total
16th BRIR	5	102	5	265	-	-	377
17th BRIR	3	56	5	166	-	44	274
20th BRIR	1	35	4	109	-	7	156
21st BRIR	7	288	8	377	1	94	775
104th Saxons	-	4	-	4	-	-	8
	16	485	22	921	1	145	1590

OUTNUMBERED TWO TO ONE
Order of the day of the 6th Bavarian Reserve Division. Extract from the army order of 20 July 1916: '*The enemy's fire was directed against the 6th Bavarian Reserve Division in particular. Late in the afternoon, this division was attacked by the XI English Corps (61st English and 5th Australian division). The attack failed along most of the 3.5 kilometre wide line north of Fromelles–Aubers that was under attack with extremely high losses on the part of the enemy. North of Fromelles the enemy broke through the division's front position in a line that was about 700 metres wide, but was immediately attacked on the flanks before the front line. All those enemies who did not save themselves by retreating were either killed or captured in the course of the night. This morning, all positions were fully under control of [our] troops, who had solved their difficult task in an excellent manner. His Royal Highness the Supreme Commander expressed he highly appreciated the division's great achievement. I thank all my troops, whose bravery and reliable cooperation made it possible to inflict a severe defeat on the attackers, although we were outnumbered two to one, and together with the division I am awaiting possible storms in the future confident of succeeding.*
St. Qu[entin] 21 July 1916
[signed] von Scanzoni.'

many ways. The approach tracks were shot up in many places, the farm (Deleval) completely destroyed. The restoration works, for which 7th Pioneer Company supported the Regiment for three days, was a major task. The repair works were hindered by the enemy's shrapnel, salvos, which followed at intervals of 20 minutes, interspersed with machine gun fire and heavy mines (mortars). The enemy's artillery, mining and rifle grenades initiated a new procedure, bombing each impact point with heavy shrapnel mines (mortars) and machine gun fire.

From the beginning of September, the enemy used heavy mines (mortars), of which about half died (blew up) in the air. There were no further ventures in the Regiment's Sector; a similar effort was made on 20 August against Sector III, in which our trenches which poked out (into the salient) were hotly engaged.

Deleval Farm near Fromelles. watercolour by Max Märtens

Those concluding paragraphs from the 16th BRIR history of 1932 are but an echo of those of the RIR 104 published in 1925 (see pages 189–90) in their reference to the neglect of their dead by the English and Australians, but naming all those years ago where the bodies of those they buried lay. The Germans were being somewhat self-righteous about the Allied behaviour. They would have known that to retrieve or bury the thousand bodies they counted on No-Man's Land would have taken great teams of men working around the clock for days right up to their wire. Something the Germans would not have tolerated. The fact that they could safely look after the Allied dead found behind their lines and on their parapets is hardly comparable.

The whole problem, of course, could have been solved if a proper truce had been agreed to, which would have made the rescue and recovery work both safe and possible. But the opportunity was lost.

In the years after the war the Imperial War Graves Commission searched for the dead and buried them in purposely built cemeteries, 'bringing in' those buried in small graveyards in the field. What happened at Fromelles to the English and Australians missing after the Battle seems to have provoked little concern. Most had their name on the wall at VC Corner, a few at Villers-Bretonneux, and the English were noted on the Loos and Ploegsteert Memorials under their regiments thus with no link to Fromelles: that was how it lay for the best part of eighty years.

But mathematics is an exact science, after all two plus two can only equal four, there is no alternative answer. So when Lambis Englezos, an Australian amateur historian greatly interested in the whole matter of Fromelles added up the number of graves of unknown Australians in cemeteries around Fromelles with the 410 interred at VC Corner, and found that this was over 160 less than the names on the memorial panels at VC Corner and Villers-Bretonneux, the search for the Missing of Fromelles began. And when he came upon the German Red Cross papers listing all those Allied soldiers that the Bavarians had buried at the time, there was very significant evidence to interest the Australian Government. In time that was supported by archaeological digs. The story of the successful search is the substance of Chapter 15.

PRINCE RUPERT OF BAVARIA
In German he was Rupprecht. He was born at Munich 18 May 1869 the eldest son of Louis III, King of Bavaria. Entering the army as a subaltern in 1886, he was in 1906 the head of the 1st Bavarian Army Corps, and in 1913 an inspector general. Rupert took the German 6th Army into Lorraine at the beginning of the war and was prominent at the first battle of Ypres. As the commander of the German forces in the sector Ypres to Arras, Rupert was in overall charge at Fromelles. He died in 1955.

In one of those quirks of history Hitler's ultimate commander at Fromelles was the direct descendant of Charles I of England and thus, according to legitimist ideas, the rightful British Sovereign as head of the House of Stuart.

Found in the Archives

The Australian Government having been convinced that there was good reason to examine further the idea of the Missing at Fromelles set in motion some work that would prove that further investigation was called for. First there was a non-intrusive examination of the site in 2007. That being positive, a UK expert in such things, Peter Barton, was commissioned to assemble a team of experts to find and then examine anything useful to the project in the Hauptstaatsarchiv Kriegsarchiv in Munich, the home of the Bavarian Division at Fromelles. In November and December 2007, this search was carried out and a 300-page Report resulted. It is from that Report that these notes are taken, together with other information throughout this book, credited and/or acknowledged to Munich Archives, to simplify the august institution's full name.

Having left the description of the five German Regiments in the action of 19/20 July to the historians, supplemented with a few Postscripts from the Report, we turn now to the activities after the battle was over when the victors must deal with the vanquished.

This essay is but a flavour of what the Investigators found in what was for them a tasting of the Munich archives, but its object is to give some background to the loss of the missing for 80 years, and finding them, then hopefully their identification , and eventually their dignified burial.

On 1 August 1916 the 6th BRD reported to Army HQ of 6th Army, one listing as informative as it is relevant. It detailed the captured equipment and prisoners as a result of the action 19/20 July. The 21st BRIR on the night captured in this order: 8 machine guns (incl 5 Lewis Guns), 20 rifles, 10 side arms, 4 officers and 250 men. Also 3 telephone apparatuses. Next to them was 16th BRIR which took 8 machine guns (incl 4 Lewis), 176 rifles, 65 side arms, 2 officers and 178 men. Then the 17th BRIR facing 61st Division captured 7 machine guns (incl 4 Lewis), 35 rifles, 25 side arms, no officers but 61 men. Also 1 telephone apparatus, 1 steel helmet, 5 tool kits for MG, 51 Lewis drums. In terms of people the totals were given as 6/10 Officers and 489/500 men, and always after the hardware captured!

On 20 July a memo, probably by Dr Ott of the Medical Company, noted that the Divisional Sector had been cleared of the enemy by 9.30 am, and some 300 unwounded and 180 wounded English prisoners had been brought in. Next, '*conditions had returned, in main, to normal. The enemy was quiet ...*' Teams from the Medical Company and the Recruit Depot were being found to recover the fallen. '*Sprayers for spraying the dead in front of our positions have been despatched.*' The German casualties he then summarized thus: died in field hospitals 25, killed in action 454, wounded 1139, and missing 158.

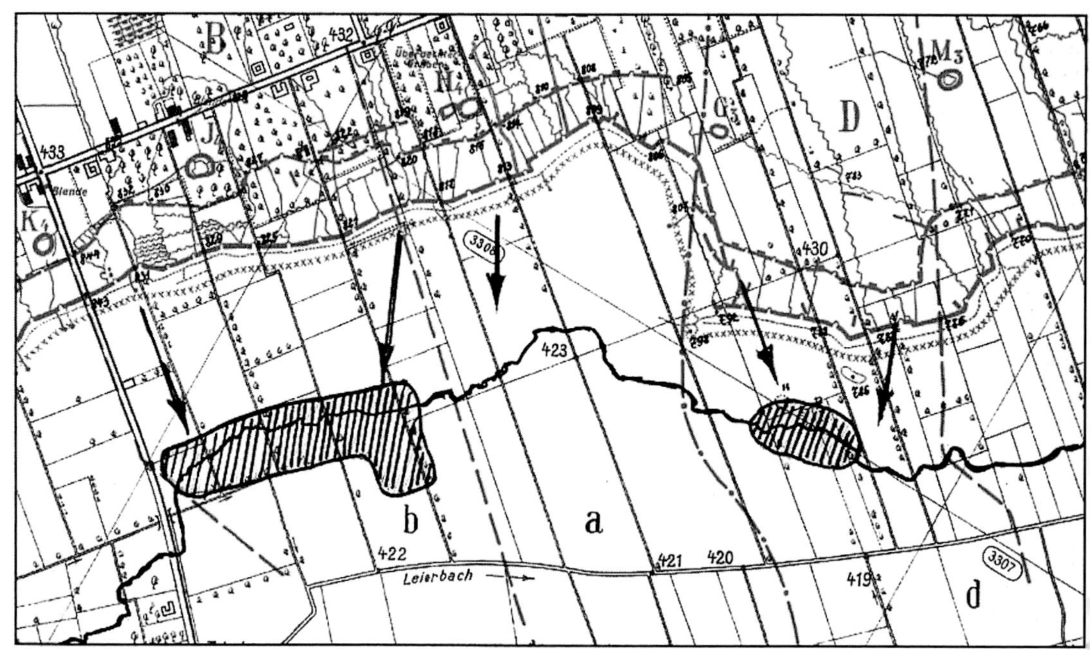

This map of the whole front line shows by arrows the first attacks from the 2/7th Warwicks on the far left, and Australian Bde on the far right. The shaded areas indicate what the English and Australians briefly held. The near total blank space at the centre indicated vividly the fate of 15th Bde.

The general situation now meant that orders had to be issued and work parties organised to move the dead.

Over at the far left, where 17th BRIR faced 61st Division, the order from Lieut von Luneschloss was blunt and to the point:

1. All bodies lying in the front lines to be collected as soon as possible, deposited in places where they are protected from the sun, and separated between English and German.
2. The trenches are to be cleaned up immediately. Booty and equipment of the dead and wounded is to be stored separately and immediately sent to the Regiment in Fournes. I especially wish to draw your attention to the fact that nobody, without exception, has the right to remove from the dead any kind of souvenir whatever these may be. Equally no one has the right to remove equipment from dead or wounded Germans.
3. I forbid any kind of seating in observation positions.
4. I shall punish any man who is found without a gas mask. No one, under any circumstances, is allowed to be without one; even putting it aside whilst working is prohibited. 21.7.16.

Later on 24 July there is this extract from a Bde order: '*English dead still remaining in and behind the trenches are not to be taken to Fournes, but buried in a suitable place between the support line and the second line positions.*' [Signed] Weissmiller.

We learn that IWGC in 1920 took a number of British bodies from the Fournes Cemetery, some 182, buried there according to a surviving sign, between 23 and 25 July. They were reburied in British cemeteries. The compiler of the Report surmises, doubtless correctly, that this is important information as it gives a date for the arrival of English bodies at Pheasant Wood ie after 25 July. This leads him to conclude that the Australian bodies, much closer to the newly dug mass graves would have been buried before the English.

As can be easily imagined, the chaos directly after the battle made many demands on the Germans. Clearing the dead was one thing but finding out about the dead where they fell was another. It would seem that many of the German Command had not sorted out in their minds that there were English and Australians. The Bavarians had, of course, only ever fought against English. This, in a sense, is no different to the English prisoner questioned by the Bavarians not even knowing what Bde was alongside his, let alone an Australian Division half a mile down the road, so to speak. But it is the nature of Germans to sort out and classify detail, and Fromelles is a classic example of this.

The 16th BRIR was particularly interested in finding out who attacked their lines. '*It is extremely important to ascertain what dead lie in front of each company sector ... findings so far suggest the composition of the English forces employed is very unusual. Effects recovered from the dead in front of company sectors, and any observations made, are to be forwarded on a company sector basis.*' Another order included '... *The Regiment is offering rewards for diligent recovery of these items ... companies are therefore asked to note the names of NCOs and men who have carried out these tasks zealously, and report them to Bn at the end of the current tour of duty.*'

Not unexpectedly the searching of the bodies of both English and Australians where they fell was the first task, then to confirm which division, brigade and battalion

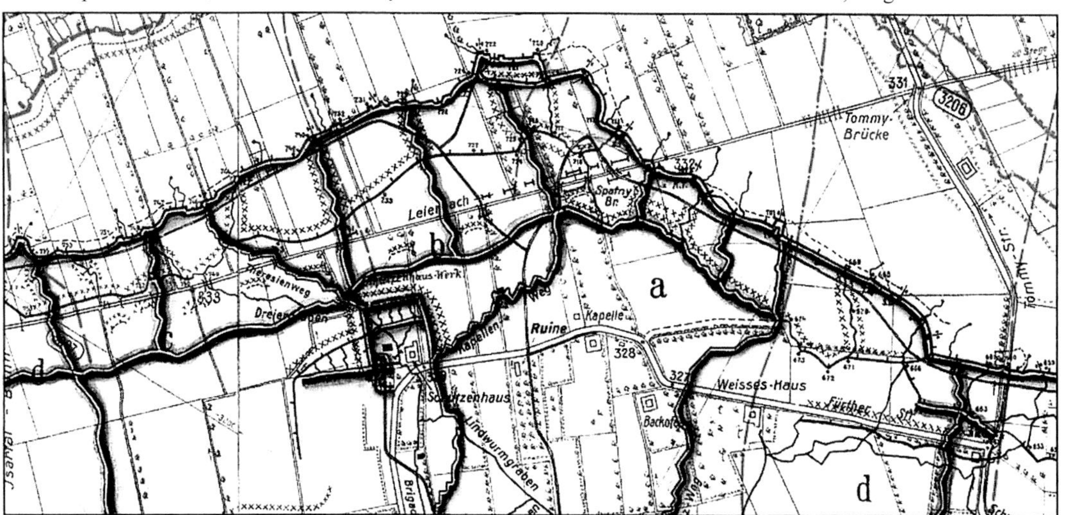

This extremely detailed map of the Sugarloaf sector illustrates dramatically the strength of the position. Note the 'threads' coming out of the front line—these were the MG and observation posts. How Allied intelligence or aerial photography missed them is difficult to understand. What is easier to understand is how the English 184th Bde and Australian 15th Bde were annihilated.

they belonged to was the next requirement. A later order asked for details of which way the dead were facing, to ascertain whether they were attacking or retreating when killed. The bodies then had to be carried back, that is those that could be. Others, one assumes, so badly damaged, were sprayed with potassium permanganate, known to Australians as 'Condies Crystals' and in every home medicine cupboard. Its red stain the badge of courage for many schoolboys braised knees. The more serious task in Flanders was to mark clearly the bodies that were unrecoverable and therefore could be a severe health risk. It did not aid decomposition as chloride of lime did, but did repel flies, but had to be repeated often.

The men of the Medical Company and Recruit Training Depot had the job of picking up the corpses. Great care had to be taken and the recovery teams were issued with protective overalls and gloves, '*they had to wear a wadding pad soaked in aluminium acetate over the nose, or a respirator ...*' and fly veils. We get some idea of the strength of the recovery teams by means of the equipment order: 70 fly veils were issued although only 25 pairs of gloves and 4 overalls were handed out!

Dr Ott ended his Report on a proud note which is dated 24 July:

The fact that a total of about 1050 wounded men were treated in the Division's hospitals between the start of the action ... and the morning of 22 July and that the hospitals now once again have a normal complement of free beds ... means that more than 900 wounded men were evacuated by hospital train or tram from 19 July ... no hold ups occurred ... The swift and sympathetic movement of the wounded, including seriously-injured stretcher cases, attests both to the tireless work of the medical personel in the first instance and to the efficiency of the motor ambulance convoy in transporting the wounded from hospitals in Haubourdin.

Earlier Dr Ott had noted that one hospital train loaded on 21 July had 107 Germans and 67 English on board.

That seems the right note to end this essay. We can visualise among the English, an Australian, William C Barry 2514, 29th Bn, severely wounded and urgently in need of hospital care. How that all happened, and that before he was rescued by the German Medics, he lay among a heap of casualties, perhaps behind the Pheasant Wood (see pages 318–28), is the pivot on which the search for the Missing began.

What else the Report collected is noted in Chapter 9 that deals with Prisoners of War, and Chapter 15 which covers the Missing at Fromelles.

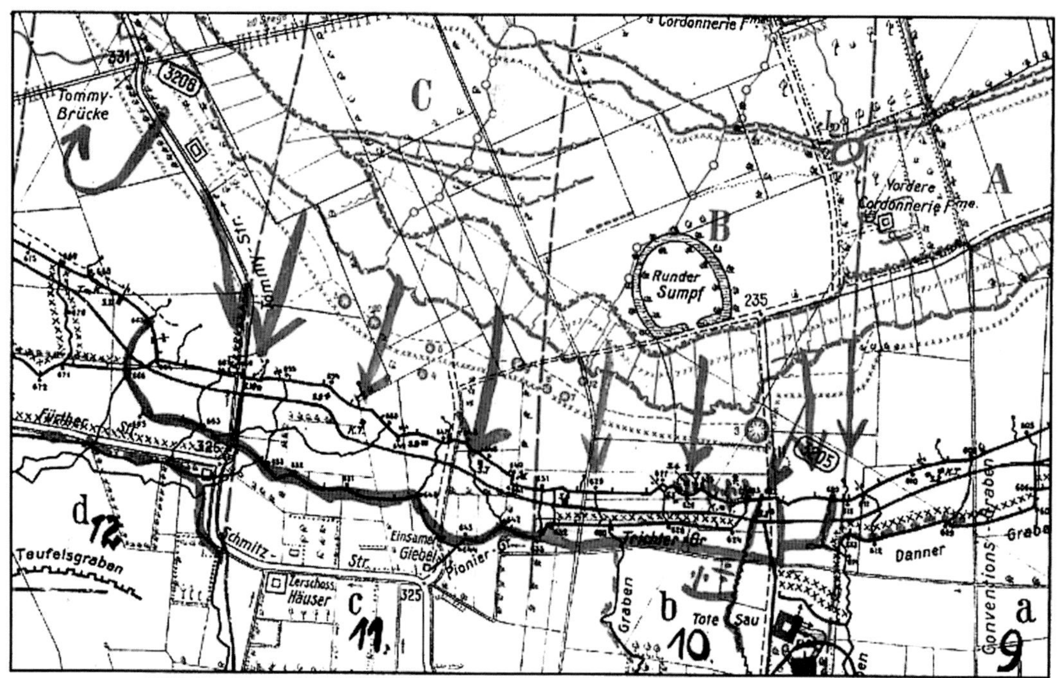

The far right of the front where 8th Bde to the right and 14th Bde to the left attacked (the thick grey arrows) with the darker line below the arrows showing the extent of the Australian incursion at its furthest, ie right along that section of the front. The 'turned back' arrow on the left would be 15th Bde, but the arrow coming in from the left arouses interest.

War forces one to think deeply

Reporting Fromelles

With masterly understatement, Dr John Williams began one of his probing studies (*AWM Journal* Oct 1993) of the media and Fromelles thus: '*If the first casualty of war is truth, then the reporting of battles must be the least trustworthy of all historical material.*'

Williams had examined the Australian, British, French and German Press accounts of 19/20 July, and when placed side-by-side one wonders if any of the reporters were (a) there, or (b) at the same place! In hindsight, the blistering accuracy of the German Communiqué of 21 July was the standard against which the reporters must be measured:

The English attack in the region of Fromelles on Wednesday was carried out, as we have ascertained, by two strong Divisions. The brave Bavarian Division against whose front the attack was made, counted on the ground in front of them more than 2,000 enemy corpses. We have brought in so far 481 prisoners, including ten officers, together with 16 machine guns.

Although this comment was in the public arena some 24 hours after the battle ceased, the Allied Press referred to 'South of Armentières' as the location: the vast majority of the war was of course fought south of Armentières. But either due to deviousness or stupidity, the word Somme was introduced. As Williams points out, it was all gracefully rolled into one: '*Gains by Allies on the Somme—Raids by Australians'* by the *Sydney Morning Herald* although the *Argus* was able to separate it out as *'Anzac Raid—On Two-Mile Front —140 Germans Captured*'. But the location had shifted to '*the region of Neuve Chapelle*'. The next Press problem was admitting that the allied forces consisted of one British and one Australian Division, and instead continually referring to '*important raids ... in which Australians took part*'. The Times on 24 July—then well and truly in possession of the German Communiqué, melted a little by having to admit that Australians were in action at Pozières, '*although three days earlier Anzac forces had joined in the local fight at Armentières*'.

According to Williams, *Le Figaro*'s correspondent or sub-editor decided to speed it up somewhat, where the attack was met by the Germans with '*violent [artillery] fire joined by machine guns ... [this]... didn't stop the Anzacs, nor the English of whom many were under fire for the first time*'. Then to use Williams' own description '*events were embroidered luxuriously*' thus:

The aim we followed was attained and heavy losses were inflicted upon the Germans ... there was no reason to hold the position ... Our men seeing with regret that the Bavarians were not counter-attacking, returned in good order, bringing back considerable booty and 120 prisoners.

It would be very difficult to describe what happened at Fromelles more inaccurately than that!

Dr Williams in scouring the German Press, particularly the *Berliner Tageblatt* and *Norddeutsche Allgemeine Zeitung*, unearthed some really surprising but not inaccurate comments about the Australians at Fromelles, together with taunts not dissimilar to those others noted that the Bavarians shouted over No-Man's Land, indicating some real *'knowledges'* of the 5th Division.

A version of what the German press said was run in the *Sydney Morning Herald* in the bottom corner of its war page of 5 August 1916, under the heading 'The Australian—a German opinion':

A Rotterdam message says, 'The Berliner Tageblatt's' correspondent on the Western Front admits that sharpshooters are specially placed behind breastworks to pick off Australian officers and adds: 'I will not say anything against the Australians. They are sturdy fellows with gold in their pockets—half-educated sons of sheep farmers, and heirs to land. We don't like their faces or eyes. They are good marksmen and fearful fighters, hard as steel but not a single Bavarian feared them as they came storming forward and crossed No-Man's Land.'

But the full version of the 'Rotterdam article' by G F Steward has some interesting extras:

Wednesday
The first German account of the Australian attack near Fromelles indicates that the German sharpshooters are now specially placed on breastworks to pick off all officers engaged in an attack.

Whilst giving an account of the English Gunners' trick to induce the Huns to leave their trenches and then pepper them with surprise hail shells, the writer, George Queri (?) headquarters correspondent of the Berliner Tageblatt incidentally gives German ideas of the Australians, that should mightily please the Anzacs.

He says: 'In the first half of July the artillery was active, but not unusually so, on the 15th the enemy sent gas out. During this we paid a visit to the enemy's trenches. They were Australians and in stronger force than usual. Next day the artillery began its great work. From their guns we received pious words from the Bethlehem Steelworks in the form of 18 pounders, 50 pounders, heavy howitzers and also 30.5 centimetre projectiles—all gifts from Bethlehem. For four days the heavy firing continued attaining the greatest fierceness on the afternoon of July 19th.

Our men were glad the attack had at last come after lying waiting so long. Brave lookouts lay on the breastworks watching the enemy. Twice these men reported they were coming, the enemy moved their fire forward and their bayonets pointed over the breastworks as though they were coming up the storming ladders. Just as we were ready to receive them a fearful fire was suddenly returned

In 1999 John Williams published *Anzacs, The Media and the Great War*, where he brought together his research and conclusions: there are 24 pages on Fromelles, elaborating on his earlier articles.

upon us. The Englishmen repeated this war game several times, supposing we should no longer believe the true alarm, but have crept anxiously into dugouts from which we have been enticed twice to receive the fearful surprise fire.

I will not say anything against the Australians. They are strong fellows, grown up with gold in their pockets, half-educated sons of rich farmers and heirs to a country. We don't like their faces and eyes. They're not the kind of people that appeal to us. Good marksmen, fearful fighters, hard as steel, but has a single Bavarian fighter learned to fear them? At seven they came storming forward but they died in fearful numbers crossing No-Man's Land. Old Bavarian and Schwabian marksmen lay upon the breastworks and left not a single officer alive to come near them. Machineguns were rushed out and used on the enemy. One jammed, but the man at the next gun discharged 14000 cartridges, blood spurting from his hands as he pressed the gun. By 9.20 two-thirds of the Division was clear of the enemy. Not a single Englishman was left standing before the trenches. The Bavarians had finished their reckoning with the enemy, and burst into singing 'Die wacht am Rhein'.

The earlier reference to sheep farmers had much to do with one of the reported battle field taunts, '*shepherd, come and be shorn*', and another '*come on, come on if you've got any pluck*'.

As far as the battle was concerned, the German Press was not bashful about the allies breaking through their lines, nor about their success in getting on top of the situation.

The losses of the English were so great we did not reckon on a repetition of the attack, which turned out to be correct.

True, it is easy to tell the truth if the victory was so obvious and overwhelming, and it is difficult how anyone, even *Le Figaro*, could have made the truth from the allies' side the least bit palatable. Luckily for the Australian Press and Government, Fromelles was swamped by Pozières, otherwise an adventurous journal like the *Bulletin* might have picked up the matter primed in the first place by the many letters written by wounded '*19th of July men*' in England from where their letters were uncensored: for an example, R St J Kennedy's letter, pages 240-41. But the evidence is that items like Cpl E A Hubbard's '*At the Front*' appeared in local papers meant little because the names of places were but dotted lines: see pages 174–76.

Bean's contribution on Fromelles as War Correspondent, rather than his later role of historian, was not much to be proud of but the best he could do at the time. We know he motored into Amiens on the evening of 20 July to file his report which he had to submit to the British Military Censor. We only know what got through by the account printed in the *Sydney Morning Herald* and *Melbourne Argus* bearing in mind their editors had worked on it also. Bean was no stranger to working with censors, and must have had a shrewd idea of what they would let through, and what they would not. This information and whatever else Bean sent ended up as the only report made on Fromelles in the Australian press. But before reading it, it is important to know what Bean wrote in his diary about the sending of this report.

I wrote a cable calling it an 'attack' and saying the losses were 'severe'. I took this to Amiens (arriving there at 8.15 pm) and I believe the censor passed it. He would not have the bombardment described as 'intense' as the 1st Army objected that there never was an intense bombardment. The other pressman (or rather Russell) had been up to 1st Army HQ so I suppose he got his telegram off before me. H Wilson got him to censor it to see that I did not say anything which disagreed with 1st Army. They say that the official communiqué calls it an 'important series of trench raids'. What is the good of deliberate lying like that? The Germans know it was an attack—they have numbers of our wounded as prisoners, we have about 100 unwounded and 30 wounded prisoners (I was told 250 but I believe this is wrong).

SYDNEY MORNING HERALD

AUSTRALIANS.

ATTACK TRENCHES.

TEMPORARY SUCCESS.

TAKE 200 PRISONERS.

(FROM CAPTAIN C. E. W. BEAN, OFFICIAL AUSTRALIAN PRESS REPRESENTATIVE.)

BRITISH HEADQUARTERS, FRANCE, July 20.

Yesterday evening, after a bombardment, an Australian force attacked the German trenches south of Armentieres.

The Australians on the left seized the German front line, and passed beyond it to the further trenches on the first system. In the centre the Australians carried the whole of the German first system, and reached more or less open country. On the right, the troops had to cross a much wider stretch between the trenches, where the Germans held a very strongly-fortified salient.

The Germans were ready for the attack and had managed to save a number of machine guns from the bombardment. In spite of very brave efforts, the troops on this flank were unable to cross the ground between the trenches, and only managed to reach the German trenches at isolated points. From these they were driven out.

This enabled the Germans to concentrate the fire of all sorts of artillery on the portion of the trenches captured. The Germans battered down their own trenches where they were occupied by our men. They also turned water from a channel down the trench on the left flank, and the Australians there, shortly after reaching the trenches, found themselves standing in water which was rapidly rising and waist high. They endured a tremendous bombardment until early the following morning, when, after eleven hours in the captured position, such Australians as retained the small remaining portion of the German line were ordered to retire.

By dint of very brave work, the engineers and infantry in the working parties had managed to get communication trenches dug completely through to the German trenches. These trenches were dug under very heavy shell fire. This work enabled the troops to carry out their retirement with a loss which is slight when the extraordinary difficulty of the operation is considered.

Among the last who returned to our trenches were eight men who said they got lost behind the German trenches, and had been wandering about till daylight in the country in the rear of the front line.

Our troops, in this attack, had to face shell fire which was heavier and more continuous than was ever known in Gallipoli. Many of them had never previously been tried. The manner in which they carried the operation through seems to have been worthy of all the traditions of Anzac. At least 200 prisoners were captured and several machine guns. Many Germans were killed. The losses amongst our troops engaged were severe.

War forces one to think deeply

Hitler and Fromelles

Writing about Hitler in the context of this book needed discipline. What he was in the years up to the end of the First World War is the man being discussed, not the man who twenty years later changed the world forever. This essay is at pains to examine Hitler's particular relationship with Fromelles.

Adolf Hitler was forever proud of his years in action with the German Army, a period according to one account, involving some 48 battles. His regiment was at Ypres, Messinés, Wytschaete, Fromelles, Neuve Chapelle, La Bassée, Arras, in Artois, Chemin des Dames, on the Somme, on the Marne and near La Montagne. Thus it could be said he served most of his time in Flanders and was at Fromelles on 19/20 July when his unit, the 16th Bavarian Reserve Infantry Regiment, had control of the Sugarloaf. And because so much survives of his memories of that time he is part of this story.

After an unhappy and desperate period as an orphan, a student and unemployed young man Hitler found the discipline and order of army life, not to say the regular meals, a wonderful relief.

We can do no better than turn to Hitler's own feelings as he expressed them in *Mein Kampf*, just over ten years later. These several paragraphs go some way towards explaining why the German army moved with the compulsion it did, as it is highly unlikely that Hitler's views were that of the minority.

Then the Balkan war broke out; and therewith the first gusts of the forthcoming tornado swept across a highly strung Europe. In the supervening calm men felt the atmosphere oppressive and foreboding; so much so that the sense of impending catastrophe became transformed into a feeling of important expectance. They wished that Heaven would give free rein to the fate which could now no longer be curbed. Then the first great bolt of lightning struck the earth. The storm broke and the thunder of the heavens intermingled with the roar of the cannons in the World War.

The War of 1914 was certainly not forced on the masses; it was even desired by the whole people. There was a desire to bring the general feeling of uncertainty to an end once and for all. And it is only in the light of this fact that we can understand how more than two million German men and youths voluntarily joined the colours, ready to shed the last drop of their blood for the cause.

For me these hours came as a deliverance from the distress that had weighed upon me during the days of my youth. I am not ashamed to acknowledge today that I was carried away by the enthusiasm of the moment and that I sank down upon my knees and thanked Heaven out of the fullness of my heart for the favour of having been permitted to live in such a time.

The fight for freedom had broken out on an unparalleled scale in the history of the world ... People dreamed of the soldiers being home by Christmas and that then they would resume their daily work in peace.

I had no desire to fight for the Hapsburg cause, but I was prepared to die at any time for my own kinsfolk and the Empire to which they really belonged.

In case those sentiments might be taken as hindsight, there has survived a photograph showing Hitler in the jubilant crowd gathered in Munich on 2 August 1914 cheering the declaration of war. Joachim Fest, in his biography of Hitler, describes it thus:

His face is plainly recognisable, the half open mouth, the burning eyes, which at last have a goal and see a future. For this day liberated him from all the embarrassments, the perplexities and the loneliness of failure.

Hitler in Munich crowd, 2 August 1914

Like so many thoughtful young men who volunteered, Hitler was moved by the patriotism involved but of course disturbed by the blunders that wasted so much of that spirit. Hardened as they became by the brutality, they were also transformed by the comradeship they found. Not a few resolved, that if they survived, they would work to change things. What made Hitler different was that he would survive and he would change things: and he never doubted that. Nobody ever recalled him complaining about the rigours of the war, although many remembered the extended lectures he gave as he sought to work out his ideas on what was wrong with the system that caused the war.

When writing *Mein Kampf* in 1925 he described vividly, proudly and characteristically his first days in the German Army, doubtless the experience and feelings of thousands upon thousands of other Germans.

On August 3rd 1914, I presented an urgent petition to His Majesty, King Ludwig III, requesting to be allowed to serve in a Bavarian regiment. In those days the Chancellery had its hands quite full and therefore I was all the more pleased when I received the answer a day later, that my request had been granted ... Within a few days I was wearing that uniform which I was not to put off again for nearly six years.

For me, as for every German, the most memorable period of my life now began. Face to face with that mighty

Volunteer Adolf Hitler, in front of the Regiments' Headquarters, May 1915
[from the Unit history of the 16th BRIR.]

struggle, all the past fell away into oblivion. With a wistful pride I look back on those days ... I recall those early weeks of war when kind fortune permitted me to take my place in that heroic struggle among the nations ... I see myself among my young comrades on our first parade drill, and so on until at last the day came on which we were to leave for the front.

At long last the day came when we left Munich on war service. For the first time in my life I saw the Rhine, as we journeyed westwards to stand guard before that historic German river against its traditional and grasping enemy. As the first soft rays of the morning sun broke through the light mist and disclosed to us the Niederwald Statue, with one accord the whole troop train broke into the strains of Die Wacht am Rhein. I then felt as if my heart could not contain its spirit.

And then followed a damp, cold night in Flanders. We marched in silence throughout the night and as the morning sun came through the mist an iron greeting suddenly burst above our heads. Shrapnel exploded in our midst and spluttered in the damp ground. But before the smoke of the explosion disappeared a wild 'Hurrah' was shouted from two hundred throats, in response to this first greeting of Death. Then began the whistling of bullets and the booming of cannons, the shouting and surging of the combatants. With eyes straining feverishly, we pressed forward, quicker and quicker, until we finally came to close-quarter fighting, there beyond the beet-fields and the meadows. Soon the strains of a song reached us from afar. Nearer and nearer, from company to company, it came. And while Death began to make havoc in our ranks we passed the song on to those beside us: Deutschland, Deutschland über Alles, über Alles in der Welt.

After four days in the trenches we came back. Even our stop was no longer what it had been. Boys of seventeen looked now like grown men. The rank and file of the List Regiment had not been properly trained in the art of warfare, but they knew how to die like old soldiers.

That was the beginning. And thus we carried on from year to year. A feeling of horror replaced the romantic fighting spirit. Enthusiasm cooled down gradually and exuberant spirits were quelled by the fear of the ever-present Death. A time came when there arose within each one of us a conflict between the urge to self-preservation and the call of duty. And I had to go through that conflict too. As Death sought its prey everywhere and unrelentingly a nameless Something rebelled within the weak body and tried to introduce itself under the name of Common Sense; but in reality it was Fear, which had taken on this cloak in order to impose itself on the individual. But the more the voice which advised prudence increased its efforts and the more clear and persuasive became its appeal, resistance became all that stronger; until finally the internal strife was over and the call of duty was triumphant. Already in the winter of 1915–16 I had come through that inner struggle. The will had asserted its incontestable mastery. Whereas in the early days I went into the fight with a cheer and a laugh, I was now habitually calm and resolute. And that frame of mind endured. Fate might now put me through the final test without my nerves or reason giving way. The young volunteer had become an old soldier.

Hitler's introduction to the full ferocity of the war was at the first battle of Ypres where the British stopped the German attempt to reach the Channel ports in October 1914. Hitler wrote that his regiment, in four days, was reduced from 3800 to 600 with only 30 Officers surviving, and four companies had to be dissolved. He received the Iron Cross (second class) in this first action at Wytschaete on 2 December 1914, and was then 25. In later life this was the only decoration he wore. On 4 August 1918, he received the Iron Cross (first class) for General Conduct as Despatch Runner, coincidentally the fourth anniversary of his enlistment.

But even in the grim *Mein Kampf* Hitler had a momentary light touch, but the conclusion he drew from the experience was of great seriousness:

I can vividly recall to mind the astonished looks of my comrades when they found themselves personally face to face for the first time with the Tommies in Flanders. After

Ernst Schmidt, Max Amann, Adolf Hitler and Foxl, probably at Fournes, Summer 1916

a few days fighting the consciousness slowly dawned on our soldiers that those Scotsmen were not like the ones we had seen described and caricatured in the comic papers and mentioned in the communiqués. It was then that I formed my first ideas of the efficiency of various forms of propaganda.

It seems Hitler was at first an orderly to Lieut Col Tubeuf of the 16th Bavarian RIR, sometimes referred to as the List Regiment in honour of its first commander, Colonel List. Hitler (No. 148, 1st Company and later 3rd Company) then became despatch runner, an extremely dangerous job requiring courage and nerves of steel: his rank was equivalent of Lance Corporal. In October 1941 he recalled one aspect of the job and what it taught him:

It's probable that, throughout the 1914–18 war, some twenty thousand men were uselessly sacrificed by employing them as runners on missions that could have been equally well accomplished by night, with less danger. How often I myself have had to face a powerful artillery barrage, in order to carry a simple postcard!

My strength lies in the fact that I can imagine the situations that troops are called upon to face. And I can do that because I've been an ordinary soldier myself.

Hitler's unit was at Neuve Chapelle in the battle of 10–14 March 1915 and throughout 1915 served in Flanders, La Bassée and Arras settling down in the Fromelles area from 8 July 1915 to 25 September 1916. Then the unit moved to the Somme and the journey there, Hitler recalled in 1942:

When we went into the line in 1916, to the south of Bapaume, the heat was intolerable. As we marched through the streets, there was not a house, not a tree to be seen; everything had been destroyed, and even the grass has been burnt. It was a veritable wilderness ...

The soldier has a boundless affection for the ground on which he has shed his blood ... Marching along the roads was a misery for us poor old infantrymen; again and again we were driven off the road by the bloody gunners, and again and again we had to dive into swamps to save our skins.

On 7 October 1916, Hitler was wounded at Le Bargur, interestingly the 5th Australian Division was opposite, and gassed 13/14 October 1918, thus spending the end of the war in hospital.

It is often suggested that Hitler was without friends in the army but the facts are otherwise. Taking the most personal first, Lieut Friedrich Wiedemann, Hitler's superior officer, who retired after the war with the rank

The Comrade

When one of us gets tired
the other will keep watch for him.
If one of us starts to feel doubt
the other suddenly laughs.

If one of us should be killed,
the other would fight like two men;
as any fighter is assigned
a comrade by God.

Adolf Hitler
Lance-corporal
14 August 1916

A surviving copy of this poem has on the reverse: *'To my comrade Max Amann as a memento'*. In the history of the 16th BRIR *Vier Jahre Westfront,* p215, Capt. Wiedemann wrote: 'Whenever someone was wounded or shot another took his place without being ordered...', his German words apparently echoing the same experience as Hitler described.

of Captain and turned to farming. When, in 1932, the history of the List Regiment was published, it contained considerable contributions by Wiedemann on the battle of Fromelles and a photograph of Hitler in May 1915. In 1934 Wiedemann joined the party and the next year became Hitler's personal adjutant, attending Hitler's first meeting with Mussolini: later he briefed Britain's Lord Halifax on Hitler's hopes for an agreement between the two countries. In this position Wiedemann was privy to all Hitler's domestic arrangements and was made a beneficiary of his will (via the party) in 1938. He discussed matters of marriage, health and even Eva Braun with his boss and admitted later in his book *Der Mann, Der Feldherr werden wollte,* that Hitler's memories of his war experiences were excellent:

I never really caught him lying or exaggerating when he told of his recollections.

It was also Wiedemann's opinion that Hess was the straightest character among the Nazi leaders: but Hitler seemed, by 1939, in Wiedemann's judgement, to be going mad. As John Toland, in his biography *Adolf Hitler,* suggests:

Ever since Crystal Night the Fuhrer seemed to inhabit an imaginary world which had nothing in common with reality and whenever Wiedemann attempted to discuss any defect in the system Hitler ignored him.

Then as Toland recorded it, the two parted:

I have no use for people in high places and in my closest circle who do not agree with my politics,' Hitler curtly told Wiedemann. 'I hereby discharge you as my personal adjutant and appoint you consul general in San Francisco. You can accept or refuse this new position.' Without hesitation Wiedemann accepted, adding that he hoped he wouldn't have to take a cut in salary. At this, Hitler's tone became milder. 'I will always keep an open ear for your financial welfare.' Thus, after four years' close association, the two war comrades parted without bitterness.

In his new position Wiedemann soon attracted the attention of the FBI for, among other things, his involvement in the behind-the-scenes peace moves between Hitler and a British group that was brought to a climax when Hess flew to Scotland on 10 May 1941.

Wiedemann was expelled from the US in June 1941 and went to Tientsin (China) to be German Consul General there. He seems to have returned to Germany in 1944 and been arrested by the Allies in 1945. At Nuremberg he was sentenced to 28 months. After that he became a farmer in southern Germany. Born on 16 August 1891, Wiedemann died in 1970.

We turn now to Rudolf Hess, Hitler's political confidant and deputy from 1933 to 1941. The experts cannot agree whether or not they knew each other whilst both were in the List Regiment. Hess was an Officer

In 1940 members of Hitler's tour party outside his billet in Fournes-en-Weppes.

The plaque, now in the Fromelles Museum

from the outset: he had been wounded at Verdun, so it is possible their paths did not cross, and Hess later left the army to join the airforce. Regardless, there can be little doubt that when they were working on *Mein Kampf* together in the Landsberg Prison they would have discussed old times in the front line.

At that point Max Amann the former Regimental Clerk with the rank of Sergeant Major, in Hitler's unit, was close by. In the group photograph of Hitler with his two army friends and Foxl, the dog, Amann is in the centre—note Hitler's hand around Amann's arm, and Ernst Schmidt is on the left: they are clearly close friends. Three weeks after the Battle of Fromelles Hitler wrote a poem *Der Kamerad* which he gave to Amann.

In the summer of 1921 Hitler apparently met Amann by accident and they compared notes. Hitler was beginning his political party and Amann trying for some office job with its attendant security. The two had been together in the same unit for four years and Hitler had observed, as he put it, Amman's *unusual ability, diligence and rigorous conscientiousness*. After some persuasion Amann became business manager of the party, Membership No 3, but on the condition that he would not be at the mercy of incompetent committees and only answerable to one person, Hitler himself. This never changed. By 1922 Amann was secretary general of the party and set about raising money for the party on the basis that to publicise their cause money was the most essential item. He saw to it that Hitler's speeches were printed and circulated. As a result of the Putsch of 1923 Amann served 6 months in Landsberg prison with Hitler. There Hitler dictated the second part of *Mein Kampf* to Amann and a secretary and when the book was finished it was Amann who decided on the simple, dramatic title *Mein Kampf* when Hitler and Hess were in favour of a long winded, verbose title.

This drawing by Hitler is listed as being of Fournes-en-Weppes and could be the rear of his billet. But it does have some things in common with the house at Haubourdin, see page 191.

1345 Froidherbe, Fournes-en-Weppes 1996. Hitler's billet in 1916

Amann published *Mein Kampf* and afterwards Hitler's speeches and texts making sure that Hitler was generously paid for all his published work. By 1933 Hitler was rich, the party had abundant funds and had its say via the *Volkischer Beobachter*, the party newspaper, which was then financially secure. Hitler himself in his recorded conversations of the 1940s, often with Amann in the audience, paid endless tributes to his friend, who had lost an arm in a firearms' accident in 1931.

As regards Amann, I can say positively that he's a genius. He's the greatest newspaper proprietor in the world. Despite his great discretion, which explains why it is not generally known, I declare that Rothermere and Beaverbrook are mere dwarfs compared to him. Today the Zentral Verlag owns from 70 per cent to 80 per cent of the German press. Amann achieved all that without the least ostentation. (22 Feb 1942)

Amann, what a jolly chap he is! Already when we were at the front, he used to let joy loose amongst us. In my unit, even at the worst time there was always someone that would make us laugh. (24 Feb 1942)

Amann's great idea was to guarantee the financial existence of the newspaper by the profits realised on the Party editions. These profits accumulated so quickly that the newspaper quickly stopped being exposed to any risks. Amann realised what a tour de force it was to maintain the house of publication during my incarceration in Landsberg. At that time, I owned part of the capital ... (27 Feb 1942)

The fact that I was able to keep the Volkischer Beobachter on its feet throughout the period of our struggle—and in spite of the three failures it had suffered before I took it over—I owe first and foremost to the collaboration of Reichsleiter Amann. He, as an intelligent business man, refused to accept responsibility for an enterprise if it did not possess the economic prerequisites of potential success. Thanks to this rule of his, the publishing firm of Eher ... developed into one of the most powerful newspaper trusts in the world. (6 May 1942)

If the Volkeischer Beobachter, which originally had merely a few thousand subscribers, has now become a gigantic enterprise, in which reckoning is by the million, we owe it first and foremost to the exemplary industry of

Reichsleiter Amann. Thanks to a quite military discipline, he has succeeded in getting the very best out of his colleagues ... (14 May 1942)

Amann's success and survival in a society riddled with Goebbels' intrigue, Himmler's butchery and Bormann's paranoia to name but three elements was undoubtedly due to his original decision of only answering to Hitler himself.

Well before it all came to an end in 1945, Max Amann was a multimillionaire, a member of the Reichstag, a general in the SS, Nazi Reichsleiter of Press Affairs and President of the Press Chamber. His publishing company, Eher, controlled 82% of the 977 papers that remained in Germany and is thought to have been the largest newspaper and publishing group in the world at that time. He had seen to it that Hitler's own wealth was considerable by designating the payments that every publisher had to make for the privilege of printing the Führer's words!

It seems amazing that not all the German press was controlled and/or owned by the Nazi Party: but of course it was all subservient. When the Nuremberg Court arraigned Amann, it could only find him guilty of having profited from the regime. He was thus stripped of his wealth, his pension and sent to the De-Nazification Court. That found him a 'major offender' and on 8 Sept 1948 sentenced him to 10 years hard labour.

Hitler's Press Chief, Otto Dietrich knew Amann well. In his relatively balanced memoirs *The Hitler I knew*, he wrote:

'The administrator of his [Hitler's] property and his money was Max Amann in his capacity as director of Eher Verlag, which published *Mein Kampf*. Once or twice a year Amann would drop in on Hitler to present his accounts. At such times he would bring up his wishes with regard to newspapers and book publishing and would ask Hitler for authority in various matters. He was seldom or never refused. Whether his unassailable position with Hitler was due to his capacity as the Fuhrer's business agent or to his having been the sergeant of Hitler's company in the First World War, was a subject much discussed among Hitler's intimates.'

Ongoing investigation into the location of the missing wealth of the Nazi Party seems to imply that Amann may

FROMELLES DRESSING STATION
Hitler's watercolour of the *'Fromelles Dressing Station'* is a good example of his work. He was basically an architectural artist and there is no evidence that he attempted to be more than that. It is obvious that the Vienna Art Academy would say that he '*showed more talent for architecture than for painting*' and thus had no place for him. His closest friend of those student days, August Kubizèk, expected him to become an architect or artist.

The Unit History of the 16th BRIR contains many illustrations by artists in the unit, but curiously none by Hitler. However there is a watercolour by Max Märtens in much the same style as Hitler, of the same subject. Hitler's view introduces a fence post and a tree through the arch and is slightly oblique to make it more interesting. There is also the figure of a horse in the arch, just sketched in. The full caption of Märtens work is: '*Shelter of the Medical Corps RIR 16 in Fromelles opposite the Regiment's Headquarters, May 1916*'. Hitler's painting is classified sometimes as 1915 and a further uncertainty is that the Headquarters were in Fournes.

well have set up Swiss bank accounts for some of Hitler's royalties from *Mein Kampf* and these funds remain, rather obviously, still unclaimed.

Every opinion of Amann during his years of power has him as 'uncouth', 'a bully', 'hardly literate' and 'generally unpleasant'. This is interestingly countered by Albert Krebs, an early leader in the Nazi Party, recalling Amann in the 1920s:

I also count it as a merit that he had a certain decency and honesty that tolerated no corruption, not just in others but also in himself.

Born a Catholic in Munich 24 Nov 1891 Amann died in poverty in Munich 30 March 1957.

Hitler at the blockhouse that saved his life, June 1940

The blockhouse discovered years later, hidden in a maize crop

The blockhouse on the Fromelles-Aubers Road 1996, a much visited tourist attraction

There is now Ernst Schmidt, variously described as a painter and master painter, about whom little has been published. A despatch runner, and corporal, like Hitler, it seems they often went together carrying messages, and some say he was Hitler's closest friend in 16th BRIR because of these shared dangers. They never lost contact, and as Hitler became rich, he helped Schmidt financially with his business and Schmidt became Mayor of his town. They were to meet up in public at Fournes-en-Weppes in 1940. Earlier, as if to make sure Schmidt was never forgotten, Hitler mentions him in *Mein Kampf.*

Towards the end of November (1918) I returned to Munich. I went to the depot of my regiment, which was now in the hand of the 'Soldiers' Councils'. As the whole administration was quite repulsive to me, I decided to leave it as soon as I possibly could. With my faithful war-comrade, Ernst Schmidt, I came to Traunstein and remained there until the camp was broken up. In March 1919 we were back again in Munich.

Although he remembered Fromelles often in his conversations it was Hitler's visit to Fromelles in June 1940 which shows the significance of that time to him. He was then conqueror of most of Europe. He went to Paris, for 21 June, so that the French might sign the surrender documents in the same train as used in 1918 for the German surrender, and the next two days he toured Paris before flying to Belgium, ending up somewhere near Fromelles for the night of 25 June.

David Irving in his *Hitler's War* gives the greatest detail of this sentimental journey:

An hour after midnight on June 25, 1940, a bugler of the 1st Guards Company took up station at each corner of the Führer's village headquarters. Seated at a bare wooden table in his requisitioned cottage, Hitler waited with Speer, his adjutants, secretaries and personal staff; he had also invited two of his fellow infantrymen from World War I to join him—one Ernst Schmidt, a master painter, and his old sergeant Max Amann, now chief of the Party's printing presses. Throughout Europe millions of radios were tuned in to this quiet forest acre. Hitler ordered the lights in the dining room switched off, and the window opened. A radio turned low whispered a commentary. At 1.35 am, the moment prescribed for the armistice to take effect, the buglers sounded the ceasefire.

It was the most moving moment of his life. Nobody would ever understand what this victory meant for him; for four years he had once fought as an anonymous infantryman, and now as Supreme Commander it has been granted to him to lead his people to a unique victory ... the Führer contentedly toured the Flanders battlefield of World War I with his old comrades Amann and Schmidt. He even found the house where he had been billeted as an infantryman and delightedly showed it to Schaub and the select handful who accompanied him on this nostalgic pilgrimage around those corners of his memory. At one point he darted off and clambered up an overgrown slope, looking for a concrete slab behind which he had once taken cover. His memory had not deceived him, for the same nondescript slab was still there and for all we know lies there to this day.

Writing much later, c. 2002, for *'After the Battle'*, Jean Paul Pallud adds some detail to Irving's account:

On Monday 24 June [Schmidt and Amman] arrived. That same day, the Armistice between France and Italy had been signed ... in Rome ... with the ceasefire due to be sounded at 1.35 am the next day, Tuesday 25 June.

That evening at Wolfsschlucht, Hitler was sitting with his entourage in the officers' mess. The windows were open and the room dark for the lights had been extinguished because of an air raid warning. At 1.35 am, from four positions around the headquarters, buglers of the 1 Kompagnie sounded 'Das Ganze Halt' (ceasefire). In the mess everyone stood to attention in complete silence. As the notes died away, Keitel said a few words and three cheers went up in honour of the Führer, the Supreme Commander ... Hitler sat in silence for a minute or so, stood up and then left. Later, both Breker and Giesler who were present testified that they had seen tears in his eyes.

John Toland in his biography adds other aspects:

Hitler himself was playing the tourist with a special group including his adjutants and his World War sergeant, Max Amann. For two days this lighthearted group was guided by the Führer around the old battlefield of the conflict that had helped lead to this one. It was a sentimental journey with Hitler enjoying every moment. He pointed out the fields of Flanders that had formerly been a hellish morass, the old trenches that had been kept as memorials and attractions for sightseers. Instead of surveying the scenes in quiet solemnity, the Führer talked interminably, explaining the minutest detail of what happened here and over there. As he drove through Lille, which he had memorialised in watercolour, a woman looking out of the window recognised him. 'The Devil' she gasped. Amused at first, he vowed he would erase that image from the minds of the conquered. The sentimental junket ended on June 26.

Hitler made his tour in an open car. He visited the German Cemetery at Fournes, a house that was an infirmary in 1916, and the billet he had shared with another in Fournes-en-Weppes, being in his day a butcher's shop with residence over. The two 'boys' were looked after by an elderly French woman who gave them nicknames—'Blackie' for Hitler and 'Blondie' for his friend. In a much-photographed ceremony, a plaque was fixed to the front of the building on 20 April 1942, Hitler's 53rd birthday: that plaque is now in the Fromelles Museum. It is also recalled that Hitler took his touring party to a block house on Aubers Ridge which he remembered as a place where he and Schmidt had had a close shave. It was not the one that is now a tourist site. In the inimical style of *After the Battle* using photographs of Hitler's tour, they found it all but hidden in a field of maize. It was on the western side of Fromelles, along rue de la Biette, until it becomes a track. A local resident remembered, in 1940 there were cars parked in the field and men walking about.

With his memory of events so vivid it would be interesting to know exactly what else he included on his itinerary: the Sugarloaf site for instance? None of the published photos give any hint of that: yet as Hitler's base for all that time, he could not have forgotten it.

Sources used for this research included:

British War Office. *Who's Who in Nazi Germany* (1942).
Bullock, Alan. *Hitler: A Study in Tyranny* (1952).
Costello, John. *Ten days that saved the west* (1991).
Davidson, Eugene. *The making of Adolf Hitler* (1978).
de Launay, J. *Hitler en Flandres* (1975).
Dietrich, Otto. *The Hitler I knew* (1957).
Fest, Joachim. *Hitler* (1974).
Hitler, Adolf (ed by Hugh Trevor Roper) *Hitler's secret conversations 1941-44* (1953).
Hitler, Adolf. *Mein Kampf* (1938).
Hoffman, H. *Hitler was my friend* (1955).
Irving, David. *Hitler's War* (1977).
Kershaw, Ian. *Hitler 1889-1936* (1998).
Krebs, Albert. *The Infancy of Nazism* (1976).
Kubizek, A. *The Young Hitler I Knew* (1954).
Maser, W. *Hitler* (1973).
McKenzie, F C. *Inside Adolf* (1993).
Pallud, Jean Paul. 'Hitler on the Western Front', *After the Battle* Issue No 117 (2002).
Pool, J & S. *Who financed Hitler?* (1978).
Roberts, S H. *The House that Hitler Built* (1937).
Shirer, William. *The Rise and Fall of the Third Reich* (1960).
Taylor, J & Shaw, N. *Dictionary of the Third Reich* (1987).
Toland, John. *Adolf Hitler* (1977).
Wiedemann, F. *Der Mann, der Feldherr werden wollte* (1964).
Williams, John. 'Words on 'a lively skirmish'' *Journal of the Australian War Memorial* No 23 (Oct 1993), p21-28.
Williams, John. 'Postscript on Fromelles', *Journal of the Australian War Memorial* No 25 (Oct 1994), p36.
Williams, John. *Corporal Hitler and the Great War 1914-18: The List Regiment* (2005)
Zentner & Bedürflig. *Encyclopedia of the Third Reich* (1991).

7

Such dreadful sights

I never thought I should ever witness such dreadful sights.
—Capt. Thomas Joseph King OBE, Roman Catholic Chaplain at Fromelles

When Wagstaff's message reached the HQs of the Brigades we can only imagine the impact. Dawn now revealed what darkness had hidden. Tivey was wondering if the number of casualties in the 8th were up to the Gallipoli rate. And Pope? If we judge by his later remarks, he was greatly peeved that his victorious 14th Brigade had to be withdrawn because the others failed. But Elliott, mercurial and marvellous, was at the Front helping back the survivors of the 15th, and all at once shaking hands, embracing, weeping and muttering that it was not his fault, *'this murderous mistake'*.

Whilst for most of the week the mornings had been misty and damp, 20 July broke clear, warm and with near perfect visibility, everybody could see and hear everything. Those things they saw and heard would visit them for the rest of their lives.

We turn first to the medical services which had been in full swing since midday on 19 July, when the victims of the early bombardment began to arrive, victims both of their own and enemy artillery it has to be said. An outline of these arrangements is essential to understanding the aftermath of the battle, supplementing it with extracts from doctors' reports and other material. The medical history of Fromelles was not brought together until 1940 with the publication of Volume II of A G Butler's *Official History of Australian Army Medical Services in the War 1914–1918*. Butler was born in Queensland in 1872 of English parents. He graduated from Cambridge with degrees in surgery and medicine in 1899. Back in Australia he joined the Moreton Regiment, he married and the couple had a daughter in 1908. He went to Gallipoli as RMO of 9th Bn, where he gained enormous respect as he did in France throughout 1916 and 1917. All this to demonstrate that when he was appointed to the task of writing the medical history he had suitable experience, both medical and military. But Colonel Butler was a doctor, not an historian, and so wanted to produce a book that examined treatments and medical progress that the extreme contingencies of war uniquely provided for. However, Bean and others who took it upon themselves to guide him wanted

HIS TRUE SELF

When, as light came up on 20 July and the party which had been trying to get the Rhondda sap across No-Man's Land was called back, Pte William Boyce 3022, 58th Bn remembered his return:

This was the time when 'Pompey' Elliott disclosed his true self ... it was breaking day when we came in and 'Pompey' Elliott was there with tears running down his face, apologising for the mix up ... I don't know how far we got with the trench it was dark ... but he was right at the head of where we started to dig our sap. He was very, very upset ... it was daylight then, 'don't blame me for this', he said 'this is wrong, it's not my fault', he was definitely very upset.

SUCH DREADFUL SIGHTS

Just after the battle the front and communication trenches were filled with either German prisoners or our dead and wounded. The first aid posts, the dressing stations and the hospitals were crowded with dying and wounded, and the 'padres' did wonderful work under very trying conditions. I met the Catholic chaplain, Father King, who had been up there three days and three nights giving spiritual ministration to the wounded members of his flock and reading burial services. 'It is too terrible,' he said to me, his eyes full of tears, 'I never thought I should ever witness such dreadful sights.'

—Capt. W J Denny
5th Division Artillery
The Diggers

FOR HUMANITY'S SAKE
25 July Routine Orders. Casualties.
(a) Units are reminded that the lists of names of killed, wounded and missing permitted on form A.F.B.213 are the lists cabled to Australia by communication to next of kin. Hence the need for humanity's sake of accuracy.
(b) Forms A.F.B.213 which are due toward the end of this week must include properly classified ('killed', 'wounded', 'missing', etc.) all those whose names are not on the last A.F.B.213 rendered. Reasonable assurance of death is required before describing anyone as 'killed'.
(c) It is reported that in the recent engagement one Battalion Orderly Room Clerk and a number of rolls went forward into the fight. This may mean loss of all records and consequent utter confusion in reporting casualties. On no account is the Orderly Room Clerk or the records to go forward so far as to risk their being lost.

THE BRITISH MEDICAL HISTORY
Published between 1922 and 1924 its Editor was Major General Sir William Grant Macpherson (1858–1927) who in his introduction states that Edmonds read both the manuscript and proof and Macpherson was '*deeply indebted to him and to his staff for valuable assistance, criticism and advice*'. This meant that Edmonds must have cleared all the medical material very early on. The work consists of four volumes of General History (2240 pages), two volumes on Diseases, two volumes on Hygiene, two volumes on Surgery and one on Pathology. In 1931 a volume dealing with Casualties and Statistics was published. Bearing in mind the quantity of maps, charts, photographs used, it is obvious no expense was spared.

NO FURTHER INCIDENT OF NOTE
In the British Medical History, Fromelles is dealt with in three pages, the vast majority concerning Australian work and casualty figures, with tables of casualties, percentage of wounds [continued opposite]

a history of the events showing more than anything else how the medical services served the AIF. With such a difference of view it is no wonder that the original two year contract in 1922 was never met, and it was not until 1938 that the first volume was published, and volume II in 1940 and III in 1943.

Why Butler floundered has been variously attributed to his own stubbornness, personality clashes and poor writing ability. But there can be little doubt that from 1922 to 1924 Butler would have been aware of the British *Medical History of the War,* some eleven volumes edited by Major General Sir William G Macpherson, covering the General History, with specialist volumes on Diseases, Surgery, Pathology and Hygiene. The thoroughness and detail of Macpherson's work is astounding and the devotion and confidence that he must have inspired in every serving doctor is obvious by the scope and quality of the information they provided while their memories were good. Butler must have wondered quite what was left to say, and the longer he dithered the more doctors died and only the statistics lived on.

The tiredness of the author is very apparent in the chapter on '*Trench Warfare and the Battle of Fromelles*'. Most of what Butler wrote of the battle was simply taken from Ellis and Bean, together with some statistics from Macpherson. In between these pieces Butler gave some important information on just how the network of medical services worked at Fromelles, as well as in the Flanders area generally during May and June. This was supported by four excellent maps, as Butler had to show exact locations of Aid Posts, roads, etc. These provide a better guide to behind-the-line areas than any map in Bean, Ellis or Edmonds. Ellis printed a list showing '*the anatomical distribution of wounds*', which means the material was available in 1919. Whereas Macpherson gave a table '*percentage of wounds according to location*' and wrote '*the officers commanding the field ambulances kept careful records of the nature of wounds...*' Macpherson also printed the '*wounded ... through dressing stations*' later reproduced by Butler. That the wounds had been examined in such thoroughness during the battle says much for the Australian Medical Services. But that others were less precise in listing the dead and prisoners led Bean to call them all casualties. It also means that as the wounds had been examined with this thoroughness at that time the rest of the material Butler quoted must have also been available then, as much of it deals with wounds. It is one of the dilemmas of Bean's history that he always used an 'all-in' casualty figure which not only gave a false picture of the event, but was a totally useless statistic.

The first part of Butler's chapter covers May and June when the AIF was new to France, and by June had sustained significant losses, mostly in raids or as a result of enemy artillery bombardment, more statistics that Bean decided not to print, but producing a figure of 7981 by his style.

Casualties of AIF on Western Front to 30 June 1916

Battle Casualties		**Non-Battle Casualties**	
Killed in action	418	Died of Disease	51
Died of wounds	178	Accidentally killed	24
Died of gas poisoning	2	Sick	5437
Wounded in action	1725	Accidentally injured	40
Gassed	9	Self-inflicted injuries	23
Shell Shock	50		
POWs	24		

Such medical services required to deal with these earlier losses meant that there was an established system by mid-July. When the 5th Division's line was lightly held by the 57th and 58th Bns, Regimental Aid Posts (RAP) were at Cellar Farm Avenue and Pinney's Avenue respectively. These cleared through Advanced Dressing Stations (ADS) at Rouge de Bout and Croix Blanche to the Main Dressing Station (MDS) at Fort Rompu, staffed by 8th Field Ambulance, and in the battle handled casualties from the left of the Australian line ie, 8th Bde. Another MDS was set up at Bac St Maur, staffed by 14th and 15th Field Ambulance and responsible for the right of the line, ie 14th and 15th Bdes. Both, according to Butler's findings, were very well equipped and safe from enemy action, and when the test came, performed brilliantly and valiantly. The real problems, or as Butler saw it '*the medical interest in the battle*', was the collecting of the wounded and their clearance first by stretchers and then by wheeled or horse drawn vehicles to an MDS. The first part depended on an enthusiastic but gradually wilting group of bearers, whilst the second part largely relied on 50 motor ambulances, 21 of which were loaned to 5th Division: Butler noted '*whose motor transport had not yet arrived*'. It was these ambulances that were often able to clear the wounded from as near to the front as Bn HQ—ie Le Trou Aid Post, in the hamlet of Le Trou, 15th Bde's Field HQ. Butler was not without an opinion about this arrangement:

> Like the plans of the battle itself the arrangements made by the ADMS (Col C H W Hardy) for clearing his front were unusual. No single field ambulance was charged with the sole duty of controlling clearance from the front, instead different sectors of it were allotted to each unit and 'definite routes were arranged and set apart.

NO FURTHER INCIDENT OF NOTE (contd)

according to locality and number of wounded treated.

The British side of things was described thus:

The number of wounded admitted to the field ambulances of the 61st Division was approximately 934. Their collection and evacuation were carried out without difficulty and smoothly. The stretcher cases were brought to regimental aid posts at Red House and Hougomont by regimental stretcher bearers on stretchers or wheeled stretcher carriers. The light cases went on foot to a collecting station at Laventie East, and were taken thence in horse ambulance wagons to a walking wounded dressing station at La Gorgue established by a detachment of the 2/3rd South Midland Field Ambulance. From there they were conveyed in cars of No. 13 M.A.C. to No. 9 and the West Riding Casualty Clearing Stations in Lillers, where they entrained. The stretcher cases were taken to an advanced dressing station at Laventie, and were then removed in the motor ambulance cars of the field ambulances to a main dressing station at La Gorgue, where a tent division of the 2/1st and 2/3rd South Midland Field Ambulances was employed. They were conveyed thence by No. 2 M.A.C. to No. 7 and No. 2 London C.C.Ss. at Merville for entraining.

There was no further incident of note during this subsidiary action, and the front over which the attack was made became quiet immediately afterwards.

THE HOSPITAL BARGES OF 61st DIVISION

20 July AM: Sent up two more barges to Merville and directed that 2 of the 3 there should be filled and sent off at once. PM: Number of wounded admitted to Field Ambulances of 61st Division since 6 pm yesterday—920, from whole army the total was 1015. The number evacuated from whole army 1228.

—War Diary. Divisional Medical Service. First Army

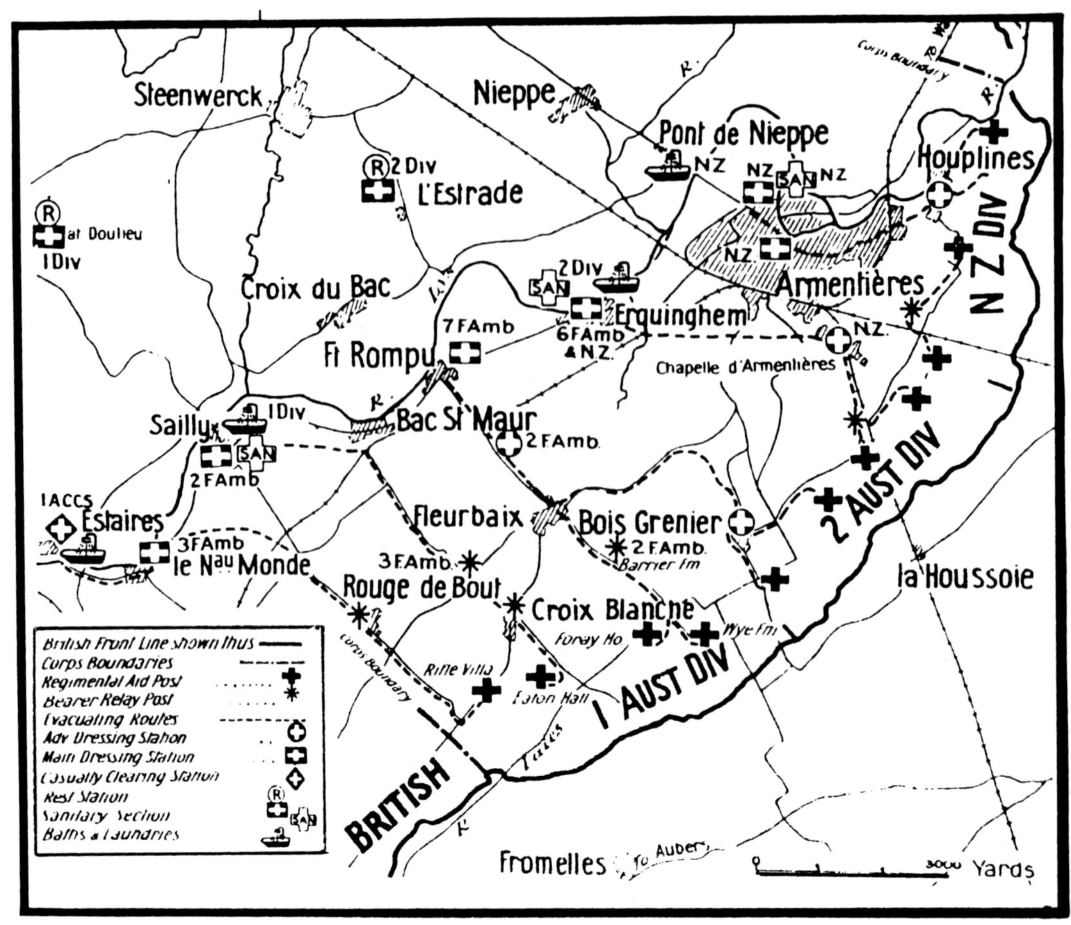

The 'Nursery' Front during the tenure of I Anzac, June 1916, showing medical arrangements.

Colonel C H W HARDY

Charles Henry William Hardy of Ballarat was born in 1861 and educated at Wesley College and Melbourne Grammar School, entering the University of Melbourne in 1879, graduating MBBS. His first appointment was in 1883 and he retired as Lieut Col AMC in 1912. He joined up in March 1915, served at Gallipoli, then Egypt, arriving in France in June 1916. In November he went down with trench fever and was in hospital in UK for three months. He never returned to action. He died on 4 April 1941.

The RPAs at Pinney's Avenue and Cellar Farm were complemented by those at Rifle Villa and Eaton Hall much further back, but described by Butler as '*all were well stocked with extra dressings and comforts*'. However, he was less pleased with the liaison arrangements between ambulance bearer officers and the RMOs: '*Appears to have been defective*', he wrote. This concerned the problems of clearing the casualties from the RAP to the loading posts, meaning that there was a huge 'log jam' at the RAPs. Hardly surprising regardless of the arrangements, when one considers the workload, and its intensity. It would seem that around midnight serious difficulties were being experienced. The 14th Bde signalled:

> *numbers of casualties exceeds the capacity of the medical staff and stretcher bearers. Our old line very full of wounded.*

To assist, a call was put out to the New Zealand Division on the left of 8th Bde and they sent '*substantial help in officers and bearers*', and to quote Butler '*the 184th Bde ... lent a hand*', a piece of information not noted by Bean, but mentioned by Ellis who also records the names of the various senior medical officers concerned in the action.

By 4.45 am however '*all was going most satisfactorily and that there were then no further bearers or medical officer wanted*'. But they had forgotten about 15th Bde no longer in action at this time like the 8th and 14th, and represented on the battlefield only by wounded and dead.

> *There is still a large number of men wounded during the action awaiting to be dealt with.*

This message, timed at 7.12 am, was two hours after the attack had been officially ended. The CO of 14th Field Ambulance came to see for himself and reported '*that whereas the wounded who had reached the dressing stations were being evacuated satisfactorily, the front line and the battlefield itself, through shortage of regimental bearers and their exhaustion, had certainly not been cleared*'. Bearing in mind the last 15th Bde attack had been at 9 pm the previous night, the twelve hour delay could not have been very helpful to the seriously

THE RMOS AT FROMELLES

8th FA: Col A E Shepherd
8th Bde: Capt. H R Catford
29th Bn: Capt. H A Irving
30th Bn: Capt. A M Langan *
then Capt. F C Wooster
31st Bn: Capt. E Russell *
32nd Bn: Capt. E W Woods (?)
14th FA: Lieut Col A H Tebbutt
14th Bde: Major H A Wyllie
53rd Bn: Capt. C Cosgrove
54th Bn: Capt. F M Farrer
55th Bn: Capt. A J Mollison (?)
56th Bn: Capt. K H Grieve
15th FA: Lieut Col A Horne
15th Bde:
57th Bn: Capt. H Rayson
58th Bn: Capt. F Boothroyd
59th Bn: Capt. G M Parker
60th Bn: Capt. F W D Collier
5th Pioneer Bn: Major E F Lind

* wounded

Scheme of clearance from Fromelles sector, July 1916.

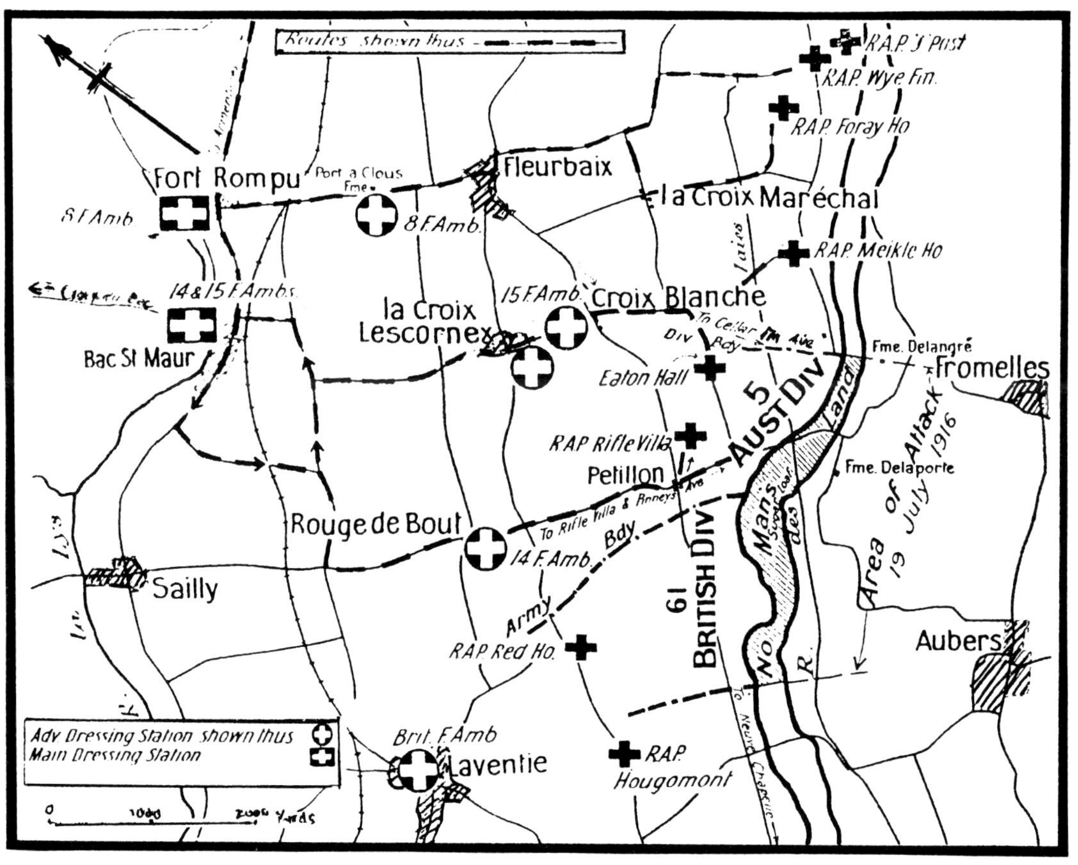

BIG CHANCE
Pte Algernon Francis Bell 3239 59th Bn was buried on the Boulogne East Cemetery (Grave VIII B 164) one of the cemeteries which took those who died of wounds in the major hospitals there. The son of William and Georgina Bell of Lakes Entrance, Algernon was a fireman aged 25, and when wounded in No-Man's Land in the first charge, took out his diary and wrote: '*July 19. 7 o'clock at night, big chance. Wounded in arm and leg. Going to try and crawl back to trenches tonight.*'

He succeeded, and survived until 24 July when he died of wounds at Boulogne.

NEW ZEALAND ASSISTANCE
While Butler made passing reference to New Zealand help only Macpherson spelt it out, they sent forward '*2 medical officers, 40 other ranks and 7 motor ambulance cars at 12.30 am on the morning of the 20th*'.

wounded, a point taken up by Butler in his summary. And one has to ask why 15th and 14th Bdes' casualties went through the same RAPs, whilst 8th Bde had its own system: just another example of the power of Tivey in lobbying for his men? There were three RMOs working at Cellar Farm on 8th Bde casualties, and five at Pinney's Avenue, both later supported by forward posts on Pinney's Avenue at the front, and Mine Avenue again at the front. The latter was abandoned when the RMO was wounded. However, due to the extraordinary efforts and bravery of everybody, the situation of the accessible wounded was reasonably satisfactory by 10 am, the trenches, dugouts and outposts having been cleared.

Firsthand reports on how this was done would have provided a gripping narrative had they been recorded within a few years of 1916. It is not clear how successful Butler was in contacting doctors who were at Fromelles, and the two he did, he used only as footnotes. However, what he did elicit from them after 25 years is of real interest.

We start with Capt. Hugh Rayson who was awarded the MC for his work at Fromelles, and when Butler found him was in a practice, Rayson and Waterhouse at Manilla, NSW. He recalled his time as RMO of 57th Bn, beginning by saying

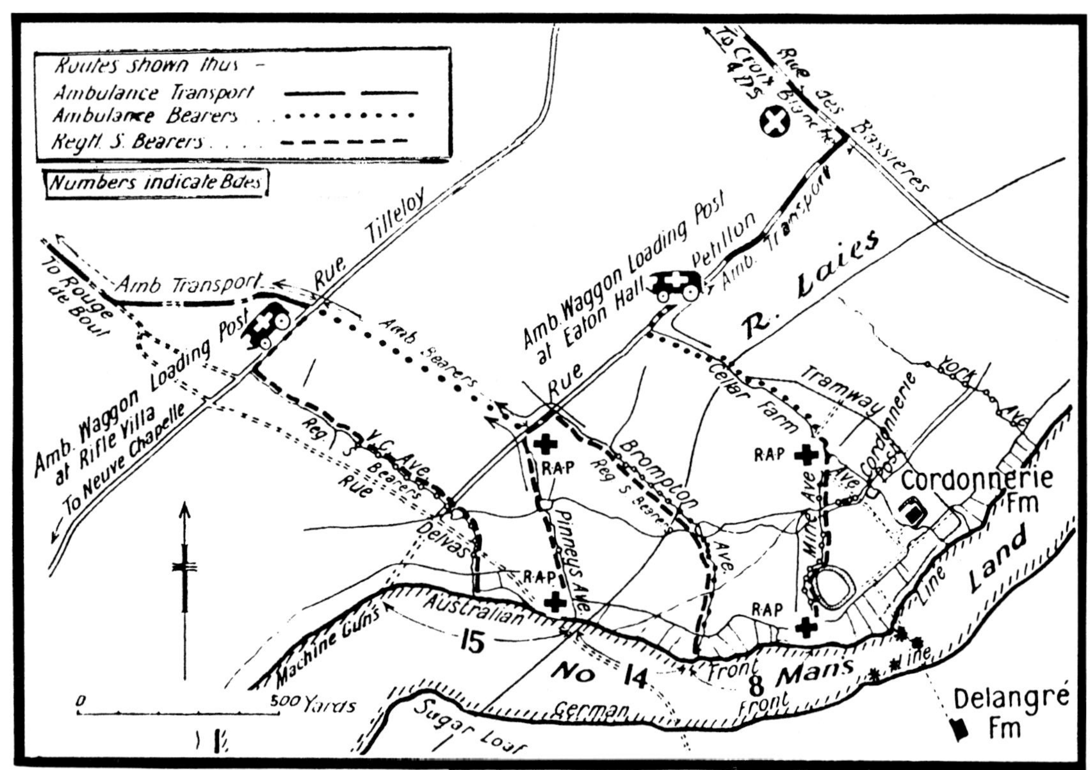

Collection and clearance at the Battle of Fromelles, 19–20 July 1916.

he had just come back (from leave?) and he went into the line with the second half of the 57th in the early hours of 20 July.

On my arrival there was a great congestion of wounded; there was a steady stream from the front line but there was great difficulty in getting them away ... owing to the shortage of bearers ...

The shortage of bearers from the front line to the Aid Post (for of course the regimental bearers were completely swamped with their task) was largely overcome by help from combatant troops after the action was over.

During the forenoon of the 20th I remember speaking to Brig General Elliott of the shortage of bearers ... he took steps immediately to have a number of men detailed for this duty, and with their assistance, the congestion was overcome. The light railway line which ran from the road near Bn HQ was of considerable help in clearing the wounded.

Wounded continued to arrive from the line in a varying stream until sometime on 21st. Just before nightfall on that day a search was made of dugouts in the line of supports and front line when a number of wounded were evacuated. During the next week wounded continued to come down as a result of the battle of 19th, these men had been rescued from No-Man's Land. As far as I can remember the last man recovered alive reached my Post 9 or 10 days after the battle. He was wounded in both legs and one arm. He told me he managed to drag himself to a shell hole in which there was a little water. He had not been able to reach the water himself, but had been able to keep his thirst down by sucking a strip of tunic which he soaked in the shell hole water; by sucking nearly continuously, he had been able to get just sufficient water to keep him alive.

An outstanding feature of my experience during the operation was the truly marvellous fortitude of the men who had been wounded. I can hardly remember one man complaining, even though in great pain. I found one man in the front line about two days after the battle who had the lower part of his face shot away; the lower and upper jaws, nose and I think one eye destroyed. By signs he made me understand that he wanted a drink. It was literally impossible to decide where to put the water bottle. And yet he was on his feet attempting to seek help.

Capt. F W D Collier had been the RMO of 60th Bn and wrote from his practice in Bank Chambers, corner Hunter and Bolton Streets, Newcastle, NSW. He and Rayson worked together until 21 July and his frank memories of the physical and practical situation complements Rayson's recollections of suffering men.

About one week before that, the 60th Bn of which I was RMO had arrived in billets ... it never went into the front line before the attack, though I had visited Rayson RMO 57th in his Aid Post just behind the support line and just off Pinney's Avenue.

On Sunday the Officers of the 60th went down to the front line to inspect where they were to attack ... there were no trenches in that area because of water, only a sandbag barricade about 9 feet high, 12 feet across at base and 6 feet across the top in two's at a time.

I had been ordered to go over with the last wave but that was changed and I was to stay back and clear up till a new position was captured, and then go over. But I had orders that my sixteen regimental

MAKE WAY PLEASE

A number of men remembered seeing a legless character in the trenches. One vivid image is that of Lieut T C Barbour: he was in correspondence with Bean about the battle and wrote:

I should very much like to know the name of the digger who after having both legs blown off, cheered on his pals, and I believe never moved until he was assured that the left flank had been carried. On my way across I met this man crawling back on his stumps, he made a plaintive request of 'make way please', polite and game to the last. He was last seen slowly moving into a sap where he no doubt perished. I heard many inquiries of him later, but he was not seen again.

NEW CEMETERIES

Routine Orders 22 July.

Cemeteries. New cemeteries have been established at the following localities:

(i) Bac St Maur (G12.d.6.2)
(ii) Sailly-sur-la-Lys (G22.c.2.6)

Should it be desired to inter more than ten corpses in either of these cemeteries at any one time, Divisional Headquarters must be advised eight hours prior to the proposed hour of interment so as to permit of special arrangements being made.

The next day, 23 July, gave a list of cemeteries available (to date) for Military burials.

i.	Estaires Communal Cemetery	
ii.	Sailly-sur-la-Lys	(G22.c.2.6)
iii.	Laventie	(G34.d.9.6)
iv.	Rue du Bois	(N2.d.3.9)
v.	Rue Petillon	(N3.b.3.3)
vi.	Rue David	(H34.d.8.8)
vii	Wye Farm	(H35.b.9.1)
viii.	Brewery Orchard	(H30.b.6.9)
ix.	Ration Farm (New)	(I19.b.8.6)
x.	Erquinghem Communal Cemetery	(H.d.4)
xi.	Bac St Maur	(G12.d.6.2)

Apart from any register of burials kept by the Cemetery Authorities, O's C Divisional Formations and Units will arrange for a proper record to be maintained of all burials in authorised cemeteries, and also of isolated burials.

WITHOUT A SINGLE HITCH

The way the British dealt with their casualties was the subject of a brief medical report sent to Mackenzie after the battle. Here, in its entirety, under the simple heading 'The 61st Division Operation for July 19', it is either an exercise in deception or a report from the only man at Fromelles on top of his job:

All arrangements worked perfectly and without a single hitch. At no period was the accommodation strained and the evacuation from the Main Dressing Stations and Divisional Collecting Station, where the slighter cases were dealt with, was most efficiently carried out by the No. 2 Motor Ambulance Convoy and No. 13 Motor Ambulance Convoy respectively. By 9.00 am on the 20th, I was able to report that the whole of the trenches were clear of wounded. The total number of wounded dealt with was 977 including 46 officers.

Signed James C Young
[signature not clear]

DISPOSAL OF EFFECTS

With the Routine Orders of 25 July came a schedule of arrangements for the disposal of the effects of Officers and Men.

The kits of deceased or missing officers were handled by Cox & Co. of 16 Charing Cross, London, whereas their 'small articles of sentimental or intrinsic value or money out of the kits' were to be sent to DAG 3rd Echelon. Kits of the sick and wounded officers went first to Boulogne then to AIF Admin HQ, Horseferry Road, Westminster, but curiously their articles of sentimental value etc. went to Cox and Co.

There was no provision for the kits of NCOs an ORs, but their 'small articles … or money out of kits' went to DAG 3rd Echelon if the owners were deceased or missing. The small articles of the sick and wounded went to D.A.D.R.T. (AMFO) Le Havre.

bearers were to go over with the last wave and collect wounded at once. I think now this was a great mistake but it was my first battle. Nine out of my sixteen bearers were knocked out soon after they jumped over and I never saw any more of them after that night. We worked all that afternoon (19th), that night and all next day without ceasing. We could not show a light and when we came to a wounded man we would ask him where he was hit and feel for his wound with hands covered in dried blood and mud. there was no time and no water to wash hands, and of course the wounded had their first dressing at the regimental aid post.

The casualties were so bad that a wounded sergeant told me that though he was twelfth man to climb the scaling ladder on the parapet he was the first one over from his ladder. The 60th went in 880 strong and came out 80 strong next am and I was senior officer of the battalion. The padre (who was in the thick of it and got the MC) and the transport officer and I were the only ones not casualties. The two officers who took over the battalion next am were both wounded and both lieutenants.

We had enough orderlies for the dressing, but the main problem was evacuation. Another problem we had was the bearers (never in action before) brought us serious cases first (those obviously dying).

These last comments were the main finding of Butler, but he was not a person to allocate blame probably being too wise in the ways of war not to understand the terrible tensions of the medical staff. However, he did not mince his words when summing up the battle:

The casualties sustained in the operation are shown in the following table. They are a measure at once of the extraordinary medical problem and of the cost to the AIF of this 'feint'—really a subsidiary attack, wholly futile and unnecessary, made by inexperienced troops against unduly distant positions with insufficient preparation, particularly by the artillery, which itself was insufficient for the enterprise. They represent a casualty list of 50 per cent of the troops engaged. Normally in the AIF the proportion of wounded and died of wounds, to killed in action, was approximately as four to one. In the 15th Brigade at Fromelles it was less than one and a half to one. This increased proportion is due to men being shot to death as they lay in No-Man's Land, or dying there through lack of assistance.

The small number of medical casualties, one officer and four other ranks wounded, is due to the comparatively slight shelling of the ambulance bearer routes in rear. Regimental bearers working in the front area lost very heavily, more so, possibly, than in any other engagement of the AIF.

It seems strange that only Butler printed any meaningful statistics about the casualties of the battle. Ellis, as already noted, only ran the anatomical distribution of wounds, but he stated that it was from a list compiled by Lieut Col Horne of 15th Field Ambulance and gave numbers, not percentages, as Butler did and who implied that the table applied to the whole division. Both Ellis' and Butler's figures are given in the margin:

Butler has seven 'sites', whilst Ellis has eight, and Ellis' figures do not produce Butler's percentages. On this whole matter Bean ducked the issue, instead supplying a list of casualties per battalion to produce the grand total of 5533, and in no way provided a definitive total of dead, died of wounds, wounded, and prisoners. He must have had access to these figures and they would have taken very little more space: in fact the one line of totals printed by Butler would have been sufficient. One must wonder about the motive for such an omission.

Casualties sustained by the 5th Division at Fromelles between noon on 19th July and 8 pm of 21st July

	Killed in action	Died of wounds	Prisoners of war	Wounded in action	Total
8th Inf. Bde ..	477	51	166	1086	1780
14th " ..	438	58	283	948	1727
15th " ..	726	98	5	904	1733
Other units ..	60	9	16	208	293
Totals	1701	216	470	3146	5553

Wounded passed through main dressing stations:-

	Walking	Sitting	Lying down	Total
8th Fld. Amb.	17	211	358	586
14th "	453	324	637	1414
15th "	347	373	557	1277
Totals	817	908	1552	3277

Reports in letters, diaries and histories about the morning of 20 July are most contradictory. The Germans said it was foggy, whilst the Australians remembered it as clear. There is confusion in many cases between the mornings of 20 July and 21 July. The latter, even to the 5th Division War Diarist became the morning after the battle. All quite understandable. Some thought the artillery bombardments continued till near noon. Perhaps it was not directed at No-Man's Land because there are so many accounts of men searching No-Man's Land for missing friends. There is little evidence that the German artillery was really concentrating on the Australian front line or behind it, as none of those doing the rescuing that morning complained of much harassment. But there had been a serious amount of German machine gun work directed at the retreating sections of 8th and 14th Brigades early in the morning.

The most insidious threat was the compulsive snipers forever in search of careless men in the trenches, stretcher

BUTLER'S LIST

Percentage of wounds according to site:

Head and neck	16.67 %
Upper limbs	31.79 %
Lower limbs	31.00 %
Thorax	7.93 %
Back	2.22 %
Abdomen	4.27 %
Shell Shock	6.12 %
	100.00

ELLIS'S LIST

Anatomical distribution of wounds:

Head and neck	328
Shoulders	99
Upper limbs	424
Chest	70
Back	91
Abdomen	48
Lower Limbs	496
Shell Shock	121
	1669

In Australia in 1978 there are still men who are in hospital from that time. I have visited patients whose periods of lucidity are interrupted by weeks and months of terror, fear that pushes them over the lip of sanity.

—Patsy Adam-Smith
The Anzacs (1978)

FELT MUCH BETTER

Under the heading 'Feeding' Col Hardy wrote: *Soyer Stoves were placed at all posts and at Main Dressing Stations to provide hot water for dressing wounds and soup for patients and personnel. These were of the greatest benefit. Men who came in shivering, cold and tired felt much better after a drink of soup.*

OUT IN NO-MAN'S LAND ABOUT TWO DAYS

On the march up to the front Freeman saw the body of a young Australian lying on the side of the road '*like a dog in the gutter*'. This caused him to resolve to kill as many Germans as he could. He recalled how the night sky was full of flares and star shells—floating down on little parachutes. This confirmed what others remembered, it being daylight at night so numerous were the flares: which was how the Germans were able to observe the feverish activity in the nights before the 19th.

Frank Freeman as a 60th man went forward on that morning '*a lovely sunny day*', full of prospects of victory because he, and all the others had been told, that they were supported by 6000 guns along a two mile front which would, before the battle, destroy all the enemy's barbed wire and clear a way through. As Freeman remembered it was in bright sunlight with a screen of dust before them that the order at last came to attack. '*The Officer shouted and we went over in three waves, three minutes apart— was in the third*'. The man on one side of Freeman fell immediately, the one on the other side shouted he was blinded, '*shell fragments - hot steel—went so close to my face I could feel the heat*'. He was hit in the foot and went down into a shell hole, '*half full of wounded, dying and dead*'. He lost consciousness. When he came to it was dark and '*complete and utter silence ... uncanny ... I'm not sure how long I was out in No-Man's Land, about two days. They took in the badly wounded first. The stretcher bearers worked for three days ... the Germans did not fire a single shot*'.

When Freeman was evacuated to Southampton, and thence to Newcastle-on-Tyne his wound had become dangerously septic. He was in hospital for 5 months, 3 in bed and 2 on crutches. At the end of that he returned to London, was fitted out in a new uniform and sent back to the 60th Battalion in France.

—Pte F E Freeman 3529, B Coy 60th Bn.

COURTESY OF ROD WILSON FROM AN INTERVIEW WITH 'FRANK' IN 1978.

parties getting too close, those salvaging rifles and the demented wounded whose insanity might have become contagious in such a situation. The moaning of the wounded and dying punctuated by shrieks of pain, calls of desperation, together with the banging together of pieces of metal by men who had no voice left, most seeking the attention of stretcher bearers, but a few pleading for executioners; that was the background noise for the rescuers.

Whilst not detracting from the bravery of the men who made the attack, they *were* driven by a certain collective compulsion to act. And there were the Trench Police behind them if at the last moment their spirits wilted or their judgement caused them to pause and think. But none of this applied to those who followed them with stretchers, who as the battle waxed and waned, went again and again looking for wounded.

And of course when the magnitude of the losses became apparent there were the others, men from all parts of the army, who in many cases just went out into No-Man's Land to do what they could, regardless of the consequences. It seems to this writer that of the many heroes of Fromelles, none were beyond these men, a feeling supported somewhat by the number of awards for gallantry given for the work. But of course by the very nature of the event what was recognised and praised was the tip of the iceberg. Butler's figures of 1552 'lying down' wounded, plus 908 'sitting wounded', plus those who died on the way back provide a figure of around 2500 stretcher cases (Bean says 2357 in the first 26 hours and by 21 July a total of 3984), over say a 30 hour period—100 an hour on average, but of course not so in reality because at peak it would have been much higher: say 400 an hour, split between three main clearing stations. Then consider two men to a stretcher, but on occasions four, and there has to be at peak, what?, eight hundred men engaged in this work. The gravity of the situation is well described by Pte Colley-Priest 6618, 8th Field Ambulance, see opposite, '*... our first taste of line work ...*' But it is the casual remarks of others in their diaries and letters that show the shock the event actually provided to the vast majority who had never witnessed such carnage. But Lieut David Doyle of 60th Bn, not quite 22, in his first battle, was coping well:

> Most awful scene of slaughter imaginable. At one time I had to get a fatigue party to clear the dead from communication trench ... we went back ... leaving dead and dying in No-Man's Land ... Of D Coy only myself and one man left. Things that impressed me were the bravery of the men ... Some horrible sights and some pitiful ones. The single

[continued page 236]

… our first taste of line work …

Private L W Colley-Priest 6618, 8th Field Ambulance, was born in 1890. He was with the unit since its inception at Malcham Park, Adelaide 4 August 1915 and went with them first to Egypt, then to France. The following section comes from a draft of the history of the unit. The history was published in 1919. Colley-Priest, who was awarded the MM died in 1927.

The following four days were quiet ones, practically no casualties passed through our station at Fort Rompu. On the 15th of July however a great number of patients arrived. Poor fellows, some of them are crippled for life. We were just beginning to realise what war means.

Those who were on duty at Port Aucluse had a rather trying time on the 18th (sic) inst, as the enemy shelled the vicinity severely. At 10 pm word came through that the Australians were doing well, a small batch of prisoners passed through the station about midnight. At 2 am word came through that every available man in the Ambulance was to proceed to the line at once. It was rather a long march, about 5 miles. The sky was lit up with flares and lights of numerous colours and the roar of the Artillery and the rattle of machine guns was terrific. The terrible battle of Fromelles (sometimes called Fleurbaix) was in progress. As we gradually got nearer the scene of action, the noise was deafening (but of course after a few more stunts we soon got used to this). On arriving at the Regimental Aid Post we found a terrible congestion of wounded. The sight was a ghastly one, and of course we were all raw recruits, in regards to this work, some of us took it rather badly. Most of the bearers worked 36 hours and many daring deeds were done by a great number of them, but they are too numerous to mention. Hundreds of wounded were lying about in the yard of the farm house (which was being used as an RAP) and along the road, so of course we all set to work immediately to get them away to a place of safety. Luckily the Loading Post was only ¾ of a mile away, and here scores of cars took the cases on. After being here about half an hour word came through that there were crowds of wounded men in the trenches needing attention. Immediately a great number of bearers went down there to get these men out. The entrance to the trenches was a narrow gap which started about ½ mile away from the RAP. I went down with a chap who had been there before, and he gave me plenty of warning when approaching dangerous places. Here we had to run like blazes as there were generally a few machine gun bullets whirring by. The sap wound in and out like a maze for about a mile and a half, and we continually passed bearers bringing out the wounded. On reaching the old front line trenches, I looked upon a terrible sight, Good God it was terrible, dead Australians lying about, in fact they were piled up four and five deep, had to pick our way over them to reach the wounded. One could scarcely call it a trench at all, as the barricades were all battered down. The trip back to the Aid Post was a strenuous one, as the sap was so narrow and had so many turns in it that it was a hard job to carry a stretcher. At some points the stretcher had to be carried over our heads, and the ground was also very uneven. I took two hours to carry a chap out of the trenches, and on arriving at the Aid Post the congestion seemed to be worse in spite of all the extra men working. A great number of the men of the Transport and Tent Division Section were stretcher bearing also. The bearers etc. continued to go down the trenches and bring up the wounded. Whilst the wounded were being brought up from the front line the Officers and men at the Aid Post did excellent work dressing the wounds etc. Major Lind, Captain Irving, Captain Wooster were on duty at the Aid Post to which I was attached. Naturally good work was progressing at the Main Dressing Station, Fort Rompu which was in charge of Col Shepherd. Every casualty passed through this station. When one considers that 8000 casualties in 36 hours in this battle, the Ambulance did excellent work in dealing with such a vast number. The 59th Battalion had a roll call in a paddock not far from the Aid Post, and it was heart rending when we were told of the very few who answered their name. At 10 pm the majority of the Ambulance bearers etc. were relieved and we proceeded back to the station at Fort Rompu for a few hours sleep. Passed crowds of troops on their way to the trenches. Naturally we all slept well and in the morning all were at work again loading and unloading cars. The yard in the Main Dressing Station was just a mass of stretcher cases, it must have been another terrible slaughter during the night. Another lot of bearers went out to the trenches again at 10 am, but fortunately on arriving at the Aid Post, they found that all the wounded had been cleared from the trenches. This was certainly excellent news, and they returned to the Dressing Station in good spirits. Although the trenches were clear of wounded there was still great congestion at the Main Station, so every one gave a hand to get the wounded attended to and placed into the Ambulance cars. Some of the poor fellows were in a bad way, as they had been lying out in No-Man's Land for 36 hours, without food or water, yet there is hardly a murmur out of them. At midday, the rush was over and all the wounded had been sent on to different hospitals. A sigh of relief seemed to go round the unit when the rush ceased and the place was clear at last. It was our first taste of line work, and was certainly a warm one and those that worked in the forward area did splendidly, as it was their christening under shell fire.

Only one casualty 13588 Pte C Beeston wounded and 6721 Pte T W Howard MM.

FROMELLES?
THAT WAS THE FINISH

Cpl Frank Parker, 634 of 57th Bn, and late of 5th Bn, made something of a reputation in the 1980s on television for his vivid phrases about the war: '*Gallipoli—only the dead forgot it*' and '*Fromelles—not a battle, a bloodbath*'. And contrary to the official view, on arrival in Marseilles, '*we had night out ... we cleared out, two or three of us ... they never missed us ... we had no money but we found somebody who did have some*'. He also had different memories about the journey north, '*they put us in cattle trucks ...*' and the billets '*... stables full of fleas, bugs ...*' and Fromelles:

> *Fromelles? That was the finish.*
> *I don't remember much about it ...*
> *I don't remember getting to Calais hospital ... I was shell shocked ...*
> *I didn't know anything about it until my brother (N. Parker 670 57th Bn) told me about it ... he was the last fella I saw ... I had a word with him before I got buried ... the word Jump ... whether somebody sung out to me to jump or whatever it was ... I couldn't get it out of my mind – jump. I was telling that to a priest in Calais, oh he said that was the good Lord looking after me ...*

Frank, who had enlisted 17 August 1914, returned to Australia 17 October 1916, and went to Caulfield Hospital for some time. His brother went right through the war. Frank, the last secretary of the 57th Battalion Association, died 21 July 1988, aged 94.

A THOUSAND BUTCHER-SHOPS

The sight of our trenches that next morning is burned into my brain. Here and there a man could stand upright, but in most places if you did not wish to be exposed to a sniper's bullet you had to progress on your hands and knees. If you had gathered the stock of a thousand butcher-shops, cut it into small pieces and strewn it about, it would give you a faint conception of the shambles those trenches were.

—R H Knyvett, 59th Bn
Over there with the Australians (1918)

> leg—the heap at Pinney's Avenue ... The wounded clutching at you as you passed.

No other Australian battalion was as untouched by the battle as the 57th, an extremely fortunate event. It could therefore put its full resources into rescuing the casualties of 15th Brigade, the biggest and most difficult rescue operation at Fromelles. Lieut L W Elliott, a 57th officer (no kin to 'Pompey') who never held back from difficult jobs, wrote telling of their efforts. His note about McCrae can be added to. In a letter to McCrae's family 'Pompey' Elliott told them that Marshall was responsible for bringing his body in: McCrae was buried at Rue-du-Bois Cemetery. Lieut Elliott's note about Carr however does not have a similar ending. Carr's name is at VC Corner.

> 20 July. Took over 300 yard line this morning. Shelled this morning. Front line is a frightful scene. Hundreds of men out in No-Man's Land, wounded and unable to be reached. Capt Marshall took out a party to help these and got in quite a number before the snipers opened up on them. Another party going out tonight. Dead men all over the place ...
>
> 21 July. Men busy getting wounded in from No-Man's Land. They had been out for 24 hours. We worked from dark till the fog lifted at 7 am. Saw Major McCrae and got his badges of rank which I handed to Capt Marshall. Most of the boys seem to have been shot in the legs and arms. They were great taking their turn with the stretcher bearers, those who were not so bad as others, volunteering to wait till next time, knowing that possibly the stretcher bearers might never come back to that particular spot again. Went out to see if I could find Eric Carr, but could find no trace. Was told after that he crawled back and was picked up by the stretcher bearers. He, with 4 bombers were the only ones of the 59th to reach the parapet. Going out again tonight to get in any survivors and identify discs of others.
>
> 22 July. Quiet day. Fatigue parties busy gathering equipment.
>
> 23 July. Quiet day. Very little shelling today. Can see one man out in No-Man's Land still. Party going out tonight.

Certainly one of those 57th Bn parties included Sgt Simon Fraser, whose letter of 31 July describing these times Bean thought so revealing of the digger spirit that he quoted it at length:

> I must say Fritz (*i.e.,* the German) treated us very fairly, though a few were shot at the work. Some of these wounded were as game as lions and got rather roughly handled; but haste was more necessary than gentle handling ... It was no light work getting in with a heavy weight on your back, especially if he had a broken leg or arm and no stretcher-bearer was handy. You had to lie down and get him on your back; then rise and duck for your life with a chance of getting a bullet in you before you were safe. One foggy morning in particular, I remember, we could hear someone over towards the German entanglements calling for a stretcher-bearer; it was an appeal no man could stand against, so some

of us rushed out and had a hunt. We found a fine haul of wounded and brought them in; but it was not where I heard this fellow calling, so I had another shot for it, and came across a splendid specimen of humanity trying to wriggle into a trench with a big wound in his thigh. He was about 14 stone weight, and I could not lift him on my back; but I managed to get him into an old trench, and told him to lie quiet while I got a stretcher. Then another man about 30 yards out sang out 'Don't forget me, cobber'. I went in and got four volunteers with stretchers, and we got both men in safely. Next morning at daylight, whilst observing over the parapet, I saw two figures in their shirts and no hats, running about half-way between our lines and the Germans. They were our captains, Cameron and Marshall, hunting for more wounded.

In Fraser's actual letter he wrote, '*and Marshall (VC) hunting for more wounded. Capt Marshall got his VC on the Peninsula and if Cameron does not get his here, well he damned well deserves it* ...' Marshall had an MC from Gallipoli, not a VC. Cameron got the MC for the work Fraser described. When Fraser turned to his diary where space was limited, his notes in part said:

19 July ... advanced down VC sap into Hell, found the advance had been a failure. We occupied our old line ...

20 July ... dead and wounded everywhere next morning ... the stretcher bearers going all day and wounded out in front to be brought in—had a good quiet day.

21 July ... Foggy morning, was going all night bringing in wounded. B Coy brought in 250. Brought up packs from Rifle Villa and had good sleep, first for three nights.

Simon Fraser's view of the German's conduct is given in the margin *Game As Lions* and *I Waved Him A Miss*—both extracts from his long letter of 31 July. For his work Fraser was Mentioned in Despatches.

The survival of men on the battlefield was astonishing. It was often noted: Lieut Doyle on 24 July '*three wounded men crawled in after being out since night 19/20th. Wonderful endurance*'. Then on 27 July, his 22nd birthday, he '*hunted up two men who had been in No-Man's Land 8 days*'.

The extraordinary story of 2nd Lieut J L Simpson of 60th Bn was remembered later in the war when he was put forward for the VC at Villers-Bretonneux in 1918. At Fromelles (he had been wounded on Gallipoli), Simpson nearly had his right arm cut off and the bones shattered. He held it on and walked all the way back, probably the length of VC Avenue to the Clearing Station. His arm was saved, but never regained its usefulness, not that that kept Simpson out of the AIF for long. After convalescence in Australia he set sail for the UK in July 1917, served a time in training activities before getting back to

... GAME AS LIONS ...

We were supporting when the charge was made, and had to hold our old line; the battalion who went over, met with too hot a reception and suffered severely, the distance was too far: when we came up the artillery were mixing things up a bit, high explosives and shrapnel were flying everywhere. We did a 200 yard sprint across the open, I did not think I could run so well ... a good few of my mates passed out that night; so far, three of my section have been killed and two wounded badly out of twelve.

For the next three days we did great work getting in the wounded from the front and I must say Fritz treated us very fairly. Some of these wounded were game as lions and got rather roughly handled, but haste was more necessary than gentle handling and we must have brought in over 250 men by our company alone.

—Sgt Simon Fraser 3101 57th Bn
(in letter dated 31.7.1916)

I WAVED HIM A MISS

Fritz has one very decent sniper in his lines; the other morning we could see a periscope up, so I tried a couple of shots at it. Fritz's sniper replied and struck the sandbag under my gun. I shifted my possy a few yards further down and just put my rifle over the parapet, when he pinged one into the sandbag alongside. Needless to say I cried 'Barley' and tried some shots with the periscope rifle, but I doubt that I hit anything.

This sniper you can tell Colin would be a great acquisition to our rifle club at Byaduk. The same gentleman, two days previously, had a shot at Sgt Major Knuckey and myself while looking over the parapet for a wounded man who was over near their trenches and over which two stretcher bearers had been hit trying to get in; we were not sure but it was a decoy, but he was brought in afterwards. Well, this sniper struck just a little too low for us, anyhow he made us get down and I waved him a miss.

—Sgt Simon Fraser 3101. 57th Bn
(in letter dated 31.7.1916)

France and those of his old mates who had survived. Simpson was killed 26 April 1918 at Villers-Bretonneux.

Those brought out by stretcher bearers and others went to the MDS at Bac St Maur or Fort Rompu, then after evaluation sent on to hospitals at places such as Calais by 21 July, or to England via Boulogne, being admitted the next day to a variety of hospitals from Chelmsford to Manchester. As the Rolls of Honour reveal, many of those who died of wounds as a result of Fromelles were thus buried in England.

Bean was much taken by a letter he had read from Pte Henry Eggin Williams 1800, 60th Bn, to his parents. He included it in his history, not however under Fromelles, but early in Volume III when writing of the character of the Digger. Williams who was 18 years old, from Palmer Street, Collingwood, wrote on 17 July:

> Dear Mother, The time is near at hand for a great offensive and, should I fall, I will be proud to know I did so in the cause of Righteousness and Justice... This will be a great blow to you, but cheer up ... Dad, I have kept your wishes, neither smoked nor taken liquor. Give my regards to all the boys and girls. So goodbye for a short time. Harry.

Bean of course did not have space to make a note about the press cutting he had in his file from *The Essex Weekly News* on 25 August. Severely wounded on 19 July, Williams was '*one of a detachment of wounded soldiers admitted 22 July*' to a hospital in Essex. In the three weeks Harry held onto his life he must have made a tremendous impression. He died 18 August and was buried at Chelmsford Borough Cemetery with Military Honours. The brass band of 2/7th Royal Scots attended, as did all the nurses and many patients, and the newspaper gave considerable space and prominence to the story at a time when the English wounded and dying from the Somme might have dominated those meagre wartime newspapers.

One of the more riveting stories of survival concerns Cpl Rowland Edward Lording 81, 30th Bn. He was born 20 June, 1899 therefore only a month over 16 when he enlisted 19 July 1915. He became a signaller with C Coy, served in Egypt before going to France and Fromelles. There, machine gun fire cut right across him and shrapnel went into his back. He was taken from the battlefield with both arms useless, both legs semi-paralysed, and with spinal injuries. In England he was in bed until January 1917, then partly mobile he was returned to Australia. It was said Lording had over 50 operations in 15 years, with 6 ribs removed and his right arm amputated. Through all this suffering he married, had three children, developed an accountancy business,

AT FRITZ'S FRONT DOOR

Cpl Thomas Clair Whiteside 2821 59th Bn was in the third wave and thus may have been in the group led by Capt. Liddelow, which got through the wire. After successfully getting across the Laies, he saw it as a lagoon rather than a river. Whiteside with some others had a clear run. They were under instructions '*not to stop at the enemy's front line, but to carry on to his supports.*' This he attempted describing his success, '*I arrived at Fritz's front door and was quizzing around to see if any of our fellows had knocked anywhere ... it was while trying to learn something ... that a sniper caught me. Got a nasty one on the head ... for a minute, thought I was done for.*'

Cpl T C Whiteside 2821, 59th Bn
3rd Southern General Hospital, Oxford, August 1916
COURTESY E WHITESIDE

After collecting his thoughts and finding a colleague interested in getting back, Clair Whiteside and Bill Skinner '*hustled like old nick ... had a machine gun turned on us two or three times'* till they got to the Australian barbed wire. Once through that they '*bawled out 59th and dropped down in a trench full of friends*'.

After treatment at Sailly, Clair Whiteside went to Boulogne and then to 3rd Southern General Hospital, Oxford, where he stayed till the beginning of September (see *Five Shillings A Day* opposite).

founded the 30th Bn Association, did work for limbless soldiers and wrote *There and Back* in 1935 under the pen name—A Tiveychoc. Writing of himself—Ted—in the third person, there can be little doubt that the writing of the book was a desperate effort to keep control of his mind: a battle he lost ten years later. The historian of 30th Bn, Lieut Col Sloan, noted in 1938 that '*Cpl "Rowley" Lording's ... wounds ... have failed completely to heal. As an example of human suffering, coupled with the determination to live, Lording's case is probably unique in the AIF*'. And Butler in the third volume of his work devoted a page to Lording: '*who deserves a special place among the immortals of the AIF*'.

Lording, racked by pain, became dependent on pain-killing drugs. His first marriage broke up, he remarried and just over a year later, on 1 October 1944, Lording died '*in tragic circumstances in a mental hospital*'. His name is not, of course, on the Roll of Honour at the Australian War Memorial, or anywhere else: but it truly belongs to Fromelles. And one has to wonder at the endurance of the first Mrs Lording in getting him through most of those years. Lording's book has a chapter on Fromelles which is terrifyingly evocative of the hours before 6 pm, 19 July 1916, as the signals company of 30th Bn makes its way forward, with wisecracks to keep its spirits up. Then:

> A red flag waves ahead. They stop for they have been warned of this—an 18 pounder in a shattered building is about to fire across the road. Bang! 'Christ! Look at that!' Somebody gasps. A rider coming from the opposite direction has his head blown off. 'Come on! Get a move on!' calls the guard with the red flag—then he sees too. Looking as white as death they go quickly past the gun and its convulsing victim. Bang! Again goes the 18 pounder—perhaps now a Fritz is dead.

Ted gets to the line, then out into No-Man's Land where the little band of signallers dig in.

> Crump! Bang! Crash! the shells fall. Zip zip zip—zip zip!! machine gun bullets kick up dirt around them ... zip zip! Bang! Another twisted heap of khaki hits the ground.
>
> It is Ted. He does not move. His cobbers crawl over to his side. 'Where d'you get it?' they ask him. His lips move, but they do not hear his reply. His arm is shattered and blood is gushing from his side. He cannot last much longer—they think he is going west ... Stan rolls him onto a ground sheet and drags him yard by yard towards the trench. Shell splinters tear through the sheet. The ground rocks from a nearby shell burst which almost covers them with mud. Stan drags him on ... At last they come to a sally port and he is carried on a duckboard into the trench. 'You've got the wind up' was Ted's gibe to Stan at Fleurbaix; now Stan has risked his life to bring Ted in.

[continued page 242]

DID ITS BEST

The signal section of 30th Bn was under Sgt T S Horgan which '*did its best to keep their telephone service going, but the continuous shelling made it impossible ...*' Part of his group was Cpl R E Lording who in his book *There and Back*, noted the others and what happened to them.

Of the other four signallers of 30th Bn, Jim S [possibly Pte J Sheehan—82] *was killed in the battle and Eric W* [L/Cpl E S Wright—70] *was wounded and taken prisoner. Wal C* [possibly Pte W A Cliffe—1333] *was wounded and invalided home soon after Fromelles, and Tom H* [Lieut T S Horgan] *went on to get his Commission and lose an arm at Villers-Bretonneux in 1918.*

FIVE SHILLINGS A DAY

After being seriously wounded at Fromelles Cpl Thomas Clair Whiteside 2821 59th Bn was sent to hospital in Oxford where he stayed until the beginning of September 1916. His letter home of that time contains an interesting note:

Was very suddenly shifted from Oxford (to 1st Aust. Aux. Hospital Harefield Mddx)—have since learned the reason why. As soon as patients are able to get about, the Australian authorities try to get them out of British hospitals for they pay the English Government 5/- a day for every Australian patient. On top of our usual pay it sucks up quite a bit ... It is much quieter at Harefield but ... little pay, 5/- a week and no pubs ... .

ODD LANGUAGES

Languages unknown to Regimental Censors. On 22 July Capt. Boase's contribution to Routine Orders was thus:

Letters in Welsh which cannot be censored regimentally should be sent under cover to the Chief Postal Censor, War Office. Letters in other unknown languages should be forwarded to the DCFC, GHQ with a memo stating the language used and the writer's unit.

... what I came away for ...

One of the best things that could happen to a wounded man was to be shipped to England, a 'Blighty' they called it, and it meant being subject to careful medical treatment and the abundant charity of the English.

At 35, Cpl Richard St John Kennedy 1302, 32nd Bn, was not easily impressed and when he wrote to his sister from Manchester just three days after the battle he was keen to put on a brave face. His long letter, here edited by about a third, describes some aspects of Fromelles not covered elsewhere, and his state of mind in England, again an interesting aspect of the overall event. Kennedy was the second youngest of eight children, and born in Hawthorn, 31 January 1881. He enlisted 14 July 1915, and two of his brothers were also in the AIF. Richard, then CQMS, was later killed near Fleurbaix on 24 June 1918 by an aerial bomb. His name is on the Villers-Bretonneux Memorial in the 32nd Battalion panel.

Dear Rene,

At last I have been through what I came away for, the result that I am now lying peacefully in Dear Old England with shrapnel wounds in both legs. So far I have had no examination and am not sure whether there is anything still in either foot ...

An hour before going into action I wrote you a letter ... and now I will relate a little of my wonderful experiences. To start with, I had a franc left, so made a good fellow of myself with my Section and we drank Best Wishes to everybody and then for the Trenches.

On our way up, about a couple of miles, the noise of the bombardment was terrible, and we had the good fortune to miss the shells. In the supports before going into the front line my star started and it never left me, and now if any man should thank God it is I, as how I got through was a mystery. Whilst waiting there, men were falling all round me, and it was hard to see these good men going and others got nervy and of course could not go on. In the front line, just before going over, one burst among six of us, and I was the only one who escaped, and it fell on me to fix them up the best way I could, as the poor old A.M.C. men and stretcher bearers were going for their lives. Then came the command 'Fix bayonets', and away over the parapet we started, and if ever there were such things as heroes, the men were, as not one flinched but followed through the opening smiling, singing and quite happy. Now came the sight, and it will live forever. The first sight I saw on ascending was the man in front of me blown to atoms, and then on the ground hundreds of my mates dead and wounded, in fact, I had to walk over them. They were in all positions, and piled in heaps, for you will understand that it was at this opening the Huns directed their chief fire.
I only got 20 yards when I got my first hit, which of course knocked me over. I still battled on and in another twenty got the heavy blow and made sure my leg was broken, and landed amongst the dead and suffering, and for the moment was stunned. On coming to, I debated whether to return or go on, but am mighty glad to say I went forward and fortunately reached the German trench safely, but was unable to go on to their second line as I couldn't crawl.

My next duty was to help to search the dugouts, but my fortunate mates had got ahead of me and settled all the swines who were left. The rest ran for their lives and got away under cover. The only thing left for me then, was to dig and help fill the sandbags which I did laying down. My mates got to the Huns' third line ... and it was now left for the reinforcements to come along and bring up ammunition, but this after a few hours failed as our trenches were blown to smithereens. Just here I want to mention the ammunition carriers, who came backwards and forwards regularly until they were also laid low ... I now struck a poor devil of a German who had crawled from somewhere unarmed. With hands in the air, he howled, 'Mercy, Comrade'. So instead of driving him through I with an N.C.O. sent him over into No-Man's Land to our lines and have been sorry ever since, as the swines when they counter-attacked drove their steel into our wounded and if ever I have another opportunity I will show no mercy but I sincerely hope that doesn't come, as I don't mind admitting I never want to go through the same again.

Richard St J Kennedy
Perth, c. 1912.
COURTESY V St J KENNEDY

My next five hours were hell on earth. As what with shrapnel, machine guns, trench mortars, liquid fire etc. flying all over you, and seeing the mates in the trenches slowly diminishing I can assure you it was enough to send one dotty. At the finish, there were in our short section of about 100 yards only twenty left, and the Germans were in the trench on our left ready to make an attack, so once again we had to stand to, with fixed bayonets, but now from the front we received word 'Every man for himself' and once again into No-man's Land. After getting tied up in both the Germans' and our own wire entanglements and falling several times I managed to reach our lines, now a mass of ruins, safely, and I doubt if half-a-dozen of us managed this. I now crawled through our communication trenches to the dressing Station ...

If we could have had the reinforcements and ammunition the trenches were an absolute certainty. If we sent word once we sent it fifty times in the last few hours, but of course it is doubtful if these brave men ever reached their destination. You would see one start, go a few yards, then drop. And others would then volunteer. They wouldn't let me go owing to my wounds, but at the finish when I had to ... I reached there after much pain and falling several times.

Don't forget the Huns got just as much as we did and their losses, like ours, would be enormous. Some of our crowd refused to take prisoners and these Huns when it comes to a fight with bayonets, are absolute cowards, and instead of fighting, throw down their arms and howl 'Mercy, Comrade'. Some of our men gave them mercy—I don't think! And after what I have seen, never again will I take a prisoner no matter how he stands.

Just before I forget, our officers were regular bricks, and the talk of them remaining in their dugouts is all rot. They were fine, and Captain White led us right to the end, and with any man in D Company will always be considered what he is, that is, a hero. I am told he went off his head but do not know for certain. I don't think there were many officers left. We won't see the casualty list here or perhaps hear anything about it, so don't fail to send me an account of the scrap ... Besides my overcoat, I am afraid I have lost everything else as they were left in our Depot, but it is very doubtful if ever I will ever see it again. My worst loss is my razors, both safety and ordinary, as here I am in a strange land with just one halfpenny to my name and that will never part from me.

To see me land in England would have done your heart good, for I hadn't a shave for five days and my clothes were torn to ribbons, owing to the barb wire, whilst my fingers were bad, and my hands and feet covered in cuts, and clothes covered in blood, with soles hanging off my boots, so there you are. Where we fought was at Fleurbaix, just south of Armentières, and next to Bois Grenier. Now that I am in England, I am able to mention the names AS THERE IS NO CENSOR. I have spent days in the trenches at both places. From the Battlefield I landed at Boulogne at 12 pm, and landed in a nice Canadian Hospital, but the next day left for Dover with thousands of wounded in a Hospital Ship ... We entrained at Dover and reached Manchester 6 am, so you see I had the rotten luck to pass through London in night time ... It is a bit hard not getting into one of the Hospitals near London, as this is not a very nice one, but I am not going to growl. The nurses are very nice and attentive, but I would have preferred the military ones. The Canadian girls were pretty.

Yesterday, my first day, some ladies gave me cigarettes which were acceptable, as I had only one left, and no tobacco. I told one girl of my not having any money and she offered me some, but I wouldn't take it ... When I do leave here I get 10 days' sick leave ... I will make for London ... I will be broke and penniless until I reach London, where I believe I can draw on my book. The Military here owe me seven quid, which I might get at the Pay Office. The people here seem very kind, and I might strike a good time yet. Besides cigarettes I struck strawberries and sweets and with a decent bed, things are not too dusty. The bed linen, like everything else here, is branded 'Chorlton House Workhouse' so you can see your darling brother Dick is really in one of these homes.

What I saw of this town dashing through in a motor I did not think much of, but I must not speak too soon. It is as you know one of the largest manufacturing places in the world. When we landed at Boulogne the aristocrats were at the station to give us chocolates and cakes which after a painful 14 hours in the train were acceptable. From there to the Hospital I motored in a swanky motor-car. The ladies were very well dressed, and some pretty. I also saw mixed bathing going on there, and it was a very beautiful place. Of course I did not see a great deal as we dashed through in a car, but I saw quite enough to give me a very good impression.

Whilst here I will write regularly but am now getting tired, as I am sitting up in the bed writing this and the leg is fairly painful ... I managed to cadge the stamp for this from a poor old Tommy. The place is packed with them, and in my ward they are a real good lot ...

I am as right as the Bank of England, and one of the luckiest men in the world. Tons of love to all.

Dick.

COURTESY V St J KENNEDY, RICHARD'S NEPHEW

EVERY DAY OF MY LIFE
Sam Benson was 6 when he said goodbye to his father, 2nd Lieut James Benson 32nd Bn. A year later a member of the South Australian police came to the Benson's door to tell Sam's mother that Lieut Benson was missing. The mother told Sam. His sister, then three, was too young to understand. But Sam understood very well, especially when he accompanied his mother to the Repatriation Department to enquire about a pension. They were told that because he was missing, pay was stopped, and until his fate was clearly established, there could be no pension. Sam recalled them saying 'how do we know he has not deserted?'.

Sam remembered what happened next: his mother '*called at a state school and said she had no money and could they give her a job. They gave her a job as janitor. I used to leave home at four in the morning with her, hail, rain or shine, and walk to the school with her*'. Sam used to pray every night for the return of his father who he remembered as a loving man and '*who took him to the football a couple of times*'. Adelaide Legacy came to the rescue after the war, even though by then Mrs Benson had lost her house, she now had a pension. Sam went to sea and by the time the second war ended he was a Lieutenant Commander, and on settling in Melbourne he began 45 years of service with Legacy, helping children of other missing men, as he had been helped. He was also in local government, a Member of Parliament, and every 19 July he placed an advertisement in the *In Memoriam* column of a Melbourne newspaper.

At Fromelles in 1991, the 75th anniversary of the battle, he was asked by the Mayor to give a speech. He confessed it was the hardest he had ever made, for behind him on the screen wall of VC Corner was his father's name, one of the 1,298 missing of Fromelles. Looking back later he told John Lahey of *The Age*:

> *It would have made a difference if my mother and I had known that my father had a grave, because there was*

[continued opposite]

And it goes on with extraordinary vividness, and at the end of the chapter Ted wrote of his rescuer:

> Stan H., who carried, or rather dragged, Ted in ... went through the war without a scratch. After bringing Ted in he went back and established, though not for long, the only signalling station of the 8th Bde in the enemy trenches that day. In a letter to Ted's people some months later he said: 'I must tell you why I have never answered your letters. I did not want to write at the time when you were under the impression I was a hero. I dragged him out, that is al—it was not a brave deed. If it has turned sorrow into happiness then I thank God I did it—for he is not forgotten by us and never will be.'

The reader is now directed to pages 240–41, *What I came away for* the story of Pte Richard Kennedy 1302, 32nd Bn, who after being wounded in both legs crawled back '*through our communication trenches to the dressing station*', and then was evacuated to England. A much different tale to that of Lording.

The extraordinary accuracy of the German body count cannot be ignored. Their communiqué of 21 July '*on the ground ... more than 2000 enemy corpses*' refers to both Australian and British dead. We know that they collected many bodies and loaded them on a train, photographed them, and then took the dead to mass graves at Pheasant Wood and elsewhere over the days after the battle. The logistic problems of their own casualties, plus almost 500 prisoners, a large proportion of whom were wounded, and the need to rebuild their parapets and repair their line generally has to reflect well on the Germans' capacity for discipline and organisation, and might go some way to explaining why the front went quiet for a while. Another reason was the Australians and British had similar problems, long lists of unaccounted for men of whom they had to collect evidence from survivors about their fate or possible resting place: an impossible task considering the events.

Pte Bill Boyce of 58th Bn, like others digging the saps across No-Man's Land recalled using bodies like sandbags, building them into walls or embankments, others into the floor '*they'll never be found, some are six feet down*'.

The next element of the aftermath of the battle is 'The Missing', which in the case of Fromelles concerns the vast majority of those who died there. This is perhaps best told by bringing together a number of different stories. The longest of these first, on pages 245–47 *I wish I could tell you more*. As well as dealing with an officer who dies of wounds at Calais, it links his story with another officer, his life-long friend who vanished, and his fate was not finally settled until October 1919 in Berlin. The personal drama that the classification of 'Missing' caused the next of kin of another officer is described in the margin article *Every Day Of My Life*. In that story we have the revelation of how the infant son of the officer who vanished at Fromelles, carried the scar all his life. Another missing officer, Captain Kenneth Mortimer, of 29th Bn, see page 173 *Always conscientious and straight forward,* was for his mother till the end of her long life 'wounded and missing': like so many others she was sure that one day he would appear at her front door.

Whilst the mother usually had other children to help fill the gap of the missing son, and the widow had his name and sometimes his children, the fiancée of the dead soldier had nothing but memories. In the style of the time many could not move on into another relationship because it seemed a betrayal, *... his loving friend...* (pages 254–55) provides a glimpse of such a tragedy.

Having now visited, so to speak, the wounded, the missing and the dead, we turn to the most controversial aspect of the battle's aftermath—the armistice suggested by the Germans before noon on 20 July, but rejected by the British and Australian HQs. Had it gone forward a huge number of wounded would have been saved, and later casualties from snipers and shells largely avoided. Depending on the length of the armistice, many of the dead might have been brought back and given proper burial, and the remains of others interred on the battlefield. Instead, men risked their lives day after day bringing in wounded, and the corpses and body pieces were left to rot in the hot summer sun. As the German war diarist observed, '*The enemy did not bother to salvage their dead, as usual*'. This was not the first time the Germans expressed this thought, as we saw at Aubers Ridge some fourteen months earlier, the same Bavarian Division stopped firing when the battlefield was so covered with British dead and dying that they thought the British should be given an opportunity to rescue their wounded and attend to their dead.

An armistice for this purpose was not a new idea for the AIF, which is one of the most troubling aspects. In Bean's Volume II on Anzac (pages 164–67) he deals at length with the 12 hour armistice on Gallipoli on 24 May 1915. The only senior officer at Fromelles who may not have heard of it could have been Tivey. There can be no doubt that McCay, Birdwood, White, Godley, Elliott and Pope knew about the arrangements on Gallipoli: it was a seminal event. Bean too had known all about it and wrote of it only a few years before he turned to writing about Fromelles. This is part of his description:

EVERY DAY OF MY LIFE (contd)
so much uncertainty about where he was killed. My mother could not get it out of her mind. It took her a long time to accept he would not return.

Then of himself, he had this to say, '*I thought of my father every day of my life*'. Captain Sam Benson CBE OStJ, RD and Bar, died 26 July 1995, quite possibly the 79th Anniversary, to the day, that the family had learned that Lieut James Benson was missing.

A GOOD HEAPING OF EARTH
Pte William Boyce 3022, 58th Bn was one of the party engaged in extending the Rhondda sap across No-Man's Land. A near hopeless job given the distance to be covered, the open ground through which it was to be dug, and that they were working in complete darkness under continuous fire. Bill remembered one grim aspect:

My job was to help dig the communication trench from our line to theirs ... and the instructions were that if the man in front of you fell, was badly wounded or dead you were to roll him to one side, the side where the firing was coming from ... in the dark you didn't have much idea ... and put a good heaping of earth over him.

A 12 HOUR TRUCE ON GALLIPOLI
Empire Day, Whit Monday, 24 May 1915. At 7.30 am an armistice was declared to enable the Turks to bury their dead which lie in heaps. Firing ceased and both sides came out of the trenches. Great fraternity existing between our men and Turks, they exchanged cigarettes, matches and money, and were talking and joking with each other like old friends instead of enemies. This is Empire Day and will be remembered by all of us who are spared to go through this war, a memory that will bring back pleasant recollections. The Turk himself fraternised freely, but the German officers held back ... Hostilities recommenced at 4.30 pm but bar a few rifle shots nothing is doing.

—L/Cpl J I Marrott 644,
13th Bn Diary
RUSI of NSW Magazine (Winter 1998)

VERY DECENT FELLOWS
Major D Glasfurd in a letter dated 21 May to his sons described this incident:

Yesterday it was rather interesting. I was up in our trenches when the Turks began to wave the white flag with red crescent ... three Turks came forward from their lines so we sent out an interpreter to meet them. The interpreter came back and said the Turks wanted to talk to an officer. General Walker went out and I went with him. We met the Turks about half way between the lines—rather nearer to Turkish lines. Every now and then there was a shot or two—sometimes a shell—but both sides practically stopped firing while we talked to the Turks. There were four of them, 2 Doctors, 1 Staff Officer and 1 Infantry Officer. They wanted to collect wounded and bury their dead. I talked French to one of the Doctors. They all seem very decent fellows. It was rather weird to stand chatting there between the two sides which have been hard at it day and night for 27 days.

COURTESY GEELONG GRAMMAR SCHOOL ARCHIVES

> The presence of several thousand dead between the crowded lines now became a matter of real anxiety to the Anzac leaders. Already in some sectors the acrid stench of corpses was never absent ... A few of the enemy's wounded still remained on May 20 between the lines, and throughout the force there was a desire to help these men ... it was certain that the Turks must be eager for the burial of their comrades, and if further time was wasted, the wounded must die. The movement for an armistice originated partly with Capt Herbert attached to Godley's staff ... who on May 20 obtained leave to go to Sir Ian Hamilton and personally press the suggestion already made by Birdwood. Hamilton, apprehensive of enemy propaganda, forbade Birdwood to open formal negotiations, but added that, if the enemy commenced the negotiations or made a genuine movement to succour his wounded or bury the dead under a Red Crescent flag, he was not to be fired upon.

One has to ask, how did Fromelles differ from this? Except the people to be rescued or buried were Australians. Bean then goes on to tell the story how after a few mistakes the Red Cross and Red Crescent flags were on No-Man's Land along with General H B Walker GOC 1st Brigade and his Staff Captain on 20 May, but when Turks were seen picking up rifles as well as wounded, the event was called off. Then further contact was made with the Turks '*after negotiations on two days at Birdwood's headquarters, an agreement was made for an armistice for burial of the dead on 24 May*'. Bean wrote:

> At 7.30 am on May 24 firing ceased and the burial parties worked all day between the lines, each interring the dead found in its own half of No-Man's Land. The written conditions were honourably observed, and, except for the burial parties, the troops in most sectors were kept in their trenches... Throughout the day the Anzac burial parties chaffed the enemy with crude tags of Arabic, exchanged souvenirs, and, when at 4.30 both sides retired to their trenches, parted as friends. The shot which renewed the conflict was not fired until 4.45, when a Turkish sniper opened.

So Godley and Birdwood who both helped that Anzac armistice now could not find the will or interest to organise another at Fromelles. As the Germans suggested it, that got around the 'legal point' put forward by Hamilton implying that any such proposal made by the allies revealed weakness of resolve. But it is clear from events prior to 19 July that the British had a history of such arrangements. Indeed, one of the most memorable truces was near Fromelles at Christmas 1914, and it was widely publicised: see page 252 *These chivalrous acts*. So Haking was not ignorant either. Nor his staff.

When this writer discovered that Bean dramatically changed his story of the event between the first and later editions of Volume III, suspicions were aroused. The further

[continued page 250]

I wish I could tell you more

When his death notice appeared in the Melbourne *Age* on the morning of 31 July 1916 there was no indication of the date or place of the battle of which 2nd Lieut Walter Hugh Vaile, 59th Bn was a victim. Curiously his seems to be the first public notice of a Fromelles casualty, yet he died five days after receiving his wounds. One can only suppose that the hospital procedures were much better organised than those on the battlefield, and telegrams were promptly despatched. In the *Sydney Morning Herald* of 1 August there was a photograph and obituary for Lieut Col Norris who had been killed in action. Most of the Fromelles casualties advertised over the next few days were, like Vaile, 'Died of wounds'. The 'Killed in Action' notices started on 2 August, although it was 5 August that the 'Official List' appeared with Vaile's name on it.

Vaile's story sadly illustrates what must have been the experience of thousands of Australian families who had to cope with the sudden disappearance of the breadwinner.

Walter Vaile was born at Greenwich, near London 30 June 1882, son of a sea captain, and as an infant in arms came with his parents to Melbourne. He was educated at Hawthorn Grammar and began work in the State Savings Bank which was expanding rapidly and offering financial security after the failure of so many banks in the 1890s. From 1912 onwards compulsory military service applied and Vaile together with many other bank officers took an active part in the Commonwealth Defence Force. By 1915 Vaile was manager of the bank in Maffra, a sizeable country town. His school friend and fellow bank manager—at Kyabram—was John Charles (Jack) Bowden. They were the closest of friends and had a shared enthusiasm for rowing, both being members of The Banks Rowing Club near Princes Bridge. Another close friend was Keith Gordon McDonald, manager of another branch of the bank: later as Captain he was Commander of B Company which had as Lieutenants—Vaile, Bowden, E T Carr, H C Howard, A D Morrow, all of whom died at Fromelles.

Bowden enlisted on 24 September 1915 and Vaile on 15 October 1915 otherwise they seemed to have done everything together.

It is for that reason their two stories

Pte Walter H Vaile, 59th Bn, 1915

Pte John C Bowden, 1915

are told here. Vaile was 34, had married Adeline (née Marshall) in 1914, and they had a son named John after John (Jack) Bowden, his godfather. Bowden was married to Jessie but they had no children. Vaile and Bowden left Australia late in December 1915.

McDonald had enlisted much earlier (25 August 1914) and served at Gallipoli, and was the only officer of B Coy 59th Bn to survive Fromelles. Thus he was able to write to Vaile's brother Guy from his hospital bed in London on 28 August 1916, explaining a little of what had happened. He had been badly wounded at Fromelles.

The night before the battle it fell to Bowden to cut ways through the wire in readiness for the charge. McDonald wrote:

Mr Bowden was out till 2 am ... and went all along our front to see if there was sufficient wire out for us to get through. Thanks to Bowden the preparation in this respect was excellent—we had no trouble in getting through the wire at all.

Had the charge followed that dawn under cover of a barrage the gaps in the wire would have been a surprise to the Germans. However they had twelve hours of daylight to concentrate their firepower on the gaps. Which is exactly what happened. Bowden led the way in the first wave and vanished. Morrow was with him and was wounded. McDonald and Vaile led the second wave: they got about half way across No-Man's Land when shot down. McDonald again:

... they were regarded as two of the 'solidest' officers ... I had to fight hard to keep them, as every Company Commander coveted them. I feel their loss as friends very much ... our company (B of the 59th) formed the first and second waves ... we had about 500 yards to cover over rough country, barbed wire, ditches, the river ... our men were magnificent—they charged in a hail of shrapnel and machine gun fire until they were practically wiped out ... I got one in the right arm before we left our trench, but it wasn't too bad, but I got it solid when about 200 yards out, through the left shoulder and out of the back. This dropped me like a log ... I was right through the Gallipoli show yet this was the severest action I've yet been in.

Another description of events came to the family from Sgt J S Aikins 3676 59th Bn in a letter 12 September 1916:

Dear Friend, I feel you will be anxious to hear of Mr Vaile and you may gather some comfort from the Enquiry account which I am able to give. But I felt somehow responsible to advise any of his friends what little I know as to how Mr Vaile received his wounds, which (I have learnt later) were fatal.

In conveying my deepest sympathy towards you, it involves the sentiments of all who knew him. He, by his genial manner and good nature, gained high favour with all whom he came in contact with. This especially applies to all the boys, in his platoon. I was his platoon sergeant.

I am at present writing in the dugout in which Mr Vaile slept the night previous to the 19th and after receiving full instructions of the Charge. At the appointed time we proceeded to our position in the firing line. As we moved to the line, the shells were bursting and crashing in all direction. After we had given the boys' final instructions, the time came to act. To be sure of anything that had happened anymore, was nigh impossible. We met such a deadly hail of bullets, shrapnel, and smoke bombs that soon the few that remained lost all touch. I was within 50 yards of the enemy's trenches and returned after 14 hours, and it was then I learnt Mr Vaile had been brought in and was wounded. We were divided on crossing a creek and the account (of the one of two of our boys who returned) was glorious. He lays great stress on the gallantry of Mr Vaile, who by his coolness set a fine example to his men.

I am not free (on account of the Censor) to say more, but I would ask you to find condolence in the fact that Mr Vaile met a gallant soldier's end. I had several narrow escapes: three bullets went through my clothing, another struck and damaged my rifle, and a piece of shrapnel struck my head, and was several times covered up by earth thrown out by exploding shells. I would be pleased to give you a fuller account on some previous occasion. Meantime with every good wish ... Yours truly, James S Aikins.

Vaile was brought in early on the morning of 20 July by Capt Norman Marshall and 2nd Lieut Bob Salmon, '*in good spirits, he had a cup of tea and was asking about Jack Bowden*'.

Vaile and Morrow were evacuated to Calais—the BEF No 3 GH, from where Matron M Harvey on 17 September writing to Walter's brother Guy, remembered the event clearly:

Lieut Vaile was as you have been informed severely wounded in the left arm and both feet. He came to us on 21 July with many other Australians and died at 11.45 pm on the 24th. Although the wounds were severe, he would I think have stood a fair chance if it had not been for the gas gangrene which set in. We had quite a number of this particular convoy who suffered in the same way.

Considering the vast numbers of gravely wounded men passing through the hospital, the individual knowledge and understanding in the Matron's letter reveals much about the Nursing Service:

Lieut Vaile was very good and brave, although so ill and was very grateful when I told him I had written to his wife to tell her that he was ill—alas unfortunately I had to write again to tell her of his passing away.

Everything that could be done for him was done, and some of his men saw his remains taken to our Mortuary and transferred to the Gun Carriage. He is buried in the cemetery which is set apart for our officers and men, and which is looked after by British Tommies.

I wish I could tell you more. We had him only 3 days, the time was so short and so much was done in the time to try and save him, but you can rest assured he died as an Englishman should, worthy of our best traditions, and he is a brother to be proud of. I could tell from the little he said he thought much of his wife and children.

Lieut Vaile was nursed by English sisters, and treated by English doctors, and a specialist came over to consult about him.

You have my deep sympathy.
Yours faithfully

Mrs Vaile had given birth to her second child, Mollie, on 4 July. Lena Vaile later told her daughter that she had sent a telegram to Walter to advise him. But after his death it, together with a letter written at the same time, were returned unopened. Apparently Walter Vaile had no doubt that his second child would be a girl, and he had in his mind already christened her. Thus he was able to write in his last letter of 12 July:

give my love to Jack and Mollie, and kiss them for me.

One can only imagine how Lena Vaile's life had changed in that year. The difference in income—Vaile enlisted as a private, and he had been a Bank Manager—let alone the change of social status. The family moved in with her late husband's sister and like tens of thousands of other war widows and orphans '*soldiered on*', because after all there was no alternative. She wore the badge of a war widow with pride until her death.

Guy Vaile set off for France in 1923 to visit the grave at Calais: a tiny snap from a Kodak pocket camera of the cemetery with its brand new headstones survives. Numerous stories are told how brothers and sisters made this pilgrimage in the twenties, to see the graves or where there was not one, stand in the place where the man they mourned went missing. '*I had to do it,*' '*I couldn't have gone on living till I searched the area,*' '*You've got to answer those questions,*' '*You have to see where they died,*' were typical remarks made about these pilgrimages.

In that burst of public grief that marked Australia in the years just after the war names were placed on Cenotaphs, Memorials, Boards. Walter Vaile was well served in this regard: and he was not untypical. His name was on the Roll of Honour Board of Hawthorn Grammar (the school closed later), on the Rowers' Memorial near Princes Bridge, on the Honour Roll of the State Savings Bank (now lost), on the 59th Bn Honour Board at Shepparton Civic Centre, and on an elegant mosaic board in the City Hall at Maffra. He was thus remembered by his school, his sport, his employer, his battalion and his adopted town.

Walter Vaile's son John never visited the grave and worked in a reserved occupation during WW2, forever bitter not that his father had died in the war, but that he had been wasted in such a useless battle as Fromelles.

Mollie, the daughter, in 1988 went to France to visit the grave. Her own daughter well aware of the emotional turmoil involved in such a pilgrimage kept in constant touch, and as it happened Mother's Day was just a few days before Mollie was due at Calais. The flowers sent for Mother's Day cheered her up considerably. The next day, for a strange moment she wondered what to do with them. Then it was obvious - take them to the cemetery at Calais. This she did, placing them against her father's headstone, tears and pride all mixed up together. '*I felt terrible, I could hardly stand up. You see, I never knew my father, and that's why I made the trip. And am so glad I did.*'

We turn now to Jack Bowden. He had vanished so completely that Jessie, his wife, despite reports to the contrary lived on in hope that he had been taken prisoner. In an effort to establish what happened to Bowden the Australian authorities traced members of his company recovering in various British hospitals. Pte John Wood 4957 (59th Bn) in Huddersfield, Pte Robert W Blackmore 3008 in County Hospital, York, Pte J A O'Neill 3093 in Harefield Hospital remembered going forward with him, but it was Pte J G Church 2020 who said most: On 4 August he was at Etaples, in hospital:

There is a creek just off the sap running out from our lines to No-Man's Land where we went across on July 19 at Fleurbaix ... I saw Lieut Bowden lying by this creek as I went over in the charge. I was about this spot for some time lying down waiting for the advance. I saw him crawl from the creek to our front line trenches and from there out of the bushes again into No-Man's Land. When last I saw him his left leg was covered in blood and his left arm strapped to his side by some of his equipment. He looked awfully bad. I did not see or hear anything more about him. He must have crawled into the bushes and died there. He was a big lump of a man, a fine strapping fellow, quiet and well liked.

On that evidence Bowden was classified 'Missing in action'. However when the lists of prisoners, dated 26.8.16, were received from the Germans via the Red Cross a number of names were listed. Some 'died of wounds' usually with a date and place of burial. Among others was the name Pte John Charles Bowden No. 1929. This caused some confusion there being no Pte Bowden missing. It took a while for somebody to realise that as Bowden had only been commissioned recently, he had not changed his identity disc—his number was in fact 1929. He was now classified as 'Died of wounds while a prisoner of war'. This was still not an answer, the German records always very precise and detailed did not explain what had happened to him. The Red Cross in Sydney wrote to Pte E Bingham 4441 (54th Bn) and Pte H H Hodson 3990 (59th Bn) both POWs in Germany for information but nothing was forthcoming.

Lieut Col Layh, CO of the 59th at Fromelles wrote in April 1917 in response to further inquiries:

Mollie Hodges, 11 May 1988
Southern Cemetery, Calais

We reported Jack Bowden as being 'killed in action' because we knew he was lying badly wounded out in No-Man's Land and we could not find him by patrolling at night, but we found out afterwards the Germans had picked him up and reported him as 'dying of wounds' after they got him. The Germans recovered his Pay Book and disc, but these were lost in transit.

By 2 January 1918, following further inquiries, Bowden was:

Officially reported as killed in action 19 July 1916. There is no question of his ever having been taken prisoner of war, this belief must have risen from the circumstances of his personal effects being picked up by the Germans in the field. There is a possibility that his body was buried by the enemy though we have never received any information to this effect.

When the war was over it was revealed that the Berlin Branch of the Red Cross did have a card for John Charles Bowden and the confusion, if there was confusion, resulted from the Germans believing him to be among those they buried in one of five large British Collective Graves outside Fasanen Wäldchen, Pheasant Wood or in a collective grave at Fournes.

What happened to the pay book and disc is unstated, but a number of such effects sent via the Red Cross did not reach their destination. In the end the Royal Prussian War Office Medical Section issued their official verdict.

Lieutenant Bowden, J C of 59th Bn fell in the neighbourhood of Fromelles on 19.7.16. Witnessed Berlin 24.10.19. (Signed) Jacobi, Lt of the Reserve.

Meanwhile Jessie Bowden (c/o W J Bowden of 34 Queen Street) had been sent her husband's effects—those he left in his billet: '1 ornament (elephant), tin box, wristwatch, one sealed paper parcel.' Jack Bowden's name is on the wall of the VC Corner Memorial. It was also on the Bank Roll of Honour, the Rowers' Memorial and on the Kyabram Memorial.

For some years the two families remembered their joint grief in a shared 'In Memoriam' notice:

BOWDEN-VAILE. In affectionate remembrance of our dearly beloved brother, Lieut John Charles (Jack) Bowden who fell in action at Fleurbaix, France on 19th July 1916, and his dear friend Lieut Walter H (Wally) Vaile who was wounded on 19th and died on 24th July 1916. Both of 59th (Inserted by Mary & Will).

Mollie married Fred Hodges and they had three daughters, Diane, Barbara and Jill. Mollie died on 23 September 1999.

INFORMATION AND PHOTOGRAPHS COURTESY MOLLIE HODGES (née Vaile)

The Padres at Fromelles

Padres were attached to Bdes rather than Bns, but this list identifies the battalions with which they were most closely associated.

29th Bn: A F Eva (CofE)
30th Bn: F P Williams (CofE)*
31st Bn: S A Beveridge (CofE)*
32nd Bn: F G Ward (CofE)*
53rd Bn: J J Kennedy (RC)
54th Bn: S E Maxted (CofE)
55th Bn: J Green (Methodist)
56th Bn: W M Holliday (CofE)
57th Bn: G W B Statt (CofE)
58th Bn: J F Huthnance (CofE)*
59th Bn: D S Brumwell (CofE)
F C Brewer (Methodist)
60th Bn: J P Gilbert (RC)
2nd ACCS: G K Tucker (CofE)
5th Div Artillery: T J King (RC)

The story of the padres who were at Fromelles could be a book in itself. The terrible challenges of the experience marked them for the rest of their lives. Among the citations in the next chapter the deeds which earned Father Kennedy the DSO, Rev. Maxted and Father Gilbert the MC are given. In the list above the names without asterisks are certain appointments, those with asterisks are educated guesses based on their names occurring in 5th Division references during the first weeks in France.

Father J P Gilbert MC, 1917
COURTESY M WOOD

James Patrick Gilbert was born on 4 August 1878 at Christchurch, New Zealand, and ordained at St Mary's Cathedral, Sydney, on 30 November 1908. He enlisted in 1916, attached to 15th Bde. Between the wars, he was a parish priest at Coogee, and during WWII and after, was Chaplain at Randwick Military Hospital. He died at Randwick on 8 September 1956, aged 81. An eyewitness of the Padre's valour at Fromelles wrote in the Melbourne Tribune, in part:

He is known by all members of the Australian forces in France, and he is always referred to as the Padre of the 60th ... On the afternoon of the start, and during the night and the next morning, he was always in the front line, heedless of the great danger he was in. He consoled the dying, and bandaged the wounded, even to the extent of tearing up his own puttees.

INFORMATION COURTESY MISSION OF SACRED HEART, NSW

After the publication of Kennedy's *The Whale Oil Guards* in 1919 it was generally classified as the unit history of 53rd Bn, perhaps because it began thus: '*This is the story of an Australian battalion. We Australians do not boast; therefore, though I may think it, I do not say it is the story of the bravest and best Anzac battalion. Incidentally, this is the story of Oswald Croshaw and other gallant men.*' Seen as the memoirs of a priest who was not shy about praising others, describing their style (or lack of it), their achievements (or absence of them), it becomes something else. He never parades his faith it is simply part of him, so it is compelling to read his tribute to another chaplain:

Another officer whose influence for good was immense was Lieut Ridley ... He is a Methodist. I am a Roman Catholic, but I say of him most sincerely that he is one of the most perfect Christians I have ever met... Brave as the bravest, cool and manly in action, beloved by officers and men. There are many Chaplains with the AIF, but I doubt if any of them has been a more successful teacher among the men of those virtues that make mortals Christ-like and heroic.

It would seem that Sgt Ridley's section reached the Laies. There he was severely wounded and had to be carried back to the Australian line. He was sent to England for treatment and returned as Lieut to the 53rd with whom at Bellicourt '*between 30 Sept and 2 Oct 1918 he displayed conspicuous gallantry and devotion to duty ... on many different occasions he organised parties for the carrying forward of ammunition and rations to the line.*'

This work was rewarded with a MC. Ridley conducted Bible Classes while with the battalion, but was not an official chaplain and although coming from a CofE background seems to have been more in the evangelical Methodist tradition in France. In later life he became a prominent Baptist preacher who kept the sword he acquired at his commissioning as '*a treasured memento of his soldierly life*'. Born on 8 Sept 1896, Ridley died on 26 Sept 1976, and left among much else, a seven verse poem: *Fromelles—a veteran's vision*; the second last verse:

Men of the old Battalion, comrades who saw and heard,
This was the birth of bloodshed for the famous Fifty-Third,
Hard were the days that followed, such as our history tells;
But not a sterner conflict than the battle of Fromelles.

Lieut J G Ridley, 53rd Bn, 1917

The most recorded padre at Fromelles was Spencer Edward Maxted. He enlisted as a private soldier on 12 September 1914 and sailed on 2 December. From 17 March 1915 he was at 1st Div HQ and two months later at Anzac HQ. On Gallipoli he served as a stretcher bearer. Just before the evacuation he was promoted to L/Cpl and in Egypt Jan 1916 he transferred to the Chaplain's Dept with the rank of Captain. As such in the Desert March he was entitled to a horse, but he chose to walk with the men. On 25 May he was attached to 54th Bn.

The manner of Maxted's death at Fromelles was noted a few days afterwards by another young chaplain, who like Maxted had come away as a private soldier attached to the AMC, believing that to be the best way of serving his fellow man. Rev. G K Tucker was made 'official' in Egypt and attached to the 2nd ACCS. His own description is an important commentary on Fromelles. On the 16 July he wrote from Sailly: '*Now that my chief work, that of looking after the wounded is near at hand, I feel somewhat fearful. God grant that I may not be found wanting ... I am ever so thankful to be allowed to do something.*' On the 17th: '*... last week ... we were ready to receive 700 patients, but now the accommodation is to be increased to 1000. I can see we shall all be very busy ... as the majority of patients will be CofE. The Colonel consulted me last week on how the mortuary tent ought to be fitted up. He is having an Altar erected and a Cross made. I shall try and keep fresh flowers there always.*'

Then on 21 July: '*... have been frantically busy ... our first patients arrived at 9.30 on Wednesday night ... until 11 am the next morning they continued to arrive. We took in 800 cases in that time. I was able to use my AMC training to some advantage.*

Rev. S E Maxted MC

We have two orderlies to two tents, each taking about thirty patients ... when one ward was full I went on to the next ... I went on in this way until 4 the next morning, and then all but one of the surgeons went to bed, so as to be ready for operations later... My services were then more needed in the dressing tent ... I was first rather fearful of undertaking the dressings but of course, the sooner the wounds can be attended to the better it is for the men. It is all very terrible ... poor chaps covered in mud and blood, with their clothes very often in ribbons ... wet to the skin ... their cheerfulness and courage is indeed wonderful ...
I cannot describe the feeling one has for these fellows. A great love seems to come into the heart for them all.
I thank God I am allowed to be with them. All but about fifty went off last night. They were sent down to the Base in an hospital train, which comes within a few yards of the hospital.
I fear there have been very serious losses and all for very little avail.
I must not, though, speak on this part of the matter.'

Two days later Tucker wrote: '*All is quiet again. Only a few patients now remain ... we are all, I think, more or less suffering a reaction ... at the time I took it all very much as a matter of course, but afterwards the awfulness of it all nearly got me down. I felt sometimes as if I could sit down and cry.*'

Then Tucker gave this news: '*I was very shocked to hear that Maxted had been killed ... he came away with the AMC, and served on the Peninsula for many months. He was the first priest in the ranks to be given a chaplaincy. After doing twenty-four hours work (chiefly stretcher bearing) on Thursday and Friday, he fell asleep from exhaustion, and was killed by a shell as he slept. He leaves a widow and young family. I remember him showing me their photos with great pride when we met in Egypt.*'

In 1930 when the Depression had reduced Australia so terribly and the men who had given so much were among the most deprived Father Tucker, as he was then known, with two others founded The Brotherhood of St Laurence in Newcastle (according

Father Tucker, 1936

to the Macquarie *Book of Events*). It became one of the great forces for social and welfare work in Melbourne, and then Australia. Father Tucker whose only real experience of the war was Fromelles, became a legend in his own time, and in a curious example of 'history repeating itself' the expansion and development of the Brotherhood of St Laurence after WWII became the responsibility of Rev. Geoff Sambell, who as padre to the 57/60 Bn in Australia and New Guinea in 1941–44, had found out much of what life was all about among the men of the 2nd AIF, not a few of them sons and nephews of '*19th of July men*'. Gerard Tucker was born 18 Feb 1885, ordained 1914, appointed OBE 1956. He died on 24 May 1974 and was buried at the Melbourne General Cemetery.

Padre A F Eva MID

CHAPLAIN'S RANKS

4th Class—relative rank of Captain
3rd Class—relative rank of Major
2nd Class—relative rank of Lieut-Col
1st Class—relative rank of Colonel
As Chaplains wear rank badges to denote their classification and relative military rank, it is incorrect to refer to them as Captain, Chaplain Captain etc. The correct mode of address is Chaplain, the Rev. ..., class ...

—AIF Order 1076, 22 Jan 1918

A MATTER OF GREAT SOLEMNITY
But the first Christmas Day (1914) was a holiday. A party of Germans came over from Fromelles and a party of ours went over to the German trenches. Here in this narrow No-Man's Land where but a week ago had been that 'clash by night', foes met as friends. The Germans agreed to bring over those of the dead which had not been buried. This was a matter of great solemnity. The grey German soldiers put the bodies on stretchers and brought them to the midst of No-Man's Land. Graves were dug there and then. Detachments of British and German troops formed up in line, and a German and an English chaplain read prayers alternatively in the two languages.

—Stephen Graham
The Challenge of the Dead (1921)

one probed the more lies appeared, and collusion in pursuit of glory and to protect reputations became obvious. No aspect of the Battle of Fromelles reveals more clearly the callous disregard of McCay for his men than this: and his attempt to shift the blame either to the British or Military Law falls apart totally as revealed by the Military Law itself, reproduced on pages 476–87. The saddest thing about this is that Bean must have known McCay was lying, and did not, or could not, turn on him and quote the Gallipoli event as a precedent in an effort to get to the bottom of the story. Painting McCay into such a corner was something Bean was always at great pains never to do. Out of the research into this event has come the long feature *The true account of the armistice at Fleurbaix*, pages 262–72. It includes some information already given in other places in this work, but repeated so that all aspects are contained in the story. This seemed the best way to handle the complexities of the event as the vast majority of this information has not been published before.

The last element of the immediate aftermath of battle are the Courts-Martial. This is a singularly difficult area to research in detail. It was ignored by Bean, but because the procedure and style of sentences says as much about the courts as the accused, it is very much part of the battle. And such offences as 'self inflicted wounds' and 'drunkenness', do reveal much about the morale of the men. On pages 258–60 *The Courts-Martial of Fromelles* tells of the proposed death sentence for a man of 55th Bn who went AWL, struck his superior officer and threatened him. There can be no doubt that if Pearce, Fisher and Hughes had

British and German meeting in No-Man's Land during the unofficial truce, Christmas 1914
Northumberland (Hussars) Yeomanry, 7th Division, Bridoux-Rouges Bancs Sector, near Fromelles

not stood against the death sentence in the forces, the generals, brigadiers and colonels of the AIF would have kept Australian firing squads busy. A fact that Ellis would have welcomed, and Bean would not have stood against, and Haig with others in the British army would have said was long overdue.

Into this same area comes *The Dismissal of Colonel Pope*, page 260, an extraordinarily vindictive act by McCay which has few parallels in the first AIF. Once again Bean is less than straightforward, being aware personally of Pope's condition—he saw him, all he could muster in a footnote was:

> Colonel Pope, on disciplinary grounds not affecting the control of his brigade during the action, was returned to Australia, but was afterwards appointed to the 52nd Bn, which he led into the Battle of Messines in 1917.

Also, one assumes, to do with discipline was the Routine Order of 27 July: '*Estaminets will, until further notice, be closed to British troops except between the hours of 12 noon to 2 pm and 6 pm to 8 pm*'. McCay took himself off on leave to the UK on 5 August and returned on 13 August, but Elliott, Tivey and Hobkirk (Pope's replacement) soldiered on drawing up their recommendations for awards—the subject of the next chapter. During that time it fell to the men so detailed to go onto the battlefield and collect from the dead their possessions, emptying their pockets and packs of personal items, cutting the cord that held their identity disc around their necks and putting the collection into a white calico bag that would in time be forwarded to the next of kin. A vivid, perhaps too vivid, recollection of this job comes down to us from Pte David Fletcher Jones (later Sir Fletcher Jones), 3546, 57th Bn, see margin *Possessions Of The Dead*. Pte Charles Henderson, 1698, also of 57th Bn recalled with great melancholy having to sprinkle lime on the bodies so as to hasten their disintegration, or as he termed it '*for reasons of hygiene*'.

Back at the various Battalion headquarters the Orderly Sergeants got out their Nominal Roll books to make some brief note against the names of the dead. These books, all still surviving, are a poignant relic of the war. In most cases in fine copperplate handwriting, the names were written in during the voyage to France, or in the first week there: number, rank, surname, initials, and remarks. The last column notes transfers out and death. There is evidence that other entries were made in pencil but rubbed out when one or other of the final ink entries were made. But one ink entry soon gave way to a rubber stamp: '*Killed in Action ——— Field*'. It was accompanied by a red

POSSESSIONS OF THE DEAD

In the quiet days that followed the massacre at Fromelles members of the 57th were assigned to collect the possessions of the dead. One of these was Pte David Fletcher Jones (later Sir Fletcher Jones):

Cpl Stan Clapton and I were out in No-Man's Land ... our job was to search each body to recover identification discs and valuables and to place each man's possessions in a suitably marked white calico bag. We were working close to the German trenches. Stan picked up a German officer's revolver and stuck it in his belt. This breach of the unwritten rules attracted immediate machine gun fire and Stan received a bullet in the chest. When a man is shot, there remains a small hole in the front and a very large one at the back. I turned Stan over and filled the large back one with my field dressing drenched in iodine. I made him as comfortable as I could, then crawled into the trenches and reported the incident to an officer. The same evening our captain accompanied me out to Stan and we put him on a stretcher. Later on the bearers told me that he died on the way to field hospital.

When I arrived at Port Melbourne on a hospital ship fourteen months later, Stan was waiting for me on the pier. He had seen my name in the list of returning casualties. I left the trenches not long after Stan. I had had doses of shell shock, falling sickness and malaria.

To his family Jones confided another aspect of this Fromelles experience, which he was never able to forget. The bodies lying out in the battlefield became filled with gases and when he rolled them over to recover their possessions, the gases caused the corpses to moan or cry out. Pte Jones was deeply marked by this and other events which persisted as nightmares for well over twenty years.

—Sir Fletcher Jones
Not by myself (1976)

These chivalrous acts

There was a history of truces on the Western Front by the time of Fromelles. The most famous being the Christmas Truce of 1914–15 which lasted till February between the British and German armies in the region of Aubers–Neuve Chapelle, near Fauquissart–the Bois de Biez, including the Fromelles area, and extending as far north as St Yves, that is a mile or so south of Messines. The history of such truces and the Christmas Truce in particular is painstakingly described in the interesting book *Christmas Truce* by Malcolm Brown and Shirley Seaton (Papermac, 1994).

One of the most important points the authors make is that there was no concealment of the Christmas Truce. Indeed the front illustration of the *Illustrated London News* January 9, 1915 is of a German soldier on one side of the barbed wire greeting two British soldiers, the caption: *The Light of Peace in the trenches on Christmas Eve: a German soldier opens the spontaneous truce by approaching the British lines with a small Christmas tree.*

Spurred by information in early December about friendly contacts between the well dug in and idle armies, the British II Corps at the behest of General Sir Horace Smith-Dorrien prepared instructions against such familiarity. The thrust of the prohibition was that unless the offensive attitude is constantly encouraged the men will fall into a *live and let live* attitude. The majority of Brown and Seaton's book comprises letters and comments by participants and witnesses of the truce, a superb commentary on what the officers, NCOs and men thought of the General's instructions: they took no notice of them! It seems Smith-Dorrien toured part of the line over the Christmas period and was '*considerably disappointed with the state of affairs*'. He had been ignored rather than disobeyed. '*To finish this war quickly*', he wrote in his report, '*we must keep up the fighting spirit and do all we can to discourage friendly intercourse. I am calling for particulars as to name of officers and units who took part in this Christmas gathering, with a view to disciplinary action*'.

However the disciplinary action hit Smith-Dorrien first. He fell out with his superior, Field Marshal Sir John French, at the end of May 1915 and was sent to East Africa. More importantly for the Fromelles story, French was soon to fall to Haig ably assisted in the task by Haking.

Whether or not Haking's ascent at this point, and his survival through the disaster at Neuve Chapelle and subsequent campaigns in Flanders, has anything to do with *official rejection of any contact with the enemy for any reason* is only guesswork. Curiously however the general attitude of Higher Authorities in regard to the Fromelles truce has distinct echoes of Smith-Dorrien's directive. Brown and Seaton quote an interesting sequence which happened a few days before Christmas, and illuminates the possibilities of 20 July 1916 at Fromelles that were lost. For despite Edmonds' protestation about there being no rights in the Geneva Convention to attend the wounded, there was a full acceptance to bury the dead, even if for hygiene reasons only.

The next morning a most extraordinary thing happened—I should think quite one of the most curious things in the war. Some Germans came out and held up their hands and began to take in some of our wounded and so we ourselves immediately got out of the trenches and began bringing in our wounded also. The Germans then beckoned to us and a lot of us went over and talked to them and they helped us to bury our dead. This lasted the whole morning ...
(Lieut G Heinekey 20 December).

There follows notes about failures of trust, usually the mark of a compulsive sniper or rogue element, always present in any army. Then another British Lieutenant in another area had this experience:

The morning after the attack, there was an almost tacit understanding as to no firing, and about 6.15 am I saw eight or nine German shoulders and heads appear, and then three of them crawled out a few feet in front of their parapet and began dragging in some of our fellows who were either dead or unconscious ... I passed down the order that none of my men were to fire and this seems to have been done all down the line. I helped one of our men in myself, and was not fired on, at all. (Lieut Sir Edward Hulse.)

Brown and Seaton then added this valuable comment:

In fact, these chivalrous acts were well within the rules of war. Armistices, properly agreed, for the burials of the dead has long been part of the accepted military code.

There can be no way that McCay with all his military and legal background could have been unaware of the Christmas Truce and the soldier's duty to dead comrades.

THE CHRISTMAS TRUCES
Contrary to general belief, this Christmas truce continued throughout the war in places. Griffith saw a meeting in No-Man's Land during 1915, with a soccer match, though some with bitter memories refused to take part. Ewart was in a similar truce the same year. Graham at Fromelles witnessed Chaplains from both sides leading prayers in No-Man's Land. In 1916 MacDougall at Loos took part in a truce—'How extraordinary', he wrote. Bradley at Hamel saw both sides waving to each other. A meeting in the middle featured at Oppy at Christmas 1917.

—Denis Winter
Death's Men (1978)

(usually) ruled line through the name. The long sad process of passing on the news now began. It seems that those who died of wounds within a few days of the battle were the first casualties reported, the hospitals being in charge of this. Next were the officers whose bodies were retrieved, then the ORs, classified under Military District, ie state of origin. The missing, which at this point included POWs, were gradually accounted for, while others shell-shocked or so badly injured they could not describe who they were, were '*traced*', and some '*returned to unit*'.

But some went somewhere else. The shell-shocked of Fromelles, 121 by one count, or if by percentage 192 (see page 233), would have initially gone to England. Those whose condition could be cured or '*improved*' might be sent back to France, the others were returned to Australia and discharged from the service because of '*war-related psychological trauma*'. How many *19th of July men* were among the 4,984 members of the AIF so classified we could never know, it being a subject nobody cared to talk about or record in much detail. In the third volume of his work Col Butler devoted a chapter to '*Moral and Mental Disorders*'.

The point made earlier about the inordinate amount of time taken by Butler to write his books is only emphasised here. Most of the senior doctors were dead, many of the records destroyed (another war was under way), and probably most of the sufferers from shell-shock and related problems were dead or so institutionalised as to have nothing to contribute. Butler too was out of date. Into 90 pages, he brought together his research and thoughts on Crime, Delinquency, Malingering, Self-inflicted wounds and Psychoses, in that order. The grouping together of crime and shell-shock in the same chapter give a very clear indication of how Butler thought. Given the attitudes of the period, it seems that Butler was battling with himself on the subject of 'neursasthenia', and whether or not the sufferers from nervous breakdown, shell-shock, hysteria, addiction, etc were just simply of weaker character. Gradually, and gradually is the word, it became accepted that an explosion nearby, a cobber blown to pieces in front of one, the prolonged absence of sleep, decent food or shelter, might affect even the most sturdy man: and that it did, was not because he was of weak character. But Butler in the 1940s was not entirely convinced. His fundamental lack of sympathy with cases of war neuroses is best demonstrated by his condemnation of Philip Gibbs' '*unwarranted reproach to the Ministry of Pensions concerning men who*', in Gibbs' words:

[continued page 256]

THE TRUCE IN 15TH BRIGADE POSITION

20 July ... This day was very quiet and spent mainly in disposing of the dead and wounded. The enemy ceased shelling our trenches as soon as our Artillery ceased firing. During the night which was fine and clear, our parties, mainly 57th Bn, brought over 200 wounded from No-Man's Land and also recovered Lewis guns. The bodies of men killed in our trenches were brought to the cemetery during the night.

21 July ... The day was very quiet. Our parties brought in some more wounded. The Germans were seen to be helping our wounded men close to their parapet. The day was spent in cleaning the kit and stores etc. from the trenches and repairing the parapets.

—15th Bde War Diary July 1916

IT WAS A BIT HARD

I was an infantryman but they had to provide all the men that survived, because there was that many wounded that the ordinary stretcher bearers couldn't cope. So we were detached for two or three days, carting wounded out. We could recover a few from No-Man's Land at night ... it was a bit hard. And the dead ... we used to get the discs and their equipment from their pockets ... and if we couldn't do anything they were left there, they weren't buried at all because sometimes the German lines were a hundred yards away, sometimes only fifty. We used to go here and come back to another place ... we made marks on old dead trees or something like that at night time ... bringing in the bodies? We couldn't cope there was that many of them.

—Charles Henderson 1698 57th Bn
Interview 1990

... his loving friend ...

James C G Downie 1097
29th Bn c. 1915

The pursuit of real information about the fate of her son began publicly when Mrs J Downie placed an advertisement in the *Argus* on 8 November 1916.

MISSING SOLDIERS: returned soldiers knowing anything of Sergeant J C Downie, D Company, 29th Battalion, reported missing in France on 19 July, are asked to kindly communicate with his mother, Mrs J Downie, Sharpe St., Geelong.

The missing man was James Charles Gordon Downie 1097, a 29-year-old woollen mill operative who had enlisted on 10 July 1915 and sailed to Egypt in November as Corporal. On 1 February 1916 he was promoted to Sergeant, and on 16 June left for France and Fromelles.

Obviously the rather stark telegram that Mr and Mrs Downie would have got from the Army (but which does not survive) was troubling, and they thought that after four months something more definite should be known, especially as the prisoners taken at Fromelles were declared in late August—early September, something that it would seem the Downies were not made aware of officially. Two letters Mrs Downie received were not much help. One was about a letter the correspondent had received, which he thought mentioned Downie being killed, but on re-reading it, this was not the case. However, he was afraid the story was already abroad so he was keen to tell Mrs Downie that the letter from his cousin did not say this, so '*I hope and trust you will get some good news of your soldier and he will come home to you in good health and strength*'. The second letter was more positive, this man's cousin, Pte K T Russell 1213, also of D Coy 29th Bn, had been reported missing, but now listed as prisoner of war. This Mr Noble of Tyabb then wrote: '*after taking the enemy trenches, the next day the commanders gave the orders to retreat. In this retreat the Australians lost heavily and I am sorry to say that I have received a letter from a friend in 44th Bn saying that D Coy, 29th Bn was wiped out ... under these circumstances there are only two chances for a missing soldier and they are killed or Prisoner of War*'. Noble then directed Mr Downie to write to the Defence Dept and the Red Cross in London. He concluded, '*will be glad to supply any other information on enclosure of a penny stamp for reply*'. The principal interest of Noble's letter is that 44th Bn was not in France but in England, thus any letter would be uncensored. This is the only way such information as '*D Coy 29th Bn was wiped out*' could get through.

Mrs Downie must have written immediately to the Red Cross in London because they cabled her on 1 January 1917 that '*as far as we know he is not a Prisoner of War*'. A month later however, the reply from the Australian Red Cross came addressed to Norman Downie, James' 30-year-old brother. The Red Cross in London had some information, from wounded D Coy men. Pte A D Cameron 1092 stated: '*I knew him well. At Fromelles there was a bit of a mix up and we got word to retire, it was a case of every man for himself. I don't think he was taken prisoner. Sgt Cole who was himself captured sent a list of men who were made prisoners that day, and Downie's name was not on the list ... I have little doubt that Downie was killed ...*'.

Pte L W Dunk 1099, and Pte C H Smith 1237 were also sure Downie had been killed by a bomb on 19 July. All these references through the Red Cross freely used 'Fromelles' or 'Fleurbaix', but right to the bitter end the Defence Department could only admit 'France'.

But three weeks later the Red Cross had unearthed another account. The London office noting that what Cpl W L Gibson 997 had to say was contrary to their previous information, they made a point of saying that Gibson '*was a careful and reliable witness*'. Gibson knew Downie '*they were both members of the original 29th Bn*' and he was wounded in the head at Fleurbaix on 19 July, and Gibson saw him on 20 July in the second line Dressing Station at Port Homrey. It was not a serious wound in Gibson's opinion. '*He was a walking case. The dressing station was well behind the line and he should not have gone missing. I am quite sure it was he*'. Gibson added, '*I was wounded the same day*'. All this must have raised Mr and Mrs Downie's hopes somewhat, but four days later the Red Cross had other reports. Pte W A Tait 1254, '*I knew Sgt Downie. He was killed at Fromelles ... on 19 July by a shell, about 4 o'clock am. He came from Geelong and was a big lump of a chap*'. (James Downie was 5'10": and weighed 11 stone, and had 36" chest). Pte W L Plunkett 1279 heard men from D Coy saying that Downie was killed.

All this caused Norman to seek contact addresses of Dunk, Smith and Gibson from the Defence Department; Dunk and Smith having returned to Australia. Despite getting contact addresses for all three, there seems to have been no replies. Mrs Downie had been in touch with other families but to no avail. One of the sisters wrote to Pte J Archer 1051 also of D Coy, and in March 1917 he reminisced about '*the last Sunday evening walk that I had with him ... along one of the many pretty walls that France is full of ... he hoped to get to Scotland, to go to a little village—Maybole—where your mother was born*'.

On 20 April 1917 James Downie the father took over the correspondence to Defence Dept but got nowhere. However, a letter to one Chaplain was forwarded to Chaplain Eva who was attached to 29th Bn at Fromelles. '*I have asked the officers of D Coy ... but they can tell me nothing further than your son went into the fight and did not return ... very probably he was killed and afterwards buried where he fell ... May God comfort you in your time of anxiety*'. It was now June 1917, and a year had passed. James wrote again on 12 Sept, and must have received some direct confirmation of his son's death because Death Notices appeared in the *Geelong Advertiser* three days later. One was from his family, his parents James and Mary, and his two sisters and two brothers. '*He gave his life for his country, his honour, faith and right*'. the other read '*A tribute to the memory of Sgt JCG Downie, (Jim), killed in action somewhere in France, July 20 1916 (previously reported missing). Lead, kindly light, midst the encircling gloom. He died as he lived—a hero and a man. Inserted by his loving friend. A Danger*'. Annie Bertha Danger of Chilwell, his fiancée, was six years younger than her beloved Jim.

James Downie's activities in Geelong were now described in the obituaries. He had worked at the Albion Woollen Mills since his boyhood in 1915 as a finisher. He was a foundation member of the Presbyterian Guild, active in the literary and Bible Study groups and a leader in football, gymnastics and cricket, being captain of Chilwell Football Club in 1911. He was also a librarian at Chilwell Free Library. The tribute concluded '*Downie's clean life helped many a comrade by its silent example. Gentle, with all his physical strength, obliging, full of sympathy for all needy ones ...*'.

Behind the scenes then followed settlement of his estate: Annie received £100, his sister Marian £25, Newtown Presbyterian Church for Sunday School £15, the Guild £10, and what was left over to his mother.

Another year went past and another brother, Walter, wrote for some information about where James was buried and '*any information that would be a comfort to the parents*'. But there was none, except what the Court of Enquiry had decided on 10 Sept 1917. The family now asked if his belongings could be sent to them, to which the reply came, '*no articles have been returned*'. And that was the end of it, well almost.

On 26 October 1921 the booklet *Where Australians Rest* was received by the Downie family, three weeks later the Memorial Scroll and King's Message, a month after that the British War Medal. In September 1922 they received the Memorial Plaque, and in February 1923 the Victory Medal. James, the father died 29 March 1922, aged 63, and Mary died 20 March 1937 aged 80. Five months earlier, on 18 November, 1936, Annie Danger had died of tuberculosis at Cresswell Sanatorium, so it was officially stated. But her family and the Downies knew she really died of a broken heart.

Annie B Danger, c. 1915

Elizabeth Douglas, the great niece of James Downie '*beginning with a couple of photographs and two death notices in the family Bible*' brought together all this material, a fuller version of which was published in the *Australian* on 11 November 1998, the 80th Anniversary of Armistice Day. Since then Elizabeth has visited Fromelles and seen the name of her great uncle on the wall at VC Corner.

PHOTOGRAPHS AND INFORMATION COURTESY E DOUGLAS

A BAD BLUE

When a reporter from the *Sydney Sunday Sun* in early April 1917 went to Randwick Military Hospital he found Cpl G P Browne 3471 54th Bn still recuperating from his wounds at Fromelles. Browne had had 14 gunshot and shrapnel wounds to his arms, leg and back, interestingly down his right side, probably indicating he was a victim of enfilade fire from the Sugarloaf. He also had been wounded in the face by a bayonet '*during a little affair with German patrols*'. Other parts of his story were as laconic. He showed the reporter the medical card some orderly had prepared and slotted into his pay book as he lay fairly motionless awaiting treatment on 20 July. '*I thought it was too good a trophy to give back, so I pinched it*', written across the corner was one word: '*dying*'. '*Colossal mistake, eh?*' and it was: George Browne lived until he was 86, having served in the militia between the wars, and 1st Anti-Aircraft Bty in Sydney during WW II.

He remembered, as had others, that '*about 20 minutes to 6 the Germans who were only about 130 yards away from our trenches held up a notice board: Advance Australia! We are waiting. You are 24 hours late*'. This knowledge, Browne was sure was due to Flemish spies. He described the setting of the sails of a windmill, the use of different coloured horses. Then he told the reporter '*You would hardly believe that we had their spies in our trenches without our knowing it?*' What did he mean? Were there locals walking through the trenches? This same preoccupation with spies got hold of Father Kennedy also. He noticed a ragged, injured local hobbling across a field behind the lines, but did nothing until he had seen him several times and looking more furtive. The man was arrested. He was the local postman, injured during his work, hence the cloth over his face, and terrified of being killed or shot by somebody. Kennedy admitted in his book that he had got it all wrong. But in dozens of accounts [continued opposite]

> had done their duty with the best of them, but now in the time of forgetfulness were forgotten, and the busy joyous selfish world passed them by, not guessing at the tragedy of these wounded souls, these nervous wrecks, these sad-eyed, stammering, wan-looking fellows, who wept sometimes in their lonely rooms and dared not apply for jobs which they knew they could not hold, even if luck gave them the chance ... Tragedies pitiable beyond words, because they have been suffered in loneliness, in the agony of long waking nights with secret fears hidden even from wives and mothers.

To which Butler wrote in reply:

> While this description conveys accurately enough, the early stage of chronic anxiety, and the final result in a few cases, it cannot be too strongly emphasised that in the great majority the condition *could* (Butler's italics) be cured and the permanent and, irreversible disorder *could* (Butler's italics) be avoided.

There was no such attitude to the man who lost an arm or a leg. But the man who lost his mind was forever suspect. Well symbolised by the initials they put on his card NYDN—'Not yet diagnosed: Nervous'. The men were sure it stood for "Not yet dead, but nearly'!

The only Fromelles casualty Butler mentioned here was R E Lording, and then in the last chapter titled *The War Damaged Soldier*. There could be no more apt example of the war damaged soldier than Lording: there also can be no more conclusive answer to the attitudes that Butler represented than Lording's end.

Generations later, Richard Lindstrom prepared *The Australian experience of psychological casualties in war 1915–1939*. This 1997 thesis is a gold mine of information, drawing on the experiences of '*over 300 Australian servicemen (most of whom were psychological casualties)*'. But more than the information is the compassion and thus the persistence in tracking down facts. Among the case studies located are several men from Fromelles. Certainly the most telling is an extract from a letter of 31 July written by Sgt L J Martin 1296, 8th MG Coy to his brother Jack. It is the most grim description of Fromelles this writer has come upon, 2300 words of absolute horror. These extracts are chosen to deal with the element of shell-shock:

> Our own little company went into battle ... a little over 100 strong ... we came out ... we could muster about twenty. We got to our firing line ... ten minutes when we lost four or five men all killed ... a shell caught two ... killed instantly ... another shell killed three outright ... the chap carrying the tripod ... was killed, the chap with the gun had ... his leg blown off, another (lost) his left leg and portion of his side.

> By the time we were to have gone over we could only muster two full teams instead of four, one or two of the chaps got shell shock and others got really frightened, it was piteous to see. One great chap got away as soon as he reached the firing line and could not be found when he was wanted. I saw him in the morning in a dug-out, he was white with fear and shaking like a leaf. One of our Lieuts got shell shock and he literally cried like a child, some that I saw carried down the firing line were struggling and calling out for their mother, while others were blabbering sentences one could not make out ...

Much of the above was quoted by Bill Gammage in *The Broken Years*, and perhaps Lindstrom found his extract in that book. But, for this part of the story, Martin's next couple of sentences from the full letter are critical:

> ... for one to get shell shock it is worse than a wound, for a wound will heal but a chap when he has lost control of his nerves takes a lot before he has got mastery of them again, and it is doubtful if he could ever be able to be relied on again. It is a thing everyone has to fight against, if, he gives in at all, he is practically done for as a fighter.

Lindstrom quotes another example, an observation by Pte O Coleman 2000, 30th Bn '*... a boy in A Coy crying all the time in a sort of hysteria that he had no ammunition. He attacked seven Germans and after he had killed them all sat down and still cried he had no ammunition ...*'.

And there were others. After the war there came to Australia Dr John Springthorpe and it was he who took on the task of caring for the mentally ill from the war at Melbourne's Mont Park. Springthorpe had been born in England, came to Australia as an infant and was educated in Sydney and Melbourne. He went with the AAMC to Egypt, returned to Australia, and then he went to England '*where he was ordered to develop ... a shell shock clinic*'. He was a specialist in mental illness and psychotherapy and at that time, November 1916, aged 65. Doubtless some of his first patients were casualties from Fromelles so his diary entry for 12 November 1916 seems a suitable conclusion to this chapter: '*The faces of the "shell shock" boys are clean, sweet, immobile young faces—faces that have looked into and tasted Hell—haunt me.*'

A BAD BLUE (contd)

of Fromelles the story: '*Padre's batman arrests postman spy*' lived on. Nobody referred back to Kennedy's own story and his remorse at his injustice.

But when on 19 July Browne was about to go forward he noticed that the bombs they had were not fused. Years later in his copy of Bean's Volume III, he wrote in the margin '*A bad blue by QM people*' and then his own footnote about his section being directed by Lieut Harris to fuse the bombs. (See page 135 for the incident of unfused bombs.)

When Browne was wounded he found a shell hole and was there for three days, some of the time sharing the space, noise and danger with a wounded Bavarian. The Australian was rescued, so it would seem, by line and harness to avoid the snipers. He went then first to Boulogne. There '*While I was at my worst*' confessed Browne, he was visited by a Salvation Army lass who introduced herself as Miss Booth. Later he thought she was probably Evangeline Booth, the daughter of the General!

George Browne was then sent to Cambridge Hospital. It was there in an effort to cure his wounds, which had been infested by flies during his three days in the shell hole, that he was given saline baths. This being a new treatment, it was deemed a suitable thing for the King to see when he visited the hospital. For years George would show friends the photograph of the event: he in the bath and King George looking at '*my wounds and tubes and things*'.

The long press interview had George Browne wounded at the battle of 'Flamelles', in Flanders and provided a hint at where it was, near Lille. '*We lost 9,000 men*' Browne told the reporter.

COURTESY G H BROWNE

The Courts-Martial* of Fromelles

As Courts-Martial are about breaches of military discipline rather than criminal acts, breakdowns in discipline, especially where they involve a group in the same unit, must highlight something else. For instance could the disobedience of so many in 5th Division Artillery have something to do with the '*shorts*'? What caused the CQMS and so many men of the 5th Pioneer Bn to challenge their officers. Sadly this detail was not located. But the general thrust and style of charges and punishments here tell their own story.

After the battle McCay issued a Routine Order part of which was titled '*the following extracts from General Routine Orders by General Sir Douglas Haig, C in C British Army in the field, are published for information and guidance and for necessary action by all concerned*'.

Paragraphs then dealt with strangers, wirecutters, telescopic sights and courts-martial. McCay then published a list of offenders and their fate. An example:

> *No 136251 Dvr J Hasemore 180th Bde RF Artillery. Using insubordinate language to an officer and using threatening language. Shot 12 May 1916.*

The next paragraph dealt with the prohibition of permanent memorials over soldier's graves: '*Forbidden until cessation of hostilities*'.

We can only surmise why McCay would select that information from an old routine order and issue it after the chaos of Fromelles.

There are 25 cases on the July Courts-Martial list, which unlike others provides no names, and only three have specific charges, although all the punishments are listed—as are the men's units. For offering violence to a superior officer a man of 10th Field Artillery received 60 days Field Punishment (FP), another in the same unit who stole something got 3 months hard labour, and another in 5th Div. Artillery Coy got 60 days for drunkenness. Out of the 25 cases, two were found not guilty. The severest punishment was 2 years hard labour in prison for a 60th Bn man for an unstated offence. The 5th Div. Artillery Coy had 7 charged, and 15th Bde had 5. No details of any of the trials, verdicts or names survive in the file. The War Diary simply said:

> *Discipline was good during the first part of the month but towards the end of the month there were a certain number of FGCMs. Vide the great event of the month was the attack made by the Division on night 19/20 July. The casualties were about 5300 for the division.*

Other than this list, only one reference to Courts-Martial survives in the 5th Division Administrative File from the pre-battle period:

> *Major R Harrison, 54th Bn, President of the Divisional Court-Martial held on 13 July to hear the case against Sgt A L Ogilvy, No 103, 14th Field Coy Engineers.*

There is nothing about a verdict nor sentence. Major Harrison was killed on 19 July.

The only Court-Martial detailed for July after the battle was in the Routine Orders of 25 July:

> *A Court-Martial was called for 10.30 am on 25 July under the Presidency of Major H T C Layh, 59th Bn, to try Pte S A Jones (No 271) and Pte W Martin (No 3354), both of 5th Pioneer Bn.*

In the 30 July Routine Orders, the results of this Court-Martial were published. Martin, who had been on a charge of, '*when on Active Service, using threatening language to his Superior Officer*', was found guilty and sentenced to three years penal servitude by Layh. McCay commuted it to 12 months hard labour. Jones was charged with '*disobeying a lawful command given by his superior officer*'. He too was found guilty and sentenced to two years hard labour, confirmed by McCay.

Then followed the Courts-Martial return for August 1916. It lists 53 cases, all but two were found guilty and given sentences ranging from a sergeant of 56th Bn being reduced to the ranks for '*neglecting to obey General Orders, demanding beer between 9 and 10 am and Military discipline*', to a man of 55th Bn sentenced first to death and then to 5 years penal servitude, and then to 2 years.

The story of Pte Clarence Merton Woods 4928 55th Bn is important because, we are told, he was the only Australian sentenced to death by an Australian Court-Martial. The fact that there was no death penalty applicable to the AIF adds a curiosity value to the case.

Woods enlisted at Holdsworthy, NSW, on 4 October 1915. He was 18 years and 5 months, single, a labourer, CofE, and his next of kin was his sister. He sailed from Sydney on 8 March 1916, and was taken on strength of 55th Bn at Ferry Post 20 April 1916. His service record is a sorry tale. Within 12 days he was in trouble for '*being late on parade, insolent to a superior officer and using insubordinate language to his superior officer*'. It cost him 5 days Field Punishment. On 19 June he sailed from Alexandria, arriving in France ten days later. As nothing is noted on his record until 8 August, we could assume he was at the Battle of Fromelles.

Woods went AWL on 4 August and was arrested four days later. On the 14 August he was charged that: '*When on active service absenting himself without leave from 9 am 4 August to 4 pm 8 August after being warned for duty*'. Then, '*striking his superior officer being in execution of his office*', and the third charge, '*using threatening language to his superior officer* [2/Lieut T C Montague], *with the words "I will knock your f--king head off"*.'

On 13 August, '*in the Field*', Woods faced a General Court-Martial

* Hyphenating of Court-Martial and Courts-Martial taken from the *Manual of Military Law* (UK War Office 1914).

ordered by Brig. Gen. C J Hobkirk (CO 14th Bde), and headed by Major O M Croshaw 53rd Bn, with members Capt. W R Sheen 56th Bn and Lieut T L Gitsham 55th Bn. He was found guilt on all charges, and sentenced '*to suffer death by being shot*'. This was confirmed by Sir H Plumer, General Commanding 2nd Army and then commuted by him to 5 years penal servitude, which was then commuted to two years by McCay. The pay of Woods, while under arrest, it was noted, being forfeited. Woods served his sentence at the Military Prison in Le Havre. He was discharged 19 May 1918 and returned to his unit. Then on 19 July—the second anniversary of Fromelles—he went AWL, evading capture until 7 August. His next release was on 2 March 1919, and he went down with influenza, then returning to the 55th Bn 13 March. He went AWL for most of that day, then after being returned to his unit, that evening he was off again, and was not arrested until 31 March. He got 28 days detention, and forfeited 96 days pay. Authorities finally got Woods onto the *Port Sydney*, 3 October. He spent most of the voyage in hospital with scabies. Back in Sydney after 5½ years, he might have seen about 2 months of service. He received the BWM and the VM.

The file reveals little else except his letter to Base Records seeking replacements for lost papers, and a lost Returned Service Badge. With '*more front than Myers*' as was the expression at the time, Woods lamented that he found it difficult to become a member of the RSSILA without them. He then gave his complete service record as '*after completing desert training ... we were shipped ... to Marseilles. Moved to the front line in the Armentieres sector. Made our first big move at Fleur Baix on 19 July 1916. Returned to Australia 13 Nov 1919*'. Further on he wrote '*I'm an invalid pensioner and utterly astounded to learn ... that the League holds no record of myself*'. Having lost the original papers, Woods lost two replacements; his application for a third came on 10 August 1960, where the file ends.

This case was highlighted by Ellis:

the first sentence of death was passed on a soldier of the Division on the 13th of August. The sentence was commuted by General McCay to a term of penal servitude, and it may be stated here that no death sentence was carried out in the Division throughout its existence.

Ellis, an unashamed advocate for the death penalty, fails to explain there was no death sentence available. Brig. General Hobkirk, an Englishman who passed that sentence, had only just taken over 14th Brigade so perhaps nobody had told him that the AIF had different rules. It is interesting to note that McCay had the final say.

It has to be said of the 51 cases found guilty, and using McCay's extract from Haig's Firing Squad list as a guide, probably 43 would have been shot had the AIF also operated British-style firing squads. An interesting aspect of the charges is the breakdown of offences. They are undated but must cover the period of the Battle of Fromelles. There are 12 AWL charges but only one desertion. The largest group are mainly disobeying orders and/or officers, with 18 others on charges of being drunk.

In terms of Brigades the 8th had five offenders, the 14th seventeen and the 15th eight. Something went wrong in 5th Division Artillery where ten men were charged, most for disobeying a lawful command of superior officer, and another four in the 5th Pioneer Bn for the same offence, including CQMS C Griffiths (229), Pte A Short (2679) and Pte J B Fallon (3052). In the Headquarters of the 15th Brigade a man got 3 months for striking a superior officer, whilst at 5th Division Headquarters a corporal got 14 days and was reduced to the Ranks for being drunk. At the end of the list, one of 5th Pioneer Bn got 2 years hard labour '*for indecently assaulting an inhabitant, namely J Singier*'. This was the third longest sentence after the man already mentioned who received 5 years, and another who had 4 years for being AWL, offering violence and threatening language to a superior officer.

But there was another type of punishment called 'Field Punishment' which could be awarded. The Routine Orders spelt out how the guilty man was to spend his 84 days.

Sapper (later L/Cpl) A W Allen No 4522. 8th Field Coy Engineers who was found guilty of being drunk while on Active Service received 84 days Field Punishment.

This consisted of the following: (a) Tied to a fixed object (in view of his comrades) for two hours for not more than three out of four consecutive days up to 21 days. As far as possible this will take place between 2pm and 4pm. (b) Total prohibition of smoking, rum ration (except in trenches) and prohibited from entering an estaminet. (c) All possible fatigues. (d) Pay. Deduction of pay for every day of Field Punishment awarded by Field General Court-Martial or Commanding Officer. (e). 6pm to 6am in guard room. The prisoner will be allowed his blankets and must sleep on the floor; if it is stone, he may be allowed straw. (f). Automatically goes to the bottom of the Leave Roster. (g) Pack drill for at least one hour. (h) Rations. Left to the judgment of the Commander of Divisions or Brigades.

An examination of subsequent months while the Division was still at Fromelles produces a not dissimilar picture to July–August, and an important follow on to the horror of the battle.

In September there were 28 general trials and another 13 for self-inflicted wounds. Of the first group, 9 were on AWL charges, 7 on striking or abusing a superior officer, 5 on general discipline charges, and among the others one was charged for attempting to commit suicide—he was found not guilty. The worst offender was from 57th Bn, he struck his superior officer, attempted to strike him again and used insubordinate language, and was sent to prison for 2 years. All but two of those on self-inflicted wounds charges were found guilty and got between 7 and 90 days Field Punishment.

In the Court-Martial lists of 5th Division in July, August, September and October, no officers appear. There are NCOs, the most senior a CQMS. So it is interesting, to put it mildly, that when on 13 October 1916 2/Lieut James Hoyle McGuire of 29th Bn was tried for striking a soldier, for being drunk and being absent without leave, to examine his punishment. He was found guilty on all charges, and all that happened was that he was cashiered. And this was signed by Haig himself on 20 October 1916. McGuire had enlisted on 1 July 1915 part of the original 29th, was No. 601 and Sgt in B Coy. He returned to Australia on 16 February 1917.

Obviously due to the huge stress at the Battle of the Somme, Haig issued a decree which McCay re-issued in Routine Orders of 30 October under the heading 'Discipline—Sleeping on Post'.

... in consequence of the frequency of cases in which soldiers posted as sentries had been found asleep at their posts, he [Haig] would in future be obliged to confirm sentences of death passed by Courts-Martial for such conduct ...

Not surprisingly, after who knows how many had been shot, somebody must have drawn Haig's attention to the fact that incompetent officers who put exhausted men on sentry duty may well have some questions to answer. Thus in McCay's Routine Order of 9 December 1916:

Fourth Army: Courts-Martial

It often happens that evidence given at Courts-Martial by witnesses discloses irregularities or breaches of discipline on the part of persons not under trial ... the accused frequently brings forward, in defence ... certain irregularities ... that he was on continuous duty for 20 hours without a rest, and that is why he could not help going to sleep. In such cases steps will be at once taken to verify the statements of the accused, and the proceedings will be accompanied by a report as to the truth of such statements.

For the record, there were 14 cases in November, whilst in December there were 13 plus another 5 for self-inflicted wounds. This caused the War Diarist to write for December '*The discipline of the Division was not so quite satisfactory as during last month, Courts-Martial showing an increase*'.

However, in February 1917 there were 29 cases.

As a footnote, when Lieut General Hobbs took over the 5th Australian Division from January 1917, his Routine Orders did not contain lists of executions in the British Army, but dealt with procedural matters at the Courts. Hobbs devoted most space to the health and the general welfare of the Division.

The Dismissal of Colonel Pope

When 5th Division went to France, Pope then temporary Colonel was given command of 14th Bde by McCay who had sacked Irving blaming him for the desert march fiasco. From the papers in the files it can be seen Pope did everything humanly possible to make his brigade's part in the attack at Fromelles a success. Unlike Elliott who openly questioned the action, there is no evidence that Pope was so minded. Anyway 14th Bde's sector was much easier than that faced by 15th Bde. Sent into attack at 6 pm on 19th and ordered to withdraw at 5.40 am on the 20th, the 14th suffered over 2000 casualties, including 496 dead.

From Bean's diary of the day we learn that on hearing of the battle he drove to Sailly arriving at 1.20 pm on 20 July. He interviewed various people including Pope, about whom he then wrote:

Pope of 14th Bde rather disgusted me by the boastful way he talked—I think he had been refreshing himself after the strain. 'Well, we were really the only Bde who didn't come back till we were told to,' he said this morning. He was rather contemptuous about Elliott and 15th Bde.

We now turn to Pope's diary of the next day:

Alleged to be drunk after lunch on Thursday. Went to sleep 3 pm. Woke at 8 am 21st. Saw Pope (Captain) off. Had bath etc. Everything quiet. When starting to prepare report on operation at 11.10 am got memo from McCay relieving me of command—as about 4.30 pm he had found me incapable of duty.

22 July. Pope (Captain) saw McCay 9 am. He says on Thursday afternoon 4.30 pm I was drunk and he knows it.

Wrote to Captains S B Pope and C E W Bean whom I saw just after (lunch) and before sleeping last Thursday.

Harold Pope was sacked unceremoniously on 22 July and sent back to Australia. McCay, despite appeals from many influential people, never changed his mind. Pope asked Birdwood for a court-martial so he could clear himself, but it was refused.

Much later as Bean worked on his story of the Battle of Fromelles he often asked those who would have been near Pope how they saw him on that day. From an interview with Cass, Bean made this note:

Cass says definitely that General Pope was all right when he left him about 2 pm on July 20th. The Brigade Major, Charteris, was of the other impression. He was the only one who was.

One has to ask, why did Bean exclude himself? In the same interview, marked confidential, Bean further quotes Cass:

Col Cass tells me that the night before the 54th had even entered the line in France Gen. McCay came to Gen Pope or himself (he is not quite sure which at this stage) and said, 'I want your Bn to do a raid tomorrow night. Col Cass or Pope answered that his Bn had never been in the trenches. How could they carry out a raid? The reply was it has got to be done and could be done all right. Then Bean adds between brackets '*There is need for care as to the exact wording of this conversation*'.

Pope had another clash with Divisional HQ on 17 July. McCay in a handwritten memo (timed 7.35 am) to Pope said:

Please refer to para 10 of instructions issued to you yesterday. You will see that you were most emphatically directed to send a patrol out last night 16/17 to enemy's line to report on its exact position and condition and to what extent it had been cut. Your front had been defined for you. Please report why this most explicit instruction was not obeyed.

Pope wrote back immediately:

... from the wording of para 10 of the instructions referred to I took it that there were patrols from whom reports were required were those usually sent out from the front trenches. 2. Seeing that troops of my Brigade were not occupying and in fact did not occupy any part of the front trenches until near day break this morning I took it this paragraph did not affect my brigade but applied only to those units who were holding the line. 3. The instructions in question reached me about 6.00 pm yesterday at which time my unit commanders were assembled to hear the orders for the proposed operation. With the exception of para 4 I read the minute in question para by para to the conference. No other construction than that mentioned above suggested itself. 4. I very much regret that if through misconstruction of an order, I have failed; but I most respectfully submit that the construction I did place on it was justified by its wording.

Pope's assertion that his men were not in the trenches and by implication Divisional HQ were not aware of this uncovers shoddy deskwork. But the fact that the Bde was on the very edge of a major action, McCay might have expected something better from Pope. One can only imagine what would have happened to 14th Bde if the attack had gone ahead on 17 July without any knowledge of the wire entanglements.

McCay made no reply.

None of this found its way into the final history, and Pope who did get back into action and prove himself exactly as he had at Gallipoli, lived the rest of his life forever marked by McCay's decision. And apart from a footnote in Volume IV Bean never again mentioned Pope.

The War Diary of the Division noted that Godley came to see McCay on 21 and 22, and that Pope went to see Birdwood on 25 July.

On 27 July the Routine Order noted: '*Lieut Col C J Hobkirk DSO, the Essex Regiment, will be granted temporary rank of Brigadier-General from date of assuming command of 14th Infantry Brigade.*' The next day, 28 July noted: '*Lieut Col (Temporary Colonel) H Pope CB relinquished command of 14th Infantry Brigade and temporary rank of Colonel on 21.7.1916.*'

All Ellis would commit to print was: '*Several important changes of command occurred shortly after the battle. Col Pope CB, relinquished command of 14th Bde ...*'

When McCay himself was replaced, the new commander of 5th Division, Hobbs, assisted by some backtracking by Birdwood found a position for Pope as commander of 52nd Bn, and after the war was fulsome in his praise of Pope's war record.

Monash seldom openly critical of McCay was sure that, in the case of Pope, McCay had been unjust.

... our old friend ...

Few men were closer to General Sir John Monash than Lieut Col (later Brig. General) J P McGlinn. Their Brigadier–Brigade Major relationship got the 4th Bde through Gallipoli in better shape than most. One of their battalion commanders was Pope, so it is no wonder when Monash heard of Pope's dismissal that he wrote to McGlinn, then on McCay's staff. McGlinn received a letter which he kept all his life; dated 2 August, it was marked 'strictly private' and began, '*My Dear McGlinn: [would you be] so kind as to drop me a private note telling me as nearly as you can feel justified in so doing, exactly what happened to our old friend , late of 4th Brigade. I am much perturbed to hear about it and have received several garbled versions of what happened ... Yours always, John Monash.*'

This concern about the fate of Col Pope was typical of Monash, and only endorsed a while later when McGlinn was evacuated ill on 9 November, never to return to the Division. On 16 November another letter, beginning *'My dear old friend'* was concerned with McGlinn's health and future career and promising to do all he could to help. No wonder McGlinn treasured this letter also: wrote Monash—*Believe me to be sincere when I say that things have never been the same since the force of circumstances has deprived me of your constant companionship and powerful help in all things.*
Yours ever, John Monash.

McGlinn also kept some letters from McCay from early 1917 when McGlinn needed every influence he could muster to get the Medical Board to clear him for active service. McCay wrote from 30 Bruton St, W Mayfair, to tell him he was taking over Salisbury, 1 May 1917, and invited McGlinn to lunch. McCay's letters began *'Dear McGlinn'* and concluded *'Yours J W McCay'* but offered him no hope. But as McGlinn ended up at an AIF Depot in England something must have been arranged. But elsewhere when it was all over McGlinn commented on McCay: '*I could not stand him ... his priggish, pedantic mannerisms.*'

The true account of the armistice at Fleurbaix

Perhaps the most memorable story to come out of Fromelles concerned the Australian officer, Major A W Murdoch of 29th Bn, walking across No-Man's Land on 20 July to talk to a German officer. His mission—to negotiate with the Germans on the bringing in of the Australian wounded. The picture of the two officers separated by the German barbed wire discussing possible arrangements, in English, on a landscape strewn with corpses and wounded, seems to represent a moment of sanity in a world gone mad. How mad that world really was, this story reveals all too clearly.

The madness, in the final analysis has to do, so we have been told down the years, with the mindless refusal of the British to consider any sort of truce. The real story is somewhat more complex.

We turn first to the only official recording of this event. It is in the War Diary of the 5th Division: note the wrong date:

SAILLY. 21.7.16. Major Murdoch 29th Bn spoke to a Bavarian Officer this morning from No-Man's Land. The officer told him we could collect our wounded if we put up a flag of truce and sent an officer blindfolded to enemy trenches. General Tivey rang up General Staff Branch who referred the question to GOC Division. General Godley, commanding 2nd ANZAC was present and he rang up 2nd Army. The MGGS telephoned about 10 minutes later that no intercourse was to be allowed under any circumstances nor could a flag of truce be entertained. General Tivey was informed by telephone and the question dropped. However, the Germans appeared to give our stretcher parties a good chance of collecting the wounded provided they did not expose themselves very prominently.

Bean noted '*that no reference to this incident appears to have found its way into the official records either of the Australian or of the German division*'. But as far as the 5th Division is concerned, that is not correct. However neither the 8th Bde nor 29th Bn War Diaries made any mention of the event.

That might have been the end of it, had not a large number of officers and men observed the event and when hearing the verdict became very angry, yet determined not to let the prohibition hamper the rescuing of their cobbers. Most attached blame to the Australian Divisional HQ, believing at that time it had some autonomy over such actions concerning Australian wounded. Later, perhaps with some justification, the British Higher Authorities were seen to be at fault. After the event, when it was not of much use, Haig made the point that although the Rule Book forbade contact with the enemy in this way, there were circumstances when this could be relaxed.

But before dealing with the machinations of the 'Higher Authorities' we should examine what happened in No-Man's Land on that sunny Thursday morning in July 1916.

At this time on No-Man's Land there were probably in the vicinity of 1,000 men so disabled by their wounds that they had no alternative but shelter in shell-holes or ditches, or in some cases, in the water of the River Laies. They would call out for help or in pain. Their hands would be seen above the edges of the hole in which they sheltered, waving to gain attention. Others silently bled to death in the grass or the river. Those alive were of course in great need of water as well as bandages.

HINDSIGHT

A distinctly important contribution to this story is The Report in 21st BRIR file found in the Munich Archives. (German time and Allied time are noted.)

Timed at 4.45 pm (3.45 pm) on 21st July, it reads: '*The enemy has been quiet by night and day. Desultory MG fire during the hours of darkness. At 10.30 am (9.30) the enemy put out a signboard with the Geneva Cross on it. Three medical orderlies then appeared in front of the enemy breastwork and began to attend to the English dead and wounded lying there. One of the orderlies was called closer and told to go back to his trenches and send out an officer to parley, if they wanted something. After immediately informing Regiment by telephone, the English officer who showed himself was told that any requests would have to be brought across by an envoy under a flag of truce. This brought no response.*

'*After about an hour we saw about eighteen men over the enemy breastwork opposite this sector. They were fired on and took cover. The English trench appeared ... to be strongly manned. At 4.00 pm (3.00), a small sign with an inscription that could not be made out appeared on the enemy breastwork in front of the left flank of the sector. Underneath the board there appeared to be a stretcher lying on the breastwork. Nothing further occurred.*'

The Report draws attention to the event described above as the morning of 21st July, whereas Bean places it in the afternoon of the 20th. As both periods were after the artillery has ceased firing, either is possible. The other problem of the German officer being Bavarian or Saxon is solved. Clearly this writer in following the idea that the Saxons who could have been in that position on 20th July afternoon, were returned to their position by 21st July, morning. The few references to Saxons recorded were, on reflection, made about the immediate post-battle period when they may have still been in position. To learn that it was the Bavarians who cared only endorses what the Report discovered in relation to the dead and wounded Australians and English. And to learn without question that Murdoch did lie to Bean, and Miles told the truth, clears up that part of the story.

There are contrary reports that shelling from both sides persisted throughout the morning, ceasing at midday according to Bean. Artillery notes indicate that was the instruction, but the mere fact we know that there were stretcher parties all over No-Man's Land in the morning runs counter to allegations of continuing artillery exchange. This is the first area of confusion: there are plenty more to come.

The story of the attempted Armistice, probably because of the controversy, was not published until 1920 when Ellis described it in *The Story of the 5th Australian Division*, working, so we are told by him only from official documents. This is his version of the event, to which the only preface needed is that Ellis, like Murdoch was of 29th Bn:

> *... the front was practically clear of wounded by 10 am on the 20th. There were still, however, hundreds of wounded in the shell-holes of No-Man's Land. It was a pitiful sight to see the hands beckoning from No-Man's Land for the assistance that could not come to them, and early on the 20th Major Murdoch, of the 29th Battalion, made a gallant but unsuccessful attempt to bring about their relief. Fashioning a rough red cross on a piece of newspaper he crossed, with Private Miles of 'D' Company 29th Battalion, to the enemy trenches and asked to see an officer. A Bavarian Lieutenant, immaculately dressed, emerged from the enemy trench, and Major Murdoch asked if an informal cessation of hostilities could not be mutually arranged to enable the wounded to be brought in. The Bavarian replied courteously enough, regretting that he had no authority to give any order to that effect and saying that he would telephone for instructions. Meanwhile, the men on both sides of the line were not slow to take advantage of the curious situation, and while our men busied themselves in bringing in wounded, the Germans exposed themselves equally freely in repairing breaches in their parapet. Major Murdoch returned unmolested to the front line, but, shortly afterwards, a few warning shots fired high indicated the enemy's intention to resume hostilities. Our men accordingly returned to their trench and the incident closed.*

As this was probably a joint effort by Ellis and Murdoch, the 'mistakes' cannot be excused nor easily explained away. Both, by 1920, must have known that the Saxons had taken over from the Bavarians, others in the line at the time knew this: but as the Saxons were widely known for their gentlemanly conduct it would not have done Murdoch any credit. Ellis' decision to omit who was responsible for not accepting an armistice is, however, his most serious flaw. Murdoch knew these facts (he had led the second wave of the 29th Bn), and whether or not Ellis was present at the time is immaterial. The discussions in the officers' mess and elsewhere over the next three years would have clearly given him all the information he required. So why did Ellis omit crucial facts? Ellis was using his history as a thesis for his law degree interrupted by the war, and he could not afford to offend anybody, least of all McCay. Supporting this fear one reads Ellis' accounts of McCay and the desert march and the last shambles under McCay at Flers with some scepticism. Both accounts when compared even with Bean are equally 'economical with the truth' if not downright and deliberately false. Another distortion, in the effort to save McCay's reputation was Ellis' assertion that '*the sick wastage of the Division (was) at a very low percentage*', when in fact it was twice that of the next highest, the 1st Division, and thus by far the worst in the entire AIF.

But we now return to the Armistice arrangements. We can see what Ellis left out or altered, as we can see the introduction into the story of Private Miles, something not referred to anywhere in the official records, except in the 8th Brigade's Decoration Book (marked SECRET) in which all those recommended for awards were listed, together with the action that warranted a recommendation, and the final decision. The very first entry on the 29th Bn page—the page for ORs that is—reads:

Pte W Miles 1178. On the morning of the 20th July he went out into No-Man's Land and searched for Capt. Mortimer. He afterwards carried water to the wounded lying there, and also carried one of his wounded comrades to our own lines. (He received no award.)

There was no mention of Murdoch in the Decorations for Officers.

Ellis, a young lawyer with his career ahead, steered clear of every controversy. His history is valuable but only officers populate the Division, and comment of legal necessity is superficial to put it politely. On the other hand, Bean seems to have been fascinated by Fromelles, perhaps because there were so many unanswered questions about the preparation, conduct and conclusion of the battle, and this catered for Bean the journalist as well as Bean the historian.

When Bean began researching this episode all he had to go on, except the War Diary, was Ellis' version of the event. Bean phoned Murdoch on 19 May 1926 to get more details of a story that one senses Bean had rather more information about than he let on.

Murdoch begins his letter, in reply, of 19 May 1926 acknowledging Bean's phone call and conversation. As we read Murdoch's correspondence with the historian his legal approach to the questions soon reveals itself as deviousness. He is aware of something that Bean seems not to be aware of, but he is not entirely sure whether or not Bean is setting a trap. But the canny Bean, as we shall see, is suspicious.

Alexander Weir Murdoch, born at Benalla in 1873, was the business manager of Prells, Importers and Exporters, of 31 Queen Street, Melbourne, but he wrote from his home address—6 Black Street, Middle Brighton:

I have to inform you that the written report given by Capt. Ellis of War Records in connection with 5th Division relating to this incident is practically correct. One thing may be added that Private Miles and myself carried as many filled water bottles as possible, distributing them to the wounded in No-Man's Land, which action was not resented by the Germans.

The interview with German officers was not marked by anything of a hostile nature. The telephone communication with German Divisional HQ was to the effect that No-Man's Land should be equally divided, the Germans taking the wounded on the half nearest their trenches and we do likewise, on condition that I was to return blindfolded and held hostage in their trenches as a bond of good faith that the condition stipulated would be carried out. Our Bde HQ communicated with Divisional HQ who would not agree to the condition laid down.

Pte Miles and myself were in No-Man's Land for about 20 minutes during which period other incidents occurred but hardly worthwhile bringing under your notice.

That last sentence must have alerted Bean. He wrote next on 22 May 1926 asking about the white flag and the Red Cross flag as he had heard that there was some confusion about which flag was carried. The introduction of the issue about flags is interesting indicating that Bean had another source of information. Or was this the trap—as the use of Red Cross flags or markings, and the use of white flags were very separate issues as far as Military Law was concerned (see pages 483, 484, 486). He also asks for the *other incidents* to assist *the writer to form his judgement.*

Two days later Murdoch replied: *I have to state the question of white flag or Red Cross was not mentioned by the Germans. In my opinion our Divisional HQ turned the matter down, not because I was to be held hostage but that our Higher Authorities thought the Germans may of had some ulterior motive. Relating to the second paragraph of your letter, to give a description would be rather lengthy and perhaps be of not much value, but I will say that the fight on both sides was a fair one and the morale of our men and the Germans good.*

Murdoch then attached a separate sheet marked 'Personal': *Perhaps in your position you might help me in securing the negative of a photograph of Miles and myself—taken by two German officers while we were in No-Man's Land, and if it is at all possible we would like to have a copy ...*

... to give you a small idea how fortunate Miles and myself were to return to our trenches. When we were interviewing the Germans, who fortunately were Saxons, a shot was fired from our lines. Possibly this did not have any ill result, otherwise we would have had to pay the penalty. With kind regards.

Curious, Murdoch now admits that he was dealing with the Saxons.

Bean tries again on the 25 June 1926, this time on the subject of water bottle distribution, whether or not Murdoch entered the German trench and how the Germans were first attracted.

Murdoch replied on 28 June, explaining that the water bottles were distributed while going across No-Man's Land, and while waiting there to which the Germans objected. To the second point, they did not enter a trench but proceeded to the barbed wire entanglement. To the third point Murdoch answered:

Yes, both lines were watching while we crossed No-Man's Land. German attention was attracted first of all by our displaying the 'Red Cross' which consisted of a newspaper pasted on board and the borders of a red cushion were used to form the cross. This was placed on top of the parapet and waved from side to side to attract German attention. When this was attained Miles and myself proceeded across No-Man's Land.

There is of course no way of knowing what information Bean picked up by chatting with survivors of the battle, and of necessity much reliance must be placed on what survives of his diaries, correspondence and notes. However, in his telling of the Armistice event there is almost nothing that cannot be tracked down to some interview or letter among Bean's papers. But for this examination what is of interest, *indeed special interest*, is the information he had but did not use.

When Bean began writing up this episode he already had some notes about it from his interviews in the field. All that he had recorded was basically critical of the British and complementary of the German behaviour.

For reasons not entirely clear, Bean was unable to locate Private Miles having assumed the man involved to be Pte H N Miles 2605 of 8th TMB, 'a draper from Warragul' despite the fact that Bean had access to the 8th Bde papers, giving the correct Miles' initial and number, in the Decorations' Book. The historian completed his piece and submitted a draft to Murdoch. Murdoch made no changes. No wonder, when we come to compare what was printed in the first edition of Volume III as against that in later editions, and against Private Miles' own story and that of other witnesses of the event.

The first version: Official History Volume III page 438. First Edition:

There followed a stillness never again experienced by the 5th Division in the front trenches. The sight of the wounded lying tortured and helpless in No-Man's Land, within a stone's throw of safety but apparently without hope of it made so strong an appeal that Major Murdoch of the 29th decided to risk his life and military career in an effort which might result in rescuing every wounded man. A Red Cross flag, improvised by tacking some red cloth upon a board covered with newspaper, was waved above the parapet in order to gain the enemy's attention, and then with a private of his battalion named Miles, Murdoch crossed No-Man's Land to the German wire. They carried with them a large number of water bottles, which they distributed to the wounded on the way over. The parapets on both sides were crowded with soldiers watching, and on reaching the enemy wire, Murdoch asked for an officer. A Bavarian Lieutenant 'immaculately dressed' emerged and Major Murdoch asked if an informal truce could be arranged to enable the wounded to be collected. The Bavarian replied courteously enough, regretting that he had no authority to give any order to that effect, and saying that he would telephone for instructions. Upon doing so, a reply was received from the headquarters of his bde or division agreeing to the proposal on condition that the Australian stretcher bearers should work only in their half of No-Man's Land, the wounded in the German half being cleared by German stretcher bearers. As a bond of good faith Murdoch, after consulting his own division was to come back blindfolded to the German trenches, to be held as hostage until the collection was finished. Murdoch at once carried back his proposal which was telephoned to McCay's Headquarters.

Lieut Col John McArthur
DSO & Bar, OBE

And there it might have ended: the first edition of Volume III of the History was published in April 1929. Much of the press coverage was centred about Bean's clearance of McCay for the desert march and for Fromelles in all its aspects. Given McCay's position in the establishment, it was not surprising that a letter from the Naval and Military Club in Melbourne over a pen name should appear:

An Officer Exonerated
To the Editor of the Argus

Sir: The resumé of Mr C E W Bean's new volume of the Official History of Australia in the War published on Saturday is interesting and enlightening. Among other things Mr Bean shows that Major General Sir James McCay was not responsible for the charge of the 2nd Infantry at Helles, the desert march of the 5th Division, or the Fleurbaix disaster. While I was not in any one of these events nor have I ever had any personal reasons for enmity against General McCay, I have long had a deep-rooted feeling against him as a leader, based solely on the statements of others. I readily admit that it is grossly unfair to form an opinion on hearsay, but the evidence against him appeared to have ample and overwhelming collaboration. My firm belief is that 90 per cent of the AIF have very bitter feelings against Sir James McCay, based on the same sort of information as that on which I based my opinion. It must be accepted that Mr Bean was in a better position than any other man to ascertain the true facts, and therefore his exoneration of the General should be sufficient and final. I feel sure thousands like myself will, when they know the truth, feel ashamed to have so utterly damned a man unreservedly. Yours etc.

'Render unto Caesar' Naval & Military Club
April 29 (1929)

Interestingly there were no supporting letters, or even contrary ones in the days following.

In London, the release of Volume III caused this paragraph in the Melbourne press:

Mr C E W Bean's third volume ... is a special feature in the newspapers. The 'Daily Chronicle' gives under headings extending across the page the story of Major Murdoch's informal truce and quotes the story to the extent of a column.

Prior to the publication of Volume III, the Australian War Memorial, then at the Exhibition Buildings in Melbourne, received a letter which started the second part of this story. The Curator wrote to the Official Historian on 25 May 1929.

Early in April ex-Sergeant W Miles (No 1178 29th Bn) wrote to the War Memorial asking if we had a copy of a photograph taken at Fromelles. Miles explained he had accompanied Major Murdoch when this officer endeavoured to arrange an armistice.

It was taken in No-Man's Land at Fleurbaix on July 21 (sic) 1916. I was attending a wounded man when the Germans called me over and we had a long talk. They then sent me back for an officer and Major Murdoch of Prells, Queen Street, came back with me. We couldn't come to terms about collecting the wounded so they told us it must be done at night. While talking to the German officer I had my photo taken repeatedly being asked to turn this way and that. Sometimes I had to hold my hands above my head. Later we were both photographed. If you should see anything like this I should be glad to know .... there were dead and wounded men everywhere around and while we were over at German's lines our men were looking over the parapet.

The Australian War Memorial drew the historian's attention to the H N Miles 2605 8th TMB being incorrect.

Then a letter arrived from ex-Sergeant W Miles of Mooroopna dated 5 June 1929 with which he enclosed a letter from Lieut Col McArthur DSO and Bar of the Drill Hall, Surrey Hills which clearly established that it was W Miles who was concerned. Miles wrote:

I have written to Major Murdoch asking him to correct the statement he went over first. I was sent back by the German officer ... and then Major Murdoch accompanied me back.

What concerned Miles most was that the mix up would spoil his claim for a pension increase so he sent his personal papers to Bean to prove his identity.

McArthur's letter was part of the support for Miles' pension claim and was a glowing tribute to a tough, reliable and courageous individual.

Bean made this note in his working papers:

Major McArthur told me that he would rather not tell me the truth about this episode which was not to the credit of our authorities—I think he meant Gen. McCay. He said Major Murdoch who is not a permanent soldier may tell you perhaps—I cannot

On 15 June 1929 Miles wrote to Treloar at the Australian War Memorial having received a reply from Murdoch.

Major Murdoch seems offended with me, but still does not admit the facts of the incident, or even that I am the person concerned, which latter is vitally necessary to me in proving my identity in my pension appeal. He then quotes others who would verify what he said, and concludes, *Once I can prove the matter to the pension board, the matter can drop as far as I am concerned. I do not want limelight.*

To his eternal credit Bean sorted through the various channels and to put it simply, found that the mistaken entry in his history had no effect on the official records where there was no confusion about who Sgt W Miles was and his service record. Bean promptly returned all Miles' papers by registered post, gumming the receipt to the copy of his letter: typical of Bean's care and consideration.

However, at this level of the story the best was yet to come. Murdoch's letter of 14 June 1929 must have crossed with Miles' letter, and he offered to help Miles in any aspect of his pension review. The rest of the letter was however singularly unpleasant and reveals finally what type of person Murdoch really was. One is now sure that Bean knew that if Murdoch was given sufficient rope he would indeed hang himself. Murdoch, now 53 years old, wrote:

Referring to the footnote on your letter, I wish you to clearly understand that in Bean's book ... the formula referring to the Fleurbaix stunt is his compiling and not mine. He referred to me for verification only.

Do not think for one minute that I am taking exception to your letter, but I wish you to understand that I am not the author of what has been done or the way in which it has been done.

The War Memorial Authorities communicated with me two or three times but I have not complied with their request. I am quite willing to do so if facts are placed before me, but I am not going to be the prime mover in placing myself in the limelight.

My opinion of the review in the 'Daily Chronicle' will deal with the Fleurbaix incident in a phrase that will not lay overdue stress on the incidents leading up to what was achieved, but more in respect to the advisability or inadvisability of carrying to completion the arrangements that were tentatively made.

With kind regards. I am yours sincerely. A W Murdoch.

Bean then wrote to Lieut Col McArthur assuring him that things regarding Miles' identity were cleared up. He then advised Miles.

In return there arrived an 18 page letter from Miles, one of those wonderful 'from-the-heart' letters that reveal the true character of the writer. It also tells us clearly much about the Battle of Fromelles. The pages were fixed together at the top, Miles having written them on a pad and torn off, the whole group at once. The complete letter follows, (some spelling and punctuation corrections have been made, principally the spelling of Murdoch and McCay). The other section of his letter is also given so as to clearly reveal the character and integrity of the little Welsh sailor, turned soldier.

Mooroopna, 30/7/29

Mr C E W Bean.

Dear Sir,

Just a few words in explanation, as to how I became interested in this matter. It is not for a desire to seek the limelight as Major Murdoch suggests [in an earlier letter] *or a wish to detract from his performance, but only to establish my identity before appealing to the board for an increase of pension. I have reason to believe that my papers are not correct, and incomplete. I was discharged medically unfit from the 21st Battn after being in the Base Hospital, St Kilda Rd for some weeks, but have no way of finding out if this period of service is attached to my 29th Battalion papers. If Miles of the 8th LTM Battery gets the credit for Fleurbaix stunt and I am listed 5th Battn you will see that my papers are in a muddle. (I was transferred to 5th Battn just before leaving the training battalion at Hurdcott, Eng., where I was a drill instructor, in Dec. 1918.) (My pension is £1-13-6 a fortnight.) I was wounded in the right side of the head and have recently spent nearly four months in Caulfield for an operation for fractured jaw. I was blown up at Polygon Wood, and reported 'Blown up and shell shock.' I was in hospital for three months all but a few days in Remy Siding, St Omer, and Calais, also resting at Trouville. That is the only time I was away from the battalion at Debnes near the coast. Now Sir, I will soon be finished this prelude to my yarn. I do not care what correction you care to make to the Official History and don't care whether my name is mentioned or not, but if you see fit to put in a word to the pension people, well, I shall be deeply grateful. Major Murdoch is a wealthy, influential businessman at Prells Buildings,*

Melbourne and I don't want to squabble with him as he may be able to injure the little pension I have got. The only child born to us since I returned, 'Aussie Miles', is a cripple and although nearly nine years old, can neither talk or walk. His condition, according to the leading doctors in Melbourne is the result of my shell-shock.

That's that.

Well Sir. Forgive the personal pronoun and here goes. Just two incidents to show that my memory of that morning is alright. Lt Col Toll, 31 Battn said just before we left the German Trench, 'Well men, no one could ask you to do more—get back to our lines, but don't bunch up,' so we went across straggling but as fast as possible. About half way across, another sniper passed me flying and sung out, 'Never knew I won a Stawell gift did you Billy?' His name was Harry Littlewood, and he is a working jeweller in Elizabeth St at present. An hour or two later Gen. McCay & Tivey (?) went along the duck boards and McCay kept on saying 'They'll get used to it.' They asked Major Murdoch how his company fared, and he called out 'fall in D Co. along the duck boards.' We fell in and Major M said to one man 'Fall in, fall in, what are you standing there for?' 'O, I'm fifteen platoon' he said and every body burst out laughing.

Pte William Miles, 8 Section, D Company, 29th Bn, Egypt 1916
COURTESY SLOUCH HAT PUBLICATIONS

A little later on I heard someone say that volunteers were being asked for to go out and get a certain Captain Mortimer who was supposed to be lying just over the parapet badly wounded. I offered and was given a red cross badge for my arm and over I went landing in a shell hole and ricking my knee. I asked two or three wounded men if they had seen Capt. Mortimer but could not find him. One man who was hit in the stomach wanted a drink but I explained that it would do him harm and cut his haversack off, as his tin of bully was hurting his back (fighting order, haversacks on back). Next man was shot in the testicles which had swollen terribly and he borrowed my knife and ripped his own pants open, and wouldn't let me touch him, his agony was great. I jumped as well as I could into another shell hole, which, however, was not deep enough to hide in, and heard some one call out from the German lines; looking over I saw a man beckoning to me. I got up and walked slowly towards him, stopping once to pick up a pair of field glasses. I stopped at the edge of his wire and the following conversation took place:

Fritz: What are you supposed to be doing?

I replied 'Tending wounded men, giving them a drink and cutting their equipment off so they will lie more comfortable till we can get them in'. He said 'You may be laying wires, this is not the 'usages' of war.' I replied 'O yes it is, the red cross is always allowed to work unmolested.' 'What did you pick up just now?' 'A pair of field glasses.' 'It might have been a bomb.' 'I'll show you I said, but he said, 'Don't put your hand in your pocket, put your hands above your head.' I did so and stood so for some time while he spoke through a field telephone to his divisional headquarters. Meanwhile two or three other officers stood on the fire step, and I was asked to turn this way and that and was photographed at least half a dozen times. There was absolutely no firing going on anywhere from the time I reached the wire. Then the gentleman who had called me over put his telephone down and turned to me. Before he could speak I asked his permission to lower my arms and he laughed and said 'I forgot, your arms must be aching.' Next question was 'What are those decorations you are wearing?' I replied unthinking 'Le Guerre Afrique.' He said 'Speak English old Chap. You were through the African war were you?' 'Yes Sir'. 'What rank are you?' 'Only a private Sir.' 'Well I want you to go back to your lines and ask an officer to come over here and we will have a 'parliament' and see if we can arrange about collecting the wounded. Will you come back and let me know what they say?' I promised to, and crossed back to our parapet. The parapet was lined with men and I had hardly stopped before someone fired his rifle off. I yelled 'Tell that b— fool to stop shooting. I've got to get back yet.' Capt. Tracy threatened to shoot any man who fired again & Col McArthur shouted for the word to be passed along to absolutely ceasefire. I then explained to Col McArthur my message and Major Murdoch came over the top to me, and we went back together to Fritz. It was explained to Major Murdoch that the German Divisional Headquarters would allow us to collect half the wounded (nearest us) and the Germans would collect the other half, if a senior officer would consent to be blind folded, taken into their trench, under a white flag, and held a hostage till the stretcher bearers had completed their work. Major M replied that he would have to see his superiors before agreeing to anything and was then requested to 'turn the other way'. I said 'Ask him for a copy Major.' He did so,

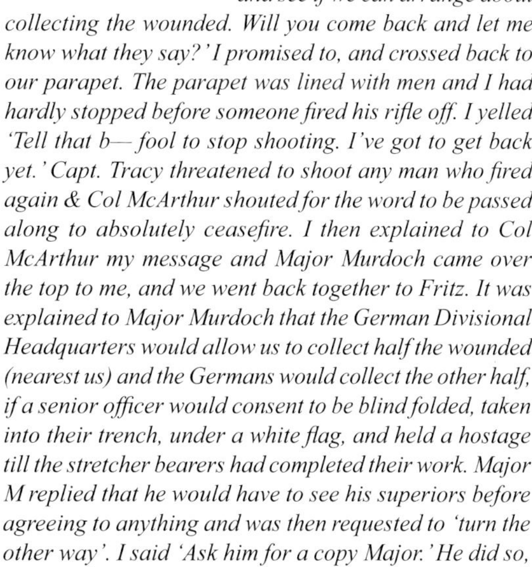

and asked where he would send it to ... He said 'Major Murdoch, Brighton, Victoria' is sufficient. We saluted all round and came back. As soon as MM mentioned the white flag we were told to come in. The stretcher bearers were made to even lift the men off the stretchers and the men hurried in. A sharp rattle of fire over our heads, and we were at it again. Next day on orders, Major Murdoch's name was altered to Weir (one of his Christian names) and mine to McKenzie. Why or wheretofore, I don't know & could never find out. Next day I was interviewed by the intelligence officer of the Oxford & Bucks who were on our left and that is the last I heard of the incident. The O & B officer particularly wanted to know if Fritz made any mistakes in his English and the only two words I found fault with were underlined.

Usages and Parliament

That Sir, is a true account. I will take a declaration on it if necessary and can find a dozen eyewitnesses to the fact that I went over first and came back for an officer.

Yours faithfully, W Miles.

**

In regard to the Sunray Trench stunt the reason Col McArthur mentions me is that I hurt my knee again there and wanted him to certify to this. I did not take part in the 29th Battn raid there as I was too small, height 5' 3', weight (then) about nine stone, now 7st 3. What Col Mc is talking about is my getting a wounded hun out of No-Man's Land. We were carrying hot boxes of tucker up to the company who relieved us <u>the morning after the raid</u>. Lt Wortley was one of the officers, but I don't know which company it was. My chum, a little Jew, Max Beth now a bookmaker at Tattersall's Club, Melbourne, couldn't get along any farther through the mud and climbed out of the sap to the harder ground on top and was instantly shot through the chest near the right shoulder. I cut his tunic open and put his field dressing and my own in the hole in his back and promised to send a stretcher for him as soon as we got back to supports. I reported the matter and went down a dug out for a sleep. Was awakened about four in the afternoon for fatigue and inquired if Beth had been brought out. Was told 'No there have been seven casualties trying to get him' Well I could tell the sniper was very close and asked how that had been carrying the stretcher. When told, I pointed out that it was exactly how a machine gun was carried and got permission from Capt. Taylor & Col McArthur to try another way. I pushed a stretcher over the top, let it fall and climbed after it, dragged it wheelbarrow fashion to Beth and placed him on it. Lt Wortley said from the trench 'You'll draw the fire get down out of it.' I replied 'Never saw him shoot a stretcher bearer yet. Keep your head down through.' Next minute Sgt Fisher peeped over the top and was killed instantly. Next Cpl Love looked over and his steel helmet went ten yards back. I dragged my mate to the communication trench where willing hands lifted him down. Waved my arm and jumped, hurting my knee again. Fritz fired the second I jumped, so he must have seen the whole performance. As soon as I got back Dr H F Maudsley cut my gum boots off, put me to bed in a dug out and gave me a pint pot of rum. Company Sgt Major Hayes came along for my regimental number and brought a drink from the Colonel. I slept all that night, and till dusk the next day when Col McArthur ordered me out of the line, injured.

At Prouville we relieved (I believe) the 23rd Londons. My platoon officer was a gentleman named Munro a bonzer little officer, game as they make them, but it was his first time in the line. As the tommies hadn't rigged even a strand of barb wire in front of the trench a patrol was ordered out and wire party put to work. I had risen to the giddy height of lance corporal by this time and as I was the only NCO available, had to go out with Mr Munro, Sgt Les Grogan, being in charge of the wiring party. He wanted to go out diamond formation with himself in the lead. We argued and finished up by going out in a semi-circle with the bulge in front, where I had a Lewis gun, and the officer next to me. It was about nine hundred yards across the valley and we were about halfway over when Fritz yelled Hala Hala and started shooting. I think I must have beaten him to it as when they got up to run the Lewis gun chopped them to pieces. Lt Munro wanted to go on and get some prisoners but I persuaded him to go a little ahead and he'd find wire. He did so and could not find a gap in it so we were compelled to return. Next night a patrol went out and was met in the long grass by Fritz suffering twenty-two casualties all between knee and ankle. Next day I was promoted corporal, my wife's allowance automatically ceased, also three kids, but Daddy was a corporal so what did it matter. The whole letter reads like a bit of skite Sir. You asked for it, so can do what you like about it.

I remain Sir, Yours faithfully, W Miles

Ex Sgt W Miles, 1178, 29th Bn, AIF

***

Mooroopna, 1/8/29

Mr Bean,

D[ea]r Sir,
It is only at my wife's request that I am forwarding the enclosed. She said 'You're a sick man Will, think of Aussie. If anything happens to you four shillings a week wont keep him.' I am sending a few names along of witnesses who, if they will, can testify that this is a true account of the armistice at Fleurbaix:

Lt Col McArthur, Drill Hall, Surrey Hills
Major Murdoch, 31 Queen St, Melbourne
RSM Jim Shean, c/o Equity Trust A & Co. Ltd, 85 Queen St, Melbourne

Sergeant Bob Rahilly, c/o SA & ASA CA Buildings, Collins Place, CI
Private J Collyer, employed by Louis Coen, Wireless Agents as motor driver
Capt. Micky Coates (still on staff. I believe at Essendon.)
Sgt W Amos, Billiard saloon proprietor, Chapel St, Prahran
Sgt Rob C Kimpton, 216 Rathmines St, Fairfield
Capt. Charles Derham (Swallow & Ariels)
Capt. Ainsley (Conn's Motors)
Capt. Ellis, Author of History of 5th Division &
Lt Jerry Davern (ex RSM, now Melbourne plain clothes police)

Yours etc, WM

It was those letters which caused Bean to entirely revise the story for the later editions of Volume III, still under 20th July 1916:

There followed a stillness never again experienced by the 5th Division in the front trenches. The sight of the wounded lying tortured and helpless in No-Man's Land, within a stone's throw of safety but apparently without hope of it, made so strong an appeal that more than one Australian, taking his life in his hands, went out to tend them. On the front of the 29th Battalion, Private Miles, an ex-sailor, who had fought in the South African War, was dodging from shell-hole to shell-hole in search of Captain Mortimer, when a voice called to him from the German lines, and he saw there an officer beckoning him. Miles walked slowly to the wire, picking up and pocketing on the way a pair of field-glasses. 'What are you supposed to be doing?' asked the officer, who spoke perfect English and was immaculately dressed. Miles said that he was tending the wounded pending such time as they could be brought in. 'You may be laying wires', said the officer, 'this is not the usages of war.' 'Oh! yes it is,' replied Miles, 'the Red Cross is always allowed to work unmolested.' The officer had seen Miles pick up some object; 'it might have been a bomb,' he said, but he hurriedly stopped the Victorian from putting hand to his pocket, and made him hold up both arms while he himself spoke through the telephone to some German headquarters. When he laid down the receiver, he asked Miles his rank. 'Only a private, Sir.' 'Well, I want you to go back to your lines and ask an officer to come over here, and we will have a parliamentaire and see if we can arrange about collecting the wounded. Will you come back and let me know what they say?' Miles returned to the Australian lines, and Major Murdoch of the 29th decided to risk his military career in an effort which might result in saving all the wounded. The parapets on both sides were crowded with soldiers watching when he returned with Miles and asked if an informal truce could be arranged. (Before they crossed, Capt. J McArthur, adjutant of the 29th, ordered all fire to cease, and a red cross flag, improvised by tacking some red cloth on a board covered with newspaper, was waved above the parapet. Meanwhile a number of water-bottles had been collected, and on the way over Miles and Murdoch distributed many of them to the wounded.) The Bavarian officer answered courteously, regretting that he had no authority to give any order to that effect, and saying that he would telephone for instructions. Upon his doing so, a reply was received from the headquarters of his brigade or division agreeing to the proposal on condition that the Australian stretcher-bearers should work only in their own half of No-Man's Land, the wounded in the German half being cleared by German stretcher-bearers. As a bond of good faith Murdoch, after consulting his own division, was to come back blindfolded to the German trenches, to be held there as hostage until the collection was finished. Murdoch at once carried back this proposal, which was telephoned in M'Cay's headquarters. (He and Miles, in spite of a remonstrance by the Germans, had, while waiting near the German wire, distributed among the wounded their remaining water-bottles.) In the meanwhile, except for the occasional discharge of a gun in the rear area, hostilities had ceased, the informal truce having spread to the whole battle-front, and the garrison of both sides were engaged—the Australians in bringing in some of the wounded, and the Germans in repairing their front trench. Near the Laies, where the Australian wounded lay thick, the Germans began to go over their parapets, apparently in order to bring in the men lying nearest to them. A message was accordingly sent by the 15th Brigade asking the artillery to stop any of its guns which was then firing.

A careful check of the Fromelles chapters reveal that Bean brought back 6 lines on page 437 and then on page 438 at the line ' … made so strong an appeal that Major Murdoch', changed that to read: ' … made so strong an appeal that more than one Australian … ' To accommodate the extra lines Bean dropped the footnote about *The Story of the 5th Australian Division* referring the reader to page 111 of that book which gave Murdoch's false story, and transfers the reference to Ellis' book to page 420, directing the reader to page 114 about another Fromelles incident. Bean also drops any reference to the German officer being Bavarian, and includes a new footnote on page 439 giving Capt. J McArthur's input, but <u>only</u> on the issue of the flag. McArthur was not mentioned in the First Edition anywhere. There were no other changes of any substance in the Fromelles chapters.

Having ascertained what actually occurred in No-Man's Land we turn now to the proposed Armistice. Although it is clear that the ultimate responsibility for the refusal to consider any arrangement clearly lay with the British, popular tradition has always blamed McCay's Headquarters.

Ellis, as we have already seen, made no reference to nor comment on the British or Australian refusal to consider a truce, and his concluding sentences were entirely untrue as he must have known.

Bean's correspondence with McCay on this subject began on 26 May 1926, thus:

Dear McCay, Among the many accounts of Fromelles, there are a certain number of references to some negotiation between the 29th Bn and the 104th Saxon Regiment concerning an armistice for picking up the wounded. As the matter was apparently referred to German divisional headquarters and to your headquarters, I would be very much obliged if you could help me by letting me know whether the matter was transmitted by you to XI Corps or First Army, and what was the principle upon which it was decided. With kind regards

Before discussing McCay's answer, we note here that Bean is aware that it was a Saxon, not Bavarian, Regiment as early as May 1926. This information he may have had from other witnesses' accounts or intelligence sources, as the Saxon Unit history was not published until 1927. It clearly states that the 104th relieved the 21st Bavarians on the night 19/20 July.

McCay would have realised that this letter required a most carefully worded reply. He doubtless knew that Bean had access to the various records and his answer could thus be verified or refuted. Curiously, nowhere in the correspondence does Bean remind McCay, that he, Bean was at Fromelles on 20 July. One has to wonder why, when such information would have surely spurred McCay to other than a legal reply. Another factor of which McCay would have been well aware was that public opinion forever blamed him for this, the desert march, Flers and Cape Helles. However much he protested his innocence in private (he went public on the issue once, to say that he would not go public) he was distrusted and hated to the end of his life. Bean's questioning, quite correctly, could never be described as sympathetic as could his correspondence with Elliott for instance. However, in all his letters to McCay over this issue he is very careful not to paint McCay into a corner, by saying he has some other information.

McCay replied on 6 June 1926 from his home at 59 Brighton Road, St. Kilda. He mentioned that he had consulted McGlinn and others '*to help or verify my recollections*':

The facts relating to the very temporary armistice to which you refer are these:

1. GHQ orders and all subordinate orders were extremely definite to the effect that no negotiations of any kind, and on any subject were to be had with the enemy.

2. It was duly reported to my Divisional Headquarters —the date I do not recall—that some arrangement had been made, apparently at first between a captain in my trenches and a German officer, for a temporary armistice for picking up wounded.

3. In view of the definiteness of GHQ orders, as soon as my Headquarters became aware of the tentative arrangement orders were at once sent to put an end to the truce, and this was done.

4. I did not refer it officially to Corps HQ, GHQ orders being too explicit to justify any such action, but I afterwards told the Corps Commander, the Army Commander about it: and they approved of the action taken.

We must not forget McCay's career cycle before the war began: from Headmaster to Lawyer to Politician to Chief of Army Intelligence to Chief Censor: as we read his various replies to Bean. There could hardly be any argument about the date that McCay could not recall, but had he 'remembered' the date it might indicate that the decision was important to him. With about half of his Division dead or wounded, on a stretch of ground easily accessible to stretcher-bearers, and with the battle lost, one might think that the General in charge of the 5th Australian Division might have cared, or even fought a corner for his troops. He might, had he one iota of charity, be seen to at least to show posterity that he tried. But of course McCay cared about nobody but himself ever: and all he could say to Bean is that two British generals later approved!

This proposition is on very shaky ground. It is obvious why Bean did not push his questioning any further. He must have known that McCay was lying, because there is no way that with his brilliant legal mind McCay would not have taken refuge behind Military Law if it cleared him of all blame. It is impossible to accept that in the ten years since Fromelles, with all his self-confessed soul-searching, McCay was not aware of the form of truce known as 'suspension of arms'. It is dealt with clearly and concisely in Chapter XIV, section III, subsections 256–260 of the *Manual of Military Law 1914* (see page 486). It is also impossible to accept that there was no copy of this manual in HQ of the 5th Australian Division, populated as it was with career British Officers under an ex-lawyer. And Section 260 leaves no doubt about McCay's guilt in this event. And in the Appendices of the Manual, No 12 even provides the internationally accepted wording for an agreement, which by its very existence demolishes totally McCay's and Edmonds' protestations (see page 487).

Anyway, the recollection McCay gives is of course at odds with the 5th Division War Diary entry given at the beginning of this story except in respect to McCay himself who is 'absent' in both cases. True McCay, for the sake of history and in 'correct form' accepts responsibility for the conduct and decisions of his staff, but the fact that he admits that he checked out the decision later with the people who it should have been checked out with on 20 July, seems to indicate fairly clearly, that he made the decision. But perhaps McCay was covering up for his staff, perhaps he was asleep, and that is no criticism.

We know McCay went to the château for a conference with Army HQ at 5 am that morning. The reference in Miles' letter to McCay coming through the trenches early on the morning of the 20th is a further time check. We can assume that he did not sleep through the battle, and because we know that all three Bde Commanders did not sleep on the night 18/19th, it might be fair to assume the same for McCay. H R Williams saw him in the line 'about noon'.

None of the domestic detail is dealt with by the War Diaries and the participants themselves do not seem to have recorded such things. However, the ever-present Captain Bean made some interesting notes in his diary of the 20 July which because his history, quite correctly, does not deal with the aftermath of battles, have not been published before. The following extracts apply to this story, other extracts are quoted where appropriate. Bean:

I reached 5th Div HQ at about 1.20 (pm) at Sailly. I went straight up to Wagstaff's room. There was a conference on and they were very busy.

Bean then collected as much information as he could for his cable which as we have seen he sent from Amiens that evening. He then visited the three Bde headquarters, 8th Bde first:

As McCay was busy I went round all 3 Bde HQs. Poor old Tivey looked quite overdone—with eyes like boiled gooseberries. He had been up two nights and been through his trenches today (quite a fair number of men were lost in our trenches this morning by German shelling). The one thing he seemed anxious to assure himself of was that his Bde had been tried as 'hard and had done as well as bdes on Gallipoli' ... And Tivey told me simply, '1700—that's about as heavy as some Bdes lost at the landing isn't it?' And so it was.

Pope of 14th rather disgusted me by the boastful way he talked—I think he had been refreshing himself after the strain. 'Well, we were really the only Bde who didn't come back till we were told to', he said this morning (sic). He was rather contemptuous about Elliott and 15th Bde.

Old Elliott was dead asleep when I called—but McCay came in and woke him up. When Elliott came out I felt almost as if I were in the presence of a man who had just lost his wife. He looked down and could hardly speak—he was clearly terribly depressed and overwrought. McCay was also, I thought, anxious about an order which he and Elliott had given for 2 Coys of the 58th Bn to support between the 14th Bde and the British.

We know from other sources that McCay also went to Pope but was unable to rouse him from his sleep and the next day dismissed him for being drunk. Pope had had an earlier run in with McCay about sending men who had never before been in trenches out on a raid some days prior, and also challenged McCay on the wording of an order (see pages 260–61).

Probably the most disturbing comment on the armistice came from General Edmonds the man in charge of preparing the British Official History. Bean submitted a draft of the Fromelles chapter to him containing at that point the first version of this story. In his letter of 27 October 1927 Edmonds was surely giving commands rather than aiding the historian:

As a matter of taste, I should omit these details. What good does it do even if true: 'legally' is wrong. The Geneva Convention gives no right to give attention to the wounded in any circumstances. (I was Secretary of the British Delegation at the Geneva Conference and an author of the official manual on the laws and customs of war.) The mistake made was asking permission to arrange a local suspension of arms. Many such suspensions were made e.g. even during the battle of Loos, when, near Hulloch, both sides ... up and removed wounded. There was another on 3 May 1918 at Villers-Bretonneux for half an hour. Of course if formations formally ask permission to arrange a suspension it must be formally refused.

Edmonds' differentiation between 'legally', the Geneva Convention and his own contribution to the Manual is difficult to sustain. There are in the Manual clear statements about attention to the wounded (and dead) which do not support his phrase in any circumstances (see page 482). But Edmonds was 'spot on' in saying that the mistake was asking permission. We can only suppose that Wagstaff turned to Godley who phoned Haking to get a decision. Had Tivey had some battle experience in such matters, he could have made his own arrangements with his German counterpart, perhaps even advising Pope and Elliott to follow suit. The success of the more experienced 61st Division in getting in their wounded might well have had much to do with their knowledge of past successes in the 'suspension of arms'.

To his credit Bean, as we have seen, did not reduce the story, and in fact when he came into possession of the real facts, added them, considerably expanding the piece. However, his attempt to be even-handed looks like compromise in the face of Edmonds this once.

In 1946 Bean published a one volume history of the war *Anzac to Amiens* and he or his editors had to summarise the armistice story in a single paragraph. This now nominated the two heroes of the episode—Pte W Miles and the German officer.

Very many wounded lay in No-Man's Land especially opposite the Sugar Loaf. Here an Australian batman, searching for his dead officer right up to the German wire, was challenged by a Bavarian officer, whose humanity now made possible an informal truce to which many Australians owe their lives.

But: the 29th Bn area was as far from the Sugarloaf as possible, and it was indisputably a Saxon officer! Anyway Murdoch did not enter the story, and McCay's 'correct form' had no place!

McArthur, Miles and Murdoch

The three main characters in the Armistice story survived the war and returned to Australia to live very different lives.

Col J MCARTHUR

John McArthur was born on 6 April 1875 at Bannockburn, Stirling, Scotland, and came to Queensland as a boy and when 19 began his military career with the Queensland Mounted Infantry. In 1899 he went to South Africa with that unit's contingent, and was invalided back in September 1900. Marrying in 1903, Isabella Agnes Bruce, they had two sons and three daughters. McArthur remained in the CMF and was transferred to Melbourne. In 1915 in the AIF, he was captain and adjutant of 29th Bn. Whatever he did in connection with the truce was never detailed by Bean, but it seems from various accounts that he was responsible for calling the line to order, ie not firing or behaving dangerously while the negotiations were under way.

When Miles thought the erroneous history of Bean would hinder his pension claim, McArthur wrote to Miles, leaving no doubt about the true story.

'It was rather surprising that another Miles has received the credit for your gallant action, when you accom-panied Major Murdoch into No-Man's Land after our dreadful experience of the night before. I remember when a volunteer was asked for, you jumped from the parapet and after having fallen, got up and although limping carried on and continued to render assistance, even after the truce had been called off. You also went out even in broad daylight and carried water to those in front of our wire, also after dark again assisted in getting in the wounded. I understand the CO had specially mentioned your work. I feel and have always felt that you deserved the greatest praise at least for what you did.'

In view of Ellis relying on serious misrepresentation of the incident, it is no surprise that McArthur gets no mention at all in Ellis' chapter. It is almost certain that McArthur was the one who saw Murdoch and Miles off on their expedition. After Fromelles, McArthur was promoted to Major and became a very considerable figure in the 5th Division. By March 1918 he was Lieut Col and had command of the 29th Bn. He earned his first DSO 28 July 1918 and a Bar to that DSO less than two weeks later. He had two MIDs. After the war, by 1926 he was Adjutant of 24th Bn at Surrey Hills, Victoria. In 1933 McArthur was appointed OBE, then retiring for a few years before signing on again in 1939 for two years at Army HQ Melbourne. He died at his home in East Kew on 22 July 1947.

The unmarked grave of William and Isobel Miles, Fawkner Cemetery

The grave of Aussie Miles, Sunbury Cemetery, Victoria.

WILLIAM MILES

William Miles, born 21 April 1880 at Caerleon, Monmouthshire, was the son of Rev. William Miles, clergyman; and Mary (née Reese). A sailor, he served in the Second Anglo-Boer War, and in 1903 came to Australia. Moving to Bendigo, he married Isobel Kathleen (Catherine) Moore from Collingwood. Her first child, Robert Percy, had been born in 1902 in Carlton. William and Isobel settled in Bendigo where he worked as a house furnisher. They had three children: William David, born in 1904; Dorothy Isobel, born in 1911; and Aussie, born in 1920.

William Miles died on 7 June 1949 at his home, 39 Emerald St, South Melbourne, aged 68, and was buried on 9 June. His occupation was given as 'permanent soldier', and he had been resident in Australia for 45 years. Aussie lived in Sunbury and died on 17 May 1988.

Major A W MURDOCH

Alexander Murdoch was born at Benalla 5 February 1873, and was educated at Scotch College. In 1905 he married Jessie Stuart Pigdon of Carlton, and their son was born in 1906 at Coburg: he also went to Scotch College. Murdoch was a Major in Egypt in 1915 and had charge of D Coy of which Pte William Miles was a member. He returned to Australia on 25 November 1917. An entry on 5 October 1917 in 5th Div Admin File explains why: '*Major A W Murdoch Bn Commander ... lacked nothing in pluck, he was physically incapable of commanding a Bn in the field.*' He was appointed Hon Major on return. Murdoch died on 24 August 1949 at his home, 8 Black Street, Middle Brighton. The one death notice in *The Age* and *Argus* on 26 August noted: 'husband of the late Jessie Stuart and father of Alexander William Murdoch. Private Cremation'.

8

At a critical moment

He assumed command of the Battalion at a critical moment.

—Brig. General H E Elliott, in his citation for Lieut Col H T C Layh's DSO at Fromelles

With the wounded in from the battlefield, as much as possible collected from the dead and their bodies covered with quick lime where practical, and prisoners lost from view (as it turned out until late August), it was time to make awards for gallantry to the survivors, and for some who did not survive.

When the proud but shattered Elliott penned his recommendation for Lieut Col Layh, his phrase—the title of this chapter—captured the essence of bravery, the action that seizes the moment, changes the situation, makes the difference, saves the life or the day: and which by the very nature of the battlefield was often just a moment. But not always. So at Fromelles there was that critical moment when Layh took control, as there was the whole long night when Father Kennedy carried wounded back to the dressing station. Deeds of bravery being not attributable to commands or coercion, but springing from values held, training acquired and experiences endured.

Capt. H T C Layh,
Lemnos, Christmas Day 1915
He received a DSO at Fromelles, another at Villers-Bretonneux and was appointed CMG for his work at Bullecourt.
AWM C1190

Recommendations were passed up from Company Commanders to Commanding Officers, thence to Brigade Commander, then to the Division and then Corps. The first medals from the deeds of Australians at Fromelles were distributed at a large parade on 3 September 1916, after a special church parade at the Divisional Bombing School where General Sir Henry Plumer GOC 2nd Army '*has kindly consented to present the ribbons*' said the Routine Order of 29 August. On 12 October another presentation of medals from Fromelles was made by General Birdwood. Such events became morale boosters for the men who received their Military Medal ribbons: which it would seem they often posted back home. Higher decorations usually took longer to go through the system. Some recipients wrote '*got a medal, but anyone would have done what I did*'. Generally speaking nobody expressed any pride in an award. But the relatives of the decorated man took another view. Their pride often had them writing to the press, but despite this, huge numbers of medals were never claimed. Ellis and the unit histories seldom went into the circumstances of an award unless it was a VC. This could not have been because

19 JULY STUNT

12 October 1916. Sir William Birdwood received us. Medals were bestowed on chaps for conspicuous gallantry on the 19th July stunt.

—Pte E C Schaeche 5444 59th Bn

WHOSE DUTY IT IS

In future the Victoria Cross or other immediate reward will not be given for the rescue of wounded excepting to those whose duty it is to care for such cases. Such attempts, more often than not, result in the death of the would-be rescuer and rescued. Moreover it depletes the fighting strength of units perhaps at the most critical moment.

—5th Division Routine Orders, 5 October, 1916

NOT WIDELY KNOWN

About a month later it was my good fortune to stand in the front rank of a hollow square—representative of every unit in the division—to witness the presentation of some fifty decorations by General Plumer.

In his brief speech to the troops General Plumer said:

That although the attack was not widely known to the public, and when the history of the war came to be written, it would probably be described as a failure. Yet, the number of decorations presented to 5th Division was proof of the importance which the General Staff attached to it, and its appreciation of the heroism displayed.

—Lieut W Smith, 53rd Bn *Reveille*, July 1936

of lack of information, but more because to pick out some for mention seemed unfair, when everybody knew that not all the brave deeds were recognised, and a few medals were not entirely deserved. As far as the Australian records are concerned, the details have always been available in Divisional papers.

Probably the recipients and their families were only aware of the official gazetted citations, inevitably some factually barren phrase like '*bravery in the face of the enemy*'. However the original recommendation was often very descriptive, and not a few relate back to previous acts or service which together with the action under review '*require recognition*' as the saying went.

For a work of this nature it would have been rewarding to be able to relate each man's bravery to a particular place or event in the battle. This proved impossible because many of the citations are missing, others are not specific and a number refer to deeds over many hours. But by collecting them together under the battalions they can be related to the known deeds of that unit described in the book, and in that way provide a view of an individual, section or company, not apparent in the general description of the battle. Whilst every effort has been made to make this list exhaustive, men transferred from other units are often classified under those units, others whose awards were made, in some cases after McCay left the Division, have only been found by chance, hence the mention of Hobbs who took over from McCay in late December 1916. This would indicate that acts of bravery ignored, or passed over, by McCay's group were submitted to Hobbs to be dealt with.

We know from the Divisional papers of August and September 1916 that 'Immediate Decorations awarded to the Division' '*in connection with the operation of 19th/20th July last*' were: DSO—4, MC—31, DCM—32, MM—49. A total of 116 immediate awards.

A number of later awards were made and where known these are marked with an asterisk. This dramatically reveals what deeds were only noted in retrospect. In the final analysis from this compilation, which includes infantry, artillery, pioneers, headquarters, and medical, the awards made as a result of the Battle of Fromelles were: DSO—9, MC—48, DCM—45, MM—63, Foreign Decorations—14, MID—38. Making an overall total of 217.

A number of unsuccessful recommendations are included in the list because they illustrate interesting aspects of the battle and if a man's deeds were of sufficient note to warrant this attention, they are important to the story.

Before describing the awards made to Infantry Battalions, it is probably important to remember the vastly different characters and circumstances involved in the three brigades. Tivey, a precise man, accountant by training and very correct, as against Elliott, large and stormy, who said what he thought, and Hobkirk who had to sort out the situation after Pope had gone, and as it would seem left no stone unturned to make sure awards were given where deserved.

8th Brigade

Among the surviving papers of the 8th Brigade is a small leather backed ledger marked 'secret'. Like a new diary it has been carefully ruled up and pages designated for the awards and honours won by the Brigade. It's notes are meagre, however Tivey did not neglect his heroes:

8th Brigade HQ

Lieut K A Goodland, Brigade Intelligence Officer '... *worked unceasingly*'. Recommended for MC: not awarded.

29th Battalion

This, the reserve battalion, was later charged with bringing up supplies and ammunition to the beleagured 31st and 32nd. The award list is surprisingly short.

Sgt R Cornish. 1467. DCM:

> *he performed consistent good work under fire ... a splendid example of courage and determination.*

Pte R H Keir* 59 must have been a remarkable man. At Fromelles he was awarded the French Croix de Guerre, the MM and was MID. Hobbs signed the recommendation that Tivey wrote:

> *This man was a bandsman, also a stretcher bearer. On the night... at Petillon, Pte Keir carried bombs and ammunition to the German trenches which were being held by our men, until the wounded started to come in. He then took up his own work and continued during the whole of the next day, going into No-Man's Land in daylight securing wounded.*

Before the war Keir, a leading member of the Malvern Tramway Band, had a significant reputation as a trombone and cornet player. He had been runner-up twice in the prestigious Ballarat South Street Competition. After the battle his CO, Col A W Bennett, wrote to Keir's father: '*I can hardly express to you ... how proud I was to have such a noble character under my command. He was always on hand in the most dangerous part*

FOUND AND LOST

At the end of Routine Orders of 23 July—

Found. Trombone in black cover. Owner apply to Divisional Headquarters.

And on the 25 July another poignant notice:

Lost. In the Rue due Bois on 20th inst, a bicycle, painted dark green with the number 552 in white and a triangle painted in red on the frame. Finder please communicate with CRE, 5th Australian Divisional Engineers.

Pte R H Keir, MM, Croix de Guerre
COURTESY SLOUCH HAT PUBLICATIONS

Major R H BEARDSMORE

Robert Henry Beardsmore was born 12 August 1873 in NSW. Enlisting in the AIF in August 1915 (he had already served with AN&ME in capturing German New Guinea) Beardsmore was wounded early on at Fromelles and did not have his wounds attended to for ten hours. On 28 July he was promoted Lieut Col and commanded 32nd Bn. In 1917 he was MID before his front line career ended in April due to health reasons, when he took charge of 5th Div. Base Depot at Etaples. After the war he, as a member of the NSW public service, had an eventful career. He died 25 Dec 1959.

Major R H Beardsmore
(see biographical note on previous page)

WHOM GROGAN CARRIED
While crossing into the German trenches Capt. B A Wark (1894-1941) was wounded in both legs, and he was carried out across No-Man's Land by Pte Grogan. Wark recovered, transferred to 32nd Bn and stayed with them till the end of the war, earning DSO in October 1917 and the VC in October 1918. He was then in temporary command. Capt. Wark's brothers, Alex and Keith, were in 56th Bn, Keith receiving the DCM at Fromelles.

WHAT NANKIVELL CARRIED
Lieut Barbour in charge of 14th Platoon had moved quickly through the enemy front line and went in search of the '*supposed support system*' and found that '*nothing of the kind existed*'. As they were in the space between 31st and 32nd Bns, Barbour decided to dig in, his men trying to raise a parapet which would protect them from rifle and machine guns. Barbour made a sketch of this position and this is what Nankivell carried back, '*though dreadfully wounded on the journey*'. Faithfully attended by such as Anderson throughout their ordeal, Barbour and the survivors just before dawn decided to return to their lines. Over half of these did not make it.

and although cut about the face, continued to work on when he could have reasonably gone to the hospital.'

Entered in the Decorations Book, the first item on the ORs page was this unsuccessful recommendation.

> Pte W Miles. 1178. '*On the morning of 20th July, he went out into No-Man's Land and searched for Captain Mortimer. He afterwards carried water to the wounded lying there, and also carried one of his wounded comrades to our own lines.*'

30th Battalion

Sent in to assist the 31st and 32nd, being the support battalion the 30th also took heavy casualties.

Major R H Beardsmore was awarded the DSO for his work in organising the digging of a sap across No-Man's Land. He was also Mentioned in Despatches.

Captain R A M Allen '*wounded in the advance but ... went forward ... later he withdrew ... but went forward again*', and Lieut I G Fullarton, '*though wounded ... he refused to go back*', the battalion Intelligence Officer, both received the MC, as did Lieut E A C MacFarlane '*conspicuous gallantry when leading a raid ...*'.

Pte F W Barrett, 354 (a runner) '*carried messages to all parts of firing line ... till he was absolutely exhausted*', Pte J G Hunter 442, '*made twelve trips across No-Man's Land*' and Pte W A Ward* 1001 '*made several trips ... later he rescued many wounded*' were all given the DCM. Barrett's was for '*conspicuous bravery throughout the fight*' and Ward's was for work on 19/20 July when he '*carried in ammunition and carried out men*' and other deeds in September.

Pte E W Hales 907 and Cpl A W Forbes 880, worked together saving the wounded: Pte H E G Staples 1614, Sgt F A Butterworth 1249, Pte J J Anderson 814, Pte T H Davies 401, Pte T C Grogan 1557 and Pte P J Nankivell 949 all received the MM. It was Pte Nankivell, D Coy runner, who was well remembered years later by his officer of the time, Lieut T C Barbour. Nankivell had vanished while taking a message back from Barbour. Then after the battle:

> *I thought I heard my name called from the vicinity of the dugout shambles. This was repeated in a feeble voice and on investigating I discovered Nankivell amongst the debris. I found him a mass of shrapnel wounds in body and legs, I could see portions of shell sticking out. To my surprise he made no mention of his terrible condition but was anxious to let me know he had delivered my message alright. In a letter he forwarded to me from hospital, he wrote ... 'I was doubtful whether I would be able to get there, but I got there.'*

Lieut Barbour in his correspondence with Bean remembered Pte J J Anderson 814 who was wounded early and he, Barbour, bound up his leg wound. Barbour also knew that Anderson received the MM.

Capt. W J R Cheeseman* was Mentioned in Despatches for: *'he was always energetic and thorough in his work and shows great offensive spirit.* 'His work on 19/20 July and other in September were what was referred to. Later Cheeseman received the DSO, MC and Legion d'Honneur.

Lieut J S Lees (KIA 20.7.1916), Lieut J W Clark and Capt. J Chapman were also MID.

Pte R H Herps 1561 and Pte E D Robinson 1263 working as a team, and Pte H McDiarmid 926, Pte E Bannister 371, and Pte J Sweeney 303, also working as a team, were all put forward for their rescuing work. No awards were given. Nor to L/Cpl E Shipp also put forward for an MM but no award was made.

Major M Purser* was Mentioned in Despatches for in the words of Tivey: '*this officer was in charge of ammunition supplies for the fighting troops. He displayed the utmost courage and coolness... though men were killed all around him, he never faltered.*' It was signed by Hobbs. He later commanded the 24th Bn at Polygon Wood and was awarded the DSO.

31st Battalion

Lieut Col F W Toll's* DSO for Fromelles was not an immediate award and was announced in October 1916. Toll himself prepared on 21 July at Fleurbaix his Report for Tivey. It was in several parts, the first dealing with the men and their deeds, the second with the battle itself, something which says much about Toll. His comments concerning the heroes of 31st Bn are used here in the absence of more formal recommendations.

For the Military Cross. At the top of Toll's several lists was Lieut G A Still, the Bn's Intelligence Officer:

> *For gallantry in organising straggling troops and advancing over open country in rear of the enemy's position, also for keeping up communications with Bde HQ by means of pigeons, and later by runners, and in German main breastworks during the night, assisting in consolidating positions won, and generally devotion to duty.*

2nd Lieut L J Trounson:

> *Showed great gallantry in maintaining a continuous service with his Lewis gun. He established himself on top of enemy's parapet and with only one man assisted materially in holding the position in German trench all night. He and his gun were literally blown out of his position.*

Capt. W J R CHEESEMAN

William Joseph Robert Cheeseman was born 12 Jan 1884 in NSW and went into business in Newcastle. He enlisted 18 Oct 1915. After Fromelles, the MC and Legion d'Honneur were for Beaumetz in March 1917. When the CO of 53rd Bn was killed at Polygon Wood September 1917, Cheeseman at 23 was promoted Lieut Col of 53rd Bn, becoming one of the youngest battalion Commanders in the AIF. Gassed at Villers-Bretonneux April 1918, he came back to lead right through till the end. In October in action at Bellicourt he saved the situation, earning the DSO, and being MID. After the war he was president of the 53rd Bn Association for many years. He died in Adelaide on 23 April 1938.

Major M Purser 30th Bn

Lieut Col F W Toll, 31st Bn
COURTESY P NELSON

2nd Lieut L J TROUNSON
Lawrence John Trounson was born at Maryborough, Victoria, 22 August 1895. He later lived at Ararat and Hollybush, Victoria. As a sergeant in 31st Bn, he arrived in Egypt in late 1915. In March 1916 he was commissioned. At Fromelles as Lewis gun officer he was seen walking forward with the gun over his shoulder, then *'setting up on a barricade of dead Germans'*. He was dislodged and the incident noted in his citation was also recorded by the German historian (see page 198), on withdrawal he carried back two other Lewis guns. Trounson, a school teacher from Victoria, was promoted Captain, June 1917, and returned to Australia, 20 August 1919. He became a salesman in Hughesdale, Victoria. Trounson died in Melbourne, 18 February 1964, aged 68.

For Distinguished Conduct Medal. CSM W McLean 349:

> *Held with great gallantry the extreme left flank of Battalions front in German main position... assisting in protection of our MG position from enemy bombers.*

Sgt F Law 246:

> *... acted with great gallantry and coolness under withering hail of artillery on the right flank. He with about ten men attacked the enemy MG position and put it out of action and captured it.*

Cpl R J Carew 43 Signaller.

> *... showed great gallantry in earlier stages of action. Although six of his comrades (signallers) were killed and wounded, he alone kept up with his CO and carried the basket of pigeons to advanced position. He then assisted in getting stragglers together. At this stage he was severely wounded in the thigh by shrapnel. He gallantly continued on, and during the night attempted to get signal communication with Colonel Cass, which only lasted a few moments. At dawn... with a revolver assisted to hold off the German bombers, and remained at his post until some of the very last... He is now in hospital.*

Sgt R J O'SULLIVAN
'For conspicuous gallantry during operations. When posted with 30 men in the main trench to link up with another battalion, he behaved in a most cool and determined manner, and held the ground allotted to him till day break'
—*Commonwealth Gazette* 14 Dec 1916

CSM R J O'Sullivan 1323 was named by Toll for the DCM but he left no description of his work. However in the records of his school, St Patrick's College, Ballarat, there is this: *'An officer and Sgt O'Sullivan were there till the last, and then brought a machine gun back to our front line and turned it on the Germans. The Sgt wasn't satisfied with that, but he goes out and brings in three wounded men.'*

For the Military Medal. Pte H G Wilson 1143, whom Toll mentioned several times. So impressed was he by Wilson's work with Pte R G Thompson in attending the wounded that Toll wrote *'with the RMO and the majority of the AMC Details being casualties ... the work of the few left was tremendous.'* However only Wilson was given the MM.

Lieut (later Captain) F Drayton* won the Croix de Guerre because as Tivey described it:

> *During the operation... this officer displayed coolness and courage of a high order... he shot a German officer... afterwards advanced with the remnants of his company to our most forward position in the German lines, and held on all night under terrific fire.*

Lieut F Drayton, 1915
COURTESY P NELSON

Major P A M Eckersley was Mentioned in Despatches, *'for his assistance in holding our advanced line.'*

Sgt (later 2nd Lieut) T R Collier* was Mentioned in Despatches because *'he was in charge of a party who laid a line from 29th Bn HQ to CO 30th Bn in the front line.'* His work on the September raids was also mentioned.

Lieut V D Bernard, *'great gallantry in re-organising scattered troops.'* Lieut R C Aland, *'his cool behaviour encouraged his men who were more or less badly shattered.'* Lieut H E McLennan *'his gallant behaviour struck me as deserving the highest praise.'* Lieut G H Wilson, *'with a few men pluckily held an exposed position.'* Lieut V L Morisset with others *'held on to first line and came through unwounded.'* Capt. C Mills and Lieut MacLeod *'did excellent work'*. These were other officers chosen by Toll for reward but none materialised. Aland received a MC later in the war.

Lieut G H WILSON
George Herbert Wilson later gave a description of how he and his team got loads of Mills bombs down the train line to 8th Bde front line: '*none of us knew how to fuse them ...*' but set to work '*under the guidance of four battalion RSMs*'. The trucks then took boxes of bombs to the line and each time brought back two shattered men ... until '*the enemy completely destroyed the trainline*'. Wilson, who was from Brisbane, later earned the MC.

Lieut Col Toll thought no less of his NCOs and men and mentioned all these for some recognition, but none were awarded medals.

Pte J J Walker, 316, *'assisted Lieut Aland carry a wounded,'* Pte D O'Connor 460 *'passed across No-Man's Land with messages three times during the night.'* Later in the war, which he survived, O'Connor became a Sergeant and was awarded MM. Pte R Eddie 663 *'This soldier a scout and of Intelligence Party acted with splendid gallantry.'* Cpl A C Day 640 *'I wish to bring to your special notice... has on several occasions shown merit of high order as a scout.'* Pte F Forder 3390, Pte R Ingram 1593, and Pte J L Fitzpatrick 1099 were all noted for their work with saving wounded.

Lieut VD Bernard, 1915
COURTESY P NELSON

32nd Battalion

This battalion in 8th Bde that was the most badly damaged and left sparse records. Only these decorations were traced.

Capt. A R White, 2/Lieut S E G Mills and Capt. R A Geddes all received the Military Cross. Captain C Q Taplin was put forward for an award but none was given. It appears that Lieut F L Krinks* later received an MC for his exploits (see page 124) including those at Fromelles.

Capt. A R WHITE
Though blown into the air by a shell in the advance, he led on through the enemy barrage till he reached their trenches where he did fine work in consolidating the position won. When the enemy counterattacked, he led a charge with fixed bayonets to create a diversion while his MGs got to safety.
—*Commonwealth Gazette* 14 Dec 1916

Sgt W Banning 274 received the Military Medal, while Sgt J S Mellish 657 and Pte H W Furze 498 were unsuccessful. Furze later received the DCM.

14th Brigade

The 14th Brigade is an interesting example of initiative at HQ. As Col Pope was sent off the day after the battle the awards had to be selected by Brig. Gen. Hobkirk who took over on 21 July. He seems to have made a real effort to ensure that full recognition was given, because the 14th is the largest of

2/Lieut S E G MILLS
... though twice wounded early ... he continued firing at his post throughout the night, displaying great personal courage.
—*Commonwealth Gazette* 14 Dec 1916

GENTLEMEN, YOUR MEN BEFORE YOURSELVES
The friendship that began by the Suez Canal between Major Oswald Mosley Croshaw a British Army Officer, and the Padre of 53rd Bn Capt. John Joseph Kennedy, the RMO of the same battalion Capt. Charles Cosgrove, and Lieut Col Bert Norris CO of 53rd, is very much a story of Fromelles.

After his education at Harrow, Croshaw had been with 19th Hussars in South Africa and in the defence of Ladysmith receiving King's and Queen's medals with six clasps. Later he served on Gallipoli and now found himself at a dead end as Bde Major Canal Defences. His old army friend Lieut Col Wagstaff organised Croshaw's transfer to 53rd Bn as 2IC, under Lieut Col Bert Norris. There he met Capt. Kennedy an Irish priest who had spent a few years in Australia, and Capt. Cosgrove a doctor from the same Catholic college in Sydney as Norris. It is clear that the three conservatives were somewhat taken by the professional soldier from Kent.

I have rarely met men of such charm of manner as Col Croshaw, wrote Kennedy, *He was brusque and harsh with people he deemed rotters. At parade he was strict but never overbearing. At mess he was an English gentleman, always courteous, a delightful host, a brilliant conversationalist, with a keen appreciation of humour, quick at repartee, a lover of music and song ...*

They went to Fromelles together where, again in Kennedy's words: *Major Croshaw witnessed more than his share of horrors. As advance Bde Major, his work was arduous and extremely perilous, while, our MO, Captain Cosgrove established himself for all time in the respect and love of the men. Gentle as a woman, he spoke cheery words of sympathy and encouragement to our poor lads ...*, of Norris, *among the fallen was our gallant Colonel*. Of himself, Kennedy gave no hint other than *never shall I forget the scenes of carnage ...*

After the battle Croshaw called a muster roll at 3 pm, 20 July: 150 men were there and five officers including Kennedy and Cosgrove, of the other [continued opposite]

the three lists. Hobkirk must have been greatly assisted by the surviving officers, because there seems to be no area neglected for recognition as is revealed not just by the infantry awards but with engineers, medical and others. Perhaps it was Hobkirk's long service in the armies of the Empire that had shown him the value of awards in terms of morale and '*espirit de corps*'. The record that survives of these deeds of gallantry in the brigade add wonderfully to the history of the battle. And the fact that Pope's brigade had such leaders as Croshaw (Norris having been killed), Cass, McConaghy and Scott was not unrelated to these honours and awards. All the battalion leaders, it should be remembered, were appointed by Irving whom McCay had sacked as a scapegoat for the Desert March.

53rd Battalion

Hon. Capt. J J Kennedy, the Roman Catholic Chaplain, was awarded the DSO. The citation had Hobkirk's and McCay's signatures:

> *At Petillon on 19th/20th July 1916, Chaplain Kennedy performed magnificent service in carrying wounded from the firing trenches to the dressing station down the first line trenches, and the remains of the communication trenches under exceedingly heavy shell fire throughout the whole night. Chaplain Kennedy frequently carried empty stretchers up to the firing line by himself, sought for and found the most urgent cases amongst the wounded, impressed anyone whom he could find (slightly wounded etc) to assist him in carrying the stretchers back to dressing station again returning to the firing line repeatedly and assisting with dressing etc. Throughout the whole action his work was invaluable and he probably saved many lives.*

Lieut O M Croshaw* CMG, late of the Queen's Own Royal Glasgow Yeomanry, received the DSO because:

> *He very ably kept the Bde Commander informed of the situation by personal visits to the advanced lines of the captured German trenches. He worked very hard to reconstruct the 53rd Battalion after it had been reduced to half its effective strength in the action on 19/20 July ... though greatly handicapped by lack of experienced officers and NCOs ... he was Mentioned in Despatches for gallantry at Fromelles.* (Hobkirk).

All these officers were awarded the Military Cross.

Capt. J J Murray, '*held his position [although] outflanked*'. Captain N D Thomson*, '*took complete charge in the trenches when ordered to retire*' (Hobkirk). 2nd Lieut T Francis, '*led a platoon.*' 2nd Lieut A E Jackson '*he showed a magnificent example to all. Not a single one of his men survived.*' 2nd Lieut N B Lovett '*... though wounded while leading ... he continued fighting all night ...*'

All the following received the DCM:

CSM S Munro* 3361 '... *for bringing out wounded men*' (Hobkirk).

Sgt F R Myers 3082 '... *showed great courage throughout the whole fight.*'

Sgt F Saunders 2665. '*ran up and down the parapet of German trenches repeatedly bombing the enemy.*' This exploit was later described as 'winning the VC but gaining the DCM' by a member of the battalion.

Pte F L Croft* 3546:

> *He accompanied his CO (Col Norris) into the German trenches... the CO, Adjutant and two others were killed ... Pte Croft taking a prisoner... before leaving he cut all the wires in the German trenches... Lieut Myers had brought this man's name to notice as being particularly cool and brave throughout... The gallantry displayed by Pte Croft on 19/20 July has only recently been brought to notice otherwise he would have been recommended at an earlier date for immediate award.*

Pte William Hobson 3025:

> *At Petillon on 19th/20th July 1916, Private Hobson worked throughout the fight under the direction of the RMO who specially singled him out for recognition from amongst the rest of the bearers, all of whom were good and worked unceasingly for over 27 hours. Private Hobson was slightly wounded on the morning of the 19th but continued to carry wounded through the communication trenches and along the front line trenches both of which were under a very heavy fire throughout the whole time and were choked with dead and wounded men, and debris of all kind. It was not until the afternoon that he permitted the RMO to dress his wound, when it appeared that he had suffered a large shrapnel wound which necessitated his immediate evacuation.*

Military Medals were awarded to the following:

L/Cpl J H Harrop* 4929: '*a medical orderly: I cannot speak too well of his bravery*' (Croshaw).

Pte F Sorton 4921 and Pte J Devery 3276A, '*the giant stretcher bearer*'—'*two stretcher bearers working together*', team work noted by Hobkirk.

Cpl V J Barkell 1305: Croshaw recommended this Corporal Signaller for MM, but it was not approved. Early in 1917 Barkell received the DCM.

Mentioned in Despatches: 2nd Lieut W C Jennings* and L/Cpl A P Anderson* 4900 on the recommendation of Hobkirk.

GENTLEMEN, YOUR MEN BEFORE YOURSELVES (contd)

three, two were later evacuated to hospital. Kennedy and Croshaw received the DSO, and Cosgrove the MC. Back in Fleurbaix just as the bombardment began on 28 July, Croshaw sure that the Germans had the range, evacuated Kennedy and other officers minutes before a direct hit destroyed their billet. In March 1917 Croshaw was wounded and MID.

The bond between the men grew and by the middle of 1917 Lieut Col Croshaw, now CO of 53rd Bn, was received into the Catholic Church. In September as the Division moved towards Polygon Wood, Kennedy recalled them walking together, *I have a presentiment that this is going to be my last fight*, the Colonel told the priest, who remembered the rest:

About midnight we moved forward to the front line. Colonel Croshaw received Holy Communion before we left the pill box. The attack came off at 5.50 am on the morning of 26th (Sept). *The last we saw of the Colonel was when he addressed the officers just before the advance, 'Gentlemen, your men before yourselves. Look to your flanks. God bless you lads till we meet again'.*

A shell burst short and gave him his passport to Eternity ... we buried him near the ruined schools on the Menin Road outside Ypres.

A tribute published in *The Times* was '... *we have lost our best friend, and the shattered remnant of our grand regiment, which he made and raised to the standard of perhaps the best fighting unit in the field, are heartbroken and disconsolate.*'

Lieut Col O Croshaw's grave is at Enclosure 21 A 21 at Bedford House Cemetery, Zillebeke. He left a widow and was aged 38.

Capt. J J MURRAY

He led the first two waves ... with great dash and skillfully consolidated the position won. Although outflanked and almost surrendered, he held onto his position with great determination. The success of his battalion was largely due to his tenacity.

—*Commonwealth Gazette* 14 Dec 1916

AN UNGAZETTED VC
Capt. Charles Arblaster of 53rd Bn earned a considerable reputation and mentions of his name occur frequently in memoirs of the battle. Kennedy wrote of him as '*my ideal officer ... clean cut, athletic and handsome ... he was a born leader of men.*' In Reveille, January 1936 he is noted as 'an ungazetted VC' and later in November 1941, a fellow officer of 53rd Bn, Major S W Evers MC recalled some of the legend: '*Capt. Charlie Arblaster (RMC Duntroon) OC D Coy and a splendid soldier, died an ungazetted VC, a prisoner at Douai. He was given a funeral by French civilians.*'

PHOTOGRAPH L & A LIGHT

The German Records reveal he died of septicaemia 24 July in a hospital in Douai behind the German lines. He had been seen wounded on a stretcher and on a tram on the night 19/20 July. His name was published on the German Death List of 26 August 1916, and he was buried at Douai North Cemetery (Row D, Grave 6), now Douai Communal Cemetery. Those possessions found on him were parcelled up in Germany but were lost in transit. They consisted of his watch, purse, pipe, mouth organ, 2 prayer books and 2 coins. His other personal [continued opposite]

54th Battalion

Led by one of the major heroes of Fromelles, Lieut Col Cass, the 54th list is the most thorough and has throughout Cass's own input: the battle, as we have seen, destroyed Cass personally, and one has to wonder why he received no formal recognition. Perhaps he refused it.

Lieut Col W E H Cass CMG was recommended for the DSO, the following citation was written by Hobkirk, and signed by McCay. Cass did not receive the award but was Mentioned in Despatches.

> *At Potillon on 19th/20th July 1916, Lt-Colonel Cass throughout the attack commanded and led his Battalion most gallantly. Through his cool and prompt steps at consolidating his left flank when the Brigade on his left retired and his counter-attacking, he enabled the 14th Brigade to maintain its position along his sector. His reports showed cool judgment and his arrangements for the eventual retirement after fourteen hours in the German trenches were well conceived and directed, all this taking place under a very heavy fire.*

Lieut W D Harris was noticed by Hobkirk for '*most energetic building up a bullet-proof parapet to consolidate the ground won*', and by Cass who put Harris forward for a DSO, '*in my opinion his wonderfully good work, splendid example and endurance, did much to inspire the whole line and is fully worthy of a DSO*'. Harris received the Military Cross.

Lieut R G Downing for '*unflinching bravery in face of overwhelming numbers ... in charge of a Lewis gun section*', the MC, the first of two.

Lieut A G Morris, '*a Scout officer [who had] gone forward in first wave*', also the MC, the first of two.

2nd Lieut A C Gunter, a '*grenadier officer*', the MC.

Hon Capt. S E Maxted, the Church of England Chaplain, he '*rendered ... services of mercy never to be forgotten by those who benefited by them*' (Bean), the MC.

All the following received the DCM.

Sgt K N Wark 2895: '*took charge of his platoon when the officer casualties had left the men of D Coy with only one officer*'.

Sgt A G Bates 1722: '*took charge of a party in the absence of any officer and constructed about 40 yards of trench to link up the 54th with the 53rd ...*'

Sgt J Cookson 1854 of Lewis Gun Section:

> he drove back the enemy's counter-attack with his machine guns ...

Pte J McCabe 1804:

did most excellent work in seconding Lieut Harris' efforts. In broad daylight he carried a wounded man from almost 300 yards in front of the position finally held.

Sgt F T Stringer 1833:

... standing on a parapet by actions and voice, he rallied together a lot of men who had been badly shaken by incessant bombing. He used his rifle freely and effectively and finally having enthused about a dozen of the badly shaken men he got them over the parapet and with a cheer led them on in counter-attack. The effect was immediate, for the Germans fled in disorder.

Stringer was also awarded the Russian Cross of St George, 4th Class.

Sgt A A Reynolds* 2199: '*a signaller*' was put forward for the DCM.

Military Medals went to:

Cpl P Mealey 4266: '*he was practically fearless*'. Pte A W Wheen 4386 a signaller of Bn HQ for '*laying and repairing telephone wires*'. Pte L P Carter-Ihnen 3272 who carried messages: '*he was cool, plucky and untiring... only a youth*'.

Cpl C R Hawke 2422.

Capt. J Hansen* for '*his work was always well and bravely done*', wrote Hobkirk, and Capt. M J Lowe* (Adjutant) '*organised parties going across No-Man's Land*', again Hobkirk's comment, both were Mentioned in Despatches.

Cass put forward some others, but it seems the deeds he specified were not recognised. 2nd Lieut H R Lovejoy* was taken prisoner and Cass thought he was worthy of some recognition. Then a group of three: '*did their duty much better in very trying circumstances than is usually expected of such junior officers. All stuck splendidly to their work*'. Cass wrote that of Lieut A H Hirst*, 2nd Lieut E S Astridge* and 2nd Lieut L Judd*, but they were given nothing.

55th Battalion

A fairly short list considering the amount of work the battalion did, and its casualties. The omission of Capt. Gibbins is extraordinary, and has to have been somebody's deliberate decision.

Lieut Col D McF McConaghy* CMG was one of the major forces in the battle, and his file contains two citations for the DSO he received. The first by Hobkirk:

AN UNGAZETTED VC (contd)

effects, simply *'a valise, brown canvas trunk, and another trunk'* were sent to Mrs C A Arblaster of 7 Errol St, Footscray.

Born at Pennyroyal, Victoria, son of Charles and Elizabeth Arblaster, Charles was 21 when he died. He had been educated at St Stephen's, Footscray, before going to Duntroon. He was OC 8th LHR MG Section, later T/Capt. and Adjutant 8th LHR on Gallipoli. Wounded there 26 September, he was evacuated to the UK and later transferred to 53rd Bn, March 1916.

Pte A W WHEEN

The MM that Arthur Wesley Wheen earned at Fromelles was the first of three (others: Beaulencourt May 1917, Villers-Bretonneux 25 April 1918), and by the end of the war he was a Lieutenant. Born 9 February 1897 in NSW, he returned to Australia in January 1919, and the next year as a Rhodes Scholar went to Oxford. Four years later he became Assistant Librarian at the Victoria & Albert Museum in London, and a few years later he translated into English *All Quiet on the Western Front*, first published in German in 1929. His translation has remained the most accepted version of the famous book. Wheen became Keeper of the Victoria & Albert Museum in 1945. He retired in 1962 and established a pottery. He died in the UK on 15 March 1971.

A SERVICE OF MERCY

In the Australian trench the scene was truly pitiful, it was packed with dead and dying men, among whom Chaplain Maxted, of Marrickville, NSW, worked in his shirt sleeves, praying with the dying and bandaging the not too severely wounded, until he was killed: a service of mercy not to be forgotten.

—Pte Joseph H Case 3057,
2nd Pioneer Bn.

Lieut Colonel McConaghy has done very excellent work in the Field. During the attack on the 5th Division opposite Fromelles on the 19th/20th July 1916, Lt Col McConaghy commanded the right sector (of the 14th Brigade attack) of the conquered ground and very ably directed its defence against numerous counter-attacks till the brigade was ordered to retire.

He commanded his Battalion in the trenches with great ability, and under his leadership it has done much good work both in construction, patrolling and in a very successful raid. He is an exceptionally good and true Battalion Commander.

The second, unsigned, adds a little more information:

At Petillon on 19th/20th July 1916, where two companies of Lieut Colonel McConaghy's Battalion (then in reserve) were ordered up to support the attack, he personally led them up and took command of the right sector. He very ably organized the defence of the new line in his sector, drove back outflanking attacks after the Brigade on the right had retired. His handling of the situation till the retirement was ordered, all under very heavy fire, was most praiseworthy.

Capt. P W Woods*, '*at the Landing, Lone Pine and who had received great praise for his organising ability in connection with the evacuation ... displayed great courage*', wrote Hobkirk. Woods received the MC, he also earned DSO and Bar; was MID four times; and was gazetted Lieut Col and commanded the Bn later. 2nd Lieut P W Chapman, '*who led boundary parties*' and Lieut W H Denoon '*who badly wounded ... [was] calm, collected and courageous*' were also awarded the MC.

DCMs went to Sgt S Colless 2808 '*utter disregard for danger*' who was later commissioned and won a MC, and to Sgt F A W Hocking 2609 '*Sgt Hocking's was the last gun to leave the C Trench ... conspicuous gallantry in organising ammunition parties for feeding Lewis and Vickers guns...*'

Pte L Chadwick 3219 and Pte J A Perkins 3150 '*worked together in placing Lieut Denoon who was severely wounded, so that he was rescued and survived*'. Both received Military Medals for this work.

Lieut C T Agassiz*, a Lewis gunner, together with Sgt J P O'Brien* 2745 and Cpl O P Martin* 1658 were all put forward by McConaghy for MID but none materialised.

56th Battalion

Interestingly two officers noted in these awards were involved in attending the 8th Brigade '*evacuation*'. Hobkirk's undiplomatic reference to this in Capt. Fanning's MID is an important footnote to the history. But perhaps what is more noteworthy

Lieut Col D McF McCONAGHY
David McFie McConaghy was born at Cootamundra, NSW on 5 April 1887. He was an accountant in Sydney before enlisting. With 3rd Bn on Gallipoli he was prominent, leading the Bn at Lone Pine: hence the CMG. After Fromelles and the DSO, he was in command of 54th Bn at Villers-Bretonneux on 9 April 1918 when the battalion headquarters was hit. McConaghy died of the wounds he received and was buried at Namps-au-Dal British Cemetery.

Lieut Col P W WOODS
Percy William Woods was born in Sydney 8 Nov 1885, and enlisted 4 Sept 1914 as a private. At the Landing he was sergeant in 3rd Bn, and a month later commissioned, and Lieutenant in August. As a platoon commander in the Lone Pine action, legend has it that his dark brown hair turned grey visibly overnight, such was the strain. He was MID for his work on Gallipoli. Transferred to 55th Bn in Egypt he was promoted Captain, and after Fromelles, Major in early 1917. He led the battalion in the capture of Doignies and second Bullecourt—his first DSO. The second was for work at Peronne in 1918: he was then Lieut Col and CO of 55th Bn. After the war Woods continued to be involved with both 55th Bn and its Association. At the Peace Day Parade in Sydney 19 July 1919 Woods led the 5th Division. He died on 5 Jan 1937.

Lieut W H DENOON
... at a critical stage he was ordered to make a counter-attack across ground swept by MG fire, on part of the enemy's trench from which we were being bombed. His attack won some 50 yards of trench before he was badly wounded.
—*Commonwealth Gazette*
14 Dec 1916

are the commendations for Pte Rowley and Pte Hellam, the first certainly, and the second probably, unsuccessful VCs.

The following officers were awarded the Military Cross:

Capt. W R Sheen: *'in bringing back elements of 8th Brigade.'*

Capt. V E Smythe *'ex-Gallipoli'* also received the Serbian Silver Medal. *'He organised a strong patrol, and maintained his position…'*. Later in the war he earned a bar to the MC.

Lieut W McI Pitt,* '… *he led two successful raids…*'.

The DCM went to Pte T C Rowley* 2436. The War Diary entry signed by Lieut Col A H Scott was first to take note of Rowley who was from Enfield, NSW, but born in Mile End, London: '… *several very brave acts and devotion to duty were noticed in the Bn, the most noticeable being No 2436 Private T C Rowley of A Coy'*. But McCay in his own handwriting put Rowley forward for the Victoria Cross. Statements were made by Capt. Fanning, and Capt. Sheen, 2nd Lieut R A Reid and CSM S M Dykes… (all now missing from the file) on or around 3 August 1916. McCay thought enough of the eventual award of the DCM to put this note in Routine Orders 19 August:

> *The GOC Division has great pleasure in promulgating the following communication from General Headquarters. Under authority granted by His Majesty the King, the Commander in Chief awards the Distinguished Conduct Medal to No 2436 Pte T C Rowley, 56th Bn, AIF.*

The extraordinary deeds of Pte Rowley were vividly described in his citation:

> *At Petillon on 19th/20th July 1916, Private Rowley, during the retirement of the 8th Infantry Brigade, proceeded to the parapet of the enemy's trench and standing up on the parapet in full view, threw grenades with such effect that the enemy had to withdraw from the parapet over which they were firing and so enabled about 80 men of the above mentioned Brigade to reach their lines in safety. The gallantry displayed by Private Rowley also prevented the enemy from gaining the head of the communication trench which had been completed across 'No-Man's Land' and so prevented the enemy cutting off the 14th Brigade's left flank thus preventing numerous casualties. Private Rowley continued throwing grenades for some three hours until his arm was so swollen that he was unable to use it. During this period Private Rowley had to retire for a fresh supply of grenades, returning alone to the enemy's parapet and continued to hold them back. By his action, he proved himself to be a man of great presence of mind and coolness and his action also denotes personal bravery of the very highest order.*

While Pte S Hellam* 2836 was originally put forward for a MM, this was later elevated to the DCM, and it would seem

Capt. W R SHEEN
For conspicuous gallantry in action. He took out a party of men during a very heavy bombardment and, by his personal example and bravery, succeeded in rallying some men who were retiring, and bringing them back to their original line. He thus secured the position against the enemy.
—*Commonwealth Gazette*
14 Dec 1916

Rue de Petillon—the main road in 5th Division area. It later became the site for Rue Petillon Military Cemetery. Elliott used this district in his citations, never Fleurbaix.
PHOTOGRAPH R LEFFLER

Pte Rowley was also awarded the Russian Cross of St George (2nd Class) which seems to have been the highest Russian decoration given to a non-officer in the AIF.

might have been considered for the VC as Hellam's citation was signed by six witnesses, including Captain Sheen and Captain Grieve, the Bn's RMO. The citation read:

> *By great initiative, personal bravery and devotion to duty, this man succeeded in rescuing several men from No-Man's Land on the morning of 21st July under heavy fire. His repeated journeys to No-Man's Land to rescue wounded, inspired his comrades and he was thus instrumental in getting more volunteers for the dangerous task of rescuing the wounded.*

Another DCM went to Cpl M Phillips 3103, '*was largely responsible for maintaining the supply of grenades across No-Man's Land and thus allowing the men holding the trenches to maintain their position*'. (see also page 139).

Sgt W Hurley* 246 '*led a bombing party and succeeded in driving the enemy back at a critical stage whilst an orderly retirement was being made*'.

Sgt J C Watt 3134 C Coy and L/Sgt H Oldham 8091 (from AAMC) for '*dressing wounded for some 20 hours without rest ... made several journeys to No-Man's Land during the early morning of 21 July to dress and bring wounded in*' were both awarded the DCM.

Military Medals went to:

Pte T Fishenden* 3039 (also MID) and Sgt T F Gordon 1363 who together were '*engaged in digging the communication trench across No-Man's Land*' (Hobkirk). L/Sgt R Stewart 1762 for '*bringing in numerous wounded men*'. Later in the war he received the DCM.

A/Sgt T R James 2706. Pte A H Clunne 4761.

Major A J Simpson,* '*when in command of the two advanced companies of the Bn, handled these with great judgement and was largely responsible for their good work and few casualties*'. This was written by Lieut Col Scott, and resulted in the Order of the Crown of Italy for Major Simpson, but not until February 1917.

Sgt M Macdonald* 760 '*a private at Lone Pine... displayed splendid courage... now a 2nd Lieut*' (Hobkirk) received an Italian Bronze Medal.

Lieut Col A H Scott,* already with a DSO from Gallipoli, was MID, but it was not a very enthusiastic citation from Hobkirk: '*he has shown himself very thorough in his methods of command*'. Also MID was Capt. C R Lucas* and CSM C E

Lieut Col A H SCOTT
Allan Humphrey Scott was born 3 April 1891 at Tumut, NSW. He went to Sydney Grammar and after school developed his ability at the high jump—6 ft in 1913, a record at the time. He worked as a clerk in Dalgetys and was a member of the 1st Bn NSW Scottish Rifles.

On 25 April 1915 as Captain in 4th Bn, Humphrey Scott reached the furthest point on the day of the Landing, thereafter called Scott's Point. His future actions on the Peninsula earned him DSO and MID. In Egypt in early 1916 he was given command of 56th Bn and he was not yet 25. He led the battalion at Fromelles and afterwards until at Polygon Wood on 1 Oct 1917 when he was shot dead by a sniper. A quiet, honest, unpretentious man, he was widely respected. Unlike his brother William, a major in 20th Bn, who later achieved some fame for probably being the model for Callcott in D H Lawrence's *Kangaroo*, and in the Second World War the hated commander of 2/21st 'Gull Force' on Ambon, taken prisoner by the Japanese in 1942.

Bock 230 '*ex-Lone Pine*'. Also mentioned by Hobkirk was Capt. F Fanning* who '... *was largely instrumental in stemming the disorder* (later altered to '*threatened disorder*') of the 8th Bdes' *retirement about 5.15 am on 20th July*'.

15th Brigade

The 15th Brigade list very much reflects Elliott's views of the world. His senior officers are noticed and thanked and at the other end of the scale those who brought in or tended the wounded got the medals. Elliott was not a great giver of medals having stated his view on several occasions that nobody should be rewarded for what they are expected to do anyway.

57th Battalion

As the least damaged battalion in the whole division, it fell to its members to be rescuers rather than warriors.

Military Crosses were awarded to: Capt. H G L Cameron*, '*coolness and daring... rescuing large numbers of wounded*'. 2nd Lieut W E S Edgar*: '*after the attack and during the three following days... went out into No-Man's Land... and brought in wounded*'. 2nd Lieut R A Salmon. '*After the attack he patrolled No-Man's Land and guided rescue parties...*'

The Distinguished Conduct Medal went to CSM J M Thorburn 656, '*the bravery and skill displayed in getting men in from the furthest point are worthy of the greatest praise*'.

A DCM later awarded to Sgt A G Ross* 752 included work he did on 19/20 July, as well at Gallipoli and on raids in September.

Military Medal to: Sgt A Strachan 2867, Cpl W S Saunders 4588, Pte J Duke 1914 and Pte W J Quirk* 3230.

Major N Marshall seemed unclassifiable even then. Already with an MC from Gallipoli, he would go on to earn three DSOs. After Fromelles Elliott wrote:

> *during and after the action ... he initiated rescue parties for wounded and personally led them close to German trenches under rifle and MG fire. It was due largely to his influence and example that so many wounded were rescued. I recommend him for...* [then in another hand, not Elliott's] *The Legion of Honour.*

And in another hand in blue crayon a large 'No'.

Mentioned in Despatches were Capt. H S Dickinson and Pte J Robertson 4576, and not forgetting Sgt Simon Fraser 3101. This tribute written by Elliott:

I INDEED RECOMMENDED YOU

McCay was relieved of his command of 5th Division in December 1916. It can therefore be assumed fairly safely that when Elliott wrote to him at that time it had something to do with McCay's change of circumstances. Elliott's letter would be with McCay's papers wherever they are, but McCay's letter survives in the Elliott file in Canberra. It reveals an aspect of the relationship between the two not visible elsewhere. It also reveals McCay's political, some might say cynical shrewdness in dealing with Elliott's considerable ego.

'I have just received your letter of the 7th. It is not often in a man's life that he receives so generous a letter, and one that makes him very proud, but yours I will keep and value—always for the splendid friendship and undeserved appreciation it expresses.

I do hope you are keeping well. I was so glad of your decoration, and know you will in turn earn the CB, for which I indeed recommended you.'

McCay thus had Elliott in his debt, and Elliott responded when the time came, but curiously only after Bean had prepared the ground.

Elliott was awarded, on 12 Sept 1916, 'the Russian Order of St Anne 3rd class with swords' gazetted 25 July 1917.

Sgt Simon Fraser, 57th Bn
COURTESY GEORGE SCOTT

> *He was responsible for some very gallant work during the period 19/23 July in leading parties into No-Man's Land and rescuing many wounded. His example has been of the greatest value to his company.*

Pte EDGAR WILLIAMS
He was born in 1884 and became Junior teacher at Long Gully, in 1900; assistant at Eaglehawk in 1904, and subsequently, Head Teacher at Mundoona North, Narrapoort and Ouyen. He was the second Principal or Head Teacher of Ouyen Primary School, where he remained until 4 September, 1915 when he enlisted—No 4621. He embarked with the 14th Reinforcements to the 5th on the transport *Themistocles* in November 1915. In Egypt, he was allotted to the 57th, but was transferred on 5 April, 1916 to the 58th. He proceeded to France and after a few days' training at Steenbecque, he entered the fighting zone. He was detailed to manage a gas apparatus, but obtained a transfer to stretcher bearer. He refused an offer to enter a school of instruction on 18 July, and came safely through the battle, but it was in rescuing wounded after the battle that he lost his life from a stray bullet. He was awarded the Military Medal for bravery in the field.

In a letter to Mrs Williams of Ouyen, his widow, Corporal Vernon wrote:

... there were many left out wounded after the attack. Private Williams worked for sixty hours getting in as many as he could. If any man deserved the VC, he did. He had not a thought for himself, so long as there were others who needed attention. His friends tried to persuade him to take some rest, but there were still two men whom he was anxious to bring in, and he refused [continued opposite]

58th Battalion

This is a curiously bare list considering what the 58th did and was expected to do.

2nd Lieut T A Fairfax* '*during work on saps across No-Man's Land moved freely about under MG and shell fire encouraging his own men until he was at last wounded*'. (Elliott). Fairfax received the Military Cross.

Pte A J Dunn* 1538 DCM '*he worked fearlessly under fire bringing wounded to the dressing station*'. L/Cpl L A Bath 2567A DCM. '*By his coolness and fine example, he steadied the men ... he went out and brought in five boxes of bombs from a dump.*'

Military Medals went to: L/Cpl H P Brandenberg 3235, Pte E Williams 4621, Pte W P McDonnell 3190, Sgt J J Charlton 2213 and Pte F C Mason 3055A.

Lieut Col C A Denehy* earned this mention from Elliott:

> *Since appointment to the command of 58th Bn on 18 July 1916, he did excellent service during the engagement of 19 and 20 July and since been invaluable in reorganizing the Bn which suffered heavy casualties in that engagement. The discipline and morale of the Bn has been improved in a most satisfactory manner under him.*

The other MID was for Cpl W J Brown* 4744 who '*with Cpl W C Davies—since KIA—rescuing wounded ... five trips before he himself severely wounded*' (Elliott). These were the stretcher bearers that went out after signalling to the Germans their mission and brought back a badly wounded man. They paused to be able to get their man into safety and a German sniper who must have been following their journey fired a single shot, killing the man on the stretcher and severely wounding Brown. The event was witnessed by many and caused great anger among the men.

Then comes the recommendation for a Victoria Cross to Major A J S Hutchinson put forward by McCay, in his own handwriting. The citation was written by Elliott. Hutchinson received nothing and was not even Mentioned in Despatches. On the file is written 'no trace of award'!

> *At Petillon on 19th/20th July 1916, Major Hutchinson displayed conspicuous and gallant leadership. On the evening of the 19th 20th*

July 1916, a message came from 5th Division that the 61st Division on our right would renew the attack at 9 pm on the Sugar Loaf Salient and notwithstanding that the previous attack by a Battalion had manifestly failed, Major Hutchinson led the two Companies of the 58th Battalion under his command in the most gallant manner under an appalling fire until he fell riddled with machine gun bullets close under the German parapet. His life and the lives of his men were gallantly given in the hope of aiding the attack of the 61st Division, which unfortunately was not made. [Enclosures—statements by Lieut H J Boyd and 2nd Lieut L H Dardier.]

59th Battalion

Perhaps like the 58th and the 60th this sparse list might have more to do with the lack of survivors rather than lack of bravery. Also of course as none of this brigade got into German trenches, most of the deeds of bravery were concerned with saving the situation and wounded.

Lieut-Col H T C Layh* was the only battalion commander in the 15th Brigade decorated as a result of Fromelles. Elliott wrote the citation for Layh's first DSO:

> *This Officer has served in the AIF with conspicuous courage and zeal since its formation in August 1914. He took part in the landing on Gallipoli where he was severely wounded. He did excellent service at Lone Pine and the Evacuation.*
>
> *Since the formation of the 15th Brigade he has been the mainstay of the 59th Battalion by his knowledge and ability. During the action of the 19th July last before Petillon he, although suffering severely from shell shock at the time, assumed command of the Battalion at a critical moment on his CO being disabled and has remained in charge ever since in front of Sailly, laboring incessantly and accomplishing successfully the very difficult task of reorganising the remnants of his Battalion into an efficient force.*

Capt. F R Hewitt: '*his cool attitude inspired his men...* [he was] *badly wounded*'. Lieut R H McC Gibbs (KIA 19.7.1916) '*when his coy commander was seriously wounded, he took charge*'. To which Elliott added: '*his calm and collected manner gave his men the impulse necessary to carry them as far as it was possible to go*'. WO D G Toohey* 659 '*organised and brought ammunition to firing line ... later brought wounded men out ... was in action again on night of 20/21st*'. Comments by Elliott; all received the Military Cross. A recommendation for Lieut D G Haddow was not successful.

L/Cpl H Schuldt 31 and L/Cpl G Every 1540 '*together they established communications under heavy fire*' (Elliott). Pte L F Harrington* 2928 '*a stretcher bearer*' and Pte E N Lowry* 3403 '*stretcher bearer... at no time has he shirked the most*

Pte EDGAR WILLIAMS (contd)

to stop until he had got them. As he was carrying one of them, he was hit in the head. He could be seen from our trenches, and was still able to walk but apparently blinded.

The children of his old school at Ouyen later obtained an enlarged framed photograph of their Head Teacher to hang in the school room as a memorial. The Education Department tribute of Williams was that he was '*a very good teacher, active, capable and conscientious*'.

Capt. F R HEWITT, 59th Bn

Frank Rupert Hewitt, later Major, came from Liverpool, served in the Boer War and with the Natal Carbineers in the Zulu Rebellion of 1906. He then went to the British Solomon Islands to manage Lever Bros Plantations. This career he left to enlist in the AIF on 16 Nov 1914. He went with the 7th Bn to Gallipoli with 1st Mobile Veterinary Section as Staff Sergeant. '*At the evacuation he was one of those who had the eerie experience of staying on for a time after the troops had left.*' He was in the last boat to leave Gallipoli. In Egypt, March 1916, he joined 59th Bn and at Fromelles was so badly wounded he was evacuated to Australia on 16 Oct 1916. After recovering he returned to Gavutu in the British Solomon Islands to resume his career.

—*Reveille* April 1934

Lieut R H McC Gibbs

dangerous tasks', Pte G Horsey 3093A, Pte A Honey 2582, Pte W J Delaney 3084, and Pte F W Whitchurch* 4638 '*showed conspicuous bravery on 19/20th*'. All these men received the Military Medal, although Harrington and Lowry are also listed as MID.

Later Whitchurch was put forward by Layh for '*a distinction*', but the following citation was crossed out and '*No*' written on it:

> *Battalion grenadier since its inception. He was through the charge of 19/20 July and showed conspicuous bravery. In October he took part in a raid and his personal example had a great influence on his men ... Since coming to the Somme ... has often inspired his men.*

Pte R E Poulter, 1915
COURTESY R H LEFFLER

60th Battalion

For the most damaged battalion there was little comfort in the list of awards. Only the combination of Lieut T Kerr and Pte R E Poulter reflected the fact that the 60th had achieved anything on the battlefield.

Military Crosses were awarded to four members of the 60th.

Lieut H Wrigley*, Adjutant:

> *... he displayed great ability in the preliminary arrangements, and at a later stage when his Bn Commander and all officers senior to him had fallen, displayed great gallantry in carrying on the attack ... until he fell severely wounded.*

Lieut J H Sterling

Lieut J H Sterling (KIA 19.7.1916):

> *... showed conspicuous bravery and coolness under the most trying circumstances. Before attacking and whilst being most heavily bombarded, he handled his men with courage and judgement. Although wounded in the neck, Lieut Sterling led his men to the attack valiantly under terrific machine-gun fire till all were casualties.*

Hon. Captain J P Gilbert*, the Roman Catholic Chaplain:

> *At Petillon on 19/20 July 1916 the Chaplain Gilbert displayed conspicuous bravery and devotion in attending to the wounded and dead under heavy machine gun fire and artillery fire. Chaplain Gilbert worked unceasingly for 48 hours after the action carrying in wounded and attending the dead, most of the time under heavy fire.*

Lieut T Kerr:

> *At Petillon on 19 July 1916 Lieut Kerr displayed conspicuous bravery and devotion to duty under very heavy artillery and MG fire. He was wounded immediately after going over the parapet in the charge but pushed on. After crossing the River Laies he organized a party and led them forward, Having got as close as possible to the German line, he found no one in front of him. His small party were the only survivors near him. He ordered them to dig in and sent back a message that he and*

Sgt W H GATES
William Howard Gates was born in Ballarat 23 June, 1892, and educated at Ballarat State School. He became a turner and fitter in that city enlisting as Cpl in Signals of 8th Bn. A Sergeant in April 1915 on Gallipoli and wounded at Krithia, Gates transferred to 60th Bn after the evacuation. He was awarded DCM at Fromelles where he was wounded again. At the end of 1917 he was commissioned and in April, 1918 promoted Lieutenant and went to 58th Bn when the 60th was disbanded. He died on 7 March 1939, and is buried at Ballarat New Cemetery.

his party were waiting and could go no further without reinforcements. These did not arrive and after waiting some considerable time he succeeded in making his way back to our parapet. After having his wounds dressed, he refused to go to hospital and remained on duty rendering valuable assistance in collecting the shattered remnants of the 60th Bn. (Elliott).

The man who carried back Kerr's message was Pte R E Poulter 2878. Kerr had found himself without paper for the message so Poulter produced his pocket New Testament and Kerr wrote on the fly leaf. '*Here with 4 men, a few yards from parapet. Must have reinforcements. Useless going on without.*' Elliott suggested a Military Medal and a Russian decoration for Poulter and he received both. Elliott wrote of Poulter:

He courageously volunteered and successfully carried an important message from the front attacking lines in No-Man's Land back 300 yards to our own trenches under withering machine gun and artillery fire. Later during the actions he showed conspicuous gallantry on many occasions in carrying messages from our firing line. (Elliott).

Distinguished Conduct Medals were awarded to three of 60th Bn.

Sgt W H Gates 34:

... during the attack on Fromelles front under heavy barrage fire, he bravely established communications across No-Man's Land ... although wounded in both legs he valiantly attempted to re-lay the signal wires until compelled to cease his attempts through complete exhaustion (Elliott)

Sgt C Johnson 1812:

... great bravery and coolness in carrying grenades and ammunition across No-Man's Land under heavy fire. He also worked unceasingly in carrying in wounded men and continued doing so for three consecutive nights under fire until he was utterly exhausted (Elliott).

CSM H N Richards 535 also received the DCM, '*when his officers became casualties, he took command ... he also did fine work carrying in the wounded*'.

Whilst Pte Poulter received the Russian Medal of St George (4th Class), Gates was put forward for the 2nd Class, one account has it that Gates rescued a Russian officer. The Serbian Silver Medal was awarded to Pte J Harrison* 36. There is a note about a Serbian Gold Medal for Sgt C P Finnie* 2924 but no trace of an award is in the file.

Three officers were Mentioned in Despatches:
Capt. M Cahill* and Lieut J H Steel.

RUSSIANS HAVE LANDED

'*The Russians have landed a force at Marseilles*' Bean wrote in his diary around 23 April. This very isolated item might explain why at Fromelles, in 54th Bn Sgt F T Stringer, in 56th Bn Pte T C Rowley, and in 60th Bn, Pte R E Poulter received Russian medals.

Their landing on 20 April 1916 was well-covered by the press. *The Illustrated War News* of 3 May carried five pictures including this one showing 'The Russians on a transport at Marseilles'.

THE ORDER OF ST GEORGE

The most prized of Russian Orders. Founded in 1769 by the Empress Catherine, it was awarded only for conspicuous bravery and was comparable to the Victoria Cross and America Medal for Valor. There were four classes of the Order.

There were also four classes of an insignia under the name of the Cross of St George, and lastly the St George's Medal which was awarded in gold and silver. The crosses and medals were bestowed upon various British Officers and men during the 1914-18 war.

The black and orange ribbon meant '*Through darkness to light*'—the black representing darkness and the orange, light.

Elliott put forward Major G G McCrae for something that would recognise not just his bravery at Fromelles, but also his work at Gallipoli which had thus far gone unnoticed:

> *This officer served in the AIF since its inception and was repeatedly recommended for his good work on the peninsula but received no reward. Upon succeeding to the Command of the 60th Battalion he effected a very marked improvement in its moral and discipline and from being the worst unit in this Brigade, it was rapidly becoming the best under his guidance. He was killed in action on the 19th July 1916, whilst gallantly leading his Battalion in the attack on the enemy's trenches near Petillon.*
>
> *I cannot speak too highly of his courage and devotion to duty.*

This earned McCrae a MID.

Less easy to understand was another recommendation for an award for Lieut Col Duigan, who was actually a member of 29th Bn. One can only suppose that Elliott called for him to come and take charge of 60th Bn where all the senior officers were lost: they had been friends since Essendon days, and after Fromelles Duigan did take command of the 60th. Wrote Elliott:

> *Owing to heavy casualties in the action of 19th and 20th July 1916 the 60th Bn was almost entirely depleted both of its officers and NCOs, including CO, 2IC, Adjutant and every Coy Commander and 2/IC. Not withstanding these difficulties Lieut Col Duigan by his ceaseless energy and ability had entirely prevented any deterioration, however slight, being manifested in the high state of morale and discipline which formerly characterised this Battalion.*

Duigan received no award.

Elliott also wrote a tribute to Major Thomas Patrick Elliott, no kin, but a man in whom he had great faith (see margin):

> *This officer was invaluable to Major McCrae in his successful efforts to raise the morale and discipline of his battalion, and gave repeated proofs of possessing the highest leadership.*

Sadly Pompey Elliott could think of no possible award for these qualities, but one supposes he just *had* to write a citation anyway.

THE GREATEST INDIVIDUAL LOSS

Major T P Elliott, then a captain, was in the 7th Light Horse. On the formation of the 15th Brigade it was considered vital to obtain a few officers of known ability to assist in laying the foundation of the various Battalions. Captain Elliott was specially asked for and his transfer was completed on 2.3.1916.

He was immediately placed in Command of a Company of the 60th Bn consisting of raw, and in many cases unpromising material. His personality was of such stirling value that from a mere formation the Company speedily became a well disciplined and trained fighting unit. Men considered incorrigible were unable to resist his authority and generally became good soldiers.

For a period he acted as Adjutant of the Battalion ... from 30.5.1916 Major Elliott acted as 2nd in Command of the 60th Bn and was responsible for most of the arrangements for the attack by his battalion at Fromelles on 19 July 1916 which were remarkably thorough and complete. He accompanied the 2nd wave of the attack and was killed while encouraging the men to move forward.

... this officer's death is the greatest individual loss the Brigade has suffered since its formation.

—Brig. General H E Elliott (undated)

SOME OPERATION PENDING

19.7.1916
My Darling Sister
Just a line to let you know all well —same with Bob, Norm and Ern. Some operation pending so must cut this short.
Your loving Brother. Tom
Love to Jackie and regards to Jack.
N.B. Don't worry about me I'll be alright. Tom.

—Major T P Elliott 60th Bn.

5th Division HQ

As the dates reveal, McCay did not get around to noticing his staff's work until 12 October 1916, which seems a very long delay.

Major (Temp. Lieut Col) Cyril Mosley Wagstaff CIE DSO RE was described by McCay thus:

> *Lt Col Wagstaff became SO 1 of this Division in Egypt in March 1916. During the period April-June 1916, the Division, in addition to being*

organised and trained, held some 8 to 9 miles of the defensive front on the Suez Canal, E of Ismailia. From 10th July till now it has held in France various sections in front of Sailly and Bac St Maur. On 19th July it took the German trenches in front of Fromelles on a front of 2000 yards and held them till the morning of 20th July. Since 20th July there have been frequent minor enterprises against the enemy by the Division, and much work has been done in strengthening and developing the Sailly Sector.

In the whole of the planning and carrying out of the training and work of the Division, Lt Col Wagstaff has been constantly active and is continually in all parts of the line. His devotion to duty, like his capacity for physical endurance, and his ignoring of danger, seems unlimited. His ability is great and his knowledge wide, accurate and thorough. He is exceptionally deserving of recognition. Brevet rank for him should be of advantage to his Corps and the Service. He so conducts himself in his relation to all ranks that he is greatly liked as well as completely respected. He is a very exceptional officer. If the Brevet be not approved, I recommend him for CMG.

Capt. (Major in AIF) Dennis Malcolm King MC was put forward by McCay for the DSO and his citation for King provides some clue to what happened with 8th Brigade.

This officer was originally Staff Captain, 1st Australian Infantry Brigade. He became Brigade Major at Lone Pine in April 1915 and thereafter to and during the evacuation at ANZAC and did constantly good work for which he was Mentioned in Despatches and ultimately awarded the MC.

He became GSO2 of this Division on its formation in March 1916 and has continued to hold that position in Egypt—March to June—and in the line in front of Sailly—July to Sept. He was SO for disembarkation of the Division at Marseilles—June/July—and his work was admirable, drawing very special commendation from the Base Commandant, Marseilles.

He has also given special attention to the organisation and carrying out of the Divisional Training Schools, with the result that large numbers of junior Officers, NCOs and men have become experts in the work taught and the efficiency of the Divisional Infantry has been greatly increased owing to his efforts.

During the operations of 19/20th July before Petillon, he was DHQ Liaison Officer with the 8th Aus Inf Bde on the left of the Division and his personal example of courage and coolness and his professional knowledge, did much to ensure the steadiness of the Brigade in question which was new to fighting, not having at most 70 of all ranks who had ever been in a campaign, and probably not 20 who had been in a serious fight.

Captain G D Smith DAQMG received the Military Cross:

Since formation ... he controlled all the necessarily hurried provision and distribution of ammunition and stores for the fight 19/20 July ... and did it admirably.

Captain R P Varwell*, originally from the Royal Irish Rifles, received the MC on Hobbs' recommendation:

Sgt A G ROSS

In John Laffin's book on Australian battlefield archaeology *Digging up the Diggers' War* (1993) he has, as in all his books on the Western Front, numerous mentions of Fromelles. He tells a story about Alexander Gordon Ross 752 57th Bn from Colac who was found by a rescue party hanging on the wire in such a state that it was felt that taking him down would only make the wounds worse. '*He begged his rescuers to shoot him ... but they were determined to bring him in ... they were without stretcher so Ross threw himself face down on the ground and instructed the others to use him as a human sledge. They tied a wounded man on his back ... and dragged the two ... across No-Man's Land.*' One does not have to have much imagination to realize the state of Ross by the time the rescue was over.

When this writer was researching the story of the 57th Bn and aware of Ross' DCM, any recommendation for the award was not located. However whilst working on this book it was, but not in the battle of Fromelles period. Doubtless Elliott had heard the sledge story but it was a repaired Sgt Ross well after Fromelles that qualified for the DCM.

During a raid made by a party of 57th Bn on the enemy's trenches near Petillon on the night of 19 August 1916, Sgt Ross displayed great gallantry in reconnaissance work before the trenches were entered ... In addition this NCO has on many occasions during the three months July to September 1916 at Petillon conducted most daring reconnaissances as a patrol leader along the enemy's wire, and has repeatedly gained valuable information. He served from the beginning to end of Gallipoli Campaign and did good service throughout.

—H E Elliott, 12 Oct 1916

Sgt Ross who enlisted 19 August 1914 returned to Australia 4 May 1917. Born in 1891 at Colac, he died in 1961 at Heidelberg.

... *utilizing zeal, energy and ability during the period when the Division was in line.* (Hobbs).

The following were Mentioned in Despatches:

Lieut Col J P McGlinn:

His arrangements for traffic control during the Petillon fight on 19/20th July were so good that not a single hitch occurred. (McCay)

Captain J M Rodd DADOS

... *he is a most valuable officer and unremitting in his devotion to duty.* (McCay)

Major F D W Thornthwaite of Ammunition Column was mentioned by Brig-General Christian.

Field Company Engineers

8th Field Company Engineers

L/Cpl G S Chisholm 4449 MM

Sgt H Hughes* 4456 MID:

cutting a sap across No-Man's Land he showed calm courage.

14th Field Company Engineers

2nd Lieut H W Fry MC (see also page 131).

... *he constructed a sap across No-Man's Land with great rapidity. The sap subsequently proved to be of the greatest value to our troops*...

Lieut L G Merkel* MID:

accompanied Cass to the German trench... and assisted in converting a drain into a fire trench.

Sgt E C Banks 14. Medal Militaire:

pegged out communication trench in No-Man's Land.

Spr C F Coulson 3994. Italian Bronze Medal.

15th Field Company Engineers

Major H Greenway* DSO.

Major Greenway was in the first landing at ANZAC and was there till the evacuation (with the exception of 6 weeks when the Brigade to which he was attached went off for a spell). He did excellent work and was twice Mentioned in Despatches; one for Lone Pine and one for the Evacuation. He was appointed Adjutant of the 5th Aust Divisional Engineers in March 1916, and in May 1916, was given command of the 15th Field Coy. Major Greenway did continuously good work in Egypt, raising and training the 15th Field Coy, in addition to carrying

Lieut Col C M WAGSTAFF
Cyril Mosley Wagstaff was born 5 March 1878 at Calcutta, educated in England, and entered the army in 1897. After a successful period at Staff College, he went to India serving on the NW Frontier, later joining the staff of Birdwood and going with him to Egypt, then to Gallipoli as GSOII, AA and QMG, With the formation of 5th Division he was appointed GSOI and thus was McCay's right-hand man. Some credit him with recognising as '*a useful idea*', another officer's suggestion to use ANZAC for the Australian and New Zealand Army Corps, and generally pushing it forward. Ellis saw him as '*a careful student of character and soon understood the Australian temperament*'. After the war he served for a time as the War Office, then in India, before returning to Britain as Commandant, Royal Military Academy, Woolwich. He died unexpectedly 21 February 1934 whilst holding that appointment. He had earned DSO, CMG, CdeG (Belgium), DSM (USA), CC (Italy) together with the India Medal and three clasps.

Lieut Col J P McGLINN
(1869–1946)
He was Monash's Brigade Major from September 1914 all through the initial period on Gallipoli and when Monash was absent for four weeks McGlinn commanded the 4th Bde. For his work at Anzac he was appointed CMG and twice MID. In March 1916 he became Assistant Adjutant and Quarter Master General of 5th Division under McCay.

the construction of hutting and Defence Lines, both of which he did with marked ability. In connection with the operations at Fromelles on 19/20th July 1916, he did excellent work in making preparations and organizing the work of the 15th Field Coy. One of his Saps was driven forward to a total distance of 687 feet, half of which was entirely new work, and the other to about 270 feet. In construction of these Saps great tenacity was displayed, for the work was continued even after the attack of the 15th Brigade had been abandoned with the object of protecting the right flank of the 14th Brigade. The situation of these Saps was particularly dangerous owing to the proximity of the Sugar Loaf. Major Greenway also displayed great ability in his dispositions for maintaining communications with the Dumps in the rear which his Company did with complete success, in spite of the repeated destruction by shell fire of both Saps and tramlines. He was again Mentioned in Despatches on January 1st 1917 for his continuous good work.

As if a DSO was insufficient for Greenway's work, Hobbs also put him forward successfully for the Order of the Crown of Italy.

Lieut L Noedl MC

... led forward a party of sappers with the attacking party and commenced work immediately...

L/Cpl A M Bowman 6081 MM. Spr W Blows 3955 MM.

5th Pioneer Battalion

CMS J H Gaylor 495 DCM

...carrying rails from dump... to the firing line ... sufficient material ... to enable a train line to be completed.

L/Cpl S Eddington 3039 MM.

L/Cpl A E Landaman 3260 MM.

5th HQ Company Signal Corps

L/Cpl J R J Burrow 3469 MM. Spr W G Duncan 3272 MM.

L/Cpl H L Pender 3672 MM.

Spr T D Henry 3493 MM (All in 4th Section)

Lieut N O'Brien* MID

Lieut H D Schroder MC. (Later 2 Bars to his MC.)

5th Divisional Trench Mortar Battery

Gnr T Crocker 393 DCM

26th Trench Mortar Battery

2nd Lieut M R Anderson. MC.

HAROLD GREENWAY
Harold Greenway was born 28 January 1887 in Sheffield, UK. After attending St Peter's College, Adelaide, and the University of Adelaide, he was BSc 1906, BE 1912, DipMines and Fellow of the SA School of Mines. He enlisted 1914 as a private, was commissioned May 1915, and promoted to Major in May 1916, commanding 15th Field Coy Engineers 1916–18. Apart from his DSO, Greenway received the Croix de Guerra and was MID five times. A mining and metallurgical engineer, he worked all over Australia, first with oil companies, later with colleries. He married the daughter of a South Australian shipping magnate in 1917.

I AM DONE
When Lieut L G Merkel in 14th Field Coy Engineers, himself only 25, had to write to the sister of Spr C P Ashdown 5363 of his unit, one judges it was difficult. *He was in my section since the company was formed and he came across from Australia with me ... he was brave and cheerful ... next to me when a shell burst wounding three of his mates and killing him ... he only said 'I am done' ... his belongings have been forwarded to his home. Regretting not letting you know before, but I have been extremely busy. Your other brother has now joined me.* Merkel was MID at Fromelles and later was awarded the Military Cross. He died in 1922 and was an engineer.

FIELD COMPANY LOSSES
Like the Machine Gun Corps, the Field Coys losses were very generalised and thus marginalised by Ellis and Bean. 8th Field Coy Bean said 'lost' (meaning dead or wounded or POW) one officer and 36 ORs: this inquiry has located the officer and 8 ORs killed and DOW. The 14th 'lost' one officer and 21 ORs, this inquiry's list has one officer and 6 ORs dead. The 15th according to Bean 'lost' one officer and 27 ORs: this inquiry has 8 ORs killed.

V5A Heavy Trench Mortar Battery

Gnr L Allen 30A. MM
Bdr J English* 4195)
Bdr A Courtney* 661) MMs Fleurbaix 16 Sept.
Gnr W F A Allan* 1466)

Field Artillery Brigades

13th Field Artillery Brigade HQ

Capt. E L Vowles* MC (per Brig Gen Bessell-Browne)

Lieut H O Caddy*. Military Order of Savoy.

> *At Fleurbaix 16/20 July he displayed zeal, energy and devotion to duty of a high order* (Bessell-Browne).

Lieut B C Handley FOO. MID.

Capt. Vowles was also Mentioned in Despatches by Brig. General Christian:

> *This officer has shown himself to be possessed of conspicuous ability, zeal and attention to duty. In Egypt he formed, organized and trained the 59th Battery of 15th F A Brigade and has fought in the Battle of Fleurbaix... He has shown himself a good administrator, disciplinarian and commanding officer. He has a good 'espirit de corps' in his command. He also rendered valuable services in command of his battery at Fleurbaix. 16-20 July 1916.*

49th Battery AFA

Lieut R W McHenry MC, '*prior to the infantry attack he observed and reported on the effect of our fire at great personal risk*'.

Bdr J Lee* 2682 Croix de Guerre (per Bessell-Browne)

25th Field Artillery Brigade

Bdr S F Chippendale 1634 DCM, '*... as a telephone specialist ... worked incessantly ... maintaining communications between trenches and battery*'. Gnr S G Robbins 1029 MM (both in 52nd Battery).

14th Light Trench Mortar

Capt. C B Hopkins (KIA 20.7.16). Sgt J M Cochrane 2800. Sgt R Ellsmore 3587—all MID.

Cpl E Rose 3132. A Belgian Croix de Guerre (all per Hobkirk).

CSM J H GAYLOR (page 295)
On 21 July 5th Pioneers recorded '*parties out all day clearing up the battlefield, salvage work and burying dead. 40 men under CSM Gaylor volunteered for rescue work in No-Man's Land. They went out in 14th Bde area but could find no wounded. 2 Lewis guns and many rifles and other salvage brought in. 1 man of party killed—only this casualty.*'

5th DIVISIONAL FIELD ARTILLERY
Mention has been found that Gnr A N Hudson* 544 received the DCM: '*At Petillon on 19 July this NCO patrolled the lines between the Bty and FOO, across open ground between the trenches ... on 9 August he also acted with great gallantry ... he is constant in his devotion to duty.*' (per Christian).

13th FIELD ARTILLERY BRIGADE
Mention has been found that Gnr C G Brown* 3480 received the DCM for work at Fromelles '*for conspicuous gallantry when maintaining communications between the FO Station and is battery during an intense bombardment. He was always the first linesman out, and displayed the greatest energy and courage*'.
—*Commonwealth Gazette* 14 Dec 1916

Capt. C B HOPKINS
Capt. Clive Boyer Hopkins, originally from Warrnambool and later of Moonee Ponds was a Duntroon graduate. Aged 20, he had given up the position of Staff Captain, 14th Bde, for the command of the 14th LTM Battery.

4th DIVISIONAL FIELD ARTILLERY
Mention has been found that Lieut Col H V Vernon* of 4th Division Ammunition Column received the DSO for work done at Fromelles. A veteran of South Africa and Gallipoli, Vernon also had two MIDs.

Royal Garrison Artillery

Cpl J T Foster 29358. MM.

4th Divisional Field Artillery

A/Bdr H D Kennedy 11350 MM. Bdr A Barwell 2110 MM (Both in 37th Bty, 10th F A Brigade).

Machine Gun Companies

5th Machine Gun Company

CSM T McKeown 30 DCM

> *...when practically surrounded he carried his gun back ... and again brought his gun into action.*

8th Machine Gun Company

Captain T R Marsden DSO.

Lieut A K Flack MC.

> *... wounded while in our trenches before infantry advanced, but took his guns into action. All his detachment was killed or wounded.*

Sgt R Webb DCM

> *When a large ammunition dump caught fire, he moved many wounded to safety ... saving their lives.*

Pte K J Vincent (also known as Minchington) 97, who was killed in the battle was noted for his bravery, but received no award, but was MID.

14th Machine Gun Company

Sgt A T Brown (later Lieut) DCM

> *when his officer was wounded, he took his guns up to the enemy trenches ... with great effect.'*

Dvr H Freeman 3472 MM

15th Machine Gun Company

Cpl E W Pinder 390 DCM

> *carried a message through heavy shell fire ... and brought back reinforcements.*

T McKeown was killed in a fall from Sydney Harbour Bridge in March 1929 [during the building of it.]
Reveille, April 1929

Capt. T R MARSDEN
For conspicuous gallantry ... he took charge of six guns in the front line, and remained in action all night. Finally with these guns, he covered the retirement of our infantry, and then carried a wounded man back across No-Man's Land. Later he went forward again, and carried in a sergeant.

MACHINE GUN COY LOSSES
The Machine Gun Coys consisted of 10 officers and between 150 to 200 ORs: the 15th MG Coy on arrival in France had 9 officers and 208 ORs. As a group neither Ellis nor Bean dealt with them in any detail and their casualties were not seriously calculated. In 1920 (Ellis) and 1929 (Bean) quoted '13 killed, 33 wounded, 8 missing' for 8th MG Coy which was unnecessarily vague, for by then everybody was accounted for. This inquiry has the number of dead as 17. In the case of 14th MG Coy Bean had 11 killed, 28 wounded and 14 missing: this inquiry has the dead at 18. For 15th MG Coy Bean had 9 killed, 26 wounded and 1 missing: this inquiry has 10 dead. As the Roll of Honour reveals the three officers of 14th MG Coy killed have their names at Villers-Bretonneux and not at VC Corner where they certainly should be. Six 8th MG Coy men were taken prisoner and nine from 14th MG Coy. It is thought that of the four 58th Bn men taken prisoner, three were machine gunners.

Lieut R A McCracken of 15th MG Coy was so badly wounded he returned to Australia 16 Oct 1916.

Field Ambulance Companies

8th Field Ambulance

Captain H R Catford RMO 8th Bde. Recommended for MC

> *on the night 19/20 July [for] his coolness and devotion to duty.* Not awarded.

Pte T W Howard 6721 MM.

14th Field Ambulance

Capt. K H Grieve RMO 56th Bn MC (per Hobkirk)

Capt. C Cosgrove RMO 53rd Bn MC.

> *carried on quite regardless of personal danger.* (Hobkirk)

L/Cpl W R Kingston 1745 DCM – '*... did very fine work at an ADS, encouraging the stretcher bearers to keep on bringing the wounded in. For two days he had practically no rest...*'.

Pte R H English 8885 MM

15th Field Ambulance

Capt. H Rayson RMO 57th Bn MC (per Elliott)

Pte H Ramsden 8792 MM.

Capt. KEITH HARVEY GRIEVE
Lieut Col Scott CO of 56th Bn wrote: '*I wish to place on record here [in the War Diary of 20 July] the valuable service of Capt. K H Grieve AMC who is attached to my Bn as Medical Officer. This Officer reached the original front firing line of the Bde sector between 10 and 11 pm on the night of 19/20 July with my first two companies. On reaching the firing line Capt. Grieve established a dressing station immediately. Owing to the battered nature of the trenches, he was unable to obtain shelter and was thus compelled to work in the open, which he continued to do, although the trenches were being heavily shelled, until the Bn was relieved on the night 21/22 July.*
I also wish to place on record the excellent work of AMC details attached to the Bn, and the Bn Stretcher Bearers who worked throughout so cheerfully and willingly without sleep.'

Capt. C COSGROVE
Charles Augustus Fitzroy Cosgrove (1885–1946) was educated at St Ignatius College, Riverview, and gained his medical degree from the University of Sydney. The *Commonwealth Gazette* 14 Dec 1916 noted: '*... he tended the wounded throughout and for many hours after the action. He was frequently under heavy fire, and carried on quite regardless of personal danger.*' After the war he went into general practice in Vaucluse, Sydney, and then in London.

Capt. H RAYSON
'*For conspicuous gallantry and devotion to duty... for several days he rendered first aid in the trenches under very heavy shell fire, and worked day and night till the wounded were finally evacuated.*'

—*Commonwealth Gazette* 14 Dec 1916

British Awards

Attempts to obtain a list of awards to the brave in the 61st British Division at Fromelles have not been all that successful, various organisations claiming that much of the material was lost during bombing of London, others that the only source is the official *London Gazette*, or that it is all too much trouble and too long ago. The notes that follow are taken from War Diaries, unit histories and similar sources mostly searched for, and supplied by the Curators of the Regimental Museums. Although the results of these recommendations are not known, the fulsome recognition of every level of bravery reveals a different British army to that too long caricatured as being staffed only by callous generals and incompetent officers.

182nd Brigade

Royal Warwickshires

In the case of the 2/7th both the CO (Col Nutt) and the GOC of 182nd Bde (Brig. General Gordon) concluded their Reports in the battle with a paragraph about '*bringing to your notice the names of Officers and other ranks who particularly distinguished themselves...*' It is almost certain that other COs also prepared such lists. None however have been located in the Warwickshire Regimental Archives, so the following information has been extracted from various histories and accounts, and War Diaries as noted.

2/6th. At a parade on 17 August '*the following NCOs were awarded the Military Medal for gallantry and devotion to duty*'. Cpl H D Brown 3529, L/Cpl C K Jones 3127, Pte J R Oliver 3532, Pte A C Weaving 3147, Pte T R B Kilner 3012. The War Diary of 24 August notes that Lieut P J Johnson was awarded Military Cross for gallantry and devotion to duty. As the units saw little action in early August all these awards might refer to Fromelles.

2/7th. On 17 August the War Diary noted '*List of 8 Military Medals to NCOs and men came out for action on 19.7.16*'. No names are given, and on 24 August '*5 ORs went up to receive Military Medals*'. On 28 August '*2/Lieuts W E Crombie (later KIA 1918 when with RAF), 2/Lieut Sturrock and CSM Marsh awarded MC*'. Again as this unit had not been in any significant action since 19/20 July, these awards are almost certainly for Fromelles, as the Unit History says three MCs were awarded for the battle.

Col Nutt received the DSO for his work at Fromelles.

Commendations were presented on 31 August to:

Cpl S A West 3738, Pte Talbot 3420, Pte A J Jones 2389, Pte Jackson 3945, Pte G T Ash 3555, L/Cpl H D Collyer 3384.

2/8th. From the Unit History we know that:

Padre Bennett '*whose work among the wounded on 19 and 20 July will always be remembered was awarded the MC—the first in the battalion*'.

Lieut Col E C Cadman received the DSO.

Capt. E H E WOODWARD
Edward Hamilton Everard Woodward's father was a colonel, his mother was the daughter of Admiral Fisher, and his wife the daughter of a Royal Navy Officer. Educated in Bristol and London, his career was in the electricity supply industry in north eastern England. He had command of Tyne Electrical Engineers RE 1929–34, later becoming a member of the British Electric Authority 1947–57. In the 1914–18 war he served first with 2/4th Glosters, later with TEERE, earning an MC in 1916, probably at Fromelles. Born in 1888, Lieut Col Woodward CBE died in 1976.

183rd Brigade

Gloucestershires

As noted in the text the records of these battalions were not located, the only surviving and significant Report being that of Lieut Col J A Tupman of 2/4th. Thus the names he mentions constitute the only recommendations found.

2/4th Gloucestershire. Capt. E H E Woodward, Lieut R G Scrase, Lieut J C James, Lieut S J Stokesbury, Cpl Porter, Cpl Squance, Pte Burge and Pte Denning.

Lieut THOMAS TANNATT PRYCE, VC, MC & BAR
Serving with the 2/6th Gloucestershire Regiment at Fromelles was 2nd Lieut Pryce, but in November 1915 he had been with C Coy of 1/6th Bn Gloucestershire at Gommecourt Wood. There on the night 25/26 he was wounded in a raid and for his bravery was awarded an MC. He was invalided to England and came back to France with 2/6th, and on 19 July, 1916 was awarded a bar to his MC *'for an act of exceptional gallantry'*.

Later he transferred to the 4th Grenadier Guards, and as Acting Captain led two platoons in an action near Vieux Berquin in April 1918. It was an extraordinary attack and defence going on for over ten hours influencing the outcome of the battle. Wrote Stephen Graham in his absorbing and brilliant *A private in the Guards* (1919): '*There never was in any annals a more marvellous stubbornness or a greater example of what discipline will do.*' Pryce was killed on 13 April and awarded a posthumous VC for his leadership and bravery.

He had been born at The Hague, Holland, 17 January 1886, and before the war he was a stockbroker from Maidenhead.

Lieut Col J A Tupman probably received his DSO for Fromelles: he was later awarded the OBE.

A press report had WO2 A E Jane being awarded Belgian Croix de Guerre for *'distinguished service, commanding and rallying his platoon.'*

2/6th Gloucestershire. Lieut T T Pryce MC (see margin).

184th Brigade

2/4th Battalion, Royal Berkshire Regiment

However in the 2/4th Royal Berks history some mentions are made. In the raid of 13/14 July, '*2nd Lieut J H Skene behaved with great gallantry. The conduct of Sgt A E Tallant who led the way over the enemy parapet, and that of CSM A Graham and Sgt H Pocock is also commended*' (Skene and Tallant were killed in the action.)

On 24 July from Battalion Headquarters, Major J H Simonds, then commanding the 2/4th wrote to HQ 184th Brigade: '*I beg to bring to your notice the names of the following Officers, NCOs and Men who were conspicuous for gallantry in the Action of July 19*'.

Capt. R Whittaker:

> *Went out with his Company under heavy machine gun fire. When, owing to heavy casualties, the Company had become somewhat scattered, Capt. Whittaker moved about under fire and collected his men and led them forward. He remained in No-Man's Land for four hours, and finding that his Company was weak and unsupported, he collected them and brought them back, together with all the wounded.*

2nd Lieut D R Gibson:

> *Led his platoon with great gallantry under heavy fire. Made repeated attempts to get through the wire gap and saved 2nd Lieut Abbott from being badly burnt through the explosion of the flares in his haversack. He afterwards led the remnants of his platoon forward by another gap, and himself patrolled some 50 yards of the German wire. He was wounded.*

2nd Lieut G S Abbott:

> *Led his platoon with splendid gallantry. Made strenuous efforts to get through the wire gap under very heavy machine gun fire. He then led the remnants towards the next gap, but was killed on the way. This officer had on many previous occasions done remarkably good work on patrols, and was a most fearless leader.*

Cpl J Powell, 3070:

> *When under heavy machine gun fire, bandaged up a wounded man, and, though wounded himself whilst doing so, finished the man's dressing after he has staunched his own wound. He afterwards got his reduced section*

away from the zone of fire in the gap and brought them back safely some hours afterwards. Has previously done very good work in patrols.

Cpl Puddle, 3409:

Dressed a wounded man under heavy machine gun fire, though wounded himself, and afterwards brought the remnants of his section into safety with great coolness. Has previously done excellent work on patrols.

Sgt F J Barrett, 986; Sgt S C Blay, 2940:

Both these NCOs got small parties forward under heavy fire to within easy distance of German parapet, and brought them back four hours afterwards, when they found themselves unsupported.

Pte E P Powell, 3366:

Went forward under heavy fire to look for remainder of attacking wave from Sgt Barrett's party. He afterwards did very good work in recovering wounded, though wounded himself.

Pte W A Hayter, 3360:

Carried out his duties as stretcher bearer during the whole day with conspicuous devotion and regardless of his own personal safety. His behaviour helped greatly to steady and encourage the men.

Dmr G Maynard, 3405:

Carried messages all day in spite of great difficulties, and carried on with the duties of the pigeon signaller when that man was wounded just before the Company went into action, taking the pigeons out with the assaulting party into No-Man's Land.

Sgt A J Dore, 3089:

During the heavy bombardment, two men of No 7 Platoon were blown over the parapet. Sgt Dore unhesitatingly jumped over the parapet and brought both men in under heavy shell fire. Their legs had been broken and they were quite helpless.

Sgt J W Lambourne, 3016:

On hearing of the death of 2nd Lieut Williams, Sgt Lambourne crawled across, under heavy machine gun fire, to his body, and searched it for documents which might prove useful to the enemy. 2nd Lieut Williams having been previously heard to express some doubt as to whether he had sufficiently emptied his pockets. During the latter part of the operations, Sgt Lambourne was of the utmost value in preserving the morale of the Company, which had lost heavily; indeed, since our first day in the trenches, Sgt Lambourne has been fearless and indefatigable in innumerable patrols and any tasks of especial danger.

L/Cpl S C Lovegrove, 5294:

This NCO was one of the leading wave of B Company, and with a few companions managed to reach No-Man's Land. Finding the assault checked, L/Cpl Lovegrove returned for further instructions no less than three times, running the greatest risks on each occasion. [He was killed in action 1 April 1917.]

Pte A E Allen, 3639:

A FOREIGNER

A newspaper article by Colonel James Digby Wyatt MC published in the *Bristol Evening Post* on 19 July 1960, the 44th anniversary of the battle, seems at first reading to be worthwhile. Wyatt was '*at the time attached as a subaltern to the 2/4th Bn, The Gloucestershire Regiment*'. But on closer examination it turns out to be made up of a few items of the 2/4th Gloucestershire Regiment and large sections of text lifted word for word from the History of 2/6th Warwickshire Regiment published 31 years earlier.

The worst example being copying exactly a paragraph describing the heroic actions of Capt. Simms of 2/6th Warwicks, and changing the name to Lieut R G Scrase commanding A Company of 2/4th Glosters! But apart from his memory or diary (which he makes no reference to) where could have Wyatt turned for information? The War Diaries were still under lock and key, and if he had gone to the British Official History, there was only ten lines, which would seem to indicate that there was not much in the official files as far as the 2/4th and 2/6th Glosters were concerned. The losses of these battalions were high, the CO of 2/6th Lieut Col F A C Hamilton was wounded, a fact Wyatt does not mention. He can only recall four names, Scrase, Lieut J C James the sniping officer who was killed, Sgt (later CSM) A Jane who '*distinguished himself, commanding and rallying his platoon*' and signals officer Lieut G D Wansbrough. Wyatt's only original information in his 3000 words was that the officers of 2/4th consisted of '*14 Glosters (including transport officer and quartermaster) and 16 foreigners*'—officers from other regiments. Wyatt was one of these, from the Northamptonshire Regiment.

THE POPPIES OF OBLIVION

This, the last part of a letter to a friend, was written on 2 June 1916 by 2nd Lieut Stephen Hewett of 2/6th Royal Warwickshire Regiment. Educated at Downside and Balliol College, Oxford, Hewett was a scholar and Hockey Blue. He was 23 when killed in action on 22 July 1916. His name is on the Thiepval Memorial.

The enjoyable things are fortunately permanent, simple, and easy to find. The complications and disorders which we make for ourselves are little things by comparison with—

'La paix de la grande nature.'

We are taught laboriously to make sorrows for one another and to tear up and harass the earth, but after a single spring the traces of the past are overwhelmed by a riot of growth 'which labours not', and in their place spring up the poppies of oblivion. The trenches which in February were grim and featureless tunnels of gloom, without colour or form, are already over-arched and embowered with green. You may walk from the ruins of a cottage, half hidden in springing green, and up to the Front line trenches through a labyrinth of Devonshire lanes. Before the summer comes again children will play between the trenches as in a garden, hide in strange hollows where old fragments of iron peep out from a wilderness of poppies and corn-flowers. Even in the shapeless ruins, where for the moment we are living, you may look up and see a swift dart from a cranny; and all is well ...

(Stretcher Bearer). Carried out wounded constantly all day under heavy shell fire. He is always to the fore and quite regardless of personal danger, and sets a splendid example to the other bearers. Worked continuously from the morning of July 19th till 7 am on the 20th, when he was completely exhausted. He also showed marked coolness when evacuating gas casualties from the Bucks line on July 18th.

Pte K W Stanwell, 3942; Pte W Norton, 3406:

Were continuously employed from 10 am till 11 pm acting as messengers backwards and forwards to the front line through heavy shell fire. Throughout they showed the greatest coolness and devotion to duty under most difficult circumstances, all telephonic communication having been cut.

The following names are brought to your attention for meritorious service during the Action of July 19th:-

2nd Lieut E C Aylett:

Mentioned for good work done throughout the attack and afterwards in recovering wounded.

Company Sgt Major A G Matthews, 2895:

Did excellent work by helping to collect the remnants of the Company under heavy fire.

Cpl Jas Pocock, 3363

Took charge of No. 12 Platoon when his senior officer and NCOs. were killed or wounded. He collected the remainder under heavy fire and brought them in safely. [He was killed in action 22 August, 1917.]

Pte L Borrett, 2856; Pte L L Martin, 2254; Pte A W Townsend, 3284:

These three men did noticeably good work in recovering and attending to wounded. All three have, in addition, done regular and reliable patrol work ever since the Battalion entered the trenches. If selection is necessary, the claims of Pte Martin are, perhaps, slightly greater than those of the other, but all have earned recognition. [Martin, then L/Sgt, DOW 11 May, 1918.]

Pte H Tee, 3593 (Stretcher Bearer); Pte R Gibbs, 3531 (Runner):

Did particularly meritorious work on July 19th, as well as on many previous occasions.

Pte T H Portsmouth, 3465:

For great coolness and disregard of personal danger while carrying messages backwards and forwards from Battalion HQ to the Front Line.

Pte W Coxhead, 5263:

This man attended to the wounded in an exposed position of the trench until himself wounded.

Cpl A F Robey, 2463:

Company Bombing NCO—led bombers forward with great coolness, and, after they had been badly cut up in the gap, kept them together for four hours under heavy fire, ready for use if required.

2/1st Buckinghamshire Battalion

These details are extracted from the Regimental Chronicle combined with other information from the unit history. The following officers were awarded the Military Cross.

Captain I Stewart-Liberty:

He displayed complete disregard of personal danger, and, by his fine example under heavy fire, gave great encouragement to his men. He kept them together in the assault under heavy machine-gun fire, and led them to the enemy's trenches. He was severely wounded.

Captain J E S Wilson (RAMC):

He went up to the front line from his aid post through a very heavy barrage in order to assist the wounded. By his pluck and skill he undoubtedly saved many lives. He afterwards controlled the evacuation of the casualties under heavy fire.

Capt. V W Ranger:

... was in No-Man's Land obtaining intelligence and communicating with Flank Battalions.

2nd Lieut A H Phillips:

He went out into No-Man's Land to reconnoitre and rally men under very heavy shrapnel and machine-gun fire. He showed great coolness and brought back valuable information.

2nd Lieut B H Drakes (E Yorks R):

He commanded the leading platoon of the assault with great dash, and, though his thumb was blown off early in the advance, he stuck to his command till again wounded in the leg after he had reached enemy's lines.

A 'half yearly honour' to use Major Christie-Miller's phrase, went to Capt. G E W Bowyer. He was adjutant and after the battle played a significant role in reorganising the Battalion.

The DCM went to RSM E Jones and to Cpl F Gurney 1694 for conspicuous gallantry during operations:

He showed the greatest courage and promptness in repairing some apparatus which had been hit by an enemy shell. He also led a bombing party in the assault with great courage.

Military Medals were received by: Sgt J Petty 2129, Signallers Cpl T Oldroyd 3321, and L/Cpl R Franklove 1636, Stretcher Bearers Cpl S R Hayers 3395 and Pte W Sanders (or Saunders) 3418.

One source has it that Lieut Col H M Williams was MID.

6th Bn, Oxfordshire & Buckinghamshire Light Infantry

Pte F W Porter, 14991, MM

Capt. IVOR STEWART-LIBERTY

Born on 16 March 1887, Ivor was the eldest son of Donald Stewart MD and Ada (née Liberty)—he assumed the additional surname Liberty by Royal Licence: his uncle Sir Arthur Liberty being the founder of the Liberty department store, Regent St, London. Educated at Winchester College and Christ Church, Oxford, he was called to the Bar by the Inner Temple in 1911. Two years later he married Evelyn Katherine Phipps, the elder daughter Rev. Canon Constantine Osborne Phipps (Canon of Christ Church, Oxford), and the sister of Charles Percy Phipps (see page 55). Ivor lost a leg at Fromelles, and when the war was over compiled *A Record of the 2nd Bucks Bn TF 1914-18*. In 1920 he was Justice of the Peace, in 1922 High Sherriff, and Lord of the Manor of The Lee, Great Missenden, Buckinghamshire, where he lived (see page 62). He later became Chairman of Liberty and Co Ltd. He died on 13 April 1952 survived by his widow and five children.

Australian and British prisoners marching through Haubourdin, 20 July 1916 en route to Lille.
TOP: AWM CO 3112. LOWER: COURTESY J-M BAILLEUL.

9

This war is awful

This war is awful for everybody who is concerned in it.

—General von Hindenburg
to Pte W C Barry, 29th Bn.

After the battle of Fromelles over 1750 Australians were classified as 'missing', so around that many households would have received that vague notification. As illustrated by the stories of James Downie (pages 254–55) and Wallace Hammond (pages 312–13) the final decision on the fate of some of the missing was prolonged and heart-breaking for relatives and friends. When the lists of prisoners taken at Fromelles first became available at the end of August and early September all the anxiety was not cured. There might be a chance that the still missing men could appear in an hospital or camp. The uncensored letters from survivors then in the UK would not have arrived in Australia ahead of the cabled prisoner lists. Then further confusion ensued as there was no place mentioned officially, and with the huge casualties at Pozières only a short time later the effect on families waiting for news must have been very destructive. Without the Red Cross and its well-monitored parcel service, and their freedom to use names of places, one wonders quite what a family might have done.

The lack of precision about numbers of prisoners is difficult to explain. Quite why Bean should note that 'about 400 [Australians] … out of the 481 prisoners taken', was surely just laziness. This inquiry has a list of 458 plus another 38 who died of wounds from Fromelles, while prisoners. Again in regard to German prisoners Bean was vague, '*the British captured 140 prisoners, of whom about 100 were taken by the 5th Division*'. Why not say '5th Division took about 100, 61st Division took about 40'—five less words! As already noted throughout this work, this consistent disregard for real figures, when real figures existed at the time, seems unnecessary, but too consistent to be accidental.

As far as the overall story of the prisoners is concerned, the capture and later career of Captain C Mills of 31st Bn is an important part of the story. He was a member of the Australian Permanent Forces, and related the circumstances of his capture to Bean. Mills had been wounded in the hand and the enemy '*all round, bombing and firing from the hip. A German under*

PRISONER BEHAVIOUR

It is interesting that around the time the list of prisoners taken at Fromelles was published, Lieut Col Wagstaff decided to issue this memo:

1. *All ranks are again warned that they are betraying their duty by giving any information other than their name and rank if they should fall into the hands of the enemy…*
2. *The following reliable information has been received:*
   i) Prisoners taken by the Germans carried on them copies of our battalion orders.
   ii) A German posing as an American interrogates all prisoners who arrive at POW camps.
   iii) The colonial troops in particular are found to give information very readily. The attention of this Division is specially directed to (iii)
3. *No documents of use to the enemy are to be forward of battalion HQ in an attack.*
4. *Every officer in immediate command of troops … will by 20 Sept communicate the foregoing to every man in his command and certify in writing … that he has done so.*

—C M Wagstaff (Lieut Col)
19 Sept 1916

MISSING

At the end of the war some 750 members of the AIF were unaccounted for, and by 1921 at the final demobilisation of the AIF there were 902 'illegal absentees'.

This photograph was published in the 16th BRIR Unit History with the caption: 'Interrogation of Australian prisoners after the Battle of Fromelles on 19 July 1916. Courtesy Lieut Spatny.'
It shows Capt. C Mills, 31st Bn (left), Capt. R A Keay, 32nd Bn (right) with officers of the 16th BRIR.
AWM 1549

officer stopped his men near me, jumped into the trench, seized me by the arm and said in English, "Why did you not put up your hands, officer? Come with me".' The next we see of Mills is in a photograph with his arm in a sling being questioned by Bavarian Officers and getting the prisoners in order for the march to Lille through Haubourdin. His version of these events given after his release is clear and straightforward as are all his statements, letters and notes.

> I was then taken under escort into their front line and along a communication trench to a farm about a mile in rear.
> (e) Were any other prisoners seen? If so, how many?
> Yes. At this farm I met three Officers and about 200 NCOs and men. All Australians.
> (f) What happened immediately after capture?
> I was not molested during my passage through the German positions. On arrival at the farm (apparently a collecting station), I was treated courteously. A German surgeon dressed my wound. I handed over the contents of my pockets at the request of an Officer and received everything back except a photo of myself taken at a studio in Melbourne, which he said he would keep as an example of the Australian uniform. The men were not ill-treated here. I was watching closely. All the wounded were dressed and those who could not walk were removed in motor ambulances. I asked that a meal should be provided for the men, but was told that there was nothing for them. They were allowed to lie down on some straw in a barn. At about midday an officer brought me a sheet of foolscap on which he had marked with colored pencils in diagrammatic form, the colors of the battalions of the 5th Divn. He said: 'This is right Captain?' I said 'I have nothing to say.' The list was correct.
>
> At about 2 pm we were marched to Lille—a long and hard march of three hours. Only one five minute's rest was allowed.

Probably because he was a professional soldier and spoke German, he knew how to get on with the Germans and being the senior officer took charge of those fit enough to march. Many photographs were taken by the Germans on the morning of 20 July, a couple show Mills and Capt. R A Keay, 32nd Bn,

EVERY AUSTRALIAN PRISONER, EXCEPT TWO

Captain C Mills OBE gave a stirring account of his experiences in Germany during and after the war to a large audience including 50 boys from Scotch College, at the Hawthorn ANA meeting on Monday evening. The lecturer was captured at Fleurbaix, spent sixteen months in German prison camps and was finally interned in Switzerland, where, after hospital treatment, he was appointed Australian representative at the British Legation at Berne to attend to the interests of Australian prisoners in Switzerland and Germany. After the armistice he was sent to Berlin to search for missing Australians, arriving there the day after the Sparticist revolution broke out. He had succeeded in getting particulars of every missing Australian prisoner except two men, whose fate remained unknown. Captain Mills said the Germans everywhere he went were looking forward to the time when they could take revenge for their humiliation. He deplored the industrial strife in Australia which was infinitely better off regards living conditions than any country in Europe ... the lecturer displayed a unique collection of German posters and other souvenirs he had obtained.

—*The Argus*, 21 July 1920

Capt. C MILLS

... Order of British Empire ... in recognition of valuable services rendered whilst prisoner of war or interned.

—*Commonwealth Gazette* 5 May 1919

leading the march (details from one photograph—pages 329 and 330). Mills did liaison work on behalf of prisoners and struck up a very good relationship with an officer in the 16th BRIR. Mills was released to Switzerland in November 1917, and returned to Germany after the Armistice for the Red Cross to trace missing Australians. He met up with his Bavarian friend who gave him a set of some 22 photographs taken at Fromelles, 20 July 1916. Mills later donated copies of these to the Australian War Memorial. For his work he was awarded the OBE, and was proud to relate that only two Australian prisoners were not traced (see margin opposite *Every Australian ...*). What the Germans learned from Mills and other officers taken at Fromelles is the substance of the feature *perhaps ... they did not know anything* (pages 309–10), gleaned from the papers in the Munich Archives.

Perhaps more important to the prisoners than Mills was Miss Mary Chomley, secretary of the Prisoners of War Department of the Australian Red Cross in London. It was she who wrote to them, and their relatives, who organised the regular and personal parcels, checked in acknowledgement cards, and so kept track of their movements. A mature, immensely capable woman who had found her work, the Red Cross files reveal her compassion, humour and the probability that she '*knew*' every prisoner. When she discovered there were two Private Antrobuses prisoner (see 29th Bn list), she admitted an error in sending one parcel only, remedied the situation, later sending books requested, and new uniforms after ascertaining the brothers' measurements. She then informed their mother. Her letters, whilst to the point, were personal. In one she wrote: '*I have been criticised for writing too friendly letters*'. One has the feeling that she and Mills had mutual friends in Melbourne

Capt. C MILLS OBE
Charles Mills was born on 17 July 1876 at Heatherton, Victoria. He began his military career with the Victorian Cadets in 1891. Then he enlisted in the Artillery in 1896, becoming Sgt Major in 1912, WO in 1915, commissioned Lieutenant May 1915 with 31st Bn. He was promoted Captain in Egypt in 1916. In 1923 Mills gave a series of lantern slide lectures '*Germany from the inside, during and after the war*'. Held in country and suburban halls, often sponsored by the Australian Natives' Association, they were free and wellnoted in the press. Capt. Mills was, for a time, with the Kooyong Regiment at Surrey Hills, and Adjutant of 4th Division Signals from 21 December 1923. From 1925 to 1936 he was quartermaster at HQ in Melbourne and retired as Lieut Col. He was twice married and died on 21 April 1937.

Australian prisoners at Fromelles, 20 July 1916. The German officer (Capt. Eckart?), third from the right, with hand raised, was the friend of Capt. Mills, who provided him with the set of photographs. When Bean chose two of the collection for his history (p199 top and 201) he made the note '*neither of them show our men as prisoners*'.
AWM A1546

MARY E CHOMLEY OBE
Mary Elizabeth Chomley was born in 1872, the daughter of Arthur Wolfe Chomley, who was the assistant Crown Prosecutor at the trial of Ned Kelly in 1880, and later a judge. She was very active in women's affairs in Victoria prior to going to London early in the war. Initially she worked at Princess Christian's Hospital for Officers, transferring in 1916, to become secretary of the Prisoners of War Department of Australian Red Cross in London, where she stayed until 1919. She had been awarded the OBE in 1918. After her work for the Red Cross she was involved in Britain in the overseas settlement of British women, and from 1928–33 president of the Women's Section of the British Legion. She later returned to Australia. Mary Chomley died in Melbourne on 21 July 1960 and was buried at St Kilda Cemetery.

TEA AND SUGAR
The full week's menu was given in the Report on Ohrdruf for the week 22–29 October 1916, of which this is part:
Sunday Breakfast: coffee, chickory, sugar.
Sunday Lunch: beef, vegetable, potatoes, onions, flour, nutritive yeast.
Sunday Dinner: flour, vegetable, potatoes, onions, fat, nutritive yeast.
Tuesday Breakfast: tea, sugar.
Lunch: same as Sunday.
Dinner: boiled potatoes, cheese.
In general terms beef was served in three lunches, salt fish in one lunch and one dinner, and sausage in one dinner. The grimmest day food-wise was certainly Saturday. Breakfast: cocoa, potato flour, sugar. Lunch: farina, mixed fruit, sugar, milk. Dinner: soya flour, nutritive yeast, vegetable, potatoes, onions, fat.

and so had an easy relationship from the start. The prisoners benefited greatly from their team work. Later when Mills was safe in Switzerland Chomley suggested that their correspondence be published. Mills was against the idea and clearly she was sad at his decision. Strangely while other correspondents' letters were kept, Mills' letters are missing. Doubtless they would have revealed the effectiveness of Mills' cooperative work with the Germans, the true extent to which Red Cross contact and food parcels ensured the survival of prisoners. The stories that follow are some of this evidence.

We turn first to an example of how the Australian Government acted in regard to just one of those captured at Fleurbaix, albeit a year after his capture.

The case of Cpl J A W Jenkins 4247, 54th Bn, caused a file to be made in 1917. It holds the 'correspondence' between the American chargé d'affaires in Berlin with the American Embassy in London, thence to Downing Street, then to the Governor-General in Melbourne (Sir R Munro Ferguson) then to the Prime Minister, and finally to the Minister for Defence. The front sheet of each group of papers, letterheading from the Governor-General's office, carries two rubber stamps at the top, the date stamp of the Prime Minister and another simply 'Concentration Camp 2nd MD'. Right at the beginning of this paper trail are printed reports compiled by the Americans in Berlin about the camps they visited as a result of '*looking after British interests*', then re-issued by His Britannic Majesty's Government and distributed. They included detailed menus and items on sale at the camps, their cost and availability. It was in the Report of 14 November 1916 that an item caught the eye of Pearce, Minister for Defence in June 1917.

> Packages. The men stated that the packages arrive regularly and take from three to five weeks to come from England ... with the exception of Corporal Jenkins, 54th Australian Infantry Regiment No 4247, and Private Hall, 3rd South African Regiment No 5727, the men are all in receipt of packages from England or Switzerland,

Pearce organised a note to the Red Cross in Melbourne to request a supply of parcels to Jenkins. In August 1917 the Red Cross in London wired back:

> ... we have been distributing food parcels regularly to ... Cpl J A W Jenkins every week since Sept 20 [1916] and we have 21 acknowledgment cards signed by him to date.

How much these parcels must have meant to Jenkins, and others, is quickly revealed by the menu at Ohrdruf Camp where Jenkins was: see margin *Tea and Sugar*.

[continued page 311]

perhaps ... they did not know anything ...

In the search for the Missing, the examination of papers in the Munich Archives on prisoners of war was regarded as most important but the Report only reproduced a fraction of the material available. The German Intelligence Officer, Capt. Lübcke seemed most keen to understand how the two divisions they had defeated were made up. To summarise, because the prisoners he had to question were, on the Australian side from 8th and 14th Bdes, and from the English 182nd Bde, he found out almost nothing about 15th Bde, and only hearsay about 183rd and 184th Bdes. He recorded, however, a lot of the opinions the Australians volunteered. Their comments about the opening of the battle demand new thinking.

Whilst the Australians succeeded in gaining a temporary foothold in one part of our trench system, the attack of 61st Division evidently broke down completely at an early stage in the face of our defensive barrage fire. This fact enables us to draw certain conclusions about the quantity of the two divisions, which, it should be noted, left in our hands prisoners from seven different Australian battalions and one British battalion.

The Germans were unable to ascertain much intelligence in regard to 61st Division. '*All that is certain is that 2/7th and 2/6th Battalions of Royal Warwickshire Regiment (182nd Bde) and 2/6th of the Gloucestershire Regiment (183rd Bde) were assaulting battalions and one of Ox and Bucks (184th Bde).*' Lübcke then introduces what surely seems new: '*when 29th Bn ... was sent forward to assist the three hard-pressed battalions of 8th Bde, its place was taken by a battalion of the Ox. and Bucks.*' We learn from Bean in fact 60th Bde (on the Australian left) had been asked to pin down the enemy with rifle and machine gun fire according to the diary of the 6th Ox. and Bucks Light Infantry: '*After the explosion of the mine, the enemy displayed much daring in his endeavour to bring fire to bear on the assaulting Australians.*' Later it assisted with artillery and machine gun support, and at the end sent '*officers and stretcher bearers to assist*'.

Lübcke managed to get a fairly accurate account of the preparations for the attack as far as 8th and 14th Bdes were concerned. He learned that '*unfortunately, according to officers, the plan went awry from the start due to an inexplicable misunderstanding. Part of the first wave of 14th Bde left its trenches at 5.30 pm (it was to leave at 5.55 pm) and some men got caught in their own artillery barrage. Unsettled by this, the first wave of 8th Bde did not leave their trenches until after their own barrage had lifted ... the 2/7th Warwicks likewise remained in their trenches until the barrage had lifted ... about 6.10 pm*'.

All this to indicate how the officers and men of the Australian Fifth Division were well aware of the shambolic start of the Battle.

Obviously the Australian officers held by the Germans were important sources of opinion as well as the general make up of 5th Division; summed up by Lübcke thus: '*The officers attribute the failure to the incompetence of the Divisional Commander. The men all say that coherent leadership was lacking from the outset ... after their Company Commander was killed as they were leaving their own trenches, some companies charged blindly and leaderless into our positions ... there were no special offensive training exercised in preparation ... The artillery of 5th Div. was specially reinforced with English heavy artillery as it had no guns over 12.5 cm / 5 inches. Our artillery* [was] *devastatingly effective, some battalions lost 50–60 ... moving up from support lines ...*'

Lübcke also found out that the orders for the attack were only disclosed to officers on 17 or 18 July, and read out to the men '*on the actual day of the attack*'. They had been assured that a massive artillery bombardment would completely flatten the German trenches ... allowing the attackers to simply walk across ... only the German front line and support trenches were to be taken and held.

Lübcke's summaries and general thoughts about the events at Fromelles are, as far as given in the Report, substantially correct, even though the battle was just over, the Germans had to remain cautious in case there was another attack. Hence his questioning about other Allied Divisions nearby. Lübcke never surmises or guesses, he must have been a formidable interrogator, hence his conclusions are most interesting; and expose from a new source, the hopeless Australian leadership:

The whole operation, according to the officers, had suffered from a lack of coherent leadership. That apart, the operation had been misconceived at the planning stage, as the order to hold the German second line trenches was fundamentally wrong. The order should have been to retire during the night to the German front line trench, and to fortify it and hold it. The greatest setback, however, was that the 15th Bde appeared to have failed completely. As a result, the attacking front was interrupted and there was no flanking cover. This was the only reason the Germans had been able to retake their front line trench and cut off the enemy units that had broken into their positions. Finally, it had been the fatal error—attributable once again to the lack of coherent leadership—for the attacking force, after it had broken into the German front line trench, to fragment into a number of smaller formations with little or no communication between them. The men had not been short of personal courage, but they were too inexperienced in combat to be able to make up for the lack of higher leadership with coherent independent action.

[continued next page]

PERHAPS ... THEY DID NOT KNOW ANYTHING (contd)

So much for the wider picture, Lübcke now assessed the Australians: *Although the Australian officers and men are in very good physical condition, they seem rather deficient in military qualities. The Australian officers are inferior in every respect to the British. As is to be expected in view of their educational background, they are completely lacking in judgement as to what is important militarily and what is not. The officers, for example, despite repeated protestations that their conscience as officers would not allow them to disclose military secrets, cheerfully dictated to us complete details of the planning and execution of the attack; and the dispositions of the units involved ... with guile we were able to extract [other] fragments of information from them. Perhaps, though, given their deficient military training, they really did not know anything.*

MEETING WITH SCANZONI

It must have been an interesting meeting that Lieut General Scanzoni had with the captured Australian Officers. He clearly belonged to a Germany, and a generation far far different from the one to come. He began: '*Report on conversations with the captured Australian officers. The officers asked not to be interrogated because, as officers, they were unable to divulge anything and were prepared to accept the consequences of their refusal, as German officers would do if captured by the British. Capt. Mills, a regular officer with 31st Bn ... proved especially talkative. He did not reproach himself for being taken prisoner ... he had done his duty and his men had acquitted themselves bravely. He had, however, committed a serious error of judgement in allowing important documents to fall into our hands, which, of course, he should never have brought over to our positions with him. The attack had been abortive, in his opinion, owing to tactical failings. There were enough troops there, they had only to be committed. The attack should have taken place over a frontage of 2½ miles ...*'

Capt. C Mills, 31st Bn 1915
COURTESY P NELSON

Mills went on to tell Scanzoni about how effective the machine guns were: '*we owed the successful defence of our positions to them and ... our artillery [and that] they were powerless against our grenadiers who headed our counter attack ... he complimented our marksmanship, but said that Australians are also very good shots; they are born hunters ...*'

With 2/Lieut Cummins 55th Bn, Scanzoni discussed Gallipoli and the Turks and the three men from 58th Bn taken prisoner on 15 July raid, '*afraid that those men had given something away and that we had forewarning of the attack*'.

Then these observations, '*All the Officers were very concerned about the fate of their men ... the American envoy* [see page 327] *had found that British prisoners in Germany were going hungry. Questions had been asked in Parliament ... The Officers were favourably impressed by our care for the wounded and treatment of the prisoners, and repeatedly expressed their appreciation. The officers say that they are all weary of the war and do not believe that it can ever be settled on the battlefield.*

'*Lieut Cummins believes that the majority of the men volunteered not ... for adventure but because they were well paid (5 marks—sometimes 6 marks—a day) and for many of them also out of patriotism.*'

The General was not without a sense of humour in this report that would go back to Army HQ. He concluded: '*Capt. Mills formed up the prisoners ready to march off and addressed a few words to them, wishing them all the best for the future and telling them that they had done their duty. Rations would not be as plentiful now as they used to be—here he jokingly remarked: don't laugh, you didn't get too much in Egypt either ...*' [signed] Scanzoni

THE 15TH BDE SURVIVOR: PTE H H V HODSON

It would appear that the only prisoner of 15th Bde taken in the attack and who survived was Pte Henry Hurlstone Victor Hodson 3990, 59th Bn, a 19 year old bricklayer from Camberwell, Victoria. Hodson enlisted 28 November 1915.

What follows is part of his account on returning to England: *I did not myself actually reach the enemy first line, being wounded by shrapnel in the head, shoulder and in both legs ...*

I was hit shortly after the start of the advance. I lay in a shell-hole with one of our own dead ... I was picked up by the Germans at about midnight on July 20. I could not walk, being paralysed down the left side.

I was removed to Lille where I was placed in hospital—an old convent that had been converted to hospital purposes. There were about a dozen of our chaps there, mostly 'Tiveys'—members of the 8th Brigade, of which General Tivey was Brigadier—all wounded. I remained in hospital at Lille about a fortnight during which time an operation was performed on my head. The food given us was good and the nurses, who were French nuns, were very attentive and kind. From Lille I was transferred to Douai. Here the food was wretched and the medical attention very poor ...

I next journeyed by train to Stuttgart, in Wurtemburg, Germany. On the train journey we received good food and accommodation. There travelled with me to Stuttgart: Pte Butler, 32nd Bn, Pte Gubbins, 55th Bn ... [Pte J Butler 1611, Perhaps G Gribbon 2728 or Pte J H Grimes 3237.]

Hodson was transferred to Holland for internment 14 April, 1918, and was repatriated to England 16 August 1918. He died on 22 July 1926, virtually the tenth anniversary of his capture.

At the end of the November 1916 Report, the Americans listed the complaints of the prisoners. The general complaints were about Sunday work, no suitable football field, inadequate clothing and delay in receiving packages. Then came three specific complaints, the first about the delay in getting money from England, the second about not being able to clean up properly after work, to which the Commandant said it was impossible to provide them with soap for this purpose and the third was by a prisoner who had his sleeve tugged by a guard: this was explained being due to the prisoner not being able to understand the instructions of the guard. Otherwise, although conditions were spartan, the Americans were reasonably satisfied with the treatment of the prisoners.

In his history of 29th Bn, *Black and Gold*, Ron Austin devoted five pages to stories of POWs taken at Fromelles, cautioning: '*the reader should be warned that the accounts... are taken from statements made ... after their release from captivity. In some cases their statements and accusations cannot be substantiated ... many ... were somewhat shameful of being captured, and ... anxious to show that they had been good soldiers.*'

The statements extracted from the POW files in Canberra tell a mixed story, usually of initial brutality, a fairly obvious reaction in the stress of battle and on a battlefield still full of danger. Then earnest medical treatment well behind the lines nearly always follows. If the prisoners were later fit for work, that work was inevitably hard labour six days a week, and the food was always insufficient in quantity and poor in quality. Pte O V Carter 1093 wrote on 15 February 1917 '*Under new scheme in England, every prisoner receives 30 pounds of feed (tinned) and 14 of bread fortnightly, and are also allowed 16 pounds extra privately, if their people wish to send to England. Every Australian has had a goat skin jacket sent to him as well as boots that lace up to the knees for the snow, and all of us are splendidly looked after by the Red Cross.*'

Still in camp two years after Fromelles, Carter wrote to his mother: '*I'll bet now that I could walk past the family of you and not one of you would recognise me. Most chaps take me for 15 years older than I am. My heart is still in the same place. In our parcels there is usually a map of Australia on a tin of "bully" and we don't 'arf worship the dearest spot on earth.*'

From the same source it was perhaps Pte E Wait, 352, who caught the dilemma of the wounded and the captor best:

> I was hit with a hand grenade ... and lost consciousness. When I recovered ... I saw men around me, but I was still rather 'fuzzy' and

RED CROSS PARCELS

Three parcels of plain food every fortnight by post ... any more food at your own expense. We will be pleased to select and despatch it for you. 100 cigarettes and 4 ozs capstan tobacco every fortnight. We will send underclothing and simple toilet necessities. When we get your measurements we will send uniform—but not tunics for officers.

Your pay will continue ... you are allowed to draw £10 a month ... you can allot £2 to Red Cross.

With each parcel there is a card to be returned with any address change given. This provides a regular check on each recipient and assists in monitoring delivery ...

—Extracts from
Official Red Cross Leaflet

A PRISONER OF WAR

On regaining consciousness after my wounds at Fleurbaix ... I was helped along by a German until we met two other Aussies, the three of us continuing to the rear of the German lines to join many Tommies and Aussies who had been caught in the same stunt. Thence we were marched to Lille, where our wounds were treated by a matron, after which we had a slice of black bread and some coffee—the first food I had had for 30 hours—and put ourselves to bed. Sleeping until 6 am I was awakened by a sparrow at the bars of the room. How I envied that bird its liberty.

After two days here, during which we received no medical attention—apparently the doctor ... had been called away to attend German wounded—we were told to dress. Entraining in cattle trucks, scantily furnished with straw we made a two days journey to Dulmen in Westphalia, being jeered at by sightseers at every stop ... Transported to camp by a civilian in a tip-dray, I was placed in a hammock to await a doctor—a Frenchman, who had been captured earlier in the field. He said I must look to God to put me right, there being no provision at Dulmen for operations.

—Pte D B Storey, 1143 30th Bn
(from Sloan, *The Purple and Gold*)

IN THE FIELD, FRANCE
On 23 August 1917 a Court of Enquiry was convened by the CO of 60th Bn 'In the Field, France', for among other things, establishing what had happened to Pte Wallace Hill Hammond, 3124. Hammond who was from Warrnambool, had enlisted 8 July 1915 and as part of 7/21st Bn reinfor-cement went to Egypt in October. On 26 February 1916 he transferred to 60th Bn. He was 19 and the oldest of seven children, and had worked as a compositor on the *Warrnambool Standard*, which probably accounts for their interest in his fate.

Initially Hammond was reported missing on 19 July, but the Enquiry decided he had been killed in action and notified the family, who placed a notice in the *Standard* on 1 September 1917.

> *Died on Service*
> *Hammond—Killed in action at Fleurbaix, France on 19th July, 1916, W H Hammond (previously reported missing) 60th Battalion, dearly loved son of Thos S and Mrs Hammond, Jamieson Street, Warrnambool.*
> *—Inserted by his parents and family*

There seems to be no indication why it took a year to reach the conclusion that Hammond was dead because the Prisoner of War lists from Fromelles were available from September 1916. Clearly the Red Cross was not entirely certain what happened, because later the *Standard* carried this poignant story:

Across the ocean's suspense and silence Mr and Mrs T S Hammond were recently prepared for the sad confirmatory news imparted to them on Tuesday last by the Vicar, the Rev. T P Bennett. Some weeks ago they received a letter through the Red Cross Society intimating that two tent mates who had been wounded on that tragic 19th July, 1916, had seen their son, Private Wallace Hammond, killed by a shell in No-Man's Land, Fleurbaix. There was, however, some slight ground for hope as the news was unofficial and it was thought that the young hero's comrades might have been mistaken in the frenzy of assault.

[continued opposite]

> did not realise my position till a German officer kicked me. He asked me if I was badly wounded. I said 'yes'. He told the men to put me in a dugout and explained to me that I could not be moved till the afternoon when some of their own wounded were going out of the line.

The medical treatment of prisoners by the Germans seems to have been exemplary, given the number of their own they had to attend. It was of particular interest when on 11 March 1918 Pte D E Neill, 1547, 32nd Bn, and Pte W C Barry, 29th Bn, returned to Melbourne and these one-legged veterans were interviewed. Barry was the author of the diary that forms the appendix of this chapter.

> Pte Neill was wounded and taken prisoner at Fleurbaix. He was conveyed to a hospital behind the lines, where one of his legs was amputated. The German doctors, he said, were very kind, and everything possible was done for him … he was transferred to the hospital camp at Laugensalza … the discipline was very strict.
>
> But we fared better than our guards in the way of food. We could not eat the rations supplied to us, but the Australian Red Cross parcels, packed with food and clothing, arrived regularly, and we had plenty to eat. We always had white bread, and this our guards never got. Then we had books to read, there being a good library of English works, supplied, I suppose, by the Red Cross … ordinary prisoners were not so well off as wounded men.
>
> Pte Barry also acknowledged the care with which the doctors treated him. They kept him four months in hospital before they amputated his leg, in the hope of saving it. He also bore out what Pte Neill had said about the excellent work by the Australian Red Cross … on one point, however, Pte Barry was very reticent, this being the behaviour of the German guards.

This '*excellent work*' included keeping a file on Barry wherein there is a letter written by him from Aachen on 18 February 1917. He had had his leg amputated on 27 October 1916:

> I am now quite well and cannot speak too highly of the kindness and attention which I received from the Doctors and nurses during the five months I was in hospital.

Of the prisoners taken at Fromelles and who later escaped, the most interesting story relates to Pte Wesley Paul Choat of 32nd Bn. He was clearly determined to get home and this may have been due to the fact that two of his brothers were killed at Fromelles. No press report makes any reference to this, but it is unlikely that in the sixteen months he was prisoner he had not been told.

The enlistment details of the Choat brothers are worth mentioning. The first to sign up was Wesley Paul Choat on 12 July 1915, he was assigned no 68. Raymond Hodden Choat enlisted 21 July 1915 and got no 67, and Archibald Percy Choat enlisted 30 June 1916 and was no. 66. They were all in the 32nd Bn and sons of Joseph and Alice Mary Choat of Francis St, Clarence Park, South Australia. Raymond was 24 when he was killed, and was buried at Rue Petillon. Archibald was 19 when he died, and his name is at VC Corner Cemetery.

On arrival in London from Holland in February 1918, Choat's fellow escapee, L/Cpl L W Pitts, 2954, 50th Bn, became spokesman:

> L/Cpl Pitts states that Pte Choat was responsible for the arrangements for their escape. Choat, during his two year imprisonment studied German to be able to travel without arousing suspicion. '*We made earlier attempts to escape but were unsuccessful ... and for those we were punished. Many of those in the camp knew of our intentions to make another attempt, but guarded the secret carefully.*'
>
> Choat raffled on old fiddle in camp, thereby raising money to pay expenses. It was impossible to wear camp clothes '*... therefore we secured the baggiest of military trousers and took out the military stripes at the sides, so when they were sewn up, they looked like ordinary workmen's trousers. We also removed the distinguishing marks on the tunics. We grew moustaches after the German fashion.*'
>
> Choat's knowledge of German was most useful. '*We noticed a policeman watching us suspiciously, and Choat asked him the way to the station. The policeman sternly asked "Who are you?" Choat replied "Belgian workmen." The policeman said "Where are you going?" Choat replied "we are going home." Choat's frankness disarmed the policeman, who indicated the direction of the station. The train travelling was difficult, but by various devices we allayed suspicion, and we feigned sleep when closely watched. Choat's disguise was perfect. He would address me in colloquial German, to which I nodded response or replied in mono-syllables. We brought a little food from the camp, and therefore it was unnecessary to visit restaurants where the absence of bread and other cards would have promptly led to our detection. Finally we reached Holland.*'

L/Cpl J W Pitts and Pte W P Choat were welcomed back to Adelaide on Sunday, 7 July 1918.

Choat added a little to the earlier story. He had also studied the stars while held prisoner and brought a compass from a Frenchman in the camp for 2/-. He also thought that, thanks to the Red Cross parcels, they ate better than the Germans. '*You can't realise how we felt as we crossed the border [into Holland]. Our next thought was food and we went to a Dutch restaurant where we had a really good feed of bread and butter.*'

Another part of this story is revealed in the Red Cross files. A few days after his arrival in Holland Choat sent a postcard to Miss Chomley: '*I have great pleasure indeed in informing you that I have, on my second attempt, succeeded in escaping from my captivity in Germany and am eagerly looking forward*

IN THE FIELD, FRANCE (contd)

Much sympathy goes out to Mr and Mrs Hammond in the loss of their first-born, who was a particularly bright youth of nineteen. Poor laddie! as he bade me a smiling good-bye, the wish was expressed that he would win the Victoria Cross. Well, he has climbed a Cross!

Mrs Hammond has done a wise and beautiful thing: she has taken to her home and heart a few weeks old baby boy. 'A child's kiss set on thy sighing lips shall make thee glad.' May this mother's heart be comforted so!

But that was not the end of it. The Base Records Office in Melbourne on 13 July 1921 wrote to Mr Hammond in the hope that he had received some information that would help in finding Wallace Hammond's burial place. Mr. Hammond wrote:

> *The last field card we had was dated 17/7/16 saying that his Battalion was going into action shortly, and the report I heard from a returned man was that they were all shot down with machine guns, crossing the river Lys, under the direction of (Officer Mackay) that is all the evidence I can give.*

No trace of Wallace Hammond was ever found so his name is in the 60th Bn panel at VC Corner Cemetery.

INFORMATION & PHOTOGRAPH COURTESY JOHN RULE

to the time when I shall be able to thank you in person for the many kind and invaluable privileges received through you … I am yours in obligation. Wess Choat'

Years later when Patsy Adam-Smith was researching her book *Prisoners of War* she interviewed Spr L Barry, 2378, 1st Field Coy of Engineers, one of the group that had included Choat and Pitts but who was recaptured. Barry related that preliminaries were organised thanks to a combination of fairly slack guards and local girls impressed by the Diggers! The only Fromelles prisoner unearthed by Adam Smith was Pte J A Giles, 4788, 53rd Bn, whose father learned of his fate in September 1916. Giles, if photographs are anything to go by, was in good health at Dulmen, Westphalia. He too was thankful for weekly parcels.

When the prisoners returned to the UK either after escaping, or when in Holland or Switzerland during the war, or on release after the armistice, all were questioned and had to give signed statements concerning their experiences. First, the events leading up to their capture, then their capture and immediate treatment, later treatment in camps and other Australians seen or noted. This sequence draws attention to an episode detailed on page 140.

> Lieut Albert William Bowman, 53rd Bn: Immediately after capture, I was taken to a dressing station in company with a few men and there met a number of wounded who were being attended to and Captain Mills and Captain Keay. Both these officers were wounded.
>
> We were afterwards marched to Lille and placed in the Citadel. During my stay there I was interrogated by a German Staff Captain, who informed me that the attack was expected and all preparations had been made to receive it. Furthermore he showed me a new copy of General Haking's Army order giving full details of the way the attack was to be carried out.
>
> From the Citadel at Lille, I was taken to Dulmen where I remained two days. On the 26th July arrived at Guntersloh, where I remained till 19th March 1917.

> Pte C A Mitchell, 53rd Bn: Lieut A W M Bowman … was a D Coy officer. I saw him running up and down the enemy second line. I was told later whilst a prisoner of war in Germany, by Corporal Kiss and Corporal Bert Horace that it was Lieut Bowman who ordered the men to surrender. They declared that Lieut Bowman himself surrendered to the Germans.
>
> Two German soldiers were escorting the officer away when our fellows shot both of them. They also threatened to shoot Lieut Bowman. I understand that both the NCOs who told me this story are now interned in Holland. While we were in Holland we all made written statements concerning this affair—of the surrender. The captain who collected these statements, I believe, was Captain R A Keay, 32nd Bn.
>
> I did not see Captain Murray at all during the engagement, but I heard while in Germany that it was really though this officer that the white flag was flown by our fellows.

A VISIT TO GERMANY

My last war experience was at Fromelles, where so many of my friends went west, Of my section of eight men who started to carry stores to the troops in the front line, five of us got through and did our little bit towards building up some kind of cover in the slimy ditches. Shortly after daybreak we were surrounded, I was badly hit and for a time remained unconscious. When we I came to my senses, I was alone and felt very sick and weak from loss of blood. I laid in the shell hole all day and towards evening started to crawl towards what I thought was our front line. I made very little progress, but on the following day as I was nearing a parapet of some kind, a German officer hailed me. He said 'Have you been out here all this time?' and I said 'Yes'. He was a decent sort and told me that he had been in New Zealand for some years: he gave me a drink and a cigarette, and advised me to rest until a prisoners' escort picked me up. I was taken to Lille, where I spent the night in great pain. On the following day I was taken to a prisoners' hospital in Douai … I managed to recover and was sent to a prison camp at Ingolstad where I was put to work and almost starved. I chummed with a 29th man named Vic Waite (352), and after we could stand our treatment no longer, decided to make a bid for liberty. We … got clean away … and we were caught … Vic was sent to Berlin and I was sent to Bavaria … when I entered Germany I weighed 11 stone; when I arrived in England I was down to 6 stone 10 Ibs.

—Cpl E R 'Tosh' Ridley, 1023, 30th Bn

[from Sloan, *The Purple and Gold*.]

> Soon after we had retired to the enemy second line, after our attempt to bomb the enemy out of the communication trench, myself and two comrades crawled out into shell-holes in front, and began to snipe [at] the enemy. I know my two comrades were both killed. I was badly wounded. I was wounded by shrapnel in the right leg and by a bullet in the head. I don't remember any more until I found myself being taken to a dressing station by the Germans on the morning of July 20. Of course I was, but then, a prisoner of war.

But the prisoner who was best remembered was surely Capt. Arblaster. One has the feeling from the statements made that his deeds and death were often the main topic of conversation during the years of imprisonment. Pte C A Mitchell, 53rd Bn:

> Captain Arblaster. He was the OC of D Coy. I saw him across in the enemy second line. At about 11 pm on the 19th July, the night following the attack, he was calling for volunteers. I made one of a party of six who volunteered to bomb the enemy out of a communication trench that was threatening our right flank (as we faced the enemy). Lance Corporal Freirat was one of that party also. We drove the enemy back until our bombs ran out. Then Captain Arblaster ordered us back to the German second line. I know that Captain Arblaster afterwards died as a prisoner of war. I was in the same ward. The French civilians subscribed and he was given a proper funeral.

L/Cpl P Freirat, 53rd Bn recalled that Arblaster was '*badly wounded ... both his arms were broken ... shot through both arms*'. And Pte A B Rankine, 53rd Bn, remembered other aspects:

> The general impression was that the Germans had got there through underground passages.
>
> Shortly after day-break Captain Arblaster lead about a dozen of us in an endeavour to bomb our way through to our own lines. We extended along the sap in open order and at the word from Captain Arblaster, made a dash for it across the open.
>
> The enemy greeted us with a fierce fusillade of machine gun and rifle fire. Though we suffered few casualties, we were driven back into the trench again.
>
> When last I saw Captain Arblaster he was lying on the parapet shot through both arms. I have since heard that he died in hospital as a prisoner of war. Captain Ranson of B Coy was alone in the trench. He went along the sap to investigate but came back shot through the arm. He then gave the order to surrender.

Overall the admiration for Arblaster seemed to outweigh the aspect of surrender which was associated with Bowman, Murray and Ranson. Arblaster's file has only his card, marked simply: '*Dead 26.8.16 at St Clotilda, Douai*'.

A REGIMENTAL ORDER HAD TO BE ISSUED

The kindness our soldiers showed towards the English prisoners can be illustrated by the fact that a regimental order had to be issued, emphasizing that our own wounded always had to be rescued before wounded enemies and that wounded enemies should be carried by unharmed prisoners in the first place. Captured officers repeatedly thanked their captors for their good treatment and care for all their wounded and captured. They were mostly of the 5th Australian Division which had already fought in Egypt and Gallipoli and that had only arrived a few days before. According to their statements the reason for our successful defence was the accuracy of the shooting of our artillery and machine guns. On the English side the leadership broke down, the attack was not led with enough intensity, they had enough troops they only had to use them.

—Capt. F Wiedemann
16th BRIR

VERY WORRIED

The prisoners were very worried about their fate. The American ambassador is claimed to have found out that the English prisoners had to go hungry in Germany. At any rate, the Australian captain who had the prisoners (among them a 65-year-old volunteer) fall in for the march-off near the division's staff headquarters felt compelled to tell his people they should accept their fate as best they could; they had all done their duty and if rations should now turn out less generous—in Egypt, however, they had not too much, either—then they should adapt to these conditions as well.

—Capt. F Wiedemann
16th BRIR

These paragraphs when compared with the Reports by Lübcke and Scanzoni on pages 309–10 reveal how closely Wiedemann, when working on his history of the 16th BRIR, stayed to the primary sources.

Two Bavarians picked me up

Just a week after his 20th birthday, Pte Thomas Dalzell Bolton 1074, a member of the original 29th Bn, was taken prisoner, suffering severe injuries to his jaw. He wrote to his old school (Geelong Grammar) from Switzerland in April 1917 to where he had been transferred after 5 months in Germany, '*now quite recovered though at present somewhat disfigured*'. Bolton, who was from Horsham, enlisted on 23 July 1915 and returned to Australia on 9 February 1919. His letter provides a detailed description of his treatment when the worst was over and he was under no duress to conceal either anger or gratitude.

Thomas D Bolton, 1913.
COURTESY GEELONG GRAMMAR SCHOOL ARCHIVES

My wound was not a very bad one, but was sufficient to put me out of action for the time being and to cause my capture. On July 19th, my battalion charged the Germans at a place called Fleurbaix at 6 o'clock in the evening, we took two lines of trenches and held them till about 2 o'clock next morning. The Germans then made a strong counter-attack and broke through our line. The part of the line I was in was cut off and surrounded so we made a charge to get back to our own lines. It was then that I was hit and knocked unconscious for the time being. A bullet passed through my right jaw, through my mouth, knocking a few teeth out, and came out on the left of my nose. Two Bavarians picked me up and half carried and half dragged me to a field dressing station behind the German lines. My wound was dressed roughly and I was then put on a stretcher and taken to another dressing station. Here I was put to bed and on waking up next morning I saw three of my company standing at the foot of my bed. They could not recognize me at first. I was then given something to eat but could not eat it as I was unable to open my mouth. Some water was poured down my throat, which was a great relief. About mid-day that same day, along with a good many others, I was packed in a railway truck and left for an unknown destination. That afternoon we landed at a place called Douai. We were taken to a big hospital called St. Clotilda Lazarette. This place had been a French convent, but the Germans commandeered it for a hospital. After we had been here a few days, I was operated on and had my wound fixed up. I spent about a month in this hospital and was treated pretty well. The food was the only fault I found here, not nearly enough. On 20th August, three of us under a guard entrained for Germany. It took us two days travelling to reach our destination. On the way we passed through Mons, Namur, and Charleroi in Belgium where all the big battles took place in 1914. We crossed the Rhine at Cologne and a fine river it is too. Well, Bochum in Westphalia, (you will find all these places on the map) was our destination. I spent another month here, in St Elizabeth's Hospital, a civilian hospital run by Roman Catholic Sisters of Mercy. Here, the treatment and food were good and I was sorry to leave, which I did on 22nd September. I was then sent to Sennelager Camp, via Padderborn in Westphalia. This camp was full of Russians, French, Belgians and British. It was one of the first prison camps formed in Germany. The camp itself was enclosed by two 9 foot barbed wire fences with two live electric wires between. In addition, guards were posted outside this, so you see there was no chance of escape. Most of the chaps in this camp had been there since the beginning and had had a pretty rough time of it. When I arrived they were getting plenty of parcels so I struck it very lucky. They gave me clothing, for I had nothing but the clothes I left the trenches with, and they shared their parcels with me. The food the Germans supplied was insufficient and not fit for pigs. You can imagine how we should have been without the parcels. The 1914 prisoners had to put up with it. We lived in low wooden huts and had vermin infested bunks to sleep in. In the morning you had to fight your way to the water taps to get a wash. The only good points about this camp were (1) we were given a hot bath once a week (2) a football ground and recreation hall were given us (3) a German clergyman who had been some time in England tried to give us a sermon in the recreation hall once a fortnight. The British and French formed an orchestra with instruments borrowed from the Germans and we had one or two very good concerts. The daily routine was as follows: breakfast at 6.30, parade at 7, dinner at 12, parade at 2, tea at 6, parade at 7, lights out at 9. All fit men were sent out to work on farms and other works. Men passed by the doctor as fit for light work had to do jobs in and about the camp. I was given a job on the parcels staff. We had to take the mail to the station in a waggon drawn by about 16 of us on a long chain and bring back the incoming mail, which we then had to sort. The distance to the station was about a mile and a half, so you can imagine the time we had pulling the old waggon. We had as many as 4000 parcels to deal with in one day (only British, of course the other nationalities did their own). Well the same thing went on day after day until the Swiss Commission came round. I was then passed for Switzerland. We entrained early one morning about the beginning of

[continued opposite]

TWO BAVARIANS PICKED ME UP (contd)

November, about 80 of us, for Constance, which we reached two days later. At Constance, we were put into German Military Barracks, and there waited for the final examination. We waited about a fortnight and during that time prisoners came in from all the camps in Germany. I suppose the total in the end was about 1,000 (all British). The French exchange came off later, and the Russians are not exchanged at all. We were then examined by Swiss and German doctors and as luck would have it I passed. I tell you it was one of the happiest moments of my life; I could not realise it at first. After the examinations were all over came the sad parting of those who had passed and those who had not. It is a terrible thing to bring men right to the border and then turn them back, several committed suicide and no wonder at it. Well, the next step as we thought was the crossing into Switzerland, but here we were mistaken. We were all put in a train and instead of going to Switzerland, were sent back to Germany, a day's journey to a place called Bastatt. We were put in a fort and kept there about three weeks. Those three weeks were the worst I spent in Germany. The Germans bullied us—we could not get our parcels, and the accommodation and food supplied by the Huns was terrible. In the end we left this hole for Constance again. On arriving at Constance we saw the Swiss train waiting for us and in another hour we were in Switzerland and as happy as little children. We were given a great reception and I never ate so much in all my life, by Jove I had a hunger. Well, I have been here about four months now and I feel as fit as when I left home. It is a very picturesque country, the mountain scenery can't be beaten anywhere. Geneva is a fine place; I spent a month there not long ago. Went down for a small operation.

—T .B.,

Hotel Berthod,
Chateau D'Oex, *20th April, 1917*
Switzerland

THE CORIAN (May 1918). COURTESY MICHAEL COLLINS PERSSE ARCHIVES CENTRE, GEELONG GRAMMAR SCHOOL

Captured at Fleurbaix

As the Germans sought to dispose themselves of the responsibility for badly wounded prisoners, some were sent to Switzerland for repatriation. Others who escaped made their way to Holland, which repatriated them to England. This selection of interviews, memories and observations provides an idea of the prisoner of war experience:

G H Reed, 54th Bn ... escaped (on second attempt) and is back in Britain ... was doing farm work at Ossenburg on the Rhine ... he was slightly wounded and captured at Fleurbaix, July 1916. (*The Argus*, 6 May 1918).

G Davison, 31st Bn ... his shoulder was smashed at Fleurbaix on 20 July 1916. He lay in a shell hole all night until captured and sent to Dulmenand. (*The Argus*, 19 June 1918).

S N Key, 54th Bn ... he was captured at Fleurbaix unwounded but underwent an operation for pleurisy and pneumonia at Dulmen Camp. He was five months in Germany before being transferred to Switzerland. (*The Argus*, 20 June 1918).

J Bolton, 31st Bn ... he was captured at Fleurbaix ... brutally hustled to the German rear despite a smashed elbow ... his health broke down ... he was sent to hospital, and when discharged refused to work and was despatched to a reprisals' camp, where he remained for eight months, suffering indignities, brutalities and discomfort, especially lack of warmth in winter. (*The Argus*, 21 June 1918).

F Hall, 32nd Bn ... was captured at Fleurbaix ...he had his leg smashed. (*The Argus*, 22 June 1918).

T Driscoll, 8th MG Coy ... had been wounded in an enemy trench ... was carried to the rear at 9 pm on 20 July by four Bavarians who wrapped him in a ground sheet and slung the sheet on a pole. At places they had to crawl on their hands and knees, but never showed the slightest hesitation ... they were rare plucky men. (Bean, Volume 3, p. 437).

R Bateram, 31st Bn ... reached the enemy's second line when his left leg was injured by machine gun fire. The wound remained undressed four days after capture. He was sent to various hospitals and eventually to Lechfeld. There Red Cross parcels were withheld for eleven weeks for the purpose of compelling non-commissioned officers to volunteer for work ... Bateram was selected in December 1916 for internment in Switzerland but was unable to travel, and he was eventually sent in the following December. (*The Argus*, 18 June 1918).

B Ross, 29th Bn ... about midnight they found me, and carried me about 4 kms in an oil sheet. (*Black and Gold*).

P C Donovan, 29th Bn ... wounded in the back by a bomb on 19 July 1916 ... struck by a bullet in the left hip the following morning. He was captured during an enemy counter-attack ... he was carried in a blanket suspended from a pole ... to a dressing station near Lille. There he lay on straw for 24 hours ... for five months he was an outpatient in Dulmen Lazarette, where a Tommy was shot dead for attempting to escape. The Germans were reluctant to give up Red Cross parcels. (*The Argus*, 18 June 1918 & *Black and Gold*).

This war is awful for everybody ...

William C Barry, 2514 29th Bn, a plumber and fitter with The Gas Company from Northcote was taken prisoner with severe wounds at Fromelles. After attempts to save his leg, the German doctor decided it had to be amputated to stop the gangrene spreading. Barry just prior to Christmas 1916 was visited in the hospital by General Von Hindenburg and recorded the event in his 'diary' which is more in the style of a memoir. The document begins with his enlistment in Melbourne in July 1915 and finishes with him having tea at Windsor Castle, personally served by Princess Beatrice, in early 1918. About 65,000 words, the diary is an extraordinary testament of survival and faith.

It is difficult to judge where or when William Barry wrote his diary. If he used notes or a pocket diary it is impossible to think he could have kept them through his period in the German hospitals. It seems more likely that after his return to England at the end of 1917 he had time to write the whole story. His memory for detail and situations is remarkable.

The extract here, some 9,500 words, gives a good idea of the extraordinary power of Barry's writing and his personal courage. The unique way he deals with the cruelties and kindnesses meted out to him during his time in Germany is profoundly moving. Although she appears only momentarily in this extract, Schwester (Sister) Franka, Barry's German nurse, is revealed as that indomitable spirit of tenderness and care that re-ignites his faith in the human race. In later life he deeply regretted that he did not contact her, but he did not know her full name or have any address, or the financial resources to instigate a search.

On 18 December 1920 Barry married Elsie May Anderson, ten years his junior; they had known each other before he went away. On their honeymoon he took ill, and other guests at the hotel consoled Elsie because 'her father was ill.' Such had been the effect of William Barry's war time experiences on his appearance. Barry on his return from the war, rejoined The Gas Company in a clerical position where he remained until his retirement on 22 September 1948. William Charles Barry was born on 22 September 1883 and died 7 February 1954.

HINDSIGHT
It was the section *In the hands of the German Red Cross*, on page 324 that began the search for the Missing of Fromelles by Lambis Englezos.

William C Barry, no 2514, A Coy, 29th Bn, early 1920s.

Landing in France

We landed at the wharf about three o'clock on Friday afternoon, but as our landing was kept a secret very few people knew we had arrived. We disembarked at five o'clock and one of the first things that I noticed was a number of German prisoners of war, escorted by French soldiers, working on the wharf. As we did not leave the wharf till eight o'clock, the band played various selections, among them being the Marseillaise, and of course the French people, who happened to be about and heard it, were delighted.

The troops moved off to the railway station at eight pm but as my company was detailed for baggage fatigue it was midnight before we got away and, as we were marching to the station, the French people were shaking hands with us as we passed them. On arriving at the railway siding everything was in darkness for fear of an air raid by the German aeroplanes. We were not very long entraining and by one am on Saturday morning we steamed off. When daylight came, and we could see about us, the country was a perfect picture and no none would ever think that there was a war on. Feeding stations were arranged for [us] at various towns and the French Red Cross ladies were very kind to us, giving freely, chocolate, cigarettes and strawberries. We met several French patrols who gave us some wine.

All the way along the line we received a great and enthusiastic reception from the people and when we reached the town of Lyons the people went mad with excitement. As soon as the train stopped a French officer rushed up and shook our Lieutenant Colonel by the hand as if they had known one another for years and then walked about arm in arm together. The French ladies could not do enough for us and after spending an enjoyable hour or two, every man was ordered to get aboard, and amid loud cheering, flag waving and singing the Marseillaise, we steamed on our way. After leaving Lyons, the country we travelled through was beautiful and there were vineyards everywhere. Late in the afternoon we passed a Red Cross train which was loaded with French wounded coming from Verdun. The spirit of those wounded Frenchmen was marvellous, and when our train came alongside them, they started to sing their national song as though there wasn't anything the matter with them.

On the Monday at midday we arrived at our destination, a little siding known as Morbeeque, and as soon as we disentrained we marched through the village in the pouring rain to our billets. Numbers one and two platoon of my company were billeted in a large barn on a farm, two miles from the main road, connecting Morbeeque with the town of Hazebrouch. It is a good idea putting the men in these billets as they are much warmer and cleaner than the tents and we have more room to move about.

The morning after our arrival at our billets we had to parade in full marching order at our battalion headquarters. I have already said that the first and second platoons were billeted two miles from the road, and that meant, we had to fall in at least one hour before the others. However we were on this game for three mornings and our captain fixed things up for us and we did our drill in a field adjoining the billet. Although we had to drill it was not very hard as it consisted of rifle shooting, bayonet fighting and lectures on the use of gas helmets.

With the gas

Monday morning about a fortnight after we arrived in France, we were marched to a large field about four miles from our billets, and an Imperial Officer gave us a lecture on the ways and means the Germans were using gas. He even had a cylinder of this compressed gas and at an order from him, every body on parade had to put on the helmets and when this order had been done a few times, the gas was turned on. The stuff is about the same colour of smoke from burning straw and came out of the cylinder with such force, that the sound resembled the hissing of escaping steam. Although my gas helmet was in first class order, I could feel the suffocating effects that the gas had. When the gas fumes had cleared away, we were ordered to remove and fold up our helmets, and then we had a practical lecture on what is known as the tear bomb. These are another inhuman device of the Germans to torture our chaps. This bomb is charged with a powerful and strong chemical which effects the eyes and when the bomb explodes, one cannot help remarking what a lovely smell of fruit, such as quinces, pineapples and pears, but in a very few minutes you are unable to see, for the chemical which has the smell of fruit, will send you blind. Now the army has got that bomb tested, for the men are issued with goggles.

Having a look around

I had not been long at this billet before I had a look around the place and it appears to me that the French people were years behind the times as far as agricultural implements are concerned and to see the farmers cutting their crops with a scythe reminded me of fairy tales. Another thing I noticed was that in the front of the farm houses was a large wooden wheel about twelve feet in diameter. A dog about the size of a cattle dog was put inside of the wheel and started trotting and the wheel began to move around on its axle. It looked like a home trainer, but it was the means the French had of getting power to grind corn or churn butter when there was no water power available. We were able to buy from the people fresh white bread, butter, eggs and coffee and many a good feed of fried eggs did I enjoy at some of these farm houses.

Estaminets

The hotels or beer shops in France are called Estaminets, where we could purchase at certain hours, wine and beer for one penny a glass, and one good thing about the beer was you could drink a ship load and it would not take any effect. We could get 'Bombard' or champagne for four and six a bottle and on pay day, or as we called it 'when the Lord fed his lambs' we celebrated some big event and had a bottle or two. Years ago the French people must have lived a very religious and pious life for, at every cross road, was an effigy of the Virgin Mary or Christ and it is a common thing to see, at the corner of the road a post as high as a telegraph pole, and a life size casting of our Saviour, crucified, in a neglected and uncared for condition, and every gate post had some kind of a religious emblem fixed to it.

Steel helmets

It was now the end of June and we were enjoying lovely weather and everybody was in the best of health. We were still in the same billet and had been issued with two gas and one steel helmets, and what drill we did, we always had to have them with us. The steel helmet resembled a basin and was rather heavy. It proved to be worthy of a place in one's kit for it saved many a man from a head wound.

Air raids

One evening my attention was drawn to the number of aeroplanes that were flying over and although we were about fourteen miles from the actual place where the fighting was, the roar of the artillery could be heard plainly. The planes which turned out to be some of the British aircraft, were that far away that they resembled flies and were attacking the enemy's lines, when all of a sudden there was a terrific roar. The Germans had sighted them and opened fire, and it was interesting to see the flash and hear the shell explode in mid air, or watch a plane dodge behind a cloud. The Germans would send up a shell thinking the plane would go straight through the cloud, only to see the plane again some distance from where the shell exploded.

On the march

Saturday morning the 7th July we were aroused at three am and were ordered to be under full marching order by six am. Everything was hustle and bustle, and by the hour named, every thing was ready for moving off. Beside our equipment including, one hundred and fifty rounds of cartridges and a day's rations, we had to carry two blankets and a waterproof sheet bringing the weight up to close on eighty pounds. As usual we were kept standing about for a couple of hours with our packs on before we moved off. The Officer in charge of us informed us, that our holidays were over and now our work was to start. We had come to France to kill or be killed and the more prisoners that we took, the more food it would require to feed them. Well the boys took it that if we took prisoners our food would be cut down and you can rest assured we did not intend to take prisoners if it could be helped.

Moving off

After standing about till eight thirty am all the division moved off and passed through the village of Morbeeque and got on the road going to the town of Merville. What with the standing about and the cobble roads the boys' feet began to give way and when we were passing through Merville it was nothing to see a couple of lads sitting by the roadside, with their boots off, and the French women with pieces of soap, soaping the chaps' socks, and their feet were blistered and chaffed like pieces of raw meat. The number of men who had to fall out of this march was awful and at ten minutes to twelve, I slung up the sponge, but joined the company at the next halt, which was at twelve o'clock and if I had known that were going to halt so soon I would have stuck to it. I noticed that all through the march Mr McCay was flying along the road in his car. After passing through the town of Estaires, and doing a little longer route march, for Mr McCay didn't think we had done enough for the day, we arrived at our billet footsore and weary after marching twenty kilometres. I felt very sore and stiff and after breakfast had to fall in with full marching order. When the battalion orders were read out Mr McCay said that he was disgusted at the way the men marched, and, if in the future any man fell out while on the march, he was liable to be immediately shot. It is all very well for anybody on horse back or in a motor car to talk like that, but it is another thing for the men on foot. As we were on the march through Estaires, a terrific battle was being fought in mid air between the rival aeroplanes and it was interesting and exciting to watch their manoeuvres.

After marching for four hours, we arrived at the village of Erkingham and there for the first time I had a glimpse of the devastation of war. The enemy, earlier in the war, had held this place and of course had done as much damage as possible. Houses were destroyed everywhere and all around, the place had been cut up with the digging of trenches. We were billeted in low wooden huts, the roof at the highest part was only six feet and they were safely hidden from view among a number of big trees. We were told that all precautions had to be taken against the aeroplanes and we were not allowed to stand about, and had to move around in two's and three's and if we saw a plane hovering around we must take no notice of it.

Off to the trenches

After staying at this place till the 10th July, we moved off early in the evening and passing through a village, which bore signs of recent and heavy fighting for every window in the place was broken and various houses were smashed to atoms, we found ourselves in open country once more, and the fields were heavily cropped and, in some places, the people had started to harvest. We had been going strong when the company was ordered to form sections, and to proceed in single file and each section was to be twenty paces apart. When we had been marching for some time, this order was again altered and the sections were reduced to five men in each, and a space of five paces between. The reason for advancing in this manner was in case the enemy started to shell us, as we were getting very close to the entrance to the communication trench at a place called Bois Grenier. All the houses and buildings along the road now was total ruins and the only living thing to be seen was the pet cat who still clung to the ruined home. The ground was full of holes, just as if someone had taken a few loads of earth away. These holes were caused by the explosions of the enemy's shells.

In the front line

Without any mishap we reached the front line of trenches and relieved the New Zealanders, who of course were not sorry to get away, but they gave us the usual sympathetic information saying everything was alright and Fritz, as we called the enemy, was very quiet and not looking for a stoush, and would not trouble us if we left him alone. As soon as we received our posts along the line, we had a look around.

The front line was built up seven feet high with sand bags filled with earth and was four feet thick. When standing on the fire step, that is a plank raised about two feet from the ground, one is able to look over the top of the parapet and see the German lines, which were, at this point, about ninety yards away. The only thing that separated us from each other was several rows of barb-wire, which was laid across No-Man's Land, as the ground between both front lines is called. We had not been in the line half an hour when the order came along the line to 'stand to' which meant every man was to be standing ready at his post. Then there was a row, for our machine guns opened fire on the German lines, just to let Fritz know we were awake and ready. We were kept standing to all night for the officers expected an attack but nothing came of it.

I get a shock

It was my turn keeping watch, for we had to do an hour's turn, when I heard a noise but could not find out what it was caused by as I could not see anything about. Presently the grass began to move and, to my disgust, two big rats appeared and bolted for their lives. It put the wind up me for a while and when daylight came, I went to see what caused the row and the only thing I could see was a piece of wood taken from a herring case and written on it in pencil was these words 'An unknown British soldier was buried here' and I came to the conclusion that the noise was caused by the rats knawing his bones. I shall never forget the first shell that Fritz sent over the following day at noon. The lieutenant and I were sitting on the fire step talking while he was busy cleaning his revolver, when all of a sudden, we heard a dull explosion then a whiz, whiz, whizzing noise passing overhead and when the shell lobbed about twenty paces from where we were sitting, there was a terrific explosion and a cloud of dust and debris went flying in all directions. Any rate nobody was hurt, the lieutenant looked at me, laughed and said he thought that he would get a move on. Then it was my turn to laugh for I had to stay where I was. It was a funny thing at this part of the line, but, Fritz's artillery would never fire, until we opened on him first. Night came on again, and at sunset, we stood to, as usual and with the exception of a star shell being fired from both lines, nothing exciting occurred.

Fritz scores

When morning broke to our surprise Fritz had scored a point during the night, for he had crept unobserved from his own line, across No-Man's Land and had hung a German flag on our barb wire. The flag stayed there all that day, till night time, and when we were 'standing to' again, a lieutenant and a private crept out from our lines to bring it in and keep it for a souvenir. But the Lewis machine gunners who were on duty, and not being informed what was doing, seeing two men moving about, immediately opened fire. The consequence was that the lieutenant was badly wounded and the private was killed. Their bodies were brought in as well as the flag. These two casualties were all we suffered at this place.

Being relieved

On Saturday night, quite unexpected, we were relieved, and after marching till two o'clock Sunday morning, we arrived at the village called Sailly. Being very tired and weary, for we had little or no sleep for five days and nights, we turned in at once and were soon fast asleep. The boys were awakened at seven-thirty and to our disgust were ordered to fall in as soon as we had breakfast, in fighting order, which meant we had to wear all our equipment, except our packs which we left behind us. After being issued with one day's ration we moved off again and after passing through the village which had been practically destroyed by shell fire, we marched in open and extended order through country that was full of shell holes and the remains of farm houses. I think we had been going for about one and a half hours, when we passed a field with a notice on a board being the words 'British Cemetery' and as I saw the number of wooden crosses, painted white, the thought flashed through my mind if it was going to be my luck to be planted there. We had not gone very much further when we passed several motor ambulances waiting along the roadside. Continuing on, we were now, marching in parties of five and each man was five paces behind the man in front, and then a space of twenty paces to the next five. An ambulance litter came round the bend of the road and a soldier was lying on it with his head bandaged, no sooner had that passed us, when several more litters came in sight. Eventually we arrived at our destination and without any delay we started fatigue duties and to carry ammunitions up to the front line trench.

I was given a trench mortar bomb and the officer in charge of us told me to take two, but, as each bomb weighed sixty pounds, I natural enough, thought one was sufficient. We had not gone many yards along the communication trench, when somebody called out 'Stretcher coming,' we had to halt to let the stretcher pass and it contained a dead man on it. We had just moved off again when the same cry went up and every few yards we had to stop and let a stretcher, with a dead man on it, go by. After going for half an hour, we eventually arrived at the front line and left our bombs and started back for more. On the way out we passed a few stretcher bearers carrying dead men. When I was making my second trip in I passed a chap carrying something wrapped up in a blanket and when he was asked what he had he answered with a gloomy look on his face 'This is all that we could find of George Challis (58th Bn KIA 15.7.1916), Carlton champion footballer.' He had been blown to pieces. Although my company was kept going for twenty four hours, without a spell and Fritz was sending over plenty of shrapnel, nobody was injured.

Back to Sailly

About eight thirty on Monday 16th July we finished our fatigue duties and were sent back to our billets and all along the road we were going along every telegraph wire was cut at each post. After having breakfast, we were allowed to have a look around the place, and it was a pitiful sight to see the way the houses had been smashed about, and, several houses that had escaped the bombardments, had the windows boarded up and post holes cut in them, so as to allow the sharp shooters in the rooms to do their work. One house that I had a look through showed signs of its tenants taking a hurried departure, as there were several pieces of furniture laying about, and on a little stand on the mantleshelf was a bouquet of orange blossom.

Monday evening was one of the times of my life that I shall never forget. As we were not on duty there was nothing much to do, only watch the different troops as they came through the village. While a party of infantry was coming through, I heard a scream of a shell passing overhead, then a terrific explosion and up in the air went two dwellings. I saw some of the lads run to the spot and found out afterwards that two men had been killed. No sooner had that shell landed, when I could hear another coming, and it seemed strange to me to see the cool and collective manner of the French women and children as they came out of their houses and hid under the hedges along the roadside. The second shell landed on a field about one hundred yards from where I was standing, fortunately with no results. As our officer thought we were in for a rough time that night, nobody was allowed to sleep inside and so we had the stars above us.

Tuesday morning we moved off again and were billeted at a little farmhouse and had to sleep under a hedge. About midnight there was a gas alarm, every man was awakened and had to put on his gas helmet, and after half an hour of this, were ordered to take them off, but I kept mine on, and was soon sound asleep again. At three o'clock there was another alarm and when the heads came around to inspect us, they found one of the boys trying to wake me, but I was safe for I had my helmet on.

19th July

Wednesday morning, 19th July, broke dull and cloudy and my company was ordered to fall in, in fighting order, and as soon as everything was ready, we moved off in the same order and to the same place as we were on Sunday. We had to do fatigue duties again till midday. On the stroke of twelve our company was ordered to leave the trenches and go back to our billets again. We had just left the trenches when our artillery opened a terrific fire on the German lines. Our bombardment lasted till ten minutes to six, then the first wave of infantry went over the top to the German lines. The 29th Battalion was moved up a little nearer and my company was billeted in a farm house. At seven o'clock there was a stir of excitement among the lads, for a party of Australians were coming along the road, in charge of a number of Germans, whom they had taken prisoners. When they passed us our lads gave a cheer, and some of our silly fools ran across the road and gave the prisoners cigarettes.

A chap and myself, feeling a bit on the hungry side, adjourned to the farm house and ordered some fried eggs and coffee and were just starting to eat them, when an order was given to fall in, without our packs. As soon as the order was carried out, we moved off to the trenches again, and when we reached the main road again, it was alive with motor ambulances bringing back the wounded. We had to advance very slowly and every wagon we passed, the driver told us that the boys had taken three lines of trenches and had Fritz on the run.

Without any excitement we arrived at the entrance of the communication trench, and here everybody was alive and busy, the wounded were being brought out and attended to as quickly as possible and were then put on the ambulances and were sent to the dressing station. I noticed several German prisoners sitting on the roadside.

Into the trenches at Fleurbaix

As soon as my company arrived we each received four Mill's bombs which we put in our pockets, and after waiting a few minutes, a pick and shovel were handed to each of us and then we moved off, and went in to the third line of supports. We had not been in the line very long before there was a gas alarm and we had to wear our gas helmets for half an hour. When all trace of gas had disappeared we were ordered to remove our helmets and march up to the front line and, as soon as it was reached, the picks and shovels were taken from us. I received a box of bombs besides two bandoliers of cartridges. About half of the company was sent over the parapet and were well in what is called 'No-Man's Land' when the party I was with was ordered to be ready, and all of a sudden Fritz opened a terrific bombardment on us and for a few minutes all was a turmoil. After Fritz had been letting it go for a few minutes he eased off and our party went over. By this time it was dark and nobody knew what to do or where to go. Eventually after a deal of trouble in crossing the barb-wire I succeeded in reaching the German lines and handed over my bombs and ammunition to some of the boys. I went back for more and returned safely. No sooner had I handed them over, when Fritz opened fire again, I was still in No-Man's Land and a lad in my platoon came up and asked me to show him the way across the wires, as he was wounded in the head and bleeding freely. After helping him on his way, I returned, only to meet another poor lad with his arm shattered and he wanted to know if there was any Red Cross men about. During all that night I never saw any, so I helped him as far as the wire entanglement and again returned. The enemy was now shelling us unmercifully and everybody was running amok with himself, for by the way they were shouting out there was nobody in charge of the men. The German artillery fire was growing fiercer every minute, in fact it was hellish—the shells were landing with great accuracy and killing the boys like flies. About ten o'clock I shifted my position and was able to get into the German trench and no sooner had I got in when a shell struck the top of the parapet with a terrific explosion. Two lads standing alongside of me started to cry for their Mothers and I told them to stop that but pray to God to get them out of this. No sooner than the words were out of my mouth then another shell hit the parapet just about my head and that was the end of everything for a while for I was unconscious.

William Barry's cloth POW label

Taken prisoner

Just about daybreak I felt my legs being roughly pulled about, and as I had regained my senses to my horror, I found myself surrounded by half a dozen Germans, who were all talking very loudly and seemed to be excited. My first thought was to speak to them, but my second one was to lay still and crack dead, which proved in my case the better plan, for one of the enemy lifted up my leg and then let it go and I let it drop as though it was broken, and without any more happening for the time they all left me. My thoughts were now to try to get back and give the alarm that the enemy had counter-attacked and were in the front line, but I must have become unconscious again, for I remembered nothing more till I woke several hours afterwards and was unable to move although was suffering no pain. Presently a number of lads came along without any equipment on, and they informed me that Fritz had retaken the trenches during the night and taken them prisoners. About five minutes afterwards another party came along in charge of two Germans with fixed bayonets and they were treating the boys cruelly by bumping them with the butts of their rifles or prodding them with the bayonets. Just then two Germans came along and on seeing me laying on the ground, one came up and spoke in good English to me, while the other was sighting his rifle and I fully expected to be shot so I drew the German's attention (who turned out to be an officer) to him and he immediately ordered him away.

Wounded

The officer after looking at my clothing informed me, to my surprise, that I was wounded and with a pair of scissors he cut the legs of my strides and showed a gaping wound in the right knee and another wound in the calf of the right leg. He then bandaged up the injuries using my field dressing and then his own. When he had finished he started to ask for information. He knew what battalion, brigade and division I belonged to and he was very anxious to know if our chaps would come back again, to which I replied that I hoped they would because I certainly could have a chance of getting back to our lines again. After trying to pump all sorts of information out of me to which I answered with the most awful lies imaginable, he wanted to know how many Australians there were in France. I promptly answered between three and five million and then the conscripts were to be called out. I cannot help laughing now when I think of the expression on his face as he exclaimed 'Was you a friawillie, a volunteer eh?' I said 'yes.' 'You Australians are b— cowards' he roared, 'we are not at war with you, but you came over here last night and went though,' here he imitated a bayonet thrust, 'while we always fight a long way off.' My German friend had lost all his kindness to me now, so I asked him if I could see a doctor. 'No' he roared 'we have too many of our own wounded to look after.' Just as he left me he said something in German to a couple of soldiers standing nearby and I got three of the worst beltings that it was possible to give a man, in fact I was knocked unconscious for more than four hours.

When I came to myself I was lying in a dug out, and I noticed that the buttons of my tunic were all undone and everything was taken out of the pockets, including my pay book, wallet and money, nearly seven pounds cash so I came to the conclusion that I had been robbed. How I put in the rest of the day I hardly remember for by now I was beginning to suffer from pain and thirst and there was nobody about. Late in the afternoon a German took my water bottle from me, and made signs he would bring it back, and as he never returned I sincerely hope that he is now pushing up daisies. As the night drew on, the pain and thirst got worse and, as I was often told that the wounded were left laying out that long that they were compelled to save and use their own urine for drinking purposes. I must admit that it is not a very pleasant idea but I afterwards met several Tommies who were compelled to do so. Late in the night or early the following morning I was roughly dragged out from the dug out by two Germans, and first thing one of them did was to take off my belt which contained my watch and other valuables. Then these two men dragged me along by the legs and arms, and when our machine guns opened fire, they left me and got for their lives and when the fire ceased they returned and the same rough handling was repeated. I think that by the way I was being moved that the parties were working in relays, for, I would be carried about three hundred yards and put down and left and it was my luck to be put down on the ground just where a party of German reinforcements halted. For when the first mob stopped I was severely kicked by several of them. At the second halt the Germans kept letting their rifles fall on me, while at the third and last halt, one German brute picked up a piece of wood six feet long and to the joy and laughter of his comrades he laid it on to my legs.

Ausweiskarte

Name Barry William C

Komp. VI Gef. Nr. 5490

Zahlkarten Nr. 10431

Zahlstelle des Kriegsgefangenenlagers Langensalza.

Unterschrift des Gefangenen:
W C Barry

William Barry's POW registration card

In the hands of the German Red Cross

Eventually without any more rough handling I was handed over to two of the German Red Cross who carried me to their dug out and gave me a piece of their black bread (and horrid tasting stuff it is) with a piece of bully beef and a drink of black coffee. The German asked me if I felt cold and I answered 'yes' and he brought me a German overcoat, it was wet with blood, but that didn't matter. He also gave me a tin of bully beef, and a piece more bread and left me propped up against a heap of earth. It was the 21st of July and the sun was shining brightly and when I was left to myself for about two hours I was able to look around, and to my horror, I was in the place where all the dead men were. I was sitting on the edge of a hole about forty feet long, twenty feet wide and fifteen feet deep and into this hole the dead were being thrown without any fuss or respect. It was pitiful to see the different expressions on their faces, some with a peaceful smile while others showed they had passed away in agony. After being in this place for a couple of hours, four Germans with Red Cross bands on their arms came out of the dug out, which was close by, and laid me on a waterproof sheet, and threading a long pole through each end, I was gently hoisted on to two of their shoulders and carried along the trench again, the two carriers being relieved every now and then.

Although our machine guns were firing all the time, without any mishap, we reached the dressing station just outside the entrance of the communication trench. At one time it had been a factory of some kind, but owing to being bombarded now and then it was in ruins. I was soon laid on a stretcher and left in the middle of the road. After laying there for a couple of hours an orderly came and took my name and particulars and fixed a tag on to my tunic. I complained to him about feeling cold and he went and brought a small oatmeal bag with which I soon rolled up the sides and made a hat of it. About midday half a dozen of us wounded chaps were put on a horse ambulance wagon and were driven to a hospital a few miles away and were all taken in and left waiting in a small room. Only the worst cases were treated here, and all the nurses and orderlies thought of was looking for souvenirs. I was now suffering great pain and was very thirsty and as there was a plentiful supply of soda water, we were given plenty to drink. I drew the orderly's attention to my foot, as it was very painful, and when he took off my boot my right instep had a nasty wound in it, making three wounds in both my legs. Our wounds were not attended to at this hospital, and the following morning we were put on the wagon again and were driven some distance to an electric tram. When I was being moved from the wagon to the tram car a big German brute walked up to me and took away my boots. As soon as we were all on the car we moved off and in a very little while we arrived at a large railway station which turned out to be Lille. We were put to bed in the waiting room and were given a bowl of soup, but our wounds were not attended to. That night I suffered great pain and thirst and of course had very little sleep. The following day after breakfast, which consisted of one slice of black bread, I thought of the tin of bully beef I still had and had just started to open it when the German sentry saw me and at once he took the lot from me, so I had to go without. We remained at Lille railway station for two days and then were put on a Red Cross train and, after a journey of a few hours, we arrived at the town of Valenciennes. We were soon put on to an electric tram and were taken to a very large and comfortable building, which was used by the French people before the war as a hospital. We were put to bed at once and were very cosy, but I could tell by the way I felt that I was in for a rough time for I was feeling very light headed. The following afternoon I was taken to the operating theatre, and as I was lying on the table with all the bandages off I was able to see all my injuries, which were a gaping wound in the left calf, right knee smashed and big toe on right foot smashed. In the room, besides the doctor and nurse, was a German officer who could speak English and a clerk who wrote down everything that was said. After my name and address were taken the officer wanted to know if I was sorry that I came to the war to which I said 'No' then he wanted to know why I came to the war, as Germany was not at war with Australia and I told him that an Australian stood by an Englishman always. As this officer found he could not get any information out of me he sneeringly remarked, 'Well you have come a long way to get your knee blown off,' but I pretended to take no notice of what he said. After the doctor had finished with me I was taken back to the ward.

Although the food was not too bad at this place, and I was attended to by the doctor about every three or four days, my condition grew worse, and it was necessary to inject morphia into my arms, to ease the pain, and make me sleep every evening. We had two German orderlies at this place who were out to get what they could and one of them took my diary from me. I don't really know if he wanted a mouse trap but he took my set of false teeth as well, for I never saw either of these articles afterwards. Once a week the German orderly would give us a post card to write home, but we were not allowed to state where we were. The only address that we were able to put on it was Pte ——— Kriegsgefangenen (meaning war prisoner) Stamlager, Wahn, which is the head base of all prison camps. The first card I sent was to my officer telling him of my whereabouts.

My health was by now broken down, besides being lightheaded, I was suffering from fever and weakness and to make things worse the cowardly orderly used to twist my leg around to make me sing songs for him, which I always did. In fact I was that low that I would tear off the dressings. One Sunday morning I was taken to the theatre and as soon as I was on the table, a cap was put over my face. I had no idea what had been done until a couple of days afterwards when my leg was being dressed by the German orderly. I noticed that a tube had been put into my leg above the knee. My condition gradually got worse and in fact I was delirious and my temperature was very high and one morning I was put on a wagon and was driven to another hospital and was x-rayed and sent back again. I shall never forget that ride for the road was cobbled and the jolting of the wagon caused me awful pain.

On September the 23rd I was taken from this hospital and sent to the Lille station again and was put on a Red Cross train, along with nine British prisoners of war. After travelling for three and a half days through Germany and along the Valley of the Rhine, which by the way the scenery was beautiful, I was well and kindly treated by the German staff on board. The train arrived at the town of Kempten in the south of Bavaria. After the Red Cross had got all the German wounded off the train and sent them to different hospitals my comrades and self were taken off and put on motor ambulance wagon and sent to a large three storied brick building and put straight to bed. During the afternoon a German who was a professional gentleman and could speak English, came and took our particulars and told us that he was the Censor and that we were allowed to write home one post card every week and two letters a month. On the following morning at ten o'clock the head doctor did his round and was accompanied by two other doctors, six nurses and two orderlies. As the staff all spoke German it was impossible to understand them, but after I had been thoroughly examined, he put me on No. 2 diet while the others were on No. 1. The food at this place was good and wholesome but of course was 'morish' (not enough). No. 1 diet got one pound of rye bread and two litres of beer per day while beside the ordinary diet I received six ounces of white bread, 1 plate of ham at 10 am, two cups of fresh milk and one pint of wine every day. But I was in such a state I was not able to eat anything for days, and to make matters worse, I was suffering from half a dozen bed sores. One afternoon a strange doctor came and saw me—I afterwards found out that he was a specialist. On the following afternoon I was taken down stairs to the operating room and put on the table. After laying there for some time watching the doctors and specialist washing their hands, the head sister, Schwester Franka, was her name and a fine girl she was, came alongside of me with a cap in her hand and, as she placed it over my face, I remembered her saying 'nix pain, nix smarten De Barry.' On the following morning when the doctor did his rounds and I was being dressed, I had three more tubes in my leg, and when the doctor who was very attentive to me used to move these tubes, the pain was fearful. Any rate with all the kind attention that I got at this place, my condition was getting worse every day and my mind was becoming very 'dopie'. I can remember one night in the middle of October, the Censor whose name was Professor Schultz, Schwester Franka and a man dressed like a priest coming to my bedside and telling me that Doctor Septz had done all he could to save my leg and the only thing that could be done was to amputate as I could not live more than a month with it on, as gangrene had set in. I had till the following night to decide, and on leaving me, the clergyman, who was the Lutheran pastor, gave me a testament with different chapter marked for me to read. On the following evening they visited me again, and enquired what I intended to do, I told them that as I was in the hands of the doctor and he knew best. The Censor produced a form and asked me to sign it giving my consent to have the operation performed. When the form was signed, the Pastor asked me if I would take Holy Communion in the morning. On the following morning, October 25th, at seven the Communion was administered. Soon afterwards I was taken down to the theatre again and the leg was amputated. I was back in the ward by eleven am and I heard afterwards that the doctor did not think that I was going to pull through. A few days after the operation I began to pull around again and my leg was healing well, in fact a fortnight after the operation I had practically finished bandaging. It was a few weeks after the operation before I was able to sit up and one morning I asked the doctor if he would get me a pair of crutches, but my foot had got stiff with being in bed so long and when I tried to stand I fell over and injured the amputation, which meant a few more stitches had to be put in, and I had to go back to bed again. In the meantime my other leg and foot had to be massaged and a very painful time I had while it was being done. The first chance I got I was up and with the help of two comrades was able to walk around the ward very slowly, and one afternoon the Pastor came and visited the ward. It was very funny to see the way he walked up to my bed, only to find I was not there, for I was at the other end of the ward playing cards with a chap in bed. The Pastor said something in German about me, and after shaking hands with all of us, he left the ward. The following evening we had a visit from the Censor and as soon as he came into the ward he said 'Where is De Barry?' I answered him and he told me that he had heard that I had been playing cards and that the Pastor had told him. He wanted to know if my mind was clear as I had given everybody a great surprise, for the doctor did not expect me to live, and as a pleasant surprise he handed me nine letters from home. This was the first I had received since the 18th July when I was in France and needless to say I was very pleased to receive them.

General Ferdinand von Hindenburg

Visited by General von Hindenburg

My health was improving daily and so was my appetite and although the food was good, I could always eat a little more which I never got except when the sister would smuggle in to me a piece of bread under her apron. One morning in the middle of December a great commotion was caused throughout the building—all the orderlies and sisters were very busy cleaning up the place for they told us that General von Hindenburg was coming that day to inspect the hospital or lazarett as it is called. At eleven am the door of the ward opened and in walked an elderly man with a grey moustache. He looked about sixty years of age, was dressed in civilian clothes and was closely followed by an orderly who called out 'Octoon' which meant 'Attention' and we all obeyed the order but the General waved his hand and said 'sit down'. He went to each bed and spoke to its inmate and when he came to me he said in splendid English 'I see young man that you have had the misfortune to lose your leg.' I answered him 'Yes, but it is all in the game.' He replied 'This war is awful for everybody who is concerned in it,' and went on.

We had a chap in our ward who was in one of the Imperial Regt., and who used to receive parcels of food and bread from his people in England. These parcels were brought into the ward by the German under officer and each article was censored before the Tommy was allowed to have it. Every loaf of bread or cake was cut up into pieces and every tin of stuff was opened. Whenever this chap got a parcel sent to him, there was a feast in our ward that night, for he always shared it with us. It was amusing to see the way the German sisters would come and see him when a parcel arrived. One day he received a number of parcels and among them was a box containing five hundred cigarettes. When the under officer had censored everything, the Tommy handed him a packet of cigarettes but the German refused to take them, so the Tommy offered them to the orderly who was standing by and he would not have them until he asked the officer. As soon as the private got the smokes and was going out of the door, the under officer put out his hand for some as well. That act just shows how frightened the Germans are of one another for they are taught to tell on each other.

US Ambassador James W Gerard, Paris, February 1917, some 6 weeks after his visit to William Barry.

Christmas

The 19th of December is always a great day among the German people, it is the beginning of their Christmas festivities and it takes the form of a number of people dressed up to represent Santa Claus and they give presents away. The day is called St Nicholas day. The celebrations were carried out in the hospital but the merrymakers were not allowed (by orders) to enter our ward. The Germans are great people for the Christmas tree, and in every ward except ours, was one gaily decorated with miniature bells, toys, etc. The day before Christmas day we had a visit from the Censor who told us that the people of the town were going to give us a treat. We were to have some cigarettes (fancy that). I had not had a smoke for months and for supper we were going to have roast stuffed venison, but no pudding. The looked for day arrived, but it was not the Christmas days that I had always been used to, for it was snowing heavily and was very cold. In the evening the German invalids had a banquet downstairs and was opened by singing one of their patriotic songs entitled 'Deutschland Uber Alles' meaning Germany over every thing. At eight o'clock our supper was brought in to us and sure enough there was a great plate for each of us of roast stuffed venison, potatoes and boiled cabbage. Later in the evening Schwester Franka gave each of us two packets of cigarettes, a present from the Doctor, as well as three apples and two small cakes. Schwester Franka came back later in the evening and distributed a large box of cigarettes amongst us, we also got an extra six litres of beer, so considering we were prisoners of war, we did not do too bad.

The following day we had another visit from the Censor and Clergyman and the Parson gave us an address in German on the birth of Christ which was translated into English by the Censor. That evening Schwester Franka came and told me that she had good news. I would be sent to England to my people before very long. I can tell you that bit of news seemed to put new life into me. My strength was coming back to me very fast and I was able to walk about the ward quite easy. On New Year's day the Parson and Censor paid us another visit, this time the Parson gave the Holy Communion and finished up with special prayers for my recovery and when he had finished we all thanked him for his kindness and attention to all of us, for besides his religious visits, he used to bring us English books to read. Two or three times several German officers came into the ward to see me and I was ordered to walk about. What this was done for I afterwards was told was to see if I was strong enough to be sent away. Every evening when Schwester Franka came to see me she always told me that I was going to be exchanged to England.

Visit from American Ambassador

At the end of the first week in January Doctor Septz was transferred to another hospital, to our disappointment, for we could not speak too well of his attention towards us. But his place was taken by another surgeon, a very kind and elderly man, who could speak English. The new man had not been with us a couple of days when he told us that we were going to be visited by 'The Ambassador of America'. Although this place was kept very clean, the morning of the visit all the orderlies and sisters were very busy tidying up the ward. At eleven o'clock the German staff accompanied by Professor Schultz and three gentlemen dressed as civilians came into the ward. We all stood to attention but were ordered to sit on our beds. The Censor asked one of the civilians if he wanted the Russian and Servian who were in the ward to leave, but he told the German to let them stop where they were. Drawing three chairs up to the first bed, the gentlemen opened their brief cases and taking out a book of papers started to ask particulars. When they had got all the information from this chap, they moved on to the next bed and so on until he came to the bed I was sitting on. After taking my name and address etc., he wanted to know how I had been treated while at that place, to which I answered that I had been well and kindly treated by everybody. The Ambassador stood up and angrily waving his hand he said 'Take no notice of these Germans, you are talking to me now' but all I could say was that I had no complaints to make. He then started to pull the bed to pieces and asked me how often were the sheets changed, four or five times a week I told him and answered the question in regards to what diet I had. He turned to the Censor and exclaimed 'This is the most extraordinary place to put Englishmen.' The Censor then told him that the building and everything in it were maintained by the 'Protestant People of Bavaria' and was known as Reserve Protestant Schule. The Ambassador then asked the doctor why my leg had been amputated so high, but as this surgeon did not perform the operation, he could not say. After enquiring if I had received any letters and parcels, he promised that he would do all in his power to send me parcels of food. He told me that as I had lost a limb I would be leaving for England very shortly. After all of us had been interviewed, and none of us could find a complaint to make, he told the German staff that this lazarett was an extraordinary place.

THE AMBASSADOR

James W Gerard was US Ambassador in Germany from 1913 to 1917. After the war began, one of his duties was to watch British interests, and that included checking the conditions of POW camps and POW hospitals. He did an enormous amount of work aided by his staff and clearly upgraded the conditions considerably. In his book *My Four Years in Germany* (1917) Gerard devotes a chapter to Prisoners of War which, while mentioning only a few camps by name, includes in view of what Germany was to become, this interesting paragraph:

As a rule, our inspectors found the hospitals where the prisoners of war were in as good condition as could be expected. I think this was largely due to the fact that so many doctors in Germany are Jews. The people who are of the Jewish race are people of gentle instincts. In these hospitals a better diet is given to the prisoners. There were of course, in addition to the regular hospitals, hospitals where the severely wounded prisoners were sent. Almost uniformly these hospitals were clean and the prisoners were well taken care of.

Gerard's care for British and Empire prisoners in Germany earned him great praise in the UK, to the extent that it was suggested a lasting memorial be set up in London to his work. In August 1917 George V conferred the Order of the Bath upon Gerard. A former lawyer, soldier in the Spanish-American War, and Judge, James Watson Gerard became a strong advocate of the League of Nations. He was active in the Democratic Party and served both Roosevelt and Truman. Born 25 August 1867, he died on 6 September 1951.

This section and the first three photographs by courtesy of Betty and Warren Leviny, daughter and son-in-law of William Barry. The whole diary has been deposited with the Australian War Memorial AWM PR00814.

Australians taken prisoner at Fromelles

29th Battalion

Name	No.	
Amy, Pte E	1057	
Antrobus, Pte A W	1968	
Antrobus, Pte H	1969	
Ballinger, Pte E	1272	*
Barry, Pte W C	2514	
Bolton, Pte T D	1074	
Brown, Pte J	1059	
Carter, Pte O V	1093	
Childs, Pte E	1094	
Cole, Sgt O S	1321	
Davidson, Pte P A	1102	†
Donovan, Sgt P C	222	
Edwards, Pte W G	2016	
Ellison, Sgt N G	1107	
Harding, Sgt T	2043	
Kearney, Pte J	288	
Lamont, Pte F H	1163	
Langmead, Pte L R	2546	
Machin, Pte H	2100	
Martin, Pte S	1192	
Mayston, Pte R S	2081	
Middleton, Pte F	2088	
Newman, CSM K F	307	
Noll, Pte E	1197	
Parry, Pte R	1211	
Phillips, Pte T J	3597	
Ross, Pte B	3890	
Russell, Pte H	1213	
Scrimgeour, Pte T	2137	†
Shiels, Pte R B	1240	
Turner, Pte H A	1255	
Tyers, Pte W	1257	
Wait, Pte E	352	
Warnock, Cpl A E	354	
White, Cpl S G	365	
Wilkin, Pte H	1269	

30th Battalion

Name	No.	
Balsdon, Pte J	2274	†
Gillingham, Pte W	1553	
Hall, Pte R E	898	
Holmesby, Pte H A	189	
Law, Pte H B	217	
McGarvey, Pte S E	721	
Pearce, Cpl H J	801	†
Phelan, Pte P J	1816	
Powis, L/Cpl C E	1601	†
Ridley, Cpl E R	1023	
Stokes, Pte S	1616	
Storey, Pte D B	1143	
Thompson, Pte L C	2170	
Wallace, Pte T	1624	
Watson, Pte N L	2475	
Wright, L/Cpl E S	70	
Wright, Pte P	1000	

Capt. C Mills, 31st Bn
AWM A1545

31st Battalion

Name	No.	
Barnett, Pte T	2872	
Bateram, Sgt R	353	
Bernard, Lieut V D	-	
Black, Pte J J	474	
Bolton, Pte J	590	
Clarke, Pte F A	560	
Collings, Pte J V	414	
Cumiskey, Pte M J	171	
Davison, Pte G	187	
Dockrill, Pte W J	39	
Downes, Pte J F	190	
Fisher, Pte E	1534	
Furlonger, L/Cpl J W	367	
Goulding, Pte J J	555	†
Graham, Pte R W	644	
Grant, Pte W J	685	
Guthrie, Pte D	3810	
Hall, Pte S	1546	
Hart, Pte G H (also known as Heaney, Pte G H	434	†
Henry, Pte R	344	
Kerle, Pte F F	516	
Knight, Pte J	2038	†
Lewis, Pte J	2481	
Marrinon, Pte J P V	254	
Mason, Pte J L	470	†
McKenzie, Pte W M	4564	
McPherson, Pte J J	3846	†
Mills, Capt. C	-	
Resch, Pte R	407	
Still, Cpl H A	802	
Terrens, Pte A J	956	†
Thomas, Pte W	959	†
Thomson, Pte G L	3547	
Thornburrow, Pte E J	763	†
Toohey, Pte M	325	
Vowles, Pte T	310	
White, Pte W	28	

32nd Battalion

Name	No.	
Ash, Pte C N	1209	†
Bartholomews, Pte H J	2283	
Bartlett, Pte C S	3014	
Bayes, Pte J F	1973	
Brooks, Pte R M J	50	
Burgess, Pte E	57	
Burrows, Pte H	1609	†
Butler, Pte J	1611	
Cahill, Pte J W	1989	†
Cahill, Pte P	1230	
Carr, Pte N T P	63	
Chesson, Pte S M	1434	
Chinner, Lieut E H	-	†
Choat, Pte W P	68	
Claxton, Pte T	1238	
Coffey, Pte A J	2004	
Colledge, Pte J R	915	
Colless, Sgt F J	1194	†
Collett, Sgt H R	855	
Corrigan, Pte A	2007	
D'Herville, Pte T A	475	
Davids, Pte T J H	473	
Davies, Pte B P	1249	
Dolphin, Pte F R	477	

A cross (†) indicates those known to have Died of Wounds received at Fromelles whilst a Prisoner of War, and are therefore also included on the Roll of Honour.
An asterix (*) indicates those who as Prisoner of War later died of illness or disease.

Dyke, Cpl W 2022 †
Dyke, Pte T D 484
Elmer, Pte T W 1618
Featherstone, Pte G H 1257
Featherstone, Pte G M 1254
Findlay, Pte P 2027
Fox, Pte F W 3112
Fursland, Pte F 98
Fuss, Pte L H 3115
Gibson, Pte G 2035
Good, Pte J McN 351
Gradwell, Pte J 1272
Grain, Pte S N 1580
Griffiths, Pte G A 1276 †
Haddy, Cpl H B 508
Hall, Pte F 513
Hard, Pte G J 281
Hart, Cpl L W 865 †
Henry, Pte J A 1284
Hill, Pte E J 1288
Hook, Pte R S W H 525 †
Hughes, Major J J -
Johnson, L/Cpl J R 969
Johnson, Pte G E 120
Johnson, Pte H P 890a
Keay, Capt. R A -
Lampe, Pte N E 123
Lamprey, Pte F A 2062
Lewis, Sgt C F 407
Luly, Sgt A E 856
McDonald, Cpl R 18
McIntyre, Pte T M 571
McKinnon, Pte D 1330 †
Messenger, Pte J A 572
Moore, Pte T 1539
Mules, L/Sgt R J 415
Murdock, Pte S 147
Neill, Pte B P 3859
Neill, Pte D E 1547
Nelligan, Pte A T 587
Nolan, Pte W 2084
Parish, Pte L W 2091
Pflaum, Pte R H 161 †
Powell, Pte R L 2387
Redman, L/Cpl T H W 167
Rice, Pte W H 604
Robinson, Cpl W 417
Russell, Pte G P 349
Seeker, L/Cpl F M 177
Shields, Pte V F S 296
Siggins, Pte H 180
Simms, Pte C G 2107
Spain, Pte J 1371
Sporsen, Pte R C 1591
Stone, Pte A D 1404
Stone, Pte C W 1375
Tilling, Pte S 345
Turton, L/Cpl F R 1064
Vardon, Pte A E 341
Voitkun, Pte A 2134
Wallis, Pte E 636
Waltke, Cpl H W 420
Warner, Pte E 202
Watson, Pte K H 640
Wolffe, Pte E O 213 †
Zachariah, L/Cpl D H M 653 †

8th Machine Gun Coy

Bernays, L/Cpl G C 94
Copley, Pte A W 913 †
Driscoll, L/Cpl T 100
Holman, Cpl W E 99
Marks, Pte C B 111
Watson, Pte S 117

53rd Battalion

Arblaster, Capt. C - †
Allen, Pte F J 4728
Arrowsmith, Pte C 3226

Capt. R A Keay, 32nd Bn
AWM A1545

Badmington, Pte R C 3486
Bailey, Cpl L F J 3235
Black, Pte S W 3010
Bowman, 2/Lieut A W M -
Breen, L/Cpl R J 4735
Campbell, Pte A 3515
Crossly, Pte H 3497
Crozier, Pte W W 3265
Davis, Pte F 1943
Dobson, Pte T H 3288
Emerton, Pte S 4772
Feeney, Pte C 2364
Freirat, L/Cpl P 1398
Giles, Pte J A 4788
Gill, Pte P J 2636
Ginn, Pte W 5367
Herket, Pte T H 3309
Keenan, Pte O 2729
Kent, L/Cpl B 3337
Killalea, Pte J F 3339
Martin, Pte F L J 3398
Mayo, Pte W B 4811
McCrossin, Pte J S 3155
McCue, Pte C J 3536
McKell, Pte A 4828
McMahon, Pte C S 3156
Mitchell, Pte C A 2734
Mollison, Pte A C 4814
Molloy, Pte J 3371
Morris, Cpl J E 3137
Myers, Pte J A 2737
Nicholes, Pte F A S 3387
Nichols, Pte F W 3388
Owen, Pte R H 3395
Pearce, Pte A J 1650
Pearce, Pte W H 3098
Quinn, Pte W 4941
Rankine, Pte A B 3412
Ranson, Capt. F R -
Riley, Pte D 4843
Robertson, Sgt E L 3516
Rolls, Pte G H 3581
Ryan, Pte J 3414
Seach, Pte C A 3430
Sharkey, Pte E 4872
Shearin, Pte E C 4862
Sim, Pte D 3468
Simms, Pte S C 1725
Simpson, Sgt H J 2414
Sinclair, Pte A A 2445
Smith, Pte R E N 3483
Smith, Pte W W 3106
Soper, Pte S 3112
Stanton, L/Cpl D P 3427
Steele, Pte J 4860
Stiles, Pte J N 4857
Stokes, Pte A C 4922
Taylor, Pte A D 4878
Turner, Pte B C 3531 †

An Australian prisoner at Fromelles
AWM 1547

Walker, Pte E E	4893	
Webb, Pte G	3151	
Wilkins, Pte H A	3467	
Willis, Pte J A	3457	
Young, Pte A E	3335	

54th Battalion

Aldham, L/Cpl J H	4627	
Armstrong, Pte J	4430	
Balcomb, L/Cpl H J	4156	
Barnett, Pte J	4732	
Barrett, Pte T	4435	
Bilbow, L/Cpl H W	1909	
Bingham, Pte E	4441	
Blacka, Pte A	3720	
Blackford, Pte C T	3625	
Bonnett, Sgt J R	3482	
Bowen, Cpl A D	2786	
Boyd, Pte A J	3010	
Bremner, Pte G	4261	
Brown, Pte R W	2572	
Brown, Pte W N	4145	
Brown, Sgt J P	2789	
Browne, Pte R B	3463	
Calder, Pte L W	4450	
Carr, Pte W D	3511	
Carter, Pte H N	4748	
Carter-Ihnen, Pte L P	3272	
Clarke, Pte B	3510	
Cobb, Pte E J	2797	
Collis, Pte D L	4459	
Costello, Pte J J	4151	
Creswell, Pte H D	4171	
Deveigne, Pte H G	2803	
Dewar, Pte R	4768	
Diamond, Pte A H L	4474	
Donaghy, Pte S	3505	
Dorey, Pte W G	4476	
Dorfman, Pte W	4477	
Dryden, Pte H	4479	
Duff, Pte A M	4189	
Duff, Pte C McM	3037	
Duncan, Pte R E	4482	
Dunlop, Pte E R	4186	
Dwyer, Pte V J	2390	
Eather, L/Cpl A E	3286	
Eaton, Pte W J P	4166	
Eaves, Pte J H	4165	†
Eyles, Pte R J	4192	
Fairweather, Pte R W	4198a	
Ferrett, Pte G A	4776	
Fletcher, Pte H P	3044	
Foley, Pte J E	4784	
Ford, Pte S W	4205	
Fry, Pte F P	4492	
Furlong, Pte J P	4782	
Gallard, Pte R M	4291	
Gibbons, Sgt B A	2817	
Gigg, Pte G	3299	
Hall, Pte W G	3474	
Hall, Pte W	4396	
Hanna, Pte L D	4226	
Hansen, Pte L H	4507	
Haslam, Pte P A	4512	
Henry, Pte G J	3647	
Hoare, Pte W M	4310	
Holloway, Pte L J W	3074	
Horne, Cpl B E	4518	
Hughes, Pte A J	4223	
Jackson, Pte A F A	4524	
Jenkins, Cpl J A W	4247	
Johnson, Cpl A M	3328	
Jones, Cpl N M	3085	
Kelly, Pte R H	4318	
Key, Pte H G	4250a	
Key, Pte S N	4815	
Kiernan, Pte L	4812	
Kiss, Pte R S	2835	
Land, Pte F J	4532	
Lawson, Pte W W	4370a	†
Lohmann, Pte H G	3563	
Lovejoy, 2nd Lieut H R	-	
Luke, Pte G M	4537	
Manley, Pte L	4538	
Martin, Pte A J	2848	
McCurley, Sgt R T	2557	
McDonald, Cpl J	1278	
McKee, Cpl A	4560	
Meyer, Pte N	4840	
Milne, Pte J D	3576	
Moir, Pte F E	432	
Moody, Pte B	3577	
Munn, Pte G	4847	
North, Pte F	4330	
O'Halloran, Pte C H	4333	
Osborne, Pte T	2934	
Paton, Pte C	2012	
Potter, Pte W A	4578	
Powell, Pte T H	4579	
Pryor, Pte H A	3639	
Reed, Pte G H	3398	
Reid, Pte A H	4304	
Richardson, Pte R B	4301	
Sargent, Cpl F H	4587	
Shepherd, Pte A J	4878	
Skea, Pte J	488	
Smith, Pte W H	2688	
Speakman, Sgt J	791	
Speer, Cpl R A	3138	
St John, Pte T	3382	
Stevens, Pte R E	3219	
Stewart, Pte D S	4600	
Summerfield, Pte H	4892	
Tate, Pte C W S	4606	†
Thomas, Pte W J	4608	†
Tilley, Pte W E	4378	
Tilney, Pte W	4326	
Turner, Pte W H	3606	
Vincent, Pte S	4379	
Waldron, Pte H	2506	
West, Pte G A	2890	
Wilkinson, Pte N	3539	
Williamson, Pte A W	4913	
Wilson, L/Cpl J H	3170	
Wright, Pte F L	3464	

Lieut G d'A Folkard, 55th Bn

55th Battalion

Name	No.	
Ashcroft, Pte H A	3210	
Austin, Cpl M J D	3230	
Barnes, Cpl J J	2502	
Barnes, Pte J J	2562	
Barry, Pte J	2382	
Bell, L/Cpl E W	1304	
Bolder, Pte A V	3490	
Bolder, Pte H D	3489	
Bolt, Cpl H T	3009	†
Bowman, Sgt D McQ	1715	
Brandson, Pte F McG	3492	
Brennan, Pte W A	4741	
Bryan, Pte R A	3767	
Cane, Pte A S	3221	*
Casey, Pte M J	3027	
Chambers, Pte F J	3032	
Coates, Pte J W	2601	
Cummins, 2/Lieut G	-	
Davis, Pte R	2341	
Deans, Pte J F	4792	
Eads, Cpl S	3086	
Ellis, Pte R C	3057	
Fairweather, Cpl A C B	1291	†
Folkard, Lieut G D	-	
Foreman, Pte W	3055	
Freeman, Pte G H	1741	
Furniss, Cpl J	2650	
Galloway, Pte J McC	3067	
Gorman, Pte R S	3810	
Gribbon, Pte G	2728	
Grimes, Pte J H	3237	
Grobert, Pte W H	3045	
Hammond, Pte J H	4828	
Harrison, Pte F G	3311	
Housego, Cpl C	3088	
Hybennett, Pte A F	3326	
James, Pte W J	3076	
Johnston, Pte W H	3253	
Jones, Pte A	3097	
Jones, Pte H L	1930	
Jones, Pte J E C	3075	
Kendall, Pte A G	3256	
Lawrence, Pte F J	3258	
Leane, Pte A C	2954	
Luland, Pte F H	4837	
Mackay, Pte J	3536	
Maher, Pte J	3885	
Mande, Pte F W	3135	
Marshall, Pte S	3861	
Martin, Pte C G	3385	
Martin, Pte W J	3375	
Mason, L/Cpl A F	1990	
Matthews, Lieut J H	-	
McCabe, Pte W J	1702	
McGoldrick, Pte C D	3124	
McInnes, Pte W J	3874	
McKenzie, Pte R	3577	
McPherson, Pte J	3355	
McPherson, Pte L A	3567	
Meyer, Pte N	4840	
Montgomery, Pte R	4854	
Morrall, Pte L A G	2860	
Morris, Pte M S	3371	
Murray, Pte D C	3883	
Nolan, Pte J	2500	
O'Brien, Pte C P	3890	
O'Neill, Pte J J	4866	*
Owens, Pte M F	3143	
Packer, Pte F R	3279	
Parsonage, Pte A R	4869	
Pattison, Pte C W	3353	
Pearce, L/Cpl O A	3200	
Purdon, Pte R A	3901	
Purdon, Pte S V	3902	
Quirk, Pte T A	3154	
Ralph, Pte V	2896	
Ratcliffe, Pte J	4882	
Reay, Pte J G	4885	†
Richards, Pte A	3419	
Rowledge, Pte A	3610	
Seinor, Pte W E	3178	
Sellen, Pte D A	4899	
Seymour, Pte A I	3920	
Seymour, Pte A J	3921	
Sherwin, Pte H A	3294	
Shirley, Sgt C	3305	
Skelly, Cpl J	3235	
Smith, L/Cpl P C	2675	
Smith, Pte F	3170	
Smith, Pte G W	3327	
Smith, Pte W G	2832	
Smith, Pte W R	2607	
Smith, Pte W R	3169	
Sparkes, Pte V E	3175	
Stringfellow, Pte G H J	3436	
Taylor, Pte A	3304	
Tharme, Pte H S	3188	
Waldon, Pte H V	3148	
Walter, Pte A B	3310	
Weddup, Pte G	3311	
Westaway, Pte H	4921	
Whitney, Pte M	3151	
Wilson, Pte F A	3197	

56th Battalion

Name	No.	
Holmes, Pte H	3555	

Capt. J H Matthews, 55th Bn

14th Machine Gun Coy

Name	No.	
Elliott, Pte J C	2640	
Gardner, Pte N L	3513	
Hart, Pte F W	3323	
McMaster, Pte G S	3118	
Newman, Pte C M	2878	
Ryan, Pte D	2806	
Temperley, Pte R E	3454	
Walker, Pte E J	2805	
Wemestad, Spr O O	6105	

14th Field Coy

Name	No.	
Mason, L/Cpl A B	5385	

57th Battalion

Name	No.	
Freeman, Pte H	1897	†
Welch, Pte W E	4934	

58th Battalion

Name	No.	
Briant, Pte C E	3239	
Dunn, Pte A H	3539	
Nash, Pte C B	1865	†
Skewes, Pte J	3449	

59th Battalion

Name	No.	
Hodson, Pte H H V	3990	

60th Battalion

None

5th Divisional Pioneer Bn

Name	No.	
Dansey, Pte H	411	

5th Divisional Engineers

Name	No.	
Thomas, Spr S	6035	

12th Bde MG Coy

Name	No.	
Gaffney, Sgt F	3749	
Harris, Pte G	1550	

10

Of your sad glory

Beside the fire at night
some far December,
We shall remember
and tell men, unbegotten
as yet, the story
of your sad glory

—Ivor Gurney,
in the trenches at
Fromelles, July 1916

The line in front of Fromelles, indeed from Armentières to Givenchy, was unchanged and largely unchallenged throughout the second half of 1916, all of 1917 and the first three months of 1918.

At that time the German strength had increased considerably as they no longer had an Eastern Front to maintain. Thus with some determination they planned a spring offensive with particular pushes in the south towards Paris, in the central region towards Amiens, and in the north towards Hazebrouck. This last front provides the end to the story as far as Fromelles is concerned. Haking had spent the last two months of 1917 and the first two of 1918 in Italy. He had been sent there with two British divisions (a third followed later) after the collapse of the Italian army at Caporetto. Now in April 1918 he was again in command of XI Corps in France. The 61st Division returned to the Laventie area after being in battle near St Quentin over the period 21 to 27 March 1918. It had been one of three British divisions facing fourteen German divisions and as a consequence was '*so badly mauled*' that it had to go into reserve: casualties were 5933. Hastily restocked the 61st was moved to Lys, west of Estaires–Laventie area and on 9 April joined again XI Corps under Haking till the end of the month, and enduring a further 2412 casualties.

On the night of 7/8 April Armentières which had been in Allied hands since 17 October 1914, was subject to a furious gas and shell bombardment. The 30 to 40 thousand shells caused terrible casualties and destruction. As dawn came up on the 8th '*which was misty ... a quiet day. Such air reconnaissances as were possible noticed no movement in the German lines. This stillness grew so uncanny that Lieut General Haking ... feared the Germans would attack just as he was getting the Portuguese out of the line*'.

The Germans swept forward right along the whole front and by the morning of 11 April had taken Messines, Armentières, Steenwerck, Estaires and were at the ramparts of Vieille Chapelle, Festubert and Givenchy. A week later they

THE ROAD TO LILLE

There is a house at a certain corner I passed of late. On it, in big white letters on a blue ground, is written 'To Lille'. Every township for a hundred miles has that same signpost, showing you the way to the great city of Northern France. But Rockefeller himself with all his motorcars could not follow this direction today. For the city to which it points is six miles behind the German lines. You can get from our lines the edge of some outlying suburb overlapping a distant hilltop.

And that is all that the French people can see of the second city of their state. The distant roofs, the smoke rising from some great centre of human activity nestled in a depression into which you cannot look; you can peer at them all day long through a telescope and wonder why it is they are stoking their chimneys, or what it is that causes the haze to hang deeply ... But for all intents and purposes that country is as much cut off from you as is the furthermost star.

But the road to the invaded country will be opened one day. An autocracy has no chance against a convinced, united, determined democracy like this. More than anything I have seen it is the surprising quiet resolution of the French which has made one confident beyond a doubt that Frenchmen will pass some day again, by no man's leave except their own, along the road to Lille.

—C E W Bean
Letters from France (1917)

A German photograph of British and Portuguese prisoners taken near Fromelles, March 1918
COURTESY J-M BAILLEUL

had closed on Ypres, had gone beyond Messines, taken Bailleul, were only five miles from Hazebrouck, had Vieille Chapelle but were still held at Festubert and Givenchy. It was a spectacular achievement, partly due to a very large artillery concentration and the fact that of the eight German divisions in the front line, and six in the second, '*thirteen came from rest*'. No such luxury was possible on the Allied side, '*the Germans ... knew that the line ... was largely held by exhausted and weakened divisions which had been withdrawn to a quieter sector*'. The Battle of Estaires, as this sector of the assault became known, began with the British First Army facing the Germans: this consisted of the I, XI and XV Corps. The XV Corps was in the Armentières area and included the 1st Australian Division under Major Gen. Sir H B Walker, the only Australian participation at this time. The XI Corps was near Neuve Chapelle and Laventie, and was all British except for the 2nd Portuguese Division which consisted of four brigades. In view of what once happened to Indian Divisions under Haking, and later the Australians, it is not without consequence that the Portuguese suffered worst here. Wrote Edmonds: '*As the fortunes of the day turned on the resistance of the Portuguese, their sector will be dealt with first. Against their three weak brigades in the front line were arrayed no less than four German divisions*'. Another historian revealed they were 5800 below strength.

Major General the Hon. Sir James McCay KCMG GB VD, General Officer Commanding the Australian Imperial Forces in Great Britain, presenting decoration to one of the Australian cadets qualifying for commissions at Cambridge
—*The Great War* (1918), Vol 11, H W Wilson & J A Hammerton (eds).

The result was a forgone conclusion with losses over 7000, and the visitor to the area today will see at the Portuguese Cemetery near Neuve Chapelle the evidence. It is perhaps not without significance that nearby is the Indian Memorial, in essence the 1915 disaster's monument. Without labouring the point too much VC Corner cemetery could in this way be classified as Haking's 1916 disaster.

The German success, although qualified in the British Official History was self-evident in the maps. The holding of Ypres was doubtless the Allies' main success and the ballooning of the line towards Hazebrouck by the Germans had been accomplished at terrible cost.

During the summer the XI Corps fought its way back towards Fleurbaix and Fromelles, and by 21 September was in possession of Sailly-sur-la-Lys, Laventie and Neuve Chapelle. The 61st Division's participation in these last battles, together with the one of 19 July 1916, and the defensive action in April caused a special bond between the Division and the town of Laventie, marked since 1935 by a plaque at the Town Hall (see page 405). But the Division now on its last legs had lost Mackenzie wounded in June, and was replaced by 59th Division, fresher and stronger. This deprived the 61st from being in the force that over the next four weeks reclaimed Fleurbaix, Bois Grenier, Fromelles, Aubers, Fournes and Beaucamps. And from being part of the XI Corps which at dawn on 17 October stood ready to liberate Lille.

As the war drew to an end, the Germans manning the fortifications around Lille pulled back into the city knowing that what had protected it over the past four years would continue to do so. The large French population and the value and importance of the city's factories and mills were, in effect, the hostages that had kept Lille largely intact throughout the war.

Thus the liberation of Lille had to be conducted with some care. The population at this time was almost entirely women, children and old men, all the able-bodied men were in German labour camps. Thus there could be no uprising, no insurrection to undermine the German forces. By the first few days of October the Germans had left Aubers Ridge, including Fromelles, Fleurbaix and beyond, and after destroying what was left of Armentières, moved back to Lille. The worn British forces, but newly energised by the scent of victory, now closed on the city. From the top of Aubers Ridge they now moved down towards Haubourdin, whilst others coming across from the west covered the northern approaches, and another group sealed off the south. The city was effectively surrounded except for an escape route on the southeast, permitted by the wily Foch, to provide a way for the Germans to save themselves and thus spare Lille. Commanding the Lille garrison was one General von Bernhardi and he showed, according to one account, '*a considerable amount of foul cunning in the last phrase of the struggle around Lille*'. This referred to Bernhardi's tactic of setting up his major artillery in Vauban Park inside the city and

Gen. FRIEDRICH VON BERNHARDI
Bernhardi was a bit more than '*cunning*'. Born at St Petersburg, Russia, in 1849, so he was now almost seventy and past his best. He had been a writer on military matters advocating war, '*the triumph of the stronger was a law of life itself*' and that '*civilisation could make progress only by warfare*'. The Great War which he was advocating in 1912 '*must be brought about by Germany*', '*she must forment trouble in the oversea possessions of the rival powers and march out with her drilled forces to world-power or downfall*'.

It was an idea that caught the imagination of one of those at Fromelles! Bernhardi died on 10 July 1930 and so missed seeing the next catastrophe that such ideas brought about. His books *Germany and the Next War* (London 1914), and *The War of the Future* (London 1920) provide more detail about his ideas.

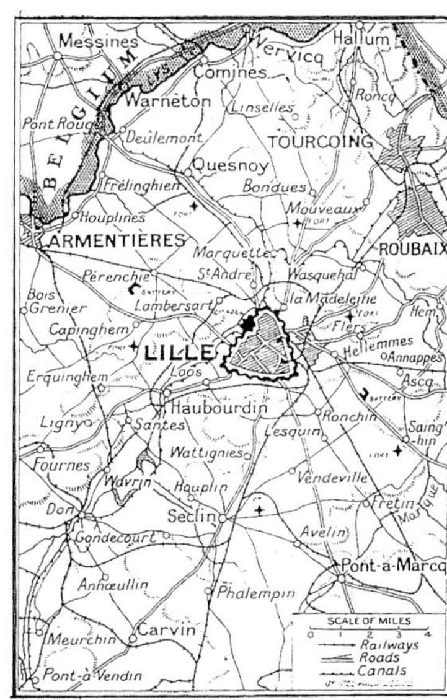

BIRDWOOD IN LILLE

The tide had now turned to such an extent that we were able to send back to Australia certain men of the AIF who had been on active service since 1914. Before the end of the month I had said goodbye to 3600 of them—an embarrassing and somewhat exhausting process, for every man wanted an autograph and a hand-shake (and such hand-shakes!) before leaving.

By the middle of October the Germans were being pressed back everywhere, and on the 15th my XI Corps, under Haking, was at a place in the Lille defences known, oddly enough, as 'Fin de la guerre'.

On Thursday, the 17 October, my Fifth Army occupied Lille.

On 20 October Clemenceau, the 78-year-old Premier of France, came to see the city of Lille which had been in German hands since October 1914 ... Dear old Clemenceau insisted on my sitting beside him as he drove to the Prefecture and Hôtel de Ville ... the streets were packed with a quarter of a million people ... Everyone wanted to shake hands or embrace us.

The next day I established my Fifth Army Headquarters at 19 Place de Tourcoing, Lille, and it was on that day, too, that M. Poincaré, the President of the Republic, made his official entry into Lille.

The Mayor and the people of Lille having expressed a desire to do honour to the British Army, a great march through the city was carried out, led by myself and staff ... in the Grande Place, the Mayor, the Bishop and the City Fathers greeted me ... they also presented me with a little crimson silk flag bearing the arms of Lille, the date and my name and an inscription of gratitude to their 'liberateurs' ... I was honoured by being made a 'Citoyen de Lille'.

When I finally left Lille I presented to the city the huge Union Jack which had flown over my headquarters, on the understanding that it should be flown in perpetuity over the Hôtel de Ville on the 17th October.

—Field Marshal Lord Birdwood of Anzac and Totnes. *Khaki and Gown* (1941)

proceeding to use up all the shells he had left. Perhaps he hoped the Allies would reply and thus destroy Lille. Depending on one's estimate of Bernhardi (see previous margin) his next move was either very clever or just '*foul cunning*'. He issued a decree that he had reached an agreement with the Allies that Lille would not be shelled, and that for their safety the entire population had to assemble at 4am on the morning of 17 October in the city squares. There, if things went wrong, they would be blown to pieces by British artillery. Under this terrible relocation a curious silence settled over the great city. The English, Scots and Welsh had no mind to pour shells on civilians, or cut their way through crowds with machine guns. But to precipitate some such action Bernhardi ordered that as dawn came up the populace at gunpoint be directed into the streets leading out of the city into the path of the British armies. An observant British airman out on dawn patrol saw the hostages waving handkerchiefs and white cloth, and advised the British forces. Thus the hostages formed a welcoming party for the liberators as Bernhardi and his men crept out. The British historian wrote: '*the Germans, however, had the humanity to leave six days' supplies behind for the inhabitants*'. By mid-morning the people of Lille lined the streets and cheered the British forward. The team that planned much of this success, under the overall stewardship of Marshal Foch was General Sir William Birdwood GOC Fifth Army, of which part was Haking's XI Corps. It was Haking who had been waiting at a place called 'Fin de la guerre', who now became the Liberator of Lille and the next day, 18 October, stood with the Mayor of the city and others to review the incoming troops. A few days later Birdwood led the Allied Parade and set up his headquarters (see margin).

When the war was over Foch went to Birdwood's HQ to thank him and through him the Fifth Army:

> Your soldiers continued to march when they were exhausted, and they fought and fought well, when they were worn out. It is with such indomitable will that the war has been won ... I am deeply sensible of the fact that Lille was delivered without damage to the town, and I am grateful for the help given so generously to the inhabitants.

Then the British historian wrote: '*So ended the Great War in the northern sector*'.

As already noted, Fromelles had a hold on C E W Bean. In his 1917 book *Letters from France* he avoids discussing it as if he is not sure how to deal with it, or because he does not understand it, yet that book carried this dedication:

General Birdwood leads the Allied parade through Lille: note the Australian standard bearer behind him.

> To those other Australians who fell in the sharpest action their force has known, on July 19, 1916, before Fromelles, these memories of a greater, but not a braver, battle are herewith dedicated.

So it is no surprise that at the very first opportunity Bean had to 'walk' the battlefield of Fromelles, he took it. It was Armistice Day, 11 November 1918, when he was there searching out the second and third line of trenches that the 5th Division never found. In some of his notes Bean refers to 'we'. Whom he had with him is not clear, but the quality of the shots tends to indicate a professional photographer, perhaps Hubert Wilkins, then an official photographer, later a distinguished Antarctic explorer. Bean examined the ditch, as Edmonds termed it, but what others called the Laies River. He stood on the remains of the Sugarloaf and looked across No-Man's Land towards the Australian lines, and looked into what was left of that fortification. But it had been wrecked or looted, and presented no permanency like the numerous blockhouses he found. All of those he photographed have since been identified as built after the battle, including the row which he located as 'north of rue Delaporte', and the remains of which today are in the Australian Memorial Park. All had been stripped of their sandbag protection and the earth coverings and there is not a person nor animal in sight. He had

MEN HE HAD SO MUCH LOVED

On the 10th [November 1918] he [C E W Bean] went north again. He had been aghast to realize that he had no single photograph of the battlefield at Fromelles ... He went on to Lille. Next morning there came the news that the war was to end at eleven o'clock ... He went out then to do what he had to do on the old battlefield at Fromelles, where, on that one night of 19/20 July 1916, the Australians had lost 5533 killed and wounded. He found what had then been No-Man's Land still littered with their remains. So for him, the war ended as he stood among the mouldering bodies of men he had so much loved.

—Dudley McCarthy
Gallipoli to the Somme

Taken 11 November 1918. This view looking NNW from the church mound shows the road that leads to the front line.
AWM EO 4032

a look at the barbed wire and found some observation posts in trees. The battlefield itself, wrote Bean, '*had become overgrown with rank grass*', and it was a grim excursion.

> *We found the old No-Man's Land simply full of our dead. In the narrow sector west of the Laies River and east of the Sugarloaf Salient, the skulls and bones and torn uniforms were lying around everywhere. I found a bit of Australian kit lying fifty yards from the corner of the salient, and the bones of an Australian officer and several men within 100 yards of it. Farther round, immediately on their flank, were a few British—you could tell them by their leather equipment. And within 100 yards of the west corner of the Sugarloaf Salient there was lying a small party of English too—also with an officer—you could tell the cloth of his coat.*

It would seem that the English officer was Capt. Harold Church who was later buried at Laventie Military Cemetery. Bean's examination of the Australian bodies, 15th Bde men found on or near the Sugarloaf, secured only two identifications. They were Sgt W Leech 3164, 58th Bn, a 24-year-old bank accountant

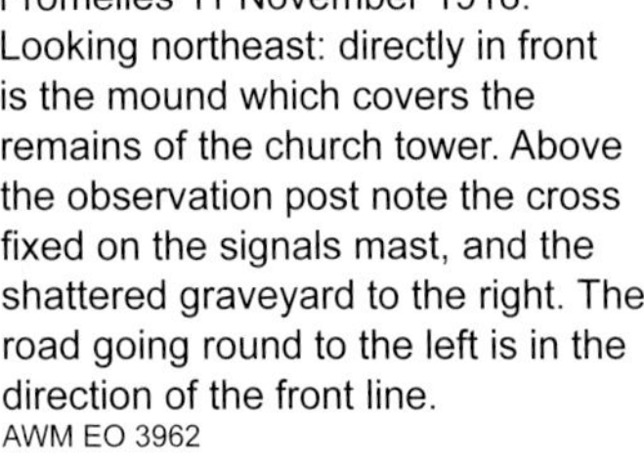

Fromelles 11 November 1918. Looking northeast: directly in front is the mound which covers the remains of the church tower. Above the observation post note the cross fixed on the signals mast, and the shattered graveyard to the right. The road going round to the left is in the direction of the front line.
AWM EO 3962

11 November 1918. The German blockhouses 'north of rue Delaporte', probably built in 1917, and the remains of which are now in the Australian Memorial Park.
AWM EO3970

from Bendigo and Pte T Aitken 3003, 59th Bn, a 35-year-old Scotsman and farmer from Moondarra, Victoria. As a result both have graves at the Pont du Hem Cemetery.

Curiously it was these finds that convinced Bean, '*it ... appears certain that no part of the enemy's line was captured, even if it was entered, by the 15th Bde in this battle*'. The finding of Church on the approaches would, to this writer, indicate that the English did not enter the German lines either.

When they were in correspondence years later, 'Pompey' Elliott in a letter to Bean dated 7 August 1926 confessed:

> *After the Armistice I was sent by General Hobbs to select a position for the 5th Divisional memorial and recommended that it should be established on the butt at Polygon Wood.*

Nephew Tunnel which runs 40° NW beneath No-Man's Land from the blockhouses in the Australian Memorial Park. In 1997, 80 years after the construction, it looked like this, but now part has collapsed. It is 38 metres long and 10 metres below the surface, 0.8 metres wide and 1.2 metres high.
COURTESY M DELEBARRE

On 11 November 1918 at the southern end of Fromelles looking southeast. The road to Aubers is to the right.
AWM EO 4033

Adding about Fromelles:

> *I regret to say that during my examination of the ground there after the Armistice I did not go carefully over the ground at all. I missed that opportunity.*

Indeed Elliott, long convinced that the thoroughness of German observation was one of the reasons for their success at Fromelles, went to the village, rather than the battlefield.

> *... the little church at Fromelles on the Aubers Ridge, overlooking our position, and which was constantly under shell fire by our guns, had actually been transformed, by the enemy, into a solid block of concrete and was used by him as an observation post from which he could command a view right into our lines and it is no doubt from this point that he observed the reinforcement of our frontlines on the day of the Battle ...*
>
> *The Church was still in its original condition a solid mass of reinforced concrete, the whole interior having been filled in. There was*

View from the Sugarloaf on 11 November 1918. Bean wrote of this photograph '*taken from the apex of the German Salient, looking north-eastwards over the ground which the 15th Australian Infantry Brigade essayed to cross. In the middle distance can be seen the channel of the small, River de Laies, in which many men were killed by machine gun fire*'.
AWM E4029

The Village Memorial. In the wake of the ruin of the village, especially the Church and graveyard, the Vicar of Fromelles, Father Dahiez, shown here, had a memorial set up where rue Delval and rue des Rouges Bancs meet: thus facing across to VC Corner Cemetery and the Australian lines
COURTESY M DELEBARRE

a little winding staircase from the rear of the church leading up to the lookout position. Near the ridge of the church there was a small space for inserting a telescope. From this spot a wonderfully accurate view of our position was revealed and it occurred to me afterwards how foolish we had been not to take advantage of the spire of the church in Fleurbaix from which a similar view no doubt could have been obtained of the enemy's position.

Clearly Pompey was not at Fromelles, but perhaps at Aubers where another church was used by the Germans as an observation post.

Bean certainly did visit Fromelles and climbed the mound of rubble that was once the church. It is clearly visible with its ruined graveyard in the view of the village. The photograph from the observation point looking down the road that leads to the battlefield forms an interesting comparison with a similar view on an old postcard—page 18.

Quite why another Australian group with Lieut S H Young as photographer visited the battlefield a year after Bean and Wilkins—13 to 15 November 1919—is difficult to judge. There was snow on the ground (eg Sugarloaf, page 190), the sky heavily overcast and the bleak winter scenery gives no hint of how the battlefield looked in July. And like Bean's observations all 32 photographs had a precise map reference and virtually all were taken of or in the German lines looking to the Allied positions, as if this team was also trying to answer some nagging questions about the battlefield. There were no views of the town, but some of post-1916 blockhouses.

Pte Ivor B Gurney 241281
2/5th Glosters c1915.

Gurney served at Fromelles and his thoughts and poems from the time are on the next two pages. Also in this unit was his lifelong friend F W (Will) Harvey, '*The Gloucestershire Poet*'. Gurney wrote of him in August 1916: '*F W H is almost certainly dead ... He went out on patrol alone, and has not returned.*' However Harvey was taken prisoner 17 August 1916, and wrote in the camps poems which he posted back to England where they were published to some acclaim. Born in 1889, Harvey, who was a solicitor, died in 1957 with a considerable reputation as a poet.

The poet at Fromelles

Ivor Gurney, now regarded as one of the important war poets, was at Fromelles with the 2/5th Gloucestershire Regiment, part of 183rd Brigade. Born in Gloucester in 1890, Gurney was a greatly gifted musician and on the brink of a substantial career when he enlisted in 1915. Although he played in the Regimental Band it seems poetry became his creative outlet in the trenches. On 10 June the 2/5th Glosters reached Laventie and stayed a week before moving to Fauquissart and into the line. Laventie was to remain the main billet for the Brigade, and many others, over the next five months. It must have been over this period that Gurney, much enamoured by the French countryside, wrote his 35-line poem *Laventie* which has two references to the Australians.

Shimmer of summer there and blue autumn mists
Seen from trench-ditch winding in mazy twists.
The Australian gunners in close flowery hiding
Cunning found out at last, and smashed in the
[unspeakable lists.

and

Café-au-lait in dug-outs on Tommies' cookers,
Cursed minniewerfs, thrust in eighteen-hour summer.
The Australian miners clayed, and the being afraid
Before strafes, sultry August dusk time then death
And the cooler hush after the strafe ... [dumber ...

and

But Laventie, most of all, I think is to soldiers
The town itself with plane trees, and small spa air;
And vin, rouge-blanc, chocolat, citron, grenadine:
One might buy in small delectable cafes there.

Of the town Gurney wrote with affection:

Laventie is a place of happy memories to many. It was a rather unique little town, built in the form of a cross, with its red brick church at the centre. Though it was only a mile or so from the front line of the Fauquissart Sector, the civilians lived on there and farmed a certain amount of land around. The town suffered considerably in 1915, when it was the scene of fierce house to house fighting, yet the billets were fairly habitable and the plane trees still stood in the streets. There are some beautiful lawns and gardens behind some of the big houses. The nights at Laventie were distinctly noisy, since eighteen pounder batteries, not to mention a fifteen inch railway gun, surrounded the village. But the place itself was seldom shelled: it seemed to be a case of 'live and let live'. If the Germans shelled Laventie, the British artillery retaliated on Aubers.

Ivor Gurney's letters from this period show that his musical ear was forever alert. For instance in his first letter after the battle (27 July) he wrote:

The machine gunners manage to make their job interesting by 'playing tunes' on their guns. As thus.

After the ordinary casual shots and steady pour, one hears: which always sounds comic, and must, I imagine require some skill.

Then Gurney described something else musical:

The infantry have to make all their fun, but, bless their hearts, there is a considerable amount when one adds it up, but their musical taste is simply execrable, and they are given to singing the most doleful-sentimental of songs. One of the worst of which is a lamentable perpetration called 'For he's a ragtime soldier,' which they have to sing on the march after being relieved. We are all fed up. How fed up you must gather from the fact that anyone who mentions home is howled down at once. ... But Gloster, like Troy in Masefield's poem, has become a city in the soul.

When the time for the Battle of Fromelles came the 2/5th Glosters was in reserve to the 2/1st Bucks—one of the assaulting battalions. It fell to Gurney's unit to come forward after the battle and bring in and bury the dead.

His ear for accents promotes an aural observation in one of his greatest poems, *The Silent One*, the first five lines:

THE CERTAIN COMRADES **(ES & JH)**

Living we loved you, yet withheld our praises
Before your faces;
And though we took your spirits high in honour,
After the English manner
We said no word. Yet, as such comrades would,
You understood.
Such friendship is not touched by Death's disaster,
But stands the faster;
And all the shocks and trials of time cannot
Shake it one jot.
Beside the fire at night some far December,
We shall remember
And tell men, unbegotten as yet, the story
Of your sad glory—
Of your plain strength, your truth of heart, your splendid
Coolness, all ended!
All ended ... yet the aching hearts of lovers
Joy overcovers,
Glad in their sorrow; hoping that if they must
Come to the dust,
An ending such as yours may be their portion,
And great good fortune—
That if we may not live to serve in peace
England, watching increase—
Then death with you, honoured, and swift and high;
And so—not die.

In trenches July 1916
(Severn and Somme 1917)

The Silent One

Who died on the wires, and hung there, one of two—
Who for his hours of life had chattered through
Infinite lovely chatter of Bucks accent:
Yet faced unbroken wires; stepped over, and went
A noble fool, faithful to his stripes—and ended.

While that might well have been a reflection of Fromelles another poem *War Books* describes a wider war: an extract:

Out of the heart's sickness the spirit wrote
For delight, or to escape hunger, or of war's worst anger,
When the guns died to silence and men would gather sense
Somehow together, and find this was life indeed,
And praise another's nobleness, or to Cotswold get hence.
There we wrote—Corbie Ridge—or in Gonnehem at rest
Or Fauquissart or world's death songs, ever the best.
One made sorrows' praise passing the Church where silence
Opened for the long quivering strokes of the bell—
Another wrote all soldiers' praise, and of France and night [stars.

Ivor Gurney being very observant and witty filled his letters from the front with wonderful descriptions of army life;

Rainy weather was our only respite, and that on claying soil how appalling! Shackles and over and underdone roast. Execrable tea, margarine crying to Heaven and the Sanitary Inspector for deracination. Bread only fit for museums. Bacon virginal—unspoiled pig. The canteen was a bright spot, but a bright spot cherished and administered by swindlers and rogues of nameless birth.

His first book of war poems, *Severn and Somme*, published in 1917 contains only two poems that are dated; *The Certain Comrades* seems certainly to relate to Fromelles. A search of the dead from the Glosters does not help with the identities of ES and JH.

Gurney survived the war physically despite being wounded and gassed, and an attempted suicide. He returned to the Royal College of Music in London and from 1918 to 1922 he published some of his finest poetry and composed his best music. The strain of the war and much else took its toll and Gurney was committed to the City of London Mental Hospital in 1922 and languished there for 15 years until he died in 1937.

Further reading:

Ivor Gurney. *Severn and Somme* (1917).
Ivor Gurney. *War Embers* (1919).
Ivor Gurney. *Poems* (1954 and 1973).
Ivor Gurney. *War Letters*, edited by K R Thornton (1983).
Michael Hurd. *The Ordeal of Ivor Gurney* (1984).
Anthony Boden (ed). *Stars in the Night: Letters of Ivor Gurney* (1986).

... the free gift of the French people ...

Part of every British War Cemetery in France, usually carved in stone at or near the entrance, is this declaration:

The land on which this cemetery stands is the free gift of the French people for the perpetual resting place of those of the Allied armies who fell in the war of 1914–1918 and are honoured here.

How this happened at Fromelles weaves together local families and Australia in a very special way. In the mid 1880s Louis Michel Descamps (1800–1885) farmed at Ennetières, 8 km northeast of Fromelles. Louis married Flavie Wattel (1809–1899) and they had three children: Emile who also farmed at Ennetières and married Caecilia Carlier; Marie who married Auguste Butin and Jules who was born in 1845 and married Eudoxie Lallemant. Jules became a farmer at Fromelles, his farm 'La Faveille' was on the road to Herlies. His position and success in the town is revealed by the fact that he was Mayor from 1877 to 1919, an extraordinary 42 years. Jules and Eudoxie had a son, Achille (1868–1955) and a daughter Marie (1871–1943). Marie married Emile Dambre (1868–1959) who had the brewery at Fromelles (see page 198).

Achille Descamps (right) with his son Canon Joseph Descamps on the day he was invested with the Legion of Honour.

Achille married Hermance Carlier (1870–1947). They lived in an handsome house in rue de Lommeries in Fromelles where their two sons, Joseph and Jean, were born in 1896 and 1899 respectively. When war overtook the area the family evacuated to Le Touquet Paris-Plage, except for Joseph who became a Lieutenant in the artillery, later being awarded the Croix de Guerre.

When the family returned to Fromelles after the war their home was a ruin (see page 199), as was the whole town, and they moved to Haubourdin so that Jean would have access to education facilities in Lille.

Achille continued to own the fields north of rue Delvas. A piece of that land he sold to the French Government in 1924, who in turn transferred it to the care of the Imperial War Graves Commission who designed and built what is now known as VC Corner Australian Cemetery, Fromelles.

At this time Joseph, back from the war, began studies for the priesthood and was ordained at the Church of St Sulpice in Paris on 28 June 1924. In the years between the wars he was priest at Tourcoing—not far from Fromelles. In the Second War, Joseph was a Captain in 302 RAL and was awarded the Legion of Honour on 4 February 1951. He continued as a priest at Roubaix and Wattrelos and died on 22 July 1979; he was buried at Fromelles. In 1984 a street off rue de Lommeries on the site of his parent's house was named rue du Chanoine Descamps in tribute to Canon Descamps, '*une grande figure de Fromelles*'.

Jean, after completing his schooling, graduated as Doctor of Law from the University of Lille in 1926, and later went into business. In 1930 he married Antoinette Scrive-Loyer and they had four children: Jacques, born 1935; Anne-Marie, born 1936; Agnès, born 1939; and Bernadette, born 1945. In the 1930s while the family was living in Lille. Jean wrote a 34-page booklet, *Historical account of the main attacks carried out by the British Army on the Armentières-La Bassée Front Line during the Great War 1914–1918,* and put together an important collection of munitions and war artifacts. Over the years he also researched and published on archaeology, local history and pottery. Jean died on 20 September 1954 in Lille.

Jean Descamps

Anne-Marie inherited from her father land adjacent to VC Corner Cemetery which included the German blockhouses in the same area that the Australians captured and held on the night of 19/20 July 1916. In 1997 she was approached by the Australian Government and agreed to the transfer of this land to the Commonwealth War Graves Commission. In 1998 this land became the Australian Memorial Park.

INFORMATION AND PHOTOGRAPHS COURTESY A-M DESCAMPS-CARRÉ

11

Choruses of silence

As you approach ... cemeteries roll into view on every hand. The dead are drawn up in solid columns to greet you as you pass ... The Army that went to guard this line is still there, still on duty ... The dead challenge the living in choruses of silence from broad fields of burial.

—Stephen Graham
The Challenge of the Dead (1921)

From late 1920 onwards those who lost next of kin in the war were sent, together with medals, death plaque and any other items due, a booklet of 72 pages titled *Where the Australians Rest—a description of many cemeteries overseas in which Australians —including those whose names can now never be known—are buried*. On the cover and title page no author's name is given, only '*Prepared under instructions from the Minister of State for Defence (Senator G F Pearce)*'. It is thought that it was written by Ambrose Pratt, the illustrations were by J G Goodchild. Whilst the idea was doubtless sincere and well meaning, it was as far as Fromelles went, and for the relatives who still had no real idea of what happened, quite useless, indeed misleading, or as the expression of the day had it, *told us nothing*.

> *Those whose dear ones were missing at Fromelles or Fleurbaix will find the cemeteries into which unknown soldiers from those fields have been gathered dealt with in the chapter upon the Rue Petillon cemetery. Other cemeteries in this area are the Anzac Cemetery and the Bonjean Cemetery at Armentières. In each case, such of the unknown who have been found are buried in cemeteries nearest the battlefield, and a tablet, with the names of all those who were reported missing inscribed thereon, will be placed on the wall of the cloister in the cemetery nearest to the battlefield on which they fell.*

The first chapter begins with the Anzac Cemetery: '*In this district, on 9 July, 1916, the Australians fought their first big battle in France*'. The typographical error of 9 instead of 19, which was hand-corrected, was not a good start.

> *For three years the line shifted but little in this area. It was held with grim resolution. In places the opposing trenches were not more than 100 yards apart. Yet, such was the strength of these trenches on the green flats, and such the unsleeping vigilance of the machine guns, that the dead in No-Man's Land could not be gathered until long after active hostilities had ceased. In many places the trenches were strengthened by shelters of reinforced concrete. One needs to see the shell holes at the Sugarloaf salient, edge to edge, of varying width and depth, to appreciate something of the violence of that fighting at Fleurbaix in July 1916...*
>
> *Many who fought in the battle of Fleurbaix are buried in Anzac Cemetery: some in the communal cemetery, near the old ruined church.*

The town memorial, Fleurbaix
11 November 1994

ANZAC CEMETERY
At Sailly-sur-la-Lys No. 255. On the north–west side of the road to Estaires from Sailly-sur-la-Lys. It was started in July 1916 as a direct result of the battle, and continued as a front line cemetery until April 1918. It was then used by the Germans as burial ground for British. There are 111 named Australian graves, among them being that of Capt. N Gibbins 55th Bn (I.A.5). This cemetery also has many 31st Bn men who are shown as killed on 21 July, which is unlikely to be correct (see page 16). When described in 1920 it was '*across the narrow, cobblestoned roadway*' from the Canadian Cemetery, that is now the busy D945 road. The French place flowers before the cross on Anzac Day and on 11 November, as they do at most of the cemeteries in this region.

Others rest at Laventie and Le Thilloy: and some were carried to the back area of Etaples.

Anzac Cemetery, Sailly-sur-la-Lys
11 November 1994

The next 'chapter'—actually 24 lines—deals with Rue Petillon Cemetery well behind the Australian front line and thus one wonders about some of the description, if not all of it.

> *A small rustic gate gives entry to the enclosure. Trees in the vicinity show effects of shell fire. A concrete 'pill box' within a few feet of the cemetery, bears the name 'Bolton Hall'.* [It was the HQ and Dressing Station of units in 1918 and known as Eaton or Eton Hall.] *Behind the German trenches was the village of Fromelles; and viewing the battlefield from this position, from the rising ground, and inside a German reinforced concrete observation post, one can understand how formidable was the task of capturing such strongholds. One 'pill box' with walls 3 feet thick is marked 'Marie haus 1916'.*
>
> *The German was already, at that early date, alive to the protection which such structures give against artillery fire. Masses of ungalvanised barbed wire of unusual strength, length, and number of spikes, added to the water ditches increased the well-nigh insuperable difficulties of attack. Such are Fromelles and Fleurbaix. Our losses at Fleurbaix were heavy—it was probably the most costly single combat in which Australians were engaged—and many a brave son is mourned as the result of the bitter struggle in this sector.*
>
> *The cemeteries are well kept, and Nature assists in veiling, if not repairing, the ravages of war.*

And that was the sum total of Fromelles. The only figure mentioned was in the beginning of the piece on Rue Petillon *one third of its 646 crosses mark Australian graves, and on some of them six or eight names appear.* As today with a total of 1507 graves, there are only 291 identified Australian graves (22 unidentified), the booklet's figures hold up, as the additional burials were mainly British. But there is no hint of VC Corner, then well and truly established, or the 1600 or so Australians not in Rue Petillon. In all fairness, the booklet does not go into great detail on other battles either, but the details of Bullecourt for instance were never as obscure at Fromelles, so relatives had information about the fate of their loved ones.

Rue Petillon Military Cemetery as drawn by J G Goodchild in 1920 and the entrance now.
PHOTOGRAPH R LEFFLER

RUE PETILLON MILITARY CEMETERY

At Fleurbaix No. 525. This is a particularly beautiful cemetery and has 1507 graves, of which 291 are of Australians, the vast majority identified, and many from 19–20 July with all battalions (except 57th) represented. Plot 1, Row K, has over 30 from 58th Bn, victims of the German raid of 15 July: one unidentified German from the raid lies with them, all their headstones close together, signifying a trench grave. Row L has 23 members of 31st Bn, victims of 19–20 July. Nearby (I.K.109) is Sergeant G D Challis 2595 of 58th Bn from 1915 Carlton Premiership side and veteran of 70 games. Chaplain Maxted MC (I.K.2) was credited with helping some 150 wounded away from the front line. In 1922 the body of Major Roy Harrison of 54th Bn (I.D.20) killed in the battle was found and identified by his silver cigarette case. 2nd Lieut Tenbosch born of British parents in San Francisco and serving in 8th Field Coy Engineers, together with a number of his men, is here (I.K.3).

The cemetery was begun in December 1914 and used by fighting units until March 1918. It was in German hands from April to September 1918. It is *irregularly arranged, because of the conditions under which it was made* and *enclosed by a low brick wall, and planted with weeping willows, mountain ash and other trees.*

Wandering the Fromelles battlefields at the same time as Pratt was Stephen Graham, and he found VC Corner.

> The flowers are withered, the thistles which gave their fragrance to the air at Ypres are white with down. Peasants everywhere are scything weeds and burning them in smoking heaps. But the trenches beyond Sailly are still shaggy-topped with teazle crowns and woolly nettle heads. One wonders how many different units at what different times occupied those 1914 trenches. Here still, one picks up old blue water-bottles and faded green straps and pouches of British uniforms. They are poor trenches—the mere staves that lined them to keep up the mud are all warped and good dug-outs are few.
>
> The Germans of course swept o'er all this in 1918. Witness the 'busted' concrete telegraph posts growing dozens of rusty iron wires from their stumps, witness the lumpy solid cement-bags by the side of the road. But between 1914 and 1918 what a history! A little way beyond the British line is a cemetery called 'VC Corner'. There are two hundred and thirty crosses and on every cross is exactly the same

> legend 'GRU. Unknown Australian Soldier'. There is no name in the whole of the cemetery. Some time some band of Australians charged here and did not come back and were not taken prisoner. Old rifles with broken rusty bayonets have been placed against the white-washed cross-surmounted entrance. Not many paces on one comes to the German line wrought in impregnable concrete, a line of snug beds in which it seems one might comfortably await the Last Day. But one concrete structure has been mined and looks as if it had been thrown bodily into the air without flying into bits. Now it stands poised upside down on a heap of dirt beside a profound pit. The Germans who were there when that happened are nearer now to the unknown Australian soldiers than we are.

Graham's reference to the upturned blockhouse describes the area that is now the Memorial Park. For years veterans visiting Fromelles unable to see any trace of the Sugarloaf took this outcrop of German concrete to be that place. What is especially interesting about Graham's description is the revelation that

STEPHEN GRAHAM (1884-1975)
Graham was a travel writer with some reputation for his books on pre-revolution Russia when he joined 2nd Scots Guards, serving with them in 1917–18 so say his biographers. But his book on this period of his life *A Private in the Guards* (1919) reaches back to Fromelles in 1914 and Festubert of 1915, and written with such understanding it is unlikely he was not there. Because of what he lived through at that time he came back in the summer of 1920 to wander the battlefields. This journey produced *The Challenge of the Dead* (1921) in which among much else he wrote of his discovery of VC Corner Cemetery, and as it was to become, the Australian Memorial Park at Fromelles.

After the war Graham continued to travel and write, and he usually produced a book a year. He died in London on 15 March 1975, aged 90.

VC CORNER AUSTRALIAN CEMETERY
At Fromelles. Memorial No. 7. Three kms north-west of Fromelles the cemetery was made after the Armistice when the bodies of 410 Australians found on the battlefield were buried in 41 groups of ten. None had been identified, so rather than have rows of near blank headstones, it was decided to use the rear wall to record the 1299 Australians who were missing. The CWGC has the list of names finalised in February 1925, and carved in June–July 1925.

The walls and buildings are all of the same fine stone work and on the lawn, gardens now mark out the areas of the graves. Two flagpoles have recently been added. The local community place flowers before the Cross of Sacrifice on Anzac Day, 19 July and 11 November.

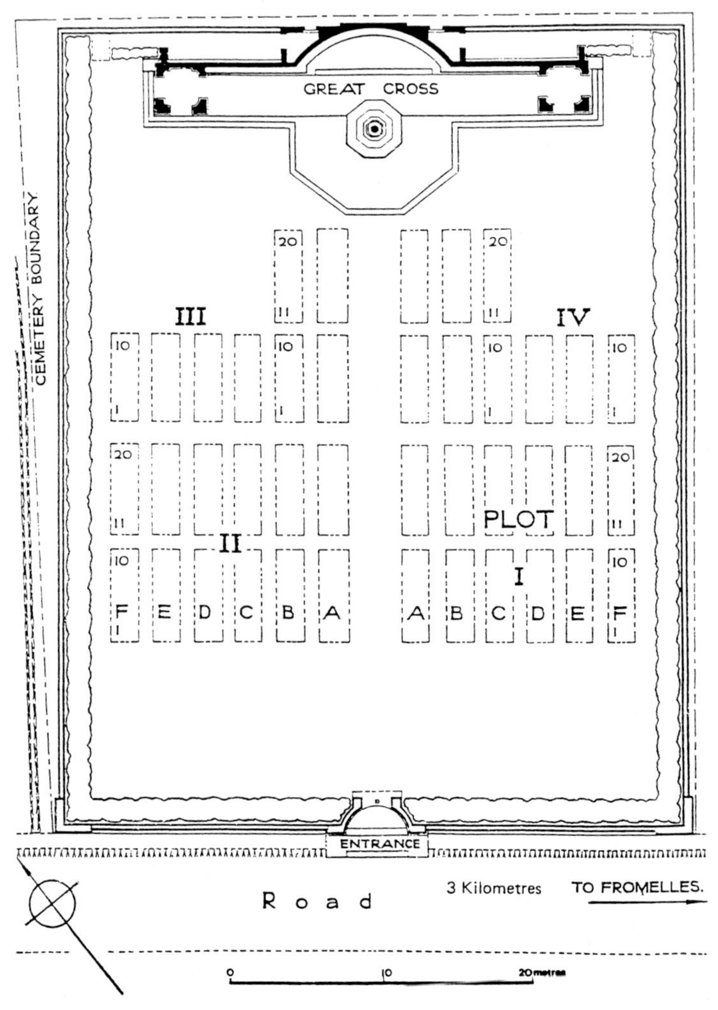

VC Corner. The layout of the graves and the plan of the whole site is a splendid example of the Commonwealth War Graves' Commission stylish yet sympathetic treatment.

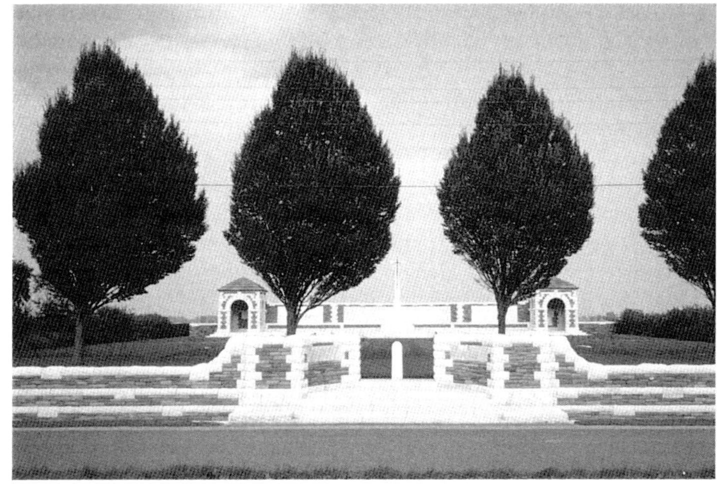

VC Corner in high summer when the contrasting stonework looks its best, as do the hornbeams.
PHOTOGRAPH R LEFFLER

VC Corner was a designated cemetery certainly in the summer of 1920.

But there were people who thought that the establishment of huge cemeteries in a foreign land was not an ideal solution. While for relatives in Britain the movement of the bodies of loved ones to their local churchyard might have been physically possible, transporting Australians, Indians, Canadians and South Africans back to their homelands was impossible. Obviously wealthy and influential people in Britain wanted to erect individual memorials, or return the body to the family mausoleum. But no:

> Reports received … indicate that the Imperial War Graves Commission does not view with favour the proposal that the bodies of soldiers who have fallen on the field of battle should be removed to their native countries … to permit a few individuals to remove the bodies of relatives would, they declare, be opposed to the spirit in which the Empire had

BURIALS

A considerable number of unknowns have been found at 36N 8.9 and 10, some of them are without doubt Australian, but at the time of collecting it was impossible to determine whether they were Australian or not, in which case they were returned as Unknown British Soldiers. Some in Rue Petillon, Y Farm, Pont du Hem, Cabaret Rouge and VC Corner Australian Cemetery, contains some 410.

About 3 years ago when the ground 36N 8, 9, 10, 14 and 15 was still in a rough state, there was every surface indication of a very heavy death roll and traces everywhere of bodies blown to pieces. A great number must still be in the ground and too deep to be located by ploughing or probing.

—Imperial War Graves Commission
23 February 1925

PACKETS OF EFFECTS

The Germans discovered two big packets of effects, and they sent the list of names which contained 194 Australians out of a total of 250 names. Of the latter, seven have graves or special crosses in several cemeteries, and the conclusion was that the effects list could not refer to the entries for unknowns supposed to have been buried in Trench Graves 2–8 according to the German Burial List.

—Imperial War Graves Commission
5 November 1928

One of the shelters at VC Corner Cemetery showing the unique stonework
PHOTOGRAPH R LEFFLER

WITHOUT CROSSES
Near the entrance to Rue Petillon Military Cemetery they lie too close to each other for it to be a coincidence and the three headstones without crosses are quite conspicuous among all the others. Cpl G Chrisp (I.K.60), Pte S R Merten (I.K.61) and L/Cpl R R Strachan (I.K.65) were all in 29th Bn, only Strachan's headstone carries an inscription: *Until the day dawns and shadows flee away*, he was 37 and from Victoria, whilst Chrisp was 25 also from Victoria and Merten 21 and from South Australia.

LE TROU AID POST CEMETERY
At Fleurbaix No. 566. It began in Oct 1914 and was used until July 1915. In November 1916 it was perhaps used again, the 56 Australians here were brought in later. Le Trou itself was 15th Bde Field HQ and a nearby aid post treated the wounded before they were sent back to the Main Dressing Station.

This extremely picturesque cemetery, reached by a small bridge over a moat, has 351 graves, 56 of them Australian, probably all from 19–20 July. Only four however are named: two each from 32nd and 54th Bns. The British identified and buried here are from 1914–15, but the Register notes that graves were brought in after the Armistice and did include fallen from 19–20 July 1916. This being so, then it would seem probable that most of the 155 unidentified graves of soldiers of the UK, and the 52 unidentified graves of Australians were from 19–20 July.

gratefully accepted the offers of Allied countries to provide land in perpetuity for our cemeteries and to 'adopt' our dead.

Much thought has been expended upon the question of the beautification of these cemeteries. Shrubs and trees will be planted in clumps and avenues, and the graves bearing headstones of uniform size and design will face towards the eastern end of the cemetery, where a huge altar stone will be erected on raised steps. Each headstone will bear the badge of the regiment to which the soldier belonged, together with his name, rank and date of death … a carved symbol of the dead man's faith and an inscription not to exceed 65 letters will be permitted.

Then they cautioned '*at present there is insufficient labour in the world to carve out the letters for the headstones and meanwhile the wooden crosses on the graves will be renewed where necessary…*'.

Later, probably due to the demand, it was proposed to charge 3½ pence per letter. The RSA protested: '*that to demand from stricken relatives a shilling or two … is unworthy of the Commonwealth*'. The Prime Minister thought it was petty and insensitive, and said so. But the Defence Authorities declared '*they are not responsible for fixing the charge, being merely agents of the Commission*'.

Meantime—in February 1919—a scheme to photograph all the Australian graves (26,000 of them) had begun and working through the summer, according to one report, took 3000 photographs. The size of the job required the appointment of 'seven more photographers', but there was no indication how many were already working on the project. The result was the supplying to the next of kin a photograph in a folder.

The authorities were trying to exclude visitors in 1919, due they said to transport and accommodation shortages, by

Le Trou Aid Post Cemetery
11 November 1994

February 1920 conducted tours for the coming spring and summer would commence from 1 March … '*accommodation at 7½ francs (6/3) for maximum of two nights at bed and breakfast*'.

In September 1921 a report was received by the Australian Government that the British were planning to cease at the end of the month exhumation of any more graves in France and Flanders. It was understood this referred to the search for some of the 125,000 British not so far recovered. Immediate protests by Canada, New Zealand and Australia caused some rethinking. To defray the cost it was suggested in Britain that French citizens should be paid a bonus for each body discovered. This brought an outcry not surprisingly, and was rejected by all the Commonwealth governments. London then decided to shift all the costs from the War Office to the Imperial War Graves Commission. In Australia, 'Billy' Hughes, the Prime Minister, in October, somewhat disgusted, '*authorised whatever expenditure is necessary for the recovery of Australian bodies*'. At this point 12,500 Australians had not been properly accounted for, as the passage of the years together with the rehabilitation and reconstruction of the battlefields made the task of identification of what was recovered almost impossible.

Around this time Donald Mackinnon, formerly Director General of Recruiting, was passing through France, probably visiting the grave of his son Brice in St Sever Cemetery near Rouen, and he wrote to friends of what he saw in the cemeteries between Fleurbaix and Neuve Chapelle:

> … the authorities have eliminated separate mounds. The soldiers are all buried under lawns, but where the head cross or stone is, a place is left vacant for flowers … roses are planted in the Rue du Bois Cemetery.

The headstone of Rev. S E Maxted at the Rue Petillon Cemetery.

The Register Entry: Maxted, the Rev Spencer Edward. Chaplain to the Forces, 4th Class, attd 54th Bn Australian Infantry. Killed in action 19/20 July 1916. Son of the late Henry Edward and Alice Rachel May Maxted; husband of Gertrude O Maxted, of corner Merrivale Rd and Nithsdale St, Pymble, NSW. Born at Sydney. 1 K 2.

RUE DAVID CEMETERY

At Fleurbaix No. 347. About 2 kms south-east of Fleurbaix, it began in Dec. 1914 and was closed Dec. 1917, but greatly enlarged after the Armistice. It contains many from 1st Middlesex Regiment who fell at the end of Oct 1914. Comparatively few of the 90 or so named AIF graves are from 19–20 July, although there is a group of 60th Bn from that date.

It is generally accepted that the vast majority of the 266 unidentified Australian graves are from the Battle, likewise a large proportion of unidentified British. Of special interest here is Pte Billy Elsdale 47th Bn (I.E.4) probably the first Aboriginal digger killed in France, 7 July 1916.

PHOTOGRAPH 12 NOVEMBER 1994

PHOTOGRAPH L ENGLEZOS

In 1932 *Crosses of Sacrifice* was published. It was subtitled 'The Story of the Empire's Million War Dead and Australia's 60,000'. The author J C Waters clearly set out to do better than Pratt and by clearly stating from where he came in the introduction, it is no wonder that the book was a great success.

> On the battlefields of Palestine, Gallipoli, France and Belgium, I have seen the cemeteries where lie those of the Empire's soldiers whose graves are known. I have seen the legion of other names upon memorial after memorial raised to the memory of the missing.
>
> Now, for the first time, I (a boy in the war years) can conceive the heart-rending torture of war.
>
> Now, for the first time, I realise the true significance of Anzac Day.
>
> And now, for the first time, I really know why, on every November 11, we stand silent for two short minutes.

As he journeyed around the battlefields of France, Waters noted the distinctive architecture of each cemetery and memorial, the particular care with the horticulture which '*wrought things of beauty, that must be an inspiration to countless generations to come*'. He recognised that the losses of Fromelles and Pozières in those few short weeks July to September 1916, '*sent a tremendous shock through the length and breath of our country*'. Of VC Corner, now built, Waters certainly caught the spirit:

> On the terrace, too, stands the Cross of Sacrifice with its bronze sword, long and slender. It rises clear above the ramparts that shelter their last encampment. Who of those 1300 commemorated there, I wonder, are sleeping in this little allotment? Who of them are out where the wheat and the oats make fairy music above their heads?

In Britain in this period many books were published on the battlefield cemeteries partially to cater for the pilgrims, visitors and tourists. One, *Silent Cities*, by S E Hurst (1929) made an

RUE-DU-BOIS CEMETERY
At Fleurbaix No. 348. Some 6 kms south-west of Armentières on the road to Bethune it was used firstly from Nov 1914 to Dec 1916, then Jan 1918 to Oct 1918. Of the 832 named graves, 242 are Australian—two long rows (Plot I, Row B and Plot II, Row A) contain men unidentified from 15th Bde (22) and 2/1st Bucks (52) whose bodies were brought from Fromelles prior to the Armistice. Major G G McCrae, CO of 60th Bn, is buried here (I.F.33). Together here are the five 57th Bn men killed on 11 July, who might, as the victims of an early German shell, be termed the first 5th Division casualties at Fromelles.

Rue-du-Bois Cemetery.
The graves of Ptes R D Bradley, I Dowsey, C Hardingham, W R Boxall and W Gregory of 57th Bn, killed in action on 11 July 1916, are the third to seventh in the front row.
12 November 1994

AUBERS RIDGE BRITISH CEMETERY

At Aubers No. 567. East of Aubers and on the east side of the road to Herlies the cemetery was made after the Armistice by the concentration of graves from smaller burial grounds all round Aubers. Of the identified graves there are seventeen Australians and 31 British who died in the Battle of Fromelles, while Plots I and II hold the unidentified bodies of the victims of 19-20 July.

The village was taken by the British on 17 Oct 1914 but lost after a few days and not liberated until October 1918.

PHOTOGRAPH L & A LIGHT

LAVENTIE MILITARY CEMETERY

At La Gorgue No. 1887. On the northeast outskirts of Laventie, it was begun by the 61st Division in June 1916 and accommodates more identified British from 19/20 July than any other cemetery. They are mostly 184th Bde including Capt. H Church (11.E.23). Attractively landscaped, there are a total of 474 graves here, some of which are for British Officers of the Indian Army and Indian troops, from Neuve Chapelle.

PHOTOGRAPH R LEFFLER

LOOS MEMORIAL

The memorial—MR 19—forms the sides and back of Dud Corner Cemetery where 1785 officers and men are buried, the great majority of whom fell in the Battle of Loos. The walls are four and half metres high and list 20,712 names—by Regiments—who have no known grave, including 330 from the Battle of Fromelles, and so is the main memorial to the British dead of that day. Four kilometres from Lens, on the northeast side of the road to Bethune, the Loos Memorial is worth a visit just to witness the enormity of the loss.

PLOEGSTEERT MEMORIAL
The Memorial—No. MR 32—is the Berkshire Cemetery Extension, and is a covered circular colonnade with the names of some 11,000, listed by regiments, carved on panels set into the walls of the colonnade. These dead are from the earliest battles in 1914 right through to the Armistice, and fell in the surrounding area. From the battle of Fromelles there are eight names, six being officers and all were with 182nd Bde. The Memorial is about 5 kms north of Armentières on the N365 to Ieper (Ypres).
PHOTOGRAPH M DELEBARRE

MERVILLE COMMUNAL CEMETERY
At Merville No. 345: with the Extension No. 346. In these two areas there are 2170 graves of British, Indians, Australians, Canadians, South Africans and Germans. During the battle of Fromelles the British Hospital was here, thus those buried at Merville are mostly classified as 'died of wounds'. The cemetery is on the northeast of the town.

effort to describe in text and photograph every cemetery and memorial, and formed a great record of the huge enterprise of commemorating and/or burying the 1,114,837 Empire dead: a task described by Rudyard Kipling as '*the biggest single bit of work since any of the Pharoahs—and they only worked in their own country*'.

As far as the British dead of Fromelles were concerned none of the places where they are buried or remembered have the same exclusivity that say Anzac Cemetery and VC Corner have for the Australian dead of Fromelles.

Of the British whose bodies were never found or identified, 330 are noted on the Loos Memorial and 8 on Ploegsteert Memorial, there are thus 217 with graves—meaning that 61 per centare noted on memorials and 39 per cent have known graves either in France or Britain. Extraordinarily similar percentages apply to the Australians of whom 1298 are noted at VC Corner, 35 at Villers-Bretonneux while 807 have known graves either in France or Britain—62 per cent and 38 per cent !

Although between the wars tens of thousands of Australians journeyed to Europe to visit the battlefields and graves, the vast majority of people intimately affected by the war never could. It was not just a matter of money, it was the time the journey took—about three months were needed because there were inevitably relatives in the British Isles to be visited.

The way Australia dealt with this was to erect in every suburb and town a memorial, some listed just the dead from the area, others listed all those who served. Honour Boards in schools, offices, churches, town halls and clubs amassed huge lists and these were displayed in the most honoured position.

In one town hall the names cover, from floor to ceiling, every wall of the foyer. Often, however, there was a call for a living memorial, and this was usually a hall for recreation purposes, sometimes attached to the school or church, but other times in the main street of the town. If possible, photographs of the men '*who went away*' were displayed, together with other photographs, framed certificates and civic tributes, almost as icons in a place of worship. Avenues of Honour were another Australian memorial: the most spectacular that at Ballarat where every man from the district who served had a tree, marked with his name and unit: the avenue stretches for 14 miles.

But none of the civic tributes had space to note where the man died. The only place for that was on the grave of his parents, his widow or his children. Thus '*In loving memory of ... killed in action 19 July 1916 at Fleurbaix*' was not an uncommon inscription in an Australian cemetery. It was the only place where such emotion could be expressed for a man who disappeared in France, as 1298 did at Fromelles.

A FATHER'S TRIBUTE
Devastated by the loss of his son, Gordon McCrae, poet and artist, designed a memorial; window and plaque in memory of Major Geoffrey McCrae, 60th Bn. They were placed in Christ Church, Hawthorn, close to where the family lived. The ceremony was on 25 March 1917, Lady Day, and the window was unveiled by Brig. General J Burston (1856–1920), a warden of the church, former Lord Mayor of Melbourne, and Commander of 7th Bde at Gallipoli. The Chaplain was Rev. F P Williams of 58th Bn, and Pte A Monkhouse 31744a, 60th Bn, the Major's last batman, had a place of honour at the service.

... that bright life ...

... there was one youngster who was a very, very fine platoon commander. He knew his men through and through. And the more he knew them the more he was filled with the same idea which has impressed hundreds of Australians here: that anything could be made of Australia.

He used to dream of what he could help to make of Australia. In the long hours of the night at Fleurbaix, when the white flares shot from behind the German parapet opposite and stooped like graceful, glinting lilies over No-man's-land, it was not these that he saw.

A patch of unkempt white wet grass was vignetted for twenty seconds till the thing fell smouldering into it, half extinguished. It lay there a few instants and died. The sandbags sprang into glaring white against the sky, and then the deep shadow of the trench rose as the flare fell and consumed them; but his eyes saw only a land of sunshine—of green and gold. A German machine-gun and then another chirruped out like a pair of canaries, ran along in step for a minute, and then died in a few resentful outbursts. The night was quiet again. And all the while this boy leaned against the parapet and thought: 'What can we make of Australia? When we get back ... ? What cannot we make of Australia?'

When he went on his short leaves from the front he used to go to any place where he thought he could pick up knowledge which would be useful for Australia—to Bournville chocolate works to find out how a factory could be run; to Liverpool to see how great mail steamers could be received; to model villages, model houses, model gardens, to see how this country and its homes might be made beautiful.

And then a German machine-gun laid him low, near Passchendaele. The head that held all that knowledge for Australia lay in the vile mud of a Broodseinde shell-crater. In the dawn, like thousands upon thousands of others, with the glowing light under the yellowing sky and the ragged grey clouds just showing through the cold vapour of vanishing dusk, that bright life with all its plans for Australia flickered out.

—C E W Bean
In Your Hands, Australians (1918)

Our Fred …

It says it all, *'Our Fred'* on the headstone of Pte Frederick Leonard Brown 3025 60th Bn, in Rue David Cemetery. He was 25 when he was killed on 19 July 1916 and *'the loved son of Mr and Mrs H L Brown'*. The simplicity of the statement, the absoluteness of the loss every parent would understand. One can imagine the Browns trying to work out an inscription. What could they say? What should they say? And then one turns to the other 'he was our Fred, that's all'. No great heroics, no noble death, no chapter and verse, no King and Country: all that mattered was that Mr and Mrs Brown were, for the rest of their lives, without their Fred.

That inscription, one of tens of thousands, came about through the work of Fabian Ware who was a Red Cross worker at the beginning of the war and later the Director of the Imperial War Graves Commission. It was his foresight and compassion that set the style and quality of British Empire war graves. Part of this style was that every headstone for general or private, British nobleman or Indian sepoy would be the same size and quality: and the unidentified body would have the same respect. At every cemetery there would be a register which included the soldier's details and those of his family if they were available. Next of kin could provide an inscription which would go at the foot of the stone. The great influence behind such phrases that would mark the cemeteries like '*Their name liveth for evermore*' was Rudyard Kipling, and it was he who pushed the idea of individual inscriptions, and was adamant that the '*headstones be equal and uniform, Field Marshal or camp follower*':

The inscriptions that follow were collected in November 1994 by the writer, except for the last seven which come from John Laffin's *We will remember them* (1995). All, of course, are for men who died in the Battle of Fromelles. Thank goodness Laffin published the 'epitaphs' (some 1320), as he calls them, which he and his wife Hazelle recorded during their many visits to the cemeteries of France and elsewhere; they are a key part of Australia's history.

When one considers that the parents who struggled with these words were all products of that Victorian upbringing which did not smile upon bearing one's soul in public, they are a revelation. On one hand the patriotic death and glory sentiments that thrust the Empire forward throughout the Victorian era, and the Biblical solace—God's will and He knows best—another driving force of the Empire. But on the other hand, as Laffin titles it, '*Profound despair and resignation*', sometimes expressed in the words of the poets, but more often in lines from their own broken hearts and now lonely lives.

Beseler, Pte G H, 31st Bn. Age 31.
In memory of my beloved son and our brother. Gone but never forgotten.
(Anzac Cemetery)

Bishop, Pte E J, 56th Bn. Age 29.
A true and noble friend.
(Croix-du-Bac)

Carnegie, Pte W L, 5th MG Coy. Age 25.
The Day Thou Givest Lord is Ended
(Anzac Cemetery)

Clayton, Pte J H, 58th Bn. Age 18.
St John C15 V13
(Rue Petillon)

Finey, Pte C L, 32nd Bn. Age 20.
[Jewish Star of David]
For God and Liberty
(Ration Farm)

Hall, 2/Lieut H J, 54th Bn. Age 22.
Do not ask if we miss him, there is such a vacant place
(Ration Farm)

Hartmann, L/Cpl S T V W, 54th Bn.
He died fighting for love and liberty
(Croix-du-Bac)

McCrae, Major G G, 60th Bn. Age 26
O Crown unfading and so early won
(Rue-du-Bois)

O'Shannassy, Pte A N, 58th Bn. Age 21.
An Anzac
(Rue Petillon)

Robin, Sgt G De Q, 53rd Bn. Age 21.
Bright, brave and true
(Rue-du-Bois)

Slattery, Pte G M, 60th Bn. Age 27.
Fiat voluntas tua requiem aeternam dona et domine
(Rue-du-Bois)

Sullivan, Pte A T, 56th Bn. Age 24.
We miss you most, who love you best.
(Anzac Cemetery)

Taylor, Capt. H, 54th Bn. Age 24.
A beautiful memory left behind. Duty nobly done.
(Rue-du-Bois)

Weller, Cpl F N, 59th Bn. Age 25.
He that liveth and believeth in me shall never die
(Croix-du-Bac)

Wootten, Pte A J, 58th Bn.
He died an Australian hero. Tis the grandest death of all.
(Rue Petillon)

Boone, 2/Lieut C A, 54th Bn. Age 31.
Death is not death to him, but glorious gain
(Anzac Cemetery)

Camps, Pte V A, 30th Bn. Age 26.
He heard the call. He gave it heed and now he sleeps in Flanders
(Rue Petillon)

Chapman, Pte J E, 31st Bn. Age 20.
Though in a foreign land you lie, our love for you will never die
(Rue Petillon)

Coulter, Pte W H, 56th Bn. Age 23.
We are thinking of you today Dear Wal, we are thinking of the past
(Rue Petillon)

Rourke, Cpl H G, 56th Bn. Age 33.
For God. For King. For Country.
(Anzac Cemetery)

Smith, Pte W N, 53rd Bn. Age 24.
These deeds which should not pass away, names that must not wither
(Ration Farm)

Winter, Pte C H, 32nd Bn. Age 28.
When could a man die better, than facing fearful odds
(Rue Petillon)

The Kennedy Crucifix

As a reflection of the spirit of the people of Fromelles, the preservation of this memorial for almost 80 years is important to record.

Lieut Paul Kennedy was killed on 9 May 1915 during the attack on Aubers Ridge, he was 28 years old and one of the four sons of Sir John Kennedy, a British diplomat (Japan, Russia, Chile, Roumania) who had died in 1912, and he was the great-nephew of the 1st Marquess of Ailsa. He was educated at Harrow and Sandhurst, joined the Rifle Bde in 1906 and went with them to Malta, Egypt and India. His body was never found and his name is on the Ploegsteert Memorial.

Two other sons also died in the war: Archibald at Mons in August 1914 and Patrick at Villers-Bretonneux 24 April 1918. All three were unmarried. The fourth son, Leo, also served and was awarded the MC. He had been a journalist with *The Times* since 1910 an occupation he returned to after the war—until 1942, when he moved to the BBC. In the late 1930s he had written *Britain faces Germany* wherein he advised his readers that Hitler meant what he had written in *Mein Kampf.*

Lieut Paul Kennedy
Killed in action 9 May 1915

Having found the graves of Archibald and Patrick, in 1921, Lady Kennedy with Leo and his sister

The Kennedy Memorial c1921

Elizabeth came to Fromelles to erect a small memorial to the memory of Paul and his friends who fought and died there. They were Lieut T F E Stanhope, younger son of the 9th Earl of Harrington who was aged 20; Lieut H R Hardinge who was the eldest son of Lord and Lady Hardinge and nephew of the Viceroy of India. Educated at Winchester, he had served in India and was aged 19. Lieut E H Leigh was the only surviving son of the Hon Sir Chandos and Lady Leigh. In the army since 1911, he was 26 years old when killed. Like Paul, all three have no known graves and their names are on the Ploegsteert Memorial.

Lady Kennedy brought with her a crucifix which had been carved in Austria, and the memorial included this under a canopy with this inscription:

To the Glory of God
and in memory
of my beloved son

Paul Adrian Kennedy commanding B Coy of the 2nd Battalion, Rifle Brigade, and his friends, Talbot Fitzroy Eden Stanhope RB, Henry Ralph Hardinge RB and Edward Henry Leigh RB as well as to all those who fell in the attack on the Aubers Ridge 9 May 1915.
Him that overcometh will I make a pillar in the Temple of my God.
Priez Pour Eux

Lady Kennedy, who was born in 1850, died in Nov 1939 '*all through the war Lady Kennedy was unwearied in different forms of war work, especially sending parcels to British prisoners of war in Germany*'. Elizabeth, her daughter, was at the front during the later stages of the war as a Red Cross nurse.

In 1955 Leo Kennedy and his daughter Clare came to Fromelles and were surprised to find that the memorial was protected by a small fence and showed all the signs of being looked after. They went to visit the priest and over lunch it was agreed that the beautiful box tree carving of Christ was a very special symbol of the losses of the Great War and should be placed '*dans le coeur de l'église toujours, visible actuallement*'.

Another crucifix was set up under the canopy and was later unveiled by the niece, Mrs Clare Heddy, who came back to Fromelles with her husband. They were welcomed by the ASBF and met among others Mr Henri Delepierre, the vice-president of the ASBF who had for the last 25 years cared for the memorial.

The Kennedy memorial is on the road from Fromelles to Sailly (rue Delvas), 250 m before the Australian Memorial Park.

The Kennedy Memorial 1990s
INFORMATION COURTESY M DELEBARRE
PHOTOS COURTESY M DELEBARRE & C HEDDY (née Kennedy).

The German Cemeteries

The bringing together of German Cemeteries in the Aubers region means that those killed on 19/20 July 1916 near Fromelles are a tiny minority among the thousands of graves that mark the German invasion of France in 1914-18. The German postcards of the period reveal the traditional village layout whilst the photographs of 1999 provide, in comparison, a somewhat bleak aspect.

Top: The Regimental Cemetery of the 17th BRIR at Aubers in 1915/16. After the war it was concentrated elsewhere.
PHOTOGRAPH COURTESY J-M BAILLEUL

Middle: The Fournes Cemetery near the village probably in 1916/17.
PHOTOGRAPH COURTESY M DELEBARRE

Lower: the Fournes Cemetery today. It has 1807 names in its Register and is 4 kms from Fromelles.
PHOTOGRAPH AND INFORMATION COURTESY J-M BAILLEUL

The German Cemeteries

Top: The Beaucamps Cemetery, probably in 1916/17.

Middle: The Beaucamps Cemetery looking towards the village which is 6 kms from Fromelles; it is the resting place of 2628 German soldiers.

Lower: The Wicres cemetery on National Route 41, 6 kms from Fromelles. Today it records the names of 584 German dead.
PHOTOGRAPHS AND INFORMATION COURTESY J-M BAILLEUL

The Origin of VC Corner

While the VC Corner Australian Cemetery is not at a corner, it takes its name from a point near the junction of Rue du Bois and Rue Delvas. About 125 yards north of this junction a communication trench ran from Rue du Bois, parallel with Rue Delvas for about 700 yards before turning south and connecting with the front line. This trench was known as VC Avenue, and was about 350 yards north west of the cemetery. The cemetery is about 50 yards in front of the Australian Line of July 1916, hence in No-Man's Land and over the area the 53rd Bn and the 60th Bn advanced.

The Victoria Crosses won in Rue du Bois are the origin of the name VC Corner and it is no wonder that the immediate area had something of a reputation for brave acts. Numerous diaries and memoirs indicate that the Australians were well aware of this association at the time. In the period we are concerned with at least 7 Victoria Crosses were awarded for gallantry in this vicinity. Considering that around 144 Victoria Crosses were awarded in Belgium and France up to 19 July 1916, it is some guidance to the scale of the battles waged within 8 miles (13 kms) of Fromelles that at least 43 of those VCs were won in this general area.

VC Corner Cemetery in the 1930s COURTESY M DELEBARRE

Although no VCs came from the 19/20 July, 1916 battle, it might be said that neglect has been overridden in a sense by the naming of the most important and the only all Australian burial ground in France—VC Corner Cemetery, where on the walls originally 1299 names of the missing of 19/20 July were recorded. This was later amended to 1298 when in 1927 the body of Major Roy Harrison of 54th Bn was found and identified. The names and deeds of the British heroes who gave the place its name are of course part of the story of Fromelles.

The first VC awarded in the area was at Rouges Bancs about a mile from the junction of Rue du Bois and Rue Delvas. On 19 December 1914, Pte J Mackenzie of 2nd Battalion, Scots Guards was helping to rescue the wounded.

On one occasion a party of stretcher bearers attempted in vain to reach a wounded man. Seeing this, Mackenzie went forward under heavy fire and carried him back from the very front of the German trenches. A second time on the same day he attempted to perform a like act of gallantry, but on this occasion he was unfortunately killed.

Two days later—21 December—at Rouges Bancs two privates of 2nd Battalion, Border Regiment were involved in further rescues.

Abraham Acton and James Smith ... went voluntarily from their trench and rescued a wounded man who had been lying exposed near the German trenches for three whole days, and later they went out a second time and brought in another wounded man into safety. The pair were under fire for an hour, but both returned safety.

Both were awarded Victoria Crosses.

It was not until May 1915 that serious fighting again took place in the Rue du Bois area. On 9 May the Black Watch (1st Bn Royal Highlanders) attacked German positions there. Leading a section of the 1st Battalion was Cpl John Ripley.

Of the whole battalion Ripley was the first man to mount the German parapet, and, standing there exposed to fire, he pointed out to others the ways through the gaps made by our artillery in the wire entanglements. This done he led his section through a breach in the parapet to the second line of trenches, and having reached his objective he set to work to make the position secure. Aided by a few men, seven or eight, he blocked up both flanks, arranged a good position for firing, and continued to defend the captured trench until all his men had fallen and he himself had been badly wounded in the head.

At the same place and about the same time L/Cpl David Finlay of 2nd Bn was in charge of a bombing party.

Leading forward a bombing party of 12 men ... he did this with the greatest gallantry until 10 of them had fallen. Then Finlay showed the stuff of which he was made. He ordered the two survivors to crawl back into safety, but he himself went forward to the assistance of a wounded man, and carried him for 100 yards under heavy fire, eventually placing him under cover.

At Rouges Bancs during the same attack Cpl James Upton of 1st Battalion, Sherwood Foresters spent the day attending wounded.

During the whole of this day Cpl Upton displayed the greatest courage in rescuing the wounded while exposed to very heavy rifle and artillery fire, going close to the enemy's parapet regardless of his own personal safety. One man was killed by a shell while in his arms. Moreover, when Upton was not actually engaged in this hazardous duty, he was bandaging and dressing the serious cases in the front of the parapet, exposed to the enemy's fire.

Upton, who came from Nottingham was known as the 'Bantam VC' due to being only 5 feet 2½ inches tall.

Near Rouges Bancs the 2nd Battalion, Lincolnshire Regiment was also in the same action. Cpl Charles Sharpe was in charge of a party sent forward to capture a portion of a German trench.

... he was first to reach it. Once there he threw his bombs with great determination and effect, and in a short time he had cleared all the Germans from a trench 50 yards long. In the end all his men had fallen, but four others came forward to assist Sharpe, and the five made another successful attack on the enemy, using their bombs with such vigour that they captured this time a trench, not 50 but 250 yards long.

Thus 4 VCs were won on one day near the corner of Rue du Bois and Rue Delvas: from then on known as VC Corner.

On 16 June 1915 L/Cpl Joseph Tombs of 1st Battalion, Liverpool Regiment (The Kings) was in action near Rue du Bois.

On his own initiative he crawled out of his trench repeatedly, and under very severe fire from heavy guns and machine guns, he rescued four wounded men who were lying about 100 yards from his trenches. One of these rescues was especially noteworthy, for Tombs dragged the man back to safety by means of a rifle sling placed around his own neck and the man's body. This heroism and devotion undoubtedly saved his life.

Australia's first VC in Europe was awarded for an act of bravery in the Fromelles area: in fact near the corner of the D176 and D222 south west of Bois Grenier. On the night of 25/26 June 1916 returning from a raid Pte W Jackson 588 of 17th Bn, after handing in a prisoner, went back to No-Man's Land three times to rescue wounded mates. The 19-year-old farmer from NSW lost an arm during his second mission but persevered and survived.

While researching the above material a full listing of the VCs from the area had to be compiled. It is surely part of the wider story, and so is included here.

1914			
15 Sept	near Festubert	1	E Harlock
29 Oct	at Festubert	2	J Hogan J Leach
23 Nov	" "	1	D S Negi
24 Nov	" "	1	F A de Pass
19 Dec	near Givenchy	1	WA McC Bruce
19 Dec	between Neuve Chapelle & Festubert	1	D Neame
19 Dec	at Rouge Bancs	1	J Mackenzie
21 Dec	" " "	2	A Acton J Smith
1915			
1 Feb	at Cuinchy	1	M O'Leary
10 Mar	at Neuve Chapelle	2	W Buckingham G S Negi
12 Mar	" " "	8	W Anderson E Barber H Daniels C C Foss W D Fuller C G Martin C R Noble J Rivers
9 May	near Fromelles	4	D Finlay J Ripley C Sharpe J Upton
16 May	near Festubert	1	F Barter
18 May	Richbourg l'Avone	1	J G Smyth
22 May	near Cambrin	1	W Mariner
26 May	Givenchy	1	L J Keyworth
12 June	"	1	W Angus
15 June	"	1	F W Campbell
16 June	near Rue de Bois	1	J Tombs
30 June	Richbourg l'Avone	1	N V Carter
3 Aug	near La Bassée	1	G A B Rochfort
25 Sept	south of Fauquissart	1	Kulbir Thapa
		1	G A Maling
25 Sept	near Cuinchy	1	A F G Kilby
27 Sept	Cuinchy	1	A A Burt
28 Sept	near Vermelles	1	A B Turner
18 Oct	Cuinchy	1	H Christian
1916			
22 June	Givenchy	2	J Erskine W Hackett
25/26 June	near Armentières	1	W Jackson (Australian)

After the battle of Fromelles, in this area, two VCs were awarded in 1917 and four in 1918.

Sources:
Sir John Smythe VC. *The Story of the Victoria Cross* (1963).
The Times History of the War.

Fromelles—after the war

After the Armistice of 11 November, the first villagers who returned were only able to find charred ruins, cracked roads, flooded trenches and concrete fortifications with the bodies of Australian, British and German soldiers left on the battlefields. To return to their homes was impossible.

A provisional church was built on rue Sotte, under the direction of Abbé Dahiez. The rubble was cleared away from the ruins and the streets by the firm, Colin of Lille. The barbed wire and the unexploded ordnance was destroyed in a place which was called the 'field of sparks' and many workers were needed to fill in the trenches and clear the back alleys. The steel and the copper kept a good number of scrap metal dealers occupied, and an explosion killed four strangers who were cutting the copper belt off some shells. Many households applied for war indemnity compensation for the destruction of their property, or for the dismantling of fortifications on their farm land.

The first stone for the new church was laid on 2 March 1924—it was consecrated on 10 April 1927.

In the same period, the mayor's office and the boys' and girls' school were rebuilt in rue de Verdun (the second storey of the Town Hall is now the Museum of the ASBF). Under the aegis of the first magistrate after the war, M Dambrine, in rebuilding the public buildings, a co-operative for reconstruction was established under a business manager and an architect with the business 'Bâtiment de Lomme' helped by many workmen from Fromelles.

In the meantime, on 15 July 1923 a war memorial was unveiled; it bears the names of 42 soldiers from Fromelles and six civilians who were victims of the Great War.

In 1925 there were only 418 people living in the village, a notable fall from the 529 who returned after the war.

INFORMATION AND PHOTOGRAPHS COURTESY M DELEBARRE

FROMELLES (Nord) - Après l'occupation Allemande - Rue du Bourg
Edit. Fruleux-Cardon, tabacs
G. Lefebvre, photo, Ascq

The Church during rebuilding, showing the location of the War Memorial and some of the graves in the churchyard.

12

What good does it do ?

I should omit these details.
What good does it do even if true…
—Brig. General Sir James Edmonds, to C E W Bean.

Now having viewed the battle first as an idea, then as a deed, and the consequences of it all—the dead, the maimed, the widowed and the orphaned, we turn to examine how the story of Fromelles was given to the public.

There was of course a considerable amount of private information in the hands of survivors and the families of the dead, information by way of letters wherein the traumatized wrote down that trauma and so passed it on. The first public showing of this, albeit stripped of personal names, units and places located by this writer was E A Hubbard's *At the Front*—pages 174–76. Doubtless other graphic descriptions found their way into country town newspapers, each alerting the local population to what had happened simply because the battalions had many of the local men serving with them. Hubbard may have had no idea of the overall battle strategy but he had an excellent grasp of the 15th Bde arrangements. The very large number of Fromelles wounded back in Australia by this time, with or without such texts, would have informed many about the battle.

The first of these robust accounts in book form was *Over there—with the Australians*, by Capt. R Hugh Knyvett (15th Bde) published in London and New York in 1918. His twelve pages from which extracts have been taken for this volume, are very much about his own experience. Apart from gossip that Knyvett would have picked up in the Officers' Mess and from other colleagues there is nothing that indicates he checked war diaries or official sources. He was seriously wounded late in 1916 and returned to Australia in January 1917. He died in New York of the flu on 15 April 1918, so never had the opportunity to write more fully, perhaps via a Unit history.

The next detailed account was in *The Whale Oil Guards*, by J J Kennedy DSO CF. His nine short pages on Fromelles as one would expect, indeed hope, were the priest's memories

THE ACCUMULATED WISDOM
Having received a part of the typescript on the Battle of Fromelles, Elliott wrote back to Bean on 17 August 1926:

I have read it through very carefully and congratulate you on the way you have pieced out the different narratives. I have nothing to add to the report itself but the following facts may be of interest to you.

Elliott then related the now famous visit of a member of Haig's staff to Elliott and his declaration about the '*bloody holocaust*'. Elliott wrote how he had been given an official booklet from the French staff, in English, which contained '*the accumulated wisdom*' of their experience thus far, one axiom of which was that an attack on a front trench line could not succeed if the distance to be covered by the attacking force was more than 200 yards.

Elliott's comment:

Bearing this in mind I myself had earlier come to the conclusion that, so far as my Brigade was concerned, if the axiom was sound, success was impossible and I was naturally greatly depressed by the prospect although naturally in loyalty to the higher command I had to carefully conceal my feelings and even my thoughts on the subject.

of the people he knew, loved, guided, converted and buried. It is also clear he was drawn to men of action spending many wonderful hours in the Officers' Mess, and by his own admission attracted to 'ne'er-do-wells' whose alcoholic condition was somewhat less glamorous than that of the officers'. The unit included a number of hopeless drunks and outstanding heroes, sometimes the same people as Kennedy was honest enough to admit. Towards the end of 1917 his health broke and in March 1918 he retired from active service. The dedication is dated 30 October 1918, and the book was published in Dublin in 1919. It is not well-written, in places he deals with himself as the padre or chaplain, other times as Father Kennedy and elsewhere as I, but it has all the warm Irishness that never despairs of the human condition. He came away from Fromelles convinced that '*our High Command foresaw the result exactly as it occurred, but it was intended to use us as a holocaust for the salvation of other divisions then hard-pressed in another part of the line. A fine compliment, forsooth!*' and he was much insulted when he read a few days later, the battle described as a raid. But Kennedy was greatly damaged emotionally by the war and this would erupt fiercely in 1920 in his next, and last attempt to deal with Fromelles and all that happened, in words.

The next account, somewhat more about the war than Father Kennedy's, was L W Colley-Priest's *The 8th Australian Field Ambulance on Active Service*. An early draft for part of this is on page 235, and does not disguise, under amusing chat, what actually happened.

Falling across these were two articles (and later two letters) in the *Sydney Morning Herald* coinciding with Peace Day and the third anniversary of the battle. The second article by Dr C MacLaurin doubtless told more people more about Fromelles than anything so far published. The attack on MacLaurin's view by a Fromelles veteran three days later seemed to confirm the still prevalent belief that Fromelles was some kind of victory.

Somebody in London had decreed that the first Peace Day should be celebrated on 19 July 1919. This extraordinary coincidence could not have been lost on survivors of Fromelles, and in Sydney on that day a first description was published under the heading *The Mystery Battle of the AIF.* It was written by Colonel Chaplain James Green who was with the 55th Bn. It became the first of three long pieces in the *Sydney Morning Herald*, which were three views of the day: the first from a padre, the second from a medical officer and the third from an infantryman decorated for his work on 19 July.

COMING HOME

And so, on 21 February 1917, the hospital train—comfortable, well appointed, and fully staffed—glided on over the rails with its complement of maimed yet happy Australians, all cheered up to be returning home … and on arrival at Avonmouth, embarked on HMAHS *Karoola* … painted white above a red water-line, with a green band—broken by three red crosses on each side—running right around the centre of the hull from stern to stern… the all Australian staff, particularly the sisters, and even the crew, capable and cheerfully ministered to the well being of the patients …

Not more than a few hours were spent by the ship at the various ports of call in Australia. Those disembarking took what might have appeared to be casual leave of their shipmates, but the parting was in fact deeply felt by all. They did not make promises to write, but just flung a 'cheerio', 'so long; or 'good luck' to one another …

Words, what words were there that could express the feelings and thoughts of these men? None. They were members of a freemasonry that had endured many partings—partings from loved ones at home, with old cobbers, with English and foreign brothers and sisters of the craft, with those 'gone west'. But their bonds of friendship, moulded in an atmosphere of mutual suffering, sympathy and good fellowship would endure. Words were unnecessary. Materially they had parted—were parting; spiritually, they were together. Life would see many reunions, and in passing they would but part to meet again.

—R E Lording (A Tiveychoc)
There and Back (1935)

Chaplain JAMES GREEN

Born in Newcastle, England, October 1864, he came to Australia in 1889. In 1900 he went to the South African War, was wounded, repatriated, re-enlisted, returned and was taken prisoner by the Boers. In 1903 back in Sydney [continued opposite]

Green began:

> Peace is celebrated today on the anniversary of the first Australian battle fought on French soil, and it is fitting that they are commemorated together—the one with its triumph and the other with its tragedy. Very little is known of the Battle of Fleurbaix. It was never fully reported for sufficient reasons. Amongst other reasons it was, perhaps, deemed inadvisable to disclose the details of our newly-arrived AIF units or the extent of our loss to the enemy. It was described in eight lines in most of the English papers, and was variously called 'a lively skirmish', a 'stirring attack' or a 'big raid ...' On strict examination Fleurbaix will probably be found to be the most expensive battle every fought by the AIF and the most desperate ... As the casualty lists of Pozières came to Australia at the same time, and there was a certain vagueness about the geographical details of Fleurbaix, there are still many people who think their sons or brothers fell at Pozières, whereas they fell at Fleurbaix.

Chaplain Green then went on to describe the arrival of 5th Division and their placement in 'The Nursery' sector. He noted that the action was static and that '*we laboured under disability of being unable to fire on Lille because of the presence of French women and children, whilst the big guns of the Lille forts could fire on us*'. He lamented the daily destruction of churches and villages and observed that '*there was the glory of being the first Australians to go into pitched battle in France, although the last to arrive*' this '*created no enthusiasm among the troops, for although eager to fight, it was felt that we had not sufficient knowledge of the intricate system of saps and trenches*'.

Overall the description of the battle was remarkedly accurate, except where Green wrote that '*many of our men got right through to Fromelles*'. The men he mentions were all from NSW which was, of course, the origin of 14th Bde, when at last '*Colonel Pope, our brigadier, gave the order to retire ... with difficulty ... our men could be induced to retire ... as they did not understand the general position*'.

Padre Green then described the armistice attempt in a different way, but very recognisable:

> ... as the battle died away a small party went out under a Red Cross flag to ask for leave to bring in the dead and wounded. They were met by a German officer, who conducted them to Headquarters, where the Boche officers at once photographed them whilst they waited for a message ... they were told that we could only get our wounded if we showed a white flag, which we, of course, refused to do ... however all through the 20 July, our bearers, at the risk of their lives, were bringing in our men ... we had a sad day of helping the wounded and burying the dead.

In the newspaper that carried Green's article, 19 July was a Saturday, there were 5 columns of 'In Memoriam on Active Service', some 300 notices. A number of stores closed for the

Chaplain JAMES GREEN (contd)
he became Senior Methodist Chaplain. On Gallipoli it may have been Green who conducted the first burial, and after the campaign he joined the 55th Bn and went with it to Fromelles. There he tended wounded men *under a barrage ... in the front line trenches*. For this and later work he received the DSO, and in 1918 was appointed CMG. These awards were for work in setting up the AIF Recreation Centre in Horseferry Road, London and work at the Front. Green returned to Sydney ill and emotionally worn out, but was always in attendance at 19 July services. He was, in the best Methodist tradition, 'good with words' and was a major force behind services dedicated to ministering to returned men unable to find their feet. He retired in 1934 and died in 1948.

A MUG SOLDIER'S FOND DREAM
Some 18 years after Fromelles S K Donnan in his letter to Bean still had strong views about the conduct of the battle. His analysis of the short-comings of McCay points positively to the reasons for the later success of Monash. Donnan's logic is unassailable:

> *As a youngster who had served a good time among engineers and surveyors on practical work on the plains I was struck with the absolute lack of knowledge and even appreciation of the technical side of things in the army. Any undertaking like this attack at Fleurbaix should have been in the hands of a man who in civil life had been in charge of big undertakings preferably of a big civil engineering character; a man who in his daily job had encountered difficulties in simple looking tasks and had to make decisions to overcome them. Such a one would know and foresee difficulties in tasks that the routine office man and amateur solder would not appreciate till it was too late. Too many men when war breaks out are given jobs on the strength of parade ground peace time advancement. I would say without knowing who was in command at Fleurbaix that the action was the result of a mug soldier's fond dream.*

Lieut General Sir Richard Haking as a member of the Permanent International Armistice Commission at Spa, Belgium 1919–20.
—*The Great War* Vol 12, H W Wilson (ed.)

day. The advertisement for Lasseters of George St, a women's store reflected the general view:

> On this day it is right and proper that the merchant should forsake his desk—that the worker should forget his work—that master and man should have one thought in common—Peace. Peace. Peace. Peace. In spirit our heroes are with us in our Triumph of Today. Let us remember them; let us vow never to forget them, for by their able sacrifice we are free, Today we celebrate Peace.

Whilst Farmers also closed, Anthony Hordern's Sale continued. In the march the men were given special permission to don their uniforms, and of this Chaplain Green remarked the next day:

> It was significant that when during last Saturday's great procession, the time arrived for a pause, while men stood with bowed heads, the 5th Division should have just reached the saluting base. What thoughts crossed the minds of the men of that division as they stood in Macquarie Street.

The 5th Division was led by Lieut Col P W Woods DSO MC, a veteran of the Landing and Fromelles, and much else. The Sunday Service was in the Paddington Methodist Church, and conducted by Chaplain Green, '*a large congregation including many returned men filled the church. Lieut J Tarn of 55th Bn read the lesson. A beautiful memorial wreath, sent by Miss Gibbins of Osborne College, Epping, whose brother fell at Fleurbaix was placed on the communal table during the service ...*' This was perhaps the first Fromelles Service held and began a tradition that has survived eighty years.

On Monday 21 July in the evening at the Sydney Town Hall there was the Naval and Military Peace Ball, attended by the State Governor, Premier, Ministers and Admiral of the Fleet. It seemed, even in its reporting not quite in line with the solemnity of the other events.

In Melbourne 7000 marched, all in uniforms with medals, and in groups: Group F led by Brig. General H E Elliott consisted of details of 8th and 14th Bdes and the whole of 15th Bde, some 47 officers and 1008 ORs. All hotels were closed and some shops, whilst others grasped for a sales opportunity like Richard's shoes—'*Great reductions today are being offered to thrifty womenfolk to celebrate peace economically*'. *The Age* newspaper carried in excess of 500 'In Memoriam on Active Service' notices, and mentioned Fromelles—*A Day of Memories*, in the news pages, but in the big double page feature on the war, no event was listed for 19 July. *The Argus* missed the anniversary altogether but reported in detail of the Farewell Dinner at the Connaught Rooms in London where under the chairmanship of Chauvel, the Prince of Wales, Monash, Rosenthal, Hobbs,

THESE HEROINES

The fierce independence of the *Sydney Morning Herald* evidenced by its publication of the Fromelles debate, had an echo in another column:

Widows, mothers, children not treated well.

Judge our indignation upon finding that these heroines who should have occupied pride of place [at the Town Hall] were relegated to the doorsteps, their view obstructed and their proper position usurped by the 'dark' aldermen of a 'dark' Town Hall and their wives and children.

Robertson, Pearce, Howse, Sir Ian Hamilton, Admiral Rose and 300 other officers wished Birdwood well.

A Peace Requiem was held at St Patrick's Cathedral, Melbourne and among those officiating was Father J J Kennedy as deacon. In the afternoon all men in uniform were admitted free to football matches. That evening in Melbourne the other side of the war's legacy surfaced. Serious rioting began and was met with a very unsympathetic police presence. This resulted in some thousands assembling the next day and marching on Victoria Barracks with the object of getting into its armoury. In the stand-off, shots were fired, both by sentries and members of the crowd, the result being the death of one of the latter, but the Barracks were not entered. On Monday 3000, mostly ex-servicemen, infuriated by the death of one of their own, marched on Parliament, to which some gained access and when the Premier, H Lawson, was receiving a deputation he was hit by a wooden inkstand and had to be evacuated. The office was trashed. Outside in the streets trams were derailed, gardens torn up, Russell Street Police Station attacked and numerous arrests made. The police, denounced by the ex-soldiers, later apologised and things settled down. Meanwhile *The Argus* had reported on Sydney's Peace Day '*City beautifully decorated. Police have quiet day*'. On Tuesday more disturbances and meetings, then:

> Many thousands of people lined the city streets this afternoon for the funeral of Pte James O'Connor, the young soldier who was fatally shot outside the barracks on Sunday evening ... the coffin was carried on a gun carriage [and draped with Union Jack and covered with wreaths]. A post-mortem examination revealed the fact that O'Connor died as the result of a shot from a revolver, and not from a service rifle. This evidence supports the contention that the shot was not fired by the sentry, but by a member of the crowd that attempted to force its way into the barracks.

The following Saturday, the *Sydney Morning Herald* printed another full column article simply headed 'Fleurbaix' by C MacLaurin, late Lieut Col AMC AIF. It began:

> I spent the terrible night of Fleurbaix in the safe if intensely busy seclusion of the Second Casualty Clearing Station where we received 801 casualties in 24 hours. Chaplain Captain Green has given an interesting account, but I think I can supplement it with some essential facts that should be known, and I certainly think the official report of that disastrous battle should be published.

MacLaurin, judging from the rest of the article, had thought long and deeply about Fromelles and was angry that so little had been made public.

Pte J O'CONNOR

James (Roy) O'Connor 5145, 22nd Bn, had enlisted 22 Feb 1916 and returned to Australia 22 July 1917. Formerly of Ballarat, his funeral left the RSL Rooms in Swanston Street, for Coburg Cemetery on 22 July 1919. Aged 22 or 24, he was buried in the Pine Ridge Roman Catholic Section (No. P482), in the grave of Ellen Flood, who had died May 1919, aged 78, and later joined by Patrick Flood, who died on 19 July 1923, aged 85, possibly Roy's grandparents.

Lieut Col C MacLAURIN

Dr Charles MacLaurin was the elder brother of Col H N MacLaurin commander of the 1st Infantry Bde who was killed on Gallipoli, 27 April 1915 at a place that became known as MacLaurin's Hill. Both were sons of Sir Normand MacLaurin, formerly a Royal Navy Surgeon, later MLC and Chancellor of the University of Sydney. Educated at Sydney Grammar, Charles completed his medical studies at Edinburgh University and by 1910 he was a Fellow of the Royal College of Surgeons of Edinburgh. He had a private practice which he left to go to the war where he was a specialist surgeon at Wandsworth Hospital and in France. Back in Australia as a result of failing health, Dr MacLaurin became senior surgeon at Randwick Hospital. When he died suddenly 20 April 1925 the *Sydney Morning Herald* wrote, '*Being a man of great culture and wide reading, Dr MacLaurin of late years turned his mind to literary work, and besides contributing articles of an historical nature to different newspapers he wrote* Post Mortem *a work that won him fame beyond Australia ... a highly gifted musician, he also had a great knowledge of and appreciation of art*'. He was 53 and was survived by his widow and daughter.

THE ARROGANT VERSUS THE IGNORANT

On 29 July after the first four weeks of Haig's personal crusade, the Battle of the Somme, when upwards of 40,000 men lay dead on the field or had been blown to bits, the C in C confided to his diary; or rather to the re-written diary that he prepared after the war for publication:

After lunch I visited HQ Reserve Army and impressed on Gough and his GSO (Neil Malcolm) that they must supervise more closely the plans of the ANZAC Corps. Some of their Divisional Generals are so ignorant and (like many colonials) so conceited, that they cannot be trusted to work out unaided the plans of attack. I then went to HQ ANZAC Corps at Contay and saw General Birdwood and his BGGS General White. The latter seems a very sound capable fellow, and assured me that they had learnt a lesson and would be more thorough in future. Luckily their losses had been fairly small, considering the operation and the numbers engaged—about 1,000 for the whole 24 hours.

[Actually, the 2nd Division attempt at Pozières Heights cost 3,500.]

All this is of importance when we consider which Australian Divisional Generals he had in mind. Commanding 1st Division was Walker, an Englishman; commanding 2nd Division was Legge, born in London and who moved to Australia when fifteen. Commanding 3rd Division was Monash, born in Melbourne who was in France from early June to 18 July before going to the UK. Commanding 4th Division was Cox of Watford, UK. The command of 5th Division was in the hands of McCay, born in Ireland and coming to Australia at the age of one.

By simple logic therefore Haig could only be referring to Legge and/or McCay. We know from the same source—Haig's diary—3 August that Gough said *'that the Australian Corps had again put off their attack. From what he said, I concluded that the cause was due to the ignorance of the 2nd Australian Division, and that the GOC Legge was not much good'*. For the record—and Haig makes no note of [continued opposite]

> The attack was to have been made on July 17, but it was put off to the 19th ... meantime we knew exactly the number of men who were to go over the top, the exact number of guns behind them, the exact sector to be attacked by each division and the exact hour of zero. And if we, non-combatants, knew these things, did others know them also? At that time Flanders was reeking with spies; half the Flemings were in the pay of both sides, and ready to sell all France for five francs.
>
> The German defences largely consisted of most tenacious mud, and great stretches of barbed wire, with hundreds of machine guns: almost between the two divisions lay the Sugarloaf, a sinister and terrible place, crowded with concrete emplacements, into which a great force of heavy artillery was to be concentrated, under British command.

He then went on to describe the bombardment, referring back to the peace concert, '*Those who heard the drums of Berlioz the other evening may multiply that colossal sound to the nth power before they can imagine the noise we sat and listened to during that awful evening. About 10 o'clock the first convoy came in, the wounded literally cock-a-hoop, "Glorious victory—hundreds of prisoners—stoush for Fritz"*' they cried as the ambulances rolled in, and we set to work.

At this point MacLaurin's narrative changes tune, the doctor takes over from the digger:

> We were operating for about 48 hours on end, but in the early morning we noticed a change in the spirits of the incoming man. They became dull and apathetic: they would not talk; not a word could we get out of them as to how the day was going. Some of them muttered, that blanky Sugarloaf.
>
> Most of the wounds were in the right arm or leg or the back, and we could infer that our boys were being enfiladed; and further, so many wounds were of such a trifling nature that it was obvious that they were being tried too severely for raw troops. So the night wore on, and by the next morning we were able to piece together the whole awful day, which so far as I know has never yet been published. Now that it is all over, and the Fifth has wiped out its failure so gloriously many a time there is no reason for further secrecy.

MacLaurin saw the battle as a series of blunders:

> ... by some awful feat of blundering the 61st had not cut their own wire ... as these fresh young English lads jumped out of their trenches they could do nothing but run up and down the line like rabbits seeking a way through; some of them tried to cut the wire, but faced a frightful blast ... until human nature could stand no more and they dropped back into shelter. Then our men toiled onwards through the mud, a great chattering on their right announced that the Sugarloaf was awake and pouring a continuous stream of bullets straight along our lines. So came to light the second awful blunder. The heavy artillery, which properly directed should, one would have thought, have levelled mountains, had actually never landed a single shell on that dreadful spot ...
>
> Even then the day need not have been absolutely lost if we brought up every reserve within reach, hurled them into the gap between the

> two divisions, and shut out the Sugarloaf ... but no reserves came, and a third most horrible tragedy was in store. Somebody again blundered, and a misunderstanding arose as to the objective.

MacLaurin's description of how the Australians unable to find the second or third line rushed on, '*and then most horrible of all, they ran into our barrage. The torrent of shells which had been protecting them suddenly turned into an engine of destruction against them ... in the morning photographs showed a line of our dead along the line of our barrage and beyond. It must be distinctly understood that our artillery were not to blame. The fault was in the impetuosity of the untrained infantry... in the midst of all this orgy of blunders and calamity, with the Sugarloaf pouring a storm of shot and shell along the lines... swarms of infantry still bravely dashed over the top, only to meet swarms of disheartened men dribbling back sick at heart, despairing, and only anxious to reach safety*'.

Dr MacLaurin concluded:

> I simply state the facts as I collected them from a great number of sources ... there can be no doubt that the effects on the morale of the 5th Division were bad ... had the Boche but known how weak we were there was nothing to prevent him from charging to the Channel. The casualties were said to be about 10,000 men of whom we heard rather authoritatively that 6850 were from 5th Division ... probably the dead exceeded 2000. It must be remembered that many of the casualties were exceedingly slight.

But the doctor who listed the blunders one by one, and told it 'as it was' reserved his one last arrow for the end of his revelation.

> To sum up, the infantry showed amazing courage, but their lack of training was their undoing ... The Australian Artillery did splendidly. The staff work all through could not be criticized, for it did not exist.

Not everybody was pleased to read what Dr MacLaurin had written. In the letters to the Editor three days later somebody who signed himself 'one of the Fifth Division' took MacLaurin to task for saying the troops were half-trained and undisciplined, and that they were moved off shortly after the 'Battle of Petillon' as he called it. However it was the longer letter from K N Wark of Crow's Nest, NSW, that decided to put things right. Wark was, of course, one of the three Wark brothers in 14th Bde and in the battle. Keith received the DCM, Blair was wounded (and later earned the VC with 32nd Bn), Alex seems to have got through unwounded. Wark gives no hint of any of this and begins:

> When those who took part in the battle ... read your issue of 19 July ... they will, I feel sure, regret that Dr MacLaurin did not leave the motive

THE ARROGANT VERSUS THE IGNORANT (contd)

it—when Legge did go forward on the 4/5 August the attack was successful.

Bearing in mind Haig's observations of 29 July and he not reaching a conclusion about Legge until 3 August, it is reasonable to suppose that he was, in his first entry, describing McCay as '*ignorant and conceited*'. Ignorant in an intellectual sense McCay never was, but conceited he certainly was. One searches all this for some overall logic. If Legge was no good, that is he made a mistake on 29 July, yet amended things to put them right a few days later, that certainly places him well ahead of a number of British Generals who never learned from their mistakes. Haking, as far as this study is concerned, being the classic example. For the record Haking was promoted a month after Fromelles, whereas Legge was returned to Australia with a CB, and badly treated for the rest of his life.

NO FEAR OF MCCAY

In private, Bean never gave any indication of admiration of, nor confidence in, McCay. Bean, on 28 June 1918 wrote to Brudenell White about the possibility of Monash becoming GOC, and White being passed over. The letter marked 'private' is of some 1500 words and is in effect an earnest essay about the future of Australia. Bean saw White as the Corps Leader, that is taking over from Birdwood and Monash as AIF Leader. Bean in later years admitted he was wrong about Monash, and that he was the right man to lead the Corps. In his letter Bean was careful to point out, '*There is no fear of McCay, nor of Legge—it is simply yourself and General Monash*'.

OFTEN PERPLEXED

Alexander Cooch, General Manager of the State Savings Bank of Victoria, published in 1934 a short history of the Bank, and remembered McCay thus:

It is related that his intellect was of such a phenomenal character that his teachers were often perplexed by his questions.

FROMELLES, 1916!
A GLORIOUS FAILURE
WHAT REALLY HAPPENED

Under those headings the Melbourne *Argus* on Saturday, 10 April, 1920, ran a 3,000 word article composed almost entirely of extracts from Ellis' *Story of the 5th Division*. It began with the two communiqués—first the German, then the British, and then a short introductory paragraph by the anonymous *Argus* writer.

In this form readers of the Argus received their first information of the great action by Australian Troops on the Western front, which has since come to be known as 'the attack of Armentières' or 'the fight at Fleurbaix', but was really 'the battle of Fromelles'. For a long time the secrecy of war kept a veil drawn over the details of this sad page in the history of the Australian Imperial Force, but closely censored letters from members of the 8th, 14th and 15th Infantry Brigades soon began to indicate that something more serious happened than was at first suggested. Since then more or less accurate accounts of the battle have been in circulation, but the most interesting features had necessarily to be withheld until after the armistice. The first consecutive record prepared from official documents and elaborated by commanding officers has been prepared by Captain A D Ellis MC, of the 29th Battalion and it is included in his 'Story of the Fifth Division'... even the most unmilitary reader will find much to stir him in this account of 'our most glorious failure'.

No other aspect of the book was mentioned in this 'review', nor any comment made.

> of this battle and its description to a more authoritative pen than that of a non-combatant, and moreover, one engaged many miles behind the lines, in consequence of which hearsay accounts only are quoted.

It might be justifiably said that the attack of MacLaurin's views were stupid, but what is interesting about Wark's letter is the parrot fashion recital of all the stock phrases. For instance '*the first intention was to induce to the Germans to divert some of their reinforcements*', '*this division was in perfect training ... and no finer disciplined force could be found in France*', etc.

From then on Wark had trouble with facts: that each brigade had a 1000 yard front, that the third line was '*some hundreds of yards to the rear, about 5 am on the 20th the left brigade received word to withdraw*', '*about 6 am the centre brigade received instructions to commence to withdraw*'. Then with this strange confession:

> It is not possible for one to criticize after actions such as this but whether the Higher Command only desired a demonstration and advertised the attack as such, or intended the attack which was eventually made, most of those who took part are not in the position to say, but it is apparent that something was wrong somewhere ...
>
> I would also like to correct a few other statements of contributors ... the attacking troops did not get cut off by our own barrage and thus become prisoners. The second German line of defence was dug into the forward slope of the ridge ... and was fully a mile or more from the front system. Thus it seems absurd that any troops would think of pushing on to it.

Wark, like the other correspondent, properly corrected MacLaurin on his statement about the withdrawal of the 5th Division and referred him, and the rest of the *Sydney Morning Herald* readers to the report by Capt. C E W Bean in London *Daily News* of 24 July 1916 '*which gives a good account of the much abused battle of Fromelles*'.

This little foray into Fromelles history doubtless fueled many discussions in smoke-filled rooms until April 1920 when A D Ellis published *The Story of the Fifth Australian Division —Being an Authoritative Account of the Division's Doings in Egypt, France and Belgium*, a very impressive book by any standard. This gave the first view of the great struggles of the Division, the first history of any part of the AIF, and settled the title for the event of 19/20 July 1916 once and for all as—'*The Battle of Fromelles*'. Admittedly Ellis by his own account was only interested in 'Official Sources' but he did include a few asides from other witnesses (see pages 262–63). To get access, his project had to be smiled upon by Hobbs and others, and was written very much within the restraints of Ellis' forthcoming legal career and ambitions. It is nonetheless, as far as Fromelles is concerned, incredibly important. When one considers that the very existence of the battle and the disaster it was, had had no press coverage before the *Sydney Morning Herald* articles one wonders the impact of Ellis' opening statements about the British and German communiqués and this searing paragraph:

> These remarks are made solely for the enlightenment of the reader, whose present knowledge may be presumed to be based chiefly on the official British communiqué ... nevertheless, the official distortion of the facts of the Battle of Fromelles has resulted in a general and profound misconception of its purposes and its gravity, and there are few incidents of the war which deserve a closer attention from the Australian public. For this reason the events leading up to the battle are here set out with some slight attention to detail.

Ellis weighed into that one source of information, the British and German communiqués, '*by no stretch of the imagination could the operations be described as "some important raids"*'. He however, like Bean, was unable to face the grim fact that the event was '*a ruse, a feint, or a pretence*'.Having personally seen the havoc of those few hours it would be inhuman to accept that view and remain sane. But grim as reality is, not all actions were great crusades of right against evil, individuals against hordes, heroes against cowards, many being just cynical arrangements to produce a reaction somewhere else ... and not always on another battlefield. Fromelles was such, and that it destroyed one way or another, 15,000 men was how it had to be, as they said then—'*c'est la guerre*'.

There is only a tinge of this reality through Ellis' description that permits him to make such observations as:

> In view of all these circumstances [the bringing together of troops and materiel] it is therefore almost certain that the enemy was well-aware of our offensive intentions. The haste of preparation necessitated by the urgent call for a diversion, thus lost the attacking side one of the chief elements of success, surprise effect. Whatever disadvantage was incurred thereby—and it was doubtless a grave disadvantage—the cause of it lay far beyond Divisional control, perhaps, indeed, beyond any human control.

And on the enemy:

> ... the German General Staff was far too astute to site its front line on the topmost crest of those ridges, for, had it done so, a slight enemy advance of a few hundred yards would have cost him his most commanding height with all its advantages of observation.

Later when Ellis came to dealing with Haking's changes of plan, or mind—depending on whether one regards him as a

19 RETURNED!

The extent of the ignorance in Australia about Fromelles is well defined by a news item in the *Argus*, 14 October, 1926:

MISSING AUSTRALIANS
Tragic Fromelles Raid
19 left out of 500

London Oct. 12

An inscription on a stone column in a war cemetery between Neuve Chapelle and Armentières modestly recounts that 481 unknown Australians are missing in that area. It is known as 'VC Corner'. It is proposed to erect the letters 'VC' at the respective ends, but during a recent visit the Commonwealth Attorney General (Mr Latham) pointed out that the tragic and most heroic and dangerous raid, in which 500 Australians went out on July 19, 1916, near Fromelles, minus identity discs and battalion colours, and all but 19 did not return, should be more fittingly emphasised. Major Phillips had undertaken to erect a commemorative tablet describing the epic so that one of the most famous incidents of the sector should not escape the notice of visitors to the battlefields of France.

A FEINT

Despite the fact that Fromelles is 40 miles (65 kms) from Pozières some never separated the two. Ernest Scott's *Australia during the War*, being Vol XI of the Official History slipped into the rut, even as late as 1936.

In less than seven weeks, at Pozières and Mouquet Farm, and in the feint at Fromelles in Flanders, they lost in killed and wounded 28,000 men. And later on in the same book '*In 1916, the first battle of the Somme and the feint at Fromelles, had cost the four Australian divisions over 28,000 casualties*'.

Thus Fromelles was not a battle of itself, but always a feint involved with the Somme.

AS WELL AS GENTLEMEN
One of the more outspoken correspondents who wrote to Bean on the subject of Fromelles was Major Robert Orlando Cowey of 55th Bn. Born in Melbourne, 15 July 1888, Cowey was at the Landing with 3rd Bn, and played a significant part in the first days. So much so that Bean in Volume 1 of his history put a footnote on page 518. *Several eye witnesses independently paid tribute to Cowey's work ...* Cowey was wounded on 28 April. Later in Egypt he transferred to 55th Bn becoming 2IC to Lieut Col McConaghy under whom he had served on Gallipoli.

I am enclosing an account of the Battle of Fromelles I put together at the request of Dr A D Ellis. Taking everything into consideration I thought and still think that it is inaccurate only in as much as it is too restrained, but Dr Ellis afterwards informed me that he would only use 'Official Records'. I do not care at present to add to what I have already set down in case I should again be disbelieved.

It will not be possible for me to give all the details as I know them on paper. You will have guessed before now that there were opportunists as well as gentlemen who made reports.

Cowey's letter like his report was bitter. He had praise for Gibbins, Wyllie and a few others, but not for Capt. Murray (see page 140). Cowey was clearly resentful of Murray, concluding his attack thus: *He has since been awarded the DSO and is presumably a respectable and prosperous citizen of the Commonwealth. Apart from the respectability I have none of the other luxuries.* Cowey then directed Bean to *Pte E Smith, my batman, a straight-forward fellow who found Capt. Gibbins commanding the left of the 14th Bde front ...* ***not*** *a certain officer whom I was astonished to hear claim the distinction later on.* Cowey concluded: *Please forgive me if I have appeared to be grumpy and brusque to you.*

There is no record of Bean's reply and the copy of Cowey's notes remain in the file. Cowey made a point of requesting that they were returned and were not copied. His letter was from Weardale, The Patch, Victoria, and dated 19 September 1926.

serious military planner, or a game player—Ellis put down the times, one by one, and then wrote: *'All this is recorded without comment'*. It was a splendid and measured comment of disgust. The detail given by Ellis would indicate he had access to 61st Division Reports which if Bean had he did not use. The reception of Ellis' book was very appreciative, *The Argus* noted '*readers received their first information ... of the battle of Fromelles*', see margin: *Fromelles 1916*. The fact that so many reviewers concentrated their attention on the Battle of Fromelles reveals the level of interest. In London it was the attempted truce that attracted attention. *The Daily Chronicle* (23 May 1920) gave under headings extending across the page, the story of Major Murdoch's informal truce and quoted the story to the extent of a column.

Ellis' treatment of McCay was gentle and polite. He stated that McCay left the Division due to '*continued ill health*', which was the official story elsewhere as against the popular belief he was relieved of his command. Anyway how come that McCay's health was good enough to see him through three English winters? Keith Murdoch wrote of his work in 1917: '*The training camps were commanded by Major-General Sir James McCay whose career included many remarkable successes. He had been a successful lawyer, politician, Minister for Defence, and banker before the war called him to field command in the Army.*' Murdoch was no admirer of McCay and in 1918 fought vigorously and successfully to keep McCay from getting command of the AIF.

Although it was never claimed to be a unit history, W H Downing's *To the Last Ridge*, published in 1920 was very much the story of the 57th Bn, and probably the master work of Australian World War One literature. Downing's chapter is headed '*Fleurbaix, otherwise known as Fromelles, Laventie and Armentières*, and like the rest of the book it was checked out by H E Elliott, who wrote in his introduction '*the accounts of Fleurbaix, the winter on the Somme, Polygon Wood ... and the Villers-Bretonneux night attack are, in my opinion, by far the truest and best I have read*'. Downing wrote no more than Knyvett, but being in reserve saw more, and writing after it was well and truly over, understood more. His grasp of all the tensions is perfectly shown in this piece:

> At a quarter to two they moved off. Shelling commenced. These were days of long and casual bombardments. Labourers were hoeing the mangold fields. Stooping men and women watched the Australians pass without ceasing their work. It may have been courage, or stolidity, or the numbness of the peasant bound to the soil, or else necessity, that

held the sad tenacious people here in such an hour of portent. Their old faces were inscrutable. They tilled the fields on the edge of the flames, under the arching trajectory of shells.

Bees hummed in the clear drowsy sunshine. There was little smoke about the cottages, where the creepers were green. The road curved between grass which was like two green waves poised on either side..

The battalions came to the four cross roads where there were trenches in the corn, by a crucifix of wood in a damaged brick shrine. There was much gun fire. They waited.

Late in the afternoon they were ordered forward. From his crucifix the Man of Sorrows watched their going. One wondered if this mild look was bent especially on those marked for death that day.

Downing's description of the battle is both compassionate and real, nothing is lost in the telling for those who were there, and for those who were not. This last piece about his Fromelles:

> The remnants of the 57th and 58th held the front line system for a further fifty days, making fifty nine in all, without relief. And the sandbags were splashed with red, and red were the firesteps, the duckboards, the bays. And the stench of stagnant pools of blood of heroes is in our nostrils even now.

But such writing did not touch one reviewer whose verdict was '*this lurid language is not flung on the pages... in order that it may sound alarm: hysteria is not portrayed that we may better love sanity and self-control... Mr Downing's nerves are evidently still jangling with his experiences... the book is badly produced and the binder seems to have run short of gum*'. But others thought much more of it, and it won the University of Melbourne's Dublin Prize in 1921.,

To the Last Ridge was reissued in 1998 and no reviewer was concerned with the binding, only with the power and presence of Downing's prose after nearly eighty years, and very many picked out passages about Fromelles.

The fourth anniversary of Fromelles was marked in the *Sydney Morning Herald* by a short piece of standard material. The next day it reported on what happened instead of a second Peace Parade: '*last night a Rally at the Town Hall for the formation of the King and Empire Alliance*'. The meeting was attended by numerous service, civic and business leaders and was part entertainment. The US Consul was in attendance so the 'Star Spangled Banner' was sung, and Major General Sir Charles Rosenthal sang 'The Death of Nelson'. All a happy echo of the Peace Ball twelve months earlier and no mention of Fromelles. But as then, once again, in Melbourne, it was very different.

On Tuesday 6 July *The Age* had carried a single notice in its Country Notes:

AT THE RISK OF DIGRESSION

In terms of research and photo-graphic content the monumental The Times *History of the War* (Twenty Volumes) is impressive, readable and valuable: it weighs 90 lbs (40.8 kgs).

It dealt with the attack south of Armentières in these words, making it much more an Australian event than the official communiqué.

The Battle of the Somme, it must always be remembered, was but part of the British operations against the Germans in France and Belgium. To remind the reader that the long line of trenches and redoubts from the east of Albert to the north of Ypres was constantly agitated by bombardments and local attack let us, at the risk of digression, relate an incident which happened south of Armentières on the 19th. At this point an Australian division, exposed to a shell fire heavier than any they had ever experienced in the Gallipoli Peninsula, followed up a heavy bombardment of the German position, which, however, had not succeeded in destroying or burying all the defenders' machine guns, by a determined attack, aided by a British division on their left. They carried the front line trenches, but were held up by those in the rear. Farther south—in the centre—the whole fortified area was stormed, and the Australians emerged into more or less open country. On the right their comrades had to cross a wide space between the front and rear lines of the system. The Germans here held a very strongly fortified salient. At places the Australians scrambled into the enemy's works, but the Germans by diverting streams of water into the captured spots made the position difficult to hold. After enduring a tremendous bombardment for 11 hours the order was given to retire. The British Engineers had constructed communication trenches along which this movement could be carried out. 200 prisoners and some machine-guns were captured, but our losses had been severe.

—*The Times History of the War*, Volume X page 112.

Chaplain JOHN J KENNEDY
Born 28 October 1881 in Ireland, John Joseph Kennedy, after education with the Christian Brothers at Dingle, County Kerry, entered a seminary and was ordained 18 June 1905. He volunteered to join a mission to Australia and became assistant priest at Wangaratta, Victoria. In Dec 1915 he enlisted as a chaplain and early in 1916 in Egypt was posted to 14th Bde, and then attached to 53rd Bn. He remained with them until the end of 1917. When his great friend Lieut Col Croshaw was killed in September, one feels not just Kennedy's health broke, but his heart also. He went to Ireland for a rest, and wrote *The Whale Oil Guards* which was published in Dublin in 1919 (see pages 363–64).

Back in Australia in late 1918 he was priest in Bendigo for two years before becoming parish priest at Myrtleford for four years. In 1920 as detailed in the text, Kennedy became the subject of great hostility, but two of his Whale Oil Guards came to his defence in letters to the press on 8 and 9 July:

I feel it necessary to say that Father Kennedy earned his DSO at the tragic Fleurbaix 'stunt' in 1916 when he practically held the front line on his own, did nearly 90 hours stretcher bearing and organizing. While still suffering from the strain of that he insisted on returning to the 53rd Bn just before the Polygon Wood 'Stunt' in 1917, and though placed under open arrest by the CO, an old Imperial Officer and his greatest friend, who thought he had done enough already, was at the jump off line ahead of the troops, and again did great work that day.

The other Whale Oil Guard simply called Kennedy '*one of the finest soldiers in that Force*'.

He returned to Ireland in 1925, later joining the American Mission, Savannah, Georgia, United States around 1926. He remained there until his death on 18 February 1957.

> Bendigo. The Princess Theatre was crowded on Saturday afternoon when the war drama 'Advance Australia' of which Chaplain Father J J Kennedy DSO is the author, was produced by young amateur performers in aid of the fund for the Bendigo Convent. About £115 was taken at the doors.

Kennedy was well known in Bendigo. He had published three novels before the war, was a good singer and organiser of concerts, and now with his war record, his sermons and lectures on the war, militarism and Ireland were well reported. Through the next two weeks city and country newspapers reported at extraordinary length, regularly 2000 words, on protest meetings about the play. Editorials as long as 1500 words condemned the author and the play. Everybody had an opinion including the Prime Minister and Senator Elliott, but like most, if not all the main critics, they had not seen it. By the nature of the one-off performance on a Saturday afternoon the only one of those public critics who had been to the play was the reporter from the *Bendigo Advertiser.*

The play concerned two brothers and a servant from the mother's home, probably in Bendigo, who went off to the war, survived Gallipoli and appear on stage together near a trench at Fromelles. The younger brother is killed, the older brother, a doctor, laments about the loss of the battle and afterwards comes to see it as due to the cowardice and inefficiency of the English Tommies. He then railed against the English class system, their patronising attitudes and much else. As might be imagined, such sentiments expoused by an Irish Catholic priest, when Ireland was fighting for Home Rule, greatly excited Empire Loyalists, Freemasons, Protestant Federationists and many others for reasons that had nothing to do with Fromelles. Due to Kennedy's bitterness about the war and some obvious historical mistakes, the play and Kennedy were publicly destroyed by innuendo and powerful political forces. Thus any debate about Fromelles, a more factually accurate play might have provoked, did not materialise. Instead the episode degenerated into something else (see '*Advance Australia*'—*The Disloyal Play*, pages 375–81) from which the only person to emerge with any credit was 'Pompey' Elliott, with Father Kennedy DSO yet another casualty of Fromelles.

[continued page 382]

'Advance Australia'—The Disloyal Play

The staging of a play written by one of the acknowledged heroes of the Battle of Fromelles two weeks before the fourth anniversary, could not have been accidental. Had the play got the reception the author hoped for, it would have run on beyond the first and only performance on the afternoon of Saturday, 3 July 1920, in the Princess Theatre, Bendigo. Thus it would have been closely associated with the battle because one of the main scenes was '*near the trenches in the battle of Fromelles*'.

One trouble with this part of the inquiry is that no text of the play seems to have survived. Kennedy lent a copy to the *Bendigo Advertiser* reporter so he could quote correctly from it, so our only source of what was said on stage is from that newspaper. Kennedy later said that the reporter had only quoted one element of the play, the parts critical of English soldiers and life. But he never offered nor quoted other parts to contradict this, even though his detractors called upon him to do so. However the Editorial in that paper two days after the review was clearly written to a pro-English agenda. Judgements on what the play was about made in other papers always related back to the *Bendigo Advertiser*. And as the trouble was more to do with what people thought (or had been told) the play said, what it was actually about was hardly an issue in the end.

Some thirty men from Bendigo and district died at Fromelles, a figure from which one could safely deduce some sixty were wounded in the battle, meaning that the best part of a hundred families would have had real knowledge of Fromelles. Their near total silence in so far as the *Bendigo Advertiser*'s columns are concerned is difficult to explain, as is the lack of any reference to the part Bendigo men played.

The play concerned an Australian woman, Mrs Fitzgerald, probably from Bendigo, widowed by the Boer War and facing the prospect of her two sons going off to the European War. The elder son was a doctor and the younger a university student. They enlisted, as did the older boy's fiancée, who was a nurse. The older son and the widow believed that the family had given enough and were unhappy about '*the rumpus in Europe! We are down here at the other end of the earth working out our own destiny.*

Father J J Kennedy DSO 1916
COURTESY MDHCC

Already our wonderful country is a nation not a mere colony. We have developed as a distinct race with our own peculiar characteristics, our own aspirations, our own ideas of liberty'.

The two brothers and a servant from the mother's house sail to Egypt, survive Gallipoli, and come together on stage again in a scene '*near the trenches in the battle of Fromelles. The doctor is dressing the wounded when a stretcher bearer brings the order to retire, as the Australian battalions have been all but annihilated because the English have failed them*'. On receipt of the order the doctor, Jack Fitzgerald, exclaims (according to the *Bendigo Advertiser*):

'*Oh hell! What a sacrifice for nothing. For myself I care not, but Australia! May God punish the cowards whose politicians summoned us from over the seas to aid them in the alleged crusade for the rights of small nations. How we have been gulled! Australia's bravest and best, abused and annihilated in order to save the dastards of the new English army who let us down every time. Curse them: curse them and the opportunists in our own land who batten on the blood of the heroes: who deceive our electors with their camouflage of patriotism, and endeavour to fetter our free Australia with the shackles of conscription. We, over here, must fight on until peace comes, or we are wiped out. Should I return to my sunny land I shall use my best endeavours to pull down jingoism and imperialism. My watchword shall be, Australia. Advance Australia.*'

Then, during the retreat, Captain Maurice Fitzgerald, the younger brother, is mortally wounded and Bill, the former servant, goes to his aid, '*I promised his lady mother I would bring him back. Damn them! Damn them! Those cold footed pommies who flunked it and let us Australians fight a whole German army*'.

In a mess room of a French billet Jack Fitzgerald and Captain Lane meet two English officers (Captain Courtney and another). The English officer observes, '*You Australians are lucky dogs. You seem to get more decorations than our fellows. You certainly get more leave. Fitzgerald, you and Lane will have a ripping time in dear old London. With your recently acquired DSOs and your good looks the girls will go mad about you*'.

Fitzgerald answered: '... *We have no love for London. We shall spend our furlough in Scotland and in Ireland. Fleurbaix burns in our minds. We have lost our brothers and comrades. They would be alive today and Fromelles would be ours were it not for the bungling and cowardice of your Tommies ... you know the story of Fromelles, and the fifth division in one night we lost 7000 men. Your division abandoned us ... and this is the account in the Daily Mail "Australian troops entered the enemy's trenches near Fromelles. There were slight casualties. Valuable information was brought back. A small number of prisoners." Ah, we were all fools: fools to be in this thing at all. I was an imperialist when I left Australia, but if spared I will go back an Australian.'*

Captain Courtney replied: '*To my shame I must admit the justice of your statements. England is degenerate and inefficient. Her lands are enclosed park lands around the castles of her Lords and capitalists. Her yeomanry is gone. In her cities her working men and women are badly housed and ill fed. The physique of her sons and daughters has been crippled, likewise their morals and mentality. Blundering politicians interfere with professional soldiers in the prosecution of the war. America may come to our rescue. If not, we are doomed.*'

These insults about English physique, mental capacity and allegations of effeminate and degenerate behaviour in the play were taken very personally because they were seen as direct comments on the relatives still living in England of the English-born people of Bendigo. Kennedy had not thought about that in the play; or later in his defence. He saw himself as an Australian speaking to Australians about the English. But the lines were forever attached to the Irish priest who wrote them, not to the Australian doctor who spoke them.

The last scene is back home, the mother mourning her lost son and Mona, the nurse, and son, Jack, marry, and Bill marries the maid. Mrs Fitzgerald's last line seems to have been '*In future, we refuse to be called British or Colonials. We are Australians*'.

The selection of the quotes may well have reflected the reporter's views and were in no way used derisively. He was most impressed, the heading was *Advance Australia. A Remarkable Play. Imperialism denounced*, and he had this to say about the production:

'*The standard of acting was highly creditable. There was not a single hitch in the performance, a fact which speaks volumes for a company of amateurs. The staging left nothing to be desired, while the realism with which the battlefield scenes were presented was an outstanding feature of the production.* [He then listed the full cast.] *Several members of the company possessed marked vocal ability, and the choruses as well as the solo items, which interspersed the acting were most enjoyable. Probably the most noteworthy of these was the song, "Advance Australia" which was written by Father Kennedy and set to music and sung by Miss V O'Donnell.* [He then listed other songs and performers.] *The humour was bright and clever. Selections were splendidly rendered by the Marist Bros Band. The management announced its intention of repeating the drama at a future day.*'

In the interval Father Kennedy spoke to the audience:

'*I take this opportunity of thanking you for your very good attendance. I hope that the drama will be a success, not only from a monetary point of view* [proceeds were in aid of a convent] *... for that seems assured, but also from an artistic point of view. I hope it will be an incentive to make us more thoroughly Australian.* [He then went on to detail how several of the cast had withdrawn a few days earlier and had to be replaced.]

I did not realise the drama had created such interest till a few of the performers resigned. Not only was there aroused a friendly interest, but also a sinister interest. A section of the community for some purpose which I cannot understand, deemed it their business to endeavour to frustrate the success of this affair. We have not done anything to antagonise them, but we can afford to despise them and ignore them. This section of the community used adverse influence, and pressed the screw on some of our erstwhile performers ... their abstention ... is not a loss ... they scarcely made themselves at home with us in our rehearsals. For success camaraderie is required. I desire to thank not only our own people for coming here this afternoon, but also the large number of those not belonging to our faith whose presence proves their friendship.'

This '*fair dealing*' with the whole event had an interesting sequel. Kennedy, when defending himself at the Returned Soldiers' Association meeting the following Thursday said, '*a reporter had come to him and congratulated him on the Australian sentiment*'. When the *Bendigo Advertiser* printed this the Editor added in—'*Our Reporter gives the lie direct to this assertion*'. But more of that in its place.

By the afternoon of the next day the storm broke. At the town hall the Masonic Lodges had a meeting and the Worshipful Master said:

'*I have heard today of a play which was staged in Bendigo yesterday and which will be looked on with shame by every loyal Britisher in Bendigo!*'

Now the play earned a new title—*The Disloyal Play*.

The *Bendigo Advertiser* on Tuesday 6 July reported '*strong indignation was expressed at a large meeting of citizens at the Beehive Exchange last night in regard to the play "Advance Australia" ... the drama as stated in yesterday's Advertiser was intensely Australian, but also provided a spirit of anti-Imperialism and was the chief topic of discussion in the city yesterday.*' The meeting was convened by A L Bolton, president of the Bendigo branch of the National Federation, and decided '*something should be done in the nature of swift retribution against the offence committed against all loyal Australians ... to prevent a repetition of the offence*'. This report gave the *Advertiser* an opportunity to re-run all the anti-English pieces quoted on Monday and to print other comments from the meeting, and run some letters, and to drop in such phrases as '*the play was written with the object of causing strife*'.

The Age, however, had another view, '*the production ... was received with enthusiasm by a packed house, and it was remarked that amongst those who most enthusiastically called for the author ... were Protestant. There was no demonstration by the audience ... People who were at the performance say that in parts it was of high standard as far as Imperial matters were affected. Portions of the play that might provide cause of complaint had been published in a section of the press, but other positions, which stood out for the Empire, these, members of the audience said, had been passed over.*'

The 1,200 word editorial in the *Bendigo Advertiser* on Wednesday, 7 July, began '*Anti-British Propaganda. Righteous indignation and anger has been aroused throughout the city and district by a theatrical production bearing the title "Advance Australia" ... from the beginning to the end the play —if it could be called a play—was a caustic amateurish caricature of English national life and an odious comparison of Australia with the Motherland ... we do not attempt to read into the manuscript ... anything in the nature of sectarianism and none who witnessed the production could possibly connect it with a desire to create religious ill feeling. In common honesty we must admit that the religious element was totally foreign to the production, and for that reason, it should be entirely kept out of the sequel and future discussions.*'

The Editor now having drawn the reader's attention to the fact that religion did not enter into it, spent the next 1,000 words reminding the readers '*Certainly the author is a priest in the Roman Catholic Church, the cast was composed practically entirely of Roman Catholics and it was produced in aid of a Roman Catholic institution, but even those phrases do not justify the production which was totally non-sectarian in character being made the basis of religious bitterness*'. And further on: '*Father Kennedy's production has incurred the withering scorn and contempt of a large section of the community, including many of his own flock, who are proud of their English parentage and nationality*'. The Editor concluded by hoping that '*official opinion will be responsible for the play being added to the index expurgations in Australia*'. That is put on the banned list in present day terms.

That tirade brought out a host of Letters to the Editor writers, most of whom hid behind anonymous titles like 'Uncle of fallen Soldier', 'Loyalist', 'A disgusted R Catholic', 'One of the 57th', 'Digger', 'Another Australian', 'Australian of British Descent', 'British Australian', and in Kennedy's favour two who signed 'Whale Oil Guard'.

The degree of ignorance, if that is what it was, was well illustrated by men who claimed to have been in the battle. Virtually everyone got the basics of the battle wrong. One early correspondent, who signed himself 'AIF' wrote: '*I was in the Fifth Division, which took part ... I beg to inform Father Kennedy that the only English troops that took part in that battle was one battalion of the King's Royal Rifles, who were not needed on account of the Australians being able to reach the enemy's third lines ... The British troops on our right did not take any part in the Fromelles stunt, therefore I cannot see how the British Tommies let us down ...*'

Editorials now appeared in the Melbourne papers and appeals were made to the Prime Minister, Billy Hughes, to censure Kennedy and attend a public meeting to declare himself on the issue. Meetings had been proposed by Empire Loyalists, Freemasons, Protestant Federationalists, Orange Order and the Returned Soldiers' Association.

The first to happen was that of the RSA at the Bendigo Town Hall on Thursday evening. It somewhat backfired partly because Kennedy was a member and he chose to attend what was billed 'The Indignation Meeting'. A number of members drew the convenor's attention to the fact that the RSA Constitution prohibiting interference in sectarian and political affairs. Another expressed the view that a representative should be sent '*to that man Kennedy*' to protest about his disloyal statements. He was told that Kennedy was a member of the branch and the member '*should have the courtesy to respect the cloth he wore*'. Another regretted the statements Kennedy made about the Tommies at Fromelles—he had been there. To which another member interjected '*This is not a branch of the Imperial League*'. Another officer who the *Age* identified as Major Roberts, but the *Bendigo Advertiser* left nameless, and who had served with Kennedy, told the meeting:

'*Father Kennedy had certainly won the DSO and the whole of his battalion felt he should have got the VC*' and '*that Father Kennedy was the only padre that held a church parade combining both Protestants and Roman Catholics.*' To which Kennedy interjected: '*At the request of the commanding officer of the battalion*'. Kennedy's own description of this was: '*... after I had celebrated Mass for the soldiers who worship at my shrine, I recited prayers common to the Christianity of all of us, and delivered a religious discourse upholding our fidelity to the God we all adored. After each such parade officers and men of 53rd Bn feelingly congratulated me on the good I have done and the healthy impression I had made.*'

Kennedy was finally allowed to defend himself saying that a very unfair procedure had been adopted to belittle him. He had had an honourable career as an Australian soldier and he thought he could express his opinion about Australia generally and Australians in particular. When he asked his Bishop if he could enlist he was refused on the score of ill health. Finally he managed to get to the front. As an officer and chaplain of the AIF he never had the slightest charge made against him of anti-imperialism or bigotry of any sort. In order to prove the esteem in which he was held he had received letters from Hobbs and other officers, when, owing to ill health he had to sever connection with the battalion. When writing the play he was not activated by any bitterness to the British Empire, but as a democrat he was not going to back down. He distrusted that Imperialism of Germany and Britain that plunged us into war in which tens of thousands of the youth of the nations of the Empire are ruthlessly sacrificed.

A member interjected. '*Is this in order?*'

Kennedy went on. '*So that you can discuss it properly you should have an explanation, otherwise you will be in the dark.*' [Hear, Hear.] Proceeding, Father Kennedy said '*he had been back twelve months and at lectures had expressed opinions as strong as those expressed in the play. What had the Press been doing that time? One of the members of the Press was a member of a certain organisation*'.

A member again rose to a point of order.

Kennedy continued on that the branch could not act against him without giving him a hearing. Then this: '*with regard to the play, the Princess Theatre was packed and there were any amount of people who could have expressed disapproval of the play. On the contrary there were none, but there was loud and occasional applause. The disapproval came soon afterwards. It was hatched and fostered by a certain section for purposes of its own. A reporter had come to him and congratulated him on the Australian sentiment.*'

It was here in the printing of the description of the meeting that the Editor inserted '*Our reporter gives the lie direct to this assertion*'.

Kennedy then loaned the reporter the manuscript, and '*The Press acted most dishonourably, for it culled out particular parts of the drama that would damage him. Parts were published to make him notorious. He did not apologise for preaching anti-Imperialism. They should not have their opinions manufactured by sectarian flag flappers*'.

Kennedy then tried to turn to the battle, '*he had the history of the war by Capt. Ellis, which stated that the 61st Division failed to gain their objective, and that the Australians suffered the casualties as he stated. The opinion had been expressed by privates and officers that if the Australians had not been let down they would not have had to pay such a tremendous toll. His opinions would never yield to the contrary.*'

Later, Kennedy defending himself, wrote: '*... I have heard officers discuss the cowardice and inefficiency of the English troops associated with us in the affair ... whether their failure was due to cowardice or to inefficiency, or to both, doesn't matter much to Australia*' It was an extraordinarily shallow remark for an intelligent, sensitive man to make. One can only assume that by then the pressure was getting at him.

'*On Anzac Day 1917 he had the honour to be elected as one of the orators at the Westminster Cathedral. Many distinguished people were present including some of our commanders from Horseferry Road. At a subsequent reception everyone had shook hands and congratulated him on the sentiments expressed and had told him it was a pity that there were not other preachers and speakers who would state that we were becoming degenerate and going down hill.*'

The upshot of the RSA meeting was to send a representative, Chaplain Captain S E Dorman, to the next Indignation Meeting the following evening. And this is the exact text of the *Bendigo Advertiser* news item for that meeting:

'*Loyal citizens are reminded of the monster patriotic meeting to be held at the Town Hall tonight at nine o'clock to express indignation at the utterances of the play "Advance Australia" staged in Bendigo last Saturday. The meeting will be addressed by Brigadier General Elliott and other speakers.*'

The huge write up of the meeting in Saturday's *Bendigo Advertiser* left no doubt where the Editor stood. Under the heading: '*Empire Loyalty. Denunciation of Play. Prime Minister's Criticism. The Road to Destruction*', it began:

'*Remarkable displays of loyalty were witnessed at a meeting of citizens in the Town Hall last night, called for the purpose of expressing detestation and abhorrence of the sentiments contained in the play "Advance Australia" produced at the Royal Princess Theatre on Saturday last in aid of the Catholic Convent Carnival, and to take steps to prevent a reproduction of the drama.*'

The fact that the meeting was chaired by the President of the Bendigo branch of the National Federation must have had something to do with something, especially as the real name of the organisation was the National Protestant Federation. As the Prime Minister, Billy Hughes, was due in Bendigo about this time they had hoped to have him on the stage. But he, and the mayor of Bendigo, conveniently had '*previous engagements*'. Hughes was campaigning in Ballarat for a crucial by-election and sent a message.

All the themes of the previous meetings were raised again and worked over, firstly by the Chairman, then Dorman, and then by Mr R Hyett, president of the Fathers' Association, '*who had three sons on active service*'. It was then the turn of Brigadier General (Senator) Elliott. He, '*with the aid of a diagram, minutely explained the movements of the opposing armies in regard to the battle of Fromelles, referred to in the play. While Elliott was speaking a youth at the back of the hall called for cheers for Father Kennedy, which were given by a section of the audience.*' Continuing, General Elliott emphasised '*that the attack was never intended to succeed. The supposed losses of the Australians, according to Father Kennedy were 7,000, whereas actual losses were 178 officers and 5,335 other ranks. The casualties were bad, but had been exaggerated by 50 per cent. It had been necessary on occasions to sacrifice the best of men so that the ultimate victory would be gained.*'

Quite why Kennedy got this wrong figure is a mystery. As he had Ellis to refer to, there is no doubt about the actual figures as quoted by Elliott. One explanation could be that Kennedy added the British casualties to the Australians which would produce a figure of 7000.

Another could be that as Ellis' figures covered noon 19 July to noon 20 July, Kennedy with his personal knowledge of later deaths added another 1500 to cover them. However in his later letter to the Catholic weekly newspaper *The Advocate* he conceded to Elliott: this was not noted in the *Bendigo Advertiser*. A few who wrote to the Editor picked up the other comments from Elliott as important: particularly '*that the attack was never intended to succeed.*' Curiously nobody in authority took up this very important remark or idea. That is it had nothing to do with the British or Australian commanders, but was all about the grim reality of tactical sacrifice.

The Advertiser report continued: '*The address of Brigadier General Elliott was keenly followed notably when he was dealing with the movements of troops. In conclusion, he remarked that he would be pleased to answer questions.*

Chaplain Captain Dorman asked whether the Australians after they had gained their objective, were compelled to retreat owing to the cowardice and inefficiency of the Tommies?'

Brigadier Elliott replied, amid cheers, '*that there had been no cowardice on the part of the Tommies. The Tommies had done their utmost.*'

Proceeding, the General said '*that he would do the author the justice of stating he had not seen the play. It was easy to take out extracts from the Bible which would have a different meaning to the full context. It was stated in the play that the Australians were fed up with English officers. Here and there they did get objectionable English officers and also some objectionable Australian officers. But they must not proceed to brand the whole of the British Army and the British nation, by isolated instances. And the same had applied to home hospitality where some behaved well and others badly.*'

When Elliott had finished, the Chairman read a message from the Prime Minister Billy Hughes: '*... I wish to assure you of my full accord with the objects of the meeting. The point to be stressed is that all this kind of talk which pervades the play, studied depreciation of Britain is Sinn Fein propaganda thinly disguised. The pretended aim is "Advance Australia", but the road along which Australia is invited to advance is the road to destruction. Australia's advancement, her independence, nay, her very existence, depends on her remaining an integral part of the British Empire ... It is only because Australia shares with the Mother Country and the other Dominions the vast burden of defence, five millions of people have been able and will be able to hold a continent that is coveted by countless millions. If therefore the author of this play is a true Australian and not a Sinn Feiner he is covertly seeking to disrupt the union which is the maintenance of that union. No man can be a true Australian who does not believe with heart and soul in the Empire, of which Australia is part.* (prolonged cheering) *The author adds to his offence by an attempt to make bad blood between the Australian soldier and his gallant comrade in arms—the English soldier ... the anti-English insinuations and suggestions of the play-writer are only another proof of the fact that his real object is to plunge a dagger into the heart of England ... the words "Advance Australia" on the lips of these people are a Judas' kiss, a betrayal of Australia, for the purpose of a bitter hatred of the Empire of which Australia is and will remain an integral part. All true Australians will beware of those who disguise under the pretense of patriotism, a seditious design, whose accomplishment would be as disastrous to Australia as defeat in war.* (cheering)'

Two motions were put to the meeting. The first to express '*detestation and abhorrence of the disloyal sentiments in the play*'. Only four dissented. The second motion was to urge the authorities '*to take such steps as necessary to prevent*' another performance of the play and '*suggests the urgent need of a more rigid censorship of plays*'. The *Bendigo Advertiser* concluded its report thus. '*The motion was carried, two women dissenting. The meeting terminated with the singing of the National Anthem and 'Rule Britannia.*'

One has the feeling that the meeting was covered by the Editor himself, whereas the reporter remained outside the Town Hall to cover the '*Counter Demonstration. Irish Element Predominates*'. It was an important report because in a quarter of the words about the meeting it told a lot about the real feeling in Bendigo.

'*By 9.15 ... the hall had been closed, the crowds that gathered around the entrances numbered some hundreds. They were a good humoured crowd and beyond a little playful barracking ... nothing of any consequence occurred ... a small group of youths and women commenced to sing "God Save Ireland". Then from all quarters streams of people flocked to the scene of the singing and the refrain was taken up with vigor ... The police closed in ... cheers for Dr Mannix, Rev. Father Kennedy, Ireland and Home Rule were given ... this was followed by further Irish songs and vociferous cheering. Hoots for Mr Hughes and Mr Bolton* (Chairman of meeting) ... *and again the singing commenced ... the police, who acted with tact and discretion ... kept the crowd well in hand.*' Later, when the speakers were leaving, '*as Mr Bolton appeared the crowd gave vent to vigorous hooting. A number of policemen (nine ... in shining helmets) surrounded Mr Bolton and as they escorted him to the Shamrock Hotel a crowd numbering some hundreds followed on behind hooting and singing Irish songs. Brigadier General Elliott walked quietly along the footpath to the hotel, and was in no way molested ...*' and then this last sentence: '*No harm was done, nobody felt aggrieved and the only tangible result will be sore throats amongst those who contributed most to the uproar.*'

After two weeks of this hammering, on the night of 19 July 1920, the fourth anniversary of

Fromelles, a Public Meeting was held in the Bendigo Town Hall, '*to express sympathy with the Rev. J J Kennedy, author of the play, "Advance Australia" ... the hall was crowded long before the time fixed for the meeting.*' This masterpiece of timing escaped the reporter from *The Argus*, and all the others, but he did detail much of what Kennedy had to say:

'*The Rev. Father Kennedy, who was received with prolonged cheering, said that he was pleased to be afforded an opportunity to vindicate his name ... Speaking of the aftermath of the play ... Kennedy said that the blast had been so furious that "Mother Argus" had come forth and protested in strong terms against it ... He resented the insinuations ... which had been made out of a spirit of sectarian hatred. The play was intended to make them glory in the fact that they were Australians and to foster a love for their country in their hearts. They, as Australians, had just as much right to criticize England and English soldiers as they had to criticize citizens and soldiers of Boston or New York. During his career as an army chaplain he had done his duty and those who had traduced him had been unable to besmirch his army service. The Union Jack obsessed the people at the head of Australia, and the Australian nation did not concern them. He had always had the greatest respect for Canadian and Scottish soldiers* (Applause). *The English soldiers with who he was associated even did what was expected of them. The military campaign at Fromelles was a hopeless bungle from start to finish. What right had the military command to sacrifice Australian divisions while the British divisions were resting behind the lines? The Rev. Father Kennedy went on to deal at length with the casualties of Fleurbaix and Fromelles and questioned the accuracy of Brigadier General Elliott's figures.*'

In doing so, according to *The Advocate*, Kennedy took a swipe at Elliott: ... '*If his military strategy was as poor as his arithmetic, I can quite understand why he did not return to Australia with a higher rank* (laughter) *I met him several times ... and from the men who served under him I heard nothing but the greatest praise ...* (applause) *as he understood Australians...*' Kennedy then expressed his sorrow that Elliott [a Nationalist senator] had represented Hughes. Elliott, who had been careful not to attack Kennedy personally, was much hurt by Kennedy's indiscretion.

The Argus continued: '*He had been associated with thousands of Australian soldiers abroad but he had heard very few express sentiments other than contempt and disgust for the British soldiers. He did not propose to give any further explanations regarding the cowardice and inefficiency of British Tommies. He repeated without the slightest apology to anybody, from Mr Hughes up, that the English soldiers were not up to their job. Australian soldiers had arrived in England on leave, footsore and dispirited, and they looked for hospitality they did not get. The Australians had been made to feel that they were of an inferior caste ... officers had been received into the houses of society but the men of the ranks faired badly ...*'

There is no point in discussing Kennedy's other theme—that Australians were treated with disdain or worse by the English populace, and thus fell pray to undesirable elements. Other comments he made, veiled in oblique references, obviously referred to the high rate of venereal disease contracted in England (much higher than that in France): it was hardly a subject to discuss in public!

While there is no evidence to confirm it, doubtless Kennedy had an Irish accent. Regardless of the fact that he moved about England in an Australian uniform and made much of being an Australian, it is fairly obvious that during the 'Troubles' in Ireland, an Irish-accented priest was hardly going to get a big welcome in London.

In conclusion, '*he would not retract one single word he had written in his play* (Cheers). *He had no intention of plunging a dagger into the heart of the Empire, as he had not the strength to do it* (Laughter) ... *He was intensely Australian and had no regrets for the happenings of the past few weeks, and was prepared if the occasion demanded, to again come on the platform and vindicate himself* (Applause).'

Two resolutions were passed: '*That the citizens of Bendigo in the public meeting affirm their entire sympathy with the Rev. J J Kennedy DSO in the cowardly attacks for political purposes made in this city against his loyalty*' (Carried with great enthusiasm). Then: '*That the sentiments expressed in the play "Advance Australia" are not disloyal and that the denunciation of Imperialism contained in the text is in accordance with Australian democracy*'. (Agreed to, with great cheering) After that, '*the singing of the National Anthem was dispensed with, and instead "Advance Australia" as composed by the author, was sung at the conclusion of the meeting*'.

When the main storm subsided, it was generally agreed the fuss had more to do with the Ballarat by-election than the prospect of an Irish takeover. It now appeared that those who promoted the indignation meetings were supporters of Nationalist Prime Minister Hughes. However, Ballarat electors rejected the Nationalist Candidate and returned D C McGrath, Labor, by a substantial majority.

As could be expected *The Advocate* covered the controversy very fully. In the 1 July issue it ran a short synopsis of the play, alerting readers to the performance and ticket prices: circle and front stalls, 3/-, stalls 2/-, gallery 1/-, which as the one performance of the play raised £115, probably means around 1000 people attended. In the 8 July issue '*an immense audience crowded the Princess Theatre ... to witness the first public performance of the play "Advance Australia". Every available seat was taken. Many patrons had ... to stand ... The play is a trenchant attack on Imperialism of any sort.'* Then they quoted *The Age* review. The issue of 15 July carried a long letter from Kennedy in his defence plus other items—around 4200 words in all. The 22 July issue had 8800 words about the final meeting under the headlines '*Triumph for Australian Sentiment. Magnificent Demonstration at Bendigo. Attacks on Father Kenendy resented. Overflow gathering of 5000.*' This last article was mostly direct reporting of what Kennedy and others said, and had almost no editorial comment. Then over the next weeks news was given of Kennedy's activities. He refused to accept the surplus monies from the sympathy meeting, and the Bendigo Committee decided to print in booklet form 2000 copies of the speeches delivered at that meeting.

Not even in the columns of *The Advocate* had anyone paused to consider Kennedy, the man, who had defied his bishop to join the AIF, gone through Fromelles, earned a DSO for his work, lost his best friend and half the men whose confessions he had heard, and with whom he had celebrated Communion in those terrible years. Irish or not, Kennedy was no different to so many who just expected much better of England and when it failed were terribly disillusioned, which was unfair rather than seditious. But some of the populace saw it as that, one suggesting that Kennedy's DSO stood for 'Dastardly Seditious Order'.

The end of the storm came when a letter Kennedy wrote to *The Argus* on August 18, was published on the 20th:

In 'The Argus' today reference is made to a letter received by the Rev. S E Dorman from Mr W A Callaway, Under-Secretary. I received a letter from the Under-Secretary demanding a copy of my play "Advance Australia". He wrote under instructions from the Chief Secretary. Being unaware of any authority he possessed to make such a demand I ignored the letter. Later two detectives called on his behalf. I assured them that I had no intention of forwarding a copy of "Advance Australia" to the Chief Secretary, nor do I intend to produce the play again. I am more than satisfied.

J J Kennedy,
St Kilian's, Bendigo,
Aug 18

An echo of this event came in May 1921 when, as the result of a debate in Parliament, there was a sharp exchange of correspondence in *The Age*. D C McGrath who had won the Ballarat seat attacked the credibility of Elliott in regard to whether or not British troops ran away, Elliott having quoted an example of when they did. McGrath reminded him of his attack on this same theme in connection with Kennedy's play. Elliott's two letters, 14 and 22 May, were clear and firm, on the subject of Fromelles and after outlining a little about the losses of 60th Bn, he wrote: '*the play was utterly false in its suggestion that the British ran away, or in any manner let us down in a discreditable manner. Moreover as this was the first action in which British troops had cooperated with Australian troops, the exclamation of the dying soldier could not ... have been uttered. For those reasons I protested against the play as a malicious endeavour to stir up bitter feeling between the peoples.*' In his second letter Elliott further cleared the air, '*At the Battle of Fleurbaix certain well-known British units were engaged with us and there was only a very limited number of them, so there is no room for mistake as to who was meant. Therefore utterances such as are put in the mouth of a dying Australian officer, accusing the British Tommies ... of the grossest and most treacherous cowardice, might well cause the deepest pain and indignation to the survivors of the heroic regiments who fought there, and the relatives of those whose bones lie upon that sodden field. This play was written by a clergyman who was present, at any rate, in the vicinity of the battle ... who therefore must have known of the falsehood of the utterance ...*'

Elliott concluded: '*It is well known to anyone who has served in the field that courage is contagious, but so also is panic, and a man may, by the association of those around him, be moved to fear equally as to the most gallant behaviour.*'

The headstone on the grave of Father J J Kennedy DSO at Westover Memorial Park, Augusta, Georgia, USA. PHOTOGRAPH OWEN MAGEE

In April 1921 there was a debate on the Defense Bill which '*provides, among other things, for the incorporation in the Defence Act of the British Army Act*'. This caused Senator H E Elliott, as he now was, to speak on an issue dearest to his heart, but it was a bitter heart. It must have been this and then a letter in *The Age* about the same issue that caused Elliott to write some 4000 words which *The Age* published on 28 May under the title *Winning the War, Australians in Conflict, Brigadier General Elliott's Story.* The theme of the letter was the Australian achievement in the war, versus the view of the British to the contribution by the colonials. In respect to Fromelles, Elliott had a few paragraphs which dealt with aspects Ellis obviously had no knowledge of. After discussing some impossible actions he was ordered to carry out on Gallipoli, Elliott wrote:

> At Fleurbaix, too, the task appeared utterly impossible, and appalling in its probable results, yet it was carried through without one murmur as far as human power could carry it through, regardless of losses.
>
> My first awakening in this regard came shortly after the battle, when I relieved with my brigade part of the Guards Division in the Valley of the Somme. In the course of conversation with the divisional commander, I happened to mention that we were fresh from the bloodbath of Fleurbaix, and he was genuinely interested, and said: '*Do you know my division was ordered to attack there not long ago and when the zero time came and we found that the enemy was fully aware of our intentions to attack, and were evidently prepared for us, we did not carry out the orders, but reported to GHQ that an attack in the circumstances was impossible, and we did not propose to go on with it*'. On my inquiring as to what happened, he replied '*Nothing*', and on my further inquiry '*Why not?*', he replied, '*the reputation of the Guards is beyond reproach. The position at Fleurbaix had been three times previously attacked, and three times the assailing troops had been driven back with terrible slaughter. When, therefore, I came to the conclusion that to carry out the attack ordered was merely to perpetuate a succession of such disasters, I refused in the circumstances to commit my troops to the attack without direct written instructions from the Commander in Chief relieving me from all responsibility in the matter.*'
>
> He further added: '*The reputation of the Australians and the courage of their leaders are now recognised as equal to the Guards or any other British division. My advice to you is this—if hereafter you receive an order which after careful reconnaissance you are satisfied is impossible you should report that fact and demand that your immediate superior should give you written instructions upon which your protest is recorded, relieving you from all responsibility.*'

Although in a sense it had nothing to do with Fromelles, Elliott's next paragraph explains much else:

> *I may add that during the remainder of war I consistently acted on that advice, and in no instance was my decision overruled by higher authority. Certainly on one occasion my brigade was immediately replaced by other troops, who were ordered to carry out the attack,*

GORDON BENNETT AND McCAY
Beginning in the issue of 24 May 1930, *Smith's Weekly* began a series of articles 'Great Deeds of the AIF', the first 21 written by Brigadier H Gordon Bennett. On Gallipoli he had commanded 6th Bn which was part of 2nd Bde of which McCay was GOC.

In the episode published on 20 Sept, Bennett had this to say of McCay's conduct at Krithia on 8 May 1915.

'*The brigadier, Colonel McCay, arrived on the scene. Walking up and down the parapet of the trench, swinging his cane, he impatiently urged the men forward. Some resented his manner, for our men needed no urging.*'

Bennett went with his men and reached a forward position.

'*Glancing back over the ground across which we had just passed we saw hundreds of huddled khaki forms lying where they fell. A subaltern named Johnston crawled up to me when the enemy fire was heaviest. Lying close to the ground, his pipe between his teeth, he said: "Sir, I wish to lodge a complaint. The Brigadier called me and my men cowards when we were back in the Tommy's Trench. I resent it." I gave him my opinion of his courage and told him to see me again about it when things quietened down.*

Before long the Brigadier came forward to inspect the front. He arrived at my position in the line just as a burst of fire was whipping up dust around us. The bullets ricochetted past with a whirr. Still the Brigadier stood there in the midst of it all as if nothing was happening.'

Once again that strange mix that was McCay—plenty of useless bravado but no feeling for other people. The Johnston referred to was most likely Lieut J A K Johnston of 7th Bn, an engineer from Williamstown, Victoria, aged 32, who died of wounds 19 May, so he never had the opportunity to proceed with his complaint. It was Major Cass, who led the 7th in that charge, and thus must have witnessed what Johnston was complaining about to Bennett. An experience which doubtless contributed to Cass's disenchantment with McCay.
[continued opposite]

although their commander had had no opportunity of making the careful reconnaissance which I had made prior to forming my decision. As for the result, I understand in one brigade they lost 700 men in about five minutes, and never gained one single yard of the enemy's position, and long afterwards when the Boche retired I beheld the melancholy spectacle of their rotting corpses fringing the edge of the enemy's impregnable wire. Yet this disastrous action was reported in Australia as a victory.

When Bean sent drafts of the Fromelles chapters to Edmonds the letter he received in return said more about British attitudes than many a learned essay on the subject. It was dated 3 November 1927.

> Without waiting for Haking's comments on Fromelles (and Gough's on Pozières) I am sending my own general comments. I have put what I think frankly as I think it would be a terrible pity if the slightest wrong impression were given by a work of national importance like your own. In a few years no one will care much about details of fighting, but the books will be read for the lessons they carry. At this distance apart, we must not misunderstand each other, and fine phrases are wasted.
>
> I hold no brief for Haking, but you should remember that his books on training written before the war were in great demand: he had been an instructor at Staff College; had in the South African War led the way in the protection of convoys, in the teeth of silly opposition of Roberts' staff, had commanded a brigade in 1914 with great success (wounded on the Aisne) and a division in 1915 with great distinction. In Sept 1915 he was selected to command a corps, and would have got the First Army (which he commanded for a time in 1916) had not Haig preferred to give it to a brother Scot, Horne.

Having 'corrected' Bean on Haking, Edmonds now set upon him for quoting Major Howard as expressing an opinion to Elliott about the forthcoming battle. Edmonds wrote to his own committee: '*Our main interest is to prevent Bean circulating uninstructed criticism of living British officers.*' Whether or not Bean used Howard's actual expression '*a bloody holocaust*' in his original text is difficult to ascertain, he modified it finally to '*Could hardly fail to end in disaster.*' Whatever Bean sent to Edmonds it still provoked this attack:

> This paragraph would mislead the ordinary reader as to the position of British Staff Officers. What members of a general's staff think does not matter and should NOT [Edmond's capitals] be disclosed. In any staff there is only one person responsible and that is the general. His staff officers are his servants. If they have doubts they can express them to him, and to nobody else (and I am quite sure this is the case in the instance you mention). If he does not accept them and they still have doubts of his wisdom, there is only one course: for them to resign. Such suggestions as 'the staff must have been acutely conscious' are most objectionable. What you take to be adverse judgment is probably the usual counter argument which some generals demand of their staff, so that all views may receive consideration. (All my generals did this.)

BENNETT AND MCCAY (contd)

Bennett's article on Fromelles, a battle at which he was not present, was a blend of Bean and Ellis, and has no information that is not from these sources. Bennett however had taken 6th Bn to the trenches at Fleurbaix in early April 1916 and organised raids on 6 June from there before going to Pozières.

BRUDENELL WHITE ON OBJECTION TO FROMELLES

Bean's inquiry to White of 27 May 1926 received this answer dated 1st June 1926:

I cannot at this stage say whether or not Gen. Birdwood's views or mine regarding the Fromelles attack had any effect on GHQ. It is quite probable. We were constantly meeting officers from GHQ and we knew Haking's keenness for what we regarded as a most undesirable operation.

PERUSED WITH INTEREST

When Bean had completed Volume III of his history he sent the text to the Secretary, Department of Defence, Melbourne with a letter dated 7 March 1928.

By the contract under which I write the Australian War History, my volumes are not subject to censorship, but, by arrangement with the Minister, I submit them to him personally before publication. He reads them, and any suggestions or comments he desires to make are of course, carefully considered ...

On 24 April the text came back with the note:

... Minister has perused with interest and has no comments to offer thereon.

THE BEAN–ELLIOTT CORRESPONDENCE

In the many letters they exchanged there was always a tangible feeling of respect between the two men. Bean in his style addressed 'Pompey' 'Dear Elliott', but 'Pompey's replies were to 'Dear Capt. Bean'. Elliott wrote from his office in RAC Building, 94–98 Queen Street, Melbourne. Phone Central 1871. Cables & Telegrams LARISTAN. Melbourne. His title was: H E ELLIOTT BA LLM Notary Public. City Solicitor.

AWARE OF THE TRUTH!
Doubtless as the result of the publication of Bean's Volume III, on 30 April 1929 somebody wrote to the Melbourne *Herald*. The letter was not published but forwarded by the Editor to Bean for comment on
2 May 1929. It read:

As a regular reader of your paper, I would like to ask the following relative to General Sir J McCay.

Can you please inform myself and many hundreds of others why General Sir J McCay was relieved of command, being sent to England after the Fleurbaix blunder. In my battalion there were 67 who answered the roll call of 1000 men.

General Sir J McCay will never be pardoned by the men lucky enough to come through unless he can make a frank statement, and let us know who was responsible. Yours faithfully, Ex-Non Com 60th Bn.

Bean replied to the *Herald* in a note marked 'Confidential' saying that '*General McCay was never aware of the whole of the facts*' and '*McCay was not relieved of his command ... he "cracked up" in the Somme winter.*' This was, of course, inaccurate. The severe winter of 1916–17 was no threat in the third week of December. Bean then wrote that '*the reader in blaming McCay is very mean, General McCay was never in a position to know who was to blame as he never had access to the higher records.*'

This view never found its way into the *Herald*, after all Bean had dealt with 'the problem' in his book.

'*... a small section of the press saw no unfairness in publishing, then and since, without verification, damning statements or implications mainly contained in soldiers' letters—the blame for the enterprise was thrown upon an unpopular but entirely innocent leader, General McCay... His security in his command was not in any way shaken by the popular error—the authorities of the AIF being well aware of the truth.*'

Bean wrote in the margin of Edmonds's letter:

> We have another account of this much more sensational and the passage is deliberately directed to draw the teeth of it.

Bean dealt with it all finally in passing on page 346 and in a lengthy footnote on page 443: but failed to use the term 'bloody holocaust' which later became a synonym for Fromelles.

Edmonds then advised Bean to leave out all reference to the attempted armistice, '*I should omit these details. What good does it do even if true ...*'. This opinion can only engender extreme scepticism about the entire British Official History as edited by Edmonds. That dealt with, Edmonds now took Bean to task on another issue:

> 'The verdict of the military student'. I suppose you mean the 'arm-chair critic' of military affairs. The only 'military students' recognised in the Army List are those at the Imperial Defence College, and the only 'students' the officers of the Staff College. The verdict of the well-read and experienced soldier would be that the experience of Neuve Chapelle, Festubert, Aubers and Loos had not been assimilated, and the troops were led forward as in open warfare, whereas they were engaged in siege warfare.

Edmonds, not a complete idiot, must have realised that '*the verdict of the military student*' was in fact Bean's view, and on this Bean did not give in and it remained—page 444.

Edmonds concluded his letter with another extraordinary statement which could have only been made by a British Empire general, rooted in a lifetime of putting down dissenting colonials.

> As a general criticism I think you look too much at the Australian Corps, without taking into account that much the same thing is going on in other Corps. The attack at Fromelles is almost identical with that of the 24th Div, the 72nd Brigade leading against the Hulloch pocket at Loos.

A year later, Edmonds, '*who had no brief for Haking*', advised Bean that he had finally tracked Haking down. '*I can't get a word out of Haking about Fromelles*', he wrote on 11 June 1928. It was too late anyway because Volume III was getting ready for the press. When finally Edmonds received it, he wrote to Bean, thus:

> I have read your Vol III with the very greatest enjoyment. It is an extraordinarily fine piece of military writing, and I wish the public would read it instead of the silly translated German stuff, like *All Quiet on the Western Front*, which is now apparently popular.

Elliott, however, had another view. He had been shown the early drafts and made comments on the action. His letter of 15 May 1929 was characteristically blunt:

> I have just read through a first time your third volume. It is a story of unrelieved tragedy but I think you have got most of the main facts relating to the fighting—correct.
>
> On the whole however it does appear to me that you have strained your conscience in the endeavour to let the Higher Command down as lightly as possible.
>
> I am delighted that you have been able to clear General McCay so completely. You have, in my opinion, however, been more than fair towards Haking in seeking excuses to palliate his responsibility in the tragedy of Fleurbaix more particularly in view of the fact which you now reveal that he was in charge of a similar operation just before this which resulted in like failure.

Elliott's comment about Haking being involved in a 'like failure' requires amplification. Bean went to great pains to describe the 'Raids at Armentières' in which the Australians were involved during June 1916. In dealing with this he wrote of the raid programme promoted by Haking in the sector south of I Anzac Corps, ie the Neuve Chapelle area. It was as part of this programme submitted around 15 June to Haig, that Haking put forward the idea of '*capturing and holding permanently ... from Fauquissart Road ... to the Sugarloaf.*' This is a very different proposition to the other raids suggested which were basically to disrupt the enemy, gain intelligence data and wreck installations that were too offensive. Because of this style they were relatively small scale, and described in the British Official History thus:

> During the twenty weeks ... 1 July ... to middle of November ... hostile trenches ... were raided on no less than 310 occasions. [Of these 204 were regarded as successful]. The troops employed varied from two platoons to two companies often with a party of engineers attached for demolition work ... in the early morning of 30 June two battalions of the 39th Division had attempted to reduce the German Salient south of Neuve Chapelle known as 'The Boars Head': trenches were taken, but had to be evacuated after two hours under concentrated artillery and machine gun fire, losses amounting to 950. The operation '*looked upon as a raid*' [Edmonds quotes], was considered by the Corps Commander [ie Haking] to have been successful.

Quite how a loss of half the men involved can be classified a success in a raid that was driven out is difficult to fathom. But it is important to note that Haking regarded it as such, endorsing Liddell Hart's wisdom that '*it matters little what the situation actually was ... all that matters is what the commander thought it was.*'

Anyway to equate a two battalion raid with a two division attack seems to be stretching the case somewhat. Few British or French generals had at that time even one victory to boast of. Whilst it is no excuse for Haking's schemes, his record was not dramatically worse than others at that time.

Brig. General Sir JAMES E EDMONDS
Born in London on Christmas Day 1861, James was the son of a master jeweller and attended King's College School, London where he attracted attention by his extraordinary memory and range of knowledge. He went on to the Royal Military Academy at Woolwich, where he was a consistent winner of prizes. In 1881 he joined the Royal Engineers with whom in 1885 he went to Hong Kong, then thought to be in imminent danger of Russian invasion. After three years he returned to the UK via Japan and the USA and became an instructor at the Royal Military Academy in 1890. In 1895 he entered Staff College. He had a great facility for languages—his best were German and Russian. These he used in later intelligence work, beginning in 1901 when he went to South Africa, later in 1904 when Britain was closely watching the Russo–Japanese war. In 1907 he moved to take charge of MOS (later known as MI5) convincing the authorities of the very substantial German espionage network in Britain.

In 1911 Edmonds was GSO1 of 4th Division and worked hard over the next three years to bring it to combat capability. However, during the retreat from Mons his health broke down and he was moved to GHQ of the Engineers where he remained for the rest of the war.

In 1919, now an honorary Brigadier General, he was appointed Director of the Historical Section, Military Branch, Committee of Imperial Defence and given the task of preparing the official history. The British History which appeared intermittently between 1922 and 1951, was subject to criticism for being too condensed, too centred on army movements and not people and action, being poorly indexed and cross referenced and too late anyway.

Edmonds was appointed CB in 1911, CMG in 1916 and Knighted in 1928. He had married in 1895 and there was a daughter from the marriage. Edmonds died at Sherborne, Dorset, on 2 August 1956.

THIS ACCOUNT ... SET NEW STANDARDS

Bean the official historian lives on through his six volumes on Gallipoli and the Western Front—'The Official History of Australia in the War 1914–18'. This account, which set new standards in the writing of war history, retains an importance in world historiography today.

The first of these standards was in level of detail. Relative to the number of troops involved, the British would have required eighty four volumes to match Bean's six and the Canadians' nine. In the event, the British account ran to sixteen volumes and the Canadian to one.

Bean's perspective was very different. His narrative switched from platoon commanders in battle to corps headquarters in the rear and all points between with the mind of the high command only one of several. He went on to describe failures in attack at length and his criticism of commanders was often biting. Above all, Bean filled his pages with soldiers; 6500 of them and each with a footnoted biographical sketch. Bean's history was, in other words, a personalised history written in a distinctive style.

That description by Denis Winter in his *Making the Legend—the war writings of C E W Bean* (1992) crisply and concisely reveals the great gift of Bean, a humanity and interest that none of the other historians could approach. On the basis that the number of men Bean mentions, it represents one in every fifty in the AIF abroad: so it is quite likely that everybody who served would have known somebody in the Official History. That must have been a great psychological boost to many of the survivors and the families of those who did not survive. It was certainly that, to the wounded nation.

Winter's choice from Bean as far as Fromelles is concerned, is mostly from the Official History, the truce episode is not from the first edition, and there are several extras from Bean's papers and other sources, notably a letter from White hugely wise after the event as ever.

The first edition of Bean's Volume III was available in March 1929, and the second in 1934: it was reprinted regularly after that. As already noted Bean changed the section of his Fromelles story in relation to the Truce, but few if anybody noticed it. All the memoirs published in the 1930s stuck with Major Murdoch's fiction and brought no new information, it having been decided that Bean not only knew it all but also printed it all.

Although there is evidence that McCay throughout the 1920s commented that he would not discuss his wartime career, the publication of Bean's Volume III brought McCay into print, and his first and last statement on Fromelles was published in *Reveille* (29 June 1929). The full text follows:

> The recently issued volume of the Official History is written by the one man in the world who knows all the ascertainable facts. In his description of Fromelles he has had before him all the official documents, records and reports, as well as many unofficial ones. He has made his account so complete, thorough and exhaustive that it would be but presumption to endeavour to improve on it. So even where his inferences and comments are not in complete accord with my own ideas, I refrain from any remarks.
>
> Before writing my real message, I desire to refer to one matter. I differ from General Haking's report that the failure was due to the Australian infantry not being sufficiently trained, and to his further statement that 'with two trained divisions the position would have been a gift after the artillery bombardment' as 'the wire was properly cut'. The wire round the Sugar-Loaf was not properly cut. That caused the failure. For this fault, neither the Division not its commander or staff were responsible. I further prefer to maintain silence about General Haking's statement that the 61st Division 'were not sufficiently imbued with the offensive spirit.' I have never believed in the method of justifying oneself by attempting to put the blame for failure on to the shoulders of others.
>
> The abiding impressions left on my mind are two—the first is the unfading memory of the heavy losses sustained by the 5th Division, a memory that has deepened with the passage of the years. The second is the recollection of the unflinching courage of the Australians who fought in the battle, a courage not surpassed on any later and more successful fields. Fromelles was a failure, and so the heroism there displayed has largely passed unrecognised. Mr Bean's volume now exhibits this bravery in its just light. I more than endorse General Haking's statements that 'the Australian infantry attacked in the most gallant manner'; and that the attack 'was carried out in an exceptionally gallant manner.' This 'ill-fated operation', as the historian calls it, the first Australian battle in France, showed the Australian solider to be second to none in courage, determination and resource. Its episodes do not yield to those of more successful subsequent encounters. None can grieve over the losses in that battle more than I—the then commander of the Division. If there be any consolation—which is doubtful—in the recollection of high-hearted courage, that consolation may well come to those whose fate and immediate duty it was to issue the orders to the 5th Australian

Division for the battle before Fromelles.—Lieut General Hon Sir J W McCay, GOC, 5th Australian Division in 1916.

Not that one would expect McCay to reflect nor offer new thoughts on his own conduct, it is important to read that he placed the blame on the uncut wire round the Sugarloaf, and the fault thus lay with the British. Considering the work Bean had put into analysing the Battle and the detail of his findings, McCay's purposely trivial summary is a most apt comment on the man's character. McCay was actually a most articulate man and could have, *had he been without blame*, prepared a dramatic defence. It would have helped the survivors and next of kin as well as himself. McCay published scores of articles in *The Argus* on all manner of subjects and given his combative nature it is folly to believe that he would not have used this talent to defend himself if he had been in the right. The simple fact has to be that he knew that he had made a mess of it all and to argue his case in public would have exposed it, and probably much more. So the clear decision was to go down as a martyr to others' 'uninformed' comment: a familiar refuge, it has to be said, for self-serving hypocrites.

A few writers over this period reflected rather than ranted, like H R Williams of A Coy, 56th Bn, in *The Gallant Company*. In the foreword by Hobbs the greatly loved little general wrote '*the best soldier's story I have ever read in Australia.*' He went on to pay tribute to the 5th Division and then direct the reader to '*the last seven paragraphs of this book. There they will find not only something well worth reading and learning, but also something to live up to.*' Williams had written strongly and well about the Australians individuality and generous spirit, and after remarking about the German's patriotism, hate and iron discipline, felt they lost because they lacked the team-work taught by sport. Then, in 1933, he concluded '*The German nations whole-hearted interest in athletics today suggests an answer.*'

The body of his book, partly from his own diary, and help from others, as far as Fromelles is concerned, does not rely on other people's versions. He had no doubt whose fault it was. '*Can the XI Corps staff absolve themselves?*' taking up strongly that the 61st Division failure to make another attempt on the Sugarloaf was the ruin of it all. '*The 5th Australian Division was sacrificed on the altar of incompetence*', Williams concluded. Williams' later book *Comrades of the Great Adventure* (1935) described billets at Fleurbaix but mentions the battle not at all.

EDMONDS' CORRECTIONS

The British Official Historian took Bean to task for elevating Fromelles to a battle: '*according to official nomenclature Fromelles is only a "subsidiary attack" like other engagements of similar nature*'.

Likewise when Bean called the Laies a river describing it as a 'straight ditch-like course', Edmonds informed him: '*The Laies IS* (Edmonds' capitals) *a ditch; it is an old artificial channel dug by local farmers for drainage purposes. Not being actually levelled, it has not a proper flow, going sometimes north, sometimes south.*'

ALL QUIET!

'*Now apparently popular*', wrote Edmonds of Erich Maria Remarque's novel of the war—*All Quiet on the Western Front* ! By the end of 1929 it had sold 900,000 copies in Germany, 300,000 in France, 300,000 in Britain and 215,000 in USA. If Edmonds had known that the '*silly translated German stuff*' had been translated by an Australian, and '*a 19th of July man*' at that, it would have surely confirmed his views about colonials in general, and Australians in particular!

Nothing, of course that Edmonds wrote, apart from remarks such as these, survives, or some might say, ought to. Other people's successful popular history is one thing academics cannot accommodate, the '*silly stuff*' especially. The translator was, as noted on page 283, Pte A W Wheen 54th Bn, and as he earned an MM at Fromelles, he is part of this story. It was he who wrote the title which was not a literal translation of Remarque's title, and it, as they say, passed into the language. It has remained through the recent new translation. A footnote that cannot be avoided—In Hitler's Germany the book was burned and the author went into exile, but he was forever thankful for Wheen's work. '*I am enraptured. It is beautiful to the utmost degree.*' Wheen wrote '*I found it easy to translate for the same reason that any other infantry private found it easy to understand.*' (see also page 448).

... THE SPOILED CHILDREN OF GHQ

The extraordinarily biased mind of Edmonds, who incidentally spent most of the war out of the line, he was only up at the cutting edge till Mons (late August 1914), is revealed methodically by T Travers in his article: 'From Surafend to Gough': *Journal of Australian War Museum No. 27*, October 1995, where he quotes interesting reports that Edmonds made to his paymasters in London. Edmonds was very much at odds with Bean over Bullecourt and its management, largely seen as a creation of General Sir Hubert Gough of 5th Army. The Australian survivors of Bullecourt forever remained angry about what they saw as British incompetence there, and that feeling was shared by Bean: after all he had witnessed it at first hand and did not rely on staff reports only.

What we learn from Travers is that Edmonds passed Bean's drafts to Gough and others for their comments and got some very self-revealing remarks back.

Gough wrote:

... the whole tone and almost all the statements of this writer are violently and personally hostile, and they constitute a veritable travesty of the facts and of history. Nothing is too far-fetched for his imaginative and poisoned mind to produce.

But as Travers points out, Bean was big enough to make adjustments in his history, and 'correct' some of his views but not alter the facts, and concedes, one feels a little grudgingly that:

In the context of historical accuracy Bean was therefore more progressive than either Edmonds or Duguid (Canadian historian).

One would hope that Australia was served better by Bean, than Britain was by Edmonds, a man who could write this paragraph:

We all feel that the historian of the AIF could afford to be a little more generous in his allusions to British units and formations. You are now aware perhaps that the home troops regarded the Australians and Canadians as the spoiled children of GHQ, who were given most rest, the pick of the fighting pitches and most of

[continued opposite]

In 1935 the publication of *There and back* by 'A Tiveychoc' was about a life wrecked by Fromelles. The author R E Lording, a signaller with 30th, told a story that attracted much attention due to his personal plight, but it did not ignite any questions about Fromelles. Nearly all the main players were now dead and the survivors kept their own counsel.

Only this memoir takes the reader into the hell and despair of those permanently maimed by the war. It is an extraordinary document, describing without self-pity the plight of the men known as *'wingies'* (without one or both arms), *'peggies'* (without one or both legs), those with ruined spines and others with gas-eaten lungs who would populate the hospitals of Australia for twenty years or more till they killed themselves or just faded away. The battle waged by Lording, from when he was only 20, against 'dope' as he called his morphia addiction, is also a story of our time. But on the very first page of Lording's memoir is the dedication so different to those in all other 'war books' that it demands mention: '*To Mrs O E H B—one of those gloriously unselfish and loving women of the war who brought a ray of sunshine, the light of hope, into those war-shattered minds groping in the darkness of mental torture and physical pain*'.

In 1938 the publication of *The Purple and Gold: a history of the 30th Battalion* was the first and only official history of a 5th Division battalion until 1992. Lieut Col Sloan devoted 20 pages to Fromelles, but most of it was from Bean or official papers, and pointedly avoided any new material. But he dealt with all ranks, casualties and medal winners, and allowed those with a special story to contribute to the appendix: the best efforts for Fromelles being stories by some taken prisoner.

The volume of the British History covering *The Subsidiary Attack at Fromelles* emerged in 1938. It, of course, had lots more important battles to deal with and for Fromelles to earn 16 pages and a map was surely due to the prominence Bean had given it years earlier. The compiler should have had access to British papers but virtually nothing is used that Bean had not found. As Edmonds had long decreed '*official histories do not have opinions*', he might have as well added 'and should not contain too much information'. The 182nd Bde gets 30 lines, the 183rd 10 lines and the 184th 26 lines: 3 officers are mentioned apart from Mackenzie and the three brigadiers. Curiously Edmonds as overall editor permitted this sentence: '*Stretcher bearers were busy, the Australians arranging a short truce in order to be able to search for and remove their wounded.*' What had happened? '*I should omit these details*', Edmonds once cautioned Bean. The only man he turned on was Monro, then long dead, '*The pity of it was that the action need not have been fought, since the First Army had perfect liberty to cancel it.*' It has to be said that if all the other material in the British Official History is as trivial as the coverage of Fromelles, then Australia's debt to Bean is beyond calculation. Because without his work on Fromelles—and all the rest of those terrible years—when the survivors and memories were still about, it would have all been lost.

In his relentless search of Haig *(Haig's Command: a reassessment, 1991)* and much else historian Denis Winter, investigated the writing of the British Official History and the part that Edmonds played in organising the material. It is a disturbing read: sifted documents, re-written diaries, destruction of contrary material, changing facts and emphasis to suit current political needs, guarding reputations '*for the national good*', locking up documents for 50 years or more, and much else.

The fact that Winter found in Australia on open access, documents to which there is no access in the UK, is an important piece of information in helping one understand the curious style of Edmonds' chapter on Fromelles. Winter explains how the system worked.

> Once these key decisions had been taken in Haig's favour, procedures for organizing and writing the histories were set up which allowed Edmonds and Committee of Imperial Defence to control every stage of production and exercise strict control over writers at all points.
>
> The process started as soon as public records returned from wartime storage ... for three years he (Edmonds) read and sorted everything. Documents considered unimportant were sent for storage ... The remainder ... sorted in 25,000 box files ... 280 drawers of maps ... together these sources comprised 25 million sheets of paper.
>
> More important than taming this mountain of paper was the separation Edmonds made between the daily narrative of the unit war diaries and the messages, orders, reports and field telegrams which formed the appendix of each diary. Edmonds extracted the latter and filed it separately under the classification number Cabinet 70. Official historians of friendly governments who were given limited access referred to this holding as 'The British Master File' and the immediate result of separating it from routine war diary material was to give Edmonds the means of controlling access to almost all the most important documents.

Winter then details how Edmonds chose his writers. Due, his friends said, to being unable to find capable people to write the narratives, he did much himself. His detractors however felt this was more due to the fact he could not get on with others when their view did not exactly coincide with his own. No wonder he was so critical of Bean expressing his opinions, quoting

... THE SPOILED CHILDREN OF GHQ (contd)

the praise—not that it was grudged. What they envied most was the corps formation of the Dominion divisions which gave them many advantages.

Travers' comment:

Much of this paragraph was false, but reveals the continuing underlying hostility of Edmonds toward Dominion forces and their histories.

All this is included here because it shows the level of Edmonds' interference and bias which is detectable in the exchanges between the two historians over Fromelles and perhaps this gives a hint of why it was below Haking to contribute or comment, and why Mackenzie and others were never canvassed for an opinion.

ON THE GROUND!

One marvels at the arrogance of Edmonds. When a reprint of Volume 1 France and Belgium 1914 was issued in 1933, he wrote a preface, the gist of which was:

Since the original edition was compiled in 1920-21, the battlefields of 1914 have been visited by many parties of British Officers, and much interesting information has been elicited on the ground ... It was therefore thought desirable to carry out a thorough revision of the text ... The maps and sketches have been revised ... and some new ones added. No such revision of the other published volumes of the history will be necessary.

THE STAR TURN

The correspondence between friends—C E W Bean and General Gellibrand, was often witty, usually wise and always affectionate. Hence this paragraph from Gellibrand on 10 March 1930:

Do you know from the military point of view I think—I am inclined to think—that so far the Fromelles account is the star turn of your history and in the years to come I shall probably kid myself that I was there, à la Geo IV and Waterloo.

POPULAR HISTORIES

Right from the outbreak of the war British newspapers and magazine publishers started to compile picture histories which were issued in weekly, fortnightly or monthly parts, and which in some cases when the war was over were reissued as bound volumes. The most important was *The Times History of the War*, twenty large volumes of patriotic flavour but an invaluable source of material. A rival—in size and treatment—was *The Great War* edited by H W Wilson which managed twelve volumes, also with many illustrations. In the early 1930s *A Popular History of the Great War* in six novel size volumes edited Sir John Hammerton (who had supported Wilson's work) was published. In this writer's view it is by far the most useful of the popular histories giving lots of detail about the movements of regiments (but no individuals) and general news of campaigns, a host of biographical material and photographs, all very well indexed.

But only *The Times* mentioned the Fromelles incident in any detail (see page 373).

MUDDLED THINKING

In the last volume of his great history, Bean tried again to sum up Fromelles. But by definition how could '*a highly trained staff*' be capable of such '*muddled thinking*'?

The tragedy of Fromelles, in which a division of the AIF lost 5,500 men, mostly in a single night, was due to muddled thinking by a highly trained staff. It was intended as a feint to keep German reserves away from the Somme battlefield. If the preparations for it, intentionally made obvious, had lasted longer they might have effected their object so long as the attack was not actually launched, but, within a few hours of its launching, the fact it was only a feint was necessarily known to the enemy. Most of the sorties at Anzac similarly made clear to the enemy within a few hours the very fact it was desired to conceal—that the real effort was elsewhere.

—C E W Bean, Vol VI (1942)

from his own observations and mentioning individuals. Sharp enough to realise that Bean, because of his contract, and being a journalist rather than an army man, Edmonds' only control was to cut him off from sources, or to be the only conduit between Bean and the approved sources.

As far as Fromelles was concerned, Edmonds, apart from getting nothing from Haking, made no mention of Mackenzie, surely the prime source of decisions, nor Brig. Gen. Carter who could have ventured a view on why his 184th Bde did not support the Australian 15th Bde. That Bean never sought to contact Mackenzie, nor raised his name with Edmonds, is one of the most troubling aspects. Only Mackenzie really knew about the 'failure' of the British, but to get information from him that contradicted McCay's story would have been very difficult to accommodate. Is this why Bean did not pursue Mackenzie? But none of this isolating of Bean required fiendish enterprise on behalf of Edmonds. All the people concerned if not still serving were enjoying considerable army pensions, and the whole lot anyway were slaves to the Official Secrets Act, which explains also the lack of input by any British officer into the story of Fromelles and Edmonds' harsh criticism of Bean for using the one story he had about a named British officer expressing a view.

All of which seems to confirm Winter's narrative about what happened when Edmonds sent approved drafts of his history to the printers.

> Edmonds had to make sure that troublesome researchers wouldn't be able to undermine the sacred text. With this in view, all drafts and narratives were retained by the Historical Branch, guaranteeing that outsiders would be denied both the detail of the original narratives and references to particular documents which were in the margins of those narratives.
>
> One more stage remained, and that the most sensitive of all. The documents themselves had to be processed in such a way that evidence for accounts different from those of the Official History was removed. Edmonds was therefore given personal authority to go through all documents bearing on the Western Front and divide them between those for burning, those for retention by the CID and a small quantity which could be safely passed to the Public Records Office, selected and arranged so as to guide researchers towards conclusions which had been built into the Official History.
>
> In this sensitive work, Edmonds had the assistance of only one higher clerical officer and three clerks, which means that his sifting took four years. It was a price Edmonds and his employers were willing to pay. The fewer the eyewitnesses and the less their grasp of what was going on, the better.

What Edmonds and his weeders took from the files of the 61st Division, its Brigades and Battalions we will never know. It has long since been established that those on such a mission are covering up something, not saving shelf space. Another factor is what was lost in the Blitz. This writer found only War Diaries and no appendices except in the case of Tupman's Report.

Since Winter published these suggestions he has come under fire for being too forthright. But as far as this work is concerned, Edmonds' own words are sufficient for a judgement: '*What good does it do, even if true*'.

On a different level, in November 1938, *Paris Match*, the French magazine published a six page illustrated feature about Fromelles—'*The Resuscitated Village*' to mark the twentieth anniversary of the 1918 Armistice. One special photograph was the old road sign: *Fromelles, 1 km, Fin de la Guerre 5 kms*, this with postcards of 1914 and 1918 and photographs of the rebuilt village. On the next pages there was a large photograph of a German cemetery, probably the one at Laventie, wherein are the dead of July/August 1918—not the Battle of Fromelles. The Editor made two references to Hitler, one that he took 10 prisoners at Fromelles in 1915. Then '*a little time later he was with his unit at Wavrin. He stayed there a year. Sometimes since then comrades and ex-officers of the Chancellor have visited the area—Fromelles, Wavrin, Beaucamps—as they have kept up contact with inhabitants there.*'

In another panel: '*For this small village, on one night, 1299 Australians fell. It is in their cemetery in the middle of fields of sugarbeet that says ... in the attack at Fromelles on 19 and 20 July 1916*'. There is also a mention of the Kennedy memorial (in French '*un Calvaire*') but no photographs of Australian nor British cemeteries.

Perhaps the most interesting photograph as far as this work is concerned is of the Girls' School Class of 1920. With not a smile among them, 29 small girls stand and sit in three rows. In the front row the youngest have signs in French, here translated: '*Godmother wanted. With gratitude to the generous Americans. 950 inhabitants—40 dead,—15 disabled. North Fromelles Red Zone. Complete devastation. Cemetery of 500 Australians.*'

The girl wanting a godmother holds the Stars and Stripes, several others have the French flag, but there are no British nor Australian flags to be seen.

THE BLOKES UP THERE

The shadow of McCay lay across the lines of men he commanded for years. In the 1990s one embittered survivor of Fromelles then himself in his late 90s suggested, '*Not that it would do much good now, they ought to dig up McCay, put him on trial, shoot him and put him back in his box.*' Then pointing to the sky, '*The blokes up there could then have a party.*'

THE AIF

Figures published in Col Butler's third volume of his Medical History give an interesting picture of the 'average digger'.

Age:	18 years	6.26%
	19 years	8.25%
	20 years	7.45%
	21–30 years	56.45%
	31–40 years	16.96%
	over 41 yrs	4.63%
Occupation:		
	Tradesmen	34%
	Labourers	30%
	Country Callings	17.36%
	Clerical	7.6%
	Professional	4.75%
	Others	5.87%
	Nurses	0.64%
Religion:		
	Church of England	49.22%
	Roman Catholic	19.26%
	Presbyterian	15.01%
	Methodist	10.19%
	Jewish	0.37%
	Others	5.96%
Marital Status [which Butler titled 'conjugal condition']:		
	Single	81.62%
	Married	17.38%
	Widowers	0.84%
	Unknown	0.16%

Brudenell White's curious silences

Bean wrote of Major General Cyril Brudenell White as '*the greatest man I have known*'. White, came out of the war with a near spotless reputation. Throughout his life he was a compulsive diary keeper, from 1895 to the day before he died in an aircraft accident in 1940 at Canberra. He made daily entries, mostly about the volume of work he had, whom he saw during the day and his own state of mind and health. He seldom philosified, was very conscious of the weather and never critical of others. A study of his diaries, their tone and the persistence of White's own style, quickly tells the reader what sort of man he was. This is well illustrated, and never contradicted by the opening page of his 1895 Diary when he was a 19-year-old bank clerk. Under *Mottos for 1895* White wrote:

Never tell a lie. Have your own opinion. Never drink or swear. Guard against immorality. Be straightforward and not afraid. Be determined. If you say a thing do it. Do all work well.

The first quarter of his first diary is in shorthand (White had won a prize for shorthand), but the rest is in longhand. Nearly every day has the words '*work right, work done well*', with mentions of tennis, horse riding, reading and doing shorthand.

For the next seventeen years White kept his diaries on a daily basis, all—apart from some early periods—in longhand. They reveal his absolute passion for work and for getting things done properly, and his concern for Ethel, his wife, and their sons and the general welfare of relatives and friends. Early in 1914 their second son was born: successive entries note that '*Ethel and baby well*', '*Ethel and small fellow well*', then '*Ethel and son well*'. By mid 1914, aware that war was on the horizon, entries include '*At office all day, all night*', then on 31 July, '*Every appearance of war*': 1 August, '*Outlook black*': 4 August, '*Conference with Prime Minister and Minister. Adoption of war measures*'. These measures were of course what Bridges, White (then Director of Military Operations and Acting Chief of Staff), Pearce and others had been working at for months, and were centred about the formation of the AIF, and mobilising 20,000 men for service abroad. On 16 August White wrote '*First night off. Did A/cs with Ethel and had some music*'. It was the last such intimate entry until the war was over.

When the First AIF sailed from Fremantle, White wrote:

1 November. A memorable day. At 6 am in glorious sunshine, warm wind and smooth sea the Orvieto led 36 transports out of King George's Sound. A beautiful sight and fitting demonstration of Britain's greatness.

In Cairo White laboured long hours on the plans for the Landing at Gallipoli, noting meetings with just about everybody, among whom once was Col McCay, and his own attendance at the Landing and afterwards. At the Landing White was near McCay and made this observation:

He was completely lost and his grip on things seemed gone. He could not orient himself. Bridges came along with his yard and a half stride and wanted to know what the hell he was doing and who were those men sheltering under the brow of Bolton's Hill? They were the 9th Bn, but McCay simply didn't know. As Bridges grew more and more angry, I saw McCay's face change. He began to get a grip on himself and before long he was in complete control, yet he was the bravest leader any man could serve under. I saw him lead his men over the top, swinging a walking stick.

From then on there can be no doubt White had an enormous work load but he still made observations, some pertinent to his work. On 4 May White wrote: '*McCay ordered off*'. A most curious entry because that was the day, according to Bean, McCay began organising the 2568 men of 2nd Bde prior to the struggle for Krithia. In actual fact McCay was not wounded till early am on 9 May. Does White's entry reveal that once again McCay was out of control? There can be no doubt about the expression '*ordered off*' because two days earlier White wrote: '*Patterson collapsed and nearly went off his head on the second night. Had to send him off.*' This has to refer to Lieut Col W G Patterson who subsequently died of illness in Australia 29 May 1916. He had returned to Australia on 3 July 1915, indicating he was put on a ship home very promptly. There are significant gaps in the Diaries during the Gallipoli campaign, mainly October and November, doubtless due to the work load. After the evacuation in December, back in Egypt, White's all absorbing task was the bringing together of the new 5th Division. He met with Godley, Birdwood, Irving, McMahon, Hobbs, Christian and Rosenthal—most one way or another, as we now know, involved in the early days of the 5th Division. White went to Alexandria on 29 March and sailed for France on the 30th. Although McCay had been in Egypt since 21 March and was in command of the new 5th Division from the 22nd, White never mentions meeting him.

Major General Sir C B B White c. 1937

Upon arrival at Marseilles, White took the train to Paris and proceeded to an unnamed HQ. On 10 June he met '*General Haking and Lawford, and General Cox (who) arrived from Egypt today.*' Over the next days he dined with Godley, rode with Birdwood, was out in the battle field in front of Messines with Gen [unnamed] and General Fanshawe, and had tea with General Plumer. Then on 24 June: '*At his command went to see the King and was invested.*'

Not much is recorded until 9 July when he lunched with Sir H Plumer. And on the next day he called on Sir H Rawlinson, and Montgomery [Rawlinson's ADC]. On 11 July from new HQ '*went out over battle field. Great din and guns. Great view of destroyed villages.*' This doubtless refers to the Battle of the Somme, where he noted that the 14 and 15 July were successful days.

On 17 July, the day originally destined for the attack at Fromelles, White makes this entry: '*Rode before breakfast. Very foggy. Good deal of rain during day. Inspected Corps Mtd Reg and Bde and Field Artillery. We go to Res Army tonight.*' White's diary is then blank from 18 July to 7 August —the period of Fromelles and the AIF entry into the Battle of the Somme at Pozières.

He returned to the pages on 9 August: '*Meeting with Army Cmdr. Then to see Gen Cox. Gen Sellheim here today to say goodbye, C in C in during afternoon but Gen and I had gone to see men in hospital. Dollman and McGlinn called.*'

While it is obvious that the huge disaster of the Battle of the Somme was more important than the attack at Fromelles, we note that White met Haking, Plumer, Godley and McGlinn, all of whom were involved at Fromelles and not Pozières. McCay is never mentioned, nor Elliott, Tivey, Pope or Hobkirk. Or for that matter Bean, to whom he loaned his car so that Bean could get up to Sailly, in the aftermath of Fromelles.

While the lack of entries in White's diary at Gallipoli can be easily explained by the fact he was in action, this cannot be the reason for the gap 18 July – 9 August 1916. White was in a comfortable HQ (his own description), near Contay, and while by no means idle, he was, as Bean's diary reveals, well-aware of Fromelles:

20 July ... this morning, on getting up and going down a little late for breakfast I heard from Smythe—he dropped the remark casually, 'The 5th Division had their little show last night'. I decided at once—if I could get a car—to run up there for the day and back. Birdwood had told me last night 'nothing for 24 hours at any rate'. White lent me his car. He said the last news has 'our men were all in the German trenches and holding on there.' 'I think they'll keep them' Butler said.

Much later on in his diaries White made these last notes about McCay and Monash: '*1 October, 1930 Heard with sorrow of death of Sir J McCay*'. and then on 3 October: '*N + another warm morning. Attended funeral of Sir Jas McCay at Church and Box Hill Cemetery. Not back till 1.15. Lunch at Club.*'

For the record he made no mention of Elliott's death and burial in March, 1931, nor of Christian's on 17 May, 1931. But on 8 October noted:

'*General Sir John Monash died at 10.55 this morning. Wrote short appreciation for Herald and Argus.*' On 11 October: '*Attended Sir John Monash's funeral in uniform lasting from 12 noon to 6.30. Long day but a wonderful tribute. Well carried out ceremony—some 300,000 people must have witnessed it. Dinner at Club and bed early.*'

In 1938, on 21 April, White wrote: '*See in this morning's paper, with great sorrow, that Talbot Hobbs died at sea yesterday. Lunch Naval and Military Club.*'

And on 12 August, 1940, White made his last entry. '*Have to go to Canberra tomorrow.*' He died together with J V Fairbairn, G A Street, Sir Henry Gullett and others the next day in a plane crash at Canberra.

Brudenell White Diaries,
State Library of Victoria
COURTESY OF LADY DERHAM (née WHITE)

THE REPUTATION OF YOUR HISTORY

Brudenell White's letter to Bean of 17 June 1932 deals with some of the latter's chapters about the 3rd Battle of Ypres. It is very revealing of White. Every attempt by Bean to criticise or comment upon the British is sternly frowned upon, and at the end of the paragraphs, White then suggests that Bean's reputation might be sullied if he does not heed White's advice. Rather manipulative one might say considering that Bean held White in high esteem.

Examples: '*I think your criticism of GHQ and the C in C is too severe and perhaps too didactic ...*' then later '*I think you might destroy the world value of your work by allowing that criticism to be too didactic.*'

Then again: '*do you think it wise to have a further hit at Gough in bringing him in a little needlessly*' then later on '*The less feeling that is shown the more unbiased will be the reputation of your history.*'

'*You have passed very skillfully over Elliott's operations and I am glad of it*' then '*But your history will be used for teaching in future and I have just a little fear that you may be regarded as condoning faults which in slightly different circumstances not easily apparent might be disastrous.*'

DESERVES GREATER EULOGY

When Brudenell White read through the chapter on Fromelles in the British history this was his opinion:

I think however that the Fromelles chapter fails to deal with the action as vigorously as it might have and its condemnation of it is far too lukewarm. I could have wished a warmer appreciation of the work done then by the AIF too. It was an outstanding piece of gallantry and deserves greater eulogy.

—Letter to A W Bazley, AWM,
3 Sept 1937

The problem of McCay

In an effort to trace the flaws in the command which led to the disaster at Fromelles it is essential to probe the character and life of James Whiteside McCay. The basic elements of his life to 1916 are covered on pages 7 and 8, in the pages describing the battle his military career is dealt with, and here we examine how he managed the years after Fromelles.

There is no doubt that in the 1920s McCay wallowed in his 'unpopularity' in firm belief that the unpopularity was due to his own wisdom being so profound and his judgements so accurate that what more could he expect from the ignorant than unpopularity? Bean in defending McCay used the issue of unpopularity as McCay saw it. But surely the crux of it was not 'unpopularity' which was just the opinion of others, the issue was McCay himself. Geoffrey Serle in his searching, sensitive biography of Monash explored McCay's character thus: '*He made his mark in Parliament by hard work, but cutting and satirically witty remarks about fellow members reduced his popularity which he always scorned to seek.*'

Apologists for McCay, of whom Bean became the public voice, whilst Pearce and Brudenell White were the private advocates, pleaded that McCay had no control over the orders handed to him by the British. Even if one accepts this, had he commanded respect from his superiors in British HQ, he could have argued his case. It was not as if he was new to such procedure. As a successful lawyer, politician and Minister for Defence, his earlier life was rooted in the business of arguing cases, defending positions, advocating causes and changing minds. Had he been, before the war, just an army officer obeying a superior officer's orders some excuse could be found. But as abundantly clear from his career up to 1914 he led, he never followed. After the war he forever took refuge in being the victim '*of the gross injustice of ... popular verdicts*' (Bean's phrase), whilst he was no more responsible '*than the humblest private*' for the disasters he presided over, which has to be one of the most illogical remarks ever made, and not in the character of Bean at all. Bean's 'apologia' for McCay, unique among his assess-ments of leaders of the AIF, can only be classified as special pleading and most probably written under pressure from Pearce and/or Brudenell White. Who else could have Bean meant when he used the phrase '*The authorities of the AIF*' to make valid this pardon? Bean knew that Birdwood never pardoned McCay.

Of the three events: Krithia, the Desert March and Fromelles over which McCay was '*loaded with blame*' (another Bean phrase), the Desert March was the one not subject to enemy activity, or a crisis situation or any other outside influence other than the transfer, by marching, of 5th Division 39 miles from one safe point to another: not terribly difficult. McCay had the time, the power, the management and others' experience of the same operation to draw upon, and still he could not get it right. No surprise then that under real stress at Krithia, Fromelles and Flers he performed even worse.

HINDSIGHT
This essay was written without the benefit of *A Turbulent Life*, Christopher Wray's highly detailed biography of McCay (see page 428), and from it dates and names have been corrected, but nothing has been deleted just because it is not noted in Wray's book. Not surprisingly, Wray does not share this writer's severe judgement of McCay, suggesting that it may have been McCay's Calvinist upbringing '*that taught* [him] *to do his duty to the end.*' valid only if one accepts the idea that ruthless ambition is a virtue. Others of us, brought up in some more humane circumstances, believe that if the ambition demands riding roughshod over others, the ambition is not worth having. If you have charge over people and they *have* to obey your orders, your responsibility for what happens is greater than theirs. You do not pull your revolver against your own men in a difficult situation when you are as lost as they are. On Anzac Day, on the day it all started, McCay showed himself as he was—contemptuous of others and mean-spirited. That was his style.

As far as Fromelles was concerned, he misunderstood the whole point of the exercise. Bean hinted at why, '*it is probably true that ... McCay welcomed the early chance of commanding his division in action.*' Perhaps this is what obscured the 'game-play' element in the attack at Fromelles from McCay. If he had understood this he would not have permitted the Australian front lines just prior to the battle to be so crammed with men that every enemy shell (and Australian shorts) caused scores of casualties.

When the battle got under way McCay permitted firstly the support battalions to go into action, and later the reserves. A few hours before dawn on 20 July the Australian line was probably held by no more than four companies. Had the Germans had the numbers of infantry to spare and been aware of this, they could have taken the entire Australian position in ten minutes as two thirds of the line had no reserves to call upon. McCay knew this, as it was his decision. Haking had no part in it.

After the battle, McCay's prohibition of a truce during which many hundreds of wounded Australians could have been brought in from No-Man's Land stands as a crime, that for anybody else would have attracted a Court-Martial.

None of this criticism is about the original order for the attack at Fromelles which may have been like so many other battle orders in the war, not very clever, it is about McCay's conduct as Commander of the 5th Division. In this he failed absolutely at every level. After Fromelles there was no redeeming incident to save his reputation. McCay's conduct should have been subject to the same sort of inquiry that went into the Gallipoli fiasco, but McCay's network protected him right to the end and beyond. For instance Brudenell White for some reason felt it necessary to go public in the Melbourne *Herald* on 16 March 1940 with this extraordinary declaration: '*Gallipoli, on the day of the landing, brings back memories of one of the greatest soldiers that ever served Australia—James McCay. In my opinion greater even than Monash*'. Quite how McCay's failures (he had no victories) were greater achievements than Monash's campaigns of 1918 escapes this writer entirely.

AWM H01890

The influence of the network of which White was part is an important footnote to the Battle of Fromelles, nobody could have had a clear conscience as far as it was concerned. The removal of Fromelles from public view, such as not having it among the battles inscribed on Melbourne's Shrine of Remembrance, is a classic example. This battle in which around 900 Victorians lost their lives is thus of less account than 'The North Sea' for instance. It was not until 1992 and 1993 when trees at the Shrine were dedicated to the 60th and 59th Bns respectively that mention of Fromelles on the plaques at the trees recorded it within the Shrine grounds.

To get a glimpse of the conduct of the men who would have been in charge of such decisions it is essential to start with some of Bean's private observations in his diary which as far as this inquiry is concerned, was primary evidence of McCay's network, and explains very clearly how McCay after destroying the 5th Division managed to get command of the main AIF training and supply base on Salisbury Plains.

Feb 16 (1917) White came back last night. I saw him today. He looked a bit worn, 'I did a great deal of rather scrappy ineffectual work, Bean,' he said to me, 'and made a few enemies.' Of course I know what he means—some of these people Legge, McCay, Anderson who are fighting for themselves ... I have no use now for the man who is not simply in this war for the winning of it. I thought Legge was once, before he spoke to me in London. No doubt Birdwood made a mistake in not telling him straight that he was not competent in the field ...

Feb 17. White ... came through the General Staff Office while I was there tonight. He said that it was a much more difficult world when you had to fight a lot of people in it. An ounce of enmity worries him more than a ton of work. He told me Birdwood wanted to continue Moore in command at Salisbury Plain—but that Legge had gathered a group of discontented people around him in London and roped in McCay; then Legge had gone to Anderson—of all people —and Anderson (who had said to Birdwood, and to White even, when over here, why don't you get rid of him? Why don't you send Legge back?) had been intriguing and sympathising with Legge, and with him had concocted and sent off a cable to Australia asking them to put McCay in charge at Salisbury Plain. Birdwood advised Australia against it but Australia disregarded the advice and put McCay in.

If I had been Birdwood I would have resigned there and then. But the little man did not—however he has written, or cabled rather, to Australia again about it ... (Bean then commented at length whether the cable Anderson sent should have gone via Birdwood—Bean's conclusion was that it should have.)

As for me—I think it is simply pitiable to see a set of straight men—White, Birdwood, Griffiths fighting a set of crooked ones (and unable to beat them because they are damnably crooked, at least Anderson is) when all the time, their whole attention ought to be concentrated upon one single object—the winning of the war.

McCay succeeded in getting command of Salisbury and remained there for the rest of the war. This extremely congenial job McCay used to the full, to promote himself, attempting in 1918 to get command of the whole AIF. This disaster was averted, thankfully, by the influence of the wily Keith Murdoch. McCay was appointed KCMG in 1918 and KBE in 1919. For his efforts on Gallipoli he had already a CB. Geoffrey Serle in his entry on McCay in ADB has McCay with a Legion d'Honneur, as does Wray in his biography also quoting the *Argus* (25 Feb 1916). The *Annuaire de la Legion d'Honneur*, the official register of living recipients, 1929 edition, does not list

McCay under Australia nor under Great Britain. Wray notes that McCay was MID in late 1916 (Flers). He had a Volunteer Decoration from 1896. It is no surprise that he was forever miffed that Monash's knighthood was a step above his.

Whilst accepting that everybody has their network and that there is nothing wrong with that, it is important to note the areas of McCay's influence in the Melbourne to which he returned in 1919.

Seemingly without relation to anything other than army jobs, McCay placed in the Routine Orders of 22 September, 1916 under the heading—Financial:

Advice has been received that 2/Lieut. N R Williams, Audit Section, AIF Administrative Headquarters, London, will shortly arrive for the purpose of effecting examinations in connection with the transactions of the Staff Paymaster ... every facility is to be afforded Lieut Williams to carry out his duties ...

Norman Rees Williams was a bit more than a passing inspector. Before enlisting Williams had been employed by the State Savings Bank of Victoria, of which McCay had been a commissioner. Williams, born in Melbourne in 1892, was educated at Castlemaine Grammar the school owned by McCay since 1885 and became the acknowledged protégé of McCay, perhaps the son he never had, and progressed steadily, partly due to his own ability, but surely McCay's stewardship was also a factor. Williams emerged from war as Lieut Col in the Pay Corps and it has been suggested that Williams '*used the Bank's passbook as a model for designing the army pay book*'. The considerable experience and responsibility in the AIF led to Williams' appointment in 1926 as Secretary to the General Manager, and three years later as Secretary of the Bank. He soon had an OBE.

The Castlemaine connections in the State Savings Bank give an interesting view of McCay's network.

From 1912 to 1914 McCay had been a Commissioner in the State Savings Bank of Victoria, an organization that had the full support of Victorian politician Harry Lawson, another solicitor from Castlemaine who defeated McCay in the 1900 State election. Lawson had been a pupil of McCay's at Castlemaine Grammar School. It is not without importance to this story that Lawson went on to be Commissioner of Crown Lands and Survey 1912–15, then Attorney-General, Solicitor-General and Minister for Public Instruction, before becoming Premier on 21 March, 1918. He remained Premier until 18 April, 1924 when he resigned and went to the Senate until 1934, getting a knighthood in 1933.

Lawson had in 1919 appointed McCay as Chairman of the Victorian Royal Commission on High Prices, which recommended the establishment of a Fair Profits Commission, at the same time McCay held an appointment as an adviser for 3 years to the Victorian Government, remaining Deputy Chairman of the State Savings Bank, and taking on the Chairmanship of the Disposals Board. Beside these well-paid jobs there was his thriving legal practice. To cope with the Melbourne Police Strike of November 1923 Monash was appointed to recruit a Special Constabulary Force, assisted by Elliott. At the end of the first week Monash went to Sydney and handed over to McCay. It was a job that suited McCay perfectly, and the only person to answer to was Lawson.

Running alongside, so to speak, was the career of George Edwin Emery, born 1859 in Castlemaine, and General Manager of the State Savings Bank from 1897 till 1929, when he retired completing 55 years service with the bank. It was Emery and McCay as Deputy Chairman from 1920, who put together the Bank's Provident Fund which began in 1922. Emery's two sons were in the AIF. He died in 1937.

Alongside Emery there was William George McBeath, born in Fitzroy in 1865, a merchant and Camberwell Councillor and Mayor for many years whilst being Chairman of Commissioners for State Savings Bank. He also held positions as chairman of Royal Commission on Navy and Defence Department 1916–18, member Business Board Defence Department 1916–18, Chairman of the AIF Disposals Board, London 1919–20, Australian Delegate to League of Nations 1924. McBeath was still Chairman of the Bank when he died on 2 April, 1931, six months after McCay. An interim Chairman ran the Bank until 1940 when Williams took over, remaining in charge until 1957 when he retired.

As a former Dux of Scotch College, McCay was always held in high regard by the school. But when the war began and McCay was to lead the 2nd Brigade, the Victorian Contingent so to speak, he assumed hero status, only added to by Gallipoli, Fromelles and Flers. The school, like the nation, was not into the business of analysing the success or otherwise of the battles. A school song was written about McCay, and when he returned wounded in 1915, legend has it that the entire school was on the wharf at Port Melbourne to greet him with the song. By the end of the war the other former Dux of Scotch, Monash, had a somewhat sounder reputation than McCay and to some extent became *the* School war hero.

While of no surprise but again reflecting McCay's character, it is interesting to note that while Monash was President of the Naval and Military Club in Melbourne from 1921 to 1930, McCay gets no mention in the Club's history, not even his death is noted.

The prospect of that death was first signalled to readers of *Reveille* in August 1930 '*we regret to hear of the serious illness ... and wish him a speedy and complete restoration to health. He has been always a generous and staunch friend of ours ...*'

McCay had been admitted to the Somerset House Private Hospital in East Melbourne where he died on 1 October 1930 of 'hypertensive renal disease' (kidney failure), as described on his death certificate. Wray quoting family connections wrote that McCay, in fact, died of cancer.

The main Australian newspapers all gave extensive coverage on 2 Oct 1930 to McCay's death the previous day, as did *The Times* of London which received its report from 'Our Melbourne Correspondent'. It pointed out that McCay was by profession a barrister and solicitor and served in both the Victorian and Federal Parliament. '*As a military commander,*' it wrote, '*he was able and vigorous, and a stern disciplinarian. He won some reputation for a remarkable series of narrow escapes from being shot.*' It then gave details of other aspects of his career not always mentioned in the Australian obituaries. For instance '*at the age of 19 he was appointed headmaster of Castlemaine Grammar School but began study of law and in 1895 was called to the Victorian Bar. That he was (for a short time) Chairman of Advisory Committee of the War Service Homes Commission and later its Business Adviser.*' It concluded that '*his good fortune and his courage made him the idol of his men. Later in the war, in Australia, he was conspicuous for his advocacy of conscription.*' No Australian paper mentioned this last point.

The *Sydney Morning Herald* pointed out that McCay was Deputy Chairman of the Savings Bank, and the only paper to put a subheading, mentioning the unmentionable: '*Led Australian Attack at Fromelles.*' From then on it was trying to be objective: '*He possessed a quality of reserve that did not make him popular with the men under his command and he was blamed for several tragic incidents in the war, such as an exceptionally gruelling and unnecessary desert march in Egypt and the awful tragedy at Fromelles, for which subsequent research by the Official Historian (Mr C E W Bean) showed he was not responsible ... (he) distinguished himself in the famous but tragic attack on Krithia. Starting the attack with a staff of 12, at the end of the day the only survivors were the commander and one signaller ... a bullet snapped his thigh bone ... for 11 years after the war Sir James McCay lived in the shadow of accusation the injustice of which he felt very keenly. This was not without its effect on his health. Happily the facts were made public during his lifetime.*' The only tribute printed was from the Minister for Defence, Mr Green.

The Melbourne *Argus* with which McCay had close links over many years carried the longest obituary by far; and noted McCay remained active in his legal practice at the same time being business adviser to the Commonwealth, and that at various times filled posts allotted to him by State Ministries.

The death notice recorded that '*he was the beloved father of Margaret and Beatrix*', that the service would be held at Cairns Church, East Melbourne and the burial would be at Box Hill, then this line: '*The funeral will not be of a military character*'. His probate papers described McCay as '*barrister of Mont Albert*'.

The *Argus* also covered the funeral on 4 October in detail, but apart from its own tribute printed no others. Of the funeral it wrote: '*Attended by a large number of leaders of public life in Victoria ... although it was not a military funeral the presence of several senior military officers in uniform, the draping of the coffin with the Union Jack and the sounding of the last post after the reading of the funeral service reminded those around the grave side of the passing of an eminent leader of the Australian Imperial Force in the Great War.*' The Scotch College flag was used as a canopy over the grave.

At the Presbyterian Cairns Memorial Church in East Melbourne the Rev. F Hagenauer pointed out that McCay had been associated with the church as a boy. Hagenauer then went on the attack, pointing out that McCay had '*faced the greatest difficulties with unwavering courage*', and that if the angry and enraged men who complained of the desert march and Fromelles had known how hard McCay fought the High Command on these issues, they would have changed their minds.

Hagenauer summed it up thus: '... *but orders having been issued Sir James McCay realised that his first duty was to obey ... he had suffered under misrepresentation for many years without complaining ... and had borne blame that was not his. He had suffered in silence until his vindication came and his name was cleared.*'

Hagenauer's eulogy, the only such tribute noted in the press was made by a man who a year later from the same pulpit attacked the politicians who deplored the activities of the New Guard in New South Wales, '*they must know that whatever semblance of order is maintained in that state is due to the New Guard.*' In Victoria something known as the White Guard (a title to do with skin colour) was standing in the wings in case order was needed to be promoted there. Throughout Australia, as elsewhere, ex-servicemen, their lives and minds hugely ruined by the war were being neglected by a Government forever overwhelmed by the task of paying Britain huge sums of money for the privilege of sending volunteers to defend the King and Empire. The unreasonableness of this meant that the Left had considerable support from former soldiers, and those who feared this most were well-established officers. It was they who set up the Old Guard—the more secret of the Rightist groups, then the New Guard—the public face of the Right which sought to rid Australia of communists, socialists and other like-minded workers organisations. This conflict divided and to a large extent neutered Australia until the Second World War. Many of those at McCay's funeral would have known all about these arrangements.

The list of Pall Bearers is interesting. In the style of the time, prominent citizens were noted first by their position then in brackets their name: Brig. General C H Foott; General Sir John Monash; Maj. General H E Elliott; Maj. General R E Williams; Maj. General J Stanley,

Chairman of the Commissioners of the State Savings Bank Sir William McBeath, Mr A S Baillieu and Mr W M Thwaites. The chief mourners were Mr Delamore McCay, Mr Heywood McCay, Mr Finlay McCay, Mr Deric McCay, and son-in-law George O Reid.

Among the congregation the *Argus* observed the following: Maj. General Brudenell White, Maj. General T H Courtney, Brig. General J P McGlinn, Leader of the Opposition (Mr Latham), H I Cohen MLC, Chancellor of the University (Sir John MacFarland), Headmaster of Scotch College (Dr W S Littlejohn), Sir Arthur Robinson, Sir Henry Maudsley, Gen Manager of State Savings Bank (Mr Alexander Cooch), Mr G W Paxton, Capt. A M Treacy, Editor of the *Argus* (Mr R L Curthoys), Mr W A Brennan (*Argus*), Mr Charles Forester, Mr H J Ramsay and Mr L Heffernan representing the RSL. (McCay was, at his death, a member of the Box Hill Branch of RSL and the cortege paused as it passed the branch for a wreath to be placed on the hearse.) A A Sleight Pty Ltd conducted the funeral.

McCay's grave (NS Presbyterian section 565), at Box Hill cemetery is the simple, standard layout and plaque for veterans of WW1. The inscription makes no reference to his family nor carries any tributes.

In the *Herald*, the obituary carried a quote from McCay on his silence. '*Having maintained my silence throughout these years, I still prefer to remain silent. My reputation as a soldier I left in the safekeeping of history. It has never appeared to be in conformity with my duty as a general officer of the AIF that I should open my mouth.*'

'Opening his mouth' on everything but himself was never a problem for McCay. In his last years every fortnight or so in the *Argus,* he sounded forth on all manner of topics: Anzac, Gallipoli, Food, Marx, Hospitals, League of Nations, Defence Policy, Paper Money, White Australia, Air Power, Rifle Clubs, State Savings Bank for example.

Why McCay never sought to defend himself, or explain his actions was doubtless because he knew that there was no plausible defence and if he exposed himself to questions he would be torn apart. And in the process so would a few other reputations.

A month after McCay's death the news found its way to Birdwood then in the last month of his best job—C-in-C India. A compulsive sender of 'sincere' messages he could well have omitted this inaccurate pretence: '*to express my deep regret at the loss of a really brave and gallant comrade who served so long with us in Gallipoli and France*'. After all McCay was on Gallipoli but five weeks and in France for only six months.

All in contrast to the weekly *Bulletin* undoubtedly the most popular magazine among the troops in the trenches during the war years.

The Bulletin magazine in the 1920s and 1930s could be relied upon to 'tell it how it is' to use the current expression. It was not overawed by McCay's brilliance or that he had just died, when it printed the following in 8 October 1930 issue:

Major General McCay who died last week aged 66 was a born soldier and a brave man—qualities which are by no means inseparable. Nevertheless he became about the most detested officer in the AIF at an early stage in the World War, and remained so to the end. It worried him, and his friends have tried to show he was maligned, their defence being that in ordering such insanities as the foredoomed Fromelles slaughter he was only obeying orders. The answer of his critics is that he should have refused to sacrifice lives to no adequate purpose, as that had been done hundreds of times in every great army, not only by officers of field rank but by NCOs, although those who have taken that kind of responsibility have usually suffered for it. A son of a manse, McCay had a fine brain of the academic type and showed the family talent for writing—two of his brothers have been editors. He was Minister for Defence 25 years ago, and in latter years was Deputy Chairman of Victoria's Savings Bank.

On another page in the same issue *The Bulletin* recorded a unique human aspect of McCay, describing what he did when he came upon a substantial two-up school in the UK camp he was in charge of. The school evacuated quickly leaving all the money on the ground, '*McCay put it into a fund for UK girls who had been too trusting with Digger lovers ... thus providing a form of assistance that could not be extended by the AIF in the ordinary course of events.*'

There remains McCay's family to briefly describe, completing these biographical notes. Boyd and Esther McCay had ten children, with one daughter dying when three, owing to a fire accident. The other girls were Leirene and Margaret. James Whiteside had six well-known brothers, probably Adam Cairns McCay (1879–1963) was the most talked about. A journalist of great talent for prose and poetry, with six languages, a bohemian lifestyle, Adam worked for a number of newspapers until he drank himself to death. Another brother Delamore William (1877–1958), also a journalist, not quite as gifted as Adam, also worked on many papers, and for a time in London. Campbell Ernest McCay (1867–1943) also wrote verse, was private secretary to W L Baillieu, politician and industrialist. Hugh Douglas McCay (1870–1953) was deputy manager of the Royal Mint in Melbourne and London. Andrew Ross McCay (1873–1958) was a senior officer with the Bank of Australasia and Walton Heywood McCay (1879–1963) was Chairman of the Rural Bank and director of land settlement in Western Australia. Thus as a family network the McCays were strong in journalism, banking, politics and the law.

McCay made his will on 19 October, 1927:

... and declare this to be my last will and testament. Having made during my lifetime due provision for my

daughter Margaret Mary McCay, I give and bequeath the whole of my estate to my daughter Beatrix Waring McCay of 7 Were Street, Brighton aforesaid barrister absolutely. I appoint my said daughter Beatrix Waring McCay to be the sole executrix of this my will.

The witnesses were W Thwaites, Solicitor of Melbourne and M O'Meara, Clerk to McCay and Thwaites, Solicitors of Melbourne.

In the best legal tradition McCay's affairs were in perfect order. His total assets were: furniture worth £6, amount of war pension due at death £9, watches, trinkets and jewellery £12, other personal effects—clothing, books and pictures £35.15.0, money in hand £7, money in the National Bank £103.12.0, his life insurance policies with AMP, NM Society and Mutual Life totalled £6,250.0.0, and the bonuses for all three were £3,578.2.0. McCay had one debt to be paid, to a Walter Collins of 16 Gray Street, St. Kilda of £118.9.9. McCay had no real estate within Victoria and probate was granted on his estate of £10,112.18.11. It was signed by Beatrix Waring Reid and George Oswald Reid. McCay's daughter had married Reid in August 1930, and while she had lived with her father in Brighton, her address, when her father died, was 7 Malvern Road, Mont Albert.

For a man whose income for at least twenty years had been substantial, and whose last ten years had been close to the financial world, McCay's 'estate' is the final evidence of his character, style and priorities.

McCay's biographer, Wray, was told by George Reid, McCay's son-in-law that when he (McCay) had been diagnosed with cancer, he decided to destroy all his correspondence, personal papers and any other records he had kept, in a backyard bonfire. Considering the amount of Australian history he had been part of, the people he knew, the records of the war he must have kept, not forgetting his considerable output of newspaper articles, it must have been a sizeable bonfire. It was also a tragic event, frustrating forever any real knowledge of the man, and the events in which he played such an important part. He had been '*cleared*' in the official history at the same time, the validity of which deep down only he could assess, and with death standing at the door, there was no point in pretending that his life was a great success. The bonfire seems to be a farewell note from a man who took everything he could out of life, and was emotionally unable to give anything back. He was a mean man, leaving nothing to the nation that had given him so much.

Pearce and McCay

Around 1938–39 Pearce turned to writing his memoirs at the behest of his friends and associates so he claimed in the introduction to the book *Carpenter to Cabinet* (1951). Also in the introduction he expressed the '*difficulty in writing a book of this kind is to know what to include and what to exclude.*' So one searches the pages for Pearce's recollections and assessments of the other members of the triumvirate that brought the AIF into being. Brudenell White always portrayed as the work horse of the group is never mentioned. Only Bridges elicits a paragraph. Pearce had just been appointed Minister for Defence. Pearce wrote: '*Among the military officers of the time, Colonel (later Major-General) Bridges attracted me most of all.*
My predecessor in office [this was McCay] *had described him to me as an impossible man. He will never give you advice suitable to the political position, he went on to say, but only that which he regards as 'sound' from the military point of view. So one day I sent for Bridges.*
I pointed out to him that I had no military experience and asked him for his advice in such circumstances as to my future actions.'

Pearce then went on to describe the three books Bridges advised him to read and study, and concluded, '*I took his advice; I did not only read those books, I studied them. To this I attribute much of the success I afterwards achieved in my administration of the Defence Department.*'

Pearce's memoirs could hardly be described as exhaustive which was a pity because few men in that period of Australian history were closer to the action. That he does not mention McCay by name is curious for McCay was always part of the political scene. Perhaps it was enough to have McCay critical of Bridges, and that when McCay as Minister should have been using Bridges' military advice, all he wanted was political advice. Very revealing indeed, Pearce had said enough.

Fromelles—the middle years

Through the 1920s and 1930s the town was slowly rebuilt, but the population hardly increased in that difficult period. Although no records seem to have survived of the number of pilgrims to the battlefields in those years, vast numbers of survivors and next of kin of those who did not survive visited France and Belgium. Given the tens of thousands of men who fought over this land, Fromelles must have been much visited. There can be little doubt that some Germans came back, anonymously as possible, to recall and reflect on days spent in the area, and just prior to the Second World War there is a memory of a busload arriving. Records do survive of some activities in Fromelles at this time, and 1938 is a good example of the rise from the ashes, albeit just before the next dark age.

In 1938 the post office was at Aubers; the postman Victor Hennebel did the deliveries—once a day. At this time there was also a public telephone box and five people were connected to the phone service.

There was an Agricultural Society under the presidency of M Louis Vermès, the Mayor. The Society of Gardeners led by M Alphonse Salomez bought and leased allotments to townspeople.

The Rural Credit Fund, run by M Georges Lerouge, offered loans to farmers and workers who could borrow money at 3% or save money with them and earn 1.75%.

The Municipal Music Group was led by M Henri Leblanc, and consisted of 30 players. The high point for them was the 'Éclair Orchestra' under the direction of Octave Equine and this continued until 1942.

The Veterans Association, under the presidency of M Eugène Leignel was very active as most of the men in the town were veterans and the Association was their club.

The Charitable Office under the auspices of the Church distributed to the homes of the poor – medicine, fuel and clothes. A dozen families were helped during this period.

Fromelles, after the surrender of France on 25 June 1940 was not, in contrast to 1914, of any strategic importance. However, several weeks beforehand, Fromelles had seen an influx of Belgian refugees on the roads, and there had been some skirmishes between French and German soldiers leading to an exodus of the population.

On 27 May 1940 the German air force bombed the roads around, and the cross-road at Fromelles. About forty bombs exploded near the presbytery and the cemetery. The British ammunition supply trucks parked in the market town were hit by the bombs. The resulting explosions of the trucks destroyed several houses and damaged many more—there were some casualties. The following day, 28 May, the Germans entered Fromelles and thus began a new occupation.

During the German occupation, a local committee and prisoners' aid group was organised and started operations in January 1942. On 31 December of that year there were still 29 prisoners of war from Fromelles in German prison camps.

On 19 July 1941, whilst escorting a squadron of bombers, Sgt Kenneth Walter Bramble of 609 (West Riding) Squadron RAF was shot down by German planes. His Spitfire crashed at Fauquissart and his body was retrieved and then buried in the British Military Cemetery at Merville (Nord). Many years later the president of the Association Antiq'Air, M Jocelyn Leclerq proposed a memorial at Fromelles to the memory of Sgt Bramble. An appeal for money for this project is currently underway.

The Germans who moved in, seemed to like the region. The Engineers and the Infantry used the old fortifications for training, and for much of the period, the village of Fromelles was occupied by reservists of the 15th Army. Until October 1942 the Germans ran a veterinary service for horses in the town.

Despite the war, Fromelles was largely untouched. The region was far from the bombing and there was no shortage of food.

The Allied bombardment of the Germans started in 1942. The people of Fromelles awoke one night to see a squadron of Lancaster bombers heading towards Germany. On the return flight, it was apparent that 10% of the planes had been shot down. It was a sight that they would see many more times.

On 8 September 1943, British planes dropped 15 bombs around Fromelles, but luckily nobody was killed. One bomb fell in a field of tobacco some 150 metres behind the Church leaving a large crater. Four more bombs exploded on the rue Sotte, towards Fournes, destroying an old block house; ten others fell without exploding, on a hangar and in the fields.

It was on Sunday 3 September 1944, after the 10 am mass, that Casimir Charlet and Emile Barbry were taken as hostages by the Germans. They were then used as human shields to cover the German retreat. After a journey of 50 kms, they were released and able to return to Fromelles unharmed.

INFORMATION COURTESY M DELEBARRE

13

An amazing outburst

> An amazing outburst during which he charged British Army Officers ... with inefficiency, was made by Brig. General Elliott.
>
> —*The Age*, 18 July 1930

To mark the 14th anniversary of the battle the Canberra branch of the RSSILA invited 'Pompey' Elliott to address them on the subject of Fromelles. By his own account, '*I went to a great deal of trouble to get lantern slides made and composed a lecture which consisted almost entirely of extracts from* [Bean's] *History.*' The immediate result was a newspaper report on the lecture headed *An echo of the war* (see margin), which later became known as *An Amazing Outburst.* Elliott was extremely annoyed at the public press and wrote to *The Duckboard*, the Melbourne Returned Soldiers' magazine, where he was sure he would be fully reported, '*I strongly suspect that as a supporter of the late Nationalist Government, their* [The Age] *correspondent regarded me as fair game to discredit in the eyes of the public by any means.*' Elliott wrote to *The Age* and took them to task, and they, who in the past had often printed hugely long letters from Elliott, now were less sympathetic and had this editorial comment:

> General Elliott is entirely mistaken in his suggestion that there has been 'deliberate misrepresentation for political ends'. No political ends exist to be served, none is under discussion. Neither do questions of accuracy concerning the data on which the lecturer relied arise. As to whether it is wise at this particular period in Australia's postwar history and in this particular month, to revive the terrible story of Fleurbaix and to reopen that awful page of war tragedy in a lecture at the Federal capital to returned soldiers, is legitimate subject for controversy.

It was an echo of the Kennedy affair, but this time Elliott was on the receiving end, however he was blaming the British authorities not the troops. Probably to make sure his true sentiments were known Elliott sent a copy of the article to the Editor of *The Duckboard*, together with the full text of his letter to *The Age* and their editorial treatment of it. '*You will note*', Elliott told *The Duckboard*, '*the heading—intended to perpetuate their previous attitude of hostility. Is it any wonder that men of decent instincts are declining to take up a public career?*'

The Duckboard ran *The Age* report, '*every word intact*', and *The Age* comment and then '*invited General Elliott to use*

AN ECHO OF THE WAR.

BRITISH INEFFICIENCY AT FLEURBAIX.

General Elliott's Charge.

CANBERRA, Thursday.—An amazing outburst, during which he charged British army officers commanding the British and Australian forces at Fleurbaix during the Great War with inefficiency was made by Brigadier-General Elliott when delivering a lecture to Canberra returned soldiers to-night.

Through this inefficiency, General Elliott said, more than 7000 men were lost to the British forces, and of this number 5533 were officers and men belonging to the Fifth Australian Division. The whole operation was so incredibly bungled that it was almost incomprehensible how the British staff responsible for it could have consisted of trained professional soldiers of considerable reputation and experience, and why, in view of the outcome of this extraordinary adventure, any of them were retained in active command. General Haking, who commanded the force, endeavored to throw the whole of the blame on to the infantry in an effort to hide his own faults. He "got away with it" for the time being, as it was placed upon General McCay, of the Australian forces. Authorities in the A.I.F. did not utter a word to raise the ban on him, in accordance with the custom of the British regular army that no criticism must be made of a senior officer. The result of the action was to cripple the Fifth Division for months, and Australia's finest officers and men perished at Fleurbaix. General Haking had undertaken the work of diverting German attention from the Somme, but apparently he formulated his attack without full knowledge of his work. The battle was the first in which the Australians took part in France, and the value of its results was tragically disproportionate to the cost. General McCay had been only a few days at the front, and as a result there was some excuse for him, but there was none for Generals Haking, Munro and Butler, who should have known all the facts. Major Howard was the only high-staff officer who appeared on the field, and he then told the speaker that he expected a holocaust. He (General Elliott) endeavored to prevent the slaughter, but apparently the generals he spoke to regarded their men as merest cannon fodder

ALL THAT MATTERS

... study of military history should be directed mainly to discover the Commander's thoughts and impressions and the decisions which spring from them ... For it matters little what the situation actually was at a particular point or moment; all that matters is what the Commander thought it was.

—B Liddell Hart
Thoughts on War

HIS ETERNAL NIGHTMARE

Herbert Scanlon enlisted as Herbert Sanlon 2807 in 22nd Bn on 16 July 1915, it was his seventh attempt. He was 16 years and 10 months old and went directly to Gallipoli. Later in Egypt he transferred to 59th Bn and went to France. At Fromelles he was badly wounded and taken to Birmingham where he was, in his own words, '*a cot case*'. He returned to Australia 16 October, 1916 permanently incapacitated. He turned to writing, publishing over some twenty years at least 21 small booklets, usually of 32 pages, of short stories, war memories and popular history. In one of these titled *Triolette* (1923) he included a story *A shattered romance*. It could be fiction or faction, but the fact that it deals with one of the persistent 'events' of Fromelles, the execution of a French spy, often described as a farmer, it is worth noting. In part, the story goes:

... and as there were others of us who had sweethearts in the village, he (Bluey) was a very handy medium for the exchange of greetings when leave from our billets was not granted. Then came the attack at Fleurbaix, with its nights of death and horror. Many of the lads who had sweethearts passed along the long road into eternal night—but Bluey survived ... he was a runner attached to a battalion that was engaged in heavy fighting at the latter end of 1916.

Manette was his sweetheart, living with her 'father'. Bluey surprised her one night after Fleurbaix on the phone speaking German. Bluey reported her to his CO and the girl and her father were [continued opposite]

The Duckboard for a full and frank description, without fear or favour, of the Battle of Fleurbaix. Readers of this journal are invited to judge cases, not by preconceived conclusions, but solely on their merits'. In *The Duckboard* for September 1930 there was Elliott's lecture text—8½ pages, around 8500 words. Elliott's introduction to his lecture was thus '*as to the conduct of the battle, Captain Bean ... who is generally most lenient towards official blundering, found himself forced to condemn it in mild but no uncertain terms ... I propose to outline the course of events ... and endeavour to show what errors were made and who was responsible for them. The facts are drawn from the Official History ... supplemented by a few details supplied from my own knowledge. I may add that I visited the field of battle after the Armistice in 1919 to verify from the enemy's point of view my own conception of the position.*'

Bearing in mind Elliott's earlier censure of Bean '*it does appear to me that you have strained your conscience in the endeavour to let the Higher Command down as lightly as possible*' it should not be a surprise that Elliott's pronouncement on Fromelles was an attack on Haking; much of which was valid, but not all of it. Elliott made much of Haking being satisfied with the resources at his disposal, and that he, Haking, had when cancellation was suggested said, '*the troops are worked up to it, were ready and anxious to do it, and a change of plan would have a bad effect upon the troops*'. To which Elliott countered '*It may be here observed that Haking spoke that which was utterly untrue and unfounded. The infantry in the line were as a fact almost unanimously against the scheme.*' Somebody must have told Haking that the artillery was ready, and the infantry. He was certainly not the type of commander who moved among his men to get their opinion, or was he such a domineering character that all wilted before him?

Searching the lecture for new information from Elliott one finds only crumbs: but some important ones. Of the heavy British artillery detailed to reduce the Sugarloaf said Elliott '*they could hardly hit it, much less subdue it, their guns being the oldest in the front. They were really afraid, as we learnt later on, of aiming at the Sugarloaf at all for fear of hitting our own lines.*'

Elliott had a few revelations about the Australians as well:

> The first wave of the 59th ... on our extreme right, got half-way across ... with small losses, the farm moat and the Laies River being bridged where required and were found to be no obstacle. This in itself shows that had No-Man's Land been half the width they could not have been

stopped. Up to then our machine guns, firing from the top of the parapet, kept the enemy quiet. At that stage, however, they met a dreadful enfilade machine gun fire from the Sugarloaf, the garrison of which, having defeated the British … now gave their attention to us. Our machine guns placed on the flank had now to lengthen their range into a protective barrage because of the danger to our own men.

The 60th, who were next on the left, got further on. A few of them got into the enemy lines and brought back some prisoners, but the great majority of this battalion were also killed or wounded long before they got to the enemy's wire.

Further on Elliott turned to the later failure:

> When the British reported they would renew their attack at 9pm and wanted help, I at once arranged with General McCay to take two companies of the 58th under a splendid Duntroon boy Major Hutchinson, and directed him to attack with them. Meanwhile I ordered the rest of my troops to try and to dig in… Unfortunately the British troops could not start. They had found the enemy fire so hot and their trenches so shattered that they could not get their men up in time. A message was sent to me to stop Hutchinson's attack, but this did not reach me till half an hour after he had gone forward … He himself fell and most of his men were slaughtered. Proper liaison measures should have prevented this catastrophe.

All that to reveal in Elliott's own words how he saw it fourteen years later. There is no hint of criticism of the British 184th Bde, but the simple understanding that '*they could not start*'. Nobody has failed anybody except in the '*liaison*' work. It is interesting that Elliott does not suggest who was at fault in that regard.

Further on Elliott mentions Cass, and it was Elliott at his best:

> Colonel Cass, who commanded the 54th magnificently throughout the fight being almost the last, with Lowe his adjutant, to withdraw. He was broken-hearted at the loss of his battalion. He had formed much the same unfavourable opinion from the outset as myself of the operation, and the thought of the awful bungling and the slaughter that resulted ruined his health and he came home.

Elliott then detailed the casualties, again straight out of Bean, and then this:

> The British units … were much weaker than ours in numbers. Their strongest battalion was about 600 in number and they had a slightly longer front upon which to attack. We cannot justly blame their failure in the circumstances. Like ourselves, they were victims of shocking generalship.

In view of what this inquiry has discovered about the British units *not* being significantly understrength it would be interesting to know what Elliott would have made of that. Under the shield of quoting Bean's piece about '*Tommies could not be relied upon to uphold a flank in a stiff fight*', Elliott said: '*But their*

HIS ETERNAL NIGHTMARE (contd)

court-martialled—Bluey gave evidence—and the two on being found guilty were blindfolded, tied to chairs and shot. Bluey was in the firing squad; he went into battle next day, got blown up, but not killed.

Scanlon wrote:

… the shell hurled him into the lap of death, but the fickle jade scorned him who welcomed her and passed him out a wreck for life, and the tap, tap of his stick will sound on the busy street, people will hurry past him; later on children will fear him. The young girls will pity him, charity will be doled sparingly to him, and his eternal nightmare will be: a blindfolded figure on a chair at twenty paces, a pressure of the trigger. Manette, his love, whose only sin was her love of country, a lifeless heap of clay'.

ON THE ROAD TO MANSFIELD

As on the road to a hundred other places in Australia, this little town memorial survives, faithfully white-washed. It remembers four who did not come back: Lieut C J Callan, died at the Hindenburg Line in 1916, L/Cpl Giles at Passchendaele in 1917, while Ptes Harris and O'Day, both of 59th Bn, died at Fromelles.

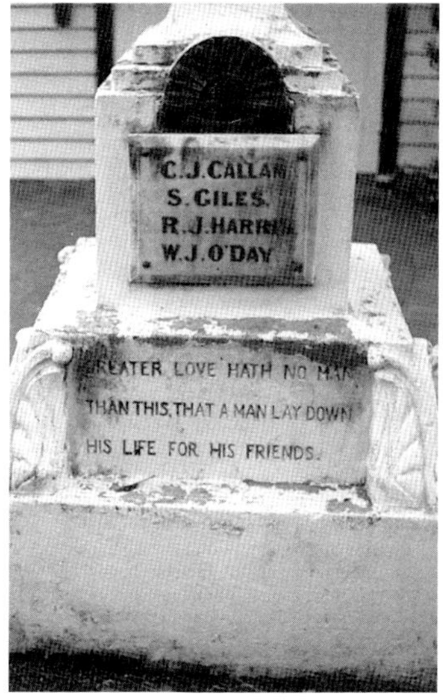

The Memorial at Panton Hills

own General Haking had cast the first stone against them, and who can blame those who followed his lead?' A very dubious and most unjust argument. Haking had said of the 61st that they '*were insufficiently imbued with the offensive spirit…*', and now Elliott is wondering if he was not a bit right ?

The last parts of Elliott's lecture were to mention first how he had spoken to Major Howard and confirmed that disaster was ahead, but '*I have never spoken to him since, or heard from him*', and secondly he summed it all up under the heading of 10 blunders:

> 1. Failure of the first duty of a commander—personal reconnaissance—resulting in selection of unsuitable ground commanded everywhere by the enemy observation and fire, and which gave no position on which to consolidate.
> 2. No-Man's Land in front of centre of attack was too wide. (This is also due to the first).
> 3. Insufficient artillery preparation, resulting in the wire being uncut and enemy front line and batteries not silenced.
> 4. Faulty division of front, the junction of units being opposite enemy's strongest point.
> 5. No arrangement for liaison between these divisions or to co-ordinate the advance itself or methods to be employed.
> 6. No sufficient arrangements for ammunition supply by aeroplanes or the like.
> 7. Gas cylinders kept in our line when it was certain that line would be bombarded.
> 8. Hurried and insufficient preparations resulting in mistakes by inexperienced junior staff officers, eg in sending up undetonated bombs. As this was the first engagement of these young officers, this danger might have been provided against by Haking.
> 9. Sending battalion staffs forward with the last wave before any lodgment had been gained in enemy's line, thus sacrificing valuable officers uselessly.
> 10. No reserves provided. Had this been done it might have been possible to push a company or two across into the space that had been gained, and by attack outwards, to have cleared the front of the 15th Brigade.

Some relentless questioning of Elliott on some of these, rather than arguing the toss about Haking might have produced some illumination on the battle. Whilst Haking might well be blamed absolutely for a number of the blunders, there are several very much in McCay's court ie 5. Surely McCay should (and could) have demanded liaison with Mackenzie. 8: hardly a matter for the Corps Commander. 9: the same, and 10! Well, whose fault was it there were no reserves? Who called for them? Who demanded them? Who authorised their use in the first instance? Not Haking that is for sure.

It was a pity that Elliott's judgement failed him because this was his last and best chance to deal with Fromelles, and

WHEN HE WAS WELL ENOUGH

Sergeant C P Finnie 2924 of 60th Bn Signallers went out in the fourth wave. When virtually all were killed, he and Sgt W H Gates returned and took out another telephone party, but all were hit and being unable to find an officer came back to the lines. For this work Gates received the DCM and Finnie was put forward for the Serbian Gold Medal, but it is not clear if he received it. He was from Nottingham, orphaned when nine, he later went to sea, ending up in Sydney, where he later became a Master mariner and ship's captain. His daughter who became a nurse and prominent in matters of social justice wrote of him:

> *He was sent to fight in France, where he was wounded. After a period in hospital he returned to active duty for a short time … but his war injuries finally led to his discharge in June 1918. When he was well enough, he and my mother married … I was born on 12 May 1919 … my mother suggested my middle name be Fleurette to honour my father's miraculous escape from death at the battle of Fleurbaix, also known as the battle of Fromelles.*
>
> *Thirty Officers and 1,000 men from 60th Bn took part … the following morning only three officers and 61 men answered the roll call. Most … were wounded, including my father who had bullets in his liver and intestines. My father survived until I was in my thirties but his personality was forever altered by his wartime experiences.*
>
> *When I was a little girl I used to see him fall on the floor in pain. My mother would get down on the floor and wrap her arms around him tightly. She said she was able to give my father some pain relief as she would feel the pain leaving him and entering her own body. He seemed to find some comfort in this.*
>
> *My father did not usually talk about his war time experiences. Except once he told me that the poppies in Fleurbaix grew more plentiful during the spring which followed the battle. This was thought to be due to the blood and flesh in the soil.*
>
> —Fleur Finnie
> *Don't Stand on the Grass* (1996)

THE 61ST DIVISION AT LAVENTIE
Surviving all that came after, the plaque on the wall of the Town Hall at Laventie shows the Division emblem together with the badges of the various regiments that made up the Division. The wording clearly refers to the Division's presence in the area at the time of the Battle of Fromelles. There is no reference to the Division's later exploits. Yet *The Times* own correspondent filed the following story, again revealing as late as 1935 ignorance of Fromelles, and even who Major General Mackenzie was.

PHOTO COURTESY M DELEBARRE

he was unable to bring to the discussion anything other than attacks on Haking and information from Bean. He had slipped into the same error as Kennedy, and got caught in the same trap: the newspaper headline, and the three-word catch phrase ... *The Mystery Battle ... The Disloyal Play ... An Amazing Outburst.*

But the offending sentence that caused Elliott the trouble nobody could argue with. It was a philosophical proposition as was Kennedy's and it was turned into a petty argument, a simple issue. The press of necessity had to do this, it is the style of newspapers: neither a vice nor virtue, just how it is. Elliott said:

> The whole operation was so incredibly blundered from beginning to end that it is almost incomprehensible how the British Staff, who were responsible for it, could have consisted of trained professional soldiers of considerable reputation and experience, and why, in view of the outcome of this extraordinary adventure, any of them were retained in active command.

Nobody knew more about the frustrations of command than Elliott. After Fromelles when he had learned you could question the Higher Authorities and live, his leadership of the 15th Bde became the stuff of legends. The men would go anywhere, do anything and at any time for him, because they knew he would never take advantage of them. In the secrecy of his letters to his wife, Elliott wrote: '*their absolute confidence in me is touching ... you must pray more than ever that I shall be worthy of this trust and have wisdom and courage given me worthy of my job.*' But that trust Elliott had secured at a high price to himself, he remained a Brigadier General throughout the war. Real men like Hobbs, perceptive enough to realise what a wonderful man was hidden inside the often very difficult Brigadier, could cope. But

61ST DIVISION MEMORIAL IN FRANCE: UNVEILING AT LAVENTIE
A plaque on the facade of the town hall at Laventie, near Lille, was unveiled yesterday in memory of the British 61st Division, which distinguished itself in the valley of the Lys in resisting the great German attack which began on April 9, 1918.

The French Army was represented at the ceremony by a company of the 110th Infantry Regiment, and the British visitors included Major-General Sir Colin Mackenzie, Brigadier-Generals Spooner and Bilton, six colonels, among whom was Sir Seymour Williams and 200 ex-servicemen. The British Ambassador was represented by Major Johnston.

The Times, Tuesday 23 April, 1935

[Brig. Gen. A H Spooner 1879–1945 had taken over 183rd Bde after Stewart left, 26 July 1916. He earned DSO and Bar and 8 MIDs, also CB and CMG. Lieut Col L L Bilton c. 1885–1954 was CO of 2/8th Worcestershires later in the war. Croix de Guerre, 2 MIDs and CMG.
Col Sir Seymour Williams 1868–1945 was CRE 61st Division and later Hon. Colonel SE Midland RE.]

**IMPERIAL PREFERENCE?
WAR SECRET DISCLOSED**
Meat supply for troops.
British Preference for Argentina.

Hobart: Thursday. An Australian War Cabinet story was told for the first time by Mr J A Jensen, when speaking on the Address in Reply in the House of Assembly. Mr Jensen said that in 1916 the Hughes Government was in power and he (Mr Jensen) was a member, a cablegram was received from the British Government, which read:

Ship 10,000,000 sovereigns: urgent: imperative: letter following explaining.

The matter was considered so important that the Cabinet meeting was held at night. Ministers realised the only gold in their possession was that held in reserve to cover the note issue, but they decided to send the gold by transport. It was done in absolute secrecy. Had it been known in Australia there would have been a panic. When they got the letter it was learned that the men at the front were badly in need of certain food, and that the Argentine was the only place it could be obtained. That country refused to take a guarantee from England for payments and declined to take English notes. The Argentine would take nothing but gold. That, Mr Jensen said, was the relief provided by Australia at a critical period. Subsequently meat was needed for the British army and navy, and the same British Government gave the contract to the Argentine because the price was ¼d per pound less than that quoted by Australia. That, added Mr Jensen, was Imperial preference with a vengeance.

—*The Age*, 25 July 1930

THE COST OF THE WAR TO AUSTRALIA
Government figures quoted in the *Sydney Morning Herald* in 1932 had it at £770,000,000. In 1936 it had risen to £868,545,231 and by the outbreak of the Second World War in 1939 it was £877,144,895.

men like White made sure Elliott never got any further: after all had he let him, Elliott may well have asked White to account for some of his decisions, a proposition that White could not countenance.

'*An Amazing Outburst*' from Elliott was as it turned out the beloved man's last outburst. He is thought to have given the same lecture to private groups in Melbourne later in 1930. He was active in the Senate until the end of the year. We know now, but none knew then that Elliott was subject to bouts of depression. disguised under an uncontroversial word—'nerves'. Surely this was a combination of the experiences in Gallipoli and France, the difficulties of keeping his legal practice going, of being a Senator, and the oncoming of the Depression. Being so conscientious Elliott aimed to do his best in every field, but like so many military men before him and after he found the abusive abrasiveness of the democratic chamber intolerable. He never understood that basic tenet of the system that you speak to create an effect, to cause some other reaction, not to tell the truth or give the facts. Many theories have been propounded for the decline of Elliott which terminated with his suicide on 23 March 1931. His network of loyal friends had kept him informed of those who had served in the 7th Bn on Gallipoli and with the 15th Bde in France. At this time scores of the old soldiers had had to walk off their farms and orchards, the suicide rate among old soldiers was very high, scarcely a week went by when there was not a story of an old soldier attacking his family or worse. Alcoholism was one plague and war-related illness was another. By 1932 over 60,000 Australians—the same number as died in the war—had died as a direct result of war wounds or illnesses linked to the war. The country was destitute of leaders of any quality and it was broke. The loyalty so readily given to the 'mother country' (see margin: *Imperial Preference*) was now a millstone, which only got heavier as Britain's plight got worse. The far right and the far left were the only places with solutions and neither were appropriate. For a man like Elliott who had cared it must have been a terrible time.

At that time suicide was judged simply as a character weakness so Elliott's critics were not surprised. However for one of his colonels it was the last straw. Layh, badly damaged in the war, was so shattered that he left his family and went to live alone in a cave in the Grampians for a year. He was joined, now and then, by other men '*in a bad way*', as the expression of the time described what nobody understood. Then the unexpected death of Cass in November robbed the survivors of Fromelles, not forgetting others from Gallipoli, of one of the most respected leaders. However as the major figures disappeared, others stepped forward.

Perhaps because somebody at the *Sydney Morning Herald* was a '*19th of July man*', Fromelles was never forgotten in that city throughout the 1930s. On prominent news pages there was the heading: 'Battle of Fromelles Anniversary'. In 1932 it quoted Bean, '*that the reason for failure seems to have been loose thinking and somewhat reckless decisions on the part of the higher staff*'. An interesting shift! The paper then observed, '*the severity of the reverse was concealed from the British public for some time*'.

It cannot have been a coincidence that this same day, 19 July 1932, was the day chosen for laying the foundation stones for Sydney's War Memorial in Hyde Park. Some 15,000 attended the ceremony but if Fromelles was mentioned in the speeches or by virtue of the date, it was not reported. One of the stone layers was Sir Philip Game, Governor of NSW, staff member of 46th Division from July 1915 to March 1916, when that Division was part of Haking's XI Corps. Game has been quoted as describing Haking as '*a vindictive bully*' and '*being really impossible, untruthful and not to be trusted*'. If he made these statements back in 1916 it is easier to understand '*his transfer out of the army against his will*' as noted in the British *Dictionary of National Biography*.

In 1936 when 19 July fell on a Sunday the paper observed 'Fromelles Anniversary Tomorrow' and whilst making no new comment about the battle noted that in Sydney the 30th Bn would lay a wreath at the Cenotaph '*in memory of comrades who fell at Fromelles*', and there would be the annual church parade at Scots Church where '*buglers will sound the Last Post and Reveille, and the pipe band will play a lament "The Flowers of the Forest"*'. This went on until 1939, and seems to have been reinstated in a smaller way after the war, at the Hyde Park Memorial. In Melbourne the 60th Bn Association never failed to hold its Fromelles Remembrance service, and place a notice in the newspaper.

Around the time Layh died, 1964, Bill Boyce of 58th Bn decided after a reflective day's fishing that he could now talk about the war to his daughters. He believed he was at last able, at seventy, to get his experiences into some perspective. Before he could only talk with others who had been through it. This was not an uncommon experience either for an old digger, or for his family.

The 50th Anniversary of the battle, 1966, was the last significant gathering of '*19th of July men*': they came together

TEN MILLION LIVES

Ten million lives were lost to the world in the last war, and they say that 70 million pounds in money were spent in the preliminary bombardment in the Battle of Ypres; before any infantry left their trenches the sum of 22 million pounds was spent, and the weight of ammunition fired in the first few weeks of that battle amounted to 480 thousand tons. ...

I do not believe that that represents the best use the world can be expected to make of its brains and its resources. I prefer to believe that the majority of people in the world in these days think that war hurts everybody, benefits nobody—except the profiteers—and settles nothing. ...

As one who has passed pretty well half a century in the study and practice of war, I suggest to you that you should give your support to Disarmament and so do your best to ensure the promotion of peace.

Field-Marshal Sir William Robertson
Chief of the Imperial General Staff
1915–18, speaking at Albert Hall,
London, 11 July 1931

BREAD

It was cruel to watch the rush for bread. These men but a few years ago were the saviours of our country, the sleek troops of war, the idol of France. They were home again—home to their sunny Australia, fresh from victories that made the world wonder. And now bread and jam—eating from the hand of charity. But there was no murmur of complaint, no talk of rebellion.

'*Well*', one said, *'a man's lucky to be alive anyway.'*

'*Yes*', said his comrade, *'but death was quick out there, Dig, and it would have been much easier to die for your country.'*

—quoted by Herbert Scanlon,
2807 59th Bn in *Humoresque*

FORTY YEARS AGO
At the Soldiers' Memorial in Bendigo, 19 July 1956:
'As the post office clock struck 5.45 pm—the hour when the 59th and 60th Battalions went over the parapet ... four men advanced to lay wreaths. [L-R]: W J Turner—60th Bn, W (Digger) Thomas—59th Bn, A Kersting—58th Bn, L Osborne—57th Bn. Mr Turner repeated the Tribute to the Fallen, the Last Post was sounded by bugler Bill Michell. Others present were A P Burns, E G Dumble and A Kirkham—57th Bn. N S Newell, E H Whinfield and W Gray—60th Bn. R H Burgess—15th MG Coy. E Timbs—14th Field Ambulance.

in Sydney at the Hyde Park Memorial. Brigadier H A Bachtold DSO MC laid the main wreath on behalf of the men who fought at Fromelles. The Eastern Command Band supplied music from the Great War period and a large part of the audience were widows and relatives of those who had not survived.

Thereafter the remembrance of Fromelles was largely in the hands of the relatives who firstly were widows, sons and daughters, and then grandsons and granddaughters: some with no more than hazy memories of an old grandfather '*who had a medal or two from the war*'.

FIFTY YEARS AGO
Fifty years ago these men with serious faces were young Diggers of the Fifth Division writing new history for Australia when its troops went into battle in France for the first time. Yesterday they stood bare headed, their faces showing the years between, as they remembered the bloody WW1 Battle of Fromelles, fifty years ago to the day ... There were still 300 survivors of Fromelles, and they were joined by 500 other officers and men of the Fifth Division who had fought elsewhere in France. They are shown ... marching to the Anzac Memorial in Hyde Park, for the special service ... the day was bleak, the trees bare and it was damp underfoot ...

—*Sydney Morning Herald*
20 July 1966

PHOTO COURTESY LATE FRANK WORMALD

A conclusion ?

It is important to note that this inquiry has produced its case against McCay largely from information available during his lifetime. Apart from his character defects, which made him totally unsuited as a leader, he was inexperienced in war and the management of a division which is precisely why Birdwood did not want him to command 5th Division preferring an English general with real experience in both these areas. When Pearce overrode Birdwood it provided the first sighting of the strength and influence of the McCay–Pearce–White group which was never accountable to anybody. During the war this was for security reasons, but after the war what reasons applied? The fact that Pearce appointed Bean and Bean's idol was Brudenell White makes it easy to see how objectivity was lost, not in the descriptions of battles, but in Bean's assessments of individuals, and in particular McCay. Bean's clearing of McCay for the Desert March, Fromelles and Flers does not stand up to the facts: but in Australia in the 1920s there could be no place for facts that in any way diminished the reputation of the AIF. Perhaps that was a necessary judgement Bean made. The new nation had suffered too much: it must not tear itself apart with inquiries into the conduct of the war.

So there was only one way to go—blame the British. One of the great attributes of British society has been its ability to deal fairly resolutely with people who '*let the side down*'. In a time of war security demanded restraint, nevertheless from 1914 onwards, thanks largely to the diversity of the British press, 'disasters' at Mons, Gallipoli and elsewhere were publicly revealed and some of those responsible rightly pilloried. Haking escaped such examination, as did many others with a worse record than his. Perhaps because he held senior appointments throughout the 1920s he had the necessary influence. However we have seen that Edmonds had no influence over him. The closer one examines Bean's treatment of the British contribution at Fromelles the more apparent it is that they told him next to nothing. Edmonds' fury about quoting a British officer's opinion reveals precisely how information *had* to be controlled. Imagine if Haking had told Bean that McCay was useless and that he did not follow orders; what would have Bean done with such information?

The egos and power plays of the Higher Authorities can only ever be the subject of opinions. Orders are different. McCay forever took refuge in this area saying he was just carrying them out as he was obliged to do. As best demonstrated during the Desert March he basically had no feeling for the men. At Fromelles it was the same, '*they'll get used to it*', he commented. The judgment of McCay has to be not on the orders he was given but how he carried them out. All five of his major recorded actions: The Landing, Krithia, Desert March, Fromelles and Flers were, as far as *he* was concerned, disasters. But when White came forward years later to proclaim that McCay was a greater soldier than Monash, it is not difficult to see who told Bean that McCay *could not* be blamed for any of the disasters that had been attached to him.

It is not easy to see how Bean could have solved this, but in a sense he did for those who would come later. He left information in his notes and files which filled in some of the gaps.

So much for the major players. Of the next rank it is clear that Harold Pope is a much neglected figure in Australian military history. His record, except for going to sleep after Fromelles, is untarnished. Did Bean leave him alone because White told him to? Bean never deals with Tivey at any depth, but Elliott was the character who appealed to him as a journalist.

The COs, arguably the most important men in the Battle of Fromelles were all mentioned, but Bean's dislike of Toll and distrust of Cass, must have robbed his narrative of much. This inquiry has sought to remedy this by including some reports which reveal the true quality of both men.

Apart from the men of the battle, there are other issues to consider. The absence of the Intelligence Summaries for all of July is without doubt curious and troubling. Did McCay destroy them? It is easy to speculate why, but all that is known is <u>that</u> they are missing. Why are the messages in and out of the Divisional HQ all neatly typed up when no others are? We have to remember that McCay was a lawyer, a politician, intelligence officer and censor in his time—so there would need to be some very convincing evidence that he did not '*organise*' the surviving files on the Battle of Fromelles. He had always been in the business of organising facts and information, and this was about protecting *his* reputation.

The Armistice is, however, the most serious issue. McCay gave some legal excuse, but here he was lying. Military Law was quite clear on the issue of '*the suspension of arms*' for the very specific purpose the German officer defined. It was McCay's neglect of the thousands of his men who lay dead, dying, wounded in No-Man's Land in those summer days that forms the most damning case against him. Hundreds of others risked their lives to bring in the wounded, and many died at this work.

Nothing can pardon McCay for that neglect.

Nothing.

Some day we will understand

Among over 200 'In Memoriam' notices in *The Register*, Adelaide, of 19 July 1920 was this:

PERRY. In loving memory of our dear brother, Private A M Perry of Naracoorte, killed at Fleurbaix, on 19 July 1916.
'*Some day we will understand*'.

That sentiment seems to be a suitable one under which to gather together miscellaneous small tributes, notes and paragraphs found along the road, so to speak. They are arranged here alphabetically and encompass eighty years of grief.

ADAM. Private John Adam 6152. 2/6th Royal Warwickshire Regiment who died 19 July 1916. Son of John and Elizabeth McAuley Adam of Grangemouth, Stirlingshire. Age 16. [CWGC Records]

ANDERSON. 2nd Lieut Edward Handfield Anderson. Born in 1886 he was educated at Melbourne Grammar School and was in their football and rifle teams. He received his commission in Egypt in March 1916 when with 57th Bn. At Fromelles on 18 July he acted as guide to 59th Bn coming into the line and when the action began the next day he advanced with them. '*He was wounded ... went out to No-Man's Land three times and brought back wounded men. The third time he was again wounded, and he persisted in going out a fourth time, though the men tried their best to persuade him not to do so: however he did go out, and was killed by machine gun fire in No-Man's Land, and was buried there.*'
[*War Services of Old Melburnians*]

BELL. A tribute of love to the memory of our dear brother Pte Harry Bell of High Street, Bendigo, who made the supreme sacrifice at Fleurbaix, July 19/20 1916.
'*Who stands if Freedom falls, who dies if England lives*'.
[*Bendigo Advertiser* 19 July 1920]

BENSON. In memory of Lieut James Benson, 5th Div, 8th Bde, 32nd Bn. Killed in action at the objective, Fromelles, France. July 19 1916.
Lest we forget. SJB. JGB. SJGB.
[*Herald Sun*, Melbourne 19 July 1994]

BESELER. In sad and loving memory of my dear brother, Private George Henry Beseler, killed in action at Pozières (France) on 19 July 1916, and loving uncle of Arthur, Hilda, Mrs D Austie, Horace, Walter and the late Private George William Wood (killed Dardanelles). Buried Sailly Cemetery in France.
My darling brother
In our hearts your memory lingers
Tender, fond and true.
There's not a day goes by, dear George
But what I think of you.
(Inserted by Mr and Mrs Wood and family, Albion St, West Brunswick)
[*The Argus*, Melbourne 19 July 1917]

BLAKE. Killed in action on 19 July 1916 (previously reported missing) George Francis, No 4737, late of 59th Bn sailed only on March 7 of the same year.
I have lost my soul's companion
A life linked with my own
Each day I miss his footsteps
As I walk through life alone
—inserted by his loving wife
[*The Age*, Melbourne 19 July 1917]

BLAKE. In loving memory of George Francis killed in France 19 July 1916 —*30 long years. Ever remembered.*
Inserted by Jean.
[*The Argus*, Melbourne 19 July 1946: this was the only WW1 notice]

[Blake was a carpenter of Footscray, aged 26. He first served with 58th Bn, then transferred to 59th. He was killed at Fromelles and buried at Ration Farm. In July 1992 the bone handle of a kitchen knife, the blade long since rusted away, with his name on it, was found on the field in front of the Sugar-loaf position by Martial Delebarre. It is now in the Fromelles Museum]

BOND. Loving memories of Pte W J Bond (Tommy) killed in France, July 19 1916. *Always remembered*—Addie
[*The Age*, Melbourne 19 July 1956]

BRUCE. Pte George Owen Bruce. Educated at Melbourne Grammar School from 1888 to 1892 he '*was a very popular boy, especially among those younger than he was, for he was of kindly disposition and hated bullying*'. After leaving school he took a great interest in militia work, holding a commission. He served in the South African War as Lieut and gained the Queen's Medal with four clasps. On his return '*he had many misfortunes*' ... he volunteered and applied for a commission, but was unsuccessful. He fought at Anzac with 8th LHR and in France with 58th Bn. When he was killed at Fromelles he was 41.
[*War Services of Old Melburnians*]

BYERS. Capt. R H K Byers of 2/4th Gloucesters who in every description of the battle was killed in the first minutes of it, is officially listed as Killed in action on 20 July.
[CWGC Records]

CAINES, Percy. Killed in action Fleurbaix 19 July 1916
Though absent, he is very near.
Still loved, still missed and very dear.
Inserted by his sister.
[*The Age*, Melbourne, 19 July 1966]

CAMERON. Cpl Ewen Alexander Cameron of Mansfield. He was a brilliant boy, gaining his Standard Certificate at the age of eight years and three months, and his Merit Certificate at eleven. He entered upon agricultural pursuits in Queensland. Returning … he commenced study again and soon became a teacher. Inspectors' reports refer to his great interest in his work and show that he was most anxious to excel. '*He was a good son and brother, never causing the least anxiety to his parents*'. Two sisters and a brother were also teachers: the brother was wounded at Fromelles. Serving with 60th Bn, Ewen was killed 19 July 1916.
[Victorian Education Dept's Record]

CHINNER. In loving memory of Lieut Eric Hardy Chinner who laid down his life at the battle of Fleurbaix, France, on 19 July 1916. [*The Register*, Adelaide 19 July 1920]

CHOAT. Pte R H Choat and Pte A P Choat of 32nd Bn, who were killed in action on 20 July 1916.
A little while and we shall meet again.
Ever remembered by their loved ones, Clarence Park.
[*The Register*, Adelaide, 19 July 1926, among over 90 notices]

COUSINS. Lieut Frank L Cousins. Born 1887, he became a teacher in 1904 at Bendigo, later taking charge of three country schools. Married with one child, he enlisted as private 17 July 1915, later transferring to 59th Bn. A sergeant, 1 April 1916, commissioned 1 June, Frank Cousins was killed 19 July 1916.
[Victorian Education Dept's Record]

CRUICKSHANKS. Sweetest memories of my darling son and our dear brother Roy, killed in action July 19 1916 (PRM) aged 17½ years.
As years roll on we miss you more
Never forgotten by his loving mother, sisters, brothers-in-law, Irene and Arthur, Lottie and Perce, Ella, only brother Cliff and sister-in-law Vera.
[*Sydney Morning Herald* 18 July 1936]

DAVIDSON. In loving memory of Pte P A Davidson, died while prisoner of war 20.7.1916. Still sadly missed. Inserted by his mother, brothers and sisters.
[*Bendigo Advertiser* 20 July 1920]

DAWSON. A tribute to the memory of Tom Dawson who was leading comedian on Harry Rickard's Tivoli Circuit for 10 years and fell fighting on the battlefield in France, July 19, 1916. '*A fellow of infinite jest. May his soul rest in peace*'.
William Maher [60th Bn]

DENNY. 2/Lieut Arnold Lorimer Denny. 6th LH and 56th Bn. Died of wounds, 26 July 1916.
[*History of All Saints' College, Bathurst*]

DOBSON. Sgt David Dobson. Born in 1867, he entered the Victoria Education Department in 1890. He served in South Africa as Lieut in 6th ACH. '*He was a very good teacher, strong and forceful, and, at all times, a zealous and vigorous worker*'. In 59th Bn as sergeant, he was killed at Fromelles and left a widow.
[Victorian Education Dept's Record]

DOWNIE. A tribute to the memory of my dear friend, Sergeant J C G (Jim) Downie, killed in action in France, 20 July 1916. 'Remembrance'. Inserted by Annie Danger.
[*Geelong Advertiser*, 20 July 1920]

ESAM. In loving memory of my brother Pte Arthur Harold Esam killed in action somewhere in France, 19 July 1916.
Forget not those who died
Now Peace does reign once more.
Remember still that lonely grave
Beyond some foreign shore.
Not marked by marble cross
Maybe not marked at all
Just buried 'neath the green grown sod
In the place they saw him fall.
Inserted by his loving sister D Mandrow, North Sydney
[*Warrnambool Standard*, 19 July 1920, one of four notices for A H Esam]

FINCH. In loving memory of my dearly beloved brother, Pte Frederick A Finch, LMG, 56th Bn. Killed in action 20 July 1916.
Another hero gone west.
Inserted by his loving brother Bert and sister-in-law Elsie.
[*Sydney Morning Herald*, 19 July 1919]

FLOWERS. Private Frank Flowers, 3512, 60th Bn, 1st AIF. Killed in action, 19 July 1916 at Fleurbaix, France. Dearly loved and loving husband of Margaret Storrie Moffat (deceased). Son of George and Catherine Flowers of Heathcote—with loving memories of our father Frank, and of his Maggie, dear mother. Nell, Mrs A C Eadie, Frank and George Flowers and families.
[*The Age*, Melbourne, 19 July 1986]

FRANKLIN. In memory of our dear boys Ptes C W (Charlie) and H L (Bert) who were killed at Fleurbaix on 19 July 1916. *Never forgotten.* [Charles Wyndham Franklin, born 1891, was a station manager in NSW, whilst Herbert Leyshorn Franklin, born 1892, was working for W D & H O Wills. Both attended Melbourne Grammar School, and both enlisted in 60th Bn. It was believed they were killed by the same shell.]

FRYER. In memory of Charlie, killed in action, July 19, 1916, at Fromelles. Inserted by his pal Mac.
[*Sydney Morning Herald* 19 July 1919]

GARRY. In loving remembrance of dear Wal, one of many victims in the Fleurbaix disaster. Fleurbaix, 19 July 1916, a day of tragic memories for the men of 15th Infantry Brigade, who were swept by a hurricane of machine gun and rifle fire, sustaining terrific casualties.
—Mother and father
GARRY. In loving memory of Pte Walter Garry (dear old Wal) who fell at Fleurbaix on 19 July 1916.
A beautiful nature, brave, kind and true.
—by Mr & Mrs F Potter and family and his old pal Tim.
GARRY. In loving memory of my dear pal, Walter Garry, reported missing on 19 July 1916.
I cannot hear your voice, dear Wally,
Your face I cannot see
But let this little token tell
I still remember thee.
—Inserted by his true mate, Corporal J M Sharples.
[*The Age*, Melbourne, 19 July 1920, among over 300 notices: another 80 on 20 July]

GIBBINS. In proud memory of my beloved brother Captain Norman Gibbins, killed in action at Fromelles, France, July 20 1916 and in memory of the gallant Australians who died with him.
'*For they shall be in the glory of it*'.
Inserted by Miss Violet Gibbins (principal), Osborne Girls' College, Epping.

GIBBINS. In proud memory of Captain Norman Gibbins, of 55th Bn, killed at the very end of the terrible fighting at Fleurbaix, July 20, 1916. Loved and admired by every soldier who knew him.
Inserted by seven of his 'lads' of the original B Coy, 55th.
[*Sydney Morning Herald* 19 July 1919]

HARRIOTT. In sad and loving memory of our dear friend, Pte Lawrence (Clarry) Harriott, 54th Bn, killed in action in France July 19 1916.
Three years have passed, our hearts still sore;
As time rolls on, we miss you more.
Inserted by his loving friends Gladys, Mr & Mrs Hopkins and family, Randwick.
[*Sydney Morning* Herald 20 July 1919. Other notices for Harriott were from his parents, his brothers and sisters-in-law, his sisters and brothers-in-law]

HENDERSON. Of William and Annie Henderson's children, four sons served abroad. Ernest Albert, born 1897 and Leslie Donald, born 1898, were the fifth and sixth sons and with the 60th Bn at Fromelles, they were both killed. The second son died of illness in 1918, and was buried in France. The third son returned to Melbourne.
[*The Ancestor* Summer 1993/94, p31]

HIGGON. Major John Arthur. 32nd, according to Bean, died of wounds, 19 July. Ellis was sure he was shot dead in the first minute of the attack. The Nominal Roll of the AIF has him KIA 20 July: as does his headstone at Rifle Farm.
HIGGON. In loving memory of my sons, Major John Arthur Higgon, Pembroke Yeomanry (late RWF) attached to 32nd Bn Australian Infantry, killed near Fleurbaix July 19, 1916, and Major Archibald Bellairs Higgon, RFA, killed at Anzac, Gallipoli, 9 Sept 1915.

HOLMES. L/Cpl Edgar C Holmes. Born 1893. He entered Teachers' College in 1909 and graduated successfully winning, in 1911, the Gladman Prize. He was BA at the University of Melbourne and studying for a degree in science when he enlisted 16 July 1915. He went to France with 59th Bn and was killed 19 July 1916. '*He was a young man of fine character, earnest, upright and faithful in the discharge of his duty... He had an assured future.*'
[Victorian Education Dept's Record]

HORSINGTON. Pte A H Horsington of 55th Bn. The CWGC Register shows that his parents lived in a house in Togo Street, Arncliffe, NSW, called 'Fleurbaix'.

HULKS. In loving memory of my dear husband and our darling dadda, Lieut Frederick Hulks, 32nd Bn, killed in action, Fleurbaix, July 19 1916. *Until the day break.* Inserted by his devoted wife Jennie and children Gloria, Phyllis and Freddie.
[*Sydney Morning Herald* 19 July 1919]

HUNTER. Robert Hunter 30th Bn is remembered on the grave of his wife and daughter at St Kilda Cemetery, Melbourne.

HUTCHESON. William Thomas Hutcheson. From time to time there passes through every school worthy of the name, a student whose undoubted mental attainments, assisted and strengthened by physical force and keen determination to get the very best of himself in every sphere of work and play, place him on a pedestal above his contemporaries. Such a one was William Thomas Hutcheson... In two short years (1910 & 1911) he was head of the Fourth and Dux of the School, and when the class rooms were left behind, a brilliant footballer, a strong runner, and an athlete to be seriously regarded whatever the sport... his regime as a Prefect at Hamilton College ... crowned with honour... At 18 years of age he was assistant Clerk of Courts at Carlton. Then he exchanged the routine of the office for camp life... in November 1915 he saw fighting in Arabia ... towards the end of June 1916 he transferred to the 58th Battalion as a Grenadier with Headquarters ... at Fleurbaix on July 19 1916 he was posted missing.
[*The Hamiltonian*, Hamilton College, Victoria 1918]

INCLEDON. Sgt Eryx Gabriel Incledon, original Anzac, killed at Fromelles 19 July 1916, beloved nephew of Mr & Mrs Harvey Walker, Clayfield. RIP.
[*Brisbane Courier* 19 July 1920]

JENKIN. Pte George Ernest Jenkin, 171, 57th Bn. He was first reported '*Missing*', then '*died, cause not stated*', then '*died as POW*', then '*DOW as POW*', to be finally listed as '*KIA*', with no body found. Quite how a 57th could have died of wounds on 19 July reflects the chaos.

JOHNSON. In memory of No 991, Cpl T N Johnson, late 42nd Battery, killed in action at Fleurbaix, 19 July 1916. Inserted by Cyril Maynard, 42nd Battery, AFA.
[*Brisbane Courier*, 20 July 1920]

LIDDELOW. In loving memory of my dear son, Captain Audrey Liddelow, CO of 59th Bn, who gave his life for King and Country at Fleurbaix on 19 July 1916. Egypt. Gallipoli. France. To him well done, good and faithful servant.
[*The Argus*, Melbourne 19 July 1926, among some 80 notices]

McCAUL. This grave of the parents of Donald Curteis McCaul at St Kilda Cemetery, Melbourne, remembers him and his death at Fleurbaix.

McKENZIE. L/Cpl Kenneth Fraser McKenzie. Born 1886 he joined the service as a junior teacher at Victoria Park School, Collingwood, in 1906 ... *a very good teacher, decisive and prompt*. He was killed at Fleurbaix, 19 July 1916.
[Victorian Education Dept Record]

McLEAN. In loving memory of our dear sons, Alex and Victor, killed in action, France, July 19, 1916.
In our dear home they are ever remembered...
Inserted by their loving parents, A and M McLean.
[*Geelong Advertiser*, 19 July 1920]

MALCOLM. In loving memory of Pte William Malcolm, killed in action at Pozières, between 19 and 20 July 1916. Inserted by his loving brother Bob and sister-in-law Mabel.
[*Sydney Morning Herald* 19 July 1919: note Pozières]

MAYES. In 2/4th Royal Berkshire, the two Private Mayes who died of wounds after Fromelles were from the same address, Haverhill, Suffolk.

MENDELSOHN. Lieut Berrol Lazar Mendelsohn. *A noble, clean and sweet life ended.* Minyon, Sydney 8 o'clock. Ullenbar, 67 Raglan Street, Mosman. Age 25.
[*Sydney Morning Herald* 4 August 1916]

MENDELSOHN. Lieut Berrol Mendelsohn. Well-known to all Fortians, and especially to swimmers ... being champion of the Bondi Club and frequently competed in our Old Boys' races... He had long been connected with naval and military affairs, while in civil life he has been since boyhood on the staff of Perdriau and Company.
[*The Fortian*, Fort St High School, Sydney, November 1916]

MORSHEAD. Sgt Ernest D Morshead. Born 1893, he entered the Victorian Education Dept in 1910 and went through the Manual Arts Course 1911-13, afterwards taking up the duties of woodwork instructor. He is recorded as an able, apt and earnest teacher. A sergeant with 29th Bn, he was killed at Fromelles, 20 July 1916.
[Victorian Education Dept Record]

MORTIMORE. In loving memory of Percy, 32nd Bn, killed in action, 19-20 July 1916.
Twenty years have passed,
Yet memories will linger
Like sweet, faded violets
we do not forget.
Inserted by his loving mother, brothers, sisters
[*The Advertiser*, Adelaide, 20 July 1936]

NITCHIE. In loving memory of my dear daddy, Pte J L Nitchie, killed in action, July 19, 1916, also my dear uncle, Pte L Nitchie, killed in action, August 4, 1916.
Though I am far away dear daddy,
And your grave I cannot see
I am always thinking of you
As you used to think of me.
Inserted by his loving daughter, little Ivy.
[*Geelong Advertiser*, 19 July 1920]

PALMER. In loving remembrance of my dear son 2892 Pte Philip Palmer, 53rd Bn, aged 19 years, late of Marrickville. *Loved by all who knew him. Only a boy, but did a man's duty.* Inserted by his loving mother and grandma.
[*Sydney Morning Herald* 19 July 1919]

PARKER. At Geelong West Cemetery, Ivan Leslie Parker, 58th Bn, probably a victim of shelling on 16 July, is remembered on his parents' headstone.

PARKINSON. Pte Edwin George Parkinson of 53rd Bn, buried at Rue Petillon was 34, the son of Mr C J Parkinson of Blackheath, England, and husband of Mrs Valerie Parkinson, of 11 rue Alphonse Daudet, Paris. Grave: I.K.13.
[CWGC Records]

PARKINSON. An affectionate tribute to the memory of Pte M G Parkinson who was killed in action at Fleurbaix, July 19, 1916.
He helped to make today.
From his friends, T and E Giblett.
[*Sydney Morning Herald* 19 July 1919]

PARTRIDGE. Sydney Carton Partridge, 3126, 58th Bn, named after 'The Tale of Two Cities' hero, died of wounds 1 September. His brother

Frank Leslie earned a DCM and was killed in action at Villers Bretonneux, 26 April 1918.

PENALUNA-ROWE. In fond remembrance of dear comrades, Pte Fred Rowe, killed in action, 19 July 1916. Also Pte Edgar Penaluna, died of wounds, 19 July 1916.
Passed away, but not forgotten,
deep within our hearts enshrined;
lived the memories of our Comrades
Always loving, true and kind.
Inserted by the members of the California Gully Free Brotherhood.
[*Bendigo Advertiser* 19 July 1920]

POLGLAZE. Charles, 2884. 59th Bn of Thornbury. K in A Fromelles, France, July 19 1916. *Remembered with respect*. Bruce Jager.
[*Herald-Sun*, Melbourne 19 July 1991]

RATCLIFF-GAYLARD. In proud and loving memory of Eric Ronald Ratcliff-Gaylard, 2nd Lieut, DCLI. Killed in action in France 19 July 1916. And his brother Cecil C A Ratcliff-Gaylard, HQ Staff, Australian Imperial Forces, killed in action in Gallipoli, 19 May 1915.
[*The Times*, London, 19 July 1921]

READ. Sgt George Reginald Read. Born 1894, he attended Melbourne High School 1908-9, and studied manual arts 1910-12. At the time of enlistment, he was a teacher of woodwork. Promoted Sergeant in 59th Bn at Ferry Post, 4 March 1916, he was wounded 19 July and died at Boulogne, 25 July.
[Victorian Education Dept Record]

RHIND. Lieut James Morison Rhind, 60th Bn. First AIF. Late 7/2nd. In everlasting memory of my brother who fell on the field of honour at Fleurbaix, France, July 19, 1916. A tribute also to his many associates of the greater Geelong and district, who died during the same engagement —*Dulce et decorum est pro patria mori* (His loving sister Ada Barbara, Karachi, Pakistan.)
[*The Argus*, Melbourne, 19 July 1956: this was the only WW1 notice]

ROBINSON. Pte Stanley Lewis Robinson. Born 1896, son of senior constable and Mrs Robinson, now of Lilydale, formerly of Wycheproof… Stanley was later head teacher at Wycheproof and later Lilydale, from where he enlisted in 31st Bn. He was killed at Fleurbaix.
[Victorian Education Dept Record]

SAINTY. Sapper Frederick Leslie Sainty. 1st Field Coy Engineers… educated at Fort Street… employed at North Sydney and Manly Electric sub-stations … he was severely wounded in action near Armentières. He died … 20 July, aged 18 years and 7 months.
[*The Fortian*, Fort St High School, Sydney, November 1916]

SCOTCH COLLEGE. In the course of this disastrous operation, Lieut Harold Cox, a veteran of the Boer War, Capt. A W Liddelow, Lieut C M Gray, L/Cpl A M Brown, Ptes C L Lake and G R Cox were all killed. Sgt A S Bishop who had served at Gallipoli succumbed to his wounds five months later.
[*History of Scotch College*, Melbourne]

SITLINGTON. Alec Frandale. On Active Service. In memory of my brother, 8th and 60th Bn, 1st AIF. Killed in the battle of Fromelles, Frace, July 19, 1916. *An original Anzac*. Inserted by Irene Bassett, 6 Gravesend St, Colac.
[*The Age*, Melbourne 19 July 1976]

SMITHS. Among the dead of 54th Bn were four Smiths with sequential numbers, so perhaps brothers and/or cousins, as family groups often organised such a sequence.
4883 Arthur Herbert, of Moree, NSW, enlisted 20 August 1915, and DOW 15 May 1917. 4884 Charles Thomas Pickering, of Greta, NSW, enlisted 13 Sept 1915 and KIA at Fromelles 19/20 July 1916 (he was a 22 year-old miner). 4885 Charles Frederick of Rozelle, NSW, enlisted 27 Sept 1915 and KIA at Fromelles, 16 July 1916. 4886 Edward George of Corrimal, NSW, enlisted 29 Aug 1915 and KIA at Fromelles, 19/20 July 1916.
[CWGC Records]

STURGEON. Killed in action in France July 20 1916, Pte William Sturgeon; also served at Indian Frontier and South Africa, held Queen's Medal with three clasps and King's Medal with two clasps: beloved husband of Mary Sturgeon, Birchgrove Road, Balmain.
He fought the fight, he stood the test.
He will be remembered as one of the bravest and the best.
[*Sydney Morning Herald* 19 July 1919]

SYDES. Sgt Maj. Charles Frederick Sydes. Born in Essex in 1885, he trained as a teacher in England, coming to Australia in 1913. He joined his two brothers already there. '*He stood 5 ft 11 ins, weighed 15 stone, when he enlisted, added another stone in camp. He was a cricketer, footballer and runner … represented his college at chess… was a first rate comic singer, ever ready to give his services in any good cause.*' In Egypt he transferred to 59th Bn … promoted Sgt, then Sgt Major, 19 April 1916. He was killed at Fromelles, 19 July 1916.
[Victorian Education Dept Record]

VINCENT. In loving memory of Pte Lawrence Stanley Vincent, killed in action at Armentières, July 1916.
He died that we may live in peace.
Inserted by his father, mother, sisters Ethel, Ruby and Rita, brother Jim and grandmother.
[*Sydney Morning Herald* 19 July 1919: note Armentières]

YOUNG, Pte James Young, 2812, 55th Bn, who died of wounds 1 October, was from Glasgow, and aged 16.
[CWGC Records]

8th BDE. A tribute to the memory of my pals of 8th Inf Bde, who made the supreme sacrifice at Fleurbaix on 19th and 20th July 1916.
Mid shot and shell, a living hell
They faced the foe that day.
Australia's sons against German guns

They fought at Fleurbaix.
They paid the price, the sacrifice
They died for you and me.
God grant them rest, Australia's best,
Who fought for liberty.
Inserted by A F Aldersley (late 31st Battalion)
[*The Register* Adelaide, 19 July 1930]

30th BN. In memory of the brave of my company, 30th Bn, who made the supreme sacrifice at Fleurbaix, July 19-20 1916. Inserted by Major B A Wark (OAS)
[*Sydney Morning Herald* 19 July 1919]

31st BN. In memory of all my chums of 31st Bn, AIF, who were killed at Fleurbaix, July 19, 1916.
Ern Hillman, late 31st Bn.
[*Sydney Morning Herald* 19 July 1919]

54th BN. In memory of the brave men of my company, 54th Bn, who made the supreme sacrifice at Fromelles, July 19-20 July 1916. Inserted by Lieut K N Wark (OAS).
[*Sydney Morning Herald* 19 July 1919]

15th BDE. A tribute to our comrades who fell at Fleurbaix, July 19, 1916. Inserted by members of the 15th Brigade Association, on behalf of their comrades.
[*The Argus*, Melbourne, 19 July 1918]

15th BDE. A tribute to the memory of the Officers, Non-Commissioned Officers and men of the 15th Brigade AIF who fell at Fleurbaix, July 19/20 1916. Inserted by GMP.
[*Hobart Mercury*, 19 July 1920]

60th Bn. A tribute to the Officers and Men of the 60th Bn, who laid down their lives at Fromelles on 19 July 1916, and other subsequent battles. *Lest we forget*. Inserted by the members of the 60th Battalion AIF Association.
[*The Age*, Melbourne, 19 July 1976]

2/6th BATTALION. The Royal Warwickshire Regiment. In proud and affectionate memory of the following officers: Capt. W Simms, Capt. T S Wathes, Capt. A E Coulton, Lieut F A Flesher, Lieut J Barron, 2/Lieut C Hurdman, 2/Lieut H Harper, and also the NCOs and men killed in action at Fromelles, France on 19 July 1916.
[*The Times*, London, 19 July 1917]

2/7th WARWICKS. H Berry, W Wale and J R Whateley were buried at Cabaret Rouge British cemetery, but due to their graves being lost, they have special memorials, 9, 7 and 10 respectively.

2/1st BUCKS BATTALION. In proud and affectionate memory of Capt. Harold Church, Lieuts C P Phipps, G W Atkinson, D G Chadwick, R B Hudson, H R N Brewin, F R Parker, the NCOs and Men who gave their lives for their country on 19 July 1916 in an attack upon the German lines near Laventie.
[*The Times*, London, 19 July 1926]

FRIENDS OF THE 15th BRIGADE
The Fromelles Service at the Shrine of Remembrance, Melbourne, 19 July 1994. Seated, far left with hat and medals, Sam Benson (see page 242–43). Then to his left, with slouch hat, Tom Brain, 60th Bn; Percy Naylor, 59th Bn, Jim Baddeley, 58th Bn and Charlie Henderson, 57th Bn; all except Jim Baddeley were at Fromelles.

Don't forget me, cobber

This phrase belongs to the Battle of Fromelles in particular, but in a wider sense to the whole AIF of the Great War. It includes that word 'cobber' now not much used, but in those days an expression of trust and friendship that any man could utter without appearing 'sissy' or dependent. It was a unique noun, it did not require, indeed could not have, an adjective like 'true mate', 'steady pal', 'good friend'. A cobber was a cobber and that was it – you just knew how to use it, to whom and when.

The poet C J Dennis knew about cobbers and war:

An' this ere Flood—I tips it must be Jim—was cobbers up in France...' and *'I've seen so much uv death—'e said, so many cobbers lyin' dead.*

The war had woven people together in such intense situations that cobbers were all important, and never more important than when one was wounded, and perhaps facing the end.

Out of such a situation came a call that was answered by Sgt Simon Fraser 3101, 57th Bn. His letter to his brother Peter found its way into the hands of C E W Bean who was so greatly moved by its sentiment and content that he quoted a large part of it in his history of Fromelles. Fraser had been going out into No-Man's Land rescuing the wounded when '... *another man about 30 yards out sang out, "Don't forget me, cobber." I went in and got four volunteers with stretchers and we got both men in safely.*'

Although Peter Corlett, the Melbourne sculptor, who had won the commission for figures at the Fromelles Memorial had already suggested one man carrying a wounded digger the figures had no particular personality in the first stages. When Peter heard the story of Simon Fraser, and was later given a photograph of the 40-year-old farmer, there was the character to match the words: mature courage, steadiness in crisis, and a sense of duty.

The sculpture, first in clay, later in bronze, shows Fraser at his work, his cobber on this trip was a man of the 60th Bn. The sculpture could therefore have no other title than: 'Cobbers'.

Who was Simon Fraser?

When Simon Fraser was born at Byaduk (25 kms from Hamilton in western Victoria) on 31 December 1876, he was the youngest of the nine children of James and Mary Fraser: he was 19 years younger than the oldest child, William. Only one of Simon's four brothers, and one of his four sisters married—both to members of the Christie family, also from Byaduk.

Sgt Fraser in bronze at Fromelles in 1998

Simon was educated at Byaduk State School and later worked on his parents' property 'Aird' at Byaduk. He joined the Victorian Mounted Rifles and was a sergeant with them for nine years. He was a member of the Byaduk Rifle Club for 11 or 12 years, and was President of the Byaduk Horticultural Society from its inception in 1906 till 1911, and then until 1915 on the committee.

When he enlisted on 13 July 1915, Simon gave his occupation as farmer, and his brother Peter as next of kin. He was 6 ft and ¾ inch (1.85 metres) tall, weighed 162 lbs (73.5 kgs), had a fair complexion, blue-grey eyes and was a Presbyterian.

At Broadmeadows Camp Simon was in the 7th Reinforcements of 22nd Battalion. He went to Egypt on the *Commonwealth* and on the formation of 57th Bn in February 1916 he joined them and was promoted to Sergeant at Ferry Post (on the Suez Canal) on 14 April 1916. He left for France on the *Kalyan* from Alexandria on 17 June 1916, disembarking at Marseilles on 24 June, and proceeding to the front line 'south of Armentières' with billets in and around Sailly-sur-la-Lys.

The 57th Battalion was in the line until withdrawn on 18 July to be in reserve. Simon Fraser, however, remained at the front to cut wire entanglements prior to the attack on 19 July. As the 57th Battalion was the only reasonably intact battalion in the 15th Brigade after the battle, they set about rescuing wounded from No-Man's Land. Of the night of 20/21 July, Simon Fraser wrote: '*was going all night bringing in wounded. B Coy brought in 250...*' His letter to his brother Peter describing these events is quoted on pages 234–35.

During leave in the UK from 16-25 September 1916 Simon Fraser visited relatives near Inverness in Scotland, and the villages where his father and uncles were born.

In December he was admitted to hospital suffering exhaustion. After recovering, he went to the School of Instruction, Balliol College, Oxford, later transfering to Trinity College.

By April 1917 he was commissioned 2nd Lieutenant and returned to France where, on 4 May, he was taken on strength of 58th Battalion. Eight days later, 12 May 1917, he was killed in action at Bullecourt. His body was never found and he is remembered at the Villers Bretonneux Memorial on the 58th Battalion Panel.

The Memorial Register reads: Fraser, Second Lieutenant, Simon. Mentioned in Despatches, 58th Bn Australian Infantry AIF. 12 May 1917. Age 40. Son of James and Mary Fraser. Born at Byaduk, Victoria.

14

A possession for ever

What these men did
nothing can alter now.
The good and the bad,
the greatness and the smallness
of their story will stand.
Whatever of glory
it contains
nothing can now lessen.
It rises,
as it will always rise,
above the mists of ages,
a monument to
great hearted men, and,
for their nation,
a possession for ever.

—C E W Bean

The quotation from Bean for the title of this chapter is set as a poem which in the passion of its words it surely is. It was the concluding paragraph of his history and refers to the whole war, but uniquely describes the dilemma of Fromelles. '*Whatever of glory it contains nothing can now lessen*', wrote Bean. This story certainly contains much glory. And '*The good and the bad, the greatness and smallness of their story will stand*': and we have seen much good and much greatness standing, usually, well in front of the bad and the smallness. And the concluding thought that the whole story is '*a monument to great hearted men, and for their nation, a possession for ever*' is a vivid a testament as could be written, and perhaps the perfect description of the monument that now stands at Fromelles.

In the first edition of this work it seemed all that could be hoped for was achieved when 'Cobbers' was unveiled at Fromelles. It had taken 80 years to get such recognition, hence the verdict then: '*the story of that monument is the conclusion of this inquiry. Perhaps it is the only answer now available.*' But no, spurred by information in these pages, the Missing at Fromelles have been found. And the installation of a second casting of 'Cobbers' at Melbourne's Shrine of Remembrance in 2008 was further proof that the story of Fromelles is not yet complete.

DON'T LEAVE ME, SIR

But the work of rescue did not cease. Two hundred men were carried in from a space less in area than an acre.

One lad, who looked about fifteen, called to me: 'Don't leave me, sir. I said, I will come back for you sonny', as I had a man on my back at the time. In that waste of dead one wounded man was like a gem in sawdust—just as hard to find. Four trips I made before I found him, then it was as if I had found my own young brother. Both his legs were broken, and he was one of those overgrown lads who had added a couple of years in declaring their age ... But the circumstances brought out his youth, and he clung to me as though I was his father. Nothing I have ever done has given me the joy that the rescuing of that lad did, and I do not even know his name.

—R H Knyvett, 59th Bn
Over there with the Australians (1918)

The creation of 'Cobbers' and its installation was, sadly, too late for '*the 19th of July men*', but not too late for many of their children and grandchildren—answers the neglect and denial of 80 years, and helps assuage the passed down bitterness. And the history is accurate, there was no need to be otherwise: there had been too much inaccurate history as far as Fromelles was concerned. Sgt Fraser *was* a 40-year-old farmer, he *was* tall and strong, he *did* carry men off the battlefield on his back, walking to the Australian lines convinced he would not be deliberately shot while engaged in this work. The only liberty taken with reality might be the wounded man clinging onto his slouch hat. But the art critic Patrick Hutchings saw a meaning:

> Corlett's sinewy sculpture is highly expressive, it shows at once the pathos of a soldier—the wounded man holds onto his hat as tightly as to the memory of home—and the heights to which a man of charity and courage can rise, as the rescuer here doggedly does.

After he was appointed Director of the Office of Australian War Graves in 1992 Air Vice-Marshal Alan Heggen became concerned that seventy-five years since the end of the Great War there was no Australian Corps memorial in France. Whilst many over the years had lamented that Australia's sacrifice in France had nothing to equal the Canadian Vimy Ridge Memorial or the South African Deville Wood, few could agree what action best symbolised the AIF. Perhaps it was the hour long TV film *Hamel - the turning point* made in 1993 for the Army Training Division by Col Kevin O'Brien that solved the dilemma. Here was an AIF victory, masterminded by an Australian, Monash, and which was to lead to greater things. Following visits to the battlefields Heggen became convinced that two events represented the Australian feat of arms on the Western Front —Fromelles and Le Hamel, 4 July 1918. Very different events to be sure, and neither given full recognition. To support this conviction Heggen co-ordinated ideas and later designs for memorials at both places. The early suggestions for the Memorial Park at Fromelles included a figure or group which would by its character need neither size nor grandeur to say what had to be said. Proposals were called for and one of these, a man carrying his wounded cobber off the battlefield by Peter Corlett was later judged absolutely right, and would be completed and installed on the 80th Anniversary of the Battle, 19 July 1996. However the shifting of funds to the hugely successful '*Australia Remembers*' commemoration centred on August 1995 meant that the project was put on hold for the next two years.

In the meantime Ross Bastiaan had made and installed one of his topographical plaques at the front of the strip of land

WE SHARED EVERYTHING

On 19 July 1916 Pte Tom Brain 2344, and Pte George Ramsay 3131A, both of 60th Bn were standing together ready for the hopover when an Australian shell fell short, near them. Tom turned to his friend and touched him asking how he was: Ramsay fell over, dead. *Not a pretty picture for an eighteen year old lad,* Tom recalled. *George was the best friend I ever had, we shared everything. His mother had died in childbirth and he was adopted by a Councillor. They asked me to write a letter ... I couldn't write a letter like that, so I saw the C of E Padre who drafted the letter and I copied it out. George's name is on the Bright Cenotaph.*

Tom was later wounded in the mouth, *Got a smack in the face, but I was walking.*, and recounted *passing 'Pompey' Elliott at VC Avenue, 25 yards from the front line tying up wounds, crying as he worked.*

Tom, whose memory of Fromelles was sufficient to reduce him to tears each time he told the story, was sure there was a truce—unofficial of course, and that McCay was the cause of all the bloodshed. One other thing he was certain of was that a French farmer who used to place '*five horses ... different colours ... in different places*' was a spy and was later shot by Australians.

Tom 'Nuggett' Brain went right through the war and came home to marry his childhood sweetheart—he had met Lila when she was eleven, and the marriage lasted 68 years. They had four children. Tom volunteered for WWII and helped in training young recruits. After numerous visits to Gallipoli and France in the 80s and early 90s, Tom died 29 March 1995. He was buried, together with his slouch hat, at Memorial Lawn Cemetery, Altona North and was the last survivor of 60th Bn.

Pte (Rtd) Tom Brain, 60th Bn at the block houses which are now part of the Memorial Park. On this 1993 tour Tom's memories of balloons, planes and smoke were a vivid recall of what he saw before being wounded.
PHOTOGRAPH D BRISTOWE

containing the blockhouses, the Office of Australian War Graves having been assured by the Mayor of Fromelles, that when the project was finally cleared in Australia he would oversee the transfer of the land. Corlett visited France in 1995 and in quiet moments at the site visualised the Park. It would be the same level as the adjacent farmland—indeed still part of it as it had always been—edged by as low and inconspicuous a wire mesh fence as practical and the majority of the ground would remain rough and the figures would stand on a small mound of concrete rubble—perhaps even rubble from demolished German blockhouses—and have a clear view of where the Australian lines once were, the destination of the figures all those years ago.

Shrine of Remembrance, Melbourne with Memorial Crosses, 1995
PHOTOGRAPH A BLANKFIELD

Whilst '*Australia Remembers*' activities were nationwide and were mainly to do with the Second World War they aroused the curiosity of the young and stirred the memories of the old. How effectively, was demonstrated, at the Melbourne Shrine of Remembrance where small wooden crosses could be purchased by anybody, marked as they wished, and then 'planted' in the Shrine lawn. The response was overwhelming. Small children thus 'remembered' their great grandfathers they never knew, and the elderly their brothers. It was interesting to see how often the word 'Fromelles' had been written on those crosses. People were not remembering: they had not forgotten.

All this interest now transferred to the 80th anniversaries for 1996, of which for Australia there were two: Fromelles and Pozières. As there would be a special service at Fromelles, the need to be there was, for some, irresistible. And rather than transcribe some routine newspaper report, the account of one such pilgrim follows. Lambis Englezos, a co-founder of *Friends of the 15th Brigade* made the journey:

> I arrived at VC Corner Cemetery early on the morning of the 19th July; it was a day I had long been anticipating. A short while later a car pulled

A BOND

Pte William Boyce 3022, 58th Bn described himself as '*a young unblooded private in a unit sprinkled with Gallipoli veterans*' who saw themselves as seasoned soldiers and were a bit aloof '*or perhaps that was my attitude*', Bill suggested. '*But after Fromelles it was different. Fromelles was a bond nothing would break, I would say.*'

Bill Boyce, formerly of 58th Bn reading a letter from the Mayor of Fromelles concerning the presentation of the commemorative medal from the town. It was presented to Bill by Martial Delebarre at Warrnambool on 27 October 1995. Bill lived to be 102, dying on 26 March 1996. He was buried at Colac.

IT WAS MURDER

The second last survivor of the Battle of Fromelles from the AIF was Fred Kelly, 53rd Bn, who served there with 14th Bde Machine Gun Company. He was also one of the last Anzacs.

Of Fromelles he said:

... I saw the worst sight I ever saw in my life. Four wounded chaps came back, they walked back. They stopped there for fifteen minutes. This chap's nose and part of his face had been chopped straight off. I put my hand out to help this chap, he said: 'don't touch me, my ribs are shattered'. That bloke's face has stopped with me all my life.

Whoever planned the battle of Fromelles was stupid, it was the greatest piece of stupidity since the Charge of the Light Brigade. We were in full view, the Germans chopped the 53rd to pieces ... Haking was a 'rat bag', it was the worst piece of strategy. It was murder, we had no chance.

—from an interview with Fred Kelly by Lambis Englezos 1998

Fred Kelly died on 26 December 1998, just nine days short of his 102nd birthday. On 14 July 1998 he had received the Legion d'Honneur.

up and out stepped Martial Delebarre. We greeted each other and made arrangements to meet that evening to 'walk' the battlefield ...

Directly in front of VC Corner Cemetery there is a ditch that runs parallel with the road ... I noticed some battlefield remnants ... live and spent cartridges, a broken SRD jar and shrapnel, a shell protruded from the embankment ... that afternoon was very warm ... I took photographs, 'fixed' some poppies to the 15th Brigade Honour Roll and sought the shade of the trees at the cemetery.

Martial arrived at the Memorial site—I noticed another figure with him and I made my way there. Martial introduced me to Mickey Flanagan, we greeted each other. He had been 'adopted' by a Fromelles family when it was learnt why he was there (see page 432). Before we set out to the Sugarloaf, Martial showed me the recently unearthed and extensive tunnel system underneath the pill boxes on the memorial site. It is little wonder that the area was never taken, the heavily fortified German lines were secure and well defended.

We made our way past VC Corner Cemetery to the point where the Laies crosses the main road, it was just after 6 pm, 80 years on. We walked along the Laies, then made our way through the wheat, across what had been No-Man's Land, we paused now and then to orient ourselves. The ground was littered with shrapnel, cartridge cases and spent bullets. Artifacts and remnants are unearthed, sown and re-sown, a continuous harvest. At the German wire ... we looked back to the Australian lines, to the distant tree lined farm house. Behind us were the Fromelles Church Tower and the Aubers Ridge. We continued on to the vicinity of the Sugarloaf ... long since levelled, covered and farmed. Some startled birds took to the air ... Not for the first time that day I thought about our dear friends, Tom Brain and Bill Boyce. By now, 80 years earlier, Tom was lying wounded, the 60th Battalion cut to pieces. Bill was at the Australian lines, soon to be sent out into the carnage, armed with digging implements, to dig a communication sap across No-Man's Land towards the Sugarloaf ...

On our way back to VC Corner, I paused once again, in the wheat field. Where there had been turmoil, terror and tragedy, there was now tranquility. I don't know why, but I called 'Coo-ee'. No birds rose, perhaps a tear. We retraced our steps, quieter, fatigued, reflective.

The evening lengthened, our attention was attracted by a strange sound. A flight of hot air balloons was approaching. A nearby balloon

The Battlefield 80 years later. The camera is looking north over No-Man's Land. The figure—Martial Delebarre—is standing at the site of the Sugarloaf: the allied front line was beyond the light coloured line —a wheat field—running across the picture.
PHOTOGRAPH L ENGLEZOS

> was 'firing up', its bright flame was clear against the fading light. The balloon rose to clear the walls of VC Corner and the telephone wires along the main road, the people waved to us. The brightly coloured balloons drifted across No-Man's Land.

80th Anniversary Service in Fromelles Church, 21 July 1996
PHOTOGRAPH A BLANKFIELD

The official services were held on Sunday 21 July. Visitors gathered in front of the Town Hall at 3.15 pm and then proceeded to the Church. It was a service of prayer—prayers for peace and for the victims of 19/20 July 1916. It began: *Vienne la Paix, may peace come on earth.* Then: *Neither time, nor distances, can obliterate Memory, whenever men accepted to die for their freedom, their country or for others, their sacrifice will not be forgotten... we are here today to pray. You came from the other side of the world to celebrate with us, on our free land, the sacrifice that your countrymen performed almost a century ago...*

The service proceeded in French and English: *Vienne la paix sur notre terre, La paix de Dieu pour les nations. Vienne la paix entre les frères, la paix de Dieu dans nos maisons.* And then Micah Chapter 4, Verses 1-4, about beating '*swords into mattocks ... spears into pruning hooks'* that *'nation shall not lift sword against nation, nor ever again be trained for war, and each man shall dwell under his own vine, under his own fig tree, undisturbed*'.

It seemed to be about peace and being left alone to enjoy the fruits of the earth, and the small community: '*we beg you Lord to grant us peace in this life ... take away anything that might endanger peace...*' And for good reason, for the people of Fromelles knew much about the alternatives.

80th Anniversary Service in VC Corner Cemetery, 21 July 1996
PHOTOGRAPH A BLANKFIELD

Then to VC Corner Cemetery where speeches were made, wreaths laid, colours presented and some pigeons released. Then people wandered about as they tend to do at such occasions, deep in their own thoughts, imagining, filling in, glad they had come. The birds had gone back into the wheat and the sun was hot. 80 years ago Simon Fraser was getting his men together for another foray into No-Man's Land. Two years on, that spirit, that resolution and courage would be here for ever.

After the anniversary the writer, then but halfway through this book, was introduced to Peter Corlett. Research into Fraser's work had located George Scott an ex-soldier from Byaduk, Fraser's home town and whose two uncles were in 15th Bde battalions. In search of photographs of these Scott discovered at Byaduk a panel of pictures of 40 Byaduk men who served, including 14 who did not return. Among those was Simon Fraser. A copy of this photograph Scott passed to the writer who showed it to the sculptor together with a description of the

THE LAST '19TH OF JULY MAN'
In an army well-populated with heroes, there could be no more fitting character than August Band to be the last '*19th of July man*'. Now in his 105th year, he was born at Mindin, west of Brisbane, on 14 December 1895. 'Augie' was a saddler when he enlisted, 13 September 1915. In Egypt in March 1916 he was

August Band, London 1917.
COURTESY A BAND

taken on strength of 15th Field Company Engineers as Driver, no 6066. With them he fought at Fromelles, Bapaume, Ypres and Somme. He was injured once when a leg was pinned under a fallen horse. 'Augie' was sent to England 'for repairs' and found himself back in the line sooner than he hoped. It was not until 8 May 1919 that he returned to Australia and he resumed work, first in a boot shop, then for thirty-five years with Queensland Railways doing their leather work. 'Augie' had married Agnes McQueen in 1924 and they had two daughters. His wife and elder daughter Valma died some years ago and 'Augie' now lives with daughter Jean and her husband Errol on their farm near Ipswich, Queensland. There 'Augie' keeps himself busy: '*he's up at 7, feeds the chooks, gets the paper from the front gate, feeds the dog, takes the wheely bin down to the gate and at 9.30 collects* [continued opposite]

work for which Fraser was Mentioned in Despatches. It caught Peter Corlett's imagination and gave his work a real-life face that had much to do with Fromelles.

In 1997 funds again became available and with Peter Corlett's proposal accepted, the land ownership transferred, the Memorial Park proceeded, now, after Alan Heggen's retirement, under the new Director of the Office of Australian War Graves Air Vice-Marshal Gary Beck. Brigadier Kevin O'Brien was appointed Special Projects Manager of the Fromelles and Le Hamel parks with the object of unveiling the Le Hamel Memorial on 4 July 1998, the 80th Anniversary of that spectacular victory, and Fromelles the next day.

A new generation of Australians interested, indeed intrigued by what the *'Australia Remembers'* project had shown them, seemed to be forming a new view. Gallipoli *was* more important than Waterloo, the battle of the Coral Sea more important than Jutland or Trafalgar. The thousands that trekked to Anzac Cove to be there as the sun came up on 25 April was a classic example of people voting with their feet. Could you be a true Australian if you had not waded out into the Aegean Sea so as to get the real view of that grim landscape? And then gone on to France and Belgium. To Villers-Bretonneux? To Peronne? To Pozières? Then if there was time, the side trip to Fromelles, where all there was to read was this carved on the back wall of the cemetery:

> In honour of 410 unknown Australian
> soldiers here buried who were among the following
> 1299 Officers, Non-Commissioned Officers and
> Men of the Australian Imperial Force killed
> in the attack at Fromelles, July 19/20, 1916.

'What happened here?' the traveller asked as he heaved himself back on the bus and looked forward to lunch at Armentières.

A 'Board of Inquiry' was organised by the RUSI of NSW which conducted, on 5 November 1997, a post-operations analysis on the Battle of Fromelles. The panel was distinguished and knowledgeable, the great sadness being that should have happened seventy years earlier. Most of the presentations were later published in the *United Services Magazine Summer 1997/98*. It had, most appropriately, as cover, the portraits of Fred Kelly as young digger and a 100-year-old veteran. Various retired or serving officers and others represented the main personalities at Fromelles, and were called upon to express their views. The chairman sometimes asked questions. While most speakers drew largely upon Ellis and Bean, one describing the Engineer and Pioneer Support produced new material from diaries of Brigadier H A Bachtold who was at Fromelles —Major Bachtold OC 14th Field Company. In a sense it was yet another endorsement of the quality of men that Col Pope had in his brigade. So perhaps by association the presentation of Col Pope's story truly caught the character of that man. He commented on the faulty maps and ill-defined objectives, he rounded on McCay on the subject of machine guns '*leaving them behind was a mistake of inexperience or incompetence on the part of the Divisional General*'. Only he drew the attention of the Board to the 'care of wounded'. He had no doubt about that either:

> he (McCay) cancelled the tentative truce as he became aware of it. He did not refer it officially to Corps HQ as the orders were too explicit to justify such action. 'Too explicit' to justify an approach verbally and if need be written approach in view of the 5000 casualties—surely humanity and concern for his men was also an explicit requirement. As it was the truce was cancelled and men perished in agony and others died trying to rescue them.

He turned to his dismissal. He quoted the despair and anguish of Tivey and Elliott, the exhaustion of Croshaw and the emotional destruction of Cass. And then this telling sentence: '*I can find no indication that he (McCay) opposed the actions at Fromelles or queried the lack of sufficient artillery and lack of time to mount the attack effectively.*' He then quoted the example of the English general, Walker, commanding the Australian 1st Division at Pozières arguing for a postponement and change of plans and succeeding. Walker was, of course, one of the English generals whom Birdwood held onto when Pearce appointed McCay despite Birdwood's opposition. But the Chairman of the Board felt in the end that most, '*if not all*', blame rested on Haking and that he '*understood*' why McCay could not question the orders. He was sure that Fromelles deserved a battle honour and quoted as a precedent a British battle honour awarded 200 years after the battle: but who should pursue the claim was not stated. The Board was then told about the Memorial Park by Brigadier Kevin O'Brien.

> Here we are in 1997, already past the 80th anniversary ... and we must now put the record straight. We have no memorial or park of any suitability for that great sacrifice. I can only presume there is some embarassment about the whole thing. We have hidden it away. It has almost been a conspiracy to hide the absolutely shameful disaster ... What we are going to do is this. We have purchased some land; the land

THE LAST '19TH OF JULY MAN' (contd)

the mail. At 4 he has a shower, then settles down to watch the news. He's in bed at 8.30, unless there are visitors'.

'Augie' apart from being a bit deaf and having 'a bung eye' which is why he gave up driving after turning 100, is in great shape and does not use a stick. Recently he told the doctor at a check up that he got a bit puffed chasing the chooks. 'You might be getting old' the doctor suggested. 'Augie' was not entirely sure that was the reason.

In October 1998, as part of its resolve to honour all those still alive, from whatever army, who fought in the defence of France in the Great War, the French Government bestowed on 'Augie' its highest award, the Legion d'Honneur. His other great honours are, of course, his Australian service medals.

August Band, Anzac Day, 1999
COURTESY E & J STEPHENS

At Fromelles, 5 July 1998. L-R: Brig. Kevin O'Brien—Special Projects Manager, Office of Australian War Graves, Mme Anne-Marie Descamps-Carré—donor of the land for the Memorial Park, Peter Corlett—sculptor of 'Cobbers', Willys Keeble—site architect, M Francis DeLattre, Mayor of Fromelles
PHOTOGRAPH T BROWN

owner has actually given the land, but we have had to pay the leaseholder ... Essentially it is a piece of the original German front line. I believe it is the piece we captured. It is an area about 100 metres long and 40 metres wide ... the section of trench we have bought is on the side of the main road and runs for 100 metres due east along the trench line, and some bunkers are still there. A national competition was held last year and a famous sculptor was commissioned to develop an idea something from this battle that we could all be proud of. It was not about victory or celebration, but about the character of the individual soldiers in those very trying conditions ... the winning design is a digger rescuing a second soldier, in the hospital carry position, stumbling along, hatless and weaponless as in those three days ...'

'Cobbers'—in clay
COURTESY P CORLETT

It must be said that in all this work on Fromelles there was no more significant moment for the writer than going to Peter Corlett's studio on 14 November 1997 and with Kevin O'Brien seeing '*Cobbers*' for the first time. The two figures in clay: the limp, hurt, trusting, thankful 60th Bn man clutching his hat, across the shoulders of the strong, focused, caring, selfless 57th Bn man who was certainly Simon Fraser right down to the slightly untidy moustache which was very much the mark of a sergeant at that time.

In the months that followed this group was transformed into bronze, emerging in its full glory for photographs at the Meridian Foundry, Fitzroy, in April 1998. From there '*Cobbers*', as it was now officially known, was taken to the Victorian Arts Centre to be unveiled on 20 April. Although the Minister for Veterans' Affairs Bruce Scott and Gary Beck were there too, perhaps the real tug that pulled the white cloth off the statue was more from Mrs Mary Falkenberg and her nephews and niece, Peter, Mark and Helen Fraser. Mrs Falkenberg who was ninety was a niece of Simon Fraser and the only family member still alive who had known him. When he went to war he left in her care his dog Laddie, writing often and giving advice on caring for it. The younger Frasers at the unveiling were the children of Robert and Heather, Robert being the grandson of Simon's brother Donald, the only Fraser boy of that generation who married.

'*Cobbers*' later went on public view at the Arts Centre over the Anzac Day period, before being flown to France. There on the site now planned and styled by Willys Keeble, it was duly installed in time for Sunday 5 July, just a few days short of the 82nd anniversary of the arrival of the 5th Division in the area. The United Mineworkers' Federation of Australia Pipe Band, some 25 strong, from Newcastle, New South Wales, touring the battlefields at the time was engaged for the ceremony. In the Great War, the Hunter Valley coal mining industry lost 353 men from the 1846 who volunteered: over 10,000 served from the Hunter Valley generally. As far as Fromelles was concerned ten Hunter Valley miners were killed and one died of wounds (see margin). Their descendants at Fromelles in 1998 began their contribution with a wreath-laying at VC Corner at 11.45 am. Then forming up and, as only a pipe band can, clad in kilts and full Scottish regalia—the Charles Edward Stuart tartan—marched along that short stretch of rue Delvas that once crossed No-Man's Land, to the Memorial Park. They led a half-guard of 10th/27th Battalion from Adelaide, followed by others caught up in the haunting strains of 'Waltzing Matilda'. The mist hanging over the cemetery seemed to lift as they moved forward adding a very special feel to the very special occasion. The weather was perfect, everybody from Fromelles was certainly there, and lots more besides. '*Cobbers*' was unveiled once again, and for the last time, by the Minister for Veterans' Affairs, Bruce Scott. The formalities complete, the band then led most of the crowd back to Fromelles where all were received by the Mayor. At last the Battle of Fromelles was finally noted, where it happened. Now it needed to be noted in Australia. Hopefully there, the last two '*19th of July men*' both over 100 years old, glimpsed the few seconds television allowed for the event.

In Melbourne on 19 July at the Shrine of Remembrance '*Friends of the 15th Brigade*' gathered as usual and heard at first hand from Peter Corlett that '*Cobbers*' was in place. It seemed strangely necessary to get such a reassurance.

UNITED MINEWORKERS'
FEDERATION OF AUSTRALIA
PIPE BAND
WORLD WAR I
BATTLEFIELD TOUR
OF FRANCE AND BELGIUM
JULY 1 - 8 1998

Hunter Valley Miners killed at Fromelles. 30th Bn: L Dryburgh, T Easton, M Hepple, J Jones. 31st Bn: J W Purcell, W B Stoddart, R Hamilton. 53rd Bn: J Goold. 54th Bn: J Brown, C T P Smith. 56th Bn: P J Penfold (DOW). Of these eleven, Purcell, Stoddart, Brown, Smith and Penfold have marked graves. The full list of Hunter Valley men killed at Fromelles totals 52, meaning some 47 have no known grave: of these, some 10 are on the list of the Missing buried at Pheasant Wood.

INFORMATION COURTESY R P LAND, D H DIAL, & I COCKRAN

Cobbers, Fromelles

'It shows, in a dramatic way, the struggle experienced to survive the chaos and terror of an early World War I battlefield, of men trying to retain their humanity in a situation that reduces them to the status of expendable "cannon fodder".'... The wounded man stubbornly holding onto his slouch hat, his connection with home and safety.'

Peter Corlett

Peter Corlett was born in Melbourne in 1944 and is creator of a number of prominent sculptures associated with Australia at War: 'Simpson and his donkey' AWM Canberra 1988, 'Man in the mud' AWM Canberra 1989, 'The Bullecourt Digger' France 1992, 'Weary Dunlop' Melbourne and Canberra 1995, 'Kokoda Memorial' Papua New Guinea 1995. His work adorns his native city showing historical identities, sports personalities, Phar Lap, mythical characters and memorable citizens.

The figures are one and a quarter life size, the overall group on the rubble base stands around 3.5 metres above the surrounding plain. Cast in bronze, it weighs around 600 kgs and took 6 months' work.

'Cobbers' by Peter Corlett.
The 2.1 metre bronze group is the centrepiece of the Australian Memorial Park at Fromelles, and was unveiled there on 5 July 1998.
PHOTOS COURTESY P CORLETT, W BELL

Cobbers, Melbourne

On 19 July 2008 at the Shrine of Remembrance in Melbourne, a second casting of Peter Corlett's inspirational statue '*Cobbers*' was unveiled before a crowd of perhaps 1000 by the Premier of Victoria John Brumby and the Mayor of Fromelles, Hubert Huchette.

Ninety-two years after the battle, almost seventy-five years since the Shrine's dedication, there was, at last official recognition of the Battle of Fromelles in Australia. Every state lost men at Fromelles, and only a few municipal memorials from the 1920s recorded the name, but the official memorials including the Shrine and the Anzac Memorial in Sydney's Hyde Park, made no mention of it.

Hence the huge significance of this 'Cobbers', a project tirelessly worked for by *Friends of 15th Brigade*—Lambis Englezos, Garrie Hutchinson and Ross McMullin.

Cobbers at the Shrine, Melbourne, 19 July 2008.
PHOTOGRAPH J CORFIELD, 19.7.08

Hubert Huchette, Mayor of Fromelles (left), and Martial Delebarre AM, Curator of the Fromelles Museum and founder of the ASBF (right), with the author. Melbourne, 19 July 2008.
PHOTOGRAPH J CORFIELD

On the subject of Fromelles ...

During the research and writing of this work in the 1990s, every reference this writer could find on the subject of Fromelles was studied, and rather than have lists of footnotes strewn throughout the book, loaded with codes and *ibid*s, it was decided to do Notes referring to the page concerned and describing in layman's language what had to be explained. This system remains, hence there is no bibliography, as all items are attributed where they are printed.

Since 2000, a number of books have appeared dealing with Fromelles, in part or in full. All writers make reference to *Don't forget me, cobber*, except one who in fact had a copy. Rather than attempt to add the contributions made by those writers into the text, here the reader is given some guide to the contents of each book so they can develop their knowledge on the subject of Fromelles.

Pompey Elliott, by Ross McMullin (Scribe, 2002, 718 pp) What Fromelles did to Elliott is the feeling of one chapter, '*The slaughter was dreadful*' in this huge and successful biography. But it might be argued that the whole of Elliott's life from 19/20 July 1916 onwards was affected by that experience. Apart from McMullin's extensive use of Elliott's papers which are very important, there are only the regular sources—'*last letters home*' at the AWM, and the few slim volumes of memoirs of the time quoted from. Naturally enough, McMullin stays within the confines of 15th Bde, except on the subject of Haking. Like so many concerned with Fromelles, the deficiency of the British, particularly promoted through the writings of Bean, is a worry. One assumes that the object of both sides in a war is to win, so Haking's advocacy in 1913 that, '*... no one can win a battle except the infantry soldier, and he cannot win except by attack,*' was proven two years later when the Germans got within sight of Paris. Later, it might be added, under the command of one of the veterans of Fromelles, the German army (admittedly supported by tanks and aircraft) attacked fairly successfully. But D-Day was another successful attack, so Haking's idea has some validity. The chapter on Fromelles is undermined by its obsession with Haking. It totally omits any criticism of McCay. Understandable, perhaps, in that Elliott's consistent defence of McCay down the years is a continuing thread in the biography of a noble character. That Elliott thought so much less of Hobbs is difficult to accommodate. Hobbs, whose patience Elliott stretched to breaking point was his commander for most of the war, and the period of Elliott's greatest successes. Hobb's handling of the blistering Reports Elliott flopped on Hobbs's desk was masterful. One wonders what McCay would have done if he got a Report on Fromelles of the same strength as those Elliott did on Polygon Wood, and Villers-Bretonneux.

Sir James Whiteside McCay—a turbulent life, by Christopher Wray (Oxford Univ Press, 2002, 250 pp). Concerned with his whole life, this well-presented volume—very good paper, excellent reproduction of photographs, very readable typeface—is only let down by the cover designer reversing McCay's photograph on the dustwrapper to fit her layout. Hence his tunic has buttons and medal ribbon on the wrong side, and his general's badge is back-to-front. The author had a long time interest in McCay being with the law firm McCay and Thwaites from 1984 on. He knew personally, McCay's son-in-law George Reid and others of the McCay family. Wray thus brings into view aspects of McCay's career to which nobody else had access. For a life so crowded with incidents, forget the turbulence, such an approach provides a good guide to how things were done in the years just before and after Federation.

Wray devotes seven chapters—127 pages—to McCay in the war. Of these, 31 pages deal with Fromelles. Apart from being a tightly written description of events, it adds no new information. Whatever McCay may have confided to his family does not impinge on the narrative, and as McCay burned all his papers as soon as he was cleared by Bean, there were no new discoveries to report. Wray being a solicitor is meticulous in assembling his sources which are considerable, and a valuable guide to much more than McCay. Wray is not given to hyperbole or colour in connection with McCay but his *Arthur Streeton: painter of light* (1993) is rather more human, but then the subject was warmer than McCay.

German Anzacs and the First World War, by John F Williams (Univ of New South Wales Press, 2003, 318 pp). Inevitably the presence of Adolf Hitler at Fromelles, and its importance to him, colours the German participation. But this deals with the Germans in the AIF not 6th Bavarian Reserve Division—dramatically illustrated by the story of Norman Meyer 4840 54th Bn, being taken prisoner at Fromelles and being interrogated by Capt. Adolf Meyer of 16th BRIR ! Williams's ability, owing to his language skills, to dig deep into both sides of the conflict makes interesting reading for those more concerned with people than grand strategies, and the Great War overall as it affected men from Monash down who had some German heritage, yet felt no loyalty to the Fatherland. The other book on this area by John Williams, *Corporal Hitler and the Great War 1914-1918* (Frank Cass, 2005, 238 pp), was written under the weight of a great personal tragedy and has none of

the lightness of touch and humanity of his *German Anzacs*. For those reading around the subject of Fromelles, the story of Hitler's long stay there—from around May 1915 to October 1916—is necessary knowledge. The problem of Hitler's history is his later status and books by 'old friends' and 'colleagues'. So how worthwhile those memories of Hitler at Fromelles are, will always be suspect, and what might have been written that was not so favourable has long since been burnt. But it is interesting to read what Williams had extracted from some of these memories. To this writer, as Chapter 6 attests, the writings of Capt. Wiedemann seem the most valid, especially as in the end his views cost him his job as Hitler's personal adjutant, but not his life—clearly both respected each other, which says something about both men and how things were all those years ago at Fromelles when both were in 16th BRIR.

Fromelles: French Flanders, by Peter Pederson (Leo Cooper, 2004, 160 pp). The only real 'pocket book' on the battle, well-produced, sturdy binding, full of photographs (33 from this work and 74 by the author), maps and a step by step guide to all the locations, where the 8th Bde started on the left, around past the Sugarloaf site to the 182nd Bde positions. The photographs of Fromelles as it is now with the various lines, landmarks and how they fit in with the present landscape are highly informative, but the smooth, almost mown fields, tend to make one forget the 8 feet and higher earthworks on each side of No-Man's Land which prevented the clear view we get today. Then, there were also abandoned orchards, random trees, some grown as wind breaks and of course, the mess of war. Thus this writer's one quibble—the use of Charles Wheeler's 'Official Painting' of Fromelles as the cover. It doubtless chose itself because it is the only picture of Fromelles in colour, but it is so misleading that one wonders what Wheeler used as reference. That is very minor ranged against the guts of the book.

The Great War, by Les Carlyon (Macmillan, 2006, 863 pp). The early inquirers into the Battle of Fromelles always included Les Carlyon. Like so many, he was struck by the lack of information, the absence of 'upfrontedness' about it, and what those screens had concealed for eighty years. Writing as only he can, Carlyon devotes the best part of three chapters to Fromelles and towards the end he writes of VC Corner Cemetery: '*A plastic poppy blows in the east wind, clattering against the concrete, and sparrows squabble and titter in a shrub in the corner, and all around are tranquil fields littered—still, and probably forever—with shells and shrapnel balls and cartridge cases and shards of iron. Look up to the ridge, and you can see the church spires of Fromelles and, to the right, Aubers. If it doesn't look much of a ridge, that's because it isn't. But when you stand on it, where the Germans were, you can count the ponies in a field near VC Corner.*'

What more is there to say? Except do not go exploring Fromelles without a photocopy of Les Carlyon's three chapters. The book might be too big and too heavy to take with you, unless you are exploring all the Western Front. Then it has to go, and as hand luggage.

Fromelles 1916, by Paul Cobb (Tempus, 2007, 252 pp). Written by a longtime WW1 enthusiast, and an Englishman whose grandfathers both served in the British Army during WW1. One hoped that that background would have spurred Cobb to write fully about 61st Division, an area neglected until this writer went to the PRO at Kew in 1994 and had a search around the papers there. But Cobb's interest is of the Australian part in the battle. To this area he adds much from sources he has found with families of men who fought at Fromelles, most importantly Lieut Col Pope: thus opening the door much wider on the unjustified dismissal of the CO of 14th Bde: the only Bde of all six who succeeded. Cobb's considered view, '*... it was more likely that he was the victim of some professional grudge or jealousy or, more likely, the casualty of a cover-up to protect McCay*', is a statement which this writer concurs, but to learn more of the circumstances is most worthwhile. The book generally is stocked with casualty tables, Orders of Battle, but ignores the Germans almost totally. The photographs, sad to say, are nearly all of Australians. With the Imperial War Museum Collection 'around the corner,' so to speak, one could have hoped the publisher would have gone in search of some new items, and 'pushed the boat out' and used some better paper on which to print them.

Fromelles, by Patrick Lindsay (Hardie Grant, 2007, 407 pp; 2nd edition 2008, 500 pp). Both editions have as their impetus the two explorations at Pheasant Wood for the Missing of Fromelles. Lindsay, an accomplished journalist and historian, as expected, catches the terrible drama of the battle in the first half. Then he turns to find the human drama of a man who had a hunch, a 'gut-feeling' about those unaccounted for in a battle that intrigued him because of the long neglect, cover up, 'too hard basket', mentality, that wanted to add nothing to what C E W Bean had written in 1929. This writer, some might say, is too close to the searcher and finder of the Missing, but hopefully those interested will find in Lindsay's work, a broad view of Lambis Englezos's obsession, together with the work of the few others who wanted to know well before the tabloid newspapers latched onto it. What is really valuable is this observant and perceptive writer's view of the work at Pheasant Wood, and the people there, not least Mme Demassiet.

Fromelles—today

For most of the period 1920 to 1960 the population of the town was just below 600, but since 1968 it has been increasing so that by 1990 another 300 people were living in Fromelles. Many of these new residents were commuters from Lille, now France's fourth city. Thus now with almost a thousand people, the population has doubled since the ravages of 1914–18. Of the houses they lived in, 50% had been built between 1919 and 1949. In 1952 the railway service to Fromelles came to an end and was replaced by a local bus service—Armentières to la Bassée and return, via a number of stops eg Bois Grenier, Beaucamps, Aubers, Herlies etc.

The French Census noted also that of the 282 buildings recorded in 1990, some 250 were inhabited by owner-occupiers, 4 were holiday homes and 7 were empty. But compared with the 1914 analysis of trades and occupations the Census returns revealed the dramatic change in life style. Now there was but one grocer, one butcher, one tobacconist, one bread shop and only two cafes. There was still one doctor and one school (with four levels). In town, four small workshops provided some local employment but there were no major employers like the brewery and mills of former times. The town of course had its town hall administration and church/welfare organisations and there was now a sports ground. Out in the fields things had also changed. Of the 854 hectares which constitute the Commune of Fromelles, 282 were devoted to cereals, 151 to vegetables, and there were only a few cows and no poultry farms.

In 1989 a group of young men from Fromelles and nearby Aubers came together to form *l'Association pour le Souvenir de la Bataille de Fromelles* (ASBF), which combined their interest in the history of the Great War and the relics in the area of that time. This brought order and support to the collection of artifacts so that a museum was established in the Town Hall. A great amount of field work was, and is, being undertaken, clearing and exploring previously deserted blockhouses, dugouts and sites. The interest of British, Australian and Germans two or three generations removed from those who fought here is reflected by the much increased volume of tourists and pilgrims. The establishment in 1998 of the Australian Memorial Park and thus highlighting the Battle of Fromelles to a new generation, has encouraged the ASBF to do more fieldwork and preserve more sites and artifacts, and to conduct tours and provide tour itineraries.

INFORMATION COURTESY M DELEBARRE

The town of Fromelles – 1997 PHOTO COURTESY PIERRE DAUMARS

15

Behind the Pheasant Wood

WITH GREAT CARE
Officers and sergeant-major-lieutenants needed to work with great care to salvage the killed, identify them in accordance with the rules, and list their personal belongings. Again, the big graveyard in Beauchamps had to be extended considerably. The killed enemies were buried in mass graves behind the Pheasant Wood.
—21st BRIR Historian, 1923

As near as can be ascertained, from aerial photographs taken between 17 June 1916 and 16 September 1918, Pheasant Wood (the Germans called it Fasanen Wäldchen) was well forested and never reduced to a typical Great War landscape. The only intrusion was the rail line cutting through the south west corner, not far from the mass graves site. The line was there before the battle and at the end of the war. The site is well clear of the front line and the forest offered cover for the Germans from many prowling, low flying British 'aeroplanes'—constantly noted in German accounts but hardly mentioned in Bean, yet vividly remembered by men who were there. It was also probably a good place to get a pheasant or two for the officers' mess.

Today the wood, or is it a forest, is dense with many trees over 10 metres high and is, as always, private property. The 1997 aerial photograph of the town (opposite) shows it on the left, beyond the church, with the south side—the location of the graves—clearly visible. The field being private land, surrounded by more private land, and nowhere near sites of fighting was not mentioned except in private letters and the 21st BRIR history of 1923 until this book did so in 2000. But it was the reference to

The 2008 Excavation.
The size and style of the archaeologists' 'encampment' behind the Pheasant Wood and over the grave sites is captured in this photograph taken from the steeple of the Fromelles Church.
PHOTO COURTESY PATRICK LINDSAY

... a total dedication ...

At the 2008 excavation, not having '*official status*', the man whose dedicated work had led to the locating of the mass graves behind the Pheasant Wood was not permitted on site. But from the movement of the archaeologists and their avoidance of eye contact, he was able to judge

PHOTOS PATRICK LINDSAY

how things were going—both at the exploratory investigation of 2007 and the excavation of 2008. The vibes were always good.

One day during the 2008 work Lambis Englezos went down to VC Corner to sit and think. There he was phoned by his son Anthony to be told that he was now a member of the Australian Defence Force: once known as the AIF. Everything was coming together.

We learn from Patrick Lindsay's *Fromelles*, much about Lambis, the restless inquirer. Lambis was born on 26 January (Australia Day!) 1953 in Salonika, Greece. His father and mother migrated to Australia in 1954, and in 1955 Lambis's brother Costa was born. They settled in Albert Park.

Later. when Lambis married Suzanne, an Australian girl of Irish descent, they settled in Brunswick and raised their family. His now considerable knowledge of the Great War was the spur to learn more and steady reading began.

It escapes both this writer and Lambis exactly when we first met, but it was probably at the Shrine on 19 July 1991. A year earlier, this writer discussed Fromelles with John Bradley, a Shrine Trustee, who put forward the idea of a service at the Shrine on 19 July 1991, the 75th anniversary of the battle. John's particular interest was that his uncle Pte Duncan Bradley 57th Bn was one of the first casualties in the Fromelles area when a shell killed five and wounded five on 11 July. The service was well-attended and this writer decided to inquire into the battle in depth. At the same time Lambis contacted the Shrine Trustees to ask if there was a tree that could be dedicated to 60th Bn in time for the publication of the Battalion's history on 26 April 1992. Without fuss, it was arrangeda tall stately *Eucalyptus maculata* was chosen and a plaque was designed and at the insistence of Lambis, the first named battle was Fromelles: the first mention in the Shrine grounds of that name. Lambis then booked another similar *Eucalyptus maculata* for the 59th Bn. Both 57th and 58th Bns still had their original trees and plaques, and later the Shrine agreed to accept matching information plaques: all, of course with Fromelles. To assist the work on the history of the 57th and 60th Battalions, Lambis arranged meetings with Tom Brain and other '*19th of July men*'. Through the 60th Bn Association, we met George Graham, another 60th Bn survivor, and via the 57th/60th Bn Association, Charles Henderson of 57th, who was also at Fromelles. Lambis by then had '*found*' at Warrnambool, Bill Boyce of 58th; these last two had the best memories. Discussion growing out of these meetings brought home the true scale of our losses: especially vivid when heard from men who were there.

In 1992 '*The Friends of the 15th Bde*' began its services. Ever since 1922 there had been a 60th Bn AIF Association, administered in its last years by Jack Kirfield. When he died in 1985, his daughter Jacqueline Todd, kept the Association going, assisted by Margaret Wood, daughter of Major Tom Kerr 60th Bn and Military Cross at Fromelles. They were persuaded to help form '*The Friends*', and so restore the services that 60th Bn and other 15th Bde units had held up until the early 1980s. Lambis found veterans and their families and brought them to the services. He searched out speakers and became the spokesman for '*The Friends*'.

[contd opposite]

Suzanne, Anthony, Lambis and Sophia Englezos, 19 July 2009

a mass grave in the memoirs of William Barry (see page 344) that attracted Lambis Englezos, and for the next seven years he pursued his 'gut feeling' that there were still unrecovered missing Australian and English soldiers at Fromelles.

After years of personal frustration working alone, Lambis's obsession interested others and together they formed what author Patrick Lindsay christened 'Team Lambis'. They were John Fielding, deputy principal of a NSW high school, and a Lieut Col in the Reserve; Ward Selby, grandson of a Fromelles veteran and mining executive whose work often took him to Europe, and of course Lambis Englezos, an art teacher at a community school and restless amateur historian. The combination of army discipline, industrial science and concentrated humane energy was what was needed.

Importantly, at the funeral service for the Unknown Soldier in Canberra on November 11 1993, Lambis Englezos escorted Reg McCarthy 7th Bn, who after the war, at 18 years of age, stayed on with the Graves Recovery Unit (GRU). He later described his work thus, '*we treated the remains like a person, someone who was there ... nobody ever cracked up under the strain of finding bodies ... we had a good sense of mateship ... I had made up my mind from the start that this was a useful thing to do.*'

When Englezos visited Fromelles for the 80th Anniversary in 1996, he was, of course, there in the summer and able to link very closely to the battle site, and walk the areas which had been but words in Bean. It was all new and vivid and he wrote of it (see pages 419–21) in a way that has a curious vision of what was to come.

But all new information did not come forward in one neat package; it was gained bit by bit from 2000 to 2008. It was near the anniversary of the battle in 2003 that the well known and respected authority on WW1, Jonathan King, published a piece in *The Australian* drawing the nation's attention to the Missing at Fromelles and the lack of interest at government level and elsewhere. Others became interested in the possibility that 161 Australians were unaccounted for from Australia's worst military disaster and things began to move.

Before then however, Englezos's persistence had ruffled feathers in Canberra, one writing to him, '*we cannot do things on your gut feelings, we need a carefully prepared, logical dossier*'. So the Team Lambis came together: the statistics were tightened up, copies of all the aerial photographs available obtained, as many references to the subject that could be found were

A TOTAL DEDICATION (contd)

This writer went to Fromelles at the end of 1994 to begin the Inquiry and the preliminary work on this book; this 'new' information shared with Lambis developed our mutual interest. Lambis brought forward his long service leave and was at Fromelles for the 80th Anniversary—19 July 1996. When he returned it was clear he '*had been taken over*' by Fromelles and the scope and content of the Inquiry benefited hugely from his research, questioning and the network he had built up with veterans, historians and friends in France.

With the publication of the first edition of this book in 2000, Lambis now had the full casualty list, and as much information as this writer could find, not least the first full translation of the German accounts of the battle, which included a reference to mass graves '*behind the Pheasant Wood*', and the diary notes of William Barry 29th Bn which mentioned burial pits. To his friends, the intensity of his interest became a little worrying but when he went back to France in 2002, Lambis felt the ground so to speak, and he got an echo back: by 2005 it was a very loud echo! Lambis's approach now became very methodical and technological, and what he achieved is the subject of this chapter.

By the middle of 2008 when the 'Missing' were no longer Missing, Patrick Lindsay wrote of Lambis: '*we should accept nothing less than a total dedication of our resources to identifying and finally laying to rest these heroes whose lives were squandered at Fromelles. It is the very least we can do for those men and their families.*'

The critical document

THE VON BRAUN ORDER 5220 OF 21 JULY 1916

Although much work had been done by Peter Barton and his team at the Munich Archives, it was when they came upon a 6th BRD '*List of English military personnel buried in the area held by this Division*' that changed things. This list gave where known names, rank, number, regiment, dates of admission to hospital, date of death and nature of their fatal wounds in campaigns up to April 1916. It seemed certain therefore that the event of 19/20 July 1916 would be covered with the same style of paperwork.

They came across an order written by Major General Julius Ritter von Braun, commanding officer of 21st BRIR. It was he who would write the history of the 21st with its reference to mass graves '*behind the Pheasant Wood*' (see page 190) '*based on official war diaries with one survey sheet and six sketches, Munich 1923.*'

The Order is headed '*Bringing up materials and recovery of bodies.*'

1. The following are assigned to the Regiment to undertake recovery of the wounded and dead:
a. 1 NCO and 24 men of the Medical Company. These will be billeted at Desprez (Eck Farm) and draw rations with the 21st Infantry Pioneer Company. They will be employed as directed by the Regimental Medical Officer.
b. Three motor lorries. These will be loaded at Brulle with screw pickets, rolls of wire and long stakes, which will be unloaded beside the light railway line, E of Fromelles, on the Mittlere Hochstrasse. The unloading will be carried out by a working party from the h-company. The lorries will then be loaded in the vicinity of the Regimental Command Post with German dead, which are to be deposited in the SE quadrant of the cemetery at Beaucamps. The Regimental Band will detail men to carry out this work as ordered by the Regimental Medical Officer, who will also arrange for the necessary supervision by a Medical Officer and other personnel, as required.

Sergeant-majors are to be in attendance during the laying-out of the bodies and will collect papers and identity discs in such a way that the personal effects and identity disc are removed from each body individually and are immediately placed in a sandbag, tied off and tagged with a cardboard or stiff paper label (pendant address label), on which the number and company appearing on the identity disc are recorded.

Each body thus registered is to be laid immediately in one of the mass graves excavated in accordance with 3 (below). The Medical Officer in attendance, who will direct the operation, is to ensure that each layer of bodies is immediately covered with a layer of earth mixed with chloride of lime, and that, when full, the grave is immediately covered over in a suitable manner. The grave sites will be allocated by the Ortskommandant [Town Major] of Beaucamps. Consecration of the bodies and the graves will take place later.

Zeltbahnen [tent squares] may be used to move the bodies, but must not be used as burial shrouds. Detached body parts are to be wrapped in cloth and buried.

The other vehicles used to transport the pioneer materials are likewise to bring back German bodies; the light railway is also to be used for this purposes as far as the halt at Beaucamps, from where the bodies will be transported on stretchers. The unloading points are to be sited to one side, fenced off at a suitable distance with barbed wire, and guarded in watches by sentries posted by the Regimental Band.

The civilian population is to be prevented from loitering and staring at the bodies.

The entire recovery operation at Beaucamps will be carried out in four hour shifts until specific arrival times are known. The sergeant-majors of the IIIrd Bn will begin at 8.00 pm today, followed by those of the 1st, then those of the IInd Bn, etc.

The English bodies will be buried in mass graves immediately to the south of Pheasant Wood. The removal of effects and identity discs, in the same way as for the German bodies, is to be carried out by the h-company, supported by one medical NCO and four men of the regiment, under the orders of the Regimental Medical Officer.

In order to expedite the rapid removal of the bodies, the dead are to be separated by nationality and laid out at depots close to the light railway, Grashof and Christuskreuz.

The misappropriation of even the most insignificant item of property from a body (German or English) constitutes robbery of the dead and will be severely punished. The collection of effects, as ordered above, may only be carried out by the sergeant-majors at Beaucamps or in the presence of a senior NCO of the h-company at Pheasant Wood.

The IIIrd Bn is to provide one section, in rotation, to assist at Beaucamps. The assistance of stretcher bearer sections from RIR 20 is requested.

2. From today, three motor lorries are assigned to undertake double trips during the night to take forward the pioneer materials (see 1 above). The h-company will provide a squad from 10 pm to carry out the unloading at Fromelles (tonight, the occupying company for the first trip, then the relieving company for the second trip).

The IIIrd Bn will provide two squads each day to load the other vehicles at Desprez when requested by the commander of the Infantry Pioneer Company. The e-company will provide two sections to unload the materials at Christuskreuz. Times to be decided by Lieutenant Marx.

3. The Ortskommandatur [Town Major's Office) at Beaucamps is to

organised. And with the Press now engaged in the discussion, Members of Parliament started to ask questions. And in reply to one which came from him via the Senate Estimates Committee, the Director of the OAWG supplied figures that Englezos had asked him for much earlier. There were 163 Australians unaccounted for—Englezos had estimated 161 (see page 437). Now for the most indisputable piece of evidence—the aerial photographs. Englezos contacted the Imperial War Museum in London in 2004, indicating his interest in the battle and the area of that interest. The Military map is a marvellous piece of basic technology. Divided into squares of 6000 yards, that is cut into four squares, then each quarter into 100 squares gives the location of the graves precisely at N.17.d.1.2., so this is what needed to be in the photograph. And it was in at least five photographs—17 June, 29 July, 1 August, 20 December 1916 and 16 September 1918. No pits in the first, but in all the rest, the last showing three still open. The clarity of the photographs is extraordinary, and turns one's thoughts back to the aerial views of the battlefield before the battle and the inability of McCay and his HQ staff to read what they were telling him—the 'second and third line of trenches' were not trenches but drainage ditches. Further evidence for the basic drift of this Inquiry.

At the same time, the Munich Archives supplied the text from 21st BRIR history as in this book and another document numbered 5220 21.7.16 which after more careful examination of these Archives in 2007 turned out to be a draft of the order from Von Braun, *The Critical Document* (see opposite). This provides all that was needed in regard to burial. Team Lambis now had real evidence to make a case that was worth consideration.

In assembling this book, many relatives of the men who were at Fromelles contributed letters and diaries, and in due course became '*Friends*'—by 2000 the services were regularly attended by 50 or more: and Fromelles always had the largest crowd. It would be fair to say that nobody at this stage had given any real thought to the idea of the 'Missing'. But when he went to Fromelles in 2002, Englezos had a full Roll of Honour and that persistent image of William Barry on the edge of a mass grave. He wrote of that visit randomly:

THE CRITICAL DOCUMENT (contd)

*have mass graves dug for approximately 300 bodies, separated by unit, but alongside one another. The officers are to be laid out separately in the centre. For the burial of the English dead, the h-company is to excavate mass graves for approximately 400 bodies. Until that time it is only to be employed on remedial works within the * position.*

Signed: von Braun.
Copies to Regiments (2), Battalions (3), Companies (14), Reg Med Off (1), IInd and IIIrd Bn Med Offs (2).

I AM BEING THOROUGH

In his position as Head of the Australian Army History Unit, Roger Lee was the man with whom the ultimate decisions rested. In retrospect it is comforting to read his remarks of 14 November 2006 to somebody who was pressing him for a result: '*I know you think I am being too deliberate and slow—I actually take it as a compliment as it also means I am being thorough. Should I at some future point recommend that a search of the site be conducted and subsequently no remains discovered, I will still be able to demonstrate that the process followed was thorough and, on the balance of evidence, the search warranted. By being able to demonstrate that, I am confident that the requests for similar actions in the future would still be treated seriously. If I just rush in and recommend we do it without thorough consideration of the evidence, I can guarantee that if the search were to prove fruitless, no such requests in the future would receive any Government support at all.*'

A German sign: To Fromelles.
AWM

> On the return visit in April 2002 ... I began to ask some questions about the missing ... one memorable afternoon, Martial and I walked the length of No-Man's Land, we started in 8th Bde lines and made our way to the Sugarloaf Salient ... there was ... battlefield debris, cartridge cases, shattered shell cases, barbed wire, dented bullets and shrapnel ... there is a constant harvest. At the Sugarloaf we found a sandbag, the hessian pattern was evident on its solid shape ... a remarkable find. During our walks I asked Martial about Pheasant Wood, whether he knew where it was ... he pointed both arms towards the village ... I wondered were there any uncovered bodies.

Trawling through the small type of this book, Englezos was attracted to the story of Lieuts Vaile and Bowden (see pages 245–47). With the newly available Red Cross Records in 2004, he managed to get copies of the British Red Cross (Berlin Branch) report on Bowden dated 27 June 1919. It explained the confusion between the German Report of finding an Australian with the disc no 1929, and the Australians looking for a Lieutenant, showing simply that Bowden after being commissioned had not changed his disc, but the crux of the German Red Cross letter of 21 January 1918 was '... *It may be assumed that possibly Lieut Bowden was buried in one of the five large British collective graves before the Fasanen Wälchen [Pheasant Wood] near Fromelles, or in the collective grave (no 1 M.4.3) in the Military Cemetery at Fournes.*' Englezos now had the vital German confirmation on the site of the mass graves. This had been published in German in 1923 and well-known to C E W Bean, as we will learn (see margin *For the fallen enemy*.

[contd page 440]

A FUNERAL

Whilst it shows the preparation for the burial of Germans at Wicres in 1915, it is reasonable to suppose that at other mass burials of their own, the Germans behaved similarly. The precise cutting of the pits must be similar to those at Pheasant Wood. Note the careful placing of the coffins, the man in the pit seems to be checking the names and hanging behind the whole group are religious standards not regimental ones. The photograph on page 359 of the cemetery at Wicres, although modern, gives an idea of the layout. None of the fallen from 19 July 1916 are thought to be buried there. An order from July 1916 on funerals provides some interesting detail:

> *For the funeral of those members of the Regiment who fell on the field of honour on 19 July, the 3rd Coy will send one section, strength 64 men, under the command of Lieut Sewald. The funeral will take place at 6.30 pm. The unit with be ready ay 6.15 pm at Fournes. Dress: Helmet, trousers in boots (gas mask). All officers, company sergeant majors and NCOs in reserve positions will also participate. The Companies will send representatives wherever men are not required to guard buildings. The Regimental band will be at the cemetery at 6.15.*
> *Signed: Luneschloss.*

The text on this German postcard is: 'The funeral of those who died in the English attack of 25 September 1915 at the cemetery of the 13er in Wicres.'
POSTCARD COURTESY J-M BAILLEUL

The mathematics of the Missing

For Lambis Englezos, his initial argument with the *status quo* was that nobody had done the maths. Bean did not, and until they were bothered by a member of Parliament, neither did the Office of Australian War Graves. The somewhat 'out of sync' office had been asked by Englezos for some support in solving the 'mystery' and they did not disguise their belief that he was wasting everybody's time. '*Every one of these names is listed as buried at VC Corner ... it contains the graves of over 400 Australian soldiers ... not a single body could be identified ... we are checking the CWGC records to see if any more information about the state of the bodies is available. However, given that not a single one could be identified suggests they had already been interfered with, eg hastily buried by Germans and tags removed and reported to the Red Cross.*'

'*If this is so,*' the Director wrote_ to Lambis, '*then that should lay to rest your belief they still remain at Pheasant Wood. Lambis, you will have to let this one go, or find some evidence for your belief. If we learn anything new, I will be in touch. Would you please distribute this message to your friends and maybe one of them can convince you as I don't seem to be able to do.*'

Of course, most of what the Director wrote was a recital of the popular version. The first sentence is wrong, the second is one of those useless 'over' or 'about' figures—the exact number was, of course, known. Bean (Vol III, p. 395) had related that on his visit to the battlefield on 11 November 1918, two bodies had been identified (p. 339) and buried—so their papers must have been with them, but as both were 15th Bde, their bodies may have been well away from the German lines, and so were untouched. The rest of the skeletons were collected and buried

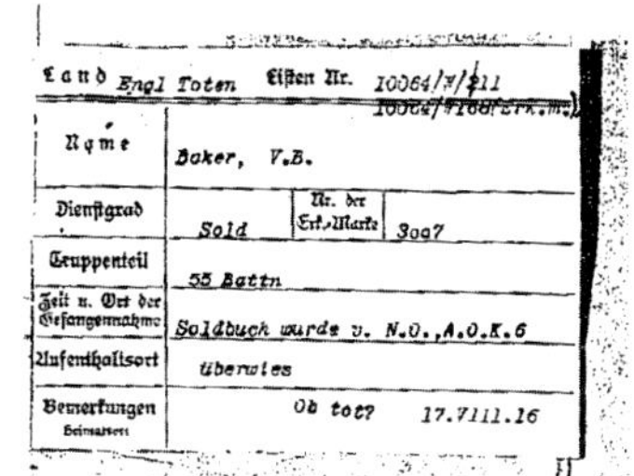

Land Engl Toten	Listen Nr. 10064/7/211	
Name	Baker, V.B.	
Dienstgrad	Sold	Nr. der Erk.-Marke 3007
Truppenteil	55 Battn	
Zeit u. Ort der Gefangennahme	Soldbuch wurde v. N.O., A.O.K.6	
Aufenthaltsort	überwies	
Bemerkungen Heimatort	Ob tot? 17.VIII.16	

The official German death list card for Pte V B Baker 3007 55th Bn which notes they have his paybook and personal effects.

at VC Corner, one assumes 410 skulls enabled a precise number to be arrived at.

The story now in the press caught the attention of Senator Mark Bishop who in 2005 at a Senate Estimates Committee asked Senator Robert Hill, the Defence Minister, to request from the Director of the OAWG the figures relating to dead, found, buried or totally missing. The Director now had to deal with the subject accurately. Very soon Senator Hill received what Englezos had sought for years: CWGC research revealed that five bodies had been found in the area in the 1920s. It was known that 410 unidentified men were buried at VC Corner, another 266 at Rue David Military Cemetery, 142 at Ration Farm Military Cemetery, 120 at Aubers Ridge British Cemetery, 72 at Y Farm Military Cemetery, 52 at Le Trou Aid Post Cemetery, 27 at Rue de Bois Military Cemetery, 22 at Rue Petillon Military Cemetery, 10 at Anzac Cemetery, and 10 at Sailly-sur-la-lys Canadian Cemetery. A total of 1131 unidentified Australians from the disaster of 19/20 July. Subtract 1131 from 1299, and less the five found in the 1920s, there were 163 'missing'. Englezos had originally felt the figure was higher—about 250. He too had not done his maths! Or was he ahead of everybody once again ? When the figure rose to 191, we wondered.

Then came the information from Jeroen Huygelier, in Belgium, and a longtime scholar on the subject of the Australians in his country during the war, that the International Red Cross had had a Wounded and Missing Enquiry Bureau during and after the war, and they had some 30,000 case files on Australians wounded or missing. As it turned out, without the public becoming aware of it, the Australian War Memorial had acquired a huge quantity of Red Cross material. Indeed on his last visit to Canberra before finalising the first edition of this work, this writer became aware of this by a remark from Ian Smith of the AWM when searching for information about Miss Chomley (page 308) and Capt. Mills—both associated with the Wounded and Missing Bureau. There was no indication then of the range of information that those files held.

However by the time Englezos learned of the scope of these files, they had been placed on the AWM's website: including not just the basic information, but also letters from troubled relatives, declarations by other soldiers and whatever else came to the Red Cross to confirm that a man was missing. Using the Rolls of Honour from this book, Englezos worked his way through the entire list of the dead at Fromelles, found or not found. It was a mammoth task but of course when it was done, it was the core of the case: the number at first count was 161.

The lists that follow take the number up to 191 Australians, because the German records give that number of men whose bodies they buried. The British Roll of Honour gives 316 names who are remembered on memorials, at Loos, Ploegsteert and Thiepval. These lists do not include the large numbers of British lost on raids prior to 19/20 July.

The Australian Missing

Name	No.
Ashworth, P A	1656
Atwell (Lee), S H	2779
Bain, W E	135
Baker, V B	3007
Balkin, M	4254
Balsdon, J	2274
Barber, W	346
Barrett, R A	3031
Batt, A G	352
Baumann, O E	10
Bell, H	191
Bennett, A	1602
Benson, G V	840
Bills, T H	605
Bishop, R C	3761
Bolt, H T	3009
Boswell, J H	891
Bourke, H J	1682
Bowden, J C	1929
Boyce, W E	1218
Breguet, J H	1983
Broadhurst, L	3013
Bromley, A C	4744
Broom, S	1522
Brumm, N L	1470
Burney, E N	1226
Burns, R D	16
Campbell, J M	495
Cartwright, T C	1235
Caswell, D	397
Chinner, E H	-
Church, C C	635
Clark, R A	4155
Clingan, A S	3168
Collier, C T	-
Connolly, W T	3585a
Corigliano, M	2011
Cozens, J A	210
Craigie, W A	4420
Cressy, H A	4179a
Crocker, J E	79
Croker, H	2010
Cuckson, W J	3032
Curran, J J	494
Dennis, S W	1252
Dewar, R A	3047
Dibben, E H	4183a
Dodd, D	4770
Doust, W H	3557
Dunn, L C	641
Dunstan, B J A	4483
Dyson, F A	3560
Esam, H	491
Fahey, P W	3060
Farlow, S	80
Fenwick, R G	882
Fitch (Ansell), A W	2825
Fletcher, F	3310
Francis, T W	2584
Gardner, H	889
Glenn, F J	1291
Gordon, J	1130
Goulding, J J	555
Grace, W A	1537
Gray, E C	20
Gray, G R	2927
Gray, S J	4296
Green, R C	1274
Greenfield, B	1275
Greenwood, P J	3115a
Griffiths, G A	1276
Grogan, V M	3114
Hale, N A	702
Harriott, L	4509
Harris, J J	3819
Hart, L W	865
Haslam, H J	1390
Hawcroft, C H	188
Higgins, W B	196
Hill, C S	842
Hoffman, C R S	2050
Holliday, C D	4801
Holmes, A	955
Holmes, J L	4305
Holst, F G	2925
Honey, G	1291
Hope, E J	4188
Hungerford, G W	3327
Hunt, T	347
Hunt, T V	1054
Hyams, S J W	2028
Irvin, D G	4807
Irving, A W J	1528
James, A M	689
Jamieson, W A	2144
Jentsch, E A	3331
Johnson, A J	2203
Johnson, R W	3367
Johnston, C D	4315
Johnston, G H	3096
Joyce, I	1624
Knable, A T	1603
Lawlor, D M	126
Leister, L	4840
Livingston, D F	1168
Loader, F O	2064
Lucre, G H	467
Maclaren, F F	2101
Magor, R H	3209
Mason, J L	470
Maudsley, R T	137
McCaul, D C	1980
McDonald, A	1553
McGuarr, R J	3873
McKenzie, A McG	1797a
McKenzie, J G	151
McLean, H	293
Mendelsohn, B	-
Mitchell, A C	2746
Moffitt, H L	-
Momplhait, A V	3282
Morgan, C	2055
Morley (Howard), J (W J)	258
Murray, C W	1590
Myers, P L	4850
Needham, A	4946
Nelson, H O	728
Nevill, J H	269
Nitchie, J L	146
Norris, I B	-
O'Donnell, S R	314
O'Donnell, W	319
Oliver, E R	316
Pagan, G	2906
Parham, E W	2092
Parker, J	572
Parry, F	320
Perry, A M	2095
Pflaum, R H	161
Pheasant, W	2462
Pitt, H C	595
Pollard, H G	324
Pretty, W H	1556
Ralston, J	1501
Randall, H J	1558
Rawnsley, A A	2392
Reid, M L	3256
Richardson, B	4581
Richardson, H	2912
Ridler, S J T	1036
Robinson, H F	1312
Ross, J H	1216
Ross, M	1040
Russell, A	4299
Ryan, D B	743
St Smith, H N	3924
Scott, J	4873
Scott, R G M	1046
Shannon, P	3433
Smith, A G	1640
Smith, G T	1245
Smith, H T	4474
Smith, J R	3983
Spence, J M	4614
Stalgis, G F	2898
Stead, J R	187
Thompson, A	2825
Toole, J	690
Tuck, A G	1252
Tucker, W C	1581
Turner, A L	39
Turner, J	767
Verpillot, A	4885
Vincent, L S	777
Wallis (Wailes), J P	4617
Walsh, L G	311
Walters, F C	1446
Wass, W	239
Weakley, P	318
Weir, A J	358
Wildman (Bradney), R R	1888
Wilkin, E F	1314
Williams, F J	3605
Williamson, A	4249
Willis, H V	983
Wilson, E R	4887
Wilson, S C	3534
Wood, A	781
Woodman, H G	794
Wynn, J C	2485
Yeo, C	795

The British Missing

Name	No.
Adam, Pte J	6152
Aldridge, Pte A	266591
Allan, Pte L W	5504
Allan, Sgt A	241891
Andrews, Pte F H	265211
Atkinson, Lieut G W	-
Austin, Pte H	266487
Austin, Sgt C	810
Avis, Pte S H	3460
Bacon, Sgt C E	267172
Badger, Pte A	2177
Bailey, Pte F W	3718
Bailey, Sgt C	3224
Baker, Pte H	200801
Baldwin, Cpl P C	6296
Baldwin, Pte H	4390
Band, A/L Sgt E	240808
Barkaway, Pte F W	267122
Barker, Pte W	201299
Barlow, Pte H	266144
Barnes, Pte G	267229
Barnett, Pte S	3367a
Barnett, Pte W H	3654
Barron, 2/Lieut L	
Bates, Pte H	3435
Battams, Cpl E C	3316
Beckett, Pte H	3456
Bees, Pte F W	200979
Beesley, Pte A	266208
Bennett, Pte H	266401
Bennett, Pte R P	6386
Bethell, Capt. T H	-
Bignell, Pte W H	6054
Billers, L/Sgt W	240420
Birchall, L/Cpl T	267143
Bird, Sgt H H	267166
Blakemore, Sgt A J	2922
Bland, Pte E J	6320
Bleaken, Pte A F	5201
Bliss, Pte P	241352
Bond, Pte A G	266731
Bone, Pte W J	266226
Bowie, Pte J L	4131
Brittle, Pte B	3872
Brooks, Pte J W	4865
Broomfield, Pte J P	5196
Brown, CSM A	3149
Bruce, L/Cpl W H V J	266515
Buckingham, Pte H	202104
Bunce, Pte J	3558
Burrows, Pte W E	201238
Byers, Capt. R H K	-
Cannon, Pte W	2923
Carter, Pte R	266618
Carver, Pte G E	267097
Casmore, L/Cpl W	266097
Castle, Pte G A	266612
Chance, Cpl J	240903
Chaplin, Sgt R W	6235
Charlwood, Pte F J	266742

The British Missing (contd)

Name	Number
Chatwin, L/Cpl A	265148
Chippett, Pte A F	265346
Christie, Pte F	267150
Clark, Pte E A P	266638
Clark, Pte H J	6206
Clarke, Pte J A	266690
Coleman, Pte E	5354
Collins, Cpl E J	1636
Collins, Pte M	267217
Cook, L/Cpl A	265265
Cook, Pte A J	3152
Cook, Pte G	266006
Cooper, Pte F	201735
Cooper, Pte V F	2349
Coull, Pte G	5598
Coulton, Capt. A E	
Cox, Pte T A	266713
Crompton, Pte H	268583
Crutchfield, Pte F	1580
Cundy, Pte E	267253
Cunningham, L/Cpl R	267218
Dale, Pte A	6066
Daniels, Pte W	4435
Darke, Pte H	4433
Darney, Pte J A	3222
Daveney, Pte T	4228
Davenport, L/Cpl H C	3492
Davey, Pte W E	5117
Davies, L/Cpl R C	267414
Davies, Pte J E	5949
Davinson, CSM F	398
Davis, Pte A	1614
Davis, Pte T H	3231
Davis, Sgt G E	1718
Dell, L/Cpl C C	266125
Dennett, Pte W	6068
Desborough, Pte T	266259
Deverell, Pte W J	5139
Dixon, Pte C	267207
Donald, Pte T	6162
Donaldson, Capt. G B	-
Downing, Pte J	3263
Drinkwater, Pte F J	265990
Dryburgh, Pte A	267224
Dwight, Pte S	3294
Eason, Pte E S	4856
Edwards, Pte A T	5109
Edwards, Pte W S T	4615
Evans, Pte J	2333
Farr, Pte H J	2828
Farren, Pte J	265409
Feltham, Pte F C	266280
Field, Pte P F	6307
Fielder, L/Cpl E C	242012
Fincher, Cpl A V	1477
Fitzgerald, Pte G W	241945
Foley, Pte W	20851
Fowler, Pte E H	266604
Galloway, Pte G	267233
Gamblin, Pte E F	6226
Gawler, Pte C S	3494
Gibson, Pte H R	265824
Goode, Pte A	3930
Grady, Pte G A	267165
Gray, Pte W	1804
Green, Pte O	2200
Greenfield, Pte E A	6079
Grieves, Pte A	4841
Griffiths, Pte C G	4951
Griffiths, Pte H	4395
Griffiths, Pte J	5958
Guntrip, Pte R W	266634
Guy, Pte J F	202023
Hadley, A/L Sgt H H	3743
Hampson, Pte E C	202767
Harding, Pte H	266654
Harper, 2/Lieut H	
Harris, L/Cpl D	5970
Hayes, Pte F H	2216
Hazelwood, Pte J	265933
Henley, Pte S	265926
Hickmott, Pte H	267263
Highnam, Pte J H	266295
Hill, Pte A	4376
Hobbs, L/Cpl W R	265291
Hodges, Pte E E	4947
Hodgson, Pte F S	266221
Hogston, Pte H W	266715
Holden, Pte B J	266662
Holly, Pte R B	5525
Holt, Pte W	266682
Hopkins, Pte B	4874
Hudson, 2/Lieut R B	-
Hughes, L/Cpl W	240322
Humphrey, Pte C J	265919
Hurdman, 2/Lieut C	
Hyett, Dmr C E	1861
Ireland, Pte D L	6170
James, Pte B	267174
Jenner, Pte A E	6314
Jephcott, Pte J	266263
Jocelyn, L/Sgt E	266351
Johns, Pte O L	5303
Johnson, L/Cpl W	4311
Jones, Pte J T	5983
Jones, Pte J W	266393
Jones, Pte J W	4825
Jones, Pte R E	2847
King, L/Cpl W A	3675
King, Pte T E	4325
Knights, Pte W	5313
Lacey, Pte E	266604
Lamb, L/Cpl W O	241019
Lamb, Pte A	3206
Lance, L/Sgt F C	265854
Langford, Lieut W J	-
Law, Pte W J	4876
Lewis, Pte E	265930
Line, Pte F W	267090
Lloyd, Pte A	3725
Lucking, Pte M	4935
Luff, L/Cpl C G	265225
Lupson, Pte G F	267236
Luxton, Pte B E	6251
Macdonald, L/Cpl A	5658
Mantripp, L/Cpl G W	8376
Marshall, L/Cpl D	267261
Marshall, Pte W J S	266764
Marslen, Pte R V	266690
Mason, Pte H	202775
McClements, Pte A	5391
McCormick, Pte W	266236
Melville, L/Cpl J	267272
Miles, L/Cpl E A	267285
Minett, Pte G H	2937
Mitchell, Pte M	241904
Moore, Cpl H	2132
Moore, Pte T	266167
Morris, Pte A H	265298
Morris, Pte A W	266197
Morris, Pte N L	2741
Munday, Pte C R	265787
Neale, Pte A G	266506
Noakes, Sgt R F	2943
Norman, Pte T G	6256
Oxlade, Cpl A E	205070
Parker, 2/Lieut F R	-
Parker, Pte T E	3940
Parsons, Pte A A	266132
Paton, Pte E	5683
Paver, Pte W	3752
Perry, Pte J W	267093
Phillips, Pte R	201152
Phipps, Lieut C P	-
Pitman, Pte E V	6324
Plowman, Pte C G	266561
Pollard, Pte A	6113
Portman, Pte A	266488
Powell, Pte W G	3821
Powley, Pte A G	6266
Pratt, Pte G E	265385
Pratt, Pte G	5687
Price, Pte H T	266714
Price, Pte P	266657
Pryde, L/Cpl J	5688
Raisey, Pte A V	3486
Ralph, Pte A J	5523
Rees, Pte W S	5962
Richardson, L/Cpl W	267290
Richings, Pte A V	1918
Routley, Pte J	3959
Rowe, Pte S A	2460
Rowson, Pte H	3904
Rudman, Capt. H E	-
Ruttens, Pte E	6123
Ryan, L/Cpl C	20871
Sanders, Pte C E	3783
Sanderson, L/Cpl D	268586
Saunders, Sgt W J	2885
Sayell, Pte A	4276
Scrase, Lieut R G	-
Scull, Pte J T	267112
Searle, Pte J J	6125
Sharlott, Pte T C	266353
Sharp, L/Cpl E	3631
Sheffield, L/Cpl S	4618
Shepherd, Pte C	268573
Sheppard, Pte H B	265192
Sheppard, Pte W J	265283
Shreeve, L/Sgt A R	267208
Simmonds, Pte J W	266619
Simpson, Cpl D	267298
Sinclair, Pte R	266692
Smallwood, Pte E	240688
Smith, L/Cpl A J V	3859
Smith, Pte H	266552
Smith, Pte J	5704
Smith, Pte W J	266681
Spooner, Pte P T	267287
Stanway, Cpl H W	265295
Starling, L/Cpl F	240909
Stephens, Sgt S	2853
Stevens, A/Cpl H	241873
Stevens, L/Cpl A F	265388
Stockham, Pte W	266734
Stoker, Pte A T	266695
Stone, Pte G C	266615
Surgenor, Pte L	6276
Sweetman, Pte A H	266591
Swift, Pte J C	265915
Symonds, Pte G	4340
Tallis, Pte T	4233
Tavenor, Pte F	266175
Taylor, Dmr G A	4369
Taylor, L/Cpl W T	240740
Taylor, Pte S	3430
Taylor, Pte T	1963
Taylor, Pte W	1857
Thom, Pte D L	5712
Thomas, L/Cpl W H	200277
Thomas, Pte S A S	3387
Thompson, Pte H F	6278
Thorne, Pte F	2659
Tilley, Pte E S	6135
Tomes, Pte H	4308
Topp, Pte A	4386
Townley, Pte F	4638
Turnbull, Pte H	267305
Twamley, Pte L	266675
Upson, Pte W T	4257
Warr, Pte B W G	4331
Waterman, Pte C S	6285
Wathes, Capt. T S	
Watkins, Dmr T	1997
Watkins, L/Cpl H P	5948
Webster, Pte F	3799
Wells, Pte H G	6339
Welsh, L/Cpl	5718
Weston, Pte L	240991
Wheeler, Cpl S	3832
Whitcroft, Pte T	266485
White, Sgt W H	2497
Whitmore, Pte H	241996
Willimott, Pte H L	5956
Willis, Cpl F J	265708
Willis, Pte F T	4207
Willis, Pte W R	4940
Winterborn, Pte J E	267217
Witten, Pte T	5528
Wood, L/Cpl S	5342
Wood, L/Sgt G E D	5430
Wood, Pte G C	2835
Wood, Pte S	266138
Woodhatch, Pte W	241887
Woodward, Pte G W C	6288
Wright, L/Cpl C H	267082

This list of 316 names comes from the Loos Memorial, the Ploegsteert Memorial and the Thiepval Memorial.

NOT A BATTLE HONOUR

When the Battle Honours were declared in 1920, the survivors of Fromelles could not believe that it was not shown against any of the battalions who had fought there. There was a 'France and Flanders' and 'Somme': these were said to cover it. The argument was that Fromelles was in Flanders and connected with the Somme campaign! Hence Fromelles is not shown on the national memorials, but in recent times it did appear on the Hyde Park Corner Memorial in London.

One of the first things '*The Friends*' attempted was to campaign for a battle honour. Representations were made by a Brigadier to the Head of the Army. Papers were gathered, a succinct Report written, and a case made. It went to Canberra and onto the desk of the man who had the power to do something about it, but who was suddenly overwhelmed by vastly more important events, and so sent the Report 'on', ending up, one assumes, in the '*too hard basket*'.

AT THE BRITISH END

The unofficial post-battle truce on 184th Bde's front was very successful. The 2/5th Glosters apparently worked day and night for four days bringing in the wounded and dead without suffering any casualties themselves. To think the same might have happened at the Australian end—but for one man's callousness.

FOR THE FALLEN ENEMY

In 1927 there had been correspondence between the Official Historian C E W Bean and the brother of Lieut Eric Chinner. Bean wrote: '*There is little likelihood of your brother having been placed in a separate grave unless he reached hospital. The History of the 21st Bavarian Regiment, which opposed him, says "For the fallen enemy, mass graves behind Fasanen Wood were arranged" [This means Pheasant Wood/Copse], I think your brother would probably have been buried behind Pheasant Copse: whether his grave has been discovered by the British grave authorities, I do not know, but if so his remains have probably been removed to VC Corner.*'

In Bowden's file, as with most others, there were letters from battle survivors describing what they saw, and desperately sad inquiries from relatives in search of some information. This pattern became immensely important in locating the mass graves. Very soon after examining the files of missing, it was clear where they had been buried. The next task was to find out if the GRU had recovered them, and if so, where did they rebury them.

To cut a very long story short, it became apparent that the GRU had not found the mass gaves at Pheasant Wood. Who knows what the site looked like or was used for immediately after the war, especially as at September 1918 these pits were still open.

With all this activity, and information moving around between WW1 buffs and experts, relatives and historians, it became increasingly obvious that something had to be done. *The Canberra Times* of 13 March 2005 spoke out: '*Opposition spokesman on veterans' affairs, Mark Bishop is among a growing group who believe a technical examination should be made of the likely mass grave site at Fromelles. Such agitation has previously met with bureaucratic reluctance, but Bishop is hopeful that Defence Minister Hill will authorize examinations, and has been heartened by the attitude of the Chief of Army Lieut Gen Peter Leahy.*'

Hill had then asked Lieut Gen Leahy, Chief of the Army, for an opinion on doing a ground scan at Pheasant Wood, and Leahy supported the idea. This persuaded all those who had to be persuaded that a presentation by Team Lambis was necessary to settle the issue, once and for all.

The result of this was a call to Englezos from the Head of the Australian Army History Unit, Roger Lee, that he had been instructed to establish a Panel of Investigation in a month's time. The homework had nearly all been done and some 20 people selected by the History Unit were called together for the presentation on 10 June 2005. The Panel included staff of the History Unit, Australian War Memorial, OAWG, the Army, and some historians including an expert in German history. While at the time it looked rather top heavy with public servants, the mix in retrospect seems to have been correct, as only the Government could negotiate at the high level necessary with Britain and France on such matters and only the Government had a diplomatic service to assist, and finally of course, only the Government could pay for the whole operation.

This was the one opportunity that Team Lambis would have to convince the unbelievers and silence the skeptics. Englezos did the speaking and Selby worked the technology. Fielding sceptical of the audience from the outset had made sure the graphics were clear and unambiguous, and the basic data was correct and seen to be so. After the general background had been described, Englezos turned to the figures showing how he had arrived at 161 missing, from the German Red Cross files and other sources. This is when a few of the panel sat up and took notice, for as Patrick Lindsay points out in his book, here were names, with service numbers, rank and battalion. This was illustrated by the German card for Jack Bowden, the Lieutenant who had not changed his identity disc and had been lost among the ORs. An onsite set of photographs recently taken by Fielding showed the undulations exactly where they should have been and Englezos finalised the presentation with a simple request, '*I believe that a non-invasive geophysical investigation of the burial sites near Fromelles is warranted.*' On the basis that they would never have another chance to present, the Team had included Fournes Cemetery and Marlaque Farm as other areas to be investigated.

Team Lambis did not walk out of the Panel of Investigation unscathed or with any feeling of optimism. It would seem those who had thought Lambis Englezos was wasting their time remained unconvinced. Others were clearly resistant to the whole idea of three non-historians fronting up with such as Powerpoint presentation. Later in the day, the Panel delivered their verdict. Not surprisingly they rejected Fournes and Marlaque Farm and of Pheasant Wood they decided:

> It was agreed that while not conclusive, sufficient evidence does exist to warrant further investigation of records pertaining to the Pheasant Wood site. Field studies are not recommended unless more compelling evidence is located to support the contention that the site was being used as a mass grave by the Germans in 1916. Should more compelling evidence be discovered, the Panel agreed to reconvene, consider the new evidence and prepare an appropriate recommendation to the Minister for further action.

AN INCREDIBLE FIND

What would be the odds of finding a small brass pendant, about the size of a 20 cent piece worn by a long dead Australian with no known grave in a field in France after some ninety winters under snow and ninety summers under crops, with ploughing and harvesting all these years? Yet a ground sweep by a metal detector around the grave sites in the 2007 investigation found two Australian good luck medallions. One was a heart-shaped Anzac badge with a coat of arms, the other was from the Shire of Alberton 1914, shaped like a horseshoe, a good luck sign.

A persistent inquirer into Fromelles because his great uncle disappeared in the battle, Tim Whitford could not believe the find at first. His great uncle Henry, one of fourteen children, was from Alberton, 4 kms south of Yarram, in Victoria. It was there that Henry's parents lived. Tim knew by research that the bodies of three other men from the area who died in the battle were accounted for—only Pte Henry Victor Willis 983 31st Bn was missing. Two things had always puzzled Tim. These were that Willis's name was not on VC Corner, but on the Villers-Bretonneux Memorial, along with a number of other 31st Bn men, and why Willis's official date of death was 21 July. Equally important, the finding of the two pendants gave further assurance that the searchers were in the right place, and influenced the decision to go along with the 'dig'. However when Henry Willis's name appeared on the German Red Cross list in relation to Pheasant Wood, Tim and his wider family knew at last what had happened to great-uncle Henry.

Left: Pte Henry Willis, 983 31st Bn.
Far Left: The Shire of Alberton pendant recovered in 2007

EVIDENCE
The 2008 Dig found two Australian rising sun collar badges, an almost complete set of the front part of the webbing equipment issued to British and Empire soldiers. This included three pouches complete with three clips of .303 ammunition in each: some heavily corroded, others better. Leather straps, that appear to be braces ... more fabric including German ground sheets, British trouser material, buckles, buttons, strap ends, part of a gas mask, a gas mask container with intact tooth brush inside, a bayonet scabbard, live .303 ammunition, a British pattern brass strap end and stud, and a match box.

Major Gen Mike O'Brien CSC (Rtd), Senior Australian Army Representative, Australian Fromelles Project Group. A specialist in logistics with the Army, he served in Vietnam with 7th Bn. Director of various studies at the Australian Defense College, he is author of *Conscripts and Regulars* and a book collector.

Tony Pollard, the leader of GUARD (Glasgow University Archaeology Research Department), has worked on battlefields in Britain and Africa, as well as with the British police as a forensic archaeologist. He and fellow archaeologist Neil Oliver were the *Two Men in a Trench* (2002).
PHOTOS PATRICK LINDSAY

So Team Lambis went home and discussed what to do next. But the Missing at Fromelles debate had gone to the press, in West Australia, South Australia and NSW, enough for Senator Bishop (Labor, WA) to speak on the subject in the Senate. People like mysteries and stories that don't quite add up. It was then learned that John Williams, the German expert on the Panel had been commissioned to go to Germany and find out what the 6th BRD had left as evidence.

Before this commission, Williams had been warm to the idea of the Missing at Pheasant Wood, but after his visit to Germany and discussions with various historians, he could see no merit in it. In the final Report he presented, the mention of Pheasant Wood as a burial ground in the 21st BRIR history was dismissed by quoting Edmonds, the Official British Historian, who wrote that Unit Histories were '*being written by fee hungry hacks*'. Williams must have missed the fact that the author of the 21st BRIR history had been the commander of the Regiment —hardly a hack. And more than that he was the author of the order that gave the instruction to '*excavate mass graves for approximately 400 bodies*'. One has to say only the men who dug the pits at Pheasant Wood, and filled them with bodies knew more about the episode than Major General Julius Ritter von Braun. But Williams formed the view that the pits might have been dug for the artillery to house Minenwerfers or some such hardware. Thus he reported to the Committee against the project going ahead. It was a sad loss to the cause.

But Government, rightly or wrongly, were taking their time working out what to do, or what not to do. They had listened carefully to Team Lambis and after a mixed report decided to go ahead and commission a non-intrusive survey. It was an adventurous thing to do. The decision to give the work to the Glasgow University Archaeology Research Department (GUARD) whose TV programme *Two men in a trench* had proved highly popular with people who watch 'thinking TV', caught the expected criticisms from those who knew more, could do it better, or cheaper. But the big thing was that the search was underway, supported by the Government. The margin note *I am being thorough* (see page 435) gives a glimpse of the process. Rough as the passage had been through the corridors of Canberra, there were facts that had to be answered and no one could ignore. There were a large number of missing bodies; mathematics had proved that. The location of the large mass graves at Pheasant Wood was proven as was, by way of the aerial photographs when they were dug. And later when they were filled in. The GRU records did not include the site as having been investigated.

The investigation of 2007 was non-invasive and produced by the use of ground penetrating radar, metal detectors and supported by general research before and after the field work, which was done by a team of six from 16 to 28 May. In the general ground sweep with the metal detectors, two significant items were found, both of which were of Australian origin but in a sense more important was the even 'scatter' of what one might call 'war debris' over the site, indicating that the surface had not been significantly disturbed since the Great War. Geophysical surveys suggested the pit filling was also undisturbed. The verdict was that the site was 'of interest', but any further work should depend on what archival records would reveal.

As always experts from near and far turned on Pollard's report. Just about every one of them could have done it better, knew more about mass graves, or had access to superior technology. Reading back over their tirades, now that they have all been proved irrelevant, is one of the bright moments of the whole business.

Lambis Englezos journeyed to Fromelles to watch the proceedings; he had long been in contact with Tony Pollard so it was a happy meeting best reflected in his same random style as in 2002. So full of joy, poetry, spontaneity, laughter and tears that they must be shared with the faithful reader who has followed the story this far. And of course there is that echo of what the man called out to Simon Fraser.

> Then in 2007 ... I had been in Fromelles almost two weeks before I went down to Pheasant Wood to make my first ever visit ... I had walked past it many many times ... the site was overgrown, the grass almost knee high. Undulations in the growth were evident, the light and the breeze indicated a rise and fall in the ground. In my strictly amateur way, I had convinced myself that this was a strong indication that this was still a burial ground ... I wasn't sure how I'd feel walking the ground, there was some apprehension, nervousness and ultimately some comfort. I felt I was in good company. I felt, sensed if you like, that they were still there.
>
> We had tried our hardest to find out if they had been recovered ... it was conceded that this had been a burial ground ... we had put forward our strong circumstantial case ... now GUARD have been sent to investigate ... thanks to the Australian Army ... who have shown imagination and sympathy for the proposal ... After all the years of research, the active discouragement, the welcomed and appreciated support, I was there with the 'boys'. I can't help it, every time I walk into VC Corner, I greet the 'boys'. There is empirical evidence, there is clear science and technology, however I was convinced that they were there, if you like, I sensed that they were there. I rested. I had made my pilgrimage.

IT IS RIGHT AND PROPER

'It is right and proper that those brave men who lost their lives at Fromelles are buried with the honour and dignity befitting their ultimate sacrifice. The new cemetery will be a lasting tribute to their bravery and a place of pilgrimage for families who lost a relative in the battle. It will ensure the memory of their actions lives on for future generations.'

Derek Twigg,
UK Veterans Minister 31 July 2008

The mass war grave was discovered by an amateur historian in Australia and confirmed by a team of archaeologists from Glasgow University on behalf of the Australian Government with support from the British Ministry of Defence and the Commonwealth War Graves Commission.

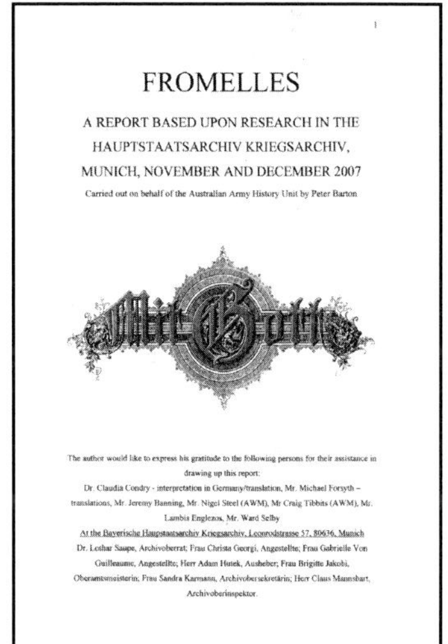

1

FROMELLES

A REPORT BASED UPON RESEARCH IN THE HAUPTSTAATSARCHIV KRIEGSARCHIV, MUNICH, NOVEMBER AND DECEMBER 2007

Carried out on behalf of the Australian Army History Unit by Peter Barton

The author would like to express his gratitude to the following persons for their assistance in drawing up this report:

Dr. Claudia Condry - interpretation in Germany/translation, Mr. Michael Forsyth – translations, Mr. Jeremy Banning, Mr. Nigel Steel (AWM), Mr Craig Tibbits (AWM), Mr. Lambis Englezos, Mr. Ward Selby

At the Bayerische Haupstaatsarchiv Kriegsarchiv, Leonrodstrasse 57, 80636, Munich

Dr. Lothar Saupe, Archivoberrat; Frau Christa Georgi, Angestellte; Frau Gabrielle Von Guilleaume, Angestellte; Herr Adam Hutek, Ausheber; Frau Brigitte Jakobi, Oberamtsmeisterin; Frau Sandra Karmann, Archivobersekretärin; Herr Claus Mannsbart, Archivoberinspektor.

THE BARTON REPORT, 2007

Commissioned by the Australian Army History Unit, the 307-page Report, plus photos, maps, and other appendages barely scratched the surface of the huge collection which was uncovered in Munich, the only fully intact (except for some post-war weeding) WW1 Archive surviving in Germany.

POUR LES SOLDATS

Having enlisted the help of the mayor of Fromelles in 2006 in finding who owned the land where the graves were, Patrick Lindsay, his wife Sarah as interpreter, and Martial Delebarre, went to the home of Pierre Jean Georges Demassiet and his wife Marie-Paule, 78 and 77 years old respectively. '*Their weathered faces brim with character, good humour and the wisdom of long experience. Pierre is a small powerful man with wispy white hair, high cheekbones and dancing impish eyes ... the Demassiets are proud farmers. They have the strong hands of those who have spent a lifetime working the land*' was how Lindsay

Mme Marie-Paule Demaisset, 2006
PHOTO PATRICK LINDSAY

described them. It fell to Martial Delebarre to explain the battle, the aftermath and how Lambis Englezos had found the site, and that they may receive a request for the site to be investigated. Marie-Paule had no trouble with that. Her family had lost two in the Great War, one whose body was not found until 1928, and the other never found at all: the names of Charles and Louis Beaussart are on the village memorial—*'Morts pour la France'*. Marie-Paule knew about family grieving: grief that was sadly added to in January 2007 with the death of her husband.

After the non-invasive investigation in May 2007, and the decision to go ahead with a 'dig' a year later, much was learned about the field. '*The land always refused to grow anything, just grass,*' Pierre had told Lindsay, mentioning also there was something strange about it ... undulations ... this

The day before my visit to Pheasant Wood, I went to Rue Petillon Cemetery ... as I made my way between the headstones I paused and looking across I saw I was beside Reverend Maxted. It was a warm day ... I had walked a fair distance. I lay down for a rest ... the grass was prickly ... I welcomed the rest and the company. I fancy I may have gone into conversational mode ... I fancy that I may have sought a blessing for the work to be done and the possible outcome. I fancied that someone might finish this work of recovery.

A lot of clever technology would be used, however ultimately it would be the clever shovel that would tell.

It was my choice to make the trip for the Investigation. I had been in regular touch with Tony Pollard and Peter Barton ... I felt I needed to be there. Resolution was close. I waited for the arrival of 'Les Angleterres'. The team were very inclusive of me - I recall these weeks with great fondness. I was an active participant. Cheap convict labour. They used a variety of clever technology to determine whether the site was 'of interest'. I never knew that archaeology was so enervating, so romantic ... the process of technology, the exacting science, the clever machinery, the shovelling, the stretching of the hamstrings, the repetition, the bagging of items, the flicking of mosquitoes, the toil - it was an amalgam of romance.

Towards the end they did a surface scan of the site using a metal detector. They plotted every item, every bullet, every shrapnel, every item. The significance of the process was that it indicated that there was a general and consistent scatter pattern across the site. The ground had not been disturbed. On the last day the scanning continued ... as I passed the detector made a loud and steady noise ... they called me to search the spadeful of earth, I found an army whistle. I was sceptical, I confess to a certain gullibility ... the whistle was too new. They had planted it, I accepted the gift with a smile. Perhaps it was a last day ritual. I thanked them. Some time later I replaced the whistle, they didn't notice and I remained in the vicinity. There was some genuine interest when the detector sang. Careless of me,

The Mayor came down, pulled some plastic cups, bottles of wine and apple juice from his backpack. We toasted and thanked each other, speeches were made. I asked Tony Pollard if he could give me a nudge, nudge, wink, wink, before I got on the plane home, leave me with some idea as to the status of the ground. He called me aside and suggested the ground was of interest. We said our goodbyes. I made my way to VC Corner Cemetery, I had made the walk many, many times. This time it was especially significant. I said hello to the 'boys' and sat on the Cross of Sacrifice, facing the etched names. I confess to an emotional release.

After the positive outcome of the non-instrusive 'dig' of 2007, and the subsequent search of the Munich Archives that had proven absolutely the work done by the Germans (details are noted throughout this work), the Australian Army was in control of the preliminary excavations of 2008 which found the Missing, GUARD had been reappointed and Englezos returned to Fromelles. It was an event he could not miss.

I returned to France for the dig. On the first day I was taken onto the site to view the work. The topsoil had been removed and the edges of the pit had been exposed. There was a distinct variation in the colour of the clay. The edges of the pit were clearly defined, there was an almost pencil line straightness to the edges. The pits had not been disturbed, they were intact.

Late on the second day of the dig, journalist Paola Totaro, was convinced that something had been found. Paola prowled and paced the fenced off press and visitor's tent area, looking across at the increased activity around pit five. Phone calls were being made, discussions were being had. Extended viewing activity and a distinct lack of eye contact as the site was being closed down for the evening, led her to believe that they had found remains.

When I arrived at the site on Wednesday morning, the third day of the dig, I was told that remains had been found. However, the 'official' announcement back home had to be made. When the team arrived, I received absolute confirmation. Tony Pollard greeted me with 'give me a hug big fella' (or words to that effect). It was a nice moment.

There was a lot of activity at the site. The police arrived to view the remains and to determine that work could proceed. Much to the consternation of the Mayor, one of the local's dogs also followed them in. There was a certain vigour and excitement and a lot of press activity. I had hoped and suggested that when remains were found that the ground would be consecrated and the work blessed by a military chaplain and local priest but that would come later.

The GUARD team had been asked to determine the status of the site and now they were to determine the state of the remains. Careful digging with trowels was the next step, as the topsoil needed to be removed from the other pits.

I saw the first remains uncovered. An arm emerged from the clay. His hand had been blown off. The human tragedy and the nature of the work to follow became more tangible. I was to make another visit to Reverend S E Maxted at Rue Petillon Cemetery.

POUR LES SOLDATS (contd)
became very noticeable especially when the grass on the site was cut very short in preparation for the second investigation in 2008. Marie-Paule mentioned that many had wanted to buy the land over the years, '*I could never understand why I needed to keep it ... but now I understand. The soldiers were making me keep it.*'

Then at the end of the 2008 'dig', when it was established without doubt that 'behind the Pheasant Wood', the killed enemy had been been buried in 1916 and were still there, Marie-Paule was the guest of honour at the closing ceremony. Lambis Englezos' dedication and work had now been rewarded. Then Marie-Paule took his hand and told him she was donating the land to the Commonwealth War Graves Commission *'pour les soldats'*.

Overshadowed in the Australian press by the bushfires of February 2009, the Press Release from the Minister for Defence, Science and Personnel, Warren Snowdon, about the Fromelles Excavation Contract disappeared from public view. It was some surprise that the GUARD team with their considerable experience and work on the project did not get the final contract, which was awarded to Oxford Archaelogy. The official statement read: '*their ability to meet the unique requirements of the project and their superior operational and management structure*.

Work on the project would begin in May 2009 and continue until Summer 2010, resulting in the creation of a new cemetery titled *'Fromelles (Pheasant Wood) Military Cemetery'* and located nearer the centre of the village. Each body will have an individual grave. Identification will be attempted by DNA and other data. The work generally will be overseen by the CWGC, and paid for by the Australian and British governments.

A MOST SPECIAL MOMENT
Of the closing ceremony, Johan Durnez, a member of the Family and Friends of the First AIF from Belgium wrote: '*... the most moving question came from an older man speaking in French ... everyone heard the soft and gentle voice ...*'

'*I ask permission to conclude this meeting with a minute of silence in honour of all those young men who died here in our community and whose graves finally have been found.*

[It] *was really a most special moment ... the generator of the pumps was turned off and then a silence fell over Pheasant Wood ...*
I am sure you can never find a better place and a better people to be guard for these eternal resting places.'

—FFFAIF,
Bulletin from Fromelles 11.6.08

... 80 years ago to the moment ...

Excuse the scribble as I am writing this on the floor of my dugout and the light is very bad. So Jack Borger finished his letter of 24 July, 1916, to his mother. A thoughtful son he had begun: *I sent Maud a cable to break the news to you of poor Jack and Tim sad end, I don't know if I have done it right or wrong ... but I thought she would break it better to you than anyone else. It was a task that I dreaded as in your weak state of health, I feared for the result: as if they were your own sons, it is awful, but it is the will of God.*

He was writing about his cousins Ptes Timothy Joseph Carey 3408a and John (Jack) Stephen Carey 3481a of 53rd Bn who had both been killed. *Jack got hit in the face with a piece of shrapnel and never moved again, killed right out just before our boys jumped over.* Of his other cousin he wrote: *Tim had joined the bomb throwers, they are the first to jump out ... Gilligan was first over, Tim went next, they only went a few yards when Tim got hit in the stomach with four machine gun bullets ... Gilligan bandaged him and Tim lived a few minutes ...* Jack then went on to describe how Gilligan had joined in the attack again, but on the way back came to see Tim, but he had died, so he took his watch to send home. (Gilligan was perhaps Pte A C Gilligan 3068, 53rd Bn.)

On the morning of 21 July, Jack '*got permission from my officers to go and make inquiry and doubly sure as mistakes are often made. I saw all the fellows who were with them and also Gilligan, there were an awful lot of our boys killed in this stunt. This has upset me awful, I am broken hearted, they were more like brothers than cousins, they were a pair of white men and the most popular pair that ever came away ... I can't put everything I would like in this letter as they are censored and we can't write what we would like. Old Gilligan acted the part of a hero as he stayed with Tim ... under very heavy fire, I heard this from many.*' Jack signed off: '*I remain your son in sorrow.*'

The body of Tim was never found and he was therefore one of those whose name is on the screen wall of VC Corner Cemetery. He was 25 and not officially declared killed in action until 2 September, 1917. The body of John (Jack), who was 32 (although shown as 23), was recovered and he was buried on the day he died in Rue-du-Bois Military Cemetery (Grave I F 16) by Padre J P Gilbert, then attached to 30th Bn.

The two boys were sons of the late Patrick Carey and Bridget Carey, of Kinchela, Macleay River, NSW. When Tim and Jack left the farm to enlist they declared themselves as labourers, but their sorrowing mother called them farmers on the forms she sent to the War Memorial. Next of kin were able to write an epitaph that would be carved at the foot of the headstone. Bridget Carey's words are among the most original and memorable: '*Will some kind mother, as you pass on, kneel and pray for my son.*' At home on the wall she hung a huge photograph of her beloved sons part of which is reproduced here, and a reminder to the generations who came later what had happened in the Great War, as far as the Carey's were concerned.

Mickey Flanagan
Fromelles, July 1996

The message did not fall on barren soil. Mickey Flanagan in 1996, a great nephew of Tim and Jack, aware that it was the 80th Anniversary of the battle, journeyed to the battlefield. At the Rue-du-Bois Cemetery in the Visitors' book he wrote:

It is 80 years ago to the moment that Private J S Carey lost his life at the battle of Fromelles. Where else should I be this day but here?. I make this journey on behalf of my late grandmother Maggie who never forgot and I placed flowers on Jack's grave for his mother Bridget who never could.

The Carey Brothers c1915
Left: Timothy Joseph Carey,
Right: John (Jack) Stephen Carey.
INFORMATION AND PHOTOGRAPHS S FLANAGAN & M DELEBARRE

The Rolls of Honour

The names that follow are the reason why all the preceding pages were written.

The British list is a product of the HMSO '*Dead of the War 1914–18*', published in 1920, checked where possible against the Commonwealth War Graves Commission Cemetery and Memorial Registers and lists in histories or archives of the British Regiments. British officers whose death was inevitably listed under the Regiment to which they belonged, rather than that in which they were serving when killed, are an area where there may be some omissions. Also due to the lack of records about the supporting and reserve battalions it proved impossible to compile their lists. This applied to the MG and Field Companies in particular, and the artillery. With the British Army then engaged on the Somme, as well as many other places, casualties of 19 and 20 July were substantial, and the official classification 'F and F' ie France and Flanders does not make it very easy to sort through the pages and pages of names involved. Hopefully British historians, now that the whole list is on CD-Rom, will be able to print off meaningful lists, something not possible before due to the huge number of British dead, and the loss of so many records in the Blitz. That said, the list here has 554 names as against the official number of 519. The British taken prisoner—thought to be about 51—was a list that evaded this research.

The Australian lists have been compiled from a number of sources—the Official Australian War Memorial list, later rendered into bronze on the walls of the Memorial at Canberra, the Nominal Roll of the First AIF on microfiche, the casualty lists in the Military Orders issued at the time of the battle, the Commonwealth War Graves Commission Cemetery and Memorial Registers, the original Nominal Roll Books of the battalions and lists in Ellis, Bean and other histories. When there was doubt about spelling, rank or date, the 'majority decision' was used. This writer felt it better to include some individuals whose details were not absolutely definite, rather than exclude them. This particularly applied to men who died of wounds. The

Anzac Cemetery, Sailly-Sur-La-Lys, November 1994

DEATH IS NOT AN ADVENTURE
This book is to be neither an accusation nor a confession, and least of all an adventure, for death is not an adventure to those who stand face to face with it. It will try simply to tell of a generation of men who, even though they may have escaped its shells, were destroyed by the war.

Lieut AW Wheen
1897–1971
MM and 2 bars
54th Bn

The introduction to *All Quiet on the Western Front,* by Erich Maria Remarque (1929), from the translation by Arthur Wesley Wheen formerly of 54th Bn, AIF, and veteran of the battle of Fromelles.

Only in the British list is the classification D—died. This was used in the HMSO List. Only in the Australian list DOW POW—Died of wounds when Prisoner of War, although there is one D POW in the British list.

KEY TO ABBREVIATIONS

D	Died
DOW	Died of Wounds
DOW POW	Died of wounds when prisoner of war
KIA	Killed in action

official view, and thus the official statistics, was that 'died of wounds' applied to those who died within 48 hours of the end of the battle. This was an unfortunate situation especially when a wounded man who had clung onto life for a week, a month, or more, before succumbing was thus never regarded as one of the dead of Fromelles. This is one of the reasons that the lists in this work total 2070 against the official figure of 1917 dead. Those dates of death are shown, for example, 23.8–23 August. Those who died of wounds when prisoner are included in the Roll of Honour. They are also shown in the POW list. Those who died of illness or disease when in the hands of the Germans are not regarded as among the dead of Fromelles.

The reader's attention is drawn to three special groups. In the 31st Bn there are 40 names officially listed as killed in action on 21 July: in the absence of any proof that this was so, they are regarded as killed in the battle of 19/20 July. In 58th Bn, there is a group of 46 who were killed in the German raid of 15 July. Because this had an important effect on later events, they are listed, but not included in the overall figure of dead from the battle of Fromelles. This same exclusion applies to the 8 of 13th Bde AFA listed as killed 18 July: see page 24.

The German lists were the most difficult. Doubtless somewhere there are lists for other BRIR regiments as good as those published by 16th BRIR. Recent research has produced overall numbers but not the individual names. Hopefully this work will encourage a researcher to compile the material. It was this writer's firm conviction, after having read of the conduct of the German soldiers at Fromelles, that a list of their dead should be included as a memorial to those men as sons, brothers, husbands and fathers from families thereafter marked by Fromelles. Doing so, however, forms no pardon for the invasion and desecration of France by Germany, and the suffering that caused.

The initials defining the cemetery or memorial are listed opposite, together with a list of UK cemeteries where those who died of wounds in British hospitals were buried. Those in search of relatives lost at Fromelles should consult the Office of Australian War Graves in Canberra, or Commonwealth War Graves Commission, Maidenhead, Berkshire, UK, which also has offices at Ypres/Ieper, in Belgium, and Arras in France.

Cemeteries and Memorials

AA Arras Road Cemetery, Rochincourt (No. Fr 1059).
AB Abbeville Communal Cemetery Extension (No. Fr 52).
AN Anzac Cemetery, Sailly-sur-la Lys (No. Fr 255).
AR Aubers Ridge British Cemetery (No. Fr 567).
BA Bailleul Communal Cemetery & Extension (No. Fr 284-85).
BH Bedford House Cemetery, Zillebeke (No. Bel. 165-67).
BO Boulogne Eastern Cemetery (No. Fr 102).
BR Brewery Orchard Cemetery, Bois Grenier (No. Fr 83).
CA Calais Southern Cemetery (No. Fr 8).
CB Croix-du-Bac British Cemetery, Steenwerck (No. Fr 1092).
CC Canadian Cemetery No 2, Pas de Calais.
CI Cité Bonjean Military Cemetery, Armentières (No. Fr 922).
CN Covin British Cemetery, Pas de Calais (No. Fr 203).
CO Corbie Communal Cemetery (No. Fr 22).
CR Cabaret Rouge British Cemetery, Souchez (No. Fr 924).
CS Canadian Cemetery, Sailly-sur-la-Lys (No. Fr 254).
CT Contal Maison Chateau, Somme.
DC Douai Communal Cemetery (No. Fr 1277).
ES Estaires Communal Cemetery (No. Fr 768).
ET Etaples Military Cemetery (No. Fr 40).
FL Flatiron Copse Cemetery, Mametz, Somme (No. Fr 453).
GZ Gezaincourt Communal Cemetery Extension, Somme (No. Fr 168).
HA Hazebrouck Cemetery (No. Fr 200).
HB Hamburg Ohlsdorf Cemetery (No. Ger 2).
HS Heilly Station Cemetery, Mericourt (No. Fr 833).
LA Laventie Military Cemetery (No. Fr 1887).
LG La Gorgue Communal Cemetery (No. Fr 354).
LI Lille Southern Cemetery (No. Fr 1027).
LM Loos Memorial (No. MR 19).
LO Longuenesse (St Omer) Cemetery (No. Fr 134).
LS Lijssenthock Military Cemetery (No. Bel 11).
LT Le Trou Aid Post Cemetery, Fleurbaix (No. Fr 566).
MB Maubeuge Centre Cemetery (No. Fr 1211).
MM Meteren Military Cemetery (No. Fr 324).
MO Morlancourt British Cemetery No 1, Somme (No. Fr 633).
MV Merville Communal Cemetery (No. Fr 345).
NC Neufchâtel Cemetery.
NI New Irish Farm Cemetery (No. Bel 96).
NW Niederzwehren Cemetery (No. Ger 3).
OV Ovillers Military Cemetery (No. Fr 393).
PH Pont du Hem Military Cemetery, La Gorgue (No. Fr 705).
PM Ploegsteert Memorial (No. MR 32).
PU Puchevillers British Cemetery, Somme (No. Fr 74).
PZ Pozières British Cemetery (No. Fr 832).
RB Rue-du-Bois Cemetery, Fleurbaix (No. Fr 348).
RC Roisel Communal Cemetery Extension (No. Fr 528).
RD Rue David Cemetery, Fleurbaix (No. Fr 347).
RF Ration Farm Military Cemetery (No. Fr 82).
RI Royal Irish Rifles, Laventie (No. Fr 706).
RP Rue Petillon Military Cemetery (No. Fr 525).
SS St Sever Cemetery, Rouen (No. Fr 145-46).
TA Trois Arbres Cemetery, Steenwerck (No. Fr 297).
TC Tyne Cot British Military Cemetery (No. Bel 125).
TD Thistle Dump Cemetery, High Wood, Longeval.
TM Thiepval Memorial (No. MR 21).
VA Valenciennes Communal Cemetery (No. Fr 1142).
VB Villers-Bretonneux Memorial (No. MR 16).
VC VC Corner Cemetery Memorial, Fromelles (No. MR 7).
VR Varennes Military Cemetery (No. Fr 41).
WA Warloy-Baillon Communal Cemetery Extension, Somme (No. Fr 43-44).
WI Wimereux Communal Cemetery (No. Fr 64).
YF Y Farm Military Cemetery, Bois Grenier (No. Fr 276).

United Kingdom

UA Fort Pitt Military Cemetery, Kent.
UB Kensal Green Cemetery, London.
UC Cambridge Borough Cemetery, Fenditton, Cambridgeshire.
UD Tottenham & Wood Green Cemetery, Middlesex.
UE Manchester Southern Cemetery.
UF All Saints Churchyard Extension, Orpington, Kent.
UG Brighton (Bear Road) Borough Cemetery, Sussex.
UH Nunhead Cemetery, London.
UI Keighley (Morton) Cemetery, York.
UJ Southend-on-sea (Sutton Rd) Cemetery, Essex.
UK Brookwood Military Cemetery, Surrey.
UL Welford Rd Cemetery, Leicester.
UM Melcombe Regis Cemetery, Dorset.
UN Stoke on Trent Cemetery, Staffordshire.
UO Epsom Cemetery, Surrey.
UP Arnos Vale Cemetery, Bristol.
UQ Lodge Hill Cemetery, Birmingham.
UR Nottingham General Cemetery, Nottinghamshire.
US Wandsworth Cemetery, London.
UT Ingham Churchyard, Suffolk.
UU Chelmsford Borough Cemetery.
UV Clacton Cemetery, Essex.
UW Sheffield (Burngreave) Cemetery, Yorkshire.
UX Portsmouth (Kingston & Milton Cemeteries), Hants.
UY Bilton (St Mark's) Cemetery, Warwickshire.
UZ Warwick Cemetery, Warwickshire.
XA Leeds (Lawn Wood) Cemetery, Yorkshire.
XB Little Wratting (St Mary) Churchyard, Suffolk.
XC High Wycombe Cemetery, Buckinghamshire.
XD Adstock (St Cecilia), Buckinghamshire.
XE Edinburgh Eastern Cemetery, Scotland
XF Hastings Cemetery, Sussex.
XG Hetten Cemetery, Durham.
XH Greenwich Cemetery, London.
XI Norwich Cemetery, Norfolk.
XJ Northampton (Towcester Rd) Cemetery.
XK Birmingham (Lodge Hill) Cemetery.
XL Cambridge City Cemetery.
XM Ipswich Cemetery, Suffolk.
XN Shorncliffe Military Cemetery, Kent.
XO Polmont Church, Stirlingshire, Scotland.

British Roll of Honour

182nd BRIGADE:
2/6th Bn, Royal Warwickshire

Name	No.	Date	Fate	Place
Adam, Pte J	6152	19	KIA	LM
Allan, Sgt A	241891	19	KIA	LM
Allan, Pte L W	5504	19	KIA	LM
Badger, Pte A	2177	19	KIA	LM
Baldwin, Cpl P C	6296	19	KIA	LM
Band, A/L Sgt E	240808	19	KIA	LM
Barron, 2/Lieut L		19	KIA	LM
Bignell, Pte W H	6054	19	KIA	LM
Billers, L/Sgt W	240420	19	KIA	LM
Bliss, Pte P	241352	19	KIA	LM
Brittle, Pte B	3872	19	KIA	LM
Brooks, Pte J W	4865	19	KIA	LM
Chance, Cpl J	240903	19	KIA	LM
Charman, Pte A W	2550	21	DOW	MV
Clark, Pte H J	6206	19	KIA	LM
Collins, Cpl E J	1636	19	KIA	LM
Cooke, L/Cpl W	3037	26.10	DOW	LG
Cooper, Pte V F	2349	19	KIA	LM
Coulton, Capt. A E		19	KIA	PM
Dale, Pte A	6066	19	KIA	LM
Darney, Pte J A	3222	19	KIA	LM
Davinson, CSM F	398	19	KIA	LM
Dennett, Pte W	6068	19	KIA	LM
Donald, Pte T	6162	19	KIA	LM
Downing, Pte J	3263	19	KIA	LM
Evans, Pte J	2333	19	KIA	LM
Farr, Pte H J	2828	19	KIA	LM
Field, Pte P F	6307	19	KIA	LM
Fielder, L/Cpl E C	242012	19	KIA	LM
Fitzgerald, Pte G W	241945	19	KIA	LM
Flesher, 2/Lieut F A		27.9	DOW	XA
Frederick, Pte G	3074	19	KIA	AR
Gamblin, Pte E F	6226	19	KIA	LM
Garbett, Cpl F	3277	19	KIA	AR
Glover, Pte A W	2825	25	DOW	LO
Green, Pte O	2200	19	KIA	LM
Greenfield, Pte E A	6079	19	KIA	LM
Grieves, Pte A	4841	19	KIA	LM
Griffiths, Pte H	4395	19	KIA	LM
Hadley, A/L Sgt H H	3743	19	KIA	LM
Harper, 2/Lieut H		19	KIA	PM
Harris, Sgt P J	2569	20	DOW	MV
Hemming, Pte B J	3268	22	DOW	LO
Hewitt, Pte W	6085	19	KIA	AR
Hillman, Sgt G	2867	19	KIA	AR
Hollier, Cpl W A	3355	19	KIA	AR
Hopkins, Pte B	4874	19	KIA	LM
Hughes, L/Cpl W	240322	19	KIA	LM
Hurdman, 2/Lieut C		19	KIA	PM
Hyett, Dmr C E	1861	19	KIA	LM
Ireland, Pte D L	6170	19	KIA	LM
James, L/Cpl J C	6246	26.8	DOW	UX
Jenner, Pte A E	6314	19	KIA	LM
Jones, Pte J W	4825	19	KIA	LM
Jones, Pte R E	2847	19	KIA	LM
Joyce, L/Cpl A H	5515	22	DOW	BO
Kenny, Pte G	3545	21	DOW	MV
King, Pte C	1660	20	DOW	LG
Lamb, L/Cpl W O	241019	19	KIA	LM
Law, Pte W J	4876	19	KIA	LM
Leishman, Pte R	6175	19	KIA	AR
Lloyd, Pte A	3725	19	KIA	LM
Lucking, Pte M	4935	19	KIA	LM
Luckman, Cpl C	3334	19	KIA	AR
Luxton, Pte B E	6251	19	KIA	LM
Major, Pte W H	3615	19	KIA	AR
Minett, Pte G H	2937	19	KIA	LM
Mitchell, Pte M	241904	19	KIA	LM
Morris, Pte N L	2741	19	KIA	LM
Newby, Pte W A	3716	19	KIA	AR
Norman, Pte T G	6256	19	KIA	LM
Peat, Pte A R	5519	22	DOW	MV
Perrins, Pte H	1794	20	DOW	MV
Peters, Pte J H	3486	19	KIA	AR
Pitman, Pte E V	6324	19	KIA	LM
Pollard, Pte A	6113	19	KIA	LM
Powell, Pte W G	3821	19	KIA	LM
Powley, Pte A G	6266	19	KIA	LM
Ralph, Pte A J	5523	19	KIA	LM
Randall, Pte E W	6117	19	KIA	AR
Reeves, Pte A E	3558	20	DOW	LG
Rowson, Pte H	3904	19	KIA	LM
Ruttens, Pte E	6123	19	KIA	LM
Sanders, Pte C E	3783	19	KIA	LM
Saunders, Sgt W J	2885	19	KIA	LM
Searle, Pte J J	6125	19	KIA	LM
Simms, Capt. W		19	KIA	AR
Smallwood, Pte E	240688	19	KIA	LM
Smith, Pte B	3497	19	KIA	AR
Starling, L/Cpl F	240909	19	KIA	LM
Stephens, Sgt S	2853	19	KIA	LM
Stevens, A/Cpl H	241873	19	KIA	LM
Surgenor, Pte L	6276	19	KIA	LM
Taylor, L/Cpl W T	240740	19	KIA	LM
Teasdale, Pte B L	3578	19	KIA	RI
Tew, Pte W E	4885	13.9	DOW	LO
Thompson, Pte H F	6278	19	KIA	LM
Tilley, Pte E S	6135	19	KIA	LM
Tipper, Pte W	6136	19	KIA	AR
Tonks, Pte W	3868	19	KIA	AR
Waterman, Pte C S	6285	19	DOW	LM
Wathes, Capt. T S		19	KIA	PM
Watkins, Dmr T	1997	19	KIA	LM
Webster, Pte F	3799	19	KIA	LM
Wells, Pte H G	6339	19	KIA	LM
Weston, Pte L	240991	19	KIA	LM
Whitmore, Pte H	241996	19	KIA	LM
Winter, Pte F	6336	12.9	DOW	LA
Witten, Pte T	5528	19	KIA	LM
Wood, Pte G C	2835	19	KIA	LM

Woodhatch, Pte W	241887	19	KIA	LM
Woodward, Pte G W C	6288	19	KIA	LM

2/7th Bn, Royal Warwickshire

Austin, Pte H	266487	19	KIA	LM
Bailey, Sgt C	3224	19	KIA	LM
Bannister, Pte W	3755	20	DOW	MV
Barlow, Pte H	266144	19	KIA	LM
Barnett, Pte S	3367	19	KIA	LM
Barnett, Pte W H	3654	19	KIA	LM
Bates, Pte H	3435	19	KIA	LM
Beckett, Pte H	3456	19	KIA	LM
Beesley, Pte A	266208	19	KIA	LM
Berry, L/Cpl H	4628	19	KIA	CR
Bethell, Capt. T H	-	19	KIA	PM
Birchall, L/Cpl T	267143	19	KIA	LM
Blakemore, Sgt A J	2922	19	KIA	LM
Campbell, Pte F	5591	8.8	DOW	MV
Chatwin, L/Cpl A	265148	19	KIA	LM
Christie, Pte F	267150	19	KIA	LM
Clarke, Pte J A	266690	19	KIA	LM
Collins, Pte M	267217	19	KIA	LM
Coull, Pte G	5598	19	D	LM
Crompton, Pte H	268583	19	KIA	LM
Cunningham, L/Cpl R	267218	19	KIA	LM
Dare, Pte L	5499	8.8	DOW	MV
Davenport, L/Cpl H C	3492	19	D	LM
Davies, Pte J E	5949	19	KIA	LM
Davies, L/Cpl R C	267414	19	KIA	LM
Davis, Pte T H	3231	19	KIA	LM
Desborough, Pte T	266259	19	KIA	LM
Dobbins, Pte J	3000	19	KIA	AR
Donaldson, Capt. G B	-	19	D POW	PM
Drinkwater, Pte F J	265990	19	KIA	LM
Dryburgh, Pte A	267224	19	KIA	LM
Farren, Pte J	265409	19	KIA	LM
Foley, Pte W	20851	19	D	PM
Galloway, Pte G	267233	19	KIA	PM
Gilbert, Sgt J T	2914	1.8	DOW	UY
Godsell, Pte H	3909	19	KIA	AR
Goode, Pte A	3930	19	KIA	LM
Grady, Pte G A	267165	19	KIA	LM
Griffiths, Pte J	5958	19	KIA	LM
Harris, L/Cpl D	5970	19	KIA	LM
Hayes, Pte F H	2216	19	KIA	LM
Hazelwood, Pte J	265933	19	KIA	LM
Holly, Pte R B	5525	19	KIA	LM
Hulligan, Pte M	268591	19	KIA	AR
James, Pte B	267174	19	KIA	LM
Jephcott, Pte J	266263	19	KIA	LM
Jocelyn, L/Sgt E	266351	19	KIA	LM
Jones, Pte J T	5983	19	KIA	LM
Kendall, Pte A	4624	20	KIA	MV
Lamb, Pte A	3206	19	KIA	LM
Lewis, Pte W J	267179	19	KIA	AR
Macdonald, L/Cpl A	5658	19	D	LM
Malin, Pte W	3896	28	DOW	UZ
Mapley, Pte A W	4209	21.8	DOW	MV
Marshall, L/Cpl D	267261	19	KIA	LM
Maxwell, Pte G	5666	25	DOW	XO
Melville, L/Cpl J	267272	19	KIA	LM
Moore, Cpl H	2132	19	KIA	LM
Moore, Pte T	266167	19	KIA	LM
Morgan, Pte R	5984	19	KIA	AR
Neale, Pte A G	266506	19	KIA	LM
Noakes, Sgt R F	2943	19	KIA	LM
Paton, Pte E	5683	19	KIA	LM
Pearman, Pte A W	2991	29	DOW	UI
Portman, Pte A	266488	19	KIA	LM
Pratt, Pte G	5687	19	KIA	LM
Price, Pte H G	6000	4.9	DOW	LO
Pryde, L/Cpl J	5688	19	D	LM
Rees, Pte W S	5962	19	KIA	LM
Richardson, L/Cpl W	267290	19	KIA	LM
Robertson, Cpl W F	5693	20	KIA	LA
Ryan, L/Cpl C	20871	19	KIA	LM
Sanderson, L/Cpl D	268586	19	KIA	LM
Sharlott, Pte T C	266353	19	KIA	LM
Sheffield, L/Cpl S	4618	19	D	LM
Shepherd, Pte C	268573	19	KIA	LM
Sheppard, Pte H B	265192	19	KIA	LM
Simpson, Cpl D	267298	19	KIA	LM
Smith, L/Cpl A J V	3859	19	KIA	LM
Smith, Pte J	5704	19	D	LM
Stanway, Cpl H W	265295	19	KIA	LM
Swift, Pte J C	265915	19	KIA	LM
Tallis, Pte T	4233	19	KIA	LM
Tams, Pte H F	3343	20	DOW	MV
Taylor, Dmr G A	4369	19	KIA	LM
Thom, Pte D L	5712	19	D	LM
Topp, Pte A	4386	19	KIA	LM
Townley, Pte F	4638	19	KIA	LM
Turnbull, Pte H	267305	19	KIA	LM
Twamley, Pte L	266675	19	KIA	LM
Wale, Pte W	266674	19	KIA	CR
Ward, L/Sgt H	3354	19	KIA	LA
Watkins, L/Cpl H P	5948	19	KIA	LM
Welsh, L/Cpl	5718	19	D	LM
Whateley, L/Sgt J R	2987	19	KIA	CR
Whitcroft, Pte T	266485	19	KIA	LM
White, Sgt W H	2497	19	D	LM

2/8th Bn, Royal Warwickshire

Lewis, Pte A V	5407	20	KIA	AR

182nd Machine Gun Company

Scudamore, Pte E F F	28575	20	KIA	CR
Thornton, Pte A	28683	20	KIA	AR
Tipple, Pte H	30525	19	KIA	CR

183rd BRIGADE

2/4th Bn, Gloucestershire

Baker, Pte H	200801	19	D	LM
Barker, Pte W	201299	19	KIA	LM
Barnard, Pte B	6328	28	DOW	BO
Bees, Pte F W	200979	19	D	LM
Bennett, Pte R P	6386	19	KIA	LM
Bland, Pte E J	6320	19	KIA	LM

Bleaken, Pte A F	5201	19	KIA	LM
Bown, Pte D B	2869	19	KIA	LA
Burrows, Pte W E	201238	19	KIA	LM
Byers, Capt. R H K		19	KIA	TM
Cave, Pte C A	6362	22	DOW	LO
Cawston, Pte H J	6249	30	DOW	LA
Chaplin, Sgt R W	6235	19	KIA	LM
Chitty, Pte A	5183	19	KIA	RB
Colbourne, Pte W	3247	11.8	DOW	MV
Cooper, Pte F	201735	19	KIA	LM
Cox, Pte H F	1580	19	KIA	LA
Critchley, Pte C	6408	2.8	DOW	MV
Daniels, Pte W	4435	19	DOW	TM
Darke, Pte H	4433	19	KIA	LM
Davey, Pte W E	5117	19	KIA	LM
Deverell, Pte W J	5139	19	KIA	LM
Driver, Pte V	5053	19	KIA	LA
Duggan, Pte W	3339	19	KIA	RB
Edwards, Pte A T	5109	19	KIA	LM
Hale, Pte P D	2827	19	KIA	LA
Hampson, Pte E C	202767	19	D	LM
Hart, Lieut R M	-	25	DOW	CT
James, Lieut J C	-	19	KIA	WI
Jay, Pte A E	4620	19	KIA	RB
Mason, Pte H	202775	19	D	LM
Mead, Pte S	4718	25.8	DOW	PU
Miller, L/Cpl H W	3597	19	KIA	LA
Moore, Pte C O	3331	29	DOW	WA
Moss, Cpl J N	6233	19	KIA	LA
Paver, Pte W	3752	19	KIA	LM
Phillips, Pte R	201152	19	D	LM
Pocock, Pte A H	20729	19	KIA	RB
Richings, Pte A V	1918	19	KIA	LM
Scrase, Lieut R G	-	19	KIA	TM
Stagg, 2/Lieut A C	-	19	KIA	MO
Sullivan, Pte H G	4623	2.9	DOW	CN
Taylor, Pte W	1857	19	KIA	LM
Thomas, L/Cpl W H	200277	19	KIA	LM
Tuke, Sgt W A B	6384	19	KIA	RB
Wheeler, Cpl S	3832	19	KIA	LM

2/5th Bn, Gloucestershire

Rowe, Pte S A	2460	21	DOW	TM

2/6th Bn, Gloucestershire

Bacon, Sgt C E	267172	19	D	LM
Bailey, Pte F W	3718	19	KIA	LM
Baker, Pte A W	4886	19	KIA	LA
Barnes, Pte G	267229	19	D	LM
Bell, Pte W	4806	19	KIA	LA
Bird, Capt. E W	-	27	DOW	GZ
Bird, Sgt H H	267166	19	D	LM
Bond, Pte A G	266731	19	D	LM
Broomfield, Pte J P	5196	19	KIA	LM
Brown, Pte E J	4837	19	KIA	LA
Butler, L/Cpl C G W	4810	20	DOW	MV
Cater, Cpl F	5940	19	KIA	LA
Charlwood, Pte F J	266742	19	DOW	LM
Chippett, Pte A F	265346	19	D	LM
Cobb, Pte H	5993	30	DOW	LO
Cook, Pte A J	3152	19	KIA	LM
Cooke, L/Cpl W	4984	10.9	DOW	CR
Cooper, Sgt S J	5937	30.9	DOW	MV
Cubitt, Pte S	5977	22	DOW	BO
Cundy, Pte E	267253	19	KIA	LM
Dixon, Pte C	267207	19	D	LM
Dore, Pte H T	5018	20	DOW	MV
Down, Lieut R H	-	17.8	DOW	PU
Eason, Pte E S	4856	19	KIA	LM
Edwards, Pte W S T	4615	19	KIA	LM
Eyre, Capt. H W	-	29	DOW	LO
Feltham, Pte F C	266280	19	KIA	LM
Fison, Lieut F H	-	19	KIA	AR
Foxon, Pte L T	3748	19	KIA	LA
Frost, Pte B	6022	19	KIA	AR
Fry, 2/Lieut L	-	19	KIA	RP
Gawler, Pte C S	3494	19	KIA	LM
Godfrey, Pte J R C	2108	23	DOW	BO
Gorrie, 2/Lieut G W	-	19	KIA	PZ
Gough, Lieut N	-	19	KIA	PZ
Griffiths, Pte C G	4951	19	KIA	LM
Gwyther, Pte C R	3876	20	DOW	LG
Hadder, 2/Lieut R	-	19	KIA	?
Hancock, Pte W S	4946	19	KIA	PH
Hawkings, Pte A G	2743	19	KIA	LA
Hickmott, Pte H	267263	19	D	LM
Highnam, Pte J H	266295	19	KIA	LM
Hobbs, L/Cpl W R	265291	19	D	LM
Hodges, Pte E E	4947	19	KIA	LM
Holden, Pte B J	266662	19	D	LM
Hooper, Pte A R	6152	19	KIA	CR
Howell, Pte E C	3592	19	KIA	RB
James, Pte C H	4957	19	KIA	PH
Johnson, Cpl E	2439	19	KIA	LA
Johnston, 2/Lieut L	-	25	DOW	MV
King, L/Cpl W A	3675	19	KIA	LM
Lacey, Pte E	266604	19	KIA	LM
Lambert, Pte W A	5958	23	DOW	MV
Langford, Lieut W J	-	19	KIA	LM
Lewis, Pte H	3858	19	KIA	LA
Lupson, Pte G F	267236	19	D	LM
Marshall, Pte W J S	266764	19	D	LM
Mathews, 2/Lieut A E	-	19	KIA	LA
Matthews, Pte H C	4887	19	KIA	LA
McCormick, Pte W	266236	19	D	LM
Miles, L/Cpl E A	267285	19	KIA	LM
Nelmes, Pte A E	4802	7.8	DOW	LG
Nicholson, Pte W I	5981	19	KIA	LA
Parsons, Pte A A	266132	19	D	LM
Pearce, L/Sgt C	4674	19	KIA	RB
Pennington, Pte T	5914	19	KIA	RB
Pike, Pte A	3448	19	KIA	RB
Raisey, Pte A V	3486	19	D	LM
Ralph, Pte C E	4932	20	DOW	MV
Rich, L/Cpl F	1962	19	KIA	LA
Robbins, Pte G H	4744	19	KIA	LA
Rolfe, Pte S	3711	19	KIA	CR
Routley, Pte J	3959	19	KIA	LM

Rudman, Capt. H E	-	19	KIA	LM
Sampson, L/Cpl H C	2685	19	KIA	AR
Sheppard, Pte W J	265283	19	KIA	LM
Shreeve, L/Sgt A R	267208	19	D	LM
Skewes, 2/Lieut A C	-	19	KIA	LA
Smith, 2/Lieut A R	-	22	DOW	WA
Smith, Pte W J	266681	19	D	LM
Spooner, Pte P T	267287	19	D	LM
Stallworthy, Sgt W J	5941	20	DOW	LA
Stockham, Pte W	266734	19	D	LM
Stoker, Pte A T	266695	19	D	LM
Sweetman, Pte A H	266591	19	D	LM
Thorne, Pte F	2659	19	KIA	LM
Whitlock, Pte E E	4071	19	KIA	LA
Willimott, Pte H L	5956	19	KIA	LM
Willis, Cpl F J	265708	19	D	LM
Willis, Pte W R	4940	19	KIA	LM
Winterborn, Pte J E	267217	19	D	LM

183rd Machine Gun Company

Bown, Pte D	2869	19	KIA	LA
Wass, L/Cpl R T	28509	19	KIA	LA
Whincop, L/Sgt H M	28606	19	KIA	LA

184th BRIGADE

2/4th Bn, Royal Berkshire

Abbott, 2/Lieut G S	-	19	KIA	LA
Barber, Pte R	3376	19	KIA	LA
Bates, Pte C	3569	19	KIA	LA
Beer, Lieut Col J H	-	19	KIA	LA
Beresford, Pte F	6670	19	KIA	LA
Blades, Pte A	6004	20	DOW	MV
Brazier, Pte E V	6610	19	KIA	LA
Brown, Pte A	6560	19	KIA	LA
Buckingham, Pte H	202104	14.8	DOW	TM
Cannon, Pte W	2923	20	DOW	TM
Church, L/Cpl F R	3760	19	KIA	LA
Cole, Pte H V	6611	19	KIA	LA
Cooper, L/Cpl A D	2963	15.8	DOW	WA
Couzens, Pte W E	3398	19	KIA	LA
Davis, Pte C	5334	19	KIA	LA
Day, Pte A	3328	20	DOW	MV
Fleet, Pte C T	6558	19	KIA	LA
Fountain, Cpl H E	3974	19	KIA	LA
Gibbons, Pte L	5277	20	DOW	MV
Guy, Pte J F	202023	14.8	DOW	TM
Hallum, Pte H	3391	19	KIA	LA
Heather, Pte J W	200319	30	DOW	?
Hollands, Pte J A	3380	19	KIA	LA
Hooper, Pte W E	5302	19	KIA	LA
Lainsbury, Pte F	5267	30	DOW	LO
Martin, Pte J W	5306	19	KIA	LA
Mayes, Pte F	6563	5.8	DOW	XB
Mayes, Pte J	6574	7.10	DOW	LG
McGhan, Pte J	6675	19	KIA	LA
Mulford, Pte F	2143	19	KIA	LA
North, Pte R	3975	10.8	DOW	LA
Painter, Pte T C	3483	19	KIA	LA
Rivers, Pte A T	3545	19	KIA	LA
Rose, Pte J	3390	19	KIA	LA
Rouse, Pte J V	5496	18.8	DOW	VR
Savage, Pte F E	2507	19	KIA	LA
Savory, Pte W J	3619	19	KIA	LA
Searle, Pte W H	5502	28.8	DOW	LA
Sellwood, Pte W G	5807	2.9	DOW	?
Smith, Cpl F	6289	19	KIA	LA
Snow, Sgt G	3800	19	KIA	LA
Stallard, L/Cpl H	5036	25.8	DOW	ET
Swain, Pte A T	5312	19	KIA	LA
West, Pte F V	6591	19	KIA	LA
Williams, 2/Lieut F C D	-	19	KIA	LA
Williams, Pte R H	6673	19	KIA	LA
Wooldridge, Pte C	3547	18.8	DOW	LG

2/1st Bn, Buckinghamshire

Aldridge, Pte A	266591	19	KIA	LM
Andrews, Pte F H	265211	19	KIA	LM
Atkinson, Lieut G W	-	19	KIA	LM
Austin, Sgt C	810	22	DOW	LM
Avis, Pte S H	3460	19	KIA	LM
Baldwin, Pte H	4390	19	KIA	LM
Barkaway, Pte F W	267122	19	KIA	LM
Battams, Cpl E C	3316	19	KIA	LM
Bennett, Pte H	266401	19	KIA	LM
Bernard, L/Cpl J	265764	19	KIA	?
Birch, Pte S A	3428	19	KIA	LA
Bond, Pte J R	2290	19	DOW	MV
Bone, Pte W J	266226	19	DOW	LM
Bowie, Pte J L	4131	19	KIA	LM
Brewin, 2/Lieut H R N	-	19	KIA	LA
Brown, CSM A	3149	19	KIA	LM
Brown, CSM R W	2982	20	DOW	MV
Brown, Pte E J	2518	19	KIA	RB
Bruce, L/Cpl W H V J	266515	19	KIA	LM
Bunce, Pte J	3558	19	KIA	LM
Butt, Pte J	5415	19	KIA	LA
Carter, Pte A G	4214	19	KIA	LA
Carter, Pte R	266618	19	KIA	LM
Carver, Pte G E	267097	19	KIA	LM
Casmore, L/Cpl W	266097	19	KIA	LM
Castle, Pte G A	266612	19	KIA	LM
Chadwick, Lieut D G	-	20	DOW	MV
Church, Capt. H	-	19	KIA	LA
Clark, Pte E A P	266638	19	KIA	LM
Clements, Pte J	5342	22	DOW	LO
Coleman, Pte E	5354	19	KIA	LM
Cook, L/Cpl A	265265	19	KIA	LM
Cook, Pte G	266006	19	KIA	LM
Cook, Pte H J	5412	19	DOW	MV
Cox, Pte J	2585	25	DOW	MV
Cox, Pte T A	266713	19	KIA	LM
Crump, Sgt J C	1579	19	KIA	AR
Crutchfield, Pte F	1580	19	KIA	LM
Damant, Pte S R	4265	25	DOW	MV
Daveney, Pte T	4228	19	KIA	LM
Davis, Pte A	1614	19	KIA	LM
Davis, Sgt G E	1718	19	KIA	LM
Dell, L/Cpl C C	266125	19	KIA	LM

Dimmock, Pte F J R	4345	25	DOW	WI
Doyle, Pte A L	5324	24	DOW	MV
Durrant, Pte E	5416	20	DOW	MV
Dwight, Pte S	3294	19	KIA	LM
East, Sgt A H	1665	19	KIA	AR
Evans, L/Cpl A	4151	19	DOW	MV
Fincher, Cpl A V	1477	19	KIA	LM
Fowler, Pte E H	266604	19	KIA	LM
Gibson, Pte H R	265824	19	DOW	LM
Gray, Pte W	1804	19	KIA	LM
Groves, Pte E W	1518	19	KIA	LA
Guntrip, Pte R W	266634	19	KIA	LM
Harding, Pte H	266654	19	KIA	LM
Harrall, L/Cpl R	3289	8.9	DOW	XC
Harris, Pte A J	4386	19	KIA	LA
Haverley, Pte C C	4377	26	DOW	LO
Henley, Pte S	265926	19	KIA	LM
Hill, Pte A	4376	19	KIA	LM
Hodgson, Pte F S	266221	19	KIA	LM
Hogston, Pte H W	266715	19	KIA	LM
Holdom, L/Cpl W J	3352	19	KIA	LA
Holt, Pte W	266682	19	KIA	LM
Hudson, 2/Lieut R B	-	19	KIA	LM
Hughes, Pte T S	5302	22	DOW	LG
Humphrey, Pte C J	265919	19	KIA	LM
Jarvis, Pte A G	2920	19	KIA	LA
Jeffs, Pte S W	4219	24	DOW	BO
Johns, Pte O L	5303	19	KIA	LM
Johnson, L/Cpl W	4311	19	KIA	LM
Jones, Pte J W	266393	19	KIA	LM
King, Pte T E	4325	19	KIA	LM
Kipping, Pte J	3019	19	KIA	LA
Knights, Pte W	5313	19	KIA	LM
Lambourne, Pte T H	1996	24	DOW	WI
Lance, L/Sgt F C	265854	19	KIA	LM
Lewis, Pte E	265930	19	KIA	LM
Line, Pte F W	267090	19	KIA	LM
Luff, L/Cpl C G	265225	19	KIA	LM
Malcolm, Pte F A	4201	22	DOW	BO
Mantripp, L/Cpl G W	8376	19	KIA	LM
Marslen, Pte R V	266690	19	KIA	LM
McClements, Pte A	5391	19	KIA	LM
Morris, Pte A H	265298	19	KIA	LM
Morris, Pte A W	266197	19	KIA	LM
Munday, Pte C R	265787	19	KIA	LM
Newson, L/Cpl F N	5358	19	KIA	LA
Oxlade, Cpl A E	205070	19	KIA	LM
Parker, 2/Lieut F R	-	19	KIA	LM
Parker, Pte T E	3940	19	KIA	LM
Payne, Pte E	2083	19	KIA	LA
Pearce, L/Cpl W C	2705	19	KIA	AR
Perry, Pte J W	267093	19	KIA	LM
Phillips, Pte F L	4336	20	DOW	XD
Phipps, Lieut C P	-	19	KIA	LM
Plowman, Pte C G	266561	19	KIA	LM
Pratt, Pte G E	265385	19	KIA	LM
Prentice, Pte H	2910	19	KIA	LA
Price, Pte H T	266714	19	KIA	LM
Price, Pte P	266657	19	KIA	LM
Savin, Pte G E	4314	19	KIA	AR
Sayell, Pte A	4276	19	KIA	LM
Scull, Pte J T	267112	19	KIA	LM
Sexton, Pte G J	1689	19	DOW	MV
Sharp, L/Cpl E	3631	19	KIA	LM
Simmonds, Pte J W	266619	19	KIA	LM
Sinclair, Pte R	266692	19	KIA	LM
Smith, Pte H	266552	19	KIA	LM
Stevens, L/Cpl A F	265388	19	KIA	LM
Stone, Pte G C	266615	19	KIA	LM
Symonds, Pte G	4340	19	KIA	LM
Tapper, Cpl J E	1634	29.8	DOW	LO
Tavenor, Pte F	266175	19	KIA	LM
Taylor, Pte S	3430	19	KIA	LM
Taylor, Pte T	1963	19	KIA	LM
Thomas, Pte S A S	3387	19	KIA	LM
Thorpe, L/Cpl A	3527	19	KIA	LA
Tomes, Pte H	4308	19	KIA	LM
Upson, Pte W T	4257	19	KIA	LM
Walker, L/Cpl A	1726	19	KIA	LA
Wallace, Pte W A	2028	20	DOW	MV
Warr, Pte B W G	4331	19	KIA	LM
White, Pte J	4189	19	KIA	LA
Williams, Pte R J	4309	19	DOW	MV
Willis, Pte F T	4207	19	KIA	LM
Wood, L/Cpl S	5342	19	DOW	LM
Wood, L/Sgt G E D	5430	19	KIA	LM
Wood, Pte S	266138	19	KIA	LM
Wright, L/Cpl C H	267082	19	KIA	LM

2/4th Bn, Oxford & Buckinghamshire

Harding, Cpl R	2191	19	KIA	LA
Jones, Pte G	2990	19	KIA	LA
Jones, Pte W J	6736	19	KIA	RB
Lunn, L/Cpl A	3560	19	KIA	LA
Reynolds, Rfn E E	6762	19	KIA	LA
Simpson, Pte G E L	4317	19	KIA	LA
Sims, Bglr T	3357	20	KIA	LG
Spratt, Rfn H F	2715	19	KIA	LA
Taylor, Pte W A	4167	19	KIA	LA
Tolley, Pte G E L	3022	19	KIA	LA
Williams, Pte R H	6673	19	KIA	LA

6th Bn, Oxford & Buckinghamshire

Barden, L/Cpl F	20413	19	KIA	RP
Bright, CSM A H	9259	19	KIA	RP
Fussell, 2/Lieut J W H	-	19	KIA	RP
Lenton, L/Cpl W H	12270	19	KIA	RP
Porter, Pte F W (MM)	14991	19	KIA	RP

1/5th Bn, Duke of Cornwall's Light Infantry

Hoskin, Pte W	2981	20	DOW	MV
Hunn, Pte N	3159	19	KIA	AR
Pomery, Pte J	2118	19	KIA	AR
Ratcliff-Gaylard, 2/Lieut E R	-	20	KIA	LA
Williams, Pte F A	1305	19	KIA	AR

61st Div Trench Mortar Bty RFA

Bridge, Gnr E	109681	19	KIA	AR

Australian Roll of Honour

8th BRIGADE

29th Battalion

Balfour, Sgt A	1364	19	KIA	CO
Barnatt, Pte G R	1062	20	KIA	VC
Batey, Pte L R V F	166	20	KIA	VC
Bell, Pte H	191	19	KIA	VC
Bowen, Pte W J	175	8.9	DOW	ES
Breguet, Pte J H	1983	19	KIA	VC
Brittain, Pte W	1361	19/20	KIA	RP
Brumm, Pte N L	1470	19	KIA	VC
Bryant, Pte A W	182	7.8	DOW	BO
Campbell, L/Sgt S G M	776	3.10	DOW	BA
Cavanagh, Pte J	213	24.8	DOW	ES
Cheshire, L/Cpl A E	1079	19/20	KIA	RP
Chrisp, Cpl G	500	19/20	KIA	RP
Clarke, Pte A	2190	25	KIA	RP
Cole, Pte R M	417	20	KIA	VC
Comb, Pte W R	800	31	KIA	RP
Cozens, Pte J A	210	19	KIA	VC
Cunningham, Pte J E	735	26	KIA	RP
Davidson, Pte P A	1102	20	DOW POW	CR
Deans, Pte A B	2008	20	KIA	VC
Downie, Cpl J C G	1097	20	KIA	VC
Edwards, Pte J B	2015	6.8	DOW	UA
Ennis, L/Cpl L J	2020	20	KIA	VC
Farlow, Pte S	80	19	KIA	VC
Francis, Pte T W	2584	20	KIA	VC
Gill, Pte R	2033	20	DOW	BA
Gordon, Pte J	1130	19	KIA	VC
Goy, Pte G	242	9.8	DOW	UB
Harland, Sgt O	253	20	KIA	VC
Haslam, L/Cpl H J	1390	19	KIA	VC
Hayes, Pte L A	568	26	DOW	ES
Higgins, Pte J I	2050	20	KIA	VC
Johnson, Pte A J	2203	19	KIA	VC
Johnson, Pte W F M	278	22.8	DOW	UC
Kennedy, Pte L F	2677	19/20	KIA	VC
Livingston, Cpl D F	1168	19	KIA	VC
Lund, Pte H	1165	19/20	KIA	RP
McIntyre, Cpl R	1173	8.8	DOW	WI
Merten, Pte S R	573	19	KIA	RP
Morshead, Sgt E D	1319	19/20	KIA	RP
Mortimer, Capt. K M	-	20	KIA	VC
Noakes, Pte N	1014	28	DOW	BO
O'Donnell, Pte S R	314	19	KIA	VC
O'Donnell, Pte W	319	19	KIA	VC
Oliver, Pte E R	316	19	KIA	VC
Parry, Pte F	320	19	KIA	VC
Pinne, Pte N E	2119	20	KIA	VC
Pollard, Pte H G	324	19	KIA	VC
Reid, Sgt J A	335	20	KIA	VC
Ross, Cpl J H	1216	19	KIA	VC
Scrimgeour, Pte T	2137	23	DOW POW	VA
Sheridan, Capt. T F	-	20	KIA	VC
Smith, Cpl P K	339	19/20	KIA	VC
Smith, Pte G T	1245	19	KIA	VC
Spooner, Cpl G W	1238	20	KIA	RP
Stone, Pte P V	682	19/20	KIA	RP
Strachan, L/Cpl R R	949	19/20	KIA	RP
Taylor, Pte J M	407	20	KIA	VC
Torbitt, Pte F A	2131	19/20	KIA	RP
Trinder, Pte W	974	26	KIA	RP
Tuck, Cpl A G	1252	19	KIA	VC
Tunbridge, L/Sgt L	976	29.8	DOW	ES
Weir, Pte A J	358	19	KIA	VC
Westmoreland, Pte H J	361	20	KIA	VC
Wilkin, Pte E F	1314	19	KIA	VC
Wills, Pte R J	651	2.8	DOW	UD
Wills, Pte G C	652	19/20	KIA	RP
Woodcock, Pte F S	1262	20	KIA	VC

30th Battalion

Abbott, L/Cpl E W	1516	20	KIA	VC
Anderson, Pte P	90	20	KIA	VC
Arkell, L/Sgt M K D	341	20	KIA	VC
Arnott, Pte C H	1968	20	KIA	VC
Aulton, Pte V H	1971	20	KIA	VC
Austin, Pte E G	593	20	KIA	RF
Balsdon, Pte J	2274	1.9	DOW POW	VB
Balsdon, Pte R H	2276	28	DOW	BO
Bennett, Pte W A	2287	20	KIA	VC
Benson, Pte G V	840	19	KIA	VC
Bourke, Pte H J	1682	20	KIA	VC
Briscoe, Pte L L	1986	20	KIA	VC
Bryden, Pte J A McG	361	23.8	DOW	RD
Burke, Pte W	609	20	KIA	VC
Callaghan, Pte J P	1998	20	KIA	VC
Camps, Pte V A	631	20	KIA	RP
Caswell, Pte D	397	20	KIA	VC
Church, Sgt C C	635	20	KIA	VC
Churchill, L/Cpl W E	382	20	KIA	RP
Coady, Sgt E	137	20	KIA	VC
Collier, Pte P	1057	20	KIA	RP
Connors, Pte W J C	130	2.9	DOW	ES
Cooper, Pte E	1251	5.8	DOW	BO
Cooper, Pte S J	633	20	KIA	VC
Costello, Pte J L	2304	4.9	DOW	RD
Cracknell, L/Sgt R B W	1025	22.8	DOW	RP
Cracknell, Pte D	2309	20	KIA	AN
Croft, Pte G	2006	20	KIA	VC
Croker, Pte H	2010	20	KIA	VC
Dalton, Pte W K	867	20	KIA	VC
Dobbie, Pte J	649	20	KIA	VC
Doyle, Pte J T	869	20	KIA	VC
Dryburgh, Pte L	406	20	KIA	VC
Easton, Pte T	2026	20	KIA	VC
Edmunds, Pte C E	2326	24.8	DOW	ES
Fenwick, Pte R G	882	20	KIA	VC
Fiddling, Pte C	1550	19	KIA	ES
Gardner, Pte H	889	20	KIA	VC
Garland, Sgt C S	2038	19	DOW	RP
Glenn, L/Cpl F J	1291	20	KIA	VC

Hart, Pte J	190	20	KIA	RF
Hawcroft, Pte C H	188	20	KIA	VC
Hayman, Pte W F	192	27.8	DOW	UB
Hedges, Pte L J	186	20	KIA	VC
Hepple, Pte M	2056	20	KIA	VC
Higgins, Pte W B	196	20	KIA	VC
Hunter, Pte R	1079	26	DOW	CA
Inglis, Pte W	686	20	KIA	VC
Jackson, Pte F H	451	20	KIA	VC
James, Pte A M	689	20	KIA	VC
Jones, Pte J	1880	20	KIA	VC
Kelly, Pte J R	915	28	DOW	BO
King, Pte C D	1096	20	KIA	VC
Laing, Pte D	2512	27	DOW	LO
Laurie, Dvr A D G	221	20	KIA	VC
Leahy, Pte R J	1104	20	KIA	VC
Leask, L/Cpl E G	1309	20	KIA	RP
Lees, 2/Lieut J S H	-	20	KIA	VC
Lucre, Pte G H	467	20	KIA	VC
Malcolm, Sgt E S	483	20	KIA	VC
Martin, Pte R L	1584	20	KIA	VC
Matthews, Pte A F	722	19	KIA	VC
Maxwell, Pte A R	3557	20	KIA	VC
McCoullough, Pte H G	1595	20	KIA	VC
McGregor, Pte T	711	20	KIA	RP
McKillop, Pte D J D	938	20	KIA	RF
McLeod, Pte A	2404	1.9	DOW	RD
McWatt, Pte J	4575	20	KIA	RP
Miller, Pte J	709	8.8	DOW	XE
Mitchell, Lieut A	-	20	KIA	VC
Murray, Cpl C W	1590	20	KIA	VC
Murray, Pte R G	930	20	KIA	VC
Nelson, Pte H O	728	20	KIA	VC
Osmond, Pte L E C	2414	20	KIA	VC
Owen, Pte W S	1326	20	KIA	VC
Parker, 2/Lieut J	-	20	KIA	VC
Pearce, Cpl H J	801	21	DOW POW	CR
Peberdy, Pte F T S	962	20	KIA	VC
Perks, Pte A J	739	20	KIA	VC
Powis, L/Cpl C E	1601	23.8	DOW POW	NW
Pritchard, Pte H E	2141	20	KIA	RP
Rawnsley, Pte A A	2392	20	KIA	VC
Reeves, Pte J	2433	20	KIA	RP
Rich, Pte D C	1134	19	KIA	VC
Robinson, Pte H F	1312	20	KIA	VC
Robson, Pte C E	746	20	KIA	RP
Ryan, Pte D B	743	20	KIA	VC
Ryan, Pte P E	1606	20	KIA	VC
Scott, Pte W F	286	30	DOW	UJ
Sheehan, Pte J	82	20	KIA	RP
Shone, Pte E	531	20	KIA	VC
Smith, Pte A J	3255	20	KIA	VC
Spence, Pte J M	4614	20	KIA	VC
Stanborough, Pte E A L	973	20	KIA	RP
Steed, Cpl F I	755	20	KIA	VC
Stephens, Pte L A	750	20	KIA	VC
Stuart, Pte R H	2163	20	KIA	RP
Sullivan, Pte C W	752	16.10	DOW	BO
Theisinger, Pte N L	1146	20	KIA	VC
Tickner, Pte F	2171	20	KIA	VC
Tisbury, Pte C F	1623	20	KIA	VC
Turner, Pte J	767	20	KIA	VC
Vale, Cpl T G	776	20	KIA	VC
Vincent, Pte L S	777	20	KIA	VC
Wall, Pte J D	783	20	KIA	VC
Ward, Pte C	2184	20	KIA	VC
Ward, Pte P R	1010	20	KIA	RP
Warrington, Pte J D	1157	22	DOW	HA
Watterson, Sgt R	582	20	KIA	RF
Watts, Pte T L	1003	20	KIA	RP
Welling, Pte E F	1311	20	KIA	VC
White, Pte R	1627	20	KIA	RP
Whitton, Pte J D G	182	20	KIA	VC
Williams, Pte A E	2188	20	KIA	RP
Willis, Sgt E E	804	20	KIA	VC
Wishart, Pte J H	1004	20	KIA	VC
Wood, Pte A	781	20	KIA	VC
Woods, Pte C A	2194	20	KIA	VC
Wymark, L/Cpl R D	789	20	KIA	VC
Wynn, Pte J C	2485	20	KIA	VC
Yardy, Pte R A	321	20	KIA	RP
Yeo, Pte C	795	20	KIA	VC

31st Battalion

Aitken, Pte C R	1113	21	DOW	BA
Anthony, Pte L	3751	27	DOW	BO
Bain, Pte W E	135	20	KIA	VC
Baker, Pte W H	184	20	KIA	VC
Barnett, Pte H E	134	20	KIA	RP
Barry, Pte W	505	19	KIA	RP
Baynes, L/Cpl F L	1523	19	KIA	RP
Bills, Pte T H	605	19	KIA	VB
Brailsford, Pte W W	1050a	20	KIA	RP
Broom, Pte S	1522	19	KIA	VC
Campbell, Pte J	29a	20	KIA	RP
Castles, Pte W E J	71	19	KIA	RP
Chalk, Pte H F	2293	20	KIA	RP
Chapman, Pte J E	166	20	KIA	RP
Charles, Pte L S	174	20	KIA	AN
Chatfield, Pte J	4989	28.10	DOW	HS
Christensen, Pte J W	1528	12.8	DOW	XF
Clements, Maj C E	-	22	DOW	BO
Coghlan, Pte J	624	20	KIA	VC
Collier, Pte A A	626	20	KIA	VC
Corcoran, 2/Lieut G F	-	30.10	DOW	HS
Cox, Lieut H	-	20	KIA	RP
Curran, Pte J J	494	19	KIA	VC
Daly, Pte L R	184	20	KIA	AN
Dank, Pte C C	320	19/20	KIA	VC
Davies, Sgt B	1517	19	KIA	AN
Dodson, Pte H E	642	20	KIA	RP
Dolan, Pte J G	1989	22	DOW	LS
Dunn, Pte L C	641	21	KIA	VB
Esam, Pte H	491	19	KIA	VC
Ford, Pte P	198	20	KIA	NI
Francis, L/Cpl W J	852	20	KIA	VC

Fraser, L/Sgt A K	200	20	KIA	AN
Gaden, Pte N	333	19/20	KIA	VC
Gavin, L/Cpl J A	482	19	KIA	RP
Goulding, Pte J J	555	19	DOW POW VB	
Grace, Pte W A	1537	20	KIA	VC
Greening, Pte J G	683	20	KIA	RP
Griffiths, Pte E B	1584	20	KIA	AN
Hale, Pte N A	702	21	KIA	VB
Hamilton, Pte R	2138	20	KIA	VC
Harker, Pte R H	345	20	KIA	RP
Hart, Pte G H	434	25	DOW POW CR	
(aka Heaney, Pte G H)				
Hicks, Pte W S	870	19	KIA	VC
Hill, Pte R	1591	20	KIA	VC
Holland, Pte T	2141	20	KIA	VC
Holley, L/Cpl C	538	20	KIA	AN
Houghton, Pte R	2340	6.8	DOW	XG
Howard, Pte R J	1619	19	KIA	RD
Hudson, 2/Lieut A	-	19	KIA	VC
Humphrey, Pte F W	342	20	KIA	VC
Hunt, Pte T V	1054	19	KIA	VC
Hyams, Pte S J W	2028	19	KIA	VC
Jeffrey, Pte G W	3549	20	KIA	VC
Jenkins, Pte A C	883	20	KIA	RP
Johnson, Pte A J	888	20	KIA	VC
Jones, Pte T W	891	20	KIA	VC
Joseph, Pte J D De P	1055	20	KIA	VC
Keen, Cpl E J	377	20	KIA	RP
Kelly, Pte F C	1706	20	KIA	RP
Kendall, Cpl H M H	365	20	KIA	VC
King, Pte S B	76	20	KIA	VC
Kippie, Pte J M	34	19	KIA	AN
Kirkaldy, Pte T D	902	20	KIA	AN
Knight, Pte J	2038	27	DOW POW DC	
Larkins, Pte J J	2148	20	KIA	AN
Leigh, Pte A D	247	20	KIA	VC
Linton, Cpl A	454	22	DOW	BA
Martin, Pte J A L	2058	19/20	KIA	VC
Mason, Pte J L	470	30.10	DOW POW VB	
Mates, Pte H C	515	20	KIA	RP
McDonald, Pte A	1553	20	KIA	VC
McDonald, Pte C G	2160	19/20	KIA	VC
McKenzie, Pte O A	1140	20	DOW	BA
McLeod, Pte H McD	1716	20	KIA	VC
McPherson, Pte J J	3846	23.8	DOW POW NW	
McReynolds, Pte F	379	26	DOW	XH
Millard, L/Cpl G P	252	20	KIA	VC
Morgan, Pte C	2055	19	KIA	VC
Morley, Pte J	258	20	KIA	VC
Nevill, Pte J H	269	20	KIA	VC
Olsen, Pte A	421	19	KIA	VC
Otterspoor, Pte F J	464	19	KIA	RP
Page, Pte P W	1735	5.8	DOW	WI
Parker, Pte E T	2396	27.9	DOW	CI
Paton, Pte A A	2508	19/20	KIA	VC
Perrin, Pte H E	1089	19	KIA	VC
Power, Pte T	330	20	KIA	AN
Purcell, Pte J W	2162	19	KIA	AN
Radford, Pte J C	288	20	KIA	VC
Rawlings, Pte F	916	20	KIA	VC
Redfern, Pte S I	1067	20	KIA	VC
Robertson, Capt. G G	-	20	KIA	TC
Robertson, Pte W C	2411	20	KIA	RF
Robinson, Pte S L	919	20	KIA	RP
Rodda, Pte B P	1604	26	DOW	LO
Ryall, Pte H	921	20	KIA	RP
Ryan, Cpl W P	1520	19	KIA	VC
Saddler, Pte H	542	19	KIA	VC
Sexton, L/Cpl J	301	20	KIA	NI
Shadforth, Pte G S	23	19	KIA	RP
Sinclair, Pte W B	1569	20	KIA	AN
Slimon, Pte R McR	2090	20	KIA	RP
Smith, Pte C J	59	20	KIA	RP
Smith, Pte J R	3983	20	KIA	VC
Spreadborough, Lieut E W	-	19/20	KIA	VC
Springfield, 2/Lieut E	-	25.10	DOW	TD
Statham, Pte G E	293	20	KIA	VC
Stoddart, Pte W B	1144	19	KIA	AN
Suffolk, Pte J J	406	14.8	DOW	AN
Sutherland, Pte G	567	19	KIA	VC
Tanner, Pte R	430	19	KIA	VC
Tedford, Pte T H	2012	19/20	KIA	VC
Terrens, Pte A J	956	21	DOW POW CR	
Thomas, Pte W	959	22	DOW POW DC	
Thomson, Pte R	962	20	KIA	VC
Thornburrow, Pte E J	763	2.8	DOW POW CR	
Tozer, L/Cpl E W	60	19	KIA	RP
Treble, Cpl A G	973	20	KIA	VC
Walsh, Pte L G	311	20	KIA	VC
Walsh, Pte T	770	20	KIA	RP
Washington, Pte D L	3059	26.10	DOW	HS
Weakley, Pte P	318	19	KIA	VC
Welsh, Pte A J J	3551	20	KIA	VC
Woodman, CSM H G	794	21	KIA	VB

Noted as KIA 21 July, see page 24

Alder, Pte R	1033	21	KIA	AN
Anderson, Pte L W	570	21	KIA	VB
Bean, Pte R A	719	21	KIA	VB
Beseler, Pte G H	817	21	KIA	AN
Bills, Pte T H	605	21	KIA	VB
Bloomfield, Pte B B	589	21	KIA	VB
Bray, L/Cpl F D	582	21	KIA	VB
Brown, Pte L C	829	21	KIA	VB
Brumby, Pte W C	585	21	KIA	VB
Cartwright, Pte A L	620	21	KIA	RP
Caughey, Pte R	3784	21	KIA	VB
Chadwick, Pte F	1004	21	KIA	RP
Cullen, Pte W	623	21	KIA	VB
Denton, Pte R G	629	21	KIA	VB
Dunn, Pte L C	641	21	KIA	VB
Farrell, Pte J S	2130	21	KIA	VB
Francis, Sgt A E	795	21	KIA	AN
Hale, Pte N A	702	21	KIA	VB
Hibbert, Pte A G	706	21	KIA	VB
Hopkins, Sgt L R	693	21	KIA	RP

Jamieson, Pte W A	2144	21	KIA	VB
Johnson, L/Cpl R	715	21	KIA	PH
Jolly, Pte W C	4231	21	KIA	RP
King, Pte F J	900	21	KIA	RP
King, Pte H	988	21	KIA	VB
Law, Pte E M W	1000	21	KIA	VB
Mackenzie, Sgt A	250	21	KIA	CR
Marcus, Pte R	732	21	KIA	VB
Oliver, Pte A	136a	21	KIA	RP
Peak, Pte S G B	739	21	KIA	RF
Pearson, Pte G C	1114	21	KIA	VB
Robertson, Pte R	3891	21	KIA	VB
Rowlands, Pte W R	1877	21	KIA	VB
Simmons, Pte W T	929	21	KIA	RP
Stiles, Pte A	944	21	KIA	RP
Taylor, Pte W	2491	21	KIA	AN
Thompson, Cpl S	803	21	KIA	RP
Warby, Pte C F	2436	21	KIA	VB
Willis, Pte H V	983	21	KIA	VB
Wilson, Pte A	799	21	KIA	AN

32nd Battalion

Allengame, Pte P H D	1966	20	KIA	VC
Ambler, Pte J L	1590	19	KIA	VC
Anderson, Pte P M	1205	20	KIA	VC
Ash, Pte C N	1209	22	DOW POW	CR
Backler, L/Cpl A H	261	20	KIA	VC
Barber, Pte W	346	20	KIA	VC
Bartlett, Pte J	881	20	KIA	VC
Batt, Pte A G	352	20	KIA	VC
Baumann, Sgt O E	10	20	KIA	VC
Beare, Sgt B	4	20	KIA	VC
Bellinger, Pte A S R J	442	20	DOW	BA
Bennett, L/Cpl A	1602	20	KIA	VC
Benson, 2/Lieut J	-	20	KIA	VC
Black, Pte J H A	42	20	KIA	VC
Blacksell, Pte W R	3023	20	KIA	VC
Blann, Pte W	43	22	DOW	BA
Bonney, Pte G E	44	19	KIA	VC
Bontoft, Pte P G	45	20	KIA	BH
Boswell, Pte J H	891	20	KIA	VC
Bottrall, Pte J	1983	19	KIA	VC
Bourke, Pte J P	885	20	KIA	VC
Boyce, Pte W E	1218	20	KIA	VC
Brooks, Pte A E	3034	20	KIA	VC
Brough, Pte N J	51	20	KIA	RF
Brown, Pte L G	2167	19	KIA	RP
Burbidge, Sgt H J C	411	20	KIA	VC
Burchell, Pte C H	450	20	KIA	VC
Burford, Pte A R E	3042	20	KIA	VC
Burney, Pte E N	1226	20	KIA	VC
Burrows, Pte H	1609	24	DOW POW	LI
Byrne, Pte J	1229	20	KIA	VC
Cahill, Pte J W	1989	3.8	DOW POW	DC
Cameron, Pte I A	917	19	KIA	VC
Cameron, Pte P	233	19	KIA	VC
Cann, Pte S I	457	19	KIA	VC
Carson, Pte D G	452	20	KIA	RP
Cartwright, Pte T C	1235	20	KIA	VC
Chinner, Lieut E H	-	20	DOW POW	VC
Choat, Pte A P	66	20	KIA	VC
Choat, Pte R H	67	20	KIA	RP
Clarke, Pte T J	1995	20	KIA	VC
Claxton, Pte M J	1239	20	KIA	VC
Cochrane, Pte W J L	73	20	KIA	VC
Colless, Sgt F J	1194	23	DOW POW	LI
Cope, Pte W V	1241	20	KIA	VC
Corigliano, Pte M	2011	20	KIA	VC
Cormack, Pte H W	1242	21	DOW	BA
Cotching, Pte G A	3073	20	KIA	RF
Cowland, Pte J J	2009	19	KIA	VC
Crawford, L/Cpl J A	77	20	KIA	VC
Creedon, Pte J V	3072	20	KIA	VC
Crisp, Pte W G	1997	19	KIA	VC
Crocker, Pte J E	79	20	KIA	VC
Croser, Pte W G	2588	19	KIA	VC
Crossman, Cpl G L	80	19	KIA	VC
Curtin, Pte F N	465	20	KIA	VC
Daniels, Pte L G	1522	19	KIA	VC
Davidson, Pte D H	469	20	KIA	RP
Davy, Pte D W	2015	19	KIA	RP
Dean, L/Cpl J	925	19	KIA	VC
Dennis, L/Cpl S W	1252	19	KIA	VC
Dillon, Pte M N H	84	20	KIA	VC
Dix, Pte B G	2913	9.8	DOW	ES
Dubois, L/Cpl B	87	20	KIA	VC
Dyke, Pte T D	484	20	DOW POW	CR
Edgley, Pte B J	487	19	KIA	RP
Emery, L/Sgt E S	13	19	KIA	RP
Feldt, Pte J J	929	20	KIA	VC
Finey, Pte C L	93	20	KIA	RF
Fisher, Pte C C	1259	20	KIA	VC
Fisk, L/Cpl L T	494	19	KIA	VC
Fraser, Pte A H	931	19	KIA	VC
Furze, Pte R A	1265	20	KIA	VC
Gibney, Pte G S D	1083	20	KIA	VC
Gillespie, Pte F	284	11.9	DOW	XI
Gillett, Pte A E	937	19	KIA	VC
Gladwell, Pte H	2036	20	KIA	BA
Gray, Pte E C	20	20	KIA	VC
Green, Cpl R C	1274	20	KIA	VC
Greenfield, Cpl B	1275	20	KIA	VC
Greenwood, Pte P J	3115a	20	KIA	VC
Griffen, Lieut R T	-	20	KIA	VC
Griffin, Pte J J	3117	19	KIA	RP
Griffiths, Pte G A	1276	20	DOW POW	VC
Gully, Pte T	941	20	KIA	VC
Hagan, Lieut T P	-	19	KIA	VC
Hall, Pte M A	1525	20	KIA	VC
Harland, L/Cpl C G	2041	20	KIA	VC
Hart, Cpl L W	865	20	DOW POW	VC
Hazell, Pte H H	571	24	DOW	CA
Hennessy, Pte W J	110	20	KIA	VC
Higgon, Major J A	-	20	KIA	RF
Hobbs, Sgt K H	405	16.9	DOW	RD
Hoffman, Pte C R S	2050	20	KIA	VC

Hollings, Pte W C	1402	19	KIA	VC
Holmes, Pte A	955	19	KIA	VC
Holzberger, Pte H W	114	19	KIA	RF
Honey, Pte G	1291	19	KIA	VC
Hook, Pte R S W H	525	22	DOW POW	CR
Hopper, Pte C L	674a	19	KIA	RP
Hounslow, L/Cpl A B	522	20	KIA	VC
Hulks, Lieut F W	-	20	KIA	VC
Humphris, Cpl B	531	20	KIA	VC
Hunt, Pte T	347	20	KIA	VC
Hutchinson, Pte J W	962	19	KIA	VC
Ingram, Pte V R	3158	19	KIA	VC
Ion, Lieut J	-	25	DOW	BO
Irving, Pte A W J	1528	20	KIA	VC
Jamieson, Pte R W	972	19	KIA	VC
Jarman, Cpl E H	866	20	KIA	VC
Jergens, Pte E W	2354	20	KIA	VC
Johnstone, L/Cpl F D	1299	20	KIA	VC
Jolly, Pte D C	3177	20	KIA	VC
Jose, Pte H N	121	20	KIA	VC
Joyce, Pte J	1624	20	KIA	VC
Judge, Pte C F	971	20	KIA	VC
Keating, Pte W	974	20	KIA	VC
Knable, Pte A T	1603	20	KIA	VC
Korber, L/Cpl A	547	20	KIA	VC
Lacey, Pte S J	977	19	KIA	VC
Lanyon, Pte C J	124	20	KIA	VC
Lawlor, Pte D M	126	20	KIA	VC
Lee, Pte J T	982	19	KIA	VC
Liddle, Pte R	3179	19	KIA	RP
Loader, Pte F O	2064	20	KIA	VC
Lodge, Pte W S	307	19	KIA	RP
Low, Pte D	663	4.8	DOW	UD
Lydiate, Pte F W	985	19	KIA	VC
Lynch, Pte T F	130	18.12	DOW	UX
Mackenzie, Pte G H	3234	20	KIA	VC
Mackness, Pte H	1009	20	KIA	VC
Magor, Pte R H	3209	20	KIA	VC
Mahoney, Pte S N	1536	20	KIA	VC
Malsch, Pte H A	1195	26.8	DOW	BO
Martin, Pte A P	135	20	KIA	VC
Mason, Pte E I	993	21	DOW	BO
Matthews, Pte H K	994	24.8	DOW	BO
Matthews, Pte P R	560	20	KIA	LT
Maudsley, Pte R T	137	19	KIA	VC
McArthur, Pte D J	1019	19	KIA	RP
McCulloch, Pte A	1011	19	KIA	VC
McGregor, L/Cpl P	2081	19	KIA	VC
McKenzie, Pte A McG	1797a	20	KIA	VC
McKenzie, Pte J G	151	20	KIA	VC
McKinnon, Pte D	1330	28	DOW POW	DC
McLean, Pte H	293	19	KIA	VC
McPhee, Pte W J O	119	20	KIA	VC
Millar, Pte G H	141	25	DOW	BO
Miller, Cpl H	576	19	KIA	VC
Miller, Pte H G J	2073	19	KIA	VC
Minter, Pte C H	144	19	KIA	RP
Mitchell, Pte A J	998	19	KIA	VC
Momplhait, Pte A V	32fc82	19	KIA	VC
Moore, Pte W R	581	28	DOW	BA
Morphett, L/Cpl A H	340	20	KIA	VC
Mortimore, Pte P	22	20	KIA	VC
Murphy, Pte J P	3227	19	KIA	VC
Murphy, Pte J T	1744a	19	KIA	VC
O'Leary, Pte H	2087	20	KIA	VC
O'Neill, Pte O R	158	20	KIA	CA
Oates, L/Cpl C N	1025	20	KIA	VC
Page, Pte A R R	1082	20	KIA	VC
Palmer, Pte W J	593	20	KIA	VC
Parham, Pte E W	2092	20	KIA	VC
Paterson, 2/Lieut A	-	20	KIA	LT
Pearce, Pte F S	672	19	KIA	RP
Pearse, Sgt J	859	19	KIA	RP
Perry, Pte A M	2095	20	KIA	VC
Pflaum, Pte R H	161	24.11	DOW POW	VB
Pitt, Pte H C	595	20	KIA	VC
Plunket, Pte C F	597	20	KIA	VC
Pretty, Pte W H	1556	20	KIA	VC
Putland, Pte A S	3869	25	DOW	BA
Quintrell, Pte R H	2391	20	KIA	VC
Randall, Pte H J	1558	20	KIA	VC
Reid, Pte M L	3256	20	KIA	VC
Ridler, Pte S T J	1036	20	KIA	VC
Riedel, Pte J B	602	21	DOW	BA
Roberts, Cpl A W	1356	20	KIA	VC
Ross, Pte M	1040	20	KIA	VC
Rostron, Pte G H	605	19	KIA	VC
Rowe, Pte J	607	20	KIA	VC
Ryan, Pte E J	1043	19	KIA	RP
Scott, Pte R G M	1046	20	KIA	RP
Searle, Pte H	1639	20	KIA	VC
Sedunary, Pte P C	3324	19	KIA	RP
Shaw, Pte H	1047	20	KIA	VC
Shepherd, Pte C F	1363	19	KIA	VC
Simon, Pte V G	1516	20	KIA	VC
Sinigear, Cpl A G	16	19	KIA	VC
Smith, Pte A G	1640	20	KIA	VC
Smith, Pte P E	621	21	DOW	BA
Smith, Pte W J	1054	19	KIA	VC
Snook, Pte G	2110	20	KIA	VC
Soans, Pte B	622	20	KIA	VC
Solomon, Pte M	1367	19	KIA	VC
Standley, Pte F W H	3283	20	KIA	VC
Stead, Pte J R	187	20	KIA	VC
Steele, Pte J N	624	20	KIA	VC
Stranger, Cpl A T	165a	20	KIA	RF
Stuart, Pte J H	1057	20	KIA	VC
Summerly, Pte M	1575	20	KIA	VC
Swanton, Pte H T	631	24	DOW	BO
Thorpe, Pte S H	2126	20	KIA	VC
Tucker, Pte W C	1581	20	KIA	VC
Tymons, Sgt J P	408	20	KIA	VC
Vincent, Pte E A	1582	20	KIA	VC
Virgin, Pte R L H	1839	31.10	DOW	HS
Wahlstead, Pte C	2135	20	KIA	VC
Walker, Sgt J	1186	20	KIA	VC

Wall, Pte L G	200	20	KIA	VC
Wallis, Pte V	2837	20	KIA	VC
Walsh, Pte R A	201	20	KIA	VC
Warner, Pte E A	203	22	DOW	ES
Warren, Pte C H	1394	20	KIA	VC
Watterson, Pte W	1385	20	KIA	VC
Webber, Pte A R B	204	19	KIA	RP
Westlake, Pte G	206	20	KIA	VC
Wilson, Pte H R	211	20	KIA	VC
Wilson, Pte V F	2143	21	DOW	BO
Wilson, Pte W W	2144	20	KIA	VC
Wilson, Sgt H	421	19	KIA	VC
Winter, Pte A V	649	20	KIA	VC
Wolff, Pte E A	213	5.9	DOW POW	DC
Zachariah, L/Cpl D H M	653	10.9	DOW POW	NW

8th Machine Gun Coy

Buckley, Pte D F	104	22	DOW	BA
Copley, Pte A W	913	25	DOW POW	VA
Davies, Pte J E L	802	20	KIA	RP
Huxley, Pte S L	876a	20	KIA	RP
Ings, Pte P E	909	20	KIA	AN
James, Pte L M	229	21	DOW	BA
Makeham, Pte J J	98a	20	KIA	RP
McDonald, Pte D C	675	2.11	DOW	HS
McKinnon, Cpl J	110	20	KIA	RP
Milton, Pte R C	31	20	KIA	RP
Minchington, Pte J A (aka Vincent J A)	97a	20	KIA	RP
Pearce, Pte W S	267	20	KIA	RP
Regan, Pte A	673	20	KIA	VC
Ross, Pte J V	113	20	KIA	VC
Stratford, Pte G J	102	20	KIA	VC
Turner, Pte A L	39	20	KIA	VC
White, Pte W J	118	20	KIA	VC

8th Field Coy Engineers

Betts, Spr S	2197	19	KIA	RP
Eadie, Spr A McK	4408	19	KIA	RD
Loader, Spr P H	4421	20.8	DOW	ES
Morrison, Cpl W J	4511	18	KIA	RP
Reeves, Spr J	4557	19	KIA	RD
Smith, L/Cpl H T	4474	19	KIA	VC
Tenbosch, 2/Lieut C P	-	19	KIA	RP
Ward, Spr R D	1153	19	KIA	RD
Young, Spr W H	4483	19	KIA	RD

18th Coy Signals Corps (8th Bde)

O'Donnell, Sgt T J	1864	20	KIA	RP

14th BRIGADE

53rd Battalion

Abbott, Pte D R L	4898	19	KIA	VC
Allan, 2/Lieut G E	-	19	KIA	VC
Allanson, Pte T H	4727	19	KIA	VC
Allen, Pte G W	3134	19	KIA	VC
Anderson, Pte F C	2101	19	KIA	VC
Arblaster, Capt. C	-	24	DOW POW	DC
Ashton, Pte E W	4729	19	KIA	VC
Aspinall, Pte F J S	3230	19	KIA	VC
Austin, Pte W J	4731	19	KIA	VC
Aysom, Pte F H	3004	20	DOW	LO
Back, Pte R C	3234	19	KIA	VC
Bacon, Pte W J	3236	19	KIA	VC
Bailey, Pte G	2468	19	KIA	VC
Bainbridge, Pte J A	1927	19	KIA	VC
Baker, Pte T N	1623	19	KIA	VC
Baldwin, L/Cpl E V	2116	19	KIA	VC
Baldwin, Pte F	3233	30.9	DOW	ES
Bancroft, Pte H W	3010	20	DOW	AN
Barrack, Sgt R G	3492	19	KIA	VC
Bartley, CQMS H H	2104	19	KIA	VC
Beck, Pte W S	3239	19	KIA	VC
Bell, Pte C F	4734	19	KIA	VC
Black, Sgt A J	2331	19	KIA	VC
Blomfield, Pte F G W	4744	19	KIA	VC
Bolton, Pte A R	3509	19	KIA	VC
Booth, Pte W S	3251	19	KIA	VC
Boyd, Pte W	3243	19	KIA	VC
Bromley, Pte A C	4744	19	KIA	VC
Bromley, Pte S R	4903	19	KIA	RF
Brown, Pte C	3007	19	KIA	VC
Bryant, Pte T S	3249	19	KIA	VC
Bryson, Cpl J B	3494	20	DOW	RB
Buckland, Sgt F A	3241	19	KIA	RF
Bugg, Pte L J	3537	19	KIA	VC
Bundy, Pte W J	3261a	19	KIA	VC
Burns, Pte A H	501	19	KIA	VC
Byrne, Pte J A	1664	19	KIA	VC
Cairns, Pte J D	3273a	19	KIA	VC
Camp, Cpl J W	3265a	19	KIA	VC
Capper, Pte A M	3266	20	DOW	BA
Carey, Pte J S	3481a	19	KIA	RB
Carey, Pte T J	3480a	19	KIA	VC
Carmichael, Pte R A	1445	19	KIA	VC
Clarke, Pte J B	3224	19	KIA	VC
Clingan, Pte A S	3168	19	KIA	VC
Coady, Pte R	3267	19	KIA	VC
Collier, 2/Lieut C T	-	20	KIA	VC
Comerford, Pte M	4755	19	KIA	VC
Connell, Pte W J	2810	19	KIA	VC
Cooke, Pte S E	4757	19	KIA	VC
Coote, Pte C G	4747	19	KIA	VC
Craig, Pte G	4751	19	KIA	YF
Crossman, Pte W	3818	19	KIA	VC
Croucher, Pte W R E	3272	19	KIA	VC
Cruickshanks, Pte R	3282	19	KIA	VC
Davies, Pte F	4934	19	KIA	VC
Davies, Pte R D	4904	19	KIA	VC
Davis, Pte F J	3297	19	KIA	VC
Dixon, Dvr F	8852	19	KIA	VC
Dodd, Pte R	2128	19	KIA	VC
Downie, Pte E L	3290	19	KIA	VC
Drane, Pte S	1186	19	KIA	VC
Duffecy, Pte T E	2494	19	KIA	RB
Duncan, Pte J A	4761	19	KIA	VC

Edwards, Pte W O	3527	19	KIA	VC	Legate, Pte C M	3366	19	KIA	VC
Evans, Pte F	4773	19	KIA	VC	Levy, Pte L H	2870	19	KIA	VC
Evans, Pte W F	4769	19	KIA	VC	Loudon, Pte J A	3367	19	KIA	VC
Flaus, Pte C H	3478	19	KIA	VC	Maher, Pte T J	4816	19	KIA	RF
Fleming, Pte H J	1651	19	KIA	VC	Main, Pte A E	3394	19	KIA	VC
Forland, Pte R C	4779	19	KIA	VC	Mainger, Pte N	4954	19	KIA	VC
Fry, Pte W	3145	26	DOW	WI	Major, Pte R	4815	19	KIA	VC
Fryer, Pte C H	3298	19	KIA	RP	Marshall, Pte J	4822	19	KIA	RF
Fuller, Pte F A	2721	19	KIA	VC	Marshall, Pte T J	4939	19	KIA	VC
Fulton, L/Cpl R J	353	19	KIA	VC	Martin, Pte C H	3355	8.8	DOW	WI
Gardiner, L/Cpl C D	2961	19	KIA	VC	Martin, Pte W	3090	19	KIA	VC
Gardiner, Pte B S W	3048	19	KIA	VC	McGrath, Pte D	3402	19	KIA	VC
Gavel, L/Cpl S J	3502a	19	KIA	VC	McHugh, Pte R B	4201	19	KIA	VC
Gearing, Pte P	3501	19	KIA	CR	McKay, Pte A J	4826	19	KIA	VC
Gilbert, Pte A	4787	19	KIA	VC	McKenzie, Pte D H	3087	19	KIA	VC
Gilmore, Pte J E	3522	24	DOW	BO	McLennan, Pte M	3368	19	KIA	VC
Gollan, Pte S J	4051	19	KIA	VC	McLeod, Cpl W E	3121	19	KIA	VC
Goold, Pte J	2443	19	KIA	VC	Meloy, Pte S A	3361	19	KIA	VC
Gordon, Pte A E	1657	23	DOW	ES	Milne, Pte J S	3380a	19	KIA	VC
Gould, Pte T H	3239	19	KIA	VC	Moate, Pte P G	2616	19	KIA	VC
Green, Pte A J	2838	19	KIA	VC	Moffitt, Lieut H L	-	19	KIA	VC
Greenwood, Pte G	2667	19	KIA	VC	Moore, Pte W	3393	19	KIA	VC
(aka Smith, Pte G)					Moran, Pte J	3553	19	KIA	VC
Grimmond, Pte R P	4789	19	KIA	VC	Morey, Pte G M	3366a	19	KIA	VC
Hall, Pte A	3341a	19	KIA	VC	Morrison, Pte M J L	2451	19	KIA	VC
Hall, Pte J	3318	19	KIA	VC	Mudge, 2/Lieut C E	-	19	KIA	RF
Harden, Pte W H	1669	19	KIA	VC	Murphy, Pte P	3545b	19	KIA	VC
Hatchett, Pte P	4613	19	KIA	VC	Murray, L/Cpl L B	3555	28	DOW	WI
Hawley, Pte M	3538	19	KIA	VC	Neil, Sgt R	2401	19	KIA	VC
Heaton, Pte W H	3336	19	KIA	VC	Nelson, 2/Lieut B J	-	19	KIA	VC
Herbert, Pte S G	3308a	19	KIA	VC	Newman, Pte B F	3412	19	KIA	VC
Higgison, Pte S P	3485a	19	KIA	VC	Nicholl, Pte J W	3587a	19	KIA	VC
Hill, L/Cpl C S	842	19	KIA	VC	Noble, Lieut W E	-	19	KIA	VC
Hillyar, Cpl A U	2152	19	KIA	VC	Norris, Lieut Col I B	-	19	KIA	VC
Hindley, Pte A R	2351	25	DOW	BA	O'Donnell, Pte W	3562	19	KIA	VC
Howatson, Pte C	3056	19	KIA	RF	Ohlson, Pte A O	3394a	19	KIA	VC
Hubbard, Pte E A	3327a	19	KIA	VC	Outlaw, Pte W S	3367	19	KIA	VC
Hungerford, Pte G W	3327	19	KIA	VC	Outram, L/Sgt L W	3391	7.8	DOW	UE
Ingram, Pte S E	2860	19	KIA	VC	Owston, Pte V M	3392	19	KIA	RF
Janes, Sgt C H	247	19	KIA	RF	Oxenham, Pte J M	3095	25	DOW	NC
Jentsch, L/Sgt E A	3331	19	KIA	VC	Pain, Pte R O C	4837	19	KIA	VC
Johnston, Pte G H	3096	19	KIA	VC	Paling, Pte G J V	3540a	19	KIA	VC
Kearney, Cpl P R	3357a	19	KIA	VC	Palmer, Pte P	2892	19	KIA	VC
Kemp, Pte L M	3368a	19	KIA	VC	Parkinson, Pte E G	3528a	19	KIA	RP
Kendall, Pte W J	3117	19	KIA	VC	Parton, Pte R	3148a	19	KIA	VC
Kennedy, Pte J V	2862	19	KIA	VC	Paulin, Capt. H	-	19	KIA	VC
Kentwell, Pte G S	3541a	19	KIA	VC	Peat, Pte W H	3580	19	KIA	YF
Kilburn, Pte W	2697	19	KIA	VC	Percy, Pte R J	2896	19	KIA	VC
King, Pte C C	3338	19	KIA	VC	Phillips, Pte J P	3422a	19	KIA	VC
Laing, Pte W L	2973	19	KIA	VC	Phillips, Pte W H	3656	19	KIA	VC
Landsler, Pte E L	3336	19	KIA	VC	Philp, Pte S	3407	19	KIA	YF
Larkin, Pte J P	4808	19	KIA	VC	Pike, Pte R	4840	19	KIA	VC
Lawler, Pte E	3076	19	KIA	VC	Plummer, L/Cpl E G	2815a	19	KIA	VC
Lawler, Pte T J	5484	23	DOW	ES	Porter, Pte W H	3397	19	KIA	VC
Lawson, Pte S	4820	19	KIA	VC	Potter, Pte W E	3395	19	KIA	VC
Lawson, Pte W R	1956b	29	DOW	WI	Poulton, Pte J W	4838	19	KIA	VC
Layton, Pte C H	4809	19	KIA	VC	Pratt, Lieut A E	-	19	KIA	PZ
Le Maitre, Pte H W	3341	19	KIA	VC	Pratt, Pte S R	2641	19	KIA	VC

Quist, Pte R G	3524	19	KIA	VC
Rickard, 2/Lieut T N	-	19	KIA	VC
Rilen, Pte R N	2196	19	KIA	VC
Roach, Pte D	2247	19	KIA	VC
Roach, Pte J	3421	14.8	DOW	UP
Roberts, L/Cpl C A	3103	19	KIA	VC
Robertson, Pte W H	2944	19	KIA	RF
Robin, Sgt G De Q	329	19	KIA	RB
Robinson, Pte W J L	4841	19	KIA	VC
Ronson, Pte W	3102	19	KIA	VC
Royan, Pte W	2900	19	KIA	VC
Sampson, Major V H B	-	19	KIA	VC
Saunders, Pte H	3442	19	KIA	RF
Scott, Pte J	3568	19	KIA	RF
Shannon, Pte P	3433	19	KIA	VC
Sharp, Pte J	4940	20	KIA	RB
Shepherd, Pte T	3448	19	KIA	VC
Sims, Pte F C	3447	19	KIA	VC
Slate, Pte E A	4870	19	KIA	VC
Smith, Pte E	3439	23	DOW	BO
Smith, Pte F W A	2910	19	KIA	VC
Smith, Pte M N	523	19	KIA	RF
Sparks, Pte J	1165	19	KIA	VC
Stacker, Pte S S	3449a	19	KIA	VC
Stapleton, Pte A E	3440a	19	KIA	VC
Staunton, Pte D J	3414	19	KIA	RF
Stephenson, Pte T W	4891	19	KIA	VC
Steuart, Pte A H	4874	19	KIA	VC
Sullivan, Pte J J	3421	19	KIA	AN
Sullivan, Pte M	3429	19	KIA	RD
Summers, Pte H	3494	19	KIA	RF
Swinfield, Pte J E	3297a	19	KIA	VC
Taylor, Pte S L	2417	19	KIA	VC
Thompson, L/Cpl P A	2034	19	KIA	VC
Thompson, Pte C	4908	19	KIA	RD
Thomson, Pte A C	4881	19	KIA	VC
Thorpe, Pte G H	4877	19	KIA	VC
Tollefson, Pte O B	3454a	19	KIA	VC
Tollis, Pte R H C	4261	19	KIA	VC
Turner, Pte A	3462a	19	KIA	VC
Turner, Pte B C	3531	24	DOW POW	CR
Turner, Pte H	3455	19	KIA	VC
Verpillot, Pte A C	4885	19	KIA	VC
Wall, Pte B	3472	19	KIA	VC
Walsh, Pte F J	3578B	19	KIA	VC
Walton, Pte T	4932	20	DOW	BA
Waters, Pte E	3515	19	KIA	VC
Watkins, Pte J E	715	19	KIA	VC
Watson, Pte J H	3576	19	KIA	VC
Watson, Pte L L	4924	19	KIA	VC
Weaver, Pte R A	3449	19	KIA	RF
Weiss, Pte F A	3578a	19	KIA	VC
West, Pte W H	4891	28	DOW	WI
Whitbread, Pte E S	3476	19	KIA	VC
Williams, Pte F J	3605	19	KIA	VC
Williamson, Pte W B	4897	19	KIA	VC
Wilson, Pte A E	4943	19	KIA	VC
Wilson, Pte A W	3474a	19	KIA	VC
Wilson, Pte E R	4887	19	KIA	VC
Wilson, Pte S C	3534	19	KIA	VC

54th Battalion

Ahern, 2/Lieut T P	-	20	KIA	AN
Anderson, Cpl D S	2560	19/20	KIA	VC
Artist, L/Cpl P	2569	20	DOW	BA
Ausburn, Pte E H	4128	19	KIA	RP
Backhouse, Pte V J	4432	19/20	KIA	VC
Balkin, Pte M	4254	19/20	KIA	VC
Ballard, Pte H A S	4730	19/20	KIA	RB
Barr, Pte P G A	3006	19/20	KIA	RB
Bayliss, Pte J	4735	19/20	KIA	AN
Bell, Pte W G	3478	19/20	KIA	AN
Bentley, L/Cpl W	3007	19/20	KIA	RB
Billington, Pte M E	4440	19/20	KIA	VC
Bishop, Pte W H	3473	28	DOW	UO
Bonnett, Pte T M	2782	19/20	KIA	VC
Boone, 2/Lieut C A	-	19	KIA	AN
Brand, Pte J J	4140a	19/20	KIA	VC
Brindal, Pte C S	3487a	19/20	KIA	VC
Brown, Pte J	4134	19/20	KIA	CR
Browne, Pte A T	4143	19/20	KIA	RF
Burgess, Pte E	4151a	19/20	KIA	VC
Campbell, Pte R A	3631	20	KIA	RP
Campbell, Sgt J M	495	19/20	KIA	VC
Cardew, Pte T L	2793	19/20	KIA	VC
Carlin, L/Cpl H	154	20	KIA	VB
Cawley, Pte H T	3630	19/20	KIA	VC
Clapperton, Pte G	4166a	19/20	KIA	VC
Clark, Pte R A	4155	20	KIA	VC
Collier, Pte L	4362a	19/20	KIA	AN
Connolly, Pte W T	3585a	19/20	KIA	VC
Conroy, Pte C W G	4460	19/20	KIA	VC
Conway, Pte J W	4357	21	DOW	BO
Corr, Pte G P	4154	20	KIA	RB
Cottle, Pte A P	606	19/20	KIA	RP
Coxall, L/Cpl T G	2387	19/20	KIA	RP
Craigie, Pte W A	4420	19/20	KIA	VC
Cressy, Pte H A	4179a	19/20	KIA	VC
Cuckson, Pte W J	3032	19/20	KIA	VC
Cutting, Pte H R	4280	19/20	KIA	RB
Daley, Pte W	3636	19/20	KIA	VC
Dalzell, Pte G T B	4763	19	KIA	TC
Davis, Pte K W	4199	22	DOW	BO
Devos, Pte J	4182	19/20	KIA	VC
Dibben, Pte E H	4183a	19/20	KIA	VC
Donnellan, Sgt R B	4181	19/20	KIA	RF
Doust, Pte R	3558	30.10	DOW	XJ
Doust, Pte W H	3557	19/20	KIA	VC
Doyle, Pte V P	4160	19/20	KIA	AN
Dunbar, Pte R	4481	19/20	KIA	RP
Dunstan, Pte B J A	4483	20	KIA	VC
Dyson, Pte F A	3560	19/20	KIA	VC
Eaves, Pte J H	4165	14.8	DOW POW	VA
Emery, Pte J	4487	10.8	DOW	UK
Evans, Pte H C	4489	19/20	KIA	VC
Ferguson, Pte T C	4207	23	DOW	ES

Flude, Pte H	3494	19/20	KIA	VC
Forrest, Pte J R	3046	19/20	KIA	VC
Fryer, L/Cpl T E	3048	19/20	KIA	VC
Gates, Pte C	4787	19/20	KIA	VC
Gaunt, Pte E G	2604	19/20	KIA	VC
Gibson, Pte W B	4947	19/20	KIA	AN
Graham, Pte H J	3543	19/20	KIA	VC
Gray, Pte G R	2927	20	KIA	VC
Gray, Pte S J	4296	19/20	KIA	VC
Green, Pte C	2406	19/20	KIA	AN
Hales, Pte A E	4221a	19/20	KIA	VC
Hall, Lieut H J	-	19/20	KIA	RF
Harriott, Pte L	4509	19/20	KIA	VC
Harrison, Major R	-	20	KIA	RP
Hartmann, L/Cpl S T V W	3061	19/20	KIA	CB
Hatter, Sgt G H	3559	3.8	DOW	XK
Hay, Pte D	4232	19/20	KIA	VC
Healey, Pte R A C	3511b	19/20	KIA	VC
Heard, Pte R F	4805	19/20	KIA	RF
Heath, Pte W F	4514	19/20	KIA	VC
Hewes, Sgt G W	515	19/20	KIA	VB
Hewitt, L/Cpl F	3067	19/20	KIA	VC
Higgins, Pte A J	4176a	19/20	KIA	VC
Hill, Pte J H	2821	19/20	KIA	VC
Hill, Sgt E	2425	19/20	KIA	RP
Holliday, Pte C D	4801	20	KIA	VC
Holmes, Pte J L	4305	19/20	KIA	VC
Hope, Pte E J	4188	20	KIA	VC
Hughes, Pte W G	1137	19/20	KIA	RF
Hurdis, Cpl J	2818	19/20	KIA	VC
Innes, L/Cpl J	4242a	19/20	KIA	LT
Irvin, Pte D G	4807	19/20	KIA	VC
Jarvis, Pte W	3328	21	DOW	BA
Johnson, Pte J	3548	19/20	KIA	RF
Johnston, Pte C D	4315a	20	KIA	VC
Johnston, Pte F	3549	20	KIA	VC
Keats, Pte P G	4528	19/20	KIA	VC
Keed, Pte A E	4811	21	DOW	BA
Kentish, Pte A	4813	19/20	KIA	VC
King, Pte H J	4816	19/20	KIA	VC
Krogman, Pte A	4253	19/20	KIA	VC
Lawson, Pte W W	4370	23	DOW POW	LI
Lee, Pte J J	4533	19/20	KIA	VC
Lee, Pte J	4822	19/20	KIA	VC
Lees, Pte P S	4534	19/20	KIA	VC
Little, L/Cpl V H	1777	19/20	KIA	VC
Maclaren-Webb, Pte P M	4324	19/20	KIA	VC
Malcolm, Pte W	3102	19/20	KIA	AN
Maxted, Chaplain S E		20	KIA	RP
Mayo, Pte B S	2850	19/20	KIA	AN
McAulay, Pte H	4391	19/20	KIA	VC
McAulay, Pte R	4270a	19/20	KIA	VC
McDonald, Pte L S R	3161	19/20	KIA	VC
McPherson, Pte D	4565	19/20	KIA	VC
Mondy, Pte C	2636	19/20	KIA	VC
Moore, Pte V H	4274	19/20	KIA	VC
Myers, Pte P L	4850	19/20	KIA	VC
Nash, Pte C E	4341	19/20	KIA	VC
Needham, Pte A	4946	19/20	KIA	VC
O'Donnell, Pte A T	3586	20	KIA	VC
Pagan, L/Cpl G	2906	19/20	KIA	VC
Paterson, Pte J	2859	19/20	KIA	BH
Pheasant, Pte W	2462	19/20	KIA	VC
Plater, Pte E	4862	19/20	KIA	VC
Preston, Pte V H G	3597	19/20	KIA	VC
Pybus, Pte A C L	3087	19/20	KIA	VC
Quihampton, Pte W	4297	19/20	KIA	VC
Read, Pte F	3127	19/20	KIA	LT
Richardson, L/Sgt H	2912	19/20	KIA	VC
Richardson, Pte B	4581	19/20	KIA	VC
Riordan, Pte W E	4583	19/20	KIA	VC
Rodda, Pte J A	4584	19/20	KIA	VC
Russell, Pte A	4299	19/20	KIA	VC
Ryan, Pte D	2678	25	DOW	BO
Sadler, Pte A A	4233	20	KIA	VC
St Ledger, Pte W J W	4601	19/20	KIA	AN
Samuels, L/Cpl A E	4315	19/20	KIA	RB
Scally, Pte F P	4872	19/20	KIA	AN
Scott, Pte J	4873	19	KIA	VC
Shaw, Pte H V	4876	7.8	DOW	XL
Short, Pte E	2726	18.10	DOW	US
Singleton, Pte A	4316a	19/20	KIA	VC
Smith, Pte C T P	4884	19/20	KIA	RP
Smith, Pte E G	4886	19/20	KIA	VC
Smith, Pte E	998	21	DOW	BO
Smith, Pte F	2876	19/20	KIA	VC
Smith, Pte H T	4526a	19/20	KIA	RF
Smyth, Pte A M	4239	19/20	KIA	AN
Spike, Pte W	4308a	19/20	KIA	AN
Starr, L/Cpl V J	424	19/20	KIA	AN
Stone, Pte J G A	4634	19/20	KIA	VC
Strangman, 2/Lieut J G	-	19/20	KIA	VC
Sweeney, Pte E	4377a	19/20	KIA	VC
Tate, Pte C W S	4606	24	DOW POW	DC
Taylor, Capt. H	-	19/20	KIA	RB
Thomas, Pte W J	4608	21	DOW POW	CR
Thomson, Pte J P	3145	19/20	KIA	VC
Tibey, Pte J	4323	19/20	KIA	VC
Toole, Cpl J	690	19/20	KIA	VC
Towne, Pte H V	4813	19/20	KIA	AN
Turner, Pte A J	2942	19/20	KIA	AN
Wailes, Pte J P (aka Wallis, Pte J P)	4617	20	KIA	VC
Walshe, L/Cpl B M	4346a	19/20	KIA	VC
Wass, Sgt W	239	19/20	KIA	VC
Watkins, Cpl H E	1846	19	KIA	RF
Watts, Sgt J H J	1644	31	DOW	BA
White, Pte E C	3152	19/20	KIA	VC
Wildman, Pte R R	1888	19/20	KIA	VC
Wilkinson, L/Cpl H M	4384	19/20	KIA	VC
Williamson, Pte A	4249	20	KIA	VC
Wilson, Pte A	1196	19/20	KIA	VC
Yabsley, Pte T W	4355	19/20	KIA	VC

55th Battalion

Anderson, Pte E L	2983	20	KIA	RP

Anderson, Pte G	3753	20	KIA	VC
Arnold, Pte J	2555	20	KIA	VC
Bagge, Pte R N	3475	20	DOW	AN
Baker, Pte V B	3007	20	KIA	VC
Baker, Pte V E	3247	20	KIA	VC
Barber, Cpl A H	2582	20	KIA	VC
Barber, Cpl R	3007	20	KIA	VC
Barnard, Pte J O	2316	20	KIA	VC
Barrett, Pte R A	3031	20	KIA	VC
Bell, Pte S	3760	20	KIA	RF
Bishop, Pte R C	3761	20	KIA	VC
Blackburn, Pte H S	3657	20	KIA	VC
Blunt, Sgt G A	4747	19	DOW	BA
Bolt, Cpl H T	3009	20	DOW POW	VB
Boyle, L/Cpl E F	2574	20	KIA	AN
Broadhurst, Pte L	3013	20	KIA	VC
Cameron, Pte R	3028	1.10	DOW	ES
Carr, Pte H	3252	20	KIA	AN
Clifton, Pte E W	4775	20	KIA	RF
(aka Leneard, Pte E W)				
Cornick, Pte R	2499	15.10	DOW	ES
Crawford, Pte C R	3262	20	KIA	AN
Crockett, Pte W J	2617	4.8	DOW	BO
Crooks, Pte T	3043	13.10	DOW	ES
Dewar, Pte R A	3047	20	KIA	VC
Duffy, Pte F	2600	7.8	DOW	UN
Egan, Pte E	4802	20	KIA	AN
Elrick, Pte J R	3228	20	KIA	VC
Eyre, Pte R H	5368	16.10	DOW	BO
Fahey, Pte P W	3060	20	KIA	VC
Fairweather, L/Cpl A C B	1291	16.10	DOW POW	HB
Ferguson, Pte P	3061	20	KIA	VC
Ferris, Pte E	3957	21	DOW	BA
Fletcher, Cpl F	3310	20	KIA	VC
Fryklund, Pte C	3520	20	KIA	VC
(aka Franklin, Pte C)				
Freeman, L/Cpl N L	3051	22	DOW	CR
Garrett, Pte W	225	20	KIA	RF
Geason, Pte P	4811	20	KIA	VC
Gibbins, Capt. N	-	20	KIA	AN
Glynn, Pte H	3517	10.8	DOW	UQ
Hancock, Cpl E F	3240	20	KIA	VC
Hare, Pte D E	3507	20	KIA	VC
Harris, Pte J J	3819	20	KIA	VC
Hester, Cpl W	3243	22	DOW	BA
Higgins, Pte S M	231	29.10	DOW	AB
Horsfield, Pte F	3090	20	DOW	CB
Ibbott, Pte A E	3539	20	KIA	AN
Jennings, Pte W J	4831	20	KIA	VC
Jones, L/Cpl W E	4820	20	KIA	AN
Lawrence, Pte F J	3258	27	DOW	CR
Leister, Cpl L	4840	20	KIA	VC
Lennard, Pte S R	4229	20	KIA	RB
Lund, Pte W	2705	20	KIA	VC
Mayer, Pte H	2873	20	KIA	VC
McGuarr, Pte R J	3873	20	KIA	VC
McLeod, Pte H J	3273	20	KIA	AN
Mendelsohn, Lieut B L	-	20	KIA	VC
Meyer, Pte E S R	3264	20	KIA	VC
Millard, Pte C W	3880	20	KIA	VC
Moore, L/Cpl E O	2739	20	KIA	VC
Munro, 2/Lieut S	-	19	KIA	VB
Murphy, Pte E P	3875	20	KIA	RP
Naylor, Sgt J	2712	27	DOW	UJ
Nelson, Cpl A E	4860	20	KIA	VC
Noldart, Sgt A S	2423	20	KIA	VC
O'Brien, Pte T F	4865	23	DOW	CA
Payne, Pte E A	2748	20	KIA	RP
Penfold, Pte N	2668	20	KIA	VC
Reay, Pte J G	4885	26.7	DOW POW	CR
Robertson, Pte A C	1168	20	KIA	RF
Rose, CSM W H C	1087	20	KIA	VC
Roth, Pte H W	4961	20	KIA	VC
Rue, Pte A E	3913	20	KIA	VC
St Smith, Pte H N	3924	20	KIA	VC
Smith, Pte A R	2784	20	KIA	AN
Starr, Pte W G	1291	20	KIA	VC
Steavens, Pte J E	3171	20	KIA	VC
Stephen, Cpl W J	2772	20	KIA	VC
Stevens, Pte G	1740	13.10	DOW	ES
Taylor, Pte J	2510	19	KIA	VC
Thompson, Cpl A	2825	20	KIA	VC
Vogt, Pte P C	1838	20	KIA	VC
Walsh, Pte P J	3952	7.9	DOW	CB
Whitnall, Pte A C	3308	20	KIA	VC
Wilson, L/Cpl D	2802	20	KIA	AN
Wood, Pte G	2039	21	DOW	BA
Young, Pte J	2812	1.10	DOW	AN

56th Battalion

Barker, Pte E	3041	20	DOW	BA
Baxter, Pte C J	1615	22	DOW	ES
Beith, Pte W	3038a	20	KIA	VC
Bishop, Pte E J	4747	3.8	DOW	CB
Bradford, Pte C	4741	21.9	DOW	ES
Brundrett, Pte H	5339	3.10	DOW	ES
Bussell, Pte R D	3012	25	DOW	UT
Carey, Pte H E E	3052a	19	KIA	VC
Clarke, Cpl E J C	3059a	27	DOW	CB
Comport, Pte A	2579	21	DOW	RB
Coulter, Pte W H	3254	20	DOW	RP
Denny, 2/Lieut A L	-	26	DOW	ES
Dodd, Pte D	4770	20	KIA	VC
Elliott, L/Cpl J R	2587	8.9	DOW	ES
Finch, Pte F A	3086a	20	KIA	VC
Geldard, Pte W H	4789	20	KIA	VC
Hall, Pte H	4802	28	DOW	CA
Hockley, Pte R R	4811	31	DOW	CB
Horsington, Pte A H	3119	20	KIA	VC
James, Pte F H	1687	20	KIA	AN
Johnston, Pte C W	2705	20	KIA	VC
Kelly, L/Cpl J	1690	20	KIA	AN
Lonsdale, Pte N	3074	20	DOW	AN
Martin, Pte F	3430	20	KIA	AN
McCann, Pte G	4848	20	KIA	AN
Miskelly, Pte J P	3609	20	KIA	RP
Oakley, Pte C V	3596	20	DOW	ES
Penfold, Pte P J	10	22	DOW	CA

Poyitt, Pte L	5193	25	DOW	BO
Purnell, Pte A	1532	20	KIA	RP
Quick, CQMS F H	3104a	20	KIA	RB
Rogers, Pte H H S	3244a	25	DOW	ES
Ross, Pte D E	4889	20	KIA	AN
Rourke, Pte H G	3242	20	KIA	AN
Rudd, Pte P M	2804a	20	KIA	RP
Rush, L/Cpl F E	4890	2.8	DOW	ES
Sturgeon, Pte W	2912	20	KIA	AN
Sullivan, Pte A T	4913	20	KIA	AN
Sweeney, Pte J L	4915	20	KIA	AN
Tuke, Pte R	3457	20	KIA	AN
Turley, Pte B L W	4924	23	DOW	BA
Walsh, Pte T	3902	20	KIA	AN
Watt, Pte J	3288	20	DOW	AN
Webber, Pte F J	4955	20	KIA	AN
Williamson, Pte A	4964	26	DOW	YF
Wilson, Pte A R	3289	9.8	DOW	WI

14th Machine Gun Coy

Briggs, 2/Lieut H F	-	20	KIA	VB
Burns, Lieut R D	-	20	KIA	VB
Carr, Pte H	3252	20	KIA	AN
Cox, Lieut A C	-	20	KIA	RB
Higgs, Cpl C	3314	24.9	DOW	RD
Hoddle-Wrigley, Lieut T	-	20	KIA	VB
James, Pte F	3347	20	KIA	VC
Jordan, Pte R	2934	20	KIA	VC
Lauder, Pte J	2722	20	DOW	AN
Lee, Pte N T	2779	20	KIA	VC
(aka Atwell, Pte S H)				
Lowe, Pte A E	2869	20	KIA	AN
Luke, Pte C S	2856	20	KIA	VC
McKay, Pte F W	3182	20	KIA	VC
Moore, Cpl C J	2394	20	KIA	VB
Richards, Sgt S	2972	20	KIA	VA
Rogerson, Pte G	3163	20	KIA	CR
Stalgis, Cpl G F	2898	20	KIA	VC
Wotten, Pte C R	3469	20	KIA	RB

14th Field Coy Engineers

Ashdown, Spr C P	5363	20	KIA	AN
Davidson, 2/Cpl G D	721	15.8	DOW	ES
Ettingshausen, Spr H V	5376	20	KIA	VC
Ferguson, Lieut J S	-	27	DOW	UB
Murray, Spr R N	5651	20	KIA	RP
Norton, Spr H	1606	19	KIA	VC
Sainty, Spr F L	2426	20	KIA	VC

14th Light Trench Mortar

Hopkins, Capt. C B	-	20	KIA	RB
Kenning, Pte J	4824	19	KIA	AN
McDowell, Pte J S P	1981	20	KIA	RB

15th BRIGADE

57th Battalion

Abrahamson, Pte A	2555	20	KIA	RB
Adams, Pte F C	1651	19.8	DOW	WI
Anderson, 2/Lieut E H	-	20	KIA	VC
Anglin, Pte M	4428	20	KIA	RB
Arbon, Pte R E	4429	19	DOW	UR
Brown, Pte W E	3035	2.8	DOW	ES
Buchan, Pte W F	4445	21	KIA	RB
Bull, Sgt W W	3036	20	KIA	RB
Clayton, Pte A N	1526	21.8	DOW	ES
Davies, Sgt H M	185	22	DOW	ES
Eldershaw, Pte A G	4963	20	KIA	RB
Farnell, Pte A E	3466	9.8	DOW	ES
Fernance, Pte A	2359	20	KIA	RB
Ferrari, Pte J W	4484	20	KIA	RB
Fraser, Pte J W	2366	9.9	DOW	AN
Freeman, Pte H	1897	14.8	DOW POW	MB
Grant, Pte S W	4500	20	KIA	RB
Ingleton, Pte C H	3840	24	DOW	XM
Jason, L/Cpl C V	2399	4.9	DOW	CR
Jenkin, Pte G E	171	19	KIA	VC
Jessop, Sgt A E	1120	13.8	DOW	ES
Kerr, Sgt A	3573	20	KIA	RB
McConnell, Pte W J N	4181	22	DOW	CA
Morrison, Pte H H	4855	27	DOW	BO
Moulton, Sgt L L	2744	26	DOW	CA
O'Brien, Pte R	3679	20.8	DOW	ES
Robertson, Pte A F	2882	20	KIA	RB
Savolainen, Pte A J	4228	20	KIA	RB
Simons, Pte J J	3608	20	KIA	RB
Strahan, Sgt A	2867	20	DOW	BA
Williams, L/Cpl E C	3653	15.8	DOW	XL

58th Battalion

KIA & DOW German Raid 14/15 July

Aitken, Pte J A	2812	15	KIA	VB
Anderson, Cpl A R G	4827	15	KIA	VB
Baker, Pte J H	3682	15	KIA	RP
Bogue, Pte T	3023	15	KIA	RP
Bray, Pte W R	2326	15	KIA	RP
Broomhall, Pte J	4024	15	KIA	RP
Bruce, Sgt G H	3026	15	KIA	RP
Bryant, Cpl N H	3027	15	KIA	RP
Campbell, Pte W	3489	17	DOW	ES
Cartledge, Pte L A	2597	17	DOW	ES
Cations, Pte W J	3485	15	KIA	VB
Challis, Sgt G D	2595	15	KIA	RP
Christie, Pte J S	3483	16	DOW	ES
Clayton, Pte J H	3709	15	KIA	RP
Clinch, Pte E	2790	15	KIA	RP
Everett, Pte G J	3506	15	KIA	RP
Farrar, Pte R C	3515	15	KIA	RP
Gannon, Pte F J	3532	15	KIA	RP
Gordon, Pte P L D	4497	15	KIA	RP
Grundy, Pte A	1770	18	DOW	LO
Gye, Pte S C	2650	15	KIA	RP
Hambling, Pte H R	3550	15	KIA	RP
Hewitt, Pte R	3035	15	KIA	RP
Johnston, Pte J H	2847	15	KIA	VB
Johnston, Pte P A	3561	15	KIA	RP
Kelsall, Pte J	3570	15	KIA	VB
Kidston, Pte E B	3057	15	KIA	RP
Lewis, Sgt H C	3166	15	KIA	RB

Lockhead, Sgt W	3167	15	KIA	VB
Lodge, Pte G L	3588	15	KIA	RP
Looney, Pte L	3562	15	KIA	RP
Mair, Capt. E H	-	15	KIA	RP
Mayo, Pte G A	3603	15	KIA	RP
Morgan, Pte J E	2720	15	KIA	VB
Muir, Pte A E	4549	17	DOW	RB
Mulconry, Pte S J	4860	15	KIA	RP
Newton, Pte T J	3196	15	KIA	RP
O'Connor, Pte J R	3515a	15	KIA	RP
O'Shannassy, Pte A N	2531	15	KIA	RP
Parker, Pte I L	3618	16	KIA	VB
Pilven, Pte H	3621	15	KIA	RP
Quinn, Pte V W	3900	15	KIA	VB
Simmons, L/Cpl E Y W	3253	15	KIA	RP
Twitt, Pte F T	3276	15	KIA	RP
White, Pte H G	2697	16	DOW	ES
Wootton, Pte A J	3668	15	KIA	RP

58th Battalion: Main Battle 19/20 July

Allen, Pte D C	401	19	KIA	VC
Allen, Pte R S	3458	19	KIA	VC
Apperley, Pte F C	2777	19	KIA	VC
Aspinall, Pte W H	3010	19	KIA	VC
Baines, Pte C V	2560	19	KIA	VC
Baker, Pte J L B	3002	22	DOW	BA
Barnes, Pte W G	3463	1.9	DOW	ES
Barnfather, Lieut A E R	-	19	KIA	VC
Bassett, CSM E A	2785	19	KIA	VC
Batten, Pte A T	4751	3.8	DOW	BO
Bird, Sgt C G	2572	19	KIA	RP
Bond, Pte W A	2577	19	KIA	AR
Bond, Pte W E E	4296	19	KIA	VC
Bowden, Pte E	4442	22	DOW	LO
Bright, Pte E H	2565	19	KIA	VC
Browne, Pte P	3043	19	KIA	VC
Bruce, Pte G O	602	19	KIA	VC
Bunn, Cpl E	3311	19	KIA	RB
Butler, Pte J T	2571	19	KIA	VC
Carr, Pte W C G	4452	31	DOW	BA
Chandler, Pte T	2597	19	KIA	VC
Chapple, Pte R C	2598	19	KIA	RF
Clarke, Pte A R	3266	22	DOW	BA
Clarke, Pte T L	3055	19	KIA	VC
Collins, Pte C	3063	19	KIA	RB
Connor, Pte A A	3496	30	DOW	CA
Coogan, Pte M T	3064	19	KIA	VC
Cooper, Pte T M	4465a	19	KIA	VC
Daly, Pte J F	4643	19	KIA	RB
Daly, Pte W W	4474	22	DOW	BA
Davis, Pte F H	4471	19	KIA	RB
Deakin, Pte G R	2616	19	KIA	VC
Dial, Pte G J F (aka Dakin, Pte G)	4470	19	KIA	RB
Dobson, Sgt W J	2148	20	DOW	ES
Duncan, Pte W	2622	19	KIA	VC
Dupe, Pte C S	3500	19	KIA	RB
Eade, Pte F	4187	31	DOW	SS
Ellis, L/Cpl A H	3125	19	KIA	VC
Ellis, Pte R P	1698	19	KIA	VC
Fair, Pte F R	4484	19	KIA	VC
Ferguson, Pte A E	3038	2.8	DOW	UE
Ferguson, Pte W	1750	19	KIA	RB
Fleet, Pte A G	3098	23	DOW	BA
Flynn, Sgt E J	639	20	DOW	AN
George, Pte W E	4797	12.8	DOW	UF
Gilchrist, Pte E M	5695	18.9	DOW	ES
Gill, Pte M W	3535	19	KIA	NI
Glew, Pte C R	3531	19	KIA	VC
Gray, Lieut C M	-	19	KIA	VC
Hannan, Sgt E	3307	19	KIA	VC
Hansen, Pte H	3016	19	KIA	VC
Hargreaves, Pte E G	3542	19	KIA	VC
Harvey, Sgt R M	2503	19	KIA	VC
Hearle, Pte E R	2599	21	DOW	UG
Hegarty, Cpl A	2857	20	DOW	AN
Hills, Pte G R	3775	1.8	DOW	CA
Hollioake, Pte P	4510	19	KIA	VC
Hunter, Pte J	4816	19	KIA	VC
Hutcheson, Pte W T	3808	19	KIA	VC
Hutchinson, Maj A J S	-	19	KIA	VC
James, Pte F	106	19	KIA	RB
Jasper, Pte B	3378	19	KIA	VC
Johnston, Cpl W	726	19	KIA	VC
Keen, Pte G C	3159	25.8	DOW	LO
Kenny, Sgt A R	3158	19	KIA	VC
Knight, Pte S	4814	19	KIA	VC
Lamb, Pte J J	3574	19	KIA	VC
Landy, Pte W J	3581	19	KIA	VC
Latta, Lieut C H	-	23	DOW	CA
Leary, Pte A B	3586	19	KIA	VC
Leech, Sgt A	3164	19	KIA	PH
Lepp, Sgt A E	4539	19	KIA	RF
Lock, Pte A A	2707	21	DOW	BO
Madgwick, Pte H W	2875	20	DOW	BO
Maxwell, Pte R	2726	21	DOW	BO
McDonald, Pte L J	3199	19	KIA	VC
McGregor, Sgt A F	2213	21	DOW	BO
McLean, Pte H W	3890	19	KIA	VC
Millich, Pte C T	3118	23	DOW	LO
Morphett, Pte G H	2647	25.8	DOW	LO
Nash, Pte C B	1865	18.9	DOW POW	CR
Nolan, Sgt W	3201	23	DOW	BO
O'Neill, Pte J F	3610	19	KIA	VC
Partridge, Pte S C	3126	1.9	DOW	LO
Payne, Pte A R	4569	19	KIA	VC
Pearson, Pte W J	1808	19	KIA	VC
Phillips, Pte W C	4567	19	KIA	RB
Plozza, Pte J	2420	19	KIA	VC
Rae, Pte W	4915	14.8	DOW	ES
Ryan, Pte J E	4576	19	KIA	YF
Scott, Lieut G N	-	19	KIA	VC
Smith, Pte C H	3256	19	KIA	VC
Smith, Pte S	4189	19	KIA	VC
Smithers, Pte R C N	2454	19	KIA	RB
Stevenson, Pte D B	4595	19	KIA	VC

Thomas, Pte D H	2812	12.8	DOW	BO
Thomas, Pte J R	3482	19	KIA	AR
Trigg, Pte R L	3681	19	KIA	VC
Watt, L/Sgt G	3288	19	KIA	VC
Whitehill, Pte J A	3281	19	KIA	VC
Williams, Pte E	4621	19	KIA	VC
Williams, Pte T E	4615	19	KIA	VC

59th Battalion

Affleck, Pte D C	3451	19	KIA	VC
Aitken, Pte T	3003b	19	KIA	PH
Allen, Cpl C P	4729	23	DOW	BA
Alliss, Pte G S	4727	23	DOW	BA
Anderson, Pte J	3003a	19	KIA	VC
Andrews, Sgt G	1503	19	KIA	VC
Armstrong, Pte L	2778	19	KIA	VC
Baker, Pte P	3453	19	KIA	VC
Balfour, Pte A G	2565	19	KIA	VC
Bambury, Pte J	762	19	KIA	VC
Barber, Pte W E	3012	19	DOW	AN
Barclay, Pte C W	3005	3.8	DOW	BO
Barker, Pte J G	1308	19	KIA	VC
Bastin, Pte W J A	2789	19	KIA	VC
Beard, Pte F A	4146	30	DOW	UD
Bell, Pte A F	3239	24	DOW	BO
Bellingham, Pte P J	2560	19	KIA	VC
Bennett, Pte C J	3240	19	KIA	VC
Benton, Pte A	2569	19	KIA	VC
Beston, Pte T J	2334	19	KIA	VC
Bethune, L/Cpl R C	3672	19	KIA	VC
Bevan, Pte G A	4973	19	KIA	VC
Bicket, Pte J A	2570	28.8	DOW	BO
Biggs, Pte W F	3022a	19	KIA	VC
Bill, Pte C	2792	19	KIA	VC
Bishop, Pte T C	3691	19	KIA	AR
Blake, Pte G F	4737	19	KIA	RF
Blee, Pte G G	3009	19	KIA	VC
Bond, Pte R R	2559	19	KIA	CR
Bond, Pte W J	3466a	19	KIA	VC
Botterill, Pte F C	4736	19	KIA	VC
Bowden, Lieut J C	-	19	KIA	VC
Boyce, Pte A J	1664	19	KIA	VC
Boyd, Pte A J	3689	19	KIA	AR
Boyd, Pte H J	2562	19	KIA	VC
Brache, Pte M W	4738	19	KIA	AR
Bradshaw, Pte F J	4749	19	KIA	VC
Breslin, Pte T	1914	19	KIA	RF
Brinckmann, Pte H C	2327	19	KIA	VC
Brown, L/Cpl A M	2584	19	KIA	VC
Brown, Pte F H	4740	19	KIA	VC
Brownridge, Pte J	1843	19	KIA	VC
Brunston, Pte H	4745	19	KIA	YF
Burden, Pte A H A	3038	19	KIA	AR
Burford, Pte J H	4762	19	KIA	VC
Butler, Pte A	3267	19	KIA	VC
Byrne, Pte F T	3321	19	KIA	VC
Cahill, Pte W P	3281	19	KIA	VC
Cain, Pte W J	3037	19	KIA	VC
Caines, Pte P C	4748	19	KIA	VC
Cameron, Pte N	2618	19	KIA	VC
Campbell, Pte A	3042a	19	KIA	VC
Cant, Pte C R	2590	19	KIA	VC
Cantwell, Pte J W	2591	19	KIA	RF
Carr, Lieut E T W	-	19	KIA	VC
Charles, Pte W S	3773a	19	KIA	RF
Christian, Pte C O J	2827	19	KIA	VC
Christie, Pte J L	3054	19	KIA	VC
Christie, Pte W J	4751	19	KIA	VC
Clark, Pte S T C	3053	19	KIA	VC
Clarke, Pte O J	4978	19	KIA	VC
Clayden, L/Cpl A J	3292	25	DOW	UB
Clements, Cpl H G	4076	19	KIA	VC
Clements, L/Cpl V J	3055	19	KIA	RP
Cobbett, Pte W	4753	1.8	DOW	CA
Coleman, Pte W J	818	19	KIA	YF
Connor, Pte E D	4783	19	KIA	VC
Cooper, Pte H A	3482	19	KIA	VC
Corin, Pte E A	3715	19	KIA	VC
Cosgriff, Pte T J	2150	19	KIA	VC
Cotter, Pte W	4462	19	KIA	VC
Cousins, Lieut F L	-	19	KIA	VC
Cox, Pte E T	2211	19	KIA	VC
Crow, Pte W F	3277	19	KIA	VC
Cunningham, Pte A J	2349	19	KIA	VC
Currie, Pte W W	4764	31.10	DOW	TD
Curtis, Pte F G	3284	19	KIA	VC
Dale, Pte F	3718	19	KIA	VC
Daley, Pte C H	3535	19	KIA	AR
Dalzell, L/Cpl B A	3299	19	KIA	VC
Daniel, Pte H G	2849	19	KIA	VC
Davies, Pte H G	864	19	KIA	VC
Davis, Pte G Y	3503	25	DOW	WI
Dewsnap, Pte J W	3027	19	KIA	VC
Dixon, Pte F A	2575	19	KIA	VC
Dobson, Sgt D	3289	19	KIA	RB
Donahoo, Pte M F	3091	19	KIA	AR
Duffy, Pte J C	1694	19	KIA	VC
Duncan, Pte G R	4790	19	KIA	VC
Dunstan, Pte E W	5375	19	KIA	VC
Dwyer, Pte F	3086	11.8	DOW	UB
Edney, Pte J E	2625a	19	KIA	VC
Ellis, Pte A W G	4075	19	KIA	VC
Elsden, Pte H R	4776	19	KIA	VC
Emery, Pte H E	3540	28	DOW	UJ
Farrelly, Pte M	3170	19	KIA	VC
Ferns, Pte W	3727	19	KIA	NI
Fitton, Pte W R	4782	19	KIA	AR
Fitzgerald, Pte J L	2474	19	KIA	VC
Flack, Pte A W	1706	19	KIA	VC
Fletcher, Pte J K	3733	19	KIA	VC
Fletcher, Pte J M	1704	19	KIA	VC
Flowers, Pte W F C	3732	19	KIA	VC
Forster, Pte H	3097	19	KIA	VC
Frazer, Pte R J	3282	19	KIA	VC
Frew, Pte L G	3519	3.8	DOW	UH
Fulton, Pte A R	3738	19	KIA	VC

Gaborit, Pte T L	3314	19	KIA	VC
Galloway, Pte T	3979	19	KIA	VC
Gandy, Pte J F	3739	22	DOW	WI
Garry, Pte W	4798	19	KIA	VC
Geal, Pte A	4821	19	KIA	VC
Gibbs, Lieut R H M	-	19	KIA	VC
Giblett, Pte C W	2639	19	KIA	VC
Gibson, Pte A L	1742	21	DOW	LO
Gilfoy, Pte H	2641	26	DOW	CA
Gill, Cpl W A	1551	19	KIA	VC
Gillespie, CSM D F	3037	27.3.17	DOW	PR
Gillies, Pte W	3071	10.8	DOW	CA
Ginman, Pte G L	3539	10.8	DOW	BO
Gittoes, Pte E C	2213	19	KIA	VC
Goldby, Sgt W	3550	19	KIA	VC
Goldie, L/Cpl C E	1553	19	KIA	VC
Goldsmith, L/Cpl R G H	3063	19	KIA	VC
Goodwin, Pte A B H	2671	19	KIA	VC
Grace, Pte G H	2798	19	KIA	VC
Gray, Pte J M	2799	19	KIA	VC
Green, Cpl S F W H	3036	19	KIA	VC
Gregory, Pte C C	3110	19	KIA	AR
Grenville, Pte V	1811	19	KIA	RB
Grumont, Sgt C A	3062	19	KIA	VC
Halloran, Pte T	3134	19	KIA	VC
Harbert, Pte H B	2173	19	KIA	VC
Harris, Pte R	2073	19	KIA	VC
Hart, Pte J E	3766	19	KIA	VC
Hart, Pte W H G	2811	19	KIA	VC
Hayes, Sgt H S	3769	19	KIA	VC
Henderson, Pte F A	3348	19	KIA	VC
Henning, Pte G E	3085	16.8	DOW	UC
Herriott, Pte W E	3364	14.8	DOW	UV
Heward, L/Cpl F H	3317	19	KIA	VC
Hills, Pte G R	3775	1.8	DOW	CA
Hind, Pte J	3066	19	KIA	VC
Hitzeroth, Pte G R	4800	19	KIA	VC
Holmes, L/Cpl E C	4115	19	KIA	VC
Holten, Pte R F	2948	19	KIA	RP
Hosie, L/Cpl G G	2844	19	KIA	VC
Hotham, Pte C J	1679	19	KIA	VC
Howard, Lieut H C	-	19	KIA	NI
Humphreys, L/Cpl H	1642	19	KIA	VC
Hunt, Sgt A	3046	13.8	DOW	UL
Hunt, Sgt W H	3357	19	KIA	VC
Hunter, Pte D	4816	19	KIA	VC
Hunter, Pte R A	3784	19	KIA	VC
Hutcheson, Pte D W	2824	19	KIA	VC
Jackson, Pte A H J	4522	19	KIA	AR
Jacobs, Pte L J	1773	19	KIA	RP
Jamieson, Pte J Y	2473	19	KIA	AR
Jennings, Pte W W A	1810	19	KIA	RB
Jessop, Pte S	1692	19	KIA	VC
Jewell, Pte H J	2957	19	KIA	VC
Johnson, Cpl R W	3367	19	KIA	VC
Johnston, Pte A A	3372	20	DOW	BA
Johnston, Pte A	3524	19	KIA	RB
Jones, Pte J	3151	19	KIA	VC
Joyce, Pte C E	36	19	KIA	RB
Kennedy, Pte J	4823	19	KIA	RF
Kerr, Pte J C	3797	19	KIA	VC
Kiellerup, Cpl O J	3160	19	KIA	VC
King, Cpl W T T	2597	19	KIA	VC
King, Pte A W L	411	23	DOW	BO
King, Pte C	1726	21	DOW	BA
Kingston, Pte W	3042	22	DOW	BO
Ladd, Pte W H	4925	19	KIA	VC
Lake, Pte C L	1712	19	KIA	VC
Lane, Pte T A	3146	19	KIA	VC
Lear, Pte I J	4130	19	KIA	VC
Lee, Pte F A	3385	19	KIA	VC
Leigh, Pte C T	4227	19	KIA	VC
Letts, Pte J	3165	19	KIA	VC
Liddelow, Capt. A	-	19	KIA	VC
Lidgett, Pte A F	4832	19	KIA	VC
Lister, Sgt R M	3812	19	KIA	VC
Love, Pte J R	3064	19	KIA	RF
Lucas, L/Sgt H S	3816	19	KIA	VC
Lynch, Pte E G	3158a	19	KIA	VC
Maddocks, Pte J H	4828	19	KIA	RF
Mann, Pte P R	3358	19	KIA	VC
Mathews, Pte A E	2723	21	DOW	AN
Matthew, Pte A D	1595a	19	KIA	VC
Maule, Pte A J	3066	19	KIA	VC
Mayo, Cpl G J	2212	19	KIA	RF
McColl, Cpl D H	4547	19	KIA	AR
McCulloch, Pte F H A	3184	19	KIA	VC
McDonald, Pte R	1678	19	KIA	VC
McEwan, Pte T M	1743	19	KIA	VC
McGhee, Pte D	3416	19	KIA	VC
McIlroy, Pte R	1791	21	DOW	ES
McInerney, Pte W J	3007	19	KIA	VC
McInnes, Pte D	2420	19	KIA	VC
McKeone, Pte J J	3408	19	KIA	VC
McLean, Pte M	4636	19	KIA	YF
McLear, Pte C W	794	19	KIA	VC
McMahon, Pte T J	3996	19	KIA	VC
McNamara, Pte C J	3120	19	KIA	VC
McRae, Pte C R	4153	19	KIA	AR
Meginess, L/Cpl F	3840	19	KIA	VC
Merton, Pte C	3178	19	KIA	VC
Miles, Pte W O'M	3575	19	KIA	VC
Milham, Pte T S	3356	19	KIA	VC
Mills, Pte L C	3582	19	KIA	VC
Mitchell, Pte A C	2746	19	KIA	VC
Mitchell, Pte A E	4845	19	KIA	VC
Mitchell, Pte S J	2714	19	KIA	VC
Montgomery, Pte W H	2217	19	KIA	VC
Moore, Pte A	1987	26.9	DOW	UM
More-Reid, Cpl G	3180	19	KIA	VC
Morris, Pte L C	2743	19	KIA	VC
Morrow, Lieut A D	-	21	DOW	BA
Mossenton, Pte H D	2635	19	KIA	VC
Mowbray, Pte A C	3063	31	DOW	UN
Murphy, Pte C	2729	19	KIA	VC
Neil, L/Cpl L J J	2406	19	KIA	VC

Newey, Pte H R	3126	19	KIA	VC
North, Pte E F	2750	19	KIA	VC
O'Day, Pte W J	1737	19	KIA	VC
O'Hara, Pte J A	3214	19	KIA	VC
O'Keeffe, Pte W P	2628	19	KIA	VC
O'Leary, Pte J	3096	19	KIA	VC
O'Meara, Pte D J	3216	19	KIA	VC
O'Sullivan, Pte W	3867	19	DOW	AN
Olston, Pte J A	4570	19	KIA	VC
Orenshaw, Cpl W H	3871	19	KIA	VC
Outen, Pte R J	3873	19	KIA	VC
Palmer, L/Cpl W E	1404	19	KIA	VC
Pamphlet, Pte J G	3860	19	KIA	VC
Parry, Pte R D	3878	19	KIA	VC
Parsons, Pte W	4864	19	KIA	VC
Pearce, Pte R V	4564	19	KIA	VC
Peiper, Pte R F	2764	19	KIA	VC
Perkins, Pte C E	2014	19	KIA	VC
Perkins, Pte E	2421	19	KIA	VC
Perrett, Pte S C	2015	19	KIA	VC
Perry, Pte R F	3448	19	KIA	VC
Phelan, Pte J F	3894	19	KIA	VC
Phelps, L/Cpl W T	2877	19	KIA	VC
Philips, Pte A E	4768	19	KIA	VC
Phillips, L/Cpl C W	4869	19	KIA	VC
Phillips, Pte A E	1804	19	KIA	VC
Pitcher, Pte B B	4911	19	KIA	VC
Polglase, Pte C A	2884	19	KIA	VC
Powell, Pte C	1755	19	KIA	YF
Powell, Pte J	2858	19	KIA	VC
Power, Sgt A C	3895	19	KIA	RF
Prescott, Pte H H P	1757	19	KIA	AR
Rabinovitch, Pte C	1798	19	KIA	VC
Rankin, Pte S	2759	31	DOW	BO
Ratcliffe, Pte F E	4570	19	KIA	RB
Raw, L/Sgt W W	3527	19	KIA	VC
Ray, Pte A W	3231	19	KIA	NI
Read, Sgt G R	3466	25	DOW	BO
Reeves, Sgt R E	1811	19	KIA	VC
Reid, Pte C J	3897	19	KIA	AR
Richardson, Pte F	4882	19	KIA	VC
Richardson, Pte J L	4515	19	KIA	VC
Ricketts, Pte L A	3224	19	KIA	VC
Roberts, Pte C E	4252	19	KIA	VC
Rogers, Pte H E	2844a	19	KIA	VC
Rosney, Pte P J	3132	19	KIA	VC
Ross, Pte R L	3568	19	KIA	VC
Ruff, Pte V H	3225	28	DOW	UC
Russell, Pte A J	2768	21	DOW	BA
Russell, Pte F G	3129	19	KIA	VC
Russell, Pte T L	2672	19	KIA	VC
Samuel, Pte E E B	3911	19	KIA	VC
Saunders, Pte H N S	3912	19	KIA	RP
Sawyer, Pte A P	4605	19	KIA	VC
Schimlick, Pte C S	4183	19	KIA	VC
Scowcroft, Pte R	2654	19	KIA	VC
Seccombe, Pte L A	5198	11.9	DOW	ES
Serong, Pte E	4590	19	KIA	VC
Seymour, Pte J A	4903	19	KIA	VB
Sibbin, Pte G S	3922	19	KIA	VC
Simmons, Pte N T	4899	19	KIA	VC
Simpson, Pte W S	3239a	19	KIA	VC
Slattery, Pte F P	1966	19	KIA	VC
Sleigh, Pte S	3244	19	KIA	VC
Sloan, Pte R	2895	19	KIA	VC
Slockwitch, Pte A	3485	19	KIA	VC
Smith, Pte J	2786	19	KIA	VC
Smith, Pte R	2268	19	KIA	RF
South, Pte F J J	3932	19	KIA	VC
Statham, Pte G W	3241	14.8	DOW	UC
Stephens, Pte W R	3944	19	KIA	RB
Summers, Pte A V	2000	19	KIA	VC
Sydes, CSM C F	3476	19	KIA	RP
Taylor, Pte N B	3915	19	KIA	VC
Thexton, Pte J W	4609	19	KIA	VC
Thompson, Pte W H	515	19	KIA	VC
Thomson, Pte E M	2811	19	KIA	VC
Thomson, Pte G J	3652	19	KIA	VC
Tolley, Pte W A	3269	19	KIA	VC
Tracey, Pte M	959	19	KIA	VC
Trost, Pte J	3956	19	KIA	VC
Tulloch, Sgt J D	3491	19	KIA	CC
Turner, Cpl S G	1284	19	KIA	VC
Usher, Pte F G	2813	19	KIA	VC
Vaile, Lieut W H	-	24	DOW	CA
Vass, L/Sgt J J	2044	25	DOW	BA
Vennell, Pte W J	3991	19	KIA	VC
Wade, Pte S V	4951	26	DOW	CA
Walker, Pte L G	3497	19	KIA	VC
Wallis, Pte R E	2926	19	KIA	VC
Walsh, Pte H R	2896	19	KIA	VC
Watson, Pte R	2831	19	KIA	YF
Watt, Pte A	3500	19	KIA	VC
Weller, Cpl F N	4669	21	DOW	CB
Wheeler, Pte W J	3669	19	KIA	VC
Whiston, Pte F	3524	21	DOW	BA
White, Sgt W J	3155	19	KIA	RB
Whitehouse, Pte C H B	3651	21.9	DOW	BO
Whitehurst, Pte J	1449	19	KIA	VC
Whylie, Pte J A	3436	19	KIA	VC
Wicking, Pte O M	3293	19	KIA	NI
Wiggins, Pte R T	3984	19	KIA	VC
Wild, Pte E V	4916	19	KIA	VC
Wilkinson, L/Cpl W B	2830	19	KIA	VC
Willey, Pte J	1789a	19	KIA	VC
Wilson, Dvr B F	3644	19	KIA	RF
Wilson, Pte W	366	18.8	DOW	RB
Windram, Pte H C	3279	19	KIA	VC
Winfield, Pte E	3966	19	KIA	VC
Witham, Cpl S	427	19	KIA	RF
Wood, Pte D	3969	19	KIA	VC
Woodcock, Pte A	3968	19	KIA	VC
Woodhouse, Pte R L	3297	19	KIA	VC
Woodland, Pte C W	3660	21	DOW	BA
Woods, Cpl W W	2202	19	KIA	VC
Yendle, Pte G	2698	19	KIA	VC

60th Battalion

Andersen, Pte C C	3998	31	DOW	XN
Anderson, Sgt R D	2452	19	KIA	VC
Andrews, Cpl W H	2554	19	KIA	VC
Armstrong, Pte J H	3681	19	KIA	VC
Arnold, Pte E J	1901a	22	DOW	BA
Arnold, Pte W S	2329	19	KIA	VC
Arnold, Pte W	1905	19	KIA	VC
Artis, Pte A	2328	19	KIA	RB
Ashley, Pte A	3009	20	DOW	BA
Ashworth, Pte P A	1656	19	KIA	VC
Bailey, Pte A J	688	19	KIA	VC
Bailey, Pte C	2849	19	KIA	VC
Bannister, Pte W H	4065	19	KIA	VC
Bannon, Pte C C	3456	19	KIA	RB
Barger, Pte W G	3655	19	KIA	VC
Barker, Pte P	4910a	19	KIA	VC
Barnes, Pte H E	2459	19	KIA	VC
Barr, Pte C C	3479	31.8	DOW	XH
Barr, Pte D	3474a	19	KIA	VC
Barr, Pte G H	3011	19	KIA	VC
Barrett, Pte B J	4431	19	KIA	VC
Bartlett, Pte D C	3768	19	KIA	VC
Barton, Pte J	4734	19	KIA	VC
Beattie, Pte W G	1160	19	KIA	VC
Beirne, Pte W B	2562	25	DOW	WI
Betancor, Pte R J	2578	19	KIA	VC
Bicket, Pte M D	3245	19	KIA	VC
Bishop, Sgt A S	1921	9.12	DOW	UW
Bishop, Pte J H	2787a	25	DOW	WI
Bleazby, Pte G	2119	19	KIA	VC
Bloore, Pte L	3248a	19	KIA	VC
Bone, Pte R H	3461	19	KIA	VC
Bonetti, Pte E E	4747	19	KIA	VC
Bowden, Pte F A	2932	19	KIA	VC
Boyd, Pte C T	2799a	19	KIA	VC
Boyd, Pte T H C	3336	19	KIA	VC
Bradley, Pte E J	761	19	KIA	VC
Bragg, Cpl A R	2564	19	KIA	VC
Brasher, Pte W	3458	19	KIA	VC
Brear, Pte C H	4438	19	KIA	VC
Brook, Pte A S	3038	19	KIA	VC
Brown, Pte F L	3025	19	KIA	RD
Brown, Pte J H	3005	19	KIA	VC
Brown, Pte P	3694	7.8	DOW	BO
Bruce, Pte W D	1768	19	KIA	VC
Bull, Pte E L	3256	19	KIA	RB
Bullen, Pte S	3035	19	KIA	VC
Butler, Pte W W C	2333	19	KIA	VC
Cahill, A/Sgt R N	2812	24	DOW	BO
Caldwell, Pte E T	2816	19	KIA	VC
Callen, Pte A	3056	5.8	DOW	UH
Cameron, Cpl C B V	3039a	19	KIA	VC
Cameron, Cpl E A	3040	19	KIA	VC
Cameron, Pte L G	4769a	19	KIA	VC
Campbell, Pte J H	3062	9.8	DOW	CA
Candy, Pte G	3060b	19	KIA	VC
Carlin, Pte G	1529	19	KIA	VC
Carroll, Pte P	1920	19	KIA	VC
Carter, Pte J	1527	13.10	DOW	LO
Cassell, Pte A	1883	19	KIA	VC
(aka Meadows, Pte R)				
Catchpole, Pte E E	1899	20	KIA	RB
Chamberlain, Pte F	2596a	19	KIA	VC
Charles, Pte H	3050b	22	DOW	BA
Christensen, Pte D	4454	19	KIA	RB
Claridge, Pte C R	2600	19	KIA	VC
Clark, Pte A	3050	19	KIA	YF
Clarke, Pte A R	3266	22	DOW	BA
Clarke, Pte T G	2830	19	KIA	VC
Clayton, Pte C J	850	19	KIA	VC
Clery, Pte A	2600a	19	KIA	VC
Clout, Pte L W F	4965	19	KIA	VC
Cohen, Pte C S	3583	19	KIA	VC
Collins, Pte G S	2835	19	KIA	VC
Condon, Pte J C	3082	19	KIA	VC
Conley, Pte J	3063	19	KIA	RF
Conway, CSM J	988	19	KIA	VC
Cook, Pte J W	3281	24	DOW	WI
Cooper, Pte H E J	3067	19	KIA	VC
Cottren, Pte A E C	3050a	19	KIA	RP
Coubrough, Pte V T J	4305	19	KIA	YF
Cowl, Pte R H	3019a	19	KIA	VC
Crammond, L/Cpl J H	2605	19	KIA	VC
Currie, Pte J	3717	19	KIA	VC
Curwen, Pte V R A	3017a	19	KIA	VC
Dalton, Pte A V W	2497	19	KIA	VC
Daly, Pte J M	3715	19	KIA	VC
Davies, Pte P G	3087	19	KIA	VC
Davis, Pte J	3289	19	KIA	VC
Dawson, Pte T J	3323	19	KIA	VC
De Lisle, Pte C V	2350	19	KIA	VC
De Melker, Sgt J H W	485	19	KIA	VC
Delaney, Pte P A	2470	19	KIA	VC
Dicker, Pte C W	3500	19	KIA	RB
Dixon, Pte F	3717a	19	KIA	VC
Docter, Pte T C	2612	19	KIA	VC
Donaldson, Pte F H	3088	19	KIA	VC
Doney, Pte A	3084	21	DOW	BA
Donohue, Pte W P	3290	19	KIA	VC
Douglas, Pte J A	1674	19	KIA	RB
Drew, CQMS E J	1150	20	DOW	ES
Dugdale, Cpl B R	465	19	KIA	VC
Easom, Pte W C	4771	19	KIA	VC
East, Pte B	1846	19	KIA	VC
Eddy, Pte R	3723	19	KIA	VC
Edwards, Pte H H	2361	19	KIA	VC
Edwards, Pte J L	3739	19	KIA	VC
Elliott, Maj. T P		19	KIA	VC
Elliott, Pte P W	3802	19	KIA	VC
Engel, Pte A F	1916	19	KIA	RF
Evans, Capt. E A		20	KIA	VC
Evans, Pte F A	4803	19	KIA	VC
Fackrell, Pte L J	1700	19	KIA	VC
Fargher, Pte P A	2022	19	KIA	VC
Fletcher, Pte E D	4911a	19	KIA	RD
Fletcher, Pte W	376	19	KIA	VC
Flowers, Pte F	3512a	19	KIA	VC

Fogarty, Pte J P	2184	19	KIA	VC
Forrest, Pte M T	3676	19	KIA	RB
Forsyth, Pte J W	3760a	19	KIA	VC
Fowler, Pte W H	3102	19	KIA	VC
Franklin, Pte C W	3105	19	KIA	VC
Franklin, Pte H L	3104	19	KIA	VC
Fraser, Pte A G	1703	19	KIA	VC
Frazer, Pte A A	4105	19	KIA	VC
Fry, Pte A G	1926	19	KIA	VC
Gibson, Cpl A E	2133	25	DOW	UE
Gibson, L/Cpl V R	1133	19	KIA	RF
Gilbee, Pte F G	4494	19	KIA	VC
Given, Pte A M	2929	19	KIA	VC
Gleeson, Pte D J	3549	19	KIA	VC
Gregory, Pte F	2802	19	KIA	VC
Griffiths, Pte C V	4793	19	KIA	VC
Grogan, Sgt V M	3114	19	KIA	VC
Groom, Pte W C	3042a	29	DOW	WI
Ground, Capt. H O		22	DOW	BA
Gunn, Pte E I	1797	19	KIA	VC
Hales, Pte H G	2363	22	DOW	HA
Hamilton, Pte H T	4505	19	KIA	VC
Hamilton, Pte W	4275	19	KIA	VC
Hammond, Pte W H	3124	19	KIA	VC
Hannan, Pte J R	1162	30	DOW	BO
Hansen, Pte J J	3006	19	KIA	VC
Harrison, Pte M	3118a	19	KIA	VC
Harrison, Pte T	3325	28	DOW	UO
Harry, Pte S H	3313	19	KIA	VC
Hart, Pte J J	3148	19	KIA	VC
Havey, Pte V	1108	19	KIA	VC
Hawkins, Pte R W	3122	23	DOW	BA
Heather, Pte H G	2815	19	KIA	VC
Heeps, Pte E S	3166	19	KIA	VC
Heggie, L/Cpl A D	3531a	19	KIA	VC
Henderson, Pte E A	3798	19	KIA	VC
Henderson, Pte L D	2603	19	KIA	VC
Hoberg, Pte T G	2871	19	KIA	VC
Holst, Pte F G	2925	19	KIA	VC
Hopkins, Pte B D	3250	19	KIA	VC
(aka Botting, Pte B D)				
Hopper, Pte H	4653	19	KIA	VC
Horsley, L/Cpl R	1241	19	KIA	VC
Hosie, Pte R W	1948	19	KIA	VC
Howes, Pte E	1946	19	KIA	VC
Humphries, Pte J H	4654	19	KIA	VC
Hussey, Pte C	2664	19	KIA	VC
Incledon, Sgt E G	35	19	KIA	VC
Irvine, Pte J McD	4824	19	KIA	VC
Jackson, Pte T	4140	19	KIA	VC
Jacobs, Pte A	3340	19.8	DOW	CA
Jenkin, Pte F H	3547	25	DOW	BO
Jewell, Sgt W B T	189	19	KIA	VC
Jones, Pte C D	1707	19	KIA	VC
Jones, Pte G	2392	19	KIA	VC
Jones, Pte H E	194	19	KIA	VC
Jones, Pte M S	3793	19	KIA	VC
Jones, Pte R	3544	19	KIA	VC
Jones, Sgt G E	798	19	KIA	VC
Jourdain, Pte A W	3155	19	KIA	VC
Kann, Pte S	3794	19	KIA	VC
Keegan, Pte W W	3141	19	KIA	VC
Kelly, Pte J	2868	19	KIA	VC
Kenny, Pte W A	3155a	19	KIA	VC
Kerr, Pte H	2486	19	KIA	VC
Kett, Pte J L	3061	19	KIA	VC
King, Pte W J	1251	19	KIA	VC
Kingham, Pte J H	1710	20	KIA	RB
Kingsford, Pte S F	3162	19	KIA	VC
Knight, Cpl P T	3552	19	KIA	VC
Lakeman, Pte S	1971	19	KIA	VC
Lancaster, Pte J W	3088a	19	KIA	VC
Latham, Pte P J	2958	19	KIA	RF
Layton, Pte W H	3566	19	KIA	VB
Le Roy, Pte A	207	19	KIA	VC
Lee, Cpl J E	94	19	KIA	VC
Lee, L/Cpl W	3071	19	KIA	VC
Leheny, Pte G D	3807	19	KIA	VC
Lennox, Cpl R T	997	19	KIA	VC
Letcher, Cpl J G	158	19	KIA	VC
Little, Pte S	4132	19	KIA	VC
Lock, Pte C W	3866	19	KIA	VC
Lockett, Cpl H	3400	19	KIA	VC
Luckhurst, Pte A G	2620	19	KIA	VC
Ludwig, Pte A E	5135	5.10	DOW	RB
Lukey, Pte C W M	3626	19	KIA	VC
Lynch, Pte M	219	19	KIA	VC
Mackay, Pte G	4834	19	KIA	VC
MacKenzie, Pte R H	2631	19	KIA	VC
Maclaren, Pte F F	2101	19	KIA	VC
Maidment, Pte H	3137a	19	KIA	VC
Maning, Pte H A B	4929	19	KIA	VC
Mannall, Pte C	2891	31.7	DOW	BO
Marshall, Pte H	1745	19	KIA	VC
Marshall, Sgt A C	3175	19	KIA	VC
Martin, Pte C J	2836b	19	KIA	VC
Martin, Pte F W	3183	19	KIA	VC
Mathieson, Pte C G	3084	19	KIA	VC
Matthews, Pte J E	3174	19	KIA	VC
Mays, Pte W H J	2644	19	KIA	VC
McCaul, Pte D C	1980	19	KIA	VC
McClaren, Pte G H	2884	19	KIA	RF
McClure, Pte W C	3858	19	KIA	VC
McCooke, Pte J	1631	19	KIA	VC
McCrae, Maj. G G		19	KIA	RB
McDermott, Pte W R P	3415	19	KIA	VC
McDowell, Sgt A H	3194	19	KIA	VC
McEwan, Pte A J	2643	19	KIA	RF
McIntosh, Sgt J D	913	19	KIA	VC
McKenna, Sgt R J	414	19	KIA	VC
McKenzie, L/Cpl K F	3208	19	KIA	VC
McKenzie, L/Cpl M	2883	9.8	DOW	CA
McKenzie, Pte J	1974	19	KIA	VC
McKenzie, Pte J	3201	19	KIA	VC
McKinery, Pte J P	1824a	19	KIA	VC
McKinnon, CSM J A	495	19	KIA	VC
McKinnon, Lieut A C		19	KIA	VC
McLean, Pte A L	3200	19	KIA	VC

McLean, Pte V H	3209	19	KIA	VC
McManus, Pte P	3831	19	KIA	VC
McManus, Pte S C	2719	19	KIA	VC
Mildren, Pte W J	4851	19	KIA	VC
Miller, Pte R C	2736	19	KIA	VC
Miller, Pte W H	2735	19	KIA	VC
Milligan, Pte W H	4547	19	KIA	VC
Mogg, Pte L	2901	19	KIA	VC
Molloy, Pte H McD	3579	19	KIA	VC
Moore, Pte J J	2648	19	KIA	VC
Morgan, Pte R E	3562	19	KIA	VC
Morley, Sgt E J	3190	19	KIA	VC
Mortimer, Cpl A E	3191	19	KIA	VC
Morton, Pte V E	3059	19	KIA	VC
Mullin, Pte H	3844	19	KIA	VC
Munro, Pte J E	1725a	19	KIA	VC
Murray, Sgt W	171	19	KIA	VC
Murrowood, Pte G T	3194a	1.8	DOW	UN
Murton, Pte H R	2904	19	KIA	VC
Nash, Pte F	3198	24	DOW	BA
Nathan, L/Sgt F J	3436	19	KIA	VC
Naylor, Pte J	4970	19	KIA	VC
Neill, Pte T	3847	19	KIA	VC
Nelson, Pte M	3197	19	KIA	VC
Newman, Pte A E	2279	19	KIA	VC
Nitchie, Pte J L	416	19	KIA	VC
Noble, Pte N J	3595	19	KIA	VC
Norris, Pte L J	2098	19	KIA	VC
Nott, Pte W E	1736	19	KIA	VC
Nunn, Pte S M	3212	19	KIA	VC
O'Connor, Pte G A	4991	19	KIA	VC
O'Grady, Pte J	4192	19	KIA	VC
O'Grady, Pte P A	3423	19	KIA	VC
O'Neill, Pte F	4867	19	KIA	VC
Olney, Pte E P	3869	19	KIA	VC
Orchard, Pte M H	4875	19	KIA	VC
Oriel, Pte W H	3100a	19	KIA	VC
Osmond, Pte W W	4268	19	KIA	VC
Paice, Pte V A G	2777	19	KIA	VC
Pattison, Pte H	3605	19	KIA	VC
Peart, Pte R C	2872	19	KIA	VC
Pegler, Pte J	2233a	19	KIA	VC
Pemberton, Pte T A	2255	19	KIA	VC
Penaluna, Pte E B	3584	19	KIA	VC
Pengelly, Pte A	4865	19	KIA	VC
Perry, Pte A J	3440	20	KIA	RB
Phillips, Pte E J	1743	19	KIA	VC
Pinniger, Pte J L	3982	23	DOW	CA
Plowman, Capt. H McD		19	KIA	VC
Pollard, Pte F J	3615	19	KIA	VC
Potts, Pte H V	2749	19	KIA	RD
Power, Pte A P	3894	19	KIA	VC
Power, Pte W H	2893	19	KIA	VC
Power, Sgt G	43a	19	KIA	VC
Pritchard, Pte H R	3115a	19	KIA	VC
Prosser, Pte R	3215	21	DOW	BA
Purcell, Pte J J	2655	19	KIA	YF
Purvis, Pte R	1748a	19	KIA	VC
Rafferty, Pte R C	4889	8.8	DOW	BA

Rahilly, Pte P V	4994	19	KIA	VC
Rainsbury, Pte G	2736a	19	KIA	VC
Rainsbury, Pte W	4769	19	KIA	VC
Ralston, CQMS J	1382	19	KIA	VC
Ramsay, Pte G S	3131a	19	KIA	VC
Rattray, Pte A A	1342	19	KIA	VC
Reeves, Pte A	3458a	19	KIA	VC
Reynolds, Pte C W	3899	19	KIA	VC
Reynolds, Pte G W	3134	19	KIA	VC
Rhind, Lieut J M		19	KIA	VC
Richardson, Pte P S	3904	19	KIA	VC
Roach, Pte E	3565	19	KIA	RF
Roberts, Pte A J	941	19	KIA	VC
Robertson, Pte W	4579	19	KIA	VC
Robinson, Pte A D	2889	19	KIA	VC
Rogers, Pte R C	3342	19	KIA	VC
Rogers, Pte S A	3139a	19	KIA	VC
Rojo, Pte E F	2786	19	KIA	VC
Roney, Pte G	3906	19	KIA	VC
Routley, Sgt R F	3243	19	KIA	VC
Rowe, Pte W A	3598	19	KIA	RD
Ryan, Pte C T	3501	19	KIA	VC
Ryan, Pte W	3244	19	KIA	VC
Salter, Pte R S	339	19	KIA	VC
Salton, Pte A	3934	10.9	DOW	ES
Santwyk, Pte H M	3134	19	KIA	VC
Sawers, Pte S S	4589	19	KIA	VC
Scott, Pte A A	2797	19	KIA	VC
Sergeant, Pte H T	2300	19	KIA	VC
Sharp, Pte H G K	3650	21	DOW	AN
Shawe, Pte W C	3249	19	KIA	RB
Sheehan, Pte F	4210	19	KIA	VC
Sheen, Pte J	1795	20	DOW	BA
Sheldrick, Pte R	2477	19	KIA	VC
Shephard, Pte G A	2776	19	KIA	VC
Shephard, Pte T H P	2778	19	KIA	VC
Shine, Pte H F	2884a	19	KIA	VC
Shore, Pte J	4239	19	KIA	RB
Shurmer, Pte R S	3885	19	KIA	VC
Silver, Pte J	2390	19	KIA	VC
Simpson, Pte J J	4909a	31	DOW	UP
Sims, Pte J E T	4939	19	KIA	VC
Sitlington, Pte A F	452	19	KIA	AA
Slattery, Pte G M	272	19	KIA	RB
Smith, 2/Lieut J H		20	KIA	RB
Smith, Pte J H A	2679	21	DOW	BA
Smith, Pte J J	3263	22	DOW	BO
Smyth, L/Sgt H B	638	19	KIA	VC
Smyth, Pte H W	3934	19	KIA	VC
Spooner, Pte E M	2663	31	DOW	UJ
Spooner, Pte J E	3941	19	KIA	VC
Sterling, Lieut J H		19	KIA	VC
Steward, Pte F J	2796	19	KIA	VC
Stobans, Pte G	2902	19	KIA	VC
Stuart-Murray, Cpl S T H	823	24	DOW	BA
Sullivan, Pte A J	2793	19	KIA	VC
Sullivan, Pte J H	3472	19	KIA	VC
Summers, L/Cpl D	635	19	KIA	VC
Terry, Pte E H	3640	19	KIA	VC

Thompson, Pte E J	3638	19	KIA	VC
Thomson, Pte C W	2033	19	KIA	VC
Tiedeman, Pte A O	3693	19	KIA	VC
Tippett, Pte H	4928	19	KIA	VC
Tipton, Pte J L	4647	19	KIA	VC
Toogood, Pte A W	4201	19	KIA	VC
Towe, Pte J	3268	19	KIA	VC
Trainer, Pte D C (aka Cook, D C)	3066	19	KIA	VC
Tredrea, Pte F S	3271	19	KIA	VC
Trehearn, Pte D Y	2913	19	KIA	RB
Tully, Pte W A	4598a	19	KIA	VC
Turnbull, Pte W R	2691a	19	KIA	VC
Underwood, Pte A C	2929	19	KIA	VC
Wallmeyer, Pte F	1784	19	KIA	VC
Walters, Pte F C	1446	19	KIA	VC
Ward, Pte R C	4933	19	KIA	VC
Wardell, Pte A P M	990	19	KIA	VC
Warren, Pte R C	3959	27	DOW	WI
Warren, Pte S M	1767	19	KIA	VC
Watkins, Pte F	3286	19	KIA	RD
Watt, Pte G D	3493	19	KIA	VC
Waugh, Pte H H	3958	19	KIA	VC
Webb, Pte T R	2910	19	KIA	VC
Whelan, Pte F J	3642	19	KIA	VC
Whelan, Pte V H	3647	19	KIA	VC
White, Pte I	3323a	19	KIA	VC
White, Pte W H	2273a	19	KIA	VC
Whitehurst, Pte J	1449	19	KIA	VC
Wickham, Pte A W F	3514	19	KIA	VC
Wilde, Pte K R	1774	19	KIA	VC
Wilkins, CQMS T G	295	19	KIA	RF
Williams, Pte H E	1800	18.8	DOW	UU
Williamson, Sgt H T	3921	19	KIA	VC
Willis, Pte J	2225	19	KIA	RF
Willox, CSM J S	727	19	KIA	NI
Wilson, Pte W	1750	19	KIA	RF
Windley, Pte H	2686	19	KIA	VC
Wood, Pte A B	2833	19	KIA	VC
Wright, Lieut E E		19	KIA	VC
Wright, Pte J R	2481	19	KIA	VC
Wright, Pte K L B	2482	19	KIA	VC
Wright, Pte R	4635	19	KIA	VC
Wyatt, Pte C J	3299	19	KIA	VC
Wynne, Pte W C	3663a	19	KIA	VC
Young, Pte W V	4639	19	KIA	VC

15th Machine Gun Coy

Barber, Pte G F T	2567	5.8	DOW	BO
Borneman, Pte J T	2795	19	KIA	RB
Brodie, Pte W R	2345	19	KIA	LA
Cox, Pte G R	2567	20	KIA	RB
Horwood, Pte C H	3136	19	KIA	RB
Jennings, Cpl G W	2637	19	KIA	RB
Lewis, Pte H E	3073	20	KIA	RB
Price, Pte A S	2733	19	KIA	RB
Shearer, Pte A	3248	19	KIA	RB
Sutherland, Pte L B	3475s	19	KIA	RB

15th Field Coy Engineers

Elliott, Spr R B	6184	20	KIA	VC
Lawler, Spr F M	5648	19	KIA	RF
Lyell, Spr J	6095	19	KIA	RB
Newton, Spr W	6096	20	KIA	VC
O'Neil, Spr J R	6245	21.8	DOW	ES
Price, Spr E S	6219	19	KIA	RB
Tickner, Spr W	6036	22	DOW	BO
Young, Spr A H	4483	19	KIA	RD

5th DIVISION

5th Divisional Pioneer Bn

Fitch (Ansell), A W	2825	23	KIA	VB
Gates, L/Cpl A	4787	28.9	DOW	ES
McGregor, Pte J R	5587	20	DOW	RB
Thompson, Pte I	2756	21	KIA	RB

5th Divisional Signals (10th HQ Coy)

Ward, Pte R D	1153	19	KIA	RD

5th Divisional Trench Mortar Battery

Doyle, Gnr T	1158	13.9	DOW	ES
Power, Gnr S R	824	1.11	DOW	RD
Ward, Gnr H W	532	27.8	DOW	ES

5th Divisional Machine Gun Coy

Carnegie, Pte W L	16	20	KIA	AN
McCawley, Pte G	3110	20	KIA	AN

5th Divisional Engineers

O'Donnell, Spr T J	1864	20	KIA	RP

5th Divisional Ammunition Column

Tipping, Gnr W	2092	21.8	DOW	ES

11th Brigade AFA

Johnson, Cpl T N	991	20	KIA	RF

13th Brigade AFA **(see page 24)**

Bowne, Sgt A E E	565	18	KIA	RP
Burling, Gnr A	3460	18	KIA	RD
Carr, Gnr C G	1238	18	KIA	RD
Everitt, Pte J S	3319	18	KIA	AN
Green, Gnr B E	3047	18	KIA	RD
Le Broeq, Gnr D T	3554	18	KIA	RD
Stevens, Gnr G E	3264	18	KIA	RD
Wheeler, Gnr W H	3702	18	KIA	RD

14th Brigade AFA

Young, Sgt F H	136	31.8	DOW	ES

4th Divisional Artillery

Thompson, Capt. C K	-	19	KIA	YF

2nd Tunnelling Company

McDonald, Spr C P	2224	19	KIA	RB

German Roll of Honour

16th Bavarian Reserve Infantry Regiment

Aicher, Pte M	9 Coy	19	KIA	22
Andessmer, L/Cpl G	8 Coy	20	KIA	25
Babl, Pte G	12 Coy	19	KIA	21
Bauer, Pte J	10 Coy	2.8	DOW	35
Benninger, Pte L	3 Coy	20	KIA	29
Bestler, Cpl O	1 Coy	20	KIA	31
Böck, L/Cpl O	1 Coy	20	KIA	28
Boedicker, Cpl R	10 Coy	19	KIA	37
Bratengeier, L/Cpl E	1 MG Coy	19	KIA	21
Braun, Pte A	11 Coy	20	KIA	33
Brenner, Pte J	10 Coy	19	KIA	22
Brummer, Pte M	6 Coy	22	DOW	19
Burger, L/Cpl J	11 Coy	19	KIA	21
Emerich, Cpl O	10 Coy	21	DOW	25
Englmann, Pte A	1 Coy	20	KIA	35
Enrainer, Pte J	9 Coy	19	KIA	24
Estner, Pte K	11 Coy	23	DOW	23
Fischhaber, Pte P	9 Coy	19	KIA	31
Frenzl, Pte G	12 Coy	20	KIA	29
Frommel, Pte M	8 Coy	20	KIA	29
Führer, Sgt Major N	11 Coy	19	KIA	28
Gartmeier, L/Cpl A	2 Coy	20	KIA	27
Gilles, Pte J	8 Coy	19	KIA	24
Gleissner, Pte F X	9 Coy	19	KIA	22
Grünwald, Pte J	9 Coy	19	KIA	23
Gumbert, Pte F	10 Coy	21.8	DOW	21
Gutbrod, Pte L	1 Coy	20	KIA	22
Härtle, Cpl A	1 MG Coy	19	KIA	25
Heiss, Pte J	3 Coy	20	KIA	22
Hitzenberger, Pte H	10 Coy	19	KIA	30
Hofmann, L/Cpl J	11 Coy	20	KIA	26
Holzner, Pte I	8 Coy	20	KIA	23
Hörath, Pte W	1 Coy	20	KIA	20
Huber, Pte J	10 Coy	19	KIA	23
Hund, Pte J	3 Coy	20	KIA	29
Ingold, L/Cpl M	1 Coy	27	DOW	22
Janssen, Pte E J A L	3 Coy	20	KIA	38
Jörg, Pte J	9 Coy	19	KIA	25
Kameter, Pte D	9 Coy	19	KIA	27
Kestel, Pte M	10 Coy	21	DOW	30
Kiebensberger, Pte K	8 Coy	23.11	DOW	22
Kling, Pte M	3 Coy	20	KIA	24
Koch, Cpl G	11 Coy	19	KIA	22
König, L/Cpl E	3 Coy	20	KIA	21
Kreutzer, Pte E	12 Coy	19	KIA	26
Kreuzpaintner, Pte A	1 MG Coy	20	KIA	23
Kronseder, Pte J	12 Coy	19	KIA	24
Kurzmaul, Pte J	1 MG Coy	19	KIA	21
Kuttroff, Lieut K	1 Coy	20	KIA	21
Lehr, Lieut M	11 Coy	19	KIA	24
Leib, Pte J	10 Coy	19	KIA	32
Leicher, L/Cpl J	3 Coy	30	DOW	30
Lerch, Pte X	12 Coy	19	KIA	21
Lösch, Pte L	1 Coy	20	KIA	22
Maas, Pte F	1 Coy	20	KIA	33
Machl, Pte J B	6 Coy	19	KIA	31
Maier, Pte M	12 Coy	20	DOW	30
Mayer, Pte L	12 Coy	20	KIA	20
Meier, Pte A	9 Coy	19	KIA	22
Möst, Pte H	6 Coy	19	KIA	23
Müller, L/Cpl F S	3 Coy	20	KIA	26
Müller, Pte M	9 Coy	19	KIA	21
Obermaier, Pte G	9 Coy	19	KIA	29
Petz, Lieut A	1 Coy	20	KIA	29
Preissel, Pte X	10 Coy	19	KIA	23
Pröller, Pte M	1 Coy	20	KIA	27
Reichenberger, Pte J	1 MG Coy	19	KIA	27
Reiser, Cpl A	6 Coy	20	KIA	24
Rieder, L/Cpl S	11 Coy	19	KIA	25
Risinger, Pte J	10 Coy	28	DOW	29
Roe, Pte J	9 Coy	20	KIA	23
Roiter, L/Cpl L	6 Coy	25	DOW	27
Ruckdäschel, Pte M	9 Coy	19	KIA	20
Ruckdäschel, Pte WH	11 Coy	20	KIA	40
Saumweber, Pte W	9 Coy	19	KIA	28
Schiessl, Pte J	6 Coy	29.8	DOW	28
Schmid, Pte J	12 Coy	19	KIA	22
Schmid, Pte J	9 Coy	20	DOW	24
Schmidhammer, Pte J	2 Coy	20	KIA	23
Schneider, Pte G	9 Coy	19	KIA	31
Schöll, Pte F	12 Coy	19	KIA	22
Schorer, Pte A	2 Coy	20	KIA	28
Schürf, Pte F	1 Coy	20	KIA	29
Seiling, Pte M	11 Coy	20	KIA	26
Sepp, Pte L	10 Coy	19	KIA	21
Simon, Cpl E	8 Coy	20	KIA	32
Sollinger, Pte J	3 Coy	20	KIA	25
Specht, Pte J	9 Coy	20	DOW	22
Springer, Pte F	12 Coy	20	DOW	27
Steinle, Pte K	10 Coy	23	DOW	20
Stiller, Pte A	10 Coy	21	DOW	32
Strasser, Pte J (from Mietenkamm)	12 Coy	19	KIA	20
Strasser, Pte J (from Pleiskirchen)	12 Coy	19	KIA	29
Strötz, Cpl J	9 Coy	19	KIA	29
Stumpf, Pte G	7 Coy	20	DOW	21
Thaller, Pte G	9 Coy	19	KIA	26
Titscher, Pte F	9 Coy	19	KIA	29
Traxinger, Pte J	12 Coy	20	KIA	27
Treiber, Pte R	1 Coy	20	KIA	27
Vogl, L/Cpl S	2 Coy	20	KIA	25
Weber, Pte L	9 Coy	19	KIA	32
Weindl, Pte S	9 Coy	19	KIA	27
Wenl, Pte L	1 Coy	20	KIA	26
Wesche, Lieut G	9 Coy	19	KIA	26
Zahn, Cpl J	12 Coy	19	KIA	26
Zeitler, Pte K	1 Coy	20	KIA	22
Zeulmann, Lieut S	2 Coy	20	KIA	26

* Figure in last column of German lists is age at death.

17th Bavarian Reserve Infantry Regiment
[3 Officers and 56 ORs = 59]

Buff, Cpl E		19	KIA	
Hehl, Sgt Major	2 Coy	19	KIA	
Mayer, Lieut F	-	19	KIA	22

20th Bavarian Reserve Infantry Regiment
[1 Officer and 35 ORs = 36]

Eichhorn, Lieut	6 Coy	19	KIA	
Weglein, Pte W		19	KIA	23
Ziegel, Sgt Major R	-	27.8	DOW	21

21st Bavarian Reserve Infantry Regiment
[7 Officers and 288 ORs = 295]

Baumgärtel, Lieut	-	19	KIA	-
Bernhart, Sgt Major A	-	20	KIA	21
Fleishmann, I		19	KIA	31
Gerngross, J	-	20	DOW	33
Keim, Lieut	-	19	KIA	-
Keller, -	-	19	KIA	-
Rosenhaupt, L/Cpl W		19	KIA	32
Schonberg, Sgt Major J	-	20	DOW	31
Wagner, Lieut	-	20	KIA	-
Wolf, Lieut	-	20	KIA	-

15 July Raid

Kriechbaum, Lieut		15	KIA	

[and 5 ORs]

104th Saxon Regiment
[4 ORs]

HINDSIGHT

The German Roll of Honour as shown for 16th BRIR was taken from their history published in 1932, and shows 107 dead. The Divisional Returns dated 1 August 1916 gives 91 killed, 392 wounded, 1 missing. The difference is clearly accounted for by those who later died of wounds. The Divisional Return for 17th BRIR was 59 killed, 116 wounded, 49 missing. Only the number of dead was available when this book was first published—as in the next two Regiments. 20th BRIR—36 killed, 118 wounded and 5 missing; 21st BRIR had 236 killed, 377 wounded and 111 missing.

The Divisional Return also gives the 17th BRIR Mining Coy as having 5 killed, 4 wounded, 5 missing. 20th BRIR Mining Coy having 3 killed. 21st BRIR Mining Coy, 6 killed, 8 wounded.

The artillery had 4 killed, 37 wounded. They lost 1 horse killed, and 10 wounded. The Pioneers, Tunnellers, Meinenwerfer crews, other miners and 2nd Bavarians add a total of 35 killed, 44 wounded and 49 missing.

Totals given:
Officers: 17 killed, 26 wounded, 2 missing.
NCOs & men: 452 killed, 952 wounded, 204 missing
[Total: 469 killed, 978 wounded, 206 missing.]
Horses: 1 killed, 10 wounded.

This was initialled by Scanzoni and sent to Army Command, 6th Army

House on Garden Street, Fromelles-Aubers, May 1916. Watercolour by Max Märtens.

The Military Law

Whilst it is easy to criticise McCay on moral grounds in regards to the Armistice, it is more important to be certain that his conduct, and that of those above and around him was outside Military Law. As a lawyer and soldier, he had the advantage of having considerable experience in both disciplines, and thus had no excuse for ignorance.

The Appendix contains extracts from the *Manual of Military Law,* published by the War Office in London in 1914, and reprinted in 1916. The selected sections given deal with several issues, but in particular aspects relative to the possible armistice at Fromelles on 20 July 1916. They are in a very real sense linked to the general proposition that war is dirty, horrible and cruel, but there are rules, and guidelines of conduct.

The means of carrying on war (page 477) and the *Killing and Disabling the Enemy Combatants* (page 478) provide a sobering view of the grim and dirty business of war. *The taking of prisoners* (pages 479) reveals the gap between the rules and conduct of both sides in this regard. But the standard it demands, some men went to great lengths to hold to, often at their own peril.

The Sick, Wounded and Dead (page 482) is relevant to the Battle of Fromelles. These selections spell out in some detail what should be done, the main thrust of which it is clear the German officer was familiar with.

The Medical Emblem (page 483) section throws some light on the Gallipoli Armistice and exactly how the Red Cross and Red Crescent were tightly protected from misuse. Miles was, perhaps because he fought in South Africa, familiar with the procedure.

The Dead (page 484) is very clear in intent and footnote (i) is worth noting.

Intercourse between Belligerents (pages 485–86) as far as Fromelles is concerned is hugely important. The German officer was familiar with the expression '*Parlementaires*' in the correct context. The whole business of '*Suspension of arms*' as detailed in para 260 is what McCay should have paid attention to. It proves absolutely that he had the right and freedom to agree to a suspension of arms. And the fact that the Manual supplies (page 487) a draft form for such an agreement is all that is needed to show how well prepared the ground was.

Lastly: *The Official Secrets Act* which has to be the most all-embracing piece of legal jargon ever devised, reveals why Edmonds was so fearful of Bean getting in direct contact with somebody who might tell him things '*he did not need to know*', and certainly should not print. It would be interesting to know if Bean was, or felt himself to be, bound by the Official Secrets Act.

The fact that the German officer used the exact phrase '*Usages of War*' reveals that he was familiar with the very latest edition. The advertisement, as the foreword to the book is called, says: '*The New Edition contains an entirely new chapter (Chapter XIV) on the laws and usages of war, which has been written by Col J E Edmonds, CB and Mr L Oppenheim LLD*'. Edmonds became the Official British Historian of the Great War, as already noted. His attempts to discipline Bean in the way he dealt with the Armistice and other matters do not sit well with some of the material he said he wrote for the *Manual*, and the attitude he later took.

The Manual is substantial, 908 pages of which 100 are the index that provides a fascinating revelation of subjects the Army of the time had a view on: Abortion, Absence without Leave, Aliens, Archives (captured), Armistice, Assassination, Balloons, Banks, Bigamy, Birth, Booty, Camp followers, Cards (cheating etc), Chaplains, Christmas Day, Civil War, Criminals, Deaf and Dumb (witnesses), Deserters, Embezzlement, Enemy, Flag of Truce, Girls, Houses, Irons, King, Language, Liquor ration, Malice, Mercenaries, Murder, Mutiny, Negroes, Newspaper Correspondents, Oaths, Opium, Parlementaire, Pawnbrokers, Pirates, Prostitutes, Rape, Receiving, Reprisals, Ruses, Shamming death, Stage plays, Suicide, Sunday, Taxes, Treason, Uncivilized Nations, Usages of War, Victoria Cross, Voting, Water, Wife, Year—to name a few. The vast majority of the subject matter of course concerns the conduct of the Army and legal information about Courts-Martial and procedures.

The First Edition was published in 1884, having been first proposed in 1879. The delay, so the preface admits, was due to various revisions of the Queen's Regulations and '*was the only complete modern treatise on the practice of courts-martial, which is almost as important as the military law itself*'. It was revised in 1887, 1894, 1899, 1907 and 1914.

Ch. XIV.

Permanent character of belligerent status.

35. It is necessary to remember that inhabitants who have legitimately taken up arms cannot afterwards change their status back to that of peaceful inhabitants. Even if they lay down their arms and return to their peaceful avocations, they may be made prisoners of war.

Fugitives and deserters.

36. Deserters and subjects of a belligerent fighting in the enemy's ranks are traitors to their country, and are, when captured, liable to the penalty for treason. They cannot be regarded as enemies in the military sense of the term and cannot claim the privileges of the members of the armed force of the enemy, but terms may be specially made for them.

Duty of officers as regards legal status of combatants.

37. It is not, however, for officers or soldiers in determining their conduct towards a disarmed enemy to occupy themselves with his qualifications as a belligerent. Whether he belongs to the regular army or to an irregular corps, is an inhabitant or a deserter, their duty is the same : they are responsible for his person and must leave the decision of his fate to competent authority. No law authorizes them to have him shot without trial, and international law forbids summary execution absolutely. If his character as a member of the armed forces is contested, he should be sent before a court for examination of the question.

(v.) *Coloured Troops.*

38. Troops formed of coloured individuals belonging to savage tribes and barbarous races should not be employed in a war between civilized States. The enrolling, however, of individuals belonging to civilized coloured races and the employment of whole regiments of disciplined coloured soldiers (*a*) is not forbidden.

IV.—The Means of Carrying on War.

Limitation of means of carrying on war.

39. The first principle of war is that the enemy's powers of resistance must be weakened and destroyed. The means that may be employed to inflict injury on him are not, however, unlimited (*b*). They are in practice definitely restricted by international conventions and declarations, and also by the customary rules of warfare. And, moreover, there are the dictates of religion, morality, civilization, and chivalry which ought to be obeyed. The means include both force and stratagem.

(i.) *The Means of Carrying on War by Force.*

General means of carrying on war by force.

40. The most important powers of resistance possessed by an enemy, in addition to the general resources of his country, are furnished by his armed forces with their military stores and apparatus, and his permanent or improvised fortresses. The means of reducing these powers of resistance are :—Killing and disabling the enemy combatants; constraining them by defeat or exhaustion to surrender, that is taking them prisoners ; and the investment, bombardment, or siege of the fortresses. How far an invader is allowed to damage, destroy, or appropriate property and injure the general resources of a country, will be considered later (*c*).

(*a*) *E.g.*, such troops as the Indian Army, the African troops of the French Army, and the Negro regiments of the United States Army.

(*b*) Hague Rules, 22. "Belligerents have not an unlimited right as to the choice of means of injuring the enemy."

(*c*) See paras. 405 *et seq.*

(i.) A.—*Killing and Disabling the Enemy Combatants.* **Ch. XIV.**

41. The international agreements limiting the means of destruction of enemy combatants are contained, apart from Article 23 of The Hague Rules, in four Declarations by which the contracting parties, of which Great Britain is one, engage:— **International agreements**

(i) "to renounce in case of war amongst themselves the employment by their military and naval forces of any projectile of a weight below 400 *grammes* (approximately 14 oz.), which is either explosive or charged with fulminating or inflammable substances"; (*a*).

(ii) "to abstain from the use of bullets with a hard envelope which does not entirely cover the core, or is pierced with incisions"; (*b*).

(iii) "to abstain from the use of projectiles the sole object of which is the diffusion of asphyxiating or deleterious gases"; (*c*).

(iv) "to prohibit, for a period extending to the close of the Third Peace Conference (*d*), the discharge of projectiles and explosives from balloons or by other new methods of a similar nature"; (*e*).

42. It is expressly forbidden to employ arms, projectiles or material calculated to cause unnecessary suffering (*f*). Under this heading might be included such weapons as lances with a barbed head, irregularly-shaped bullets, projectiles filled with broken glass, and the like (*g*); also the scoring of the surface of bullets, the filing off the end of their hard case, and smearing on them any substance likely to inflame a wound. The prohibition is not, however, intended to apply to the use of explosives contained in mines, aerial torpedoes, or hand-grenades. **Prohibited means of killing. Arms which cause unnecessary suffering.**

43. The use of poison and poisoned weapons is forbidden (*h*). By analogy this prohibition has been extended to the use of means calculated to spread contagious diseases. **Poison, &c.**

44. The deliberate contamination of sources of water by throwing into them corpses or dead animals is a practice now confined to savage tribes. There is, however, no rule to prevent measures being taken to dry up springs, and to divert rivers and aqueducts.

45. Train wrecking, and setting on fire camps or military depôts, are legitimate means of injuring the enemy when carried out by members of the armed forces.

46. Assassination, and the killing and wounding by treachery of individuals belonging to the hostile nation or army, are not **Assassination.**

(*a*) Declaration of St. Petersburg, 1868. For a list of parties to the Declaration, see Appendix 1.

(*b*) Hague Declaration, 1899. For a list of parties to the Declaration, see Appendix 2.

(*c*) Hague Declaration, 1899. For a list of parties to the Declaration, see Appendix 3.

(*d*) That is until the next Peace Conference has completed its labours.

(*e*) Hague Declaration, 1907. For a list of parties to the Declaration, see Appendix 9. It may be remarked here that hardly any of the Great Powers have signed this Declaration; it is, therefore, practically without force.

(*f*) Hague Rules, 23 (*e*).

(*g*) The use of soft-nosed and explosive bullets is already provided against in the Declaration referred to in para. 41 (ii) above. According to the French *Manuel*, p. 14, it must not be accounted reprehensible if irregular troops raised in haste to oppose an invader should in default of regulation ammunition and bayonets make use of small shot and the cutting tools which are available in the country. This, however, goes too far, since "cutting tools," include saws and the like which would cause "unnecessary suffering," and are therefore forbidden.

(*h*) Hague Rules, 23 (*a*).

Ch. XIV. lawful acts of war, (*a*) and the perpetrator of such an act has no claim to be treated as a combatant, but should be put on his trial as a war criminal (*b*). Measures should be taken to prevent such an act from being successful in case information with regard to it is forthcoming (*c*).

Outlawry. **47.** As a consequence of the prohibition of assassination, the proscription or outlawing of any enemy, or the putting a price on an enemy's head, or any offer for an enemy "dead or alive" is not permitted.

Quarter. **48.** It is forbidden to declare that no quarter will be given (*d*).

49. It is hardly necessary to state that the custom is now obsolete by which quarter could be refused to the garrison of a fortress carried by assault, to the defenders of an unfortified place who did not surrender when artillery was brought against it, and to a weak garrison who obstinately and uselessly persevered in defending a fortified place against overwhelming forces.

Killing of surrendered combatants. **50.** It is forbidden to kill or wound an enemy who having laid down his arms, or having no longer means of defence, has surrendered at discretion (*e*).

51. This prohibition is clear and distinct; there is no question of the moment up to which acts of violence may be continued without disentitling the enemy to be ultimately admitted to the benefit of quarter. War is for the purpose of overcoming armed resistance, and no vengeance can be taken because an individual has done his duty to the last but escaped injury (*f*).

Infractions of laws of war. **52.** Few wars have occurred without both belligerents making mutual charges of breaches of the laws of war (*g*). Such charges as have been proved have almost invariably been shown to have been the deeds of subordinates who have acted through ignorance or excess of zeal; they have more and more rarely been deliberate acts. Care must therefore be taken that all ranks are acquainted with the laws of war and that they endeavour to observe them.

53. A belligerent is not justified in at once dispensing with obedience to the laws of war on account of their suspected or ascertained violation on the part of his adversary (*g*).

(i.) B.—*The Taking of Prisoners* (*h*).

Changes in treatment of prisoners. **54.** Few of the customs of war have undergone greater changes than those relating to the treatment of prisoners. In antiquity war captives were killed, or at best enslaved; in the Middle Ages they were imprisoned and held to ransom; it was only in the seventeenth century that they began to be deemed prisoners of the State

(*a*) Hague Rules, 23 (*b*). For instance, it would be treachery for a soldier to sham that he was wounded or dead, or to pretend that he had surrendered, and afterwards to open fire when the enemy came up to him.

(*b*) See para. 441 *et seq.* below.

(*c*) In 1806 an offer to assassinate Napoleon was made to the British Government by a foreigner. The man was detained (the law not permitting of his punishment) and the French Minister of Foreign Affairs was informed.

(*d*) Hague Rules, 23 (*d*). Formerly it was held that the general duty to give quarter did not protect an enemy who had personally violated the laws of war, who had declared his intention of refusing to grant quarter, or of violating those laws in any grave manner, or whose government or commander had done acts which justified reprisals. (See paras. 452–460.) The American "Instructions" recognized the refusal of quarter in certain circumstances (arts. 60–63).

(*e*) Hague Rules, 23 (*c*).

(*f*) An individual who refuses to cease firing, after a general surrender has been made by his commander, forfeits his privileges as a combatant.

(*g*) For further examination of this question see *post* paras. 435 *et seq.*, "Means of securing legitimate warfare."

(*h*) The British instructions with regard to prisoners of war are contained in "General rules for prisoners of war interned in the United Kingdom."

and not the property of the individual captors. Even during the wars of the nineteenth century they were often subjected to cruel neglect, unnecessary suffering, and unjustifiable indignities.

The persons who may claim the privileges of prisoners of war.

55. The written laws regarding prisoners of war are contained in Articles 4 to 20 of The Hague Rules, in certain paragraphs of the Geneva Convention, and in the Convention concerning the Rights and Duties of Neutral Powers and Persons in war on land.

56. Every member of the armed forces, if he falls into the hands of the enemy, has a claim to be treated as a prisoner of war, unless he has committed a war crime (*a*).

Followers.

57. It is expressly enacted that followers of armies—such as newspaper correspondents, reporters, sutlers, and contractors—who are captured and retained, can claim to be treated as prisoners of war, provided they can produce a certificate from the military authorities of the army they are accompanying (*b*).

Civilian.

58. In addition to the members of the belligerent forces and the civilians who accompany armies by permission of the military authorities, the following are liable to be made prisoners :—

(i) The Sovereign and the male members of the royal family, the head of a Republican State, and the Ministers who direct the policy of a State, although as individuals they may not belong to the army.

(ii) Civil officials and diplomatic agents attached to the Army.

(iii) Persons whose activity is of service in the war :—such as higher officials, diplomatic agents, couriers, guides, etc. ; also all persons who being at liberty may be harmful to the opposing State :—such as prominent and influential political leaders, journalists, local authorities, clergymen, and teachers, in case they incite the population to resistance (*c*).

(iv) The mass of the population of a province who rise to defend their territory before it is invaded by the enemy (*d*).

59. In some cases it may only be found necessary to detain such persons for a period.

60. Although The Hague Rules do not contain anything regarding the treatment of private enemy individuals and enemy officials whom a belligerent thinks it necessary to make prisoners, it is evident that they also can claim all the privileges of prisoners of war. Such individuals are not civil prisoners ; they are taken into captivity for military reasons, and they are therefore prisoners of war.

Special treatment of military attachés and diplomatic agents of neutral Powers.

61. It is contrary to usage to take prisoners military attachés or diplomatic agents of neutral Powers, who accompany an army in the field, or are found in a captured fortress, provided they are in possession of papers of identification and take no part in the hostilities. They may, however, be ordered out of the theatre

---

(*a*) See para. 441 *et seq.*

(*b*) Hague Rules, 13. Without such certificate they are liable, if found in the theatre of war, to arrest as suspected persons.

(*c*) As regards civilian inhabitants of occupied territory who are requisitioned, impressed, or hired to act as transport drivers, as labourers to construct fortifications or siege works, and in similar capacities which assist the army, or who voluntarily perform such services, and who are captured whilst so assisting : the enemy may detain them temporarily, requisition their services (see, however, paras. 383–91), or release them as he thinks fit. But he may not retain them as prisoners of war (see para. 207 (i), last three lines). There is of course no necessity for such civilians to wear a "fixed distinctive sign, recognizable at a distance" (see para. 22).

(*d*) See para. 29 above.

Ch. XIV.

of war, and if necessary, handed over by the capturing Power to the Ministers of their respective countries (*a*).

Wounded and sick.

62. Wounded and sick when captured are prisoners (*b*), but the members of the medical personnel are not as a rule made prisoners (*c*).

Chaplains.

63. Chaplains attached to armies, so long as they confine themselves to their spiritual duties, cannot be made prisoners of war (*d*); if they are captured they must be released under conditions similar to those applicable to the medical personnel.

Deserters from the enemy.

64. Deserters from the enemy should be treated as prisoners of war, unless special circumstances render it desirable to liberate them. Deserters and subjects of a belligerent captured in the ranks of the enemy have, as already pointed out, no right to claim treatment as prisoners of war, or the benefit of the laws of war.

Prisoners who enter neutral territory.

65. Prisoners of war, even if sick or wounded, who escape into the territory of a neutral Power, or are brought into it by troops taking refuge in such territory, do not necessarily acquire their complete liberty (*e*).

General position of prisoners.

66. Prisoners of war are in the power of the enemy Government, and not of the individuals or units capturing them, and they must be humanely treated (*f*).

Right of interrogation.

67. Every prisoner is bound to give, if questioned on the subject, his true name and rank. In case he refuses to do so, he is liable to have the privileges curtailed which are due to prisoners of his class (*g*).

68. The right of interrogation is not limited to name and rank, yet a prisoner is not bound to reply to other questions. It is permissible to employ every means, provided they are humane and not compulsive, to obtain all the information possible from prisoners with regard to the numbers, movements, and location of the enemy. A prisoner cannot, however, be punished for giving false information about his own army (*h*).

Private property of prisoners.

69. According to The Hague Rules all personal belongings of prisoners of war, except arms, horses, and military papers, remain their property (*i*). In practice personal belongings are understood to include military uniform, clothing and kit required for personal use, although technically they may be the property of Government (*j*).

(*a*) A British naval attaché and two American military attachés with the Russian forces captured by the Japanese at Mukden were, after a report had been made to the Minister of Foreign Affairs, Tokio, sent to Japan and handed over to the Ministers of their respective countries. (Ariga, pp. 122, 123.)

(*b*) Geneva Convention, art. 2.

(*c*) See para. 184 *et seq.*

(*d*) Geneva Convention, art. 9.

(*e*) See para. 490 *et seq.*, for the discussion of this situation.

(*f*) Hague Rules, 4.

(*g*) Hague Rules, 9.

(*h*) The shooting of a prisoner for such reason is, as *Kriegsbrauch*, p. 16, says, "cowardly murder."

(*i*) Hague Rules, 4. According to the opinions expressed at The Hague Conference, 1907, *Actes*, Vol. III, pp. 20, 107, field glasses, range finders, maps, bicycles, and other objects used for military purposes, and means of transport also remain their property. See, however, para. 71. Nothing was said about saddlery and harness, but they would naturally follow the fate of the horse to which they belong, whilst ammunition should seem to be included under "arms." Prisoners may of course be called upon to prove that the field glasses, etc., are really their private property.

(*j*) After the battle of the Sha Ho some Japanese soldiers compelled Russian prisoners to give up good boots and take their worn out ones in exchange. This was admitted to be irregular, but was excused on the ground that the men did not take the boots to enrich themselves, but in order better to serve their country. (Ariga, p. 161.) Similar stories are narrated of the Germans in 1870-1. (See Letters of Major von Kretschmann, Latreille's French translation, p. 382.)

Ch. XIV.

VI.—THE SICK, WOUNDED AND DEAD.

International agreements.

174. The treatment of the sick and wounded of armies, the privileges of the personnel charged with their care, the special immunities of the establishments and buildings in which they are attended, and the obligations with regard to the dead are dealt with in the "Convention for the Amelioration of the Condition of the Wounded and Sick in Armies in the Field" of the 6th July, 1906, generally called the "Geneva Convention" (*d*). The duties of neutral Powers as regards sick and wounded who are permitted to enter their territories are dealt with in the "Convention concerning the Rights and Duties of Neutral Powers and Persons" (*e*).

(i.) *The Sick and Wounded.*

Care of sick and wounded obligatory.

175. The first and most important obligation is that sick and wounded persons belonging or officially attached to armies must be respected and taken care of, without distinction of nationality, by the belligerent in whose power they may be (*f*).

176. As this obligation might prove too onerous for a victor left in possession of a battlefield covered with the wounded not only of his own but also of the enemy's army, it has been agreed that a belligerent who is compelled to abandon sick or wounded to his foe must, so far as military exigencies permit, leave behind with them a portion of his medical personnel to take care of them, and the necessary material (*g*).

(*d*) Printed as Appendix 4. The original Convention of 22nd August, 1864, still holds good between Powers which were signatories of it and have not ratified or adhered to the late Convention. (See art. 31 of the 1906 Convention.)

(*e*) See para. 493 *et seq.*

(*f*) Geneva Convention, art. 1 (para. 1). A wounded man who continues to act in an actively hostile manner is not entitled to claim protection.

(*g*) Geneva Convention, art. 1 (para.

Sick and wounded are liable to be made prisoners.

178. Sick and wounded who are captured are prisoners of war; they have no privileges different from those of unwounded and healthy prisoners beyond that of proper medical attendance. In particular they have no right to claim exchange or release because they are unfit for active military service. Exchanges or releases, however, may be made, or sick and wounded may be handed over to a neutral State, by mutual agreement between commanders (*b*).

Search for and protection of wounded.

179. After an engagement the commander in possession of the field must take measures to have search made for the wounded and to protect them against acts of pillage and maltreatment (*c*).

180. Measures must also be taken to punish very severely any such acts whether committed by persons subject to military law or by civilians (*d*).

Nominal rolls to be sent to enemy.

181. A nominal roll of all wounded and sick who have been collected must be sent as early as possible to the authorities of the country or army to which they belong. The proper channel for sending this information to the enemy is the Prisoners of War Information Bureau (*e*).

(*b*) Geneva Convention, art. 2. As regards the action of the neutral State in such a case, see para. 498 below.

(*c*) Geneva Convention, art. 3.

(*d*) Geneva Convention, arts. 3 and 28. Although Great Britain signed and ratified the Convention with reserve of art. 28 (which binds the signatory Governments to undertake the legislation necessary for the above purpose), as it was not possible to commit Parliament to any particular course for which legislation was not already available, there is no doubt that the required amendments of existing laws so as to include civilians, will in the course of time be approved. Commanding officers can meantime deal with offenders as marauders. (See para. 448.)

(*e*) Geneva Convention, art. 4 (para. 2).
For details of the Bureau, see paras. 102–12.

(vi.) *The Medical Emblem.*

The Red Cross on a white ground.

210. The mark which has been adopted to indicate the medical service of armies is a Red Cross on a white ground (*b*). This sign, by the provisions of the Geneva Convention, must not be used except to protect and indicate the medical units and establishments and the personnel and material accorded privileges by the Geneva Convention (*c*).

Permission of military authority.

211. In no case can the sign be recognized unless it is used with the permission of competent military authority. The permission is signified either by a written authorization, or by an official stamp on the sign (*d*).

The flag.

212. Medical units and establishments must hoist the Red Cross flag. It must be accompanied by the national flag of the belligerent to whom the unit or establishment belongs, unless the unit falls into the hands of the enemy. In this situation the Red Cross flag alone will be flown (*e*).

(*b*) Turkey, however, uses a Red Crescent, and Persia a Red Sun. In addition to flying the Red Cross flag, military hospital ships must be "painted white outside with a horizontal band of green about one metre and a half in breadth," and officially recognized hospital ships equipped by private individuals or societies, white with a similar horizontal band of red. (Hague Convention, 1907, for the Adaptation of the Principles of the Geneva Convention to Maritime War.)

(*c*) Geneva Convention, arts. 18, 23, and 27. Arts. 23 and 27, which forbid the use of the Red Cross emblem except to indicate the Army Medical Service, have not yet been signed and ratified by Great Britain, but the powers to accept these articles have been obtained by the enactment of the Geneva Convention Act, 1911 (1 and 2 Geo. V.), and the formalities involved in the notification of their acceptance at Berne will be carried out in due course. Until the passing of this Act, the full title of which is "An Act to make such amendments in the Law as are necessary to enable certain reserved provisions of the second Geneva Convention to be carried into effect," there was no municipal law in Great Britain to prevent the use of the Red Cross on white ground as a trade mark, a merchandise mark, or as a badge of a sisterhood or friendly society, or by any individual who chose to adopt it. The Act makes it unlawful "for any person to use for the purpose of his trade or business, or for any purpose whatsoever, without the authority of the Army Council, the heraldic emblem of the red cross on a white ground formed by reversing the Federal colours of Switzerland, or the words 'Red Cross' or 'Geneva Cross.'"

Existing rights in the emblem or words as a trade mark are permitted to continue for four years. It may be remarked that if within four years there should be war with a Power which has accepted these Articles and has completed the arrangements for forbidding the use of the emblem and words, it may become advisable to make provision under Martial Law to extinguish any existing rights to their use forthwith and to provide penalties.

(*d*) Geneva Convention, arts. 19, 20, and 21.

(*e*) Geneva Convention, art. 21. A rigid *plaque* may be used instead of a flag (Geneva Conference, *Actes*, p. 196). There is no indication how the two flags are to be associated. In most armies the two flags are flown on separate poles which are sometimes crossed. When both flags are hoisted on the same pole, the Red Cross should be uppermost (Field Service Regulations, part II, sect. 85, 2).

214. The persons protected by the Geneva Convention (*b*), in order to secure the privileges conferred by it, must wear fixed permanently to the left arm an armlet (brassard) with the Red Cross on a white ground, delivered and stamped by competent military authority (*c*). Such persons must, if they do not wear a military uniform, be in possession of a certificate of identity (*d*). **The brassard.**

215. The material of the medical service must, in order to obtain the benefits of the Convention, be marked with the Red Cross on a white ground (*e*). **Marking of material.**

(*b*) That is to say, those engaged exclusively in the collection, transport, and treatment of the wounded and the sick, and in the administration of medical units and establishments and the personnel of Voluntary Aid Societies of the belligerents and neutrals who fulfil the conditions laid down in paras. 190–93.

(*c*) Geneva Convention, art. 23. Under the Geneva Convention of 1864 (art. 7) the brassard could be slipped on and off as it was merely "allowed" (*admis*) and no directions were given as to how it should be worn. It must now be "fixed" (*fixe*), because it would be gravely inconvenient if it could be put on and taken off too easily (Geneva Conference, 1906, *Actes*, pp 194–261).

(*d*) There is no authorized form for certificates of identity. The use of certificates may lead to frauds unless there are marks on them by which the bearer can be recognized as the rightful owner. A certificate without such mark of recognition must be carefully scrutinized and steps taken to verify the rights of the bearer to be in possession of it. Finger-prints, photographs, and signatures are the most suitable recognition marks; but there may be difficulty as regards entering finger-print records or photographs; and in some countries signatures may not always be obtainable. There should, however, be no difficulty in noting distinguishable marks, such as scars on the face, loss of fingers or portions of fingers, etc., and the apparent age, height, colour of eyes and hair. Efforts are being made to obtain some definite international understanding with regard to the details which should be noted on a certificate of identity.

(*e*) If the material is marked with the Geneva Cross only, it cannot well be accepted as private property belonging to a Voluntary Aid Society, as the Cross is the distinctive mark of the medical service of armies (Geneva Convention, arts. 18 and 19). To obtain the extra privileges referred to in para. 209 the material of Voluntary Aid Societies should be marked, in addition to the Geneva Cross, with the name of the Society or some other means of identification.

The size of the Cross is not laid down. It was proposed at the Geneva Conference, 1906, that all the vehicles of the medical service should be painted white and should have on them as large a Red Cross as possible. Practical and economic objections led to the proposal being rejected (*Actes*, p. 194).

(vii.) *The Dead.*

Examination, protection, and burial of the dead.

217. The dead must be protected against pillage and maltreatment (*g*).

218. The military identification marks or tokens found on the dead must be sent to the authorities of the army or country to which they belong as early as possible (*h*).

219. Before the dead are buried or cremated they must be carefully examined to see that life is extinct (*i*).

220. The articles of personal use, valuables, letters, &c., found on a field of battle or left by wounded or sick who die in medical establishments or units must be collected and transmitted to the persons interested, through the authorities of their own country (*j*).

(*f*) Geneva Convention, art. 26

(*g*) *ibid*, art. 3.

(*h*) *ibid*, art. 4. The Prisoners of War Information Bureau is the proper channel for the transmission. (See paras. 102–112.)

(*i*) Geneva Convention, art. 3. There is, however, no obligation to bury or cremate them, although the principle that even the enemy's dead should be given burial is generally admitted.

(*j*) Geneva Convention, art. 4. This would also appear to be the duty of the Prisoners of War Information Bureau.

Ch. XIV.

VII.—Intercourse between Belligerents.

(ii.) *Parlementaires and Flags of Truce.*

Parlementaires.

224. The usual agents in the non-hostile intercourse of belligerent armies are known as parlementaires (*c*).

225. Their duties include every form of communication with the enemy in the field. For example, the conveyance of a letter, or of a simple verbal message; a summons to surrender; negotiations for suspension of hostilities or for capitulation; settlement of the exchange of prisoners. Arrangements may be made through parlementaires for the appointment of plenipotentiaries or agents for any purposes of special importance (*d*).

Inviolability.

226. Whilst in the performance of their duties, provided their conduct is correct (*e*), they are entitled to complete inviolability (*f*).

227. It is of the utmost importance that every soldier in an army, from the highest to the lowest, should be thoroughly acquainted with the privileges of parlementaires and with the proper mode of receiving them, so that no untoward incident can possibly arise.

Credentials of parlementaire.

228. According to the Hague Rules, a person to be regarded as a parlementaire must be authorized by one of the belligerents to enter into communication with the other and must present himself under cover of a white flag (*g*).

Signification of the white flag.

229. Since time immemorial a white flag has been used as a signal by an armed force which wishes to open communication with the enemy. This is the only signification that the flag possesses in International Law. The hoisting of a white flag, therefore, means in itself nothing else than that the one party is asked whether it will receive a communication from the other. It may, perhaps, only indicate that the party which hoists it wishes to make an arrangement for the suspension of arms for some purpose; but it may also mean that it wishes to negotiate for surrender. Everything depends on the circumstances and conditions of the particular case. For instance, in practice, the white flag has come to indicate surrender if hoisted in the course of an action by individual soldiers or a small party. Great vigilance is always necessary, for the question in every case is whether the hoisting of the white flag was authorized by the commander.

(*a*) For good faith in other matters see para. 140 above.

(*b*) See paras. 105-106 as regards intercourse concerning wounded and prisoners.

(*c*) It has been thought desirable to adopt this word, for which the ancient verb "to parley" would seem good authority, from the Hague Rules; it is current in all other armies in addition to an expression for "flag of truce." The use of the latter term by British manuals in the past to mean indifferently both the envoy and the emblem, and sometimes to mean only the envoy, and at other times the envoy and his attendants, has given rise to some confusion. The use of the expression "bearer of a flag of truce" to signify the principal agent is also misleading, as he is seldom the actual bearer of the flag. See note to arts. 32, 33, 34 of the Hague Rules in Appendix 6 to this chapter.

(*d*) The punishment for sending a flag of truce to the enemy "treacherously or through cowardice" or "without due authority" is given in A.A. 4 (3) and 5 (4).

(*e*) See Hague Rules, 33 and 34, and para. 251 below.

(*f*) Hague Rules, 32.

(*g*) Hague Rules, 32.

Intercourse between Belligerents.

(iii.) *Armistices.*

Nature and kinds of armistices.

256. During the continuance of war belligerent forces have sometimes occasion to suspend active operations within the whole or part of the region and theatre of war. The mutual agreements made for such temporary cessations of hostilities are known, in the wider sense of the term, as armistices. Although all armistices are essentially alike, in so far as they consist in cessation of hostilities, three different kinds must be distinguished, namely, suspensions of arms, general armistices, and partial armistices (*d*).

257. The Hague Rules (*e*) distinguish only between general and local armistices, apparently comprising both suspensions of arms and partial armistices under the term "local armistices."

Suspensions of arms.

258. A suspension of arms is essentially a military convention of very short duration, concluded between commanders of armies or detachments in order to arrange some pressing local interest: most frequently to bury the dead, or to collect and succour the wounded (*f*), or sometimes to exchange prisoners, or to permit conferences, or to enable a commander to communicate with his Government or a superior in order to request or obtain orders (*g*).

259. A suspension of arms applies only to the troops under the command of the officers who agree to it.

260. Suspensions of arms have nothing to do with the war generally, nor with political purposes, since they only serve a pressing military interest of local importance. For this reason every commander of a force is, so far as the enemy is concerned, supposed to be competent to agree upon a suspension of arms, and no ratification on the part of superior officers or other authorities is required. Such an agreement is therefore in all circumstances and under all conditions binding, although a subordinate commander who enters upon it without instructions may be held responsible by his superior.

(*d*) Five expressions have in the past been used in the British Army to signify a cessation of hostilities falling short of peace:—Truce (as in the "History of the War in South Africa," Vol. II, p. 501), local truce, armistice, cessation of hostilities (as in the convention made after Majuba in 1881), cessation of arms (as in the negotiations preceding the surrender at Saratoga), and suspension of arms. Yet they do not appear to have been employed with any exactitude, and even a further expression, a "cease fire for three hours" has not been unknown. Other languages have no exact terminology either: the Germans speak of *Waffenruhe* and *Waffenstillstand*, without exactly distinguishing between them, and *Kriegsbrauch* uses the term *Waffenstillstand* only. The French instructions distinguish between *armistices* and *suspensions d'armes*. It has been found advisable to follow the practice of the more authoritative publicists in distinguishing three different kinds of armistices as in the text

(*e*) Art. 37.

(*f*) *E.g.*, at the siege of Port Arthur authority was given to the divisional generals of the Japanese army to arrange suspensions of arms for the removal of the dead, if they judged fit, without reference to the commander-in-chief. (Ariga, p. 294.)

(*g*) Thus a suspension of arms was agreed upon at the siege of Belfort on 13th February, 1871, in order to allow the commandant to receive instructions from the French Government (see App. 16); and on 9th August, 1898, the Governor of Manila requested a suspension of arms from Admiral Dewey which would allow him to receive instructions from Madrid.

APPENDIX 12.

FORM OF SUSPENSION OF ARMS FOR THE BURIAL OF THE DEAD, ETC.

General A.B., commanding the British forces at and General C.D., commanding the forces at agree as follows:—

Art. 1. A suspension of arms for the space of three hours, beginning at ten o'clock and ending at one o'clock on this day of is agreed to for the purpose of burying the dead and withdrawing the wounded.

Art. 2. The beginning of the suspension of arms shall be notified by two white flags hoisted simultaneously, the one within the British lines, and the other within lines. The white flags shall continue flying during the suspension of arms, and such flags shall be lowered simultaneously as a signal of the conclusion of the suspension of arms.

Art. 3. All firing shall cease during the suspension of arms.

Art. 4. The British troops shall not, during the suspension of arms, advance beyond the line, and the troops shall not advance beyond the line. The space between the two lines shall be open to all persons engaged in burying the dead, or in attending to the wounded, or on carrying away the dead or the wounded, but to no other persons.

Official Secrets Act, 1911.

[1 & 2 GEO. 5 c. 28.]

An Act to re-enact the Official Secrets Act, 1889, *with Amendments.* [22nd August, 1911.]

Wrongful communication, &c., of information.

2.—(1.) If any person having in his possession or control any sketch, plan, model, article, note, document, or information which relates to or is used in a prohibited place or anything in such a place, or which has been made or obtained in contravention of this Act, or which has been entrusted in confidence to him by any person holding office under His Majesty or which he has obtained owing to his position as a person who holds or has held office under His Majesty, or as a person who holds or has held a contract made on behalf of His Majesty, or as a person who is or has been employed under a person who holds or has held such an office or contract,—

(*a.*) communicates the sketch, plan, model, article, note, document, or any information to any person, other than a person to whom he is authorised to communicate it, or a person to whom it is in the interest of the State his duty to communicate it, or

(*b.*) retains the sketch, plan, model, article, note, or document in his possession or control when he has no right to retain it or when it is contrary to his duty to retain it:

that person shall be guilty of misdemeanour.

Notes

No references are given to the Fromelles' chapters by A D Ellis or C E W Bean. Most of the quotes in italics are from these sources. Most items in the margins are sourced; the few that are not is because the source could not be traced.

xxii John McCrae was Lieut Col in Canadian Medical Corps and died 28 Jan 1918. He was aged 46 and came from Ontario. He was buried at Wimereux Communal Cemetery Grave IV H 3.

p. 1 Anzac loss is from Bean, Vol II, p. 909: 7594 of this figure were killed. Later research by A Ekins (1998) raises the figures to 28,150 and 8709. Fromelles' figure is from Bean, Vol III, p. 442.

p. 3 See T Travers, *The Killing Ground* (1987) for comments on Haking.

p. 5 Ellis and Bean. Michael Piggott's exhaustive guide to Bean's papers (AWM 1983), makes no mention of Ellis.

p. 6 Security breach. Neither Ellis nor Bean seem to consider this a threat or even possibility at Fromelles when writing their official story.

p. 7 XI Corps Order. Mackenzie's Report to Haking. PRO Kew UK WO95 3033.

p. 8 McCay on AIF Nominal Roll is shown as of 2nd Inf Bde RTA 19.4.19./ No decorations are shown.

Mrs Julia McCay died of heart failure 13 July 1915 unexpectedly at Richmond, and she was buried at Castlemaine: the children were then 18 and 14. [*The Argus*, 14 July 1915]. McCay's father died 1 Sept 1915.

Captured documents. Ex-5th Division Memo No. 3, 7 July 1916.

p. 13 Mrs Pearce. *The Argus*, 14 July 1915: group of letters regarding her 'German background'. Her relationship to Mrs Monash. Searle, *John Monash* (1982), p. 205.

p. 15 German casualties: in pencil in the margins of the German Unit Histories that Bean used are calculations which clearly reveal Bean knew the exact figures.

p. 23 Conan Doyle quotes: *The British Campaigns in France and Flanders 1915* (published 1917). Chapter 2: 'Neuve Chapelle and Hill 60'.

p. 28 Verdun Casualties: Edmonds' last volume. *'What went wrong'*, Edmonds, Vol II (1915), p. 335.

p. 30 Somme casualties: West Yorkshire from Max Plowman, *A Subaltern on the Somme* (1927). It is probable that 60th Bn had more than 360 wounded: but that is the total reported in Military Orders.

p. 36 UK Unit War Diaries, PRO Kew, UK. 182nd Bde. WO95 3054. 2/6th Warwicks WO95 3056. 2/7th Warwicks WO95 3056. 2/8th Warwicks WO95 3057. 183rd Bde WO95 3058. 2/4th Glosters WO95 3060. 2/6th Glosters WO95 3062. 184th Bde WO95 3063. 2/4th Royal Berks WO95 3065. 2/1st Bucks WO95 3066. 2/4th Oxon & Bucks WO95 3067.

p. 44 Tunnellers. See 3rd Aust Tunnelling Coy. R Macleod, 'Phantom soldiers', *Journal of the Australian War Memorial*, No. 13 (Oct 1988). Bean Vol VI, p. 949-67.

p. 48 Royal Warwickshire Regiments, see H T Chidgey, *Black Square Memories* (28th RWR) (1924). Cornish Bros. *History of 2/6th RW 1914-19* (1929).

p. 51 Tupman's Report. PRO Kew WO95 3060.
'They know what...' see Lawrence Housman (editor), *War Letters of Fallen Englishmen* (1930). Also *The Poppies of Oblivion*, p. 302.

p. 53 184th Bde see G K Rose, *The Story of the 2/4th Oxfordshire and Buckinghamshire Light Infantry* (1920). J C Swann, *Second Bucks Battalion.* 2/4th Bucks Battalion Record. 2/1st Bucks Battalion Record.

p. 64 61st Division PRO Kew, UK. HQ War Diary WO95 3033 (includes Mackenzie's Report).

p. 69 Haking and Portuguese, April 1918. *Reveille*, Dec 1929.

p. 70 Mackenzie KCB. *The Times*, 3 June 1918, p. 10.

p. 71 Stewart at Chitral: John Harris, *Much Sounding of Bugles* (1975); Sir George Robertson, *Chitral* (1899). Carter in Africa: The Relief of Kumasi. Alan Lloyd, *The Drums of Kumasi* (1964).

p. 78 Lieut Gen. H B Walker, see *Reveille*, 1 Dec 1934.

White-McCay on Desert March. AWM 3DRL 606 243A.

p. 84 Desert March. See also Bert Bishop, *'The Hell, The Humour and the Heartbreak': A Private's View of WW1* (1991), Chapter 5, p. 31 onwards.

p. 89 The Australian Boot. See Ernest Scott, *Official History* Vol XI, p. 258 & 545.

p. 90 Cancelled Raids: AWM 3DRL 606 243A.

p. 93 *'Spies all over the place'*, AWM 2DRL 171.

p. 96 17 July. Pending the attack, the previous day Tivey had asked McCay if he could use *'one company of the 3rd Bn to construct a communication trench across NML after the fourth wave had gone over.'* McCay advised that it was impossible in daylight.

p. 109 The main extra source of material for this chapter was AWM 3DRL 606 243A, Bean's papers.

p. 111 H Brewer's diary: Mitchell Library, Sydney (see also on p. 137).

p. 112 South African War: Senior officers from 5th Division who were there included: Tivey, Elliott, Christian, Cox-Taylor, McGlinn, Wieck, Cass, Toll. Also Birdwood, Bessell-Browne, Brudenell White (too late for action).

p. 118 F W Toll. AWM 3DRL 606 95.

p. 120 W Smith, see *Reveille*, 1 July 1936.

p. 122 *'In no way ...'* AWM MSS 1365.

p. 125 J W Clark, see *Mufti*, 1 July 1937.

S K Donnan letters to Bean. AWM 2DRL 712 (also on pages 137–39, 140–41, 142 & 361).

C H Lorking: AWM 3DRL 7953 44 and 606 240.

p. 127 14th Bde. Ranging through from July to November 1916, *The Sydney Mail* published many photographs of officers and men killed or decorated in the Battle of Fromelles. Whilst not all 14th Bde, they all seem to be from NSW.

Among the dead of the 53rd was Harry Paulin, born in England in 1872. He was a horse groom until joining the Life Guards at 17. His career in the British Army was marked by awards and promotions in gymnastics, musketing, horse-manship and he became champion Guardsman in Life Guards. As Staff Sgt Major, Paulin was posted in 1912 to Australia. In 1914 he enlisted and went with 7th LHR to Gallipoli and was commissioned there. By the end of April 1916 he was Captain Paulin: his nickname was 'Ironsides'.

p. 128 W E H Cass. See *Argus*, 20 April 1935 article by Helena Cass about Lemnos where she was a nurse. Was this where she met Cass? She died on 21 November 1965 and was buried in her husband's grave at the Melbourne General Cemetery. The grave is sheltered by a large pine tree and carries the simple inscription: 'A soldier who loved his men'.

p. 131 *'Rum was issued...'*, AWM 3DRL 606 240.

p. 132 *'The ditch was full...'* AWM 3DRL 606 240.

p. 137 H J Maynard. *'Cookers'*: another article by him in *Reveille* appeared in May 1935. Maynard settled in the UK and invited 55th Bn cobbers to visit him if they came to the UK.

p. 141 I B Norris. Much of this article from *Our Alma Mater*, the school magazine of St Ignatius College (Riverview), Sydney.

p. 142 N Gibbins. AWM 3DRL 696 243A. See *Wartime* No. 26, T Luckins, 'Gates of Memory'.

p. 145 *'Foreman'*: AWM 3DRL 606 261.

p. 146 G G McCrae: AWM 1DRL 0427.

p. 148 *'No one moving'*. AWM 3DRL 606 123.

p. 150 A W Liddelow. For his service prior to Fromelles, see AWM 1DRL 0417 Diary/Notes.

p. 152 Bean first draws attention to the existence of summer time when describing events in early May 1916, referring to a German artillery salvo at 7.40 pm: *'In the German records the hour appears as 9.40, the enemy time (Mid-European time plus one hour of daylight saving) being then two hours in advance of the British. The British and French advanced their clocks on June 14.'* And later: *'Clocks had been put back an hour on Oct 1.'*

p. 155 C E Gatliff: AWM 1DRL 0309.

p. 159 Engineers/Pioneers. See F H Stevens, *The Story of the 5th Pioneer Bn* (1937).

p. 164 Elliott's letter: AWM 3DRL 3856 item 10.

p. 170 J C Stewart/57th Bn: DRL 606 70. E Tivey/8th Bde: 3DRL 606 52.

p. 171 *'Old Elliott'*: AWM DRL 606 52.

p. 173 K M Mortimer. Purser in *Reveille*, July 1935. T Luckins, 'Gates of Memory'.

p. 177 Hubbard's four other articles on Fromelles were only located as the first edition was nearing completion; they are now published here.

p. 179 *'High Morale'*: AWM 3DRL 1722 10-11.

p. 180 The German Army: extracted from *German Army Handbook*, April 1918 and other sources.

p. 183 *'Photograph by German intelligence officer'*. This is one of a group of around 22 photographs given to Capt C Mills by a German officer and later donated to the AWM. The series is A1544-1566.

p. 184 Letters from Soldiers. The widely known *Kriegsbriefe gefallen studenten* (1928) seems to have no letters refering to Fromelles and only a few from men in Bavarian units. Smaller books published by various German Jewish communities did have letters concerning Fromelles, and one from Nuremberg, included profiles. All names were included in *Ein Gedenkbuch* (1932) which listed the 12,000 German Jews who died on active service 1914-18.

p. 188 T M Pflaum: AWM PRO 0503. See also *History of Elder Smith.*

pp. 215-16 Reporting Fromelles: AWM 3DRL 606 52. Rotterdam article: Translation by courtesy of Mrs P Hocking, daughter of Lieut L Stillman of 60th Bn (29th at Fromelles). He obtained the translation in the UK in 1916.

p. 219 Hitler in *Mein Kampf* gives the date of being wounded as 7 October. Other 'authorities' persist with 5 October.

p. 225 Butler. See Bernard O'Keefe, 'Butler's medical histories', *Journal of the Australian War Memorial* No. 12 (April 1988), p25-34.

p. 230 *'Big Chance'*. AWM 2DRL 176.

p. 231 *'Make way'*: AWM 3DRL 606 243A. Drs Rayson & Collier, AWM 41 3/11.19 & 41 1/5.14.

p. 232 *'without a single hitch'*, PRO Kew UK WO95 3038.

p. 235 Langford Wellman Colley-Priest wrote and published *The 8th Australian Field Ambulance on active service ... Aug 4 1915 to March 5 1919* (published in Sydney in 1919, 74 pages with a Roll of Honour).

p. 236 E T W Carr. His brother R I C Carr was killed at Gallipoli 29 June 1915, and he was killed along with seven other officers of the 59th. He and Lieut Gibbs were said to have been killed on the German wire, see James Affleck, *Geelong Grammarians at the Great War* (1999).

p. 237 Fraser: AWM 1DRL 0300.

p. 239 *'Did its best'*. Lording only gave initials, and all but 'Jim S' were easy to trace. *Reveille* June 1931.

pp. 245-47 J C Bowden. AWM 1DRL 428.

pp. 248-49 *Australian Churches at War* (1980) and *Padre* (1986) by Michael McKernan provide much background but mention only Maxted, Green and Tucker of the Fromelles group. Other sources are Tucker's two books, *As private and Padre with the AIF* (1919) and *Thanks be* (1954). For Ridley see Harold Evans, *Soldier and Evangelist* (1980), also Diary AWM 2DRL 0775. Kennedy and Tucker are in the *Australian Dictionary of Biography*.

p. 256 L J Martin, 6-page letter, AWM 1DRL 0483.

p. 257 Shellshock: while researching for this book the writer came across actual cases where the health of the children of men 'blown up' at Fromelles was clearly seriously affected.

p. 260 Pope: Bean's comments AWM 3DRL 606 243A.

p. 261 McGlinn's file at AWM 3DRL 632 item 78.

pp. 262-72 *'The true account ... '* Main source AWM 3DRL 606 243A. Miles' pension etc AWM 3DRL 606 145. Edmonds *'I should omit'*, AWM 3DRL 7953 34. McArthur's comments AWM 3DRL 606 145. Red Cross and Murdoch AWM 3DRL 606 31. McArthur see *Australian Dictionary of Biography* and *Reveille*, August 1933. The MGGS at Haking's HQ was Major General C H Harrington. Photographs of Murdoch and Miles: Bean noted '*the officer acting for us in Germany would look for them*'.

p. 271 *As a matter of taste*, AWM 3DRL 7953 34.

p. 273 H T C Layh. Whilst a trusted leader and soldier, 'von Layh' (his nickname) was not popular with officers nor men. Lieut Doyle wrote in his diary for 19 July '*very little humour—Best—the fat major blown into 6 ft of mud and water*'. This was the 'shell shock' referred to by Elliott. See also *Australian Dictionary of Biography*. 5th Division citations. AWM 28 18.7.1916 - 22.7.1916 etc.

pp. 275-76 R H Beardsmore, see *Australian Dictionary of Biography.* T C Barbour AWM 3DRL 606 243A. W A Ward ex-Sydney CofE Grammar School (Shore). Also Sloan, *The Purple and Gold* (1938).

p. 277 W J R Cheeseman, see *Australian Dictionary of Biography.* J Chapman, ex-Sydney CofE Grammar School (Shore). L J Trounson, see *Victoria: The Education Department's Record of War Service* (1921), p188.

pp. 278-79 P A M Eckersley and V D Bernard, ex-Ipswich Grammar School, Queensland. R C Aland, ex-Toowoomba Grammar School. H E McLennan, ex-Brisbane Grammar School.

p. 280 J J Kennedy, see *Australian Dictionary of Biography*. T Francis, ex-Ipswich Grammar School, Queensland.

p. 281 F Saunders and J Devery, see *Reveille*, Jan 1936.

pp. 282-83 Arblaster AWM 1DRL 928. *'An ungazetted VC'* AWM 1DRL 428. Lesley Light during her trip to northern France in 1999 observed that several recent visitors to the Douai Cemetery had noted in the visitors' register that they had come to pay their respects to Capt Arblaster. Maxted's MC is not on the *Commonwealth Gazette* listing, nor was a citation located in the file. Curiously most information was 'second-hand'. Note from Cass, AWM MSS 1365. A C Gunter ex-Brisbane Grammar School, and K N Wark ex-All Saints' College, Bathurst, NSW.

p. 283 A W Wheen, see *Australian Dictionary of Biography.* Also *Reveille*, 1 March 1935. *Wartime* No 42.

pp. 284-85 P W Woods and D McF McConaghy see *Australian Dictionary of Biography.* Woods also in *Reveille*, 1 Feb 1933, and obituary in *Reveille*, 1 Feb 1937; McConaghy's widow was noted as attending Woods' funeral. P W Chapman ex-The Armidale School, NSW. W McI Pitt, ex-Sydney Grammar School.

pp. 286-87 A H Scott and W Scott see *Australian Dictionary of Biography.* A J Simpson and C R Lucas, ex-Sydney Grammar School. F Fanning, ex-St Ignatius College, Sydney. H G L Cameron, ex-Melbourne Grammar School. McCay's letter to Elliott, AWM 3DRL 606 271. W E S Edgar ex-Scotch College, Melbourne. R A Salmon, ex-Ballarat College, Vic. H S Dickinson, ex-Wesley College, Melbourne.

pp. 288-89 E Williams, *Victoria: The Education Department's Record of War Service* (1921), p. 97. C A Denehy, ex-Parade College, Melbourne. R H McC Gibbs, ex-Caulfield Grammar School, Melbourne.

p. 291 H N Richards, ex-Wesley College, Melbourne.

p. 292 J H Steel, ex-Caulfield Grammar School. G G McCrae, ex-Melbourne Grammar School. T P Elliott, AWM 3DRL 2872. See *Wartime* No 24.

pp. 294-95 J P McGlinn, See *Australian Dictionary of Biography*. 'Mention' (A N Hudson, C G Brown, H V Vernon) were later 'finds' and have not been located and so confirmed from main lists. They were all 'later' awards. H L Pender, *Victoria: The Education Department's Record of War Service* (1921), p170.

p. 297 MG Coy figures. Some from Nominal Roll Book held by Australian Archives, Melbourne.

pp. 297-98 H R Catford, ex-Wesley College, Melbourne. C Cosgrove, ex-St Ignatius College, Sydney; also Jenny O'Neill, *The Flying Cosgroves* (1996).

pp. 300-02 2/4th Royal Berkshire list, Courtesy of the Royal Gloucestershire, Berkshire & Wiltshire (Salisbury) Museum. T T Pryce, see E Wyrall, *The Gloucestershire Regiment in the War 1914–18* (1931).

p. 307 Red Cross files. AWM 1DRL 428. C Mills, AWM 9317/3/118, AWM 9312/3/59, AWM 933/2/19.

p. 308 J A W Jenkins, Australian Archives MP367/1/ D 563/3/12. Mary Chomley, see *Wartime* Nos 21 and 41.

p. 311 POW Statements, AWM 30 series.

p. 316 T D Bolton, see also R Austin, *Black and Gold*, p. 218; *The Corian* (Geelong Grammar School), May 1917, p. 58; James Affleck, *Geelong Grammarians at the Great War* (1999).

p. 337 Bean's visit to Fromelles. AWM 3DRL 606 117.

p. 338 Photographs (at AWM) taken after the war. Bean/Wilkins: E04029 (11 Nov 1918), Young/ E5776-5807 (14–15 Nov 1919).

p. 342 Cemeteries: the numbers after the name of the cemeteries and memorials are the official number of the CWGC and this will facilitate finding the register and making inquiries. Full list on page 449.

p. 348 S Graham, see *Who's Who* and *Who Was Who*.

p. 349 *Packets of Effects*: AWM 3DRL 606 243A.

p. 363 *'Accumulated wisdom'*: AWM 3DRL 606 261.

p. 370 A D Ellis, see *Mufti*, 1 Aug 1936. Ellis' memories of Fromelles, a review that merely repeats what he wrote in 1919 and includes no new information.

p. 381 J J Kennedy. In November 1920, undeterred by the '*Advance Australia*' turmoil, Kennedy staged another play, 'a grand Irish drama', *The Desmonds of Dingle*, in Bendigo, again at the Princess Theatre. Billed as a 'sporting drama', it caused no comment, and had two performances.

pp. 383-84 Edmonds: AWM 3DRL 7953 34.

pp. 384-85 H E Elliott on Vol III, AWM 3DRL 606 261.

p. 385 *'Boar's Head'*. Edmonds, 1916, Vol. 2, p. 544.

p. 389 Gellibrand to Bean: AWM 3DRL 6673 Item 492.

p. 392 Brudenell White, see Bean, *Two men I knew* (1957).

pp. 392-93 C B B White. See Rosemary Derham, *The Silence Ruse* (1998).

p. 395 Bean Diary 1917: AWM 3DRI 606 70. Legion d'Honneur. The 1929 Register has Legge and Gellibrand under Australia; and Monash, Glasgow and Rosenthal under Great Britain. Of those mentioned in this work, Haking, Pearce, Cheeseman and S B Pope received the Honour.

p. 398 Delamore and Heywood McCay were brothers, Finlay and Derek were nephews and Reid was a son-in-law. The Victorian Government was not represented because of the 'official reason', McCay had belonged to the government 31 years ago. The Federal Government opposition was represented by Latham, who managed, on 31 October, to get motion through Parliament '*in appreciation of McCay's services*'.
Hagenauer. Another of his controversial views was that the First World War was a Papal-Kaiser intrigue to conquer the world.
The names on the Melbourne Shrine are: upper level, Front: Amiens, Villers-Bretonneux. Left: Messines, Ypres 1917. Right: Mont St Quentin, Hindenburg Line. Rear: Pozières, Bullecourt. Lower level, front: Landing at Anzac, Sari Bair. Left: Cocos Islands, North Sea 1915-1918. Right: Romani, Gaza-Bethsheba. Rear: Megiddo, Damascus.

p. 399 McCay's Office: The brother of W Thwaites was married to McCay's sister. O'Meara was a relation of his late wife. His will was made long before he took ill.

p. 401 Elliott's lecture: Notes in Canberra file. AWM 41 216 21 carries this note: *'This was given to me by General Elliott in 1930 at the Royal Military College, Duntroon,* A G Butler.'

p. 404 Colin Perceval Finnie, enlisted 5.7.15 RTA 31.8.18. Hon Lieut 15.7.17.

p. 408 Lower photo. Tall man with glasses front row, far right is A L Glover 2642 58th Bn.

p. 423 'Augie' Band died 31 October 2002. He was aged 105.

p. 453 2/1st Bucks. Additonal KIA Quale, 2nd Lieut CP. Wilson, Lieut J E S (RAMC).

p. 454 Duke of Cornwall Light Infantry. 'went out to western front as pioneers 61st Div May 1916. When moving to front line they were shelled. 1 officer, 4 ORs killed. 16 ORs wounded.' Regimental History.

p. 471 Jones, Sgt G E. Stained Glass Window, Church of Christ, Mitcham.

pages 501, 503 Manning Clark quotes from *Speaking out of turn* (1997).

INDEX

This index contains all people mentioned in the text and margin notes except for the list of prisoners of war on pages 329–32. The page number in bold denotes a photograph, and the number underlined indicates a major biographical article on the person concerned. The index does not include the rolls of honour, nor the notes on pages 488–91.

Author's thanks and notes

ONE CANDLE
The whole point of writing a history is to present the past as a book of wisdom for those now living; to increase the number of mourners and decrease the number of mockers; to increase the number of lovers and believers.

There is a Chinese proverb: it is better to light one candle than to curse the darkness.

—Prof Manning Clark
Sydney, 31 August 1987

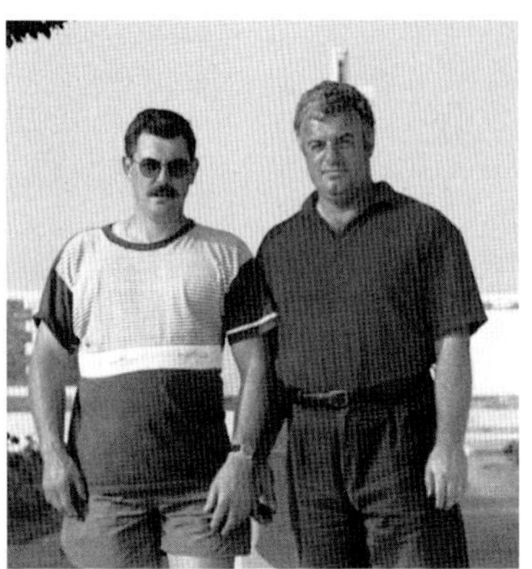

Martial Delebarre and Lambis Englezos, Fromelles, July 1996

Isabelle Costa de Beauregard, Melbourne Shrine, 19 July 1993
PHOTO P BLANKFIELD

When one attempts such a book as this, the help, encouragement and co-operation of others are often the only things that keep one going. In this case, my son Justin, to whom this volume is dedicated, never wavered. All along the way he searched for anything and anybody connected with Fromelles with huge success. When the final drafts were typed, he made the text into pages, and the pages into a book. He organised the Rolls of Honour and compiled the index and cast a critical, professional historian's eye over my history and notes.

Back in 1994 when it seemed possible that the Australian War Memorial might provide a small grant to help with my research, my friends John Morgan and John Bradley wrote sufficiently enthusiastic references that Dr Peter Stanley and his committee were persuaded. I thank them all most sincerely and trust that this volume meets their expectations. I apologise for the length of time it has taken.

Critical to keeping going was the energy, networking and friendship of Lambis Englezos, who as a co-founder of '*Friends of the 15th Brigade*', brought to my sometimes wavering spirit exhortations to keep at it. Our many discussions about Fromelles helped sort out times and motives, resolve contradictory accounts and understand some of the characters. Lambis introduced me to veterans, recorded their memories, brought them to our services and thus I am hugely thankful to have known men such as Frank Parker, George Graham, Arthur Ebdon, Charles Henderson, Tom Brain, Bill Boyce, Bob Barclay, Ernest King and Percy Naylor—just to list those who were at Fromelles from the many veterans we have met over recent years.

Another mainstay of the work has been Isabelle Costa de Beauregard-Robertson, formerly Consul General of France in Melbourne. From that position, she gave '*The Friends*' enormous help, encouragement and was so generous with her time that the old diggers became 'her boys' in a very special way. Her interest in the Great War as it affected her country meant that she knew instinctively why we Australians on pilgrimage to the battlefields of France, even after all this time, still weep when we walk up and down between the rows of headstones in those beautiful, sad war cemeteries. That *sympathique* was critical and was added to by Martial Delebarre, curator of the Fromelles Museum, when he acted as guide to Lambis on the 80th Anniversary of the Battle, and later supplied me with much information and many photographs, especially those relating to his home town and its past. As a small boy, he said, he would cycle past VC Corner Cemetery unable to understand why the Australians had buried their people here in France. His friend, Jean-Marie Bailleul has also helped with photographs and information about Aubers area generally. Anne-Marie Descamps-Carré whose family had much to do with the Australian presence at Fromelles also provided photographs and important information. I am also grateful to Jeroen Huygelier for his analysis of events.

For aspects of the British side of the story, I am indebted to the curators and archivists of the Museums of the Regiments involved: Oxfordshire & Buckinghamshire (Richard Jeff), Royal Warwickshires (Vanessa Harber), the Glosters (Col D E Whatmore) and Royal Berkshires (Major P J Ball). When in Kew, London, at the Public Record Office in late 1994, the staff seemed to be engaged in a contest about who could be most helpful to colonials. My research benefited much from this attention. Cameron Simpson loaned me some very useful books which particularly helped in putting together the British Roll of Honour.

The window provided by the translations of the German accounts of the battle enables English readers for the first time to visit the other side of No-Man's Land. I was fortunate to have Barbara Sauer, a Bavarian, to do most of this work. Her origin and personal interest has caught I believe much of the spirit of those times, and she was able to make sense of expressions which were related to the Munich area from where many of the Germans who were at Fromelles came. What she was unable to do before returning to Germany has been translated by Jock Burns whose help has been, on the historical level —wonderful; and on the philosophical level—tremendously important. Waldemar Dabkowski translated another portion and Nicole Boelhoff translated the letters in the German chapter. Others working in the German area have generously shared their research with me, especially Harry Taplin, who found much of the original material and supplied me with it. For his forthright comments and scholarly work I must also thank John Williams.

At the Australian War Memorial Research Section Ian Smith has been most helpful in guiding me in the right direction and Bill Fogarty and Ian Affleck were very helpful with photographs. The staff at the Office of Australian War Graves in Canberra have given much help in the self-imposed task I

LEGACY

When researching the work of the Australian Tunnellers for this book I found that they numbered among them, Francis Samuel Broome Rickards. A sapper in the 3rd Australian Tunnelling Coy, number 8130; he enlisted 1 June 1917 so was not at Fromelles. From 1946 onwards I knew him as 'Tex' Rickards, owner of Rickards Advertising Service of 377 Little Collins Street, Melbourne. Via Legacy he gave me my first job as office boy; later he allowed me to write for radio and press, and to do programmes and articles as well as advertisements. He was an honest and widely respected man, strong on friendship, loyalty and country, he wore his RSL badge every day with real pride. A small man, he dressed in a dapper style—spats in winter, and rather British we thought in those days when that was a plus. 'Tex' was my introduction, other than my father, to the strength of the old digger network. As my father was never able to explain to me how it all came about, I picked up what I could from 'Tex': not war stories, but that style of judgement of other men, that war had taught both my father and 'Tex': that is, *would you want him next to you in the trench?*

I was in 'Tex's' trench for five years till I left to travel. He invited me back afterwards, but I thought it sensible to move on.

That I found 'Tex' again while doing this book was a happy event, and to mention him here is a long overdue thank you for his tolerance and patience with the somewhat lost youth that Legacy passed on to him in 1946.

Dick Leffler, Fromelles, 1994
PHOTO R LEFFLER

set myself, that is to locate the grave or the memorial of all who died at Fromelles. The superb collection of World War I material held by the State Library of Victoria, both in printed and manuscript form, were vital sources of information and memories of Fromelles. Without their most helpful staff I doubt if I would have found a fraction of what came down from 'the stacks'. The help from the staff at the libraries of the University of Melbourne, Monash University, La Trobe University and Deakin University is also gratefully acknowledged.

Kevin O'Brien when he was working with the Office of Australian War Graves in charge of the Fromelles Memorial Park project provided invaluable information and contacts, also special help with the conduct of artillery, signals and intelligence services in battle. Our joint work together on the booklet for the Memorial Park previewed some of the new information we unearthed, and which is now more fully dealt with in this inquiry. Kevin's encouragement and enthusiasm throughout has been an immense help.

Historians are like deaf people, they answer questions nobody has asked them.

—Leo Tolstoy
(quoted by Prof Manning Clark)

The list of those whose fathers, uncles, grandfathers, great-uncles or great-grandfathers went through Fromelles and who helped me with letters, diaries, papers, photographs, maps and memories is considerable. All material used is credited and I trust that seeing the items in print will form an appropriate tribute to those concerned. For special items, helpful advice and much else, I have to thank Jacqui Todd (née Kirfield), Secretary of '*Friends of the 15th Brigade*', Margaret Wood (née Kerr), the late Mollie Hodges (née Vaile), Betty Leviny (née Barry), Elizabeth Douglas, Robert Fraser, Owen Mortimer, Keith Hubbard, Bob Bryant, Ron Austin, Geelong Grammar School Archives, Scotch College Archives, Allan Blankfield, Ross McMullin, Keith Rossi, Peter Corlett, Willys Keeble, George Scott, Sue Flanagan, the late Dick Leffler, Betty Whiteside, Allan Box, Patricia Hocking (née Stillman), Andrew Barnes, Owen Magee, Geoff Browne, Kath Martin, Harry Quick, Wayne Gardner, Peter Liddelow, David Huggonson, Vic Kennedy, Lesley and Amrit Light, Archive of the Catholic Archdiocese of Melbourne (Rachel Naughton) and Michelin (Sally Abbotts).

Special thanks are due to Hinn and Piphâl Thann in Canberra whose warm hospitality after a long day in the front of the microfilm or microfiche reader was very welcome, and to Noel Robinson for her valued support over the years this work has taken.

At the 'coal face', these last two years has been Carol Huntington who typed the vast majority of this book from my handwritten pages. My gratitude to her is profound. Also thanks to Lyn Hewat and others at the Ivanhoe Copy Centre whose care with old photographs, fragile books and crumbling papers has been an important contribution.

Cobbers unveiling: Melbourne Arts Centre, 20 April 1998.
R-L: The Hon Bruce Scott—Minister for Veterans Affairs, Air-Vice-Marshal Gary Beck—Director of Office of Australian War Graves, Peter Corlett—sculptor, Robin S Corfield.

... and thanks for this edition

My cobber Lambis Englezos thought enough of this book to take it to Melbourne University Press and canvass the idea of publishing a second edition. I wondered if I could catch again the spirit of Fromelles after ten years, and so update, correct and generally improve my first effort. My son Justin was certain I could with his help as I had for the first edition. The combination seemed to give MUP some confidence so we went ahead, adding in a chapter about the Missing at Fromelles found by cobber Lambis! Patrick Lindsay, Mike O'Brien and Tim Whitford helped with information for this chapter, and in their different ways proved that behind the Pheasant Wood there was a significant piece of Australian history. I am very grateful to MUP for taking me on, in particular Tracy O'Shaughnessy for her early interest and Kabita Dhara for bringing the book together.

Justin typeset the whole book, slotted in new photos, endured my changes of mind, updated the index and Rolls, and encouraged me to keep at it, so in a very real sense, this is *his* edition. My gratitude to him is thus boundless.

After the unveiling of *Cobbers* on 19 July 2008, in the park surrounding the Shrine of Remembrance, in Melbourne, the '*Friends of 15th Brigade*' held their annual service in the Shrine. The speakers were Martial Delebarre AM, President of the *Fromelles Weppes Territorials Memoriale* and Major General Michael O'Brien CSC (Rtd), the Australian Army Project Commander at Fromelles. The Blessing was given by the Rev Lieut Col Graham Redfern and wreaths were laid by the Mayor of Fromelles (Hubert Huchette), Martial Delebarre and Robin Corfield on behalf of '*The Friends*', shown here with his son Justin. Brig Keith Rossi (Rtd) recited the Ode and Luke Glasson, Australia Army Band, sounded the Last Post and Reveille.

THE MIEGUNYAH PRESS

This book was designed by Robin S Corfield
The text was typeset by Justin Corfield
The text was set in 11 point Times with 13 points of leading
The text is printed on 115 gsm Chen Ming matt art paper